The Origins of Inequality, and Policies to Contain It

The Origins of Inequality, and Policies to Contain It

JOSEPH E. STIGLITZ

OXFORD
UNIVERSITY PRESS

OXFORD
UNIVERSITY PRESS

Great Clarendon Street, Oxford, OX2 6DP,
United Kingdom

Oxford University Press is a department of the University of Oxford. It furthers the University's objective of excellence in research, scholarship, and education by publishing worldwide. Oxford is a registered trade mark of Oxford University Press in the UK and in certain other countries

Published in the United States of America by Oxford University Press
198 Madison Avenue, New York, NY 10016, United States of America

British Library Cataloguing in Publication Data

Data available

Library of Congress Control Number: 2024932973

ISBN 9780198799580
ISBN 9780198799597 (pbk.)

DOI: 10.1093/oso/9780198799580.001.0001

Printed and bound in the UK by
Clays Ltd, Elcograf S.p.A.

Preface

Inequality is now recognized as one of the defining challenges of our age. It has played a central role in the dramatic changes in politics in the U.S. and elsewhere. In a December 2013 speech, President Barack Obama promised to make it the center of focus for the remaining years of his term, as he described "a dangerous and growing inequality and lack of upward mobility."[1,2]

A Long Neglect

But until recently, economists had relatively little to say about the subject. In few if any of the major graduate programs in economics was there even a small unit on inequality. Indeed, American economists, with a few exceptions, have not only ignored inequality; they have even denigrated a concern over inequality, encapsulated in Nobel Prize winning economist Robert Lucas' famous quip, "Of the tendencies that are harmful to sound economics, the most seductive, and in my opinion the most poisonous, is to focus on questions of distribution."[3] In macro-economics, the representative agent model—which assumed inequality simply didn't matter—predominated.

In recent years, all of this has changed, partly because of the enormous increase in inequality within most countries, which has been documented by a large number of works. While economists have long paid careful attention to poverty, increased availability of data on incomes at the top have provided us with a better picture of just how extreme inequality has become.

The Many Dimensions of Inequality

There are, of course, many dimensions to inequality and its increase in recent years: more money at the top, more people at the bottom, an evisceration of the middle. Each has its own explanation. Discrimination, lack of educational opportunity, and, especially in the U.S., lack of access to health care and a deficient bankruptcy code may be more related to the bottom; deficiencies in corporate governance and regressive taxation, to the excesses at the top; globalization to the plight of the middle.

[1] He went on to say, "I believe this is the defining challenge of our time: Making sure our economy works for every working American." See Obama (2013). Obama has emphasized his concern about inequality on several other occasions, including in his January 28, 2014 State of the Union address (Obama, 2014), and in a December 6, 2011 speech at a high school in Osawatomie, Kansas.

[2] Similar concerns were raised at Davos, the annual meeting of the global elites, where business leaders have listed inequality as the world's most pressing problem. The World Economic Forum's January 2015 discussion paper (Samans, Blanke, Corrigan et al., 2015) set the tone for the meetings that year.

[3] Lucas, 2004.

While discussions often focus on inequality of income, wealth, and opportunity, other inequalities are even greater—for instance in health, related in part to the lack of access to medical care, but also to diet and other aspects of lifestyle.

When I was chief economist of the World Bank, we conducted a huge survey of some 10,000 poor, in an exercise called "the voices of the poor."[4] We asked, what aspects of their deprivations did they find most oppressive. Of course, they mentioned the lack of income. But they also noted the lack of security (physical and economic) and the lack of voice. Similar concerns arise in developed countries, especially with cutbacks in the welfare state and its system of social protection. There is a two-way relationship between the lack of voice—political power, or even access to justice—and economic inequality. Lack of voice weakens support for systems of social protection and equality of voice and even access to justice.

The Importance of a Theoretical Framework

Recognizing the magnitude of inequality and some of its key dimensions is necessary, but not sufficient, to deal with it. One has to have a good grasp of the economic, political, and social forces that have given rise it. There have been a number of attempts, especially by empirical economists, to parse out one aspect of inequality or another, to ascertain, for instance, the role of education (Goldin and Katz, 2008), or of globalization (see the discussions in Stiglitz, 2006a, 2018a), or of financial markets (Galbraith (2012), or of skilled-biased technological change (for a critical survey, see Card and DiNardo, 2002)—changes in technology which increase the demand for skilled workers relative to unskilled. But for reasons that will be made clear later in this volume, none have provided an adequate *systemic* view; while each has told part of the story, none seems up to the task of providing a holistic framework to understand what is going on. There have been a few attempts to explain the causes and/or to prescribe solutions to a more popular audience.[5] But, there have been few attempts to provide comprehensive theoretical frameworks explaining in particular the growth of wealth inequality.

Some 50 years ago, I developed what remains as the canonical model for analyzing the intergenerational distribution of income and wealth (or, more broadly, advantage and disadvantage) across generations, within which one could easily analyze equilibrium wealth and income distributions.

While economists have long been concerned about the determinants of the factor distribution of income (i.e., between capital and labor), influenced in part by Marxian analysis which saw inequality through class lenses, until my paper, published in *Econometrica* in 1969 and a more extended presentation to the 1966 meetings of the Econometric Society in San Francisco, little had been written about the determinants of the distribution of income and wealth *among individuals*. That work provided one of the first, and until relatively

[4] Narayan, Patel, Schafft et al., 2000.

[5] See, for instance, Galbraith (2012); Stiglitz (2012a, 2015h, 2019a); Atkinson (2015); Stiglitz, Abernathy, Hersh et al. (2015); and Stiglitz, Stetter, Dougherty et al. (2019); Reich (2015); Milanovic (2010, 2016); Bourguignon (2012); Bourguignon and Scott-Railton (2015); Piketty (2014, 2019); Noah (2012); and Wilkinson and Pickett (2010). (Several of these works do contain within them theoretical frameworks which I comment upon extensively below.)

recently, one of the few, general models within which the dynamics of inequality could be examined.[6]

That paper built on a body of work on growth theory that was then developing in Cambridge, Massachusetts and Cambridge, UK. I got my Ph.D. from the former (studying under the father of modern growth theory, Nobel prize economist Robert Solow) and spent a couple years in the latter (first under a Fulbright Fellowship, then as a research fellow at Gonville and Caius College), where I worked with Nobel Prize economist James Meade, a to-be Nobel prize economist James Mirrlees, Frank Hahn, Nicholas Kaldor, Joan Robinson, David Champernowne, and a host of others who were deeply concerned about inequality. Their influence will be evident in what follows.

At the end of my 1966 paper (written mostly while I was in Cambridge, UK) I argued that to explain the persistence of inequality, one needed to introduce uncertainty—randomness in the returns to capital or other key variables. A decade earlier, David Champernowne had provided a set of theoretical conditions under which a stochastic model would give rise to an equilibrium income or wealth distribution, and I then showed that the model I had created in fact satisfied those conditions. Shortly thereafter, while working in Kenya at the Institute for Development Studies at the University of Nairobi under a grant from the Rockefeller Foundation, I met another young economist from Cambridge who shared many of my interests, David Bevan. In the 1970s, with both of us in Oxford,[7] we collaborated in using continuous time stochastic processes to analyze equilibrium wealth distributions, the insights of which are central to this book.[8]

Unfortunately, at the time we did our work, interest in inequality had waned—even as inequality was beginning to soar. It was to be close to a third of a century later that such models were once again used to study wealth inequality. Meanwhile, while the focus of much of my research was elsewhere (especially on the consequences of imperfections of information), the growing inequality continued to be a major pre-occupation of mine, as evidenced in many of the chapters of this book—it was, after all, the reason I had entered economics in the first place. With my becoming a member and then chairman of the Council of Economic Advisers under President Bill Clinton,[9] and then chief economist of the World Bank, it was at the center of much of my work on economic policy.

The Origins of This Book

While much of the economics profession had studiously avoided thinking about inequality, with the devastating effects of the Great Recession, this was no longer tenable. About a decade ago, my research focus again turned to inequality. In 2011, I wrote a popular article in *Vanity Fair,* "Of the 1%, for the 1%, and by the 1%," which, capturing the mood of

[6] In one sense, it provided the micro-foundations for Champernowne's earlier (1953) work providing the theoretical foundations for the Pareto-tail of the income distribution.

[7] He at St. Johns College, I, first at St. Catherine's College (at the invitation of (now Lord) Nicholas Stern, who I had also met in Nairobi), and then as Drummond Professor at All Souls' College.

[8] See, in particular, chapters 12 and 33.

[9] While most of those in Clinton's cabinet professed a deep concern about inequality, many had other policy priorities—including financial market deregulation and lowering capital gains taxes—the effects of which was to increase inequality. Robert Reich, Secretary of Labor, was a major ally within the Administration in advocating for measures that might militate against the growth of inequality. For a discussion of these debates, see Stiglitz (2003a).

the time, in the post 2008 crisis, went viral.[10] The title reflected the new societal divisions, not based on class, but on income and wealth, and between a very small group at the top, and the large numbers below. I wanted, too, to emphasize that the observed inequalities were not just the product of market forces, but of government policies, which in turn were shaped by the "1%."[11] And finally, in a major change in economic perspectives, which typically emphasize trade-offs—one can have more equality only if one gives up on economic growth—I argued that the economy and our society suffer as a result of this inequality. This is even so for many in the 1% itself.

My long-time editor at Norton, Drake McFeely, urged me to expand these ideas into a book, which I did the next year: *The Price of Inequality: How Today's Divided Society Endangers Our Future*. There I explained in greater detail the adverse effects of inequality, in all of its dimensions, emphasizing in particular the adverse effects of inequality generated by rent-seeking and exploitation; and laying out a comprehensive economic agenda for dealing with it. It emphasized the importance not just of redistribution, the long-time concern of those concerned with inequality, but of policies which might alter the distribution of *market* incomes, now often referred to as *pre-distribution*. Articulating the nexus between political and economic inequality, I suggested that the problem was not the economics, the measures that could be undertaken to reduce inequality, but the politics, getting those measures adopted.

That book was followed by four others directed at popular audiences, one based on a series of articles written for *The New York Times*, *Vanity Fair*, and other newspapers and periodicals, *The Great Divide: Unequal Societies and What We Can Do about Them* (2015h); one centered (like much of the discussion in this volume) on the growth of market power, *People, Power, and Profits: Progressive Capitalism for an Age of Discontent* (Stiglitz 2019a); and two focused on policy, written for important think tanks in the U.S. and Europe, *Rewriting the Rules of the American Economy: An Agenda for Growth and Shared Prosperity* (Stiglitz, Abernathy, Hersh et al., 2015)[12] and *Rewriting the Rules of the European Economy* (Stiglitz, Stetter, Dougherty et al., 2019).[13]

Undergirding the analyses and policy proposals of those books was a large body of academic work conducted over the years. My own work has been theoretical, based on the empirical findings and insights of others. It is necessary to understand how our economic system works—how and why it generates the level of inequality that it does—if we are to devise policies to respond to it. Small experiments (the random control trials that have become popular in recent years) can give us insights into how individuals' and firms' behavior might change, but they can't address how the economy system as a whole might

[10] Reprinted in Stiglitz (2015h).

[11] In two of my recent books, with co-authors from the Roosevelt Institute and the Foundation of Progressive Studies in Brussels, I have explained how the rules of the game have reinforced inequality—and how those rules of the game need to be changed if we are to contain it. See Stiglitz, Abernathy, Hersh et al., (2015) and Stiglitz, Stetter, Dougherty et al., (2019).

[12] With N. Abernathy, A. Hersh, S. Holmberg, and M. Konczal, written for the Roosevelt Institute, the think tank growing out of the Presidential Library of Franklin Delano Roosevelt. Published by W. W. Norton.

[13] Written with Ernst Stetter, Carter Dougherty, Stephany Griffith-Jones, Isabel Ortiz, Jeronim Capaldo, Daniela Gabor, and Margit Schratzenstaller-Altzinger, written for and with the Foundation for European Progressive Studies, a confederation of progressive European think-tanks. Also Published by W. W. Norton.

respond. For that, one has to have a broader understanding of the system as a whole, something that can only be provided by a more general theory, of the kind that we try to provide here.

This book brings together my earlier work, developing it further, on the basis of new research, and especially to reflect the changes in our economy and our understandings of it and inequality that have occurred in the intervening years.

Key Changes in the Economy and Our Understandings of Economics

I want to call attention to several of these changes, which I will elaborate upon in later chapters. Some 60 years ago, a great economist, Nicholas Kaldor, Professor at Cambridge, put forward a set of "stylized facts" (Kaldor 1957) meant to capture the essence of key macroeconomic features of the economy. One of these, he argued, was the constancy of the share of labor and the capital output ratio. And when I was a graduate student, many a model was constructed to explain these seeming facts. But again, in a little anticipated change, it turned out that that the share of labor started to decrease, and, depending how measured, significantly so. So too, the wealth–income ratio started to increase. Then, what seemed remarkable was the constancy of the share of labor and the capital output ratio. Now, what seems remarkable is how rapidly the share of labor seems to be declining and the wealth output ratio seems to be increasing.

The new empirics present some deep quandaries. As Chapter 10 explains, it is virtually impossible to reconcile these and other "facts" concerning what has been happening with the distribution of income with the standard competitive model that has long been the cornerstone of economics.

That model had already been under attack for decades, with the development of information economics, showing that even small imperfections of information could have devastating effects on all of the standard results, including those on the efficiency of markets. Even the result that markets "clear"—that prices and wages were such as to ensure that supply equaled demand—were undermined, as it was established that competitive markets could be associated with unemployment and credit rationing. Information asymmetries—where some individuals know more than others—not only enable some to exploit others but can give rise to persistent market power.[14] Game theory provided additional tools for analyzing markets with imperfection competition. Behavioral economics questioned the premises of rationality that dominated competitive analyses. Understanding of the limits of markets led to a renewed emphasis on institutions.[15]

[14] For a broad review, see Stiglitz (2002a).

[15] Important strands of nineteenth and early twentieth century economics had emphasized the importance of institutions (Veblen 1899; Commons 1931; Hamilton 1919), but then there developed a strong school of economics that argued that economic outcomes are determined by the underlying fundamentals of preferences and technology: markets see through institutional arrangements. For instance, while it might *seem* that sharecropping undermined incentives (since tenant farmers received only a fraction of their efforts), a deeper understanding of the implicit or explicit contractual arrangements suggested otherwise (Cheung 1969). One of my early contributions was to argue that sharecropping *did* matter; it was a natural institutional arrangement arising out of imperfections of information and incompleteness of risk markets (the absence of insurance), but the design of this institution did attenuate incentives (1974b). I thought of this work as providing the foundations of a new institutional economics, where the institutions themselves could be explained; but where the details of the institutions themselves had consequences. In the latter part of the twentieth century, this became a major theme in the "new

There were other changes in the economy in the decades after World War II. Workers started living longer, pension funds grew into the trillions of dollars, and so life-cycle savings became important. Thus, while before there was a simple division between "workers" and "capitalists," now, workers were substantial owners of capital. A decrease in the interest rate helped workers who were borrowers, but hurt workers who were depending on interest from bonds for their retirement. A major aspect of inequality was the division of wealth between life-cycle savings and dynastic savings.

The corporate sector changed too, as did the financial sector and its role in the economy, and in inequality. Some of the highest paid individuals were CEOs and Wall Street executives. They were compensated in new ways, by stock options. The disparity between executive pay and that of the average worker increased. And now, while many of the very rich were those who inherited their money, there were also substantial numbers who had made fortunes during their lifetimes.

A central theme of this volume is that these changes in our economy, and in our understandings of the economy—the imperfections of markets, the limitations of competition, the importance of institutions—are critical to understanding the new stylized facts, and in particular to understanding the growth of inequality.

From My 1969 Paper to an Understanding of What Is Happening in the Economy Today

When I began work on this book, I wondered: Would my earlier paper be useful in understanding what had happened? Was it necessary to make marked changes in that framework? While the overall framework has proven remarkably robust, this book highlights some of the critical ways that the earlier theory had to be changed.

In my earlier work, there were no monopoly profits, no land rents, or even intellectual property rents. Like much of the work in growth theory at the time, I simply assumed that markets were competitive.[16] Now, I believe that explaining what has been happening to the distribution of income entails understanding what is happening to these variables—why monopoly profits and land rents are increasing and what are consequences; and much of Part II of this book does that.

To understand the growth in inequality among individuals, one has to understand the determinants of the distribution of returns to different factors, to capital and to labor, and the growth of land rents and monopoly profits; but the central message of my earlier paper is that one has to go beyond that, to understand the evolution over time of the ownership of different factors. Thus, this book shows how these new understandings of how our macroeconomy is functioning can be integrated into a simple model of the dynamics of wealth ownership.

institutional economics." (Coase's theory of the firm [1937] was an important forbearer of the new institutional economics. See also Coase [1992, 1998]; North [1990, 2006]; Ostrom [2005]; and Williamson [2000].)

[16] And, from a technical point of view, that output was produced by a constant-returns-to-scale production function, with capital and labor being the two inputs.

The Two Foundations of Our Analysis

Central to the approach of this book are two foundational ideas:

(a) While every market economy will be characterized by some degree of inequality, the extent of inequality in the U.S. today is not an inevitable consequence of capitalism—it the result of the policies that have been adopted, the rules and regulations, the laws governing corporations, competition, and labor markets, financialization and globalization.

(b) At any moment, we can think of inequality as arising from a tug of war between forces pulling the economy apart (centrifugal forces) and pushing it together (centripetal forces). If left unperturbed, there would be equilibrium wealth distribution in which the opposing forces were just balanced. It described the equilibrium as the result of a balancing of centrifugal and centripetal forces—forces pulling the economy apart and those pushing it together. As the economy changes, these forces will inevitably change, resulting in the economy evolving from one equilibrium to another. This provides a framework both for understanding changes and for devising policy responses: first, examining how various structural features of the economy affect the balance between these centripetal and centrifugal forces, then identifying the ways, for instance, that the centrifugal forces have strengthened and the centripetal forces have been weakened, and finally formulating policies that work in the opposite direction.

Our approach suggests an answer to the question "What is to be done?" lies somewhere between the two extremes, one suggesting that the problems are inherent with capitalism[17]—the analysis presented here suggests that they are not—and the other that minor tweaks to the system—for instance, better and more equal access to education—will suffice. The analysis presented here suggests that they will not.

The view reflected in the models presented here is that there are strong natural forces for intergenerational transmission of advantage and disadvantage, both "nature" and "nurture," which are pervasive and persistent, but that there are public policy interventions that can, over time, lead to a more equalitarian society. We argue further that the extent of inequality today in the U.S. is as much a result of the "laws of man" as the laws of nature: they are the consequence of policies, what we have done and what we have not done—for instance, weakening the bargaining power of workers, failing to enforce competition laws and adapt them to the twenty-first century, and managing globalization in ways which serve corporate interests rather than those of workers or consumers. The analytics presented here suggest that matters may get worse, and that

[17] This is the perspective taken on by Piketty [2014), whose book not only provides a wealth of data documenting the increases in inequality and the other stylized facts to which I referred earlier, but includes a theoretical framework explaining the increase in inequality. The possibility that was at the center of his analysis, that the wealth and income of capitalists would grow relative to the size of the economy was one I had already considered in my 1966 and 1969b papers, but rejected as part of a long-run equilibrium, simply because the law of diminishing returns would imply that the return on capital would diminish—to the point where such growth in capitalists' wealth could not be sustained. Later chapters will explain further the sense in which his theory is a special case of these more general theories, and why I and most others have found his explanation unpersuasive.

there are policies that could simultaneously reduce inequality and improve economic performance.

The purpose of this book, however, is not to develop that policy agenda—that is the task I have undertaken in the series of books and articles over the past few years to which I referred earlier. Rather, it is to develop the broad analytic framework that describes the creation and perpetuation of inequality, within which one can better analyze the consequences of inequality and what can be done about it.

Structure of the Book

The book is divided into three parts. The first contains much of the intuitive analysis, a series of papers written to be more accessible, and published in places like *Scientific American* or *The National Tax Journal.*

Part II begins with two of my older articles on inequality, because they provide the foundations of my more recent work and goes on to present the more general theories of inequality that I have developed over the past half-decade. They describe the strong forces leading to the growth of inequality, they explain why inequality persists, they describe how the growth of market power leads to increases in inequality both directly, but also indirectly through the political process—generating still more rents for the wealthy. As bad as things are now, we suggest that things may get worse, as a result of AI and robotization—one of the chapters in Part II provides the basic analytics enabling us to begin to ascertain what the effects of these upcoming changes in technology might be.

One of the reasons for working so hard to formulate coherent models of the determinants of inequality is to assess the consequences of policy. Only through a comprehensive model of the economy can one ascertain in particular whether a particular policy will be successful in the long run, as behaviors change in response. For instance, a tax on capital could lead to less savings, depressing wages, and increasing inequality. Whether that is the case is a subtle and complicated matter—it turns out that under quite general conditions the effects will be perverse. But at the same time such adverse consequences are not inevitable: we show that there are policy designs—for instance, using the proceeds of the capital tax to invest in human capital—which under quite general conditions reduce inequality and increase the well-being of workers.

Part III presents a selection of some of my earlier papers on certain aspects of inequality, from mobility, to discrimination, to its implications for macroeconomics and for economic efficiency, to the consequences of inheritance taxation, to the economics of opportunity. Rereading them today, the issues are as germane now as they were when I wrote them.

Before each part, I provide an introduction setting the scene for the papers to follow.

A challenging aspect of this book is that while my 1966 and 1969 papers provide an over-arching framework for conceptualizing what has been happening to the distribution of income and wealth, much of the "action" occurs in the details—in, say, the growth of monopoly or land rents or the increased financialization of the economy, and I do not attempt to incorporate all of these into a single model of the twenty-first-century economy. I believe, however, that such a model would necessarily have to be so complex that it would have provided little insight into what is going on. By contrast, I believe that far more insight can be had by first building the scaffolding, the overall framework, and then constructing a series of simple models illuminating different parts of the framework—each tailor-made to shine a light on the question at hand.

The previously published papers included in this volume are reprinted largely as they were originally published, with minor modifications to avoid excessive repetition (there still remains some unavoidable repetition, necessary to put the analysis of that chapter into context). In many cases, since the papers came out, an extensive literature has developed. For instance, there is now a large empirical literature reinforcing the conclusions here that much of the increase in wealth is not associated with an increase in the capital stock. I have not attempted to incorporate references to this literature in the articles, though in the introduction to the chapters and the parts I provide some discussion of what is now, fortunately, growing into a large literature.

A Final Word

When I began my research into the dynamics of income inequality a half century ago, I did so because I thought the level of inequality I observed then seemed intolerable. As a young economist, I wanted to understand the forces that gave rise to it, in the hope that by understanding those forces, we might do something about it. I had not realized then that I was living in the golden age of capitalism—that inequality was at the lowest level ever in modern times. We are still far from fully understanding the forces that give rise to inequality. For decades, the field was left untilled, and in the intervening years, inequality has grown far worse. The work of Piketty, Atkinson, Saez, Chetty, Milanovich and so many others has given us a far firmer empirical basis for understanding inequality. There remains the theoretical challenge of making sense of all of this. I hope that this book may be a small contribution in helping us move forward on this important task.

Contents

Introduction and Overview of the Volume

This book presents an analytic framework for understanding the origins of inequality—for understanding why it has persisted and why it has grown worse—a framework within which we can ascertain the effects of alternative policies, and which might suggest additional policies for containing it.

In a sense, it represents the culmination of some six decades of work on inequality, all of which began when, in my third year at Amherst College, I decided to switch from the study of mathematics and physics to economics: I kept thinking about the massive inequalities and social maladies—discrimination, episodic unemployment, labor strife—that I had seen so vividly as I grew up in Gary, Indiana in the 1940s and '50s. I wanted to do what I could to construct "another world." I was an activist—I had been President of the Student Council, gone down South to advance integration, joined in Martin Luther King's march on Washington in August 1963. When I went to MIT, I found a cohort of like-minded graduate students, including George Akerlof, with whom I shared the Nobel Memorial Prize in economics in 2001, and Mrinal Datta-Chaudhuri, from India, and from whom I learned more vividly about an oppression quite different from what I had seen in the U.S., that of colonialism. We discussed and debated the relationship between what we were being taught as graduate students, and what we had seen with our own eyes and what we read from critics of the system. They didn't always jibe.

We appreciated our teachers' attacks on Milton Friedman and the Chicago school, that suggested that one should leave everything to the market. We *knew* that that was wrong. But we were discomfited by the neoclassical models that were at the core of our instruction, for were they correct, with few exceptions, markets might work as well as the conservatives claimed. And I particularly was disturbed that so little attention was paid to inequality. It was as if they were claiming it didn't matter, at least not for economics. I *felt* that that too was wrong.

Thus, began two interrelated strands of my lifetime research agenda: *explaining* the pervasive inequalities that mark our societies, and more broadly, the distribution of income; and *reconstructing economics*, making clear what was wrong with the neoclassical model, and why it was that markets often did not bring about the economic nirvana of Pareto efficiency that was claimed. Adam Smith had suggested that the pursuit of self-interest (sometimes called greed) would lead, *as if by an invisible hand*, to the well-being of society. My work[1] had shown that the reason that the invisible hand sometimes seemed so invisible was that it simply was not there: whenever information is imperfect or asymmetric (with some individuals knowing some things that others don't) *or* markets are incomplete—that is *always*—markets are not Pareto efficient, that is, there are interventions to the market, based on the same limitations, the limited information or the limited markets, which could make some individuals better off without making anyone else worse off.

[1] In particular, my paper with my Columbia colleague Bruce Greenwald (1986).

The Origins of Inequality, and Policies to Contain It. Joseph E. Stiglitz, Oxford University Press. © Joseph E. Stiglitz (2025).
DOI: 10.1093/oso/9780198799580.003.0001

While both of these strands are reflected in the chapters that follow, this book is mostly about economic inequalities.

At the time, the other major center of economic research was Cambridge, England, and there a group of scholars was intensely focused on understanding inequality. Having decided to write my thesis on growth and inequality, I got a Fulbright Fellowship to Cambridge, where I completed my dissertation shortly after turning 23. Several of the leading lights there were as convinced as I was that something was wrong with the neoclassical model, and that inequality mattered a great deal for the behavior of the economic system. Their main focus, however, was on differences in savings rates. That was the aspect too that had been emphasized by Hirofumi Uzawa, a distinguished Japanese economist with whom I had gone to study briefly in Chicago in 1965, and who became a lifelong friend.[2] Such differences are important,[3] and can in part be explained by differences in income and wealth. But the chapters below explain why the consequences of inequality are far broader.

A year after coming back from Cambridge, I got my first glimpse of inequality and poverty in the developing world, with a trip to Hong Kong, Thailand, and India—seeing firsthand the extremes I had only read about. It made a lifelong impression and gave me new insights into both the failures of markets and into the nature of inequality. When, two years later, Jim Coleman at the Rockefeller Foundation asked me to go to Kenya, to the Institute of Development Studies and the University of Nairobi, I jumped at the chance. While this book is primarily about inequality in developed countries, my close study of inequality in the developing world helped shape my thinking.[4]

I couldn't, of course, foresee what would happen to inequality in the ensuing decades. I hadn't realized that when I was growing up in Gary, Indiana, it was the golden age of capitalism: inequality would only grow and grow and grow. As I explain below, there were other unexpected changes in the overall economy, some the causes of the increased inequality, some the consequences. This book seeks to create models which can help parse out these different forces.

This is largely a book about theory, and like any theory, it abstracts from many details. Inequality has many dimensions—not just economic but political and social—and we make no pretense to be comprehensive. Even within the narrow domain of economics, we will not be able to touch on some of the most important aspects, for instance, those associated with location. We hope, however, that our narrower focus enables us to more deeply understand at least some of the key drivers of today's inequality and some of the consequences.

1 Contrasting Perspectives on Inequality

The chapters below illuminate several of the major controversies in the theory of income and wealth distribution and in the design of policies to address inequality.[5] In this

[2] We edited a book together (Stiglitz and Uzawa, 1969).

[3] And play an important role in several of the chapters below, in particular, Chapter 29.

[4] And is particularly evident in Chapters 7, 23, 25–27.

[5] As I noted, this book focuses on theory. There are also a large number of controversies in the empirics of inequality—for instance, in the magnitude of the increase in inequality, with some claiming that correctly measured the increase in inequality is much less than others and the decline in the share of labor is smaller, and

introduction, I summarize these themes and what our analysis has to say about them, with references to where the details are presented given in endnotes.

There are nine themes, in particular, to which we call attention.

The first controversy relates to whether or not inequalities arise out of natural competitive economic forces and represent "just deserts." Do inequalities mostly result from differences in societal contributions, with those who are wealthy justly so because they have contributed more? Or are they mostly an outcome of the exercise of market power, for instance by capitalists vis-à-vis workers or by CEOs vis-à-vis other corporate stakeholders? Or do they arise as a result of some other form of exploitation—discrimination or taking advantage of uninformed consumers or engaging in some deceptive practice?

The second controversy is about whether what really matters is inequalities in outcomes, individuals' income, wealth, or health; or inequalities in opportunities, the chances society provides to different individuals.

The next three controversies concern the relationship between economic performance and inequality. The third controversy is about whether economics should just focus on doing whatever it takes to increase the size of the economic pie—leaving the issue of how the pie is divided to politics.

The fourth controversy surrounds an alternative reason that economists might not need to spend much attention on inequality: if a rising tide really lifts all boats, all will benefit as we increase GDP.

And the fifth controversy is over the extent to which national income (or better, some appropriate measure of well-being)[6] is likely to decrease—or increase—if we adopt policies that reduce inequalities.

Sixth, the volume considers whether the inequalities currently observed in a capitalist economy such as that of the United States are an inevitable feature of capitalism. In particular—and this is the seventh controversy—we examine whether the capitalist system (the market economy) is characterized by ever-increasing inequality or whether there is an equilibrium wealth distribution. If there is such an equilibrium, one would expect inequality to stop increasing at some point as it reaches some kind of balance point; without such an equilibrium, disparities in wealth might continue to grow indefinitely if there are no policies put in place to limit them.

The eighth controversy that the book analyzes surrounds why workers are getting a smaller share of the economic pie, and capitalists a larger share. The different perspectives on this follow naturally from the different perspectives on whether inequality is largely a matter of exploitation or just deserts. Is the declining share of labor, for instance, the steady erosion of the bargaining power of workers and the growth of monopoly power in the corporate sector? Or is it the result of "natural" economic forces working in a competitive market: Does it have something to do with changes in the relative scarcity of capital? Or

in the sources of inequality, with some claiming, for instance, that increases in dispersion of wages across firms is of far greater importance than the increase in dispersion within firms. At appropriate points in the book, we will comment on those issues, but it is not the objective of this book to resolve those disputes.

[6] There is by now a large literature pointing out that GDP does not provide a good measure of societal well-being. For the most part, we elide the issues raised by that literature, noting only that some of the specific policies discussed in the ensuing chapters may induce an even greater reduction in inequalities in well-being than in inequalities in income. See Stiglitz, Fitoussi, and Durand (2019a, 2019b) and Stiglitz, Sen, and Fitoussi (2010).

does it have something to do with the innovation process, with robots replacing workers and decreasing especially the value of unskilled workers?

Finally, the book asks: is it useful in understanding the evolution of inequality to think of "classes"? Or is class analysis an outmoded nineteenth-century Marxian notion?

2 Just Deserts or the Exercise of Power?

One of the longest standing controversies in the economics of inequality is the *justifiability* of inequalities—a question that relates, in turn, to their origin. Today, there is consensus that certain kinds of inequality are unfair. For example, no one can easily defend the inherited inequalities of feudalism. In Europe, perpetuators of the system during the feudal era suggested that they were preordained, but with the Enlightenment such justifications no longer held much weight. But even as the Enlightenment demolished the mystical justification for feudalism, the defenders of the old order proved adaptable: they now suggested that changing these long-standing orders would lead to social havoc, with an unacceptable price to be paid. In the eighteenth and nineteenth centuries, feudalism faded, but industrialization was accompanied by persistent and growing inequality. New explanations—or justifications—had to be found for these disparities.

Two broad strands of thought emerged. One sought to understand the evolving distribution in terms of exploitation and market power (Karl Marx), the other in terms of social contribution (the marginal productivity theory). Marx (1818–83), focusing on the inequality between capitalists and workers, argued that the former achieved their riches through the exploitation of the latter: the real source of "value" in an economy arose from the labor of workers.

The latter theory argued that inequalities arise naturally in a competitive economy because of differences between individuals or families in their assets, abilities, and preferences. Some, for instance, may save more, work harder, or have greater talents; those individuals who contributed more would be rewarded with greater income; those who saved more would, over time, have more wealth. Wealth disparities would be especially great if those with higher income also saved more. This perspective is associated with neoclassical economists, such as John Stuart Mill (1806–73), and has been the dominant theory in the Anglo-American world over the past century and half. Nassau Senior (1790–1864), the first holder of the Drummond Chair of Political Economy at Oxford in 1830, argued that inequality arose from the greater *abstinence* of the wealthy, who abstained from consuming to increase their wealth, with the increasing wealth increasing productivity and wages, from which all would benefit—an early version of trickle-down economics.[7] In this view, the wealthy were justly rewarded for their abstinence.

[7] Perhaps ironically, those who seek to explain the growth of inequality through differential savings (e.g., my teacher at Cambridge, Nicholas Kaldor and, more recently, Thomas Piketty) are thus more in the tradition of Nassau Senior than of Karl Marx.

Nassau Senior was the first holder of the Drummond Chair in Political Economy at All Souls College, the first chair in economics in the English-speaking world, established in 1825. (I held that chair in the 1970s.) The difference in political perspectives between Senior and Marx was stark: Senior opposed even mild reforms like child labor laws and the Factories Act of 1847 (sometimes known as the "Ten Hours Act") because of their adverse effects on the return to capital.

Of course, as wealth gets passed on from one generation to the next, the wealth of succeeding generations cannot be attributed to *their* efforts; it is just the result of their "choosing the right parents," or as one billionaire put it, the outcome of the sperm lottery. The high income and wealth of those who come by their position through inheritance can no more be described as a "just desert" than those in the feudal era who came to their position by right of birth. And in our twenty-first-century meritocracy, similar concerns are being raised: the children of the well-educated, wealthy, and well-connected have a better chance of getting the qualifications necessary to succeed in today's economy.

The two perspectives are not, of course, mutually exclusive: part of the fortune of Microsoft's Bill Gates may have arisen from the social contribution of his firm's personal computer operating system; but this was greatly amplified by the firm's exercise of market power, including through practices that were ruled anticompetitive by courts in three continents.

As another example: In many countries (and, among the advanced countries, especially in the U.S.), individuals and corporations may initially attain their wealth through an innovation or other important social contribution. But then, they use that wealth to exert large political influence, and in turn use that influence to further enrich themselves. They achieve this further enrichment both by ensuring that the "rules of the game" favor them and by gaining preferential treatment from government (subsidies, contracts, obtaining public assets at below-competitive prices, selling goods and services to the government at above-competitive prices).

The two views on the origins of inequality provide not just alternative descriptions of the origins of inequality but different normative perspectives, with inequality in the former case being malignant, in the other, more benign, with clear implications of policy.[8]

This book argues that neoclassical theory may provide only limited insight into what has been happening. Though we may not be able to precisely parse out the relative importance of exploitation (broadly interpreted), it clearly plays an important role in current inequalities, especially as we see current wealth and income inequalities at least in part as a legacy of earlier inequalities. Slavery was not a voluntary transaction—physical force was used; and much of America's inequality originates from such abuses of power. Many of Russia's oligarchs obtained their wealth by what can best be described as stealing it from the state, as Canadian minister of finance Chrystia Freeland described in her 2000 book, *Sale of the Century*.

Unless there is a perfect market, returns to different factors, individuals, and corporations may differ markedly from their social return—from their "just deserts." And a perfect market would require perfect competition, perfect information, and perfect rationality. This is a supremely unlikely combination that is all but impossible in the real world. Yet the "perfect markets" competitive model—which makes all of these assumptions—is still used as grounds for most economic analyses, including those attempting to understand changes in inequality. In the real world, CEOs may garner for themselves more than a perfect market would grant them, and workers may get less. Most labor markets are not well described by the competitive model, and employers often engage in practices that reduce workers' market power. The distribution of income between workers and corporations is

[8] Though the analysis below explains why inequality, even when it arises out of "just deserts," may have adverse effects on economic performance.

obviously affected by the rules governing collective bargaining—individual workers have little bargaining power against corporations. The extent to which governments adopt and enforce laws enabling unionization and enhancing workers' bargaining power affects the share of national income accruing to workers, and thus the degree of income inequality.

Discrimination based on race and gender has played an important role in U.S. inequality, and the extent of that discrimination has been affected both by the rules that have attempted to circumscribe it and how they are enforced.[9]

Market power (in other words, corporate or monopoly power) is another important deviation from the competitive paradigm, with both distributive and efficiency implications.[10] If the ownership of the monopolies is concentrated (as it is), monopoly power leads to inequality. The power to raise prices means, in effect, that real wages (wages adjusted for the costs of the goods and services that individuals purchase) are lower than they otherwise would be—workers are worse off. The existence and persistence of market power reflects the importance of the rules of the economy (discussed in detail in this volume): markets on their own are not naturally competitive. But countries can adopt rules that make the economy more competitive than it would be otherwise.

Recent years have seen multiple demonstrations of how unregulated or under-regulated corporations can exploit a host of consumer and worker vulnerabilities—pushing dangerous, addictive products (like cigarettes, opioids, and carbohydrate-rich foods and drinks), dishonestly selling polluting diesel cars, and, in the financial and private for-profit education sectors, engaging in a wide range of deceptive and exploitive practices.

This book explains why it is hard to reconcile key observed phenomena with competitive equilibrium analysis, and thus with the "just deserts" interpretation. The competitive model cannot explain, for instance, the increase in the wealth-to-income ratio even as wages stagnate, the fall in the share of labor, and the seeming rise in the profit rate. That model too can account for only part of the increase in the value of wealth in the U.S.[11] Instead, a model in which there has been an increase in exploitation and rents (returns in excess of what would emerge in a competitive market) better explains the unequal outcomes of today's economy.

The book goes further in showing the interaction between, say, market power and wealth distribution: it explains why an increase in market power today is associated with an increase not only in inequality in incomes today, but an increase in inequality in *wealth* today and in the future—which in turn implies even greater inequalities in income in the future.

It explains too some of the reasons for the increase in the market power of corporations and the weakening of the market power of workers. These imbalances are partially a result of changes in technology and the structure of the economy but are also partially (and perhaps largely) a result of changes in laws and how they are enforced. Legislation has failed to keep up with changes in the economy, including the innovativeness of those in the corporate sector in exercising, extending, and amplifying their market power. Thus, this book

[9] Discussed in Part III.F. Again, no one would claim that the income differentials arising as a result of such discrimination reflects "just deserts." It is just another aspect of "exploitation."

[10] The issues discussed in the following paragraphs are discussed much more extensively in Chapter 16 and in Stiglitz (2019a).

[11] These are among the stylized facts that describe what has been happening to the economies of advanced countries in recent decades. See Chapter 10 below.

traces the changes in inequality not just to the laws of nature—to changes in technology or preferences, traditionally described as the fundamental "drivers" of the economy—but to the "laws of man." It thus emphasizes an institutional perspective that has gained increasing recognition in recent years.[12]

While I focus on exploitation that is the result of increases in corporate market power and a diminution of workers' bargaining power, exploitation can take on other forms. There is, of course, a long tradition of such exploitation: cigarette companies making cigarettes more addictive and denying their adverse health effects; snake-oil companies pretending that there are medicinal benefits from their products. But modern technology has allowed this to be done on a scale that is perhaps unprecedented:[13] the drug companies creating the opioid crisis, as they too claimed that their products were not addictive; the for-profit education sector exploiting the desire of poor but uninformed students to get ahead, to "sell" them education products that do not advance their careers, leaving them with debts but little more; or the food-processing and sugar-intensive soft drink companies pushing high-carbohydrate products that are addictive and have led to the epidemic of childhood obesity and diabetes.

The financial sector has excelled in exploitation—evidenced in the financial crisis of 2008 and its aftermath. It pushed mortgages that were beyond individuals' ability to pay and credit cards with fine print that resulted in the unwary paying billions in hidden fees.

We explain how those who excel in exploitation—not those who excel in providing the goods and services that enhance long-run prosperity—may become wealthy. In this sense, there is a fundamental difference between what contributes to the wealth of a nation and what contributes to the wealth of an individual. While the "just deserts" theory argues that the two are coincident, the exploitation theory argues that much of the wealth of the individuals at the top comes at the expense of the wealth of the nation, of the well-being of other citizens, and of the overall economic and societal performance. It has weakened health, contributed to instability, and led to an overall worsening of well-being. We show, for instance, how financial market deregulation and other financial policies have led to an increase in land rents. Similarly, the increase in market power has led to an increase in the capitalized value of corporate monopoly profits, thereby leading directly to an increase in wealth and income inequality. The increase in market power directly harms overall economic performance, as it distorts resource allocations. (The central theorems in economics arguing that markets are efficient require that markets be competitive.) But the increase in rents and corporate power has a powerful indirect effect. High land rents are associated with higher value of land; higher corporate profits are associated with higher values of stocks. The increased value of these alternative stores of value "crowd out" real capital accumulation, investments in plants and equipment and R&D, resulting in wages and growth that is lower than it otherwise would be.[14]

The rules of the game, which are set largely through a political process, clearly have a central role in the determination of inequality. But the political process itself is affected

[12] As we noted in the Preface, while there is a long tradition in economics emphasizing the importance of institutions, in the era in which neoclassical economics reigned, their role was denigrated, and the emphasis was placed on the underlying drivers. Information economics helped explain institutions like sharecropping and their effects both on efficiency and distribution. See Stiglitz (1974b) and Part III.C. below.

[13] And behavioral economics has provided firms with new tools for exploiting individual vulnerabilities.

[14] See Chapters 15–18 in this volume.

by societal inequalities—especially in polities like the U.S. where money matters. Thus, economic inequality gives rise to political inequality, and the wealthy can use their disproportionate political power to set rules which exacerbate such inequalities. The interaction between economic and political inequalities can shed light on why some advanced economies—facing similar technologies and preferences—can differ so in the extent of inequality. The Scandinavian countries, for instance, have a low level of economic inequality, giving rise to a politics which supports rules sustaining greater equality. The U.S. with its extremes of economic inequality has a politics which reflects that, providing ample scope for the wealthy to exercise political influence through campaign contributions, and thereby giving rise to rules that in turn lead to more inequality (a tax system that taxes those at the top at lower rates than those below; financial liberalization which provided banks ample opportunity to engage in exploitation; labor laws and laws governing globalization that undermined workers' bargaining power). The analysis shows that the underlying economic forces can result in quite different equilibria—in a politics that is consistent with rules that sustain low inequality or in one which gives rise to rules leading to a high level of inequality.

2.1 Just Deserts in a Twenty-First-Century Economy

There is another critique of the "just deserts" perspective: each individual's economic contribution is itself to a large extent a result of collective efforts, not just of his own efforts. This is most easily seen by contemplating the productivity of a talented person living in a war-torn or otherwise dysfunctional State. But more generally, any individual's productivity depends not just on the country having a good legal framework (a rule of law), fairly and efficiently enforced, but also on having good infrastructure and other skilled people with whom to interact, all of which depend on the State. In the twenty-first century, productivity depends heavily on technology, and much of the advance in technology rests on research that is in whole or in part financed by government and occurs in public research institutes and universities. Parsing out the individual's marginal contribution from that of those provided collectively is impossible. But it is clear that private corporations appropriate for themselves much of the returns from these societal contributions, especially in areas of science and technology.[15] That is why some have suggested that the government make a greater effort at appropriating for the public the returns to publicly funded research, putting the proceeds into a sovereign wealth fund, the benefits of which would be shared more equally.

3 What Matters, Inequality in Outcomes or Inequalities in Opportunities?

In recent decades, there has been a raging debate about what matters more, inequalities in outcomes (the distribution of income or wealth) or inequalities in opportunities. One

[15] Thus, if the U.S. government had appropriated for the public a fraction of the social returns emanating from its helping fund the internet, today's distribution of wealth might look markedly different. Similarly, if the government had taken and/or retained equity positions in the enterprises which it helped finance or bail-out (Federal Express, Tesla, virtually all the major banks), the government's balance sheet would look markedly different.

perspective holds that if everyone, no matter the income and education of their parents, has the same opportunity, that's all that counts.

The other perspective argues that both inequalities of outcomes *as well as inequalities of opportunity* are important; both shape the nature of our politics and society and the two are in practice inseparable. Inequalities in outcomes—the income and wealth that individuals receive—reinforce themselves, with those with greater income and wealth giving greater opportunities to their children. Societies with greater inequalities in income and wealth almost *inevitably* are societies with greater disparities in opportunities. The advantages that better-off parents can give to their children (or the disadvantages that those less-well-off bestow on theirs) cannot ever be fully undone by the state. Moreover, if the rungs of the ladder are further apart, it is harder to climb up the ladder. The causality, of course, goes both ways: societies with greater disparities in opportunities are likely to generate greater disparities in incomes and wealth.

The evidence supporting the perspective that both forms of inequality are important is compelling. Among advanced countries, those with more inequality of incomes have less economic opportunity. This relationship has been replicated over different sets of countries (and within different regions within a country) and different time periods.[16]

For those who have thought of the U.S. as a land of opportunity—the American Dream is a dearly held ideal—data on economic mobility has been devastating. The life prospects of a young American are more related to the income and education of her parents than in most other advanced countries. Only Italy and the UK even come close to providing so little opportunity.

There are, moreover, even ambiguities in what we should mean by "equality of opportunity." Preferences—our ability and willingness to seize opportunities when they present themselves—are themselves partly or largely inherited. Our ability to take advantage of opportunities, to exert efforts, might rightly be thought of as part of the circumstances that we inherit.[17]

4 Does a Rising Tide Lift All Boats?

There is a collection of arguments put forth especially by those on the Right suggesting that economics need not—or even more strongly *shouldn't*—devote attention to inequality. The first is that if one grows the economy, everyone benefits. President Kennedy famously said, "A rising tide lifts all boats."[18] This view has subsequently become associated with "trickle-down" economics—giving money to the top benefits everyone in society, provided only that it helps the economy grow. There never was any theoretical argument or empirical analyses behind such contentions, and the evidence is overwhelming that that has not been the case in recent decades. The economy has grown, those at the top have done very well,

[16] The relationship was first developed by Miles Corak of the Graduate Center at CCNY (Corak, 2013), and is presented in Chapter 4. Chetty, Hendren, Kline, and Saez (2014) have shown that there exists a similar relationship within the United States. In the empirical work, inequality in income is typically measured by the Gini coefficient and inequality in opportunity is generally measured by the extent of intergenerational mobility.

[17] These issues are discussed more fully in Chapters 6, 22, and 23.

[18] Kennedy, 1963.

but those elsewhere have not—with incomes in the bottom of the distribution stagnating or even declining.

5 Should Economics Just Focus on Maximizing the Size of the Economic Pie?

There is another argument that economists often put forward for not paying attention to inequality. Many claim that good policy entails just focusing on efficiency—maximizing the size of the economic pie. If one doesn't like the distribution of income that emerges out of a competitive process, one should simply impose lump-sum taxes—taxes that don't distort behavior—to redistribute income. It was this belief that underlay Nobel Prize winner Robert Lucas' inveighing against discussions of inequality mentioned in the Preface. Lucas called the focus on inequality "poisonous." But this book, and my earlier work, explain why issues of distribution and efficiency cannot be separated.[19] It is not just that lump sum taxes don't exist.[20] It is that the distribution of income affects the performance of the economic system, an idea that we elaborate on in the next section.

6 The Big-Trade Off vs. the Big Price

Traditionally, even economists who were concerned about the social, political, and moral consequences of inequality worried that there might be a high cost of doing much about it. As Arthur Okun, chairman of the U.S. Council of Economic Advisers under President Lyndon B. Johnson argued, there was a trade-off—one could have more equality, but only at a cost of lower growth or lower GDP. Indeed, he called this *The Big Tradeoff* (Okun, 1975). The argument was that to reduce inequality, one had to impose progressive taxes; such taxes attenuated incentives, with adverse economic effects. People saved less and worked less.

Beyond the increasing recognition of the role of market power, other forms of exploitation, and other sources of "rents" in generating inequality discussed earlier, perhaps the most important change in perspectives about inequality is the development of theories and a body of evidence showing that equality and economic performance may be complementary.[21] This was the central theme of my earlier book, *The Price of Inequality*: We pay a high price for the high levels of inequality that divide our society—not only politically and socially, but even economically. That is, one can simultaneously reduce inequality and increase economic performance. This is especially so when inequality reaches the

[19] The idea that one can separate the analysis of efficiency and distribution—that any Pareto efficient distribution can be achieved through a competitive equilibrium with lump sum redistributions—is referred to as the "Second Fundamental Theorem of Welfare Economics." (The First Fundamental Theorem asserts the efficiency of competitive markets.) Thus, the work referred to in this subsection represents effectively the repeal of the second welfare theorem. For earlier discussions, see Shapiro and Stiglitz (1984) and Stiglitz (1994b).

[20] Part of the reason is that the government doesn't have the information required to levy the requisite lump sum taxes. Taxes are imposed on income and consumption, and such taxes are necessarily distortionary, at least to some extent. This was one of the important insights of Sir James Mirrlees (1971), work for which he received the Nobel Prize. See also Stiglitz 1982e, 1987a, Chapter 36, and the large literature cited in those papers.

[21] For an overall discussion, see Stiglitz (2012a). For a more recent presentation of empirical evidence, see Ostry, Loungani, and Berg (2019).

extremes that it has in the U.S. Of course, this perspective is a natural consequence of those presented in previous sections: If inequalities arise as a result of market failures, for instance from exploitation that distorts the economy, policies that reduce such exploitation can improve economic performance and increase equality. Even when inequality arises just from the growth of land rents—with land disproportionately held by the wealthy—policies that capture those land rents by taxation for public use can have triple benefits: a direct reduction in inequality, an improvement in growth and equity from well-targeted public expenditures, and an increase in private investment, as the lower value of land "crowds out" less investment. More generally, taxing the "rents" the growth of which has played such an important role in the growth of inequality—whether they are land rents or monopoly profits—can reduce inequality without any distortionary costs. Even better, in some cases such taxation may reduce incentives for rent-seeking and increase productive investments.

There are other aspects of inequality where government interventions can lead to both less inequality *and* improved economic performance. Consider inequalities arising from lack of access to opportunity—with those borne to parents of limited means not being able to reach their full potential. Some of this arises from inherent imperfections in capital markets, limiting individuals' ability to borrow to invest in human capital and to divest themselves of the risks of such investments.[22] The provision of free education to those whose parents have limited resources increases equality of opportunity, equality of incomes, and increases efficiency.

Increases in inequality can exacerbate the consequences of imperfect and asymmetric information. This is most evident in poor agrarian economies where, because of inequalities in land ownership, large fractions of the population work under sharecropping arrangements, facing an effective tax rate of 50 to 70%.[23]

Behavioral economics has also called attention to some of the systemic effects of pervasive inequality on individual and societal performance, including a lack of aspirations of those at the bottom, a discouragement of effort,[24] a sense of entitlement of those at the top, and difficulties in cooperation.[25]

Today, the perspective that there is a high price of inequality (Stiglitz, 2012a) has now become mainstream.[26] I believe that helping bring about this change in perspective may have been one of the most important contributions of my research and writings on inequality over the past half century.

[22] These market imperfections are inevitable, a result of costly, imperfect, and asymmetric information. Understanding these market imperfections and their consequences has been at the center of my broader research agenda.

[23] These costs are often referred to as "agency costs," because they arise when one individual works for (i.e., is an agent of) another, rather than working for themselves. See in particular Part III.C.

[24] An aspect of "efficiency wages"—where (absolute and relative) pay affects performance. I developed these theories while I was at the Institute for Development Studies in Nairobi in 1969c, and subsequently published the analyses in a series of papers: See Stiglitz (1974c, 1982f, 1992b, 2009b, 2013b), Shapiro and Stiglitz (1984), and Nalebuff, Rodriguez, and Stiglitz (1993). See also Akerlof and Yellen (1990).

[25] See Demeritt, Hoff, and Stiglitz (forthcoming), part of the growing literature focusing on the endogenous determination of preferences and behavior. (See, for example, Hoff and Stiglitz (2010, 2016).)

[26] See, for example, Ostry, Berg, and Tsangarides (2014), Ostry, Loungani, and Berg (2019), and the references cited there.

7 Is Extreme Inequality an Inevitable Feature of Capitalism?

Critics of capitalism claim that inequality is an inevitable and necessary feature of capitalism. Capitalism is based on *individual* efforts—their work, savings, and entrepreneurship. In a society where everyone's income is the same, there would be little incentive to work or to save. More recently, Thomas Piketty has argued that not only is capitalism inevitably marked by high levels of inequality, but that the level of inequality is ever increasing: because of the higher savings propensities of capitalists, and because of the high return on savings, in excess of the rate of growth, the share of national income going to capitalists is increasing unless government intervenes to lower the after-tax rate of return to capital.

This book argues, to the contrary, that while market economies will have some level of inequality, the currently observed high and increasing levels of inequality are not an inevitable feature of capitalism. Inequality is greatly affected by the rules of the game. One aspect of those rules is tax and expenditure policies—in other words, how progressive they are. But another aspect of those rules is our legal and economic framework, which may or may not restrict, for instance, the ability of corporations to exploit consumers through market power or deceptive practices; or workers through an imbalance of bargaining power. The legal framework can also, through corporate governance laws, enable corporate executives to extract more corporate income for themselves. Similarly, rules governing globalization and monetary policy may affect the bargaining power of workers.[27]

As I have put it elsewhere, *inequality is a choice*—a choice made largely through the political system which sets the rules.[28] The problem is thus not with the "laws of economics" and the economic system "capitalism," but with politics and the political system. Some form of a market economy is essentially necessary to manage a complex modern economy, and as we noted earlier, capitalism might even function *better* with rules that result in greater equality.

But critics of capitalism might legitimately respond: Capitalism is an economic *and* political system. The economic inequalities to which it gives rise inevitably give rise to political inequalities, which result in rules favoring the capitalists. This may be true, but it begs the central question: can one have a sustainable political and economic system, a democratic market economy, with a modicum of inequality—a level of inequality markedly less than that in the U.S.? This book argues strongly in the affirmative. As we have already observed, there can be multiple political and economic equilibria, in some of which inequality is much less than in others; the U.S. may be in a "high inequality" equilibrium;[29] other countries, such as those in Scandinavia, may be in a sustainable equilibrium with less inequality.

History, however, is always unfolding. Technology and politics are ever-changing. Some societies, such as Sweden, that seemed to have been in a low inequality equilibrium have seen inequality increase—though to levels that are still markedly below that of the U.S. This evolution is what critics of capitalism would have predicted. But it may also be possible,

[27] See Stiglitz, Abernathy, Hersh et al. (2015) and Stiglitz, Fitoussi, and Durand (2019a).

[28] Stiglitz (2015h).

[29] Whether such an equilibrium is sustainable in the long run within a democratic institutional framework is a question that rightly is now being extensively discussed. In Stiglitz (2019a) I argue that it requires sufficient progressive taxation so that there cannot be a buildup of wealth inequality.

going forward, that as technology and society evolve, there may be sustainable alternative political and economic arrangements, with high standards of living but lower levels of inequality—for example, arrangements in which cooperatives and nongovernmental organizations play a more important role than they currently do. Sweden, too, may have been influenced by the ideas that came to dominate in the 1980s in the more capitalistic societies, in the "neoliberal era," that the gains in productivity from less progressivity in tax and expenditure policies and deregulation and privatization are so great that essentially *everyone* would be better off. Ideas matter; and as these ideas have increasingly come to be discredited, even in the capitalist societies where they had dominated, they will have less sway elsewhere, and this may make the more equalitarian social and political equilibrium more sustainable.

Unfortunately, it is only possible in this volume to hint at these possibilities, what it would take to create a society with a far higher degree of equality—in all the relevant dimensions, and in a sustainable way. This book does, however, lay important groundwork for taking the next step in realizing such possibilities.[30]

8 Balancing of Centrifugal and Centripetal Forces

Another question, related to that about the inevitability of inequality in capitalism, is whether capitalism is necessarily marked by *ever-increasing inequality*, in the absence of government intervention, or whether there is an equilibrium income and wealth distribution.

This book takes the latter view: at any moment of time there is an equilibrium toward which the economy is converging. The equilibrium results from a balance between *centrifugal* forces pulling the economy apart, and *centripetal* forces limiting the ever-increasing inequality.[31] These centrifugal forces include the randomness of good fortune and the ability of the wealthy to use their wealth and connections to obtain higher returns than available to others. Of course, these centrifugal and centripetal forces are always changing. In this view, central to understanding recent increases in income and wealth inequality is examining the changes in the centrifugal and centripetal forces. It is, in fact, easy to identify changes in policies and in the structure of the economy that have weakened the centripetal forces and strengthened the centrifugal forces, resulting in the economy moving (rapidly) toward a new equilibrium with greater inequality. The observed increase in inequality reflects a transition from the old equilibrium to the new; but the fact that inequality has increased in recent decades does not mean that it is ever-increasing.

30 I also explore these possibilities briefly in *People, Power, and Profits* (Stiglitz 2019a).

31 Earlier, Champernowne (1953) (who was still teaching at Cambridge when I went there as a graduate student, and with whom I interacted as I began my own work in this area) provided a set of conditions on the mobility matrix—describing the probability that the child of an individual in say the *i*th decile would have wealth in the *j*th decile—which would generate an equilibrium wealth distribution with the shape observed. But he did not provide any structural model explaining why those conditions should be satisfied, nor did he provide any analysis of the relationship between income (wage) distributions and wealth distributions. This was the contribution of my 1966, 1969c, and 1978 papers as well as that of Bevan (1974) and Bevan and Stiglitz (1979), investigating the evolution of the distribution of wealth as families transmitted wealth to their heirs, with bequests depending both on inheritances, wages, and the return to capital. (See Chapters 8, 9, and 33 below.) At a technical level, we also introduced the use of diffusion stochastic differential equations. Since then there has been further work in this area, noted in the introduction to Part II.

Similarly, understanding why the U.S. is marked by greater inequalities than other advanced countries is largely a matter of understanding why the rules and policies in the U.S. enhance the centrifugal forces and weaken the centripetal forces. So too policy centers around identifying changes that would strengthen the centripetal forces and weaken the centrifugal ones. This book argues that there are a host of changes in policies that could reverse the growth of inequality, creating a more equalitarian society.

By contrast, the central tenant in Piketty's work (2014), is that capitalism (without government intervention) is marked by ever-increasing inequality: the wealthy transfer large amounts to their children, a process which leads, he suggests, to their getting an ever-increasing share of national income when the rate of return on capital is greater than the rate of growth of the economy—what he describes as the normal state of the capitalist system.

I had considered a very similar dynamic—the possibility that, for a time, the wealth of the wealthy would grow so fast that there would be increasing income and wealth inequality—in my earlier work (1969b, 1978) and in work with David L. Bevan (Bevan and Stiglitz, 1979).[32] In this work, we concluded that there were strong forces limiting the growth of wealth inequality. One such force was a diminution in the marginal return to capital (under the law of diminishing returns) as the capitalists' capital accumulates relative to output or labor. Eventually the rate of return would fall to a low enough level that the rate of growth of capitalists' capital was equal to or lower than the growth of the economy—and inequality would stop increasing. In this sense, Piketty's analysis is not internally coherent.

We had not centered our attention on the forces for growing inequality that Piketty had emphasized for two other reasons. First, we noted other forces limiting the growth of inequality, including (a) the division of wealth among multiple heirs; and (b) the regression toward the mean in abilities. Secondly, it was hard to account for the increase in inequality that began to appear in the latter part of the twentieth century by changes in the variables that are at the center of Piketty's analysis—if anything, an increase in retirement/lifetime savings by workers reduced the gap in savings between capitalists and workers. There were, however, a host of changes that had increased the centrifugal forces that we had identified and reduced the centripetal forces. Hence, we thought our framework did a better job of accounting for what was observed, and gave accordingly better, and more comprehensive, guidance on how to contain the growth of inequality. Piketty's analysis focused on one central instrument, reducing capitalists' return on capital through capital taxation. Chapter 13 shows, in fact, that unless well designed, such taxes can be counterproductive, explaining why such taxation needs be accompanied by public expenditures.

Piketty did not refute our analytics, but rather argued that *historically* the rate of return has remained larger than the rate of growth. In this view, the period after World War II was a historical anomaly, the result of social solidarity brought on by World War II. I believe it is correct to call attention to the differences between that era and that of the last 40 years. But the differences entail more than lower taxes on capital (on which Piketty focuses). They also involve changes in the structure of the economy and the rules governing it. We may have only limited scope in undoing the effects of changing structures, but there is considerable scope for undoing the rules—including the rules that have increased corporate market

[32] Reprinted here in slightly modified form as Chapters 8, 9, and 33.

power and weakened that of workers—and adopting new rules that at least partially undo the effects of structural changes in the economy contributing to growing inequality.

Piketty's analysis, looking at the *seeming* returns to capital, confounds what are two distinct kinds of economic returns—the returns to investments in productive capital, in capital goods, plants and equipment, and R&D; and monopoly profits and other forms of what economists refer to as "rents." I argue that the seemingly high current returns to capital include significant amounts of rents, including returns associated with the exercise of market power, and that increases in these rents have more than offset decreases in the returns to real investments, so that overall returns have not diminished.[33] But if this is so, it means, for instance, that stronger antitrust laws and better labor legislation could lower the returns obtained by capitalists, thereby reducing inequality.[34]

This analysis is important not only because it gives us an understanding of the growth of inequalities but also, as we have repeatedly emphasized, of what we might do about it. For instance, based on his analysis, Piketty (2014) argued that to curb ever-increasing inequality we must impose global capital taxes that significantly reduce the return to capital (so the after-tax return is below the rate of growth). Since the prospect of imposing such global taxes is dim, the prospects for curbing the growth of inequality—in this perspective—are bleak. In contrast, the work presented in this volume shows not only that ever-increasing inequality is *not* an inevitable feature of capitalism, but also, as we have noted, that Piketty's solution may even make matters worse, as it could lead to decreased capital accumulation, which in turn would lead to lower wages. A capital tax with proceeds distributed as lump sum payments to workers, while seemingly equalitarian, leads to greater inequality, but a capital tax with proceeds invested in human capital in an equalitarian way leads to more equality. At the same time, I present a variety of policies that can reduce inequality from the extremes of today, by, for instance, changing key rules governing the market economy.

9 Capital Accumulation vs. Innovation

Focusing on one major divide in society, that between "capital" and "labor," we have already noted a major set of disagreements—between those who see the return to capital largely as simply its competitive return, corresponding to the social marginal productivity of capital, and those who see much of the income of capitalists as derived from one form of exploitation or another, and affected greatly by the rules of the game that affect permissible levels of exploitation and relative bargaining powers.

But there is another somewhat more subtle and complex distinction: between those who see the relative shares of workers and capitalists as largely driven by *accumulation*—driven

[33] In economics, the term capital has multiple meanings. We refer to investments in, say, machines and factories as capital investments. This is real capital. But we also refer to an individual's financial wealth as their capital. The returns to financial wealth can include capital gains. The value of a monopoly is the value of the entire stream of returns it earns, which includes the return on its physical capital, any capital gains it might earn on any assets it sells, and its monopoly profits.

[34] Matters are still more complicated: observed returns to capital also include returns to bearing risk. Improvements in financial markets should have led to lower returns to risk bearing, further decreasing the average return received by capitalists—weakening the force for inequality that is at the center of Piketty's analysis. But changes in the rules of the game may have had just the opposite effect: capital market, financial market, and trade liberalization may have exposed countries to greater risk, thereby increasing the amount of risk to be borne and accordingly the risk premia. See Chapter 10.

by changes in the relative supplies of capital and labor determined by how much individuals and corporations save—versus those who see it as largely a result of *innovation* and the effect of innovation on the relative returns of capital and labor. If, for instance, firms invest in labor replacing robots, then wages will fall. One perspective focuses on the determinants of savings; the other on the determinants of the nature of innovation—whether there is a focus on saving labor or capital. Earlier work (such as that of Robert M. Solow) focused on accumulation, with innovation "fixed," so that changes in the savings rate led to changes in the long-run scarcity of capital and the distribution of income.[35]

But the pace and nature of innovation is clearly not fixed. It is *endogenous*, a result, at least in part, of decisions made by firms: how much to innovate, and on what to spend scarce R&D resources. Most vividly, as attention has focused on climate change, there has been a burst of innovation in renewable energy. So too, if capital is scarcer—as reflected in a higher share—it will induce firms to innovate more to increase the productivity of capital. That increase in productivity will in turn at least partly offset the effects of the decrease in savings that led to the increased share of capital.

We establish, though, a stronger result. *In the long-run equilibrium*, it is the innovation process itself which drives the economy and determines the share of capital—that, and nothing else (at least in these simple models.)[36] Everything else adjusts to accommodate. Explaining how and why this occurs is somewhat complex and is therefore postponed until later in the book (Chapter 17).

10 Classes, Meritocracy, the 1%, and "We're All Middle Class Now"

A dominant view in the nineteenth century and well into the twentieth was that society was divided into classes, with relatively little mobility from, say, the lower to the upper. The lower classes relied on their wages to live and spent most of what they earned; the upper class lived off inherited wealth. These socioeconomic classes differed in many other ways: in the UK, one could identify an individual's class background by his speech. Their interests and preferences differed, too.

By the middle of the twentieth century, at least in the U.S., the conception grew that, with few exceptions, everyone was middle class: it was as if there was one happy family, with small distinctions between lower- and upper-middle classes. That, like the American Dream and the notion that the U.S. was a land of equal opportunity, was a myth. Statistics on the country's inequalities, a selection of which is presented later in this book, show the extent to which that was so. But it was a useful myth, especially in engendering the kind

[35] The impact of the decrease in the amount of capital relative to labor depends on how easy it is to substitute labor for capital. If it is very hard to substitute, then wages will fall a lot, and so the share of labor will fall. Technically, we measure the ease of substitution by the elasticity of substitution, and if that elasticity is less than unity, the share of labor falls.

[36] There are two kinds of technical progress—that which increases the productivity of labor and that which increases the productivity of capital. Which is chosen by the economy is determined by the relative shares. It has long been recognized that long run equilibrium requires that there be *only* labor augmenting technological change, that is, the economy *must* "choose" to have pure labor-augmenting progress—so the long-run distribution of income must be that which induces the economy to make that choice. Accordingly, changes in the distribution of income in the long run (in the competitive model) are determined by changes in the share required to induce pure labor augmenting technological change.

of solidarity needed in time of war. It was useful, too, for the elites, for it took the attention of ordinary citizens away from their current plight and helped them focus on *what might be.* It even helped in engendering support for policies that were of benefit to the elite, such as the reduction of the estate tax.[37] With the high threshold of $11.7 million in 2021 (below which no inheritance taxes are due)—compared to $600,000 just two decades ago, in 1997—few Americans are at risk of paying the tax;[38] many have nevertheless acquiesced to its reduction. (Despite its high threshold and the many loopholes that enable tax avoidance, the tax nonetheless generates substantial revenue because of the extremes of the country's inequalities in wealth.)

When I wrote my 2011 *Vanity Fair* article, "Of the 1%, by the 1%, for the 1%," I wanted to highlight these myths, emphasizing that those at the top had a disproportionate share of income, wealth, and political power. It was too much of a stretch to say that these individuals were *just* middle class.

A related myth developed: that those at the top got there out of merit. We are not like "Old Europe" with its inherited aristocracy; we are a "meritocracy." But as I explain below, the chance of getting into that meritocracy for those with parents at the top is so much greater than for those with parents in the bottom that the U.S. is more akin to a largely inherited plutocracy. In this plutocracy, those with wealth typically "work"—they are not the idle rich, the clippers of coupons, the caricature of the nineteenth-century society. But even the nature of their work sets them apart from those in the rest of society.

The models presented here, for the most part, take a narrow economic perspective on these issues. They explain the "fat tail" distributions, in which so much of the wealth is in the hands of those at the top. Some of the models generate the high correlation between wages and wealth that have been observed in the data. In this way, they stand in marked contrast to the "class models" (including that of Piketty) where wages are irrelevant for capitalists.

For the most part, the models here do not attribute the differences in wealth to differences in "behavior," for instance, higher savings rate, as suggested by standard class analysis. And if there are differences in behavior, they are more the consequence of differences in wealth than the other way around—individuals save more when they become wealthy.[39] But almost surely, an approach such as taken in this book (and in virtually all of the economics literature) that looks solely at economic determinants of behavior—how behavior is driven by income and wealth—underestimates the role of the social transmission of advantages and disadvantages, which is at the core of perspectives that emphasize class.[40] As a major strand in twenty-first-century behavioral economics (Hoff and Stiglitz, 2016; Demiritt, Hoff, and Stiglitz, forthcoming) emphasizes, preferences and behavior are

[37] And its actual elimination for one year, 2010.

[38] The top tax rates have also come down, from 55% to 40%. During World War II and the years afterwards, including the periods with the fastest economic growth, the top marginal tax rate was nearly 80%.

[39] See, in particular, the discussion in Chapter 11.

[40] Early work focusing on growth and distribution, such as that of Kaldor (1955a), Uzawa (1961, 1963), Pasinetti (1962), and Stiglitz (1967) took an explicitly class-based approach. The contrast between these approaches, and that of Solow (1956), which ignored the role of distribution in aggregate behavior, is noteworthy. For a long time, the mainstream of macroeconomics seems to have followed Solow, especially with representative agent models; but eventually, attention had to be paid to the large fractions of the population that were credit constrained—with aggregate behavior more consistent with the older class models than the representative agent models. See, for example, the HANK models (Kaplan, Moll, and Violante, 2018). These models incorporate credit rationing, the importance of which had, of course, been recognized by an earlier generation of macro-models. See,

endogenous—shaped by those around us, by our society—and there may be certain patterns that give rise to higher incomes for the individual (e.g., greater thrift, more focus on education),[41] while other patterns lower the incomes of others (e.g., discrimination).

Our educational system, the basis of our meritocracy and our system of opportunity, may in fact play a central role in the preservation and amplification of our inequalities, both because access to the institutions of higher learning that signify "merit" is disproportionately limited to the children of those with high income and education; and because those institutions not only provide connections that enhance later opportunities, but also help share preferences and behavior in ways that sustain their economic position. The central role played by meritocracy in the perpetuation of inequalities explains, in turn, the correlations between wealth and wages—in form, it is different from classical class analysis, but in substance not.

In short, while traditional class analysis does not provide a good account of economic inequality in the U.S. and most other advanced countries today, it is wrong to pretend that there are not important distinctions—the most important separating those at the *very* top from the rest. And while much of the differences in behavior (say savings or investing in their children) are a result of the economic position of those at the very top, the economic and social position of their parents matters as well.

11 Beyond Economics: The Social Implications of Inequality

This volume focuses mostly on the economics of inequality, describing the origins of economic inequalities, their consequences, and what can be done about them. But as the above discussion hints, the consequences of inequalities, especially when they reach extremes, go well beyond economics: they affect the nature of democracy and society. Especially when inequalities arise from exploitation, there is a moral dimension that cannot be ignored. The fact that I say little about these issues in this book does not mean that I think they are unimportant. Rather, it is that I have discussed them elsewhere. This book focuses on the analytics of inequality. The following paragraphs encapsulate some of the key aspects of the social dimensions of inequality and elaborate on the discussion of the preceding section.

Traditional economics assumes that decision-makers have exogenous preferences (that is, they're just given at birth, unaffected by one's parents and surrounding) and behave rationally. However, sociologists, social psychologists, and behavioral economists[42]

for example, Greenwald and Stiglitz (1987a, 1988b, 1990b) and Stiglitz and Weiss (1992), but seemingly forgotten in the interim.

More recently, Rinaldo and Milanovich (2020) have tried to distinguish among societies on the basis of the correlation between wages and wealth. In the extreme version of the class-based models referred to earlier, workers have no wealth and those with wealth have no wage income. In the Solovian/representative agent models, wealth and wages are perfectly correlated. Rinaldo and Milanovich suggest that western Europe and Northern America are less class based than other regions. This downplays the role of wealth in meritocracies in acquiring high paying jobs in, say, the U.S., the extent to which wealth inequalities are perpetuated through meritocracy, and the differences in the magnitudes in wealth inequalities and their consequences across societies.

[41] This, of course, was the gist of Max Weber's famous 1905 work *The Protestant Ethic and the Spirit of Capitalism*.

[42] Especially what is sometimes called "strand two," deriving its roots from sociology and social psychology and emphasizing that preferences are shaped by our culture and society, including the nature of the inequalities within it. See Hoff and Stiglitz (2016) and Demeritt and Hoff (2018).

acknowledge that society shapes what individuals want and how they think and have documented that the socio-economic position of one's parents affects preferences, cognition, social norms, and societal divides and interactions. How we see the world and how we behave are shaped by our society and our place within it, even as individuals shape society.

There is in particular increasing evidence that societies with greater inequality, and greater *inherited* inequalities, differ in important ways from societies with less inequality because of the impact of inequality on the behavior of individuals within these societies—both those at the top and the bottom.

There are multiple social mechanisms through which societal inequalities increase. A person's beliefs about his or her relative standing (which is affected by parents' relative standing), beliefs about competence (which is affected by poverty), and perceptions of others' perceptions of oneself affect aspirations, how immediate rewards are weighed against those that might accrue in the future (referred to as "present bias"), and the willingness to take risks. Large disparities between groups in parental wealth and income can lead to large disparities between groups in perceptions of own competencies and in aspirations. Importantly, these differences in perceptions and aspirations have consequences for individual choices, leading to behavior that reinforces inequalities.

There are other behavioral consequences of inequality: As we noted earlier, those who grow up wealthy may have a sense of entitlement and may be more prone to break the rules.[43] A society cannot function well, of course, if the rich and powerful think they are above the law.

At the same time, poverty—including relative poverty (being born at the bottom in a highly unequal society)—affects performance and social outcomes through multiple channels that sociologists and behavioral economists consider but which traditional economics omits.

Most obviously, poverty leads to stress. A central constraint recognized in behavioral economics but left out of standard economics is our limited bandwidth (cognitive capacity). With more resources devoted to day-to-day survival, the poor have fewer resources available to think about the long run. They have fewer mental resources available for making the kinds of "good" decisions that advance their interests over the long run.[44]

There is a literature, too, that emphasizes that individual well-being is related to an individual's *relative* standing (for example, consumption or income relative to the average consumption or income).[45] A concern about relative standing may lead to excessive consumption—and debt. As a result, individuals who are attempting to keep up with the Joneses experience high levels of stress.[46]

[43] Piff, Stancato, Côté et al. (2012) provide evidence that the rich violate traffic laws more than others do and engage in other anti-social behavior more.

[44] Shah, Mullainathan, and Shafir (2012); Mani, Mullainathan, Shafir, and Zhao (2013); Mullainathan and Shafir (2013). A large literature has developed on this subject in recent years, documenting the effects and attempting to understand better what drives them. For instance, poverty impairs the quality of decisions (Haushofer and Fehr (2014)).

[45] In macroeconomics, it goes back to Duesenberry's relative income hypothesis, which he used to explain savings behavior (Duesenberry 1949). More recent work on the behavioral implications of this hypothesis for labor supply and savings includes Stiglitz (2008d) and Arrow and Dasgupta (2009). Robert Frank (2005) has explored these and many other implications.

[46] For a discussion of related ideas and empirical evidence, see, for instance, Palley (2008) and Bricker, Krimmel, and Ramcharan (2020). Many have argued that excessive debt played a role in the 2008 crisis. See Sufi and Mian (2015).

The disparities may also lead to a sense of grievance. Together, these factors may undermine poor individuals' sense of agency and that too may aggravate disparities in performance.[47] Inequality may thus decrease the performance of those at the bottom, without improving the performance of those at the top. Indeed, the performance at the top may also be impaired.

Large inherited inequalities also affect social interactions in ways that can make them self-perpetuating. Not surprisingly, large and growing income inequality has led in the U.S. (and elsewhere) to extensive and increasing income segregation, with high-income families living in different locations than those with lower incomes, with effects that are larger for Black families than for white families.[48] With education provided locally, income segregation tends to create large differentials in educational quality, which themselves create large differentials in opportunity and outcomes.

Economic segregation also means, of course, less social interaction across income classes—less intermarriage and less understanding between individuals who differ in economic background. There is evidence from a natural experiment that regular interactions in small, fixed groups of young people working together to achieve common goals changed the behavior of rich children; they became more generous, less discriminatory, and more willing to play with poor children.[49] In the absence of government intervention, increasing income segregation makes such interactions rarer.

These aspects of societal inequality—and their role in the transmission of inequalities across generations—are fundamental to understanding the perpetuation of inequality in our society. And yet, as important as they are, they necessarily will be given short shrift in the theoretical formulations that follow.

12 The Origins of Inequality and What to Do about It: A Taxonomy

This book develops a set of theoretical models providing insights into the forces that give rise to inequality. But, of course, the real objective is insights into what can be done to reduce inequality. When I began my study of inequality, the focus was on redistributive taxation. But especially in recent years, the set of interventions has expanded greatly.

Two broad distinctions have proven useful. First, there are policies that affect the *market* distribution of income. Second, there are those that entail *redistribution*, either through taxation or expenditure policies. Programs like social insurance, safety net programs, and publicly provided health care have large impacts on what matters—the distribution of

[47] Of course, such inequalities relate not just to income and wealth, but also to caste, race, and ethnicity. See, for example, Steele and Aronson (1995); Hoff and Pandey (2006, 2014); and Hoff and Stiglitz (2010).

That perceptions of unfairness can lead to less work effort is one of the pillars of efficiency wage theory, with adverse effects on "morale," as we noted in fn. 25. This can be especially so if there is a perception of discrimination. See Stiglitz (1973d, 1974d) and Part III.F. below.

[48] See Reardon and Bischoff (2011).

[49] The evidence emerged from a decision of the Supreme Court in New Delhi that required elite private schools in Delhi that exist on land leased from the state in perpetuity at highly subsidized rates to reserve 20% of seats for students from households earning under $2,000 per year (Rao, 2019). The elite schools had to admit a randomly selected set of poor applicants and could not charge them any fees. The policy changed the composition of cohorts that began preschool in 2007 and later.

well-being.[50] Even regulatory policies can have large redistributive consequences: it is the poor who often suffer the most from environmental degradation.

There are, of course, a myriad of policies that affect the market distribution of income (sometimes referred to as "pre-distribution" policies).[51] Again, we can divide those into two categories: those that affect the distribution of the ownership of assets, and those that affect returns.

A key determinant of the distribution of assets—one on which my research has been particularly focused—is the intergenerational transmission of assets, and more generally, of advantages and disadvantages: the transfer of human and financial capital, of connections and social capital, and even modes of behavior that lend themselves to economic success. We discuss here too the countervailing forces, the public provision of education and inheritance taxation. While those with more financial capital tend also to have more human capital—and pass those advantages onto their children—public policy can weaken these links.

Given the distribution of these "assets," we think of market forces—the law of supply and demand—as determining the returns on the assets and thus the distribution of income. But here again there are two approaches to which our earlier discussion has already called attention. There is, for one, the standard competitive model. Then there are more recent approaches—including some I have emphasized throughout my work—which highlights market imperfections, and especially market power and the rents it generates, whether that market power arises from asymmetries in information or barriers to entry.

As we observed above, pervasive discrimination (ethnic, racial, and gender) has played an important role in societal inequalities in many countries. And it has been a particularly key feature of American inequality. Understanding discrimination takes us, of course, beyond the standard competitive economic model, as the discussion later in this book makes clear;[52] addressing these inequalities may require policies that go beyond standard interventions in competitive economies.

Whether the economy is or is not perfectly competitive, *rules* matter. As Chapter 5 emphasizes, markets don't exist in a vacuum. Rules affect whether firms are allowed to pollute or to discriminate, what happens when a firm or an individual goes bankrupt, who gets to make decisions within a firm, and the extent to which workers are exposed to competition from cheap labor abroad. They affect whether firms can collude to raise prices, whether they can exploit consumers and get away with it, and whether workers can get together to countervail corporate market power. Thus, rules and regulations are an important set of instruments affecting the distribution of income and wealth—and even more so, the distribution of well-being.

Traditional distribution theory largely takes the demand and supply curves for labor and capital as given, but they are greatly affected not only by rules and regulations, but also by

[50] Formally, the book is about the distribution of income and wealth, but well-being is what we should really be interested in—including health and security. For extended discussions, see Stiglitz, Sen, and Fitoussi (2010); Stiglitz, Fitoussi, and Durand (2019a, 2019b).

[51] Redistributive taxes can, of course, affect the market distribution of income, and the design of taxation needs to take that into account, which early work in optimal taxation failed to do. But see Stiglitz (1982e, 1998a, and especially Chapter 19 below).

In the policy arena, the distinction between redistribution and pre-distribution is made in Chapters 5 and 19 (based on Stiglitz (1998c) and Hacker and Pierson (2011)).

[52] See Chapters 34 and 35, and the introductory discussion to that part of the book.

tax and expenditure policies, and indeed every aspect of public policy. A standard aspect of public sector economics is to analyze the *incidence* of such policies, that is, how they may induce behavioral changes that affect relative returns. For instance, a tax on capital may so reduce the supply of capital that workers may be worse, even if the proceeds of the tax are redistributed to them. This volume describes instances of this—but also describes how there may be packages of policies, such as a tax on capital with the proceeds spent on education, that unambiguously increase workers' well-being. The composition of public expenditures may affect the market distribution of income. The composition may do so directly, as it affects demand for different factors of production, and indirectly, as it elicits changes in the demand and supply of private goods by market participants—at the same time that it directly impacts the well-being of the recipients. Moreover, government programs, like the public option for health care, can affect the competitive landscape, and thus market power and rents.

One set of determinants of inequality that has not received sufficient attention is the institutions for the sharing and shifting of risk and the policies that affect the magnitude of risks that society faces. Some individuals are going to have "good luck," others bad. Obviously, inequalities in well-being at a given moment are affected by the extent to which those who are experiencing bad fortune can obtain insurance; markets, for reasons that are now well understood, do a far from perfect job in providing insurance, and in most advanced countries, social insurance plays an important role.[53] With imperfect insurance, seemingly random events can have important consequences for the determination of the distribution of income and wealth, and the models of this book help explain why. By the same token, public policy can affect the extent to which markets *create* and *manage* risks, and the extent to which risks are socially absorbed. The failure to regulate the financial sector adequately exposed the country to enormous risk. So too, in developing countries and emerging markets, liberalizing capital markets has exposed those countries to high levels of risk. Risk has a direct effect on inequality in increasing dispersions in income; but it has a systemic indirect effect—in markets, those bearing risk—disproportionately the rich—get rewarded for doing so. Increasing risk thus leads to an increase in these individuals' income, increasing inequality.

Another area that has not received sufficient attention, which I discuss extensively in this volume, is the role of public policy in steering technology.[54] There has been much concern of late about the threat of technology replacing labor, increasing unemployment—especially among workers of limited skills—or reducing their wages. But changes in technology don't just happen. They are, especially in modern economies, shaped by public policy, for instance tax and monetary policies, which affect the relative cost of labor and capital, and government research policies. Such policies can encourage more resources to be devoted to enhancing the productivity of workers or to "saving the planet" from environmental catastrophe, rather than replacing unskilled labor through robotization, driving down unskilled wages or driving up unemployment among those with less skills.

In short, *every* aspect of public policy that touches on *any* aspect of economic behavior or individual well-being has distributive consequences, both direct and indirect. The

[53] For the limitations in insurance markets, see, for example, Rothschild and Stiglitz, 1976 and Arnott and Stiglitz, 1988b, 1990. For the role of social insurance and government in risk-bearing, see Chapter 37 below and Stiglitz, 1993a.

[54] See Chapters 17 and 18 below and Korinek and Stiglitz (2020).

economic theorists' comparative advantage is identifying these multitudinous effects. We have more instruments at our disposal for addressing inequality than we may have imagined.

13 Using the Taxonomy to Understand Increasing Inequality

The taxonomy I've just provided is useful not only for thinking of various interventions through which increasing inequality can be contained, but in providing us a lens through which we can understand the marked increase in inequality over the past half century in the U.S. and many other countries. As Chapter 10 emphasizes, many of the models constructed in the middle of the last century were designed to explain the constancy of the relative shares of income between capital and labor. By contrast, those presented here are constructed to help us explain not only the changes in the shares but the increased dispersion of income and wealth. While this book does not attempt to parse out the contribution of the different factors—in fact, the models show that different factors are so inextricably linked that such a parsing is not possible—the analysis calls attention to several aspects of our changing economy and society, several of which have not been given the attention they deserve in the empirical literature explaining the growth of inequality. That literature has, not surprisingly, called attention to those factors (like skill-biased technological change or globalization) that might shift the demand and supply curves, and thus affect relative returns to different factors in a competitive economy. But that literature neither explained the direction of technological change[55] nor how the rules of the economy, such as those governing globalization, shaped the growing inequality.[56]

There have been changes in the structure of the economy, in the structure of society, and in policies, themselves endogenous and affected by politics, which in turn is affected greatly by economic inequalities, as we have repeatedly noted. Economic inequalities inevitably get translated into political inequalities. The models not only identify the effects of policy changes (like reduced tax progressivity) on inequality *today*, but also trace out the evolution of the impacts over time, as a new, more unequal equilibrium wealth distribution is created.

In *People, Power, and Profits: Progressive Capitalism for an Age of Discontent* (Stiglitz, 2019a), and in several of the chapters below, I argue that one of the major sources of the increase in inequality is the growth of rents, and especially rents associated with market power and exploitation (see also Philippon, 2019). This increase in market power is partly a result of changing judicial interpretations of competition laws, partly a result of a failure to enforce these laws, and partly a failure of these laws to keep up with the changes in the economy—the new threats to competition, including innovation in how to better create market barriers and amplify market power. The structural changes in the economy, including the shift from manufacturing to a service-sector economy in the last three decades or so, not only affect demands for different factors but also the competitive landscape, in numerous ways sketched out (briefly) in the chapters below. Forces interact: the

[55] Emphasized in Chapters 17 and 18.

[56] A subject to which much of my earlier work was devoted. See, for instance, Stiglitz (2002b, 2018a, 2019a, 2008c, 2018d) and Stiglitz and Charlton (2005).

move toward a service sector economy would, on its own, have made wage compression (which reduces differences between wages paid to workers of different skills) and unionization more difficult; but globalization, as it was managed (as I argued in *Globalization and its Discontents Revisited* (Stiglitz, 2018a)), weakened workers' bargaining power and made unionization still more difficult; but then on top of all of this, the influence of corporate money in politics led to labor legislation weakening still further workers' bargaining power and making unionization even more difficult.

So too the move to a knowledge economy and the rapid changes in the economy may increase the value of information; and if that is so, those who are more connected, and can otherwise obtain better information will do better. The returns on capital of the wealthier may be higher than the rest, and this can lead to sustained inequalities. With the differentials increasing, wealth inequalities will increase.

Strikingly, as the models in this volume illustrate and some commentators have observed, some of the changes in society that might have been thought to have brought about greater equality, at least of opportunity, have had just the opposite effect. Meritocracy seems better than inherited privilege; but when "merit" is associated with educational credentials that are, because of their costs, mainly accessible to the children of the rich, meritocracy creates a system which facilitates the transmission of advantage from one generation to another. The lack of support for good public education, as well as the curtailing of other equalitarian health, education, and nutrition policies—all part of the cutback in the role of the state—all weaken the most important force countervailing inequality. At the same time, the assortive mating associated with attendance at elite educational institutions leads to still more inequality in the distribution of household income—and over time, to even greater inequalities in the equilibrium distribution of income and wealth.

Recent decades have been marked not only by an increase in inequality, but also by a slowing of the rate of growth—particularly striking given that we are supposed to be in an era of innovation. The theories presented here suggest that this is not just an accident of history: As we noted earlier in this Introduction, equality and growth and efficiency are complements. Societies with unequal access to education are not using their human resources efficiently. Societies with high levels of exploitation—with high rents generated, for instance, from market power—are not efficient. And, as the chapters in this volume illustrate, the growth of "rent-capital"—the capitalized value of rents, regardless of their source—crowds out productive capital.

These are just some of the ways in which the models in this book shed light on the marked changes in the economy over the past half century.

14 Principal Insights

It is always difficult to summarize a work such as this into a few paragraphs: if I could, there presumably would not have been the need for a book of this length. Still, it is important to grasp the central insights, which will be developed and embellished in the subsequent chapters:

1. **The best way to understand the observed growth of inequality is as a movement from one equilibrium income and wealth distribution to another.** In

equilibrium, there is a balance between centrifugal forces (pulling the economy apart and leading to greater inequality) and centripetal forces (pushing it together, reducing inequality). A framework for understanding what has moved us toward a more inegalitarian equilibrium is to identify changes in these forces during the last third of a century—the increases in the centrifugal forces and the diminution in the centripetal forces. And a framework for thinking about policies to create a more equal society consists of asking how we can enhance the centripetal forces and weaken the centrifugal forces (Chapter 12). There are some natural stabilizing forces, preventing ever-increasing wealth inequalities—if the capital accumulated by capitalists were to grow faster than national income, with diminishing returns, eventually the return to capital would decrease. Bad policy—regressive taxation—could overcome this natural equalizing force, enabling ever-increasing inequality. And there are some limitations in the convergence process, such that even without stochastic returns, wealth inequalities may be preserved: the rich may be able to obtain higher returns on their investments (through investments in information or insider information), with wealth begetting more wealth, and the rich may have significantly higher savings rates than ordinary workers (Chapter 11). But even here, there is not normally ever-increasing divergence: there is an equilibrium wealth distribution.

One of the ways in which these dynamic growth models with nonlinear savings and returns functions differ from the standard macroeconomic models is that there is not a unique steady state equilibrium—indeed, there are, even in the simplest of models, an infinity of steady states, each with a different wealth distribution. History matters—it can determine which of these equilibria the economy is in. And policy matters, too—it can move the economy to an equilibrium with less inequality.

2. **The analysis of the determinants of wealth and income inequality is naturally decomposed into the determinants of inequalities in factor endowments and an analysis of the returns to factors.** The latter is further decomposed into (a) the determinants of factor shares (labor versus capital) and of skill premiums (relative wages) in well-functioning competitive labor markets, including the role of technological change and international economic integration; and (b) other determinants of differentials in factor returns, including market imperfections and the rules governing the economy. Earlier discussions of inequality focused primarily on relative factor shares (the distribution between "capital" and "labor") and the "skill premium," and largely in the context of competitive markets. These earlier discussions' analysis is an ingredient in our broader analysis, which includes a simultaneous dynamic analysis of the distribution of factor endowments and factor returns; and in the latter, we place much more emphasis on market failures and institutional design and changes.

The inequality-induced institutional changes and changes in the rules of the game began apace as part of the Reagan–Thatcher revolution. Every aspect of the market game—including the conduct of monetary policy, and especially globalization—has changed in ways contributing to greater inequality. Rewriting the rules once again could lead to a marked increase in the equality of market incomes, imposing less of a burden on redistributive policies.

For the most part, I do not address the origins of the institutional changes,[57] nor do I examine the changes in any detail (though I do discuss them in Chapter 5). Instead, I focus on the *consequences* of these changes: how wage inequalities to which they may give rise get translated into wealth inequalities, through the intergenerational transmission of financial wealth, leading to the perpetuation of income differences, and, through the transfer of advantages intertemporally through human capital, to even larger wage differences. In principle, equal access to good public education could partially offset this effect. But in practice, in the U.S., it appears that unequal provision of public education may reinforce it and may increasingly being doing so—another illustration of the importance of institutional design and change.[58]

The next several points focus on some of the key determinants of factor returns going beyond those relevant in the standard competitive model.

3. **Changes in technology (such as skill-biased technological change) cannot explain the large gap between the growth of average worker productivity and average compensation.** Moreover, there are natural market forces that should limit such skill-biased technological change: as the share of unskilled labor decreases, the incentive for skill-biased technical change decreases. At the same time, we show that it is not so much capital accumulation and savings and the elasticity of substitution between capital and labor (the extent to which an increase in capital relative to labor decreases the share of labor, as emphasized by Robert Solow) or differences in savings propensities (as emphasized by Nicholas Kaldor), but the process of innovation itself that determines the long-term *factor* distribution of income.[59] But it also needs to be recognized that the market itself is not efficient in the allocation of resources to research and development: there are excessive efforts at replacing labor, leading to a too-high unemployment rate and too-low wages (and correspondingly insufficient resources devoting to addressing climate and other environmental problems). Again, government policies may either exacerbate or mitigate these market distortions.[60]
4. **There are multiple determinants of changes in wage inequalities.** Skill-biased technological change is one possible determinant, but so are institutional changes, such as unionization and labor legislation, and policy changes, such as those governing globalization. Thus, this book is very much in the institutionalist tradition,

[57] Stiglitz, Abernathy, Hersh, et al. (2015) and Stiglitz, Stetter, Dougherty, et al. (2019) describes at length many of the key changes in the rules governing the economy over the past 40 years and their impacts. My earlier work tried both to show that institutions (like sharecropping in agriculture) mattered and to identify some of the forces giving rise to observed institutions. See, for instance, Stiglitz (1974b, 1975b) and Braverman and Stiglitz (1982, 1986a) and Chapters 25 and 26 below.

[58] Education also performs a screening role—differentiating the more able from the less able, and this screening role may be as or more important than human capital in giving rise to wage differences. To the extent that that is so, education may lead to more inequality and lower (net) output. See Stiglitz (1975a), Weiss (1988, 1995).

There are complex interactions between inequality, the availability of private education for the rich, and the political determination of expenditures on public education. See Stiglitz (1974h). There is now a rich literature exploring these questions more deeply, especially empirically. Space limitations prohibit giving it the attention it deserves.

[59] As we argued earlier in this introduction, *over the very long run* what is crucial in the determination of the relative share of labor may be the shape of "innovation frontier," the trade-off between labor and capital augmenting technological change. Changes in the innovation frontier drive changes in the distribution of income.

[60] These ideas are developed in Chapters 17 and 18.

in contrast to standard neoclassical economics, which often seemed to suggest that institutions don't matter—one just needed to look to "demand and supply." Institutions matter because of the host of often interrelated considerations typically excluded from neoclassical analysis: imperfections of information, incompleteness of markets (including risk markets), imperfections of competition, transactions costs, and a host of other market failures. Labor markets are far from perfectly competitive, and that's why workers' bargaining power is so important. By pitting American workers against low wage workers abroad, trade liberalization undermined workers' bargaining power, almost surely contributing to a lowering of wages.

5. **Not only has workers' bargaining power decreased, but corporate market power has increased.** These changes in power relationships have contributed to the increase in corporate profits and inequality. Changes in the structure of the economy (the move to the service sector economy) and changes in technology (network effects in the digital economy) have contributed to this outcome. Not only have competition laws failed to keep up with these changes—and with the innovativeness of corporations in creating, augmenting, and extending their market power—but also changes in the rules of the game, often through court decisions, and how they are enforced have given companies freer rein in the pursuit of market power. Moreover, policy and political economy have played a perverse role in at least some countries. Low corporate tax rates create greater incentives to engage in rent-seeking behavior. There may be multiple equilibria, one with progressive taxation and low rent-seeking, and another with less progressivity and more rent-seeking (Chapter 16).
6. **There has been a large increase in rents in the economy—land rents, intellectual property rents, and monopoly profits—and the increase in these rents has played an important role in the growth of inequality.** The source and consequences of the growth of these rents and their capitalized value are central to an understanding of the growth and consequences of inequality (Chapters 14 to 16)—points elaborated on below. At the same time, there are a large number of stylized facts describing the economy that are hard to plausibly reconcile with the standard competitive equilibrium model with just capital and labor, but are easy to understand once one extends the analysis to rents (Chapter 10).
7. **The increased market share of rents is an important contributor to the growth of inequality.** Ownership claims on rents are unequally distributed, leading to greater inequality in wealth today, a pattern reinforced over time, in subsequent generations, through the intergenerational transmission of advantage (Chapter 12). And with greater "rent-wealth," there will be lower levels of real investment, so wages will be lower than they otherwise would be (Chapter 13). The distinction between *wealth* and *capital* is central (Chapter 11). Wealth has been growing much more rapidly than capital; indeed, in some countries, there may even be a decrease in the ratio of capital to income and the ratio of capital to effective labor, helping to explain wage stagnation.[61]

[61] This distinction between wealth and capital helps explain the conundrums in Piketty's analysis. For a more extensive discussion, see the introduction to Part II.

8. **An important dimension of wealth inequality today is associated with the distinction between life-cycle savers and capitalists (dynastic savers).**[62] Even though today, workers, through their retirement funds, own a substantial amount of wealth, bequests—inherited wealth—remain important, with a significant fraction of the wealthy gaining a significant fraction of their wealth through inheritance (see Chapter 13). Capital and inheritance taxes, even with proceeds fully redistributed to workers, may leave workers worse off because of adverse incidence effects—a lower level of capital accumulation, and thus lower wages. But if the proceeds are invested in human capital and infrastructure, wealth inequality can be reduced (Chapter 19). At the same time, the increased importance of life cycle savings implies that the distributive consequences of certain policies are markedly different today than they were in an earlier era: it used to be that a lowering of interest rates helped borrowers (who were relatively poor) at the expense of lenders (who were relatively rich). Now, lowering interest rates has two additional effects, seen most evidently in the post-Great Recession policies of quantitative easing: retirees, depending on interest on government bonds were hurt; the wealthy, who own the overwhelming share of equities, were the great beneficiaries.
9. **Public policy affects income and wealth inequality in multiple ways.** Public policy affects not just relative supplies and demands, but the competitiveness of markets, relative market power, and the productivity of different factors. Loosening the reins to anticompetitive practices is one obvious example. Financial market liberalization may have provided more opportunity for banks to exploit the poor.[63] Moreover, this book's analysis shows how a lowering of collateral requirements or an increase in credit supply gives rise to an increase in land value, which directly benefits landowners, who are disproportionately the rich; and how loose monetary policy (such as quantitative easing) disproportionately benefits the owners of equity (the rich) at the expense of life-cycle savers, simply because of differences in the form in which they hold their wealth (Chapters 13 and 15). Moreover public policy affects the direction of innovation; while current policies encourage robotization and other changes that "save" labor and lead to lower wages, there are alternative policies which would have the opposite effect. And public policies can either aggravate or mitigate the intergenerational transmission of wealth and more broadly, of advantage and disadvantage. It will become clear that, in spite of rhetoric to the contrary, much of public policy exacerbates rather than reduces inequality.
10. **While some public policies in the past may have contributed to the increase in inequality, there is ample scope for policies to create a more egalitarian society.** Such remedies are possible even in the face of robotization, which so many seem to be dreading (Chapter 18). Earlier in this introduction, we provided a taxonomy of such policies, in particular, those that affected the distribution of market incomes (pre-distribution) and those that redistributed market incomes; those that changed the distribution of market income by changing asset ownership and those

[62] At least for some countries, there appears to be an increase in inherited inequality relative to life-cycle inequality (Bowles and Gintis (2002) and Piketty (2014)). But there is not unanimity about this conclusion. See, in particular, for the U.S., Wolff and Gittleman (2014). Our model enables us to ascertain the conditions under which either result might be expected.

[63] See, for instance Stiglitz (2010a).

that changed the returns to assets. For instance, beyond public investments and the role of government in setting the rules of the game, especially important are redistributive taxes (Chapters 19, 21, 32, 33, 36) and redistributive expenditure policies (Chapter 12, 19, 27, and 37), including investments in children and strong systems of social protection; macro-stabilization policies—it is the poor that bear the brunt of economic downturns (Chapters 30 and 31); and policies to confront discrimination (Chapters 34 and 35).

11. **Increasing equality may improve economic performance, as the discussion above has highlighted.** This is especially true of policies that reduce market power or that tax land rents, providing greater incentives for capital accumulation (Chapter 14), or which curb the artificial increase in land prices through the excessive expansion of credit and financial market liberalization (Chapter 15), or which enhance economic opportunity. Further benefits are attained through the reduction of "agency costs" that arise in the presence of excessive inequality (Chapters 24–26). Policies that contribute to an increase in equality of opportunity can also lead to an increase in equality of outcomes (equality of income and wealth). But as we emphasized earlier in this Introduction, a singular focus on opportunities is misguided: opportunities and outcomes cannot simply be separated. This book also provides an analytic framework for assessing whether one society is more equal than another, or one society has more equality of opportunity than another (Chapters 20–22). If we are to reduce the pervasive inequalities in our society, we must take a multi-pronged approach, doing what we can to reduce both inequalities in outcomes and inequalities in opportunities. And if we do so, in some of the ways suggested in this book, we are not only likely to see smaller disparities between the rich and poor, but better economic performance. I also believe it would lead to greater social cohesion and better functioning democracies—but demonstrating that would take us beyond the subject of this book.

This book thus provides a holistic but "high level" view of the inequalities in our society—a view which is more nuanced than either of the perspectives that prevailed in earlier eras: that they arose "naturally" from competitive forces, on the one hand, or from a power struggle between capitalists and workers—with the former typically prevailing—on the other. Market forces are at play—but they are shaped by power, expressed both within the economy and within politics, and with the two being intimately intertwined. Understanding the drivers of inequality in all of this complexity is essential—otherwise, there is the risk that well-intentioned policies will not only fail but could even backfire. But understanding the drivers of inequality in all of this complexity helps us see both the many factors that have contributed to its growth in recent decades and the multiple instruments that are available to turn the tide.

Few doubt that today, the United States and much of the world face an inequality crisis. That crisis in turn plays a central role in the crisis in democracy confronting so many countries. For decades, the mainstream of economics paid little attention to inequality. Some claimed it was unimportant, at least for understanding how the market economy functions. Others, like Lucas, argued that focusing on inequality was dangerous—it was "poisonous." This has left the economics profession ill-equipped to address this central crisis in our society.

Much has happened since I began tilling these fertile fields—inequality has grown so much worse, and a growing number of economists are, at last, turning their attention to study it in all of its dimensions. They have contributed enormously, especially to our detailed empirical knowledge. Still, with limited exceptions, few have tried to provide an overall account of how our economic and political system gives rise to inequality, such as I have attempted to do here—culminating (and completing for the moment at least) a research project that I began some 55 years ago. My hope is that such an account will help in constructing the multi-pronged, comprehensive, and concerted policy response that will be needed if we are to contain this inequality and preserve our democracy.

Acknowledgments

As I noted in the beginning of this introduction, I have been engaged in the research described here for more than 50 years, and in that time I have accumulated a long list of debts, impossible to summarize in a few pages. In any attempt to do so I will undoubtedly fail to do justice. With these misgivings in mind, I have to begin with my teachers and co-authors (particularly of the papers reprinted here).

The beginnings of this book can be traced to my M.I.T. doctoral dissertation on Growth and Inequality, and I owe an enormous debt to my advisors Robert Solow, Paul Samuelson, and Ed Kuh.

It is a cliché—but still true—that one learns as much from one's classmates as one's teacher; but several of my classmates were particularly important in reinforcing my belief in the importance of inequality and the failings of the competitive model that was the mainstay of economic analysis at the time. I want to particularly acknowledge George Akerlof, with whom I shared the Nobel Prize. We spent many hours as graduate students (and ever since) talking about imperfect information, inequality, the limits of standard economic theory, and a wide range of other topics. One of the topics we discussed early on was the relationship between distribution, growth, and stability, reflected here in Chapter 29.

I wrote most of my Ph.D. while on a Fulbright at Cambridge in 1965–66. Inequality and deficiencies in capitalism were at the center of much of the discussions, and I owe a great deal to the late Frank Hahn, Michael Farrell, Joan Robinson, Nicholas Kaldor, David Champernowne, and James Meade, as well as to lively conversations with younger colleagues, Bob Rowthorne, Agit Singh, David Newbery, James Mirrlees, Geoff Heal, and especially Tony Atkinson, who devoted his life to understanding inequality, and who was among the first students I tutored at Cambridge. Chapter 18 is devoted to his memory. Two visitors at Cambridge during the time I was there were also influential: Peter Diamond and Kenneth Arrow.[64]

I owe an especial debt to David Bevan, whom I first met in 1969 while we were both working in Kenya, which had just recently acquired its independence. The friendship and collaboration we began then continued as I spent four years at Oxford. Chapter 9, where we develop the equilibrium theory of the distribution of income and wealth based on the balancing of centrifugal and centripetal forces, exemplifies the fruit of that collaboration. Much of this book represents an elaboration of that work.

[64] He had also been my teacher at MIT. Later he would be a colleague, friend, and co-author.

I also owe an especial debt to Michael Rothschild, both for our work together in understanding how markets with imperfect information are so different from those with perfect information—even a little bit of information imperfection can have a large effect and give rise to market power and exploitation; and in developing a methodology of assessing whether one distribution is more unequal (or riskier) than another.

As I noted in the beginning of this introduction, I was drawn into economics by a concern about inequality and a desire to figure out what we could do about it. It was thus natural that one of the questions to which I would turn was how to design redistributive tax systems. I was lucky that the topic was front and center at Cambridge during the time I studied there, with pathbreaking contributions made by Mirrlees and Diamond, and I was doubly fortunate to work closely with both of them. Over the subsequent years, in my research on redistributive taxation I was joined by a number of collaborators: two from Cambridge—Dasgupta and Atkinson; Yale University students Steven Slutsky and Richard Arnott; and Dagobert L. Brito and Jonathan Hamilton. This theoretical work naturally morphed into more policy-oriented work, some reflected in the chapters below. While I wrote less about expenditure policy, social insurance, and inequality, I need to acknowledge my collaboration with Larry Lau, Eytan Sheshinki, and Jungyoll Yun. I have learned a great deal from each of them. Volume 5 of *Selected Works* contains more of my papers in these areas. Here, I want to acknowledge also the influence of David Bradford, Nick Stern, Jim Poterba, Michael Boskin, and Martin Feldstein.

I've had an enormously fruitful lifetime collaboration with Ravi Kanbur, who studied with me at Oxford. Chapters 6 and 22 present some of our analysis of mobility: when can one say that one economy is better at providing opportunity than another.

George Akerlof, with whom I shared the Nobel Prize, spent many hours when we were graduate students and since talking about imperfect information, inequality, the limits of standard economic theory, and a wide range of other topics. One of the topics we discussed early on was the relationship between distribution, growth, and stability, reflected here in Chapter 29.

I continued to work closely with Avi Braverman after he completed his thesis with me at Stanford, as he went to the World Bank, and particularly on questions of sharecropping, including impacts on inequality and innovation, incorporated here in Chapters 25 and 26.

When I went to work as an advisor to President Clinton, I was lucky to be able to recruit one of Harvard's brightest students, Jason Furman, and we became friends and collaborators. (He went on to become chairman of the Council of Economic Advisers under President Obama.) Among the many, many topics we worked on together was the relationship between unemployment and inequality, in a paper presented to the annual meeting of central bankers at Jackson Hole, an excerpt from which is contained in Chapter 30.

Over the past decade, Anton Korinek, who studied with me at Columbia, has been a collaborator on work on macroeconomic externalities and on technological change. We've been particularly engaged in the question of the impact of changes such as artificial intelligence on distribution, and what can be done about it. Chapter 18 reprints one of our joint papers on the subject.

More recently, as the UN worked to formulate a set of agreed goals for the international community, I worked with Michael Doyle, my colleague at Columbia's law school and political science department and former Assistant Secretary General of the UN, to make sure that among the sustainable development goals was one focusing on poverty. Chapter 7 was written together to advance that objective. Inequality was included in the SDGs as SDG 10.

Throughout the book, one will see references to joint work with my numerous co-authors, including Richard Arnott, Kaushik Basu, Mike Boskin, Dagobert L. Brito, Partha Dasgupta, Domenico Delli Gatti, Avinash Dixit, Aaron Edlin, Shahe Emran, Mauro Gallegati, Sanford Grossman, Jonathan Hamilton, Karla Hoff, Larry Lau, Barry Nalebuff, Peter Neary, Patrick Rey, Alberto Russo, Steve Salop, David Sappington, Carl Shapiro, Karl Shell, Eytan Sheshinski, Steve Slutsky, Nicholas Stern, Andrew Weiss, and Jungyoll Yun.

While over my career, I've worked in many areas—taxation, industrial policy, economics of information, macroeconomics, development—all of them touch on inequality: I've been concerned about how the economic system works, and an essential part of that is understanding how the fruits of that system are distributed. I've been concerned too about how public policy, and especially tax policy can be used to achieve more egalitarian outcomes. There are several areas just touched upon in this book, but which still have greatly influenced my general thinking about inequality: intellectual property, development, macro- and financial stability, and the transition from Communism to a market economy. My thanks to my collaborators in these areas, including Stefano Battiston, Andrew Charlton, Sergio Godoy, José Antonio Ocampo, Shari Spiegel, Richard R. Nelson, Claude Henry, Stephanie Griffith-Jones, Antara Haldar, Marcus Miller, Arjun Jayadev, Kevin Murdoch, Thomas Hellman, Mario Cimoli, Giovanni Dosi, Achal Prabhala.

In addition to these there is a long list of individuals to whom I am indebted for each chapter, acknowledged in the published versions of the papers from which the chapters are derived.

The social consequences of inequality is an area I just touch on in this introduction and briefly discuss in the ensuing chapters, but I think it is a crucial topic and hope that economists will devote far more attention to it in the future. My thinking in this area has been greatly shaped by an ongoing research project with Karla Hoff and Allison Demeritt.

While most of this book is devoted to theory, there has always been a close dialogue between theory and policy, evident hopefully throughout the book. In my years in the Clinton Administration and the World Bank I had the good fortune to work with dedicated public servants and great intellects, who enhanced my understanding of inequality both within America and globally. I want to acknowledge invaluable conversations with Nancy Birdsall, François Bourguignon, William Easterly, David Ellerman, Robert Greenstein, Isabelle Guerrero, Roumeen Islam, Branko Milanović, Alicia Munnell, Peter Orszag, Martin Ravallion, Robert Reich, Lyn Squire, Marilou Uy, Michael Walton, and a host of others too numerous to name.

After I left the World Bank, there were several groups with whom I was particularly engaged in discussions of inequality. One was the Roosevelt Institute (whose influence is particularly apparent in Chapter 5): I wish to acknowledge Felicia Wong, Nell Abernathy, Adam Hersh, Susan Holmberg, and Mike Konczal. Our work together led to *Rewriting the Rules of the American Economy: An Agenda for Growth and Shared Prosperity*. I subsequently worked with the Foundation for European Progressive Studies (FEPS) on a parallel book for Europe (with Carter Dougherty). Thanks to Ernst Stetter, David Rinaldi, and the entire FEPS team.[65]

[65] See Stiglitz with Abernathy, Hersh, et al. (2015) and Stiglitz with Stetter, Dougherty, et al. (2019).

A third group was Economists for Peace and Security, chaired for a long time by James Galbraith and more recently by Linda Bilmes (who co-authored *The Three Trillion Dollar War*).[66] They have long kept a spotlight on the multiple factors going into political stability, of which equality is one.

A fourth was the Commission on the Measurement of Economic Performance and Social Progress, which I co-chaired with Jean Paul Fitoussi and Amartya Sen, and its successor, the High-Level Expert Group on the Measurement of Economic Performance and Social Progress at the OECD, which I co-chaired with Jean Paul Fitoussi and Martine Durand. Among the most intensely discussed topics were those associated with inequality, and these have had a great deal of influence in my thinking on the subject. Besides those already mentioned, I note the contributions of Alan Krueger, especially on matters of subjective well-being and economic mobility, Angus Deaton, especially on matters of subjective well-being and health, Nick Stern (who succeeded me as chief economist of the World Bank and with whom I had worked since our time together in Kenya in 1969), on issues related to the environment, and Yann Algan and Bob Putnam, on inequality, social capital, and trust.[67]

Finally, in the aftermath of the 2008 financial crisis, I was asked by the President of the General Assembly to chair a Commission of Experts on Reforms of the International Monetary and Financial System.[68] Among the topics discussed was the relationship between inequality and instability. Again, I wish to thank all the Commissioners and rapporteurs for their insights, some of which are reflected in the discussions below.[69]

In addition to these, there are a host of NGOs, governments, and international organizations I have worked with over the past two decades in the fight to achieve greater economic and social justice. While the focus of my interactions was social change, in each of these encounters I learned something more about how our economic system worked in ways that preserved and increased societal inequities, and what we might do about it. To single out a few people: Damon Silvers at the AFL-CIO, Lawrence Mishel at the Economic Policy Institute, Lori Wallach at Public Citizen's Global Trade Watch, Winnie Byanyima at Oxfam, Mark Weisbrot at the Center of Economic Policy Research, Kristalina Georgieva at the IMF, and U.S. Senator Elizabeth Warren.

In this book, I have drawn heavily on the scholarship of the large number of economists who have turned their attention in recent years to inequality—after decades of neglect; sometimes just through their writing, often through that as well as more personal interactions. Besides those already mentioned, I want to acknowledge Paul Krugman, Thomas Piketty, Janet Gornick, Enrico Giovanni, Gabriel Zuchman, Emmanuel Saez, and John Roemer. Anyone studying mobility today will have been influenced by the work of Miles Corak, Raj Chetty, and Bashkar Mazumder.

I have had the good fortune to have been able to work at some of the leading research universities around the world—MIT, Yale, Princeton, Stanford, Oxford, Cambridge, and now Columbia. Each has provided fertile grounds for research, for interactions with colleagues, and excellent students. For more than two decades now, Columbia has been my home, and I especially want to acknowledge the support the university has provided that

[66] See Stiglitz and Bilmes (2008).

[67] The reports of the two groups were published as Stiglitz, Sen, and Fitoussi (2010) and Stiglitz, Fitoussi, and Durand (2019a).

[68] Report available as United Nations (2010). See the report for the list of commissioners.

[69] Especially in Part III.D of this book.

enabled the completion of this book. I have had long discussions on many of the topics covered here with long-time colleagues and friends, including Ned Phelps, Glen Hubbard, and Geoff Heal.

Columbia has also provided me with students and post-docs, who both motivated me and from whom I have learned so much, several of whom have gone on to be co-authors and who I have already acknowledged. I want to mention in particular Martin Guzman, who, following his post doc, co-authored much of my more recent work in macroeconomics. Martin went on to become the Minister of Economy for Argentina, where he had to deal firsthand with the inequalities associated with a pandemic coming on top of a debt crisis.

I especially want to thank Bruce Greenwald, whose collaboration goes back four decades, with whom I've taught courses for two decades, and whose insights into the inefficiencies of market economies in the presence of incomplete markets and imperfect information and the economic consequences of structural transformation—both in theory and in the particulars of the transformation—including on inequality—through which our economy is now going have been invaluable.

Over these many years, I have been the beneficiary of research support from many foundations, including Rockefeller, Ford, Hewlett, Mott, FEPS, Japan International Cooperation Agency (JICA), and the National Science Foundation. I particularly gratefully acknowledge support from the Institute for New Economic Thinking (INET), which enabled me to complete this project. INET, through its president Rob Johnson, not only provided financial support but a forum for dialogue on the issues discussed in this book, particularly through its Commission on Global Economic Transformation, which I co-chaired with Michael Spence.

An especial thanks to the many research assistants who have worked with me on this project, including Parijat Lal, Victoria Mooers, Ricardo Pommer Muñoz, and Haaris Mateen (with whom I am currently working on a project that extends the results of Chapter 12).

I owe a particular debt to my staff, Caleb Oldham, Chloe Oldham, Sofia Bennett, Susanna De Martino, and Gabriela Plump, and especially my publications manager Andrea Gurwitt. Eamon Kircher-Allen again did the impressive job he has done with my other recent books in pulling everything together, managing the whole project, and editing.

PART I
BROADER PERSPECTIVES

Introduction to Part I

Part I presents six articles written for more popular audiences plus one written explicitly for this volume. It begins with an article published in *Scientific American* that both presents some of the basic statistics of the growing inequality and diminishing opportunity and the skeletons of the analytic arguments that will be fleshed out in the rest of the book, for instance, the role of market distortions, the "rigged economy," in giving rise to inequality.

This is followed by a short article, based on a lecture given to the National Tax Association, summarizing the alternative interpretations of why inequality has increased. Most of these contain some grain of truth, but I explain why some of the most popular explanations fall short in giving us an adequate understanding of what is going on—essential if we are to devise policies to effectively address inequality. This chapter in particular critiques the notion that unfettered inequality is an inevitable consequence of contemporary capitalism, and provides an alternative, new framework for analyzing changes in income and wealth distribution. By thinking of these distributions as a result of changing centrifugal and centripetal economic and political forces—forces pulling the economy apart or pushing it together—we can identify changes in our economic and social structure that may have played a central role in the creation of today's high level of inequality, and we can analyze the potential impacts of alternative policies. Specifically, this chapter continues the argument of Chapter 1 that much of the increase in inequality is associated with the growth in rents—including land and exploitation rents (e.g., arising from monopoly power and political influence).

The third chapter was written for a volume on *Rethinking Capitalism*, edited by Mariana Mazzucato and Michael Jacobs. Especially in Europe, the 2008 crisis inspired a re-evaluation of capitalism. Since the early 1970s a substantial body of research had undermined Adam Smith's presumption in the efficiency of the market economy—the invisible hand which was supposed to make sure that the pursuit of self-interest led to the wellbeing of society was invisible because it was not there. Still, it was not until the crisis that it became clear just how inefficient and unstable an unregulated market economy could be.

But even advocates of market efficiency never claimed that the distribution of income that would emerge out of the market was socially desirable. The advocates of many of the "neoliberal reforms" (supply side economics in the U.S., Thatcherism in the UK) was that, somehow, all would benefit from the growth that would result from free markets through trickle-down economics. This chapter presents some of the evidence that that has not happened in the U.S. and most other advanced countries, gives some of the evidence on the growth of rents as a key explanation, describes some of the theory and evidence on the adverse economic effects of inequality, and concludes with a brief discussion of some of the policies that might reduce inequality.

Chapter 4 takes up one central theme of the previous chapters—that inequality is not an inevitable feature of capitalism, that it is not determined by the laws of nature but by the laws of men, and in particular, by the rules, regulations, and policies governing the economy. This chapter is based on a set of excerpts from *Rewriting the Rules of the American Economy*, a report I wrote (with Nell Abernathy, Adam Hersh, Susan Holmberg, and Mike Konczal) for the Roosevelt Institute—a think tank that grew out of FDR's presidential library. In the book, we argue that one of the major sources of increases in inequality is that the underlying rules of the economy have been rewritten over the past 40 years to advantage the 1%, and now have to be rewritten again. The book provided a progressive agenda to simultaneously reduce inequality and increase growth based on rewriting the rules of the economy. This report in turn was based partially on the analytic work contained here, in this book.

Rewriting the Rules received an unusual amount of attention—so much so that it has been followed by two sequels, *Rewriting the Rules of the European Economy*[1] and *Rewriting the Rules of the Korean Economy*.[2] As we note in the preface to the edition published by W.W. Norton (co-authored with Felicia Wong, President of the Roosevelt Institute):

> *The New York Times* called it "an aggressive blueprint for rewriting 35 years of policies that ... have led to a vast concentration of wealth among the richest Americans and an increasingly squeezed middle class." *Time* magazine said *Rewriting the Rules* revealed a "secret truth" about inequality. The Ford Foundation called the report a "landmark." Of course, politicians listened, too. Senator Elizabeth Warren lauded the report as "groundbreaking." Advocates, labor leaders, members of Congress, and presidential candidates called, requesting briefings and discussions and further explications of "the rules." Importantly, they saw the report as a call to action: what could we do, specifically, now, to begin to create a stronger economy?

As we note in the Introduction to this volume, while we focus on the U.S., what has happened here has also occurred in many other countries around the world. The international rules of the game have also been changed, often under the influence of the same misguided economic theories, reflecting the same ideologies and similar economic interests. In some cases, America has been seen as a role model; in others, it has used its influence at the World Bank, the IMF, the WTO, the G-20, and in other international settings to induce, and in some cases, effectively to force the kind of changes that led to more inequality and poorer economic performance in the United States on other countries.

The next chapter, written with Ravi Kanbur of Cornell and published in *Vox,* which attempts to make technical papers more accessible, situates some of the current policy discussions in a historical context. Growth theories traditionally focus on the Kaldor-Kuznets stylized facts, formulated in the 1950s—for example, the constancy of the share of labor and the capital-output ratio and the decline of inequality in the advanced countries. These no

[1] Stiglitz, Stetter, Dougherty, et al., 2019.
[2] Park, W.-S., B. Y. Cheon, et al., 2018.

longer hold; and new theory is needed to explain what is occurring. The chapter argues that new models need to drop competitive marginal productivity theories of factor returns in favor of rent-generating mechanisms, which are greatly affected by the "rules of the game," as described in Chapter 4. They also must model interactions among physical, financial, and human capital that influence the level and evolution of inequality. A third key component will be to capture mechanisms that transmit inequality from generation to generation, the subject of much of Part II of this volume.

Most of the work in the measurement of inequality has focused on a static picture—the distribution of income or wealth at a moment in time. But views about the "fairness" of an economic system also entail an assessment of social mobility. We are concerned about inequality of opportunity, as well as inequality of outcomes. This chapter flags the importance of this issue, which will be taken up in greater detail in Part III.B.

The final chapter of Part I was written in the fall of 2013 as the world was engaged in a debate over the new Sustainable Development Goals (SDGs). The success of the earlier Millennium Development Goals (MDG) had made a convincing case for the efficacy of the role of the UN in setting global norms. The MDG's commitment, made at the onset of the new millennium, to reduce poverty by half by 2015 had led to a global focus on poverty reduction. The goal was more than achieved, though poverty reduction in China played a disproportionate role, and the numbers for Africa were disappointing. There was a consensus that the new global goals should be more comprehensive and apply, in some way, to both developed and developing countries.

The growing inequality in the U.S., China, and many countries around the world suggested that the reduction in inequality should be one of the central goals. Michael Doyle, formerly Assistant Secretary General of the UN and a colleague of mine at Columbia University (in both the Law School and Political Science Department) and I teamed up to push for the adoption of an inequality goal as part of the SDGs. We received push back from an unexpected quarter: while President Obama had said that reducing inequality was one of the central issues facing the U.S., the United States opposed the inclusion of inequality as a goal, I suspect because it did not want to draw global attention to this critical weakness in America's economic, political, and social system. Not only was inequality high, there was every reason to believe that it would increase.

This chapter was written as part of our effort to get inequality adopted as a SDG. We wanted to show both the economic and political consequences of inequality. One of the reasons that the UN had originally been created was to reduce conflict. The chapter summarizes not just the economic consequences of inequality (discussed elsewhere in this book), but also the political consequences, including for conflict. It reviews literature suggesting that particular kinds of inequities (e.g., "horizontal," across ethnic groups) are especially important drivers of conflict.

By determined and concerted campaigning, we were able to overcome the opposition of the United States and some other developed countries, and an inequality goal was included in the SDGs: "Reduce Inequality within and among countries."

As we discuss elsewhere in this volume, however, there are many ways of assessing the extent of inequality. In this chapter, we argue that attention should be centered on extreme inequality, and we suggested a particular measure, the Palma ratio, the ratio of share of the richest 10% of the population to that of the poorest 40%. The reason for this is that, as Jose Gabriel Palma of Cambridge University argued, the middle of the society regularly gets for itself a relatively constant share of national income. Countries really differ in how the remainder of the "pie" is divided between the top and the bottom. It is thus a more sensitive measure: the Palma ratio for South Africa, for instance, is eight times that of Sweden or Norway, while the Gini coefficient is a little more than twice as large.

While the UN adopted an inequality goal, it decided to focus attention again on the bottom—not the very bottom, as it had done with the Millennium Development Goal (the elimination of extreme poverty), but the bottom 40%. The goal adopted was: "By 2030, progressively achieve and sustain income growth of the bottom 40 per cent of the population at a rate higher than the national average."

The chapter argues that beyond setting particular goals for the reduction of inequality, it is important to have national dialogues focusing on inequalities, spearheaded, we suggest, by commissions to be established in each country, "to assess and report on the effects" of these national inequalities. We believed that the many dimensions of societal inequalities had long been neglected, and shining a spotlight on the subject would inevitably lead to greater efforts to reduce societal inequality.

1
A Rigged Economy and What We Can Do about It

Americans are used to thinking that their nation is special.[1] In many ways, it is: the U.S. has by far the most Nobel Prize winners, the largest defense expenditures (almost equal to the next 10 or so countries put together), and the most billionaires (twice as many as China, the closest competitor). But some examples of American Exceptionalism should not make us proud. By most accounts, the U.S. has the highest level of economic inequality among developed countries. It has the world's greatest per capita health expenditures yet the lowest life expectancy among comparable countries. It is also one of a few developed countries jostling for the dubious distinction of having the lowest measures of equality of opportunity.

The notion of the American Dream—that, unlike old Europe, we are a land of opportunity—is part of our essence. Yet the numbers say otherwise. The life prospects of a young American depend more on the income and education of his or her parents than in almost any other advanced country. When poor-boy-makes-good anecdotes get passed around in the media, that is precisely because such stories are so rare.

Things appear to be getting worse, partly as a result of forces, such as technology and globalization, that seem beyond our control, but most disturbingly because of those within our command. It is not the laws of nature that have led to this dire situation: it is the laws of humankind. Markets do not exist in a vacuum: they are shaped by rules and regulations, which can be designed to favor one group over another. President Donald Trump was right in saying that the system is rigged—by those in the inherited plutocracy of which he himself is a member. And he is making it much, much worse.

America has long outdone others in its level of inequality, but in the past 40 years it has reached new heights. Whereas the income share of the top 0.1% has more than quadrupled and that of the top 1% has almost doubled, that of the bottom 90% has declined. Wages at the bottom, adjusted for inflation, are about the same as they were some 60 years ago! In fact, for those with a high school education or less, incomes have fallen over recent decades. Males have been particularly hard hit, as the U.S. has moved away from manufacturing industries into an economy based on services.

1 Deaths of Despair

Wealth is even less equally distributed, with just three Americans having as much as the bottom 50%—testimony to how much money there is at the top and how little there is at the

[1] Originally published in 2018 as "A Rigged Economy and What We Can Do about It," *Scientific American*, November, 56–61. Reproduced with permission. Copyright © 2018 Scientific American, a Division of Springer Nature America, Inc. All rights reserved. I am greatly indebted to Madhusree Mukerjee, an editor with Scientific American, and Debarati Ghosh for editorial assistance.

The Origins of Inequality, and Policies to Contain It. Joseph E. Stiglitz, Oxford University Press. © Joseph E. Stiglitz (2025).
DOI: 10.1093/oso/9780198799580.003.0002

bottom. Families in the bottom 50% hardly have the cash reserves to meet an emergency. Newspapers are replete with stories of those for whom the breakdown of a car or an illness starts a downward spiral from which they never recover.

Fading of the American Dream

Contrary to popular belief, equality of opportunity in the U.S. is lower than in most advanced countries—and it is declining. A 2017 report by economist Raj Chetty and others indicates that an American born in 1940 was almost certain to become more prosperous than his or her parents. Someone born in 1980 is just as likely to be worse off, however. Declining equality of opportunity stems in large part from the high cost of higher education, coupled with spiraling economic inequality. Statistics from the World Inequality Database show that since about 1970 the income of the top 1%, corrected for inflation, has quadrupled, whereas that of the bottom 90% has stagnated. Men with only high school degrees have seen their incomes drop.

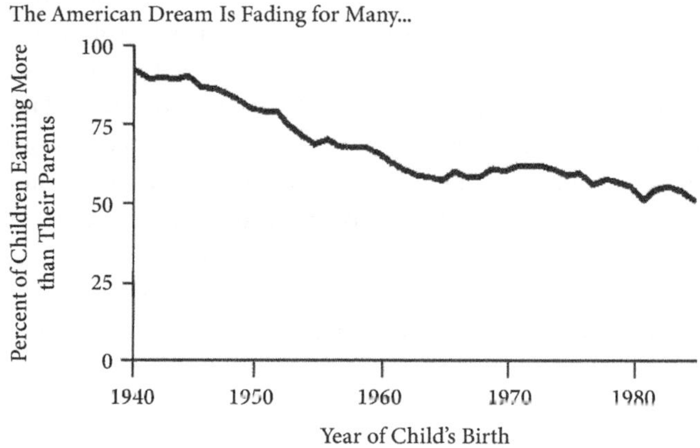

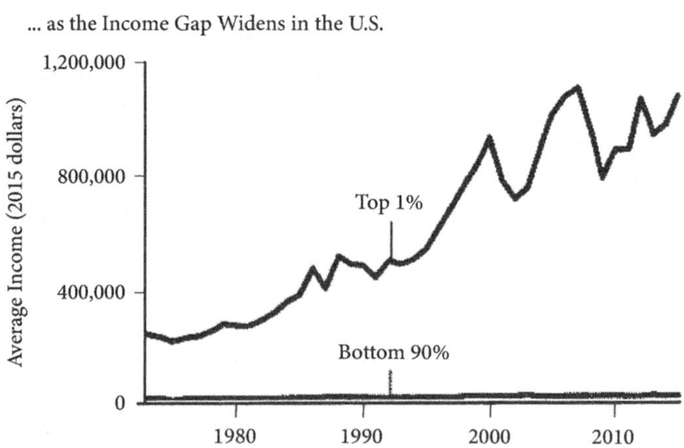

Sources: Chetty, Grusky, Hell, et al., The fading American dream: Trends in absolute income mobility since 1940, *Science*, vol 356; April 26, 2017 (child–parent wealth comparison): World Inequality Database (90% vs. 1% wealth trend data).

In significant part because of high inequality, U.S. life expectancy, exceptionally low to begin with, is experiencing sustained declines. This in spite of the marvels of medical science, many advances of which occur right here in America and which are made readily available to the rich. Economist Ann Case and 2015 Nobel laureate in economics Angus Deaton describe one of the main causes of rising morbidity—the increase in alcoholism, drug overdoses, and suicides—as "deaths of despair" by those who have given up hope.

Defenders of America's inequality have a pat explanation. They refer to the workings of a competitive market, where the laws of supply and demand determine wages, prices, and even interest rates—a mechanical system, much like that describing the physical universe. Those with scarce assets or skills are amply rewarded, they argue, because of the larger contributions they make to the economy. What they get merely represents what they have contributed. Often, they take out less than they contributed, so what is left over for the rest is that much more.

This fictional narrative may at one time have assuaged the guilt of those at the top and persuaded everyone else to accept this sorry state of affairs. Perhaps the defining moment exposing the lie was the 2008 financial crisis, when the bankers who brought the global economy to the brink of ruin with predatory lending, market manipulation, and various other antisocial practices walked away with millions of dollars in bonuses just as millions of Americans lost their jobs and homes and tens of millions more worldwide suffered on their account. Virtually none of these bankers were ever held to account for their misdeeds.

I became aware of the fantastical nature of this narrative as a schoolboy, when I thought of the wealth of the plantation owners, built on the backs of slaves. At the time of the Civil War, the market value of the slaves in the South was approximately half of the region's total wealth, including the value of the land and the physical capital—the factories and equipment. The wealth of at least this part of this nation was not based on industry, innovation, and commerce but rather on exploitation. Today we have replaced this open exploitation with more insidious forms, which have intensified since the Reagan–Thatcher revolution of the 1980s. This exploitation, I will argue, is largely to blame for the escalating inequality in the U.S.

After the New Deal of the 1930s, American inequality went into decline. By the 1950s inequality had receded to such an extent that another Nobel laureate in economics, Simon Kuznets, formulated what came to be called Kuznets's law. In the early stages of development, as some parts of a country seize new opportunities, inequalities grow, he postulated; in the later stages, they shrink. The theory long fit the data—but then, around the early 1980s, the trend abruptly reversed.

2 Explaining Inequality

Economists have put forward a range of explanations for why inequality has in fact been increasing in many developed countries. Some argue that advances in technology have spurred the demand for skilled labor relative to unskilled labor, thereby depressing the wages of the latter. Yet that alone cannot explain why even skilled labor has done so poorly over the past two decades, why average wages have done so badly, and why matters are so much worse in the U.S. than in other developed nations. Changes in technology are global and should affect all advanced economies in the same way. Other economists blame globalization itself, which has weakened the power of workers. Firms can and do move abroad unless demands for higher wages are curtailed. But again, globalization has been integral to all advanced economies. Why is its impact so much worse in the U.S.?

The shift from a manufacturing to a service-based economy is partly to blame. At its extreme—a firm of one person—the service economy is a winner-takes-all system. A movie star makes millions, for example, whereas most actors make a pittance. Overall, wages are likely to be far more widely dispersed in a service economy than in one based on manufacturing, so the transition contributes to greater inequality. This fact does not explain, however, why the average wage has not improved for decades. Moreover, the shift to the service sector is happening in most other advanced countries: Why are matters so much worse in the U.S.?

Again, because services are often provided locally, firms have more market power: the ability to raise prices above what would prevail in a competitive market. A small town in rural America may have only one authorized Toyota repair shop, which virtually every Toyota owner is forced to patronize. The providers of these local services can raise prices over costs, increasing their profits and the share of income going to owners and managers. This, too, increases inequality. But again, why is U.S. inequality practically unique?

In his celebrated 2013 treatise, *Capital in the Twenty-First Century,* French economist Thomas Piketty shifts the gaze to capitalists. He suggests that the few who own much of a country's capital save so much that, given the stable and high return to capital (relative to the growth rate of the economy), their share of the national income has been increasing. His theory has, however, been questioned on many grounds. For instance, the savings rate of even the rich in the U.S. is so low, compared with the rich in other countries, that the increase in inequality should be lower here, not greater.

An alternative theory is far more consonant with the facts. Since the mid-1970s the rules of the economic game have been rewritten, both globally and nationally, in ways that advantage the rich and disadvantage the rest. And they have been rewritten further in this perverse direction in the U.S. than in other developed countries—even though the rules in the U.S. were already less favorable to workers. From this perspective, increasing inequality is a matter of choice: a consequence of our policies, laws, and regulations.

In the U.S., the market power of large corporations, which was greater than in most other advanced countries to begin with, has increased even more than elsewhere. On the other hand, the market power of workers, which started out less than in most other advanced countries, has fallen further than elsewhere. This is not only because of the shift to a service-sector economy—it is because of the rigged rules of the game, rules set in a political system that is itself rigged through gerrymandering, voter suppression, and the influence of money. A vicious spiral has formed: economic inequality translates into political inequality, which leads to rules that favor the wealthy, which in turn reinforces economic inequality.

3 Feedback Loop

Political scientists have documented the ways in which money influences politics in certain political systems, converting higher economic inequality into greater political inequality. Political inequality, in its turn, gives rise to more economic inequality as the rich use their political power to shape the rules of the game in ways that favor them—for instance, by softening antitrust laws and weakening unions. Using mathematical models, economists such as myself have shown that this two-way feedback loop between money and regulations leads to at least two stable points. If an economy starts out with lower inequality, the political system generates rules that sustain it, leading to one equilibrium situation. The American system is the other equilibrium—and will continue to be unless there is a democratic political awakening.

Global Inequality Trends

Inequality has increased in most advanced countries because of factors such as globalization, technological change, and the shift to a service-based economy. It has grown fastest in the U.S., however, according to the World Inequality Database. That is because rules have been rewritten to make them more favorable for the rich, while being disadvantageous to everyone else. Large companies have been allowed to accrue more power over the market, whereas the influence of workers has shrunk. Taxation and other policies have consistently favored the wealthy.

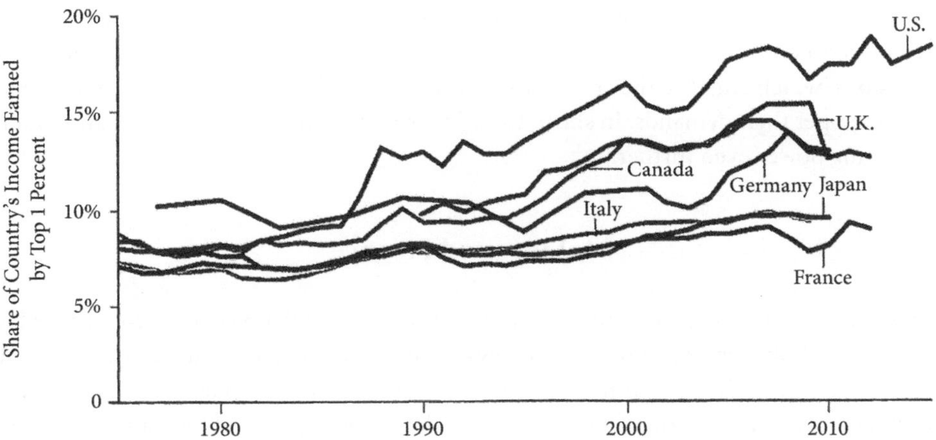

Sources: Economic Report of the President, January 2017: World Inequality Database.

An account of how the rules have been shaped must begin with antitrust laws, first enacted 128 years ago in the U.S. to prevent the agglomeration of market power. Their enforcement has weakened—at a time when, if anything, the laws themselves should have been strengthened. Technological changes have concentrated market power in the hands of a few global players, in part because of so-called network effects: you are far more likely to join a particular social network or use a certain word processor if everyone you know is already using it. Once established, a firm such as Facebook or Microsoft is hard to dislodge. Moreover, fixed costs, such as that of developing a piece of software, have increased as compared with marginal costs—that of duplicating the software. A new entrant has to bear all these fixed costs up front, and if it does enter, the rich incumbent can respond by lowering prices drastically. The cost of making an additional e-book or photo editing program is essentially zero.

In short, entry is hard and risky, which gives established firms with deep war chests enormous power to crush competitors and ultimately raise prices. Making matters worse, U.S. firms have been innovative not only in the products they make but in thinking of ways to extend and amplify their market power. The European Commission has imposed fines of billions of dollars on Microsoft and Google and ordered them to stop their anticompetitive practices (such as Google privileging its own comparison-shopping service). In the U.S., we have done too little to control concentrations of market power, so it is not a surprise that it has increased in many sectors.

Rigged rules also explain why the impact of globalization may have been worse in the U.S. A concerted attack on unions has almost halved the fraction of unionized workers in the nation, to about 11%. (In Scandinavia, it is roughly 70%.) Weaker unions provide workers less protection against the efforts of firms to drive down wages or worsen working conditions. Moreover, U.S. investment treaties such as the North Atlantic Free Trade Agreement—treaties that were sold as a way of preventing foreign countries from discriminating against American firms—also protect investors against a tightening of environmental and health regulations abroad. For instance, they enable corporations to sue nations in private international arbitration panels for passing laws that protect citizens and the environment but threaten the multinational company's bottom line. Firms like these provisions, which enhance the credibility of a company's threat to move abroad if workers do not temper their demands. In short, these investment agreements weaken U.S. workers' bargaining power even further.

4 Liberated Finance

Many other changes to our norms, laws, rules, and regulations have contributed to inequality. Weak corporate governance laws have allowed chief executives in the U.S. to compensate themselves 361 times more than the average worker, far more than in other developed countries. Financial liberalization—the stripping away of regulations designed to prevent the financial sector from imposing harms, such as the 2008 economic crisis, on the rest of society—has enabled the finance industry to grow in size and profitability and has increased its opportunities to exploit everyone else. Banks routinely indulge in practices that are legal but should not be, such as imposing usurious interest rates on borrowers or exorbitant fees on merchants for credit and debit cards and creating securities that are designed to fail. They also frequently do things that are illegal, including market manipulation and insider trading. In all of this, the financial sector has moved money away from ordinary Americans to rich bankers and the banks' shareholders. This redistribution of wealth is an important contributor to American inequality.

Uneven Distribution of Global Growth

Globalization has benefited millions of the poor in emerging economies, particularly in China. Data compiled by economist Branko Milanovic and displayed in the *World Inequality Report 2018* demonstrate, however, that between 1980 and 2016, the steepest gains went to the world's top 1%, which captured more than a quarter of the growth in the global economy. In early 2018 Oxfam International reported that just 42 individuals have as much wealth as the bottom 50% put together. The middle classes in the U.S. and western Europe have benefited the least from global growth, as have the world's poorest.

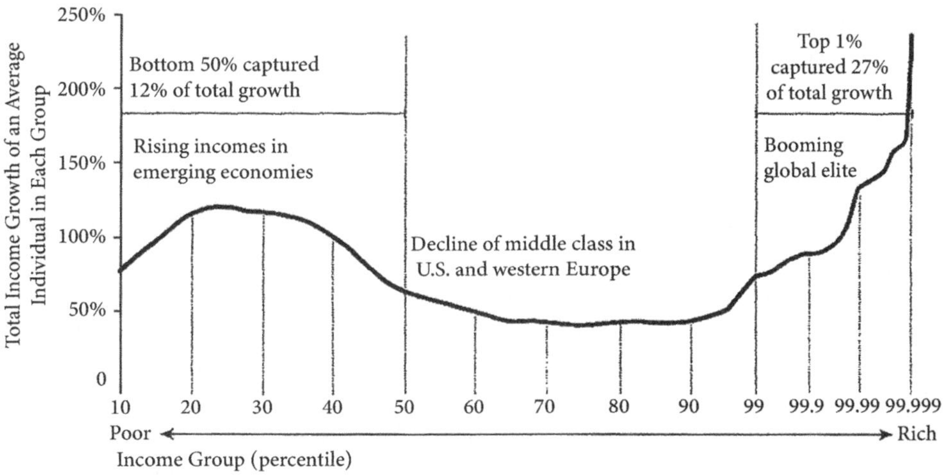

Sources: World Inequality Report 2018. World Inequality Lab, 2017; Branko Milanovic.

Other means of so-called rent extraction—the withdrawal of income from the national pie that is incommensurate with societal contribution—abound. For example, a legal provision enacted in 2003 prohibited the government from negotiating drug prices for Medicare—a gift of some $50 billion a year or more to the pharmaceutical industry. Special favors, such as extractive industries' obtaining public resources such as oil at below fair-market value or banks' getting funds from the Federal Reserve at near-zero interest rates (which they relend at high interest rates), also amount to rent extraction. Further exacerbating inequality is favorable tax treatment for the rich. In the U.S., those at the top pay a smaller fraction of their income in taxes than those who are much poorer—a form of largesse that the Trump administration has just worsened with the 2017 tax bill.

Some economists have argued that we can lessen inequality only by giving up on growth and efficiency. But recent research, such as work done by Jonathan Ostry and others at the International Monetary Fund, suggests that economies with greater equality perform better, with higher growth, better average standards of living and greater stability. Inequality in the extremes observed in the U.S. and in the manner generated there actually damages the economy. The exploitation of market power and the variety of other distortions I have described, for instance, makes markets less efficient, leading to underproduction of valuable goods such as basic research and overproduction of others, such as exploitative financial products.

Moreover, because the rich typically spend a smaller fraction of their income on consumption than the poor, total or "aggregate" demand in countries with higher inequality is weaker. Societies could make up for this gap by increasing government spending—on infrastructure, education, and health, for instance, all of which are investments necessary for long-term growth. But the politics of unequal societies typically puts the burden on monetary policy: interest rates are lowered to stimulate spending. Artificially low interest rates, especially if coupled with inadequate financial market regulation, often give rise to bubbles, which is what happened with the 2008 housing crisis.

It is no surprise that, on average, people living in unequal societies have less equality of opportunity: those at the bottom never get the education that would enable them to live up to their potential. This fact, in turn, exacerbates inequality while wasting the country's most valuable resource: Americans themselves.

5 Restoring Justice

Morale is lower in unequal societies, especially when inequality is seen as unjust, and the feeling of being used or cheated leads to lower productivity. When those who run gambling casinos or bankers suffering from moral turpitude make a zillion times more than the scientists and inventors who brought us lasers, transistors, and an understanding of DNA, it is clear that something is wrong. Then again, the children of the rich come to think of themselves as a class apart, entitled to their good fortune, and accordingly more likely to break the rules necessary for making society function. All of this contributes to a breakdown of trust, with its attendant impact on social cohesion and economic performance.

There is no magic bullet to remedy a problem as deep-rooted as America's inequality. Its origins are largely political, so it is hard to imagine meaningful change without a concerted effort to take money out of politics—through, for instance, campaign finance reform. Blocking the revolving doors by which regulators and other government officials come from and return to the same industries they regulate and work with is also essential.

Beyond that, we need more progressive taxation and high-quality federally funded public education, including affordable access to universities for all, no ruinous loans required. We need modern competition laws to deal with the problems posed by twenty-first-century market power and stronger enforcement of the laws we do have. We need labor laws that protect workers and their rights to unionize. We need corporate governance laws that curb exorbitant salaries bestowed on chief executives, and we need stronger financial regulations that will prevent banks from engaging in the exploitative practices that have become their hallmark. We need better enforcement of antidiscrimination laws: it is unconscionable that women and minorities get paid a mere fraction of what their white male counterparts receive. We also need more sensible inheritance laws that will reduce the intergenerational transmission of advantage and disadvantage.

The basic perquisites of a middle-class life, including a secure old age, are no longer attainable for most Americans. We need to guarantee access to health care. We need to strengthen and reform retirement programs, which have put an increasing burden of risk management on workers (who are expected to manage their portfolios to guard simultaneously against the risks of inflation and market collapse) and opened them up to exploitation by our financial sector (which sells them products designed to maximize bank fees rather than retirement security). Our mortgage system was our Achilles' heel and we have not really fixed it. With such a large fraction of Americans living in cities, we have to have urban housing policies that ensure affordable housing for all.

It is a long agenda—but a doable one. When skeptics say it is nice but not affordable, I reply: We cannot afford to *not* do these things. We are already paying a high price for inequality, but it is just a down payment on what we will have to pay if we do not do something—and quickly. It is not just our economy that is at stake; we are risking our democracy.

As more of our citizens come to understand why the fruits of economic progress have been so unequally shared, there is a real danger that they will become open to a demagogue blaming the country's problems on others and making false promises of rectifying "a rigged system." We are already experiencing a foretaste of what might happen. It could get much worse.

Widening Wage Gap

Since about 1980 the productivity of American workers has doubled, according to Josh Bivens and others at the Economic Policy Institute. But wages for production and nonsupervisory workers have stagnated, with virtually all the gains from increased productivity going to investors and owners. Salaries for the top 1%, including corporate executives and finance professionals, have, however, gone up—by more than 150% between 1979 and 2012. The increasing wage gap plays a significant role in spiraling inequality.

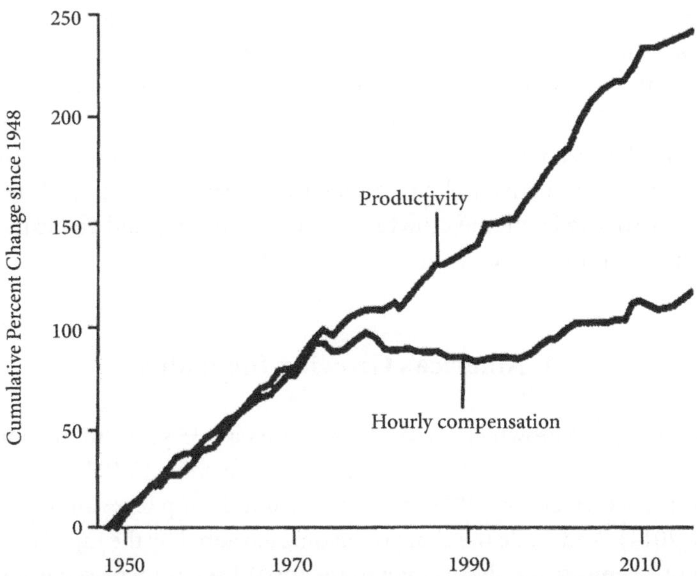

Sources: Raising America's pay: Why it's our central economic policy challenge, by Bivens, Gould, Mishel, and Shierholz, Economic Policy Institute, June 4, 2014; *The State of Working America*, by Lawrence Mishel, Josh Bivens, Elise Gould, and Heidi Shierholz, 12th edition, ILR Press. 2012.

2

The Origins of Inequality, and Policies to Contain It

This chapter, written in response to an invitation from the *National Tax Journal*, and originally presented at the meetings of the National Tax Association in Santa Fe, November 14, 2014, provides an overview of my theories of inequality, in particular, in juxtaposition with those of Thomas Piketty, whose 2014 book *Capitalism in the Twenty-first Century* was then receiving enormous attention.* It critiques the notion that unfettered inequality is an inevitable consequence of contemporary capitalism and provides an alternative, new framework for analyzing changes in income and wealth distribution. By thinking of these distributions as the result of changing centrifugal and centripetal economic and political forces, we can identify changes in our economic and social structure that may have played a central role in the creation of today's high level of inequality, and we can analyze the potential impacts of alternative policies. Specifically, I suggest that much of the increase in inequality is associated with the growth in rents—including land and exploitation rents (e.g., arising from monopoly power and political influence).

1 America's Growing Inequality

America's inequality has grown enormously over the past 35 years, to the point where the upper 1% receives more than a fifth of all the nation's income.[1] Wealth inequality is even greater: the top 1% own about 42% of the wealth, and the top 0.1% alone own 22% (Saez and Zucman, 2014). And while the share of income garnered by the top 1% has doubled in the last third of a century, the share going to the top 0.1% has increased even more, going up nearly threefold as of 2013 (Piketty and Saez, 2003, with tables updated to 2013).

The recession made all of this worse. Ordinary Americans were hurt badly by the loss of jobs and houses, and according to the Piketty and Saez data, the typical American didn't see any recovery even after the recession officially ended: 91% of all the increase in the first three years of the "recovery" went to the top 1%. An economy that is not creating benefits for most of its citizens is a failed economy.[2] The impact of the recession on wealth inequality was even more devastating, with median wealth sinking back to levels of 25 years ago, 40% below pre-crisis levels (Boshara, Emmons, and Noeth, 2014; Bricker, Dettling, Henriques, et al., 2014).

Most disturbing were two points that I emphasized in one of my previous books: America has the highest level of inequality of any of the advanced countries, and America has

* Originally published in 2015 as "The Origins of Inequality, and Policies to Contain It," *National Tax Journal*, 68(2): 425–48. Reprinted with permission.

[1] Piketty and Saez (2003), with data updated through 2013.

[2] Stiglitz, Sen, and Fitoussi (2010) discuss the fact that GDP is not a good measure of economic performance.

The Origins of Inequality, and Policies to Contain It. Joseph E. Stiglitz, Oxford University Press. © Joseph E. Stiglitz (2025).
DOI: 10.1093/oso/9780198799580.003.0003

among the lowest levels of equality of opportunity (Stiglitz, 2012a).[3] As I put it, the American Dream is largely a myth. Of course, some very talented individuals do rise from the bottom to the top, and this fact is an enormous strength of the country. But the life chances of a young American are more dependent on the income and education of his or her parents than is the case in other advanced countries—even most of those in old Europe.

What has happened in America has reversed long-standing beliefs about both the nature of American society and the evolution of economies. We believed we had become a middle-class society and the strength of the middle class was the strength of America. Not only is the middle class shrinking in size—with more people in poverty—but the incomes at the top have pulled away from those in the middle. While the average productivity of workers has doubled since 1970, wages for many workers have barely increased.[4]

While most serious economists have always been skeptical of notions of trickle-down economics—that if the top does well, so does the rest of society—what has happened in the last third of a century bears testimony to just how wrong that theory is: those in the middle have had stagnant incomes for a quarter of a century, and the wage of a full-time male worker, adjusted for inflation, is lower than it was 40 years ago.[5]

In the middle of the twentieth century, Nobel prize-winning economist Simon Kuznets argued that while there is growing inequality in the initial stages of development, eventually inequality is reduced. There is a plausible argument for this pattern: industrial wages exceed agricultural wages, so that with urbanization and industrialization, as more and more people go from low-income rural to more highly paid urban jobs, standard measures of inequality increase. Eventually, urbanization dominates. With so few in the rural sector, their relatively low incomes have little impact on inequality and, finally, incomes in the rural sector increase. America seemed to follow this pattern—until around 1980. In the years after World War II, the agricultural sector shrank rapidly (dropping below 2% of employment by the twenty-first century),[6] and America became a middle-class society. All parts of the society saw their incomes rise, but those at the bottom saw their incomes rise faster than those at the top.

Since 1980, Kuznets's vision has been destroyed. The growth of the economy as a whole was slower than in the decades after World War II and it was not shared prosperity. This, in part, accounts for the new agenda being put forward by some: rather than relying on trickle-down economics, this alternative vision says we can and should build the economy from the middle, as we did in the period following Word War II.

There is a simple interpretation of what happened: There is always some inequality, Earlier, we noted that as the economy went through the transformation from agriculture to manufacturing, some individuals in some places were better able to take advantage of the new opportunities. This led to new and growing inequalities, until again, those behind finally began to catch up. This same pattern has been unfolding, especially since the mid

[3] There is much additional literature on the subject, including Jäntti, Bratsberg, Røed, et al. (2006) and Corak (2013).

[4] Shierholz and Mishel (2013) discuss how real U.S. wages have stagnated for decades. Adjusted for inflation, average hourly earnings of production and non-supervisory employees have decreased some 30% since 1990; see "Average Hourly Earnings of Production and Non-Supervisory Workers." Federal Reserve Bank of St. Louis, http://research.stlouisfed.org/fred2/series/AHETPI/.

[5] "Historical Income Table P-36." U.S. Census Bureau, http://www.census.gov/hhes/www/income/data/historical/people/.

[6] "Percent of Employment in Agriculture in the United States." Federal Reserve Bank of St. Louis, http://research.stlouisfed. org/fred2/series/USAPEMANA.

to late 1970s, as the global economy moves from manufacturing to the knowledge-based, service-sector economy.

These are global forces, which affect different countries differently, partly because they each start in a different position: some are more manufacturing dependent, some have a more educated labor force, better able to make transitions. But both globally and nationally, these underlying forces are transformed, amplified in some cases, muted in others. Globalization, itself affected by changes in technology which have reduced costs of transportation and communication, has, however, been shaped by changes in international agreements. These have, by and large, amplified the effects in advanced countries, while creating new opportunities everywhere, but especially in emerging markets.

Piketty and I share the view that Americans often have an American-centric view, trying to blame or credit one party or another with the positive and negative changes in our economy. Piketty's book, as well as my earlier work, in effect, warns us against this reasoning, as there appear to be global forces at work.

But at this point our analyses differ. Piketty claims that it is innate properties of capitalism—the excess of the interest rate over the growth rate—that drives the long-term growth of inequality. He suggests that a high and even growing level of inequality is essentially an inevitable consequence of capitalism. (There are some policies—like a global capital tax—which might arrest it; but this policy on which he focuses the most seems totally out of reach.)

I argue, to the contrary, that policies within each country are crucial, and they can—and have—affected the growth of inequality. Some countries have more inequalities in market income, more increases in market income, more inequality in after-tax and transfer incomes, more increases in after tax and transfer income than others. Among the advanced countries, the U.S. is an "outlier": it begins with a higher level of market income inequality than others; and then it does less to "correct" it. And as inequality in market incomes has grown, there have been moves to lower tax rates at the top.

The fact that even with these global forces there are marked differences in outcomes means that something else is at play than just the global forces we have identified and, in particular, that policies matter. I thus argue that the levels of and changes in inequality are not the inevitable consequences of capitalism itself but how market economies are structured. (Piketty, with his focus on the *inevitability of the increase in inequality under capitalism* (unless there is a global capital tax), is thus less interested in the variants of capitalism, such as American-style or Scandinavian-style capitalism than in the underlying forces of capitalism itself.)

Piketty sees the period after World War II—the period in which I grew up and which I didn't realize at the time was the golden age of capitalism—as unusual, as an exception to his almost iron law of capitalism. I see it as another illustration of my main thesis: with the right policies in place, inequality can be kept in check, and even brought down, and this is so even in the presence of underlying forces that might lead to greater inequality.

The strongest evidence in support of my perspective is that inequality is so different in countries with similar economic structures. The laws of economics operate similarly on both sides of the Atlantic. Yet America's inequality is greater than elsewhere, and those countries that have followed America's economic model have seen a similar (but not quite as great) increase in their inequality. Of course, what happens here has effects elsewhere;

our policies are contributing not only to inequality here, but also to inequalities abroad. Thus, I would argue that the real issue is not capitalism in the twenty-first century, but politics in the twenty-first century.

A major thesis of this chapter (and of this book as well as my earlier 2012 book *The Price of Inequality*) is accordingly that inequality is a *choice*, albeit one we make within our political system. Our inequality is not, for the most part, the result of inexorable economic laws. Rather, it is the consequence of our policies, and in turn, a reflection of our politics. Of course, there are economic forces at play that are dividing the country, but these forces are shaped by—and sometimes driven by—our policies.

There is a vicious circle in our democracies. Wealth and income inequality translate into political inequalities, especially in the United States, where our legal framework provides great scope for the influence of money. But then these political inequalities translate back into more economic inequalities.

There is a second major theme: Ever-rising inequality is depressing not only for what it would imply for our society and our democracy, but even for our economy. There has been a marked change in thinking about the consequences of inequality. It used to be thought that to do anything about inequality would require higher taxes that would weaken incentives and thereby weaken the economy. Arthur Okun, chairman of the Council of Economic Advisers under President Johnson, referred to this as "the big trade-off" (Okun, 1975). By contrast, the major thesis of my book *The Price of Inequality* (and of many chapters of this book as well) is that we are paying a high price for inequality—at least at the extremes it has reached in the United States and in the way that it has been generated. We could have a stronger economy, higher growth, and less instability if only we did something about our outsized inequality. This view has now, in fact, become the mainstream view, with support from the IMF (Berg and Ostry, 2011) and others (e.g., Galbraith, 2012).

In this chapter, I focus on two questions: What has given rise to this inequality? What can be done about it? In particular, is rising inequality largely the inevitable consequence of market forces (capitalism in the twenty-first century), about which there is little we can do, at least little in the realm of practical politics?

2 The Causes of the Increase in the Wealth–Income Ratio

2.1 Piketty's Narrative

Piketty presents a simple story of growing inequality. If those at the top save all of their income, their wealth grows at the rate of return on capital (r), and if r is greater than the rate of growth of the economy, wealth grows faster than income as a whole, and so too for their income (so long as the rate of return on capital does not diminish—which he suggests has not happened and is not likely to happen). He interprets the increase in the wealth–income ratio observed in many advanced countries as providing support for this hypothesis. He also sees the increase in the wealth–income ratio as essentially an increase in the capital–income ratio, and thus what economists would call capital deepening.

2.2 Skepticism about This Narrative

Many economists have been skeptical of this story on several grounds. Piketty's theory focuses on inherited wealth, and yet some (perhaps many) of those at the top of the income distribution did not inherit their wealth. The savings rate, *s*, even at the top, is far from 1: best estimates put the number around 0.35 (Carroll, 1998; Dynan, Skinner, and Zeldes, 2004; Piketty and Zucman, 2014). If that is the case, then *r* can be considerably greater than *g*, and yet *sr*—which would determine the pace at which the wealth of the capitalists would accumulate—will be less than *g*. Many at the top seem not to invest their money well, with investment and consumption often becoming blurred as their wealth is put into extravagant houses, horses, wineries, and art. The upshot is that wealth is often not perpetuated. As I observed in a paper presented at the 17th World Congress of the International Economic Association (Stiglitz, 2016a):

> John D. Rockefeller was America's first billionaire. At death, in 1937, his assets amounted to 1.5 percent of GDP. Had his assets grown at the rate *g* (the rate of growth of the economy) they would be worth today some $340 billion. If *r* (the relevant rate of return) were just 1 percent more than *g*, their family wealth should have grown to $680 billion. If, using numbers that Piketty might say are still conservative, but more realistic, the disparity between *g* and *r* is 2 percent, their wealth would have been $1. 3 trillion. Instead, the total value of the family assets is estimated to be $10 billion—less than 1 percent of the predicted amount—divided among almost 300 members (Roberts, 2014).[7]

2.2.1 The Rate of Interest Is an Endogenous Variable

Most importantly, the rate of interest is an endogenous variable. One of the most deep-seated beliefs among economists is the law of diminishing returns. Surely, with all of this capital deepening that Piketty suggests has been happening, the rate of return on capital should fall. If it doesn't, we have to rethink our basic models, and in ways far more profoundly than those offered by Piketty.

2.2.2 The Puzzle of Movements in Factor Returns

There are other disquieting aspects of growing inequality, especially in America, but also elsewhere, that are hard to reconcile with standard economic theories. Normally, capital deepening would be expected to raise labor productivity, and thereby wages. But wages have stagnated. (The numbers are even worse if the wages of the top 1% are excluded—the pay of bankers, CEOs, etc.—in which case there has been a dramatic decline in the income share of wages (Giovannoni, 2014, 2015).) While some have talked a lot about skill-biased technological change (which would increase the productivity of some workers at the expense of others), one can show in the standard model that average and marginal productivity—and in competitive markets, therefore the average wage—should have still increased.

[7] It appears from this story that Piketty's analysis seems to have overestimated "*r*," overestimated the extent to which returns were reinvested, and underestimated the importance of the division of wealth among one's heirs.

2.2.3 The Puzzle of the Pace of Increase in the Value of Wealth

One thinks of wealth accumulation as a steady process, of setting aside some of one's income every year, not consuming it, but rather investing it. But with America's low savings rate (the average net national savings rate of the United States over the period 1970–2010 was 5.2%),[8] one can account for only about half of the increase in the value of wealth.

2.2.4 Long-Run Determinants of the Wealth–Income Ratio

Finally, Piketty takes a long-term perspective, and it is therefore natural to ask: what determines the wealth–income ratio in the long run? Is it conceivable that the parameters describing the economy have changed, say, over the past 40 years, in ways that would lead to an increase in the wealth–income ratio, especially of the magnitude observed in some countries? Economists have formulated a large number of growth models (all within the neoclassical tradition, where output is a function of capital and labor, but differing in the determinants of savings). In each model, the equilibrium capital–output ratio increases with the savings rate and decreases with the long-run growth rate.[9] In the United States and many other countries, the savings rate has decreased, while the growth rate has fluctuated, increasing in the years after World War II, and again in the Clinton years, but diminishing more recently. But the movements in the wealth–output ratio do not seem to reflect these changes well, either qualitatively or quantitatively.

2.3 Capital Is Not to Be Confused with Wealth

There is a simple resolution to these conundrums. Much of the increase in wealth has little to do with savings in the usual sense. Rather it is the result of capital gains—especially the increased value of land—and an increase in the capitalized value of other rents. It is a mistake to confuse capital with wealth. Capital is, of course, an aggregation, somehow, of different capital goods. For purposes of assessing control over resources, a natural way to aggregate is to use market values. But market prices may or may not be a good way of aggregating these factors of production for purposes of assessing whether "inputs" into the production process have increased, and quantifying whether they have increased more than the supply of labor (i.e., whether there has been capital deepening).[10] The value of houses soared in the years before the crisis; this is part of our "capital stock." But no one would say that the capital input into the production process increased commensurately. Quite the contrary, the relevant measures of plant and equipment may have increased relatively little compared to GDP. In some countries, they may even have declined.

[8] Part, but only part, of the "wealth residual" (the unexplained portion of wealth accumulation) can be explained by net capital inflows.

[9] The long-run growth rate in turn is the sum of the long-run rate of increase of the work force plus the rate of labor augmenting technological progress.

[10] Domestic capital deepening could also occur because of inflows of foreign capital, but such inflows do not change the basic picture described here.

2.4 The Significance of Land

The distinction between wealth and capital is especially evident once land is taken into account. The value of land on the seashore may be going up, but that doesn't mean, in a real sense, the country is "wealthier" (though obviously, the owners of that land have more paper wealth). Since land is not increasing, if land is a factor of production (which it is, at least when it comes to the production of housing services, which constitute a quarter of GDP), then if we are to talk about an aggregate input, we have to weigh together the fixed land supply with increasing capital. When we do this using the best national income accounting ("aggregation") techniques, it turns out that the aggregate input ("land plus capital") is actually diminishing relative to GDP, at least for some advanced countries.

Similar to the increase in real estate values is the increase in the value of depletable natural resources, like oil, gas, iron, and copper. Economic theory (Hotelling, 1931) predicts that the price of these natural resources should increase over time; such increases are essential to efficient allocation of these resources over time, and would occur even in the absence of their increasing scarcity relative to labor, capital, and other inputs. Globally, much of the inequality at the top is related to ownership and control of such resources, including oil-rich sheikhs in the Middle East and the Russian oligarchs. (And, of course, this oil and mineral wealth gets translated in part into real estate wealth, as they demand residences in London and New York and homes in the Riviera and Southampton.)

The fact that capital in any productive sense is not increasing as fast as wealth helps explain part of the anomalies; it could help explain the failure of the return to capital to fall, or even the failure of wages to rise as much as one would have expected.

2.5 Exploitation Rents

But there is, I believe, something else going on: an increase of what might broadly be called exploitation rents. With the large inequalities that marked early capitalism in the eighteenth and nineteenth centuries, two broad strands of thought emerged: one seeking to understand the evolving distribution in terms of exploitation and market power, the other in terms of social contribution (the marginal productivity theory, what I will refer to below as the "neoclassical model," which is the standard one taught in conventional economics courses). There is some truth in both views. In some parts of the economy, there is strong competition, with factor prices reflecting productivities, but in others, competition is more limited. The incomes of those who enslaved others in the United States and elsewhere was a result of oppression and exploitation, but the exploitation continued long after, with discrimination still a part of the American economy.

In the late nineteenth and early twentieth centuries, there was much concern about "monopoly capitalism." Rockefeller and Carnegie made their fortunes through monopolies. Today's capitalism is different, and perhaps in some areas even more immune to anti-trust laws. Network externalities have given real market power to a few firms and the move to a service-sector economy may have resulted in greater scope for more local market power.

Many of the rents are derived from the use of political influence. The railroad barons of the Gilded Age made their fortunes in part through land grants from the U.S. government. Some of the top fortunes today can be traced either to the exploitation of market power or to grants of rents from the government. In many cases, the different forms of rents interact. Grants of zoning variances create wealth for real estate moguls; the provision of the 2003 law providing coverage for drugs for Medicare recipients—which said that the U.S. government, the largest purchaser of drugs in the world, could not bargain over prices—provided an estimated trillion dollars to the drug companies; preferential provisions of the tax laws provide trillions more to other special interests; and the giving away of the country's natural resources (or sales at below competitive prices) provides trillions more. The financial sector combines a variety of forms of exploitation rents, which have contributed to inequalities both at the top and the bottom: predatory lending and abusive credit card practices provide rents derived from exploiting the poor based on imperfect information and knowledge; market manipulation, evidenced in the LIBOR and FOREX scandals, also generates rents based on imperfect and asymmetric information, but this time mainly exploiting others who are better off; the huge interchange fees associated with credit and debit cards provide rents based on market power related to the control of the payments mechanism. Insider trade and the sophisticated front running associated with high frequency trading (Lewis, 2014; Stiglitz, 2014a) generate other forms of rent, as does the trading in credit default swaps and derivatives, based on non-transparent over-the-counter trading. As the financial sector grew to account for 8% of GDP, garnering for itself 40% of all corporate profits in the years before the crisis[11]—with little to show for its activities in terms of improved economic performance, either in growth or stability—it has become increasingly hard to reconcile its returns with the neoclassical model.

2.6 Evidence in Support of the Exploitation Model

Though there is no way to "prove" which model—the exploitation model or the neoclassical model—provides more insights into the origins of our increasing inequality, a number of pieces of "evidence" are suggestive. If we look at the Forbes 100 list of the wealthiest people, it is striking that it does not include those who have made the most important contributions to the advances in our standards of living—the discoverers of the transistor or the laser, those whose insights led to the invention of the computer, the Internet, or advances in modern medicine, or the discoverers of DNA. They do include those who have made important contributions to commerce, but their wealth is often the result of amplifying these contributions through the exertion of market power—as in the case of Bill Gates. The basic laws of competition limit the wealth that any individual can, in a short period of time, accumulate without the exercise of some monopoly power. Similarly, if we look across sectors of the economy, it is remarkable how in so many rent seeking (either based on the exertion of private market power or extraction of rents from the public sector through the exercise of public influence) is so evident: agricultural, health, natural resources, telecommunications, and high technology.

The recession provided more evidence. Bank officials, whose contributions to society, and even to their firms, were clearly negative, nevertheless received huge bonuses—a disconnect between compensation and contributions. But for those who had studied

[11] "Table 6. 16D. Corporate Profits by Industry." National Income and Product Accounts, Bureau of Economic Analysis, http://www.bea.gov/National/nipaweb/SelectTable.asp.

executive compensation, this had long been evident. There was no increase in productivity of managers that could justify the huge increases in their compensation over the past 35 years. Moreover, the form of compensation—linked to stock market prices, as much determined by changes in interest rates and other factors well beyond the control of the executives as by performance—showed that there was not even an attempt to closely link contribution and pay.

Piketty, with his co-authors, provided further evidence. Looking across countries, they observed that increasing taxes at the top did not lead to slower growth (Piketty, Saez, and Stantcheva, 2014). Under the neoclassical model, one would have expected the higher taxes to discourage effort and thus lower growth; under the exploitation model, higher taxes might discourage rent seeking, but this could even be good for the economy.

Most importantly, though, the exploitation model provides a ready interpretation of the seeming anomalies uncovered earlier. When the rights to rents can be bought and sold, they get capitalized. Increases in monopoly power show up simultaneously in higher profits, lower wages, and a higher value of "capital." If mining companies get more access to valuable natural resources on government-owned land at below-market prices—or the gap between what they have to pay and the fair market value increases—then the value of these mining companies increases. Changes in bank regulations, which allow them to undertake more risk, increase the chances of a bailout and thus the expected value of transfers from the government. The value of these transfers will be capitalized in the value of the banks, and thus the change in regulations will be reflected in an increase in the value of these institutions. One should not misread this as an increase in the wealth of the country. In each of these instances, the true wealth of the economy is unchanged or diminished. An increase in monopoly power shifts wealth from workers to the owners of the firms with market power, but the decrease in the wealth of workers is not recorded, while the increase of the value of firms is. Because of the market distortion associated with the exercise of market power, societal welfare is actually lowered. Increased transfers of money from the public to the private sector similarly increase the wealth of the banks but decrease the wealth of taxpayers. The former is recorded, the latter is not, and because of the distortion, overall wealth is lowered.

The exploitation theory can thus simultaneously explain the increase in the wealth–income ratio, the stagnation of wages, and the failure of the return to capital to fall. Much of the story of the increase in inequality in the United States is the increase in the wealth–income ratio, without a decrease in its return. Simple arithmetic means that if that happens, the share of capital in national income increases; since capital is more unequally distributed than labor, it follows that such a change would result in an increase in the measured inequality of income. These factors explain what might account for the increase in the wealth–income ratio and what might simultaneously account for the seemingly paradoxical failure of the return to capital to fall. But what gives rise to the increase in both land and exploitation rents? I will have a few words to say about this later in the chapter.

But this is not the full story, for as noted earlier, there has been an increase in concentration of wealth among capitalists. We also need to better understand the determinants of the rate of interest to see why it might not have fallen in the way expected, and why, since the middle of the twentieth century, there has been an enormous increase in life-cycle savings. We need to understand better the relationship between life cycle and inherited wealth. It turns out that these three issues are closely related.

3 The Determination of the Return to Capital

3.1 The Importance of the Savings Rate of Capitalists

Central in Piketty's explanation of the growth of the capital-(wealth-)output ratio is the observation that the return to capital exceeds the rate of growth. Earlier, I suggested that so long as the savings rate of capitalists is less than unity, what matters is the relationship of sr to g, where s is the fraction of their income that they save. The wealth of capitalists increases at the rate of sr, so only if sr is greater than g will inherited wealth increase faster than national income. But sr could plausibly be less than g even if r is greater than g. Indeed, that is the case for the numbers provided by Piketty and Zucman cited earlier for the United States.[12] Moreover, as capital accumulates, one would expect r to decline. Economic theory ought to explain whether, in the long run, sr could plausibly remain above g.

In fact, standard growth theory provided an answer to these questions a half century ago. I used such theories to develop a theory of the distribution of income and wealth among individuals in my Ph.D. thesis.[13] In the long run, if all individuals save the same fraction of their income (as in the classic Solow (1956) model that defined neoclassical growth theory), then in the long run, $sr < g$.[14] With s being around a third, all that is required is that the rate of return to capital be less than three times the rate of growth; most studies suggest that this is the case now and the general theory argues that this will be true over the long run.

I showed that under this condition, if all families had the same wage, divided their income equally among their children, and had the same number of children, then wealth would eventually be fully equalized, regardless of the initial distribution of income. I had shown that what mattered was not the relationship between r and g, but between sr and g, and in the long run, inequalities would not persist because sr would be less than g (even though r would be greater than g) in these simple models. There are, however, other forces giving rise to inequalities, which I discuss in the next section.

3.2 The Implications of Differences in Savings between Capitalists and Workers

First, I note that there are other frameworks generating somewhat different results. In the battles in the middle of the twentieth century over different views of growth, the Cambridge School (United Kingdom) argued that a better model than the Solow neoclassical model hypothesized that capitalists save a far larger fraction of their income than workers. In the long-run equilibrium, $s_c r = g$, where s_c is the savings rate of capitalists. The rate of interest in long-run equilibrium was greater than the rate of growth, by just enough to offset the fact that capitalists save less than all of their income. In the long run, contrary to Piketty, the wealth of capitalists grows at exactly the same rate as the economy.

[12] With the savings rate at the top of the income distribution around 1/3, and g around 2.8%, $sr < g$ so long as $r < 8.4\%$, which it clearly is on average.

[13] This work was presented in 1966 to the meetings of the Econometric Society in San Francisco, and subsequently published (in abbreviated form) as Stiglitz (1969b).

[14] Solow showed that $sY/K = g$, where Y/K is the output capital ratio. But $Y = wL + rK$, where w is the wage rate, so it is immediate that $g = sr + (swL/K) > sr$.

As I showed in Stiglitz (1969b), this has, however, a disturbing implication: any initial inequalities in wealth ownership (among the capitalists) are preserved. There is neither a tendency for wealth inequalities to increase or decrease. But if there is variability in the returns to capital, then inequalities in wealth grow increasingly large over time. The fact, however, that those at the very top of the wealth distribution in the United States are not those who have had wealth accumulate over multiple generations suggests that this is not a good model for understanding the distribution of wealth, at least in the United States.

3.3 Life-Cycle Savings and Taxes

Late-twentieth-century capitalism in the United States and many other advanced countries was accompanied by an enormous increase in life-cycle savings, as life expectancies grew far faster than retirement ages. The increase in (private) retirement savings was somewhat dampened by the growth of public retirement programs but increased with the shift from defined benefit programs to defined contribution systems.[15] One might have thought that these large amounts of retirement savings would have driven down the return to capital—perhaps even making $s_c r < g$, just as in the neoclassical model—leading toward the equalization of wealth. And that may have happened in the middle of the twentieth century.

But two forces worked in the other direction. First, and perhaps most importantly, changes in tax laws meant that the very rich actually faced lower tax rates than the not-so-rich, so that for them, s times their after-tax returns was greater than the rate of growth. (We will return later to a more extensive discussion of taxation.)

Secondly, in the long run, there is a balance between dissaving of the retired and the saving of the young. In the long-run equilibrium, it turns out that even with life-cycle savings, $s_c r = g$. The capital stock, rates of return to capital, and wage rates are all determined by the savings behavior of capitalists. Life-cycle savings "crowds" out capitalists' savings. The greater the life-cycle savings, obviously the smaller the share of the country's wealth that is owned by the plutocrats—but that is the only effect.[16]

4 Centrifugal and Centripetal Forces

The best way of thinking about the changing distribution of income and wealth is to think of the economy being pulled apart by centrifugal forces—creating more inequality—at the same time that there are underlying centripetal economic forces dampening inequality. The equilibrium distribution of income and wealth reflects a balancing of these centrifugal and centripetal forces. Over time, the strength of, say, the centrifugal forces may increase, and this will lead to an increase in inequality. Such an "equilibrium" theory provides a better

[15] The shift from defined benefit to defined contribution systems would not have resulted in a change in wealth but a change in who controlled it if the former had been fully funded. In defined benefit programs, the wealth would have resided within corporations. It would be a difficult task to attribute this wealth to the eventual recipients.

[16] This result is developed in Stiglitz (2016a) but was anticipated in Pasinetti (1962).

approach to thinking about what has been going on in recent decades than the notion that there are certain inexorable forces in capitalism leading to ever-increasing inequality. Rather, changes in economics and in policies have changed the balance between the two sets of forces. By identifying what these forces are, one is in a better position to "rebalance" the economy.

The fact that wealth compounds at the rate of interest obviously is an important centrifugal force, but the fact that only a fraction of wealth is reinvested and that $sr < g$ in the basic neoclassical model means that wealth compounds at a rate slower than the growth of the economy; limitations on savings thus act as a centripetal force, as does the fact that the wealth accumulated by any generation is normally divided among multiple heirs.

The variability of returns to capital also leads to wealth and income inequality. Those who are lucky will give more wealth to their children, and if their children are also "lucky" they will be able to bequeath more to their children. In 1953, a brilliant colleague at Cambridge (United Kingdom), David Champernowne, formulated a simple stochastic model generating income and wealth distributions with fat-tails (more wealth in the extremes of the distribution than one would have expected with, say, a lognormal distribution) (Champernowne, 1953). In Stiglitz (1969b),[17] I then showed that a stochastic variant of my neoclassical model satisfied the Champernowne conditions.

Subsequently, in Bevan and Stiglitz (1979) (see also Bevan, 1979), I used more advanced techniques (employing diffusion models) to demonstrate that the level of inequality decreased with the size of $g—sr$ and increased with the variability of returns. But, as I noted earlier, r itself is an endogenous variable, affected, for instance, by the savings rate itself. In Part II of this volume, I show that the level of wealth inequality increases with the share of capital. The observed increase in the share of capital would thus be expected to lead to more inequality in wealth. If the elasticity of substitution is less than one,[18] an increase in the capital–effective labor ratio (e.g., as a result of an increase in the savings rate or a reduction in the population growth rate) will lead to a decreased share of capital and less inequality. Of course, just the opposite happens if, in spite of the increase in the wealth–income ratio, the capital-effective–labor ratio declines, so long as the share of rents doesn't increase too much. Either way, it reinforces my earlier conclusion: one cannot understand what is happening to inequality of wealth without taking into account the growth of rents.

Wage dispersions—especially in the extremes—give rise to wealth inequality. Those at the bottom accumulate no wealth, while those at the very top save enough not only for their retirement, but to pass on wealth to their heirs. If the wages of children were the same as those of the parents, wealth inequality would simply reflect these underlying wage disparities (compounded by the good and bad luck of the random returns on capital). But there is a process of regression toward the mean, and a faster pace of regression will result

[17] This is the unpublished version of Stiglitz (1969b), which I presented at the December 1966 meetings of the Econometric Society in San Francisco.

[18] The elasticity of substitution describes how easy it is to substitute capital for labor. When the elasticity is low, an increase in capital (relative to labor) so diminishes the return to capital that the overall share of capital diminishes. The capital–effective labor ratio takes account of the fact that because of technological change, one worker today may be the equivalent of two workers earlier.

in less wage and wealth inequality. The aphorism "rags to riches and back to rags in three generations" reflects this perspective.

The fact that the rich save so much more than the poor is a centrifugal force, as those who get large incomes (as a result of high wages or a high return on investments) will save more to pass on their wealth to their children. If the savings function (giving savings as a function of income or wealth) is S-shaped, then it is possible that the two-class model described earlier (a capitalist class whose income is largely based on wealth that saves at a high rate, and a working class with more limited savings, mostly for retirement) provides a good description of the economy. The inequality of wealth is not caused by the differences in savings functions—all individuals could have the same savings function—but the differences in savings rate simply reflect the endogenous distribution of income and wealth.

Dispersions in family size and in inheritance customs and law can also affect inheritances and wealth inequality. Primogeniture gives rise to high levels of inequality. If there is a high variability in family size, then, even with equal division, there will be a large dispersion in inheritances.

This framework allows us to think about how changes in the economy, society, and policies may have affected the centripetal and centrifugal forces. With the very rich paying a smaller tax rate on capital than the less wealthy, the centrifugal force of wealth-compounding has increased. In the standard neoclassical model, capital taxation reduces the variability of returns and hence tail-inequality. Thus, a reduction in the average taxation of capital (even without the regressivity currently observed) leads to more inequality (unless offset by a corresponding fall in the before-tax return—see below).

There are many ways in which rich parents can transmit advantages to their children, including by providing them with a better education. Public education can thus be an important equalizing force. But if there is economic segregation (and there is evidence of an increase in such segregation), if schools are locally funded, and if schools in rich communities provide a better education than those in poor communities, then there will be more intergenerational transmission of advantages. The equalizing force of "regression toward the mean" will be dampened, as it will if there is more assortative mating, as a result of the rich and talented being more segregated into schools that are different from those attended by others.

The fact that advantages are transmitted across generations implies, of course, that societies, such as the United States, with high levels of economic inequality are likely to be marked by low levels of economic opportunity, a relationship that Krueger (2012) has labeled the Great Gatsby curve,[19] which has been shown to hold within the United States (Chetty, Hendren, Kline, and Saez, 2014). This is especially the case in the absence of government actions to "level the playing field," by providing all children, regardless of the income of their parents, access to good education and health care. Programs like Head Start are designed to partially undo some of the disadvantages facing the poor, and there is some evidence that such programs work (Heckman, 2011; Heckman, Pinto, and Savelyev, 2013). By the same token, the increase in inequality in the United States in recent years suggests that going forward there will be still greater inequalities of opportunity, which will then translate into still greater inequalities in income and wealth.

[19] Krueger's remarks were based on the work of Corak (2013).

5 Explaining the Increase in the Price of Land

Earlier, I argued that the basic neoclassical model could only explain part of the increase in income and wealth inequality. Much of the growth in inequality and the increase in the wealth–income ratio are related to an increase in rents and land values. In the middle of the last century, land was essentially dropped out of the models used by economists. After all, agriculture, the source of the major demand for land, had shrunk to a very small fraction of GDP. But as I noted earlier, housing services are an important component of GDP, and land values, especially in our urban areas, are an important part of housing services. Indeed, with urbanization, one would expect an increase in land values.

But there is more going on: land is a store of value. The value of land today is largely dependent on its expected value tomorrow, ad infinitum. This means that land prices are largely untethered. Rising expectations can, at least for a while, be self-fulfilling. Land bubbles have marked capitalism from its early days, and we have been going through just the latest instance.[20] But even when there is a "correction," there is no assurance that the economy is not off on another bubble-path.

One of the main drivers of land prices (or the value of other non-produced assets) is credit availability. As quantitative easing made so abundantly clear, a flood of liquidity can drive up asset prices. This is especially easy because, as I noted, land prices are largely untethered. If credit is made available to those with collateral and provided at interest rates below the expected rate of return, there will be a heavy demand for those assets (like land) that can easily be used as collateral. Thus, changes in monetary and regulatory policies that lead to an expansion of credit will contribute to an increase in the value of land—to an increase in "wealth"—but not necessarily to an increase in the country's real capital stock.

Such monetary policies can contribute at the same time to growth in income and wealth inequality, and the mechanism by which this occurs represents a fundamental change in our understanding of the structure of the economy. In the nineteenth century, analyses of monetary policy focused on impacts on creditors and debtors. The election of 1896 was fought on this issue: moving to the bimetallic standard would lead to higher prices, reducing the value of the debts owed by farmers to the banks. Thus, loose monetary policy was seen as pro-equality.

Similarly, in the post-World War II era, looser monetary policies were associated with faster economic growth and higher employment, driving up wages. The excessive focus on inflation contributed to a ratcheting down of wages; when a recession occurred, wages stagnated, and workers did poorly. But as soon as the economy started to recover and unemployment fell, central banks, focusing on inflation, would raise interest rates, preventing workers from recovering in the upswing what they had lost in the recession.

Keeping interest rates close to zero seems to have contributed to wealth inequality, too. While this policy didn't stimulate the economy much (as predicted—though it may have prevented the economy from falling into an even deeper downturn), it hurt owners of

[20] Technically, they could be prevented if there were markets for land going out infinitely far into the future. The equilibrium conditions requiring the returns to land (rents plus capital gains) to equal the returns to capital goods imply that if the price is not "right," bubble prices can't be sustained, as demonstrated in the last episode. Formal models showing this have been developed by Hahn (1966), Shell and Stiglitz (1967), and Stiglitz (2016a).

short-term government bonds—older, risk-averse people who had acted conservatively—but helped the owners of equity, disproportionately the very rich. Earlier, I talked about two types of wealth holdings: life-cycle and inherited. While the proportion of wealth in life-cycle savings may be far higher than seventy-five years ago, there are important compositional differences in the two kinds of wealth holding. The very rich are able to bear more risk and disproportionately own equities, so the low-interest policy of the Federal Reserve, which advantaged equities, improved the fortunes of those at the top.

6 Explaining the Increase in Exploitation Rents

There are several reasons for the increase in exploitation rents, some of which were noted earlier in this chapter, including that changes in technology gave more scope for network externalities, and thus for market power. But there are other institutional and societal forces at play. Changes in mores led corporate executives to exploit weaknesses in corporate governance laws, and the weakening of unions meant that they were less able to check these abuses. An unintended consequence of the 1993 tax change—effectively imposing taxes on high executive pay unless it was performance related—was to encourage seemingly performance-related executive pay. Executives discovered new non-transparent ways of increasing their incomes, including by diluting shareholder holdings. Accounting rules gave them ample scope for doing so. Globalization—in the asymmetric way that it was done, without appropriate safeguards—and declining unionization weakened the bargaining power of workers. Deregulation of financial institutions allowed them to engage in more exploitive activities.

There were some opposing changes, but these proved less powerful than had been expected. Laws against discrimination and affirmative action programs did allow a larger number of minorities and women to be more successful; yet the average Black–white gap in incomes remains unchanged, that in wealth has increased, especially after the recession, and the gender gap remains large.

Finally, there is little doubt that there has been an increase in the influence of money in politics. And because the size of government itself has increased, there are more opportunities and incentives for the wealthy and corporate interests to engage in rent seeking in the public sphere. The deregulation movement itself, especially in the financial sector, can be viewed as part of this rent-seeking agenda. President Eisenhower, in his farewell address, effectively warned against such rent seeking on the part of the military industrial complex. But the list of successful rent seekers today is much larger, including the drug companies as well as those in oil, gas, and mining, and the financial sector.

Public policy has affected inequality in other ways. In some periods, there has been lax enforcement of anti-trust laws, and even the limited rules governing, say, the financial sector. Lowering taxes on the wealthy may have actually encouraged rent seeking. It takes effort (and in some cases, rather unpleasant effort) to engage in rent seeking. Since so much of the return to rent seeking goes to those at the very top of the income distribution, when their tax rates are lowered, the benefits of rent seeking, relative to the costs (especially the personal costs) may be lowered.

7 Taxation and Other Public Policies

The previous section outlined some of the ways that public policy in recent years has contributed to the increase in inequality. In fact, every law and regulation and every policy potentially has an impact on inequality. Markets don't exist in a vacuum, and our laws and regulations determine how they operate. A bankruptcy law, such as ours, that gives owners of derivatives first claim helps derivatives; a bankruptcy law, such as ours, that makes student loans almost undischargeable even in bankruptcy, discourages borrowing for education and thus impairs upward mobility on the part of those who need loans to obtain a good college education.

So too for every expenditure program. Australia provides income contingent loans to every university student. Other countries provide large subsidies that lead to lower tuition. With a university education increasingly necessary for economic success, a tuition-financed system such as ours makes a university education less accessible in the United States than in other countries, reduces upward mobility, and thereby contributes to inequality.

Taxes in particular can have a large effect on inequality, as I noted earlier, but as always, one has to pay particular attention to tax-shifting. Consider, for instance, Piketty's central model in which capital accumulation is the result of capitalists saving a fraction (all) of their wealth. If in this world a tax is imposed on capital, the amount of savings/investment will be reduced, and the return to capital will increase. In the short run, Piketty is right that there will be a reduction in the capital–output ratio and a reduction in the extent of inequality among capitalists. But the lower level of investment will lead to a higher return to capital, and in the long run, the after-tax return will be exactly the same as before. There is no change in income and wealth inequality among capitalists. Moreover, because the capital stock is lower, wages will be lower. It can be shown (Stiglitz, 2016a) that even if all the tax proceeds are redistributed to workers, they can be worse off. Quite different results are obtained if the tax is imposed on inheritances (and even better, if one taxes the returns to capital that are not part of life-cycle savings).

But full shifting only occurs in this special model, and only if the government does not invest some of the proceeds. If it does so, particularly in investments that increase workers' productivity (either investments in human capital or in technology or infrastructure that are complementary with labor), then wages can rise and the standard of living of workers can improve.

My analysis has shown that tax structures that tax inheritances and exempt life-cycle savings from interest income taxes can also improve the distribution of income and wealth.[21] The earlier discussion emphasized, too, the importance of progressive capital taxes, and how our current tax structure, which is regressive at the top, may itself be contributing to the growth of wealth inequality at the top.

Some have argued against the taxation of capital (and inheritances) on the grounds that such taxes are inefficient. The returns to capital consist of four parts: (1) the pure rate of

[21] Even in this case, however, one has to be attentive to tax shifting, as such taxes might encourage a shift toward the transfer of human capital. But provided there is a good public education system, the effects of this shift will be limited.

interest—the T-bill rate; (2) the return to risk—related to the β of the asset; (3) the excess returns from the ability of the investment manager (presumably, what he is compensated for, and typically referred to as the α); and (4) rents—some of these excess returns may be related to the exercise of monopoly power or other aspects of rent seeking.

In this parsing, at most, it is the first that should not be taxed on the standard efficiency grounds that differential taxation distorts the economy, and in recent years, these returns have been very, very low. Increases in taxation of the second component (so long as there are adequate provisions for loss offsets) actually increase efficiency; well-designed higher taxation provides better risk sharing, which is especially important in the context of imperfect risk markets (Domar and Musgrave, 1944; Stiglitz, 1969a). The third component should be included in labor income, and subject to the progressive income tax. If some individuals consistently get higher risk-adjusted returns to capital, those higher returns should be ascribed to their "labor services." Indeed, those in Wall Street always claim that is why they should be well compensated. (The preferential tax treatment of carried interest is one of the ways that our tax system leads to more inequality.) The fourth component should be taxed at very high rates.

There is a practical challenge in parsing out the components, but, at the very least, this parsing of the nature of the returns to capital should make it clear that the returns to capital should be taxed, and possibly at rates even higher than those imposed on conventionally measured labor income. If one cannot parse out the different components, then the tax rate imposed should reflect the relative importance of the different components even if one were not concerned with redistribution.

Finally, I want to link this discussion with the earlier analysis of increases in wealth inequality, which showed that the increases are closely related to increases in land prices. Piketty's recent book noted the enormous increases in the wealth–output ratio in most capitalist countries in the last third of a century. But these increases have been partly, and in some cases largely, related to increases in the value of land. A tax on the return to land, and even more so, on the capital gains from land, would reduce inequality and, by encouraging more investment into real capital, actually enhance growth. This is, of course, an old idea, promoted most famously by Henry George (1879).

In concluding this section, let me digress briefly. The standard argument against differential taxation is based on Atkinson and Stiglitz (1976),[22] in which we showed that if there is an optimal income tax, then no differential taxation on commodities is desirable. An implication is that, treating consumption at different dates as different commodities, one should not impose an interest income tax, which changes the relative price of consumption at different dates. That model entailed special technical assumptions (e.g., about the separability between consumption of all goods and leisure) that limit its applicability. Beyond that, several factors are omitted from this model.

First, there are no inheritances. If there were, and they were observable, then they would normally be taxed. How they should be taxed within the standard social welfare framework is a more complicated matter.

Second, there are no rents. As explained above, much of the seeming return to capital is actually rents, and the Henry George principle says that such rents should be taxed at 100%.

[22] The result was subsequently generalized in Kaplow (2006b).

Third, in the Atkinson–Stiglitz framework, individuals differ in only one respect—their output per hour. But skill mixes are far more heterogeneous, and tax policy (encouraging, say, some kinds of investments and discouraging others) can affect the before-tax distribution of income just as it can affect the after-tax distribution of income.

It is, in fact, desirable for government not to just rely on ex post redistribution but to design tax and expenditure policies, to the extent possible, that create a more equalitarian pre-tax and transfer distribution of income, reducing the burden imposed by redistributive taxation.[23]

8 Concluding Comments

Piketty's book provides us with a wealth of data to interpret. It had been widely recognized that inequality in most advanced countries had been increasing markedly since 1980. It had also been widely recognized that inequality was lower in the period after World War II than it had been, say, in America's Gilded Age or in the years just before the Great Depression. The juxtaposition of those two observations leads to a natural question: Was this period that I referred to earlier as the golden age of capitalism a rare exception the result of the unusual solidarity brought about by World War II, including policies like the GI bill that provided a free college education to everyone who had fought (which was essentially every young able-bodied man)? Or did the policies that began to be instituted in the 1980s represent an aberration of the trend that Kuznets had earlier identified—of economic advances being associated with greater equality?

The general theories that I have discussed in this review, while they cannot provide a definitive answer, provide some hints. In the absence of changes in policies, such as lowering taxes on capital, standard models would not imply either the increase in the wealth–income ratio or the increase in inequality that has been observed. The standard economic model will not suffice.

One set of changes that I have not discussed are changes in technology. Technological change has made labor more productive, and at least in some areas, like computing, there have been enormous increases in the productivity of capital. Some types of labor have had their productivity increased more than others.[24] Still, there should have been an increase in average wages paid (given that the rate of return to capital has remained roughly constant).[25] And these changes in technology cannot explain why there should have been such an increase in the gap between average wages (or compensation) and productivity.

This leaves two other partially related sets of explanations: (1) an increase in rents[26]—an increase in land rents and land values, and an increase in exploitation rents and

[23] Stiglitz (1998a, 2015d) provides a more extensive discussion of the issues.

[24] Although such skill-biased technological changes may have played an important role in explaining wage inequalities before 2000, it is hard to see how they can account for what has happened since. It is also hard to reconcile the timing of changes in wage rates with changes either in technology or globalization. Shierholz, Mishel, and Schmitt (2013) provide a more extensive critique and review of the literature.

[25] This is proven in Stiglitz (2016a).

[26] There is one further category of rents that has increased—those associated with intellectual property. While important, they do not seem to be the primary drivers of the observed increases in inequality. Part of the increase in intellectual property rents is associated with the move to a knowledge economy, but part of the increase is the result of stronger intellectual property laws. While there is a debate about whether this has led to more innovation (there are reasons to believe it may have had exactly the opposite effect), it is clear that the "enclosure of the

an associated increase in wealth that represents the capitalization of those rents; and (2) changes in public policies which are, on balance, inequality-increasing. I have shown how a variety of policies—most importantly, tax, education, anti-trust, monetary, corporate governance, and regulatory policies—may have contributed to recent increases in inequality.

Americans still like to see themselves as the middle-class families of the 1950s. That period, as Piketty has reminded us, was unusual, and much has happened in the last half century. The set of policy and structural changes brought on in the 1980s, here and abroad—deregulation, globalization, the lowering of marginal tax rates—did not bring about the burst of growth that had been hoped for in the United States and other advanced countries. Growth, in fact, has been markedly slower than in the decades after World War II, and the benefits of what growth there has been have gone to those at the top of the income distribution.

The title of Piketty's book and much of his analysis suggests that it is capitalism that is at fault, that this is just the way that market economies work. My analysis of market models suggests that there is no inherent reason that there should be the high level of inequality that is observed in the United States and many other advanced countries. It is not a necessary feature of the market economy. It is politics in the twenty-first century, not capitalism, which is at fault. Market and political forces have, of course, always been intertwined. Especially in America, where our politics is so money-driven, economic inequalities translate into political inequality.

There is nevertheless considerable hope. For if the growth of inequality was largely the result of inexorable economic laws, public policy could do little more than lean against the wind. But if the growth of inequality is the result of public policy, a change in those policies could lead to an economy with less inequality, and even stronger growth.

knowledge commons" (to use Boyle's term) has generated more measured wealth, appropriating benefits that would have otherwise been shared in society (Boyle, 2003; Stiglitz, 2014c).

3

Inequality and Economic Growth

1 Introduction

This chapter was written for a volume on "rethinking capitalism" (Mazzucato and Jacobs, 2016).[1] Especially in Europe, the 2008 crisis inspired a re-evaluation of capitalism. Since the early 1970s a substantial body of research had undermined Adam Smith's presumption in the efficiency of the market economy—the invisible hand which was supposed to make sure that the pursuit of self-interest led to the wellbeing of society was invisible because it was not there. Still, it was not until the crisis that it became clear just how inefficient and unstable an unregulated market economy could be.

But even advocates of market efficiency never claimed that the distribution of income that would emerge out of the market was socially desirable. The claim here was weaker: that somehow, all would benefit from the growth that would result from free markets through trickle-down economics. This chapter presents some of the evidence that that has not happened in the U.S. and most other advanced countries, gives some of the evidence on the growth of rents as a key explanation (a theory which while will be further advanced in later chapters), describes some of the theory and evidence on the adverse economic effects of inequality, and concludes with a brief discussion of some of the policies that might reduce inequality.

In the middle of the twentieth century, it came to be believed that "a rising tide lifts all boats": economic growth would bring increasing wealth and higher living standards to all sections of society. At the time, there was some evidence behind that claim. In industrialized countries in the 1950s and 1960s every group was advancing, and those with lower incomes were rising most rapidly.

In the ensuing economic and political debate, this "rising-tide hypothesis" evolved into a much more specific idea, according to which regressive economic policies—policies that favor the richer classes—would end up benefiting everyone. Resources given to the rich would inevitably "trickle down" to the rest. It is important to clarify that this version of old-fashioned "trickle-down economics" did not follow from the post-war evidence. The "rising-tide hypothesis" was equally consistent with a "trickle-up" theory—give more money to those at the bottom and everyone will benefit; or with a "build-out from the middle" theory—help those at the center and both those above and below will benefit.

Today the trend to greater equality of incomes which characterized the post-war period has been reversed. Inequality is now rising rapidly. Contrary to the rising-tide hypothesis,

[1] Reprinted with permission from Michael Jacobs and Mariana Mazzucato (eds.), *Rethinking Capitalism: Economics and Policy for Sustainable and Inclusive Growth*, pp. 134–55, Oxford: Wiley-Blackwell.

The author is indebted to Eamon Kircher-Allen and Deberati Ghosh for research assistance. Financial support from INET and the Roosevelt Institute Project on Inequality, supported by the Ford Foundation, the Bernard and Irene Schwartz Foundation, and the John D. and Catherine T. MacArthur Foundation, is gratefully acknowledged.

The Origins of Inequality, and Policies to Contain It. Joseph E. Stiglitz, Oxford University Press. © Joseph E. Stiglitz (2025).
DOI: 10.1093/oso/9780198799580.003.0004

the rising tide has only lifted the large yachts, and many of the smaller boats have been left dashed on the rocks.

The trickle-down notion—along with its theoretical justification, marginal productivity theory—attempts both to *explain* inequality (why it occurs)—and to *justify* it (why it would be beneficial for the economy as a whole). This chapter looks critically at both claims. It argues in favor of alternative explanations of inequality, with particular reference to the theory of rent-seeking and to the influence of institutional and political factors, which have shaped labor markets and patterns of remuneration. And it shows that, far from being either necessary or good for economic growth, excessive inequality tends to lead to weaker economic performance. In light of this, it argues for a range of policies that would increase both equity and economic wellbeing.

2 The Great Rise of Inequality

Let us start by examining the ongoing trends in income and wealth. In the past three decades, those at the top have done very well, especially in the U.S. Between 1980 and 2014, the richest 1% have seen their average real income increase by 169% (from $469,403, adjusted for inflation, to $1,260,508) and their share of national income more than double, from 10% to 21%. The top 0.1% have fared even better. Over the same period, their average real income increased by 281% (from $1,597,080, adjusted for inflation, to $6,087,113) and their share of national income almost tripled, from 3.4% to 10.3%.[2]

Over the same 34 years, median household income grew by only 11%. And this growth actually occurred only in the very first years of the period: by 2014 it was only 0.7% higher than in 1989, after peaking in 1999.[3] But even this underestimates the extent to which those at the bottom have suffered—their incomes have only done as well as they have because hours worked have increased. Median hourly compensation (adjusted for inflation) increased by only 9% from 1973 to 2014, even though at the same time productivity grew by 72.2% (Figure 3.1). (To understand how significant this divergence of productivity and wages is, consider that from 1948 to 1973 both increased at the same pace, about doubling over the period.)[4] And these statistics underestimate the true deterioration in workers' wages, for education levels have increased (the percentage of Americans who are college graduates has nearly doubled since 1980, to more than 30%),[5] so that one should have expected a significant increase in wage rates. In fact, average real hourly wages for all Americans with only a high school diploma have decreased in the past three decades.[6,7]

[2] Piketty and Saez, 2003 (updated). Figures are in real 2014 dollars and include capital gains.

[3] Source: U.S. Census Historical Table H-6. It should be clear that median wages could have declined, even though in a panel study, most individuals (families) would have seen an increase in their wages, if there were a sufficiently large number of new entrants into the labor force, and if these new entrants had much lower skills/education than those previously in the labor force.

[4] See Bivens, Mishel, Shierholz (2015).

[5] U.S. Census Data on educational attainment, http://www.census.gov/hhes/socdemo/education/(accessed December 22, 2015).

[6] See Economic Policy Institute (2015).

[7] At one time, such results were explained as a result of skill-biased technical change (see Violante, 2008), in which case those without skills would see their wages decline, but those with skills should see their wages increase. But an (appropriately) weighted average wage should still rise (see Stiglitz, 2016a). Data over the last 15 years, however, during which even the wages of skilled workers have stagnated, implies that something else is going on.

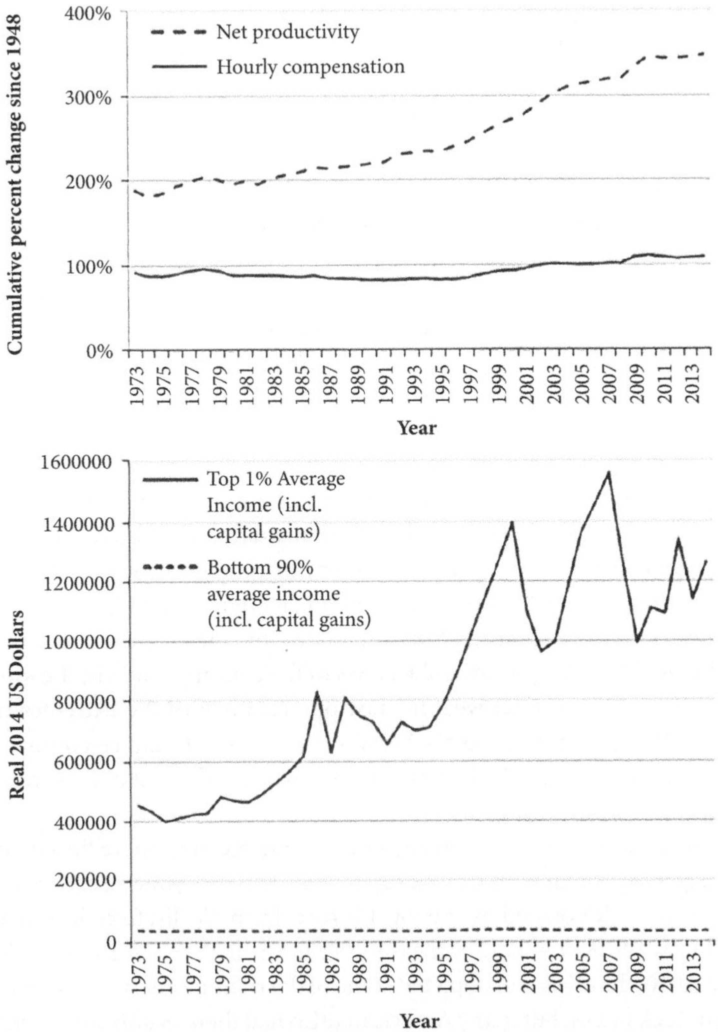

Figure 3.1 Wages, productivity, and average incomes in the U.S. (1973–2014).

Notes: (top panel) Data are for average hourly compensation of production/nonsupervisory workers in the private sector and net productivity of the total economy. "Net productivity" is the growth of output of goods and services minus depreciation per hour worked. EPI analysis.

Sources: Economic Policy Institute (top panel; based on data from the BEA and BLS); The World Wealth and Income Database. Facundo Alvaredo, Tony Atkinson, Thomas Piketty, Emmanuel Saez, and Gabriel Zucman (bottom panel).

In the first three years of the so-called recovery from the Great Recession of 2008–9—fully 91% of the gains in income went to the top 1%. By 2014, the rest of the income distribution had experienced a bit more of a boost, but even accounting for that, 58% of the gains in total income have gone to the top 1% since 2009. (During that period, the income of the bottom 99% has grown by just 4%.)[8] Presidents Bush and Obama both tried a trickle-down strategy—giving large amounts of money to the banks and the bankers. The

[8] Piketty and Saez, 2003.

idea was simple: by saving the banks and bankers, all would benefit. The banks would restart lending. The wealthy would create more jobs. This strategy, it was argued, would be far more efficacious than helping homeowners, businesses, or workers directly. The U.S. Treasury typically demands that when money is given to developing countries, conditions be imposed on them to ensure not only that the money is used well, but also that the country adopts economic policies that (according to the Treasury's economic theories) will lead to growth. But no conditions were imposed on the banks—not even, for example, requirements that they lend more or stop abusive practices. The rescue worked in enriching those at the top; but the benefits did not trickle down to the rest of the economy.

The Federal Reserve, too, tried trickle-down economics. One of the main channels by which quantitative easing was supposed to rekindle growth was by leading to higher stock market prices, which would generate higher wealth for the very rich, who would then spend some of that, which in turn would benefit the rest.

These trickle-down policies were relatively ineffective—one reason why seven years after the U.S. slipped into recession, the economy was still not back to health. As Wray and Nersisyan (2016) argue, both the Fed and the Administration could have tried policies that more directly benefited the rest of the economy: helping homeowners, lending to small and medium-sized enterprises and fixing the broken credit channel.

Wealth is even more concentrated than income—by one estimate more than 10 times so. The wealthiest 1% of Americans hold 41.8% of the country's wealth; the top 0.1% alone control more than 22% of total wealth.[9] Just one example of the extremes of wealth in America is the Walton family: the six heirs to the Walmart empire command a wealth of $145 billion, which is equivalent to the net worth of 1,782,020 average American families.[10]

Wealth inequality too is on the upswing. For the four decades before the Great Recession, the rich were getting wealthier at a more rapid pace than everyone else. Between 1978 and 2013 the share of wealth owned by the top 1% rose dramatically, from less than 25% to its current level above 40%; the share of the top 10% from about two-thirds to well over three-quarters.[11] By 2010, the crisis had depleted some of the richest Americans' wealth because of the decline in stock prices, but many Americans also had their wealth almost entirely wiped out as their homes lost value. After the crisis, the average wealthiest 1% of households still had 165 times the wealth of the average American in the bottom 90%—more than double the ratio of 30 years ago.[12] In the years of "recovery," as stock market values rebounded (in part as a result of the Fed's lopsided efforts to resuscitate the economy through increasing the balance sheet of the rich), the rich have regained much of the wealth that they had lost; the same did not happen to the rest of the country.[13]

[9] Saez and Zucman, 2014. As the authors show, wealth share estimates vary slightly depending on how and whether capital gains are included in the estimate.

[10] Harkinson, 2015.

[11] Saez and Zucman, 2014.

[12] Saez and Zucman, 2014.

[13] That this is the case can be clearly seen by examining what has happened to different kinds of wealth since the end of the crisis. Stocks, which are disproportionately owned by the wealthy, have done very well. Stock market values in the United States increased by $13 trillion from January 2009 to December 2013, according to data from the Center for Research in Security Prices. Meanwhile, home values, which account for much of middle-class wealth, have not enjoyed a strong recovery: 13.4% of American homes were still underwater as of the third quarter of 2015, according to real estate company Zillow—their owners owe more on their mortgages than the market says their houses are worth. For a concise discussion of this, see Dreier (2014).

Inequality plays out along ethnic lines in ways that should be disturbing for a country that had begun to see itself as having won out against racism. Between 2005 and 2009, a huge number of Americans saw their wealth drastically decrease. The net worth of the typical white American household was down substantially, to $113,149 in 2009, a 16% loss of wealth from 2005. But the recession was much worse for other groups. The typical African American household lost 53% of its wealth—putting its assets at a mere 5% of the median white American's. The typical Hispanic household lost 66% of its wealth.[14]

Probably the most invidious aspect of America's inequality is that of opportunities: In the U.S. a young person's life prospects depend heavily on the income and education of his parents, even more than in other advanced countries.[15] The "American dream" is largely a myth.

A number of studies have noted the link between inequality of outcomes and inequality of opportunities.[16] When there are large inequalities of income, those at the top can buy for their offspring privileges not available to others, and they often come to believe that it is their right and obligation to do so. And, of course, without equality of opportunity those born in the bottom of the distribution are likely to end up there: inequalities of outcomes perpetuate themselves. This is deeply troubling: given our low level of equality of opportunity and our high level of inequality of income and wealth, it is possible that the future will be even worse, with still further increases in inequality of outcome and still further decreases in equality of opportunity.

2.1 A Generalized International Trend

While the U.S. has been winning the race to be the most unequal country (at least within developed economies), much of what has just been described for it has also been going on elsewhere. In the past 25–30 years the Gini index—the widely used measure of income inequality—has increased by roughly 29% in the United States, 17% in Germany, 9% in Canada, 14% in UK, 12% in Italy, and 11% in Japan (Figure 3.2).[17] The more countries follow the American economic model, the more the results seem to be consistent with what has occurred in the United States. The UK has now achieved the second highest level of inequality among the countries of Western Europe and North America, a marked change from its position before the Thatcher era (Figures 3.2 and 3.3). Germany, which had been among the most equal countries within the OECD, now ranks in the middle.

The enlargement of the share of income appropriated by the richest 1% has also been a general trend, and in Anglo-Saxon countries it started earlier and it has been more marked than anywhere else (Figure 3.3). In rich countries, such as the U.S., the concentration of wealth is even more pronounced than that of income and has been rising too. For instance, in the UK the income share of the top 1% went up from 5.7% in 1978 to 14.7% in 2010, while the share of wealth owned by the top 1% surged from 22.6% in 1970 to 28% in

[14] See Taylor, Kochhar, Fry, et al. (2011).
[15] Corak, 2013.
[16] Corak, 2013.
[17] OECD Income and Poverty Statistics, available at http://stats.oecd.org/Index.aspx?DataSetCode=IDD#. See also OECD, 2015.

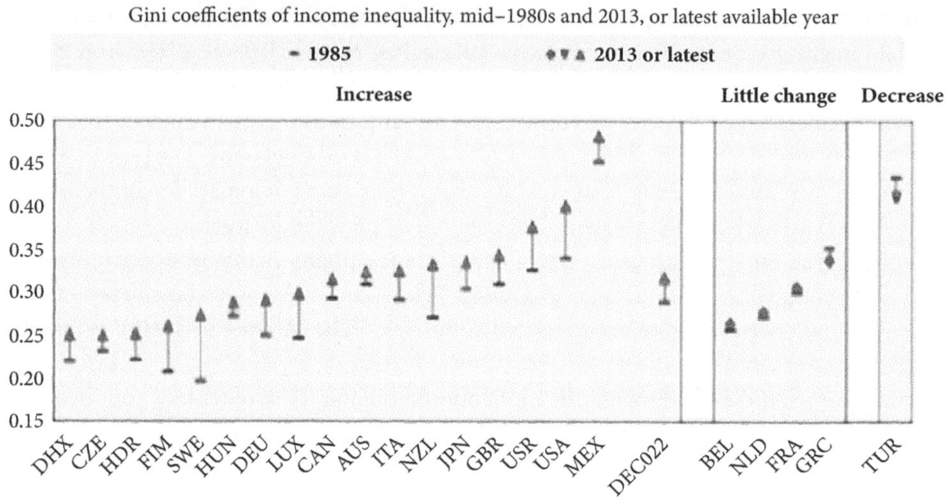

Figure 3.2 Gini coefficient of income inequality in OECD countries (after-tax and transfer).
Note: income refers to disposable income adjusted for household size.
Source: OECD, *In It Together: Why Less Inequality Benefits All*, 2015.

2010 and the wealth share of the top 10% increased from 64.1% to 70.5% over the same period.[18]

Also disturbing are the patterns that have emerged in transition economies, which at the beginning of their movement to a market economy had low levels of inequality in income and wealth (at least according to available measurements). Today, China's inequality of income, as measured by its Gini coefficient, is roughly comparable to that of the United States and Russia.[19] Across the OECD, since 1985 the Gini coefficient has increased in 17 of 22 countries for which data is available, often dramatically (Figure 3.2).

Moreover, recent research by Piketty and his co-authors has found that the importance of inherited wealth has increased in recent decades, at least in the rich countries for which we have data. After displaying a decreasing trend in the first post-war period, the share of inheritance flows in disposable income has been increasing in the past decades.[20]

3 Explaining Inequality

How can we explain these worrying trends? Traditionally, there has been little consensus among economists and social thinkers on what causes inequality. In the nineteenth

[18] Piketty, 2014, supplementary materials, Tables S9.2 and S10.1: piketty.pse.ens.fr/en/capital21c2, (accessed April 14, 2016).

[19] The comparison is made using World Bank data. Some caution should be exercised in comparing different countries' Gini coefficients: in addition to the well-known flaws in the measure, different databases have used slightly different methodologies or income data to arrive at their respective figures, and thus figures are different depending on the data source. Nevertheless, many different studies confirm these broad trends.

One should also be particularly cautious in interpreting differences in Gini coefficients between developed and developing countries. Kuznets (1955) put forward a persuasive set of reasons that one might expect inequality to increase in the initial stages of development, as some parts of the country and some groups in the country are better able to seize new opportunities and pull away from others. Eventually, the laggards catch up. China's growth in inequality over the past 30 years is consistent with Kuznets hypothesis; that of the advanced countries is not.

[20] Piketty and Zucman, 2015.

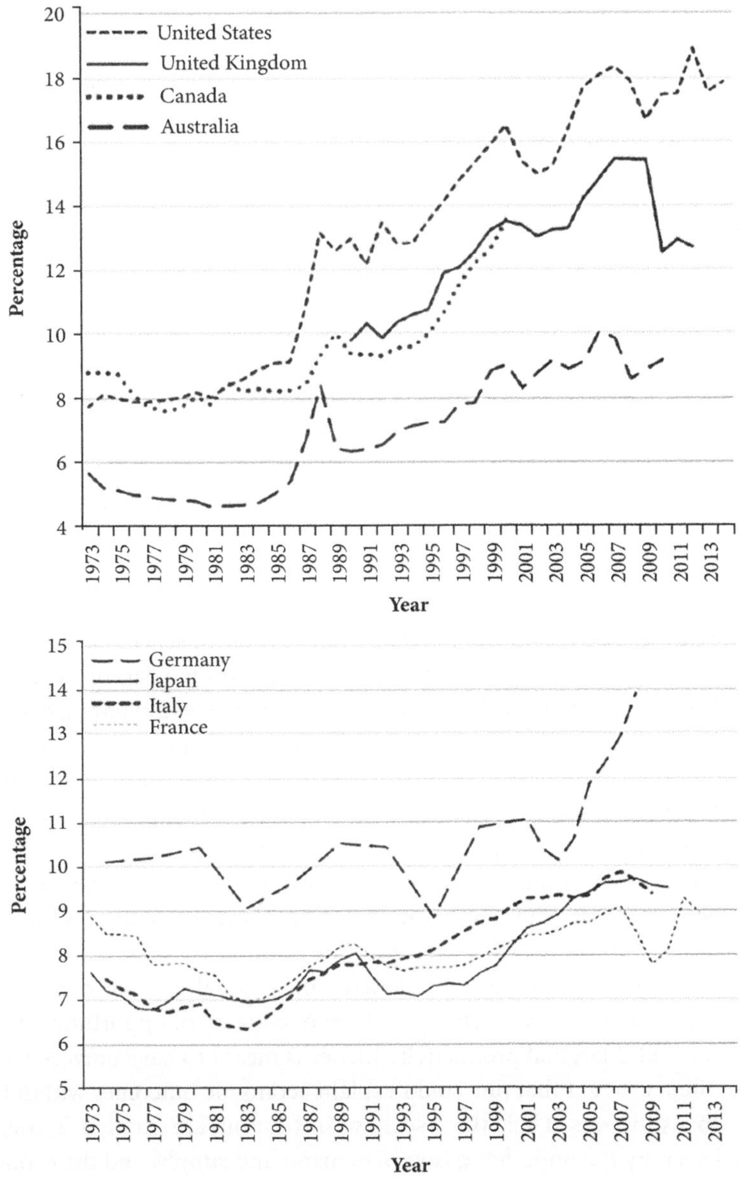

Figure 3.3 Income share of the richest 1% in some major industrialized countries.
Source: The World Wealth and Income Database (latest data available at http://www.wid.world/).

century, they strived to explain and either justify or criticize the evident high levels of disparity. Marx talked about exploitation. Nassau Senior, the first holder of the first chair in economics, the Drummond Professorship at All Souls College, Oxford, talked about the returns to capital as a payment for capitalists' abstinence, for their not consuming.[21] It was not exploitation of labor, but the just rewards for their forgoing consumption. Neoclassical economists developed the marginal productivity theory, which

[21] See Senior (1836).

argued that compensation more broadly reflected different individuals' contributions to society.

While exploitation suggests that those at the top get what they get by taking away from those at the bottom, marginal productivity theory suggests that those at the top only get what they add. The advocates of this view have gone further: they have suggested that in a competitive market, exploitation (e.g., as a result of monopoly power or discrimination) simply couldn't persist, and that additions to capital would cause wages to increase, so workers would be better off thanks to the savings and innovation of those at the top.

More specifically, marginal productivity theory maintains that, due to competition, everyone participating in the production process earns remuneration equal to her or his marginal productivity. This theory associates higher incomes with a greater contribution to society. This can justify, for instance, preferential tax treatment for the rich: by taxing high incomes we would deprive them of the "just deserts" for their contribution to society, and, even more importantly, we would discourage them from expressing their talent.[22] Moreover, the more they contribute—the harder they work and the more they save—the better it is for workers, whose wages will rise as a result.

The reason why these ideas justifying inequality have endured is that they have a grain of truth in them. Some of those who have made large amounts of money have contributed greatly to our society, and in some cases what they have appropriated for themselves is but a fraction of what they have contributed to society. But this is only a part of the story: there are other possible causes of inequality. Disparity can result from exploitation, discrimination, and exercise of monopoly power. Moreover, in general, inequality is heavily influenced by many institutional and political factors—industrial relations, labor market institutions, welfare, and tax systems, for example—which can both work independently of productivity and affect productivity.

That the distribution of income cannot be explained just by standard economic theory is suggested by the fact that the *before*-tax and transfer distribution of income differs markedly across countries. France and Norway are examples of OECD countries that have managed by and large to resist the trend of increasing inequality (Figures 3.2 and 3.3). The Scandinavian countries have a much higher level of equality of opportunity, regardless of how that is assessed. Marginal productivity theory is meant to have universal application. Neoclassical theory taught that one could explain economic outcomes without reference, for instance, to institutions. It held that a society's institutions are simply a façade; economic behavior is driven by the underlying laws of demand and supply, and the economist's job is to understand these underlying forces. Thus, the standard theory cannot explain how countries with similar technology, productivity, and per capita income can differ so much in their *before*-tax distribution.

The evidence, though, is that institutions do matter. Not only can the effect of institutions be analyzed, but institutions can themselves often be explained, sometimes by history, sometimes by power relations, and sometimes by economic forces (like information asymmetries) left out of the standard analysis.[23] Thus, a major thrust of modern economics is to

[22] For a recent application of this argument in defense of inequality, see Mankiw (2013).

[23] I recognized this early in my own work on information asymmetries, in a major controversy with Steven N. S. Cheung over whether the institution of sharecropping (which I argued could be explained by information asymmetries) mattered (see Cheung, 1969; Stiglitz, 1974b). North (1990) has perhaps done more to bring institutional analysis into the mainstream than anyone else.

understand the role of institutions in creating and shaping markets. The question then is: what is the relative role and importance of these alternative hypotheses? There is no easy way of providing a neat quantitative answer, but recent events and studies have lent persuasive weight to theories putting greater focus on rent-seeking and exploitation. We shall discuss this evidence in the next section, before turning to the institutional and political factors which are at the root of the recent structural changes in income distribution.

3.1 Rent-Seeking and Top Incomes

The term "rent" was originally used to describe the returns to land, since the owner of the land receives these payments by virtue of his ownership and not because of anything he *does*. The term was then extended to include monopoly profits (or monopoly rents)—the income that one receives simply from control of a monopoly—and in general returns due to similar ownership claims. Thus, rent-seeking means getting an income not as a reward for creating wealth but by grabbing a larger share of the wealth that would have been produced anyway. Indeed, rent-seekers typically destroy wealth, as a by-product of their taking away from others. A monopolist who overcharges for his product takes money from those whom he is overcharging and at the same time destroys value. To get his monopoly price, he has to restrict production.

Growth in top incomes in the past three decades has been driven mainly in two occupational categories: those in the financial sector (both executives and professionals) and non-financial executives.[24] Evidence suggests that rents have contributed on a large scale to the strong increase in the incomes of both.

Let us first consider executives in general. That the rise in their compensation has not reflected productivity is indicated by the lack of correlation between managerial pay and firm performance. As early as 1990 Jensen and Murphy, by studying a sample of 2,505 CEOs in 1,400 companies, found that annual changes in executive compensation did not reflect changes in corporate performance.[25] Since then, the work of Bebchuk, Fried, and Grinstein has shown that the huge increase in U.S. executive compensation since 1993 cannot be explained by firm performance or industrial structure and that, instead, it has mainly resulted from flaws in corporate governance, which enabled managers in practice to set their own pay.[26] Mishel and Sabadish examined 350 firms, showing that growth in the compensation of their CEOs largely outpaced the increase in their stock market value. Most strikingly, executive compensation displayed substantial positive growth even during periods when stock market values decreased.[27]

There are other reasons to doubt standard marginal productivity theory. In the United States the ratio of CEO pay to that of the average worker increased from around 20 to 1 in 1965 to 354 to 1 in 2012.[28] There was no change in technology that could explain a change in relative productivity of that magnitude—and no explanation for why that change in technology would occur in the U.S. and not in other similar countries. Moreover, the

[24] Bakija, Cole, and Heim, 2012.
[25] See Jensen and Murphy (1990).
[26] Bebchuk and Fried, 2006.
[27] Mishel and Sabadish, 2012; Bivens and Mishel, 2013.
[28] AFL-CIO, 2013.

design of corporate compensation schemes has made it evident that they are not intended to reward effort: typically, they are related to the performance of the stock, which rises and falls depending on many factors outside the control of the CEO, such as market interest rates and the price of oil. It would have been easy to design an incentive structure with less risk, simply by basing compensation on relative performance, relative to a group of comparable companies.[29] The struggles of the Clinton administration to introduce tax systems encouraging so-called performance pay (without imposing conditions to ensure that pay was actually related to performance) and disclosure requirements (which would have enabled market participants to better assess the extent of stock dilution associated with CEO stock option plans) clarified the battle lines: those pushing for favorable tax treatment and against disclosure understood well that these arrangements facilitated greater inequalities in income.[30]

For specifically the rise in top incomes in the financial sector, the evidence is even more unfavorable to explanations based on marginal productivity theory. An empirical study by Philippon and Reshef shows that in the past two decades workers in the financial industry have enjoyed a huge "pay-premium" with respect to similar sectors, which cannot be explained by the usual proxies for productivity (such as the level of education or unobserved ability). According to their estimates, financial sector compensations have been about 40% higher than the level that would have been expected under perfect competition.[31]

It is also well documented that banks deemed "too big to fail" enjoy a rent due to an implicit state guarantee. Investors know that these large financial institutions can count, in effect, on a government guarantee, and thus they are willing to provide them funds at lower interest rates. The big banks can thus prosper not because they are more efficient or provide better service but because they are in effect subsidized by taxpayers. There are other reasons for the super-normal returns to the large banks and their bankers. In certain of the activities of the financial sector, there is far from perfect competition. Anti-competitive practices in debit and credit cards have amplified pre-existing market power to generate huge rents. Lack of transparency (e.g., in over-the-counter CDSs and derivatives) too have generated large rents, with the market dominated by four players.[32] It is not surprising that the rents enjoyed in this way by big banks translated into higher incomes for their managers and shareholders.

In the financial sector even more than in other industries, executive compensation in the aftermath of the crisis provided convincing evidence against marginal productivity theory as an explanation of wages at the top: the bankers who had brought their firms and the global economy to the brink of ruin continued to receive high rates of pay—compensation which in no way could be related either to their social contribution

[29] I had written a series of theoretical and policy papers arguing this in the 1980s. See, for example, Nalebuff and Stiglitz (1983b) and Stiglitz (1987c).

[30] The author was a participant in some of these battles. For a more extensive discussion of them, and their consequences, see Stiglitz (2003a). There were other later battles concerning, for example, in pay and other reforms in corporate governance. For a discussion of the kinds of reforms in tax and corporate governance laws that might make a difference, see Stiglitz, Abernathy, Hersh, et al. (2015).

[31] Philippon and Reshef, 2012.

[32] Baker and McArthur, 2009. For a different view, see United States Government Accountability Office (2014), United States General Accounting Office, which argues that funding advantages existed before the recent financial crash but have disappeared afterwards.

or even their contribution to the firms for which they worked (both of which were negative). For instance, a study that focused on Bear Sterns and Lehman Brothers in 2000–8 has found that the top executive managers of these two giants had brought home huge amounts of "performance-based" compensations (estimated at around $1 billion for Lehman and $1.4 billion for Bear Stearns), which were not clawed back when the two firms collapsed.[33]

Still another piece of evidence supporting the importance of rent-seeking in explaining the increase in inequality is provided by those studies that have shown that increases in taxes at the very top do not result in decreases in growth rates. If these incomes were a result of their *efforts*, we might have expected those at the top to respond by working less hard, with adverse effects on GDP.[34]

3.2 The Increase in Rents

Three striking aspects of the evolution of most rich countries in the past 35 years are: (a) the increase in the wealth-to-income ratio; (b) the stagnation of median wages; and (c) the failure of the return to capital to decline.[35] Standard neoclassical theories, in which "wealth" is equated with "capital," would suggest that the increase in capital should be associated with a decline in the return to capital and an increase in wages. The failure of unskilled workers' wages to increase has been attributed by some (especially in the 1990s) to skill-biased technological change, which increased the premium put by the market on skills. Hence, those with skills would see their wages rise, and those without skills would see them fall. But recent years have seen a decline in the wages paid even to skilled workers. Moreover, as my recent research shows,[36] *average* wages should have increased, even if some wages fell. Something else must be going on.

There is an alternative—and more plausible—explanation. It is based on the observation that rents are increasing (due to the increase in land rents, intellectual property rents, and monopoly power). As a result, the value of those assets that are able to provide rents to their owners—such as land, houses, and some financial claims—is rising proportionately. So overall wealth increases, but this does not lead to an increase in the productive capacity of the economy or in the mean marginal productivity or average wage of workers. On the contrary, wages may stagnate or even decrease, because the rise in the share of rents has happened at the expense of wages.

The assets which are driving the increase in overall wealth, in fact, are not produced capital goods. In many cases, they are not even "productive" in the usual sense; they are not directly related to the production of goods and services.[37] With more wealth put into these assets, there may be less invested in real productive capital. In the case of many countries where we have data (such as France) there is evidence that this is indeed the case: a disproportionate part of savings in recent years has gone into the purchase of housing, which has not increased the productivity of the "real" economy. In the United States, matters

[33] See Bebchuk, Cohen, and Spamaan (2010).
[34] Philippon and Reshef, 2012.
[35] This section is based on Stiglitz, 2015a.
[36] Philippon and Reshef, 2012.
[37] Though they may be reflected in GDP and may be related in particular to the value of housing services.

are even worse, with measures of aggregate capital—including housing—increasing more slowly than income.

Monetary policies that lead to low interest rates can increase the value of these "unproductive" fixed assets—an increase in the value of wealth that is unaccompanied by any increase in the flow of goods and services. By the same token, a bubble can lead to an increase in wealth—for an extended period of time—again with possible adverse effects on the stock of "real" productive capital. Indeed, it is easy for capitalist economies to generate such bubbles (a fact that should be obvious from the historical record,[38] but which has also been confirmed in theoretical models.[39]) While in recent years there has been a "correction" in the housing bubble (and in the underlying price of land), we cannot be confident that there has been a *full* correction. The increase in the wealth–income ratio may still have more to do with an increase in the value of rents than with an increase in the amount of productive capital. Those who have access to financial markets and can get credit from banks (typically those already well off) can purchase these assets, using them as collateral. As the bubble takes off, so does their wealth and society's inequality. Again, policies amplify the resulting inequality: favorable tax treatment of capital gains enables especially high after-tax returns on these assets and increases the wealth especially of the wealthy, who disproportionately own such assets (and understandably so, since they are better able to withstand the associated risks).

3.3 The Role of Institutions and Politics

The large influence of rent-seeking in the rise of top incomes undermines the marginal productivity theory of income distribution. The income and wealth of those at the top comes at least partly at the expense of others—just the opposite conclusion from that which emerges from trickle-down economics. When, for instance, a monopoly succeeds in raising the price of the goods which it sells, it lowers the *real* income of everyone else. This suggests that institutional and political factors play an important role in influencing the relative shares of capital and labor.

As we noted earlier, in the past three decades wages have grown much less than productivity (Figure 3.1)—a fact which is hard to reconcile with marginal productivity theory[40] but is consistent with increased exploitation. This suggests that the weakening of workers' bargaining power has been a major factor. Weak unions and asymmetric globalization, where capital is free to move while labor is much less so, are thus likely to have contributed significantly to the great surge of inequality.

The way in which globalization has been managed has led to lower wages in part because workers' bargaining power has been eviscerated. With capital highly mobile—and with

[38] See Reinhardt and Rogoff (2009).

[39] See, for instance, Hahn (1966); Shell and Stiglitz (1967); Stiglitz (2015a).

[40] As we noted earlier, skill-biased technological change might be able to explain declines in unskilled labor; but it is hard to reconcile either the timing of wage changes, or the stagnation even of skilled wages in recent years, with such theories. Moreover, *average* wages should have increased. It is, of course, possible that average productivity increased while marginal productivity did not. (This cannot, of course, happen in the Cobb–Douglas production function so beloved by macroeconomists.) But I have seen no evidence for this sudden change in technology—and no theory for why this might have happened.

tariffs low—firms can simply tell workers that if they don't accept lower wages and worse working conditions, the company will move elsewhere. To see how asymmetric globalization can affect bargaining power, imagine, for a moment, what the world would be like if there was free mobility of labor, but no mobility of capital. Countries would compete to attract workers. They would promise good schools and a good environment, as well as low taxes on workers. This could be financed by high taxes on capital. But that's not the world we live in.

In most industrialized countries there has been a decline in union membership and influence; this decline has been especially strong in the Anglo-Saxon world. This has created an imbalance of economic power and a political vacuum. Without the protection afforded by a union, workers have fared even more poorly than they would have otherwise. Unions' inability to protect workers against the threat of job loss by the moving of jobs abroad has contributed to weakening the power of unions. But politics has also played a major role, exemplified in President Reagan's breaking of the air traffic controllers' strike in the U.S. in 1981 or Margaret Thatcher's battle against the National Union of Mineworkers in the UK.

Central bank policies focusing on inflation have almost certainly been a further factor contributing to the growing inequality and the weakening of workers' bargaining power. As soon as wages start to increase, and especially if they increase faster than the rate of inflation, central banks focusing on inflation raise interest rates. The result is a higher average level of unemployment and a downward ratcheting effect on wages: as the economy goes into recession, real wages often fall; and then monetary policy is designed to ensure that they don't recover.

Inequalities are affected not just by the legal and formal institutional arrangements (such as the strength of unions) but also by social custom, including whether it is viewed as acceptable to engage in discrimination.

At the same time, governments have been lax in enforcing antidiscrimination laws. Contrary to the suggestion of free-market economists, but consistent with even casual observation of how markets actually behave, discrimination has been a persistent aspect of market economies, and helps explain much of what has gone on at the bottom. The discrimination takes many forms—in housing markets, in financial markets (at least one of America's large banks had to pay a very large fine for its discriminatory practices in the run-up to the crisis) and in labor markets. There is a large literature explaining how such discrimination persists.[41,42]

Of course, market forces—the demand and supply for skilled workers, affected by changes in technology and education—play an important role as well, even if those forces are partially shaped by politics. But instead of these market forces and politics balancing each other out, with the political process dampening the increase in inequalities of income and wealth in periods when market forces have led to growing disparities, in the rich countries today the two have been working together to increase inequality.

[41] America's mass incarceration policies have also been an important instrument of discrimination. See Alexander (2010).

[42] For a recent account of this literature, see Basu (2010). See also Stiglitz (1973d, 1974d).

4 The Price of Inequality

The evidence is thus unsupportive of explanations of inequality solely focused on marginal productivity. But what of the argument that we *need* inequality to grow?

A first justification for the claim that inequality is necessary for growth focuses on the role of savings and investment in promoting growth and is based on the observation that those at the top save, while those at the bottom typically spend all of their earnings. Countries with a high share of wages will thus not be able to accumulate capital as rapidly as those with a low share of wages. The only way to generate savings required for long-term growth is thus to ensure sufficient income for the rich.

This argument is particularly inapposite today, where the problem is, to use Bernanke's term, a global savings glut.[43] But even in those circumstances where growth would be increased by an increase in national savings, there are better ways of inducing savings than increasing inequality. The government can tax the income of the rich and use the funds to finance either private or public investment; such policies reduce inequalities in consumption and disposable income, and lead to increased national savings (appropriately measured).

A second argument centers on the popular misconception that those at the top are the job creators, and giving more money to them will thus create more jobs. Industrialized countries are full of creative entrepreneurial people throughout the income distribution. What creates jobs is *demand*: when there is demand, firms will create the jobs to satisfy that demand (especially if we can get the financial system to work in the way it should, providing credit to small and medium-sized enterprises).

In fact, as empirical research by the IMF has shown, inequality is associated with economic instability. In particular, IMF researchers have shown that growth spells tend to be shorter when income inequality is high. This result holds also when other determinants of growth duration (like external shocks, property rights, and macroeconomic conditions) are taken into account: on average, a 10-percentile decrease in inequality increases the expected length of a growth spell by one half.[44] The picture does not change if one focuses on medium-term average growth rates instead of growth duration. Recent empirical research released by the OECD shows that income inequality has a negative and statistically significant effect on medium-term growth. It estimates that in countries like the U.S., the UK and Italy, overall economic growth would have been six to nine percentage points higher in the past two decades had income inequality not risen.[45]

There are different channels through which inequality harms the economy.[46] First, inequality leads to weak aggregate demand. The reason is easy to understand: those at the bottom spend a larger fraction of their income than those at the top.[47] The problem may be

[43] I've argued elsewhere (2015e) that the problem is not really a savings glut: there are huge needs for investment on the global level. Unfortunately, the global financial system is unable to intermediate—to ensure that the available savings is used to finance the real global investment needs. The consequence is the "paradox of thrift": savings leads to inadequate aggregate demand.

[44] Berg and Ostry, 2011.

[45] Cingano, 2014.

[46] The discussion below emphasizes three channels. There are others. The increased instability noted earlier has adverse consequences for growth. Extremes of inequality, especially when they seem unjustified, undermine societal trust, and this hurts growth. To the extent that inequality arises from distortionary rents, these distortions also hurt economic performance.

[47] Dynan, Skinner, and Zeldes, 2004.

compounded by monetary authorities' flawed responses to this weak demand. By lowering interest rates and relaxing regulations, monetary policy too easily gives rise to an asset bubble, the bursting of which leads in turn to recession.[48]

Many interpretations of the current crisis have indeed emphasized the importance of distributional concerns.[49] Growing inequality would have led to lower consumption but for the effects of loose monetary policy and lax regulations, which led to a housing bubble and a consumption boom. It was, in short, only growing debt that allowed consumption to be sustained.[50] But it was inevitable that the bubble would eventually break. And it was inevitable that when it broke, the economy would go into a downturn.

Second, inequality of outcomes is associated with inequality of opportunity. When those at the bottom of the income distribution are at great risk of not living up to their potential, the economy pays a price not only with weaker demand today, but also with lower growth in the future. With more than one in six American children growing up in poverty,[51] many of them facing not just a lack of educational opportunity but also a lack of access to adequate nutrition and health, the country's long-term prospects are being put into jeopardy.

Third, societies with greater inequality are less likely to make public investments which enhance productivity, such as in public transportation, infrastructure, technology, and education. If the rich believe that they don't need these public facilities and worry that a strong government which could increase the efficiency of the economy might at the same time use its powers to redistribute income and wealth, it is not surprising that public investment is lower in countries with higher inequality. Moreover, in such countries tax and other economic policies are likely to encourage those activities that benefit the financial sector over more productive activities. In the United States today returns on long-term financial speculation (capital gains) are taxed at approximately half the rate of labor, and speculative derivatives are given priority in bankruptcy over workers. Tax laws encourage job creation abroad rather than at home. The result is a weaker and more unstable economy. Reforming these policies—and using other policies to reduce rent-seeking—would not only reduce inequality; it would improve economic performance.

It should be noted that the existence of these adverse effects of inequality on growth is itself evidence against an explanation of today's high level of inequality based on marginal productivity theory. For the basic premise of marginal productivity is that those at the top are simply receiving just deserts for their efforts, and that the rest of society benefits from their activities. If that were so, we should expect to see higher growth associated with higher incomes at the top. In fact, we see just the opposite.

5 Reversing Inequality

A wide range of policies can help reduce inequality. Policies should be aimed at reducing inequalities both in market income and in the post-tax-and-transfer incomes. The *rules of*

[48] This and other arguments in this section are developed at greater length in my book *The Price of Inequality* (Stiglitz, 2012a).

[49] Jayadev, 2013. See also United Nations (2010) and Stiglitz (2010a).

[50] See for example Barba and Pivetti (2009).

[51] The reported rate as of 2018 was 17.5%. See "Child Poverty in America 2017: National Analysis," Children's Defense Fund, September 12, 2018, https://www.childrensdefense.org/wp-content/uploads/2018/09/Child-Poverty-in-America-2017-National-Fact-Sheet.pdf.

the game play a large role in determining market distribution—in preventing discrimination, in creating bargaining rights for workers, in curbing monopolies and the powers of CEOs to exploit firms' other stakeholders and the financial sector to exploit the rest of society. These rules were largely rewritten during the past 30 years in ways which led to more inequality and poorer overall economic performance. Now they must be rewritten once again, to reduce inequality and strengthen the economy, for instance, by discouraging the short-termism that has become rampant in the financial and corporate sector.[52]

Reforms include more support for education, including pre-school; increasing the minimum wage; strengthening earned-income tax credits; strengthening the voice of workers in the workplace, including through unions; and more effective enforcement of anti-discrimination laws. But there are four areas in particular that could make inroads in the high level of inequality which now exists.[53]

First, executive compensation (especially in the U.S.) has become excessive, and it is hard to justify the design of executive compensation schemes based on stock options. Executives should not be rewarded for improvements in a firm's stock market performance in which they play no part. If the Federal Reserve lowers interest rates, and that leads to an increase in stock market prices, CEOs should not get a bonus as a result. If oil prices fall, and so profits of airlines and the value of airline stocks increase, airline CEOs should not get a bonus. There is an easy way of taking account of these gains (or losses) which are not attributable to the efforts of executives: basing performance pay on the relative performance of firms in comparable circumstances. The design of good compensation schemes that do this has been well understood for more than a third of a century,[54] and yet executives in major corporations have almost studiously resisted these insights. They have focused more on taking advantages of deficiencies in corporate governance and the lack of understanding of these issues by many shareholders to try to enhance their earnings—getting high pay when share prices increase, and also when share prices fall. In the long run, as we have seen, economic performance itself is hurt.[55]

Second, macroeconomic policies are needed that maintain economic stability and full employment. High unemployment most severely penalizes those at the bottom and the middle of the income distribution. In a recession, workers are suffering thrice over: from high unemployment, weak wages, and cutbacks in public services, as government revenues are less than they would be if economies were functioning well.

As we have argued, high inequality has weakened aggregate demand. Fueling asset price bubbles through hyper-expansive monetary policy and deregulation is not the only possible response. Higher public investment—in infrastructures, technology and education—would both revive demand and alleviate inequality, and this would boost growth in the long and in the short-run. According to a recent empirical study by the IMF, well-designed public infrastructure investment raises output both in the short and long term, especially when the economy is operating below potential. And it doesn't need to increase public debt

[52] Stiglitz, Abernathy, Hersh, et al., 2015.

[53] In the last chapter of my book *The Price of Inequality* (2012a), I outline 21 such policies, affecting both the distribution of income before taxes and transfers and after.

[54] See, for instance, Nalebuff and Stiglitz (1983b).

[55] See, for example, Stiglitz (2003a). More recently, I and my colleagues at the Roosevelt Institute have explained how other changes in tax and regulatory policy have contributed to short-sighted and dishonest corporate behavior (see Stiglitz, Abernathy, Hersh, et al., 2015).

in terms of GDP: well-implemented infrastructure projects would pay for themselves, as the increase in income (and thus in tax revenues) would more than offset the increase in spending.[56]

Third, public investment in education is fundamental to addressing inequality. A key determinant of workers' income is the level and quality of education. If governments ensure equal access to education, then the distribution of wages will reflect the distribution of abilities (including the ability to benefit from education) and the extent to which the education system attempts to compensate for differences in abilities and backgrounds. If, as in the United States, those with rich parents usually have access to better education, then one generation's inequality will be passed on to the next, and in each generation, wage inequality will reflect the income and related inequalities of the last.

Fourth, these much-needed public investments could be financed through fair and full taxation of capital income. This would further contribute to counteract the surge in inequality: it can help bring down the net return to capital, so that those capitalists who save much of their income won't see their wealth accumulate at a faster pace than the growth of the overall economy, resulting in growing inequality of wealth.[57] Special provisions providing for favorable taxation of capital gains and dividends not only distort the economy, but, with the vast majority of the benefits going to the very top, increase inequality. At the same time they impose enormous budgetary costs: 2 trillion dollars from 2013 to 2023 in the U.S., according to the Congressional Budget Office.[58] The elimination of the special provisions for capital gains and dividends, coupled with the taxation of capital gains on the basis of accrual, not just realizations, is the most obvious reform in the tax code that would improve inequality and raise substantial amounts of revenues. There are many others,[59] such as a good system of inheritance and effectively enforced estate taxation.

6 Conclusion: Redefining Economic Performance

We used to think of there being a trade-off: we could achieve more equality, but only at the expense of overall economic performance. It is now clear that, given the extremes of inequality being reached in many rich countries and the manner in which they have been generated, greater equality and improved economic performance are complements.

This is especially true if we focus on appropriate measures of growth. If we use the wrong metrics, we will strive for the wrong things. As the international Commission on the Measurement of Economic Performance and Social Progress argued, there is a growing global consensus that GDP does not provide a good measure of overall economic performance.[60]

[56] International Monetary Fund, 2014. Note that the balanced budget multiplier itself provides a framework in which governments can increase investment and stimulate the economy today, without incurring any increase in current deficits—but lowering future deficits and the debt/GDP ratio.

[57] Piketty, 2014.

[58] More precisely, these are the estimated costs ("tax expenditures") associated with these special provisions. See Congressional Budget Office (2013). This figure includes the effects of the "step-up of basis at death" provision, which reduces the taxes that heirs pay on capital gains. Not including this provision, the 10-year budgetary cost of preferential treatment for capital gains and dividends is $1.34 trillion. These calculations do not, however, include the value of the fact that the tax on capital gains is postponed until realization.

[59] See Stiglitz (2014e).

[60] The Commission's report was released in 2009, and published as Stiglitz, Sen, and Fitoussi (2010). The OECD has since continued work in this vein with its Better Life Initiative https://www.oecd.org/statistics/better-

What matters is whether growth is sustainable, and whether most citizens see their living standards rising year after year.

Since the beginning of the new millennium, the U.S. economy, and that of most other advanced countries, has clearly not been performing. In fact, for three decades, real median incomes have essentially stagnated. Indeed, in the case of the U.S., the problems are even worse and were manifest well before the recession: in the past four decades average wages have stagnated, even though productivity has drastically increased.

As this chapter has emphasized, a key factor underlying the current economic difficulties of rich countries is growing inequality. We need to focus not on what is happening on average—as GDP leads us to do—but on how the economy is performing for the typical citizen, reflected for instance in median disposable income. People care about health, fairness and security, and yet GDP statistics do not reflect their decline. Once these and other aspects of societal well-being are taken into account, recent performance in rich countries looks much worse.

The economic policies required to change this are not difficult to identify. We need more investment in public goods; better corporate governance, antitrust and anti-discrimination laws; a better regulated financial system; stronger workers' rights; and more progressive tax and transfer policies. By "rewriting the rules" governing the market economy in these ways, it is possible to achieve greater equality in both the pre-and post-tax and transfer distribution of income, and thereby stronger economic performance.[61]

Acknowledgments

The author is indebted to Eamon Kircher-Allen and Deberati Ghosh for research assistance. Financial support from INET and the Roosevelt Institute Project on Inequality, supported by the Ford Foundation, the Bernard and Irene Schwartz Foundation, and the John D. and Catherine T. MacArthur Foundation, is gratefully acknowledged.

life-initiative.htm) and its High-Level Expert Group on the measurement of economic and social progress, convened in 2013. (Report released in November 2018 as Stiglitz, Fitoussi, and Durand, 2018, and later published as Stiglitz, Fitoussi, Durand, 2019a.)

[61] See Stiglitz, Abernathy, Hersh, et al. (2015).

4

Alternative Theories of Inequality

Historical and Theoretical Perspectives, Causes, Consequences, and Policies

Inequality, especially in the United States, has the multiple dimensions—soaring income and wealth inequality at the top, the evisceration of the middle, and an increase in poverty of the bottom; there are inequalities in health and opportunity, in voice in the political system and even access to justice.[1,2]

[1] Chapter based on a chapter of the same title originally published in *The Great Polarization: Economics, Institutions, and Policies in the Age of Inequality*, edited by Rudiger L. von Arnim and J. E. Stiglitz, Columbia University and the Initiative for Policy Dialogue, 2021.

[2] In this chapter, we provide some of the standard data supporting these conclusions. One of the big advances in the economics of inequality in the past decade is the increased availability of data, especially making use of administrative data, such as tax records. Much of the data cited below relies on four major sources: LIS Cross-National Data Center (Luxembourg Income Study) https://www.lisdatacenter.org/; the world inequality database https://wid.world/; a UN data base https://www.wider.unu.edu/project/wiid-world-income-inequality-database; and a Harvard database focusing on mobility https://opportunityinsights.org/. There are also some websites which have assembled data on inequality in a useful and thoughtful way. See, for instance, that of the Peterson Institute (https://www.piie.com/microsites/how-to-fix-economic-inequality) and that of CORE—Economics for a changing world (https://www.core-econ.org).

There is a broad consensus that inequality has increased over the last couple of decades and that inequality—both in market income and in after tax-and-transfer income—is larger in the United States than in other advanced countries. But there are some, especially on the Right, who contend that inequality is less than these numbers suggest and has increased less. While this chapter makes no pretense to provide a comprehensive view of the data, and our theoretical models would still be relevant even if the increase in inequality was more limited than these data suggest, it might still be useful to review some of the points in contention.

Inequality in market income. Current estimates rely heavily on income tax data. There are, of course, reporting problems, perhaps especially significant at the very top and the very bottom. But the incomes of those at the bottom is sufficiently small not to affect the overall picture. On the other hand, there are reasons to believe that there is significant underreporting at the top, partly because much of their income is in the form of capital gains, and only realized capital gains are reported. Indeed, individuals have an incentive to realize losses and not gains, providing a further bias to the reported data. Critics note that changes in the tax law (particularly the 1986 bill) resulted in incentives for CEOs and other corporate executives to get more of their compensation in cash and less in shares and other forms of compensation that were not reflected well in income tax data. Accordingly, the subsequent increase in reported income at the top did not really reflect an increase in inequality. But inequality at the top continued to grow in subsequent years. Not including capital gains, as Auten and Splinter (2019) effectively do in their analysis, is to leave out an important part of income, and because capital gains accrue disproportionately to the top, estimates based on such a construction of income may vastly underestimate inequality. In particular, as our later analysis emphasizes, the value of a corporation can increase not just because of invested earnings, but also because of an increase in market power (monopoly profits) or the value of its real estate holdings. For a further discussion of tax evasion and the measurement of inequality, see Alstadsaeter, Johannesen, and Zucman, 2019.

A second factor that has some bearing on the measured degree of inequality among households is that there have been changes in household formation (e.g., whether individuals marry), and these changes have affected differently those at various points in the income distribution. The adequacy of various procedures to account for these demographic changes seems to be a point of contention. In any case, however, this cannot account for the measured increase in inequality in the upper tail of the distribution. Nor does it provide any explanation of why lower income individuals are less prone to be married; for many it may be that they feel that they cannot afford to marry: the manifold consequences of income inequality may induce even greater inequalities in well-being.

The Origins of Inequality, and Policies to Contain It. Joseph E. Stiglitz, Oxford University Press. © Joseph E. Stiglitz (2025).
DOI: 10.1093/oso/9780198799580.003.0005

The objective of this chapter is to provide a somewhat more systematic overview of the various theories of the origins of inequality than that provided in earlier chapters, sometimes conflicting, sometimes complementary, and in doing so, to provide some of the descriptive statistics illustrating its various dimensions. Understanding the origins of inequality (the title of Chapter 2) is important if we are to design effective policies to reduce it. Policies to reduce wage disparities may differ if low returns to labor are a result of poor education, or corporate market power or economic rules that have weakened the bargaining power of workers. This is particularly so as we consider its most socially and morally objectionable aspects and those with the most adverse economic consequences. If inequalities arise out of exploitation, say out of the use of power (as in the case of slavery), it's a far different matter than if they arise, say, because some individual has made an invention that has enriched all of society or because some individuals have saved more than others.

A single chart, Figure 3.1 from Chapter 3, illustrates what has been happening in the U.S. over the past half century. It shows the average income of the bottom 90% and that of the top 1%, on the same scale. While increases in the bottom 90% are imperceptible, that's not true for the top.

As we noted in the introduction to the volume, while earlier discussions of inequality focused on *factor distribution*—what determined the distribution of income between say capital and labor—this book[3] is more broadly concerned with *the distribution of income among individuals*. That in turn is related to (a) the distribution of factor endowments, for example capital and skills among individuals; and (b) the distribution of returns on factor endowments, for example the returns to capital and the skill premia—the difference in wages (related, in a competitive world, to differences in productivity) between highly skilled and less skilled individuals.

Thus, the research agenda is divided into two (interrelated) parts: ascertaining the distribution of "endowments"—why some have so much more human or financial capital than others and why have these disparities been growing; and ascertaining the distribution of factor returns—why, for instance, at least according to most accounts, is the share of labor diminishing?

Inequality in after-tax and transfer income. Here, one of the critical issues is the treatment of the large increases in payments under Medicare and Medicaid. When appropriate account is taken of the costs of providing medical services, except in one year, when there was an extension of drug benefits to Medicare recipients, real expenditures on health care have gone down. It is hard to see how decreases in real health care benefits can contribute to slowing down the pace of increase in market-income inequality.

Inequality in wealth. Here, the fact that so much wealth at the top is held-off shore (Zucman, 2013, 2015), in trusts, and in assets (like paintings) that are hard to evaluate, or even detect, suggests that wealth inequality may be much larger than the standard numbers suggest.

Inequalities in well-being. Later in the chapter we will discuss some of the inequalities in key factors affecting well-being, such as health. There are still others, such as insecurity. Many of these inequalities, to the extent that they can be measured, appear greater than inequalities in income and appear to have risen even more.

For further discussions, see the online appendix to Piketty, Saez, and Zucman (2018).

[3] I view one of the contributions of my 1966 and 1969b articles was to change the focus from distribution of income among factors—understandable from the "class analysis" that had played such an important role during the previous century—to the distribution of income and wealth among individuals. But the discussion of this chapter and elsewhere in this book suggests limits to such an individualistic analysis: economic outcomes are affected not just by individualistic actions but also by the rules of the game, which are set collectively, by a political process, where ideology and class interests play important roles. See also Becker (1967).

1 Alternative Perspectives: Ever Growing Inequality vs. an Equilibrium Wealth and Income Distribution; Inequality as "Just Deserts" vs. Inequality as Exploitation

In recent years, there have been two distinct perspectives on inequality: One, most associated with Piketty (2014), holds that inequality is an innate aspect of capitalism; indeed there is an innate tendency within capitalism itself for ever increasing inequality—matters will get worse *unless there is strong government intervention*. The other view, dating back to Champernowne (1953), and developed further by Stiglitz (1966, 1969b, 1978, 2015a), and Bevan and Stiglitz (1979) (the basis of Chapter 9), is that there is, in any era, an equilibrium income and wealth distribution. We argued that the economy was best described as having an equilibrium—a balance between centrifugal forces pulling the economy apart, including the randomness of good fortune and the ability of the wealthy to use their wealth and connections to obtain higher returns than available to others, and centripetal forces limiting the ever-increasing inequality. In this view, recent increases in income and wealth inequality reflect a weakening of the centripetal forces and a strengthening of the centrifugal forces. At the center of the analysis of America's increased inequality is thus an attempt to understand the changing balance of centrifugal and centripetal forces.

By contrast, the central tenant in Piketty's work is that the wealthy transfer large amounts to their children, a process which leads, he suggests, to ever increasing inequality when the rate of return on capital, r, is greater than the rate of growth of the economy, g—what he describes as the normal state of the capitalist system. When $r > g$, their wealth (and therefore their share of national income) will grow faster than national income. The process as he describes it has been criticized (correctly I believe) in not being internally coherent. Indeed I had considered a very similar dynamic in my earlier work (Stiglitz, 1969b) and in work with Bevan (Bevan and Stiglitz, 1979), and concluded (in contrast to Piketty) that there were strong forces limiting the growth of wealth inequality, including (a) the division of wealth among multiple heirs; (b) the regression toward the mean in abilities, and (c) a diminution in the marginal return to capital that would result (under the law of diminishing returns) as the capitalists' capital accumulates relative to output or labor, eventually bringing the rate of return to a low enough level that the rate of growth of capitalists' capital was lower than the growth of the economy.

1.1 Politics, Economics, and Inequality

Both of the two key determinants of inequality are, of course, greatly affected by politics. Labor, anti-trust, and corporate governance laws have large implications for the distribution of factor incomes; inheritance taxation and education policies are at the center of the intergenerational transmission of advantage and disadvantage. Of course, ever growing inequality gives rise to political demands to curb it, and thus, in a broader political-economic analysis, there may still be some kind of equilibrium even were Piketty's economic analysis to be correct.

As we shall see, *some*, but not all, of the changes in wealth and income dynamics are political, for example the result of changed tax structures. It is important to understand what policies may have contributed to the growth of inequality, and what policies might bring us to an equilibrium with less inequality.

1.2 Inequality and Exploitation

There is another dichotomy in modeling inequality: between analyses which seek to interpret changes within the context of a competitive model, and those which put market power and exploitation at the center. This goes to one of the key longstanding controversies in inequality: whether it arises from "just deserts" or exploitation.

One of the longest standing controversies in the economics of inequality is the *justifiability* of inequalities—related in turn to their origin. No one could easily defend the inherited inequalities of the feudal period. Those at the time suggested that they were preordained, but with the Enlightenment such justifications no longer held much weight. The best that the defenders of the old order could do was to suggest that changing these *natural* or long-standing orders would lead to social havoc, with an unacceptable price to be paid.

As new inequities emerged in the eighteenth and nineteenth centuries, new explanations had to be found. Two broad strands of thought emerged: one seeking to understand the evolving distribution in terms of exploitation and market power (Marx), the other in terms of social contribution (the marginal productivity theory). Marx, focusing on the inequality between capitalists and workers, argued that the former achieved their riches through the exploitation of the latter: the real source of "value" in an economy arose from the labor of workers.

The alternative theory argued that inequalities arise naturally, in a competitive economy, because of differences in their "social contributions," that is, in the marginal value of what they bring to the marketplace. These differences, in turn, are related to preferences and abilities—some, for instance, may save more, work harder, have greater talents. This theory is associated with neoclassical economists, such as John Stuart Mill, and became the predominate theory in the Anglo-American world over the past century and half. Nassau Senior, the first holder of the Drummond Chair of Political Economy at Oxford in 1830, argued that inequality arose from the greater *abstinence* of the wealthy, who abstained from consuming to increase their wealth, with the increasing wealth increasing productivity and wages, from which all would benefit—an early version of trickle-down economics.[4] In this view, the wealthy were justly rewarded for their abstinence.

The two views on the origins of inequality provide not just alternative descriptions of the origins of inequality but give rise to different normative perspectives with clear implications for policy, with inequality in the former case being malignant, in the other, more benign.[5]

[4] Perhaps ironically, those who seek to explain the growth of inequality through differential savings (e.g., Kaldor and Piketty) are thus more in the tradition of Nassau Senior than of Karl Marx.

Established in 1825, the Drummond Chair in Political Economy at All Souls College (which I held in the late 1970s), was the first chair in economics in the English-speaking world. The difference in political perspective between Senior and Marx was stark: Senior opposed even mild reforms like the Child Labor Act and the 10 Hours Act because of their adverse effects on the return to capital.

[5] Though the analysis below explains why inequality, even when it arises out of "just deserts" may have adverse effects on economic performance.

The two perspectives are, of course, not mutually exclusive: part of the fortune of Microsoft (Bill Gates) may have arisen from the social contribution of its PC operating system; but this was greatly amplified by its exercise of market power, including through practices that were ruled anti-competitive by courts in three continents. As another example: in many countries (and, among the advanced countries, especially in the U.S.), individuals and corporations, who may initially have attained their wealth through an innovation or other important social contribution, then use that wealth to exert large political influence, and then use that influence to further enrich themselves, both by ensuring that the "rules of the game" favor them and by preferential treatment from government (subsidies, contracts, obtaining public assets at below competitive prices, selling goods and services to the government at above competitive prices).

Though we may thus not be able to parse out precisely the relative importance of exploitation (broadly interpreted), it clearly plays an important role in current inequalities. Slavery was not a voluntary transaction—physical force was used; and much of America's inequality originates from such abuses of power. Many of Russia's oligarchs obtained their wealth by what can best be described as stealing it from the state, in what Chrystia Freeland, formerly Canada's foreign minister, described in her 2000 book as "the sale of the century."

Outside of a perfect market—with perfect competition, perfect information, perfect rationality—returns to different factors, individuals, and corporations may differ markedly from their social return (from their "just deserts"). CEOs may be garner for themselves more than they would in this ideal world, workers may succeed in getting for themselves less. Most labor markets are not well described by the competitive model, and employers have often engaged in practices that reduce workers' market power. The distribution of income between workers and corporations is obviously affected by the rules governing collective bargaining—individual workers have little bargaining power against corporations. The extent to which governments adopt and enforce laws enabling unionization and enhancing workers' bargaining power affects the share of national income accruing to workers, and thus the degree of income inequality.

Discrimination based on race and gender has played an important role in U.S. inequality, and the extent of that discrimination has been affected by social norms, by the rules that have attempted to circumscribe it and how they are enforced.

Market (corporate or monopoly) power is another important deviation from the competitive paradigm, with both distributive and efficiency implications. If the ownership of the monopolies is concentrated (as it is), monopoly power leads to inequality. The power to raise prices means in effect that real wages are lower than they otherwise would be—workers are worse off. The existence and persistence of market power again reflects the importance of the rules of the economy: markets on their own are not naturally competitive. Countries can adopt rules that make the economy more competitive than it would be otherwise.[6]

Recent years have seen multiple demonstrations of how un- and under-regulated corporations can exploit a host of consumer and worker vulnerabilities—pushing dangerous

[6] Adam Smith in *The Wealth of Nations* (1776) explained that "People of the same trade seldom meet together, even for merriment and diversion, but the conversation ends in a conspiracy against the public, or in some contrivance to raise prices." There are both natural and man-made barriers to entry that enable market power to be sustained. Indeed, Stiglitz (1987e) showed that even arbitrarily small fixed, sunk costs can sustain high levels of profits in equilibrium.

addictive products (like cigarettes, opioids, and carbohydrate rich foods and drinks), dishonestly selling polluting diesel cars, and, in the private for-profit education and financial sectors, engaging in a wide range of deceptive and exploitive practices.

While my earliest work focused on inequalities arising in a competitive model, I soon realized how unrealistic and unrobust that model was. Even a little bit of information imperfection changed the results dramatically, leading to outcomes that were more akin to those associated with markets with high levels of imperfect competition and market power.[7] It is hard to reconcile key observed phenomenon with the "just deserts" interpretation based on a theory with perfect competition where each is rewarded according to his "contribution," but a model in which there has been an increase in exploitation and rents (returns in excess of what would emerge in a competitive market) is broadly consistent with what has been observed. I have thus increasingly become convinced that a significant part of the increase in inequality has to do with an increase in the market power of corporations and the decrease in that of workers, especially unskilled workers (Stiglitz, 2019a).

Still, even in a world of imperfect competition, the forces identified in the competitive model play an important role, so we begin our discussion with the determinants of inequality in that framework.

2 The Distribution of Factor Incomes in a Competitive Model

The rich own more capital, get a better education, have better health, and get more opportunities: these are among the reasons why they are rich. They get richer still by increasing their ownership of financial and human capital, increasing the returns they get on their assets, and more broadly, their opportunities relative to others—a process we will describe in greater detail later in this chapter. They also get richer when the returns to capital or CEO pay or the returns to skills increase; they get relatively richer when the share of capital increases. Thus, the study of inequality and its changes begins with an analysis of the distribution of factor incomes. There are two key parts of this analysis: the distribution of income *among* workers—the differences in pay of skilled vs. unskilled workers—and the distribution of income *between* workers and capital.

Competitive analyses focus on changes in factor supplies and demand. The story is simple: if there is increased scarcity of the factors owned by the rich, their factor prices will increase, and inequality will increase. There are two key questions: the distribution of labor income, including between skilled and unskilled labor, and the share of income going to capital.

2.1 Skilled vs. Unskilled Labor

Such a demand and supply analysis has been used to explain the skill premium, the higher income earned by skilled workers relative to unskilled workers. "Skilled biased technological change" has increased the productivity of skilled workers relative to unskilled workers,

[7] See, for example, Diamond (1971) and Stiglitz (1985b).

so it is claimed.[8] This translates into an increase in the demand for skilled workers relative to unskilled workers, and an increase in the skill premium. This effect is so strong that (it is alleged) it has overcome a countervailing supply effect: that a larger fraction of the population is getting more educated, so that in the absence of such changes in relative productivities, the skill premium would have decreased.

The skilled bias theory lost favor as the primary explanation of the growth of inequality, especially in the years following the global financial crisis, as wages of even college graduates seem to have stagnated.[9] In any case, it can only explain (part of) the change in the distribution in incomes; it cannot explain, say, the decreasing share of labor and the relative stagnation of average wages.

2.1.1 Endogenous Factor Bias

The literature on skilled biased technological change, for the most part, has not addressed the question of why technological change has been skilled bias.[10] Normally, in stable systems, one would think that research would try to offset factor scarcities: if some factor is becoming more expensive, research would be directed at economizing on the use of that factor. While the processes may be slow, they should again work to limit ever-growing inequality.[11]

2.1.2 The Role of Globalization

Globalization—lowering barriers to trade particularly between developed and less developed countries—predictably leads in the advanced countries to lower returns to labor relative to capital and to lower unskilled wages relative to skilled. Increased imports of unskilled intensive goods reduce the demand for such labor in developed countries, lowering their wages.[12] In the 1990s and early years of this century, advocates of globalization typically argued that skilled bias technological change played a more important role than globalization, but this presumption has come to be questioned, especially with the work of Autor and his colleagues on the "China shock."[13] This work has, moreover, made clear that the underlying hypothesis of the competitive model that labor is mobile, getting quickly reallocated in responses to changes in demand, is *not* valid.

[8] For a survey of what has become a large literature, see Acemoglu (2002).

[9] The skill premium seems also to have decreased See, for example, Shierholz and Mishel (2013) and Shierholz, Mishel, and Schmitt (2013).

[10] There is an old literature on endogenous factor bias, and a more recent literature. See, in particular, Chapters 18 of this volume (based on Stiglitz, 2006b), building on early work by Kennedy (1964), Samuelson (1965), Drandakis and Phelps (1966), von Weizsacker (1966), and others cited in those chapters. See also Acemoglu (1998, 2002, 2010), Acemoglu and Restropo (2018), and Barrales-Ruiz, Mendieta-Muñoz, Rada, et al. (2022).

[11] However, the dynamic process may not be stable if the elasticity of substitution is greater than unity, and the economy can set off on a divergent path (see Stiglitz, 2014a and Chapter 17 below).

[12] This was the fundamental insight of Samuelson and Stolper (1941) and Samuelson (1948). It is remarkable that those who seemingly believed in competitive markets ignored or denied this effect, arguing that somehow, even without government intervention, trickle-down economics would ensure that everyone would be better off. Trickle-down fails, of course, not just for globalization but also for technological change. See Chapters 17 and 18 below.

[13] Autor, Dorn, and Hanson (2013, 2016). The impact of the China shock and trade integration with less developed countries may have passed, with the growth of protectionism in the U.S. and the slowing of trade relative to GDP.

2.2 Explaining the Changing Shares of Capital and Labor

In the competitive theories, the second key question is explaining the increasing share of capital, which is central to the growth of income inequality. The increasing share of capital plays such an important role because inequality in wealth is so great, so if there is a relative increase in the return to capital, income inequality will increase.

Figure 4.1a shows the high level of inequality in overall wealth holdings, increasing over time, with today the top 1% owning upwards of 40% of all wealth, twice their share in income.[14] Figure 4.1b makes the same point perhaps more poignantly by observing that in 2019 just eight men in the U.S. owned as much wealth as the bottom 50%—some 165 *million*.

There are three strands of thought (within the competitive paradigm) attempting to explain the growing share of capital—one emphasizing the role of globalization, a second a change in the relative supply of capital, and the third changes in technology.

Globalization. Trade integration between developed and developing countries would (as we've discussed in the previous paragraphs) increase the relative return to capital in the advanced countries. There is one problem with this theory: the *marginal* return to capital (say for a safe asset) has actually gone down.

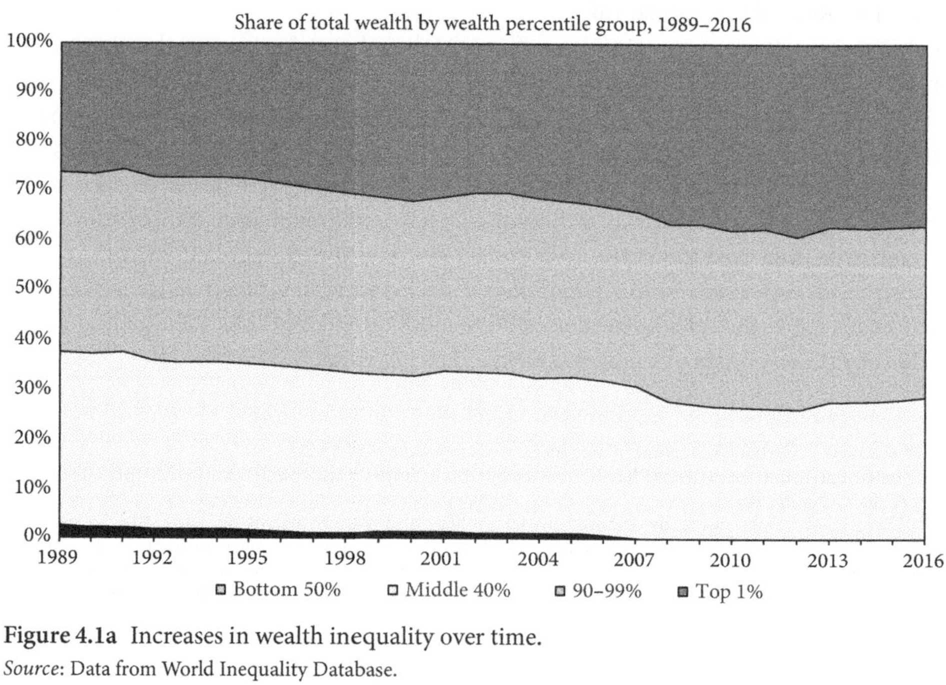

Figure 4.1a Increases in wealth inequality over time.
Source: Data from World Inequality Database.

[14] As in the case of data on income inequality, there are controversies about the extent of the increase in wealth inequality—with the data shown here showing a greater increase than that based on survey methodologies. For a review, see Kopczuk (2015). The data here capitalizes reported returns (naturally, called the capitalization method), and as discussed in Kopczuk, the capitalization method finds a larger recent increase in the share of wealth owned by the top 1% than the Survey of Consumer Finance finds, but otherwise the data sources show broadly consistent trends over time. In particular, both methods show that wealth concentration has increased since the 1980s. See Zucman (2019).

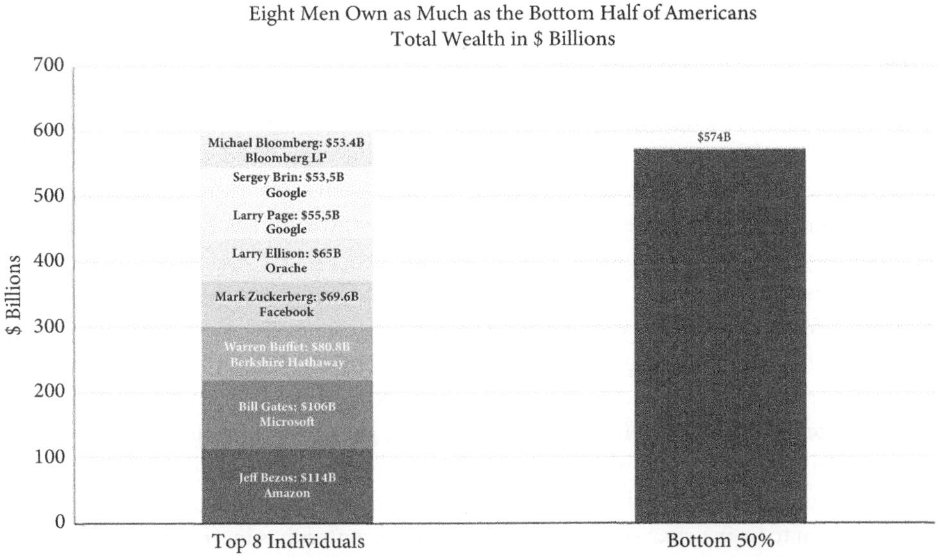

Figure 4.1b Extremes in American inequality.

Note: The data for the bottom 50% exclude wealth in automobiles, which constitutes a large fraction of the wealth of those at the bottom; however, such wealth does not in general provide much buffer for individuals against shocks they experience, nor does it help much in their meeting needs like retirement. (Automobiles alone constitute nearly two-thirds of the wealth of the bottom 50%, which itself says a lot). At the same time, financial wealth is even more inequitably distributed than these numbers suggest. The Federal Reserve's Distributional Financial Accounts provide more comprehensive wealth estimates. This figure is similar to one that appears in Institute for Policy Studies, "Wealth Inequality in the United States" (2020), which is based on previous years of the same publicly available data.
Source: Bottom 50% data from Federal Reserve Board, 2019 Survey of Consumer Finances. Top 4 data from the 2019 Forbes 400 list.

Changes in relative supply. Some, like Piketty (2014) have argued that the supply of capital has increased relative to that of labor.[15] This view is supported by policymakers like Ben Bernanke, former chairman of the Federal Reserve Board, who have talked about a savings glut. But an increase in the capital labor ratio should be associated with a rise in average wages, and if anything, wages appear to be relatively stagnant. Moreover, one would have expected the share of capital would *decrease*. The vast majority of empirical studies suggest that the elasticity of substitution (which measures how easy it is to substitute capital for labor) is less than unity,[16] which implies that if there were a savings glut, or an increase in the capital per worker, the share of labor should have increased.

In fact, at least in many countries, including the U.S., probably the capital labor ratio has decreased. One can trace out, from national income data, the increases in the capital stock and compare that with the increase in the labor supply and income. National income accounts suggest that capital (as we normally measure it) has been not keeping pace with

[15] In the presence of innovation, what matters is the "effective" capital and "effective" labor supplies.

[16] See Arrow, Chenery, Minhas, and Solow (1961); Young (2013). It should be noted that some authors have recently argued otherwise. See, for example, Mallick (2012). Those who argue that the elasticity of substitution *must* be greater than one because we have seen an increase in the share of capital even as the capital output ratio has increased are arguing in a circular way: they ignore the measurement problems associated with measuring both capital and its share. As Chapter 10 (based on Stiglitz, 2015a) points out, the capital stock is not well approximated by measures of wealth. See the discussion below.

the growth of the national income, let alone the labor supply.[17] At the same time, there is compelling evidence (including that presented by Piketty) that there has been an increase in the wealth income ratio. There is a simple resolution to the seeming contradiction of an increase in the wealth income ratio occurring simultaneously with a decrease in the capital income ratio: wealth can increase with an increase in (the capitalized value of) rents—land rents, intellectual property rents, or monopoly rents. Because the capitalized value of rents has been increasing (the value of non-produced assets), wealth has been increasing even as capital may have decreasing.[18]

An increase in land rents can, of course, be accommodated within a competitive framework. While land rents were important in the early development of the economics discipline—in a time when agriculture was the predominant sector—land seemed sufficiently unimportant in a manufacturing economy that most models simply ignored it. This was a mistake, because a large fraction of expenditure goes to housing and commercial real estate, and in an increasingly urbanized society, land rents become particularly important. Transportation costs are significant as are the economies of agglomeration—individuals and firms want to be in urban centers, and land in such centers has increasingly high value.[19]

But what has been happening to the price of land is about more than urbanization and demographics: At least some of the increase in land values is a consequence of the conduct of monetary and financial regulatory policy, which has led to an appreciation in the value of certain non-produced assets, most importantly land, thereby contributing to the growth of wealth inequality.

Still, the increase in land rents can account for only part of the disparity between changes in wealth and changes in capital.[20] At least a significant part has to do with an increase in monopoly and other forms of "exploitation" rents, to which I turn later in this chapter.

Technological Change. There is a third possible explanation within the competitive paradigm for the changing share of capital: (endogenous) technological change, which may, for instance, have increased the *effective* labor supply (through labor augmenting technological progress) relative to capital; and this could be true even if there were a (slight) increase in the supply of capital relative to workers. If the elasticity of substitution between capital and labor is less than unity, a decrease in the ratio of capital to *effective* labor supply would increase the share of capital—consistent with what is observed. But the marginal return to capital should have then increased, and yet the safe return to capital seems to have decreased.[21]

Interestingly, in the standard induced technology model, in the long run, the share of labor is driven by the "innovation locus" giving the trade-off between labor and capital augmenting technological change. The long-run equilibrium share of labor is the share which induces pure labor augmenting technological change.[22] Over the long run, *changes*

[17] Taking into account labor augmenting technological progress, which we discuss more fully in the following paragraphs.

[18] Thus, at the heart of the inability of Piketty's theory to explain the "stylized" facts of growth and inequality is this distinction between *wealth* and *capital.* See Stiglitz (2016a). A more extensive discussion is included in the NBER paper by the same title, Stiglitz (2015a).

[19] There is a large literature describing the link between land rents, transport costs, and agglomeration economies. See, for example, Arnott and Stiglitz (1979, 1981), Krugman (1991), Fujita, Krugman, and Venables (1999), and Glaeser and Gottlieb (2009).

[20] There is a growing consensus on this (see, e.g., Robbins, 2019). Rognlie (2015), however, attributes much of the increase in the observed wealth income ratio to an increase in real estate.

[21] There are other reasons why this explanation is suspect: if anything, the pace of innovation has slowed in the last 40 years, not increased.

[22] For there to be a steady state growth path, technological change has to be pure labor augmentation.

in the factor distribution of income between capital and labor are then driven by changes in the innovation locus, and neither by globalization nor changes in the relative supply of capital or labor.[23]

It can be shown that, in general, the market determination of the factor bias of technological change is not socially optimal—indeed there is a presumption that it leads to excessive innovation replacing unskilled workers resulting in excessive unemployment. Moreover, those who make the decisions about the choice of technology—the managers and capitalists—may do so to enhance their own welfare, at the expense of workers, and this may be so even in a decentralized economy without collusion.

There is thus a role for government to try to shift the direction of innovation in ways that enhance the return to labor relative to capital, and unskilled labor relative to skilled labor.[24] Unfortunately, government policy may be doing exactly the opposite, with higher taxes on labor than on capital and with suppressed interest rates, especially in the period after the 2008 economic crisis.

2.2.1 Risk

Most of the standard models ignore risk. Different kinds of assets yield different returns. Normally, risk would increase expected returns, and that will affect (average) wealth dynamics. If ρ is the average after-tax rate of return, including compensation for bearing risk, and if s_p is capitalists' saving rate, then the average rate of accumulation of capital of capitalists is $s_p\rho$, and if that exceeds the rate of growth of the economy, g, then capitalists' capital will increase relative to the size of the economy. But as a matter of theory, were that to occur, eventually ρ would fall, so that eventually $s_p \rho \leq g$. If $s_p \rho < g$, their wealth, relative to the size of the economy, will diminish. As we noted earlier, that seems to be what has been happening in the U.S. and some other advanced countries. To put rough numbers on this, if $g = 2\%$, $s_p = 0.3$, then so long as $\rho < 0.066\%$, capitalists' wealth is increasing less rapidly than national income. And remember ρ is the *after tax* average return.

Of course, even if for capitalists as a whole, $s_p\rho < g$, for the richest of the rich, who often have a higher savings rate and a lower tax rate, just the reverse may be true.

It is natural that the rich own the riskier assets—they are better able to bear the risk.[25] And it is natural that the riskier assets yield a return higher than the safe assets—otherwise even the rich (who we assume are risk averse) would not be willing to hold them. If that is the case, then there can be growing inequality among the rich, with the richest of the rich pulling away from the others. Still, there may be centripetal forces preventing an ever-increasing concentration of wealth at the very top.[26]

Changes in policies will, of course, affect the risk premium (the disparity between ρ and the safe rate of return). Exposure of the economy to greater risk may lead to higher

[23] So too, in the long run, the distribution of labor income between skilled and unskilled labor depends on the innovation locus. If skilled and unskilled labor are two distinct groups of individuals growing at the same rate, then the long run share of each is such that the rate of change of labor augmenting technological progress for each type is the same. Again, long run changes in the labor distribution are related to changes in the innovation locus or changes in the underlying demographics. An extension of these models then can generate an equilibrium level of unemployment, through a Phillips curve giving the rate of change of real wages as a function of the unemployment rate or a non-shirking constraint, as in the Shapiro-Stiglitz (1984) model.

[24] This was one of the interesting suggestions made by the late Tony Atkinson in his last book (Atkinson, 2015).

[25] The riskiness of an individual's portfolio depends on his (relative) risk aversion. While there is a broad consensus that individual's absolute risk aversion declines with wealth (individuals are willing to hold absolutely more risky assets), there is at least a strand of thought which argues that relative risk aversion increases with wealth, and if that is true, then the average return of wealthier individuals would be lower than for less wealthy

risk premium, or a lowering of the degree of progressivity of the tax system leads to high *after-tax returns.*[27]

At first blush, some of the data looks consistent with this picture. Figure 4.2 shows the large differences in the portfolios of the rich and the poor; the top 1% holds half of the stock shares, but only 5% of the debt.[28]

Not only do those at the top have higher wage incomes and own more capital, they get a higher return on their capital, because they invest a higher proportion of their wealth in higher return assets.[29] Figure 4.3a shows the (real) return on T-bills (the figure shows the return on the 10-year inflation indexed Treasury bond)—for the past decade real returns have been under 1%, and sometimes negative.[30] Figure 4.3b shows the observed real returns to corporate equity, typically varying between 8% and 10%. It is clear that there is a large

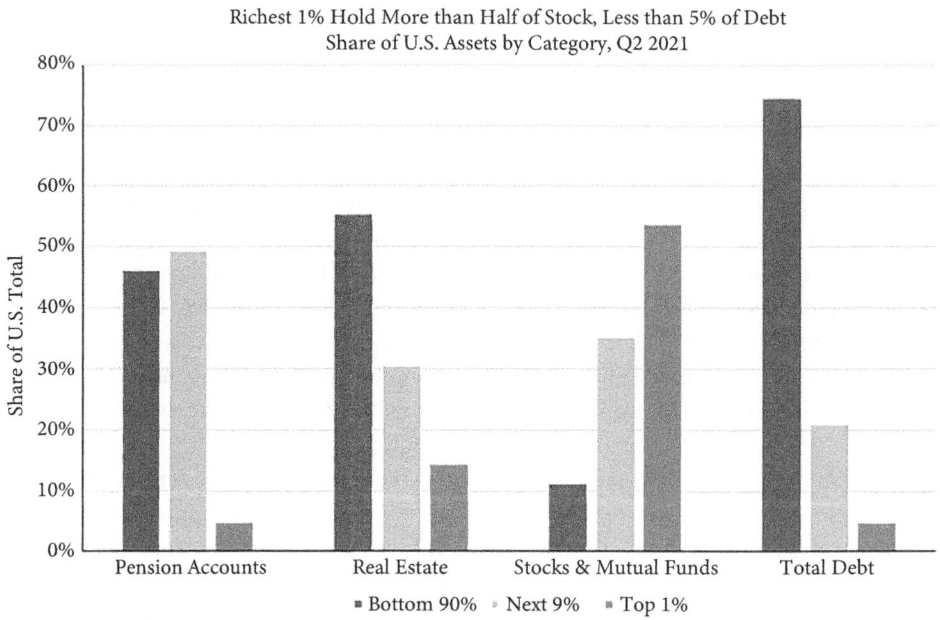

Figure 4.2a The rich own disproportionately higher yielding assets.

Note: This figure is similar to one that appears in Institute for Policy Studies, "Wealth Inequality in the United States" (2020), which is based on a previous quarter of the same publicly available data.
Source: Federal Reserve Board, Distributional Financial Accounts, Q2 2021.

individuals. The data suggest otherwise: These effects may be undone by tax provisions. See Arrow (1965), Stiglitz (1969a, 1972d), and Cass and Stiglitz (1972).

26 These centripetal forces include social norms whereby many of the richest donate large fractions of their wealth to charity, including the foundations which they create, and that, with regression to the mean, their children may not have the same talents and squander the family fortune. The mathematics behind these processes is described in Chapters 9 and 12 below, based on Bevan (1974), Stiglitz (1978, 2015a), and Bevan and Stiglitz (1979).

27 With substitution and income effects offsetting, it could also lead to lower savings rates.

28 As we noted earlier, this may be partly because of differences in risk aversion. But it may also have much to do with tax provisions—the greater importance of the preferential treatment of capital gains for the rich.

29 They may also get higher returns from their ability to better allocate their funds within any asset class: given their larger portfolios, they may have access to better information. It has been hard to get definitive data verifying this. A theoretical analysis is presented in Chapter 11.

30 The return on a short-term government bond minus the rate of inflation would give a similar picture.

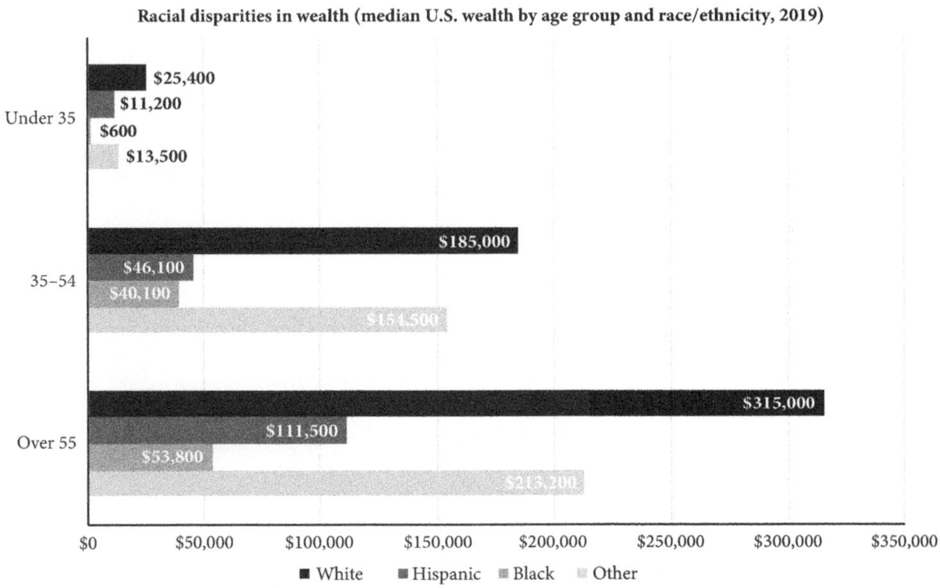

Figure 4.2b Racial disparities in wealth.

Note: This figure is similar to one that appears in Peterson Institute for International Economics, "How to Fix Economic Inequality?" (2020), which is based on the same publicly available data. Median wealth by age group and race and ethnicity in 2019 dollars.
Source: Federal Reserve Board, 2019 Survey of Consumer Finances.

Figure 4.3a Ten-year Treasury inflation-indexed security, constant maturing.

Note: Monthly average, January 2003 – June 2020. Not seasonally adjusted.
Source: Federal Reserve Board, retrieved from FRED, Federal Reserve Bank of St. Louis.

Figure 4.3b Corporate Profits rate (with inventory valuation and capital consumption adjustments).

Note: Quarterly average, January 2003 – January 2020. Corporate profits after tax, with Inventory Valuation and Capital Consumption Adjustments, divided by GDP.
Source: U.S. Bureau of Economic Analysis, retrieved from FRED, Federal Reserve Bank of St. Louis.

discrepancy, and one which has increased in the years immediately following the 2008 crisis, with inflation-indexed returns on government bonds turning negative.

There is something curious about this result. The economy's ability to manage risk over time has increased, as new risk instruments have increased. During the period of the Great Moderation, from 1983 to 2008, it is hard to see why the risk premium should have increased. In some instances (say the risk premium on Greek bonds) it shrank to absurd levels. The implication is that the disparity in observed returns to stocks and bonds cannot be explained just by an (increasing) risk premium; it has to do with something else: the increase in rents (monopoly returns), the subject of the next section.

3 The Distribution of Factor Incomes and Wealth in an Economy with Market Power

The previous section explained how the competitive model attempts to explain the changes in inequality, and in particular factor incomes and shares that have occurred in the U.S. and other advanced countries in recent decades. The conclusion I have reached is that the facts are not consistent with any reasonable competitive model. This brings us to the second major strand of thought described earlier, which sees inequalities as arising in part from exploitation of some individuals or groups of individuals by others. This exploitation can take on many different forms.

3.1 Discrimination

Slavery and the inequalities today which can be traced to slavery is the most obvious example of exploitation-driven inequality, but there are more and less subtle forms of exploitation. In South Africa, the dominant whites passed laws restricting blacks from engaging in farming, forcing them in effect into working the mines. Restricting opportunities is a time-honored way of exploitation.[31] There are myriad forms of discrimination, whether it's on gender, race, or ethnicity. Those who are discriminated against have lower wages and wealth. Figure 4.2b, for instance, shows the large disparities in wealth between Hispanics, African Americans, and Whites. While income disparities were reduced after the passage of the Civil Rights bills in the 1960s, progress later stalled, and predatory lending, with a sometimes racial-bias, contributed to an increase in wealth inequality in the years after the Great Recession.[32]

While some seem to have suggested that wage discrimination could not persist in a competitive economy (Becker, 1957) that conclusion is wrong (see Arrow, 1972a; Stiglitz, 1973d, 1974d; Hoff and Stiglitz, 2016; and Part III.F of this volume). If, for instance, there are imperfections of information or other market imperfections, the discriminated against group may not invest in high-quality education because employers *presume* that they haven't and don't pay them accordingly. Those presumptions are, of course, then consistent with what is observed, as those who (correctly) believe that they will be discriminated against may not make the investments that would enable them to be more productive.

But while discrimination can thus exist and persist in competitive models with imperfect information, in practice, much of the observed discrimination relates to imperfections of competition. One group can *effectively* collude to advantage themselves at the expense of others, exemplified by Jim Crow in the South. In economies with imperfect competition—all economies—it is easy for discrimination to persist and to be self-perpetuating. Those who break the norm of discrimination will themselves be punished. Game theory and behavioral economics have given us tools within which we can understand better these patterns of discrimination.

In such situations, government actions to bar discrimination can enable the economy to move from an equilibrium with discrimination to one without—and in doing so increase output and efficiency (a general result when inequalities arise from exploitation). In the U.S., public policy has had ambiguous effects in recent decades. While affirmative action, desegregation, and other programs designed to reduce discrimination (as well as other civil rights programs designed to extend equality of political rights) bore some fruits in their earlier days, in the presence of counterforces, progress slowed and in some cases was reversed.[33] These same forces led to mass incarceration, further impeding progress.[34] Meanwhile, economic segregation increased, even as there was some slight progress in racial integration, with the result that inequalities in access to education may have increased. To deal with the long legacy of discrimination, government today will have to take a far more active stance than just prohibiting it, or even just insisting on affirmative

[31] See Wilse-Samson (2013). There are a number of papers on the broad theme of restricting opportunities as a way of exploitation. See, e.g., Naidu (2010), Acemoglu and Wolitzky (2011), and Naidu and Yuchtman (2013).

[32] See, for example, O'Flaherty (2015) and Stiglitz (2018c).

[33] Harris and Curtis (2018), Stiglitz (2018c), and the references cited there.

[34] Alexander (2010).

action. There will need to be large federally funded education programs, along the lines of the GI bill after World War II, ensuring all those in discriminated groups (such as African-Americans and Native Americans) can obtain all the education for which they are qualified at the best institutions for which they are qualified, and if the private labor market is slow to ensure full employment for these groups, government programs need to step into the breach.

3.2 Growth in Market Power

One of the most important sources of growth in inequality is the growth in market power, especially in the U.S., where an increasing part of GDP is in sectors where only a few firms predominate.[35] There have been changes in the structure of the economy that have led to increased market concentration and market power, for instance the growth of sectors in which network effects predominate (so all individuals want to be on the same network, like Facebook), making competition virtually impossible; or the growth of the digital/innovation economy, in which marginal costs are low relative to fixed costs (again, precluding competition).[36]

A particularly problematic aspect of the change in market structure is the transition to the service sector economy, from manufacturing (and from agriculture, which predominated before that). The natural unit of production in the service sector is smaller than in manufacturing, there is more accountability of individual contribution, and more product differentiation. Competition may as a result be limited, and wage compression (where differences in wages are less than differences in productivities) reduced. The result is both more rents and more earnings dispersion: on both accounts inequality may increase.

3.3 Other Explanations of Increases in Corporate Market Power

A few firms may not only have more market power, the successful firms have also learned how to exploit this market power, to extend it and make it more durable. Contractual arrangements of the kind used by Microsoft[37] and American Express[38] leverage existing market power to create barriers to entry which enhance their market power and make it more lasting.

[35] For a more extensive treatment of these topics, see Chapter 16 below, Philippon (2019), and Stiglitz (2019a).

[36] As the industrial economy developed, many worried that the high fixed costs associated with manufacturing would act as a barrier to entry, and believed that the world was evolving toward "monopoly capitalism" (Baran and Sweezy, 1966) with imperfect competition (see also Robinson, 1933). As it turned out, with globalization, the fixed costs associated with manufacturing were sufficiently limited that in most sectors a moderate to high level of competition was viable.

[37] For instance, Microsoft bundled its browser with its operating system, effectively killing its competitor Netscape. It was willing to do so—effectively to give away its browser—out of fear that a competitor browser might be used to undermine its market power in PC operating systems. It used other techniques to undermine competition—spreading fear that there would be problems of interoperability. Its actions were ruled to be anti-competitive in both U.S. and Europe. (For full disclosure, I was an expert witness in antitrust actions taken against Microsoft in Europe, U.S., and Korea.)

[38] Essentially the same contractual arrangements were used by Visa, Mastercard, Sabre, and Amadeus (the latter two are airline reservation systems) to restrict those that used their platforms from passing on the high charges they imposed for the use of their platforms to their customers, thus short-circuiting the workings of the price system. (At various times, I was an expert witness in competition proceedings in these cases.) A 5–4 Supreme Court decision in 2018 (with the business-friendly Republican justices in the majority) ruled (in *Ohio vs. American Express*) that the anti-competitive contracts were not, in fact, anti-competitive.

But firms have also learned other techniques of exploitation both of market power and of consumer vulnerabilities. The Silicon Valley firms have learned how to extract information from their customers, which can be used for price discrimination—transferring, in effect, wealth to them from their customers.[39] Data is the new natural resource, and they have ruthlessly exploited their control over it.

Behavioral economics has also provided firms with new tools for exploiting individual vulnerabilities. There is, of course, a long tradition: cigarette companies making cigarettes more addictive and denying their adverse health effects; snake-oil companies pretending that there are medicinal benefits from their products. But modern technology has allowed this to be done on perhaps an unprecedented scale: the drug companies creating the opioid crisis, as they too claimed that their products were not addictive, the financial sector pushing mortgages that were beyond individuals' ability to pay or credit cards with fine print that resulted in the unwary paying billions in hidden fees, or the for-profit education sector exploiting the desire of poor but uninformed students to want to get ahead, to "sell" them education products that do not advance their careers, leaving them with debts but little more; or the food processing and sugar-intensive soft drink companies pushing high carb products that are addictive and have led to the epidemic of childhood obesity and diabetes.

But even as technology and market structure changed in ways which may naturally have led to more concentration of market power, and even as firms were innovative in devising new ways of extending, augmenting, and perpetuating market power, not only didn't public competition policy fail to keep up, but efforts by big business and conservatives to weaken anti-trust policy met with considerable success.

3.4 Weakening of Worker Power

Unions—the institution through which workers engage in collective action—have traditionally provided a check against some of the abuses of corporate power. Another change in the economy has been a weakening of unions, partly as a result of new legislation, partly as a result of the way existing legislation has been implemented, partly as a result of a change in market structure (toward sectors in which unions have been historically weak), and partly as a result of globalization, which has, in effect, pitted unskilled workers in advanced countries against the far more numerous unskilled in the developing countries and emerging markets. Firms can move abroad, hire cheap labor, and then ship the goods back to the advanced countries; this means workers' jobs are under constant threat, and this too has weakened workers' bargaining power.[40] And the limited ability of unions to protect workers in the face of this onslaught has weakened the attractiveness of unions—a downward vicious circle weakening workers' position.

Other factors may have contributed to workers' weaker bargaining power: for instance, the growth of certain contractual arrangements—non-compete clauses and dispute resolution through compulsory arbitration, rather than through courts, without the possibility

[39] In doing so, they destroy the key efficiency properties of the market economy, which requires that all individuals and firms face the same prices. Earlier, I had argued that perhaps the most important inefficiencies associated with market power was this price discrimination. Stiglitz (1977a).

[40] Making matters even worse is that investment agreements, typically part of trade agreements, actually give firms stronger property rights investing abroad than investing at home. One explanation for why corporations put such store in such agreements is that they undermine workers' bargaining power, lowering wages at home. See Stiglitz (2008c, 2018a, 2018d).

of class action—have weakened workers' market power just as new contractual forms discussed earlier have strengthened corporate power in markets for goods and services.[41]

Public policy has played a large role (Stelzner, 2017). Labor legislation and its interpretation and enforcement have made collective action by workers more difficult. The minimum wage has been eviscerated—in 2020, adjusted for inflation it stood at the same level that it was more than 60 years ago—as has hours and pay legislation (e.g., governing overtime.) (See Figure 4.4.)

3.5 Other Important Deviations from the Competitive Model

This section has focused on an important set of deviations from the competitive equilibrium analysis: pervasive market power and exploitation. But there are many other assumptions that go into the competitive model, and each has its implication for inequality. Most importantly, the model assumes full employment; the persistence over long periods of time of unemployment itself suggests limitations to that model. As we noted, an increase in unemployment weakens workers' bargaining power, and other things equal, leads to lower real wages.[42] The shift of focus in monetary policy to fighting inflation (beginning

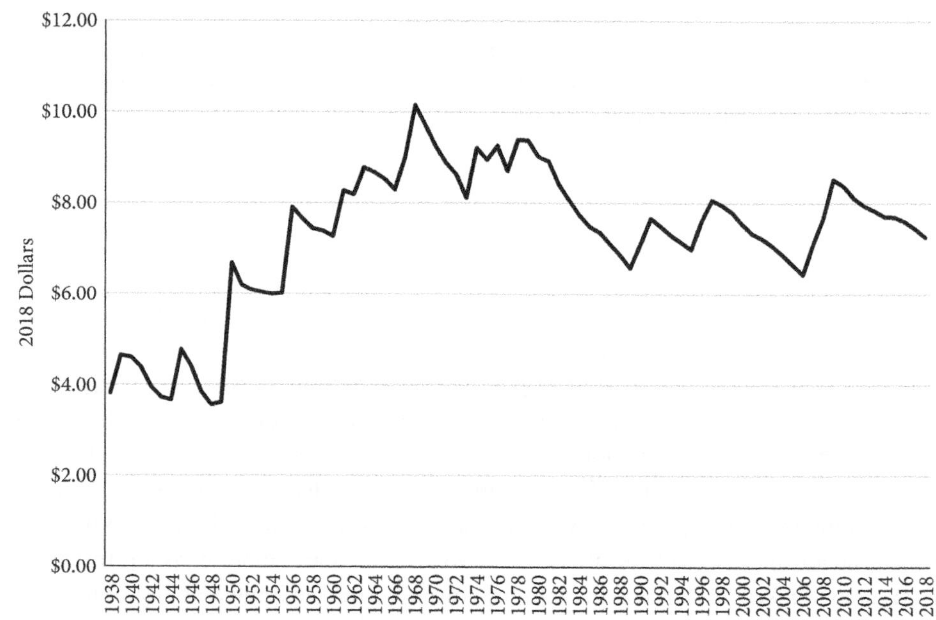

Figure 4.4 U.S. Real Federal minimum wage.

Note: Federal minimum hourly wage for nonfarm workers, dollars per hour, annual, 1938 – 2020. Inflation measured using CPI-U. A similar figure, drawn from the same public data, appears in Cooper (2019). The figure here differs slightly fromthat Cooper (2019), which instead uses the CPI-U-RS and is shown in 2018.
Source: Federal minimum wage rates from U.S. Department of Labor, retrieved from FRED, Federal Reserve Bank of St. Louis. CPI-U from U.S. Bureau of Labor Statistics.

[41] See Stiglitz (2021) and the other papers in that volume.

[42] Of course, other things are seldom equal; the lower employment/capital ratio in a downturn will, with diminishing returns, result in a higher marginal product of labor. This chapter focuses on long run trends, but cyclical movements in real wages may provide evidence about what happens as a consequence of economic changes that

in the 1980s), rather than creating growth and ensuring full employment, the average unemployment rate is higher than it otherwise would have been, putting downward pressure on wages.[43] So too, austerity policies, or more generally worries about deficit spending, have sometimes weakened fiscal stimulus when it is badly needed, prolonging downturns and exacerbating unemployment.

4 Rents and Macro-economic Puzzles

Our discussion so far has explained why one cannot understand today's inequality without looking at rents and exploitation and has noted some of the changes in the economy responsible for the increase in these rents. Indeed, it is hard to make sense otherwise of the overall macro-data. We note some stark "stylized" facts, in addition to the relative stagnation of wages, which stand in marked contrast to those presented by Kaldor (1957), which asserted, in particular, the constancy of relative shares and the capital output ratio:[44]

(a) There has been a marked increase in the wealth income ratio in countries around the world. This was, of course, one of the main themes of Piketty's (2014) book, illustrated by Figure 4.5. In the U.S., the wealth income ratio went from around three in 1975 to five in 2016. But, as we have noted, this has occurred even as the capital income ratio has fallen.

(b) There has also been a seeming increase in the returns to capital, illustrated in Figure 4.3a and Figure 4.6 by U.S. corporate profits as a share of GDP, up markedly from an average 6% for the half century beginning in 1950 to consistently more than 8% since the early 2000s (average value 2000–19 of 8.37%), and more than 10% in some years.

(c) In spite of high profits, business investment (as a share of GDP) has been low, plunging from a high of 7% in the 1960s to around 3% in the years after the Great Recession. (See Figure 4.7.)

(d) While average wages have been stagnant, those at the top have done very well. Those areas of the economy where inequality has grown the most—for instance, in finance and CEO compensation—are areas where rent-seeking seems prevalent. It is in

result in higher level of sustained unemployment—further deviations from the economy's production possibilities curve. Here, the evidence is ambiguous, with real product and real consumption wages sometimes moving in different directions, and with correlations differing across countries and periods. Overall, there is less cyclical movement than standard competitive theory would suggest. See Greenwald and Stiglitz (1988a). Phelps and Winter (1970), Stiglitz (1974c), and Greenwald and Stiglitz (2003b) identify some factors that determine cyclical movements in real wages (and thus the distribution of income) in models of imperfect information (costly search and costly labor turnover). These factors also would affect the long run distribution of income, implying, for instance, that changes in search and turnover costs might affect the distribution of income. That would, of course, also be the case in standard bargaining models.

Of course, over time, both capital accumulation and the pace and direction of technological change are endogenous, and, as fn. 10 points out, it is the drivers of this that may in the long run determine the factor distribution of income.

[43] See Stiglitz (2010a).

[44] For a more extensive discussion of the contrast between the new stylized facts and the old, see Chapter 10.

Figure 4.5 Time Series of Wealth income ratio (U.S. and other advanced countries).

Note: Net private wealth is equal to private assets minus private debt. Net national wealth is equal to net private wealth plus net public wealth.
Source: World Inequality Database, World Inequality Report 2018.

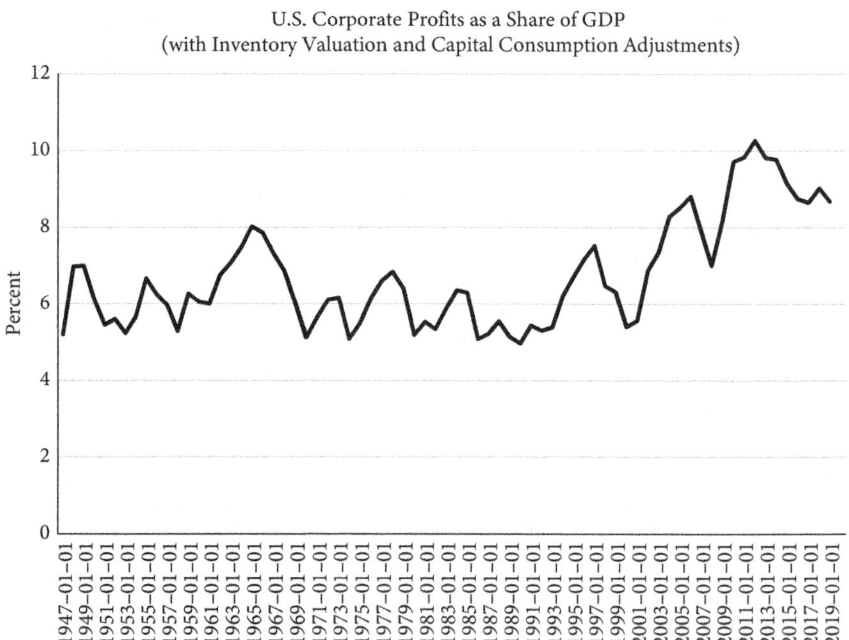

Figure 4.6 U.S. corporate profits as a share of GDP.

Note: Annual average, 1947-2019. Corporate profits after tax, with Inventory Valuation and Capital Consumption Adjustments, divided by GDP.
Source: U.S. Bureau of Economic Analysis, retrieved from FRED, Federal Reserve Bank of St. Louis.

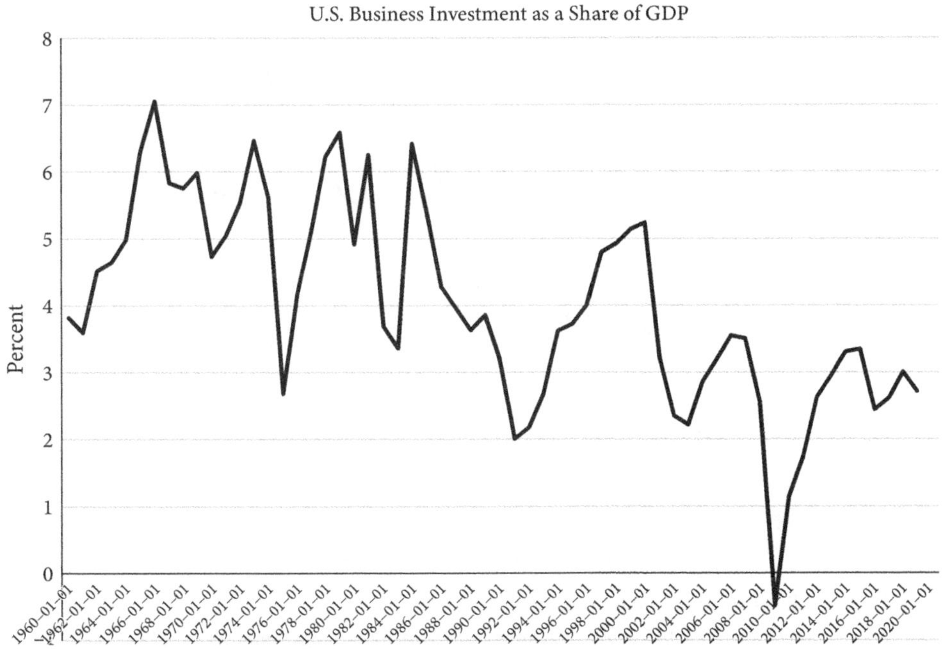

Figure 4.7 U.S. business investment as a share of GDP.
Note: Annual average, 1960-2019. Net private domestic business investment divided by GDP.
Source: U.S. Bureau of Economic Analysis, retrieved from FRED, Federal Reserve Bank of St. Louis.

fact impossible to understand the increase in CEO compensation on the basis of a standard competitive neoclassical model, where pay is related to social marginal productivity. There is no evidence that productivity has increased anywhere to the extent that pay has increased; nor is there any evidence that the disparity in pay between American CEOs and those elsewhere in the advanced world can be accounted for by differences in productivity. Moreover, looking at the compensation schedules, it is clear that pay is based on factors that are totally unrelated to the CEOs' contribution: an airline company's profits will go up when oil prices decline, and so then will his pay; but the executive typically played absolutely no role in the determination of the price of oil.[45]

(e) There is growing disparity in compensation even at the top, illustrated in Figure 4.8a, showing how the top 0.1% has seen their incomes grow so much faster than even the top 1%, and Figure 4.8b, which shows how CEO pay has increased even faster than those in the top 0.1%. But intrafirm inequalities in compensation may not be as important as cross-firm inequalities. Furman and Orszag (2018a, 2018b) have argued that wages (of individuals of any measured skill level) are correlated with firm profitability, typically interpreted as "productivity." The

[45] This was one of the central themes of my book *The Price of Inequality* (Stiglitz, 2012a). In Nalebuff and Stiglitz (1983a, 1983b) we explained how one could and should design compensation schemes that provided better incentives with lower risk than those commonly employed by firms. When I have explained this to CEOs, those who have understood the analysis shrugged it aside: it is clear that their objective is to extract as much from other corporate stakeholders without their objecting.

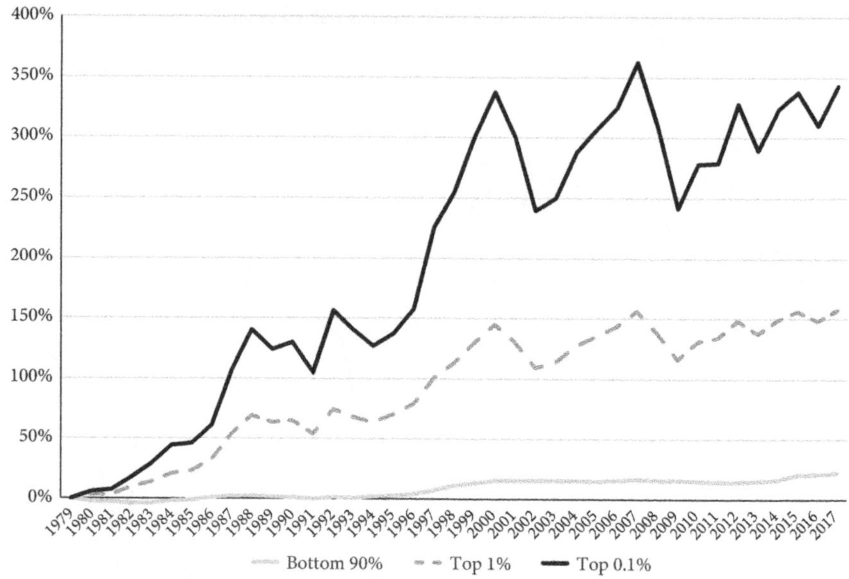

Figure 4.8a Increase in earnings at the very top.

Note: Cumulative percent change in real annual earnings by earnings group, 1979-2017.
Source: Data from Economic Policy Institute, "Top charts of 2018" (2018), where a similar figure using the same data set appears; this data is adapted from Mishel and Wolfe, "Top 1 Percent Reaches Highest Wages Ever—Up 157 Percent Since 1979" (2018).

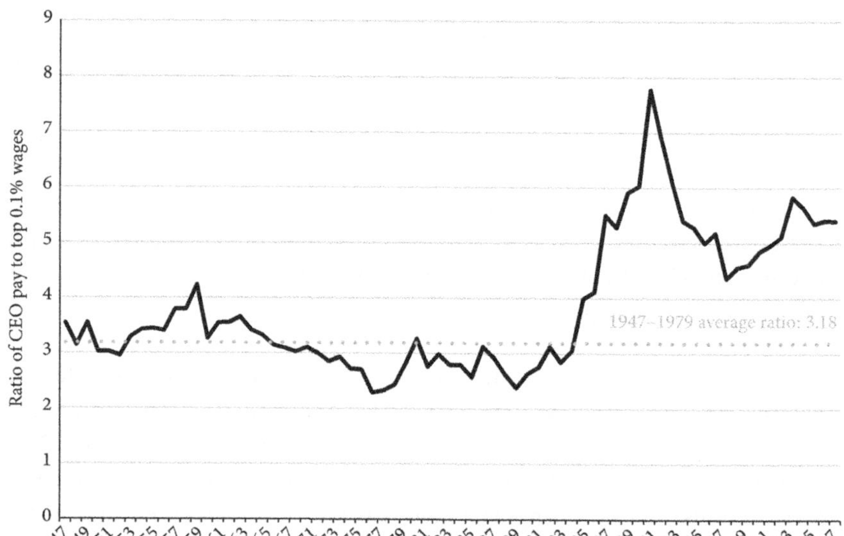

Figure 4.8b Comparison of CEO compensation with top 0.1% wages, 1947–2017.

Source: Data from Mishel and Wolfe, "CEO compensation has grown 940% since 1978" (2019), where a similar figure using the same data set appears; this data is Mishel and Wolfe (2019)'s analysis of data on top 0.1% wages from Mishel and Wolfe, "Top 0.1 percent reaches highest wages ever—up 157 percent since 1979" (2018) and extrapolation of Kaplan, "Executive Compensation and Corporate Governance in the U.S.: Perceptions, Facts and Challenges" (2012) CEO compensation series.

interpretation of these cross-firm inequalities in productivity remains unsettled—is it measurement error?[46] Is it really true that some firms are persistently more efficient than others—that knowledge about technology, including managerial practices, diffuses so slowly? Or is it that differences in profitability are related not so much to differences in productive efficiencies but to differences in market power? (The seeming persistence of differences in "measured" productivity across firms is, itself, testimony that the standard neoclassical model, in which knowledge disseminates freely within a country, may be wrong.[47]) I suspect that the observed differences in profitability most likely are at least in part attributed to differences in market power—highlighting the importance of rents which we stress here. However, that leaves open the question of why firms with market power seem to share some of their rents with their workers—is it because of efficiency wage effects?[48] And/or because at least part of the knowledge about how to maintain and extend market power resides in the workers—the high-paid workers in part are holding their employer as hostage?

(f) The flip side of so much money going to workers at the top is that the rest have not done well—as illustrated in Figure 3.1 of Chapter 3. Political dissatisfaction has been centered around males and especially among those with only a high-school education. Figure 4.9a gives us a feeling why—median income of a full-time male worker (and the full-time workers are the lucky ones) is the same as it was more than four decades ago (adjusting for inflation) and matters are even worse for those who have not graduated from college (Figure 4.9b).[49]

(g) The share of labor and capital—appropriately measured—has been declining, matched by an increasing share of rents. There is a way of getting at the magnitude of the increase in aggregate rents: look at the share of labor and the share of capital. The residual—what is left over—is the share of rents. Neither of these calculations are straightforward. Standard data on labor includes, for instance, anyone who gets

[46] That is, it is possible that the workers of the same education level that work in the more profitable enterprises are in fact more productive. Recent econometric studies have attempted to correct for this possibility.

Vertical disintegration of firms—contracting out, for instance, janitorial services—may simultaneously reduce within firm wage dispersion (offsetting in part the effect of soaring CEO pay) and increase cross-firm dispersion. Such vertical disintegration must, of course, itself be explained. It may be that those managing firms realize that localized efficiency wage effects (where workers' performance is particularly sensitive to the wages of those around them) means that janitors in high wage firms get paid more; vertical disintegration may enable them to obtain the janitorial services at lower wages.

[47] There is, in fact, ample evidence against that hypothesis, as discussed, for instance, in Stiglitz and Greenwald (2014).

[48] The efficiency wage hypothesis (discussed further in fn. 50) argues that productivity is affected by the wages an employee receives. As we noted earlier, individuals may be more sensitive to the wages of others around them—in the same firm—than to wages more generally, and this may result in paying higher wages even to less skilled workers. So too, workers' productivity may be sensitive to whether they are being treated fairly, and if the firm is paying senior management high levels of compensation and paying out large dividends, then fair treatment may require higher wages. For a more extensive discussion of efficiency wages, see Stiglitz (1974c, 1987b, 2009b), and Akerlof and Yellen (1990).

[49] As Binder and Bound (2019) point out, "[W]hen analyzing secular change in labor market outcomes conditional on educational attainment, it is important to consider the possibility that the underlying skill composition of the less-educated population has changed over time. This is especially relevant when considering the high-school-dropout and high-school-degree-only populations, which have shrunk in size over time relative to the college-educated population.... Regardless, our analysis fails to find evidence that the no-college population of men has become increasingly negatively selected on labor market skills since the 1980s."

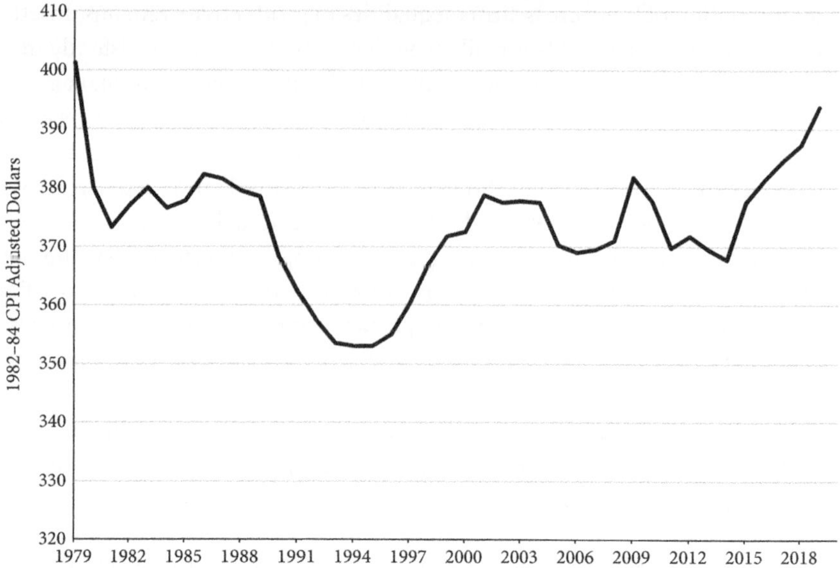

Figure 4.9a Median real income of full-time male workers.

Note: Annual Men age 16 and over. Wage and salary workers employed full-time. Median usual weekly real earnings.
Source: U.S. Bureau of Labor Statistics, retrieved from FRED, Federal Reserve Bank of St. Louis.

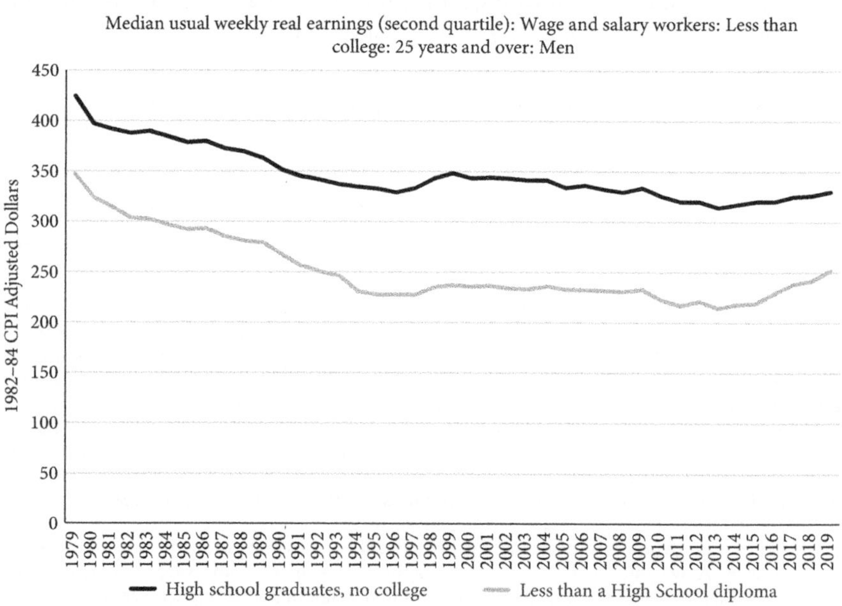

Figure 4.9b Median real weekly earnings of non-college educated male workers[a]

[a] Since the percentage of population in each of the two groups in the figure has changed, some of the changes in each group may be a result of compositional changes.

Note: Annual, not seasonally adjusted. Men age 25 and over. Wage and salary workers employed full-time. Median usual weekly real earnings.
Source: Earnings data from U.S. Bureau of Labor Statistics, retrieved from FRED, Federal Reserve Bank of St. Louis. CPI data from Federal Reserve Bank of Minneapolis.

> paid a W-2—who is an employee.[50] CEOs and bankers are, in this sense, workers—they work for others; but they are not workers in the sense that economists typically use the term to describe "laborers." If we exclude the top 1%, we get a number closer to what we would normally mean by laborers, as Figure 4.10 shows.[51]

Constructing an imputed share of capital is only slightly more difficult. From the national income accounts, we can calculate how much has been added to the capital stock each year. (We need to estimate depreciation to know much pre-existing capital has worn out. We can similarly calculate intangible forms of capital.) We know, from data in the financial market, the "risk-adjusted required return" on this capital, and multiplying the two together generates the competitive return to capital, as in the work of Simcha Barkai of the London Business School.[52]

Barkai shows that the share of capital is down substantially; the share of labor is down substantially; and that means the share of rents is up substantially. But just as the rich own a disproportionate share of the high yield-high risk assets, they own a disproportionate share of the high rent assets. An increase in rents redounds to their benefits—it increases inequality.

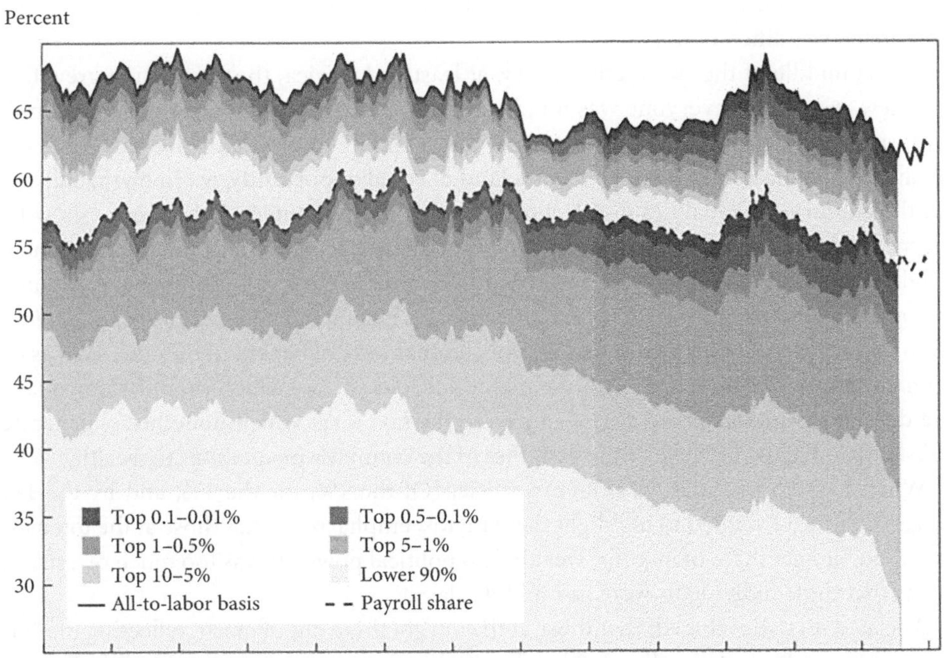

Figure 4.10 Share of labor income in non-farm business sector.

Note: Labor share includes all proprietors' income without Inventory Valuation and Capital Consumption Adjustments.

Source: Elsby, Hobijn, and Sahin (2013).

[50] Labor income also includes an imputation for labor income for the self-employed.

[51] Giovannoni (2014). Similar but less dramatic results are obtained by Barrales and von Arnim (2017) looking at just the corporate sector.

[52] Barkai (2020).

5 Inequality in the Long Run, the Perpetuation of Inequality, and the Economic Consequences of Inequality

We began our analysis of the drivers of the increase in inequality by focusing on the distribution of factor returns: the increase in the returns to factors owned by the rich relative to those of the rest would naturally generate increasing inequality. The second part of the analysis entails explaining differences in the ownership of factors, and in particular the perpetuation of inequality through the intergenerational transmission of advantage and disadvantage, the vicious circle whereby the children of the poor have poorer health, poorer education, less opportunities, and inherit less capital than those at the top.

5.1 Classes, Meritocracy, the 1%, and "We're All Middle Class Now"

A dominant view in the nineteenth century and well into the twentieth was that society was divided into classes, with relatively little mobility from say the lower to the upper. The lower classes relied on their wages to live and spent most of what they earned; the upper class lived off inherited wealth. These socio-economic classes differed in many other ways: in the UK, one could identify an individual's class background by his speech. Their interests and preference differed too.

By the middle of the twentieth century, at least in America, the conception grew that, with few exceptions, everyone was middle class: it was as if there were one happy family, with small distinctions between lower and upper middle classes. That, like the American dream and the notion that the U.S. was a land of equal opportunity, was a myth. Statistics on the country's inequalities, a selection of which are presented in this book, show the extent to which that was so. But it was a useful myth, especially in engendering the kind of solidarity needed in time of war. It was useful too for the elites, for it took the attention of ordinary citizens away from their current plight and helped them focus on *what might be*. It even helped in engendering support for policies that were of benefit to the elite, such as the elimination of the estate tax. With the high threshold (below which no inheritance taxes are due), few Americans are at risk of paying the tax, a tax which nonetheless generates substantial revenue because of the extremes of the country's inequalities in wealth.

When I wrote my 2011 *Vanity Fair* article, "Of the 1%, for the 1%, and by the 1%" (Stiglitz, 2011c) I wanted to highlight these myths, emphasizing that those at the top had a disproportionate share of income, wealth, and political power. It was too much of a stretch to say that these individuals were *just* middle class.

A related myth developed: that those at the top got there out of merit, reflecting the "just deserts" view of inequality discussed earlier in this chapter. We were not like "old Europe" with its inherited aristocracy; we were a meritocracy. But as we will explain below, the chance of getting into that meritocracy for those with parents at the top was so much greater than for those with parents in the bottom that it was still apt to refer to the U.S. as largely an inherited plutocracy. In this plutocracy, those with wealth typically "work"—they are not the idle rich, the clippers of coupons, the caricature of the nineteenth-century society. But even the nature of their work sets them apart from those in the rest of society.

The analyses presented here for the most part take a narrow economic perspective on these issues: the equilibrium theory balancing centrifugal and centripetal forces can, for instance, explain the "fat tail" distributions, in which so much of the wealth is in the hands of those at the top and can generate the high correlation between wages and wealth that has been observed in the data; but, for the most part, the analyses do not attribute the differences in wealth to differences in "behavior," as suggested by standard class analysis; and if there are differences in behavior, they are more the consequence of differences in wealth rather than the other way around. But almost surely, such an approach underestimates the role of the social transmission of advantages and disadvantages, which is at the core of perspectives which emphasize class.[53]

5.2 The Intergenerational Transmission of Advantage and Disadvantage

The theory of the *distribution of factor endowments* is concerned with the intergenerational transmission of advantages and disadvantages[54] through the transmission across generations of abilities and preferences (e.g., for work vs. leisure or consumption now vs. consumption in the future), the intergenerational transfer of financial and other assets, and the provision of human capital. Wealthy parents naturally provide advantages to their children—better education, health, and, in an economy where connections matter (that is, all economies) connections.[55] Sometimes governments reinforce these "natural" patterns, sometimes they lean against them, for instance by providing compensatory education for the poor (that is education that attempts to make us for differences in home background). If left to themselves, many among the rich would be quite willing to ensure that their children had all the advantages of society, sending their children to expensive schools that the poor could not afford, creating an elite meritocracy that few children of the poor could enter. Meritocracy legitimates a system of inherited privilege. Under meritocracy, the children of the rich must work for their place in society, unlike the old systems where societal positions were simply inherited. But they may not have to work hard: in the U.S. a child of the poor who does well at school has poorer life prospects that a child of the well-off who does

[53] Early work focusing on growth and distribution, such as that of Kaldor (1955a), Uzawa (1961, 1963), Pasinetti (1962), and Stiglitz (1967) (reprinted as Chapter 28) took an explicitly class-based approach.

The contrast between these approaches, and that of Solow (1956), which ignored the role of distribution in aggregate behavior, is noteworthy.

For a long time, the mainstream of macroeconomics seems to have followed Solow, especially with representative agent models; but eventually, attention had to be paid to the large fractions of the population that were credit constrained—with aggregate behavior more consistent with the older class models than the representative agent models. See, for example, the HANK models (Kaplan, Moll, and Violante, 2018).

These models incorporate credit rationing, the importance of which had, of course, been recognized by an earlier generation of macro-models, but seemingly forgotten in the interim. See, for example, Stiglitz and Weiss (1992) and Greenwald and Stiglitz (1987a, 1988b, 1990b).

More recently, Ranaldi and Milanovic (2020) have tried to distinguish among societies on the basis of the correlation between wages and wealth. In the extreme version of the class-based models referred to earlier, workers have no wealth and those with wealth have no wage income. In the Solovian/representative agent models, wealth and wages are perfectly correlated. Ranaldi and Milanovic suggest that western Europe and Northern America are less class based than other regions.

This downplays the role of wealth in meritocracies in acquiring high paying jobs in, say, the U.S., the extent to which wealth inequalities are perpetuated by serial correlation in wage disparities, and the differences in the magnitudes in wealth inequalities and their consequences across societies.

[54] There are still other dimensions to the intergenerational transmission of advantages and disadvantages. Below, we make brief reference to the transmission of cultural norms. There is increasing awareness of the importance of location—where an individual is born makes a large difference to an individual's life prospects; and this is true both within and between countries.

[55] All of this is part of what is sometimes referred to as social capital.

comparatively poorly.[56] Of course, with greater income, health, and education differences among parents, there is likely to be greater differences among children.[57] This is especially problematic in countries like the U.S. and UK where large fractions of children grow up in poverty.[58]

High-quality public education—starting before kindergarten[59]—and public programs ensuring access to health and adequate nutrition could in principle go some way in leveling the playing field. On the contrary, when public education is local, and there is extensive geographical segregation based on income, education, and wealth, then public education itself may preserve, and possibly exacerbate, the inequalities that arise otherwise from the intergenerational transmission of advantage.[60] The U.S. demonstrates how important these early inequities are: even though the most selective colleges (like Harvard and Yale) are need-blind that is they accept students regardless of their financial need, filling in the gap between the posted price of the college and what the family can pay out of their endowment—and even though these colleges make a concerted effort to recruit individuals from lower socio-economic groups, typically a very small percentage of the student body comes from the bottom half of the country.[61] Even very bright students have a big handicap in overcoming backgrounds (either from the family or from elementary and secondary schooling) that put them at a competitive disadvantage, especially in academic endeavors.

Of course, parents, in the decisions about how many children to have and how much to invest in each child, have significant effects on the intergenerational transmission of inequalities; those decisions are affected by economic variables—the direct and opportunity costs as well as income—as well as cultural and societal norms, though those too can change over time.[62,63]

[56] See, for example, Chetty, Friedman, and Saez, et al. (2020) who note that lower-income students with the same test scores as higher-income students have lower incomes in their early 30s. It also describes how even once one controls for the college attended, a student from a poor family still makes less than a student from a rich family that went to the same college. For a broader discussion of meritocracy, see Markovits (2019).

[57] A number of studies show the relationship between parent incomes and child educational attainment. See, for example, Akee, Copeland, Keeler, et al. (2010). Haveman, Sandefur, Wolfe, and Voyer (2004) have attempted to trace the impact on disparities in educational attainment as income inequality has increased.

[58] The 2018 U.S. poverty rate for children under age 18 was 16.2% (most recent year available, using Census's Official Poverty Measure) from Semega, Kollar, Creamer, and Mohanty (2019). 2018–19 UK poverty rate for children under age 18 was 20% (defined as children living in households with income below 60% of the median): Francis-Devine (2020).

[59] See, for example, Heckman (2011).

[60] Economic segregation in the United States has become worse in recent decades. Bischoff and Reardon (2011) and Taylor and Fry (2012). Owens et al. (2016) show the increasing economic segregation between schools and school districts.

[61] Chetty et al. (2020) find that "Among 'Ivy-Plus' colleges (the eight Ivy League colleges plus Duke, MIT, Stanford, and the University of Chicago), more students come from families in the top 1% (annual family income above $532000 in 2015 dollars) of the income distribution (14.5%) than the bottom half of the income distribution (13.5%)." The paper also finds that only 3.8% of students come from the bottom quintile at Ivy-Plus schools.

[62] Becker and Tomes (1979, 1986, 1994) extensively explore the economic determinants of these decisions; but curiously, Becker railed against economists attempting to understand preference formation (see Stigler and Becker, 1977). Only recently has behavioral economics turned to study them in the context of endogenously determined preferences. See World Bank (2014), Hoff and Stiglitz (2016), and Demeritt, Hoff, and Stiglitz (forthcoming).

The fact that preferences are endogenous and affected by one's surroundings undermines the neat distinction made by Roemer (1998) between "circumstances" and "effort" as determinants of outcomes (incomes)—with individuals being held accountable for differences arising from efforts, and with society attempting to ensure that there is equality of opportunity, that is, equal outcomes for equal efforts, by offsetting differences arising from differences in circumstances.

[63] Cultural norms can disadvantage individuals in a variety of ways, for example making them more reluctant to take certain jobs that are viewed to be "gender inappropriate," even when those are the only or best paying jobs available.

The previous sections of this chapter have looked at inequalities in income and wealth. There are also huge inequalities in virtually every aspect of life that affects well-being: in voice, security, access to justice, opportunity, and health. When I was chief economist of the World Bank, we had a major project to ascertain what aspects of poverty—besides basic economic deprivation—were of most concern to the poor themselves. Their answer: insecurity and lack of voice.[64] Lack of access to justice contributes, of course, to a sense of insecurity. And the mass incarceration that marks the U.S. and the deprivation of voting rights for many of those who have served time contributes to the lack of voice and the perpetuation of the system of mass incarceration.[65] Here, I note only two dimensions of inequality that are closely linked to income and wealth inequality and economic performance.

5.2.1 Health Inequalities

Especially in the United States, where there is no universal access to health care, there are large disparities in mortality (life expectancy) related to income and education. Figure 4.11a shows, for instance, the large disparities in life expectancy across income.

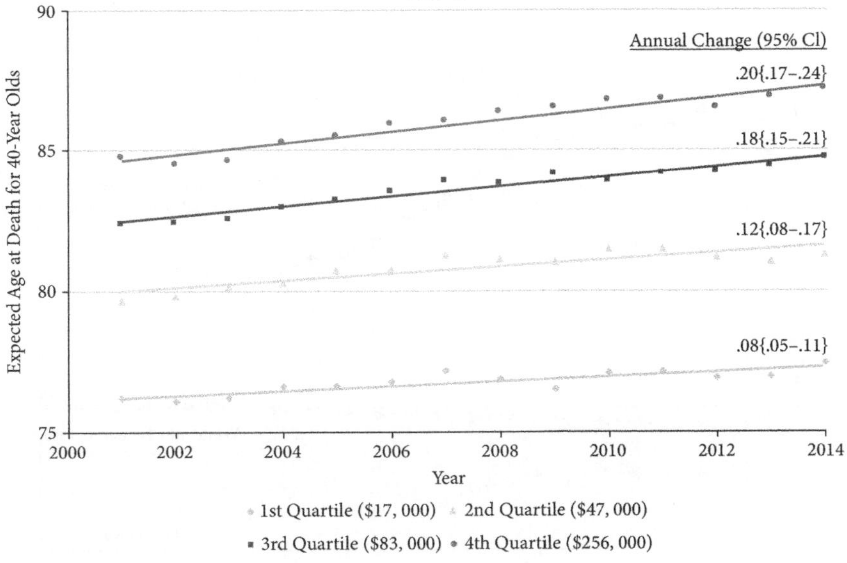

Figure 4.11a Disparities in life expectancy.[b]

[b]Chetty, Stepner, Abraham, et al. (2016) and Belluz (2018).*Note*: Mean quartile income across 2001-2004 (population weighted, rounded to the nearest thousand dollars) in parentheses.
Source: This figure is similar to one that appears in Chetty et al (2016), "The Association Between Income and Life Expectancy in the United States, 2001-2014," which is based on the same data, available from The Health Inequality Project.

Needless to say, societies with a multiplicity of cultural norms can generate persistent inequalities. If some groups put a higher value in school performance, putting pressure on their children to do well in academic studies and providing them at home with more tools to succeed, they may, on average, perform better. More of their children will make it to the good schools, and given the differences in the qualities of school, more of their children will succeed in becoming among the high-income earners of the next generation.

[64] See, for example, Narayan, Patel, Schafft, et al. (2000).

[65] The lack of equal access to justice obviously also contributes to inequality, in all of its manifestations. In the lead up to and during the Great Recession, many who did not owe any money were thrown out of their homes. See Stiglitz (2015b).

There are feedback loops between economic and health inequalities, overall life expectancy, and economic performance. One of the reasons that life expectancy in the U.S. has been declining (Figure 4.11b) is lack of access to health care and lack of opportunity. Poor health impairs economic opportunity; but lack of opportunity leads to what Ann Case and Angus Deaton (2015, 2017) have called *deaths of despair*—the epidemic like increase in deaths from alcoholism, drug overdose, and suicide (Figure 4.11c), of a kind that I have only once before seen, when, as Chief economist of the World Bank, life expectancy declined with the dissolution of the Soviet Union, accompanied by a fall of some one-third in measured GDP. As Case and Deaton document, matters have become worse with each cohort, and are worse in those parts of the country in which there is less economic opportunity.

5.2.2 Inequities in Opportunities

As inequality in income and wealth began to increase in the U.S. and many other countries in the late 1970s and early 1980s, popular rhetoric, especially among the Right, began to emphasize the importance of *opportunities*. Individuals might differ in their income and wealth, but so what if that was a result of hard work and effort. What mattered, in this view, was that everyone should have the same chances. As we noted earlier, the founding myth of the United States was that it was a land of opportunity—the American Dream—and the argument was that that was still true. A closer look at the data suggests otherwise,

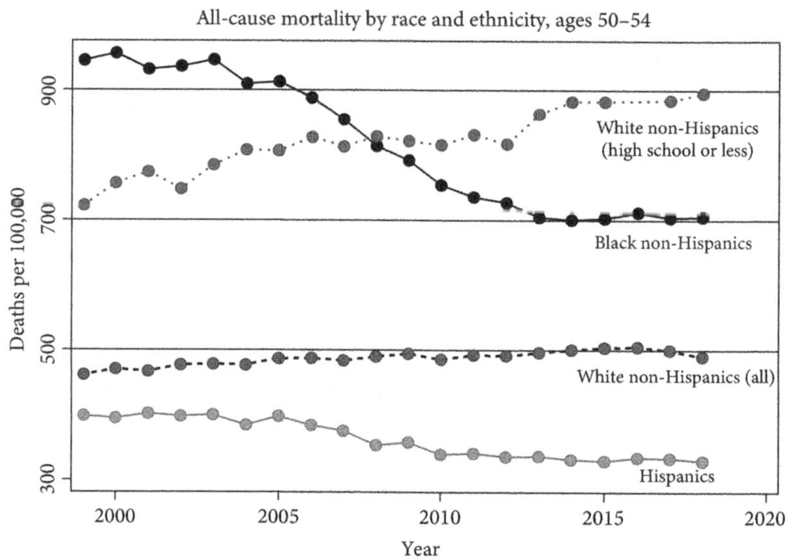

Figure 4.11b Increase in mortality by race and ethnicity.

Note: 1999–2018. Four states (GA, OK, RI, SD) do not provide education on death certificates in the early 1990s, and thus are excluded through 2004. Case and Deaton (2017) exclude these states in all years, but the publicly available NVSS records do not contain state of death from 2005 onward. Consequently, in this version all states are included from 2005 forward.

Source: Data from CDC-Wonder Underlying Cause of Death Files, National Vital Statistics System individual death records, and the March Current Population Survey as provided by CEPR. This figure is similar to one that appears in Case and Deaton (2017), which is based on the same publicly available dataset. Updated through 2018 using code and data appendix for Case and Deaton (2017) (available online).

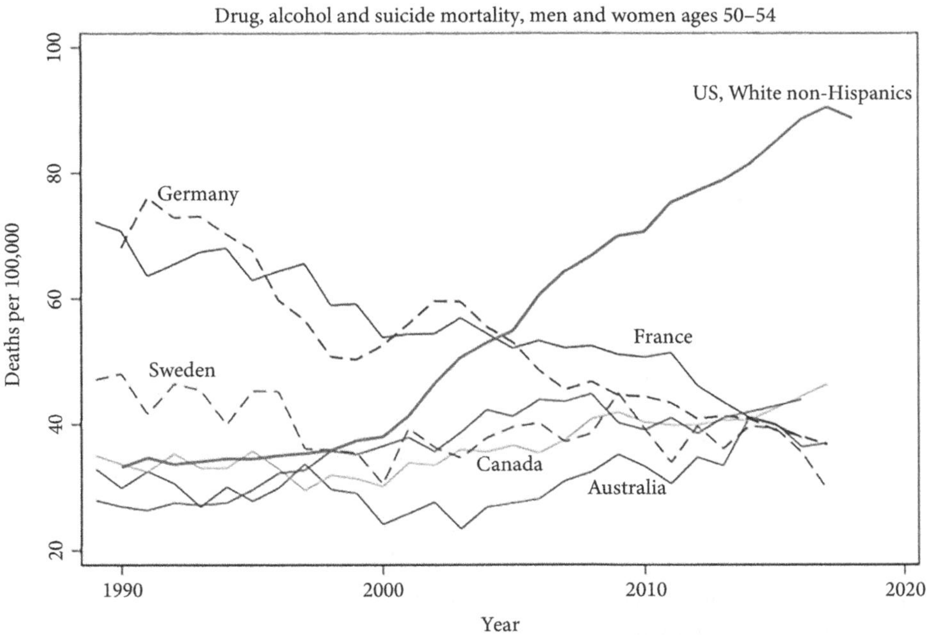

Figure 4.11c Increases in deaths of despair in the U.S.: While drug, alcohol, and suicide mortality declined in other countries, it sourced in U.S.

Note: 1989-2018.

Source: Data from CDC-Wonder Bridged Race Population Estimates, World Health Organization Mortality database, and United Nations World Population Prospects 2019. This figure is similar to one that appears in Case and Deaton (2017), which is based on the same publicly available dataset. Updated through 2018 using code and data appendix for Case and Deaton (2017) (available online).

that the life prospects of a young American are more related to the income and education of his parents than in most other advanced countries—Italy and UK providing the only "competitor" for the position of *least* opportunity.

Figure 4.12a below shows the relationship between income inequality (measured in the standard way by the Gini coefficient) and opportunity (measured by 1—the correlation between the earnings of the parent and the child; when the correlation is zero, the social mobility measure is "one"). Two key insights emerge from the figure: there are large disparities *among advanced countries* in both inequality and opportunity, emphasizing the role of *policy* in determining each, a major theme of my earlier work on inequality; and countries, like those in Scandinavia, that have low levels of inequality have high levels of opportunity.

Similar patterns exist within the United States. The work of Chetty and his co-authors (Chetty, Hendren, Kline, and Saez, 2014) shows the large variation in intergenerational mobility across the United States, with low levels of mobility in the South and certain parts of the Midwest, locations noted for their lower incomes.

Figures 4.12b and 4.12c graphically illustrate both the diminution in opportunity over time and the lower level of opportunity in the U.S. compared to other countries. Figures 4.12b shows that America is distinctive in having few people at the top whose fathers were in the bottom quartile of the income distribution, while 4.12c shows the diminishing fraction

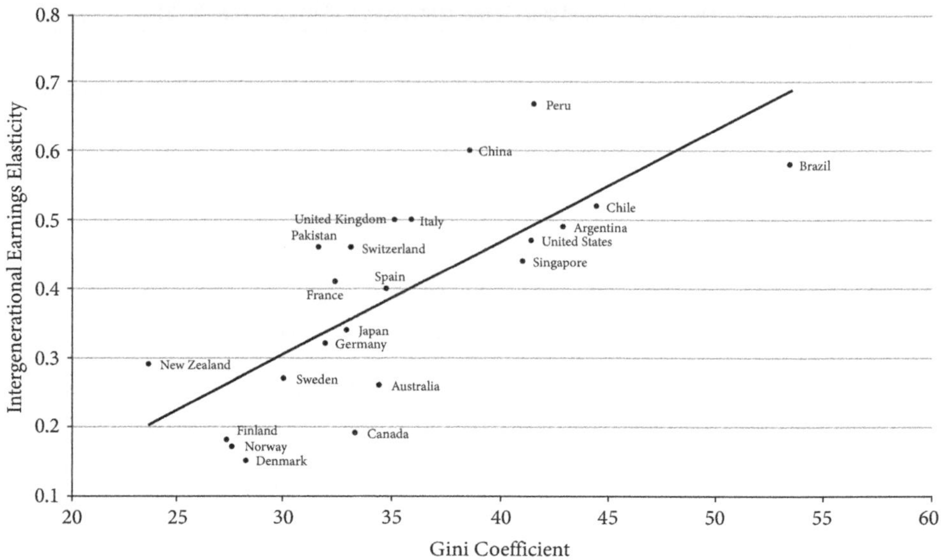

Figure 4.12a Relationship between opportunity (mobility) and inequality.

Note: Line is the least squares fitted regression.
Source: Intergenerational earnings elasticities (between father and son earnings) as listed in Figure 1 of Corak, "Inequality from Generation to Generation: The United States in Comparison," (2016). Gini coefficient from World Bank, World Development Indicators, most recent year available. World Bank estimates are not available for New Zealand and Singapore; instead, World Institute for Development Research (WIDER) Gini estimates are used, accessed from the World Bank's All The Ginis Dataset.

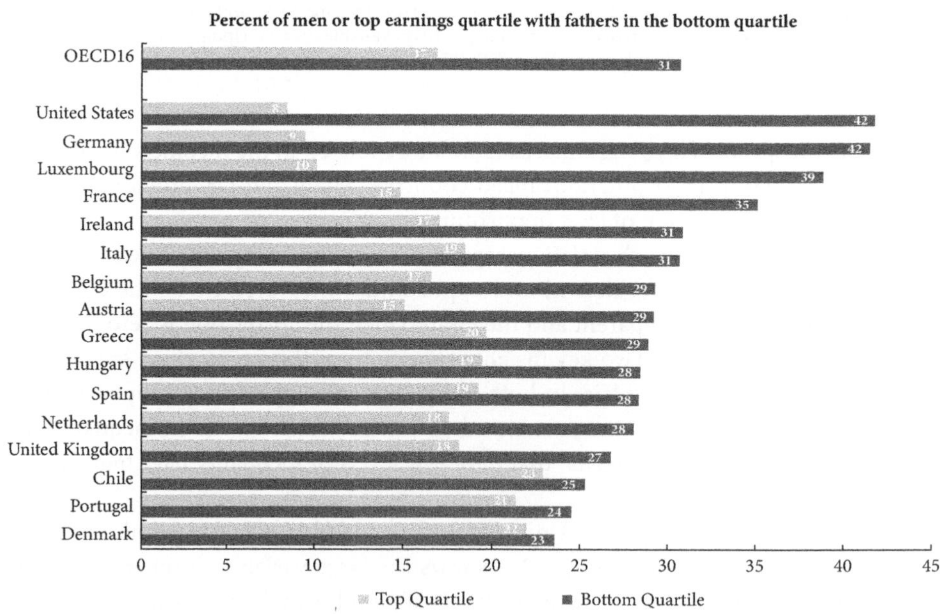

Figure 4.12b America ranks low in opportunity: Percentage of men in bottom or top earnings quartile with fathers in the bottom quartile.

Note: Calculations based on 2011 data. Chile refers to 2009 data. Numbers shown on bars are rounded.
Source: This figure is similar to one that appears in Peterson Institute for International Economics, "How to Fix Economic Inequality?" (2020), which is based on the same data, available in Organization for Economic Cooperation and Development (OECD), "A Broken Social Elevator? How to Promote Social Mobility," (2018).

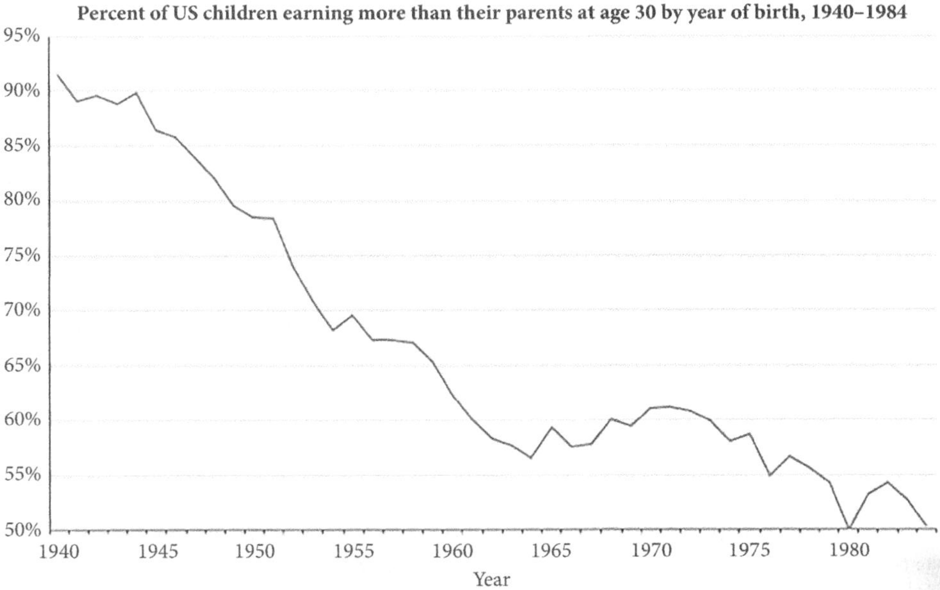

Figure 4.12c Diminishing opportunity: Percentage of U.S. children earning more than their parents at age 30 by year of birth, 1940–84.

Note: Children's Income is the sum of individual and spousal income at age 30, excluding immigrants after 1994. Parental income is the sum of the spouses' income for families in which the highest earner is ages 25–35.
Source: This figure is similar to one that appears in Peterson Institute for International Economics, "How to Fix Economic Inequality?" (2020), which is based on the same data, available in Chetty et al, "The fading American dream: Trends in absolute income mobility since 1940" (2017).

of children earning more than their parents at the age of 30. The latter result reflects the combined effect of less upward mobility and slower growths in income.

The intuition for the strong correlation between inequalities in outcomes and inequalities in opportunities is that if the rungs of the latter are further apart, it is harder to climb up the ladder; and those societies that have done well in public education and offering opportunity for all succeed in getting better outcomes. One simply cannot separate out "opportunities" from "outcomes." As we have emphasized elsewhere, there is inevitably high levels of intergeneration transfer of advantage and disadvantage, not only in resources and connections, but in the preferences and modes of behavior.[66]

This discussion highlights the *average* relation between the income of a child and his parents; but such averages masks deeper structures: there can be poverty traps—with those at the bottom finding it particularly hard to get into the middle class—and wealth traps—with those borne to privilege likely to have a life in the elite. (The formalization of these dynamics through a mobility matrix, and the ranking of mobility matrices—when can we say that one society is unambiguously more mobile than another—are discussed in Chapters 22 and 23.)

[66] See our earlier discussion in this chapter of Roemer, and the more extensive discussion of the notions (and measurement) of income and opportunity elsewhere in this volume.

5.3 Location

A factor that is increasingly recognized as related to all of the inequalities that we have described is location—where people are born and live affects their life prospects in many ways: access to quality education and jobs, and especially in the U.S. with its systemic racism, for African-Americans, the extent of discrimination. Location is also tied up with wealth accumulation through homeownership and the large differentials in capital gains associated with home ownership. The competitive equilibrium theory, discussed earlier in this chapter as the economists' "benchmark model," *assumes* that labor is highly mobile, so that locational differences in wages couldn't persist. But they do, and these differences have come to play an increasingly important role in inequalities in the U.S. and some other countries. Locations suffering, for instance, from deindustrialization systematically and persistently lag behind in incomes.[67]

5.4 Putting It All Together: The Dynamics of Factor Endowments and Factor Shares

We began the analysis with a discussion of the determinants of the factor distribution of income in a competitive model. But that, we noted, in the long run depends on the aggregate accumulation of human and financial capital, and that depends on the behavior of households, and importantly, on their transmission of human and financial capital from one generation to another. The aggregate changes are nothing but the sums of the changes within the households. Modeling macro dynamics and micro dynamics simultaneously and in a consistent manner generates a simultaneous set of stochastic differential (or difference) equations, which, under some simplifying assumptions, can be solved for the steady state (Stiglitz, 1966, 1969b, 1978, 2015a, 2021; Bevan, 1974; Bevan and Stiglitz, 1979).

As we noted earlier, the equilibrium depends on the balancing of centrifugal and centripetal force, and the analysis has identified some of the critical forces and how they have changed. Each change can be analyzed in terms of its impact on the centripetal and centrifugal forces in the economy. "Noise," for example randomness in returns, associated with a riskier environment is a key centrifugal force. Increases in noise, for example as a result of less progressive capital taxation or greater financial and trade liberalization, lead to more inequality. Good public education, the universal provision of high-quality health care and strong progressive redistributive taxes constitute centripetal forces; the weakening of either will lead to more inequality. Some changes, such as reductions in capital taxation or making them less progressive both increase the economy's centrifugal force and reduce the centripetal force, increasing inequality on both accounts.

With inequalities in wealth playing such a central role in inequalities in income, an increase in the share of capital naturally strengths the centrifugal forces in the economy, leading to more inequality. (For the precise formula, see Chapter 12 below.)

But the share of capital is, of course, itself endogenous. Standard growth theory related the long run distribution to the effective capital labor ratio, which in turn was related to

[67] See Delli Gatti, Gallegati, Greenwald, et al. (2012a) and Autor, Dorn, and Hanson (2016). These inequalities have large political consequences. See Autor, Dorn, Hanson, and Majlesi (2020).

the savings rate and the growth rate. In Solovian economics, an increase in the aggregate savings rate or a reduction in the rate of growth of the labor force or the rate of labor augmenting technological progress results in an increase in the capital–effective labor ratio, and a diminution in the share of capital, if the elasticity of substitution is less than unity. Distribution may affect the savings rate, as in Kaldor's analysis.

But earlier in this chapter we discussed models of endogenous growth, where the long run equilibrium share of capital is determined by the innovation locus, that share which just generates pure labor augmenting technological progress. In any case, for any given innovation locus, the long run capital output ratio is such to ensure constancy of the effective capital output ratio.[68] In this model, it is only changes in the innovation frontier that change the long run distribution of income; while changes in the aggregate savings rate or the rate of growth of the effective labor supply generate changes in the capital output ratio, but not in the distribution of income. (See also Chapter 17 below and Barrales-Ruiz, Mendieta-Muñoz, Rada, et al. (2022).

The dynamics of inequality perpetuation that we have just described applies as well to economies with imperfections of competition. Now, however, there is another source of disparity in the economy: the ability to engage in exploitation and rent seeking, which may be a quite different "skill" than the ability to generate conventional returns to capital. Moreover, those with market power typically work hard to maintain their market power, creating entry barriers and reducing opportunities for others. It is another instance where wealth and power begets more wealth and power. And it is why competition policy should be viewed with the ambit of equality-generating policies.

Moreover, an increase in the market power of corporations and a weakening of that of workers diminishes the share of labor, and, following the above analysis, thereby increases the economy's centrifugal forces, leading to, for instance, a fatter tailed wealth distribution.

5.5 The Consequences of Inequality: Poorer Economic Performance

There is a fundamental consequence arising from the difference in perspectives on inequality provided in this chapter vs. the standard competitive model: in that model, greater equality can only be achieved by intervening in the market economy, and such interventions have a cost. Arthur Okun, chairman of the Council of Economic Advisers under President Johnson, described this as "the big trade-off" (1975). By contrast, if inequality arises from exploitation and other imperfections in markets, and if it is associated in the inequalities in health and opportunities that we have just described, then there exists policies (to be described in the next section) which increase economic performance and reduce inequality—a prediction consistent with the empirical evidence presented by Ostry, Berg, and Tsangarides (2014) and Ostry, Loungani, and Berg (2019) and consistent with the historical experience of the U.S., where the period after World War II was marked by low

[68] If s is the average savings rate, a function of the share of labor, S_L, which in the long run is determined as in the text at $S_L{}^*$, then $s(S_L{}^*) / g = K/Y$, where K/Y is the capital output ratio and g is the long run rate of growth, equal to the rate of labor force growth plus the rate of labor augmenting technology progress. sY/K is sometimes referred to the warranted rate of growth, g as the natural rate of growth. Equilibrium entails the two equaling each other.

If $y(\kappa)$ is output per effective unit of labor, where $\kappa = \mu K \lambda L$ is the effective capital labor ratio, then $Y/K = \mu f(\kappa)/\kappa$. Endogenous technological progress increases μ to the requisite value.

and decreasing inequality and faster growth, compared to the decades that preceded and followed.[69]

6 Historical Perspectives

Inequality has not always been as high as it is. Writing in the middle of the twentieth century, Nobel-prize economist Simon Kuznets suggested that while in early stages of development inequality would increase, later it would decrease. (Kuznets, 1955) The argument was simple: early on, some parts of the economy pull ahead, taking advantage of the opportunities afforded by modernization (at the time, industrialization and urbanization). Later on, others catch up, and the lagging part of the economy increases its share. As he was writing, the evidence supported his hypothesis; but he could not have understood what was to happen a couple of decades later—the sudden and large increase in inequality, especially in the U.S. (though the pattern is present elsewhere, though diminished in magnitude), evidenced in Figure 4.13. (While these charts show the dramatic increase in wealth of the top 1% and the even more dramatic increase in that of the top 0.1%, other measures of income and wealth inequality show similar patterns.)

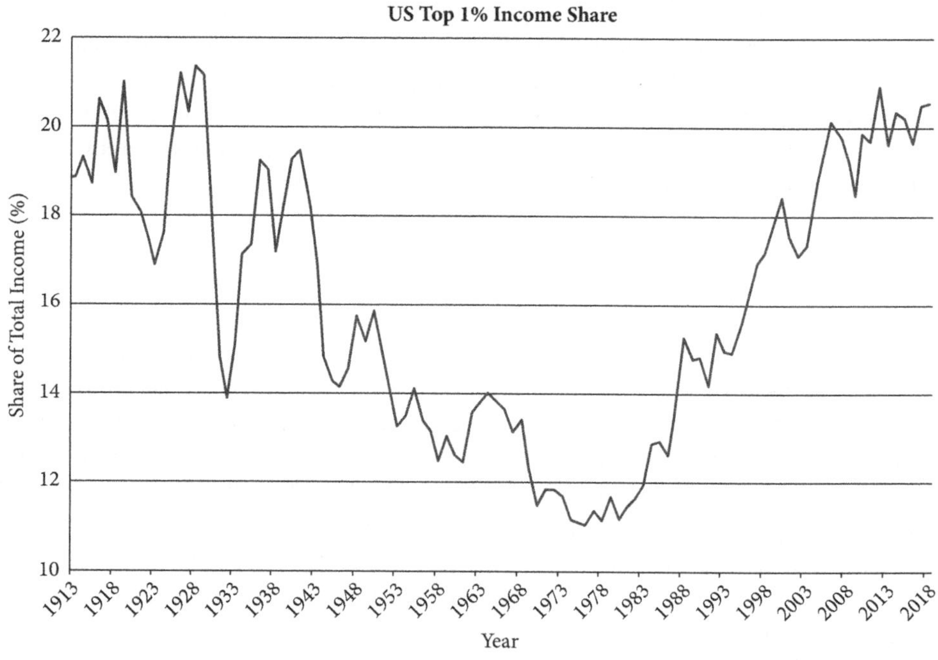

[69] This is also consistent with the experience of East Asia, where equalitarian policies were associated with high growth.

Earlier growth theories argued that *in the short and medium term* growth depended on savings, and the rich saved a larger fraction of their income than the poor, so that greater inequality was good for growth. The experience of East Asia showed (a) government policy can increase savings rates among the entire population; (b) public savings and investment are crucial, and these can be funded by progressive taxation; and (c) the benefits of greater equality in terms of human capital formation, trust and stability, etc. dominate.

See World Bank (1993), Birdsall, Ross, and Sabot (1995), Stiglitz (1996), and Stiglitz and Uy (1996).

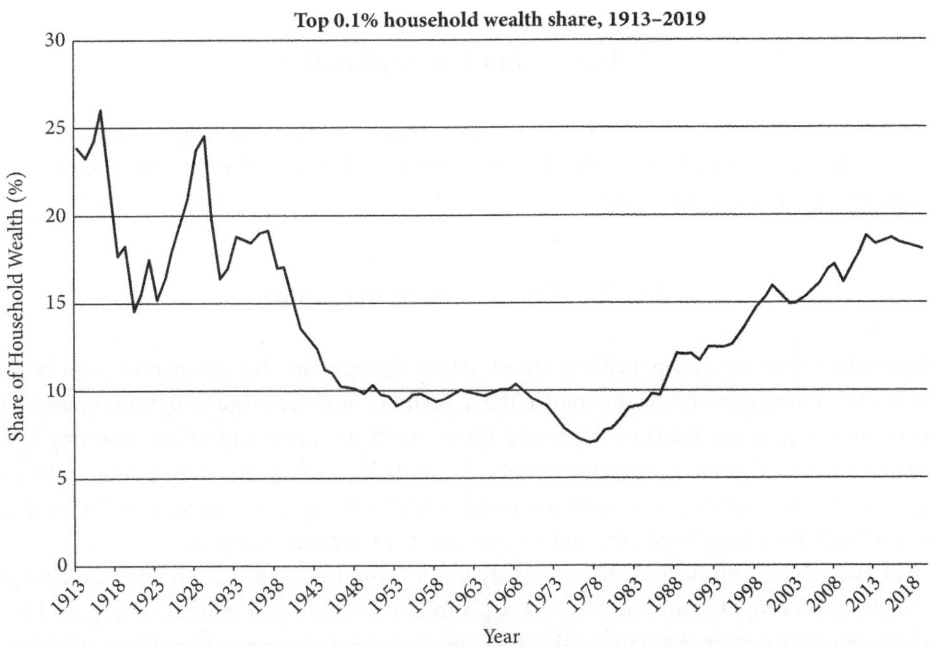

Figure 4.13 Decline and subsequent growth in inequality in income and wealth.

Notes: (a) Pre-tax national income, 1913–2018. Adults age 20 and over. Income equally split in couples. (b) Share of household wealth. Adults over age 20. Wealth equally split in couples. (c) Share of household wealth. Adults over age 20. Wealth equally split in couples.

Source: (a) World inequality Database. (b) This figure is similar to figure VI Saez and Zucman (2016). Updated using data from Piketty, Saez, and Zucman (2018), Appendix Tables II, table TE1. (c) This figure is similar to figure I Saez and Zucman (2016). Updated using data from Piketty, Saez, and Zucman (2018), Appendix Tables II, table TE1.

The question is why? The alternative perspectives, outlined earlier in this chapter provide us alternative hypotheses: Piketty's view that growing inequality is an inevitable feature of capitalism (in the absence of, say, a tax on capital that would lower the after-tax return to capital) is that the decline in inequality from the beginning of the Great Depression until the mid 1970s was an historical aberration, brought about particularly by the solidarity following from World War II.

By contrast, the equilibrium theories argue that we have moved (or are moving) from one equilibrium distribution to another, with the new equilibrium income and distribution far more unequal than the earlier prevailing one. While formal models using, say, stochastic diffusion equations focus on analytic issues—what kinds of changes in the relevant "parameters" of the economy, both those related to structure (say the advent of globalization) and policy, for example, marginal tax rates at the top, lead to what kinds of changes in the equilibrium wealth distribution—a deeper analysis requires an understanding of the intellectual, social, economic, and political forces that have led to these changes, including the changes in policy.

In this respect, the two perspectives are in accord: social, economic, and political forces in mid-twentieth century, such as the greater solidarity brought about by World War II, led to policy changes that, in turn, led to a more equalitarian (equilibrium) income and wealth distribution. While a fuller exploration of these historical forces would take us beyond this chapter, we provide some speculative observations in the next section.

7 Power, Politics, and Policy

The different theories we have outlined have markedly different implications not only for the consequences of inequality for the economy, but also for the effectiveness and desirability of different policies.

7.1 Policies to Reduce Inequality

Models focusing on competitive markets stress changes in the balance of supply and demand.[70] These are important; particularly germane are the large structural changes in the economy, in some parts of the world the move from a rural agrarian economy to an urban industrial economy, in more advanced countries, as they move from a manufacturing economy to a service and innovation economy.[71] Changes in preferences, technology, and globalization have been central to these structural transformations.

But as we have emphasized here, equally if not more important are how these changes have affected competition, how they have given rise to rents and market power, and how the economic rules of the game—those governing, for instance, competition and labor

[70] Thus, policies that provide more access to higher education not only reduce inequalities in human capital—thereby directly reducing income inequalities—but also (in these models) reduce the skill premium. But if human capital and labor are substitutes, the increase in the "effective" labor supply may, if the elasticity of substitution between capital and effective labor is less than unity, reduce the share of labor, thereby contributing to an increase in overall inequality.

[71] There are, in addition, large transitional effects of such structural transformations, which go beyond our long run equilibrium analysis. See Delli Gatti, Gallegati, Greenwald, et al. (2012a, 2012b).

relations—have changed. Thus, changes in technology, including transportation costs, might have led, on their own, to greater inequalities in competitive markets; but the inequalities may have been compounded by changes in corporate market power, changes which, in turn, were affected both by the changes in technology and policy changes, for example the weakening of competition laws and their enforcement.

The different theories not only direct attention to different variables but provide different predictions as to the consequences of government interventions attempting to improve the distribution of income and wealth. The competitive theories, for instance, imply that tax interventions to reduce inequalities may have adverse incentive effects—which may be so large as to undo the intended benefit. Moreover, short run effects—focusing on changes in the distribution of factor incomes today, *given* the distribution of factor endowments—may be different from the long run effects, when the distribution of factor endowments change. A long run analysis needs to focus on the changes in economic structure and policy that change the balance between centrifugal and centripetal forces, leading to an equilibrium characterized by greater or less wealth inequality.

Critics of policies that might lead to greater equality often stress the possibility of these long run adverse effects which undermine the short run positive effects, making the measures counterproductive in the long run. But this should be only the beginning of the analysis. For instance, a tax on capital, the proceeds of which are redistributed to workers, under quite general conditions leads to greater inequality. The question is, are there sets of policies—policy "packages"—for instance, a capital income tax the proceeds of which are used for investments in human capital and/or infrastructure, which reduce inequality and improve economic performance, not just in the short run (when factor endowments are given), but also in the long run (when they change). The answer is, under quite general conditions, yes (Chapter 19 below). And this is especially so if there are other market failures such as imperfect capital markets. The existence of competition does not mean that there are no other market failures which contribute both to economic inefficiency and inequality.[72] Because of imperfect information, capital markets are inherently imperfect, and this will result in especially the poor investing too little in education. Egalitarian public education can as a result both reduce inequality and increase economic performance.

Well-designed tax and expenditure policies can have a direct effect on inequalities in opportunities and outcomes and their perpetuation (whether markets are competitive or not). Regressive taxes[73]—where those at the top pay a lower percentage of their income in taxation than those with lower income—clearly result in more inequality in after-tax disposable income. (The effects are obvious in the short run, but the effects can compound over time, as the rich reinvest their higher disposable incomes.) By contrast, progressive expenditure policies—where the government, for instance, finances health care for all—can result in greater equality of well-being, and again, over the long term, greater equalities in income and wealth.[74]

[72] Indeed, with imperfect information and incomplete markets (and information is always imperfect and markets are always incomplete), competitive markets are not in general Pareto efficient. See Greenwald and Stiglitz (1986).

[73] For a recent discussion, see Saez and Zucman (2019b).

[74] Ascertaining what is *truly* progressive is often difficult. Medicare, the program providing health insurance for those over 65, some claim is regressive, because "as a result of relatively regressive financing mechanisms and the higher expenditures and longer survival times of wealthier beneficiaries" (McClellan and Skinner, 1997). Similarly, providing highly subsidized university education is often claimed to be regressive, since those receiving

In the United States, there is evidence that safety net programs have helped reduce poverty—mitigating the inequality at the bottom. See Figure 4.14.

Inheritance taxes and the structure of public education are, of course, two of the major determinants of inequalities in income and opportunity. Though good public education could play an important role in offsetting inherited inequalities, in practice it often seems to reinforce them, especially in a country such as the U.S. marked by extensive economic segregation and with locally provided education—where communities in which the poor live also provide poorer educational opportunities. If public education is to offset inherited advantages and disadvantages, there has to be a significant compensatory element—there has to be more spending on the poor than on the rich.

Many seeking to create a more equal society have focused their efforts on education. But while that will go some way to improving matters, it will not suffice. Ironically, while public discussion has focused on equalizing opportunities through education—equalizing intergenerational transfers of human capital—in many countries, and especially the U.S., there have been great efforts on the part of one party to increase *inequalities* in the intergenerational transfer of financial wealth, through lowering (or, for a brief one year, under the administration of President George W. Bush, eliminating) the inheritance tax. Not surprisingly, such policies result in the growth of inequality. More broadly, regressive taxation—taxing those at the top at a lower rate than those below—both enables and incentivizes those at the top to grow richer relative to those below (Figure 4.15).

While there are a host of policies that can increase equality of income, wealth, and opportunity within a competitive framework, the possibility of doing so—and even further

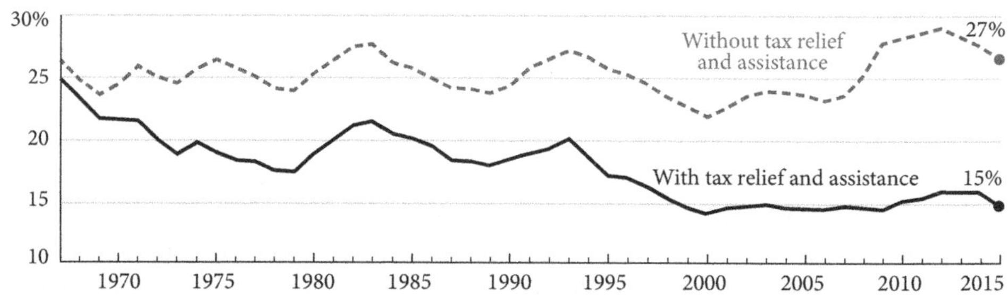

Figure 4.14 U.S. poverty levels with and without tax relief and government assistance programs, 1967–2015.

Note: Refers to market income poverty and supplemental poverty measure (post-tax-and-transfer). Based on Wimer et al, "Trends in Poverty with an Anchored Supplemental Poverty Measure" (2013), updated November 2016 as reported in Furman, "Combating Inequality: Social Safety Net" (2017).
Source: Reprinted by permission, Peterson Institute for International Economics, "How to Fix Economic Inequality?" (https://www.pile.com/microsites/how-fix-economic-inequality), 2020.

the subsidy will, on average, have higher incomes in the future. It is more equitable, it is claimed, to provide loans, and especially income contingent loans, where repayment is made conditional on the income the individual actually earns. On the other hand, children of the poor may be reluctant to borrow significant amounts of money, even when repayment is made income contingent, so that any loan program may be a barrier to upward mobility. For a discussion of these loan programs, see Stiglitz (2014g, 2016c) and Chapman, Higgins, and Stiglitz (2014).

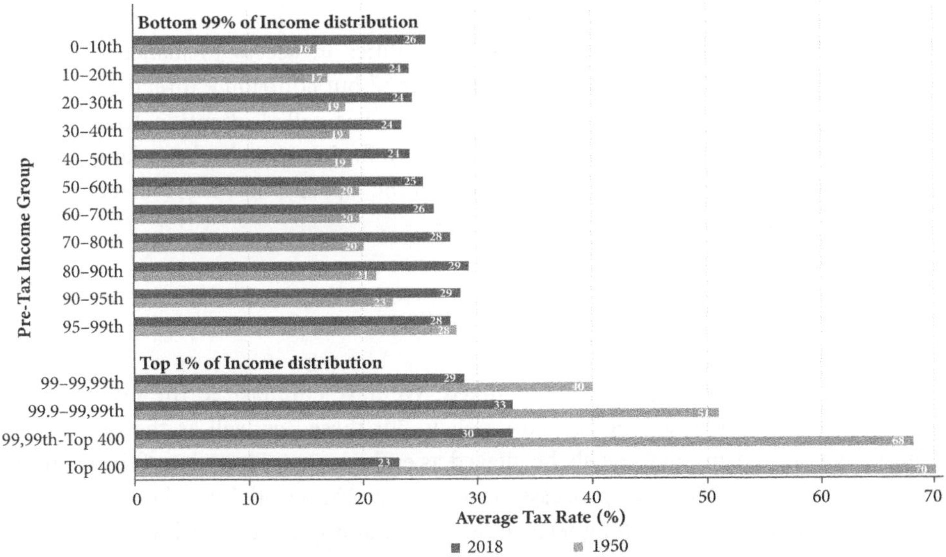

Figure 4.15 Average tax rate by pre-tax income group in the United States, 1950 and 2018.

Notes: Tax rate includes all federal, state, and local taxes. Taxes are expressed as a fraction of pre-tax income. 0–10th percentile denotes the bottom 10 percent of the income distribution. Top 400 refers to the Forbes list of the 400 highest earning Americans.

Source: This figure is similar to one that appears in Peterson Institute for International Economics, "How to Fix Economic Inequality?" (2020), which is based on the same data, from Saez and Zucman "The Triump of Injustice" (2019), Appendix Tables C1, C8, D1.

increasing efficiency and growth—is even greater in real world economies marked by high levels of rents and exploitation. Curbing monopoly power gives a double dividend of eliminating a distortion and increasing equality. Tax increases at the top may in fact be salutary, because they may discourage rent-seeking. There can even be a triple dividend: the reduced value of rent-capital (the capitalized value of rents) induces more capital accumulation, increasing wages.

7.1.1 Complexity in the Design of Equalitarian Policies

Because the poor have different assets, policies which are seemingly neutral can have large distributive effects. The fraction of their income that is, on average, derived from labor is higher than that from capital, so that any policy which adversely affects the return to labor relative to capital has adverse distributive consequences. Similarly, we noted that the rich own disproportionately assets which yield returns in the form of capital gains, so that the lowering of the capital gains tax was inequality-increasing. And to the extent that the capital gains arise from land or other fixed assets, the lower tax rate is de facto a lowering of taxes on rents—thus having no direct incentive effect, but possibly having an adverse effect in inducing lower capital accumulation (with high rent-wealth substituting for capital). So, too, monetary policies like QE (quantity easing), the effect of which is to increase the price of equities, increases wealth inequality, even if it might have some benefits in increasing employment.

7.1.2 Interactions between Social and Economic Inequalities

Earlier in this chapter we discussed how inequalities in access to justice and health care not only give rise to inequalities in "well-being," but contribute directly in inequalities in income and wealth. Behavioral economics has called attention to how social interactions—especially excesses of inequality—may, for instance, lead to a lack of aspiration at the bottom and/or a sense of entitlement at the top, and how these affect economic performance and the perpetuation of inequalities.

7.2 Politics and Economics

Politics and economics are inextricably linked: We have emphasized the importance of the rules of the game and more broadly policy. But these—as well as the evolution of technology—should simultaneously be viewed as endogenous. The rules of the economic game are set through political processes (see Stiglitz, 2012a; Stiglitz, Abernathy, Hersh, et al., 2015; Stiglitz, Stetter, Dougherty, et al., 2019; and Chapter 5 below). While rules matter even in competitive economies, the rules themselves affect the extent to which an economy is marked by exploitation. We've already noted multiple examples: competition policy, policies aimed at reducing discrimination, and monetary policy. Regulations could have prevented some of the worst instances of exploitation discussed earlier in this chapter. Sometimes, the legal framework has exacerbated problems: America's system of mass incarceration provides an obvious example. But there are many more subtle examples. The country's 2005 bankruptcy law made it virtually impossible for students to discharge their debt, even when they go bankrupt, encouraging exploitation by the for-profit universities. That same law made bankruptcy in general more difficult, encouraging predatory lending. Corporate governance laws provided CEOs with the freedom to construct "incentive" compensation schemes which directed an increasing fraction of corporate revenues toward top management—without leading to any commensurate improvement in corporate performance. Accounting laws and legislation enabled corporations not to meaningfully disclose the full value of the benefits they were conferring on their executives.[75] Laws weakening workers' bargaining power or consumers' ability to get redress from corporations that have exploited them through class action suit contribute too to inequality.

7.2.1 Wealth Inequality and Inequalities of Power

Perhaps the most important inequalities are inequalities in power, inequalities that are exhibited in day-to-day interactions, interactions in every sphere of society, in the workplace and in politics. Such inequalities undermine the nature of democratic politics and society. Large inequalities of economic power get translated—especially in a political system which allows money to matter as much as that of the U.S.—to inequalities in political power; and that means those with money have the ability to get the economic rules of the game written in their favor, perpetuating and exacerbating these economic, political, and power inequalities.[76] Chapter 16 below shows that there may be multiple political and

[75] See Stiglitz (2003a).

[76] Sometimes, individuals with particular interests collude in the political sphere (in ways which would be illegal in the economic): they form industry associations to lobby for special benefits. Sometimes they agitate

economic equilibria: one with a high level of inequality, generating rules that sustain that inequality, and another with a low level of inequality, giving rise to rules that sustain the more equalitarian society. It is even possible that there is ever-increasing inequality—as the rich get richer, they use their power to continually reset the rules to advantage themselves more.[77]

Most fundamentally, inequality may thus affect the nature of society and democratic politics—elsewhere I have suggested that it is even hard for a system of checks to balances to work over the long run if inequality is too high: those at the top will prevail (Stiglitz, 2019a).[78] On the other hand, there *may* be political forces that prevent this, at least in nominally democratic countries, provided that the influence of money in politics can be curtailed: eventually, in one way or another, the voice of the vast majority, whose interests are not served by growing inequality, gets heard.

8 Concluding Remarks

In this chapter I've attempted to provide a concise summary of the major strands of thought that have affected our understanding of inequalities. There is a close connection between our understanding of the causes of inequality (say in income and wealth) and that of its consequences and what can and should be done about it. The neoclassical theory which argued income differences were a result of differences in individuals' societal contributions suggested that individuals were getting their "just deserts," and that there would be a cost to reducing inequality. But when inequalities are attributed to a variety of market failures and distortions, reducing these would actually both improve economic efficiency and reduce inequality. Inequality arising out of discrimination and the abuse of market power are obvious examples. But so too are inequalities of opportunities arising out of lack of access to education: many children of the poor are never able to fully live up to their potential.

There are a multitude of policies which have contributed to the growth of inequality, and a multiplicity of reforms which can help reduce it. Our richer discussion of the sources of inequality, going beyond the competitive model, has identified a richer set of policies for

for political action with an understanding of their shared interests, for example lobbying for less progressive taxation. Elites and the wealthy also shape the cognitive frames in which policies are evaluated: the competitive model became the dominant paradigm, and it shaped policies, and those policies often advanced the interests of the elites—even if they would have argued that that was not their motivation. But almost surely, because the policies were in their interests, they saw the benefits more clearly than the costs; had decision making been more in the hands of those who were adversely affected, not only might the limitations of the dominant paradigm have become more extensively recognized, but it is possible that different decisions might have been made. We are now beginning to become more aware, for instance, that policies which increase the risk exposure of an economy (such as capital, financial market, and trade liberalization) may disadvantage those least able to bear risk (the poor) and even advantage those more able to bear risk (the rich). Only recently has there been awareness of how meritocracy, as structured in the U.S. today, may be perpetuating inequalities, as we noted earlier.

[77] This conclusion, of the possibility of ever-increasing inequality, is similar to that of Piketty (2014), but he bases it on arguments concerning the basic structure of a capitalist economy (that the rate of return will be greater than the rate of growth), which we have questioned.

[78] A side-effect of inheritance taxation is that it may result in more inequality in consumption—inheritances sometimes smooth consumption intergenerationally. More important than inequalities of consumption are inequalities in wealth, especially because of the role that such inequalities play in giving rise to inequalities in political power. Moreover, there are other policies that can offset any adverse effects on inequalities of consumption.

reducing inequalities, including those associated with reducing the market power of corporations, increasing that of workers, and addressing a host of other "market failures." In *The Price of Inequality* and *People, Power, and Profits* I lay out more fully the agenda. Here, I summarize with a brief taxonomy, building off the analysis of this chapter, and illustrate with a few examples. Inequality can be reduced either by reducing inequalities in market incomes (what is commonly called now pre-distribution); or by redistribution. Inequalities in market income are affected by inequalities in ownership of assets—affected, for instance, by inheritances, itself affected by inheritance taxation, and the provision of public education (human capital)—and the relative returns to and property rights in different assets. Here, we have emphasized the importance not only of "demand and supply," but of market power, the balance between the power of large corporations and workers. A host of rules and regulations—labor legislation, corporate governance, and competition laws—affect this balance. The conduct of monetary policy affects the average level of unemployment, and the bargaining power of workers. Tax and technology policy affects the factor bias of technological change.

Redistribution, in turn, can take multiple forms: progressive taxation or progressive expenditures. There is, of course, no neat separation: if the government pays higher salaries to its workers, it will drive up wages and increase the share of labor. What government spends money on affects the demands for workers of different skills.

Central to our analysis has been thinking of there being, at any moment of time, an equilibrium income and wealth distribution, where centripetal and centrifugal forces are balanced. Regressive taxation acts as a centrifugal force, fattening tail-inequality, while more progressive taxation reduces income and wealth inequality at the top; better public education acts as a centripetal force, pulling the economy toward greater equality, and inheritance taxation—if the proceeds are well invested in education and public goods, like infrastructure—can both help prevent the creation of an inherited plutocracy and increase the wages of workers.

Perhaps the most important lesson of this chapter is that the level of inequality is not an inevitable feature of capitalism, but is greatly affected by the rules of the game—by, of course, tax and expenditure policies (i.e., how progressive they are), but also by the legal and economic framework, which restricts, for instance, the ability of corporations to exploit consumers through market power or deceptive practices or workers through an imbalance of bargaining power; or which, through corporate governance laws, restricts the ability of corporate executives to extract more of corporate income for themselves. Similarly, rules governing globalization and monetary policy affect the bargaining power of workers.

In this perspective, capitalism might even function *better* with rules that resulted in greater equality. As I have put it elsewhere, *inequality is a choice.* (Stiglitz, 2015b). The problem is not with the economic system "capitalism," but with the political system which sets the rules. But critics of capitalism might legitimately respond: capitalism is an economic and political system; the economic inequalities to which it gives rise inevitably give rise to political inequalities, which results in rules favoring the capitalists.

During the past 40 years, in the U.S. the rules have been rewritten to favor those at the top—and this increase in inequality has been accompanied, perhaps not surprisingly, by a slowing of growth and (until the pandemic) the largest economic downturn since the Great Depression. The United States is paying a high price for its inequality—it is dividing society, undermining the country's democracy, and weakening the economy.

9 Appendix: Some Global Perspectives

This chapter, and most of this book, focuses on inequality within a country—indeed, most of the analysis is conducted for closed economies. This chapter has illustrated what is happening by looking at data from the United States, partly because it is the most extreme. (Medical doctors look to pathology to understand what happens in a normal body, and extreme pathologies often bring the greatest insights. This may also be true in the study of inequality.)

As we have already noted, there are marked differences in the level of inequality around the world. Figure 4.A1 shows graphically these disparities—very high levels in U.S., Brazil, Russia, and a few other countries, and low levels in Northern Europe.

Globally, wealth inequality is even more extreme than it is in the U.S. Every year, Oxfam reports on wealth concentration at the very top: how many of the richest people have as much wealth as the bottom 50%, roughly 3.8 billion people. In 2010, when they first issued the report, it was 388; by 2018, it was only 26. Their 2019 report[79] includes statistics like: The world's 2,153 billionaires have more wealth than the 4.6 billion people who make up 60% of the planet's population; and the richest 1% in the world have more than double the wealth of 6.9 billion people.

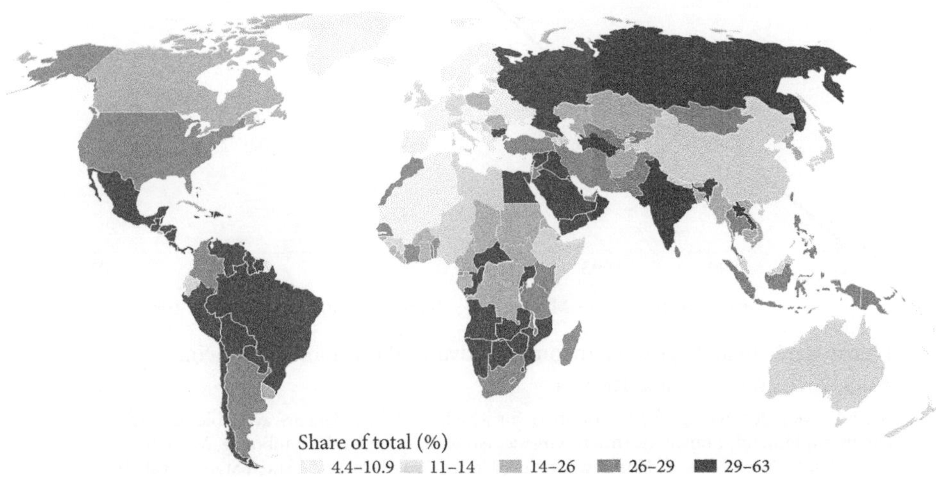

Figure 4.A1 Top 1% national income shares around the world.

[79] See Oxfam (2020), "Time to Care."

Figure 4.A2 shows the systematic "pulling apart" of the advanced economies of the advanced countries, with those at the top seeing incomes increase markedly, with those at the bottom doing far more poorly, and stagnating in the years after the Great Recession. We have repeatedly remarked that inequality in the U.S. is larger than elsewhere, though inequality is growing in most countries around the world. Still, there were a few countries which (at least at the time that chapter was written) were seeing a decrease in inequality. Figure 4.A3 compares the relative stagnation of the bottom 50% of the U.S. with the admittedly slow growth (40% over 35 years) in Europe. Figure 4.A4 provides a dramatic illustration of the consequence: while in 1980, the bottom 50% had a significantly smaller share of national income than the top 1%, by 2015 the numbers had more than reversed. By comparison, while the share of the top 1% has increased and the bottom 50% decreased, the latter still have a markedly larger share.

Finally, Figure 4.A5 shows that inequalities in wealth are across the board larger than inequalities in income—and the U.S. stands out in both dimensions among advanced countries—U.S. inequalities in wealth are particularly noteworthy, with 79% of the wealth being held by the top 10%, more than 50% greater than the OECD average.

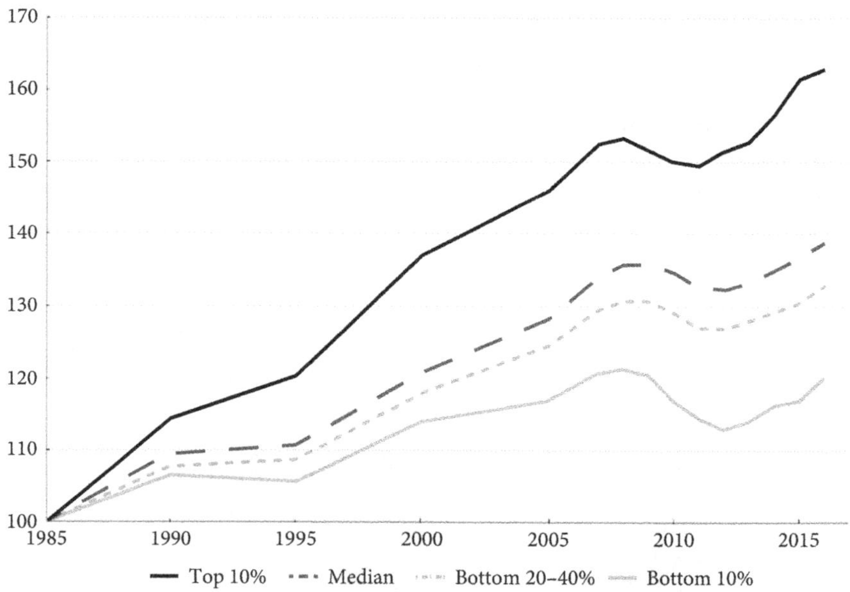

Figure 4.A2 Real disposable income in advanced economies by income position, 1985–2016 (index: 1985=100).

Note: Unweighted average for 17 countries for which long-term data are available: Canada, Denmark, Finland, France, Germany, Greece, Israel, Italy, Japan, Luxembourg, Mexico, Netherlands, New Zealand, Norway, Sweden, United Kingdom, and United States. Available dataset includes Mexico, which is not an advanced economy.

Source: Peterson Institute for International Economics, "How to Fix Economic Inequality?" (2020), based on Organization for Economic Cooperation and Development (OECD), "Under Pressure: The Squeezed Middle Class," (2019).

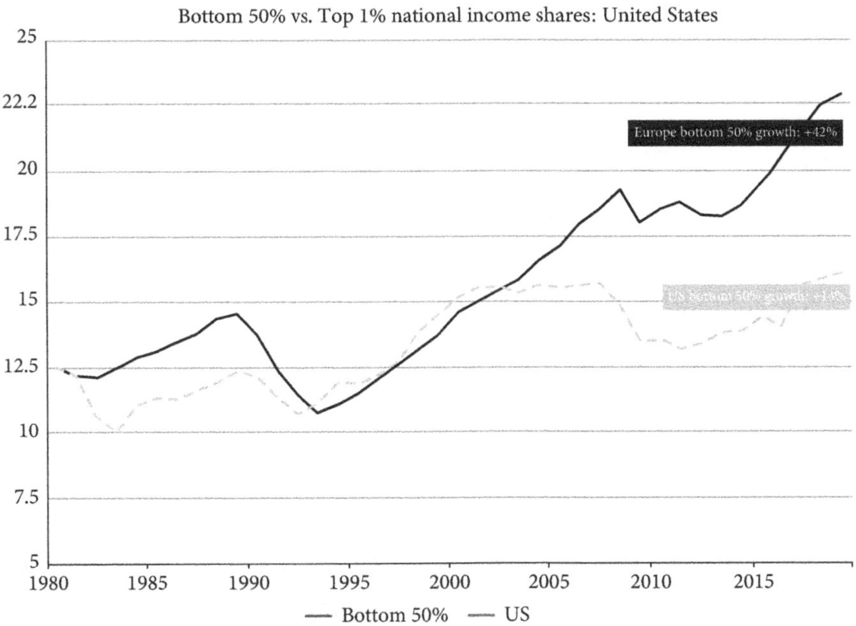

Figure 4.A3 Average pretax income growth of bottom 50% of population relative to 1980 U.S. vs. Europe.

Note: 1980-2019.

Source: This figure is similar to one that appears in Blanchet, Chancel, and Gethin (2019). For the Europe line, this figure uses the Europe average pre-tax national income of the bottom 50% series publicly available from WID.world; this series is very similar but not identical to the Europe series Blanchet, Chancel, and Gethin (2019) constructed and used in the original figure. For the US line, this figure uses the 2020 update of the Piketty, Saez, and Zucman (2018) publicly available data; Blanchet, Chancel, and Gethin (2019) use the original Piketty, Saez, and Zucman (2018) data.

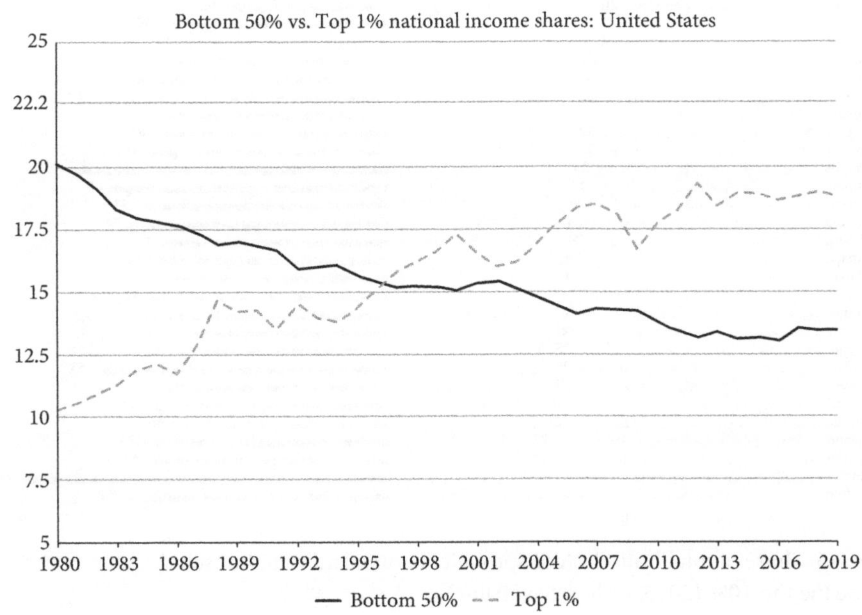

Figure 4.A4 Pretax share of national income 1980–2017 U.S. vs. Europe.

Note: 1980-2019.

Source: This figure is similar to one that appears in Blanchet, Chancel, and Gethin (2019). For the Europe lines, this figure uses the publicly available WID.world series of Europe pre-tax national income shares of the bottom 50% and top 1%; these series are very similar but not identical to the Europe series Blanchet, Chancel, and Gethin (2019) constructed and used in the original figure. For the US lines, this figure uses the 2020 update of the Piketty, Saez, and Zucman (2018) publicly available data; Blanchet, Chancel, and Gethin (2019) use the original Piketty, Saez, and Zucman (2018) data.

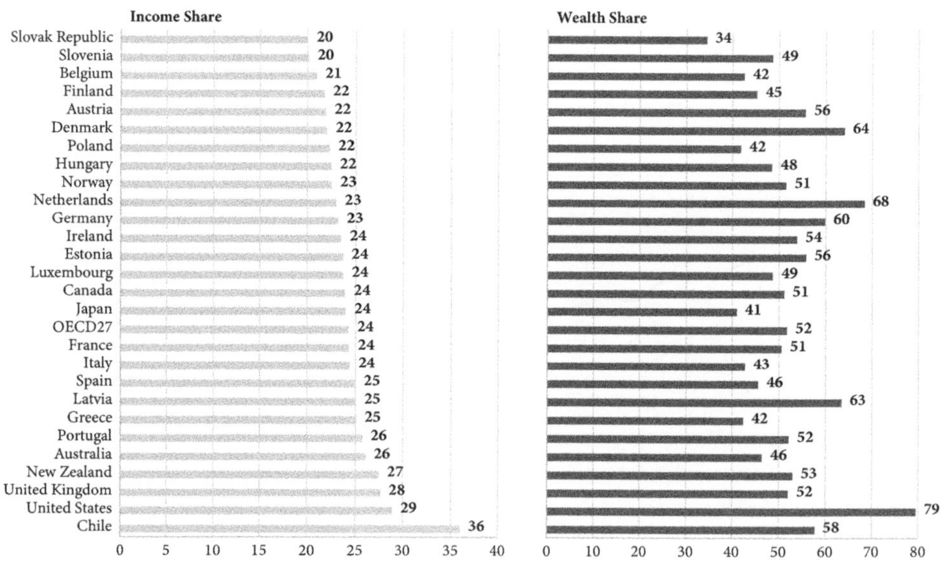

Figure 4.A5 Share of total household disposable income and total household net wealth held to be the top 10% (2015, or latest available).

Note: The OECD average is the simple country average. Data refer to the share held by the richest 10% of households in the case of wealth; and by the richest 10% of individuals in the case of income. Numbers shown on bars are rounded.

Source: Peterson Institute for International Economics, "How to Fix Economic Inequality?" (2020), based on Organization for Economic Cooperation and Development (OECD), "Society at a Glance 2019: OECD Social Indicators," (2019).

5

Rewriting the Rules of the Economy and the Shaping of American Inequality

This chapter is based on a set of excerpts from *Rewriting the Rules of the American Economy*, a report I wrote, with the assistance of Nell Abernathy, Adam Hersh, Susan Holmberg, and Mike Konczal, for the Roosevelt Institute—a think tank that grew out of Franklin D. Roosevelt's presidential library.[1,2] The book, as we noted in the introduction to this part of the volume, provided a progressive agenda to simultaneously reduce inequality and increase growth based on rewriting the rules of the economy.

As we note in the introduction to the volume, while we focus on the United States, what has happened here has also occurred in many other countries around the world. The international rules of the game have also been changed, often under the influence of the same misguided economic theories, reflecting the same ideologies and similar economic interests. In some cases, America has been seen as a role model; in others, it has used its influence at the World Bank, the IMF, the WTO, the G-20, and in other international settings to induce, and in some cases, to effectively force on other countries the kind of changes that led to more inequality and poorer economic performance in the United States.

This chapter is an edited and updated version of a set of excerpts of *Rewriting the Rules*.[3]

***

The economic experiences of the last 35 years have pulled the rug out from under many of our traditional economic conceptions. When President Kennedy said that "a rising tide lifts all boats," he gave voice to a theory of progress that had guided thinking in economics and policy for years.[4] But the experiences of the last third of a century show that we cannot take shared growth for granted.

We have created a so-called market economy that is rife with distortions that enrich the top and stifle long-term growth. The slowing of our economy and the increase in inequality are two sides of the same coin. Changes instituted over the last 40 years have led to an increase in shortsighted behavior, with less spending on the kinds of long-term investments, including investments in people, that would generate high rates of sustainable growth. This short-term behavior has created an unstable economy, manifested in the 2008 crisis. And in spite of the reforms enacted since the crisis, there is no assurance that there will not be a repeat.

[1] Reprinted with permission from the Roosevelt Institute.
[2] Published as Stiglitz, Abernathy, Hersh, et al. (2015).
[3] The excerpts are not presented necessarily in the order in which they appear in the book.
[4] John F. Kennedy Library. N.d. "JFK on the Economy and Taxes." Retrieved, May 5, 2015 (http://www.jfklibrary.org/JFK/JFK-in-History/JFK-on-the-Economy-and-Taxes.aspx).

The Origins of Inequality, and Policies to Contain It. Joseph E. Stiglitz, Oxford University Press. © Joseph E. Stiglitz (2025).
DOI: 10.1093/oso/9780198799580.003.0006

1 The Sources of Our Problem

The American economy is not out of balance because of the natural laws of economics. Today's inequality is not the result of the inevitable evolution of capitalism. Instead, the rules that govern the economy got us here. Markets do not exist in a vacuum: they are shaped by our legal system and our political institutions, by our rules and regulations. The roots of America's dysfunction lie deep in the rules and power dynamics that have prioritized corporate power and short-term gains at the expense of long-term innovation and growth. The outcomes shaped by these rules and power dynamics do not make the economy stronger; indeed, many make it weaker.

We can change those rules using what we have learned in economics. Best of all, changing the rules to promote economic stability for American families will actually be good for the economy. The notion that we have to choose between economic growth and shared prosperity is false.

This is good news. Inequality—at the level and of the type that we see today—is a choice. When the rules no longer work, it's time to rewrite them. (Here we take a comprehensive view on the rules: they include, too, the institutions designed to implement and oversee the rules and the policies that govern the economy, from those on the conduct of monetary policy to those that relate to the level and direction of investment.)

2 A Historical Perspective

The problems we face today are in large part the result of economic decisions we made—or failed to make—beginning in the late 1970s. Our economy was more balanced in the decades prior to 1980 and functioned remarkably well during the middle of the twentieth century. Faced with the disaster of the Great Depression, Franklin D. Roosevelt put into place a series of major policy changes to counteract the overwhelming and harmful effects of unregulated banks and stock markets. The Federal Deposit Insurance Corporation ensured the safety of bank deposits; the Glass–Steagall Act separated deposit-taking banks from those engaged in investment activities, so that banks couldn't use federally insured money for high-risk speculation; the Securities and Exchange Commission enforced new market and securities laws designed to protect ordinary investors, preventing market manipulation and insider trading; and the National Labor Relations Act gave workers the right to bargain collectively. The combination created what John Kenneth Galbraith called "countervailing power" and enabled the country to avoid financial crisis for half a century.[5] In this golden age of capitalism the country's economy grew faster than in any other era, and while incomes grew at the top, middle, and bottom, those at the bottom saw their incomes grow faster than those at the top.

Of course, even in the golden age of capitalism, markets and the economy were not perfect. Systematic discrimination against women and people of color meant that large groups of Americans were shuttled into low-wage jobs, like domestic or janitorial work, that were not protected by unionization. African-Americans were excluded from higher education and home loan programs designed to provide opportunity to middle-income Americans.

[5] Galbraith, John Kenneth. 1952. *American Capitalism: The Concept of Countervailing Power.* Boston, MA: Houghton Mifflin. The first financial crisis after 1929 was the S & L crisis of 1989, the result of the deregulation of the 1980s.

Deprivations faced in one generation have consequences for later generations. Beginning in the 1950s, the civil rights movement fought for and made progress on desegregation, antidiscrimination, and voting access. Mobility increased during that generation, but these steps forward have not been enough. Progress has been met by obstacles, and mobility has stalled.

2.1 Deregulation and Market Fundamentalism

In the 1980s, under the influence of supply-side economic theories developed during the previous decade discussed earlier in this chapter, and driven by conservative ideology and special interests, American policymakers began to deregulate the economy.[6] The results were disappointing: as we have noted, the hoped-for supply-side responses were not forthcoming, tax revenues fell, and we experienced lower growth and more instability.

But in spite of the failures of supply side policies, the power of "market fundamentalist ideology" persisted, infecting even centrist Democrats. The 1990s and 2000s brought other sweeping changes influenced by this ideology, including unbalanced trade agreements, further deregulation of the financial sector, and further lowering of taxes on capital (dividends) and on capital gains. The adverse effects on inequality were obvious and turned out to have strong political consequences.[7] But there were also adverse effects on macroeconomic performance. The deregulated finance sector incentivized short-termism among corporations. Much of the growth we saw in the 1990s turned out to be unstable, built on asset bubbles—first the tech bubble, then the housing bubble. The "great moderation" turned out to be a phantasm: instead of new economic insights (for instance, concerning the conduct of monetary policy) leading to a better-managed economy, we had more instability, slower growth, and more inequality.

2.2 Changes in Technology and Globalization

At the same time, there were changes in technology and globalization, the closer integration of the countries of the world. These advances were supposed to increase standards of living, not pose a threat to middle-class life, and they might have done that had we managed them well. But the widely accepted premise was that unfettered markets would automatically make all of us better off, and that premise turned out to be woefully wrong. There were significant job losses in the American economy and downward pressure on wages, and government did little to nothing to alleviate the suffering and to help either people or communities that were losing jobs.

Moreover, globalization and technological change were not just things that happened. Both were shaped by our policies. We could have had more advances reducing the usage of carbon, rather than of unskilled labor. Globalization needn't have undermined the bargaining power of workers as much as it did.

[6] Some aspects of deregulation, such as in airlines, actually began a little earlier. Airline deregulation did not bring about the kind of competitive market for which the deregulators had hoped, and therefore discredited the theory of contestability underlying deregulation, but the really adverse effects of deregulation began with the deregulation of the financial system.

[7] Discussed further in Stiglitz (2010a, 2012a, 2018a, 2019a).

The culmination of all these factors is the high-rent and high-exploitation American economy that has not been working for most Americans.

In short, 35 years of supply-side thinking and the corresponding set of rules has reshaped all aspects of our economy and society and led to slower growth and unprecedented inequality.

3 New Understandings about the Economy

We are fortunate, however, that advances in economic thinking over the past half century enable us to rewrite the rules of the economy once again, but this time in ways that promote sustainable shared prosperity.

In particular, there has been a radical shift in economic theory since the middle of the twentieth century, allowing us to better understand the strengths and limits of markets.

The rules shaping our current economy were informed by an economic orthodoxy that we now know is incorrect and outdated. "Supply-side" economics posited that constraints imposed by regulations and disincentives imposed by taxes and a generous welfare system were limiting growth—a sharp break from earlier decades, when Keynesian economists emphasized insufficient demand as the limiting factor. All of this was allegedly to encourage more work and savings. The premise was that lowering taxes would increase growth and all would benefit. Ronald Reagan argued that growth would increase so much that tax revenues would increase even as tax rates decreased. Supply-side ideas led not only to deregulation and lower tax rates on top incomes and on capital, but also to cuts to social welfare programs and public investments. The results are now in: We cut top tax rates and repealed regulations, but the benefits didn't "trickle down" to everyone else. These policies increased wealth for the largest corporations and the richest Americans, increased economic inequality, and failed to produce the economic growth that adherents promised.

3.1 Failure of Textbook Explanations of Inequality

Textbook models trying to explain inequality focus on a simple theory: each individual receives returns commensurate with his or her social contributions. Differences in individuals' incomes are then related to differences in productivity, skills, and effort, and changes in the distribution are attributed, for instance, to changes in technology and to investments in human and physical capital. Following such an analysis, much of the wage inequality that emerged in the latter part of the twentieth century was attributed to "skill-biased" technological change, the fact that changes in technology put a greater premium on certain skills, and that individuals with those skills did better than the rest. The argument went that these skills were acquired through education, over the long run, wage premium would induce more young people to acquire these highly valued skills, and as they did so, the premium would be reduced. The high level of the education premium reflected a mismatch between the needs of the new technologies and our labor force.

These were important insights, and certain policies followed: providing a larger proportion of the population with these skills would reduce inequality. But there are serious deficiencies and limitations in these theories. Skill-biased technological change, for example, cannot explain why highly skilled workers have had to move into lower-skilled jobs. It cannot explain what has been happening to wages in the past decade—even skilled workers are not doing well. Nor can it explain the magnitude of the rise of pay at the top—including CEOs and those in the financial sector—or the yawning gap between the growth in productivity of workers as a whole and average wages. Historically, wage and productivity growth moved in tandem, but this has not been true for the last third of a century.

3.2 The New Institutionalist View vs. the Traditional Model

Of course, inequality and how the overall gains from growth get distributed among individuals are complex phenomena caused by a number of factors. Technology, globalization, shifting demographics, and other major forces are important, and parsing out the relative contributions of different factors is not simple. But these forces are largely global in nature. If they are the primary drivers, all advanced countries should be similarly affected. But among advanced economy countries, the U.S. has the highest level of inequality, so the explanation for the outcomes we see in the United States cannot lie solely or even principally in global factors.[8] Moreover, not even the effects of global forces are out of our control. Their impact can be changed significantly by the policy decisions we make. Given the failings of the older models, we need an alternative explanation for the extreme inequality we see today.

Our institutionalist approach is based on two simple economic observations: rules matter and power matters. This approach began with a set of insights from academic research. Over the past four decades, economists have increasingly drawn attention to the many ways that the standard model, which assumes perfect information, perfect competition, and perfect risk markets. This new view has shown that even when markets are fully competitive, there can be "market failures," important instances where government intervention is required to ensure efficient and socially desirable outcomes.

In sum, while both the traditional and institutionalist economic approaches explain some of what has been going on, the latter theory is increasingly compelling.

3.3 The Key Role of Rents in Explaining Inequality

Rewriting the Rules argues that more recent theories suggesting that inequality is growing because wealth is growing faster than income—so owners of wealth are getting an increasing share of national income—are at best incomplete. The increase in wealth arises not from savings but from an increase in the value of existing assets. Much of the increase in wealth is attributable to the increase in the value of fixed assets and not the reflection of an increase in productive value. The most obvious and widespread example is the massive rise in real estate values. If the value of real estate increases thanks only to the rising price

[8] Organisation for Economic Co-operation and Development, "Income Inequality," https://doi.org/10.1787/459aa7f1-en (accessed August 10, 2021). The last year for which comparable data is available is 2017, though the United States showed no sign of losing this distinction as of 2021.

of the property it sits upon and not to physical improvements, this does not lead to a more productive economy; no workers have been hired, no wages paid, no investments made. In economic terms, this gain is simply an increase in "land rents." Some of this increase in the property value is a natural consequence of urbanization, but much is due to the *financialization* of the economy, including the increased supply of credit—credit that typically goes to those that already have wealth.

Land rents are the most obvious source of rents in the economy, but economists have identified many others, including monopoly profits, drug pricing, patents, and other forms of intellectual property.

If monopoly power increases, monopoly profits will increase, and so too will the value of the monopolies—the measured wealth of the economy. But the productivity of the economy will decrease, and so too will the value of wages adjusted for inflation. Inequality will also increase.

There are many other examples of such "exploitation" rents.

Changes in the rules that structure the economy can lead—and plausibly have led—to an increase in these rents and their capitalized value. For instance, if the concentration of the banking system increases such that more banks are "too big to fail," meaning their individual failure could jeopardize the entire financial system, the value of banks will increase, not because the bigger banks will become more efficient, but because increased monopoly power and expectations of a government bailout at some point in the future will increase their value.

3.4 The Distinction between Capital and Wealth

In this analysis, we make a distinction between capital and wealth.[9] Only an increase in the former necessarily encourages growth; because wealth may increase simply because there has been an increase in rents, the productive capacity of the economy may not be increasing in tandem with measured wealth.

Understanding this distinction between wealth and capital is pivotal: If inequality were the result of an increase in capital, we should also have seen an increase in average wages and a decline in the return to capital. Neither of these has been observed. Something else is going on—the increase in rents. We refer to the capitalized value of rents as Rent Capital.

3.5 The Adverse Effects of Increasing Rents

The value of Rent Capital has been increasing so much in some countries that wealth may have increased but the real capital stock has decreased—and this by itself would have lowered wages from what they otherwise would have been. But the growth of rents may itself have played a direct role in the decrease in real investment: those wishing to hold capital, say for retirement, can do so by holding on to Rent Capital rather than making productive investments in the economy. And finally, the distortions associated with many forms

[9] We elaborate on this distinction in Chapter 6 of this volume.

of Rent Capital, in particular those associated with market power, actually weaken the economy and increase inequality.

4 Solutions

Rewriting the Rules suggests a comprehensive menu of answers, demonstrating that, in fact, there are some things—in fact, many things—we can do to fight inequality *at the source*, which would at the same time create a more stable and faster-growing economy.

4.1 Pre-Distribution Rather than Re-Distribution

Creating shared prosperity is not just a matter of *redistribution*—redistributing after-market income through taxes and transfers—though that is very important. We must also increase wages, well-being, and ultimately economic and political power for the majority of Americans.

4.2 Minor Tweaks Won't Do

We cannot afford to go forward with minor tweaks and hope that they do the trick. We know the answer: they will not, and the suffering that will occur in the meantime is unconscionable.

Policies that focus only on the symptoms of our dysfunctional economy—for instance, on remedying the worst extremes of inequality—will not change the way today's economy is structured nor tackle the reasons that our economy seems to generate more inequality than the economies of any other advanced countries.

4.3 Growth and Equality Are Complements

We do not need to circumscribe our efforts to promote shared growth simply out of fear that such efforts will necessarily damage overall economic performance. Recent research has identified the many channels through which greater inequality hurts economic performance, and why it is that higher GDP growth does not necessarily benefit large swaths of the population[10]

4.4 Rewriting the Rules Once Again

We can, moreover, reshape the intermediating structures that determine how global forces manifest themselves. We can improve economic security and opportunity by tackling the technocratic realms of labor law, corporate governance, financial regulation, trade agreements, codified discrimination, monetary policy, and taxation.

[10] See, for example, OECD (2014) and Ostry, Berg, and Tsangarides (2014).

The experience of the last 35 years, across many nations, suggests that the rules of the economy, including those of finance, corporate governance, and international trade, all can be rewritten to promote growth and shared prosperity rather than channel more wealth and opportunity toward those who already have the most.

Here, we are emphasizing a critical role of government which has not received the attention it should, especially by those who argue for leaving everything to markets: Markets don't exist in a vacuum; it is government that structures markets and sets the rules and regulations under which they operate. Rules and institutions are the backdrop of the economy, and the ways we set these rules, and keep them up to date and enforce them, have consequences for everyone.

4.5 Taking a Long-term Perspective

This is not just about the present, but the future. The policies of today are "baking in" the America of 2050: unless we change course, we will be a country with slower growth, ever more inequality, and ever less equality of opportunity.

Inequality has been a choice, and it is within our power to reverse it.

6

Wealth and Income Distribution

New Theories Needed for a New Era

With Ravi Kanbur

Six decades ago, Nicholas Kaldor (1957) put forward a set of stylized facts on growth and distribution for mature industrial economies.[1] The first and most prominent of these was the constancy of the share of capital relative to that of wealth in national income. At about the same time, Simon Kuznets (1955) put forward a second set of stylized facts—that while the interpersonal inequality of income distribution might increase in the early stages of development, it declines as industrialized economies mature.

These empirical formulations brought forth a generation of growth and development theories whose object was to explain the stylized facts. Kaldor himself presented a growth model which claimed to produce outcomes consistent with constancy of factor shares, as did Robert Solow. Kuznets also developed a model of rural–urban transition consistent with his prediction, as did many others (Kanbur, 2012).

1 Kaldor-Kuznets Facts No Longer Hold

However, the Kaldor–Kuznets stylized facts no longer hold for advanced economies. The share of capital as conventionally measured has been on the rise, as has interpersonal inequality of income and wealth. Of course, there are variations and subtleties of data and interpretation, and the pattern is not uniform. But these are the stylized facts of our time. Bringing these facts center stage has been the achievement of research leading up to Piketty (2014).

It stands to reason that theories developed to explain constancy of factor shares cannot explain a rising share of capital. The theories developed to explain the earlier stylized facts cannot very easily explain the new trends, or the turnaround. At the same time, rising inequality has opened once again a set of questions on the normative significance of inequality of outcomes versus inequality of opportunity. New theoretical developments are needed for positive and normative analysis in this new era.

What sort of new theories? In the realm of positive analysis, Piketty has himself put forward a theory based on the empirical observation that the rate of return to capital, r, systematically exceeds the rate of growth, g; the famous $r > g$ relation. Much of the commentary on Piketty's facts and theorizing has tried to make the stylized fact of rising share of capital consistent with a standard production function $F(K, L)$ with capital "K" and labor

[1] Written with Ravi Kanbur. H. Lee Professor of World Affairs, International Professor of Applied Economics and Management, Professor of Economics at Cornell University and CEPR Research Fellow. Originally published on August 18, 2015 as "Wealth and Income Distribution: New Theories Needed for a New Era," *Vox EU*.

The Origins of Inequality, and Policies to Contain It. Joseph E. Stiglitz with Ravi Kanbur, Oxford University Press.
© Joseph E. Stiglitz (2025). DOI: 10.1093/oso/9780198799580.003.0007

"*L*." But in this framework a rising share of capital can be consistent with the other stylized fact of rising capital-output ratio only if the elasticity of substitution between capital and labor is greater than unity, which is not consistent with the broad empirical findings (Stiglitz, 2016a). Further, what Piketty and others measure as wealth "*W*" is a measure of control over resources, not a measure of capital *K*, in the sense that that is used in the context of a production function.

2 Differences between *K* and *W*

There is a fundamental distinction between capital *K*, thought of as physical inputs to production, and wealth *W*, thought of as including land and the capitalized value of other rents which give command over purchasing power. This distinction will be crucial in any theorizing to explain the new stylized facts. "*K*" can be going down even as "*W*" increases; and some increases in *W* may actually lower economic productivity. In particular, new theories explaining the evolution of inequality will have to address directly changes in rents and their capitalized value (Stiglitz, 2016a). Two examples will illustrate what we have in mind.

- Consider first the case of all sea-front property on the French Riviera.

As demand for these properties rises, perhaps from rich foreigners seeking a refuge for their funds, the value of sea frontage will be bid up. The current owners will get rents from their ownership of this fixed factor. Their wealth will go up and their ability to command purchasing power in the economy will rise correspondingly. But the actual physical input to production has not increased. All else constant, national output will not rise; there will only be a pure distributional effect.

- Consider the case where the government gives an implicit guarantee to bail out banks.

This contingent support to income flows from ownership of bank shares will be capitalized into the value of these shares. Of course, there is an equal and opposite contingent liability on all others in the economy, in particular on workers—the owners of human capital. Again, without any necessary impact on total output, the political economy has created rents for share owners, and the increase in their wealth will be reflected in rising wealth inequality. One can see this without going through a conventional production function analysis. Of course, the rents once created will provide further resources for rentiers to lobby the political system to maintain and further increase rents. This will set in motion a spiral of increasing inequality, which again does not go through the production system at all—except to the extent that the associated distortions represent a downward shift in the productivity of the economy (at any level of inputs of "*K*" and labor).

Analyzing the role of land rents in increases in inequality can be done in a variant of standard neoclassical models—by expanding inputs to include land; but explaining increase in inequality as a result of an increase in other forms of rent will need a theory of rents which takes us beyond the competitive determination of factor rewards.

3 Differences in Inequality: Capital Income vs. Labor Income

The translation from factor shares to interpersonal inequality has usually been made through the assumption that capital income is more unequally distributed than labor income. Inequality of capital ownership then translates into inequality of capital income, while inequality of income from labor is assumed to be much smaller. The assumption is made in its starkest form in models where there are owners of capital who save and workers who do not.

These stylized assumptions no longer provide a fully satisfactory explanation of income inequality because: (i) there is more widespread ownership of wealth through life-cycle savings in various forms including pensions; and (ii) increasingly unequal returns to increasingly unequally distributed human capital has led to sharply rising inequality of labor income.

Sharply rising inequality of labor income focuses attention on inequality of human capital in its most general sense:

- Starting with unequal prenatal development of the fetus;
- Followed by unequal early childhood development and investments by parents;
- Unequal educational investments by parents and society; and
- Unequal returns to human capital because of discrimination at one end and use of parental connections in the job market at the other end.

Discrimination continues to play a role, not only in the determination of factor returns given the ownership of assets, including human capital; but also on the distribution of asset ownership.

- At each step, inequality of parental resources is translated into inequality of children's outcomes.

An exploration of this type of inequality requires a different type of empirical and theoretical analysis from the conventional macro-level analysis of production functions and factor shares (Heckman and Mosso, 2014; Stiglitz, 2015a).

In particular, intergenerational transmission of inequality is more than simple inheritance of physical and financial wealth. Layered upon genetic inequalities are the inequalities of parental resources. Income inequality across parents, due to inequality of income from physical and financial capital on the one hand, and inequality due to inequality of human capital on the other, is translated into inequality of financial and human capital of the next generation. Human capital inequality perpetuates itself through intergenerational transmission just as wealth inequality caused by politically created rents perpetuates itself.

Given such transmission across generations, it can be shown that the long-run, "dynastic" inequality will also be higher (Kanbur and Stiglitz, 2015). Although there have been advances in recent years, we still need fully developed theories of how the different mechanisms interact with each other to explain the dramatic rises in interpersonal inequality in advanced economies in the last three decades.[2]

[2] For early discussions of such transmission processes, see Stiglitz (1969b) and Bevan and Stiglitz (1979).

4 High Inequality: New Realities and Old Debates

The new realities of high inequality have revived old debates on policy interventions and their ethical and economic rationale (Stiglitz, 2012a). Standard analysis which balances the tradeoff between efficiency and equity would suggest that taxation should now become more progressive to balance the greater inherent inequality against the incentive effects of progressive taxation (Kanbur and Tuomala, 1994).

One counter argument is that what matters is not inequality of "outcome" but inequality of "opportunity." According to this argument, so long as the prospects are the same for all children, the inequality of income across parents should not matter ethically. What we should aim for is equality of opportunity, not income equality. However, when income inequality across parents translates into inequality of prospects across children, even starting in the womb, then the distinction between opportunity and income begins to fade and the case for progressive taxation is not undermined by the "equality of opportunity" objective (Kanbur and Wagstaff, 2014.

5 Concluding Remarks

Thus, the new stylized facts of our era demand new theories of income distribution.

- First, we need to break away from competitive marginal productivity theories of factor returns and model mechanisms which generate rents with consequences for wealth inequality.

  This will entail a greater focus on the "rules of the game" (Stiglitz, Abernathy, Hersh, et al., 2015).
- Second, we need to focus on the interaction between income from physical and financial capital and income from human capital in determining snapshot inequality, but also in determining the intergenerational transmission of inequality.

Third, we need to further develop normative theories of equity which can address mechanisms of inequality transmission from generation to generation.[3]

[3] Developments in this area are exemplified by Roemer and Trannoy (2014).

7
Eliminating Extreme Inequality
A Sustainable Development Goal, 2015–30

With Michael Doyle

1 Introduction

This chapter was written in the fall of 2013 as the world was engaged in a debate over what should be included in the new Sustainable Development Goals (SDGs).[1] The success of the earlier Millennium Development Goals (MDG) had made a convincing case for the efficacy of the role of the UN in setting global norms. The MDGs' commitment, made at the onset of the new millennium, to reduce poverty by half by 2015 had led to a global focus on poverty reduction. The goal was more than achieved, though poverty reduction in China played a disproportionate role, and the numbers for Africa were disappointing. There was a consensus that the new global goals should be more comprehensive and apply, in some way, to both developed and developing countries.

The growing inequality in the U.S., China, and many countries around the world suggested that the reduction in inequality should be one of the central goals. Michael Doyle, formerly Assistant Secretary General of the UN and a colleague of mine at Columbia University (in both the Law School and Political Science Department) teamed up to push for the adoption of an inequality goal as part of the SDGs. We received push back from an unexpected quarter: while President Obama had said that reducing inequality was one of the central issues facing the U.S., the United States opposed the inclusion of inequality as a goal, I suspect because it did not want to draw global attention to this critical weakness in its economic, political, and social system. Not only was inequality high, there was every reason to believe that it would increase.

This chapter was written as part of our effort to get inequality adopted as an SDG. We wanted to show both the economic and political consequences of inequality. One of the reasons that the UN had originally been created was to reduce conflict. The chapter summarizes not just the economic consequences of inequality (discussed elsewhere in this book), but also the political consequences, including for conflict. It reviews literature suggesting that particular kinds of inequities (e.g., "horizontal," across ethnic groups) as especially important drivers of conflict.

[1] Written with my Columbia University colleague, Michael Doyle, Professor of International Affairs, Law and Political Science and former Assistant Secretary General of the UN. Originally published in 2014 as "Eliminating Extreme Inequality: A Sustainable Development Goal, 2015–2030," Ethics and International Affairs, 28(1): 5–13. The authors have benefited from the research assistance of Alicia Evangelides, Eamon Kircher-Allen, and Laurence Wilse-Samson.

The Origins of Inequality, and Policies to Contain It. Joseph E. Stiglitz with Michael Doyle, Oxford University Press.
 DOI: 10.1093/oso/9780198799580.003.0008

By determined and concerted campaigning, we were able to overcome the opposition of the United States and some other developed countries, and an inequality goal was included in the SDGs: "Reduce inequality within and among countries."

As we discuss elsewhere in this volume, however, there are many ways of assessing the extent of inequality. In this chapter, we argue that attention should be centered on extreme inequality, and we suggested a particular measure, the Palma ratio, the ratio of the richest 10% of the population's share of gross national income divided by that of the poorest 40%. The reason for this is that, as Jose Gabriel Palma of Cambridge University argued, the middle of the society regularly gets for itself a relatively constant share of national income. Countries really differ in how the remainder of the "pie" is divided between the top and the bottom. It is thus a more sensitive measure: the Palma Ratio for South Africa, for instance, is eight times that of Sweden or Norway, while the Gini coefficient is a little more than twice as large.

While the UN adopted an inequality goal, it decided to focus attention again on the bottom—not the very bottom, as it had done with the Millennium Development Goal (the elimination of poverty), but the bottom 40%. The goal adopted was: "By 2030, progressively achieve and sustain income growth of the bottom 40 per cent of the population at a rate higher than the national average."

The chapter argues that beyond setting particular goals for the reduction of inequality, it is important to have national dialogues focusing on inequalities, spearheaded, we suggest, by commissions to be established in each country, "to assess and report on the effects" of these national inequalities. We believed that the many dimensions of societal inequalities had long been neglected, and shining a spotlight on the subject would inevitably lead to efforts to reduce societal inequality.

At the United Nations Millennium Summit in September 2000, UN member states took a dramatic step by putting people rather than states at the center of the UN's agenda. In their Millennium Declaration,[2] the assembled world leaders agreed to a set of breathtakingly broad goals touching on peace through development, the environment, human rights, the protection of the vulnerable, the special needs of Africa, and reforms of UN institutions. Particularly influential was the codification of the Declaration's development related objectives, which emerged in the summer of 2001 as the now familiar eight Millennium Development Goals (MDGs), to be realized by 2015:[3]

1. Eradicate extreme poverty and hunger.[4]

    - Halve the proportion of people living on less than a dollar a day and those who suffer from hunger.

[2] General Assembly Resolution 55/2, "United Nations Millennium Declaration," UN document A/RES/55/2, September 8, 2000,www.un.org/millennium/declaration/ares552e.pdf.

[3] As announced in the appendix to the "Road Map Report," UN document A/56/326 of September 6, 2001. The UN member states tasked the UN Secretary-General with preparing a "road map" that would develop and monitor "results and benchmarks" ("Follow-up to the Outcome of the Millennium Summit," UN document A/RES/55/162, December 18, 2000). For an analysis of the origins and significance of the MDGs, see Doyle (2012).

[4] The original indicator was $1 a day, which has since been raised to $1.25 to reflect inflation.

2. Achieve universal primary education.

    - Ensure that all boys and girls complete primary school.

3. Promote gender equality and empower women.

    - Eliminate gender disparities in primary and secondary education preferably by 2005, and at all levels by 2015.

4. Reduce child mortality.

    - Reduce by two-thirds the mortality rate among children under five.

5. Improve maternal health.

    - Reduce by three-quarters the ratio of women dying in childbirth.

6. Combat HIV/AIDS, malaria, and other diseases.

    - Halt and begin to reverse the spread of HIV/AIDS and the incidence of malaria and other major diseases.

7. Ensure environmental sustainability.

    - Integrate the principles of sustainable development into country policies and programs and reverse the loss of environmental resources.
    - By 2015, reduce by half the proportion of people without access to safe drinking water.
    - By 2020, achieve significant improvement in the lives of at least 100 million slum dwellers.

8. Develop a global partnership for development.

    - Develop further an open trading and financial system that includes a commitment to good governance, development, and poverty reduction—nationally and internationally.
    - Address the special needs of the least developed countries, and the special needs of landlocked and small island developing states.
    - Deal comprehensively with the debt problems of developing countries.
    - Develop decent and productive work for youth.
    - In cooperation with pharmaceutical companies, provide access to affordable essential drugs in developing countries.
    - In cooperation with the private sector, make available the benefits of new technologies—especially information and communications technologies.

As UN Secretary-General Kofi Annan later described them, the MDGs were a remarkable effort in international coordination. They established common ground among competitive development agencies, inspired concerted action by international organizations and national governments, and offered an opportunity for citizens to insist that governments focus on the "we the peoples" they claimed to represent. In short, they transformed the agenda of world leaders.[5]

The MDG record has been mixed. Some goals, such as halving the proportion of people living in extreme poverty, have been met at the global level, but none have been fulfilled in all countries. Others, such as universal access to primary education, are unlikely to be achieved by 2015.[6]

However, while the accomplishment of these goals would have been an impressive achievement, even taken together they do not represent a complete or comprehensive vision of human development. They were constrained by what the member states could agree upon in 2000 and, in particular, they lacked a vision of equitable development.[7] As the international community thinks about the set of goals that will follow the MDGs, it is time to address that shortcoming by adding the goal of "eliminating extreme inequality" to the original eight.

2 Why Inequality Matters

Every country has a distinct political economy that shapes the extent and effects of inequalities; each requires separate assessment. The marked differences in the extent and nature of inequality across countries demonstrate that inequality is not just determined by economic forces; it is shaped by politics and policies.

Full equality is not the goal. Some economic inequalities may be conducive to economic growth. Other inequalities may not be worth addressing because doing so infringes on cherished liberties. While the precise point at which inequalities turn harmful may differ from country to country, once inequality becomes extreme, harmful social, economic, and political effects become evident. Extreme inequalities tend to hamper economic growth and undermine both political equality and social stability. And because inequalities have cumulative economic, social, and political effects, each of these contributing factors requires separate and concerted attention. We turn first to the economic arguments for reducing extreme inequalities, and then to the political and social arguments.

2.1 Economic Arguments

Economists of widely differing philosophical outlooks agree that inequalities of incomes and assets have harmful economic effects.[8] Increasing inequalities, with top-heavy income distributions, lessen aggregate demand (the rich tend to spend a smaller fraction of their

[5] Annan and Mousavizadeh, 2012, pp. 244–50.

[6] United Nations 2013a, pp. 4–5.

[7] The original goals did not include access to reproductive rights, which was corrected in 2005. See General Assembly Resolution 60/1, "2005 World Summit Outcome," UN document A/RES/60/1, paragraphs 57(g) and 58(c):mdgs.un.org/unsd/mdg/Resources/Attach/Indicators/ares60_1_2005summit_eng.pdf. These goals also lacked the governance goals being considered today. See the Report of the High-Level Panel of Eminent Persons on the Post-2015 Development Agenda (2013), Annex II, p. 50.

[8] For a more thorough discussion of the adverse economic consequences of inequality, see Stiglitz (2012a).

income than the poor), which can slow economic growth. The attempt of monetary authorities to offset these effects can contribute to credit bubbles, and these bubbles in turn lead to economic instability. That is why inequality is often associated with economic instability. In this perspective, it is not a surprise that inequality reached high levels before the Great Recession of 2008 and before the Great Depression of the 1930s.[9] Recent International Monetary Fund research shows that high inequality is associated with shorter growth cycles.[10]

Much of the inequality observed around the world is associated with rent-seeking (for example, the exercise of monopoly power), and such inequality manifestly undermines economic efficiency. But perhaps the worse dimension of inequality is inequality of opportunity, which is both the cause and consequence of inequality of outcomes, and causes economic inefficiency and reduced development, as large numbers of individuals are not able to live up to their potential.[11] Countries with high inequality tend to invest less in public goods, such as infrastructure, technology, and education, which contribute to long-term economic prosperity and growth.

Reducing inequality, on the other hand, has clear economic as well as social benefits. It strengthens people's sense that society is fair; improves social cohesion and mobility, making it more likely that more citizens live up to their potential; and broadens support for growth initiatives. Policies that aim for growth but ignore inequality may ultimately be self-defeating, whereas policies that decrease inequality by, for example, boosting employment and education have beneficial effects on the human capital that modern economies increasingly need.[12]

Gaps between the rich and the poor are partly the result of economic forces, but equally, or even more, they are the result of public policy choices, such as taxation, the level of the minimum wage, and the amount invested in health care and education.

2.2 Political and Social Arguments

Gaps between the rich and the poor are partly the result of economic forces, but equally, or even more, they are the result of public policy choices, such as taxation, the level of the minimum wage, and the amount invested in health care and education. This is why countries whose economic circumstances are otherwise similar can have markedly different levels of inequality. These inequalities in turn affect policy-making because even democratically elected officials respond more attentively to the views of affluent constituents than they do to the views of poor people.[13] The more that wealth is allowed unrestricted roles in funding elections, the more likely it is that economic inequality will get translated into political inequality.

[9] Stiglitz, 2012a Ch. 4, pp. 83–117.

[10] Berg, Ostry, and Zettelmeyer, 2012. For a more theoretical treatment of the links between inequality, instability, and human development, see Stiglitz (2012b).

[11] Easterly, 2007. The Council on Foreign Relations has reported that there are enormous gaps in American students' achievement depending on their socioeconomic background, and found that parental wealth exerts a stronger influence on achievement in the United States than in almost any other developed country. See Council on Foreign Relations (2013).

[12] Easterly, 2007.

[13] Bartels, 2008.

As noted, extreme inequalities undermine not only economic stability but also social and political stability. But there is no simple causal relation between economic inequality and social stability, as measured by crime or civil violence. Neither form of violence correlates with Gini indices or Palma ratios (the top 10% of the population's share of Gross National Income (GNI) divided by the poorest 40% of the population's share of GNI).[14] There are, however, substantial links between violence and "horizontal inequalities" that combine economic stratification with race, ethnicity, religion, or region. When the poor are from one race, ethnicity, religion, or region, and the rich are from another, a lethal, destabilizing dynamic often emerges.

Drawing on 123 national surveys in 61 developing countries, one study carefully documents the effects of inequalities in assets among ethnicities. For a typical country with average values on all the variables accounting for violence, the probability of civil conflict in a given year is 2.3%. If the level of horizontal asset inequality among ethnic groups is increased to the 95th percentile (and the other variables remain at their average values), the probability of conflict increases to 6.1%—more than a twofold increase. A similar comparison focused on differences in income among religious groups shows an increase from 2.9% to 7.2%—again, more than twofold.[15] Another study using similar methods finds regional disparities in wealth to be correlated with an especially high risk of conflict onset in sub-Saharan Africa.[16]

Using a different methodology that focuses on geographical disparities in income that are linked with ethnic differentiation, rather than surveys to measure inequalities, other authors confirm the dangers of large horizontal inequalities. Focusing on the post-cold war period (1991–2005), Lars-Erik Cederman, Nils Weidmann, and Kristian Gleditsch divide the total sum of economic production in a given ethnic settlement area by the group's population size to get ethnic group-specific measures of per capita economic production. They find that both relatively poorer and relatively richer ethnic groups have higher likelihoods of experiencing civil war. Demonstrating that not just ethnographic factors are at work, they show that the richer (or the poorer) the ethnographic group is, the greater the likelihood of the extreme groups experiencing civil war with other ethnographic groups.[17]

3 The Many Dimensions of Inequality

Just as discussions of poverty and poverty reduction expanded from a single-minded focus on income to many other dimensions of deprivation—including health and the environment—so too did they evolve in the case of inequality.[18] Indeed, in most countries it appears that inequalities in wealth exceed those in income. Especially in countries

[14] We would prefer a measure of post-tax (after all income and other taxes) and post-transfer incomes (after housing, child care, social security, and other subsidies), but this is not yet widely available.

[15] Østby, 2008.

[16] Østby and Strand, 2013.

[17] Cederman, Weidmann, and Gleditsch, 2011.

[18] The World Bank's classic study Voices of the Poor highlighted that the poor suffered not just from a lack of income but from insecurity and a lack of voice. This was subsequently reflected in the decennial World Bank's World Development Report on Poverty in 2000. The International Commission on the Measurement of Economic Performance and Social Well-Being (Stiglitz, Sen, and Fitoussi, 2010) emphasized that metrics of performance (including output and inequality) had to be expanded beyond just conventional measures of GDP and/or income. The OECD has carried on this work in their Better Living Initiative, including the construction of the Better Life

without adequate public health systems, a Palma ratio reflecting health status would almost surely show even greater inequalities than a Palma ratio for income. A Palma ratio based on exposures to environmental hazards would likely demonstrate a similar trend.

One of the most pernicious forms of inequality relates to inequality of opportunity, reflected in a lack of socioeconomic mobility, condemning those born into the bottom of the economic pyramid to almost surely remain there. Alan Krueger, former Chairman of the U.S. Council of Economic Advisors, has pointed to this link between inequality and opportunity.[19] Inequality of income tends to be associated with less economic mobility and fewer opportunities across generations. The fact that those born into the bottom of the economic pyramid are condemned to never reach their potential reinforces the correlation between inequality and slower long-term economic growth.[20]

That these dimensions of inequality are related suggests that focusing on one dimension at a time may underestimate the true magnitude of societal inequalities and provide an inadequate basis for policy. For example, health inequality is both a cause and consequence of income inequality. Inequalities in education are a primary determinant of inequalities in income and opportunity. In turn, as we have emphasized, when there are distinct social patterns of these multiple inequalities (for example, those associated with race or ethnicity), the consequences for society (including social instability) are increased.

4 Measuring the Goal

We propose that the following goal—call it "Goal Nine"—be added to revisions and updates of the original eight: Eliminate extreme inequality at the national level in every country. For this goal, we propose the following targets:

- By 2030, reduce extreme income inequalities in all countries such that the post-tax income of the top 10% is no more than the post-transfer income of the bottom 40%.
- By 2020, establish a public commission in every country that will assess and report on the effects of national inequalities.

There is a growing consensus that the best indicator for these targets is the Palma ratio, which effectively focuses on extremes of inequality—the ratio of incomes at the very top to those at the bottom.[21] In many countries around the world it is changes in these extremes that are most noticeable and most invidious, while the share of income in the middle is relatively stable.[22] All countries should focus on their "extreme" inequalities, that is, the

Index. An important part of the agenda of the OECD High Level Expert Group on the Measurement of Economic Performance and Social Well-Being is the construction/evaluation of alternative measures of inequality.

[19] Krueger, 2013.

[20] Corak, 2013.

[21] Cobham and Sumner, 2013a. The Palma ratio is "the ratio of the top 10% of population's share of gross national income (GNI), divided by the poorest 40% of the population's share of GNI." We would prefer a measure of post-tax (after all income and other taxes) and post-transfer incomes (after housing, child care, social security, and other subsidies), but this is not yet widely available.

[22] This is not true, however, for all countries. In the United States, for instance, there has been a hollowing out of the middle class, with a declining fraction of the population between, say, twice and half median income and a declining fraction of income going to this group. It has long been thought that a stable democracy depends on

inequalities that do most harm to equitable and sustainable economic growth and that undermine social and political stability. A Palma ratio of 1 is an ideal reached in only a few countries. For example, countries in Scandinavia, with Palma ratios at 1 or less,[23] do not seem to suffer from the liabilities associated with extreme inequalities. Indeed, in some accounts they seem to benefit from a positive "equality multiplier" across the various aspects of their socioeconomic development, making them efficient and flexible as well as equitable and stable.[24]

But countries differ not just in how unequal they are now but also in their culture, tolerance of inequality of various kinds, and capacity for social change. Hence, the more important target is the second one: a national dialogue by 2020 on what should be done to address the inequalities of most relevance to the particular country. Such a dialogue would draw attention to the policies in each country that exacerbate inequality (for example, deficiencies in the education system, the legal system, or the tax and transfer system); those that simultaneously distort the economy and contribute to economic, political, and social instability; and those that might most easily be altered.[25]

Support for reducing extreme inequalities is widespread.[26] In a letter to Dr. Homi Kharas, lead author and executive secretary of the secretariat supporting the High-Level Panel of Eminent Persons on the Post-2015 Development Agenda, 90 economists, academics, and development experts urged that reduction in inequality in the post-2015 development framework be made a priority, and suggested that inequality be measured using the Palma ratio.[27] They argue—consistent with our analysis—that inequality threatens poverty eradication, sustainable development, democratic processes, and social cohesion.[28]

Awareness of the adverse effects of inequality has moved beyond academics and social activists. A July 2013 speech by U.S. President Barack Obama outlined the role of inequality in creating credit bubbles (like the one that precipitated the Great Recession) and the way it deprives people of opportunity, which in turn fosters an inefficient economy in which the talents of many cannot be mobilized for the good of all.[29] And Pope Francis, in his address in the Varginha slum of Rio de Janeiro on World Youth Day 2013, emphasized the need for greater solidarity, greater social justice, and special attention to the circumstances of youth. And, again consistent with the studies cited earlier, he declared that peace cannot be maintained in unequal societies with marginalized communities.[30]

a thriving middle class. If so, the decline of the middle class should be of special concern. (For a fuller discussion of these issues, see Stiglitz (2012a). Part of the national dialogues on inequality that we recommend below would focus on the nature of the inequality that is emerging in various countries.

[23] Palma, 2011.

[24] Moene, 2013.

[25] For instance, in the United States, such a dialogue would note inequalities in access to education and health; a bankruptcy code that gives first priority to derivatives and makes student loans difficult to discharge, even in bankruptcy; a tax system that taxes income of the rich derived from speculation at much lower rates than wage income; a minimum wage that, adjusted for inflation has not increased in half a century; and a system of social protection that does a much poorer job in "correcting" inequalities in income than systems in other advanced industrial countries. It would analyze the extent to which disparities in income are a result of differences in productivities, with differences in productivity in turn partly explained by disparities in access to quality education; the extent to which disparities in income are related to rent-seeking; and the extent to which such disparities can be accounted for by inheritances.

[26] Cobham and Sumner, 2013b.

[27] See the March 19, 2013 letter to Dr. Homi Kharas of the Brookings Institute from 90 economists, academics, and development experts supporting the use of the Palma ratio as a measure of inequality.

[28] Obama (2013).

[29] Shear and Baker, 2013.

[30] Pope Francis, 2013.

There are many dimensions to inequality—some with more invidious effects than others—and many ways to measure these inequalities. One thing is certain, however: sustainable development cannot be achieved while ignoring extreme disparities. It is imperative that the post-MDG agenda have as one of its central points a focus on inequality.

PART II
THE BASIC THEORY

Introduction to Part II

Part I provided the basics of the economics of inequality—a brief description of what has been happening, especially in the U.S., combined with the key insights into the drivers of this increase in inequality and what can be done about it. Much of the analytics are based on simple models of the economy that are presented in this part of the volume. It is divided into two parts, my basic earlier theoretical studies, followed by my more recent contributions to the subject.

Early Studies

I entered economics largely motivated by my concerns about inequality. The activism of the 1960s, of which I was a part, naturally led me to want to do something about it. President Kennedy talked about addressing the long-standing poverty that marked Appalachia;[1] but I was more ambitious—I wanted to do something about the pervasive inequality throughout the country, a sample of which I had witnessed growing up in Gary, Indiana. But we could only do something about inequality if we understood its origins, its drivers. In short, we needed a better understanding of its determinants. While economists, such as Cambridge economists Nicholas Kaldor and Joan Robinson (with whom I studied as a graduate student in 1964–65), had discussed the distribution of income among *factors*, that is, the distribution between capital and labor, I was more interested in the distribution of income among individuals. Why did so many people have so little capital, for instance, and so few had so much?

This was a subject which had almost gone unstudied, at least in the years leading up to my graduate studies.[2] It was necessary to think of this in a dynamic context, with the income and wealth of one generation affecting that of the next. The contrast between Gary, Indiana, where I grew up, and Amherst College, where I did my undergraduate studies, illuminated the process. Most of my well-off college classmates had parents and grandparents who were also well-off. We might talk about rags to riches and back to rags in three generations, but the reality was that there was more persistence in wealth than that adage suggested. It was

[1] In fact, there is some evidence that he may have been less concerned about inequality more broadly, as reflected by his use of the phrase, "a rising tide lifts all boats."

[2] It was a topic not addressed in any of the classes I took, but one of my thesis supervisors, Robert Solow, had written his thesis on the subject, and it was a concern too of two of my soon-to-be colleagues at Cambridge, James Meade and David Champernowne.

natural, as I thought about the matter as part of my Ph.D. dissertation, to begin by thinking of the Solow dynamic aggregate model that dominated the economics profession at the time. His work, and virtually all of the work that followed, paid no attention to distribution; indeed, the assumptions they made meant that distribution had no consequence for the aggregate.

I saw, however, how one could look at the dynamics of different dynasties within the Solow framework, constructing a macroeconomic model based on the micro foundations of the underlying households in the economy.[3]

My goal was to identify the forces that led to wealth convergence or divergence, and to ascertain whether there was an equilibrium wealth distribution. The first fruits of that research were first presented at a research seminar in Cambridge in the spring of 1966. As a young graduate student, the enthusiastic response of the assembled "greats" in economics of the time, including David Champernowne, and James Meade (later to get the Nobel Prize) were heartening. At the time, there were two mail deliveries a day in Cambridge, and the Cambridge dons often used the mail to carry on written arguments with each other. I received a multi-page note from Meade the next day, with a long set of queries and suggestions. The revised paper became part of my thesis, was presented at the Econometrics Society meeting in January 1966, and part of it was subsequently published in *Econometrica* in 1969 (reprinted as Chapter 8). Somewhat to my surprise, in the simplest models, with no uncertainty, no matter how unequal was the initial wealth distribution among families, eventually there was convergence—and fairly rapidly. On the other hand, in a simple "capitalist" model, where all of savings was done by capitalists, there was neither convergence nor divergence: whatever the initial distribution, it persisted.

Here and in later chapters, we will show that many of these results are quite robust. For instance, we can show that the results also hold if the savings rates are not fixed, but determined to maximize intertemporal utility, or (following Pasinetti) if workers save.

Five key sources of persistent inequality are identified in the paper: persistent wage (ability) differences, inherited across generations, non-linear savings functions, differences in savings behavior (between capitalists and workers, or, as we will refer to them in later chapters, dynastic savers and life-cycle savers), alternative patterns of inheritance to the equal division assumed here, and stochastic returns. Later chapters will take up in greater detail each of these.

But it was the last of these that I found most interesting: a few years before, David Champernowne (1937, 1953) had developed a theory of equilibrium income distribution using standard Markovian probability theory. He had identified a set of conditions under which the tail of the distribution had a Pareto tail—a fatter tail than the normal distribution. But he had not provided any theoretical basis for why the Markov transition matrix should satisfy those conditions. It turned out easy to establish that in the discrete time analog to my model with random returns to capital, the Champernowne conditions were satisfied. The intuition was simple: there was always a probability that someone would be lucky and get an outsize return, and that so would his children, and his grandchildren, etc. For those

[3] A few years later, the drive to provide micro foundations of macroeconomics provided the basis of what was called at the time the revolution in macro-economics. As Bruce Greenwald and I subsequently argued, much of the work, from new classical to real business cycles onwards, chose the *wrong* micro foundations, based on the increasingly discredited perfect markets model, with perfect competition, perfect information, perfect rationality, etc. See Greenwald and Stiglitz (1987b), Stiglitz (2018e).

lucky enough, return to capital will dwarf wage income. Hence, the process for large wealth is largely multiplicative, and it is easy to show that such processes give rise to a Pareto tail.

(The Pareto (or Pareto Levy) distribution is such that, for large values of wealth the percentage of the population with wealth great than W is approximately βw^{α}, with $0 \leq \beta \leq 2$, i.e. the log of the fraction is (approximately) linear in the log of wealth.)[4]

Thus, one of the directions which my research took in the following years was to explore in greater detail the way that a balancing of centrifugal forces—pulling the economy apart, such as random high returns by the wealthy—and centripetal forces (pulling the economy together, the regression toward the mean of ability, the division of wealth among multiple heirs, the equalization process of public education) can give rise to an equilibrium distribution of wealth. This is the thrust of Chapter 9, written with David Bevan, who I had first met when I was doing research in Nairobi in 1969, and who had gone on to write a doctoral dissertation on precisely that topic. When I visited Oxford in 1974, we began a fruitful collaboration. By moving from the discrete time Markovian model of Champernowne that I had used in my 1969 paper, to continuous time stochastic processes, we were able to get further insights in the equilibrium wealth distributions that might emerge and the critical parameters that might determine the degree of inequality.[5]

We establish that an equilibrium wealth distribution exists if $sr < n$, where s is the savings rate, r the return on capital, and n the rate of growth (here just the rate of increase in the population).

Here, we use the model to calculate the variance of income, wealth, and consumption, and to see how it is affected by parameters in the economy or policy. For instance, other things being equal, the greater the disparity between the rate of growth and sr the more equal the distribution. In the more recent work, described below, I was able to confirm that one should expect that the critical condition $sr < n$ be satisfied, and, noting that the

[4] There were others who studied the Pareto distribution, including Mandelbrot (1961) whom I got to know while I was at MIT. See also the early work of Simon (1955) and Wold and Whittle (1957).

[5] Since our work in the early and mid-70s, several others have used diffusion models to study inequality. See, for example Achdou, Buera, Lasry, et al. (2014), Achdou, Han, Lasry, et al. (2022), Gabaix et al. (2016), and Nirei and Aoki (2016), Benhabib, Bisin, and Zhu (2015). There are many technical and economic differences between the models we examined in our earlier work and these studies; for instance, we do not require reflecting barriers even though for large values of wealth there is negative drift; and we ground much of our analysis on standard growth theory, deriving key parameters determining the strength of centripetal and centrifugal forces endogenously.

The cited papers as well as virtually all of the other earlier literature (see, e.g. Champernowne, 1953) generate an equilibrium wealth distribution with a Pareto tail employ a reflecting barrier below and proportionate shocks with a negative drift at the top. Stiglitz (1966, 1969b) provided plausible microeconomic foundations; but in the discussion in Chapter 12, as well as in some of our earlier work, we show how the assumption of the reflecting barrier below can be dropped with the assumption of strictly positive wages. Some of the literature, such as Gabaix et al. (2016) replace the assumption of an asymptotic negative drift with assumptions of random deaths (dynasties simply end) and births, with the distribution of wealth among the births being more equalitarian than among those dying.

Achdou et al. make the important contribution of explicitly deriving savings behavior with boundary constraints, deriving high limiting values of marginal propensities to consume (low or zero bequests).

Gabaix et al. (2016) make the important contribution of analyzing speeds of convergence to the long run distribution, but within a model without both wage and capital income. They emphasize the importance of what they call scale and type dependencies to obtain plausible speeds of convergence, which they note was missing from many of the earlier models generating Pareto tail distributions. However, even our earlier models (Stiglitz, 1978) embraced simple versions of these dependencies, reflected in the heterogeneity of individual abilities and the dependence of the variability of the return to capital depending on portfolio allocations, and that depending in turn on wealth. The discussion of Chapter 12 highlights too some of the rapid—in some cases, discontinuous—changes that have helped bring about the large changes in the observed wealth distribution.

long run value of r is endogenous, relate the extent of inequality as measured by the Pareto tail to the underlying fundamentals (Chapter 12).

More broadly, Chapter 9 reviews the role of intergenerational transfers in determining inequality (in contrast to life-cycle inequality, the inequalities that arise as individuals save for their own retirement). It distinguishes, for instance, between (largely) unintended bequests, where individuals save for retirement, but die earlier than the longest contingency upon which they planned for, and planned bequests, noting that the incentive effects on the former are likely to be weak. The importance of such "unplanned" bequests will have increased as life expectancies have increased far faster than the retirement age. And while annuity markets have improved, they still are imperfect.

A large part of wealth inequality arises from inheritances (in the U.S., by some estimates at much as two-thirds),[6] and much of that is planned, and that is what the central model of the chapter allows us to analyze. The methodological innovation of Chapter 9 (along with Chapter 33 below) was to introduce the use of diffusion equations to study the long-run stochastic equilibrium, combining results from stochastic differential equations with those of long run growth theory.[7] The power of this technique in enabling us to derive simple expressions especially for tail inequality is illustrated in Chapter 12 below. At the same time, more conventional approaches using stochastic difference equations enable us to derive strong results relating the long-run variance of wealth to key structural and behavioral parameters of the economy.

[6] See Alvaredo, Garbinti, and Piketty, 2017. There are both methodological and problems in ascertaining the fraction of wealth attributable to inheritances, resulting in considerable disparities in estimates. See Feiveson and Sabelhaus (2019). Wolf and Gittleman (2014) suggest that inheritances play a smaller role. Chapter 13 below provides a model incorporating both life-cycle and dynastic savings.

[7] Since our work in the 1970s, there appears to have been a hiatus of some decades before economists and mathematicians returned to the subject. In the years after the Great Recession, there was a blossoming of research. See Benhabib and Bisin (2018) and the references cited therein.

Of the cited papers, the closest in spirit to our analyses is Benhabib, Bisin, and Zhu (2011) who provide a richer model of the evolution of income over an individual's lifetime with bequests, but apart from that, formulates a dynamic model that is essentially the same as Bevan (1974, 1979), Stiglitz (1978), and Bevan and Stiglitz (1979). Unlike Chapter 12 and our earlier work, they and the other cited papers do not, however, relate the returns to factors to aggregate behavior (that is, the average value of wage income or the return to capital does not depend on the average value of the capital or wealth labor ratio) and hence don't obtain simple representations of either the variance of income and wealth or the Pareto tail parameter of the kind we derive. They *assume* a structure of autocorrelation of wages, while we derive that structure from underlying assumptions concerning the stochastic processes governing regression toward the mean in ability (and in more general formulations, investments in human capital). They consider, on the other hand, more general distributions than the diffusion process we employ in our continuous time analysis (though our discrete time analysis is more general), invoking general mathematic results of Saporta (2004, 2005) that were not available at the time that we did our earlier work; but again, our use of diffusion processes allows us to derive explicit expressions for the Pareto tail, with results that are consistent with the more general analytic qualitative results that they provide.

They, and much of the rest of the literature on inheritances, derives bequest functions based on individuals evaluating their own lifetime consumption and a "utility of bequest," with that utility unrelated to the circumstances (income, wealth, or "utility") of the recipient. While that greatly simplifies the analysis, there is evidence that those giving bequests do take into account the circumstances of the recipients. This is important, because it provides the key motivation in our analysis for bequests—those with high income and wealth know that their descendants are likely to be worse off than they are. I do not believe, however, that the models formulated here adequately reflect these concerns—an important avenue for future research.

Curiously, most of the subsequent literature did not cite our earlier work (though Becker and Tomes (1986) did make reference to it, and this work in turn has been cited by most of the serious literature in this area). It may be that it was written too far in advance of the growth of interest in the subject. (The fact that Bevan and I published our joint paper in what appears today to be an obscure journal, *The Greek Economic Review*, may not have helped, but Bevan's work in the *Economic Journal* and my work in a major International Economic Association Volume and distributed as a National Bureau of Economic Research paper provided a more accessible source.

Recent Advances

As I note in the introduction to the volume, given the enormous increase in inequality in the years after 1980, it was natural for me to ask, could the models I had constructed earlier help us understand what was going on? How did they need to be changed to accommodate or explain what was going on. Piketty's work provided an additional spur: his conclusions (based in part on enormous historical work across many countries) was that there would be ever-increasing inequality, and that the only way to combat it was through a global capital tax. These results stood in marked contrast to Bevan and Stiglitz, Champernowne, and the final part of Stiglitz (1969), which suggested that there was an equilibrium income and wealth distribution; and to the results of the first part of Stiglitz (1969b) (Chapter 8 above) which showed that in a model where everyone is identical and there were no stochastic elements, the economy converged to equality regardless of the initial wealth distribution. The result of that model is obviously wrong; the model is useful because it forces us to think about the forces that give rise to the persistent inequalities that we observe. The models presented here show that there is indeed a presumption that there is an equilibrium wealth distribution.

Chapter 10 begins by looking at the new "stylized facts," broad descriptions of the macroeconomic variables that relate to distribution. These I contrast with those that characterized the era in which I had begun my writing. The models that were successful in explaining the latter facts—for instance, the constancy of the share of labor and of the capital–output ratio—were, at least on the face of it, inconsistent with the new facts, such as the diminution in labor's share and the increase in the wealth–income ratio.

Moreover, the new stylized facts seemed to counter conventional wisdom: For instance, the claim was made that the wealth–income ratio (interpreted to be the capital–income ratio) was increasing, even as the return to capital did not fall and wages were relatively stagnant. Standard assumptions concerning diminishing returns implied that if the capital–income ratio rose, wages had to rise and the return to capital had to fall. But the facts suggested otherwise.

Chapter 10 argues that such an analysis, like my earlier models, leaves out one important factor: rents, both land rents and monopoly rents. One of the most important contributions then of the following chapters is to add rents to the theoretical analyses.

If one confuses returns to capital goods and rents, it might even look as if returns on capital are increasing, or at least not diminishing, when in fact the return on capital and the share of capital, properly measured, is decreasing. Similarly, wealth includes the capitalized value of rents (including the value of land), and thus exceeds the value of the capital stock—and if rents are increasing over time, the gap between the two will increase over time. If one confuses capital (meaning physical capital goods, like plant and equipment) with wealth, then when wealth goes up, one might think capital was increasing, even though it was decreasing. These simple insights go a long way in explaining the seeming anomalous stylized facts. Thus, Chapters 14–16 explore models where rents play an important role, where the growth of rents crowds out capital—so the increase of rents is part of the explanation for the slow growth of capital and wages. The chapters describe the role of policy in the growth of these rents—and how alternative policies can curb rents and reduce inequality.

But before looking more carefully at how rents change the general theory of income and wealth distribution, I wanted to revisit the basic model without rents and with no stochasticity. First, I wanted to see if there were further results that had eluded me some years earlier that I could now derive. For instance, dictates of modern macroeconomics say that savings behavior needs to be *derived* from utility maximizing behavior. Earlier, it was permissible to simply assume a fixed savings rate. I wanted to show that the results I had derived earlier could be derived (at least in steady states) from utility maximizing individuals/dynasties.[8] Not surprisingly, the answer, shown in Chapter 11, was yes.

Our earlier analysis had also established that in the basic model, where everyone has the same savings rate, there is always wealth convergence, regardless of the initial conditions. But in Chapter 11, we show that with more general savings functions, wealth inequality can persist even if all individuals have identical productivities and savings functions, in particular, if those with higher incomes/wealth have a higher savings rate or if wealth begets wealth, that is, higher wealth individuals are able, over a range at least, to obtain higher returns. Of course, if individuals differ in productivities and/or savings rates, there will be an equilibrium wealth distribution, and Chapter 11 provides a simple characterization of the equilibrium. We show that there may be multiple long-run equilibria; for instance, an equilibrium with a low capital–labor ratio, generating low wages but a high share of labor, sustained by a low average savings rate; or an equilibrium with a high capital ratio, with a high share of capital, sustained by a high average savings rate. Indeed, we show that there may be an infinity of long-run equilibria and the distribution of wealth matters—emphasizing the lack of robustness of standard macro models, especially those based on the representative agent model.

In Chapter 12 I returned to the analysis inequality in the presence of uncertainty, developing further the framework I originally explored in the 1970s with David Bevan (Chapters 9 and 33), developing the central framework to much of this book: There is an equilibrium wealth distribution that represents a balancing out of centrifugal forces (the random elements that mean, in particular, that some at the top get lucky, increasing their wealth still further) and centripetal forces—bringing the economy closer together, associated with, for instance, the division of wealth among one's heirs and the likelihood that the children of the very talented will be less talented (the rags to riches and back to rags in three generations).

There was one important new insight: if one focused on the long-run equilibrium, the rate of return on capital was endogenous, and one could use the long-run macroeconomic equilibrium condition to strengthen long run results about the determinants of inequality.[9]

We derive a simple expression for the tail inequality as a function of just the rate of growth and the share of capital. When the production function is Cobb–Douglas, this provides a complete characterization of the tail inequality. When it's not, changing the savings rate or the tax rate will change the capital–labor ratio, and that will change the share of

[8] As I note in the chapter, both empirical research and behavioral economics have questioned whether savings behavior derived from the standard intertemporal utility maximization model with constant discount rate and time separable utility provides a better description of actual savings behavior than alternative hypotheses. In the chapter, we are able to go beyond time separable utility functions with fixed discount rates.

[9] A critical condition in our earlier work was that $sr < n$ (otherwise there would be ever increasing inequality). Our analysis showed that that would in general be the case. This also established that the concerns raised by Piketty about ever increasing inequality, which required that $sr > n$, might have some validity in the short run, but not in the long.

capital, and that will have an indirect effect on the long-run equilibrium distribution of wealth. But with the new general formula, if one knows the elasticity of substitution, so one knows the extent to which the share of capital will change, one can ascertain the overall effect on the equilibrium wealth distribution of, say, a tax on capital. The chapter shows that, provided the elasticity of substitution between capital and labor is not too small, a tax on capital will reduce inequality.

Perhaps the most important contribution of the chapter is the attempt to explain the observed increase in wealth inequality: what changes in our economy and in our society have led to an increase in the centrifugal forces and a weakening of the centripetal forces?

As we noted earlier, since our earlier work and that of Bevan, there have been a number of attempts to use stochastic differential equations to model equilibrium wealth and income distributions, most focusing on entrepreneurship, and, following Champernowne's earlier work, making use of a reflecting barrier to ensure the existence of a steady state. These models do generate a Pareto distribution. But while the tail of the wealth distribution is Pareto, the whole distribution is not a Pareto distribution. The chapter, following our earlier work and forthcoming work of Mateen and Stiglitz, provides a more realistic and more general model which does not require the use of the artifice of a reflecting barrier and which generates a tail which is asymptotically Pareto for high levels of wealth, but which can generate a distribution for lower levels of wealth which is more in accord with observed data.

Chapter 13 focuses on the other major source of inequality—the difference between life-cycle savers and dynastic savers (those whose wealth is, at least in large measure, derived from inheritances.) Again, we are able to get a remarkably simple results, characterizing the ratio of life cycle to total wealth as a function of the rate of growth of the economy, the ratio of the savings rate of life-cycle savers to that of dynastic savers (which can be related in turn to differences in their preferences, including time discount factors), and the share of capital. We identify tax and expenditure policies which can successfully reduce the share of inherited wealth—showing that a simplistic policy of taxing capital or inheritances and distributing the proceeds to workers actually is counterproductive, but if the revenues are used to invest in human capital or infrastructure, workers can be better off and inequality reduced.

The chapter introduces one more possibility: the possibility that all individuals are essentially similar, but only when they become sufficiently well off do they become dynastic savers. We develop a simple statistical equilibrium where there is an equilibrium fraction of the population in each group.

Chapters 11–13 explore how different aspects of savings and individual heterogeneity interact to determine the equilibrium wealth distribution—Chapter 11, for instance, based on non-linear savings functions and Chapter 13, based on differences between families that only save for their retirement and those that leave bequests.

The following three chapters takes up the observation that a large proportion of the increase in wealth is related to the increase in rents. Chapter 13 retains the assumption of competition but looks at real estate—land rents. But while it was understandable why land was ignored in earlier neoclassical models (including Solow's, and those, like my own, trying to explain inequality), focusing on a twentieth-century manufacturing economy where agriculture was a small share of GDP, it was a mistake: About a quarter of GDP represents housing services, of which land rents represent a significant proportion. And agglomeration economies, captured in part by land rents, are even more important in a modern industrial and innovation economy.[10] Population increases and urbanization too have contributed to the growth of the price of land at certain locations. We develop several models explaining the determination of the price of land, demonstrating why much of the increase in wealth would go into the value of land.

Using overlapping generations models (including the variant developed in Chapter 13), we show how capital gains on land can "crowd out" capital accumulation. Taxing land rents can reduce inequality directly and indirectly, through inducing more capital accumulation, thus increasing wages.

The analysis shows the unstable dynamics associated with land prices, especially once one takes into account the interactions between capital gains in land and capital accumulation. The models suggests that *some* of the increase in wealth income ratios observed in recent years may in fact be only temporary: there may be (and there evidently have been) bubbles.

Chapter 15 shows that the financial sector, sometimes aided and abetted by government, through changes in financial regulations, in particular concerning collateral requirements, may have contributed significantly to the increased value of land.

We explain why the composition of wealth between capitalists and life-cycle savers are different; and financial and monetary policies that differentially affect different assets can have accordingly a marked effect on wealth distribution. More generally, we argue that the way our credit system functions (or malfunctions) has played an important role both in the increase in the wealth–income ratio and in the increase in wealth inequality. We describe certain reforms to our monetary system—an electronic payments system, a system of trade chits, and credit auctions—that would result in greater macro-stability and greater equality, with smaller rents being garnered by the financial system and less savings being diverted to increased holdings of non-produced assets like land.

Chapter 16 then turns to the increase in the value of shares (equity) arising from increased market power giving rise to increased pure profits. The chapter discusses many of the factors contributing to these increased profits, and how these increased rents lead to lower levels of capital accumulation. As in Chapter 13, increased taxes on rent (increases in the corporate profit taxes) may, accordingly, lead to higher wages. The latter part of the chapter focuses on political economy. In earlier work (Stiglitz, 2012a) I had talked about there being multiple political/economic equilibria. The rules of the game determine the distribution of income. But the rules of the game are set by politics, and economic inequality inevitably gets translated into political inequality. Thus, I argued, there could exist an equilibrium with low inequality, where the equalitarian polity supporting rules that generate high levels of equality. But there could be another equilibrium with a high level of inequality, where the rich use their influence in politics to obtain rules that sustain the inequality. I suggested that such a model might help explain the difference between some of the Nordic countries, with their high levels of equality, and the U.S.

This chapter presents a more formal model of the two-way relationship between economic and political power, set in the context of the debate over the corporate income tax. With a high corporate income tax, those in different industries have little incentive

[10] See, for instance, the discussion below, Venables (2012), Stiglitz and Greenwald (2014), and the references cited there.

to engage in rent seeking: most of what they obtain will be recaptured by the government. Conversely with a low corporate income tax, there will be a high level of rent seeking.[11] But now, think of the effort devoted to lobbying about the level of the corporate income tax: when rents are high, it pays to lobby strongly for a low tax rate, and conversely when rents are high. There is thus a {high tax, low rent} equilibrium and a {low tax, high rent} equilibrium, with inequality higher in the latter than in the former.

This chapter is an example of an analysis of a *simultaneous* and *interdependent* political and social equilibrium of a kind I had analyzed earlier with Hoff (2004, 2008) in the context of a transition from Communism to a market economy, and discussed further in the context of inequality in *The Price of Inequality*: economic inequality leads to political inequality, affecting the setting of the rules of the game, which can perpetuated and enhance economic inequality. There can be multiple societal equilibria.

History matters in determining which equilibria one is in, though in ways which are often complex. In Western Europe, the shortage of labor arising from the bubonic plague led, with a lag, to increased wages and a breakdown of the feudal system. But in parts of Eastern Europe, it appears that the shortage of labor led to tighter controls on labor, a strengthening of feudalism, as the dominant elites had to take stronger measures to preserve their positions. America's system of slavery, with its long aftermath of economic, racial, and social inequities, has much to do with, on the one hand, the relatively high returns to labor (so manpower was valuable) but on the other hand the inability to obtain cheap labor within competitive markets, especially given the unattractive nature of the work. The plantation owners turned to exercise of force, rather than to markets—a dramatic illustration that one cannot understand present-day inequalities simply in terms of the competitive market paradigm.

History matters in another way: it shapes the evolution of technology, the subject of the next two chapters.

Dark Clouds over the Future

Chapters 17 and 18 focus on technology and innovation. A major source of inequality in wages, it has been argued, is "skilled bias technological progress," which increases the demand for skilled labor (and hence its wage) relative to that of unskilled labor (see Chapter 4). But the nature of technological change is *endogenous*, the result of decisions of firms about how to allocate scarce research dollars. Chapter 17 asks, how do we explain the bias of technological progress and is there anything government can do to change it? We show that what emerges from a competitive market equilibrium is *biased*—excessive investment in, say, innovation replacing unskilled labor. Worse, we suggest that certain government policies, such as the persistently low interest rates after the onset of the Great Recession, may have exacerbated the bias, achieving perhaps a limited short-term gain in employment at a long-term cost.

The effects of such policies—like the effects of events like the bubonic plague—may be long lasting. If researchers and innovators are induced to develop new labor-saving technologies, when subsequently interest rates rise, the new technologies remain available; the

[11] This is a result discussed earlier by Piketty, Saez, and Stantcheva, 2014.

demand for labor remains less than it otherwise would have been. As researchers and innovators have *learned* how to reduce labor, they may continue their efforts in this direction, so even after the financial impetus to save labor has been weakened, labor-saving innovation continues.[12] By the same token, the Covid-19 pandemic is likely to have long-lasting effects on technology—on the capacities to interact at a distance—with evident effects on the distribution of income, increasing disparities in incomes and well-being between those with skills and in occupations where such new technologies can be employed and those where they cannot.

The chapter emphasizes, too, a quite different equilibrating force at play when the pace of job creation differs from that of the increase in the labor force—an adjustment of technology, creating more jobs out of any given level of savings. But the dynamics of adjustments with endogenous technology are markedly different from those associated with the standard neoclassical model: when the equilibrium is stable (and it may not be), the adjustment may be oscillatory, rather than monotonic. (Obviously, when the process is subject to stochastic shocks, it is even more likely that the economy will exhibit marked fluctuations.)

Today, there is considerable worry about artificial intelligence and robots replacing workers and driving down wages. Chapter 18, written with Anton Korinek for an NBER conference on artificial intelligence, provides an analytic framework with which to analyze the relevant issues. It argues that, broadly, while the market equilibrium may result in workers being worse off, there are tax and other interventions (e.g., in the rules governing intellectual property) that can ensure that everyone is better off. It also points out that there are circumstances in which privately profitable innovations can actually make society as a whole worse off, reinforcing the conclusion of the previous chapter that there is a presumption that the rate and patterns of innovation are not socially optimal, with room for government intervention.

More recent work, not included in this volume, with Anton Korinek has explored how government can and should steer innovation in directions which are more socially desirable—recognizing that offsetting the distributive consequences of, say, labor-saving innovations may be costly, or impossible. Other recent work, in particular, has noted that there are cross-border redistributive effects—developing countries whose main asset may be a large endowment of unskilled labor are likely to be particularly hurt by unskilled-labor-saving innovation; and under current political arrangements, little will be done to offset these distributive effects.[13]

Going forward, there are additional concerns about how the evolution of technology may worsen the distribution of income, highlighted in on-going work with my long-term collaborator Bruce Greenwald. Consider, for instance, the pandemic induced changes in technology, which have allowed many skilled workers to work from home. This reduction in commuting time can be viewed as a major increase in standards of living for those in jobs which can be done remotely. So too, the reduced cost of access to certain services—particularly saving time—is of particularly value for high wage workers. These innovations thus reduce the demand for unskilled transportation services as they increase the real wages of skilled workers.

[12] See Atkinson and Stiglitz (1969) and Stiglitz and Greenwald (2014).

[13] The same holds for other innovations, for example those replacing fossil fuels with renewable energy.

More broadly, the innovations of the early twentieth century shifted the economy toward manufacturing, sectors in which there was (eventually) global competition, with workers working in production units which were (eventually) easy to organize, and the growth of union power not only partially offset corporate power but led to wage compression. Moreover, the need for worker discipline and skills led to a demand for public education. The machines augmented the productivity of workers.

Current innovations, including AI and robotization, may be leading to labor-replacing machines. As the economy moves to a service sector economy, competition may be more limited; and even more so with technologies marked by high fixed costs and lower marginal costs; with unionization more difficult and corporate market power enhanced, the share of labor could decline further and disparities among workers increase further.

Finally, this book does not discuss the large adjustment costs associated with the new technologies. These have been evident in the deindustrialized parts of Europe and the United States: large numbers of workers have found it difficult to shift into the sectors of the economy that are expanding and have experienced significant income losses (lower wages and higher levels of unemployment). In earlier research (delli Gatti, Gallegati, Greenwald, et al., 2012a, b), we highlighted that imperfect labor mobility can lead to unemployment—not only in the sector adversely affected, but throughout the economy, as those in that sector decrease their demand for goods and services; moreover, in these circumstances, *more* flexible wages may weaken the economy—as workers see their incomes fall even more, their demand for goods and services declines even more; but Keynesian structural policies—in particular, helping workers adjust to the new technology—can help restore full employment. These are all important topics, particularly relevant as one tries to understand today's inequalities, but they take us beyond the analyses of this book.

Taxation

In Part I, I discussed extensively how public policy can reduce inequality. Chapters 16 and 17 show the role that antitrust and monetary/financial policy plays in generating inequality. There, and in Chapter 15, I show how tax policies—including land taxation—can reduce inequality.

Public finance economists, of course, always focus on the overall incidence of taxes; changes induced by the tax may undermine the direct effects of a policy. Of particular concern is that a tax on capital will so reduce savings that wages will fall: workers will be worse off, and inequality may even increase.

The trade-off was at the center of much of traditional development theory, where there was also a concern that lower savings will lead to lower growth. Chapter 13 formalizes the analysis of these trade-offs. While it is clear that wages in the long run may be lower with redistributive taxation, it is a more subtle matter to ask, taking into account the lowering of the wage, if the proceeds of a tax on profits are distributed to workers, are they better off? The disturbing, but seemingly quite general, result is that they are worse off. (Indeed, in the two-class model, with life-cycle and dynastic savers, it turns out that there is full shifting: the after-tax returns to the dynastic savers is unchanged.)

We are able to show, however, in Chapter 13 that if the proceeds of the tax are invested, in particular in human capital, provided only that the return to human capital is high enough, then redistributive taxation on capital and inheritances enhances workers' welfare and can reduce inequality.

I first established this result in a paper written in memory of my co-author in some of my earlier papers on optimal taxation, Tony Atkinson. We had written a paper (Atkinson and Stiglitz, 1976) showing that if utility functions were separable between leisure on the one hand and consumption goods on the other, and if the relative productivities of different individuals were fixed, then optimal taxation entailed no commodity taxation.[14] An easy reinterpretation of the model held that consumption at different dates should be treated like consumption of different commodities; and that implied that there should be no interest income tax. As a matter of policy, the conclusion was one with which I could not disagree more. In Chapter 19, I set about explaining why. Several of the arguments I put forward have important implications for standard optimal tax theory: With restrictions on the set of taxes that can be imposed, the imposition of an interest income tax has general equilibrium distribution effects; it reduces the burden imposed on (costly) redistributive taxation. Thus, even if there is a deadweight loss associated with an interest income tax, it may be socially desirable. To put it another way, an interest income tax may reduce the distortion associated with self-selection (or incentive-compatibility or collateral) constraints. It is an argument for *pre-distribution*, doing what one can to reduce inequalities in market income.

This argument also has important implications for public expenditure policy and the desirability of taxes that might undermine productive efficiency (which Diamond and Mirrlees (1971) had argued should be preserved even in the presence of distortionary consumption taxes). Government needs to take into account the distributive consequences of its policy—it should be willing to accept some distortions in productive efficiency if doing so improves the market distribution of income/relaxes the self-selection constraints, and long run returns may differ from the pure rate of time preference.[15]

But perhaps the most important reason for taxation of capital and inheritances is that in the real world, there are important differences in societies where inheritances play a large role in generating wealth inequalities, especially because inequalities in wealth almost inevitably get translated into inequalities in political power. (I elaborate on these issues in the introduction to Part III.E., on inheritances, which includes two of my earlier papers on that topic.)

Piketty in Retrospect

As I noted in the Preface, while concerns about inequality never were far from the center of my research agenda, it was not until my 2011 *Vanity Fair* article "Of the 1%, by the 1% and for the 1%" that it became one of the foci of attention, leading to my 2012 book *The Price of Inequality*. A couple years later, Thomas Piketty's *Capital in the 21st Century*, with its wealth of data and powerful theory of ever-increasing inequality, seized the attention of those concerned about growing inequality.

[14] In later work, I showed that this result extended to all Pareto efficient tax structures.

[15] Of course, there were some technical assumptions—the separability of preferences between leisure and goods—that were essential to the Atkinson-Stiglitz result, but are clearly not satisfied. The chapter includes a discussion of the optimal structure of taxes under more plausible assumptions.

Some 60 years earlier, Nobel Prize economist Simon Kuznets (1955) had argued that, while in earlier stages of development, inequality would grow, eventually inequality would fall. There was a simple intuition behind Kuznets' finding: in the early stages of development, some regions and some groups in the population seize the new opportunities afforded, say by the industrial revolution. They forge ahead and become wealthy. Cities, in particular, become the locus of high incomes, while the agrarian rural sector lags behind. Eventually, those left behind catch up and those in the lagging agrarian sector represent an increasingly small proportion of the population. As this happens, inequality falls.

While in the golden age of capitalism, between the end of World War II and, say, 1980, the period in which Kuznets was writing, inequality in the advanced countries was at historical low levels, and in some places continued to decline, Kuznets' Law clearly no longer applies. Beginning in the 1980s, inequality began to increase, and especially so in the twenty-first century.

Piketty argued that the decades following World War II were an historical anomaly, the one period in which capitalism was not characterized by a high level of inequality. Going forward, we should expect their share of national income will grow at the rate of $r-g$, where r is the return on capital and g is the growth rate.

Anecdotes aren't proofs, but they sometimes can alert us to factors that might have escaped attention in a simple model. John D. Rockefeller was America's first billionaire. At death, in 1937, his assets amounted to 1.5% of GDP. Had his assets grown at the rate "g" and if, using numbers that Piketty might say are still conservative, but realistic, the disparity between g and r is 2%, then their wealth would have been \$1.3 trillion. Instead, the total value of the family assets is estimated to be \$10 billion—less than 1% of the predicted amount—and this wealth is divided among almost 300 members.[16]

Earlier in this introduction and in the introduction to the volume, I noted that Piketty's conclusion stood in contrast to those I and others had reached, about there being an equilibrium wealth distribution. Indeed, I noted that his analysis could be viewed as a special case of the more general models I had considered, but I had focused my attention on non-divergent trajectories. Here, I want briefly to explain why—and why his results seem inconsistent with what has been happening.

Piketty's analysis, like that of Chapter 13, is based on a two-class model, capitalists who save everything, so their wealth grows at the rate of return on capital, r; and workers, who save essentially nothing.[17] Because capitalists' capital is growing at the rate r, and the rate of return is *assumed* not to diminish[18] if $r > g$, capital grows faster than the economy, consistent *if one assumes that wealth and capital are the same*, with the observation that the wealth–income ratio is increasing. It also means that the share of national income going to capitalists, rK/Y, is increasing (with an obvious limit of 1), at the rate we noted before of $r - g$.

[16] Roberts (2014). It appears that Piketty's analysis seems to have overestimated "r," overestimated the extent to which returns were reinvested, and underestimated the importance of the division of wealth among one's heirs.

[17] In Chapter 13, we allow workers to save, and so long as their savings rate is not too high, it has no effect on the analysis.

[18] Piketty devotes much of his efforts to looking at the historical record, but what is recorded in the data is not just the return to capital, but also to market power and other forms of rents. If market power increased over time, even as the return to capital diminished, the observed average return might not diminish. Our analysis is consistent with this interpretation.

But the rate of savings of even the top 1% is markedly lower than 1[19], sufficiently lower that for plausible values of r and g, capitalists' capital is growing more slowly than output. This is, of course, perfectly consistent with an increase in the wealth–income ratio—once we recognize the difference between wealth and capital and the increasing disparity between the two, emphasized in Chapter 10.

Most importantly from an analytic perspective, there is a basic incoherence between the assumptions that the disparity between wealth and capital are not important and that the rate of return is not declining. For if capital were even approximately growing at the rate of wealth,[20] so that the capital–income ratio were significantly increasing, it would imply that the (effective) capital–labor ratio would be diminishing, and that would imply—in a competitive economy—that the rate of return on capital would diminish. And it would continue to diminish until the rate of growth of (capitalists') capital and income were equated, implying that the share of capitalists' income can't increase forever.[21]

Where we agree with Piketty is that the period after World War II was, in many ways, a historical anomaly, at least in part because the rules of the game that undergird the economy in that period, the importance of which we have emphasized throughout: there were not just very progressive taxes, but also anti-trust laws were more strongly enforced, the excesses of financialization were curbed by regulation, corporate governance kept the excesses of CEO's in check, and labor legislation had not yet curbed the powers of unions and collective bargaining to the extent that is the case today.

[19] Saez and Zucman (2014) estimate that the average saving rate for the wealthiest 1% of Americans was 36% from 1986 to 2012. Dynan, Skinner, and Zeldes (2004) also obtain high savings rates for the rich—but far lower than unity. Chapter 10 explains that with such savings rates, the after-tax average rate of return on capital would have to be implausibly high for the rate of growth of capitalists' capital to grow faster than the rate of growth of the economy.

[20] Piketty himself recognizes the possibility that there can be an increase in the value of land, but quickly dismisses its historical importance (though he notes that that does not mean that its importance might rise in the future): "the increase in the value of pure land does not seem to explain much of the historical rebound of the capital/income ratio [sic]" (Piketty 2014, p. 198).

[21] There is one more disturbing aspect of his analysis: its implications for the distribution of wealth among capitalists. The rate of growth of the economy will, if there is labor augmenting technological progress, be greater than the rate of growth of the population, hence if $r > g$, $r > n$. If the population growth rate of capitalists is not greater than that of the workforce in general, that means that there will be ever increasing divergence among capitalists: those who are richer initially will see their wealth grow faster than those who are less rich. If returns are stochastic, matters are even worse—even with zero drift (no regression toward the mean, i.e., $r = n$) there is ever-increasing inequality in wealth among the capitalists.

This seems inconsistent with the claims made by Piketty, who says that among those who hold wealth "the distribution of wealth tends toward a long-run equilibrium and that the equilibrium level of inequality is an increasing function of the gap $r - g$ between the rate of return on capital and the growth rate.... The greater the difference $r - g$, the more powerful the divergent force. If the demographic and economic shocks take a multiplicative form (i.e., the greater the initial capital, the greater the effect of a good or bad investment), the long-run equilibrium distribution is a Pareto distribution (a mathematical form based on a power law, which corresponds fairly well to distributions observed in practice). One can also show fairly easily that the coefficient of the Pareto distribution (which measures the degree of inequality) is a steeply increasing function of the difference $r - g$" (Piketty 2014, pp. 363–4).

PART II.A

EARLY CONTRIBUTIONS

8

Distribution of Income and Wealth among Individuals

1 Introduction

Although the recent literature has abounded with alternative theories of distribution of income among factors of production, there have been few attempts to develop a theory of distribution of wealth and income among individuals.[1,2,3] The purpose of this study is to isolate some of the economic forces which in the long run tend to equalize wealth and some which tend to make it less evenly distributed. In particular, we examine the implications for distribution of alternative assumptions about the form of the consumption function, the heterogeneity of labor skills, inheritance policies, and the response of the reproduction rate to different levels of income.

We begin by considering a simple model of accumulation, with a linear savings function, a constant reproduction rate, homogeneous labor, and equal division of wealth among one's heirs. In such an economy, if the balanced growth path is stable, all wealth and income is asymptotically evenly distributed, with the possible exception, in the case of negative savings at zero income, of a group with zero wealth. In the process of accumulation, there may, however, be a period during which wealth becomes less evenly distributed. We then show that the basic conclusions are unaltered under a variety of alternative savings assumptions, where savings is a function of wealth or of the distribution of income, or where savings is a nonlinear concave function of income, and that variable rates of reproduction make no difference at least to the asymptotic results. The effects of alternative taxes on the speed of equalization are investigated in Section 2.3 and in Section 2.4 we consider a simple example to see the order of magnitudes of time that are involved in the equalization process.

In the remaining sections of the chapter, we investigate the "forces for inequality": heterogeneity of labor force, class savings behavior, and alternative inheritance policies.

[1] Originally published in 1969 as "Distribution of Income and Wealth Among Individuals," *Econometrica*, 37(3): 382–97. *Econometrica* is published by John Wiley & Sons Ltd on behalf of The Econometric Society. Reprinted with permission.

[2] This chapter is a revised version of a paper presented to the December 1966 meetings of the Econometric Society and of Chapter IV of my doctoral dissertation submitted to M.I.T. I am indebted to A. Atkinson, D. Champernowne, F. H. Hahn, E. Kuh, J. Meade, P. A. Samuelson, and R. M. Solow for their comments and suggestions. Financial support was provided in part by grants from the U.S.–UK Educational Foundation, Gonville and Caius College, Cambridge, and the National Science Foundation.

[3] Notable exceptions to this are the works of Champernowne (1953) and Mandelbrot (1961), but their work suffers from the deficiency that the distribution of income is determined by a stochastic process, the character of which seems to have little to do with economic processes themselves. They seem to have little to say about, for instance, the relationship of the distribution of income among factors to the distribution of income among individuals.

The Origins of Inequality, and Policies to Contain It. Joseph E. Stiglitz, Oxford University Press. © Joseph E. Stiglitz (2025).
DOI: 10.1093/oso/9780198799580.003.0009

2 The Forces for Equality

2.1 The Basic Model

In this section (and throughout the chapter), it will be convenient to think of society as divided into a number of groups; all the members of any one group have the same wealth but groups differ in their per capita wealth holdings.

We assume that labor is homogeneous (all workers receive the same wage). Thus, all the members of any one group have the same income as well as the same wealth. Each factor is paid its marginal product. We assume a concave, constant returns to scale production function;[4] if y is output per man and k is the aggregate capital–labor ratio, then

$$y = f(k), \quad f'(k) > 0, \quad f'' < 0. \tag{8.1}$$

If w is the wage rate, and r the interest rate,[5]

$$r = f'(k), \quad w = f(k) - kf'(k). \tag{8.2}$$

If y_i is the income per capita of group i, and c_i is the capital per man, then

$$y_i = w + rc_i. \tag{8.3}$$

Savings per capita is assumed to be a linear function of income per capita. Hence if s_i is the per capita savings of group i, m the (constant) marginal propensity to save, and b the per capita savings at zero income, then

$$s_i = my_i + b. \tag{8.4}$$

Reproduction occurs at a constant rate n, there is no intermarriage between income groups, and wealth is divided equally among one's offspring. These assumptions ensure that the proportion of the population in each group, a_i, remains constant.

We can now write down the basic equation of per capita wealth accumulation for group (8.5):

$$\frac{\dot{c}_i}{c_i} = \frac{s_i}{c_i} - n = \frac{b + mw}{c_i} + mr - n. \tag{8.5}$$

Moreover, if we let K_i be the total wealth holdings of group i, and define:

$$k_i = K_i/L = a_i c_i, \tag{8.6}$$

it is clear that

$$k = \sum k_i = \sum a_i c_i. \tag{8.7}$$

[4] Satisfying the Inada derivative conditions.

[5] For most of the analysis, all we require is that the interest rate be a declining function of the capital–labor ratio and that the wage rate be an increasing function of the capital–labor ratio.

Then the differential equation for aggregate capital accumulation is

$$\dot{k} = \sum \dot{k}_i = \sum a_i \dot{c}_i = b + mw + mrk - nk. \tag{8.8}$$

Observe that *the aggregate capital accumulation behavior is independent of the distribution of wealth.* This is an essential result of the linearity assumption.

In analyzing this model, we shall first discuss the aggregate balanced growth paths and their stability. We shall then discuss the conditions under which a given group is in equilibrium, that is, has unchanging per capita wealth. Next, we will consider short and long run movements in the wealth distribution. Finally, we will investigate what these results imply for movements in the distribution of income.

2.1.1 Aggregate Balanced Growth Paths

If the economy is in balanced growth, $\dot{k} = 0$, that is,

$$my = nk - b. \tag{8.9}$$

In the case of $b = 0$, a strictly proportional savings function, this is simply the "Solow" equilibrium. If $b > 0$, there is a unique value for which $my = nk$, that is, a unique aggregate balanced growth path. If, on the other hand, $b < 0$ (at a zero income a negative amount is saved), then there will in general exist two balanced growth paths.[6]

If there is only one balanced growth path, it is globally stable, since for capital–labor ratios greater than that of the balanced growth path, savings per capita is less than that required to maintain the same capital–output ratio with population growing at the rate n. The converse follows for capital–labor ratios less than that of the balanced growth path.

On the other hand, if there are two balanced growth paths (Figure 8.1), the lower one will be locally unstable and the upper will be locally stable. Differentiating the capital accumulation Equation (8.8) with respect to k and evaluating it at $\dot{k} = 0$, we obtain:

$$\frac{\partial \dot{k}}{\partial k} = mr - n. \tag{8.10}$$

The balanced growth path is stable or unstable as $\partial \dot{k}/\partial k$ is less than or greater than zero. The slope of the my curve is mr, and n is the slope of the $nk - b$ curve. Since my is concave, it is clear that the lower intersection must have $mr > n$ and the upper intersection must have $mr < n$.[7]

Thus, to the left of the lower equilibrium, savings per man is less than that required to sustain that capital–labor ratio, and hence the capital–labor ratio falls (continually).[8]

[6] These results are contingent on the concavity of the production function and on the production function satisfying the Inada conditions.

[7] In the singular case of a tangency between the my curve and the $nk - b$ curve, where the upper and lower equilibria merge together, we have a stable–unstable equilibrium: stable with respect to upward deviations, unstable with respect to downward deviations. In this equilibrium, $mr = n$, the rate of profit is equal to the rate of growth divided by the marginal propensity to save.

[8] What happens when $k = 0$ is a question which we shall postpone for the moment. Negative k is possible only if there exist foreign countries from whom one can borrow. For a long-run savings function it may well be argued on the basis of econometric evidence that b is zero; we prefer, however, to keep the analysis as general as possible.

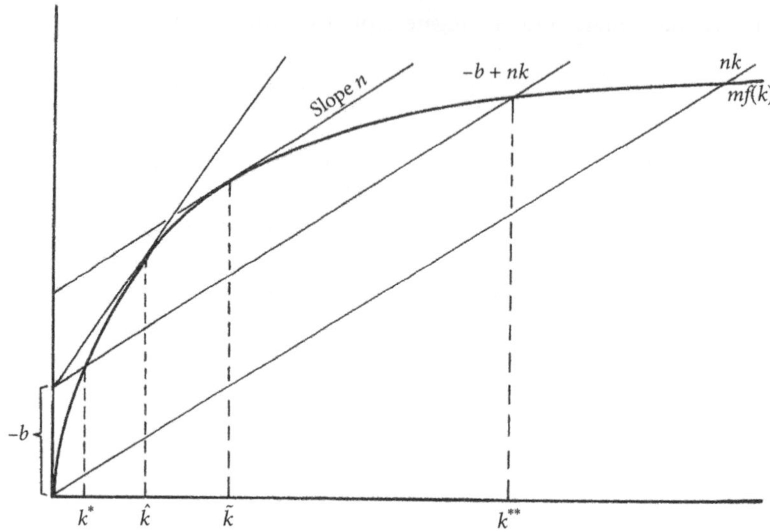

Figure 8.1 Balanced growth paths with linear consumption functions.

Above the lower equilibrium, but below the upper equilibrium (between k^* and k^{**} on Figure 8.1) the reverse situation holds, so that the economy has an expanding capital–labor ratio. Finally, above the upper equilibrium (k^{**}), the economy has a declining capital–labor ratio.

2.1.2 Equilibrium for Wealth-Income Groups

Having analyzed the aggregate properties of the model, we turn now to investigate the behavior of the separate wealth-income groups.

It should be clear that for any given aggregate capital–labor ratio k, there can exist at most only one group, with per capita wealth c^*, which is in equilibrium, that is, only one group whose per capita wealth is neither increasing nor decreasing. We require $\dot{c}_i/c_i = 0$ or

$$c^* = \frac{b + mw(k)}{n - mr(k)}. \tag{8.11}$$

(Observe that c^* is a function of k.)

If we define (see Figure 8.1)

$$w(\hat{k}) = f(\hat{k}) - \hat{k}f'(\hat{k}) = -b/m \tag{8.12}$$

and

$$r(\tilde{k}) = f'(\tilde{k}) = n/m, \tag{8.13}$$

then, because of concavity of $f(k)$, $k^* < \hat{k} < \tilde{k} < k^{**}$ and if

$$\begin{array}{llll}
k < k^*, & my + b - nk < 0, & mr - n > 0, & mw + b < 0; \\
k^* < k < \hat{k}, & my + b - nk > 0, & mr - n > 0, & mw + b < 0; \\
\hat{k} < k < \tilde{k}, & my + b - nk > 0, & mr - n > 0, & mw + b > 0; \\
\tilde{k} < k < k^{**}, & my + b - nk > 0, & mr - n < 0, & mw + b > 0; \\
k^{**} < k & my + b - nk < 0, & mr - n < 0, & mw + b > 0;
\end{array} \tag{8.14}$$

it immediately follows that for any given k, there is a unique wealth-income group in equilibrium, and that $c^* > 0$ if $k < \hat{k}$ or if $k > \tilde{k}$, but $c^* < 0$ if $\hat{k} < k < \tilde{k}$.

It should be observed, however, that in the first case, with $k < \hat{k}$, groups with per capita wealth less than c^* have decreasing per capita wealth, while if $k > \tilde{k}$, groups with per capita wealth less than c^* have increasing per capita wealth. (The converse is true for those with per capita wealth greater than c^*.) In the intermediate case, all groups with wealth greater than c^*, and, in particular, all groups with positive wealth holdings, have increasing per capita wealth.

2.1.3 Movements in Distribution of Wealth

We examine now how the distribution of wealth changes over time. Without loss of generality, we consider the case of two income groups. We wish to know whether c_1 is growing faster or slower than c_2, given that $c_1 < c_2$. If it is growing faster, then the ownership of wealth (at least in a relative sense) is becoming more "equalitarian"; if it is growing slower, it is becoming less "equalitarian." But

$$\dot{c}_1/c_1 - \dot{c}_2/c_2 = (b + mw)(1/c_1 - 1/c_2). \tag{8.15}$$

Hence, if $b + mw > 0$, the ownership of wealth becomes (relatively) more equalitarian, while if $b + mw < 0$, it becomes "worse." If $b = -mw$, there is no change in the (relative) ownership of property. Hence, to the left of $\hat{k}$ the ownership of capital is becoming more uneven; to the right it is becoming more even.

The economic reasoning behind this result should be clear. If $b + mw$ is equal to zero, increasing per capita wealth by a given percentage increases savings (mrc_i) by the same percentage, but it also increases the savings required to sustain that per capita wealth (nc_i) by the same percentage, so that whatever c_i happens to be, there it remains. If $b + mw$ is positive, increasing per capita wealth by a given percentage increases (per capita) savings by a smaller percentage, while the savings required to sustain that per capita–wealth ratio goes up in proportion to c_i, and conversely for $b + mw$ less than zero.

Thus, if the economy asymptotically converges to the upper equilibrium in the long run, there must be an equalitarian distribution of wealth, since at the upper equilibrium the wealth per man of the poorer groups grows faster than that of the richer groups. Indeed, if the economy is in balanced growth we can rewrite Equation (8.15) as

$$\frac{\dot{c}_i}{c_i} - \frac{\dot{c}_j}{c_j} = (n - mr)k\left(\frac{1}{c_i} - \frac{1}{c_j}\right). \tag{8.16}$$

Since the condition for stability for aggregate equilibrium is $n - mr > 0$, we have the general proposition that, *if the economy is at a stable equilibrium, the distribution of wealth must eventually be equalitarian.*[9]

But at the lower equilibrium, those groups with initial per capita wealth less than the equilibrium will grow continually poorer, while those groups with initial per capita wealth greater than the equilibrium will grow continually richer. This follows from

$$\begin{aligned}\dot{c}_i &= mw + b + mrk^* + m(c_i - k^*)r - nk^* - n(c_i - k^*)\\ &= (c_i - k^*)(mr - n) \gtreqless 0 \quad \text{as} \quad c_i \gtreqless k^*.\end{aligned}$$

(And of course, those with more initial per capita wealth have a faster rate of growth of per capita wealth.)[10]

Thus it should be clear that although the fact that each of the individual groups is in equilibrium implies that the aggregate is in equilibrium, the converse is not true. The aggregate can be in equilibrium while the distribution of wealth is changing.

We are finally ready to fully describe movements of the distribution of wealth in our economy.

(i) There exist in general two balanced growth paths,[11] along which the capital–labor ratio, output–capital ratio, wage rate, etc., are all constant.
(ii) The one corresponding to the higher capital–labor ratio is stable both with respect to the aggregate (locally) and with respect to the component income classes (globally). If the overall capital–labor ratio is increased or decreased (provided it does not fall below k^*), the economy returns to the balanced growth path, and if individual income classes are perturbed, the economy eventually returns to the equalitarian state.

[9] Thus, the fact that poor individuals have a lower average propensity to save than that of rich individuals does not necessarily mean that over time the distribution of wealth will become more disparate. See Friedman (1957), especially chapter IV.

[10] If there is a lower bound on the amount of capital that one can hold (an upper bound on indebtedness), then we must modify our savings functions. Assume that the lower bound is zero. Then

$$\begin{aligned}s_i &= b + mw + mrc_i, \qquad & c_i > 0,\\ s_i &= 0, & c_i = 0.\end{aligned}$$

We assume that there are two groups, a "poor" group with zero wealth and with a of the population, and a "rich" group with $1 - a$ of the population and all the capital. Then

$$\begin{aligned}\dot{k} &= (1 - a)(b + mw) + (mr - n)k\\ &= (1 - a)b + mf(k)(1 - a\alpha(k)) - nk = \Psi(k)\end{aligned}$$

where $y = w + rk = f(k)$ and $\alpha(k) = w/f(k)$. Then $\Psi'(k) = mf' + kf''am - n$. Hence, for $k < \tilde{k}$, $\Psi'(k) < 0$, and thus there can exist at most one equilibrium with $k > \tilde{k}$.

But since $\Psi''(k) = mf''(1 + a) + f''kma$, which depends on the third derivative of $f(k)$, there may exist more than one solution with $k > \tilde{k}$.

If the elasticity of substitution equals one, then there will exist at most two solutions, since the capital accumulation equation is identical to that examined earlier, with m replaced by $m(1 - a\alpha)$.

We can extend these results to the case where the lower limit of per capita wealth is not zero, but e. Then, in the balanced growth path, we can show that $k = ae + (1 - a)((b + mw)/(n - mr))$. We can show, as above, that there can exist at most one solution to this equation for $k > \tilde{k}$.

[11] There will be one if $b \geq 0$. If the Inada condition is not satisfied and the production function is not concave, then, of course, there may exist more or fewer equilibria.

(iii) The one corresponding to the lower capital–labor ratio is unstable, both with respect to the aggregate and with respect to the component income classes. If the aggregate k is decreased, it continues to decrease (forever); if it is increased, it continues to increase until it arrives at the upper equilibrium. If individual income classes are perturbed from the equal distribution position in such a way that the aggregate capital–labor ratio remains constant, the classes with per capita wealth greater than the overall capital–labor ratio continually increase their per capita wealth. The converse is true for those with less wealth than the "average."

(iv) If the economy is initially within the region between k^* and $\hat{k}$, then the overall capital–labor ratio is increasing and the economy eventually arrives in a state with completely equal distribution of income and wealth; but until the overall capital–labor ratio becomes equal to $\hat{k}$, the relative distribution of wealth becomes more uneven.[12]

(v) For all capital–labor ratios greater than $\hat{k}$, the distribution of wealth becomes (relatively) more even, eventually reaching complete equality.

2.1.4 Movements in the Distribution of Income

The adaptation of these results to movements in the distribution of income is straightforward. If the elasticity of substitution of the production function[13] is equal to one, then the analysis carries over exactly. If the elasticity of substitution is less than one, for instance, then

(a) in the region $\hat{k} < k < k^{**}$, the decreasing share of capital and the equalization of its ownership both serve to equalize the distribution of income;

(b) in the region $k > k^{**}$ the increasing share of capital and the equalization of its ownership offset each other; eventually, of course, the equalization tendencies dominate;

(c) in the region $k^* < k < \hat{k}$, the decreasing share of capital and the increasing spread in the ownership of capital offset each other; eventually, the economy moves into the region $\hat{k} < k < k^{**}$;

(d) in the region $k < k^*$, the increasing share of capital and the increasing spread in its ownership both serve to make the distribution of income more unequal.

The case of elasticity of substitution greater than unity may be analyzed similarly.[14]

2.2 Alternative Savings and Reproduction Assumptions

The question naturally arises as to what extent the results obtained in the previous section depend on the particular assumptions made there. In this section, we show that the basic

[12] Perhaps one should not draw morals about the real world from such simple models. If the distribution of wealth appears in the short run to be becoming more uneven, do not lose hope in the capitalist system. Eventually (which may be a long time), the economy may lead to an equalitarian state, by its own accord.

[13] It should be noted that none of the results thus far has depended on the shape (except that f is concave and satisfies the Inada conditions) of the production function.

[14] So far we have assumed that there is no technological change. Hence, in the long run, all incomes (in steady state paths) are constant. If there is technological change, in the case of nonproportional linear savings hypothesis, we must make some adjustments in the analysis. But the basic qualitative results will, of course, be unaffected by Harrod neutral technical change.

presumption for equalization obtains under a wide variety of specifications of savings and reproduction behavior.

2.2.1 Nonlinear Savings Functions

Let savings per capita of the ith group be a nonlinear function of income per capita of the ith group, $s(y_i)$. Then, for any given aggregate capital–labor ratio, k, there may be any number of income classes which are in equilibrium, that is, for which $s(y_i) = nc_i$. But if the savings function is convex or concave there can be at most two groups, since

$$\frac{d^2\,[s\,(y_i) - nc_i]}{dc_i^2} = s''r \gtrless 0 \quad \text{as} \quad s'' \gtrless 0. \tag{8.17}$$

But while aggregate savings behavior is independent of the distribution of income when the savings function is linear, it is not when the savings function is nonlinear. In general there will be any number of balanced growth paths, that is, capital–labor ratios for which

$$s\,(w(k) + r(k)c_i) = nc_i, \tag{8.18}$$

where $k = \sum a_i c_i$. But if the savings function is concave, and the proportion of the population in each of the income groups is fixed, then there can be at most three balanced growth paths. Two will have only one class present and one will have two classes present.[15]

The two one-class equilibria have exactly the same stability properties as in the linear case, and nothing more need be said about it here. The two-class equilibrium has, as one might expect, properties of both the lower and upper equilibrium one-class economies; if part or the entire lower class is disturbed, so that their wealth per capita is less than that in equilibrium, they become increasingly poorer and if they become slightly richer (in per capita wealth terms) than in equilibrium, they become increasingly richer, until they "merge" with the upper class. Of course, we have been assuming throughout this process that as individuals shift their class membership the aggregate capital–labor ratio changes in the appropriate way. As a larger proportion of the population join the upper class, the aggregate capital–labor ratio must rise. But as it rises, it leads all the other members of the lower class out of equilibrium, and since the lower equilibrium is unstable, there is no mechanism for them to reach equilibrium. It is unlikely then that any two-class equilibrium situation could ever be maintained for long.

Hence, in this model as in the linear model first examined, if the balanced growth path is stable, there is a tendency in the long run for the equalization of wealth and income—with the possible exception of a group (in an underdeveloped economy perhaps almost the entire economy) whose wealth is at some lower bound (zero, or the upper bound on indebtedness).

15 The one class cases require $c_i = k$. Hence we require $s\,(w + rk) = nk$. But since $s(k)$ is a concave function of k, and nk is a linear function of k, there can be at most two solutions.

In the two-class case, let a per cent of the population be in the lower equilibrium and $(1 - a)$ in the higher. Let $\bar{k} = ac_1(k) + (1 - a)c_2(k)$ where $c_1(k)$, $c_2(k)$ are the solutions to Equation (8.18) for given k. Then $dc_i/dk = -s'(c_i - k)f''/s'r - n$. For the lower class, $c_i < k$, if the savings function is concave, $s'r > n$. The converse holds for the upper equilibrium. Hence $dc_i/dk < 0$ and $d\bar{k}/dk < 0$. There exists at most one k for which $\bar{k} = k$. As in the linear case, there is of course one further possibility existing (provided that at "very large incomes" savings becomes approximately proportional to income)—the poor could reduce their capital to a lower bound of, say, zero while the rich become increasingly richer.

2.2.2 Savings as a Function of Wealth and Income

Recent investigations into savings functions have indicated that savings may be a function of wealth as well as income, for example, $s = b + my + zc$ so

$$\dot{c}_i/c_i = \frac{(b + mw)}{c_i} + mr + z - n. \tag{8.19}$$

The analysis proceeds exactly as in Section 2.1 of this chapter, and Equation (8.19) is identical to (8.5) with n replaced by $n - z$. If z is positive, then it is as if the rate of population growth is smaller than it actually is, so that the equilibrium capital–labor ratio is higher, r is lower, w is higher, etc. The more reasonable assumption is to make z negative, indicating that the more wealth one has, for any given income, the less one saves (as for instance some of the life-cycle stories suggest); then it is as if n is higher, that is, the equilibrium capital–labor ratio will be lower, wages will be lower, and the profit rate will be higher.

An alternative formulation of savings behavior is the following: individuals have a desired wealth–income ratio, given by q^*. If the wealth–income ratio is less than the desired, they accumulate. If it is greater than the desired, they decumulate. We may write the adjustment process as

$$\dot{c} = h(c^* - c), \tag{8.20}$$

where

$$c^* = q^* y = q^*(w + rc). \tag{8.21}$$

Substituting, we have

$$\dot{c} = h[q^*(w + rc) - c] = hq^* w + (q^* rh - h)c. \tag{8.22}$$

Since $k = \sum ac_i$,

$$\dot{k} = hq^* w + (rq^* h - h)k = hq^* y - hk. \tag{8.23}$$

There is a unique balanced growth path, with $q^* = y/k$, and it is stable. Moreover, for any given aggregate capital–labor ratio, there is at most one c for which $\dot{c} = 0$:

$$c = \frac{q^* w}{1 - rq^*}. \tag{8.24}$$

This is meaningful only if $r(k) < 1/q^*$, that is, for very low capital–labor ratios there exists no positive c for which $\dot{c} = 0$. In all cases, however, the poor accumulate capital faster than the rich, since

$$\frac{\dot{c}_1}{c_1} - \frac{\dot{c}_2}{c_2} = hq^* w\left(\frac{1}{c_1} - \frac{1}{c_2}\right) \tag{8.25}$$

and eventually all wealth is evenly distributed.[16]

[16] In the original, there was a discussion of a classical savings function. This discussion is now part of later chapters.

2.2.3 Variable Rates of Reproduction

In this subsection, we assume that the rate of reproduction of the ith group is a function of its per capita income $n_i = n(y_i)$. For simplicity, we shall revert to the linear savings assumption. It is clear that different groups will in general have different rates of reproduction and the group with the highest rate of reproduction "dominates" the entire population. All groups except the dominant one asymptotically "disappear." Assume there are only two groups—the rich and the poor. If the rich reproduce more quickly than the poor, then although it is true that "the poor have ye always among you," in a relative sense they disappear. On the other hand, even if the rich reproduce more slowly than the poor, so that they become an infinitesimal part of the population, they may still have more than an infinitesimal part of the wealth of the total economy. To see this, if K_r is the capital of the rich and K_p that of the poor, and a is the proportion of the rich (asymptotically $a = 0$), then

$$\frac{d\,ln(K_r/K_p)}{dt} = \frac{\dot{a}}{a(1-a)} + \frac{\dot{c}_r}{c_r} - \frac{\dot{c}_p}{c_p} = (mw + b)\left(\frac{1}{c_r} - \frac{1}{c_p}\right) + (n_r - n_p).$$

By assumption, $n_r < n_p$. If the economy is in an unstable equilibrium, $b + mw$ is negative so the wealth of the rich may be growing faster than that of the poor.

But if the economy is in a stable equilibrium,

$$\frac{d\,ln(K_r/K_p)}{dt} < 0,$$

so that asymptotically, the rich are infinitesimal not only in numbers but also in total wealth holdings, relative to the total economy.

2.3 Taxation and Equalization

Taxes for redistribution do more than just redistribute income today—they increase the rate at which wealth is equalized. To see this, consider the effects of a proportional income tax, in which all the proceeds are divided equally among the citizens.

If group i's before tax income is $y_i = w + rc_i$, its after tax income is

$$y_i' = (w + rc_i)(1 - t) + t(w + rk)$$

and hence the per capita wealth accumulation behavior of the economy remains unchanged. The relative movements in per capita wealth of two groups are given by

$$g_c = \frac{\dot{c}_i}{c_i} - \frac{\dot{c}_j}{c_i} = (b + mw)\left(\frac{1}{c_i} - \frac{1}{c_j}\right) + mrtk\left(\frac{1}{c_i} - \frac{1}{c_j}\right), \qquad (8.26)$$

and the change in the speed of equalization from the no-tax situation is

$$\Delta g_c = mrtk\left(\frac{1}{c_i} - \frac{1}{c_j}\right). \qquad (8.27)$$

Again, we observe that for "high" k, the poor increase their per capita wealth relative to the rich, until incomes and wealth are completely equalized, while for "low" k the rich grow richer relative to the poor. But note the two effects of the income tax:

First, the critical k which determines whether there is wealth equalization or not is lower, since now the condition is not $b + mw = 0$, but $b + mw + mrtk = 0$. In fact, at a tax rate greater than $1 - (n/mr)$, even at the lower balanced growth path equalization of wealth will occur.

Second, the rate at which equalization occurs is increased (or, if the distribution becomes more uneven, it does so at a slower rate than in the absence of the tax).

Similarly, the effects of progressive income taxes, profits taxes, and wealth taxes may be analyzed. It can be shown that for taxes of the same revenue the redistributive effects of either a profits tax or a progressive income tax are greater than those of the proportional income tax.

2.4 The Speed of Equalization: An Example

In this section we shall work through an example to give the rough orders of magnitudes of the time involved. We take the Cobb–Douglas production function, $y = k^{\alpha}$. If $b = 0$, the differential equation for the aggregate capital–labor ratio is

$$\dot{k} = mk^{\alpha} - nk.$$

This can easily be solved explicitly for $k(t)$:

$$k(t) = \left\{\left(k(0)^{1-\alpha} - \frac{m}{n}\right) e^{(\alpha-1)nt} + \frac{m}{n}\right\}^{1/(1-\alpha)}$$

so that

$$\lim_{t\to\infty} k(t) = \left(\frac{m}{n}\right)^{1/(1-\alpha)} = k^{*}.$$

If we use as our definition of distance from equilibrium $V(k) = (k(t) - k^{*})^{2}$, then the rate of change of $V(k)$ is given by

$$\frac{d\ln V(k)}{dt} = -2\frac{k\left(mk^{\alpha-1} - n\right)}{\left\{\left(k(0)^{1-\alpha} - m/n\right) e^{(\alpha-1)nt} + m/n\right\}^{1/(1-\alpha)} - (m/n)^{1/(1-\alpha)}}.$$

On the other hand, the differential equation for per capita wealth of group i is

$$\dot{c}_i = mw + (mr - n)c_i = mk(t)^{\alpha}(1-\alpha) + \left(m\alpha k(t)^{\alpha-1} - n\right)c_i$$

so

$$c(t) = e^{-\int_0^t (n - m\alpha k(v)^{\alpha-1})dv}\left[c(0) + \int_0^t mk(\tau)^{\alpha}(1-\alpha)\, e^{\int_0^{\tau}(n - m\alpha k(v)^{\alpha-1})dv}\, d\tau\right].$$

If the economy is in aggregate equilibrium, this takes on the simple form

$$c_i(t) = (c_i(0) - k^*)\, e^{(mr-n)t} + k^*$$

or

$$c_i(t) = (c_i(0) - k^*)\, e^{(\alpha-1)nt} + k^*.$$

If we use as our measure of inequality of wealth the variance

$$V(c) = \sum_i a_i(c_i(t) - k)^2,$$

we can immediately calculate the speed of equalization when the economy is in aggregate equilibrium:

$$\frac{d\, lnV(c)}{dt} = 2(\alpha - 1)n.$$

It should be noted that the speed of equalization depends only on the rate of growth and the share of labor, and in fact is proportional to each.

To get an idea of the numerical values, let us assume that $\alpha = .25$, $n = .01$, and $m = .2$. Then the "half-life of wealth inequality" is 46.2 years, that is, in 46.2 years, the variance in wealth is reduced in half. If, on the other hand, $k = .8k^*$, so $V(k) = .04k^*$, it takes 46.4 years for $V(k)$ to be reduced in half (i.e., for $k = 0.8586k^*$).

We have already noted that the speed of equalization is very sensitive to n and α. If, for instance, the rate of growth increases from 1% to 2%, the "half-life" is reduced from 46.2 to 23.1 years.

3 Forces Tending to Preserve Inequality

In the first part of this chapter, we have identified some strong long-term forces leading the economy to equalization of wealth and income. There are, on the other hand, several forces tending to preserve inequality in wealth and income. The forces that we shall focus on in particular are (a) heterogeneity of the labor force, (b) "class" type savings behavior, and (c) alternative inheritance policies.

3.1 Heterogeneous Labor Force

In this section we assume that some labor is more productive than other labor and receives, accordingly, a higher wage. We further assume that different kinds of labor are related to each other in a "pure labor augmenting way" so the ratio of the wage of any two groups is constant, and there is no intermarriage between groups. We revert to the assumption of a constant rate of growth of population and a linear savings function.

If p_i is the number of efficiency units incorporated in each member of group i, it is easy to show that in equilibrium c_i, per capita wealth of the ith group, is a linear function of p_i:

$$c_i = \frac{b + mp_i w}{n - rm}.$$

Thus, for any given distribution of productivities, we can derive the resulting asymptotic distribution of wealth. If $g(p)$ is the density function of p, then the density function of c is

$$\frac{n - rm}{mw} g\left(\frac{c(n - rm) - b}{mw}\right).$$

If productivities are normally distributed, wealth will be normally distributed; if productivities are lognormally distributed, wealth will also be distributed lognormally (but a three parameter lognormal function).

Further insight into this economy may be had if we assume that the economy has only two classes—an efficient class with $p = 1$ and an inefficient class with $p < 1$. The economy is on a stable balanced growth path; thus $n - mr > 0$ and $b + mw > 0$. Then, if p is sufficiently small, that is, $p \leq -b/mw$, all of the capital will be owned by one class. In fact, if $p < -b/mw$, the poorer class actually goes into debt to the richer class, and there exists an equilibrium per capita debt of the poorer class. The rich save enough to lend to the poor and sustain the capital–labor ratio.

If $p < -b/mw$, but a constraint is imposed on borrowing (say, no borrowing is allowed at all), then we have a two-class economy in which the poor consume everything and the rich (the capitalists) consume a proportion of their income. Denoting the efficient group by a subscript one,

$$\dot{k} = a_1 \dot{c}_1 = a(mw + mrc_1 - nc_1 + b).$$

In balanced growth $\dot{k} = 0$, so

$$r = \frac{n - (a(b + mw)/k)}{m} = \frac{n}{m} - \frac{ab}{mk} - \frac{aw}{k}.$$

If aw/k, the wage income of the rich divided by the *total* capital stock, is small and $b = 0$, we see that $r \approx n/m$, *the rate of profit is equal* (approximately) *to the rate of growth divided by the propensity to save* (of the "rich"), exactly the result of the Cambridge theory of distribution[17]

3.2 Class Savings Behavior

The presence of different classes in the economy with different savings behavior may also give rise to disparities in the distribution of wealth. Consider a two-class economy: a capitalist class which does not work and saves s_j of its profits, and a workers' class which derives

[17] Pasinetti (1962).

its income from wages plus return on the capital previously saved and saves s_i of its income (regardless of the source). Models with this savings behavior have been investigated by Pasinetti (1962), Meade (1963), Samuelson and Modigliani (1966), and Stiglitz (1967). Because of the linear savings assumption, the aggregate capital accumulation behavior is independent of the distribution of wealth. Thus, there is at most one two-class balanced growth path (i.e., a balanced growth path with both capitalists and workers present). Along this balanced growth path, $r = n/s_j$. It is easy to see that distribution of wealth among the capitalists is a historic accident, and, as in the Kaldorian case with savings out of wages equal to zero, increases in the capital of one capitalist occur at the expense of other capitalists. All "workers," on the other hand, have the same wealth and income asymptotically, since for any group,[18]

$$\begin{aligned} \dot{c} &= s_i w + s_i r k_w + s_i r (c - k_w) - n k_w - n (c - k_w) \\ &= (s_i r - n)(c - k_w), \end{aligned} \tag{8.28}$$

where k_w is the capital per man owned by workers. Since $s_i < s_j, s_i r - n < 0$, so that if any labor group has per capita wealth greater than the average, k_w, its per capita wealth declines. The converse holds for any labor group with less per capita wealth than the average.

There also exists a unique balanced growth path with only workers present (the "dual regime" of Samuelson and Modigliani (1966)). But this case is identical to that investigated above in Section 2.1 with $b = 0$, for which we have already shown that asymptotically all wealth is evenly distributed.

3.3 Primogeniture

So far in this chapter we have considered only cases where wealth was divided equally among one's children. Without going into a detailed exposition of alternative inheritance programmes, let us consider the case perhaps most contrary to that which has been discussed thus far, that of primogeniture (all wealth being left to the first-born son). To carry through the analysis we shall need to introduce some further simplifications, and shift the analysis to discrete time.

We consider a period in which the population doubles itself. Each "family" has exactly two sons and two daughters. For simplicity, we shall say that children are born at the end of the period. Everybody lives for only one period, parents dying after giving birth to their quadruplets. We shall examine only equilibrium paths. Then, at the beginning of any period one half of the population has zero capital. Of the remainder, one half are born to fathers who were first born, one half to fathers who were not. (1/2)(1/2) of the population has $b + mw$ wealth per capita. Of the remainder, one half are born to fathers who were first born and one half to fathers who were not, so (1/2)(1/2)(1/2) of the population has $b + mw + (1 + mr) \times (b + mw)$ wealth per capita. And so on.

[18] Since in balanced growth, $\dot{k}_w = s_i w + s_i r k_w - n k_w = 0$.

If we number our groups from the poorest to the richest, then the ith group has $(1/2)^{i+1}$ of the population (where the 0th group has zero wealth) and has a per capita wealth of

$$\frac{(b+mw)\left[(1+mr)^i-1\right]}{(1+mr)-1}=\frac{b+mw}{mr}\left[(1+mr)^i-1\right] \qquad (i=1,\ldots n).$$

If we compare any two groups, their ratio of per capita wealth is

$$\frac{(1+mr)^i-1}{(1+mr)^j-1}.$$

For large i this yields the distribution function of an asymptotically Pareto form:

$$g(c>c^*)\approx \gamma c^{*-ln2/ln(1+mr)},$$

where $ln\,\gamma = ln\,\frac{1}{2}[1-(ln(b+mw/mr)/ln(1+mr))]$ and where $g(c>c^*)$ is the proportion of the population with per capita wealth greater than c^*. To see this, note that the proportion of the population in the ith group is always equal to the proportion in all groups whose index is greater than i. For large i, $(1+mr)^i-1$ is approximately $(1+mr)^i-1$ so the proportion of the population whose wealth is greater than $(1+mr)^i\,(b+mw)\,/mr$ is $1/2^{i+1}$, and the result is immediate. If $mr=.6$ (recall that r is the rate of return over a generation, for example, if the rate per year is 0.05, a generation is 30 years, then $r\approx 4.48$), then the exponent of c is 1.48, an empirically reasonable value.[19]

3.4 Other Sources of Inequality

Among the more important sources of inequality not discussed here are the following:

(a) Life-cycle savings. If individuals save over their lifetime in a manner suggested by the life-cycle hypothesis, the age distribution will be one of the prime determinants of the wealth distribution. There is some evidence to support this (see, e.g., Lapman, 1962).

(b) Stochastic elements. Throughout the above discussion, we have made the assumption, conventional in growth theory, that there is no randomness in the rate of return on capital, in the rate of reproduction, etc. We have already noted that the theories of income inequality of Champernowne (1953) and Mandlebrot (1961) are based primarily on stochastic models. Champernowne and Mandlebrot have shown, for instance, that if: (i) $c(t)$ is a Markovian sequence in discrete time, (ii) for large c, $ln\,c\,(t+1)-ln\,c\,(t)$ is a random variable independent of $c(t)$, (iii) for

[19] To derive the aggregate capital–labor ratio of the economy, k, observe that k is simply a weighted sum of c_i, where the weights are proportions in the population. If $\frac{1}{2}(1+mr)$ is less than unity, the infinite sum converges to $k=b+mw/(1-mr)$. If we rewrite this equation as $b+my=k$ and observe that $n=\Delta L/L=1$ in our discrete model, we obtain exactly the Solow growth equation—aggregate equilibrium is unaffected.

large c, $E(c(t+1) - c(t))$ for given $c(t)$ is negative, and (iv) for small c, the transition probabilities are such that not all $c(t)$ can become zero, then c (for large c) would have the Pareto distribution. They unfortunately have not provided any economic justification for these assumptions. A slight modification of our model can, however, provide us with an economic motivation for them. If, for instance, we assumed that the rate of return on capital is a random variable, uncorrelated with the amount of wealth an individual owned (at least for large c) but with an average value equal to the marginal product of capital, then (in the discrete time analog of our model of Section 2.1), all the Champernowne conditions are satisfied, provided only that the economy has a sufficiently large[20] capital–labor ratio.

[20] In the terminology of Section 2.1, provided $k > \tilde{k}$.

9

Intergenerational Transfers and Inequality

With David L. Bevan

1 Introduction

Why are the rich so rich?[1] And why are the poor so poor? This question has puzzled thinkers for millennia.[2] Yet our understanding of the processes which generate wealth inequality is still extremely limited. Some view inequality as an inherent consequence of the necessity to provide incentives in market economies; attempts to reduce inequality may have, in this view, significantly deleterious effects on the level of national income. Others view inequality as resulting from monopolies (often government-granted), in which case the elimination of monopolies would increase both equality and economic efficiency. Still others view inequality as arising simply out of random processes (luck); there would neither be a gain or a loss in efficiency from reducing it. Thus, the effect of any particular policy measure designed to reduce the degree of inequality will depend on the underlying structural determinants of inequality, and it is important to obtain a better understanding of these.

This task is, however, a difficult one. The data are extremely sparse and empirical work requires considerable perseverance as well as ingenuity. This paucity of evidence does, of course, leave the theorist a field uncluttered by too many awkward facts; he can be fairly uninhibited in his construction of models. Nonetheless, working models of inheritance are almost as rare as good data. Recently, however, there have been several attempts to remedy this deficiency; this chapter attempts to survey and put into perspective a number of these attempts. Most of these models do not, at least as presently formulated, seem completely consistent with the "stylized facts" of wealth inequality. We conclude our discussion with some conjectures on why this may be so and on some suggestions for future research.

[1] Reprinted from *The Greek Economic Review*, 1(1), August 1979: 8–26. At the time of publication, the authors were affiliated with St. Johns and All Souls Colleges of Oxford, respectively. The authors would like to express their appreciation to John Flemming and Tony Atkinson for helpful discussions. Research support from the National Science Foundation is also gratefully acknowledged. Part of the paper was written while Stiglitz held the Oskar Morgenstern Distinguished Fellowship at Mathematica and was visiting professor at the Institute for Advanced Studies, Princeton. An earlier version of the paper was presented at the American Economic Association Meetings, Chicago, August 1978.

[2] Although, with a sufficiently low discount rate, there is a view that the present discounted value of "welfare" inequality is less than it appears at present. Cf. "The meek shall inherit the earth."

The Origins of Inequality, and Policies to Contain It. Joseph E. Stiglitz with David L. Bevan, Oxford University Press.
 DOI: 10.1093/oso/9780198799580.003.0010

2 Life-Cycle Theories of Wealth Distribution

There are two broad categories of models for explaining the wealth distribution: life-cycle models and inheritance models.[3] As is well known, differences between the patterns of consumption and income generate patterns of wealth accumulation and decumulation. Then, the distribution of life-cycle savings will depend on the age distribution of the population, as well as on the distribution (for any given age) of differences in the patterns of lifetime consumption and earnings. Although the magnitude of this inequality should presumably be directly related to the magnitude of differences in wages,[4] it is likely to be affected by a number of other features of the economy:

(a) The introduction of a social security program should reduce the amount of life-cycle savings.[5] Since benefits increase less than proportionately to lifetime incomes, this should have a more marked effect on the poor, thus increasing observed wealth inequality. If, however, we include the (expected) present discounted value of social security payments in the measure of an individual's wealth, the social security program probably decreases wealth inequality.
(b) The introduction of privately funded pension schemes will have similar effects.
(c) More generally, since in the absence of annuities, individuals have to save against the contingency that they live a long time, improvements in annuity markets are likely to decrease life-cycle savings. Since annuities are mainly purchased by the wealthy, this may decrease wealth inequality.[6]
(d) The availability of better rental markets for housing and the ability to reduce equity holdings in housing by obtaining a mortgage should again reduce the need for savings for retirement. The effect of this on wealth distribution is ambiguous: if the income elasticity of housing is less than unity, there will be a proportionately smaller reduction in wealth holding of the wealthier, and this will tend to increase inequality; but to the extent that there is a larger proportion of home-owners among the wealthy, this will tend to decrease inequality.

Clearly, some of wealth inequality is due to life-cycle inequality. The difficulty is assessing how much. In principle, this is an easy question: all we have to do is to find out the

[3] For an early attempt to see the implications of the life-cycle model for the wealth distribution, see Stiglitz (1966).

[4] But inequality in life-cycle wealth, as measured by (say) the coefficient of variation, will not, even for a given cohort, be precisely equal to that of observed wages. First, individuals differ in their savings rate; secondly, the distribution of lifetime wages is likely to have a lower coefficient of variation than the distribution of wages observed at any moment of time; and thirdly, savings rates are not necessarily constant, independent of income levels. The first effect would imply that wealth inequality is greater than wage inequality, the second that it is smaller, and the third is ambiguous, depending on whether savings rates increase or decrease with (lifetime) income.

[5] Unless retirement ages are reduced significantly.

[6] If individuals knew precisely how long they would live, then annuities would make no difference; individuals could as well simply spread their wealth over their retirement years. But since death is stochastic, individuals always have to keep a reserve against the contingency that they live a long time. The problem (after retirement) is formally analogous to the optimal depletion of a stock of a natural resource, when a substitute with zero cost of production will be discovered, at some unknown date in the future. The question is, what effect does uncertainty about the date of death have on the amount of wealth accumulated at the date of retirement? The presumption is that this increases the demand for wealth, but there may be conditions under which the reverse happens. For a discussion within the context of natural resources, see Dasgupta and Heal (1974) and Stiglitz and Dasgupta (1981).

distribution of incomes (over lifetime) and consumption and calculate from that the distribution of life-cycle savings. To do this, properly, of course, would require following a large panel of individuals over their lifetime. Since this has not been done so far, we must rely on indirect evidence for assessing the relative importance of life-cycle savings. This is of three sorts: (a) How much of aggregate savings can be explained by a life-cycle model? Although several such calculations have been made (see, e.g., Tobin, 1967, Farrell, 1970), they required such strong assumptions as to cast doubt on the credence of any results obtained; (b) Has the wealth distribution changed qualitatively in the way predicted by changes in the characteristics of the economy, of the kind discussed above? Although some changes have occurred, they do not (yet) seem to be as large as they would be if life-cycle savings were the only (or primary) determinant of the wealth distribution; (c) Can the life-cycle model explain the tail of the wealth distribution, the large percentage of wealth owned by the upper 1–2% of the population? The answer seems to be no, not under any plausible hypothesis concerning the distribution of lifetime wages and savings patterns (see Flemming, 1976).

3 Inheritance Models: Unplanned Bequests

Thus, to understand wealth inequality, some reliance must be placed on models of inheritance. We distinguish here between two kinds of such models: those in which bequests are planned and those in which they are unplanned.

There are two important reasons that individuals have unplanned bequests. First, because of the imperfect annuity markets referred to earlier, and because death is stochastic, at the time of death they will always have some wealth. Secondly, because of imperfect rental markets for housing, and other durable assets, some individuals at death will own houses (or other assets). Since the magnitude of the inequality of wealth is much larger than can be explained by such assets themselves, this may contribute to inequality, but is clearly not important in explaining the tail of the distribution.

The imperfect annuity market can, however, give rise to significant inequality. For individuals who inherit more (because their father died early) will wish to save more for their own retirement, spreading the increased consumption completely over their life. If they have, say, a constant elasticity utility function, they will have, at each date, proportionately more wealth than their friends who inherited nothing. Thus, if they too die early, their children will inherit proportionately more. This will give rise to a wealth distribution which is Pareto in the tail (see Stiglitz, 1976b). Moreover, the degree of inequality will be increased if the size of families, among whom the wealth is divided, is also stochastic. This model can, we suspect, go a long way in explaining the degree of wealth inequality.

The extent that wealth inequality arises out of life-cycle savings or unplanned bequests has some important implications for inheritance tax policy: for, *to the extent that inheritances are unplanned, the imposition of an inheritance tax will have no incentive effects* (*e.g., on work effort or risk taking*) *and such taxes are non-distortionary.*[7]

[7] This assumes that the individual puts zero value on the inheritance received by his descendants, an assumption that is probably closer to the truth than the opposite prevailing assumption, that individuals care as much for their descendants as they do for themselves.

4 Incidence of Non-Distortionary Inheritance Taxes: Balanced Growth Path Incidence

The fact that such a tax is non-distortionary does not mean that it has no effect on the economy. If the average savings rate out of inheritances differs from that out of income as a whole, an inheritance tax[8] will change the aggregate savings rate of the economy; this change in the aggregate savings rate will change factor prices and the distribution of income between capital and labor. This, in turn, may have a significant effect on the distribution of income and wealth in long-run equilibrium (see Stiglitz, 1966, 1976b, 1978).

For instance, if the savings rate of the wealthy is higher than the average of the population, the decrease in the equilibrium supply of capital will, if unskilled labor has a higher degree of complementarity with capital than does skilled labor, increase relative wage differentials, and this will increase the inequality in (lifetime) wealth. The fact that an inheritance tax could actually increase inequality because of the change in the capital–labor ratio is not necessarily to be taken as an argument against it; for there may be other instruments available to the government to offset this, in particular, government monetary and debt policy. Stiglitz (1976b) has argued, accordingly, that in assessing the effects of such taxes, one should employ balanced growth path incidence, where the effects on capital accumulation are neutralized by appropriate government policy.

5 Planned Bequests

Although some bequests are of the unplanned variety, many bequests are planned, and the remainder of this chapter is devoted to exploring the implications of planned bequests.[9]

First, we need to ask, why would an individual plan to leave something to his heirs? Even if individuals are altruistic, and have a utility function in which the welfare of their immediate heirs enters directly, say in the form:

$$U_t = u_t + \left(\frac{1+n}{1+\delta}\right) U_{t+1} = \sum_{r=t}^{\infty} \left(\frac{1+n}{1+\delta}\right)^{r-t} u_r, \tag{9.1}$$

where u_t is the utility associated with the direct consumption of the t-th generation, U_t is the (total) utility of the t-th generation, $(1 + n)$ is the number of children an individual has and δ is the discount rate, then an individual would only leave a bequest if, in the absence of the bequest, he believed that his heirs would be worse off than himself.[10] But with technological progress, the descendants are likely to be better off. Thus, planned bequests can only be generated if

[8] Keeping government expenditures fixed and compensating for the increased revenue from the inheritance tax by a *uniform* decrease in income taxes.

[9] For a more extensive treatment of some of the topics discussed in this section see Bevan (1974, 1979) and Stiglitz (1978).

[10] If $1 + r = \frac{1+\delta}{1+n}$, where r is the rate of interest. If $1 + r > \frac{1+\delta}{1+n}$, even if wages are not rising, there will be some bequests. Given the rise in wages the difference between $1 + r$ and $\frac{1+\delta}{1+n}$ cannot, however, come anywhere near explaining the magnitude of bequests.

a) One expects one's descendants to have a lower wage, that is, there is a wage distribution, and one's children's relative wage (relative to the mean) is not only lower than one's own, but sufficiently lower to compensate for the secular increase in wage rates.
b) One has inherited some wealth, the benefits of which, if one is altruistic, one desires to share with one's descendants. But one inherits wealth only under two conditions: (i) unplanned bequests from one's parents as described in Section 3; (ii) planned bequests.

There are two important implications of this line of reasoning: If all bequests are planned, then the distribution of bequests (inheritances) must simply be related to the wage distribution; but even if there were no wage differentials, then the occurrence of some unplanned bequests would, in subsequent generations, give rise to planned bequests. More generally, in planning one's pattern of life-cycle savings, with stochastic death, the realization that one's children will benefit from an early death may have an important effect on the levels of savings. In such situations, even with unplanned bequests, an inheritance tax has a distortionary effect and may have a significant effect on aggregate savings, possibly more significant than when inheritances are totally planned.[11]

To the extent that bequests are planned, they represent intra-family redistribution; thus, *taxing inheritances may actually increase inequality in consumption;* this can be seen most simply by considering a polar case; assume that the interest rate is zero and the growth rate is zero (or more generally, the interest rate is equal to the growth rate); then if inheritances are abolished, the distribution of lifetime consumption will be equal to the distribution of lifetime incomes, while with inheritances, the inequality of lifetime consumption will be smaller, because of intra-family redistribution.

If the interest rate exceeds the growth rate, then an individual who happens to receive a higher-than-average wage can sustain a permanently higher level of consumption for his descendants, and thus with inheritances, the inequality in consumption may exceed the inequality of wages.[12]

Thus, to assess the effect of inheritance taxation on the distribution of wealth and consumption, we need explicitly to formulate a model exploring the interactions between wages and bequests.

6 Wealth Distribution Arising from Planned Bequests

We now attempt to formulate a model in which the distribution of wealth arises completely from the planned decisions of altruistic individuals toward their descendants. There are two parts to such a model as follows.

[11] The reason for this is that, with completely planned bequests, motivated by an attempt to redistribute income between oneself and one's less fortunate heirs, there is an income effect and a substitution effect from the tax which operate in opposite directions. But with stochastic death, the substitution effect would seem to dominate. Consider, for instance, individuals who have inherited nothing. They would plan to leave nothing to their heirs; part of the expected return, however, from savings is the expectation that, if one does die early, one's savings will be of some value, although less than if one survived. An inheritance tax reduces the value of savings, and thus discourages lifetime savings.

[12] For instance, those whose wages exceeded mean wages could always buy a perpetuity which grew at the rate of growth of the population (so per capita, all heirs would have their consumption increased by the same amount).

6.1 Wage Dynamics

First, we need to relate the wages (or ability) of the child to that of the parent. Two polar models have been investigated extensively in the literature, one where the child's ability is unrelated to that of the parent, and the other where it is perfectly correlated (cf. Stiglitz, 1969b). A more reasonable specification, however, would take account of the stochastic nature of the relationship between the ability of the parent and the ability of the child.

If we describe the economy as if there were a discrete number of ability levels (wage groups), the ability (wage) distribution at time $t+1$ is related to that at time t by

$$x_{t+1} = Dx_t, \tag{9.2}$$

where $\underline{x}_t$ is the vector describing the ability distribution, i.e. x_{it} is the proportion of the population at date t in the ith ability group and D is a Markov matrix; d_{ij} specifies the proportion of those whose parents are in ability level i who will be at ability level j. The steady state ability distribution is given by the solution to

$$x^* = Dx^*$$

and it can be shown that, under fairly weak conditions,

$$\lim_{t\to\infty} x_t = x^*.$$

The nature of the wage distribution can be related to properties of the matrix D. Much of the earlier literature on stochastic models of wealth and income distribution was essentially concerned with finding restrictions on the matrix D which ensured that the distribution which was generated had particular properties, for example had a Pareto tail (cf. Champernowne, 1953; Mandelbrot, 1961). Usually, little attempt to provide an explanation of why these conditions should be satisfied in any economic model was made.

The approach which we describe below represents an attempt to relate the notion of "regression toward the mean" to the long-run ability (wage) distribution.

We postulate that[13]

$$A_{t+1} = \beta_t(A_t) + z_t(A_t), \quad Ez_t = 0 \tag{9.3}$$

the ability, A, of the child is related to that of his parent, but there is "noise" in the relation, described by the random variable z.

If β_t is linear and constant over time, Equation (9.3) becomes

$$A_{t+1} = \beta A_t + \nu + z_t \tag{9.3$'$}$$

Taking expectations, we can derive a difference equation for mean ability,

$$\bar{A}_{t+1} = \beta\bar{A}_t + \nu \tag{9.4}$$

[13] This specification is Markovian: it is only the parents' ability which affects the child. This seems reasonable, but more general specifications can also be handled. The technique employed below follows closely that used in Bevan (1974).

Thus mean ability converges to

$$\overline{A}^* = \frac{\nu}{1-\beta} \tag{9.5}$$

More interesting, however, is the fact that we can derive a similar difference equation for the variance of A, if

$$\begin{aligned} E\left[(z_t - \overline{z})^2\right] &= \sigma_z^2, \quad \text{for all} \quad t, A \\ V_A^{t+1} &= \beta^2 E\left[A_t - \overline{A}_t\right]^2 + \sigma_z^2 \\ &= \beta^2 V_A^t + \sigma_z^2 \end{aligned} \tag{9.6}$$

We can again solve for the steady state solution

$$V_A^* = \frac{\sigma_z^2}{(1-\beta)^2} \tag{9.7}$$

Hence we obtain the coefficient of variation:

$$\frac{\sqrt{V_A^*}}{\overline{A}^*} = \frac{\sigma_z}{\nu}\sqrt{\frac{1-\beta}{1+\beta}} \tag{9.8}$$

Notice that (9.3′) can be rewritten as

$$A_{t+1} = \beta A_t + (1-\beta)\overline{A}^* + z_t \tag{9.3″}$$

and $1-\beta$ determines the speed with which ability regresses toward the mean.

Even if it were thought that the difference equation was basically genetically determined, it could be affected by social policy; for instance, coeducational residential colleges may increase the tendency for assortive mating (more able males marrying more able females). This may lead to an increase in β, that is, the ability of the son is likely to be more highly correlated with the ability of his father. Note that such a policy change will increase the variance of ability.[14] (Conversely compensatory educational policies may reduce the variance in wages, if wages are just a function of ability.)

If we postulate further that

$$A = \ln w \tag{9.9}$$

and that z is normally distributed, then it immediately follows that in steady state, A will be normally distributed, and wages will be lognormally distributed.

For many purposes, it is easier to work with a continuous approximation to the difference Equation (9.3); thus, we write:

$$dA = \beta(A)dt + zdt, \tag{9.10}$$

where dA represents the change in ability level (wage). We continue to assume that the "noise" is normally distributed; more specifically, we postulate that Equation (9.10) is a diffusion process. This allows us to solve explicitly for the distribution of wages at each date,

[14] Assuming σ_z is invariant.

and, in particular, for the steady state distribution. This steady state distribution depends on the two functions $\beta(A)$ and $z(A)$. If we set $A = ln\, w$ then, if $\beta(A)$ and $z(A)$ are both constants, independent of A, we obtain a lognormal wage distribution (Stiglitz, 1978). This is the continuous time analog to the earlier result.

This model is consistent with the observed patterns of regression toward the mean and indeed it was this which motivated the original formulation of the model; for our purposes, it makes no difference whether this regression is related to genetic or environmental factors, or to mating patterns which are imperfectly assortative.

6.2 The Bequest Behavior

The bequest of a parent will be a function of his lifetime wage, his inheritance, and the return he has received on his capital.[15]

$$B_t = B(w_t, B_{t-1}, r_t). \tag{9.11}$$

Equation (9.11) is a dependent stochastic process, that is, the stochastic process for w, given the function B, generates a stochastic process for B_t. Thus, Equations (9.11) and (9.3) together with a relation between ability and wages, generate a steady state distribution $F(w, B)$ of wages and wealth.

In principle, the bequest function can be derived from the expected utility maximization behavior of the individual, knowing the stochastic process generating the wage distribution, and knowing that his heirs will be solving a problem analogous to the one he is presently solving.[16] If there are borrowing constraints (since the low ability children would like to borrow against the future higher income of their descendants) these ought to be taken into account in the solution. This turns out to be a difficult problem to solve in general, and so we have (reluctantly) taken two alternative approaches. The first is to investigate the consequences of certain simple rules, for example linear bequest functions; the second is to assume that the individual solves the optimal bequest problem, slightly incorrectly, substituting the mean value of each of the variables for the distribution (i.e., as if, in Equation (9.3), he postulated that $z_t = 0$).

[15] This obviously oversimplifies, by assuming that we can reduce the individual's wage earnings to a single number, w, and similarly for his return on capital. If there were no uncertainty, or if there were perfect risk markets, this could clearly be done; but more generally, bequest behavior will depend on the wage received at each date of his life and on the return received on each investment made.

[16] Some readers of earlier versions of these models have expressed concern over the fact that, in this formulation, parents do not know the ability of the child before they make their bequests. If they did, then the bequest would be a function of the ability (wage) of the child as well as of the parent. This complicates the analysis but will not alter its structure: it will still be impossible for an individual to know the ability of his children's children (or grandchildren). However, this modification would imply (when the bequest function is derived from an expected utility maximization problem) that parents ought to leave different amounts to children whose abilities differ. There is some fragmentary evidence that parents do this to a limited extent at most. This can be reconciled with the model presented here in several ways: (a) since wages are an imperfect surrogate of ability, if parents distributed according to true ability (which they knew) there might still be only a weak statistical relation between wages and bequests; (b) parents may be concerned with the incentive effects associated with compensatory bequests; (c) parents may feel a "moral obligation" to treat their children alike (just as firms often treat workers whose productivity differs the same) but they still may take into account the average level of ability of their children in determining the (uniform) bequest to give their heirs.

If we postulate that (9.11) is a linear function (as before), then we may write:[17,18]

$$B_t = s_1 w_t + s_2 B_{t-1} + s_3 r_t B_{t-1} \tag{9.12}$$

We again take expectations to obtain the difference equation for the mean of B,

$$\overline{B}_t = s_1 \overline{w}_t + s_2 \overline{B}_{t-1} + s_3 E r_t B_{t-1} \tag{9.13}$$

If we now postulate that the distribution of r_t is uncorrelated with the wealth of the individual and invariant over time, we obtain that the mean of B converges to

$$\overline{B}^* = \frac{s_1 \overline{w}^*}{1 - s_2 - s_3 \overline{r}} \tag{9.14}$$

Similarly, we can derive a difference equation for the covariance of wealth and wages:

$$\begin{aligned} E\left[\left(B_t - \overline{B}_t\right)\left(w_t - \overline{w}_t\right)\right] = E\Big[& s_1 (w_t - \overline{w}_t)^2 + s_2\left(B_{t-1} - \overline{B}_{t-1}\right)\left(w_t - \overline{w}_t\right) \\ & + s_3\left(r_t B_{t-1} - \overline{r}\overline{B}_{t-1}\right)\left(w_t - \overline{w}_t\right)\Big] \end{aligned} \tag{9.15}$$

To solve this, we have to recall our difference equation for w_t or A_t. Although the more natural specification is (9.3″), with z assumed normal, and the relationship between A and w given by (9.9), to solve (9.15) we need to assume:

$$w_{t+1} = \hat{\beta} w_t + \hat{v} + z_t \tag{9.3‴}$$

(This can be thought of as a linearization of the difference equation obtained by substituting (9.9) into (9.3′).)

Then (9.15) can be rewritten

$$\operatorname{cov}(B_t, w_t) = s_1 V_w^t + \hat{\beta}(s_2 + s_3 \overline{r}) \operatorname{cov}(B_{t-1}, w_{t-1}) \tag{9.16}$$

where we have made use of the fact that

$$w_t - \overline{w}_t = z_{t-1} + \hat{\beta}(w_{t-1} - \overline{w}_{t-1})$$

and where we have assumed

$$\operatorname{cov}(z_{t-1}, B_{t-1}) = 0$$
$$\operatorname{cov}(r_t, z_t) = 0$$

$$\operatorname{cov}(r_t, w_{t-1} \times B_{t-1}) = \operatorname{cov}(r_t, B_{t-1}) = 0$$
$$E[r_t z_{t-1} B_{t-1}] = E[r_t]\, E[z_{t-1}]\, E[B_{t-1}].$$

[17] This assumes that the effect of r_t depends on the wealth the individual has invested; in this simple model, the only relevant wealth which is invested (beyond life-cycle savings) is his inheritance.

[18] We have written this equation without an explicit stochastic term (other than through r). This is a convenient simplification; the reader may easily introduce such a term, which may for instance represent variations in the number of children. Randomness in savings may also be easily incorporated.

Putting it all together gives

$$V_B^t = s_1^2 V_w^t + s_2^2 V_B^{t-1} + s_3^2\left(\bar{r}^2 V_B^{t-1} + \sigma_r^2 E\left[B_{t-1}^2\right]\right) + 2s_1\hat{\beta}\left(s_2 + s_3\bar{r}\right) cov\left(B_{t-1}, w_{t-1}\right) + 2s_2 s_3 \bar{r} V_B^{t-1} \tag{9.17}$$

Hence, the variance and covariance converge to

$$\text{cov}^*(B, w) = \frac{s_1 V_w^*}{1 - \hat{\beta}\left(s_2 + s_3\bar{r}\right)} \tag{9.18a}$$

$$V_B^* = \left\{V_w^* s_1^2\left(1 + 2\hat{\beta}\left(\frac{s_2 + s_3\bar{r}}{1 - \hat{\beta}\left(s_2 + s_3\bar{r}\right)}\right)\right) + s_3^2\left(\sigma_r^2 \overline{B}^2\right)\right\}\left(\frac{1}{1 - s_2^2 - s_3^2\left(\bar{r}^2 + \sigma_r^2\right) - 2s_2 s_3\bar{r}}\right) \tag{9.18b}$$

$$V_w^* = \frac{\sigma_z^2}{\left(1 - \hat{\beta}\right)^2}. \tag{9.7″}$$

This completely describes the asymptotic distributions. Policies can affect the savings parameters (s_1, s_2, and s_3), and the variance of wages and r (redistributive taxation). In the long run, these changes may give rise to changes in the aggregate capital stock (Equation (9.14)) and, in a closed economy, this will change factor prices and shares and hence inequality. These long-run general equilibrium effects may not only alter quantitatively the results, they may actually reverse the sign, so a tax on inheritances which reduced wealth inequality in the short run may increase it in the long run.

To gain some further insight into the model, let us simplify by assuming that individuals save a given fraction of their total lifetime income, and divide it equally among their children. Then

$$B_t = \frac{s\left(w + rB_{t-1}\right) + B_{t-1}}{1 + n},$$

so

$$s_1 = s_3 = \frac{s}{1 + n}, s_2 = \frac{1}{1 + n}.$$

Moreover, let us assume $\sigma_r^2 = 0$. Then (9.18a) and (9.18b) simplify to

$$\text{cov}^*(B, w) = \frac{\left[\frac{sV_w^*}{1+n}\right]}{1 - \hat{\beta}\left(\frac{1+sr}{1+n}\right)} \tag{9.18a″}$$

$$V_B^* = V_w^*\left(\frac{s}{1 + n}\right)^2\left(1 + 2\hat{\beta}\left(\frac{1 + s\bar{r}}{1 + n - \hat{\beta}(1 + s\bar{r})}\right)\right)\left(\frac{1}{1 - \left(\frac{1+s\bar{r}}{1+n}\right)^2}\right) \tag{9.18b″}$$

$$\rho^2 = \frac{(1 + n)^2 - (1 + sr)^2}{(1 + n)^2 - \hat{\beta}^2(1 + sr)^2} \tag{9.18c}$$

If n and r are small

$$\rho^2 \approx \frac{2(n - sr)}{1 - \hat{\beta}^2} \tag{9.18c''}$$

and

$$V_B^* \approx \frac{V_w^* s^2(1 + n + \hat{\beta}(1 + sr))}{2(n - sr)(1 + n - \hat{\beta}(1 + sr))} \tag{9.18b''}$$

Observe that the inequality of wealth increases with the savings rate and interest rate, and decreases with the reproduction rate, and with the speed of regression toward the mean.

The variance in consumption can also be calculated, under these special assumptions, from

$$C_t \equiv (1 - s)(w_t + r_t B_{t-1}) \tag{9.19}$$

$$V_C^t = (1 - s)^2 \{V_w^t + 2\bar{r}\,\mathrm{cov}(B_{t-1}, w_t) + \bar{r}^2 V_B^{t-1}\} \tag{9.20}$$

Simplifying further, as before, by letting $s_1 = s_3 = \frac{s}{1+n}$, $s_2 = \frac{1}{1+n}$ and $\sigma_r^2 = 0$, we obtain

$$V_C^* \approx (1 - s)^2 V_w^* \left\{1 + \frac{2\bar{r}s}{1 + n - \hat{\beta}(1 + s\bar{r})} + \frac{\bar{r}^2 s^2(1 + n + \hat{\beta}(1 + s\bar{r}))}{2(n - sr)(1 + n - \hat{\beta}(1 + s\bar{r}))}\right\} \tag{9.21}$$

This equation makes clear the critical determinants of the variance of consumption (which we would consider, for many purposes, more relevant than inequality in income or even of wealth itself). The first of the critical parameters is the magnitude of inequality of wages. This we have related to the speed of regression toward the mean (coefficient $\hat{\beta}$) and the random component in ability transmission (σ_z^2). The speed of regression toward the mean enters in a second way (besides through its effect on V_w^*): when abilities are more highly correlated, there is more "compounding" of savings, and, if the rate of interest is positive, this increases inequality. Thus, the higher the rate of interest and the lower the rate of reproduction, the greater the inequality.

The effect of s is itself ambiguous. On the one hand, if the speed of regression toward the mean is fast and the rate of interest is low, then it serves to reduce inequality: able individuals share their good fortune with their descendants, who are likely to be less able than they. But if the rate of interest is high, relative to the rate of reproduction, and the speed of regression toward the mean is low, then it serves to increase consumption inequality.

Thus, if r is small, it is clear that the variance of C is reduced as a result of inheritance compared to what it would have been without (which would have been just V_w^*) and the abolition of inheritances would increase the inequality in consumption. Of course, prohibitively high inheritance tax rates generate no revenue; they simply force the individual to consume his income during his lifetime. Small tax rates will generate some revenue and may reduce inequality of consumption.[19]

[19] If one's objective is minimizing the variance of consumption, there exists an optimal inheritance tax rate to do this. See Stiglitz (1978).

As we shall note below, one has to be somewhat careful with this kind of comparative statics exercise. As we mentioned, the behavioral parameters (e.g., savings rates) may, in fact, be affected both by governmental policies and by the non-behavioral parameters. Thus, changes in r and β may well give rise to changes in savings rates.

Similar results obtain if we use the continuous time approach. Thus, focusing on the special case with zero variability in the rate of return on capital and the rate of reproduction, and where a constant fraction of lifetime income is left as a bequest, we obtain:[20]

$$\dot{B} = sw + (sr - n)B$$

where

$$d\,ln\,w = -(1 - \beta)\,ln\,w dt + \tilde{z}dt.$$

These equations can be solved simultaneously for the wage and wealth distribution. As before, to obtain solutions, a linear approximation to these equations must be taken. When that is done, results closely parallel to those for the discrete model described above are obtained (see Stiglitz, 1978).

The intractability of the theoretical model in its general form, and the necessity therefore of working with linear approximations, has led us to attempt a numerical simulation. We considered a large number of alternative specifications of the parameters of the problem (the interest rate, the utility function (which we parameterized by a constant elasticity utility function), the discount factor (δ in Equation (9.1)), the regression factor (β), and the coefficient of variation in wages). We have also considered the effect of imposing a borrowing constraint on individuals.[21]

The results of this exercise are complex, and are described in greater detail in Bevan (1979). Here, we draw attention to five aspects of them.

First, the results are very sensitive to the value assumed for the elasticity of the marginal utility of consumption, η. For example, lowering η from 4 to 1 may raise the sensitivity of the average level of bequest to changes in the after-tax rate of interest by a factor of 100.

Second, for plausible values of η, the average level of bequest is very sensitive to other parameter values, particularly to the rate of interest (a typical result with $\eta = 2$ would have a rise of one-tenth of a percentage point in the interest rate raising the average bequest by an amount equal to average annual earnings).

Third, inequality in wealth is sensitive to the shape of the upper tail of the earnings distribution. Working with a lognormal distribution, it is difficult to generate a tail in the

[20] To see this, write

$$B_t = \frac{s(w_t + rB_{t-1}) + B_{t-1}}{1 + n}$$

$$\Delta B_t = \frac{s(w_t + rB_{t-1}) - nB_{t-1}}{1 + n}$$

$$\approx (s - n)(w_t + rB_{t-1}) - nB_{t-1}.$$

[21] In the simulations, attention was focused on sets of parameters which yielded reasonable values of aggregate savings. This was an important restriction, implying that we had one fewer degree of freedom.

Table 9.1 Percentage of population in various wealth ranges: Simulated vs. actual

wealth range*	Simulated** (lognormal)	Simulated** (Champernowne)	Actual***
10–25	2.80	1.34	6.38
25–50	1.26	1.12	1.72
50–100	0.10	0.62	0.70
100–200	0	0.14	0.16
200 +	0	0	0.10
Average wealth	1.18	1.29	2.12
R^2 wealth/wages	0.052	0.034	?

* Times median wages
** $\beta = 0.5$, elasticity of marginal utility of 2, $\delta = 1/3$. Lognormal has median 1, standard deviation in the logs 0.39, $r = 4.5\%$. Champernowne has median 1, other parameter 3.37, $r = 4.5\%$. Rate of growth of per capita earnings and population both = 2%.
*** Derived from Atkinson and Harrison's estimates for UK wealth distribution, 1966.

wealth distribution which is sufficiently "fat," for reasonable values of the parameters. An earnings distribution with a Pareto tail (such as the Champernowne distribution) offers a much better fit[22] (see Table 9.1).

Fourth, the relation between wealth inequality and consumption inequality is very complex; they may easily move in opposite directions. This is partly due to the rather low correlation between inheritance and earnings even when earnings are themselves heritable to a high degree.

Finally, the borrowing constraint plays a crucial role. When it is set at zero, the large majority of individuals (typically 80–95%) are constrained to leave no bequest. If it is relaxed somewhat, so that negative bequests are possible up to some (reasonable) finite amount, the majority then proceed to make the maximum negative bequest, and a very different wealth distribution is obtained. This is not a surprising result under the present assumptions: it is due partly to limited altruism but mainly to the growth in per capita earnings over time. It does mean that analytic models which ignore the constraint (such as the one outlined in our first approach) must be treated with some caution.

7 Concluding Remarks

These models, simple as they are, enhance our understanding of the process of wealth determination, and have some important implications for policy. They also raise some questions requiring further exploration.

It seems likely that there are several processes at work determining the wage and wealth distribution. Much of wealth accumulation may be for life-cycle purposes, but the tail of the distribution—in which a great deal of wealth is concentrated—probably cannot be related to life-cycle savings. Secondly, the tails of the wage and wealth distributions are fatter than can be explained by a conventional model of regression toward the mean.[23] A fat tail in the

[22] Recall that the model is required to explain the top 1–2% of the wealth distribution only, the bulk of the remainder being adequately explained by models of the life-cycle type.

[23] There are other mechanisms which generate Pareto tails, related to primogeniture and stochastic death (unplanned bequests), but it is unlikely that these account for the observed distribution (see Stiglitz, 1969b, 1978).

wealth distribution can, through the transmission mechanism we have described here, be related to a fat tail in the wage distribution; but then, how do we explain these extremely high incomes? They may reflect the fact that in certain types of activities, in particular, in certain types of inventive and entrepreneurial activities, the returns have extremely large (possibly infinite) variances. They may, however, simply be the outcome of "lotteries" with no economic effects other than on income distribution.

The point of making these distinctions is that the effect of taxation may be markedly different on different kinds of savings. For instance, the taxation of extremely large inheritances will not have the serious distortionary effects that the critics of the tax seem to claim if these are generated by windfall gains; while the consequences, both positive and negative, of inheritance taxes for upper-middle-income individuals, in the (log) normal part of the income distribution, may be significantly different from those for the very wealthy. The design of the inheritance tax structure ought to take this into account.

The design of tax policy needs to take some further aspects into consideration. First, the models we have formulated are characterized not only by a steady state distribution, but by a set of stochastic difference (differential) equations. Two economies might have the same steady state distribution but differ in these dynamic equations; they may differ, in other words, in the degree of intergenerational mobility. There is a widespread view that social mobility is good. Can this be related to more basic ethical postulates (e.g., to utilitarianism), and what implications do these dynamic aspects have for the design of policy?

Secondly, there is a widespread view that "it is better to give than to receive." Gifts, in a utilitarian context, are doubly blessed: for both the giver and the receiver obtain utility from them. Does this suggest that government policy ought to encourage these gifts, rather than discourage them?

Finally, although from a utilitarian point of view, it is natural to focus on the distribution of consumption, it is not clear that this fully captures the nature of inequality in our society; there are reasons why one may oppose inequality of wealth, even if consumption were equalized, for example because of the abuses of power to which it may give rise.

These are all considerations which a fuller Taanalysis of public policy toward inheritance and the inequality of wealth would need to take into account.

PART II.B
RECENT UNPUBLISHED CONTRIBUTIONS

10

Explaining the New Stylized Facts of Growth and Distribution

Some 50 years ago, economic theorists tried to develop explanations for what were then viewed as the stylized facts of growth and distribution, articulated by Nicholas Kaldor.[1,2] Among the central facts was the constancy of the capital–output ratio and the relative shares of capital and labor.[3]

Today, there seems to be a new set of stylized facts—some contradicting the old—that have to be explained.[4] This chapter first sets out these stylized facts, explains why they are not only markedly different from the old, but also why they require a new set of theories: they at least seem to violate some longstanding hypotheses, such as the law of diminishing returns, and are hard to reconcile with a wealth of empirical observations, for example concerning the elasticity of substitution between labor and capital and the relative stagnation of average wages. Most importantly, the standard models cannot explain the growth of the wealth–income ratio, as described, for instance, in the empirical work of Piketty (2014).

The central thrust of this chapter is to show that these stylized facts are inconsistent with standard neoclassical growth theory, but that the quandaries thus posed can be resolved by observing that if there are rents in the economy, wealth will exceed the capital stock by the capitalized value of these rents. We show that a model incorporating growth in rent-wealth can go a long way in explaining the new stylized facts, including how it can be the case that the capital–income ratio goes down at the same time that the wealth–income ratio increases.

After laying out the stylized facts in Section 1, Section 2 uses variants of the standard neoclassical model to show their inconsistency with that theory. We first show that wealth has grown far faster than can be accounted for by data on capital accumulation from national income accounts, that *if* the capital–output ratio had increased, an appropriately weighted average wage would have had to have increased—contrary to what has been observed, and that the declining share of labor could only be reconciled with the large increases in average labor productivity if a huge and so far unexplained gap had opened up between movements in marginal and average productivities during the last 40 years (in contrast to previous decades where the two moved in tandem). Finally, we establish that in the long run under the standard model of intertemporal optimization, workers' wages should have (on average) gone up significantly.

[1] Revised, edited, and updated version of a paper originally distributed as "New theoretical perspectives on the distribution of income and wealth among individuals: Part I. The Wealth Residual," NBER working paper 21,189, May 2015.

[2] Kaldor (1957). For a recent review of the attempts to explain these facts, see Jones and Romer (2010).

[3] Other facts included the constancy of the rate of growth of output and capital and of the return on capital.

[4] This chapter focuses on advanced countries. A slightly different analysis would be required for developing and emerging countries, though the theoretical formulations presented here are general.

The Origins of Inequality, and Policies to Contain It. Joseph E. Stiglitz, Oxford University Press. © Joseph E. Stiglitz (2025).
DOI: 10.1093/oso/9780198799580.003.0011

The rest of the chapter then shows how introducing rents into the standard model can explain the stylized facts. Section 3 introduces land, and discusses the challenges posed by aggregating land and productive capital, and those measures reflecting "control over resources" (conventional wealth measures) are not appropriately used as inputs into production functions. Section 4 discusses why rents have increased. The final section explains why wealth generated by rents is so different from wealth associated with productive capital, why an increase in rents may, if for instance associated with market power, lead to an increase in measured "wealth" but a decrease in real capital, and in productivity and wages.

Later chapters of this part of the volume provide the detailed modeling of the various drivers of the increase in rent-wealth.

1 The New Stylized Facts

Like the old, stylized facts, the new, stylized facts are grounded in certain empirical observations.[5] Among these are the following (some of these "facts" are truer for some countries than others; and there are a few country exceptions):[6]

(a) Growing inequality in both wages and capital income (wealth), and growing inequality overall.[7]
(b) Wealth is more unequally distributed than wages.
(c) Average wages have largely stagnated, even as productivity has increased, so the share of capital—or more accurately, the share of income going to factors other than labor—has increased.[8]
(d) Wealth is positively correlated with wages, and other indicators of well-being are positively correlated with both, so that inequalities in standards of living, by most accounts, are even greater than in income. Given that inequality in each of the components of income (wages and capital) is increasing, given the positive correlation between the two, and the increasing relative importance of the more unequal component, capital, is also increasing, it is, of course, not surprising that there would be an increase in overall level of income inequality.[9]
(e) In many countries there have been significant increases in the ratio of wealth to income.[10]
(f) The return to capital has not declined, even as the wealth–income ratio has increased and as average wages have stagnated.

[5] Other stylized facts have also been seemingly rejected by the data: the rate of growth of output, for instance, has been highly variable. Some of these observations are discussed at greater length in Chapter 4.

[6] Obviously, in a world of globalization, factor payments in different countries are related—in the limiting case, with no trade barriers factor prices would be equalized (Samuelson, 1948). There is, however, considerable evidence that the world is nowhere near this limiting case.

[7] Reflected not just in growing Gini coefficients, but an increasing share of income going to those at the very top. For up-to-date data, see the latest statistics from the OECD, the World Inequality Data base, and the LIS data base.

[8] See Shierholz and Mishel (2013) and the more extended discussion in Chapter 4. For instance, wages of production and non-supervisory employees on private non-farm payrolls in constant 2018 dollars was lower in 2018 than in 1973. Desilver (2018) based on BLS data. (The share of production and non-supervisory employees was little different at the two dates.)

[9] The only way that this could not happen is that there would have been a significant decrease in the correlation between wages and capital or between the return to capital and the level of capital. In fact, there is some evidence of an increase in the correlation. See Alvaredo, Atkinson, Piketty, and Saez, 2013.

[10] See Piketty (2014) and Piketty and Zucman (2014). For the UK, Germany, and France, the wealth–income ratio rose from about 300–360% in 1970 to 377–618% in 2010. The U.S. had a relatively small increase, from 399% to 456%.

1.1 Ambiguities in Data

In the discussion below, we will note that many of these stylized facts are contested, or at the very least, there is debate about the interpretation of the data. Most importantly, we'll observe that what is usually classified as the return to capital actually includes elements of "rents," pure profits and the return to land, and we noted in Chapter 4 that what is usually classified as the return to workers includes returns to CEOs, bankers, and others whose income is probably not appropriately classified as "labor income." Their income is certainly not "labor income," which we usually think of as going to workers.[11]

1.2 The Puzzles Presented by the New Stylized Facts

Economists had worked hard to explain the *old, stylized* facts, and Solow, Kaldor, and a host of other economists produced a variety of models doing so. The theories they developed in response—and indeed, other theories developed over the past 200 years—are challenged by the new stylized facts. They cannot explain the markedly different *new* stylized facts. It would seem that a new set of theories is required.[12]

(i) The standard theories predict that the capital–output ratio is eventually a constant, seeming to contradict the observation of an increase in the wealth–output ratio.

(ii) Standard growth theory begins with the observation that r, the rate of return on capital, is an *endogenous* variable. Among the most basic laws of economics is the law of diminishing returns. If capitalists continue to invest at a rate faster than the growth of the labor force,[13] then the rate of return to capital should diminish.[14] If the rate of growth of capital is greater than that of the economy, g, the output–capital ratio will decline, and if the average productivity of capital (the output–capital ratio) decreases, *normally* the marginal productivity will decrease. In the Cobb–Douglas production function—the special parameterization so loved by macroeconomists—average and marginal returns move in tandem, so that a fall in the average productivity of capital would be accompanied by an equiproportionate fall in the marginal productivity. In the case of an elasticity of substitution less than unity, supported by most of the empirical evidence, the fall in the marginal productivity is larger. Thus, explaining how the output–capital ratio could decrease while the rate of return to capital is unchanged is particularly difficult.

[11] There are other ambiguities about the measurement of the returns to capital that we noted in Chapter 4. What might be thought of as the real "pure, risk free" return to capital—reflected in the real returns to short-term U.S. government bonds—has gone down, especially since the 2008 crisis; in some years it has been negative. At the same time, we'll observe later that what is often referred to as the average return to capital (including a risk premium and many elements of rents) has gone up. An important question is: How does one reconcile these two trends?

[12] See Chapter 4 for some of the supporting data/graphs and a slightly more extended discussion of some of these puzzles.

[13] As we shall note below, what really matters is the growth of the effective labor force, the sum of the labor force growth rate and the rate of labor augmenting change.

[14] It is worth noting that in standard models, the condition $r \geq g$ must be satisfied if the economy is intertemporally efficient. If Piketty's analysis were correct, where he claims that if $r \geq g$ there will be ever-increasing inequality, it would imply that, except in the limiting case where $r = g$, *any efficient economy would be characterized by ever increasing inequality.*

(iii) Standard theories suggest that if the capital–output ratio increases, it is because there has been an increase in the capital–(effective) labor ratio. An increase in the capital–(effective) labor ratio should be associated not only with a decrease in the return to capital but also with an increase in wages; but as we have noted, wages have stagnated.

(iv) More generally, virtually any production model with technological change will associate a relatively constant return to capital, an increasing capital–labor ratio and technological progress with significant increases in the average wage rate.

(v) And while most (but not all) studies of the elasticity of substitution suggest that it is less than unity, capital deepening would imply an increasing share of labor—contrary to the new stylized facts.[15]

(vi) It is hard to reconcile the increase in the capital–income ratio with national income account data on savings. Those data allow us to estimate what has been happening to the real capital stock, and that has not been increasing as rapidly as the value of wealth. There is a large unexplained component—a disparity between wealth and capital—which we call the *wealth* (or wealth-income) *residual.*

(vii) While the share of corporate profits has increased, suggesting a high rate of return to investing, the level of investment (measured by the share of investment in GDP) has remained low.

1.3 Other Stylized Facts

These are not the only stylized facts that need to be explained. There is a large literature trying to explain the *shape* of the income and wealth distribution, for example why the tails of the distribution are Pareto (fat-tailed) and why, at lower levels of income, the income distribution seems to be described by a lognormal distribution.[16]

Any micro-founded macro-theory purporting to explain the stylized macro-facts has to simultaneously explain these features of the income and wealth distributions as well as the macroeconomic trends described earlier.

1.4 What Theory Can and Cannot Tell Us

Theory, together with empirical studies, can shed some light on alternative hypotheses. We can test the *logical* consistency of the arguments. It can allow us to ascertain whether certain observed results can *plausibly* arise with "reasonable" assumptions. We can ascertain whether certain outcomes are *inevitable* (under a given set of hypotheses) or only arise

[15] See Arrow, Chenery, Minhas, and Solow (1961); Young (2013). A good review of the literature (Knoblach and Stockl, 2020) concludes "the empirical evidence increasingly favors a below-unity elasticity of substitution in the broad range of .4 to .7." It notes that earlier estimates entailing a misspecification of technological progress resulted in biasing the estimates towards unity. See Chirinko (2008) and Knoblach, Roessler, and Zwerschke (2016).

It should be noted that some authors have recently argued otherwise. See, for example, Mallick and Mohsin (2007). Those who argue that the elasticity of substitution *must* be greater than one because we have seen an increase in the share of capital even as the capital–output ratio has increased are arguing in a circular way: they ignore the measurement problems associated with measuring both capital and its share, the subject of much of the discussion below.

[16] See Aitchison and Brown, 1957; Lebergott, 1959. We will touch on these issues in the next chapter.

under certain parameter values. We can undertake coherent thought experiments to see what might happen if some policy were to change, for example a tax were to be imposed on the return to capital.

Standard growth theory has developed under a set of hypotheses about the nature of production (constant returns to scale, two factors of production—one, labor, which is exogenous, the other, capital which is endogenous). A central result has been that only if technological change is labor-augmenting will the economy converge in the long run to a steady state with a fixed capital–output ratio; and models have been formulated that show that if there is a choice of technological change (between labor and capital-augmenting technological change), then so long as the elasticity of substitution is less than unity, the economy converges to labor-augmenting technological change.[17] These are all logical propositions. We *assume* that we can ignore land, that we can describe the economy *as if* there is a single aggregate capital stock, and that the economy is competitive. We know that in some places and in some sectors land is important and markets are not competitive, and we know that as a matter of theory, the conditions under which we can aggregate the myriad forms that capital can take into a single aggregate, "*K*," are highly restrictive.[18] We know these models represent gross simplifications, but we may hope that we can ignore those details in getting an overview of the overall economy, in our analysis of macroeconomic variables like the share of labor.

If the predictions of the theory are inconsistent with what is observed, then we need to inquire which of the simplifications have to be discarded and attempt to construct a more general theory. That is what this book attempts to do, introducing land, rents, and imperfections of competition into the standard model to provide better insights into what is happening, particularly to the distribution of income and wealth.

But we know that even then the model may not be up to the task of explaining what is going on: We know too that there are other limits to the standard model. The shifts of technology with the industrial revolution and the IT revolution may, for instance, not be captured well within such a framework. Technological change can change the productivity of different factors as well as elasticities of substitution among them.[19] Moreover, the essence of capitalism has been structural change—moving from an agrarian economy, to an industrial economy, to a service and innovation economy. Standard growth models, and especially those focusing on steady states, especially can't capture the consequences of the transitions, which may play an important role in the recent growth in inequality. These are important caveats, which for the most part we put aside here.[20]

[17] See Stiglitz (2014d) and the references cited there. The paper also shows that if the elasticity of substitution is greater than unity, the steady state equilibrium is unstable. See also Acemoglu (2002, 2010).

[18] The conditions under which such aggregation would yield a production function with the properties usually assumed are restrictive. See Stiglitz (1974a) and the references cited there. Even if there is a single capital malleable capital good ex ante, once a machine has been constructed, with a given labor requirement, it can't be converted into a capital good with a different labor requirement. The dynamics of an economy with "putty clay" are markedly different from those of the standard neoclassical model, implying that that model does not probably provide a good description of short run dynamics, even if it provides insights into long run behavior. See Cass and Stiglitz (1969).

[19] See Atkinson and Stiglitz (1969) and Stiglitz and Greenwald (2014). See also Acemoglu and Restrepo (2018).

[20] In Delli Gatti, Gallegati, Greenwald, et al. (2012a, 2012b) we provide a beginning of such a theory, and in Stiglitz (2015h) I provide a discursive interpretation of the implications of the transition from a rural agrarian economy to an urban industrial economy based on joint work with Bruce Greenwald.

2 An Analytic Perspective on the Key Anomalies

In this section, we elaborate on these puzzles, providing the resolution in the next section.

2.1 The Wealth-Accumulation Residual

Here, we focus on the last of the puzzles: how we can reconcile the magnitude of the increase in wealth (capital) with national accounting data on savings. Just as a matter of national accounting,

$$\frac{d}{dt}(ln\,K) \equiv \left(\frac{dK}{dt}\right)/Y\beta, \tag{10.1}$$

where $\beta = K/Y$ is the capital–output ratio, and

$$\frac{d}{dt}\left(ln\left(\frac{K}{Y}\right)\right) \equiv \left(\frac{dK}{dt}\right)/Y\beta - g, \tag{10.2}$$

where $g = d\,ln\,Y/dt$, the rate of growth of the economy.

$\frac{\frac{dK}{dt}}{Y}$ is the ratio of net investment in the economy to GDP. While that number varies greatly, for the U.S. between 1970 and 2019 it averaged 7.7%. The wealth–income ratio varied too, from around 4 in 1970 to about 4.3 in 2010.[21] Thus, treating for the moment "K" and "W" as identical, Equation (10.1) implies that capital would grow at the rate of around 1.85% (higher in 1970 when $\frac{\frac{dK}{dt}}{Y}$ was higher and β was lower). With the average growth rate of the economy over the period 1970–2010 being 2.8%, (10.2) predicts a decline in the wealth–income ratio, at an average annual rate of somewhat more than 1%, in contrast to the observed increase. If these numbers were accurate, the observed increase in wealth–income ratios must come from somewhere else than the steady accumulation of capital goods.[22,23]

This is what we referred earlier to as the "wealth-accumulation residual" (analogous to the Solow residual—Solow had shown that capital accumulation could account for only a small fraction of the increase in productivity; the rest had to be explained *somehow*). We will argue below that there is a simple explanation of the residual—the increase in the capitalized value of rents, including land rents.

Other data series yield a similar result—that the *capital–output ratio* (measured from the NIPA accounts) *has decreased*, although at a somewhat lower rate than the above calculation would suggest. For instance, the standard Penn Tables have capital growing in constant

Similarly, the assumption of a fixed rate of growth of population is hardly plausible *for the long run*. Already, in many developed countries, the rate of growth of the population has decreased markedly—in Japan it is negative. It too should be viewed as an endogenous variable.

21 See Piketty and Zucman (2014).

22 This can be expressed in another way. The average annual increase in the value of wealth for the U.S. Piketty and Zucman (2014) estimate to be 3.0%, considerably in excess of the above estimate of the increase in the capital stock. (Piketty and Zucman (2014) suggest that savings accounts for 72% of the increase in the wealth–income ratio, somewhat greater than the rough estimates above.)

23 It could, of course, come from an increase in the price of capital goods relative to consumption goods. But in fact, the price of investment goods relative to consumption goods has fallen by 2/3 since 1970, making the puzzle all the greater. (Based on FRED data.)

dollar terms at the rate of 2.6% between 1970 and 2010,[24] suggesting a net savings rate plus capital inflows of somewhat greater than 10%; while the U.S. Bureau of Economic Analysis had GDP growing at a slightly higher rate,[25] resulting in the capital–output ratio *declining* at an annual rate over the period of 0.247%. Another data series, from the University of Groningen, shows that between 1970 and 2017, the capital stock (at constant prices) went up by a factor of 3.12, while output went up by a factor of 3.68, for a marked decline in the capital–output ratio.[26]

We can reframe Equation (10.2) to ask, what is the critical net savings rate such that there is an increase in the "real" capital–output ratio? Let g^* be the "natural" rate of growth of the economy, the sum of the rate of growth of population (work force) and the rate of labor augmenting technological progress, $\gamma = W/Y$, the wealth–income ratio, $\xi = K/W$, the ratio of the value of produced capital to wealth (which includes land), and s is the net savings rate; then

$$\frac{d}{dt}\left(ln\left(\frac{K}{Y}\right)\right) = \frac{sY}{K} - g^* = \frac{s}{\gamma\xi} - g^*, \quad (10.3)$$

so that capital deepening (defined as an increase in the capital–output ratio) occurs if and only if

$$s > g^* \gamma\xi. \quad (10.4)$$

The United States is an open economy, and there have been considerable capital inflows. These have varied considerably at a percentage of GDP. Assume capital inflows equal iY. Then

$$d\,ln\,(K/Y)\,/dt = (s+i)\,Y/K - g^* = (s+i)\,/\,\gamma\xi - g^*. \quad (10.3')$$

Thus, if it were assumed that the U.S. growth over the last 40 years was close to its natural rate, 2.8%, $\gamma = 4$, and $\xi = 1$ (land is an unimportant), $s \approx 5\%$,[27] and a reasonable value of $i \approx 0.02$, then $d\,ln(K/Y)/dt \approx -1\%$.[28] Even taking account of capital inflows, the capital–output ratio falls at the rate of about 1% per year.[29] To put it another way, assuming a more

[24] Feenstra, Inklaar, and Timmer (2015), available for download at www.ggdc.net/pwt.

[25] U.S. Bureau of Economic Analysis, Real Gross Domestic Product [GDPCA], retrieved from FRED, Federal Reserve Bank of St. Louis; https://fred.stlouisfed.org/series/GDPCA, January 6, 2020.

[26] Their estimate of the 2017 capital–output ratio is 3.17, markedly below the Piketty estimate of the wealth–income ratio, reinforcing the conclusion of the importance of rents. Source: https://fred.stlouisfed.org/series/RGDPNAUSA666NRUG and https://fred.stlouisfed.org/series/RKNANPUSA666NRUG, downloaded March 15, 2020.

[27] Piketty and Zucman (2014) present data showing that the average net national savings rate of the U.S. over the period 1970–2010 is 5.2%.

[28] This would imply that the observed rate of growth is slightly less than its natural rate, since there is negative capital deepening.

[29] We obtain similar results if we postulate particular behavioral models. Take a simplified version of the model that seems to underlay Piketty's analysis, a Kaldorian savings model (Kaldor, 1957), where capitalists save a fraction s_p of their income and workers nothing. For simplicity, assume the *after-tax* rate of return on capital is 5% and $s_p = 0.4$, consistent with the data discussed earlier. Then capital would increase at the rate of $.05 \times .4 = 0.02$. If the growth rate were greater than 2%, the private capital–output ratio would be declining.

Similar results hold if there are some savings out of wages. As Pasinetti (1962) notes, a more reasonable model divides income according to whom it accrues, that is, interest and wage income accruing to workers is treated

reasonable value of $\xi = 0.8$, s would have to be great than 6.4% in order for the capital–output ratio to increase. In short, it is hard to generate plausible increases in the *real* capital stock that could account for the observed increases in the *wealth–income ratios* in recent decades.[30]

There is still a different way of looking at the puzzle of the increase in wealth–output ratios. Over the past 60 years, a wide variety of models describing the growth of the economy have been formulated. In each, in the long run (steady state) there is a particular capital–output ratio. In each, changes in the underlying parameters (the rate of growth of the labor force, the rate of growth of labor augmenting technological progress, and savings behavior) can explain a change in the long run capital–output ratio. The question is, have there been any changes in these parameters sufficient to explain/account for changes in the capital–output ratio and the factor distribution of income of the magnitude observed?

For instance, in the Solow growth model, the long run capital–output ratio is given by s/g^*, where again g^* is the long run growth rate, equal to the rate of growth of labor supply plus labor augmenting technological change, and s is the (net national) savings rate.[31] g^* has varied, for instance increasing in the 1990s and the first part of this century, while the savings rate (in the U.S.) has decreased, which would suggest a *decrease* in the long run capital–output ratio, not an increase—let alone an increase of the magnitude asserted.[32,33]

All of these are different ways of making the same point: one cannot understand what is happening to macro-economic variables like wealth–income ratio, capital income, and capital–labor ratios if one assumes that capital and wealth are the same concepts.

2.2 Can Wages Fall, the Capital–Output Ratio Increase, and the Return to Capital Not Fall as k Increases?

The previous section argued that in none of the standard models of economic growth can one plausibly obtain an increase in the equilibrium value of the capital–output ratio of the magnitude observed *if we interpret wealth as capital.* If one interprets "W" as capital, then there has been not only an increase in the capital–output ratio, but also in the

similarly. In Chapter 13, we assume workers save for their retirement, while capitalists save to pass on money to their heirs. In later chapters, we also sketch a model in which the division of society into these different groups arises endogenously.

30 Short run fluctuations in the wealth–income ratio are dominated by capital gains and by cyclical movements in income. The marked changes in the wealth–income ratio in the U.S. before and after 2008 highlight these points.

31 In the Kaldorian model, the long run capital–output ratio is given by $s_p S_K/g^*$, where S_K is the share of capital. At least in some of the countries reporting large increases in the wealth–income ratios, those increases are out of proportion to plausible changes in s_p, S_K, or g.

32 For instance, between 1960 and 2000, the savings rate for the Unites States fell from 8% to 2% while the rate of growth increased from 2.3% to 4.1%. If these were permanent changes, then the long run capital–output ratio would have fallen by a factor of almost 8. (Observed growth rates will, of course, be higher than g^*—the sum of the rate of growth of population and labor augmenting technological progress—if there has been capital deepening, less than g^* if the reverse has been happening.) A fuller analysis would have to take into account changes in capital inflows; but these cannot account for what has been observed.

33 Matters are no better if we view the savings rate as endogenous, determined by intertemporal utility maximization. Then, the critical variable is the intertemporal discount rate, and again, it is hard to see changes in that variable of the magnitude that would account for changes in the observed capital–output ratio. And if there had been a change in intertemporal preferences, they could only impact the aggregate capital–output ratio through an observed increase in the savings rate; but, to the contrary, the aggregate savings rate has declined.

capital–labor ratio. Our ultimate objective is to understand the distribution of income, both among individuals and among factor shares. We now ask, can wages fall (as they have been doing) as the capital–labor ratio, *k*, increases, *within the standard neoclassical model*?[34]

Some have suggested that changes in technology may have advantaged some types of labor—skilled workers—and disadvantaged others.[35] While the timing of the changes in the share of labor and the decrease even in wages of relatively skilled labor in more recent years argues against skill biased technological change as the major, or at least sole, explanation of changes in distribution,[36] here we focus on the analytics.

We establish two general results: in the standard model with just capital and labor, if there has been an increase in *k*, *an appropriately weighted average wage must increase; and at least one type of labor must see an increase in their wages.* The fact that both skilled and unskilled labor seem to be confronting stagnant wages suggests that something else is going on.

2.2.1 An Appropriately Weighted Average Wage Must Increase

Assume output, Y, is a function of aggregate capital, K, and several different types of labor: $Y = F(K, L_1, L_2, \ldots)$ is constant returns to scale. In the following discussion, we will simplify and assume only two types of labor. Constant returns to scale (CRTS) implies that

$$F_{L_1} L_1 + F_{L_2} L_2 + F_K K = F,$$

so

$$F_{L_1,K} L_1 + F_{L_2,K} L_2 + F_{KK} K = 0,$$

Diminishing returns implies $F_{KK} < 0$, which is why if there is only one type of labor $F_{LK} > 0$: an increase in capital must increase the marginal productivity of labor, and the wage. Here, it is clear that the wage of one of the two types of labor could go down as K increases, that is, for some i, $F_{L_i,K} < 0$

But consider the average wage, $\overline{w}$:

$$\overline{w}(K) = (F_{L_1} L_1 + F_{L_2} L_2)/L$$

where $L = L_1 + L_2$.

$$\overline{w}'(K) = \frac{(F_{L_1,K} L_1 + F_{L_2,K} L_2)}{L} = -\frac{F_{KK} K}{L} > 0.$$

The weighted average wage must increase when capital (the capital–labor ratio) is increased.

[34] Exactly the same analysis holds with technological change, where we focus on the effective capital–labor ratio.

[35] The first to propose the idea of skill-biased technological change was Griliches (1969). See also Krusell, Ohanian, Rìos-rull, and Violante (2000), Autor (2002); and Autor, Katz, and Kearney (2008).

[36] See Card and DiNardo (2002) and Shierholz, Mishel, and Schmitt (2013) and the references cited there.

This result is strengthened if we assume that over time there is both an increase in k and in the quality of the labor force. Let ω be the proportion of high skilled workers.[37] Then

$$\frac{d\overline{w}}{dt} = \overline{w}'\frac{dK}{dt} + (F_{L_1} - F_{L_2})\frac{d\omega}{dt} > 0.$$

Data for the United States, for instance, shows otherwise: an essentially stagnating average wage rate, certainly not increasing in pace with the rate of labor augmenting technical change—quite different from what one would expect during a period which the capital–output ratio has increased—if we interpret "wealth" as capital.[38]

2.2.2 Movements in Average Productivity

Unfortunately, we typically cannot observe marginal productivities directly; but we do have data on average productivities, $\overline{P} = F(K)/L$. It should be obvious that (if nothing else changes) $\frac{d\overline{P}}{dK} = \frac{F_K}{L} > 0$, that is, average productivity should increase with capital deepening. Direct data on average productivity is consistent with this hypothesis.

Thus, if we are to believe in the competitive determination of wages, given the large disparity in the movement of, say, the average productivity of the bottom 99% and their average wage, then somehow a huge gap between movements in marginal and average productivities must have opened up—a gap that has yet to be explained.[39]

2.2.3 Technological Change and the Factor Price Frontier

The factor price frontier gives the maximum return to one factor that can be obtained, given the compensation of the other factors. Technological changes move the factor price frontier outward. It is almost thus obvious that if the return to capital remains unchanged, then at least the wage of skilled or unskilled labor (or both) must increase.

[37] The result follows immediately upon observing that we can write:

$$\overline{w} = F_{L_1}\omega + F_{L_2}(1-\omega)$$

and treating K and ω as functions of time.

[38] Shierholz and Mishel (2013) show that between 2001 and 2012, average real wages in the private sector increased at an average annual rate of 0.07%. More recent data between 2006 and 2019 suggest a slightly faster increase of 0.67% (based on U.S. Bureau of Labor Statistics, Average Hourly Earnings of All Employees: Total Private [CES0500000003], retrieved from FRED, Federal Reserve Bank of St. Louis; https://fred.stlouisfed.org/series/CES0500000003, January 5, 2020 and U.S. Bureau of Labor Statistics, Consumer Price Index for All Urban Consumers: All Items in U.S. City Average [CPIAUCSL], retrieved from FRED, Federal Reserve Bank of St. Louis; https://fred.stlouisfed.org/series/CPIAUCSL, January 5, 2020. U.S. Bureau of Labor Statistics, Consumer Price Index for All Urban Consumers: All Items in U.S. City Average [CPIAUCSL], retrieved from FRED, Federal Reserve Bank of St. Louis; https://fred.stlouisfed.org/series/CPIAUCSL, January 5, 2020.) At the same time the quality of the labor force, as measured by the average number of years of schooling, has increased, and the average productivity of the labor force has increased, at a rate far greater than the increase in wages, suggesting a decrease in wages per efficiency unit. (According to WID, the average number of years of schooling has increased from 12.7 years in 2001 to 13.3 years in 2012. https://ourworldindata.org/grapher/mean-years-of-schooling-1?tab=chart&country=USA.)

[39] That is, Giovannoni (2014) noted that between 1980 and 1990 the share of the bottom 99% of workers has gone down by over 20%, which means that the ratio of their average wage to their average productivity has gone down by the same amount. More dramatic results are observed if we look at broad categories of workers like production and non-supervisory workers, where (real) wages have stagnated over the past 40 years, while average productivity has doubled.

Note too that skill-biased technological change might explain why there might be marked disparities in movements in median wages and average productivity; but it does not explain the phenomenon just described.

It is possible to show further that if the return to capital remains unchanged, the appropriately weighted *average* wage would have to increase.[40] Again, it is not easy to reconcile observed patterns of changes in factor prices with the theory.[41]

Of course, technological change can be such as to reduce the demand for labor at a fixed capital stock—what Hicks (1932) called labor-saving innovation. The return to capital would increase. But under standard growth models, the response would be an increase in the pace of capital accumulation, partially—and in some cases more than fully—reversing the decline in wages.[42] Indeed, in those models where the long run rate of return is driven by the pure rate of time preference, in the long run, a one-time labor-saving innovation must increase the average wage and leave the interest rate unchanged.

3 The Resolution of the Seeming Paradox: There Is More to Wealth than Capital

The previous two sections argued that it is hard to reconcile the new stylized facts with virtually any form of the standard growth model *under the assumption that the increase in wealth corresponds to an increase in productive capital.* What, then, is going on?

The most plausible hypothesis is that wealth (*W*) and capital (*K*) are markedly different objects, and that wealth can be going up even as capital (as conventionally understood) is going down. If capital is not going up much (or even going down) in tandem with the increase in the effective labor supply, it would explain why the interest rate (the return to capital) has not gone down and why wages have not gone up as much as might be expected.

There are many forms of wealth that are not produced assets. Some of the increase in wealth in recent years is, for instance, associated with an increase in the value of land. The increase in the value of land does not, however, mean that there is *more* land, and that therefore the productivity of labor should go up. And an increase in the value of land does not mean that the marginal productivity of capital should decrease. Once we sever the relationship between *K* and *W*, all the paradoxes described in the previous section disappear.

[40] For simplicity, assume that only the productivity of skilled workers (denoted with subscript 1) increased. Let λ = the productivity of a skilled worker. If $\frac{dF_K}{dt} = 0$, $F_{KK}\frac{dK}{dt} + F_{1,K}\lambda L_1 \frac{d\ln(\lambda)}{dt} = 0$, and normalizing L at unity, $\frac{d\overline{w}}{dt} = (F_{1,K}\lambda L_1 + F_{2,K}\lambda L_2)\frac{dK}{dt} + (F_{1,1}\lambda L_1 + F_{2,1}L_2)\lambda L_1 \frac{d\ln(\lambda)}{dt} + F_1 L_1 \lambda \frac{d\ln(\lambda)}{dt}$. Using the properties of constant returns to scale production functions and the condition that F_K is unchanged, we can show that $\frac{d\overline{w}}{dt} = F_1 L_1 \lambda \frac{d\ln(\lambda)}{dt} > 0$.

[41] The analysis of capital-augmenting technological progress is somewhat more complicated. First, the "volume" measure of the capital stock discussed below is supposed to adjust for differences in quality of capital. Whether it does so adequately is beyond the scope of this chapter. Secondly, with capital-augmenting technological progress, there is no steady state. Short-term capital-augmenting progress, by increasing the effective capital stock, would have been expected to have an unambiguously positive effect on wages.

[42] A "labor augmenting" technological change may or may not be labor saving. If there were a single type of labor, then labor augmenting technological change increases the effective labor supply, and, everything else being the same, would reduce the effective capital–labor ratio, and hence the wage *per effective labor unit.* But each worker would represent a larger number of effective labor units, so whether the wage per worker increases or decreases would depend on the elasticity of substitution. Only if the elasticity of substitution is substantially below unity would wages fall.

3.1 Wealth as a Measure of Control over Resources

The standard wealth-income measure is constructed by adding up the money value of wealth and dividing it by the money value of income. Tracing how that ratio and the ownership of that wealth evolves over time captures something that is important in our economy and how it is changing: control over resources. But the measure of wealth so constructed is *not* a good measure of the relevant inputs into the production process—wealth could be going up, and yet any reasonable measure of inputs could be moving in the opposite direction, as we have just seen.

Moreover, changes in the wealth distribution, so measured, do not even necessarily reflect well the distribution of "well-being." For example, the bundles of goods bought by those at different income/wealth levels may differ—indeed, in some of the models below, the increase in wealth is closely linked to the increase in the price of a good which is consumed only by the rich, so that the increase in inequality in well-being is lower than the increase in money-wealth.[43] At the same time, the concentration of wealth may have much to do with the concentration of political power, and significant increases in the concentration of wealth may have a more distortionary effect on our politics and society than the raw numbers suggest. In addition, one of the concerns of those in the middle and bottom of the income distribution is lack of security; an increase in wealth enhances security, contributing enormously to an increase in well-being.

3.2 Index Number Problems and Wealth as a Measure of Productive Inputs

The concepts "wealth" and "capital" are thus different, and there are difficult measurement problems involved in each. Both are aggregates, and an aggregate constructed for one purpose may not be appropriate for another. The "volume" of capital goods resulting from saving out of national income (letting consumption goods be the numeraire) will be affected by changes in the price of capital goods relative to consumption goods. And the *effective* increase in "K" will also be affected by capital-augmenting technological change. (Indeed, the two issues are closely related; because there are constant changes in the design of capital goods, one has to establish a "hedonic" index of equivalency.) If the only capital good were computers, the increase in the "volume" of K from a given amount of savings would have increased enormously over time. In calculating aggregate "K", we have to add up capital of different types, whose relative prices and productivities are changing over time.[44]

But even abstracting from these subtleties, and assuming that there was a single capital good, K, and a single fixed factor, land, T, we can easily see that movements in K do not adequately summarize what is happening to aggregate input (relative to labor).

[43] These problems are similar to those that have arisen in the measurement of poverty, with Pogge and Reddy (2010) arguing that standard estimates do not adequately reflect differences in prices faced by the poor—a claim that Martin Ravallion (2002) has disputed, illustrating that these index number problems are both difficult and contentious.

See, in particular, the discussion of positional goods in later chapters.

[44] I am very indebted to Paul Schreyer of the OECD, who concludes his discussion of these issues (personal note to author) by observing "the distinction between the wealth and production aspects of capital is indeed important and a story about 'W' does not immediately translate into a story about 'K.'"

If land is a factor of production,[45] then wages will be related to inputs of both K and T. There are two marked changes for the standard two-factor (capital and labor) analysis. First, with two factors, capital and labor are always complements, as we have noted. With three factors, capital and labor can be substitutes (e.g., labor replacing robots). In that case, an increase in capital can lower wages. Secondly, if T is fixed and labor supply increases, then the increase in K has to be proportionally greater—possibly much greater—than the increase in labor supply to ensure that wages increase, to offset the failure of T to rise.

In short, we need to add up K and T somehow to ascertain what is happening to the aggregate "non-labor" input, which we will refer to as C. How we add the two together—and how K and T interact in the production process—matters a great deal. And what makes sense for one purpose or in the context of one model or an economy with one technology may not in another.

If T and K were additive in the production function, that is, $Y = F(K + T, L)$, then aggregate input, C, simply adds K and T up linearly.[46] In the case of France, for instance, this aggregate "C" has been going up more slowly than GDP, even though K has been going up *slightly* faster than GDP.[47] (See Figure 10.1.)[48]

On the other hand, we could have a production function of the form:

$$Y = F(C, L) \tag{10.5}$$

where now

$$C = K^{\zeta}T^{1-\zeta}.\ 0 \leq \zeta \leq 1 \tag{10.6}$$

K and T can be thought of working together to produce "capital services" via a Cobb Douglas production function. Then, since T is fixed,

$$\frac{d}{dt}(ln\ (C)) = \zeta\frac{d}{dt}(ln\ (K)). \tag{10.7}$$

Now, C is increasing if K is increasing, but whether it is increasing faster or slower than GDP depends on the relative weights assigned to the two inputs, ζ. With even a relatively high value of ζ, C/Y appears to be declining for France.

[45] As we noted earlier, although land is not very important in most industrial processes (certainly not as important as it is in agriculture), housing services represent an important component of GDP, and land is an important input into real estate. Even so, lack of availability of land has proven to be an impediment to development and industrialization in certain places, for example in India.

[46] We note that this is not a plausible production function, since if that were the case, there shouldn't be any changes in the relative price of T and K, since they are perfect substitutes.

[47] In the U.S., where K has arguably been going up more slowly than Y, it is obvious that $K + T$ must be going up more slowly than Y.

[48] Similar results hold for the two other countries for which we have been able to obtain comparable data, Australia and Korea, from the OECD. Land accounts for a large part of national wealth—at current prices, between 40% and 60%—and the wealth output ratio excluding land has been rising, while the ratio including land has been falling. I am indebted to Paul Schreyer for this data.

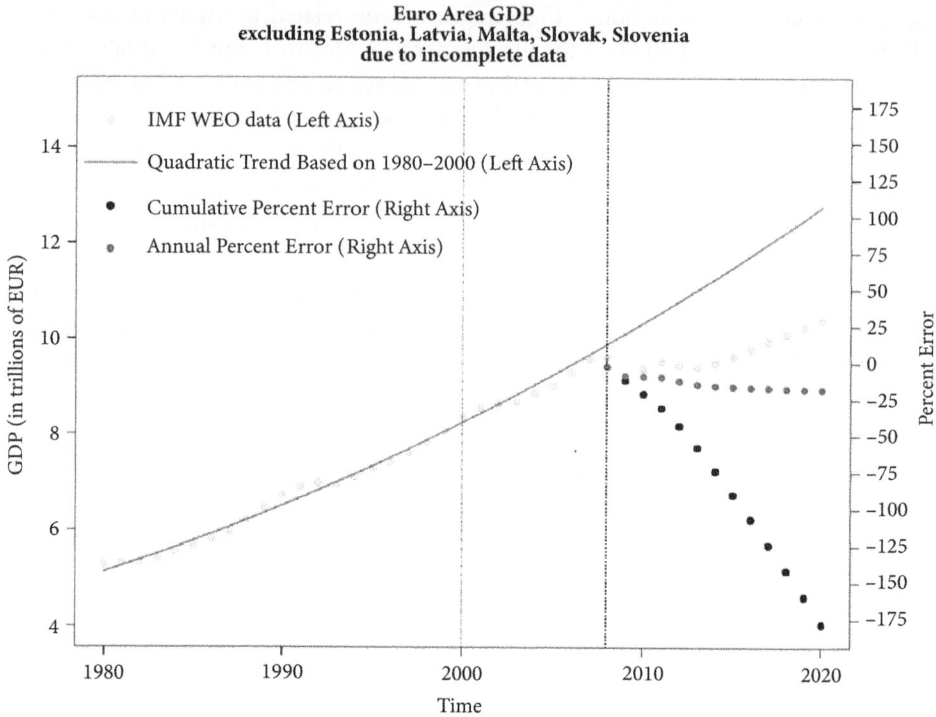

Figure 10.1 Time series of capital, output, and capital plus land (at fixed prices).
Source: OECD.

The production function defined by Equations (10.5) and (10.6) has one very interesting property. Consider the rate of change of wealth, $W = K + pT$:

$$\frac{d\,ln\,(W)}{dt} = \xi\frac{d\,ln\,(K)}{dt} + (1 - \xi)\,\frac{d\,ln\,(p)}{dt} \tag{10.8}$$

where it will be recalled

$$\xi = K/W. \tag{10.9}$$

But in a competitive economy

$$p = [(1 - \zeta)/\zeta]\;K/T, \tag{10.10}$$

so, substituting into (10.9), we obtain (as expected) $\xi \equiv \zeta$, a constant, so that

$$\frac{d\,ln\,(W)}{dt} = \frac{d\,ln\,(K)}{dt}$$

and

$$\frac{d}{dt}\,(ln\;(C)) = s/\beta \tag{10.11}$$

and

$$\frac{d}{dt}\left(ln\left(\frac{C}{Y}\right)\right) = \frac{s}{\beta} - g \tag{10.12}$$

Thus

$$\frac{dW}{dt} > 0 \text{ if } s > g^{*}\beta\zeta, \tag{10.13a}$$

while

$$\frac{d}{dt}\left(\frac{C}{Y}\right) < 0 \text{ if } s < g\beta. \tag{10.13b}$$

As we noted, for the United States, the latter inequality is clearly satisfied, while for plausibly small values of ξ, so is the former. For plausible values of the parameters, *one can simultaneously have an increasing wealth–income ratio and a decreasing capital–income ratio*. This is the situation that prevails today in many countries.

Thus, while this Cobb–Douglas model of capital services can easily explain a divergence between an appropriate measure of aggregate-capital-to-income and wealth–income ratios, with one rising and the other falling, it can't actually explain the divergence between wealth and the physical capital stock itself, K.

To explain the divergence between K and W more generally, we need to employ more general models of capital services, e.g. with an elasticity of substitution not equal to one. Depending on the elasticity of substitution between K and T, the rate of increase in W can be much larger or smaller than that in K. Assuming an elasticity of substitution between T and K that is low would imply that as K/T increases, p increases, and clearly, if it increases enough, W/Y can increase even though K/Y is decreasing.

This analysis makes clear that different indices, different measures of wealth and capital (C), can differ not just in the magnitude by which they change over time, but even in the direction of change; and an appropriate measure of aggregate input could have gone down even though the standard measure of wealth increased.

4 Parsing Out the Wealth Residual

We argued in Section 2.1 that it is hard to reconcile national savings data with the observed increase in wealth. There was what we referred to as the "wealth residual." There are, in fact, several reasons that W can increase without a concomitant increase in K, besides an increase in the value of land. There could be (a) an increase in the value of other inelastically supplied factors[49] (b) an increase in the value of intellectual property; or (c) an increase

[49] In the short run, there can be capital gains on producible assets as well, but such large increases cannot be sustained in the long run, since they will elicit a supply response. Some of the increase in "seeming" wealth that occurred in the U.S. prior to the 2008 crisis may have been attributable to capital gains on buildings (though it is difficult to parse out such capital gains from capital gains on land). But the "correction" brought down the implied price of building to or below the reproduction cost. If we take consumption goods as our numeraire, the price of capital goods could increase or decrease, though such changes typically are of a limited magnitude in the absence of technological change; with technological change, there can, of course, be significant changes in appropriately measured prices.

in what might be called "exploitation" rents. Exploitation rents, in turn, can be a result of "market power" or of political power and influence or in regulations, which give say corporations greater freedom to exploit others. Indeed, it was in the context of exploitation by corporate or other special interests of the public that the term rent-seeking first got coined. The deviations from the competitive benchmark that we are interested in here take on many forms besides that classically associated with imperfect competition in product or labor markets. Exploitation can, for instance, arise through corporations taking advantage of vulnerabilities of individuals, their lack of information or human foibles.

There is a long tradition of referring to income generated not from activities that add to the nation's economic pie as *rents*. Rent-seeking activities, directed at getting a large slice of the nation's economic pie, often diminish the size of the pie. There is an increasing consensus that much of observed inequality—especially at the top—is associated with rent-seeking, including the exercise of monopoly power.[50]

For brevity, we will refer to the *capitalized* value of rents as *rent-wealth*. Claims on future rents, including those associated with that market power, can be bought and sold, and thus, once created, are much like any other form of wealth from the perspective of the owner—but, of course, not from the perspective of society as a whole.

After discussing land rents in the next subsection, the following three sub-sections explore various forms of rent-seeking that diminish national income because of the distortions associated with rent-seeking, including the direct expenditures necessary to garner the rents. We then consider two other potential sources of an increase in rent-wealth.

4.1 Changes in Rents on Land and Other Non-produced Assets

As population increases, the scarcity value of particularly attractive sites (like land in the Riviera) becomes greater. Much of the value of land today is in urban areas; as the population in key urban centers increases,[51] the value of land in these cities increases.

There is considerable evidence that recent decades have shown "a historically unprecedented boom in global house prices.... Rising land prices explain about 80 percent of the global house price boom that has taken place since World War II."[52] The increase in land prices thus accounts for some—and in some places much—of the increase in wealth and wealth–income ratios.

[50] Piketty, Saez, and Stantcheva (2014) provide an interesting empirical test, pointing out that increases in tax rates at the very top are *not* associated with slower rates of growth. See Stiglitz (2012a, 2019a) and the references cited there for evidence that rents have grown and have become an important source of income at the very top and for a broader discussion, including the many forms that rent-seeking takes in a modern economy. (See also the discussion of monopoly rents below.)

The timing of increases in the share of capital are perhaps more consistent with those being explained by rapid changes in the degree of exploitation than by sudden changes in the effective capital–labor ratio. Typically, changing effective factor supplies occurs only slowly (except in times of war), while policy/legal changes that affect distribution can occur quickly. (Note that most changes in technology are embodied, and thus enter the economy only slowly, as new capital replaces the old; and even disembodied changes take time to diffuse through the economy.)

[51] Itself an endogenous variable. Changes in preferences (for instance for local public goods) and technology can lead to increased agglomerations, with an increase in land values. See, for instance, Arnott and Stiglitz (1979, 1981). Changes in technology and the structure of demand may have also contributed to an increase in agglomeration economies. See, for example Venables (2012).

[52] See Knoll, Schularick, and Steger (2014, 2015).

There can be an increase in the value of *any* asset fixed in supply: The wealthy strive not just to own homes in the Riviera but also Renaissance paintings. Thus, the discussion of positional goods in later chapters applies to these other assets as well as to land.

In a world with increasing population, and fixed supplies of depletable natural resources, the value of these resources can also be expected to increase.[53]

4.2 Changes in Market Power

Underlying the Solow growth model and the Stiglitz (1969b) model of equilibrium income and wealth distribution is the assumption of competition. But if monopoly power of firms increases—evidenced by higher market concentration (and other indicators of market structures associated with limited competition) in some three-fourths of American industry, higher profit rates in the corporate sector[54] at the same time that risk-adjusted rates of return have declined, and higher mark-ups—it will show up as an increase in the income of capital (an increase in the income of the owners of the firms with market power), and the present discounted value of that will show up as an increase in wealth, and in particular in what we have called rent-wealth.[55]

The magnitude of the associated increases in the capital–wealth ratio from even a small increase in market power can be significant. A permanent increase in the share of "capital"[56] by just 1% would, when capitalized at a real discount rate of 1.5%, imply an increase of the wealth–income ratio of 67%; an increase of market exploitation leading to an increase in the share of "capital" by 5% would lead to an increase in the wealth–income ratio by a factor of more than 3.[57]

There is also a large literature discussing why we might expect an increase in monopoly power in a modern economy, for example as a result of network externalities (Katz and Shapiro 1994) and the fixed costs associated with research (Dasgupta and Stiglitz, 1980a), or the transformation of the economy towards the service sectors that may have increased the importance of local monopolies (Greenwald and Kahn (2009)). (Many of these arguments, however, are inconsistent with the assumption of a constant returns to

[53] Hotelling (1931) showed that if the cost of extraction of a depletable natural resource were zero, its price would rise at the rate of interest (which in an efficient equilibrium is always greater than or equal to the rate of growth). His analysis has since been embedded within general equilibrium intertemporal models; see, for example Stiglitz (1974f, 1974g) For the most part, Hotelling's predictions have not been borne out, perhaps because markets have not anticipated well innovations, like renewable energy, and the discovery of new sources of fossil fuels, like shale gas and oil. For most recent evidence, see Anderson et al. (2018).

[54] By a variety of measures. Tobin's q, the ratio of market value to "book value," the depreciated value of the firm's assets, has also increased. Similarly, the increases in Tobin's q cannot adequately be explained by changes in taxes. As we discuss below, some of the increased returns can be attributed to a decline in workers' bargaining power. See Brun and Gonzales 2017 and Stiglitz (2019a) and the references cited there.

[55] See Stiglitz (2019a) and Phillipon (2019) and the references cited there, including Furman and Orszag (2018a, 2018b).

As we have already noted, it is hard to reconcile the large divergence between average compensation and productivity of workers *without* assuming an increase in market power of firms or a decrease of that of workers.

As de Loecker and his colleagues have shown (de Loecker et al., 2017, 2019), there has been an increase in mark-ups, consistent with the hypothesis of increased average market power.

[56] We use quotes to remind the reader that we are including in the share of capital monopoly rents.

[57] Actually, the increase in the wealth–income ratio is even greater than these calculations would suggest, since, as we note in the next paragraph, the distortion in the economy lowers the magnitude of the denominator.

scale production function.[58]) There has also been extensive innovation in the ability to create, sustain, and exploit market power. Artificial intelligence and Big Data have enabled firms to engage in price discrimination, extracting more of individuals' consumer surplus, enhancing their profits even as new distortions in the economy are created.[59]

Finally, market-power-rents can increase as a result of weaker enforcement of competition laws, or a failure of competition laws to keep pace with changes in the economy, including innovations by the private sector in their ability to create and maintain market power (e.g., through the design of anti-competitive contracts). The nexus between politics and economics is a theme running throughout this book: economic power gets translated into political power, which in turn shapes the economic rules of the game, including those related to ensuring competition the markets.

4.2.1 Exploitation of Workers

If firms have market power over their workers (monopsony power), then that too will give rise to rents, which will be capitalized in wealth. Again, this is a transfer of resources from workers to corporations—a non-zero sum transfer because of the resulting distortion in the economy. There is ample evidence that changes in labor law and its implementation, globalization, and the weakening of unions have all contributed to the weakening of workers' bargaining position.[60,61]

4.2.2 Abuses of Corporate Governance: Simultaneous Exploitation of Consumers and Shareholders

Within corporations, CEOs, and senior management have extensive market power vis-à-vis other corporate stakeholders.[62] Especially in the U.S., CEOs have shown an ability and willingness to take greater advantage of deficiencies in corporate governance laws to appropriate for themselves more of the value of corporations. This *should* lead to a decrease in the market value of firms relative to what it otherwise would be (with the value of what management has appropriated for itself not reflected in standard accounts of a nation's wealth). There is, however, considerable evidence that because of the lack of transparency of the manner in which they appropriate these returns, markets typically do not fully reflect the dilution in shareholder value (e.g., associated with stock options), or at least do not do so quickly.[63] Moreover, much of the compensation takes the form simply of a transfer of ownership claims on the returns to the firm, so that the value of the firm itself is not reduced. Note further that if this rent appropriation by managers is labeled as "compensation," then

[58] Moreover, the hypothesis of the increased role of fixed costs is inconsistent with the observed decline in the investment GDP ratio—if that were the only important change in the economy.

[59] Stiglitz (1977a) observed that the main distortions associated with monopoly arose from their use of costly and imperfect mechanisms of discrimination in order to extract more consumer surplus. Standard efficiency requires all individuals to face the same prices. For a more extensive discussion of these issues, see Stiglitz (2019a).

[60] Indeed, Stelzner (2015) argues that much of the increase in inequality can simply be explained by changes in labor laws and the way they are enforced. For a more extensive discussion of the role of globalization in weakening workers' bargaining position, see Stiglitz (2017b, 2019).

[61] Moreover, economists have gradually come to recognize the extent to which imperfect mobility of workers (both across space and across sectors) gives rise to monopsony power, even where there are multiple employers within a community. Non-compete clauses and collusion among employers have also played a role in weakening workers' bargaining power. See Krueger and Ashenfelter (2018), Starr (2019), and Harris and Block (2021), including the introductory essay Stiglitz (2021).

[62] Again there is a large literature explaining the sources of this market power and providing evidence of its extent. For a simple theoretical model, see Edlin and Stiglitz (1995).

[63] See, for example, Stiglitz (2003a).

the wage share is increased. This is consistent with the results noted earlier suggesting a marked decline in the wage share if the upper one percent of "wage earners" are excluded.

4.3 Increases in Exploitation Rents

While the rents generated by the exploitation of market power are the most obvious example of exploitation rents, there have been considerable advances in the ability of corporations to exploit consumers. Tobacco, food, and pharmaceutical companies have, for instance, developed more addictive products—all the while denying their addictiveness—that enrich corporate coffers while imposing considerable harms on the consumer-victims. Developments in marketing, AI, and behavioral economics have enriched the tools available to corporations to take advantage of consumers. Behavioral economics has exposed a large number of "irrationalities" in individuals' behavior, instances for example in which individuals systematically overestimate some risk and underestimate others. Corporations have now begun systematically to exploit such irrationalities to increase their profits. Imperfect, and especially asymmetric information, gives rise not just to imperfections of competition, but to an enhanced ability of corporations to exploit consumers and to engage in discriminatory pricing.

4.3.1 Exploitation Rents in the Financial Sector

The financial sector exemplifies many aspects of what has occurred. Elsewhere, we and others (Galbraith (2012)) have, for instance, focused on the role of the financial sector in increasing inequality. The financial sector grew before the 2008 crisis from 2% to 8% of GDP. The sector's profits grew to absorbing 40% of all corporate profits. There are reasons to believe that much of this might be associated with exploitation rents (including those associated with market manipulation, insider trading, predatory lending,[64] and anti-competitive practices arising from their control of the payments mechanisms, giving rise as well to abusive practices in credit and debit cards, etc.) and capitalized in the value of wealth. Though there was some increase in the amount of wealth to be managed, the increase in the wealth–income ratio was not so substantial to account for the increase in the share of the financial sector; nor can that sector's remuneration be accounted for by the improvements in their management of the funds, and even less so, by any improvement in overall economic performance.[65] These increased profits were due not just to market power in the conventional sense, but their ability to exploit the public sector (discussed further below), asymmetries of information and vulnerable consumers. If, for instance, the financial sector improved its ability to exploit the poor through predatory and discriminatory lending practices and abusive credit card practices (and the resulting profits were not bid away because of imperfections of competition), then there would be an increase in standard metrics of wealth. But, of course, the increased wealth of the banks comes at the expense of the decreased well-being of those they exploit.

[64] See, for instance, Valenti and Schultz (2016) for a discussion of the impact of predatory lending practices.

[65] Indeed, the extensive research on efficient markets has questioned the value-added of the wealth management services of the financial sector: ordinary investors would have done as well or better simply by buying indexed funds.

4.4 Political Power, Inequality, and Rents

There is an exercise of political power in each of the areas of exploitation we have described. Regulations (anti-trust laws) might have prevented or at least circumscribed the exercise of market power, the exploitation of information asymmetries, or taking advantage of consumer ignorance or human foibles. Changes in regulations—deregulation, the weakening of anti-trust laws, granting more power to CEOs, changing legal frameworks to the disadvantage of workers—all have led to more "profits," to more corporate rents, and thus to increased rent-wealth.

In addition, of course, traditional corporate rent-seeking takes the form of corporate subsidies and tax preferences (sometimes grouped together as corporate welfare and amounting to tens of billions of dollars in the U.S. every year). It includes instances where the government pays more for what it buys or sells government assets (like oil leases) at below fair-market prices.

4.4.1 Successful Corporate Rent-Seeking: Transfers from the Public Sector to the Private

There are more subtle forms of "exploitation." Government allows too-big-to-fail banks. The value of those banks is higher than they otherwise would be, *because of government risk-absorption.* But the contingent-liability of the government is not capitalized, and because this liability doesn't show up in the national balance sheet, it appears as if the wealth of the economy has increased. But with appropriate metrics (where the decreased wealth of tax-paying citizens, as a result of the increase in the expected present discounted value of the higher taxes that they will have to pay to bail out the banks), just the opposite would have happened: we would have recognized that because of the distortions associated with too-big-to-fail banks, the productive capacity of the economy has been diminished; that the bail-outs are Pareto-inefficient, and that the wealth of the economy has been diminished.[66]

4.5 Information and Knowledge Rents

Earlier, we explained how firms can generate rents by creating and exploiting information asy mmetries. In a modern economy, there are many other ways by which knowledge and information differentials can give rise to rents. Insider trading and market manipulation (e.g., in the LIBOR and Foreign Exchange markets) are the most obvious examples. There are reasons to believe that much of the profits generated by high frequency trading is a sophisticated form of front-running, taking advantage of differential access to information. (Stiglitz, 2014c, and the references cited there). These information rents are often primarily distributive, increasing incomes of some individuals at the expense of others. In many cases, they lead to Pareto inefficiency.[67] High-frequency trading may result in diminished incentives to gather information which may lead to a more efficient economy. Because the

[66] This discussion raises similar issues as those the Commission on the Measurement of Economic Performance and Social Progress discussed in moving economic activities from the public to the private sector. (See Stiglitz, Segal, and Ananda, 2010.)

[67] See, e.g. Stiglitz (1975a).

incentives to engage in *productive* information gathering are reduced, the overall efficiency with which capital is allocated is reduced. Thus, net national income is reduced, even if the "wealth" is increased, because of the capitalized value of the increased rents (profits) of the high frequency trading firms.[68]

4.5.1 Intellectual Property

There is another, closely related and increasingly important category of assets, intellectual property. Here, there have been three factors contributing to the increased market value of intellectual property: there may be more knowledge; the value of any "piece" of knowledge increases as the size of the economy (other inputs) increase; and more of knowledge has been privately appropriated, and hence shows up in wealth data.[69] Knowledge that is freely available increases output, but doesn't show up in anybody's balance sheet and therefore would not normally be reflected in the national accounts as wealth, except to the extent that the knowledge increases the return to and therefore the value of capital goods. (With competition, the additional returns may even be bid away.) But changes in the intellectual property regime (what Boyle, 2003, refers to as the enclosure of the knowledge commons) enables corporations to better appropriate for themselves the value of knowledge, and in some cases, even appropriating the value of preexisting knowledge; this increases *their* wealth, at the expense of the wealth and well-being of others. But our system of accounts only records the increases in the former, not the decreases in the latter.[70] Because more restrictive intellectual property rights result in a less efficient use of knowledge, the long-term productive capacity of the economy is diminished—even as measured wealth increases.[71]

4.6 Changes in Discount Rates and Risk Management

There is a further reason for an increase in the value of wealth without a concomitant increase in the *physical* productive capital stock: A decrease in the interest rate (normally associated with capital deepening) should lead to an increase in the value of any asset with a fixed stream of returns.[72]

[68] Stiglitz, 2014b.

[69] See, for instance, Henry and Stiglitz (2010) and the works cited there.

[70] Moreover, the charges imposed for the use of knowledge lower GDP, and thus a change in the intellectual property regime extending rights to enclose the knowledge commons can both increase the measured value of wealth and lower the value of GDP: the wealth–income ratio will accordingly rise.

The privatization of public knowledge (such as the patent granted for basmati rice, eventually overturned) or the granting of "excessive" intellectual property (patents that are excessively broad, such as covering all four-wheeled self-propelled vehicles, or copyrights that are excessively long, such as extending 70 years beyond the death of the writer) can be viewed as a special case of exploitation rents discussed above.

There is one more form of rents associated with intellectual property that has almost surely grown over time: that generated by brand names, especially the identification of a product with say a sports star.

[71] Note, however, that in those situations where intellectual property rents increase as a result of increased investments in research, the increased measure wealth does correspond to an increase in the productive capacities of the economy. In this sense, an increase in intellectual property rents differs from the exploitation and political rents discussed in earlier subsections, where increased wealth of some comes at the expense of the well-being of others.

[72] A change in interest rates may also induce large changes in the relative price of different goods and in the price of capital goods relative to consumption. This was the essential issue in the Cambridge–Cambridge controversy some half a century ago, where it was observed that the value of capital and the choice of technique may be non-monotonic in the interest rate. See Sraffa (1960) and Stiglitz (1974a). Thus, in models with the production

In the private sector, the relevant discount rate is the after-tax return, so that there are two offsetting effects on the value of wealth of an increase in a tax on capital. In the limiting case where the tax rate on capital and the tax rate on profits are the same and before-tax returns are unaffected by the tax changes, the value of an asset yielding a before-tax return of R every year would be unchanged, that is:

$$V = \frac{(1-t)R}{(1-t)r} = R/r.$$

The value of assets facing an average tax rate greater than that relevant for the discount rate will go down; and conversely if the average tax rate is smaller. Thus, if corporations are able to take advantage of extensive loopholes to lower their average tax rate below the marginal tax rate facing investors, which appears to be the case,[73] the value of wealth will increase. But, of course, the increase in measured wealth as a result of the opening up of loopholes is nothing more than a transfer from the rest of society to the owners of the corporations, with the subtraction of others' wealth (say, the increase in the present discounted value of taxes that they will have to pay or the present discounted value of the value of reduced benefits they receive not recorded in the national wealth accounts).

Changes in risk management and the ability to absorb risk can also have effects on the wealth–income ratio.[74] At the same mean and variance of the return to an asset, such changes lead to an increase in the certainty equivalent return, and therefore of the market value. If the improved risk management/ability to absorb risk leads to a lower effective discount rate, the increase in market value can be even larger.

There can also be countervailing general equilibrium effects. Individuals may reallocate more of their wealth to assets with a higher risk and higher mean return, that is, assets which (on average) have a *lower* capital–income ratio.

5 Why Rent Wealth Is Different from Capital

While an increase in capital increases productivity, with consequent beneficial effects on wages, an increase in rent-wealth can have just the opposite effect. There are two critical aspects of an increase in rent-wealth: (a) a redistribution from the rest of the economy to the successful rent-seekers; and (b) possibly a change in the economy's overall productivity (well-being). An increase in land rents (with land fixed in supply) represents an example of a pure redistribution: the increase returns to the owners of land comes at the expense

of commodities by means of commodities, the economy at a low interest rate and a high interest rate may look the same (the same technologies are employed), while at an intermediate interest rate a different technology is employed. Even if the value of wealth has changed in going from the low to the high interest rate, there has not been capital deepening, at least in any meaningful *real* sense.

[73] While the nominal corporate income tax rate was 35%, the average effective corporate tax rate before the 2017 tax bill was passed was 27%, and a large fraction of multinationals paid a far smaller fraction of their global profits in taxes.

[74] While financial markets often claim that their innovations have enhanced the ability to manage risk, the extent to which this is the case remains debated. Some of the financial innovations may have actually increased risk (Stiglitz, 2010b). Some of the financial innovations may have led to the creation of pseudo-wealth—wealth based simply on differences in perceptions in beliefs (Guzman and Stiglitz, 2014); while other innovations, like improvements in the ability to sell short, may reduce market values (Scheinkman and Xiong, 2003). Chapter 15 shows how changes in financial market regulations can affect the value of assets.

of the owners of other factors of production. But most of the forms of rent described in the previous section represented *distortions* to the economy—inefficiencies that lowered productivity, even if they resulted in an increase in rents, and therefore of "wealth." Further, in Chapters 14 and 16, we will show that an increase in rent-wealth serves as a substitute in individuals' portfolios for capital accumulation, so that an increase in rent-wealth may naturally lead to a decrease in K (and thus in the real productivity of the economy).

Relatedly, in most of the instances of an increase in rent-wealth described below, the increased returns are *attributed* to the firm, and are added to the return to capital. But they are not really a return to the firm's investment in capital goods, but rather a return, say, to its market power, including its investments in creating barriers to entry. The result is that the value of the firm will exceed the value of its invested capital. The ratio of the market value of capital goods to its replacement value is often referred to as Tobin's q,[75] and is typically measured by taking the ratio of the market value of a company to (the depreciated value of its) capital stock. In a competitive economy in equilibrium, with no rents and monopoly profits, $q = 1$. If $q > 1$, it pays firms to invest; the greater q, the greater the incentive to invest. But in a world with market power (and/or other forms of exploitation), q, as conventionally measured, will be greater than 1. But that says nothing about the *marginal* return to investment, that is, how the value of the firm will be affected by an increase in the capital stock. For a firm with market power, further investment, increasing output, will lower prices, and though sales will increase, overall profits may decrease. Thus, an increase in q will not necessarily be associated with increased investment.

In situations where an apparent increase in wealth is associated with decreased well-being, a change in the flow of resources that accrues to "capital" (but might better be ascribed to, say, the owners of monopoly power) gets capitalized in wealth, but the present discounted value of the decreased flow to the rest of the economy is not reflected in our standard wealth metrics. *We don't, for instance, value the change in the stream of tax revenues to the government or the expenditures by the government or the reduced wages accruing to workers as a result of increased market and political exploitation.* Thus, some of the increase in wealth as conventionally measured has as much to do with our accounting frameworks as with anything else.

6 Concluding Remarks

This chapter began by describing a new set of stylized facts—different from those which were the focus of discussion in the middle of the twentieth century. We suggested that, no matter how good the standard model in any of its variants might be in explaining short-term movements in the economy, it could not explain these long-term trends. That theory argues that the increase in wealth and the wealth–income ratio is related to the slow and steady setting aside of income for the creation of more round-about means of production (to use Böhm-Bawerk's term), to enhance the capital deepening of the economy and thus the productivity of labor. But that theory can only explain a fraction of the increase in wealth or in the wealth–income ratio. This unexplained component of the

[75] See Tobin and Brainard (1977), though the idea has earlier antecedents. See, in particular, Kaldor (1966).

increase in wealth per capita (or wealth relative to income) we referred to as the *wealth* (or wealth-income) *residual.*

We have argued that there is a simple explanation of the increase in the wealth–income ratio: an increase in the value of rents, a concept that plays little or no role in modern neoclassical theory. We have, in turn, provided several complementary explanations of this increase in rents (and the associated increase in wealth, that is, the capitalized value of these rents), most importantly, land rents, exploitation rents, and intellectual property rents. Once we recognize the presence of rents, it becomes clear that *wealth* and *capital* are two distinct concepts, which unfortunately are often conflated. In particular, it is wrong in general to use "wealth" as the measure of capital as an input into a production function; while there are complex issues concerning the aggregation of, say, land and physical capital, linear aggregation, using relative prices as weights, is not an appropriate aggregator.[76] Later chapters will explore land rents in greater detail. Here, we have noted that the increase in exploitation rents, including those associated with the exercise of market power, actually diminishes economic productivity: the wealth–income ratio increases both because the numerator is larger and because the denominator is smaller.

Once one recognizes the growing importance of rents and the distinction between wealth and capital, many of the new stylized facts and the anomalies with which we began this chapter are easily explained: wages can be stagnating, or even declining, because the capital–output ratio is declining[77] or because workers' bargaining power is decreasing (the deviation between their marginal product and their compensation is increasing), or for both reasons. The return to capital may not be declining because the capital–output ratio is declining and/or because what we are measuring is not the *marginal return to capital* but an average return, which includes monopoly and other exploitation rents, which have been increasing. The share of wages may be declining because rents are seizing a larger share of national income and/or because the capital–income ratio is declining and the elasticity of substitution is less than unity (consistent with most of the empirical evidence).

6.1 Two Alternative Perspectives: Marx vs. Smith

Neoclassical theory sees differences in income as related to differences in the social contributions of individuals and the assets that they control make. And hence, the neoclassical theory of wealth inequality focuses simply on the transmission of ownership of assets across generations and the determinants of relative returns to different factors, based on the relative supplies of different factors, technology, and preferences. But changes in these standard variables not only provide an inadequate explanation of the growth of the wealth–income ratio; they also fail to provide a convincing explanation of changes in the wealth and income distribution. We have explained that even if technical change were skilled biased, changes in wealth–income ratio should be associated with an increase in the *average* wage.

[76] And accordingly, studies that look at what happens to relative shares as the wealth/income ratio changes to make inferences about the elasticity of substitution are misguided.

[77] As we have emphasized, once one moves away from a two-factor production function to a production function with three or more factors (capital, labor, and land), then capital and labor may not be complementary, so that an increase in the stock of capital does not necessarily increase wages. Still, for much of the discussion we shall assume that capital and labor are complementary. Chapters 17 and 18 discuss more explicitly the possibility that capital and labor are substitutes (e.g., labor-replacing robots).

Nor can other changes in technology, robotization and a change in the substitutability of capital and labor, provide a convincing explanation of the new stylized facts.

This chapter has shown that one cannot understand the stylized facts, including growing inequality, without a greater understanding of rents, what gives rise to them, and how they evolve over time. Standard neoclassical theory simply is not up to the task. We've described the many different forms of rents. We use the term *exploitation rents* in a more general way—beyond just the obvious one of monopoly and political power. It includes discrimination, taking advantage of imperfections in corporate governance laws and of asymmetries in bargaining power between workers and firms, and a variety of forms of exploitation by the financial sector, including market manipulation, insider trading, predatory lending, and abusive credit card practices. We have explained why there are reasons to believe that, at least in some important sectors, there has been an increase in market power, and in the ability and willingness to engage in exploitation. Indeed, some have suggested that a defining characteristic of at least American-style capitalism in the twenty-first century is the growth of a new form of corporate control, different from the managerial capitalism that defined the mid twentieth century, dominated by rent extraction (engineered via the financial sector) out of the corporate sector.[78] A casual look at those who are among the wealthiest (on say the Forbes 100 list) confirms that rents have played an important role in wealth inequality.

Some, perhaps much, of what has occurred is related to the political process. Political decisions affect not just the redistribution that occurs at any moment through the tax system, but also the before-tax-and-transfer distribution of income. Some of the rent-seeking within the political process is well-known—encapsulated in the term "corporate welfare."[79] Equally important, the scope for rent-seeking within the private sector is affected by the legal framework (anti-trust, corporate governance, labor, and bankruptcy laws and how they are enforced). Most importantly, the increase in inequality in income and wealth, at least in some countries, has translated into increased inequality in political power, reinforcing already existing economic inequalities.

A second explanation of the "wealth" residual—a second important form of rents—and the one upon which we focus in Chapter 13 is the increase in land rents. There is an easy way of addressing the inequality that arises as a result of capital gains on land: to tax capital gains, especially those associated with increases in land values. This, of course, has long been part of the progressive tax agenda—advocated in the nineteenth century by Henry George (1879). In later chapters, we show that such taxes, by encouraging individuals to put their savings into more productive forms, can, under some circumstances, not only lead to lower inequality, but also to higher incomes because they lead to higher levels of investment. We will also show how financial policy (e.g., excessive expansion of credit) can give rise to increases in values of land, enhancing wealth inequality.

[78] See, for instance, Mason (2014, 2015). He points out a striking number of ways in which this new form of capitalism is different from either twentieth-century managerial capitalism or the capitalism reflected in the neoclassical model, and describes the financial system more as a mechanism for distributing cash out of the corporate sector than of raising funds for the corporate sector, the traditional "intermediation" role described in standard textbooks.

[79] Defense contractors and pharmaceutical industries benefitting from being overpaid; mining, oil, and gas benefitting from receiving natural resources at below market prices; the agricultural sector from direct subsidies; steel and a host of others from trade protection, preferences hidden within the tax system, and a myriad of other forms of corporate welfare.

So too, regulatory and tax policies can curb inequalities that arise out of a variety of forms of exploitation.

But before turning to these issues, we need to explore more fully the determinants of the equilibrium distribution of income and wealth among individuals, the subject of the next several chapters.

Appendix A1 Missing *Real* Capital: The Destruction of human and other forms of capital in recessions[80]

In the chapter, we discussed the problem of the wealth residual—the disparity between wealth and measured capital. There, we focused on long run secular trends. There is a related set of problems in the measurement of wealth and capital over the business cycle: observed changes in the capital stock as conventionally measured leave unexplained much of the changes in the output in the short run as well as much of the longer-term adverse effects, especially of deep downturns. Those wedded to neoclassical theory are forced to interpret these movements as unexplained negative level and trend "productivity shocks," as if the economy experienced episodes of collective amnesia, in which knowledge of how to transform inputs into output seemingly disappears.

In this appendix, we take a closer look at what happens to wealth (capital) in a recession. As we shall see, many of the effects have strong distributional implications.

Recessions destroy capital and impede its accumulation. We can trace out the consequences for plant and equipment, as revealed by investment data.[81] (Even then, we may not do so fully: we don't adequately monitor maintenance expenditures.)[82] But we don't adequately trace out what is happening to other forms of capital, and in particular, human capital. There are several important effects.

The first has to do with education, and here, the effects would appear to be ambiguous: Increased competition for jobs lead to greater incentives for formal education while reduced employment opportunities reduces incentives but also reduces opportunity costs. Moreover, with a prolonged downturn, many can't afford to stay in school. Many worry that if they have to borrow to go to school, if they can't get a job, the debt burden will be enormous.[83]

[80] Excerpted from Stiglitz (2016b), with slight modifications. These ideas have been subsequently elaborated on in Stiglitz, Fitoussi, and Durand (2018, 2019b).

[81] We could also measure the increased *market* value of capital (including the increased value of equities) but (for reasons explained in greater length in Stiglitz, 2016a), that would not be a good measure of the change in wealth. The economic downturn worsens the bargaining position of workers, lowering their real wage (increasing the ability of firms to "exploit" workers). The resulting increase in the value of *measured* capital is offset by a corresponding decrease in the present discounted value of wages (human capital), but the latter is typically not recorded. (Shapiro-Stiglitz (1984) provides a formal model showing how higher unemployment lowers the real wage.)

[82] Thus, traditional analyses describing the decline in productivity in recessions as a result of labor hoarding may not be quite correct: some of the labor was spent in maintaining plant and equipment—doing maintenance that had been deferred during the preceding boom. The resulting increase in the "true" value of capital is not captured in GDP statistics. By the same token, the markedly different patterns of productivity in recent downturns—reflecting ruthless management that quickly trims any unneeded labor—may not be as positive as the numbers on their face suggest: they do not capture the impacts on the maintenance of either human or physical capital stocks.

[83] These effects are obviously stronger in countries like the U.S., where children and their parents have to pay the bulk of costs, where tuition is high and there is greater reliance on loan programs where repayments are not

In practice, it appears that in normal downturns, the first effect (increased demand for education as a result of a lowered opportunity cost) dominates, but in more extended downturns such as the Great Recession of 2008, at least in the U.S., over time the second effect may have become more important, especially for advanced (graduate) education.[84]

Other Hidden Losses

In addition to the unmeasured change in societal wealth from these changes in investments in formal education, there are several other effects.

First, there is a reduction in the quality of education as government cuts back on funding, not only for tertiary education, but also for primary and secondary.

Secondly, other government cutbacks affect both learning and future productivity: Reduced access to health care and nutrition on the part of the poor can have life-long effects, including in the ability of children to learn; and these effects become especially important as the number of children living in poverty increase with an economic downturn.

Perhaps the most adverse effects are related to a decrease in job experience (learning on the job)—long recognized as a major part of human capital. There are especially adverse effects on young people who can't get jobs: in a period in which they should be accumulating skills and work experience, their skills atrophy. Several studies[85] have documented that those entering the labor market at a time when unemployment is high experience significantly diminished lifetime incomes. And when these adverse effects are aggregated over the large fractions of young people who face extended unemployment (youth unemployment in Europe as a whole was persistently almost 25% in the years following the onset of the 2008 Recession, and in the countries most afflicted by the euro crisis, over 50%) one obtains significant losses in human capital.

But this is not the only loss: Those in their 50s and early 60s are forced to retire early. They had productive skills (human capital) which, in more normal times, would have yielded returns for years to come. As a result of the crisis, all of this human capital is written down to zero—or would be if we had a good set of accounts.[86]

contingent on the borrower's income. In the case of the U.S., further discouragement results from a bankruptcy law that says that student debt cannot be discharged even in bankruptcy. (See Stiglitz, 2012a.) Still a further adverse effect arises from the particular way that government support is provided: by states, who have balanced budget frameworks, and who, accordingly, typically cut back support for higher education in a recession, forcing much higher tuitions. This was especially true in the 2008 recession, because of its severity and duration. For a discussion of the impacts on tuition and student indebtedness, see Stiglitz (2013c).

[84] Note that in any case, the market for education is distorted: there may either be too much or too little investment in education. Because of signaling/screening effects as well as societal benefits arising from a more educated populace, social returns to education may be greater or less than the private returns.

[85] Khan, 2010; Brunner and Kuhn, 2010; Taylor, 2013.

[86] There is another effect in those countries where there has been a cutback in pensions and/or where individuals rely on their own savings: many who would have retired are forced to keep working (often at low skilled jobs), as their retirement income becomes greatly diminished (especially with quantitative easing, those who had put their money into "safe" assets—government bonds—saw their incomes eviscerated). Our standard metrics do not do a good job in capturing the adverse welfare effects of the recession on these individuals.

There are a further set of complex adverse welfare effects, with potentially important implications for the stock of human capital. As the elderly who otherwise would have retired seek jobs, there are search externalities on other job-seekers. (See Greenwald and Stiglitz, 1988d.)

When there is a deep and prolonged downturn, these effects on human capital can be very significant; and it would seem that the adverse effects far outweigh the positive effects that might arise from more extended enrollment in school. This is certainly consistent with negative hysteresis effects associated with extended periods of unemployment, and with econometric studies suggesting that prolonged downturns lead to a decrease in potential growth.[87] These unobserved wealth effects help explain why effects of downturns persist.[88]

A2 Estimating the Size of the Missing Capital—the Magnitude of Capital Destruction in a Recession

We can get a rough order-of-magnitude *estimate* of the magnitude of the capital destruction in a recession by estimating the difference between where the economy would have been, in the absence of the recession, and how it actually evolved. See Figures 10.A1 and 10.A2, which show that six years after the crisis GDP in the United States was some 15% below what it would have been in the absence of crisis—in Europe some 17% lower. The total *cost* of the crisis in terms of lost output is truly enormous—depending on the discount rate, possibly well in excess of $100 trillion. (A 15% permanent loss in a $15 trillion economy growing at 2% with a discount rate of 3%—twice the real return on government T-bills—amounts to a loss of $22.5 trillion.)[89]

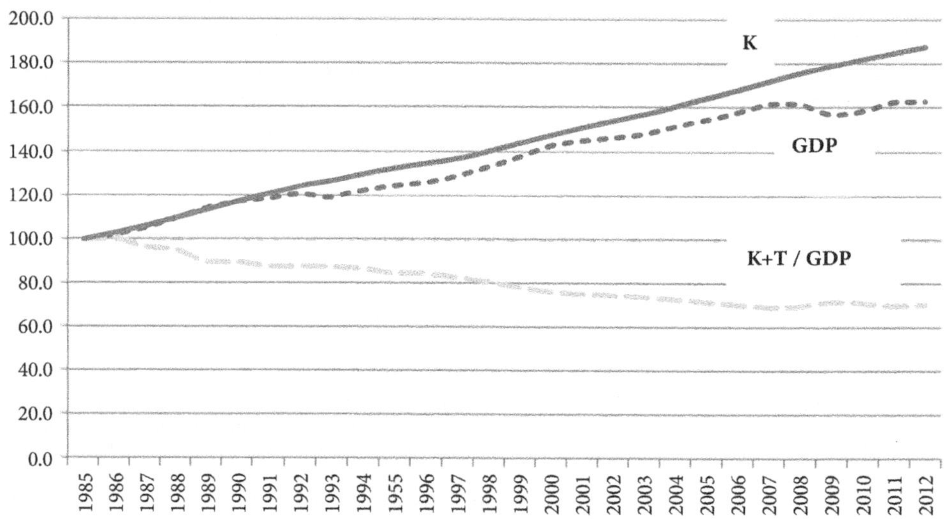

Figure 10.A1 USA growth below trend.

[87] Reifschneider, Wascher, and Wilcox, 2013.

[88] There is a literature suggesting that the economy's dynamics exhibit near unit roots. Thus, once the economy gets displaced to a lower GDP, if there is any return to where it was before, it is very slow. See Campbell and Mankiw (1987).

[89] As Stiglitz, Sen, and Fitoussi (2010) point out, GDP does not provide a good measure of the loss of well-being: it does not, for instance, include any valuation of the increased insecurity that the downturn has brought. Cutbacks in public programs are valued at the reduction in the value of the inputs, not the value to citizens of the services provided.

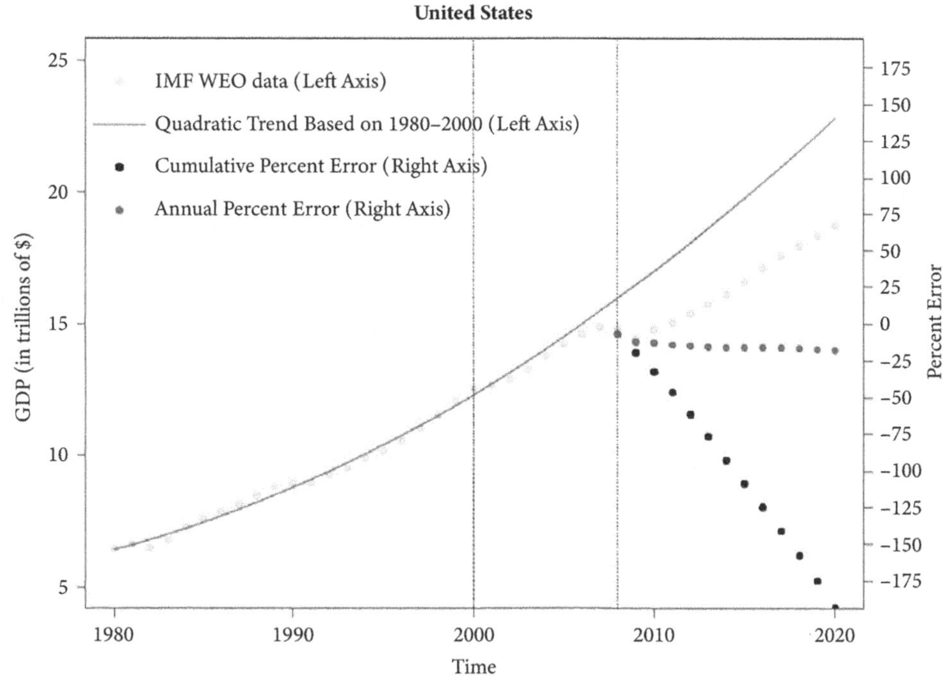

Figure 10.A2 Europe growth below trend.

We can in principle measure the delta in "normal" capital *K* (the difference between what *K*, as conventionally measured, would have been but for the recession and actual *K*); that is, we can estimate, the consequences of reduced investment to the capital stock. Similarly, we can estimate the delta in normal human capital ("education") as conventionally measured, that is again, the difference between what the level of human capital, as conventionally measured, would have been, in the absence of the recession, and its actual level.[90] We can then estimate the predicted effect of these changes on output. (For instance, if lower investment has decreased the capital stock from what would normally have been the case, in the absence of the recession, by some 1%, then if the share of capital is 0.25, standard analyses would suggest that output would be some 0.25% lower than it would have been on the normal path.)

The difference between the decline in GDP (relative to the normal path) that can thus be accounted for and the actual decline in output (relative to the normal path) is the result of missing "dark matter"—analogous to Solow's residual. The present discounted value of the difference is the value of the *missing capital.*

Back-of-the-envelope calculations suggest that the magnitude of this missing capital is enormous. *True* GDP is the sum of consumption plus *true* investment plus government expenditures (plus, in an open economy, net exports). *True* investment is the difference in *true* wealth. We have been ignoring the effect of the downturn on *hidden wealth*, and thus

[90] As we have noted above, there may be significant measurement errors in both variables, for example because of hard-to-observe changes in maintenance.

on *true investment.* The decline in GDP in the Great Recession was, accordingly, much greater than the standard numbers suggest.

There is an important agenda going forward of trying to parse out this missing capital.[91] Our earlier discussion helps identify some of this missing capital, but there are other capital losses that are harder to measure. Bankruptcy results in a loss of organizational capital, including the tacit knowledge that resides within the bounds of a firm. In recent years, there has been increasing recognition of the role of social capital for the well-functioning of the economy, and there is some direct evidence of the erosion of social capital as a result of long-lasting deep downturns. Trust is too important, and the behavior of the banks in the years before the crisis undoubtedly led to an erosion of trust.

Even if we can't precisely parse out the components of this missing capital, the loss is real and needs to be taken into account. It provides a further rationale for governments to take strong countercyclical measures. And changes in this missing capital and its composition can play an important role in changes in inequality, both in the immediate aftermath of a crisis, and in the long run.

[91] The problem is analogous to that posed by Solow in his classic 1957 paper. He showed that one could explain only about an eighth of the growth of output per capita by an increase in the capital–labor ratio. The rest was called "the residual," and considerable efforts were made in subsequent years to explain the residual, for example the movement of labor from less productive sectors (agriculture) to more productive sectors, the shortening of hours of work, and, most importantly, technological change.

11

Generalizing the Basic Model

Inequalities in Equilibrium Wealth among Individuals with Heterogeneous Abilities and General Intertemporal Preferences

1 Introduction

This is the first of seven chapters extending my earlier work and that with David Bevan to explain the equilibrium wealth and income distribution.[1] We strengthen and deepen our original results, showing the far more extensive conditions under which wealth inequality can persist and analyzing more precisely the determinants of its magnitude.

This chapter is conducted within the neoclassical framework of Stiglitz (1969b), where output depends on capital and labor through a constant return to scale production function and factor prices are determined in competitive markets, and there is no uncertainty. In this framework, an increase in the capital–output ratio necessarily is associated with a decrease in the return to capital in the long run. Our models explicitly require micro- and macro-consistency: increased accumulation leads to lower returns, until the condition that the rate of return is greater than the rate of growth is no longer satisfied.

We begin by reviewing our earlier generalization of the standard Solow model in which all individuals (dynastic families) save at the same rate and have the same wages, but in which they begin with different endowments of (per capita) capital. Nonetheless, the long run equilibrium entails complete equality.

The main objective of this chapter is to test the robustness of this result. Chapter 8 noted that if different families have different abilities (wages) or savings rates, there will not be wealth convergence. We described the resulting equilibrium wealth distributions. Here, we provide a fuller characterization of the equilibrium wealth distributions, showing, for instance, that, even without such wage inequality, with more general savings functions, *there may exist an infinity of equilibrium income and wealth distributions.*

On the other hand, we show that the results of Chapter 8 continue to hold (not surprisingly) if instead of assuming that the savings rate is simply given, we assume that it is derived as a result of intertemporal utility maximizing dynasties.

The chapter is divided into two parts (besides this introduction and a conclusion). In Section 2 we set up the basic model, a variant of the Solow model, in which we identify the conditions under which there can be sustained inequality. In Section 3 we show that analogous results hold with dynastic families maximizing intertemporal utility.

In the following chapters, we explore several important extensions to this analysis: introducing randomness in returns, more elaborate models of savings (for instance, where some individuals are simply life-cycle savers and others are dynastic savers, focusing on future

[1] Revised version of part of a paper originally distributed as "New theoretical perspectives on the distribution of income and wealth among individuals: Part II. Equilibrium Wealth Distributions," NBER working paper no. 21190, May 2015.

The Origins of Inequality, and Policies to Contain It. Joseph E. Stiglitz, Oxford University Press. © Joseph E. Stiglitz (2025).
DOI: 10.1093/oso/9780198799580.003.0012

generations) and various sources of rents, and analyzing the implications of endogenous innovation.

2 Basic Model: Generalizing Solow to Heterogeneous Dynastic Families

The basic model is a variant of the Solow growth model, where we think of the economy as consisting of dynastic families, leaving equal bequests among their children.[2] For simplicity, we initially ignore technical change. The models in this chapter assume competition. Our focus is analyzing the role of intertemporal/intergenerational transfer of assets in determining the long-run wealth distribution.

The evolution of wealth per capita for the *i*th family is described by the differential equation:

$$\frac{d}{dt}(\ln k_i) = \frac{s_i y_i}{k_i} - n_i, \tag{11.1}$$

where y_i is the *i*th family's income (per capita)

$$y_i = w_i + r_i k_i, \tag{11.2}$$

where w_i is the *i*th family's wage, r_i is its return on capital, and k_i is its capital (per capita). We assume that there is perfect inheritance of both labor market and capital market productivity. n_i is the *i*th family's rate of reproduction.

An essential part of the analysis is macro- and micro-consistency: The aggregate capital stock, K, is the sum of the capital owned by each family, K_i,

$$K = \sum K_i . \tag{11.3}$$

So too that aggregate labor force L is the sum of the labor supplied by each family, N_i. The aggregate capital–labor ratio, k, then is just $k = \frac{K}{L}$. We assume a neoclassical production function where output per worker is $f(k)$. The aggregate k (the aggregate capital–labor ratio[3]) determines the average return on capital, r, and wages:

$$r_i = \rho_i f'(k) \tag{11.4a}$$

$$w_i = v_i\,(f(k) - f'(k)k), \tag{11.4b}$$

where ρ_i is the *relative* return to the *i*th family's investment (some families are able to obtain a higher return from their investments than others, with $f'(k)$ being the *average* marginal return across all families)[4] and where v_i is the *relative* return to the *i*th family's labor (some

[2] This section repeats the analysis of Chapter 8, which provides the basic framework for this and following chapters.

[3] When, later, we introduce labor augmenting technological change, k will stand for the capital–effective labor ratio.

[4] That is, in the obvious notation, $E(\rho) = 1, E(v) = 1$, Since the wealth distribution is itself endogenous and may vary over time, this formulation is not quite precise. More generally, the average value of the marginal productivity of capital is $\frac{\sum \rho_i K_i}{K}$, which obviously depends on the wealth distribution.

families receive higher wages—payments per unit labor—than others, with $f(k) - f'(k)k$ being the *average* wage across all families).

The evolution of each family's wealth per capita, $k_i = \frac{K_i}{L_i}$ is simply given by

$$\frac{d\ln k_i}{dt} = s\frac{w_i}{k_i} + \left(sr - n_j\right), \tag{11.5}$$

using the fact that

$$\frac{d\ln K_i}{dt} = s_i\left(w_i + rk_i\right)/k_i,$$

where n_j is the rate of growth of the jth family ("dynasty") and where for simplicity we assume the ith family saves a fraction s_i out of income (more generally, their savings function might, for instance, differentiate among the sources of income).[5]

2.1 Identical Savings and Heterogeneous Abilities

Assume, as in Solow and Chapter 8, that a *constant* fraction of income, s, is saved, and w, s, r, and n are the same for all families. Then

$$\frac{d}{dt}\left(\ln k_i\right) - \frac{d}{dt}\left(\ln k_j\right) = sw\left(\frac{1}{k_i} - \frac{1}{k_j}\right), \tag{11.6}$$

There is convergence of the wealth distribution: regardless of initial distribution of wealth, there will eventually be equality of wealth. This result holds no matter what the value of s and how it is determined. The speed of convergence is proportional to sw.[6]

If s, r, and n are the same, but w_i differs across families, then in steady state the wealth distribution corresponds precisely to the wage distribution. Asymptotically,

$$\frac{k_i^*}{k_j^*} = \frac{w_i}{w_j}. \tag{11.7}$$

If wages are log-normally distributed, so will wealth.[7]

Formally, the discussion above focuses on the transfer of financial assets, but an important aspect of income and wealth inequality is the provision of human capital (education), which is partially provided privately and partly publicly. At a basic level, the models presented here can easily be adapted to accommodate human capital. Inequality in resources

[5] This could either be because of institutional factors or because, as in the models of later chapters, there are separate stochastic processes governing the evolution of wages and capital.

[6] In the long run equilibrium, $sf(k) = nk$, or $sf(k)k = swk + sr = n$, so sr is always less than n, the rate of growth. While Piketty, in his analysis, emphasized the relationship between the rate of return and the rate of growth (with capital growing faster than income if the rate of return exceeded the rate of growth), it is clear that what matters is not the rate of return, r, but sr; and we have shown that, in the long run, in the standard Solow growth model, sr *must* be less than the rate of growth, not greater, as he hypothesized. Chapter 14 analyzes a two-class (capitalists and workers) model.

[7] In Stiglitz (1969a) we describe an array of other possibilities, including divergent paths. Here, we focus on what we consider to be the central cases. See also the discussion below.

gets translated into inequality in wages, and through that can be perpetuated. On the other hand, we can think of publicly provided education as a public transfer of wealth from one generation to the next. The effect on the equilibrium distribution of wealth will depend on how progressive the taxes are that finance it and how regressive[8] the human capital allocations are.[9]

2.2 Generalized Savings Functions: Multiplicity of Steady State Distributions of Income

Critical to the convergence result was the assumption that the savings rate, the rate of return to capital, and the reproduction rate do not depend on income (i.e., if individuals all receive the same wage, on k_i). Indeed, if that is the case, even with identical individuals (families), there can exist multiple steady states. Thus, let savings be just a function of y, and y is just a function of k, $f(k)$, so we write $s(f(k))$; there can be multiple values of k for which $s(f(k))f(k) = n(k)k$.[10] Figure 11.1 shows a case where the savings function is such that the savings rate is low for low incomes, and then the marginal savings rate increases. As Panel B of Figure 11.1 illustrates, there can be a low-level equilibrium k^*, where the savings rate is low, and another stable one k^{**} where the savings rate is high. Similar results hold if, above a certain level of income, the rate of reproduction (rate of growth of labor supply) falls.[11]

But under these circumstances, not only can the economy be trapped in a low equilibrium, so can families, and there can exist a multiplicity of equilibrium distributions of wealth and income, even for a given level of aggregate income.

To see the conditions under which these results obtain, assume the economy is in steady state, with a given r. Assume first that income is equally distributed. Then a steady state requires

$$s(y(k))\,y(k) = nk, \tag{11.8}$$

and it follows directly that there can exist multiple steady states if the savings rate increases sufficiently with income:[12]

[8] That is, the extent to which the children of the rich and better educated themselves get a better education. In the U.S.'s largely locally managed and financed education system, with the country's high level of economic segregation, the rich, living in rich ghettos, get transferred to them more human capital than the poor, living in their poor ghettos.

[9] Detailed modeling is, however, quite complex, for unlike financial capital, human capital is subject to diminishing returns and interacts strongly with the intergenerational transmission of abilities, described below. Moreover, the public and private provision of human capital may be largely substitutes, with the allocation of intergenerational transfers between human and financial capital the result of a maximization problem, but one in which norms and sociological concerns enter in important ways, with a great deal of weight being placed on children's ability to get a good job, since that plays a more important role in the determination of an individual's place in society than just income alone.

[10] More generally, we can let the savings rate depend on the interest rate, which depends on k, the wage rate, which too depends on k, and income from capital. Thus, the steady state savings rate depends on k, $s(k)$, and there can be multiple values of k for which $s(k)f(k) = n(k)k$.

[11] In the more general case, there can exist more than two equalitarian steady state equilibria.

[12] Straightforward logarithmic differentiation of sy/k generates $S_K(1+\eta) - 1$. sy/k is monotonical in k if condition (b) is not satisfied, so there can be at most one value of k for which $sy/k = n$.

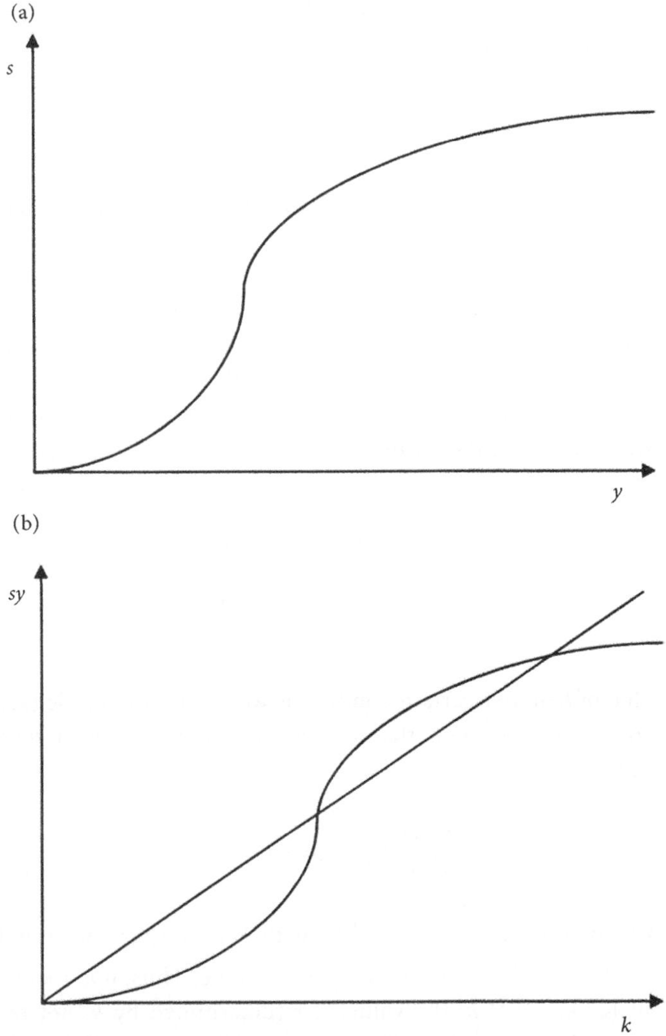

Figure 11.1 If the savings rate or the reproduction rate are a function of k (of the level of income or of any other variable affected by the capital labor ratio) there may exist multiple steady states. Panel A: Savings rate is low for low income but high for high incomes. Panel B: Multiple equalitarian steady states.

For the existence of multiple equalitarian steady state equilibria, we require

(a) $s(0)\,r(0) < n$ *and* $\lim \frac{y(k)}{k} < n$ *as* $k \to \infty < n$

or

(b) $Z \equiv S_K(1+\eta) - 1$ changes sign as k increases at least once.

where S_K is the share of capital and $\eta \equiv \frac{d\,ln\,s}{d\,ln\,y}$, the income elasticity of the savings *rate.* A sufficient condition for (b) is that the elasticity of substitution of the production function be less than unity and $\eta \geq 0$, for then for small k, $Z < 0$ while for large k, $Z \geq 0$.

Note that in the savings function of Panel A of Figure 11.1, η is low for low and high values of y, but high for intermediate values of y. That means that even for a unitary elasticity of substitution, Z will be negative for low and high values of k, but will be positive for intermediate values of k, provided only that

$$\max \eta\,(y(k)) > \frac{S_L(k)}{S_K(k)},$$

where in the obvious notation, $S_L = 1 - S_K$, and we have noted that the shares depend on the capital–labor ratio k.

More interesting though than the existence of multiple equalitarian steady states is the existence of *multiple equilibrium wealth distributions*. There is, in fact, an infinity of possible equilibria distributions of wealth. Assume, for instance, that there are only two groups in the population, with a proportion of the population in the high wealth group being denoted by γ. The savings rate of any family depends on k, the aggregate capital–labor ratio, which determines the wage and interest rate, and the family's own k_i. Then $\{k_H, k_L, k, \gamma\}$ constitute an equilibrium if

$$d\ln k_i/dt = ws\,(k,k_i)\,/k_i + rs\,(k,k_i) - n = 0 \tag{11.6$'$}$$

$$k = \gamma k_H + (1-\gamma)\,k_L. \tag{11.9}$$

Thus, for any value of k, under certain conditions we can find multiple (stable) values of k_i satisfying (11.6′). To see this, note that for fixed k, w and r are given. $s(k,k_i) \equiv s(w(k) + r(k)k_i) = s(y_i)$, and

$$\frac{d\ln(sy_i)}{d\ln(k_i)} = (\eta + 1)\,S_K^i. \tag{11.10}$$

This expression is identical to that for $\frac{d\ln(s)}{d\ln(y)}$, with S_K, the share of capital, replaced by $S_K^i \equiv \frac{rk_i}{y_i}$, the share of capital in the ith individual's income. Thus, if $k = k_i$, the expressions are identical, but for $k_i > (<)\ k$, the value of r (determined by k, not by k_i) is higher (lower). Thus, given the savings function of Figure 11.1, there will in general be multiple value of k_i, for any value of k, for which (11.6′) is satisfied. In particular, this will be true if

$$Z_i \equiv [\eta\,(y_i) + 1]\,S_K^i - 1 \tag{11.11}$$

changes sign at least once, for some value of k_i, given $r(k)$ and $w(k)$.

Our earlier discussion made clear that that is likely to be the case. Thus, for small k_i, Z_i will be negative, while if max $\eta\,(y_i)$ is large enough, for intermediate values of k_i, Z_i will be positive.

Figure 11.2 shows the implications for the case where $s\,(0)\,r(k) < n$, which will hold for large enough k. Then if the savings rate increases enough for large y_i, then there will exist a two-class equilibrium, with $k_L = 0$, and

$$w(k^*)\,s\left(w(k^*) + r(k^*)\frac{k^*}{\gamma}\right) = \left((n + s\left(w(k^*) - r(k^*)\frac{k^*}{\gamma}\right)\right)r(k^*)\,k^*. \tag{11.12}$$

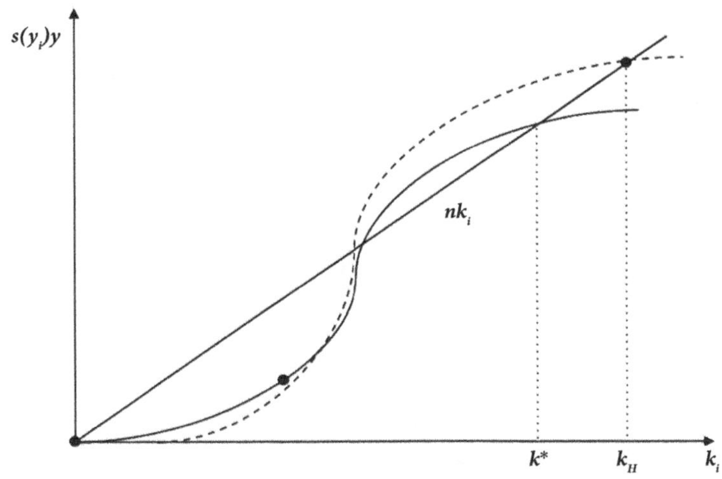

Figure 11.2 At any value of k, there may be multiple values of k_i which are sustainable. The solid curve gives saving, $s(y(k))\,y(k)$ as a function of k, showing the (multiple) steady states where $sy = nk$. The dashed curve takes k as given, and shows *individual* savings, $s(y_i)\,y_i$ as a function of k_i. The dashed curve lies above (below) the solid curve as $k_i > (<)k$. This implies that $k_H > k^*$. The proportion of the population that hold wealth is given by $\gamma = \frac{k^*}{k_H}$.

For any k^*, we solve (11.12) uniquely for the equilibrium value of γ.[13] As Figure 11.3 illustrates, an increase in k^* leads to a decrease in k_H and an increase in γ, in the fraction of the population in the economy that are capitalists.[14]

2.2.1 An Example

Assume that $s(y) = 0$ for $y < \hat{y}$ and $s = s_c$ for $y > \hat{y}$. Then for k such that $w(k) < \hat{y}$, that is, $k < w^{-1}(\hat{y})$, $k_L = 0$, and $k_H = \frac{k}{\gamma}$. From (11.6″) below, $\gamma = \frac{[n-r]k}{s_c w}$. For there to be an equilibrium wealth distribution, we require that $0 < \gamma < 1$, i.e. $\hat{k} < k < \hat{\hat{k}}$ where $\hat{k} \equiv f'^{-1}\left(\frac{n}{s_c}\right)$ and $\hat{\hat{k}} \equiv min\left\{w^{-1}(\hat{y}), k_0\right\}$ where k_0 is the solution to $s_c f(k_0) = nk_0$. It is easy to show that so long as $\hat{y}$ is large enough (so that those who only earn wages don't save) but not too large (so that the capitalists do save), there can exist an equilibrium wage distribution.

2.3 Wealth Begets Wealth

We have assumed so far that all individuals receive the same return on capital. But it is possible that the return that the ith family receives on its investment is

[13] So long as $s' \geq 0$, since for given k, there is then a unique solution to (11.12).

[14] An increase in k increases or decreases y_i at any value of k_i as $(-k + k_i)f''$ >or< 0. Thus, for large k_i, y_i is decreased, so $s(y_i)y_i$ is shifted down, as depicted in Figure 11.3, provided only that $\eta + 1 > 0$. The figure also makes clear that for a high enough value of k, there may not exist any value of k satisfying (11.6′).

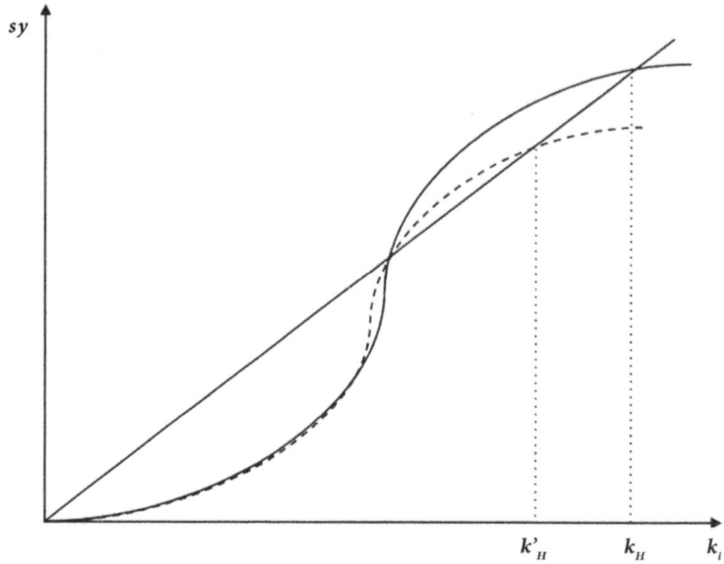

Figure 11.3 An increase in the capital labor ratio will change the values of the sustainable k_i. An increase in k lowers the return to capital, so a large k lowers income and total savings, resulting in a lower value of k_H. (Corresponding to any sustainable set of $\{k_i\}$ there is a distribution of the population among the groups which supports the hypothesized value of k.).

an increasing function of its wealth and the aggregate capital–labor ratio of the economy[15,16]:

$$r_i = r(k_i, k). \tag{11.13}$$

Returns to investment are related to the investments one makes in acquiring information, and the optimal investment in information is a function of the size of one's wealth (simply because information is a fixed cost).[17]

Assume all families have the same wage, savings and reproduction rates. Again, let the proportion of the population in the high wealth group be denoted by γ. Then $\{k_H, k_L, k, \gamma\}$ constitute an equilibrium if

[15] It is not inevitable that there be such a relationship: Though information is a fixed cost, one can imagine a financial market which amortized these fixed costs uniformly, in which case those with large amounts of wealth would obtain the same returns as those with lesser amounts of wealth (putting aside the slight differences that might arise from non-linear transactions costs). But, again, because of imperfections of information, there are costly agency problems, and those with enough wealth may be able to mitigate these agency problems by running their own investment fund. As we comment later, the markets for information may be an important driver in current inequalities.

[16] Some of the higher average returns of the wealthier may be a result of their being better able to bear risk. This is consistent with the hypothesis of decreasing relative risk aversion and is supported by evidence on portfolio composition, which shows that richer individuals hold a larger portion of their portfolios in equity.

[17] It might seem that portfolio managers could, in principle, avail themselves of the same advantages of scale and market it to ordinary customers. But ordinary individuals cannot screen between fund managers that have been lucky and those that have been skilled, and portfolio managers know this.

$$\frac{d}{dt} ln\,(k_i) = \frac{ws}{k_i} + sr\,(k_i, k) - n = 0, \tag{11.6''}$$

and (11.9) continues to hold. Thus, for any value of k, we can again find multiple (stable) values of k_i satisfying (11.6″), provided only that

$$sy_i\,(\eta + S_K^i)\,(1 + \zeta) - nk_i$$

changes sign for different values of k_i, where $\zeta = \frac{d\,ln\,(r)}{d\,ln\,(k_i)}$ is the elasticity of returns to capital with the size of capital and S_K^i is the share of capital income for the *i*th individual. In particular, this must be true at the values of k_i for which (11.6″) holds, which means that

$$sy\,[\eta + S_K)\,(1 + \zeta) - 1]$$

must change signs for different values of k_i, for given k. If we assume that ζ is low (or zero) for low values of k_i (there is a minimal threshold below which the amount of capital has little effect on the return), and asymptotically, ζ is also low (or even negative) (there are managerial problems in managing large amounts of wealth, and limits in the ability to exploit arbitrage opportunities), then there will be multiple values of k_i for which (11.6″) is satisfied, provided only that there is a value of k_i for which ζ is large enough, that is, $> (1/\eta + S_K) - 1$.

There will then exist at least two (stable) values of k_i for which (11.6″) holds, and there is then a value of γ which generates the assumed value of k through (11.9).

Since there exists a (two) income wealth distribution for every value of k (within a range), there exists an infinite number of equilibria wealth distributions. (And in general, there can exist, for any k, more than two values of k_i for any value of k satisfying (11.6″) implying an even larger range of equilibrium wealth distributions.)

A recent study based on Norwegian data confirms a key implication of this model: Individuals earn markedly different returns on their wealth, these differences cannot be explained by portfolio allocations between safe and risky assets and are positively correlated with wealth and are persistent over time.[18]

2.4 An Alternative Formulation

There is an alternative discrete time formulation that simply captures the results of the previous subsections. Assume a member of generation t takes the wealth that he has inherited, k_{it}, adds to it his income, $y_t \equiv w_{it} + r_t k_{it}$, and decides how much to consume and how much to give as a bequest to his heirs, $B_{it} = B\,(k_{it}\,(1 + r_t) + w_{it})$. The bequest has to be divided among his $1 + n$ heirs, so

[18] See Fagereng et al., 2019. The latter properties could be the result of (as here) higher wealth *inducing* higher returns, or because (as possibly in the models of the next chapter) some families have a higher ability in earning returns, and this generates the higher wealth.

$$k_{it+1} = \frac{B\left(k_{it}\left(1+r_t\right)+w_{it}\right)}{(1+n)}.$$

Normally, we would expect B to be S-shaped; with bequests being small when $k_{it}\left(1+r_t\right)+w_{it}$ is small, and as $k_{it}\left(1+r_t\right)+w_{it}$ gets large, B' asymptotes to a value $b^* < 1$. It is clear that at any given k^*, there is an equilibrium wealth distribution, with some individuals having $k_i^* = 0$ (no inherited wealth) while others have $k_i^* = k_H > 0$, with $k^* = \gamma k_H$, where as before, γ is the fraction of the population in the upper income state, and k_H is the solution to

$$k_H = \frac{B\left(k_H\left(1+f'(k^*)\right)+\left(f(k^*)-k^*f'(k^*)\right)\right)}{(1+n)}.$$

For any k^*, there is a corresponding value of k_H, and an associate value of $\gamma = \frac{k^*}{k_H}$. In short, there are an infinite number of equilibrium wealth distributions.

2.5 Heterogeneous Savings and Abilities

Here, we investigate what happens if those with greater ability (productivity) save a higher proportion of their income, consistent with the model of the previous sections, where the savings rate increases with income.[19] We again consider a two-class model. w is the wage per efficiency unit, and group i has productivity v_i. Group i has a higher productivity than group j, and a higher savings rate: $s_i > s_j$.

Since group i will own a disproportionate share of the capital, if the share of capital is high, the aggregate savings rate will be high. This means that there can be multiple steady states, if the elasticity of substitution is greater than one. To see this, we write the aggregate dynamics as

$$\frac{d}{dt}ln(k) = s_w\left(\frac{w}{k}\right)+s_c r-n = s_w\left(\frac{y}{k}\right)+\left(s_c-s_w\right)r-n, \tag{11.14}$$

where s_c is the weighted average savings rate out of capital and s_w is the average savings rate of workers:

$$s_c = s_1\pi+s_2\left(1-\pi\right)$$
$$s_w = s_1\alpha+s_2\left(1-\alpha\right),$$

where π is the fraction of capital owned by group 1, α the share of labor income going to group 1. α depends just on the relative productivities and the relative size of the two groups. On the other hand, s_c depends on π. In steady state, π is constant, and that means k_i must increase as the same rate as k_j. It is straightforward to show that (recalling that v_i is the *relative* productivity of the ith family's labor):

[19] This section is adapted from Stiglitz (1966). In an unpublished comment on an earlier version of that paper, James Meade explored a similar model with a Cobb–Douglas production function, and I am greatly indebted to him for discussions after presenting some of these results in a seminar in Cambridge in the spring of 1966.

$$\begin{aligned}\tfrac{d}{dt}(\ln k_i) - \tfrac{d}{dt}(\ln k_j) &= w\left(\tfrac{s_i v_i}{k_i} - \tfrac{s_j v_j}{k_j}\right) + r(s_i - s_j)\\ &= \left(\tfrac{k_i^*}{k_i}(n - s_i r) - \tfrac{k_j^*}{k_j}(n - s_j r)\right) + r(s_i - s_j)\\ &= \left(\tfrac{k_i^*}{k_i} - \tfrac{k_j^*}{k_j}\right)(n - s_i r)\Big) + \left(r\left(1 - \tfrac{k_j^*}{k_j}\right)(s_i - s_j)\right)\end{aligned} \tag{11.6'''}$$

(assuming that $n - s_i r > 0$), which is, of course, the same as the earlier expression when $s_i = s_j$. But when $s_i > s_j$, it is possible that if $k_j > k_j^*$, $\frac{k_i}{k_i^*} > \frac{k_j}{k_j^*}$, and for k_i to be still growing faster than k_j.

We can show that $\frac{d}{dt}(\ln k_i) - \frac{d}{dt}(\ln k_j)$ is greater than, equal to, or less than zero as $\left(\frac{rk}{w}\right)(s_i - s_j)$ is greater than, equal to or less than $\alpha\left(\frac{s_i}{\pi}\right) - (1 - \alpha)\left(\frac{s_j}{1-\pi}\right)$.

This in turn means that in steady state[20]

$$\left(\frac{rk}{w}\right)(s_i - s_j) = -\left\{\alpha\left(\frac{s_i}{\pi}\right) - (1 - \alpha)\left(\frac{s_j}{1 - \pi}\right)\right\}. \tag{11.15}$$

If individuals had the same productivities and same savings rate, then wealth would be distributed according to the size of the group—that is, there is no wealth inequality. If a group has a higher savings rate, then it will have a higher share of wealth, as expected. And if the groups have the same savings rates, but different productivities, then wealth per capita will have the same distribution as productivities, as we have noted earlier. Thus, (11.15) encapsulates all of the earlier results.

It also follows from (11.15) that π is an increasing (decreasing) function of k as the relative share of capital increases with k, that is, as the elasticity of substitution is greater (less) than unity. Take, for simplicity, the case with unity elasticity of substitution. Then (11.15) can be solved for π^*, thus determining s_c. From (11.14) there is then a unique value of steady state k. But since $\frac{ds_c}{dk} > 0$ if the elasticity of substitution is greater than unity, the derivative of $s_w\left(\frac{y}{k}\right) + (s_c - s_w)r$ with respect to k may be positive for some values of k, if s_1 is sufficiently greater than s_2, and then there may be multiple steady states, that is, multiple values of $\{k, \pi\}$ satisfying (11.14) and (11.15): there are multiple values of wealth inequality consistent with the underlying parameters. Higher values of k support greater wealth inequality.[21]

2.5.1 Taxation

In Stiglitz (1969b), it was shown that the speed of convergence increased with a proportional income tax with the proceeds redistributed uniformly.[22] It is straightforward to show that a progressive income tax of the same total revenue increases the speed of convergence even more.[23]

[20] The analysis can easily be extended to the case where group i not only has, say, a higher savings rate and a higher labor productivity, but also a higher return on capital. It should be obvious that that results in that group having a still higher share of capital.

[21] Though this result is thus consistent with two of the stylized facts noted earlier (an increase in the wealth–income ratio and an increase in wealth inequality), it hypothesizes an elasticity of substitution greater than unity, which the weight of empirical evidence argues against.

[22] In the next chapter, we will consider a stochastic equilibrium, where the centripetal force—called the drift—is a key variable in determining the level of inequality. An income tax increases the magnitude of the drift.

[23] By the same token, a profits tax at the rate τ increases the rate of convergence by an amount equal to $sr\tau\left(\frac{1}{k_i} - \frac{1}{k_j}\right)$, that is, by exactly the same amount that an income tax at the rate τ. But obviously, the income tax raises far more revenues: for a tax of the same revenue, a profits tax is far more equalizing than an income tax.

3 Intertemporal Utility-Maximizing Dynastic Households

In spite of the development of behavioral economics which has established that individuals make their decisions based on simple behavioral rules such as those employed in the previous section, it has become fashionable, especially in macroeconomics, to derive the savings rate as a solution to an intertemporal maximization problem. The standard model makes strong and unrealistic assumptions, such as that utility functions are time separable with a constant discount rate, and that families maximize a dynastic utility function. (Later chapters consider life-cycle savers.) It is straightforward to show that if everyone is identical (also a standard assumption), the savings rate is simply a function of k. But that assumption won't do here, where we wish to consider whether, in fact, there will be an equilibrium wealth distribution or whether there will be convergence to equality. The full solution to the rational expectations dynamic equilibrium (where individuals correctly anticipate the dynamic path of wages and interest rates) is, in general, complicated, for the distribution of wealth will affect the aggregate savings rate, and that in turn determines the evolution of w and r over time. It is implausible that, under general conditions, individuals would be able to calculate this rational-expectations dynamic equilibrium. And even less likely once we take into account the randomness of technological change, heterogeneity of preferences, and the uncertainty about changes in the rules of the game set by political processes. Indeed, even in the best of circumstances, the conditions under which the economy converges to a rational expectations equilibrium are highly restrictive.

If, somehow, the economy did converge to a steady state, then, of course, the perfect foresight-rational expectations equilibrium *going forward* might make sense. For simplicity, ignoring uncertainty (as in the rest of this and the next chapter), we can establish the result that *the only long run steady state equilibrium entails wealth convergence.*[24] With the standard assumptions on intertemporal utility described earlier, with everyone having the same utility functions, and for simplicity assuming that there is no technological change, if there exists a steady state,

$$f(k^*) = \delta - n, \tag{11.16}$$

where δ is the pure rate of time preference. But with w and r fixed, every family is solving the same intertemporal maximization problem, and each therefore converges to the same steady state, with $k_i = k^*$.

3.1 Non-separable Utility Functions

It is more plausible that preferences are not time-separable. For simplicity, assume that they take the recursive form (Koopmans, 1960):

$$W_{t+1} = W(C_{t+1}, W_t). \tag{11.17}$$

[24] The shape of observed savings functions has to take into account uncertainty and the role of precautionary savings. Boundary values—limits on the amount that individuals can borrow—play an important role. See the discussion in later chapters.

The key property of (11.17) is that in steady state, the marginal rate of substitution between consumption in time $t+1$ and earlier periods ($\mathbf{C}_t$) is a function of C^* denoted by $\delta(C^*)$. Thus, in steady state

$$\delta(C^*) = \delta\left[f(k^*) - nk^*\right] = f'(k^*) - n. \tag{11.18}$$

It should be apparent that if $\delta' < 0$ for some values of C, then there can exist multiple long run steady state equilibria. But it is still the case that if there is a steady state, then all families will face the same return to capital, and they all therefore must converge to the same C^*; that is, the same value of k_i^*.

The possibility of multiple solutions to (11.18), that is, multiple steady state values of δ, is important, however, in the context of models later in this book, where the equilibrium wealth distribution depends on the centripetal forces at play—that is, on the equilibrium value of δ. There may be multiple equilibrium wealth distributions, even in an economy with a given set of preferences and technological parameters.

3.2 Differences in Preferences

If families differ in their intertemporal preferences, however, there won't be convergence. Assume there are two groups of families, one with a higher pure rate of time preference than the other. There can then exist a steady state equilibrium where the interest rate is determined by the family with low time preference, δ_L, and the high time preference family is at the boundary value where they consume all of their income (assuming that families cannot borrow, or that there is a finite borrowing limit). The equilibrium is then described by

$$f'(k^*) = \delta_L - n \tag{11.19}$$

$$k_H = 0 \tag{11.20}$$

$$k^* = \gamma k_L, \tag{11.21}$$

where, in the obvious notation k_L and k_H are the per capita wealth of the high and low time preference families (rather than, as earlier, they represented the per capita wealth of the low and high wealth dynasties), respectively: *the distribution of wealth is determined by the distribution of time preference.* In the long run, the family with the lowest time preference has all the wealth, and all the other families have no wealth, consuming all of their income in each generation.

4 Concluding Comments

The models presented here extend the analysis of Stiglitz (1969b) in several important directions. They show that if there are differences across dynasties, passed on (perfectly) from generation to generation, then the earlier result of convergence of wealth, regardless of initial conditions, no longer holds: there can exist multiple equilibrium wealth distributions. We have provided some simple characterizations of these wealth distributions, in terms of differences in abilities, rates of return on investments, and savings rates.

Perhaps most interesting are the results that even if there are no ex ante differences among individuals, the equilibrium may be characterized by wealth inequality: those who wind up wealthy save more and have a higher return on their investments than those who, by dint of bad luck, have inherited low levels of wealth. We have shown, in particular, how the fact that wealth may beget wealth—with those at the top of the distribution receiving higher returns to capital than others, because connections may give them inside information or because, given their wealth, it pays them to invest more in getting information that allows them to have a higher return—may lead to sustained inequality, even when there are no dynastic differences in savings rates.

Introducing heterogeneity changes one of the key results of standard growth theory: there may now exist multiple steady state equilibria, and associated with the different steady states, a different wealth distribution.

We set the analysis in the context of simple savings models, where dynasties save a particular fraction of their income. Some recent literature has been critical of such arbitrary savings functions, insisting that they be micro-founded. The literature in behavioral economics has countered that simple behavioral rules may provide a better description of behavior than that derived from complex optimization problems. And this may be especially true when those optimization models begin with simplified assumptions which can be rejected empirically, such as time separable utility functions.

We nonetheless show that our results can easily be motivated by dynasties maximizing intertemporal utility. We show, moreover, that there may be multiple equilibria in a simple model without time separability, or in a model with time separability, but with different rates of time preference, undoing a central result in analyses assuming separability.

While the models in this chapter provide insights into the limitations of the wealth-convergence theorem, their main role is to set the stage for the stochastic models to which we turn in the next chapter.

Appendix Extension to Technological Change

The model can be extended to labor augmenting technological change, where now k denotes the capital stock per effective worker, $\frac{K}{La}$, where a is the number of efficiency units associated with any worker (at a given time). Then, instead of (11.5) we have

$$w_i = av_i\left(f(k) - f'(k)k\right). \tag{A11.1}$$

Nothing else in the analysis changes. Now the rate of growth of the economy, g, is given by

$$g = (1 - S_k)(n + \lambda) + \frac{S_k sf(k)}{k}, \tag{A11.2}$$

where λ is the rate of labor augmenting technological change, equal to $\frac{d\,ln(a)}{dt}$ and where S_K is the share of capital. (By constant returns to scale, the sum of the shares of capital and labor equal unity.) In the long run

$$g^* = n + \lambda = \frac{sf(k^*)}{k^*}. \tag{A11.3}$$

Since none of this affects (11.6), it is still true that, under the stipulated conditions, the distribution of wealth depends only on the distribution of wages. In the long run, neither r nor g, nor the difference between r and g, has any impact. Indeed, looking more closely at (11.6), we see that not even the speed of convergence depends on r, g, or $r - g$.[25]

Later models will show that these results are quite general.

[25] Except indirectly: k affects both sw and r.

12

Equilibrium Income and Wealth Distributions

Balancing Centrifugal and Centripetal Forces

1 Introduction

The previous chapter expanded on Stiglitz (1969b) in describing the strong force in the economy for convergence of wealth.[1] But wealth inequality persists. And even when families differ systemically in their productivities, wealth inequality appears to be far greater than wage inequality. While one of our models, in which the savings rate of higher-income individuals is higher, can partially explain this greater wealth dispersion, it does not fully account for the degree of inequality, especially once one considers that abilities are not perfectly inheritable.

This chapter builds on the "micro-founded" macroeconomic model of the last chapter, where aggregate dynamics result from aggregating the dynamics of the individual households (dynasties). The first part of Chapter 8 described an important centripetal force in the economy, bringing wealth together, as each generation must divide its wealth among its heirs; but there are important centrifugal forces as well: some individuals, for instance, may have good luck and achieve a very high return on their investments or have highly compensated talents, and it is possible that the same will happen to their children. If they pass some of that good fortune onto their children, their children will be wealthier. While the convergent process described in the basic model ensures that the effect of such good fortune attenuates over time, even as it does, new stochastic events create new inequalities. An equilibrium distribution of wealth exists when the two sets of effects, which we can think of as centrifugal and centripetal forces, are just balanced. We show that there is, under plausible conditions, such an equilibrium.

In this equilibrium, those who are lucky—either because they have high ability (high returns on their human capital) or high returns on their financial capital—save for future generations, knowing that their heirs will be less lucky. *On average*, though, the very rich, who have inherited considerable wealth from their parents, are decumulating, because they are less able and received a lower return on their capital than their forefathers. They leave less to their heirs, eating into their inherited capital, but spread out their wealth over future generations. This is what prevents inequality from growing ever larger. If their children in turn have the misfortunate of still lower wages or returns to capital, their consumption will be lower than that of their parents. What enables consumption per capita to be constant *overall* is that at the same time there are families whose incomes are increasing; and what enables the average savings rate to be constant is that offsetting the decumulation of those just described is the savings of those at the bottom and middle. Those in the middle

[1] Originally "New theoretical perspectives on the distribution of income and wealth among individuals: Part II. Equilibrium Wealth Distributions," NBER working paper 21190, May 2015. This chapter builds off of work presented in Chapters 9 and 33.

The Origins of Inequality, and Policies to Contain It. Joseph E. Stiglitz, Oxford University Press. © Joseph E. Stiglitz (2025).
DOI: 10.1093/oso/9780198799580.003.0013

may be saving, knowing that there may be a rainy day, and they want to anticipate the bad fortunes that may occur in the future. There are also some from poor and low-wage families who have "struck it rich," enjoying either higher wages than their parents or well-above average returns to capital. In these families, there is an increase in consumption per capita.

Macro-micro consistency entails that all the accumulations and decumulations just offset each other, and the postulated r^* is the rate of return on capital, given the equilibrium capital–labor ratio. A value of r^* that might have been associated with an ever-decreasing consumption or increasing consumption (because it was higher or lower than the pure rate of time preference) in a representative agent model is not in this model simply because of the heterogeneity of the population and the shocks to which they are exposed.

Using long-run equilibrium conditions allows us to extend the earlier studies of equilibrium wealth distributions,[2] deriving simple formulae for variances and covariances and the tails of the wealth distributions, which enable us to describe how inequality is affected by changes in the key parameters of the economy, as well as by various taxes.

The chapter is divided into three sections. In the first, we present the basic model where the only source of variability is the return on capital. In the second, we focus on variability in wages. In Section 4, we use these models to discuss the centripetal and centrifugal forces at play in recent years—to identify changes that might account for the increased inequality. Readers wishing to skip the details of the mathematics may go directly to Section 4.

2 The Basic Stochastic Model: Variable Returns to Capital

We begin with the basic dynastic equilibrium model of the previous chapter:

$$\frac{d\ln k_i}{dt} = \frac{sw_i}{k} - (sr - n_i), \tag{12.1}$$

where, it will be recalled, k is the capital–labor ratio, s the savings rate, w the wage, r the return on capital, n the rate of growth. In the model of this chapter (unlike the analysis of Chapter 10) there is no distinction between wealth and capital. The price of capital goods in terms of the consumption numeraire is unity, and there are no sources of rents. Throughout, we could have as well used the symbol "W" representing wealth for "K" representing capital.

To hone in on the issues at hand, we assume wages for all dynasties are the same and there is no labor augmenting technological progress,[3] which in turn implies that the long-run growth rate g^* is just the rate of growth of the population, n. This was the case examined in Chapter 8, where regardless of the initial wealth distribution, with everyone obtaining

[2] This and the next section also incorporate previously unpublished results in Stiglitz (1966) and extends Bevan and Stiglitz (1979) (Chapter 9) and Stiglitz (1978) (Chapter 33). Bevan (1974, 1979), Stiglitz (1978), and Bevan and Stiglitz (1979) appear to be the first to use diffusion models to study inequality. In the subsequent years, Pareto results have frequently emerged in models with heterogeneous agents. For a recent treatment, see Nirei and Aoki (2016).

I am also indebted to Haaris Mateen for extensive discussions on these topics.

[3] Identical results hold if there is labor augmenting progress, in the analysis of the detrended distribution of wealth. We would then replace in the equations below n with $g = n + \lambda$.

the same returns on their capital, there is convergence. We assume now that the return to capital of each family is stochastic, with an i.i.d. distribution.

Then, even if there were no wage inequality, there would be persistent wealth inequality. Families that had a run of good luck—high values of r—would have accumulated far more wealth than those who had a run of bad luck. The wealth accumulation equation is given by[4]

$$dk_t = (sw - \mu k_t)\, dt + \sigma k_t dZ_t, \tag{12.2}$$

where σ the risk is associated with the return on capital and is assumed proportional to r :

$$\sigma = r\underline{\sigma} \tag{12.3}$$

and where μ is the rate at which there is regression to the mean (the drift in the stochastic process), with those with high levels of capital per capita "drifting" back to the long-run equilibrium value and where μ is

$$\mu = n - s > 0. \tag{12.4}$$

(12.2) is a modification of a standard geometric diffusion process. It can be shown nonetheless (using a continuous time extension of the Kesten–Goldie theorem[5]) that *the stationary wealth distribution has an asymptotic Pareto tail*—for these rich individuals, wages become negligible, so wealth changes effectively in a multiplicative way. The whole distribution, of course, is not a Pareto distribution—and, of course, the wealth distribution is not a Pareto distribution.[6]

Letting $c_t = ln\, k_t$, for large k (12.2) can be rewritten (using Ito's Lemma)

$$dc_t = \left(-\mu - \frac{\sigma^2}{2} + swe^{-c_t}\right) dt + \sigma dZ_t. \tag{12.5}$$

For large c, the term we^{-ct} goes to zero, while for small k, swe^{-ct} becomes unbounded, ensuring a positive drift.[7] The value of the Pareto coefficient on the distribution of k—the measure of tail inequality α—is given by

$$\alpha = 1 + \frac{2\mu}{\sigma^2}. \tag{12.6}$$

An increase in α represents a decrease in inequality. For $1 \leq \alpha \leq 2$, the range of many of the estimated values, inequality is so high that the variance is infinite.[8] (12.6) gives the

[4] Z is a standard Brownian motion, i.e. $dZ_t \equiv \lim_{\Delta t \to 0} \varepsilon_t \sqrt{\Delta t}$, where ε_t here is normally distributed with mean zero and unit variance.

[5] See Kevei (2016).

[6] Thus, this work uses a geometric/multiplicative process with an additive term in continuous time that is different from most of the work using diffusion equations to study income distribution, for example those mentioned in Gabaix (2009). We also do not need to employ reflecting barriers, as is conventional in this literature. But see discussion below.

[7] This is why we don't need a reflecting barrier in this formulation. The additive term *swdt* is sufficient.

[8] See Gabaix (2009) and the references cited therein. Typically, the wealth Pareto coefficient is estimated to be around 1.5.

natural result that (tail) inequality decreases with the drift and increases with the variance of returns.

Using the conditions for long-run equilibrium,[9] $sf = nk^*$ (where, it will be recalled, f is output per capita, a function of just the capital–labor ratio, k):

$$D^* \equiv \alpha - 1 = 2s^2 \frac{1 - S_k}{S_k^2 n \underline{\sigma}^2}, \tag{12.7}$$

where S_k is the share of capital.[10] This gives the value of the tail inequality simply in terms of three key parameters—the savings rate, the rate of growth, and the variance of returns, plus the share of capital. In long-run equilibrium, the *size of the difference between the rate of return and the rate of growth* does not appear as a determinant of tail-inequality, simply because the rate of return is itself an endogenous variable, depending on the parameters describing the economy. In case of a unitary elasticity production function, the share of capital, S_k, is also a given, so in that case, we can completely describe tail inequality in terms of exogenous parameters. Not surprisingly, in that case, an increase in the share of capital increases tail-inequality, as does an increase in the growth rate and a reduction in savings rates. The latter result might seem surprising: after all, an increase in the savings rate reduces the drift, which by itself should increase inequality. But in the long run, it also reduces the interest rate, and we have assumed that there is a fixed coefficient of variation in the returns to capital: a lower return to capital thus means a lower variance of return, and (12.7) says that that effect predominates.

Of course, in more general models with s, n, $\underline{\sigma}$, and S_k endogenous, (12.7) still holds, but it is a more complicated matter to ascertain the effect of a change in a parameter (s or n) on tail-inequality.[11]

2.1 Comparative Statics: An Increase in n

In analyzing the comparative statics effects of an increase in the growth rate, one has to ascertain the direct impact and the indirect impact, through the effect on the long-run equilibrium. Thus, a very partial equilibrium analysis would note that an increase in the growth rate (n) leads to an increase in the "drift" and thus a reduction in inequality. But an increase in n has two further effects in the long run. It increases the rate of return on capital (since the equilibrium capital–labor ratio is reduced), which has just the opposite effect on drift; but if, as we assume, the coefficient of variation in returns is constant, a higher rate of return is associated with more variability, and this leads to *more* inequality. Equation (12.7) provides a simple formula showing how all of these effects get balanced off against each other.

Thus, an increase in n leads to more inequality, if factor shares remain the same and S_k is fixed. But an increase in n will normally change the factor distribution. An increase in

[9] $D^* = 2(n - sr)/r^2\bar{\sigma}^2 = 2n(1 - rk/f)/r^2\bar{\sigma}^2 = 2s^2(1 - S_k)/S_k^2 n\bar{\sigma}^2$.
Because α is greater than 1, the law of large number applies, and k converges to k^*, so in analyzing asymptotic distributions, we can assume that r and S_k taking on their asymptotic values.

[10] (12.7) can be shown to be equivalent to Equation (33.21′) in Chapter 33 (which was derived directly from the Kolmogorov equations.)

[11] Except when the elasticity of substitution is unity, S_K is a function of k, which is just a function of s/n.

n leads to a decrease in k, and hence an increase in the share of capital if the elasticity of substitution is less than unity. If the elasticity of substitution is less than unity, this reinforces the direct effect. There is thus a critical value of the elasticity of substitution ε, $\varepsilon^* \equiv \frac{1}{1-S_k} > 1$, such that for any k (and therefore S_k),

$$\frac{\partial \alpha}{\partial n} < 0 \text{ or } > 0 \text{ as } \varepsilon < \text{ or } > \varepsilon^*. \tag{12.8}$$

Provided the elasticity of substitution is not too great, an increase in the growth rate increases tail inequality.[12] Another way of putting the result is that, assuming that the elasticity of substitution is fixed and less than one, there is a critical $k^*(\varepsilon) \equiv S_k^{-1}(1 - 1/\varepsilon)$ such that if $k > k^*$, an increase in the growth rate increases tail inequality.

2.1.1 Endogeneity of *s*

This analysis has, however, assumed that the change in n—with all the consequent changes in, say, the rate of return to capital, the variability of return to capital, and the "drift" of the stochastic process—will leave the savings rate unchanged. In the short run, that may be true; in the long run, we might expect changes, but economic theory provides us with little guidance, with income and substitution effects typically pulling in different directions, and with ambiguous effects of changes in uncertainty.[13]

We have not formally modeled the impact of an increase in n. The higher n leads to higher interest rates, increased variability of returns, and a larger drift. (The effect of the latter on optimal savings has not been well-studied. Those who inherit a lot of wealth will expect their descendants to be less well off, so that should induce a higher savings rate. On the other hand, it means that, at any level of wealth and wage, a dynasty's expected present discounted value of wealth will be lower, so that might induce lower savings.) The next section shows that there is a presumption that if the increase in the growth rate leads to a decrease in the savings rate, the overall adverse effect of the increase in the growth rate on inequality is worsened; but if it leads to an increase in the savings rate (which the analysis of the next section is likely to be the case) then this secondary effect will partially offset the direct effect.

2.2 Comparative Statics: An Increase in *s*

Similarly, a very partial equilibrium analysis would observe that an increase in the savings rate reinforces any differences in wealth that arise, that is, the drift is reduced so inequality increases. But the fuller analysis provided by Equation (12.7) notes that not only is the variance of returns lowered in the long run (because r itself is lower), but an increase in s leads

[12] Since as k increases, S_k increases if the elasticity of substitution is greater than unity, if the elasticity of substitution increases with k, there can be ranges of k for which an increase in the growth rate increases inequality and others for which the opposite is the case. Obviously, for a constant elasticity of substitution production function, when k is small (and hence S_k is small), corresponding to a high value of n, an increase in n increases tail inequality, and conversely when k is large (and hence S_k is large), corresponding to a low value of n, an increase in n decreases tail inequality.

[13] See, for example, Rothschild and Stiglitz (1971) and Diamond and Stiglitz (1974). For instance, the effect of an increase in uncertainty may depend on properties of the utility function (like U''') about which we have little information.

to an increase in k, which, if the elasticity of substitution is greater than unity, increases S_k, which in turn increases inequality. These competing effects balance out so that *provided*[14]

$$\varepsilon < \varepsilon^{**} \equiv \frac{2 - S_k}{S_k} \geq 1,$$

an increase in the savings rate leads to decreased inequality in wealth (in the tail). Again, this can be put slightly differently: if the elasticity of substitution is fixed and less than unity, there is a critical value of k, $k^{**}(\varepsilon) \equiv S_k^{-1}(2/1 + \varepsilon)$, such that if $k > (<)\, k^{**}$, an increase in s decreases (increases) inequality.

Changes in the U.S. and many other advanced countries associated with a decrease in both the savings rate and n would thus pull in different directions.

Similar results obtain if the sole source of variability in inheritance (per capita) is the result of variations in family size. Ignoring the (important) problems posed by the discreteness of family size and the limited range of family sizes, but assume family size is described by a standard stochastic process, with $\sigma = n\underline{\sigma}$, then we obtain:

$$D^* = 2\frac{1 - S_k}{n\underline{\sigma}^2}. \tag{12.9}$$

A decrease in n would thus again lead to a lower level of tail inequality, provided that the elasticity of substitution is not too much in excess of unity. Similarly, a decrease in the variability in family size (at any value of n) would lead, as expected, to less wealth inequality.

2.3 Capital Taxation

A tax at the rate τ^c on the return to capital, with proceeds redistributed to workers leaves the aggregate capital accumulation equation and therefore the steady state unchanged, but increases the speed of convergence:

$$\frac{d\ln(k_i)}{dt} - \frac{d\ln(k_j)}{dt} = s(w + \tau^c rk)\left(\frac{1}{k_i} - \frac{1}{k_j}\right).$$

Now for higher income individuals,

$$\frac{d\ln(k_i)}{dt} \approx sr(1 - \tau^c) - n,$$

and if we have stochastic returns to capital, as before, the Pareto coefficient will be described by the same equations as before, except now:

$$D^* = 2s^2\frac{1 - (1 - \tau^c)S_k}{S_k^2 n(1 - \tau^c)^2\underline{\sigma}^2},$$

where, it will be recalled, S_k is the before tax share. The capital tax reduces tail-inequality, because it reduces the variability of returns. The capital tax also increases the magnitude of

[14] The logarithmic derivative of D^* with respect to s is $2 - \frac{(2-S_K)(1-\frac{1}{\varepsilon})}{1-S_K}$.

the drift. These results hold, however, only if the share of capital is unchanged. This will be true if the production function is Cobb-Douglas or if, as in the Solow model, everyone saves the same fraction of their income, k and hence the share of capital, will remain unchanged. But if the fraction of income saved by higher income individuals is higher, then redistributive taxation will lower the average savings rate associated with any income/wealth distribution, and this will increase tail inequality, if the elasticity of substitution is less than one. If the elasticity of substitution is low enough, it is possible that tail-inequality may actually increase. But these adverse effects can be offset if the government invests enough of the proceeds of the tax, so that there is no adverse effect on k. Indeed, if the government invested all of the proceeds, and the savings rate out of capital is less than unity, then not only would wages be increased and income inequality reduced, but so would wealth inequality be reduced.

2.4 Imperfect Competition

The above analysis assumes competitive markets. If the return to capital exceeds its marginal product (implying, in a constant returns to scale technology, that wages are lower), the analysis is little changed. We simply replace (12.7) with (12.10):

$$D^* = 2s^2 \frac{1 - mS_k}{m^2 S_k^2 n \underline{\sigma}^2}, \tag{12.10}$$

where m measures the extent to which the return to capital exceeds it marginal product. It immediately follows that an increase in market power (m) leads in the long-run equilibrium to an increase in tail-inequality.

3 Variable Wages

Assume wages for each family are determined by the *same* stochastic process, with regression toward the mean, that families optimize intergenerational utility and that there is a lower bound on wealth (individuals can't borrow more than a certain amount).[15] The latter assumption turns out to play an important role in the determination of wealth and consumption inequalities. Then there exists an equilibrium wealth distribution which is related to the nature of the stochastic process of wages, the intertemporal/intergenerational discount factor, the interest rate, the degree of altruism across generations, and the elasticity of marginal utility.

The usual process of regression toward the mean leads to an earning distribution. Using a standard diffusion model, we can generate a lognormal earnings distribution.[16]

We now investigate how we can go from that earnings distribution to determine the wealth distribution. High ability/wage individuals save a lot because they rationally expect

[15] The details of this model are set forth in Chapter 9. The notion of regression toward the mean is well-established, dating at least back to Galton (1886). See also Dewey (1889). As we explain below, there may be some forces weakening, and even reversing, regression toward the mean (referred to below as "trend reinforcement").

[16] A slight modification of the model in the previous section can be used (as in Chapter 9) to generate the earnings distribution: the model described above provides the dynamics of "skill" levels, which in turn can be

their children to face lower wages.[17] If some of those who have thus saved are lucky and have high returns to their investment, wealth inequalities will increase even more. Eventually, of course, some descendants will be less lucky both in being born with more limited abilities and getting lower returns on their investments. This regression toward the mean, plus the division of wealth among one's heirs, results in their being an equilibrium wealth distribution, whose properties we analyze in this section.

More formally, we can solve for the optimal savings as a function of the wealth of the individual, *K*, his wage, *w*, and the interest rate *r*. For simplicity, assume the economy is in steady state, with a constant aggregate capital–labor ratio. Some families (dynasties) may be saving, some dissaving, but we assume that there are enough that the law of large numbers means that everything nets out: net capital accumulation is just enough to keep the capital–labor ratio constant. Savings, how much of one's lifetime wealth one bequeaths to one's heirs, will be a function of the known stochastic processes and preferences[18]:

$$s(K, w; r^*, \beta, \delta, \underline{\sigma}),$$

where at any moment, the individual's lifetime wealth, consisting of his inherited capital, here denoted by *K*, and his lifetime wages, *w*, is the outcome of the wage and capital stochastic processes, with the coefficient of regression toward the mean in the

translated into earnings differentials. The mathematics is the same, with now

$$dA_t = -\beta\left(A - \overline{A}\right)dt + \sigma_A dZ_{wt}$$

where *A* is some measure of ability and where is the extent of regression toward the mean ($\beta = 0$ means that there is no regression toward the mean). Individuals with above average ability on average have less able descendants (regression toward the mean). We can solve for the equilibrium distribution of *A*. The faster the regression toward the mean and the less the "noise" (σ_A), the lower the level of inequality.

A is unobservable. What is observable is wages, or income, which are some function of *A*, say $ln\, w = A$. Simple models of ability distribution give rise to normally distributed abilities, and if $w = ln\, A$, lognormal distributions of wages (incomes), often said to describe the wage distribution apart from the top (Aitchison and Brown, 1957). But there is no reason that the transformation of "ability" into "productivity" doesn't occur through a different process, giving rise to, say, a fatter distribution of wages, for example the Champernowne (1953) distribution and, of course, the earnings differentials associated with particular skill differentials may change over time. (The Champernowne distribution has cumulative form $F(y) = 1 - \frac{2}{\pi} tan^{-1}\left(\frac{u}{y}\right)^{\eta}$ where $F(y)$ is the proportion of individuals whose earnings are less than *y*, *u* is the median, and η is a constant, related to the coefficient of the Pareto tail.)

[17] This is a natural extension of Friedman's permanent income hypothesis to an intergenerational context where parents are concerned about the well-being of their children.

The Bevan-Stiglitz model, like the later work of Becker and Tomes (1979, 1986, 1994), entails endogenous decisions concerning bequests, where individuals assess the value of bequests in terms of impacts on later generations (a quite different approach from that of Piketty and Saez (2013) described below.) But unlike Becker and Tomes, we do not endogenize fertility decisions. And none of the studies fully incorporate interactions between human and financial capital and the investments in children that are publicly provided. On this, we side with Arthur Goldberg (1989) who argued that what he referred to as more "mechanical" models (for instance, with savings rate and fertility rates described by pre-specified stochastic processes) may provide more insights than those that try to endogenize all the relevant variables. Indeed, modern behavioral economics goes further: it suggests that the simple models may provide a more accurate description of the economy. Ironically, some of the principle "predictions" of the Becker-Tomes model which they argued showed the power of their model have subsequently been questioned. For instance, they suggest that "fertility is positively related to the wealth of parents" and that consumption "would not tend to regress at all among rich families who leave gifts and bequests to their children." More recently, Lindahl, Palme, Sandgren-Massih, and Sjögren, 2014) have provided an empirical test of the model on Swedish data, which rejects the model.

[18] We explicitly note only δ, but obviously, the elasticity of marginal utility also matters, as Chapter 9 emphasizes.

wage equation given by β, the pure rate of time preference (which reflects how concerned each generation is about the next) by δ, and the coefficient of variation on returns by $\underline{\sigma}$.[19]

In discrete time, the individual's lifetime wealth, $W_{t+1} = w_t + (1 + r^*)k_t$ where k_t is the wealth the individual has inherited. If each generation has $1 + n$ children, then

$$k_{t+1} = s\,[w_t + (1 + r_t)\,k_t\,]\,]/\,(1 + n), \tag{12.11}$$

where r_t is i.i.d. distributed with mean r^* and standard deviation $\sigma = r^*\underline{\sigma}$. As in Chapter 9, we assume that the stochastic difference equation for wages is given by

$$ln\, w_{t+1} = \beta\, ln\, w_t + (1 - \beta)\, E\, ln\, w + z_t, \tag{12.12}$$

where $Ez_t = 0$.

Obtaining general solutions to (12.11) and (12.12) when s is itself the solution to the intergenerational optimization problem is, not surprisingly, difficult. Chapter 9 describes several approaches, some involving numerical solutions for particular parameterizations. We will not repeat the discussion, but here, and later in the chapter, we comment on two specific aspects, the role of borrowing constraints and the challenge of "fat-tails."

3.1 Role of Borrowing Constraints

In the absence of borrowing constraints, those with low inheritances (either financial or ability) would like to share their poor fortune with their successors. Knowing on average that their heirs will be better off than they, they would like to consume beyond their total lifetime wealth, leaving debts to be paid by their heirs. In most countries, however, individuals cannot do that, so there is a limit to their bequests. They cannot leave a negative bequest. In stochastic models, this acts as a reflecting barrier. If they have misfortune, individuals may dissave, until they have nothing left. Only when they have good fortune—say a high wage—can they again begin to save.

Heuristically, the solution to the optimization problem consists of two parts: for $W \leq W^*$, savings (transmission of wealth to the next generation) is zero; for $W > W^*$, savings increases in wealth (in some calculations, in a nearly linear way). The problem is analogous to that of running an optimal agricultural stockpile (buffer), which I studied with David Newbery (Newbery and Stiglitz (1981, 1982a). One cannot have negative stockpiles.[20]

[19] The individual's "state" variables are K and w, and the two are governed by different stochastic processes, so it is not necessarily the case that savings would depend just on total wealth, rather than the composition of that wealth.

[20] This highly non-linear savings function is markedly different from that postulated by Milton Friedman, who argued that individuals saved a constant fraction out of their lifetime income (wealth). Friedman had obviously ignored these non-negativity constraints.

3.2 Calculation of Wealth Inequality and Its Relationship to Wages: Discrete Time Model

Besides the numerical simulations, Bevan and Stiglitz (1979) (Chapter 9) provide explicit formulae for the relevant variances and covariances, based on a linearization of Equations (12.11) and (12.12).

$$k_t = s_1 w_t + s_2 k_{t-1} + s_3 r_t k_{t-1} \tag{12.13}$$

and

$$W_t - \overline{w} = z_{t-1} + \hat{\beta}\left(w_{t-1} - \overline{w}\right) \tag{12.14}$$

$\hat{\beta}$ represents the force of regression toward the mean. $\hat{\beta} = 1$ means that there is no regression toward the mean: next period's wage on average is this period's wage. On the other hand,

$\hat{\beta} = 0$ means that this period's wage has no effect on next period's wage. We assume that z is uncorrelated with either K or r. The coefficients s_i represent the net transmission of wage, wealth, and interest income from one generation to another, and take into account the division of wealth among heirs (i.e., savings divided by $1 + n$, where n is the number of heirs). Equation (12.13) reflects the possibility of different inheritance policies with respect to an individual's own wages and the financial wealth that he inherits, but we later simplify for the special case where $s_1 = s_2 = s_3$.

We can solve (12.13) for the steady state value of k^*, which we write as (where w^*, k^*, and y^* now represent the average value of wages, per capita wealth and per capita income across families):

$$(1 - s_2)\, k^* = y^* \left[s_1 (1 - S_k) + s_3 S_k\right]. \tag{12.15}$$

To simplify what we shortly see as quite complicated formulae, we assume a Cobb–Douglas production function, with S_K fixed. That enables us to simply solve for r^* from (12.15):

$$r^* = S_k (1 - s_2) / \underline{s}, \tag{12.16}$$

where $\underline{s} = s_1 (1 - S_k) + s_3 S_k$, the average savings rate out of capital.

When S_K is fixed, we can write the key variance/covariance equations in terms of underlying parameters:[21]

$$\text{cov}^* (k, w) = \frac{s_1 V_w^*}{1 - \beta\left(s_2 + \frac{S_k}{\underline{s}} (1 - s_2)\, s_3\right)} \tag{12.17}$$

[21] This analysis goes beyond that of Chapter 9 by using the steady state conditions to solve for the values of the endogenous variables $\{r, w\}$.

Note that (12.17) holds even when S_K is not fixed, but then the steady state value has to be solved for in (12.15). The comparative statics are more complicated, because changes in, say, savings rates affect the equilibrium share of capital. We ignore this effect below.

and

$$V_k = \frac{s_1^2 V_w \left[\frac{1+\hat{\beta}(s_2+s_3 r^*)}{1-\hat{\beta}(s_2+s_3 r^*)}\right] + s_3^2 r^{*2} \underline{\sigma}^2 k^{*2}}{1 - s_3^2 r^{*2} \underline{\sigma}^2 - (s_2 + s_3 r^*)^2}, \tag{12.18}$$

where r^* is given by (12.16), which, in the central case where all the savings rates are the same, becomes

$$V_k = \frac{s^2 V_w \left[\frac{1+\hat{\beta}(s+S_k(1-s))}{1-\hat{\beta}(s+S_k(1-s))}\right] + S_k^2 (1-s)^2 \underline{\sigma}^2 k^{*2}}{1 - s^2(1-2S_k) - S_k^2(1-s)^2(\underline{\sigma}^2+1) - 2sS_k}. \tag{12.18$'$}$$

Note that the variance only exists as long as $V_k > 0$. The numerator in (12.18′) is always positive. Therefore, the variance exists if[22]

$$1 > s^2(1-2S_k) + S_k^2(1-s)^2(\underline{\sigma}^2+1) + 2sS_k$$

and

$$V_w^* = \frac{V_Z}{1-\hat{\beta}^2}, \tag{12.19}$$

where V_Z is the variance in the underlying wage process and

$$w^* = (1 - S_K)\left(\frac{1-s_2}{\underline{s}}\right)^{\frac{S_K}{S_K-1}}. \tag{12.20}$$

We can also calculate the correlation coefficient

$$\rho \equiv \frac{\text{cov}^*(k,w)}{\sigma_k \sigma_w} = \frac{s_1\sqrt{1 - s_3^2 r^{*2}\underline{\sigma}^2 - (s_2+s_3 r^*)^2}}{\sqrt{s_1^2\left(1-\hat{\beta}^2(s_2+s_3r^*)^2\right) + \left(1-\hat{\beta}(s_2+s_3r^*)\right)^2 s_3^2 r^{*2}\underline{\sigma}^2 k^{*2}}} \tag{12.21}$$

3.2.1 Comparative Statics

A few comparative statics results may be derived from (12.18)–(12.20):

(a) As expected, weaker regression toward the mean (higher β) leads to higher covariances and correlation coefficients and a higher variance k (both because the variance of w is increased, and also because of the slower regression toward the

[22] Note that in the continuous time formulation used earlier (with no variance in wages), the variance of wealth was always infinite. In the continuous time formulation, the magnitude of tail inequality increased with $\bar{\sigma}^2$ and with the share of capital. So too here, with a large variance of returns or with a large share of capital the variance of capital is infinite. In particular, as the share of capital approaches unity, the required variance of returns under which the variance of capital is infinite goes to zero. On the other hand, if $\bar{\sigma}^2$ is small enough, then so long as $S_k < 1$ the variance of k is finite.

The discussion below further amplifies on the similarities—and in some cases differences—between the comparative statics in the continuous time and discrete time versions.

mean, those who have higher wages in one period have, on average higher wages the next).

(b) Not surprisingly, an increase in the variance of the underlying wage process increases the variance of wages and capital. It has, however, no effect on the correlation coefficient between k and w.

(c) Focusing on the central case where $s_1 = s_2 = s_3 = s$, an increase in the savings rate increases the covariance of k and w and the variance of k, provided the variance of r is not too large. If there is variability in the returns to capital, then there are complex interactions, with an increase in savings lowering the return on capital, and hence (as in the previous section) the variance of the return on capital, mitigating to some extent the direct effect.

(d) An increase in the variability of r increases the variance of k but reduces the correlation coefficient.

(e) An increase in the share of capital increases the variance of 1. An inheritance tax (or a tax on capital) lowers the share of capital as received by capitalists at any k, *assuming that the average savings rate is unchanged* (and, correspondingly, that the before tax rate of return on capital is unchanged). That means that if there is no change in savings rates, long-run wealth inequality is reduced. (Our earlier discussion highlighted the ambiguous effects of changes in rates of return and uncertainty.) A higher inheritance tax also shifts the savings function down (at each k and w), because the need for putting aside to benefit future descendants who might be worse off is reduced, because of the public redistribution. In the limiting case of a near 100% tax on inheritances, s would presumably fall close to zero, and inequality of consumption will be higher than for the case with $s > 0$.[23]

Of course, all the results need to be qualified because the savings rate itself is endogenous and in general the aggregate savings rate might change (though our earlier discussion made clear the direction of change was ambiguous). This is even more important in the context of variable w than earlier: parents with high wage incomes know that it is likely that their descendants will have a lower wage. This is especially so if there is a faster pace of regression toward the mean (a lower value of $\hat{\beta}$). A faster pace of regression toward the mean would induce dynasties save more in an attempt to smooth consumption across generations. This would normally offset the direct effect, but if the variance of r is very large, then the indirect effect on savings would reinforce the direct effect.

Plausibly, if rich families have strong feelings of intergenerational equity, to guarantee that future generations have as high a standard living as the current—even taking account the redistributions they will receive, which will be based on average wealth holdings/transfer—will require a higher savings rate. If that happens, the higher savings rate will reinforce the partial equilibrium effects of the inheritance tax to decrease inequality. Alternatively, the savings rate could decrease: parents' sense of equity toward future generations is not so strong that when the trade-off between current and future generations changes, so does their sense of what they want to leave their children. The lower

[23] See the discussion in Part III.E. for why even if that were the case, an inheritance tax still might be desirable.

savings rate drives up the before tax interest rate. The limiting case is one where the before tax interest rate is driven up so much that the after-tax interest rate remains unchanged.[24] In that case, the lower savings rate will undo some or possibly even all of the equalizing effects of the tax.[25]

In our economy, r is sufficiently small that families would have little incentive to save if they knew that their children were going to be as well off as they.[26] For instance, assume a dynastic family maximizing intertemporal family utility, with future families' utility discounted at a factor δ. If they treat their descendants with the same weight as they treat themselves and they knew their children were going to have a wage the same as theirs, they would take any wealth and spread it among all future generations. In the limiting case where they had strong egalitarian feelings, they would spread it so that their children are in the same position as they are, that is, if $r = n$, they would save all of their wealth, so that all of their children would be in exactly the same position as they (a peculiar stance, since they would then not enjoy the good luck of having wealth.) If $\delta < 1$, so future descendants get less weight than the current generation, it would seem that those who are lucky and have high wages would set aside something for future generations, so long as $r > n$.

The important point is that what matters are the *behavioral* responses, not responses that should be assumed on the basis of some hypothetical intertemporal dynastic maximization model. And it would be wrong to infer the aggregate responses by assuming a representative agent in the absence of uncertainty. The uncertain evolution of future generations' well-being is an essential part of the savings decision. The wide range of estimates of interest elasticity of savings for individuals in different circumstances suggests caution in prediction. The failure of the aggregate savings rate to change in response to large changes in the tax rate—in the U.S., the savings rate went down as the tax rate went up—suggests that institutional factors (like individuals current mortgage commitments, savings plans for which they are signed up at work) may drive savings behavior, at least in the short run and possibly in the long. These institutional factors may differ, of course, markedly across countries. In the long run, adjustments may occur which reflect underlying beliefs and preferences. But those beliefs and preferences are themselves endogenous.[27] For instance, in countries where there is a high level of youth unemployment, children are increasingly living with their parents until sometime in their thirties. It is conceivable that bonds across generations are strengthened, especially as compared to those in a country where it is more common for children to leave home earlier and live at some distance from parents. Changes in intertemporal preferences—a weakening of bonds across generation—could result in more inequality in consumption.

[24] This is the case we explore in detail in the next chapter.

[25] It becomes more difficult in this context to determine what will happen to the overall level of consumption inequality as a result of an increase in a tax on capital or inheritances, which in a partial equilibrium setting lowers the return to capital. (See Chapter 9.)

[26] What matters, of course, is the rate of return relative to the rate of discount. The relevant unit of time is a generation, some 30 years, and the rate of return over that period is not insignificant.

[27] Recent strands of research in behavioral economics have stressed the endogeneity of preferences. See, for example, Hoff and Stiglitz (2016).

3.3 Continuous Time Formulation

We can, as before, write down a continuous time formulation:

The wealth stochastic process is as before:

$$dc_t = \left(-\mu - \frac{\sigma^2}{2} + swe^{-c_t}\right) dt + \sigma dZ_t, \tag{12.22}$$

where the evolution of w is governed now by the stochastic process driving A (with $A = ln\, w$):

$$dA_t = -\beta (A - \underline{A})\, dt + \sigma_A dZ_{wt}. \tag{12.23}$$

We assume that the underlying Brownian stochastic processes are uncorrelated.

The pair of coupled stochastic differential equations gives rise to the equilibrium wealth and wage distribution in which some rich families are in the process of decumulating wealth, and some are saving. The economy as a whole is in macroeconomic equilibrium. It can be shown that the steady state wealth distribution indeed has an asymptotic Pareto tail through a usage of the Kesten-Goldie theorem. Intuitively, in the limit as capital $k \to \infty$, the Pareto tail of capital dominates the lognormal tail of wages. In fact, the tail inequality coefficient is the same as before.

3.3.1 Explaining the Magnitude of the Tail-Inequality

Bevan (1979) argues that the standard diffusion model does not adequately explain wealth inequality, but that a model generating a simplified two-parameter version of the Champernowne (1953) wage distribution provides a good description of the wealth distribution, "performing markedly better than the lognormal." Such a distribution can, of course, be generated from the underlying normal ability distribution derived earlier, simply by assuming that wages are a more complicated function of A (rather than the simplistic assumption that $w = ln\, A$ that we assumed).[28]

But there are other ways of obtaining fatter tails to the distribution, related to the discussion of the previous chapter. Bevan and Bevan and Stiglitz assumed that the return to capital did not depend on one's wealth; but in Chapter 11 we explained how "wealth begets wealth," and those at the top might be expected to receive higher returns. Moreover, what matters is after tax returns, and in the U.S. and some other countries, de facto top marginal tax rates are *lower*, because of provisions which favor the rich (e.g., more of their income is in the form of capital gains, as we noted in Chapter 4[29] which receives favorable treatment, both because it is typically taxed at a lower rate and because taxes are only levied upon realization),[30] they are in a better place to engage in tax avoidance (e.g., through cross-border tax arbitrage in companies that they own that operate in multiple jurisdictions), and they make greater use of tax paradises.

[28] See the discussion in fn.15 above.

[29] See also Saez and Zucman (2019b).

[30] And in many countries, such as the U.S., totally escapes taxation when the asset is passed on to one's heirs, through a provision which is called step-up-of basis upon death.

4 The Centrifugal and Centripetal Forces in the Economy

The previous discussion highlighted the robust conditions under which the economy converges to an equilibrium wealth (and wage) distribution and provide a framework for understanding the forces that can lead to an equilibrium wealth distribution that is more or less unequal. We can ask, for instance, what changes in (a) the process of intergenerational transmission of advantage; (b) in markets; and (c) in public policy have occurred which affect the asymptotic distribution? We can categorize factors affecting the equilibrium wealth distribution as those that affect the drift, the centripetal forces, and those that affect variability, the centripetal forces. Some of the changes that we describe below increase both the dispersion and reduce the drift, increasing inequality on both accounts; some exercise their effects primarily on the drift, others on the dispersion; and in the case of still others, there may be countervailing forces, leaving the net effect on the equilibrium wealth and income distribution ambiguous.

More dispersion of returns to capital and wages will lead to more dispersion of wealth. The increasing dispersion of wages (the explanation of which we address elsewhere in this book, and which has been a subject of an extensive literature) increases the centrifugal force in the economy, leading to more inequality. So too more dispersion in reproductive rates and savings rates will lead to greater dispersion in wealth. If some families have a small number of children, inheritances will have to be divided among a smaller number, and so wealth (per capita) increases. In particular, if richer families have smaller families, then there will be more wealth inequality.[31]

The second major set of determinants is "drift"—the extent of the persistence of differences in returns and wages. Thus, one of the factors limiting the build-up of ever-increasing inequality is that the children and grandchildren of those who made a fortune typically have a greater likelihood of squandering the family fortune than magnifying it, reflected in the adage, from rags, to riches, and back to rags in three generations. Higher savings rates overall weaken the centripetal forces, leading to more inequality.

Changes in the *average* value of various variables, in particular, the return to capital, can have a significant effect on drift. Institutional and demographic changes can affect both savings rates and reproduction rates, thereby affecting the return to capital. For instance, increased longevity and the institutionalization of private pensions have increased life-cycle savings, and if that life-cycle savings doesn't just "crowd out" capitalist savings (as it does in the model of the next chapter), it will lead to lower interest rates, accelerating the drift, lowering equilibrium inequality.

The model helps frame a discussion of other forces that could lead to greater inequality, by focusing on the underlying drivers, the level of dispersion of wages and returns to capital, the perpetuation of those differences, and the transmission of advantages and disadvantages across generations.

[31] But the boundary value condition, where there are no children, has just the opposite effect, if those without children give their estate away. Similar results hold if wealthy individuals decide not to give a large proportion of their wealth to their children.

4.1 Intergenerational Transmission of Advantage

If the very rich can use their wealth, and more broadly the position in society that that wealth gives to them, to get higher returns to their capital and access to better jobs for their children ("rents" in the labor market, above normal returns in the capital market), then wealth will become more concentrated. This has, of course, always been true—connections matter, and connections are passed on across generations; but if the extent to which this is true changes, then there will be a change in the equilibrium distribution of income and wealth.

One might have thought that in a meritocratic society these connections would matter less, and that may indeed be the case in countries, like those in Scandinavia, which take meritocracy seriously. But in countries like the U.S., there is little evidence that the importance of connections has significantly decreased. Indeed, ironically, in an imperfect meritocracy, the importance of connections may actually be increased. For instance, increasingly to get a good job one needs an internship, which is often unpaid. Not only can the children of the less affluent not afford these internships, but it often takes connections to even get this unpaid work.[32]

The use of connections to get access to jobs becomes more important when jobs are rationed, that is, there is unemployment. If macro-economic policies are run in a way that results in persistently higher unemployment, one might expect inequality to increase, not only as a result of the direct impacts on wages, but also as a consequence of the indirect impacts we have just identified through the intergenerational transmission of advantage.

Connections matter in another sphere: politics. In many countries, those with connections are able to extract rents from the public.[33] This is true even in democracies, though it has to be done in a more "rule based" way: the manner in which the banks first "purchased" deregulation, and then received mega-bailouts, is a case in point.[34]

How wealth begets wealth is well understood and has been extensively discussed in the previous chapter. So too, how those in poverty become trapped there is well understood: Those near bankruptcy have to pay higher interest rates, making their descent toward the bottom even steeper.[35] Their attempts at survival occupy so much of their energies that they cannot think about the long term; and accordingly, they do not make the long-term investments that would increase their incomes.[36]

[32] Perlin (2011). For a broader discussion of meritocracy, see Markovits, 2019.

[33] Much of inequality in many countries is related to privatizations and the sale of public assets at below market prices. But there are many others. Sometimes the transfers occur in a more indirect way: the government issues a banking license to someone that is politically connected; the "private" bank lends money to favored parties to purchase the state assets that are being privatized. Restrictions on who can bid ensure that the prices are below what they would be in a competitive market. Much of the Russian oligarchy was created in this way.

To the extent that connections can be purchased, this just reinforces the increasing (private) returns associated with wealth ownership.

[34] See Johnson, Simon, and Kwak (2010) or Stiglitz (2010a).

[35] Battiston, Delli Gatti, Gallegati, et al. (2012) refer to this as trend reinforcement.

[36] Mullainathan and Shafir (2009); Mani, Mullainathan, Shafir, and Zhao (2013); and Demerritt, Hoff, and Stiglitz, forthcoming.

4.1.1 Explaining Increased Inequality in a World with Near Zero Interest Rates

Those without wealth cannot get access to credit markets (or can do so only at very high interest rates).[37] This becomes especially important in an era of super low interest rates and with large gaps between average returns and the rates at which the very rich can borrow.

But this in turn raises two fundamental issues:

(a) How can we explain the seemingly high persistent average returns to capital? Our usual models differentiate between "labor" and "capital" and, with the "savings glut," it would seem that the return to capital should have plummeted. Shouldn't that mean that the share of capital would have plummeted too?[38]

(b) In an era in which interest rates are near zero, how can the inequality of income and wealth increase? And especially so as risk premia seemed to decrease as interest rates fell and as the economy got better at managing risk? In Piketty's analysis, this period of low interest rates should be an era of wealth convergence. But instead, there was wealth divergence.

In the following paragraphs, we suggest answers to these questions—answers which tell us something about today's income and wealth inequality.

4.1.2 Knowledge and Inequality

The scarce factor in our economy would seem not to be capital, but knowledge. Capital flows relatively freely across borders; yet differences in per capita income persist, and largely because of impediments to the free flow of knowledge. The banks' manipulation of the LIBOR and foreign exchange markets as well as insider trading scandals exemplify the returns that can be obtained from information asymmetries[39]—even information asymmetries deliberately created by the market. While these were *outside the law*, there are pervasive opportunities to do similar things (with perhaps slightly lower returns) *within the law*. It is the belief that there are returns to knowledge that motivates those who manage capital to invest so much in the acquisition of knowledge, and to work so hard to keep what they know secret.[40] But not everyone has equal access to knowledge; and in markets timing is critical: knowing something slightly before others can yield large (private) returns.[41]

[37] Theories of asymmetric information and imperfect risk markets have helped explain this seeming market imperfection.

[38] Under the assumption of an elasticity of substitution less than unity. See the discussions in earlier chapters.

[39] It should be noted that only the most egregious examples of the use of inside information are illegal and get prosecuted.

[40] As it is sometimes put, "knowledge" is both power and money. For a broader discussion, see Stiglitz and Greenwald (2014).

Interestingly, the efficient markets hypothesis suggested such investments yielded no return: information disseminated perfectly and instantaneously throughout the economy. But why then would rational individuals invest so much money in gathering information? See Grossman and Stiglitz (1980a). The evidence, however, is that markets are not informationally efficient, and that means there are returns to investment in information/knowledge. See Shiller (2002).

[41] Especially if other market participants are overconfident or unaware of their informational disadvantage. Note again these are private returns, not social returns. See Stiglitz (1982a). Differential access to technology and information processing abilities has similarly given rise to rents in equity markets, especially more recently, in high frequency trading. See Stiglitz (2014c) and the references cited there.

4.1.3 Risk Taking

Given the asymmetries of information—those without access to special information know the equity markets can be a stacked game—and given that less well-off individuals are more risk averse, it is natural that the richest individuals own a disproportionate share of equities; and if equities have a higher return than safer assets, then, on average, those at the top will see their wealth grow on average faster than those lower down. Moreover, as wealth increases, individual's ability to absorb risk increases. (This affect could be partially weakened over time by improvements in the management of risk, so that the overall portfolio risk—which is what matters for the evolution of wealth inequality—is reduced. But these improvements would in turn lead to a still further increase in overall risk taking. While the presumption is that the net amount of risk taking would still increase with wealth, what happens to the difference in returns obtained by the rich and poor is not so clear.[42])

Further, Chapter 11 explained why wealthier individuals should have a natural advantage in obtaining higher returns—it pays them to be more informed, and thus the risk they perceive when buying, say, an equity portfolio may be lower.

4.1.4 Education as a Mechanism for the Transmission of Advantage

If richer individuals (high wage individuals) invest more in the human capital of their children, so their children have higher average wages (at any level of ability), the pace of regression toward mean will be slowed and there will be more wealth inequality.

High quality public education can counter this force, ensuring that everyone faces a more level playing field. If the educational system did this, it would be the most important centripetal force for equality in our society.

But in a society, like the U.S., where there is a reliance on local funding for schools, if there is more economic segregation,[43] then there will be more inequality in the transmission of human capital. So too if greater reliance is placed on tuition for financing tertiary education, in the absence of adequate scholarships; and this is even true if debt financing is made available, unless the debt repayments are income contingent, as in Australia. Higher interest rates charged on student loans will lead to more inequality of human capital; so too would the passage of a bankruptcy law that makes student debt not-dischargeable even in bankruptcy (as the U.S. has done with a series of laws dating to the 1970s, the most recent expansion of which was the Bankruptcy Abuse Prevention and Consumer Protection Act of 2005).

4.1.5 Demography

If, for some reason, there was an increase in assortive mating, with those with high wages (productivities) marrying others with high wages, then arguably, the pace of regression toward the mean might be slowed. If previously, alpha males chose mates based on looks, rather than on characteristics that drove market returns, then the pace of regression toward the mean in wages would presumably be faster. If one organizes tertiary education to

[42] If everyone had the same constant degree of relative risk aversion, then as the economy got wealthier, there is no presumption that wealth inequality would change. But if there is decreasing relative risk aversion (consistent with a larger fraction of wealthy individuals' portfolios being allocated to the high risk assets), then the disparity in portfolio allocations could either increase or decrease, depending on the relative pace of the change with an increase in wealth.

[43] Evidence is that economic segregation has increased. See Bischoff and Reardon (2011).

increase the likelihood of assortive mating on the basis of market productivity, then the pace of regression toward the mean will be slower.

The OECD (2011) has called attention to the role of changing social patterns (e.g., in family structure and household formation) on income inequality among households. These patterns translate, over time, into wealth inequalities. For instance, if there are some households with two earners and only one child, they are likely to pass on to their child more wealth than is the case for households with two or more children and only one earner. Patterns, such as those emerging in the United States, where those at the bottom of the distribution are less likely to get married are likely associated with less transmission of human capital across generations at the bottom, leading to more wealth and income inequality.[44]

4.1.5.1 Differences in Norms and Social Customs

Differences in norms and social custom can lead to more wealth dispersion, especially by weakening drift at the top: if some groups in society save more, then they will have more wealth.

But one has to be careful in interpreting observed differences: in the next chapter we present a model with non-linear savings in which ex ante everyone is identical, but those who are wealthy have a higher savings rate *because they are wealthy.* That is, differences in wealth lead to differences in savings rate (which, of course, reinforce and sustain those differences in wealth), in contrast to the Kaldor/Marx (or Piketty) perspective, in which it is differences in savings rates which give rise to differences in wealth. This may be especially so if, as we have suggested, the returns to capital are higher for those with more wealth; for then, their incentive to save may be higher.[45]

These forces work at the bottom of the distribution as well as at the top. Thus, it is possible that there is a poverty trap. Those with low income and capital save little, but if one could somehow increase their income and wealth enough, they would move out of this poverty trap.

Other changes in norms can reinforce the intergenerational transfer of advantage and disadvantage. If growing up in a stable, two-parent home provides some educational advantage, then recent trends which show a diminution in marriage rates and stability in the bottom half of the income distribution (partially perhaps a result of their deteriorating living conditions) would exacerbate disparities.

4.2 Changes in Markets

Changes in markets may also lead to changes in the equilibrium wealth distribution.[46] Better insurance and annuity markets mean that individuals have to accumulate less precautionary and retirement savings. There is large variability in the time of death, and those who die early with large amounts of precautionary and retirement savings leave more

[44] Greenstone and Looney (2012).

[45] Chapter 11 showed how under these conditions one could get an equilibrium wealth distribution even without dispersion in the return to capital.

[46] We focus in this section on changes in markets other than the widely discussed ones affecting wage inequality, such as skill biased technological change, globalization, etc. discussed more extensively earlier (for instance in Chapter 4).

to their children.[47] Better rental markets or reverse mortgages mean that the elderly are less likely to hold large amounts of real estate wealth—passing on less to their heirs upon death.[48] An increase in the difference between life expectancy and the age of retirement[49] and an increase in the variance of the age of death will lead to more wealth inequality.[50]

4.2.1 General Equilibrium Effects and Multiplicity of Equilibrium

Early developments in growth theory noted that if there is a difference in consumption patterns of the rich and the poor, with the rich preferring capital-intensive goods, multiple equilibria could easily arise: There is one equilibrium with a high return to capital and low wages where capital-intensive goods are predominately produced and consumed, and another one with a low return to capital and high wages where labor-intensive goods are predominately produced.[51]

Analogous effects arise in the models under study here. Assume that the rich prefer commodities the production of which requires more capital and is associated with more risk. But as we saw earlier, the rich have a greater tolerance for risk and consume disproportionately capital-intensive goods. There is an equilibrium in which the rich get a larger share of the economic pie, so that the overall structure of production is such as to increase the demand for the capital and risk bearing services of the rich—thus leading them to have higher incomes.

But the rich can themselves move the economy toward the high risk-high return to capital equilibrium. Assume that they control the choice of technology within the firm. Reflecting their greater ability to bear risk, they choose a riskier technology, inducing (on average) more risk in corporate shares. The market equilibrium will entail a higher "price" for risk, therefore higher average incomes of those at the top who, on average, are more able and willing to bear risk.

"Innovations" like structured finance can similarly give rise to a shift in average income toward the top and an increase in wealth inequality. It increases the supply of safe assets, and increases the risk associated with the residual. The former reduces the returns to the assets held by ordinary individuals (the life-cycle savers) and increases those held by dynastic savers.[52]

4.2.2 Structural Transformation

The economy is going through a structural transformation, from a manufacturing economy to a service-sector-based economy. The *transformation* itself can have large distributive effects. (Greenwald and Kahn, 2009) Some individuals are better able to make the transformation, to seize the new opportunities. They will do well. Others will be left behind.

[47] These are sometimes referred to as "unplanned bequests," but that is not quite an accurate description: individuals should take this risk into account in their savings decisions. See Chapter 9.

[48] It is worth noting that there are large differences across countries in the relative role of rental markets vs. home ownership. In Germany, homeownership is relatively low.

[49] This variable is critical in the life-cycle model described in the next chapter. In the absence of annuity markets, individuals care not just about the mean life expectancy; the variability in life expectancy will also affect savings rates—and therefore the importance of life-cycle savings.

[50] Chapter 8 constructed a simple model of stochastic death which gives rise to a Pareto tail, which is consistent with the above observations.

[51] See Solow (1961), Uzawa (1961, 1963), Stiglitz and Uzawa (1969).

[52] Of course, if the generalized Modigliani–Miller theorem held (Stiglitz,1974a) held, structured finance would not alter the general equilibrium. Stiglitz explains why the conditions required for the MM theorem to hold are not likely to be satisfied.

The result is that there can be an increase in inequality—an explanation similar to one originally posed for the Kuznets curve in earlier stages of development.

But the level of inequality in the new *equilibrium* may differ as well. For instance, because the size of the production unit in services is smaller, it may be easier to identify the individual contribution of any particular individuals (as opposed to in the assembly line, where it is virtually impossible). When it is possible to easily observe differences in productivity, market wages will do so (Stiglitz, 1975a).

It is even possible that the range of observed productivity differences in certain areas of services is greater than in the arena of manufacturing. The assembly line provides a constraint on what any individual worker can do. Certain parts of the service sector are particularly affected by being part of the "winner take all economy"—the best soccer players and opera singers can get paid multiples of the average.

The winner-take-all effect is also important in the growing parts of the economy where fixed costs are more important and as a result of Bertrand competition, the firm with the lowest costs or best products wins the entire market—or the best ability to engage in discriminatory pricing and other monopolistic and exploitive practices (Stiglitz and Greenwald, 2014). The owners and key employees of these firms do extraordinarily well.

Moreover, vertical disintegration—firms buying janitorial services from others—may result in more wage inequality. Efficiency wage effects are almost surely stronger within firms than across firms: individuals worry about equity (wage differentials) *within their own firm*, resulting in even janitors in higher paying enterprises getting paid more.[53]

Unionization will often prove more difficult in this new context; unions have traditionally pushed for wage compression.

Finally, many of the key services are very local in nature, and there may be more monopoly power in the provision of these services than in more homogeneous commodities or manufactured goods.

In short, the distribution of equilibrium wages (and therefore wealth) may differ as production technologies change and the variance in returns on capital can increase. In primitive agriculture, holding land quality constant, the main difference in productivity may have been related to physical strength. As agriculture developed, differences may arise as a result of the ability to process weather and other information, to know the right time to plant and the right kinds of fertilizer to use. As agriculture develops still further, and these knowledge functions are routinized, differences in productivity may actually be reduced.

Other large structural changes, such as globalization, have contributed to an increase in inequality, through a variety of channels that are illuminated by our model, weakening the centripetal forces and increasing the centrifugal forces. For given differences in abilities and skills, in advanced countries, globalization leads to greater disparities between wages of skilled and unskilled workers. This then translates directly into greater wealth inequality.

Financialization and financial globalization leads to greater risk—greater variability in the return to capital—which again translates directly into greater inequality.

Both financialization and globalization may contribute to an increase in the return to and share of capital. Globalization is partly the result of changes in technology—lower costs of

[53] Efficiency wage theory says that worker's productivity increases with the wage paid. There are a large number of reasons why this may be so.

transportation and communication. But it is also a result of changes in policy, described below: one could have structured globalization in ways which would have resulted in less inequality.

4.2.3 Increasing Market Power

Earlier, we explained how, not surprisingly, an increase in corporate market power leads to an increase in the equilibrium level of wealth and income inequality (e.g., Equation (12.10)). Similar results hold for a weakening of workers' market power. There are multiple changes in the structure of the economy which have led to such changes, some (such as the increasing importance of fixed costs such as research relative to marginal costs, and the move to a service sector economy) have been discussed above, while others are discussed in Chapter 16 below. As we note in the next subsection, public policy has played an even more important role—evidenced by the fact that the increase in market power appears to differ markedly across different advanced countries with similar technologies and demand structures.

4.3 Changes in Public Policy

Public policy has a major impact on each aspect of the generation of wealth inequality described above. We've already noted several: how the design of the education system affects dispersion in human capital, a key driver in income and wealth inequality; how the rules governing globalization affect wage dispersion; so too, how government engagement in structural transformation can affect geographic income and wealth dispersion; and how regressive taxation at the top increases top tail wealth inequality. Here, I note eight further points.

First, the provision of public annuities reduces the need for individuals to save for retirement. But since most countries only provide limited public annuities, there are differential effects across the income distribution: It partially accounts for the essentially zero savings for retirement for the bottom part of the population. Hence, overall, wealth inequality (which is traditionally measured excluding implicit social security wealth) is probably increased. (While social security may have as a result increased wealth inequality, it markedly reduced inequalities in consumption and well-being—an important lesson for interpreting data on changes in wealth inequality.[54]) Other social protection programs may have similar effects: they reduce the need for precautionary savings, and that effect is likely to be larger on lower income individuals.[55]

Secondly, taxation of capital and especially of bequests has both an income and a substitution effect reducing bequests, and thus the transmission of inequality. A lowering

[54] There are other important caveats in interpretation: if people live longer, spending a larger fraction of their life in retirement, lifetime savings will increase, and even if there were no inequality in lifetime well-being, there would be large increases in wealth inequality. It should be clear, however, that the increase in wealth inequality, especially at the top, cannot be explained by changes in lifetime savings.

[55] Somewhat offsetting this effect is that because lower and middle income individuals may have much less savings than they otherwise would, with imperfect annuity markets, there is less dispersion in wealth holdings caused by the random timing of death. But since even before the advent of social insurance, retirement and precautionary savings of these individuals were limited, this effect is probably not significant.

of the tax on capital would be expected, in the "basic model," to lead to an increase in wealth inequality. Thus, the marked lowering since 1980 in these taxes may have played a significant role in the increase in wealth and income inequality.[56]

Progressive capital taxes reduce wealth inequality, as we have seen. Changes in taxation in the United States have reduced progressivity. Indeed, today those with very high incomes pay much lower effective tax rates on their income than those with lower incomes. In the models explored here, if the taxes at the top are low enough, this can in fact give rise to an ever-increasing level of wealth inequality.[57]

Thirdly, monetary policy, whether intentionally or not, affects the distribution of income and wealth. Quantitative easing (QE), by lowering interest rates and increasing equity prices, increased the wealth of the wealthy individuals who own the bulk of equities. Differences in portfolio composition (described in Chapter 4) are understandable: wealthier individuals are better able to bear risk, and accordingly will put more of their wealth into high risk equities. Low interest rates hurt retirees who had put their savings into what they thought were prudent investments, government bonds. Lower interest rates encourage firms to use more capital-intensive technologies, reducing the demand especially for low-skilled workers.[58]

Traditionally, the central distributional conflict confronting monetary authorities has been seen as that between debtors and creditors, with low interest rates benefiting the former at the expense of the latter. But today, the conflict is often between owners of equity and owners of short-term debt. The impact on wealth distribution may be driven by differences in portfolios.

Public policy affects the relative returns to different classes of assets and the riskiness of these assets. Preferential treatment of capital gains taxes is of most value to the rich, and hence this tax policy not only benefits the rich, but also may lead to greater disparity in ownership patterns—so that monetary policies like QE have a greater impact increasing inequality than they otherwise would.[59]

Fourth, we note that any change in markets or public policy which affects the distribution of wages will (according to our basic model) affect over time the distribution of wealth. There is an extensive recent literature on the determinants of wage dispersion, discussing, for instance, how globalization and skill biased technological change may have led to greater wage inequality. But the extent to which this is true is not just determined by market forces, but how those market forces are shaped by public policy, for example the rules governing unionization and globalization and science policy—the direction of research

[56] There is an important caveat to this conclusion, in at least some of the models we have examined. In, for instance, the model examined in the next chapter with dynastic savers, there is full shifting; thus, the lowering of the tax rate simply leads, in equilibrium, to a lowering of the before tax return—with the after tax return unaffected. We describe how these adverse incidence effects can be reversed.

[57] And even more so, if those at the top can attain higher returns than others. The critical condition is that the top savings rate, s_t, times the after tax return obtained at the top, $r_t(1 - \tau_t)$ be greater than the reproductive rate at the top n_t.

[58] There are, in addition, macroeconomics (which go beyond the scope of most of the models constructed in this book). If monetary authorities tighten whenever wages start to rise, the effect will be a ratcheting down of the wage share. See Chapter 10 of Stiglitz (2012a) and Stiglitz (2015a) for a more extensive discussion of the distributional effects of monetary policy.

[59] Similarly, limitations on loss offsets may be less binding on high wealth investors, who always have assets with returns against which they can offset the losses; and hence these provisions may similarly have asymmetric effects.

that is encouraged.[60] Weaknesses in corporate governance in the U.S. have allowed corporate executives to seize for themselves an increasing share of the corporate revenue stream, at the expense of both wages of ordinary workers and investment (and hence future wages).

Fifth, changes in policy affect not just the distribution of wages *among* workers, but also the distribution of factor incomes *between* workers and capitalists. For instance, changes in labor law have weakened worker's bargaining position (Seltzner, 2015), and investment agreements giving corporations stronger property rights abroad than they have at home have an indirect effect of further weakening it (Stiglitz, 2018a). Weakening of antitrust laws enable those who control certain assets to reap a larger share of national income, increasing prices, and lowering workers' real wages.

The rules of globalization too have weakened workers' bargaining power. There are ways that globalization could have been managed that would have had less adverse effects.[61] Financial globalization—capital market liberalization—has exposed domestic financial markets to more volatility. Our model explains how such volatility translates into higher levels of equilibrium wealth and income inequality.

Deregulation more generally has opened up more opportunities for rent-seeking and exploitation—and when workers are exploited more by firms (such as banks engaging in predatory lending or abusive credit card practices) their real income goes down and the share of "capital" (including the rents achieved through this exploitation) increases.

So too, a major structural change in the economy is the move toward a knowledge economy. Differences in productivity are related to differences in knowledge, but who appropriates the returns is in fact at least partly a matter of public policy. The design of the patent system can make a big difference: under current arrangements, much knowledge that is produced through public investments in research is effectively privatized by corporations.

Sixth, again, there are important general equilibrium effects. A policy like capital market liberalization exposes a country to more risk, thus increasing the demand for "risk absorption services." It is the wealthy that disproportionately provide those services. The returns to risk-absorption increase, that is, the income of the wealthy, better able to manage risk, increases. Thus, a change in policy that increases risk increases the Pareto tail and increases the share of national income going to the rich.

Seventh, as Chapter 5 emphasized, markets don't exist in a vacuum. They have to be structured, by laws and regulation. How they are structured affects market income and after-tax and transfer income. And the two cannot be separated. The tax system obviously affects behavior in ways which affect market income. Stiglitz, Abernathy, Hersh, et al. (2015) argue that it is changes in these rules in the U.S. and elsewhere that accounts for much of the change in inequality, and it does so in ways into which this model helps provide insights, the underlying drivers of inequality (the underlying wage distribution), the intergenerational transmission mechanisms (with impacts on drift) and the centrifugal forces associated with greater variability.

Eighth, while the previous discussion emphasized the rents associated with market power and other forms of *economic* exploitation, and how that contributes to income and

[60] As we have already noted, low interest rates encourage labor-saving innovations. A carbon tax would have encouraged more resource saving innovation, and less labor-saving innovation. See Chapters 17 and 18.

[61] For example, through the impact of investment agreements. See the discussion in Chapter 4 and the references cited there.

wealth inequality, there are also rents directly associated with political power (that is, not through shaping the rules of the market), for example, through subsidies, preferential tax treatments, government purchasing goods and service at prices above a competitive level or selling assets (like natural resources) at prices below a competitive level. Since political power is related to wealth, this kind of political rent seeking, accruing only to some of the wealthy, increases wealth inequality both through reducing "drift" and increasing dispersion.

Finally, if we endogenize the *political* equilibrium, we can again get multiple equilibria, in one of which there is greater economic equality, resulting in a political equilibrium which supports rules leading to more equalitarian incomes, and in the other, there is greater inequality, supported by a political equilibrium which produces rules supporting that higher level of inequality. We formally model this in Chapter 16.

4.3.1 Cyclical Effects

The models of this chapter are concerned with the long-run evolution of the wealth distribution. Yet, one cannot separate the consequences of economic instability from the long-run analysis, particularly in the presence of asymmetries in impacts and hysteresis effects. It is those at the bottom that suffer the most from economic fluctuations (see, e.g., Furman and Stiglitz, 1998), and in the boom, they do not make up for what they lose in the recession (especially if monetary authorities follow the kinds of policies described earlier). Instability may thus contribute to income and wealth inequality—the 2008 economic downturn being a case in point.[62] The extent to which this is so depends, of course, on both the strength and design of automatic stabilizers, like unemployment insurance, but also the strength and design of discretionary policies. (Policies, such as undertaken in the U.S. in the aftermath of the 2008 crisis, which bailed out banks but did little to help homeowners contributed to the increase of inequality generated by that recession.)

4.3.2 An Overview of the Changing Balance between Centrifugal and Centripetal Forces in the Economy

Three of the key centripetal forces in the economy may have weakened in recent decades, especially in the United States: the tendency for smaller families has weakened the effects of division among heirs;[63] the reduction of progressivity of the tax system—to the point where at the upper reaches it has become regressive—may have changed the stochastic process describing returns from one characterized by mean reversion to one characterized by trend reinforcement; and the equalizing effect of public education has been weakened with increased economic segregation and increasing disparities between schools attended by the children of the rich and that of the poor. Meanwhile, some of the centrifugal forces may

[62] It should be pointed out, however, that these effects are not unambiguous, since many economic fluctuations are associated with stock market crashes that especially adversely affect those at the top. Income and wealth inequality fell after the stock market crash of 1929. The 2008 crisis may have especially adversely affected workers because of the disproportionate effect on housing wealth, and government policies which restored stock market wealth more effectively than housing wealth.

[63] The role of fertility decisions in driving wealth inequality is complicated and somewhat contested. While there is some evidence that children are "normal" goods, that is, an increase in income/wealth would, by itself, lead to slightly larger families (Black et al., 2013; Lovenheim and Mumford, 2013), on average with higher incomes women's education is higher, so the opportunity cost of children is higher and family size lower. In general, it would appear that the latter effect dominates today. For Sweden, Elinder, Erixson, Waldenström (2018) conclude "variation in the number of children" by wealth has no significant effect.

have become stronger—wage disparities have increased, with stagnation, or even decreases, in real wages of those at the bottom and soaring increases at the top; assortive mating combined with greater female labor force participation has led to an increasing divide between families with two high income earners and at most one child, and those with one breadwinner, often working at low wage jobs; differentials in access to health care between the top and the bottom are one factor contributing to large observed differences in health status, reinforcing earnings differentials; and an increased scope for rent seeking described in other chapters of this book and elsewhere too may have contributed to increases in incomes at the top. The centrifugal force associated with dispersion in returns too have almost surely increased.

Given all of this, it is not surprising that there has been increased disparity in the income and wealth distribution.

5 Concluding Comments

The models presented in this chapter help focus on a critical question in today's society: the transmission of advantages across generations.[64]

The intergeneration transmission of advantage, whether accomplished through transfer of financial wealth, human capital, or "connections," is important because societies in which positions are in an essential way based on inheritance are fundamentally different from those in which positions arise from individual's own efforts and abilities. Such societies cannot claim that there is a level playing field, that there is equality of opportunity. There is already ample evidence that this is true in the U.S., with the children of the rich who perform poorly in school ending up with higher incomes than the children of the poor who do well; and with a young American's life prospects being heavily dependent on the income and education of his parents.

For more than two centuries, there has been an attempt to break away from a feudal system in which a child's position in society is pre-ordained by that of his parent and move to a meritocratic system where it is determined by the child's own ability. In many respects we have succeeded, but perhaps not as much as we had hoped: the evidence is that even in a society like the United States avowedly committed to meritocracy, inherited advantages play a key role, and more than a role than can be explained by the process of transmission of genes. The models presented here help explain why that is so.

We should also be concerned with wealth inequality, however it is generated, because societies in which there are large wealth (and income) inequalities function differently from more equalitarian societies. There are social and political consequences. It is worth noting that the attack on monopolies and trusts in the Progressive era was more motivated by concerns about their political and social consequences than the market distortions to which they gave rise.

[64] While in most our analysis, we make simple and we believe plausible hypotheses about the savings behavior of individuals, it should be clear that similar results would hold in a model in which capitalists maximize their intertemporal dynastic utilities, and workers maximize their life-time utilities, as we showed in Chapter 11. Indeed, the model may even be consistent with one in which all workers maximize dynastic utilities, but for those workers with low wages and capital, the borrowing constraint is binding, as noted earlier in the chapter.

This chapter has shown that in the natural stochastic extension of the standard growth model, there exists an equilibrium wealth distribution. This result stands in marked contrast to that of Piketty who has argued that capitalism is associated with ever increasing inequality. The reason is simple: in the models investigated here, even for the rich, the savings rate times the return on capital is less than the growth rate (which in the simplified models without technological change, is just the rate of growth of the population). So long as there is diminishing returns to capital deepening, it cannot be that as the wealthy accumulate more and more, the rate of return does not decline. The fact that it has not declined in the way expected can be explained: it is possible (and from the data, seems quite plausible) that the capital–effective labor ratio (taking into account labor augmenting technical progress) has actually decreased, at least in the U.S. and some other advanced countries; and/or it is possible that while the pure returns to capital may have decreased, monopoly and other rents (which show up as non-labor returns) have gone up, a possibility we explore further in Chapter 16.

But our analysis also exposes the possibility of ever-increasing inequality at the top, at least for an extended period of time, based not on the average return to capital in general, but on the returns obtained by those at the top, who because of informational advantages and/or greater willingness to undertake risk and/or because of de facto regressive taxation (they can more effectively engage in tax avoidance and tax evasion activities, bringing down their effective tax rates) may have far higher after tax returns to capital. (Similar results showing the possibility of ever-increasing inequality are obtained in the "classical" savings model of Appendix 12.2, where workers saving nothing; all of savings are done by capitalists.)

We have been able to derive simple closed form expressions for the level of tail-inequality in terms of the underlying properties of household behavior (savings and reproduction) and technology (most importantly, relative *shares* and the variability in returns). This has allowed us to derive precise results about the effect of different forms of taxation on tail-inequality.

The results again can be contrasted to those of Piketty, who has emphasized the importance of the difference between the return to capital and the rate of growth. Because we argue that the return to capital in the long run is an endogenous variable, our formulae emphasize the importance of the underlying parameters, like savings rates and growth rates.

Some policies that might seem to reduce inequality may, because of the shifting of taxes and expenditures, may have a more ambiguous effect. For instance, in our central model where everyone saves the same percentage of their income, a capital tax redistributed to workers reduces tail-inequality; but if the savings rate increases with income and the elasticity of substitution is sufficiently small, a capital tax redistributed to workers may increase tail-inequality.

In the next chapter, where wealth inequality is associated with the difference between dynastic and life-cycle savers, we will show that workers will actually be worse off, if the proceeds are distributed to them as pure transfers, but if the proceeds of the tax are spent on education, there can be unambiguous reductions in inequality.[65]

[65] By contrast, taxes on the return to land (discussed in later chapters), including capital gains, reduce wealth inequality and, under certain conditions, even lead workers to be better off.

The models presented here help us understand how changes in the underlying key parameters, such as savings rates, bequest behavior, and reproduction rates, and the differences among families with respect to these variables affect the equilibrium wealth distribution. Throughout our analysis, we have also emphasized the key role of policies in determining inequality, and we have delineated in particular the effect of changes in taxes on the equilibrium level of inequality. Just as we argued in Chapter 10 that one could not explain the increase in the wealth–income ratio solely within a neoclassical model (without rents), so too one cannot fully explain the increase in wealth inequality within a neoclassical model (without rents), such as we have presented here. Chapters 14–16 will explore in greater detail some of the determinants of the magnitude of rents in some very simple models.

I also do not believe that we can account well for changes in inequality solely in terms of changes in the structural parameters of the economy (preferences and technology). Policy has made a crucial difference. Section 4 described how many of the policy changes in recent years had strengthened the centrifugal forces and weakened the centripetal forces. But that raises a deeper question: why have we adopted such policies? Thus, in the end, to understand the growing inequality in America and other advanced countries, one has to come to terms with *politics*, and how economic inequality translates into political inequality, which in turn leads to policies which reinforce the economic inequalities.

Because so much of the increase in inequality in income and wealth is related to changes in policies, changes in those policies may be able to ameliorate this growing inequality. If we believe that there are large costs to our economy, our democracies, and our societies of this growing inequality, then at the very least, we should ask, are there changes in policy which will slow down this increase in inequality, and perhaps reverse it. An understanding of the forces that may be contributing to the growing inequality, such as that we have attempted to provide here, is a first step in constructing such a policy agenda.

In fact, there is a long list of policy changes—changes in legal frameworks, taxes, and expenditures—which would lead to less inequality in both the short run and the long, and simultaneously increase economic performance.[66] It is not the lack of knowledge that is preventing these actions from being undertaken. It is politics, a politics shaped by inequality of political power which follows from and can amplify inequalities in economic power.[67] The growing inequality in American society is thus a reflection as much of democracy in the twenty-first century as it is of capitalism in the twenty-first century.

[66] See, for example, Stiglitz (2012b) and Piketty (2014). Such changes affect both the distribution of income and wealth at any moment of time as well as the dynamics that describe the evolution of those variables. This chapter has taken technology as exogenous, but as Braverman and Stiglitz (1989) point out, technology and technological change itself is affected by societal inequalities. Sharecropping is a prevalent tenancy arrangement in economies with large disparities in land ownership, but not otherwise. But the choice of technology at one moment affects the distribution of income and wealth and wealth dynamics, and even the nature of technological change.

[67] The points raised here (and similar points made elsewhere in this chapter) are echoed in Suresh Naidu's excellent review of Piketty (2014).

Appendix 1 Alternative Formulations of the Wealth Generating Process

In Chapter 9, we presented a slight variation of the model in Section 3.3, where individuals add to what they inherited a fraction of their income, s, but pass on their inheritances—with per capita wealth (capital) then being given by

$$k_t = \frac{s\,(w + r\,k_{t-1}) + k_{t-1}}{1+n}. \tag{A12.1}$$

This implies in the steady state $sr = S_k n$. This formulation allows us to explicitly analyze the effect of the growth rate (the rate of growth of the population). In the special case where $\underline{\sigma}^2 = 0$, we can obtain simple formulae for the variance of k, the covariance of k and w, and the correlation coefficient between k and w.

$$V_k^* = V_w^* s^2 \frac{1+n}{1+n-\widehat{\beta}(1+S_k n)} \frac{1}{(1+n)^2 - \left(1+(S_k n)^2\right)}. \tag{A12.2}$$

The comparative statics with respect to the share of capital and regression to the means are even simpler than in the model in the text: an increase in the coefficient of regression to the mean (a lowering of β) lowers wealth inequality as does an increase in n.

And an increase in the share of capital or the savings rate increases wealth inequality.

Appendix 2 The Basic Kaldor Model

The formalization of the classical savings model where workers save nothing is usually attributed to Kaldor (1955a).[68] Using the notation of the chapter, we write:

$$\frac{d}{dt}(ln\ k_i) = s_{pi} r_i - n_i, \tag{A12.3}$$

where we continue to focus on the case where there is no labor augmenting technological progress, so that in the long run, $g = n$, and where s_{pi} is the savings rate of the ith capitalist dynasty. It is easy to translate these results into the more general case.

Assume s_p, r, and n are the same for all families. *Then relative wealth of all families would remain the same; any initial inequality of wealth would be perpetuated*, a result which contrasts starkly with that of the Solow model, where any initial differences in wealth asymptotically have no consequences:[69]

$$\frac{d}{dt}(ln\ k_i) - \frac{d}{dt}(ln\ k_j) = 0. \tag{A12.4}$$

[68] For a two-sector version, see Uzawa (1961).

[69] This result was originally derived in Stiglitz (1969a). One of the motivations of this appendix is to reconcile these results with those asserted by Piketty (2014) in a seemingly similar model.

Note that this is true regardless of the value of r, n, or s_p—that is, the relationship between the interest rate and the growth rate has nothing to do with relative wealth inequality. *Wealth inequality is unrelated to $r—g$.* It is just a matter of history.

In the long run there is a simple relationship between the rate of interest and the rate of growth:

$$s_p r = n, \tag{A12.5}$$

so r is greater than rate of growth, but in spite of this, there is no *further* concentration of wealth.

A2.1 Heterogeneous Savings Rates

Assume, on the other hand, that families differ in their savings rate, that is, s_i for some family is greater than for some other family. Then its relative wealth will grow without bound. *There is ever increasing wealth concentration at the top.*[70]

As we noted earlier, any coherent model must reconcile macro-variables with the micro-analysis, that is,

$$\frac{dK}{dt} = \sum_i \frac{dK_i}{dt} = \sum_i s_i r K_i = r \sum_i s_i K_i = r s^* K,$$

where

$$s^* \equiv \sum_i s_i K_i / K$$

is the weighted average savings rate. There is not only increasing wealth concentration at the top, but also an increasing average savings rate, an increasing capital–labor and capital–output ratio, and a diminishing rate of return on capital.

But r, K/Y and s all approach asymptotically limiting values given by r^{**}, $(K/Y)^{**}$, s^{**}, respectively. Then asymptotically all of wealth is in hands of the families with the highest savings rate, and

$$s^{**} = s_i, \tag{A12.6}$$

$$r^{**} = \frac{n}{s^{**}} = f'(k^{**}) \tag{A12.7}$$

and

$$(K/Y)^{**} = f(k^{**})/k^{**} \tag{A12.8}$$

The long-run equilibrium is dominated by the family (families) with highest value of s_i.

[70] This is a result which is consistent with Piketty's conclusions, but it arises not from the relationship between the rate of interest and the rate of growth but from differences in the rate of savings among *different* capitalists.

A2.2 Stochastic Returns to Capital

We return to the basic model where all capitalists save at the same rate s_p. Assume that there exists a *macroeconomic* steady state with all families having the same savings rate, returns on capital, and reproduction rates, and that the economy is in that steady state. Then the drift of the diffusion equation, $\mu = 0$ and the stochastic differential equation describing the *i*th dynasty's growth in wealth per capita is (instead of (12.2)):

$$dk_t = \sigma k_t dZ_t \tag{A12.9}$$

The variance of per capita wealth is ever increasing.

13

Wealth Inequality

Life-Cycle Savings vs. Inherited Wealth

1 Introduction

A key concern about the growing inequality in the United States and other advanced countries is the worry that we are giving rise to an inherited plutocracy.[1] Piketty (2014) emphasized that if $s_p = 1$ and the rate of interest were greater than the rate of growth, inherited wealth would increase over time both absolutely and relative to national income. On the other hand, the fact that individuals are living longer and must save for their retirement means that life-cycle savings are also increasing, reflected in part in the huge increase in pension funds.[2] In this chapter, we construct a simple model incorporating both inherited and life-cycle savings, describing the equilibrium distribution of income and wealth, and in particular, between inherited wealth and life-cycle wealth.

We are able to obtain simple formulae describing the equilibrium share of wealth held by life-cycle savers. Using these formulae, we can easily ascertain the effects of, say, tax policy or changes in the parameters of the economy. We show that an increase in the savings rate of workers (as a result, for instance, of encouraging them to save more) has no effect on output per capita, but does increase the share of wealth of life-cycle savers. Life-cycle savings crowds out inherited savings. On the other hand, a tax on capital (even if it is paid disproportionately by the rich capitalists, with proceeds paid out to workers, and so would therefore be viewed as progressive) will be so shifted that capitalists are unaffected and workers' income, including transfers, actually goes down, as does their share in national wealth. But these adverse incidence effects are far from inevitable: the revenues raised from taxation can be used for investments, either in human or physical capital. There are expenditure policies which can ensure that the capital tax increases equality. This bears out a general theme of this book: tax and expenditure policies have to be constructed to consider general equilibrium incidence effects, and the two sets of policies have to be considered together.

The chapter is divided into three parts, beyond the introduction and conclusion. The first is based on the standard neoclassical model with fixed savings rates and with the proceeds of any capital or inheritance tax distributed to workers. In the second, we allow some or all of the proceeds of taxation to be invested in education or infrastructure (public investments that increase the productivity of private investments). In the third section, we allow the distribution of the population between life-cycle savers and capitalists to

[1] This chapter is a revised and edited version of parts of papers originally distributed as "New theoretical perspectives on the distribution of income and wealth among individuals: Part III. Life Cycle Savings vs. Inherited Savings," NBER working paper 21191, May 2015; Stiglitz (2018b) and Mattauch, Klenert, Stiglitz, and Edenhofer (2019), reprinted here as Chapter 19). Parts of this were also published in Stiglitz (2016a).

[2] See Milevsky and Huang (2011). For statistics on the size of pension funds, see OECD (2013).

The Origins of Inequality, and Policies to Contain It. Joseph E. Stiglitz, Oxford University Press. © Joseph E. Stiglitz (2025).
DOI: 10.1093/oso/9780198799580.003.0014

be endogenous, with the two groups having identical savings functions. The only difference is that when wealth is low enough, bequests drop to zero. With stochastic returns, individuals move between the two groups. In the final section of the chapter, we comment on how the models may provide insights into understanding the growth of wealth inequality.

Appendix 1 shows that the analysis is unaltered if we had assumed utility maximizing workers and capitalists. Appendix 2 presents the proof of the adverse effect of capital taxation on workers. Appendix 3 discusses the limiting case of the model where there are no capitalists.

2 Basic Model

We assume two groups: There are workers who live two periods and save for their retirement.[3] Their savings are referred to as "life-cycle savings." Then there are the capitalists, who save a fixed percentage of their income, s_p.[4] For simplicity, we use a discrete time model.

As in the previous chapter, output is produced by means of a neoclassical constant returns to scale production function $Q = F(K, L)$, where K is the capital stock and L the labor supply (there is full employment). $k = K/L$ is the capital–labor ratio. $Q/L = F/L = f(k)$ gives output per worker as a function of the capital–labor ratio. $f' \geq 0, f'' \leq 0$. The return to capital is f', and the wage rate is $f - kf'$. We assume that the number of capitalists and workers increase at the same rate, n (assumed here to be exogenous). For simplicity, we ignore labor augmenting technological progress, though it is straightforward to bring it into the analysis.

The difference equations describing the evolution of the economy are given by:[5]

$$(1 + n)\, k_{t+1}^{c} = \left(1 + s_p f'(k_t)\right) k_t^{c} \tag{13.1}$$

and

$$k_{t+1}^{w} = s\left(r\left(k_{t+1}\right)\right) w\left(k_t\right), \tag{13.2}$$

where k^w and k^c are workers' and capitalists' capital (per capita), respectively, where we have allowed the savings rate of workers to depend on the (rationally expected) interest

[3] In that sense, the model is similar to that of Pasinetti (1962), where there are two classes too. Later in the chapter, we model workers' savings behavior (life-cycle savings). See also Samuelson and Modigliani (1966), Stiglitz (1967, 1969b), and Judd (1985). More recently Baranzini (1991), Michl (2009), Stiglitz (2015c; 2016a, 2018a), Mattauch, Edenhofer, Klenert, and Bénard (2016), and Klenert et al. (2018) have analyzed related models in which workers save in a life-cycle fashion.

[4] s_p can be derived endogenously, if, as in the standard representative agent model, families maximize dynastic utility.

[5] Notice that for capitalists, savings are defined as the *addition* to their wealth, while for workers, since each worker starts life (in this model) with no wealth, savings are their total wealth. (There are alternative formulations based on gross savings generating similar results.)

rate,[6] and where

$$k_t = k_t^w + \beta k_t^c, \tag{13.3}$$

where β is the ratio of capitalists to workers. (By assumption capitalists supply no labor). Here, β is assumed to be fixed.

These equations fully describe the dynamics, given an initial value of workers' and capitalists' capital.[7] In the steady state, $k^{(c^*)} = k_t^c = k_{(t+1)}^c$ and similarly for k_k^w. Hence, from (13.1)

$$n = s_p f'(k^*) = s_p r, \tag{13.4}$$

where k^* is the steady state value of k and $f'(k^*)$ is the steady state return on capital, equal to r.[8] The steady state level of capital (and the equilibrium interest rate) is determined simply by capitalists' saving propensity. If $f'' < 0$, k^* is uniquely determined.

If workers save more, the economy does not become richer; income does not go up; wages do not increase. All that happens is that they increase their share of total capital.[9]

For later reference, we note that

$$\frac{d\,ln\,k^*}{d\,ln\,(n/s_p)} = -\sigma/S_L, \tag{13.4'}$$

where σ is the elasticity of substitution and S_L is the share of labor (assuming perfect competition). An increase in n/s_p lowers the equilibrium capital–labor ratio by an amount which is proportional to the elasticity of substitution (obviously, if the elasticity of substitution is zero, there is no change), and inversely proportional to the share of labor.

The steady state capital of workers (life-cycle capital) is given by

$$k^{w^*} = s(k^*)\,w(k^*). \tag{13.5}$$

Hence

$$\frac{k^{w^*}}{k^*} = \frac{s(k^*)\,w(k^*)}{k^*}. \tag{13.6}$$

[6] This assumes that the fraction of an individual's income that is saved is just a function of the interest rate, consistent with homothetic preferences. We could have employed a more general savings function: $s(w_t, r_{t+1}) = s(k_t, k_{t+1})$ where the savings rate depends not only on the rate of return on capital (which depends on k_{t+1}) but also on wages, which depend on k_t. Little here depends on the precise form of s, though we will observe that some results do depend on whether the savings rate increases or decreased with k_{t+1}. Note that in steady state, an increase in k will be associated with an increase in wages and a decrease in interest rates. Total savings will increase with k so long as the substitution effect of the decreased interest rate is not too large.

[7] As Hirano and Stiglitz (2019) show, there can in general be an infinite number of trajectories consistent with rational expectations. This follows from the fact that there may be more than one solution to (13.2) for k_{t+1}^w for any $\{k_t, k_t^w\}$. (Substituting (13.1) into (13.2), we obtain $k_{t+1}^w = s\left(k_{t+1}^w + \beta\left(1 + s_p f'(k_t)\right) k_t^c/(1+n)\right) w(k_t)$). The reason is that if workers expect a high interest rate, they will need to save little for their retirement—but then the interest rate will be high; but if they expect a low interest rate, they will need to save a lot, but then the interest rate will be low.

[8] Note that all variables are measured over a generation, which is the basic time unit of analysis.

[9] Of course, there is a limit to the share of capital that they can hold—it has to be less than unity. This constraint plays an important role in the analysis below.

Using (13.4) this can be rewritten:

$$\frac{k^{w^*}}{k^*} = \frac{s\,(k^*)\,w\,(k^*)}{f'^{-1}\left(\frac{n}{s_p}\right)} = n\frac{s\,(k^*)}{s_p}\frac{1 - S_k}{S_k}. \qquad (13.7)$$

The ratio of wealth of life-cycle savers to that of capitalists (or to total wealth) depends on the relative savings rates, the relative shares, and the growth rate. Given the savings and production functions, inequality is just a function of (n/s_p). Using (13.4′), we can calculate:

$$d\ln\frac{k^{w^*}}{k^*}\Big/ d\ln\frac{n}{s_p} = 1 + \nu - \frac{1 - \sigma}{1 - S_k}, \qquad (13.7'),$$

where $\nu = d\ln s/d\ln r$, the interest elasticity of savings[10], noting that an increase in n/s_p increases the return on capital, by (13.4). Thus, if

$$\sigma < S_K - S_L\nu, \qquad (13.7'')$$

an increase in n or a lowering of s_p increases wealth inequality because the induced indirect effect in lowering the share of labor exceeds the direct benefit of, say, the lowering of the savings of capitalists. The critical value of σ is lowered if $\nu > 0$, because the increased return to capital induces more savings on the part of workers, partially offsetting the adverse effect of the lowering of workers' (share of) income.

If the savings rate of workers increases, for instance because of increased expected retirement longevity,[11] workers' wealth increases proportionately, while aggregate wealth remains unchanged. By the same token, in this model, if the generosity of social security increases, so the savings rate of workers decreases, workers' wealth (excluding their claims on social security) decreases proportionately, while aggregate wealth remains unchanged (in a pay-as-you-go system).

There is an important qualification to this analysis: workers' savings has to be low enough so that, on their own, they do not drive the rate of return below n/s_p. For if they do, then the life-cycle savers eventually drive out the capitalists.[12] It would appear that this condition is normally satisfied.[13]

[10] If workers' intertemporal utility functions are Cobb–Douglas, then $s' = 0$. If workers' utility function is such that $U = \min\{C_t, C_{t+1}\}$, then $(1 - s)w = s(1 + r)w$, or $s = 1/[2 + r]$, so (13.7) can be rewritten $k^{w^*}/k^* = n\frac{1}{2}s_p + n$ $1 - \frac{S_k}{S_k}$. In this case, an increase in s_p reduces the share of inherited wealth provided the elasticity of substitution is not too small.

[11] Incorporating such a change formally in the model is not easy, for it entails moving from a two-period model to, say, an n period model, where the individual works n_1 periods and is retired for $n - n_1$ periods. The key insight, though, that the rate of interest is set by the savings rate of capitalists remains valid.

As we have noted earlier, there are a number of other factors that could affect life-cycle savings—the adequacy of provision of health care for old age, the efficiency of annuity markets and the extent to which they are affected by asymmetries of information, and uncertainties both about retirement age, rates of return to capital, and life expectancies. In practice, there are other institutional factors: most individuals save through retirement programs, and the rules and regulations concerning those retirement programs can have first order effects on the amount set aside.

[12] The critical condition is that $s\,(k^*)\,w\,(k^*) < k^*$, or that $\frac{s(k^*)}{s_p} < \frac{S_k}{n(1-S_k)}$. If $n = 1, s_k = 0.2$, then the condition becomes $s\,(k^*) < 0.25s_p$. If population growth slows, it is even more likely that the condition will be satisfied.

[13] For more extensive discussions of the boundary condition, see Mattauch, Klenert, Stiglitz, and Edenhofer (2019).

2.1 The Effect of Taxation

If we impose a tax on capital at the rate τ^c, we obtain instead of (13.4):

$$n = (1 - \tau^c) s_p f'(k^*), \tag{13.4a}$$

or

$$r = \frac{n}{(1 - \tau^c) s_p}. \tag{13.4b}$$

Where it will be recalled r is the before tax rate of return ($= f'$). This implies that *the after-tax return to capital is not affected by the tax*. There is, in effect, full "shifting." As the tax rate increases, the equilibrium capital stock diminishes.[14]

The before tax return $f'(k)$, of course, increases:

$$\frac{d\,ln\,r}{d\,ln\,\tau^c} = \frac{d\,ln\,f'}{d\,ln\,\tau^c} = \frac{\tau^c}{1 - \tau^c}, \tag{13.8}$$

and the equilibrium k decreases

$$\frac{dk^*}{d\tau^c} = \frac{f'(k^*)}{(1 - \tau^c) f''(k^*)} < 0. \tag{13.9}$$

2.2 Capital Taxation with Proceeds Distributed to Workers

To ascertain the effect on the wealth distribution, we have to specify what happens to the tax revenue. Assume it is redistributed to workers. Then the transfer T (per capita) is given by

$$T = \tau^c r(k^*) k^*. \tag{13.10}$$

Thus, workers' lifetime income is given by

$$Y^W = w(k^*) + T. \tag{13.11}$$

[14] We should emphasize that this result is not general. In Chapter 15, we consider, for instance, a model in which capitalists have a choice of assets to hold, and in equilibrium, they hold all of the risky assets. In a generalization of that model, it is easy to show that a tax on the excess returns to capital over the safe interest rate leads to more risk taking, that is, a shift in their portfolio to higher return assets. (Domar and Musgrave, 1944; Stiglitz, 1969b). If these assets are complements to labor, that shift by itself may increase wages. We note later too that taxes on capital gains in land may redirect investment into forms that are more complementary with labor.

Noting that in our simplified model, the saving rate depends only on the after-tax rate of return, and from (13.4a) that is unchanged, and letting s^* denote that value of s, (13.6) can be rewritten as

$$\frac{k^{w^*}}{k^*} = \frac{s^*}{k^*} Y^W. \tag{13.12}$$

Then, to ascertain the effect of an increase in the tax rate on the share of inherited wealth, we simply have to ascertain the sign of

$$\frac{d\left(\frac{s^*\left(w(k^*)+T\right)}{k^*}\right)}{d\tau^c} \tag{13.13}$$

An increase in the tax rate lowers the wage, but at least for low τ^c increases the transfer. But it is possible to show that the former effect dominates:

$$\frac{dY^W}{d\tau^c} = \left(-k^* f''(k^*) + \tau^c \left(k^* f''(k^*) + f'(k^*)\right)\right) \frac{dk^*}{d\tau^c} + r(k^*)\, k^* \tag{13.14}$$

The sign of (13.14) is thus that of $\frac{\tau^c\left(f'(k^*)\right)^2}{(1-\tau^c)f''(k^*)} < 0$ for $0 < \tau^c < 1$. ($\frac{dY^W}{d\tau^c} = 0$ at $\tau^c = 0$.)

Hence, *the loss in wages is always greater than the benefit from the transfer.*

It follows that

Proposition 13.1 An increase in the interest income tax with proceeds distributed as lump sum payments to workers always increases the relative importance of inherited wealth and has an adverse effect on the distribution of consumption (well-being): workers are worse off while capitalists are unaffected.[15]

Since the after-tax interest rate facing capitalists is the same, their flow of consumption (in steady state) is unaffected. Workers' lifetime utility is a function of their income, Y^W, and the interest they receive on their savings (after tax). We have already shown the derivative of Y^W with respect to τ^c is negative (except at $\tau^c = 0$, where it is zero). But because the after-tax return the worker receives from his investment is unaffected, workers are unambiguously worse off.

Thus, in the case that would *seem* to be the most favorable to workers—where all the proceeds are redistributed to them—their income is reduced, their welfare is reduced, and inequality is increased.

[15] Since s is fixed, and Y^w falls, k^{w^*} falls, while k^* increases. We can rewrite (13.7) with taxes as $k^{w^*}/k^* = ns(k^*)/s_p(1 - \tau^c)(1 - s_k/s_k + \tau^c)$ where S_k is the share of capital before tax.

2.3 Inheritance Tax with Proceeds Distributed to Workers

Assume now that only the return on inherited wealth is taxed. Life-cycle savings is exempted, for example through IRA accounts. (13.4a) continues to hold: k^* is the same function of τ^c. Now, we have a somewhat more complicated problem:

$$\text{Ţ} = \tau^c r(k^*)(k^* - k^{w^*}), \tag{13.15a}$$

where

$$k^{w^*} = s(k^*)(w(k^*) + \text{Ţ}). \tag{13.15b}$$

Substituting (13.15a) into (13.15b), we obtain:

$$k^{w^*} = \frac{s\left(\frac{n}{s_p(1-\tau^c)}\right)(w(k^*) + \tau^c f'(k^*)k^*)}{1 + s\left(\frac{n}{s_p(1-\tau^c)}\right)\tau^c f'(k^*)} = \frac{s\left(\frac{n}{s_p(1-\tau^c)}\right)(w(k^*) + \frac{n\tau^c}{(1-\tau^c)}k^*)}{1 + s\left(\frac{n}{s_p(1-\tau^c)}\right)\frac{n\tau^c}{(1-\tau^c)}}, \tag{13.15c}$$

where we have made use of the fact that the before tax interest rate (which is the interest rate received by workers) is $\frac{n}{s_p(1-\tau^c)}$ so $\frac{dr}{d\tau^c} = \frac{r}{1-\tau^c}$. We have already shown that as τ^c increases $w(k^*) + \tau^c k^* f'(k^*)$ decreases. Similarly, as τ^c increases the denominator increases at a fixed s. Moreover, at fixed k^*, k^{w^*} increases with s. Hence, so long as $\nu \leq 0$ (or more generally, not too large), k^{w^*} decreases; but if the elasticity of substitution is greater than a critical threshold (less than unity) then the share of life-cycle wealth increases nonetheless; but if the elasticity of substitution is very small, it can decrease.[16]

Now, however, the effect on relative consumption (well-being) is more ambiguous. In particular,
at $\tau^c = 0$, using (13.9):

$$\frac{dY^W}{d\tau^c} = \frac{dw}{dk^*}\frac{dk^*}{d\tau^c} + r(k^*)(k^* - k^{w^*}) = -k^{w^*} f'(k^*) < 0. \tag{13.16}$$

The adverse effect on wages is the same as before, but now the transfers are smaller. On the other hand, workers' lifetime utility if a function of their income and the return to capital:

$$V(r(k), Y^W)$$

V is the indirect utility function.[17] Hence we show in Appendix 13.2 that[18] at $\tau^c = 0$,

$$\frac{dV}{d\tau^c} = 0. \tag{13.17}$$

That is, the loss in income is precisely offset by the increased return to capital.

16 Now $\frac{k^{w*}}{k^*} = \frac{ns\left(\frac{1-S_k}{S_k}+\tau^c\right)}{s_p(1-\tau^c)+s(k^*)\tau^c n}$. So long as $s_p > ns$ and $\nu \geq 0$ the direct effect of an increase in taxes is to increase the relative importance of life-cycle savings. If the elasticity of substitution is greater than one, the indirect effect is also positive.

17 We can in principle derive the savings functions from V.

18 We have made use of the fact that for an indirect utility function, $\frac{\partial V}{\partial r} = k^{w^*}\frac{\partial V}{\partial Y^W}$.

But for τ^c small but > 0, $\frac{dV}{d\tau^c} = V_Y \tau^c \frac{f' dk^{c*}}{d\tau^c} > 0$, provided only that ν, the interest elasticity of savings, is not too positive and the elasticity of substitution is low enough.[19] What is critical in determining the welfare of workers is the tax transfers of capitalists to workers. As τ^c increases slightly, k decreases, and normally k^{w^*} decreases as well, since wages decrease. The delicate question is the balance of the two. If the elasticity of substitution is low enough, k^{w^*} falls by more than k, and that means the transfers increase, and workers welfare is increased.

On the other hand, for high enough tax rates, eventually k^* falls below k^{w^*} (k^{c^*} becomes zero), and the economy switches to a one class economy, with only life-cycle savings, with

$$s\left(k^{w^*}\right) w\left(k^{w^*}\right) = \frac{k^{w^*}}{1+n}.$$

We refer to the critical tax rate as τ^c_{max}. Clearly, because wages are lower than they were in the initial equilibrium and there are no transfers, workers' incomes are lower. But though wages are lower, the interest rate they receive on their savings is higher. But we can establish that workers are always better off in the two-class equilibrium with inequality than in the one-class equilibrium without inequality.

In the obvious notation, we write:

$$V(\tau^c_{max}) - V(0) = r\widehat{\tau^c}\,\widehat{V}_Y \int_0^{\tau^c_{max}} \frac{dk^{c^*}}{d\tau^c}\, d\tau^c = -r\widehat{\tau^c}\,\widehat{V}_Y\, k_0^{c^*} \leq 0,$$

where $k_0^{c^*}$ is the value of k^{c^*} when $\tau^c = 0$, $\widehat{\tau^c}$ is an intermediate value of τ^c, $0 \leq \tau^c \leq \tau^c_{max}$, and $\widehat{V}_Y$ is an intermediate value of V_Y between that at $\tau^c = 0$ and τ^c_{max}.

While a small inheritance tax, the proceeds of which are used to finance transfer payments to workers, may increase workers' welfare, a high enough tax lowers welfare.[20] (We rush to add that the next section will show that if the proceeds are spent on public investments, then even a high inheritance tax can be welfare increasing.)

Similarly, aggregate workers' consumption (per capita) C^w decreases with the tax:

$$\begin{aligned} C^w &= f(k) - nk^* - (1 - s_P)\, r(1 - \tau^c)k^{c^*} \\ &= f(k^*) - nk^* - (1 - s_P)\, n\, k^{c^*}/s_p \\ &= f(k^*) - nk^*/s_p + (1 - s_P)\, nk^*_w/s_p, \end{aligned}$$

[19] We establish the result by showing that under the specified conditions $\frac{d^2V}{d\tau^{c2}} > 0$.

These results can be seen best when ν is very negative. Then, as the tax rate increases, the before tax interest rate increases, and k^{w^*} decreases, because the savings rate is reduced; if it decreases enough, k^{c^*} could increase, and thus the transfer payments made to workers could increase, possibly more than offsetting the lowering of wages.

It should be noted that here ν represents the *total* change in workers' savings rate as the interest rate changes. If the savings rate also depends on the level of transfers (i.e., is affected by the level of income), that effect is also included.

[20] This analysis assumes that social welfare is only assessed from the perspective of workers (who receive no inheritances.) It ignores the welfare of the capitalists. If their well-being were also included within the social welfare function, the optimal tax would obviously be different. Note the steady state income of the capitalists always decreases with taxation, that is, $\frac{d}{d\tau^c}((1 - \tau^c)\, rk^*) = (1 - \tau^c)(f'(k^*) + f''(k^*)\, k^*)\frac{dk^*}{d\tau^c} - r(k^*)\, k^* = \frac{f'(k)f'(k)}{f''(k)} < 0$, but so does income per capita.

so

$$\begin{aligned} dC^w/d\tau^c &= \left(f' - n/s_p\right) dk/d\tau^c + (1 - s_P)\, n/s_p(dk_w^*/d\tau^c) \\ &= [\tau^c/(1 - \tau^c)]n/s_p\, dk/d\tau^c + (1 - s_P)\, n/s_p(dk_w^*/d\tau^c) < 0, \end{aligned}$$

so long as the savings elasticity is not too positive.

2.4 Inequality among the Rich and Progressive Capital Taxation

A progressive capital income tax can affect the degree of inequality among the rich—in this model, among the capitalists—as we noted in the previous chapter.[21] The argument for a progressive capital tax is strengthened if we look more carefully at the nature of the *measured* returns to capital. In economists' simplest models, all capital receives the same returns. If returns are stochastic, then it is simply luck that determines who gets high returns. If that were all that there were to the matter, a progressive tax on the rate of return to capital in excess of the average return (with offsets for returns below that level) would be welfare increasing, if capitalists were risk averse. If savings were elastic in the certainty equivalent return, then savings would increase, and workers would be better off.

The high average returns received by capitalists could reflect their greater willingness to take risk, and represent a return to risk taking, as reflected in the differing portfolio compositions noted in Chapter 4. If capital markets are imperfect (so risk is not fully diversified) and individuals are risk averse, riskier investments will yield higher returns than safe. A proportional capital tax on *excess returns* (over the safe rate of interest) would, under these circumstances, increase risk taking, and thereby average (before tax) incomes of the capitalists at any given level of wealth. The capitalists' accumulation Equation (13.1), and the equilibrium condition (13.7) relate to the *average* returns: they have to be large enough to endow the next generation with the same wealth per capita of the present. The higher average returns lead to more capital accumulation, depressing marginal and average returns. Hence, k^* is increased and workers benefit from higher wages.

There may, however, be other possible explanations for above average returns. The returns could represent greater skill at investing, in which the returns ought to be viewed as a return to labor, not as a return to capital, and taxed accordingly.[22] (Lower returns to capital for workers, in our model, affects the distribution of wealth between life-cycle savers and capitalists, depending on whether workers' interest savings elasticity is positive or negative; but even if it reduces wealth inequality—as will happen when the interest elasticity is negative, that is, workers have to save more to smooth their income across time—the lower returns reduces their welfare.)

Finally, the returns could in part be a return to exploitation. To the extent that that is the case,[23] then a progressive tax would discourage such rent seeking behavior, increase economic efficiency, improve the well-being of those who are being exploited, and reduce overall inequality. We pursue this interpretation further in Chapter 16.

[21] An earlier version of the ideas in this section were delivered as a keynote address at the National Tax Association annual meetings, Santa Fe, November 2014.

[22] This is particularly relevant given the literature which has suggested that the *pure* returns to capital should be taxed at a zero rate, based on a misinterpretation of the Atkinson-Stiglitz (1976) result. See also Stiglitz (2015d) and Chapter 19 below.

[23] We cited evidence that that was the case earlier.

3 Public Investment

We extend the analysis of the previous section in two critical ways: the revenues from the capital or inheritance tax are spent to public investment, for example in education or infrastructure; and we introduce utility maximizing workers and capitalists.[24]

As we showed in earlier chapters, the latter extension is straightforward, and does not change the analysis is any fundamental way. Capitalists maximize a standard intertemporal utility function with discount factor $1/\delta$. We normalize by assuming workers have a (fixed) population of unity, capitalists of N, so capitalists' consumption is NC_c. We simplify the analysis by assuming the government simply wishes to maximize workers' steady state consumption or utility.[25] We assume, for simplicity, that the labor supply is fixed (at unity as well).[26]

But allowing government to invest the revenues from capital taxation does fundamentally change the results. Recall the central message of the previous section: a capital or inheritance tax in a two-class economy so lowers wages that workers are (normally) worse off, even taking into account the transfers they receive. But if the revenues are spent on human or physical capital, wages may actually be increased, and workers unambiguously better off.

3.1 Public Revenue Spent on Education

First, we assume all revenues from taxation are spent on education. Later subsections will generalize the results. Then output, Q, is a constant returns to scale function of (private) capital, K, and effective labor, which is a function of investment in human capital per capita. Noting that labor supply has been normalized at unity, and assuming for simplicity that there is no labor growth, the effective labor supply can be written as $\phi(K_g)$, with $\phi'(K_g) \geq 0$ and $\phi''(K_g) \leq 0$. So the overall (constant returns to scale) production function can now be written

$$Q = F(K, \phi(K_g)). \tag{13.18}$$

Investments in education increase productivity, but there are diminishing returns. Because of constant returns to scale in capital and effective labor, we can write:[27]

$$Q = \phi f(K/\phi) = \phi f(k), \tag{13.19}$$

[24] Thus, we generalize Mattauch, Edenhofer, Klenert, and Bénard (2016) and Mattauch, Siegmeier, Edenhofer, and Creutzig, et al. (2018). Their models used logarithmic utility functions for both capitalists and workers, which naturally generate the kinds of fixed savings rates assumed by the earlier literature. Mattauch et al. (2017) focused on ascertaining the conditions under which in equilibrium all capital was held by workers. Here, we assume that the tax rates on capital (or on capitalists) are low enough that this is not so.

[25] Similar results obtain if we analyze more generally Pareto efficient tax structures, or tax structures which maximize a more general inequality averse social welfare function, so long as the disparity between the two groups is large enough, so that the marginal social utility of consumption of capitalists relative to that of workers is small enough.

[26] Thus, while earlier sections focused on the issue of the labor supply elasticity, here our concern is on savings. Results on the desirability of capital taxation would be strengthened by allowing a positive labor supply elasticity.

[27] We assume for satisfies the usual Inada condition, $\lim f'(k)$ as k goes to zero is infinity.

where $k = \frac{K}{\phi}$ the capital–"effective labor" ratio. We assume a tax rate of τ on the net return to all capital.[28]

We now modify our earlier analysis in three ways: we assume the rate of growth of the population, n, is zero, we allow for depreciation at the rate η, and we assume that capitalists maximize an intertemporal utility function of the form $\sum \frac{U(C_t)}{(1+\delta)^t}$, that is, a time separable utility function, where C_t is the t-th generation's consumption and δ is the pure rate of time preference. This implies that in long run equilibrium k is given by:

$$r \equiv (1-\tau)(f' - \mu) = \delta, \tag{13.20}$$

where, as before, r is the (after-tax) rate of return on capital,[29] μ is the rate of depreciation[30] and the tax is applied only to net returns. The after-tax net return to capital is simply related to the pure rate of time discount. (13.20) determines the equilibrium value of k as a function of τ (given η and δ):[31]

$$k = f'^{-1}\left[\frac{\delta}{1-\tau} + \mu\right] \equiv \psi(\tau), \tag{13.21}$$

with $\psi'(\tau) = \delta/(1-\tau)^2 f'' = -\frac{km\sigma}{S_L} < 0$,

where $m = \frac{f' - \mu}{f'}$, the ratio of the net to the gross marginal return to capital.

We denote by k_0 the value of k when $\tau = 0$: $k_0 \equiv \psi(0)$. Tax revenue is $\tau\,(f' - \eta)\,K$, all of which is spent on public education. Hence

$$K_g = \tau(f' - \mu)K = \frac{\tau\delta}{1-\tau}K = \frac{\tau\delta}{1-\tau}\,\psi(\tau)\,\phi(K_g). \tag{13.22}$$

There is a unique solution for K_g for any give τ if τ is small or if $\zeta < 1$, where $\zeta = \frac{d\ln\phi}{d\ln K_g}$, the elasticity of productivity with respect to investments in human capital. We can then solve (13.22) for K_g as a function of τ:

$$K_g = \Omega(\tau) \tag{13.22$'$}$$

with

$$dK_g/d\tau = \frac{\delta\psi(\tau)\,\phi(K_g)}{(1-\tau)^2}\{1 + \tau\frac{f' - \eta}{f''k}\}/\{1 - \zeta\}. \tag{13.22$''$}$$

An increase in the tax rate has two effects: a direct effect, increasing revenue, and an indirect effect, a reduction in the capital stock, which can reduce the total tax revenue. The direct effect is greater than the indirect effect so long as the tax rate is small. For small tax rates, $dK_g/d\tau$ is approximately $\delta\psi(0)\,\phi(0)$.

[28] Again, similar results obtain if one can differentiate between taxes on capital for workers and that of capitalists (e.g., a tax on life-cycle savings vs. a tax on inheritances), or if capitalists engage in some tax avoidance activities, to convert some of their capital income into what appears as wage income.

[29] With no depreciation, $r = 1 - \tau f'$.

[30] The large number of variables appearing throughout the book makes it necessary for us to use the same symbol for different variables in different chapters. In the previous chapter μ was the drift of the diffusion process.

[31] Throughout the analysis below, we assume we are in an equilibrium in which there are capitalists. See Pasinetti (1962), Samuelson and Modigliani and Samuelson (1966), Stiglitz (1967, 2015d), and Mattauch, Klenert, Stiglitz, and Edenhofer (2022).

As in the previous section, we assume that worker savings are given by $s_w(r)w$,[32]

$$w = \phi(K_g)\, g(k) = \phi(K_g)\,(f - kf'), \tag{13.23}$$

where $g(k) \equiv f - kf'$ is the return per unit of effective labor. Hence from (13.22) and (13.23) w depends just on τ. An increase in the tax rate (from $\tau = 0$) increases K_g and hence $\phi(K_g)$—the efficiency units per worker; but it lowers k and hence g, the wage per efficiency unit. As before,

$$(d\ln g/d\ln k)(d\ln k/d\tau) = -\,(k^2 f''/w)\left(\frac{f'(k^*)}{(1-\tau^c)f''(k^*)\,k}\right) = (S_K/1-\tau^c)\,S_L. \tag{13.23'}$$

At $\tau = 0$, $dw/d\tau = \phi'(0)\,\delta\psi(0)\,\phi(0)\,g(\psi(0)) - \delta\phi(0)\,\psi(0) = \delta\psi(0)\,\phi(0)\,[\phi' g(\psi(0)) - 1]$, which is positive provided only that the return to investments in human capital are large enough, that is,

$$\phi' > \frac{1}{g(\psi(0))}.$$

We can now solve for workers' steady state utility, $V^w = V^w(w, r)$, which depends just on $\{w, r\} = \{w, \delta\}$ which from (13.23) depends just on τ. It is thus apparent that *a small tax always improves workers' welfare, so long as the return on capital is large enough.*

We can now calculate the optimal tax, which maximizes w (using (13.21), (13.22″) and (13.23):

$$\begin{aligned}\frac{dw}{d\tau} &= g\phi'\frac{\delta\psi(\tau)\,\phi(K_g)}{(1-\tau)^2}\{1 + \tau\frac{f' - \eta}{f''k}\}/\{1 - \tau\zeta\} - \frac{\phi\psi\delta}{(1-\tau)^2} \\ &= \frac{\delta\psi(\tau)\,\phi(K_g)}{(1-\tau)^2}\;\frac{1}{1-\tau\zeta}\left[g\phi'\left(1 - \tau\frac{m\sigma}{S_L}\right) - (1 - \tau\zeta)\right] \\ &= \frac{\delta\psi(\tau)\,\phi(K_g)}{(1-\tau)^2}\;\frac{1}{1-\tau\zeta}\left[g\phi' - 1 - \tau\left(\left(\frac{m\sigma}{S_L}\right)g\phi' - \zeta\right)\right].\end{aligned}$$

$g\phi' - 1$ is the net productivity of investment. $\left(\frac{m\sigma}{S_L}\right)g\phi' - \zeta$ reflects the erosion of the tax base (the decrease in wages from the tax incidence effect). Hence the optimal tax rate is given by:[33]

$$\tau^* = \frac{g\phi' - 1}{g\phi'\frac{m\sigma}{S_L} - \zeta}.$$

[32] If they don't, then $K_w = S(w, r)$, and the analysis proceeds much as below.

[33] Obviously $0 \le \tau^* \le 1$. We assume $\phi' > 1$; $0 \le \zeta \le g\phi'\frac{m\sigma}{S_L}$.

A tax levied only on the capital earnings of capitalists would be even more favorable to workers.

The result that there must be an optimal tax can be established even more easily. We know that there exists a τ_{max} such that at above or that level, $k_c = 0$, implying $K_g = 0$, implying that the wage is lower than at = 0.

Thus, the optimal tax rate is higher the higher the marginal return on public investment, provided $\frac{m\sigma}{S_L} > \zeta$; the higher the *elasticity* of return on public investment, ζ, and the lower $\frac{m\sigma}{S_L}$, that is, the lower the elasticity of substitution (a high elasticity of substitution entails a large change in k in order to restore the capital market equilibrium condition (13.20); the higher the share of labor; and the lower is m.

We can also easily solve for what happens to the wealth distribution at the tax rate increases:

$$K_w = s_w(r)\phi\left(K_g\right)g(k) = s_w(\delta)\,\phi\left(K_g\right)g(\psi(\tau)), \tag{13.24a}$$

using (13.20) and (13.21), implying that K_w also depends just on τ. On the other hand,

$$K = k\phi = \psi(\tau)\,\phi((\Omega(\tau)), \tag{13.24b}$$

which also just depends on τ, so we can directly calculate K_w/K as a function of τ, and just through the effect on k:

$$\frac{K_w}{K} = \frac{s_w(\delta)\,g(\psi(\tau))}{\psi(\tau)}.$$

We have already established that an increased tax lowers k. Straightforward calculation establishes that

$$d(K_w/K)/d\tau > \text{ or } <0 \text{ as } \sigma > \text{ or } < S_K. \tag{13.25}$$

When the elasticity of substitution is large (greater than the share of capital), then the ratio of g to k decreases with k, and hence increases with the tax rate: the tax increases wealth equality; but when the elasticity of substitution is low, the adverse effect on capital accumulation of the capital tax on the returns to labor outweighs the direct effect of the capital tax, and even inequality is increased by the capital tax.

3.2 Transfers and Capital Augmenting Public Investment

These results assume that all of the proceeds of the tax go to investments in human capital, and there is no productive public investment to augment the productivity of capital goods and no transfers. More generally, the total income of a worker with transfers but net of labor taxes t are given by

$$W = \phi(f - kf') + \tau r K_P - K_g - K_{PI} - t, \tag{13.26}$$

where K_{PI} is investment in public capital goods allocated to augmenting capital productivity, and K_P represents, as before, just private capital. In this section, K_g represents investments in human capital. Output is a CRTS function of effective labor, K_{PI} and K_P:

$$Q = F\left(K_P, K_{PI}, \phi\left(K_g\right)L\right). \tag{13.27}$$

We already know that a tax only used to finance lump sum transfers to workers worsens workers steady state utility and we have provided general conditions under which if tax revenues are invested in human capital, workers' welfare is improved and inequality reduced.

3.2.1 Limiting Case: Public and Private Capital Goods Are Perfect Substitute

Assume now that the production function is

$$Q = F(K_P + K_{PI}, L), \tag{13.27a}$$

that is, that public and private capital goods are perfect substitutes, and that the government takes the revenue from the capital tax τ and the labor tax t and invests it in public goods. Assuming now no investments in human capital, no transfers and taxes on labor, and normalizing again labor supply at unity, and so letting $k = K_P + K_{PI}$, in steady state, we then have

$$K_{PI} = \tau(f'(k) - \mu) \tag{13.28}$$

and

$$k = K_P\,(1 + \tau(f'(k) - \eta)). \tag{13.29}$$

In an equilibrium with capitalists, (13.24) still holds, so we can express:

$$K_P = \frac{\psi(\tau)}{1 + \tau\,(f'(\psi(\tau)) - \mu)'} \tag{13.30}$$

giving K_P as a decreasing function just of τ. A two-class equilibrium requires, of course, that

$$K_P \geq sg\,(\psi(\tau)). \tag{13.31}$$

As before, for large enough τ the two-class equilibrium doesn't exist, and because $K_P < k$, the critical value of τ is smaller.

Workers' welfare increases with k, and since k decreases with τ, that means capital taxation, invested in capital goods which are a perfect substitute for private capital, lowers workers' welfare.

3.2.2 Wage Taxes

This result, though, hinges on our assumption that we not employ taxes on workers. Assume now we impose a tax on capital and/or capitalists sufficiently high that we move from a two-class economy to a one-class economy. Our earlier analysis suggested that without public investment, workers would be worse off. With appropriately designed worker taxation using for public investment, however, they will be better off. Workers' utility is $V(w(k) - t, r(k))$, where $s(w(k) - t) = k$. For simplicity, we assume a fixed savings rate (as would arise from a logarithmic utility function).[34] Then

$$\frac{dk}{dt} = \frac{s}{-ksf'' - 1} = \frac{s\sigma}{rsS_L - \sigma}.$$

If r is large enough ($> \frac{\sigma}{sS_L}$), then an increase in t leads to an increase in capital stock, and thus an increase in wages. Substituting the equilibrium capital accumulation equation into the indirect utility function, we obtain

$$V\left(\frac{k}{s}, r(k)\right),$$

which is maximized when $-sf''\,k = 1$, or

$$r = \frac{\sigma}{sS_L}.$$

At each value of k, workers are obviously better off, because the consumption that is available doesn't have to be divided with the capitalists. Moreover, the level of k which optimizes workers' welfare will not in general be the level of k generated in the two-class model by capitalists' saving behavior.

3.2.3 Private-sector Capital Augmenting Public Investment

If all tax revenues go to public capital that *augments* the productivity of private capital, then $Q = F\left(H\left(\frac{K_{PI}}{K_P}\right)K_P, L\right)$.[35] We assume $H(0) \equiv H_0 > 0$, and z as z approaches infinity is $H_{\lim}$ and bounded, where[36] for purposes of this chapter only, $z \equiv \frac{K_{PI}}{K_P}$, the ratio of public capital to private capital. In equilibrium the effective capital–labor ratio is determined so that:

$$(Hf'(k) - \mu)(1 - \tau) = \delta. \qquad (13.21')$$

where now $k = H(z)K_P$. For future reference, we noted that wages are just equal to $g(k) = f(k) - f'(k)k$, whereas before, $f = F/L$.

Since public investment is financed by a tax on the return to capital, in steady state (assuming public capital has the same depreciation rate as private)

$$\mu K_{PI} = \tau K_P[Hf' - \mu], \qquad (13.32)$$

implying that z is given by

$$z = \tau[Hf'(k) - \mu]/\mu. \qquad (13.33)$$

[34] The results though are perfectly general.

[35] This formulation is chosen so that the production function is constant returns to scale. It is assumed that the government does not appropriate directly the returns to public capital goods, but rather, the returns are appropriately by the owners of capital goods (just as the returns to human capital are appropriated by workers).

[36] In the previous chapter, we defined z as the ratio of private to public capital. It is more convenient here to express the ratio of private capital to total capital.

(13.21′) and (13.33) can be solved simultaneously for k and z as a function of τ. Substituting (13.33) into (13.32′) we obtain:

$$z(1-\tau) = \tau\delta/\mu, \tag{13.34}$$

which (as expected) implies that at $\tau = 0$, $z = 0$, and as τ approaches 1, z approaches infinity. (13.36) can be solved for z as a function of τ, and substituting back into (13.32) gives k as a function of τ. Straightforward differentiation then yields the results that at $\tau = 0$,

$$Hf''dk/d\tau = \delta[H'(0)f' - \mu]/\mu Hf''(1-\tau)^2. \tag{13.35}$$

Hence, provided $H'(0)$ is large enough ($> 1/f'(k_0)$), where k_0 is the equilibrium capital–labor ratio when $\tau = 0$, it is desirable to tax capital to investment in capital-augmenting investment. On the other hand, as τ approaches unity, z approaches infinity (from (13.33)) and k approaches zero (from 13.21′), that is, w approaches zero. Therefore,

There exists a strictly positive optimal wage maximizing capital tax $0 < \tau < 1$, provided only that $H'(0)$ is large enough.

Since the after-tax return remains fixed at δ, the tax rate which maximizes workers' wages also maximizes their well-being.[37]

The central point is simple: while a capital tax the proceeds of which are simply distributed to workers hurts workers because of adverse incidence effects, under quite general conditions,[38] with an equalitarian social welfare function it is desirable to impose a tax on capitalists' return to capital, and with large disparities in income between capitalists and workers, strong equalitarianism, and high productivity of investments in human capital, in capital goods which increase the productivity of private capital good or even are just substitute for private capital goods, the optimal tax on capital may be very high.

4 Toward a More General Model

The previous section assumed that society is composed of two groups of individuals, workers who engage in life-cycle savings, and capitalists who pass on wealth from one generation to the other. We have for the most part ignored the kinds of inequalities within each group that were the focus of the previous chapter. Obviously, we could combine the analyses: wage inequalities will give rise to inequality in life-cycle savings and inherited inequalities passed on from one generation to the other, as described earlier. Random returns on investment provides a centrifugal force to the economy.

Here, we discuss models in which there are not two distinct classes of individuals; all individuals are the same ex ante, but the observed behavioral differences arise simply

[37] If we imposed a tax on the return to capital of capitalists only (e.g., by exempting life-cycle savings), (13.32) has to be altered, to subtract out workers' holdings of $\mu K_{PI} = \tau(K_P - sw)[Hf' - \mu]$.

[38] The result can be shown to hold with more general utility functions for capitalists (e.g., recursive Koopmans functions, so that the long run interest rate need not be invariant to tax policy). It also holds with different specifications of taxation, for example a wealth tax on capitalists, or a tax on intergenerational transfers, rather than a tax on their net income.

because of individual's wealth. Assume, for instance, that providing bequests is a "luxury" good, and that when individuals' wealth exceeds a certain level, they begin to act like capitalists, transferring part of their lifetime wealth (including what they inherited from their parents) on to their children.[39] On the other hand, with stochastic returns to wealth, the wealth of dynastic families can fall below that critical threshold, in which case they stop providing inheritances: their only savings would then be life-cycle savings.

In particular, let us assume savings of any individual are a function of his end of period wealth, which is just his wage and the return on the capital from the previous period: $s(W_t)\,W_t$, where

$$W_t = w_t + (1 + r_t)\,k_t. \tag{13.36}$$

But assume $s(W_t)$ is S-shaped, the extreme version of which would be $s = s_0$ for $W \leq W^*$ and $s = s_1 \gg s_0$ for $W > W^*$.[40] Then there exists a two-class equilibrium. To see the nature of the equilibrium, assume initially that there is no uncertainty, and a fixed fraction of the population ϑ are in the upper income group. Then

$$s_i\,(w\,(k) + (1 + r\,(k))\,k_i) = (1 + n)\,k_i,\ i = 0, 1, \tag{13.37}$$

$$k = \vartheta k_1 + (1 - \vartheta)\,k_0. \tag{13.38}$$

For each value of ϑ, there is a different equilibrium, that is, $k_i = k_i\,(\vartheta)$. For instance, if $s_0 \approx 0$, (13.37) can be approximated by

$$s_1\,((1 + r\,(k))\,k/\vartheta) = (1 + n)\,k. \tag{13.39}$$

Here, it is not that the workers have a different savings *function* from that of the capitalists; it is only that their income is low, so they save little.[41] Most importantly, we have (as we did in Chapter 11) endogenously *derived* a two-class model out of a S-shaped savings function.

Now, let us assume that there is variability, for example in the rate of return. A few families in the lower class have the good fortune of having a run of good luck and cross the critical W^* threshold, while a few families in the upper class have the bad fortune of having a run of bad luck and move into the lower class. The fraction of those crossing depends, of course, on the risk associated with the return to capital, the average value of those returns, and the distance of the average member of the class from the critical threshold. We thus write, in

[39] Similar results obtain if individuals are altruistic, and maximize a dynastic utility function, but there are borrowing constraints. Then, to a first approximation, below a certain level, there are no bequests, but bequests increase with wealth above that level. (As we noted in Chapter 12, normally, the problem is analogous to solving an optimal stockpiling problem, studied in Newbery and Stiglitz, 1981, 1982a.)

[40] This particular formulation has the characteristic of a jump in the level of savings. A formulation with similar consequences is $s(W) = s_0$ for $W \leq W_1$; $s(W)W = s_0W_1 + s_1(W - W_1)$ for $W_1 \leq W \leq W_2$; and $s(W)W = s_0W_1 + s_1(W_2 - W_1) + s_2(W - W_2)$ for $W \geq W_2$, with $s_1 >> s_0$ and $s_1 >> s_2$.

[41] On the other hand, if $\vartheta = 0$, we obtain the discrete variant of the Solow model. With enough variability, this is not a stable equilibrium.

reduced form:

$$\varkappa_1 \vartheta = \varkappa_0(1 - \vartheta), \tag{13.40}$$

where $\varkappa_1$ is the probability of an upper-class individual falling below the threshold W^*, and $\varkappa_0$ is the probability of a lower class individual making it into the upper class, with $\vartheta = 1/(1 + (\varkappa_1/\varkappa_0))$. Hence

$$\vartheta = 1/\,(1 + (\varkappa_1/\varkappa_0)). \tag{13.41}$$

We can now solve (13.37), (13.38), and (13.40) simultaneously for $\{\vartheta, k_1, k_0, k\}$, and we can analyze how various changes in the economy might affect the distribution of wealth in the tails and the distribution of income. The solution clearly depends on the stochastic processes governing the relevant variables. And using this model, we can analyze the effects of policy on the proportion of the population in each group as well as the magnitude of the tail inequality.[42]

More broadly, we can envisage changes in policy, behavior, and technology (the savings functions, the stochastic processes) that could move the economy from one in which most individuals are in the "upper group" (the middle-class society of the past) to one in which most are in the lower group (the "99%/1% society" of the present). Financial sector "innovations" that encouraged those at lower wealth not to save and regressive capital taxation might, for instance, accomplish this.

5 Concluding Comments

A central concern in the growth of wealth inequality is whether an increasing fraction of wealth will be controlled by a class of wealthy "capitalists," passing their wealth down from generation to generation. This picture contrasted markedly with the more hopeful note that emerged in the middle of the last century, that an increasing fraction of wealth would be held by ordinary citizens for their own retirement. As pension funds and IRA accounts built up, the latter view gained in ascendancy. But in spite of the growth of such accounts, and despite firms switching from defined benefit programs to defined contribution systems, the increasing concentration of wealth at the top seems to belie this notion of the creation of a "people's capitalism."

[42] Assume, for instance, that we impose a *progressive* tax on capital, such that all the wealthy pay the tax at the rate τc, with all the proceeds redistributed to workers in the lower class. Converting back to the continuous time formulation and using the diffusion model introduced earlier, we obtain the result that *so long there is not full shifting of the tax, the tax reduces tail-wealth inequality.* We can rewrite the equilibrium condition for group 1 in the continuous time formulation as $r\rho = n - rs_1\,(1 - \tau^c)$, where $\rho = \vartheta\frac{1-S_k}{S_k}$, the ratio of factor shares times the proportion of the population in the upper group, itself an endogenous variable. Hence if missing inequality, it is the case that an increase in τc with proceeds distributed to workers makes it more likely that someone of the lower class moves up to the upper and someone of the upper moves down to the lower, but the former effect is stronger than the latter, as one might expect, from (13.41) $\frac{1-S_k}{S_k}$. So long as the elasticity of substitution is not too low, $r\rho$ increases. There is some shifting, but not complete shifting. Hence the drift, $n - rs_1\,(1 - \tau^c)$ increases (consistent with the hypothesis that $\varkappa_1$ increases). At the same time, the variability in net returns, decreases.

The effect on the distribution of income is more complicated. If $\frac{1-S_k}{S_k}$ increases, there are more individuals in the upper group, but the differences in income between the two groups is smaller, so long as the elasticity of substitution is not too small.

The models here analyze the equilibrium wealth holdings between these two classes of wealth-holders. We obtain a remarkably simple formula of considerable generality,

$$\frac{k^{w^*}}{k^*} = n\frac{s(k^*)}{s_p}\frac{1 - S_k}{S_k}.$$

In the case of a competitive market with a Cobb–Douglas production function, with capitalists' savings rate fixed, and with workers' preferences being described by logarithmic utility functions, so s and S_k are fixed, this gives a closed form solution to the relative shares in terms of the parameters of behavior (preferences) and technology.[43,44]

Contrary to the suggestion of Piketty (2014), the share of wealth of the capitalists does not increase without bounds and the relationship between the rate of return and the rate of growth does *not* play a key role in the long run (partly because in standard growth models, the rate of return on capital is itself an endogenous variable).

The comparative statics of the model are much as one would expect. In the case of Cobb–Douglas production functions, the relative role of life-cycle savings increases with the rate of growth,[45] with the savings rate of life-cycle savers relative to capitalists, and with the share of labor.[46] Thus, the reduced share of labor, the reduced rate of growth, and the reduced savings rate of workers can all help account for a reduced share of life-cycle savings.

Throughout our analysis we have emphasized the importance of taking a general equilibrium perspective. Some policies that might seem to reduce inequality may, because of the shifting of taxes and expenditures, have a more ambiguous effect. For instance, because of tax shifting, the taxation of the return to capital would exacerbate the problem of inherited wealth *even if the proceeds were fully redistributed to workers.* There is a presumption that workers are worse off and inequality increases.

But these adverse effects arise because capital taxation reduces capital accumulation, and this gives rise to an adverse incidence effect. This adverse effect can be completely offset if the government takes the proceeds and invests them either in human or physical capital. Indeed, we have shown how taxation combined with public investment can then be used to reduce the level of inequality and increase the welfare of workers.

In an earlier chapter we explained that it was hard to account for the increase in the wealth- income ratio in a standard neoclassical model. Similarly, I think it's hard to account for the increase in wealth and income inequality in a standard neoclassical model, of the kind present in the previous chapter.

A major omission in these models (and a major lacuna in my earlier 1966 and 1969 papers) was rents, both land rents and those associated with market distortions, deviations

[43] As we noted, in the more general case, s and S_k have to be solved for simultaneously.

[44] As we note in Appendix 13.1, the results are far more general. The savings behavior of capitalists can be derived, for instance, from intertemporal utility maximization.

[45] This is the one result that may not be intuitive. In the more general case, sw/k depends on what happens to w/k as k increases; and this depends on whether the elasticity of substitution is greater or less than the share of labor. An increase in n, keeping everything else constant, leads to a higher equilibrium rate of return and therefore a lower equilibrium value of k.

[46] However, as we noted, matters are not quite so simple, because the savings rate of life-cycle savers may itself be an endogenous variable, affected by the growth rate and capitalist's savings. In the simple case of logarithmic utility functions, this will, of course, not be the case. Another key variable is the ratio of the share of labor to that of capital, which too can be affected by these variables.

from the competitive paradigm, such as monopoly power. If these rents are appropriated disproportionately by the wealthy, and if the share of these rents in national income increases, then it is to be expected that income and wealth inequality will increase.

In the next three chapters, we present alternative theories of the determination of rents, including those associated with land. We believe may provide a better description of what has been happening than the standard neoclassical models which have ignored them.

Appendix 1 Intertemporal Utility Maximizing Workers and Capitalists

In the text, we provided a simple model where capitalists and workers each have fixed savings rate. This would be the case, for instance, if both capitalists and workers have logarithmic utility functions. Assume the capitalist owns a capital stock K_t^c and maximizes intertemporal utility given by

$$\sum_{t=0}^{\infty} \frac{1}{(1+\rho_c)^t} ln\left(C_t^c\right),$$

Then

$$\frac{C_{t+1}^c}{C_t^c} = \frac{1+(1-\tau)\, r_{t+1}}{1+\rho_c}.$$

Or in steady state:

$$\rho_c = (1-\tau)\, r_{t+1},$$

And everything proceeds as in the text, substituting ρ_c for n/s_p. Indeed, exactly the same results hold in steady state regardless of the form of the utility function.[47]

Similarly, workers maximize

$$ln\left(C_t\right) + \frac{1}{1+\rho_w} ln\left(C_{t+1}\right).$$

generating

$$s_w = \frac{1}{2+\rho_w}.$$

In this case, the savings rate depends just on the rate of time preference, and $\nu = d\, ln\, s/d\, ln\, r = 0$. In the more general case, workers maximize:

$$U\left(C_t\right) + \frac{1}{1+\rho_w} U\left(C_{t+1}\right).$$

[47] In the more general case, the savings rate will be sensitive to the interest rate.
As we have noted elsewhere in this book, the assumption of time separability of consumption is important in this analysis.

For some U, $U' > 0$, $U'' < 0$, yielding:

$$U'(C_t) = (1 + (1 - \tau)\, r_{t+1})\, U'(C_{t+1}) / 1 + \rho_w$$

or

$$U'((1 - s)\, w) = (1 + (1 - \tau)\, r_{t+1})\, U'(sw(1 + (1 - \tau)\, r_{t+1})) / 1 + \rho_w,$$

from which we can directly calculate ν.

Appendix 2 Derivation of the Effect of an Increase in Capital Taxation on Workers' Utility

$$\frac{dY^W}{d\tau^c} = \frac{dw}{dk^*}\frac{dk^*}{d\tau^c} + r(k^*)\,(k^* - k^{w^*}) + \tau^c\, r\{k^{c^*}/(1 - \tau^c) + dk^{c^*}/d\tau^c\},$$

where

$$k^{c^*} = k^* - k^{w^*} = \frac{k^* - sw(k^*)}{1 + s(k^*)\,\tau^c f'(k^*)}.$$

and where we assume that $k^* > k^{**}$, the value of k for which $k^{**} = sw(k^{**})$ (which, in turn, requires that the tax rate not be too high). Then, using standard properties of the indirect utility function[48] and the fact that in steady state:

$$[dV/d\tau^c]/V_Y = \tau^c\, r dk^{c^*}/d\tau^c$$
$$= (\tau^c r^2/(1 - \tau^c)\,(1 + s(k^*)\,\tau^c f'\{1/f'' + sk^*_w - \nu s[w + k_{c^*}\tau^c f']\}.$$

Thus, if $\tau^c = 0$, $dV/d\tau^c = 0$; if $\tau^c > 0$, $dV/d\tau^c < 0$ if ν is not too negative and the elasticity of substitution is high enough; $dV/d\tau^c > 0$ if ν is not too positive and the elasticity of substitution is low enough. If ν = 0, there is a critical elasticity of substitution (depending on the parameters of the problem) below which workers' welfare improves.[49] This result may seem surprising, given that a low elasticity means a large adverse effect on wages. But a large elasticity of substitution also means that capitalists' capital falls, and thus the inheritance tax transfer from capitalists to workers, and it is this effect which dominates.

48 After taking into account the cancelation of several terms, and the expressions for $\frac{dk^{c^*}}{d\tau^c}$, $\frac{dk^{w^*}}{d\tau^c}$, $\frac{dk^*}{d\tau^c}$, and $\frac{dr}{d\tau^c}$.

49 $1/f + sk_{w^*} = \frac{fk}{f'w}\left\{-\sigma + s(\frac{k_w}{k})S_L\frac{f'}{k}\right\} = \frac{fk}{f'w}\left\{-\sigma + s^2\frac{S_L{}^2}{S_K}r^3\right\}$, so workers' welfare depends on whether

$$\sigma < \text{or} > s^2\frac{S_L{}^2}{S_K}r^3.$$

Appendix 3 Conditions in Which the Two-Class Model Degenerates into One Class

There is an important constraint in the model of Section 2: $k^* \geq 0$, that is, the solution to (13.1), giving k^*, must be greater than the solution to (13.2) giving k^w. As workers' savings increase, for fixed savings of capitalists, the equilibrium value of k^* doesn't change; workers' savings crowds out capitalists' savings. We can solve for the boundary condition in which $k^c = 0$. Mattauch, Klenert, Stiglitz, and Edenhofer (2019) have done that, for the special case where both capitalists and workers have logarithmic utility functions.

Then

$$s^W = \frac{1}{2 + \rho_W},$$

where ρ_W is workers' pure rate of time discount (see Appendix 13.1), and the long run condition for capitalists is the same as before. Thus, the lower the discount rate, the more workers save, and the more likely is it that capitalists are totally crowded out.

In the model of Section 3 where the proceeds of capital taxes are invested in human capital, the long run equilibrium value of $k^*(\tau)$ is given by (13.23) and K_g by (13.25). Thus, the boundary value between the two class and one class regime is given by the values of τ for which

$$s^w g'(k^*(\tau))\,\phi\left(K_g\,(\tau)\right) = \psi(\tau). \qquad \text{(A13.1)}$$

In general, the higher s^w the lower the maximum value of the capital tax rate at which a two-class equilibrium exists, for increasing workers' savings rate increases workers' holdings of capital, while increasing the tax rate reduces the aggregate level of the capital–effective labor ratio.

14

The Role of Land in Creating Wealth Inequality

1 Introduction

In Chapter 10, we noted that standard neoclassical models assuming competitive markets could not explain the increase in the wealth–output ratio observed in the U.S. and many other advanced countries.[1] That model also could not adequately explain the growth of wealth inequality that has been observed.

Central to our resolution of both puzzles was the understanding that wealth and capital were different concepts. The source of the disparity between the growth of wealth and the growth of productive capital is the growth of rents. In this chapter, we look at the consequences of an increase in the *value* of land—not associated with any increase in the *amount* of land or of the productivity of the economy.[2]

We present a series of models that might account for much of the increase in the value of wealth taking the form of an increase in the price of land. These models not only help us understand the increase in the wealth–income ratio, but also the increase in wealth inequality.

This chapter is divided into four sections besides this introduction and a conclusion. In Section 2, we present the simplest model with land rents, showing that the increase in wealth may be markedly greater than the increase in capital. Section 3 examines land as a positional good, deriving a similar result that increases in wealth are greater than increases in capital. Section 4 investigates the dynamics of land prices, showing that in a natural formulation, bubbles can easily arise, and along such "bubble paths," wealth may increase, even though capital (per capita) is decreasing. Wealth accumulation in the form of land crowds out real capital accumulation. Eventually such land bubbles break—inevitably at great cost to the economy. In the fourth section, we return to the model of Chapter 13, where we looked at the distribution of wealth between life-cycle savers (workers) and capitalists, and examine the effects of land on inequality in such an economy and the policies which might mitigate the adverse effects.

[1] Revised and edited version of a paper originally distributed as "New theoretical perspectives on the distribution of income and wealth among individuals: Part IV. Land and Credit," NBER working paper 21192, May 2015.

[2] We also noted in Chapter 10 that there has been an increase in other forms of rents, and when capitalized, these too give rise to an increase in wealth. We discuss these further in Chapter 17.

The Origins of Inequality, and Policies to Contain It. Joseph E. Stiglitz, Oxford University Press. © Joseph E. Stiglitz (2025).
DOI: 10.1093/oso/9780198799580.003.0015

2 A Simple Model with Land Rents

The simplest model is one in which the rents associated with land are fixed and last in perpetuity, while the production of industrial goods requires no land. Then a slight decrease in the (long-term real) interest rate can lead to a large increase in the value of land.[3] Thus, national output is given by

$$Q = F(K, L) + R, \tag{14.1}$$

where Q is total output, K is productive capital and L is labor, for the moment assumed fixed, F is constant returns to scale, and R is the fixed return to land. Then the value of wealth, W, is given by[4]

$$W = K + \frac{R}{r} = K + R/F_K, \tag{14.2}$$

where r is the rate of interest (return on capital, equal to F_K) so that

$$\frac{dW}{dK} = 1 - \frac{RF_{KK}}{F_K^2} > 1. \tag{14.3}$$

If F is, for instance, a unitary elasticity of substitution production function, with coefficient on capital of α, then

$$\frac{dW}{dK} = 1 + \frac{R}{Q}\frac{1-\alpha}{\alpha}. \tag{14.4}$$

If, for instance, $R/Q = .3$ and $\alpha = .2$, then $dW/dK = 1 + 1.2 = 2.2$: the increase in wealth is more than twice the increase in productive capital.

2.1 The Effect of Taxation

Henry George (1879) was a great nineteenth-century progressive economist who argued in favor of the taxation of land. The big advantage of land taxation is that it has no adverse incentive effects, and the revenues can be spent in a progressive way.[5]

If the return land is taxed, then W and K are more closely aligned. If the returns to land are fully taxed (as they would be with the Henry George tax), W and K would be fully aligned. This follows directly from rewriting (14.2) as

$$W = K + \frac{(1-\tau^L)R}{r} = K + (1-\tau^L)R/F_K, \tag{14.2'}$$

where τ^L is the tax rate on the returns to land.

[3] If R is the rent from the land, and r is the real interest rate, then the value of land $VT = R/r$, so that there is an equiproportionate increase in the value of land from a decrease in the real interest rate.

[4] This analysis applies to a comparison across steady states with different K.

[5] Interest in the land tax was revived by Arnott and Stiglitz (1979, 1981).

3 Positional Goods

Similarly, if land serves as a *positional* good, there can be an increase in the value of land, without any increase in the productive potential of the economy. Rich individuals compete for houses in the Riviera. As the rich get richer, they compete more vigorously for this real estate, and the price of this fixed asset increases, without any increase in "real" output.

Assume there are some assets in fixed supply which are valued because of the signal they provide concerning one's economic position, and that do not affect production of conventional goods. Assume all the wealth of the economy is held by the rich (an assumption which does not depart too far from reality) and that the demand by the rich for these goods is given by $M(W, p)$[6] with $M_W > 0$ and $M_p < 0$, with the equilibrium given by

$$M(W, p) = pT, \tag{14.5}$$

where p is price of land, T, which is fixed supply, and $W = K + pT$. For simplicity and without loss of generality, we choose units so $T = 1$. Equation (14.5) can be solved for p as a function of W, and K can then be solved for

$$K = W - p(W). \tag{14.6}$$

Then

$$\frac{dK}{dW} = 1 - p' = 1 - \frac{M_w}{1 - M_p} < 1. \tag{14.7}$$

As wealth increases, part of that wealth is reflected in an increased value of land, meaning that the capital stock increases more slowly. If the wealth elasticity of the demand for positional goods is large enough and the price elasticity is small enough, then an increase in W may be associated with a decrease in K.

3.1 Wealth Inequality

In the model just presented, what matters for land prices is the wealth of the wealthy—since it is only they who demand land (as a positional good). Assume a simple two-class model (as in Chapter 13), but that (as before) only the wealthy demand land. Then an increase in the fraction of the wealth held by the wealthy, Υ (i.e., an increase in wealth inequality) will lead to an increase in the price of land, and instead of (14.5) and (14.6) we now have:

$$M(\Upsilon W, p) = pT \tag{14.5'}$$

and

$$K = W - p(\Upsilon W). \tag{14.6'}$$

[6] All of these results are equally valid if land is demanded by the wealthy for *any* reason. All that is required for our formal analysis is that the poor (workers) do not demand land. It should be obvious, however, that our results extend to any model in which workers also demand land, so long as their (per capita) demands are less than that of the rich (the capitalists).

It follows that an increase in wealth inequality leads to higher land prices and, for any given W, a lower equilibrium value of K.

We can see this even more forcefully in the kind of two-class model that we formulated in the last chapter, and which will explore further in Section 5. Assume that a society is more unequal, in the sense that there are fewer capitalists (a smaller fraction of the population are capitalists). A key result of the last chapter is that the aggregate capital–labor ratio is determined just by the time preference (or savings behavior) of capitalists. Recall Equation (13.3) from the previous chapter, which we rewrite as:

$$k_t = k_t^w + \beta k_t^c,$$

where β is the ratio of capitalists to workers. With fixed time preference of capitalists, k^* is fixed, and with workers saving only in the form of capital (they do not value the positional good land at all) k^{w^*} is also fixed, which means that the wealth per capita of capitalists increases inversely with β: the fewer the capitalists, the higher their per capita wealth. If we assume that there is a positive wealth elasticity for land among the capitalists, then a natural formulation of the demand function for land is

$$\beta M((pT + k^* - k^{w*})/\beta, p) = pT. \tag{14.5''}$$

Implying that an increase in β (a decrease in inequality) would lower the land price if

$$1 - \varsigma < 0 \tag{14.8}$$

where $\varsigma = \frac{d \ln M}{d \ln W}$, the wealth elasticity of the demand for land, that is, if the wealth elasticity of land is greater than unity, then a decrease in the proportion of the population that are capitalists leads to an increase in the price of land, and to an even greater inequality in wealth holdings. The wealth of the capitalists (per capita) is $(k^{c^*} + pT)/\beta$, the derivative of which with respect to β is negative, and in absolute value larger because of the effect on land prices. Thus, having few capitalists leads not only to each having more capital per capita and more land per capita, but also to a higher land price, while life-cycle savings of workers (per capita) remains unchanged. Accordingly, the gap between the (per capita) wealth of capitalists and workers increases.

3.2 Inequality in Well-being

While in this and other models in this section, the increase in wealth may be largely (or entirely) due to an increase in land values, one might ask: does this lead to *real* inequality? After all, the rich consume the positional goods. The increase in land values affects them, and them only. Workers are only affected to the extent that the increase in land values crowds out capital accumulation, so K decreases (or does not increase as much as it otherwise would), as in the model of Section 5. Without land, a decrease in K leads to a decrease in wages (capital and labor have to be complements); with land, it is possible that capital could be a substitute for labor (labor replacing robots).

While this conclusion is true in the simplified model we have constructed here, it is natural that there be a direct spill-over to workers from the increase in the price of land. Assume, for instance, landlords/capitalists rent out some of their land to workers, at a rental rate which increases with the price of land p. Then, policies and behavior which lead to an increase in p disadvantage workers.[7]

Still, the observation that the increase in land prices (or of other positional goods) disproportionately affects the wealthy has several important implications. First, it reminds us that in making comparisons across different income groups, we have to take into account the different market baskets of goods that they consume. The increase in the relative prices of positional goods means that there may not have been as large an increase in inequality as would appear to be the case. But there are important effects going the other way (but not included in our model), and which almost surely predominate—for instance, the increased insecurity that the non-rich face, not adequately reflected in income statistics.

Secondly, it helps explain differences in savings behavior both over time and across income levels. To achieve "success" as demonstrated by acquiring expensive positional goods may require more savings (more wealth) today than when the price of such goods was lower.[8]

Thirdly, by the same token, patterns of inheritances and lifetime giving too may be endogenous, affected in particular by such changes. If increases in real estate prices make it difficult for even reasonably successful workers to purchase a home that they and their parents believe is appropriate to their station in life, wealthy parents will provide larger intra vivo transfers. Note that, in part at least, the direction of causality has changed: greater wealth and wealth inequality arising from an increase in real estate prices has led to greater inheritances and intra vivo transfers across generations among the top.[9] Greater disparities beget greater disparities.

3.3 Foreign Ownership

The demand by foreigners for positional goods may lead to an increase in the wealth of the citizens of a country as well as to an increase in wealth inequality. Assume, as above, rentiers own all the positional goods (land in the Riviera). A sudden and unanticipated increase in the desire for these pieces of land by foreigners increases their value, and the wealth of those who happened to own this land; and if those within the country who own the land are the wealthy, it will contribute to the increase in inequality within the country. This seems to have been a factor increasing inequality within several countries.[10]

[7] A full equilibrium analysis would require us to include workers' demand for land in the determination of the price of land, Equation (14.5). Note that a progressive land tax—levied only on large land holdings—would reduce the demand for land by the wealthy, lower the price of land, and therefore increase the well-being of workers.

[8] It has been argued that high savings rates in China are at least partially explained as part of the competition for wives in a country where female infanticide has created a shortage. See Wei and Zhang (2011).

[9] The increase in the price of land is only partially explained by the discussion of this section. Chapter 16 argues that the expansion of the credit supply provides an important part of the explanation.

[10] Not only do the wealthy get wealthier, ordinary citizens in a real sense get poorer: as we noted in the previous subsection, the increase in land prices will almost surely translate into an increase in their cost of housing.

4 Bubbles: The Dynamic Instability of the Market Economy

Bubbles are a pervasive and recurrent aspect of market economies. The breaking of bubbles is almost always followed by a recession. The recurrence of bubbles and their relationship to the ensuing downturns has long been noted (see Kindleberger, 1978). While an explanation of that lies beyond the scope of this chapter (and this book, which focuses on models in which there is full employment), it is important to understand why it is that market economies are prone to having bubbles. Indeed, while the 2008–9 recession may have represented a "correction" of the real estate bubble that led to it, the economy may not have fully corrected the price of real estate.

Hahn (1966) and Shell-Stiglitz (1967) showed the dynamic instability of the economy with heterogeneous capital goods in the absence of a full set of futures markets extending *infinitely* far into the future (or without perfect foresight extending infinitely far into the future). The steady state was a saddle point.

The underlying economics is simple: in competitive equilibrium, demand equals supply for every good (asset) at every date. Individuals allocate their consumption over time within a lifetime budget constraint. In models with infinitely lived agents (or with overlapping generations, but with the economy going on infinitely far into the future) one can only be sure that one's consumption plans are consistent with one's lifetime budget constraint if there are markets going infinitely far into the future. If there are markets going only a finite distance into the future, one's plans can appear totally consistent over that finite horizon; but at some time beyond that horizon it may turn out that they are inconsistent.[11] The mathematics of the saddle point says that one has to be extremely precise in one's current estimates of the infinite future—a slight error in today's prices, for instance, leads one eventually far away from the long run steady state.[12]

Macroeconomics of the past four decades has essentially assumed this problem away. Of course, one has to admit that there are not futures markets going infinitely far into the future (or for every state of nature)—indeed, futures markets go only a little way into the future. Of course, one should admit that there are repeated instances of bubbles, where markets seem to have miscalculated, and the economy appears to have been on a trajectory that is inconsistent with long run equilibrium—there are massive corrections, crises, bankruptcies, etc. But this empirical reality is shunted aside, and theory has focused on a special case where all individuals are identical (the representative agent model), individuals know this, and reflect upon what the equilibrium trajectory must look like, knowing that everyone is like themselves. In short, they focus on a market economy in which markets are inessential, because there would be no trade in them if they existed. Once one recognizes, though, that there are large differences in individuals, that no individual knows the preferences and beliefs about the future of all others, then this "trick" won't work. To solve for the equilibrium, each individual has to know the preferences of all other individuals, eviscerating the virtue of decentralization through markets. There is no way one can escape

[11] More generally, these macroeconomic inconsistencies play a central role in Guzman and Stiglitz's (2020) dynamic disequilibrium theories.

[12] Though in models with a single individual—or equivalently, a representative agent—the individual himself has the information required to ensure that his behavior is consistent with the transversality condition, this is not the case in more realistic settings with heterogeneous agents. See the discussion in the next paragraph.

confronting the consequences of the absence of futures markets extending infinitely far into the future—including the inherent instability of market economies.

The saddle-point property has been viewed almost as a "virtue" in more recent dynamic macro models: it ensured that there was a determinate path for the economy, given the relevant state variables. By contrast, here, we argue, as Hahn (1966) and Shell-Stiglitz (1967) did earlier, that in the absence of a futures markets extending infinitely far into the future, there was no way that a decentralized economy could be sure that it was on the saddle-point trajectory. And if it missed the trajectory by even a slightest amount but kept along a trajectory in which the arbitrage (equal return) condition was satisfied, then the economy "exploded"—or more accurately, eventually there would be a breakdown, a moment in which the arbitrage condition would not be satisfied; individuals' plans would be not be fulfilled.[13]

Defenders of the market economy might say, "Don't worry. Markets are forward looking, enough so that they will quickly discover the errors of their ways, and make a quick and relatively costless correction." History suggests otherwise: even shortly before the real estate bubble of the early 2000s broke, the "market," the vast majority of economists and pundits, and even economic leaders like the head and former head of the Federal Reserve Board, Ben Bernanke and Alan Greenspan, denied that we were on a bubble-trajectory—indeed, they often went so far as to suggest one can't rely ascertain whether one is on a bubble-trajectory until the bubble breaks. (See Stiglitz, 2010a.)

Here we explore these instabilities in a simple model with land.[14] The same result on dynamic instability noted by Hahn and Shell-Stiglitz also holds for a model with capital and land, with the two state variables being K, the stock of capital, and p, the price of land. We extend the production function in the straightforward way so that $Y = F(K, L, T)$, where, as before, T is the supply of land and L is the supply of labor, and F is constant returns to scale.[15]

There is a delicate problem: if there is labor force growth (or even labor augmenting technological progress), the land–labor ratio goes to zero. Under normal assumptions about the production function, the return to land itself would go off to infinity. This problem can be "solved" by assuming just the right amount of land augmenting technological progress.[16] At first blush, this seems unpersuasive: why should nature produce land augmenting technological progress in just the right amount to sustain a steady state? But upon reflection, it may not be so coincidental, once we introduce a theory of endogenous factor bias (see Chapter 17). We know that the bias is determined by relative factor shares, and if the

[13] See Guzman and Stiglitz (2020). This paragraph summarizes one aspect of the critique of the representative agent models with rational expectations (DSGE models). See also Stiglitz (2011b, 2018e). There is also a large literature explaining the instability of such models. See Guernerie (1992).

[14] Discrete time models can give rise to somewhat different results—the economy is still not stable, but there is a possibility of an infinite number of rational expectations paths, neither converging to a steady state nor exploding, but with booms and busts, all contained within a limited range. See Hirano and Stiglitz (2020).

[15] For simplicity, we assume that F_K approaches infinity as K approaches zero, and that the marginal product of capital falls to zero only as K approaches infinity.

[16] Alternatively, we could assume—contrary to fact—that there is neither labor force growth or labor augmenting technological progress. But doing so would present its own problems. In the Solow growth model, in the long run, the capital output ratio equals s/n, that is, as n goes to zero, s/n goes to infinity; and with standard production functions, this means that the marginal product of capital goes to zero. If there is a fixed asset, land, yielding a given return (as in Section 2), and the value of that asset goes off to infinity. Essentially, the model breaks down.

elasticity of substitution is less than one, as land becomes more scarce, there are greater incentives for land augmenting technological progress.[17]

In this section, we investigate two alternative approaches. The first entails assuming a conventional production function (without land), but the existence of land as a store of value. The second assumes a fixed rate of land augmenting technological change, equal to n.

4.1 Non-productive Land

In this case, output is just a function of K and L, as in the models explored earlier in this book, and there is a fixed supply of unproductive land, which we normalize at unity and whose price, relative to the numeraire, produced goods, is p.[18] It is only a store of value; it doesn't even perform the role of a positional good, discussed earlier in the chapter. The key equilibrium condition is that the return to holding land and capital must be the same, that is, since land is non-productive,[19] its entire return is its capital gain, $\frac{d}{dt}(ln\, p)$, and the equilibrium condition is

$$\frac{d}{dt}(ln\, p) = (F_K - \mu). \tag{14.9}$$

where μ is the depreciation rate and F_K is the gross return to capital.

The short run dynamics are described by (14.9)) and a capital accumulation equation. Since our objective is to show how land taxation can increase growth and reduce inequality and to demonstrate the instability of the dynamical system, we employ the simplest savings model, where workers do not save and only capitalists save and they save a fixed fraction, s_c, of "full *net* income" including capital gains but netting out depreciation.[20] (This is called the Haig-Simons definition of comprehensive income (1921, 1938), and was employed earlier in the analysis of dynamic systems by Shell, Sidrauski, and Stiglitz, 1969).[21]

$$\frac{dK}{dt} + T\frac{dp}{dt} = s_c\left(F_K K - \mu K + T\frac{dp}{dt}\right). \tag{14.10}$$

The RHS of (14.10) is net savings (as seen by the individual, not according to the national income accounts). This goes into an increase in the value of land ("land savings") and capital accumulation.

Substituting (14.9) into (14.10), we obtain (again using the normalization that $T = 1$):

$$\frac{dK}{dt} = s_c(F_K K - \mu K) - (1 - s_c)\frac{dp}{dt} = (s_c K - (1 - s_c)p)(F_K - \mu). \tag{14.11}$$

[17] See, for example, Stiglitz (2014d), Chapter 17 below and the references cited there.

[18] Similar results hold for a model with money, such as that formulated in the next chapter.

[19] Similar results hold for the model of Section 2, where land yields a fixed return, unaffected by the amount of capital and labor. In that case, instead of (14.9) we obtain $\frac{d}{dt}(ln\, p) + R/p = (F_K - \mu)$.

[20] In this chapter, we use the symbol "s_c" for the savings rate of capitalists, rather than that used in the previous chapter, s_p, simply to remind us that savings is a fraction of *total* income including capital gains.

[21] Similar results can be obtained if we assume savings are a fixed fraction of total national income (including capital gains). In the next subsection, we consider a quite general savings function.

Equations (14.11) and (14.9) provide a pair of differential equations fully describing the dynamics of the economy.

4.1.1 Steady States

Figure 14.1 shows the steady states, given by the solution to the loci

$$F_K = \mu \quad (\text{The } \dot{p} = 0 \textit{ locus}) \tag{14.12a}$$

and

$$p = s_c K/(1 - s_c) \quad (\text{The } \dot{K} = 0 \textit{ locus}). \tag{14.12b}$$

We define K^* as the value of K solving (14.12a), where the net return to capital, $F_{K-\mu}$, is zero. The $\dot{p} = 0$ *locus* is a vertical straight line, while the $\dot{p} = 0$ *locus* is an upward sloping straight line. Note that any value of p along $K = K^*$ is an equilibrium, since $dp/dt = 0$ when $K = K^*$.

4.1.2 Dynamics

The dynamics are easy to describe and are also depicted in Figure 14.1: To the right of $K = K^*$, p is decreasing (the net return to capital is negative) and to the left it is increasing. Above the $dK/dt = 0$ locus, but to the left of K^*, K is decreasing, while above the $dK/dt = 0$ locus, to the right of K^*, K is increasing. Conversely, below the $dK/dt = 0$ locus, but to the left of K^*, K is increasing, while below the $dK/dt = 0$ locus, to the right of K^*, K is decreasing.

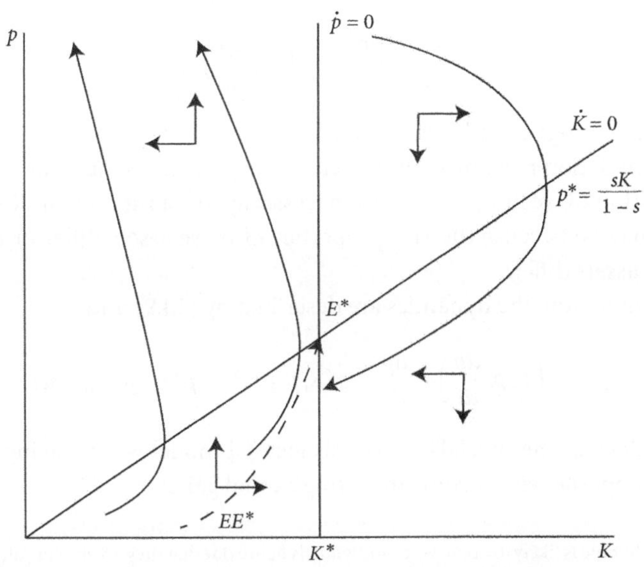

Figure 14.1 Dynamics with land and a simple savings function: Any $\{p, K\}$ along K^*E^* is a stable equilibrium. Any $\{p, K\}$ along that line above E^* is unstable –with a slight decrease in K below K^* the economy diverges. Any K above K^* converges to K^*. Any $\{p, K\}$ with $K < K^*$ and p below EE^* converges to a $\{p, K\}$ along $\{p^*, K^*\}$. Any $\{p, K\}$ with $K < K^*$ and p above EE^* diverges.

Let $p^* \equiv sK^*/(1-s)$. K^* in combination of any value of $p < p^*$ is a stable equilibrium; K^* and any value of $p \geq p^*$ is an unstable equilibrium. The saddle point trajectory EE^* divides the bottom quadrant (below $dK/dt = 0$ and to the left of K^*) into a convergent and non-convergent region. Below EE^*, paths converge to $K = K^*$. Above EE^*, they diverge.

Dividing (14.9) by (14.11), we obtain the slope of the trajectories:

$$\frac{dp}{dK} = \frac{p}{s_c K - (1 - s_c)\, p}, \tag{14.13}$$

which is finite below the locus $p = s_c K/(1 - s_c)$. But $\dot{K}$ approaches zero as K approaches K^*, so the trajectories approach K^* only asymptotically. We can similarly show that if $K_0 > K^*$, and p_0 is above the $dp/dt = 0$ locus K will converge to K^*; but K will initially increase, before decreasing to K^*.

Thus, there are an infinity of stable equilibria, in all of which the level of income is the same, but in which there can be markedly different values of wealth, $K + pT$. pT is indeterminate. But if $K_0 < K^*$ and the initial price is too high (above EE^*), the economy experiences a bubble—the price of land rises, and as it does so, it crowds out capital accumulation, leading to an even faster rate of growth of land prices, until the whole thing comes crashing down. The equilibrium conditions simply can't continue to hold.[22]

4.1.3 A Generalized Savings Function

The special savings function employed was chosen because it simplified the dynamics. In the more general case, the system is even less stable. Assume a quite general savings function—net savings are a function of capital (which determines income), the value of land, and capital gains.[23]

$$\frac{dK}{dt} + \frac{dp}{dt} = s\left(K, p, \frac{dp}{dt}\right), \tag{14.14}$$

K and p affect savings both because they increase the income and wealth of the individual. This formulation recognizes, however, that aggregate savings may differ depending on the composition of wealth (i.e., it is not necessarily just a function of $K + pT$, aggregate wealth). This may be because the risk properties of these assets differ or the individuals who own these assets differ.

With this formulation, the dynamics are described by (14.9) and

$$\frac{dK}{dt} = s\left(K, p, \frac{dp}{dt}\right) - \frac{dp}{dt} = s\left(K, p, p\left(F_K - \mu\right)\right) - p\left(F_K - \mu\right). \tag{14.15}$$

Our earlier model was the special case of this general model where savings are a fraction of capitalists' comprehensive income including capital gains.

[22] Of course, the bubble is likely to break when individuals figure out that they are moving along an inconsistent path. In the case of the real estate bubble of the first decade of the twenty-first century, it was remarkable how long it took for the "market" to realize this: the crash occurred a couple of years after real estate prices stopped increasing.

[23] We continue with models that are outside of the standard framework of intertemporal utility maximization, because the standard intertemporal utility maximization models assume away the essential problem that we wish to investigate here, as we have already noted. Besides, these simple savings model may provide a better representation of how the economy actually behaves. An alternative framework where individuals operate with a finite horizon is provided by the overlapping generations model of Section 5.

There are two possible (sets of) steady states. One is given by the solution to (14.12a) and

$$s\left(K^*, p^*, 0\right) = 0. \tag{14.15}$$

If we assume (at $dp/dt = 0$), $s_K > 0$ and $s_p > 0$ (in the absence of capital gains, an increase in wealth of any form leads to increased savings),[24] then (at least near $K = K^*$) the $\dot{K} = 0$ curve is downward sloping. The steady state equilibrium is locally unstable. The steady state equilibrium may be globally unstable (Figure 14.2a); or the dynamics may be oscillatory, as illustrated in Figure 14.2b, and the economy may converge to a limit cycle.[25] In particular, if the $\left.\frac{dp}{dK}\right|_{\frac{dK}{dt}=0}$ locus hits the vertical axis, then the dynamics are constrained. Its behavior is that of an economy with no land, since by (14.9) on $p = 0$, $dp/dt = 0$, so p remains at 0. Over the long run, $0 \leq K \leq K^{**}$ where K^{**} is defined by $f(K^{**}) = \mu K^{**}$ (i.e., the capital stock that would result if the savings rate were unity). p is non-negative. We can trace out a single oscillation along the path that begins say at $K = K^*$ and p very small. Such a path cannot hit the K^{**} boundary or the horizontal axis. If the value of p when it returns to K^* is lower than the initial p, then subsequent oscillations are arbitrarily close to the initial oscillation. If the value of p when it returns to K^* is greater than the initial p, all paths must be contained within the bound defined by this oscillation, a straightforward implication of which is that there must be a limit cycle.[26]

The second possible steady state is defined by $p = 0$ and $s\left(K^{***}, 0, 0\right) = 0$. (Recall that $\frac{dp}{dt} = p\left(F_K - \mu\right)$ so that $\frac{dp}{dt} = 0$ for $p = 0$ for all finite values of $F_K - \mu$.) If $s_k > 0$, so long as p is constrained to be zero, the dynamics are stable. But if p is ever perturbed above zero, the dynamics described earlier become applicable.

4.2 Land Augmenting Technological Change

In this section, we assume that land is productive and the *effective* land supply increases at the rate n. The equation describing the equalization of returns to land and capital now takes on the form

$$\frac{dp}{dt} = pF_K - F_T. \tag{14.16}$$

In steady state, $\frac{d \ln p}{dt} = n$.

[24] Here $s_p \equiv \frac{\partial s}{\partial p}$ is effectively the marginal propensity to save from an increase in "land wealth." (This should not be confused with the symbol used in the previous chapter for the capitalists' savings propensity), though clearly the two are not unrelated.)

[25] The dynamics are locally oscillatory if $\left(s_K\left(K^*, p^*, 0\right) - p^* F_{KK}\left(K^*\right)\right)^2 < 4\left(-s_p\left(K^*, p^*, 0\right) p^* F_{KK}\left(K^*\right)\right)$.

[26] Note that $\left.\frac{dp}{dK}\right|_{\frac{dK}{dt}=0} = -\frac{s_K - pF_{KK}(1-s_3)}{s_p + (F_K - \mu)s_3}$. If as K gets small, s_p remains greater than $(1 - s_3)(F_K - \mu)$, then the $\left.\frac{dp}{dK}\right|_{\frac{dK}{dt}=0}$ locus will hit the vertical axis. (s_3 is the (marginal) savings out of capital gains. It is natural to assume that $0 < s_3 < 1$).

Along any trajectory, $\frac{dp}{dK} = \frac{dp/dt-dt}{dK/dt-dt} = \frac{p(F_K-\mu)}{s-p(F_K-\mu)}$ which for $K > 0$ goes to zero as p goes to zero, so long as $s(K, 0, 0) > 0$.

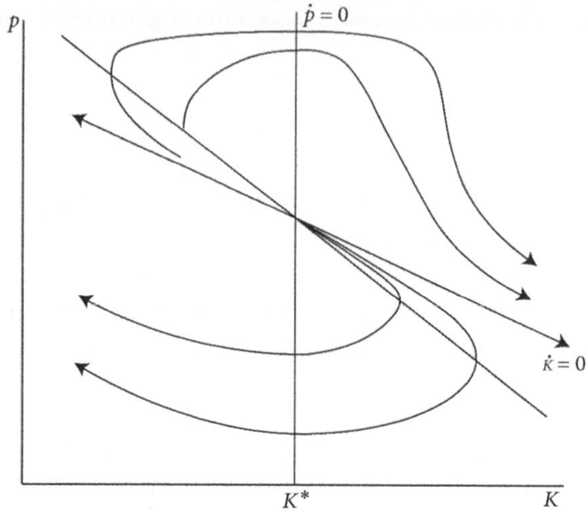

Figure 14.2a Dynamics where savings depends on portfolio composition as well as capital gains: unstable equilibrium.

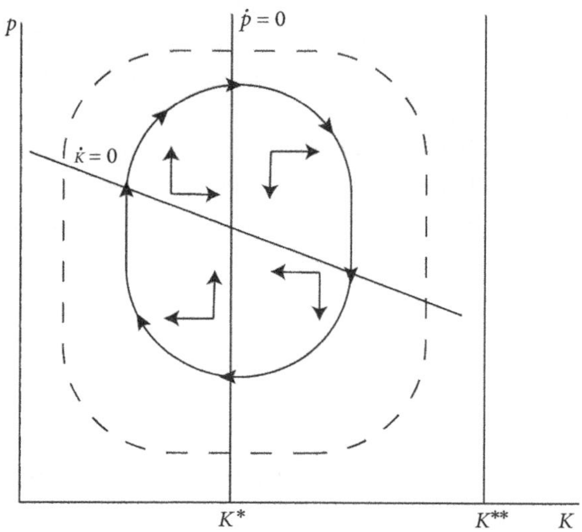

Figure 14.2b Dynamics where savings depends on portfolio composition as well as capital gains: limit cycles.

Because the rate of land augmenting technical progress is n, one unit of land becomes more valuable over time—the number of equivalent units of land grows at the rate n. With labor and land both growing effectively at the rate n, we can express everything in per capita terms. Redefining units so that $\widehat{T}$ is a unit of effective land, so that the supply of effective land is growing at the rate n, and denoting f (as before) as output per unit effective labor, which is a function only of the capital labor and capital land ratios. But since labor and land are increasing in tandem, we can express f simply as a function of the capital–labor ratio k. Then $f_{\widehat{T}} = F_{\widehat{T}} = F_T e^{-nt}$. We e define the price of a unit of effective land, q by:

$$q = e^{-nt}p, \tag{14.17}$$

so that

$$\frac{d}{dt}(ln\ q) = \frac{d}{dt}(ln\ p) - n = F_K - \frac{F_T e^{-nt}}{q} - n. \tag{14.18}$$

Then the *capital arbitrage equation* can be rewritten:

$$\frac{d}{dt}(ln\ q) = \frac{d}{dt}(ln\ p) - n = f_k - \frac{f_{\hat{T}}}{q} - n. \tag{14.19}$$

The dynamics are described by the capital arbitrage equation and the equation describing capital accumulation. To simplify our analysis, for the remainder of this section we assume $\mu = 0$ and we assume that a constant fraction of all income (including capital gains), s, is saved.[27] We can write (14.10) as:

$$\frac{d}{dt}(ln\ K) + \frac{pT}{K}\frac{d}{dt}(ln\ p) = s\left(\frac{F(K, L, T)}{K} + \frac{T}{K}\frac{dp}{dt}\right) \tag{14.20}$$

or in our normalized units:

$$\frac{d}{dt}(ln\ k) = s\frac{f(k)}{k} - \frac{(1-s)\left(qf_k - f_{\hat{T}}\right)}{k} - n. \tag{14.20'}$$

4.2.1 Steady States

The steady state is given by the solution to the loci along which $dq/dt = 0$ and $dk/dt = 0$.

In steady state, $\frac{d}{dt}(ln\ q) = 0$, so $f_k - n = \frac{f_{\hat{T}}}{q}$, or

$$q = \frac{f_{\hat{T}}}{f_k - n} = \Phi(k) \text{ for } k < k^{**} \equiv f_k^{-1}(n). \tag{14.21}$$

$\Phi' > 0$ provided only that

$$\frac{f_{\hat{T}k}}{f_{\hat{T}}} > \frac{f_{kk}}{f_k - n}. \tag{14.22}$$

Under natural restrictions, the limit of Φ as k goes to zero is zero, and as k goes to k^{**} is infinity. In Figure 14.3, we have drawn the upward sloping $\Phi(k)$ curve.[28] Above the curve, q is increasing; below it is decreasing.

[27] If, instead, we had assumed that a constant fraction of capitalists' income was saved, as in the preceding section, we replace, in (14.21), the average product of capital with the marginal product of capital. In the case of a Cobb–Douglas production function, the marginal product is S_K times the average product, where S_K is the share of capital.

[28] A sufficient condition for this is that land and capital are complements.

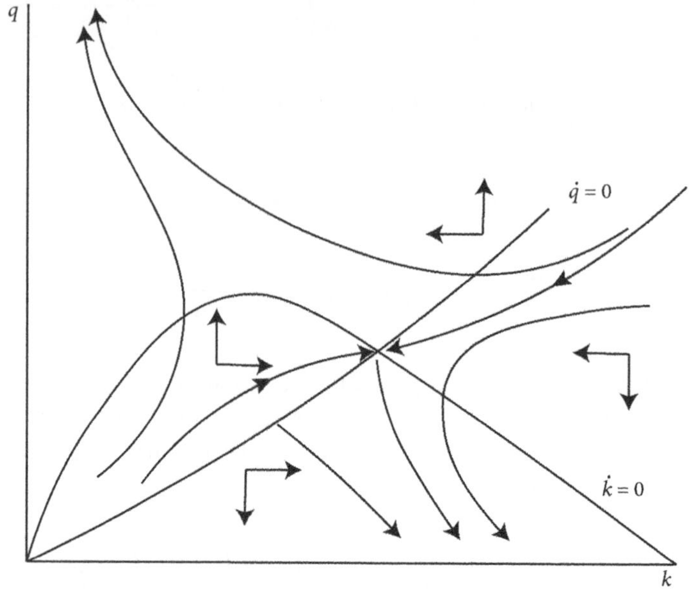

Figure 14.3 Dynamics with land augmenting technological progress. The equilibrium is a saddle point. In the absence of futures markets extending infinitely far into the future, the dynamics are unstable. If the initial price is too high, in finite time the bubble explodes.

The $\dot{k}=0$ locus is given by

$$q = \frac{sf(k) + (1-s)f_{\hat{T}} - nk}{(1-s)f_k} \equiv \psi(k). \qquad (14.23)$$

Under natural restrictions, $\psi(0)=0$, and for large enough k, the numerator of (14.23) becomes negative. Define k^{***} as the solution to[29]

$$sf(k^{**}) + (1-s)f_{\hat{T}} = nk^{***}. \qquad (14.24)$$

Hence ψ is the inverted U shaped locus depicted in Figure 14.3. It is easy to show that the Φ locus cuts the ψ locus from below and there is a unique equilibrium. Above the locus, dk/dt is negative, below it is positive.

If land prices are too high, for ownership of land to generate the same returns as capital, the price of land has to increase. On the other hand, if q is above both the $dk/dt=0$ locus and the $dp/dt=0$ locus, it means that the increase in the value of land ("savings" in this sense) acts as a substitute for real capital accumulation, and k accordingly diminishes. *The result is that the steady state equilibrium is a saddle point, as depicted in the figure.*

With futures markets extending infinitely far into the future, q is set along the trajectory converging to the steady state, that is, there is a unique value of q for each k such that the economy converges to the steady state.

[29] If there is more than one solution, k^{**} is defined as the smallest.

Without futures markets extending infinitely far into the future or infinite foresight, there is no reason to believe that the transversality condition will be satisfied. But along the paths which satisfy the short run arbitrage equation but do not converge to the long run equilibrium because the initial price is too high, the price of land eventually increases super exponentially.[30] As a result, in finite time, the "bubble" will be "corrected." But it can be a long time. And even when there is a "correction," it may still be on a "bubble path." The price of land falls, but to a level still above the convergent path.

Note that on the trajectories in which the price of land "explodes," eventually the increase in the value of land crowds out capital accumulation—the capital stock declines, *even though wealth continues to increase.* Indeed, as k gets small, virtually all of wealth is in the value of land, and thus wealth increases at the rate of $n + \frac{d}{dt}(ln\ q) = n + f_k - \frac{f_{\hat{T}}}{q}$. Above the $dq/dt = 0$ locus, $qf_k > f_{\hat{T}}$ so that wealth is unambiguously increasing (and even increasing per capita). Indeed, the wealth–income ratio (as usually defined, where income ignores capital gains) goes off to infinity.

Does this explain the observed increase in wealth–income ratio? It seems that this is at least a better explanation than the alternative *theory of an ever increasing "true" effective capital–labor ratio.*

4.3 Taxation

In this section, we ask, what happens when we impose taxation on capital gains at the rate τ^{cg} and/or the returns to land at the rate τ^{L}. The capital arbitrage equation now becomes

$$(1 - \tau^{cg})\frac{dp}{dt} = pF_K - F_T(1 - \tau^L). \qquad (14.16')$$

In steady state, the price of land is going up at the rate n, so in the steady state (using our normalized units)

$$(1 - \tau^{cg})\,nq = qf_k - f_{\hat{T}}(1 - \tau^L) \qquad (14.16'')$$

or

$$q = \frac{f_{\hat{T}}(1 - \tau^L)}{f_k - (1 - \tau^{cg})\,n}. \qquad (14.21')$$

To complete the analysis, we need to specify what is done with the revenues raised by the tax. Assume that the proceeds of the tax are redistributed to consumers so (in the model of the previous section, where savings depend only on comprehensive aggregate income) savings are unaffected, and the dynamics are affected only through the effects of taxation on capital gains themselves, that is, on nq.

[30] When the price is too low, eventually, the price may shrink to zero. For the rest of the analysis, we ignore this case.

Then the capital accumulation equation becomes:[31]

$$\frac{d}{dt}(\ln k) = s\frac{f(k)}{k} - \frac{(1-s)\left(qf_k - \left(1-\tau^L\right)f_{\hat{T}}\right)}{k\left(1-\tau^{cg}\right)} - n, \qquad (14.20'')$$

so in steady state:

$$q = \frac{\left\{\frac{[sf(k)-nk]}{(1-s)(1-\tau^{cg})}\right\} + \left(1-\tau^L\right)f_{\hat{T}}}{f_k}. \qquad (14.23')$$

The steady state is given by the solution to (14.21′) and (14.23′), giving the locus of $dq/dt = 0$ and $dk/dt = 0$ with land and capital gains taxes.

The land tax lowers the $dq/dt = 0$ and the $dk/dt = 0$ locus, but the former more than the latter (simply because the denominator in the former is smaller than in the latter). As Figure 14.4 shows, this means that an increase in a tax on the return to land leads to an increase in the capital–labor ratio and an increase in wages,[32] validating the common presumption that savings diverted into land investment (or speculation) is money that could otherwise have gone into real investment.

The analysis of the effect of a capital gains tax is more complicated. It can be shown that a capital gains tax increases capital accumulation provided $f_k > \frac{n}{s}$ (or is not too much smaller) and $f_{\hat{T}k} > 0$ (land and capital goods are complements, or not too strong substitutes).[33]

4.4 Comparative Statics with Optimizing Dynastic Savers

If we assume instead of individuals saving a fixed from of their income that they maximize dynastic savings, then as before, using continuous time, setting the depreciation rate at

[31] Noting that savings are reduced by the reduced after tax comprehensive income (by *scg*) but the value of land holdings still increases by nq. In deriving (14.21"), we have made use of (14.16") to solve for capital gains (nq):

$$nq = \frac{qf_k - f_{\hat{T}}\left(1-\tau^L\right)}{\left(1-\tau^{cg}\right)}.$$

[32] Assuming that capital and labor are complements. See the discussion earlier in the chapter.

[33] Substituting (14.20′) into (14.21′), we obtain

$$sf - nk - (1-s)\frac{nf_{\hat{T}}\left(1-\tau^L\right)}{f_k - \left(1-\tau^{cg}\right)n} = 0,$$

from which we can directly calculate $\frac{dk}{d\tau^{cg}}$, the sign of which depends on the sign of

$$-[sf_k - n - (1-s)n\frac{1-\tau^L}{f_k - \left(1-\tau^{cg}\right)n}\left\{f_{\hat{T}k} - \frac{qf_{kk}}{1-\tau^L}\right\}.$$

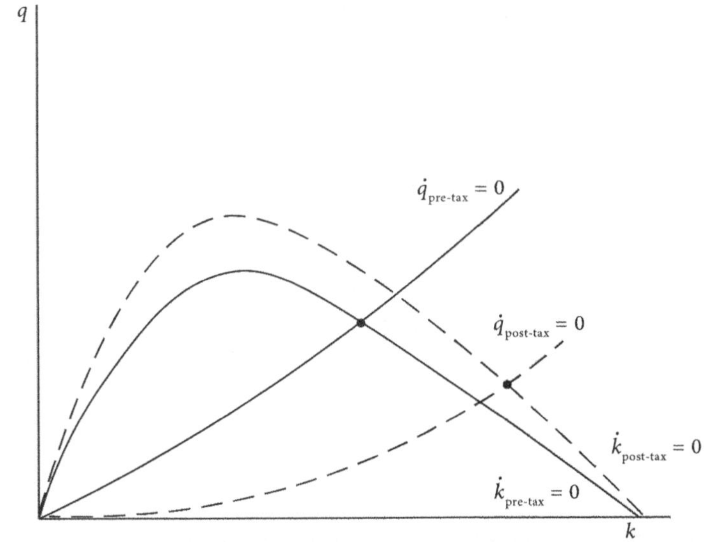

Figure 14.4 Impact of an increase in a land tax. The $\dot{q} = 0$ locus shifts down and the equilibrium value of k increases.

zero, we obtain in steady state:

$$f_k = \delta + n, \tag{14.25}$$

Equation (14.25) and the capital arbitrage equation (14.21′) define the equilibrium. It is straightforward that a tax on land or on capital gains increases the equilibrium q, but leaves k^*, the capital–labor ratio, unaffected. As before, however, workers are better off. Wages are unaffected.

On the other hand, in a two-class model, with dynastic savers and workers doing no savings, while wages unaffected, the transfers workers receive from the taxes increases their incomes and consumption. (Obviously, the dynamics, including the stability analysis, differs. For reasons that we have already explained, this model is not particularly useful in understanding the dynamics of adjustment when there is not a full set of futures markets extending infinitely far into the future.)

5 Land in a Life-Cycle Model

In Chapter 13, we formulated a life-cycle model, and used it to explain the division of wealth between capitalists and workers (lifetime savers). It is easy to incorporate land into this framework. Now, however, because land is a store of value that is alternative to capital, there is an important question: could savings that otherwise be used for capital accumulation be deflected into land, thereby *harming* workers?

5.1 Pure Life-Cycle Model

We begin our analysis with the case where there are *only* life-cycle savers, but there is a fixed asset, which we will call land. For simplicity, we focus only on the steady state.[34] For simplicity, we assume no population growth but there is depreciation of capital (so there has to be some gross savings in steady state).

The variables of interest can all be expressed as functions of k, the capital–labor ratio, simply because the land–labor ratio is fixed. The returns to land must equal the returns to holding capital. In steady state, the price of a unit of effective land, denoted by q, will be constant. Letting f_T denote the marginal return of a unit of land, which in steady state is constant, the capital arbitrage equation still has to be satisfied, which implies that[35]

$$q = \frac{f_T}{f_k - \mu}, \tag{14.26}$$

where, as before, μ is the rate of depreciation of capital, so $f_k - \mu$ is the net return to capital; and

$$s(w(k), r(k))\, w(k) = k + \frac{f_T}{f_k - \mu}, \tag{14.27}$$

in the obvious notation, where wages and returns to capital are functions of the capital stock per capita, and where we have normalized the land supply (per capita) at unity. Workers save a fraction of their wage income, with the fraction depending on their wages and the rate of return to capital. Savings are put either into capital goods or into land holdings.

It is useful to rewrite (14.26) to focus on "savings in capital." Normalizing the supply of land per capita at unity, we have

$$\Omega(k) \equiv s(w(k), r(k))\, w(k) - \frac{f_T}{f_k - \mu} = k. \tag{14.27a}$$

Any value of k solving (14.27a) is a steady state equilibrium.

There can be multiple equilibria, as illustrated in Figure 14.5. As k increases, wages increase, and savings increase, so long as the substitution effect is not too great. The slope of the LHS can be greater or less than unity, and can vary with k, so that the LHS can cross the 45 degree line more than once.[36] There is a natural sense in which stability requires that the savings curve cut the 45 degree locus from above, that is, the increase in savings *into capital* from an increase in the capital stock is less than the increase in the capital stock itself.

[34] For a more complete analysis of this model, see Stiglitz (2010b). Similar results hold with money, rather than land.

[35] Because there is no labor force growth and no land augmenting technological progress, the amount of land and "effective" land are identical. For notational simplicity, we drop the caret over T.

[36] As long as $ds/dk > 0$ and $f_{TK}/f_T < f_{KK}/f_k$, the LHS of (14.27a) is increasing. More generally, it can be either decreasing or increasing.

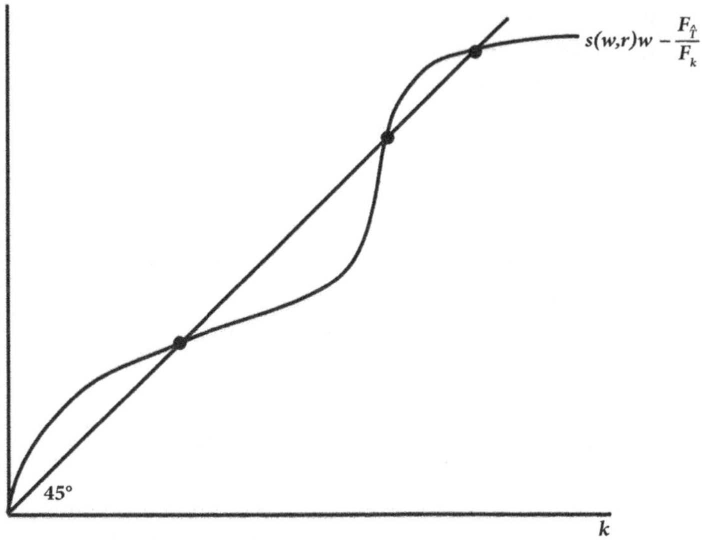

Figure 14.5 Multiple steady states in life-cycle models.

Looking across (steady state) equilibria, it is clear that, letting W denote wealth per capita.

$$\frac{dW}{dk} = \frac{d}{dk}\left(k + \frac{f_T}{f_k - \mu}\right) = 1 + q\left[\frac{f_{Tk}}{f_T} - \frac{f_{kk}}{f_k - \mu}\right]. \tag{14.28}$$

If

$$\frac{f_{Tk}}{f_T} - \frac{f_{kk}}{f_k - \mu} > 0, \tag{14.29}$$

then W increases more than k, that is, as the capital stock increases, so do land values. That will always be the case if T and k are complements.

By the same token, we can ask what happens if there is an upward shift in the savings function, that is, the savings function is given by $\gamma s(w(k), r(k))$. Then

$$\frac{dk}{d\gamma} = \frac{sw}{1 + q\left[\frac{f_{Tk}}{f_T} - \frac{f_{kk}}{f_k - \mu}\right] - sw' - w\frac{ds}{dk}} \tag{14.30}$$

which is positive for a stable equilibrium, and again, (14.28) implies that the increase in wealth is normally greater than the increase in k. Some of the increased savings goes into an increased value of land, reducing the benefits that otherwise would have accrued to a higher savings rate.

5.1.1 Taxing Capital

A tax on the return to wealth (both land and capital) will shift the function $\Omega(k) = sw - f_T/f_k$ up or down depending on whether s is decreasing or increasing in r, which implies that in a stable equilibrium, it will lead to an increased or decreased value of k depending on whether s_r is greater or less than zero. The change in wealth will typically be larger than the change in k (so long as inequality (14.29) is satisfied). But, as we have noted earlier, while in a two-factor production function, a decrease in k necessarily leads to a lower wage, now it may not. Capital and labor may be substitutes rather than complements.

5.1.2 Taxing Land

It is easy to see that in this model, a tax on the value of land the proceeds of which are distributed to workers results in an increase in investment and a reduction in the return to capital (in a stable equilibrium).[37] If $F_{KL} > 0$ (labor and capital are complements) wages will rise.[38] A fortiori, if the tax revenues are fully invested, wages go up even more.

5.2 A Two-Class Model with Land/Money

In this section, we extend the model of Chapter 13 where there are both life-cycle savers and dynastic savers to incorporate land or money. The capitalists' long run equilibrium wealth accumulation equation is described by

$$r = (1 - \tau)(f_k - \mu) = \delta, \qquad (14.31)$$

where τ is the tax rate on the return to capital and δ is capitalist's pure rate of time preference. The rate of interest is given by (14.32), and with land fixed, that implies a particular value of $k = k^*$, as in our earlier analysis. We similarly rewrite the steady state wealth equation for workers as

$$W^w = s(w + \Gamma). \qquad (14.32)$$

where Γ is the tax transfers workers receive and where, as in Chapter 13, workers' wealth (per capita) is given by W^w. Workers' savings rate can be either fixed or a function of the interest rate or even a function of the interest rate and their income. Since k is the only state variable, we can write the savings rate simply as a function of k. In steady state, the return to capital and the return to land (the return to each of the assets) is the same, which implies that the price of land is as before and total wealth is:[39]

$$W = k + q, \qquad (14.33)$$

where now W is total wealth (per capita).[40]

[37] The value of land is $(1 - t^L)\frac{f_T}{f_k}$. The reduction in f_k will normally partially offset the tax, so that the value of land will not go down commensurately with the reduction in $1 - t^L$.

[38] Recall that capital and labor can be substitutes (robots replacing human labor). From the fact that F_K is homogenous of degree zero, $F_{KK}K + F_{LK}L + F_{KT}T = 0$, so if $F_{LK} < 0, F_{KT} > 0$—land and capital have to be complements.

[39] Recall the normalization that the land supply is unity.

[40] Where we have again chosen units so that the land per capita is unity.

In steady state, (14.33) can be solved for the equilibrium value of wealth, since $q^* = \frac{f_T}{f_k - \mu}$ is also just a function of k. Hence, the steady state equations for life-cycle wealth relative to total wealth W^* is now in the absence of taxes and transfers just

$$\frac{W^{w^*}}{W^*} = \frac{s(k^*)\,w(k^*)}{W^*} = \frac{s(k^*)\,w(k^*)}{q + k^*}. \tag{14.34}$$

Changes in worker savings have no effect on total wealth but increase the share of that wealth they hold; an increase in capitalists' savings rate (a lowering of their time preference) leads to an increase in k, with an effect on wealth that is normally greater than the increase in k because of the increased value of land, as in the earlier model. Thus, the effect on inequality is greater than in a world without land.

Again, in this model, we can easily study the effect of various forms of taxation on the distribution of income and wealth (between capitalists and life-cycle savers); these effects are markedly different than in the pure life-cycle model of the previous sub-section because of tax shifting. Land taxation has no effect on k^*, hence no effect on wages; it simply leads to a diminution of the value of aggregate wealth—the value of land.

But a land tax at the rate t^L generates an annual rent of $t^L F_T$ distributed to workers, whose net income is thus $F_L + t^L F_T$. Since a land tax leaves k^* unchanged, and hence $w = F_L$ unchanged, it is clear the higher the land tax, the better off are workers. There is an increase in equality, with the share of total wealth held by life-cycle savers increasing.

Inheritance and capital taxation, as in Chapter 13, lead to an increase in the before tax return on capital, lowering k. If capital and labor are substitutes, then capital and land have to be complements, so the aggregate value of wealth is reduced by more than the reduction in k.[41] The reduction in k increases wages (because capital and labor are assumed substitutes). The effect on transfers is ambiguous, but if the capital and land tax is small, the direct effect of the increase in wages dominates. But if capital and labor are complements (as in the standard two-factor model), the opposite may happen.[42] Workers are worse off because wages are lowered, and again, if capital and land taxes are small the direct impact on wages dominates. But this adverse incidence effect can be offset (as we showed in Chapter 13) if the proceeds of the tax are invested in human capital or public infrastructure.

5.2.1 A Two-Class Model with Land as a Positional Good

We return now to Section 3, where capitalists hold land as a positional good. We replace the arbitrage equation (14.26) with an equilibrium condition recognizing the non-pecuniary benefits of owning land, a generalization of the model of Section 3:

$$M(W^c, F_T/q - f_k) = 1, \tag{14.35}$$

where as before q is the price of land, f_k is the return on capital and f_T is the return on land, and W_c is the wealth of capitalists. The earlier model is one in which there is

[41] That is, F_T, the return on land, is reduced, and since the relevant discount rate is the after tax rate of return, which is unchanged, the value of land is reduced.

[42] The revenue from the capital tax, $f_k - \eta_k$ decreases if the share of capital decreases as k decreases, but may increase otherwise. The revenue from the land tax $t^L F_T$ decreases if capital and land are complements, and increases if they are substitutes.

no non-pecuniary benefit, so the pecuniary returns to the two assets have to be the same. The intertemporal arbitrage equation of capitalists sets k^*, as before, so (14.35) can be solved for q. Presumably q will be higher than it was before, so inequality would be greater than it was in our earlier model.

6 Concluding Remarks

This chapter has considered a series of models within which we can ask: why might the price of land have increased in recent decades, what implications does this have for capital accumulation and inequality, and if the effects are adverse, what can be done about it?

The standard neoclassical assumption of an aggregate production function which is constant returns to scale in capital and labor—ignoring the limited supply of land—made some sense, as the economy switched from agriculture to manufacturing. But housing is an important component of GDP, land (or space) is an important element of residential value, and because transportation costs are significant, so is location. Hence it is not surprising that land rents would increase, and especially as changes in the economy (both as a result of changes in the structure of production and preferences) may lead to increases in the importance of the economics of agglomeration.[43]

Even if land were not to get more valuable over time as a result of increased agglomeration economies or population pressure, capital accumulation itself—with the resulting lowering of the return to capital—could increase the present discounted value of land because of the decrease in the discount rate, so that the value of wealth would increase more rapidly than the increase in the capital stock.[44] As we observed in Chapter 10, a measure of wealth is *not* a good measure of capital inputs.[45]

Matters may be worse than this standard analysis would have suggested: We have, for instance, considered land as a positional good—the value of beach front property in the Riviera or in Southampton increases with wealth and wealth inequality. Indeed, the effects are reinforcing.

In a variety of contexts, we have explained how this increase in the value of land can crowd out capital accumulation, making the economy in a fundamental sense poorer even if the value of wealth has increased. It is not just that measured wealth may increase even as the productive capacity of the economy decreases; the increase in land values, the source of the disparity, *causes* the decrease in productive capacity. This formalizes the insight of Chapter 10 and is a theme to which we will return in later chapters. This decrease in capital accumulation, in turn, leads to lower incomes per capita and lower wages.

There is a natural policy implication of this analysis: that if we could decrease the value of land, we could increase capital accumulation and hence wages.[46] We show that a tax on land (or on the capital gains on land, for example in models where part of the return to land is its

[43] See the discussion of Chapter 10 and the references cited there.

[44] As this chapter has emphasized, this is not inevitable: if land and capital are substitutes, the decreased return on land can dominate the lowered discount rate.

[45] There is one perverse possibility, where the increase in the value of wealth understates the increase in productive capital, and that is where capital and land are substitutes, so that capital accumulation leads to the reduction in land rents, so much so that the value of land actually decreases in spite of the lower discount factor.

[46] Again, there is a caveat: this assumes that capital and labor are complements. In a three-factor production function, we have noted that they may be substitutes.

increased scarcity value relative to produced goods) can do this. Thus, we reinforce Henry George's conclusion about the desirability of a land tax: not only is it desirable because the supply of land is inelastic (and thus such a tax is non-distortionary), but because it results in higher levels of national income and greater equality.

In Chapter 13, in a two-class model without land, we observed, by contrast, that a tax on the return to capital or an inheritance tax, with proceeds passed on to workers (i.e., not invested in either physical or human capital), actually increased inequality and made workers worse off. The taxes discouraged savings, and the resulting decrease in capital lowered wages more than the value of the transfers. Though it is still true that savings are discouraged and income per capita is lowered, it is not necessarily the case that wages are lowered, especially so if investment is in human replacing robots (as discussed further in Chapter 18).[47]

We have explained too why land bubbles are a natural part of market economies (in the absence of futures markets extending infinity far into the future); and even when there are "corrections," there is no assurance that the market will not once again go off on a bubble path. Indeed, in the absence of infinite foresight into the future, it seems implausible that the market would find just the right price that converges to the steady state; ever so slight deviations from that "right price" can eventually lead to an exploding bubble. On such bubble paths, wealth, as conventionally measured, may increase, even as the real wealth of the economy—the capital stock (per capita)—diminishes.

Instability, of course, can impose particularly large costs on workers, a subject we discuss further in Part III.D.[48]

While markets on their own have thus a proclivity for instability, monetary and financial policy are supposed to stabilize the economy. In practice, though, much of the observed macro-instability is a result of misguided monetary and regulatory policies—for instance, allowing excessive credit creation and its allocation to mortgages, resulting in a real estate bubble, exemplified by what happened in the years prior to the 2008 crisis. These policies also contributed to the increase in inequality over the period. The next chapter explores these issues.

[47] As we noted repeatedly, in a three-factor model, results are more ambiguous: capital and labor can be substitutes (in a two-factor model they are always complements). This is the case, for instance, for labor replacing machines (like robots). Then, the decrease in capital accumulation raises wages and workers benefit from both the transfers and from the decreased capital accumulation. See Chapter 18.

[48] As we have noted elsewhere, whether recessions lead to an increase in *measured* inequality depends on the measure one employs and subtle differential effects on labor vs. capital. For instance, profits, being a residual, may decline more than wages in an economic downturn.

15

The Role of Credit and the Financial System in Creating Wealth Inequality

1 Introduction

The connection between the growth of inequality and the financial sector has long been recognized (Galbraith 2012).[1] This chapter presents a simple model showing how monetary and financial policy contributes to wealth inequality and provides a set of policy responses.

Monetary and financial policy has multitudinous effects. Most directly, it affects a key price in the economy—the interest rate—and the availability of credit;[2] and the interest rate and credit availability affect the price of assets, the level of economic activity, and the level of inflation. What matters is not just the amount of credit that is available, and the terms on which it is available, but how credit gets allocated, and as we will see, these key decisions have contributed significantly to inequality.

1.1 Macro Management and Inequality

Monetary authorities, however, view their main responsibility is macro management—ensuring full employment without inflation; and any increase or decrease in inequality is viewed as collateral damage or benefit. Moreover, they claim that when they do their job, maintaining full employment and preventing inflation, they are promoting equality and the well-being of ordinary citizens.

When they succeed in promoting full employment, there is some truth in such claims. Whatever the effect of a major economic downturn on measured inequality,[3] the impact

[1] This chapter is a revised and updated version of "New theoretical perspectives on the distribution of income and wealth among individuals: Part IV. Land and Credit," NBER working paper 21102, May 2015. It also draws upon Stiglitz (2015c), originally presented as a keynote address to The Ninth Biennial Federal Reserve System Community Development Research Conference, April 3, 2015; and Stiglitz (2018f, 2017a), published in a festschrift in honor of Deepak Nayyar.

[2] More conventional economics focuses on *money*. In modern economies, where money is created through the banking system, what matters is not the liability side of banks' balance sheets or the money supply, but the credit that they make available. That is what determines what households and firms can buy, thus driving the demand for both produced and non-produced goods. As we explain below, banks can create money essentially out of thin air, which is why the regulations/policies that limit or facilitate their ability to do so are so critical.

[3] The effects can be ambiguous, because a severe economic downturn hurts workers and capitalists alike; the impact on inequality depends on the differential effects, which may vary from economy to economy and from time to time. The 2008 crisis led to increased wealth inequality, because so much of the wealth of those in the middle and bottom was held in the form of housing, and real estate prices plummeted. In addition, the way the recovery was managed disproportionately benefitted the top: 91% of the gains in the first three years of the recovery went to the top 1% of the population; and as we explain below, Quantitative Easing (QE) increased the wealth of those at the top. This helps explains why the recovery was so anemic.

The Origins of Inequality, and Policies to Contain It. Joseph E. Stiglitz, Oxford University Press. © Joseph E. Stiglitz (2025).
DOI: 10.1093/oso/9780198799580.003.0016

on workers' well-being is severe, as they lose jobs and face increased insecurity.[4] Moreover, if governments cut back on the provision of basic services on which they depend (such as education and health), in response to decreased tax revenues, as happened in the euro crisis, the effects can be devastating.[5]

Still, there are different ways of moving the economy towards full employment; some are more likely to succeed than others; some are more likely to be accompanied by an increase in inequality. When the increase in inequality is large, it can undermine efforts to increase aggregate demand and employment, simply because the marginal propensity to consume of the rich is so much lower than that of the rest of society. Increases in inequality and especially declining incomes of workers and retirees have feedbacks, depressing aggregate income still further. (See the discussion in Part III.D.) Thus, for example, low interest rates depress the consumption of retirees who are dependent on interest, and in deep downturns, this effect may be comparable to or even larger than the increase in investment (which may be nil, when uncertainty is sufficiently large, because then the interest elasticity of investment may be low).[6]

By the same token, some of the channels by which traditional monetary policy exerts its effects are inherently associated with increases in wealth inequality, especially at the top, rendering them less effective than is sometimes claimed. One of the justifications put forward by the Fed for the quantitative easing was that the decrease in interest rates increased wealth. Consumption, and thus aggregate demand, increases with wealth. But QE's wealth effects worked largely through a change in share prices. While the returns for life-cycle savers holding bonds went down, the lower cost of and return to debt led the price of equities to increase. We noted in Chapter 4 that there were large differences in portfolio composition between the rich and the poor. As one would expect, the rich hold more of their wealth in risky assets, like equities. Any policy which differentially benefits those assets held by capitalists leads to greater inequality.[7] Because it was mostly the wealth of the wealthy that increased, the impact on aggregate demand was much smaller than it would have been if wealth-inequality had not increased.[8] QE was thus just another variant of "trickle-down" economics, and not surprisingly, it was remarkably ineffective: If the marginal propensity to consume out of wealth of the wealthy is low—which may

[4] See, for example, Stiglitz, Stetter, Dougherty, et al. (2019).

[5] See, for example, Stiglitz (2016d), Stiglitz, Stetter, Dougherty, et al. (2019).

[6] Moreover, with large fractions of the population being target savers—saving to finance a down payment on a house, the college education of their children, or for retirement—a lowering of the interest rate induces lower consumption (higher savings) among those still in the workforce, as well as retirees dependent on interest income.

None of these distributional and behavioral subtleties are well-captured in standard DSGE models, though they are partially (but imperfectly) captured in more recent heterogenous agent New Keynesian models (HANK). But such models, for instance, do not address the central issue of this chapter, the allocation of credit to *non-produced assets*. See Kaplan, Moll, and Violante (2018).

[7] In a model with life-cycle savings (as presented in Chapters 13 and 14 and discussed below), where there is a choice among asset holdings, the composition of wealth-holdings will differ between the capitalists and life-cycle savers, simply because the two groups will differ in their ability and willingness to bear risk and because they face different tax rates, so after tax returns differ. Monetary, financial, and fiscal policy affect simultaneously differences in portfolio composition between capitalists and workers and, because of the differences in the mean and standard deviations of returns of different assets, the equilibrium wealth distribution.

[8] The advocates of QE focused on the wealth effect, which, as we've suggested, may be limited. But there is another effect, the cash flow effect, which, especially in a world of credit rationing, can overpower the wealth effect. Retirees depending on interest saw their incomes reduced. To the extent that they expected lower interest rates to prevail in the future, it became even more important for them to husband their funds today and reduce consumption.

be especially so if the low interest rates are announced to be temporary, so that there is a significant risk that the value of the assets may decrease when interest rates return to more normal levels[9]—then the impact on aggregate demand will be weak, possibly more than offset by the reduced consumption of lower income/wealth individuals who depend more on interest payments. It is thus not surprising that many studies have found that QE had very limited impacts on aggregate demand, though a large impact on wealth inequality.[10]

1.2 Access to Credit and Inequality

Monetary and financial policy affects not just the overall level of credit availability but also who gets access to credit,[11] and access to credit can affect both economic outcomes and opportunities. Indeed, the system by which credit is allocated may be one of the main sources of wealth and income inequality: if a favored few get access to credit, then their wealth increases relative to those without such access. If access to credit is limited to those who are already wealthy, inequalities are perpetuated, and there will be limited opportunities for entrepreneurship by those born of limited means.

Russia provides the quintessential example of the role of finance in creating inequality: It was through the banking system that the Russian oligarchy was largely created. Bank licenses were granted to some politically connected individuals. Those with banking licenses could use that power to obtain loans that enabled them and their associates to buy enormously valuable state assets as they were privatized. Limited access to funds meant that competition in the privatization auctions was limited, and thus those with access to funds could acquire the state assets at far below fair market value.[12]

In a less dramatic way, wealth inequality in the United States and other advanced countries is linked with the financial system. If much of the growth of wealth is related to an increase in credit (or other changes in the financial system); if access to credit is based on collateral or connections; and if the assets which have benefited from the increase in credit (or other changes in the financial system) are disproportionately owned by the rich, then it should be apparent that these increases in credit and

[9] In fact, in perfectly functioning markets, an interest rate policy that is announced to be temporary should have a minimal effect on long-lived assets. Asset prices should have been anticipated to return to more normal levels when the intervention was reversed, and knowing this, the price now should not have increased much. Thus, there should not have been much wealth effect. If, for some reason, markets did not fully reflect this reasoning, then rational owners of these inflated assets would still know that there was a risk that they return to more normal values; thus, their wealth would be viewed as riskier, and under plausible conditions accordingly their marginal propensity to consume out of this increased wealth would be small. (See Rothschild and Stiglitz, 1971.) For further discussion, see Stiglitz (2015e).

[10] On the limited impacts for aggregate demand, see empirical work by Chen, Cúrdia, and Ferrero (2012) and theoretical work by Woodford (2016). For impacts on inequality, see Beraja, Fuster, Hurst, and Vavra (2019).

[11] In standard neoclassical models, everyone has access to credit; all that matters is the interest rate charged. But in the presence of imperfect information, credit is typically rationed. The theory of credit rationing (e.g., Stiglitz and Weiss, 1981) based on asymmetric information provided an explanation for pervasive credit rationing. In the presence of such credit rationing, the expected return of even the marginal individual who gets access to credit may be substantially in excess of the cost of capital (the interest he has to pay), so that one's future economic prospects depends critically on access to credit. Stiglitz and Greenwald (2003a) analyze how changes in monetary and financial policy translate into changes in credit availability.

[12] This was especially the case in countries that restricted foreign bidders. For a more extensive treatment, see, for example, Freeland (2000).

other changes in the financial system may have played a major role in the increase in wealth and income inequality.[13] By the same token, if the financial sector discriminates in providing mortgages, those who are in the discriminated-against group won't have opportunities to participate in the increase in wealth associated with a housing boom. Historically, American financial institutions engaged in massive discrimination (both "red-lining," excluding largely African-American communities, and charging higher interest rates to Hispanics and African-Americans than comparably risky whites), but remarkably, 40 years after civil rights legislation outlawing such discrimination, major American banks were still engaged in discriminatory practices, especially in the form of predatory lending.[14]

Discrimination is, of course, only one of many forms of exploitation in which the financial sector has engaged. They have used their market power to extract "rents" out of the rest of the economic system. While the next chapter explores in greater detail the role of rent-seeking involving exploitation of market power in the creation of inequality, here we focus in particular on the rents associated with the creation of credit. Of course, the adverse effects on inequality of exploitation directed at the poor—discrimination, predatory lending, and abusive credit card practices—are also significant, but beyond the scope of this chapter.[15]

This chapter focuses on two key ways by which the financial sector affects inequality: (a) excessive expansion of credit leads to higher prices of land, crowding out capital accumulation; workers are worse off, those at the top better off; and (b) the rents associated with credit allocation go to financiers. Financial deregulation has contributed to growing inequality both by contributing to excessive credit creation and enabling the bankers to garner for themselves more rents. The chapter describes a set of reforms addressing both channels through which finance contributes to inequality. It also describes an alternative approach to monetary policy which would lead to greater macro stability—and since macro-instability gives rise to inequality, this too would contribute to greater equality.

[13] This is especially so if the changes in policy were not fully anticipated, or more generally, were viewed to be uncertain. The uncertainty in the changes in policy increases the variability of asset prices, making these assets even more differentially attractive to the rich, so that when the favorable policies are adopted (e.g., financial sector deregulation changes the rules to allow for greater expansion of credit), the benefits accrue disproportionately to the rich.

Much of economic analysis is conducted in the context of policy changes that are either temporary (and known to be temporary) or permanent (and known to be permanent). In reality, there is always uncertainty, both because circumstances change and political control changes. In contestable democracies, major parties differ in their views on a wide range of policies, and when control shifts from, say, the left to the right or vice versa, there are a wide range of possible alterations in policy. Market participants know this, and policy makers too can and should take into account the alternative strategies by which market participants might respond to these uncertainties. See Korinek and Stiglitz (2008). For an application to dividend taxation, see Korinek and Stiglitz (2009).

[14] See, for example, Stiglitz (2010a).

[15] Also beyond the scope of this chapter are several other ways by which the financial system's behavior affects inequality. The decisions made by our financial institutions shape our economy—they're supposed to do that, of course, because they are responsible for allocating scarce capital. But, even in a competitive capital market, they can do that in ways which benefit disproportionately capitalists and the rich. If they allocate more resources to riskier investments, the price of risk will increase (to induce wealth-holders to bear that risk), and that will benefit the wealthy, who are better able to bear this risk. It is easy to show that this feedback mechanism can give rise to multiple equilibria—a high risk equilibrium where capitalists do well, choosing to hold risky assets and rewarded for their willingness to do so, to bear risk, and a low-risk equilibrium. The parallel to Uzawa's (1961) model with capitalists having a higher savings rate—increasing the demand for the capital intensive good, and hence the return on capital—should be clear.

Later in this chapter we will note still other ways in which the financial sector perpetuates inequality, such as the predilection of bankers to provide credit to those similar to themselves.

1.3 A Key Limitation

The models that we explore here are all full employment models, so they do not assess the critical trade-offs associated with short run macroeconomic management—for instance the social benefits of increased employment among workers generated by QE policies which lead to increased wealth inequality. The analysis already presented suggests that once the distributional effects of such policies are taken into account, and particularly once the analysis is conducted within more realistic macro models incorporating credit and equity rationing and cash flow and uncertainty effects, the short run benefits may be smaller than is typically alleged.[16]

This chapter, by contrast, focuses on long run impacts—and here, we see that some policies associated with the easing of monetary policy may not stimulate capital accumulation in the long run; quite the contrary, especially in models with land, increased land values resulting from looser monetary policy may crowd out capital accumulation and lead to lower wages, as we saw in the last chapter. Similar results hold here even without land—just with the presence of market power. These effects—the emphasis that the major impact of monetary policy, at least under certain circumstances, may be on the prices of non-produced assets rather than the output of produced goods and services—are also of relevance for short run analysis, and again highlight the limitations of monetary policy in stimulating the economy and reducing unemployment, especially in a severe downturn. If correct, it suggests too that even in the short run the adverse effects of monetary policy on inequality may dominate. These are questions which we hope to pursue in future research.

In the following chapter, we'll identify some further adverse effects of loose monetary policy: increased incentives to replace labor with machines, reducing employment and wage prospects in the medium term. We need to emphasize, however, that well-designed fiscal, financial, and banking policies can countervail these untoward effects, for example through directed lending programs that allocate more resources to labor intensive investments that increase the overall demand for labor, and especially unskilled labor.[17]

1.4 Organization of the Chapter

This chapter is divided into two major sections. The first describes how credit creation can lead to changes in asset prices—in particular the price of land—and wealth inequality, focusing in particular on the role of collateral constraints. It thus builds on and extends the models of Chapters 10 and 14 on the relationship between wealth and capital accumulation, explaining how wealth can increase even when the capital stock decreases,

[16] By the same token, there are many specifics of the conduct of short run monetary policy which affect the distribution of income, both in the short run and the long. Inflation targeting, where monetary authorities focus on inflation rather than unemployment, results in higher levels of unemployment; this weakens the bargaining power of workers, resulting in lower wages. Lower wages and less employment obviously mean that workers do more poorly. When governments persistently follow such policies, the share of wages is likely to be lower over the long run. A full analysis of these short run effects of monetary policy requires the construction of a short run macro model, a task beyond the scope of this chapter.

[17] Such directed credit has been criticized as distorting the market; but that criticism is based on two premises that we discredited earlier in this book: that the market is efficient, and that one can separate distributional issues from issues of efficiency.

as a result of an increase in the value of land. In these models, changes in monetary and financial policy are the exogenous variables driving the changes in the economy.

The second section considers a set of major policy reforms intended to reduce the rents appropriated by the financial system through its control of the means of payments (the credit and debit card system) and credit creation. The public appropriation of these rents, through the proposed reforms, could have a direct impact on inequality; but even more important, we show that these reforms can lead to greater macro-stability, which itself has significant distributive consequences.

2 Credit, Collateral, and Wealth Inequality

We have argued (in Chapter 10) that much of the growth of wealth is associated with the increase in rents and their capitalized value. In the last chapter, we focused on the increased value of land and other fixed assets. The demand for land and other assets depends itself on the availability of credit—a fact that was made abundantly clear by recent experiences with Quantitative Easing.

Standard macroeconomic and monetary models have given short shrift to the existence of a non-produced asset other than money. Thus, a change in monetary or financial policy can only have an effect either on the quantity of produced goods or the price of money relative to produced goods—conventionally measured inflation. In recent years, however, large changes in base money have had little effect on inflation, but have had a large effect on the price of other assets, including land.[18] Consistent with recent experiences, we assume that an increase in, say, credit availability or other changes in financial or monetary policy *only* affect the price of *other* non-produced assets—the polar assumption to that of the current standard literature.

2.1 The Role of Collateral

In the models below, collateral will play a crucial role. It allows those with wealth to borrow more—to amplify their wealth. And it allows banks to "safely" expand the supply of credit (money). Because of the key role that the concept of collateral plays, we need to say a word about what makes for collateral and the drivers of collateral requirements. Individuals put up collateral as a guarantee that they will repay a loan; it's an asset that can easily be seized if the debtor fails to fulfill his obligations.

What is accepted as collateral is both a matter of law and economics. Critical is the value of the collateral in the event of a default. For an asset to serve well as collateral requires that its value not be too variable, and in particular not be positively correlated with the level of economic activity (and hence the risk of default). Assets, the value of which may vary with the business cycle or with potential structural change act as poorer collateral than those whose values is stable.

[18] The next chapter will explore impacts on the value of monopoly and oligopoly rents.

There are two more aspects of collateral. A short-term government bond would seem to provide good collateral, but the question is: why borrow against this collateral, rather than sell the bond, necessitating borrowing less. Part of the answer is that the provision of collateral is intended to change the order of seniority in the event of bankruptcy: those with collateralized loans get paid off (up to the value of the collateral) before those without collateral. Of course, moving someone to a more senior position implicitly moves other creditors to more junior positions, and that would imply the firm would have to pay higher interest rates on those loans. This is essentially another form of capital restructuring, and according to the generalized Modigliani–Miller Theorem (Stiglitz, 1974e), this should make no difference. But the MM theorem does not hold in the presence of information asymmetries and bankruptcy costs—and both of these are ever present. Thus, changing corporate financial structure, including by changing seniority structure, does matter, and this is especially so in the presence of incomplete contracts: effectively one can "cheat" some of those whose claims become more junior, because they had not fully structured their debt contracts to make their interest payments contingent on such actions.[19]

Finally, there is the issue of control: the value of an asset to an individual or firm may be greater than the market value, because the individual believes that he can extract more value out of the asset. While the asset is provided as collateral, the individual or firm can still control the asset (subject to certain restrictions), and thus, there is a residual value to the original owner that goes beyond what he could have obtained had he sold it now. (Control, of course, is not relevant in the case of government bonds.)

The fact that land, and certain other assets, can be used as collateral makes them particularly attractive and may increase their value; but the value associated with the ability to be used as collateral will depend on the financial system. If, for instance, banks do no lending based on collateral, then there is no extra value associated with those particular assets that can be used for collateral; but if they do, the easier access to credit for those who have collateral, the higher these assets will be valued (say, relative to their financial returns).[20] This will be evident in the model presented in the next subsection.

2.2 Organization of This Section

We explore three different models highlighting how credit creation leads to increased inequality. In the first two, a non-produced good (land) is central. Increased credit increases the value of land and depresses capital accumulation, thereby hurting workers. In Section 2.3, land has an intrinsic value to some wealthy, for example as a positional good; while in Section 2.4, land is just another store of value, so that all that matters is the pecuniary return to land, its rent plus capital gains. The third section instead considers a life-cycle model with capital and labor as the only factors of production and assumes that the ownership of capital can be used for collateral.

[19] I also suspect that there is more than a little market irrationality: many, perhaps most, market participants do not fully grasp the full consequences of collateralized borrowing.

[20] By the same token, the more assets that are accepted as collateral, the lower will be the "collateral premium" attached to any particular asset.

2.3 Credit and the Value of Land

In this section, we provide a bare-bones model that may capture some of what has been going on through the expansion of credit, in particular allowing the financial system to lend more. There are two approaches, yielding similar results: lowering, say, banks' capital adequacy requirements, allowing them to lend more on the basis of their existing capital; or reducing collateral requirements for lending.[21] Here, we simply assume that the banking system provides credit based on collateral.[22] When the price of land in the Riviera goes up, the banks are willing to lend more. If the banks are willing to lend more, the price of land in the Riviera goes up. It is a decision of the banks (itself a function of decisions of the central bank) concerning amounts and terms (interest rates and collateral requirements) of credit availability that drives the price of land (real estate).

We modify the model of the last chapter by assuming three distinct classes of individuals—workers who just consume, capitalists who save out of profits, own enterprises and invest only in capital goods, but have no access to credit, and rentiers, who own land.[23] Their demand for land depends on W^T, the wealth of the rentier, p, the price of land, c, the amount of credit that is available, and r, the interest rate (the opportunity cost of owning land, for the moment taken as given): $M\left(W^T, c, p, r\right)$, with the equilibrium condition now being given by

$$M\left(W^T, c, p, r\right) = pT = W^T + c, \tag{15.1}$$

where W^T is just the value of the land minus what they owe in credit: $W^T = pT - c$. Substituting into (15.1) we obtain:

$$M(pT - c, c, p, r) = pT. \tag{15.1'}$$

[21] The close relationship between the two is seen if we formulate the capital adequacy requirements in risk-adjusted terms. Collateral requirements effectively change the risk-weight associated with a loan.

[22] Here, we follow most of the literature in assuming that the collateral requirement is exogenously fixed, and ask what happens when the requirement is changed. Of course, in a fully rational model, the collateral requirement is endogenous. That was the case in the early analyses of credit with collateral (Stiglitz and Weiss, 1986), in which collateral also served a somewhat different function than described earlier—it could mitigate both the adverse incentive and selection effects that could arise in the presence of asymmetric information, for instance conveying information about the likely riskiness of the borrower.

In the short run, there is evidence that collateral requirements do not change in the way that standard theory would have predicted or in the ways that one would have expected a prudential regulator to respond to changing circumstances. Indeed, the Federal Reserve lowered the down payment required on housing as the bubble took off in the early years of this century, when, had they taken any account of the increased likelihood of there being a bubble with a subsequent fall in prices, they should have done just the opposite.

[23] The model is obviously stylized, and can easily be generalized. We have assumed, in particular, that capitalists-entrepreneurs are the only ones who do *real* savings, while landowners/rentiers simply buy land, and that credit is only provided to the latter rather than the former. These simplify the analysis without changing the qualitative results. In the final sub-section, we allow credit against capital goods as collateral.

Following our earlier discussions on collateral, here are good reasons why land should serve better as collateral than capital goods—capital goods tend to be constructed for specific purposes, and are less malleable, less alterable to other uses, with often large asymmetries of information concerning the prospects of returns not only in the intended use, but also in alternative uses.

There are also good reasons that the provision of credit often gets reflected in land bubbles (or bubbles in other assets that are fixed in supply): when the price of capital goods exceeds the production costs, the supply will increase, and this limits the extent to which the price (relative to the price of consumption goods) can rise or the duration of any bubble associated with a produced good. (Nonetheless, bubbles of produced goods do occur—the tech bubble in the nineties and the tulip bubble in the seventeenth century being the most famous instances. These bubbles are testimony to market irrationality but are likely to be short lived.)

As in the previous chapter, we normalize by setting $T = 1$. We can solve for the price of land as a function of the interest rate and credit availability:

$$p = \psi(c, r) \tag{15.2}$$

with

$$\frac{dp}{dc} = \frac{M_c - M_W}{1 - M_W - M_p} > 0. \tag{15.3}$$

provided only that the demand for land (the positional good) increases more with the provision of credit (which is tied to the purchase of land as collateral) than with an increase in wealth;[24] and that an increase in wealth is allocated only partly to an increase in the demand for land.

The wealth of the rentiers is entirely driven by the provision of credit:

$$W^T = p - c = \psi(c, r) - c. \tag{15.4}$$

To close the model, we need an additional equation describing capital accumulation, and thus the determination of the rate of return r. We take the simplest version, due to Kaldor (1957). Capitalists-entrepreneurs save a fraction of their gross income, s_p, putting their money into capital goods:

$$\frac{dK}{dt} = s_p rK - \mu K, \tag{15.5}$$

where μ is the depreciation rate,[25] so in steady state (we continue with the assumption of the previous chapter that population is fixed, and there is no technological change; both assumptions can be changed, as in the previous chapter).[26] This implies that

$$F_K(K^*, L) = \frac{\mu}{s_p}. \tag{15.6}$$

In this model, the provision of additional credit has *no* effect on the equilibrium capital stock. For simplicity, we assume that the interest rate charged for borrowing to purchase land, r, is equal to the real return on capital, which is given by (15.6) and unaffected by c.[27]

[24] The denominator of (15.3) is naturally positive: otherwise, an increase in the price increases the value of the demand for land more than it increases the value of the land itself. Sufficient conditions for this are that $1 > M_W$, that is, that not all of increased wealth is spend on land purchases, and $M_p < 0$, an increase in the price of land (relative to consumption numeraire) reduces the demand for land.

[25] r is now the gross return to capital. We could rewrite all of these equations based on net savings and net income, without changing any of the results. We could also employ more generalized savings functions, including (as we have shown in earlier chapters), savings functions that are derived from explicit utility maximization. Our formulation at different points in this book differs; in each case, we choose the formulation that allows us to focus best on the central issues of concern.

[26] To repeat the model of the previous chapter: Land is assumed to be unproductive, and demanded just for its consumption (including positional) value. Output is produced by a constant-returns-to-scale production function, $Q = F_K(K^*, L)$ and $r = F_K$.

[27] Since the risk properties of the two assets are likely to be different, the interest rate charged on credit to buy land could differ from credit to buy capital goods. The results are obviously unaffected if there were a fixed

We thus obtain from (15.1′), letting $W = W^T + K$, the sum of the wealth of the rentiers and the capitalists,

$$\frac{dW}{dc} = \frac{dW^T}{dc} = \frac{-\left(1 - M_c - M_p\right)}{1 - M_W - M_p}. \tag{15.7}$$

An increase in credit increases wealth through an increase in land prices but has no effect on the capital stock. Since it is only the wealthy who own the land and that get access to credit, all of the increase in wealth (capital gain) goes to the wealthy rentiers. Monetary policy, here interpreted as an increase in credit c, *causes* both the increase in (non-productive) wealth and the increase in wealth inequality. But while wealth has increased, wages and capital accumulation are unaffected. (Later sections will show that in more general models, capital accumulation and wages are likely to decrease.)

2.3.1 Adverse Effects on Workers

This analysis ignores, however, the effect of the increase in land rents on the well-being of workers. Assume that workers' demand for housing (land) is a function of p and w. Assume, for simplicity, that though their well-being depends on p, their aggregate demand for land is so small that it has a negligible effect on p. Then it is straightforward that an increase in credit availability makes workers worse off and rentiers better off.[28] In the long run, monetary policy (making credit more available) does not lead to higher growth or high GDP per capita. It leads to higher wealth, but only through higher land prices, and this benefits only the rentiers at the expense particularly of workers.[29]

2.4 Credit and the Creation of Land Bubbles and Inequality

In this sub-section, we consider a simple extension of the model of Section 4 of the previous chapter to incorporate credit. The central message is that excessive credit creation may lead to a diversion of savings into land accumulation, and this crowds out capital accumulation, lowering wages and worsening inequality. Excessive credit creation can also lead to a land-bubble, which explodes within finite time.

For reasons already explained in the previous chapter, we assume land augmenting technological progress at the rate n, the rate of growth of population that (in the absence of labor augmenting technological progress, which we assume for convenience, is zero) equals the long run rate of growth of the economy, g. To simplify, we assume that there is no consumption value to land.[30]

differential return, and, with some increase in complexity, can be generalized. We ignore this distinction for the moment, but see the next subsection.

In the next section, we will assume that the bank-lending rate, say for the purchase of land, is set by the government and that $r \leq F_K$.

[28] If capitalists' well-being also depends on land-consumption, they too are worse off. If capitalists' savings propensity depends on the price of land, then there will be an additional effect from the interaction of the land price and the capitalists' savings rate.

[29] We have assumed that the economy is always at full employment, so aggregate demand does not matter. The rentiers may spend more the wealthier they are, so that through this indirect effect, an increase in credit leads to an increase in aggregate demand. For reasons we have explained elsewhere, however, easier monetary policy may, in the short run, actually lead to a contraction in aggregate demand.

[30] To recall the details of that model, output was a constant returns to scale function of land, T, labor, L, and capital, $K : Q = F(K, L, \chi T)$, where χ reflects land augmenting technology progress.

The return to holding land ρ_T is then the capital gain on land, the yield on land, F_T, and the option that owning land provides to get access to funds at a low rate, which for simplicity we assume is zero, to buy more land:[31]

$$\rho_T = (1+\alpha)\left(\frac{d\ln p}{dt} + \frac{F_T}{p}\right), \tag{15.8}$$

where here owning a dollar's worth of land allows one to borrow enough to increase one's land holdings to $(1+\alpha)$, on each unit of which one obtains a return which is equal to capital gains plus rents.

If there is an unanticipated change in the rules of the game—say a lowering of the collateral required for a loan—then there will be an increase in the price of land: those who are lucky enough to own land at that moment receive a large capital gain. Such a change could be motivated by a perceived improvement in the ability to manage risk, or by political influence, with the financial industry persuading politicians that such a change would allow a more efficient capital market. Of course, such a change in the regulations regarding lending does not increase the amount of real resources available in the economy, even if it might allow banks to lend more, and thereby might increase the profitability of banking. The direct impact inevitably will be on the prices of non-produced assets. Assume, as in the models we are exploring in this chapter, the economy is at full employment. If financial regulations were eased, banks could lend more, given their deposits and net worth. If banking is profitable at the margin, each bank would believe such a policy would be desirable, and each would try to lend more. But if they all started to lend more, either the demand for non-produced assets increases (as here), raising the price of land, or there would be excess demand for produced goods, and the Fed would have to raise interest rates, to tighten credit in a fully offsetting way.[32]

The change in collateral requirements has, of course, large distributive consequences. If, for instance, before the change in collateral requirements land was mostly owned by the rich (say because of risk properties which made the asset relatively more attractive to them), then the rich will be the beneficiaries of the change in asset prices: wealth inequality will increase.

As more credit is provided, the price of land will be bid up[33], and in equilibrium:

$$pT - c + \alpha(pT - c) = pT. \tag{15.9}$$

[31] Obviously, at a zero interest rate there is credit rationing. As we discuss later, there will be credit rationing so long as the interest charged is less than the return to holding land, which, by the capital arbitrage condition, has to be equal to the return to holding capital, F_K. (In the previous section, it will be recalled, we assumed that $r = F_K$.)

[32] Obviously, if banks can create money and charge for it more than they have to pay depositors, banking will be highly profitable and there will be incentives to enter. We assume that banking authorities control entry into banking, and, either directly or indirectly (e.g., through reserve requirements) the supply of credit c.

[33] In standard monetarism, it is the price of produced goods relative to money that increases. Non-produced goods (land) plays no role. The model we posit here takes the opposite stance: the price of produced goods (in nominal terms) remains unchanged; it is only the price of non-produced goods that changes. Later in this chapter we explain why, as a polar model, we believe ours comes closer to describing today's reality than the conventional one. More importantly, so long as some of the increased credit goes to increased demand for non-produced assets, the effects we describe will be present, and indeed will dominate as the central bank "sterilizes" the effects on produced goods.

The first two terms, $pT - c$, are landlords' demand for land out of their own net wealth, while $\alpha(pT - c)$ is their demand for land based on borrowing, using land as collateral. The total has to add up to the value of land. (15.9) can be solved for p as a function of c.

$$\frac{(1+\alpha)c}{\alpha T} = p. \tag{15.10}$$

If α is fixed,

$$\frac{d\ln p}{dt} = \frac{d\ln c}{dt}. \tag{15.11}$$

Equations (15.8) and (15.11) determine the rate of return on land; that is, in this model, monetary/financial policy (the choice of α and the rate of credit expansion, $\frac{d\ln c}{dt}$) determine the price of land and the returns on investing in land—thereby affecting investment in capital goods, as we shall shortly see. If monetary authorities don't get policy right, wealth/savings will be diverted from productive investment to holding land. And such policies will lead to lower wages and more inequality. Traditionally, monetary/financial policy has ignored this effect, with its focus on the effect for the demand for produced goods. As we shall see, the effects on the demand for non-produced assets are of first order importance.

2.4.1 Steady State Analysis

We begin by analyzing the steady state, where, crucially, credit increases at the rate of growth. Then, as before, assuming a constant rate of land augmenting technological change at the rate n, in the long run equilibrium, the price of land will increase at the rate n. As in Chapter 14, defining q as the price of an "effective" unit of land, in equilibrium, the return to land must equal the return to capital, so

$$\frac{d\ln q}{dt} + \frac{f_{\hat{T}}}{q} + n = \frac{f_k}{1+\alpha}. \tag{15.12}$$

where, it will be recalled, f is output per capita, a function of the capital–labor ratio, k (and since the *effective* supply of land is increasing at the same rate, this is proportional to k). $f_{\hat{T}}$ is the return to an "effective" unit of land, also just a function of k.[34] In steady state, $\frac{d\ln q}{dt} = 0$, which means that the credit supply has to increase at the rate n (from 15.11) and

$$\frac{f_{\hat{T}}}{q} = \frac{f_k}{1+\alpha} - n, \tag{15.13}$$

defining q as a function of k and the collateral requirement α. In particular, it is clear that for fixed k, as α increases, q increases: the price of land increases with the ability to borrow against it.

To close the model, we need to provide a theory of capital accumulation. This can be done in any of a number of ways, as we have illustrated in earlier chapters, and the previous subsection of this chapter. We could have, for instance, dynastic savers maximizing intertemporal utility, with a pure rate of time discount of δ, determining the

[34] Recall that the price of land at time t is $p(t) = q(t)e^{nt}$ because of the land augmenting technological change.

marginal return to capital, and hence k^*. Then, from (15.13), there is a simple relationship between q and α, and as in the previous subsection, a change in α has no effect on capital accumulation—it only affects the value of land, and the magnitude of wealth inequality.[35]

Alternatively, as in the previous chapter, we assumed that there was a fixed savings rate out of income. That leads to a capital accumulation equation identical to that of Chapter 14, except now the equation for capital gains is given by (15.12), reflecting the ability to leverage land:

$$\frac{d\ln k}{dt} = s\frac{f(k)}{k} - \frac{(1-s)\left(\frac{qf_k}{1+\alpha} - f_{\hat{T}}\right)}{k} - n. \tag{15.14}$$

Setting $\frac{d\ln k}{dt} = 0$, we can again solve for q as a function of k, for a given α, and then solve that and (15.13) simultaneously for $k^*(\alpha)$. It is easy to show that *increased leverage leads to a decreased level of capital accumulation and lower wages*—just the opposite of the advocates of financial market liberalization.

Similarly, we can assume instead that there is a single group of capitalists/rentiers, who save a fixed fraction, s, of their *full* income, which includes capital gains. Instead of (15.14) we obtain

$$\frac{d\ln k}{dt} = s\frac{f_k k + f_{\hat{T}}}{k} - \frac{(1-s)\left(\frac{qf_k}{1+\alpha} - f_{\hat{T}}\right)}{k} - n, \tag{15.15.}$$

with precisely the same result: Making the market more efficient, in terms of "using capital more efficiently," reducing collateral requirements and increasing leverage, simply leads to increases in the value of land and crowds out capital, leading in turn to a lower capital–labor ratio and wages.

2.4.2 Dynamics

The dynamics are the same as described in the previous chapter. Given the saddle-point trajectories, for a given k_0, unless q_0 is set precisely correctly, the economy will not converge to the steady state, and may well go off on a bubble-path. To ensure stability may require careful adjusting of all of the elements of monetary and financial policy.

But now, return to (15.11), which provides a dynamic equation for p. Clearly, if $\frac{d\ln c}{dt} > n$, the value of land increases relative to capital, and asymptotically, the return to land is just its capital gain (and all wealth is in the value of land). With q/k ever increasing, we see from (15.14), assuming that as k goes to 0 rents go to zero, that

$$\frac{d\ln k}{dt} \to f_k\left[s - (1-s)\frac{q}{k(1+\alpha)}\right] - n < 0 \tag{15.14'}$$

or

$$\frac{dk}{dt} \to -qf_k\frac{1-s}{1+\alpha}, \tag{15.14''}$$

[35] Interestingly, income inequality is unchanged, with wages, the return to capital, and land rents all fixed.

implying that k hits zero in finite time: excessive expansion of credit leads to a real estate bubble that breaks in finite time; the arbitrage equations can't be satisfied for economically relevant values of the variables.

While I don't put much store in this model in the long run—keeping credit growing at a higher rate than the rate of growth of the economy would seem to be an invitation for a disaster—the point that high credit expansion leads to large capital gains on land, crowding out capital accumulation, has general relevance.[36]

Note that along such a trajectory the ratio of the (full) income of capitalists to that of workers will be increasing, provided that the elasticity of substitution is not too high.

$$\frac{Y_K}{Y_L} = \frac{F_K K\left(1 + \frac{p}{K}\right)}{F_L L}. \tag{15.16}$$

where Y_K is the (full) income of capital and Y_L that of labor.

Trajectories where there is a rapid expansion of credit shift the income distribution towards capitalists. This simple model is consistent with the stylized facts described in Chapter 10, including an increasing value of the wealth–income ratio.[37]

2.4.3 The Division of Rents between Banks and Capitalists/Rentiers

In the model of this section, so far we have assumed that there is a government owned or regulated bank that charges an interest rate of zero. So long as the interest rate charged is less than the (marginal) return to capital f_k there will be an unlimited demand for capital, and there will have to be rationing, even with collateral requirements.[38] (At an interest rate equal to f_k, demand is indeterminate, since investors are indifferent between borrowing and not.) The analysis above will be essentially unchanged if the bank charges a higher interest rate, r_b, except that the value of land will be lower and the bankers' profits higher. The equation giving the equality of returns is now

$$f_k = (1 + \alpha)\left(\frac{d\ln p}{dt} + \frac{F_T}{p}\right) - \alpha r_b, \tag{15.17}$$

implying that (changing to efficiency units of land) now, in steady state

$$q = \frac{f_{\hat{T}}}{\frac{f_k + \alpha r_b}{1+\alpha} - n}, \tag{15.18}$$

making it clear that the higher the interest rate charged, the lower are land prices. Since the interest payments are simply a transfer between rentiers and financiers, if their savings

[36] We could similarly analyze the consequences of the rate of growth of credit being less than the rate of growth of the economy, but in practice, governments tend to expand credit at a rate equal to or greater than the rate of growth of the economy. This may be because of political pressures—both financiers and rentiers benefit from increased credit expansion. Workers lose, but their voice is typically not so influential. (If the rate of increase of credit is permanently lower than the rate of growth of the economy, asymptotically, credit becomes unimportant: the "real" equations drive the evolution of k and q.)

[37] Obviously, to fully explain the stylized facts, we have to introduce (labor augmenting) technological change.

[38] This stark result is the result of our ignoring uncertainty. If the returns to land or capital are uncertain, then the demand for credit will decrease as the interest rate increases. At any level of credit creation, given the "regulation" about collateral requirements, there is an equilibrium level of r_b; a change in the availability of credit, and thus in r_b, will affect the relative price of land.

rates are the same, at any value of q, the equilibrium k will be the same. This, together with (15.18) means that charging a higher interest rate leads to greater capital accumulation—in the long run, workers benefit because of the lower equilibrium land prices.

Because at any interest rate below f_k, there is excess demand for credit, the presumption is that in the absence of government regulation, with credit expansion being constrained by government through one instrument or another, competition among borrowers will drive the interest rate up to f_k—banks will get for themselves the returns from their government granted right to create credit. Section 3 of this chapter will discuss how the government can re-appropriate for itself these rents.

2.5 Credit Creation, Monetary Policy, and Inequality in a Life-Cycle Model

A slight variation of the *life-cycle model* of the last chapter allows us to explore in more detail some of the distributive consequences of a change in monetary policy that results in lower lending rates. We show that lowering interest rates is good for workers, not because of the long-standing view that workers are, on average, debtors—in life-cycle models on average they are providers of capital. Rather, lower interest rates are shown to encourage capital accumulation, and this leads to higher wages, and if the elasticity of substitution is less than unity, workers' receiving a larger share of national income.

The issues can be seen more clearly in the context of a model where we assume only two factors of production, capital and labor, and[39] where the *ownership* of capital ("equity in capital") can be used for collateral.

Assume that workers are very risk averse, while the capitalists, who are substantially wealthier, are (close to) risk neutral. We assume that the government issues a fixed number of bonds B; each bond pays a fixed (real) amount, r_g, which is controlled by the government (monetary authority). We assume that the returns to capital are variable, so that all the capital is owned by the capitalists (they are the owners of equity), and all government bonds are owned by workers. We refer to the random return on capital by $\tilde{r}$, its expected value by

$$r = E(F_K). \tag{15.19}$$

Again, for simplicity, we assume that capitalists save and reinvest *all* of their gross income, and the law of large numbers holds, so that we can describe the macroeconomic equilibrium by

$$s_p r = s_p E(F_K) = \mu, \tag{15.20}$$

where, as before, s_p is the (gross) savings rate of capitalists and μ is the rate of depreciation. For the rest of this section, we assume for simplicity that $s_p = 1$. The results can easily be generalized. Also for simplicity, we continue with the assumption made earlier that the rate of growth of the population is zero.

[39] Unlike the previous section. Earlier, we provided an explanation for why land might better serve the function of collateral. The assumption that capital goods or equity claims on "capital" are used as collateral is only being made to simplify the analysis.

The price of the bond is π. Thus, the real rate of return to holding a bond is $\frac{r_g}{\pi}$. Because of risk aversion, $\frac{r_g}{\pi}$ can be substantially below $E(F_K)$, the expected return on capital, and workers will still hold their wealth in government bonds. On the other hand, so long as $\frac{r_g}{\pi}$ is less than $r = E(F_K)$ no capitalist will hold a government bond. The price of the bond adjusts so that all of workers' savings are held in bonds,[40] that is, if we assume a constant savings rate of s_w out of first period income (net of taxes), then (in our discrete time model):

$$B\pi = s_w(w - \tau), \tag{15.21}$$

where w is the wage and τ is the lump-sum tax. Interest on government bonds is financed through these lump sum taxes. (Not surprisingly, the structure of taxation matters.)

$$r_g B = \tau. \tag{15.22}$$

Combining (15.21) and (15.22), we obtain:

$$B\pi = s_w(w - \tau) = s_w(w - r_g B) \tag{15.23}$$

so

$$\pi = s_w\left(\frac{w}{B} - r_g\right). \tag{15.24}$$

It can be shown that equilibrium requires $\pi = 1$,[41] that is,

$$B = \frac{s_w w}{1 + s_w r_g}. \tag{15.25}$$

Now, a change in r_g financed by a tax on labor leaves the returns to capital unchanged (Equation (15.20)), and that means that K^* is unchanged and w is unchanged; but it necessitates a change in B and τ. In particular, it can be shown that an increase in r_g leads to an increase in τ.[42] It thus leads to decreased first period consumption, but to increased second period consumption.[43] Since across steady states, all profits are invested, each period wage income equals aggregate workers' consumption, where C_1 is workers' consumption while working and C_2 is consumption when retired:

$$C_1 + C_2 = w, \tag{15.26}$$

the steady state utility of workers is maximized at $r_g = 0$ (when in effect individuals face the same constraint as the societal constraint (15.26)).[44]

40 We again normalize the labor supply at unity.

41 Second period consumption is just $B + r_g B$, i.e. letting C_t equal consumption in the tth period of the individual's life, and focusing on the steady state,
$C_1 + C_2 = (1 - s_w)(w - \tau) + \tau + B = w - s_w(w - \tau) + B = w$, from which (1.25) follows immediately.

42 $\tau = r_g B = s_w r_g \frac{w}{1+s_w r_g} \cdot \frac{d\ln(\tau)}{d\ln(r_g)} = 1 - \frac{s_w r_g}{1+s_w r_g} = \frac{1}{1+s_w r_g} > 0.$

43 $C_2 = (1 + r_g)B = (1 + r_g)\frac{s_w w}{1+s_w r_g} \cdot \frac{d\ln C_2}{d\ln r_g} = \frac{r_g}{1+r_g} - \frac{s_w r_g}{1+s_w r_g} = \frac{r_g(1+s_w r_g - s_w - s_w r_g)}{(1+r_g)(1+s_w r_g)} = \frac{r_g(1-s_w)}{(1+r_g)(1+s_w r_g)} > 0.$

44 The individual maximizes $U(C_1, C_2)$, subject to the constraint $w = C_1 + \frac{C_2}{1+r_g}$. Steady state utility is obviously maximized when the individual solves this problem with $r_g = 0$, that is, where $U_1 = U_2$. One could conduct a full dynamic analysis, rather than focusing on steady states, with much the same results. Focusing on steady states greatly simplifies the calculations.

In this model, the T-bill rate is totally divorced from the (expected) rate of return on capital. We can, however, link the two, by assuming that the government, while borrowing from workers (who are engaged in life-cycle savings) is willing to lend to capitalists at a rate that is equal to or greater than that rate. For simplicity, we assume that there is a single rate, but that the government rations the amount it is willing to lend to capitalists, since so long as $r_g < E(F_K)$, risk neutral capitalists will want to borrow as much as possible. Part of the way it rations credit is to require collateral. Hence, allowing capital to be used as collateral, if a unit of capital allows a firm to borrow α, the overall expected return to a dollar of accumulation is $E(F_K)(1+\alpha) - \alpha r_g$. In effect, the government borrows from life-cycle savers at the rate r_g and on-lends the money to capitalists in a rationed way.

In the short run, with K fixed, a lowering of r_g leads to an increase in the net income of capitalists by an amount proportional to the amount lent to capitalists and a reduction of the income of life-cycle savers/workers by a corresponding amount. It is, in effect, a direct transfer from workers (life-cycle savers) to capitalists.[45]

Note that in this model, the distributive consequences of a lowering of the interest rate are the opposite of that derived in conventional "class" analysis, where workers are seen as debtors and capitalists as creditors. In that model, a lowering of the interest rate hurts capitalists and helps workers. Here, workers and capitalists are both owners of capital, but different kinds of capital. A lowering of the interest rate helps owners of equity and hurts those who hold government debt. This model seems to be a better description of the modern economy, and in this model, lowering interest rates unambiguously contributes to growing inequality, at least in the short run.[46] (In a still more general model, with many periods in an individual's working life: in younger periods, individuals are borrowing to buy a house or to pay for the education of their children, while in subsequent periods, they are repaying what is borrowed and then saving for retirement.)

Over the long run, when K adjusts, matters are quite different. The capital accumulation equation entails profits being reinvested. For simplicity, we continue to assume that all of profits are reinvested, that is, $s_p = 1$. Gross returns on capital are $F_K K$, but capitalists have borrowed additional money to invest. Since for every dollar of their own money they have invested, they have borrowed α, if K is the level of the capital stock, the amount borrowed is $\frac{\alpha K}{(1+\alpha)}$, and capitalists' income, all reinvested, is $F_K K - \left\{\frac{\alpha K}{(1+\alpha)}\right\} r_g$. With α fixed, in equilibrium, a lowering of r_g increases the return to investing. The long run equilibrium condition is now modified to

$$F_K - \frac{\alpha r_g}{1+\alpha} = \mu. \tag{15.27}$$

Defining $\nu \equiv \frac{\alpha r_g}{1+\alpha}$, it is easy to show that

$$\frac{dK}{d\nu} = \frac{1}{F_{KK}} < 0. \tag{15.28}$$

[45] In practice, the government does not lend to capitalists, but banks do. But the central bank lends to the banks and sets the interest rate at which money is provided to the banks. When the interest rate is lowered, it enables banks to lend to capitalists at a lower rate. At the same time, the central bank's "profits"—which are turned over to the fisc and allow either an increase in public expenditures or a reduction in taxes—will be lowered. In stylized form, our model captures this.

[46] This model, however, abstracts from Keynesian aggregate demand effects, which are the central motivation in lowering interest rates. We have assumed a full employment neoclassical economy.

As r_g or α increases, K decreases. The latter may seem surprising, since more leverage one might assume leads to more investment. The previous section explained why that reasoning was in general wrong: there, greater leverage could just increase the price of land, displacing capital. Here, we provide a second reason: in general equilibrium, more leverage, *at a fixed interest rate*, means the capitalists pay out more to others, so there is less to invest. As always, one shouldn't confuse partial and general equilibrium results.

Because of (15.28), wages go down as r_g increases, and accordingly, so does workers' wellbeing. Interestingly, this is so even if the government returned all the interest payments it receives from lending to capitalists back to workers. Workers' total income would then be

$$T = w + K^{*}\nu. \tag{15.29}$$

Moreover, using (15.28)

$$\frac{dT}{d\nu} = \frac{\nu}{F_{KK}} < 0 \text{ for } \nu > 0. \tag{15.30}$$

Hence, from the perspective of maximizing workers' total income, it is optimal to set $\alpha = 0$, that is, no leverage.

3 Who Gets the Rents Associated with Credit Creation?

We observed in the previous section that the rents associated with credit creation are garnered either by the rentiers or financiers, depending on the setting of the lending rate. While that model was highly idealized, in practice, there appear always to be rents associated with credit creation.

A natural question is: Why not have an auction of credit, so there won't be any rents?

Part of the answer is provided by the theory of information asymmetries: Stiglitz-Weiss (1981) and a large subsequent literature have explained why the provision of credit cannot be auctioned.[47] Those that know that they are unlikely to be able to pay back the loan—say with a small probability of a very large return but a high probability of a zero return—may be willing to bid the highest.[48] There has to be an allocation process, entailing judgments about who is most likely to repay. But if that is the case, then who controls the allocation process makes a difference. Because it is a difficult task, entailing difficult judgments, it is natural that it be entrusted to those who are better educated, to the elites. But the elites are better judging those that are similar to themselves; there is an additional element of risk in judging those that are different, that is, not members of the elites. Moreover, there are shared judgments about risks and values. Not surprisingly, then, they allocate capital to

[47] Adam Smith (1776) recognized the problem far earlier: "If the legal rate ... was fixed so high ... the greater part of the money which was to be lent, would be lent to prodigals and profectors, who alone would be willing to give the higher interest. Sober people, who will give for the use of money no more than a part of what they are likely to make by the use of it, would not venture into the competition...."

[48] With limited liability, the consequences of not repaying a loan are limited. The provision of collateral affects the extent of adverse selection and incentives, but not enough to eliminate the problem. See Stiglitz and Weiss (1986).

those that are similar to themselves and who have shared perspectives on the world—even when and where connected lending is prohibited;[49] and, of course, even more so when connected lending is allowed. In this manner, inequality builds on itself.

Underlying the rents associated with credit creation is government. To understand this, we need to recall how credit gets created: a bank lends "money" to say a firm, simultaneously creating on its balance sheet an asset (the loan) and a liability (the deposit). The borrower values the deposit because it can write a check against the deposit, knowing that it will be honored. It is like cash. And the merchant who accepts the check does so because it has faith in the bank; but the faith in the bank is *really* trust in government, that the government has done its job of regulating and supervising the bank, to ensure that the bank has the capacity to honor the check, and that should it turn out that the bank can't, the government will step in. In short, the check is accepted because of trust in government. Thus, underlying credit creation in our private banking system is the government. And the rents associated with credit creation that are appropriated by private banks are really rents associated with this trust.[50]

In the introduction to this chapter, we commented on the role that banks with their control of access to credit played in creating Russia's oligarchy. In Western countries, there is a need for more subtlety, but the consequences for the creation of wealth inequality may be similar, if not as extreme. The financial sector has become one of the major sources of the increase in inequality: Much of the wealth at the top as well as the lack of wealth at the bottom is a result of their ability to appropriate the rents associated with credit creation and their control of the electronic means of payment as well as in their exploitative activities.

Much of the discussion in the aftermath of the 2008 crisis was focused on curbing the multiple abuses that were so dramatically exposed in that crisis, based on market exploitation (see, e.g., Stiglitz, 2010a).[51] Here, we focus on another issue: curbing the rents that accrue to the sector, while at the same time improving the overall performance of the economy and the well-being of consumers. Even if we can't fully appropriate for public purpose these rents, it doesn't mean that there aren't *excessive* rents built into the financial system.[52] In the next two subsections, we describe briefly two ways of reducing the excessive rents accruing to the financial sector.

3.1 The Public Option

Rents accrue to the private financial system because of natural barriers to entry (e.g., associated with imperfections and asymmetries of information), strategic barriers to entry (e.g., anti-competitive actions taken by those in the financial sector), and regulatory barriers to entry.[53] In the absence of any barriers, presumably rents would be competed away (though

[49] Even if connected lending is restricted, so banker A can't lend to himself or his relatives, banker A can lend to the relatives of banker B, and banker B can lend to the relatives of banker A.

[50] This is especially so, through the privatization of gains and the socialization of losses that has become a regular feature in economies with too-big-to-fail banks.

[51] There is an especial concern about the frequency of certain practices, such as predatory lending and abusive credit card practices, which have particularly deleterious effects on the poor. See the references in earlier footnotes and Akerlof and Shiller (2015).

[52] In particular, most of the rents do not appear to be "differential rents," rents associated with bankers' greater ability to assess and manage risks—as evidenced by the repeated failures in lending.

[53] Some of the ideas in this section are elaborated in Stiglitz (2019a).

such competition does not assure economic efficiency). In the next section, we describe how, even if there are, say, natural or strategic barriers to entry, government can capture much more of the rents associated with credit creation in general than it does now.

Here, we describe how competition from the government can drive down rents, and in the process enhance societal welfare. Consider, for instance, the allocation of credit for mortgages. Today, such allocation is not based on judgment so much as credit scoring. It is an information intensive process, involving the processing of information about the incomes of the borrower and the values of the properties being acquired.

An alternative to the current system in which the private sector gathers this data, processes it, and then awards mortgages is one in which the government stands willing to provide a mortgage to anyone who, say, has paid taxes over the past five years, in an amount related to the value of the property and his income. We refer to it as the public *option*, because the government doesn't force individuals to take this mortgage: the government just provides an additional option to those provided by the private sector. Competition from government drives down the rents that the financiers receive and allows the public to appropriate some of the residual rents for itself: both taxpayers and homeowners are better off. The government could even provide far better mortgages than those that the private sector makes available—providing better risk sharing.

There are several intrinsic reasons that government has an advantage in providing mortgages. Government entities have the best data: through the income tax system, it has a complete history of income, and through property registries, of real estate transaction prices.[54] The government is in the best position to enforce the debt contract, partly because the incremental cost of collecting mortgage payments through the income tax system is negligible. For all these reasons, the administrative costs for such a system are likely to be very low, so that mortgages could be provided at an interest rate only slightly greater than that paid on government debt.

The government has a second fundamental advantage: While the objective of the private sector is to maximize its profits (rents), which entails taking advantage of individuals ignorance and vulnerabilities, their weaknesses in risk assessment, their lack of bargaining power, and the imperfections of competition, in principle at least the government's objectives are more benign—simply to increase the well-being of citizens. Thus, in the run-up to the Great Recession, the financial sector discriminated against minorities—simply because it thought it could get away with it; it developed "innovative" mortgages—involving shifting more of the risk to homeowners, and resulting in millions of them losing their homes, and bringing about the greatest downturn since the Great Depression. By contrast, using information easily at its disposal, government could construct a system of income contingent mortgage loans (where payments each year would depend on the family's income that year) that would be far better than the current system in managing the risks of home ownership.[55]

[54] The 2008 crisis also revealed important agency problems within the private sector, especially associated with securitization (associated with asymmetries of information, both moral hazard and adverse selection) which gave rise to significant fraud on the part of originators, borrowers, and sponsors. The remedies that were intended to mitigate these agency issues (the put-back mechanism, and legal remedies such as fraud) proved ineffective, all the more so as those in the financial sector refused to honor their contracts, and the legal remedies for addressing these breaches of contract turned out to be slow, costly, and of only limited effectiveness.

[55] For a discussion of the merits of income contingent loans, see Chapman, Higgins, and Stiglitz (2014).

Thus, with the public option, the huge rents and the associated inequality of the private mortgage system with its predatory, discriminatory, and exploitive lending could be greatly reduced, and the enormous waste of resources as financial institutions look for those upon whom they can prey would also be reduced. Better lending and better designed mortgages would contribute too to macro stability. Citizens would benefit in having better designed mortgages, at lower interest rates—and would benefit too from the greater macro stability that would ensue.[56]

3.2 Restoring Domestic Control over Credit Creation and Capturing Excessive Financial Sector Rents

We've described several of the ways by which the financial system creates inequality—most notably, through excessive credit creation that inflates the price of land, crowding out capital accumulation and lowering wages, with the rents associated with credit creation going to the bankers and those who own the banks. There are several other channels that have been documented, such as the excessive credit creation that can create credit bubbles, which when they break impose high costs on society, and in particular on workers; and the multiple abuses, forms of exploitation, to which we have alluded to repeatedly, such as predatory lending—which simultaneously contribute to economic instability.[57] At the same time, the financial sector has used its control of the electronic means of payments to inhibit the movement to a far more efficient way of settling accounts—and to extract enormous rents out of merchants and induce consumers to pay usurious interest on their credit cards. Of particular concern is that the sector seems to be earning these excessive rents, without performing the societal functions that banks were supposed to perform, for example, lending to small and medium sized enterprises, or providing well-designed mortgages, enabling families to manage the risk of homeownership.[58]

In this section, we propose a simple set of reforms—a full move to an electronic payments system and an auction of the *right* to issue credit by banks—which would reduce these excessive rents, enable better macro management of the economy, and therefore enhance economic stability, promote transparency, and help curb many of the financial sector's exploitive activities.

3.2.1 Electronic Payments Mechanisms

One of the main functions of money is that it serves as a medium of exchange, enabling transactions.[59] Historically, gold was used. It was replaced by currency, which in turn was largely replaced by checks. Today, however, transactions can be performed much more efficiently on digital platforms; electronic transfers are extraordinarily cheap. That should

[56] One concern is, would it be political acceptable for government to undertake foreclosure for non-payment? Of course, with better lending practices and better mortgages, including income contingent mortgages, there would be a much smaller necessity of foreclosure. But the fact that in other domains, the government has been forceful in taking actions in response to non-payment (e.g., of taxes) suggests that this would not be a problem.

[57] In many parts of the world, the financial sector also facilitates money laundering, tax avoidance and evasion, and other anti-social activities, which have a disproportionate adverse effect on the poor.

[58] See the discussion of the previous subsection.

[59] The invention of money, enabling more efficient exchange than simple barter, is viewed as one of the great advances of mankind. See Weatherford (1997) and Ferguson (2009).

have led to the dominance of electronic payments as a medium of exchange. A main impediment has been the market power of the financial sector: banks and credit card companies use that market power to charge prices for the services of electronic payments platforms that are considerably in excess of marginal or even average costs. Regulators, legislatures, and courts in antitrust actions have begun intervening to curtail the fees and certain other abusive practices used to maintain and extend their market power, with some success in certain jurisdictions (e.g., Australia). This has helped some countries to make great strides towards a cashless economy.[60]

A digital platform for all transactions, run, say by the Central Bank, would have the numerous advantages to which we referred earlier. It can, for instance, facilitate greater transparency (thus limiting some of the nefarious activities which the current financial system seems to support, as evidenced by the Panama and Paradise Papers[61]). This chapter focuses, however, on credit auctions, which can be facilitated by an electronic payments mechanism, and on how such auctions can simultaneously reduce the rents appropriated by the financial sector and promote macro stability.

3.2.2 The Limitations of Current Monetary Tools

We begin by discussing the limits on current monetary tools. In a modern economy, central banks and financial regulators regulate banks' creation of credit, but they do so only indirectly. For instance, the *maximum* amount of credit that banks can create is controlled by the central bank, through, for instance, reserve and capital adequacy requirements. The central bank can also affect the magnitude of credit creation indirectly, by changing the opportunity cost of lending, the return on T-bills.[62]

Even though the instruments available to the Central Bank are imperfect, they are supposed to regulate the economy *in just the right amount*, so there is a Goldilocks economy, neither under- nor overheated but "just right." It is apparent that they have often failed to do so. The economy is often over- or underheated. Sometimes there is too much credit creation, leading to an excess of aggregate demand, and prices rise; there is inflation. Sometimes there is too little credit creation and too much of what credit is created goes to the purchase of pre-existing assets; as a result, there is a lack of aggregate demand, and there is disinflation, sometimes even deflation, and unemployment. Sometimes monetary policy has fed asset bubbles, the breaking of which (and they inevitably do break) is a major source

[60] In Denmark, only an estimated 20% of retail transactions use cash (Danish Payments Council, 2016), and in Singapore, less than 40% of all transactions use cash (Thomas, Jain, and Angus, 2013). In India, charges for electronic payments between an individual and merchants from whom purchases have been made have been essentially eliminated, reflecting the negligible costs of electronic payments.

[61] Electronic money has a further advantage, especially in countries where small businesses predominate—it significantly curtails the extent of tax avoidance. Rogoff (2017) has emphasized the importance of electronic money for curbing tax avoidance and other crimes, and for giving space for negative interest rates. Elsewhere (Stiglitz 2016b), I have argued that the benefits of negative interest rates have been greatly exaggerated.

There is concern in some jurisdictions where discriminated against groups don't have debit or credit cards that for a store not to take cash is discriminatory. In the proposed reform, everyone would have access to the digital platform.

There is also concern in non-democratic societies that requiring electronic transactions provides another surveillance tool.

On the other hand, the pandemic has thrown the benefits of cashless transactions into sharp relief.

[62] Greenwald and Stiglitz (2003a) emphasize that credit creation is affected both by central bank policies and the policies of the financial regulators, for example with respect to capital adequacy.

of volatility. Thus, monetary and financial policy[63] helped create the housing bubble, the breaking of which was pivotal in generating the 2008 crisis. After the 2008 crisis, there was a massive increase in the Fed's balance sheet and liquidity, as the Fed pumped money into the economy. But relatively little of this went to buy goods and services produced in the United States, so in spite of the huge expansion of the money supply as conventionally measured,[64] the economy remained weak.

This failure of monetary policy to stabilize the economy is partly a result of the often noted "long and variable lags" associated with monetary policy, with monetary authorities having to base their actions on predictions concerning the future course of the economy; the central bank has to forecast what GDP will be over the next eighteen months or so, to know how much money (credit) to allow to be created today. There is always error in such forecasts.[65]

But more important, for our purpose, is *instrument uncertainty*, the "noise" in the link between what monetary authorities do and GDP. Particularly after the Great Recession, the link between standard monetary variables, the money supply and the nominal interest rate, and economic activity seemed weak. At the very least, the stability of the relationship between money, interest rates, and economic activity was questionable, making the formulation of monetary policy difficult and making monetary policy a far from perfect tool for macroeconomic stabilization.[66]

In short, monetary authorities are unable to control the supply of money or the interest rate in such a way as to stabilize the economy anywhere near to the extent that would be desirable and should be possible. For instance, there may still be extended periods in which there is a deficiency of domestic aggregate demand—a deficiency that seemingly could be easily corrected since there are credit-worthy individuals and firms who would like to spend but cannot get access to credit. A near-zero T-bill rate, however, does not mean businesses can get access to credit at such a rate—or at any rate.

3.2.3 Controlling the Supply of Credit: A Hypothetical

Matters might be different if there were a single source of credit, a Government Bank. The Bank could add "money" into the economy, lending money to a small enterprise who will use the funds to make an investment that it otherwise would not have been able to make, thus stabilizing the economy. The Government Bank simply puts more "money" into the

[63] Including inadequate regulation and supervision and allowing banks to vastly increase mortgage credit through securitization.

[64] The assets of the Federal Reserve increased from around $850 billion in 2007 before the crisis to $4.5 trillion in 2015. There were similar increases in Japan and by the ECB. M2 increased from $7.4 trillion to $12.3 trillion.

[65] Lags are important, because in their absence, monetary authorities could observe the consequences of, say, a particular level of M (money supply) or interest rate or regulatory intervention, and adjust policy in response. With long lags, the danger is that monetary policy will be tightened, just when it should be loosened. Longstanding critics of discretionary policy argued that that was typically the case, so that it would be preferable to stick to a simple rule, and not attempt countercyclical policy. The evidence, however, is that discretionary macro-economic policy has resulted in greater economic stability. (See Clarida, Gali and Gertler, 2000, and references therein.)

[66] See, for example, Stiglitz (2018f). Part of the reason is that the links posited in the standard monetary models, for example between interest rates and consumption, aggregate demand, and output are tenuous at best, with theoretical foundations not based on a twenty-first century economy where credit, not money, is needed for transactions (and in fact relatively few transactions are mediated by money as conventionally defined); where most transactions are exchanges of assets, not purchases of newly produced goods and services; and where the opportunity cost of "money" is not the interest rate, but (for most accounts by value) the difference between the T-bill rate and the money market rate, a number which is very small with little cyclical significance. See Greenwald and Stiglitz (2003a).

bank account of the enterprise, which the enterprise can then use to make the investment. Of course, in providing credit there is always a risk of non-repayment, and standards have to be established for evaluating the likelihood of repayment and charging an interest rate to compensate for that risk.

In recent decades, faith in government's ability to make such evaluations has diminished, and confidence has been placed in the private financial system.

3.2.3.1 Problems of Delegating Credit Creation to the Private Sector

The 2008 crisis, as well as other frequent crises that have marked the last third of a century, has (or at least, should have) undermined that confidence.[67] Arguably, not only did the banks not make good judgments—as evidenced by the massive, repeated bailouts—but they systematically failed to fulfill what they should have seen as their major responsibility, providing credit to create new jobs and expand enterprises. By some accounts, such "real" lending amounts to just 3% of their activities; by others, to some 15%. But by any account, the activities of banks, including bank finance, have been directly elsewhere.[68]

There were always obvious problems in delegating the power of credit creation, backed by government, to private institutions: They could use their power to benefit their owners. If they made bad loans, the government might have to engineer a bailout. Governments have tried to circumscribe the most obvious abuses, for instance connected and excessively risky lending, through regulations and supervision. But these regulations didn't address one of the key underlying problems: Credit is scarce and rationed, so giving private banks the right to create credit with government backing gave rise to the possibility of their capturing enormous economic rents.

3.2.4 Credit Auctions

In spite of the problems in doing so, the government may still want to delegate responsibility for making credit decisions to private enterprises, *if* the government can assure sufficient accountability for the *allocative* decisions.[69] Auctioning the right to provide credit

[67] There have been numerous instances in which widespread judgments have been questioned (especially with hindsight, but often even at the time the loans were made, by those outside the banking sector), including at various times those associated with over-lending to fiber optics, to fracking, to housing in the runup to the Great Recession, to Latin America or East Asia. Of course, these mistakes do not in themselves establish that there were flaws in lending practices or that decisions concerning whether or not to obtain further information were themselves "unreasonable." They show that ex post judgments were wrong. But they do not establish that ex ante they were unreasonable, on the basis of information available at the time. At least in some cases, such as the excessive lending to Latin America in the 1970s and to housing in the years prior to the 2008 crisis, there is a considerable body of evidence that at the time the loans were made the risks were excessive. See, for instance, Stiglitz (2010a) and especially Shiller (2002). In the housing crisis, there is also considerable evidence of fraudulent behavior on the part of key market participants, including banks and credit rating agencies, whose reports underpinned beliefs about the risks associated especially with securitized products. See Financial Crisis Inquiry Commission (2011). Flawed incentive systems help explain these failures. (See Nalebuff and Stiglitz, 1983a; Stiglitz, 2010a.)

[68] See, for example, Kay (2015) and Turner (2015).

[69] A main concern with government allocation of credit is that it can too easily get politicized. While in the presence of imperfect information and incomplete markets there is no presumption that the banks' allocation of credit to maximize its profits will be socially desirable, it may be possible to address some of the major market failures by restrictions on the allocation of credit. Such restrictions already exist, even in largely market economies, such as the U.S. (the CRA requirements to provide credit to underserved communities), but even more so in economies where government takes a more active role in development, as in East Asia (Stiglitz and Uy, 1996).

among adequately capitalized, regulated, and supervised banks[70] is one way of doing so.[71] The banks would then undertake the process of credit screening—allocating credit on the basis of *their* judgments about repayment capacity, within the constraints that the central bank may impose (designed to ensure that the credit gets allocated in socially productive ways) as well as monitoring and enforcement. The winners of the credit auction simply transfer money from their account to the accounts of the borrowers they deem to be the most creditworthy.[72]

Arguably, there are enough sufficiently well capitalized participants in the financial sector that the rents remaining with the financial sector after this auctioning process would be minimal—certainly less than under current arrangements.

With credit auctions, government controls the aggregate supply of credit *directly*, rather than relying on indirect instruments; but the microeconomic decisions of who gets the credit is delegated to the private banks, subject to certain restrictions that the government may impose. Because the government controls directly the quantity of credit, macro stability will be enhanced.[73]

The magnitude of net credit to be added each month will be determined by the country's central bank on the basis of its assessment of the macroeconomic situation—that is, if the economy is weaker, it will provide more credit to stimulate the economy.[74] Accordingly, even with a system of delegated credit allocation, the Central Bank can control the magnitude of credit creation with some precision—and thereby the level of macroeconomic activity.

4 Macroeconomics and Inequality

That the financial system is a major driver of inequality in our society is now well accepted. Many of the ways in which it did this received extensive attention in the aftermath of

[70] Supervision and regulation mitigate the consequences of asymmetric information; these, together with the requirement of sufficient net worth ensures that the risk of non-repayment of the money auctioned off is limited, thus alleviating the concerns about auctions noted earlier. (Supervising a limited number of banks is clearly far more feasible than close supervision of a myriad of individual borrowers.) Without these provisions, the credit auction to banks would encounter the same problems confronting credit auctions more generally.

[71] There are many details about the design of the auction process, some of which we touch upon in Stiglitz (2017a). To avoid the possibility of banks (the buyers of the right to issue credit) speculating, buying up credit now against the chance that its price will be higher at a later date, and thereby adding uncertainty to the amount of new credit actually issued to producing enterprises for purposes of investment, the right to issue credit would be date-stamped, that is, banks would have the right to issue new credit, but only for a specified period, for example three months.

[72] And they would not have purchased the right to issue credit if they did not intend to issue credit (putting aside concerns about option value and speculation, addressed in an earlier footnote).

[73] In Stiglitz (2017a) we provide conditions under which such a credit auction can ensure greater macro stability than controlling the interest rate, show how the analysis can be extended to an open economy, and explain how the system can be used to encourage more socially productive investments (when social and private returns differ) In particular, constraints can be imposed on lending for the purchase of land, reducing the extent to which land appreciation crowds out productive investment, as described in Section 2 of this chapter.

[74] The system is symmetric. The central bank may decide that there is too much money in the economic system—that is, the banks are lending too much, using "money" that they receive in repayment to make new loans. In that case, the government can buy back rights to issue credit: they buy back the money that they have allowed the banks to effectively manage on their behalf. Again, there can be an open auction for those most willing to give up rights to issue credit. This would literally drain money out of the banking system. (Note that under current arrangements, central banks add to or subtract from the ability and incentive of banks to lend by buying or selling bonds (through auctions). They effectively use a very indirect mechanism of control rather than a more direct mechanism.)

the 2008 crisis: underregulated banks with market power took advantage of that market power, information asymmetries, and individual vulnerabilities to engage in a wide variety of exploitive activities, a large fraction of which moved money from the bottom of the economic pyramid to the top.[75] Banks engaged in racial and ethnic discrimination, further exacerbating inequalities in those important dimensions. The financial sector persuaded the poor to borrow beyond their ability to pay, and then charged them usurious interest rates.[76] Changes in bankruptcy laws making it ever harder to discharge debts distorted the incentives of banks, diverting attention from ensuring that lending was prudential to pushing loans on the unwary, and created a system of partial indebted servitude, where workers spend a large fraction of their life working just to satisfy what they owe the banks (Stiglitz, 2012a). Struggling to survive, they have no ability to make investments that would help them emerge from such poverty, and indeed, even to think long-term.[77]

All the advances over the past half century in markets, including financial markets, and in our understanding of markets have *not* led to greater macroeconomic stability—in fact, quite the opposite. (This stands in marked contrast to the insights provided by Keynesian economics, which did lead to greater macro stability.) The financial sector used its political influence to push for deregulation, and the instability to which financial deregulation gave rise had particularly deleterious effects on workers.[78]

This chapter has analyzed only a few of the mechanisms by which the financial sector contributes to inequality, but those we have analyzed have, to our knowledge, not been adequately investigated before. In particular, we have focused on one central aspect of today's financial sector—its ability to create credit—and the connections between land, collateral, the financial system, and inequality. It builds off the results of the last chapter, and helps set the scene for the next: Chapter 14 explained how increasing land values could crowd out capital accumulation. Here, we have shown how excessive credit expansion can contribute to increasing land values.

The links between monetary and financial policies and rent-capital are complex. Thus, financial liberalization and deregulation, allowing greater expansion of credit, for example by lowering collateral requirements, rather than enhancing growth and efficiency, has had just the opposite effect—and simultaneously increased inequality.

We saw too how the delegation of money creation to private banks can give rise to large rents to the financial sector, rents which directly contribute to inequality, but also do so indirectly through their effect on capital accumulation; but attempts to curb those rents by limiting the interest rates charged by banks may lead to an increase in rents of rentiers.[79]

[75] Banks and others in finance also engaged in activities that exploited other well-off individuals, for example their market manipulation and sophisticated versions of front running and insider trading.

[76] Usury used to be forbidden, but part of financial deregulation was allowing lenders to take greater advantage of borrowers by charging high interest rates.

[77] See, for example, Mullainathan and Shafir (2009, 2013), Mani, Mullainathan, Shafir, and Zhao (2013), and Kaur, Mullainathan, Oh, and Schilbach (2019).

[78] They are the least able to cope with the consequences, so suffer particularly in the downturns. Small and medium sized firms also have a hard time weathering downturns, and since banks know this, the greater the instability, the less available will funds be to SMEs, and the higher the interest rate that lenders will charge. Thus, instability reduces access to funds for new enterprises, reducing opportunity. The nexus between inequality and instability is explored further in Part III of this book.

[79] As we saw in the last chapter, these adverse effects can be offset by appropriate taxation. Ironically, in the United States, the period of financial deregulation was also a period in which the taxation of land rents, especially the capital gains on land, was reduced, reinforcing the adverse effects on capital accumulation.

The models we have presented generate dynamics that are consistent with many of the key observations made in Chapter 10—a rising value of wealth, with stagnant wages and capital accumulation. Misguided monetary policy can, moreover, generate bubbles, of the kind discussed in the previous chapter. If unstable bubbles are to be avoided, there must be careful control of monetary policy—one cannot simply rely on self-regulation.

With this enhanced understanding of these mechanisms, we have proposed several major reforms which will reduce the extent to which the sector contributes to inequality.[80] More generally, properly designed financial, monetary, and tax policies can curb rent-capital and thus contribute to equality.[81]

Even with these reforms, though, the financial sector is likely to enjoy substantial rents: an essential function of the financial sector is gathering and processing information; the informational advantage thus derived inevitably gives it market power, of a kind that standard anti-trust laws have found hard to curb.[82] In the last chapter, we saw that land taxes can promote greater equality by encouraging more real capital accumulation; the benefits of high taxes on profits in the financial sector are even greater, as we have noted: the rents accrue to those at the top, and the rent-capital arising from the financial sector crowds out real capital—high profits taxes reduce those rents and the value of the associated rent-capital.

4.1 From the Traditional Model of the Financial System to a Twenty-First-Century Model

The analysis of this chapter differs markedly from standard monetary economics, where there is no discussion of its impact on asset prices, and in particular of non-produced assets, and it is simply assumed that money creation normally translates into an increase in the demand for produced goods, thus stimulating economic activity, reducing unemployment, and helping workers. It is only in anomalous situations, like a liquidity trap, that that does not occur. This chapter has focused on the more realistic setting where there are also non-produced assets (such as land), emphasized that it is credit, not money, that should be the center of attention in macroeconomics, has highlighted how changes in credit creation can hurt workers, and has shown how a host of government policies can curb financial sector rents and regulate better the creation of credit and its use.

Because these results run counter so much of conventional wisdom concerning monetary policy, in these concluding remarks, we review some of the important ways that our analysis differs from the more conventional approaches to macroeconomics. One of the important differences, to which we alluded in the beginning of the chapter, is that we look at the long run effects. Many of the concerns we raise are also relevant in the short run.

[80] Some have suggested that some of the adverse effects that have been observed in recent years were unintentional. But many of the current monetary and financial policies were adopted at the behest of the financial sector. It was clear—even at the time the policies were adopted—that they would lead to greater inequality and instability. See, for example, Stiglitz (2003a).

[81] So too competition policies which reduce rent-capital associated with monopoly profits, the subject of the next chapter, contribute to an increase in equality.

[82] Well-designed corporate profits taxes can capture much of these rents. (The older literature on the corporation income tax viewed the tax as a tax on capital in the corporate sector, but a more careful examination of the tax, with its provisions for deductibility of interest and depreciation, suggests it is to a large extent a tax on pure profits. See Stiglitz (1973e, 1976f).)

In particular, the fact that the expansion of credit may go disproportionately to increase the demand for non-produced assets, rather than the demand for produced goods and services, has been evident in the massive expansion of liquidity in the aftermath of the 2008 financial crisis and the onset of the pandemic. Wealth inequality increased dramatically, with only a muted response in the intended effect, increasing employment and economic activity.

We note too some of the key changes in the financial system in recent decades—changes which more conventional monetary policy has not always adequately taken into account—and their relationship to our analysis.

Before turning to an analysis of how our framework differs from more traditional approaches, we make two key observations: In our model, credit is at the center, not money; and credit creation is *not* about intermediation. And the key divisions in society which should be the center of distributional analyses in monetary policy are not so much about debtor/creditor relationships but about the ownership of *different* assets, the prices of which are differentially affected by monetary policy.

4.2 Changing Perspectives on the Financial System: The Role of Intermediation

The standard (nineteenth-century) model of the financial system is that it intermediated between savers and borrowers, between farmers who had more seed than they wanted to plant or consume, and between those who wanted to plant more seed than they had. The financial system was thus essential in *translating* the "abstinence" of the savers into productive investments. But this model of a "seed" financial system does not describe our modern financial system. Credit, giving one party the ability to spend more than his income, is created out of thin air, under the credibility of the banks and the governments that back them up, and limited only by regulatory authorities, the policies of central banks, and the incentive structures provided to the financial sector and those who work there. Indeed, in recent years, on net, the financial system has not even raised capital for the corporate sector. It is more accurate to describe it as disintermediating than intermediating.

4.3 Changing Perspectives on the Financial System: Money as a Medium of Exchange

Monetary theory for the past 80 years has been largely based on the demand for money as a medium of exchange—to facilitate transactions—with government controlling the supply of money through open market operations and monetary regulations (like reserve requirements). While such a theory might have been relevant at the time it developed, it clearly is not today. What matters for the purchase of produced goods or non-produced goods, for that matter, is not money but the availability of credit—claims that can be used to buy either produced or non-produced goods. That's why we've focused on the consequences not of an increase in money, but of an increase in credit. And the two do not necessarily move in tandem.

4.4 Changing Perspectives on Key Divisions in Society

We have also explained that the traditional division of society into the owners of capital and workers or creditors and debtors no longer seems *fully* appropriate, given the large amount of life-cycle savings, as discussed in earlier chapters. Key divisions are between capitalists, who pass on their wealth from generation to generation, and workers who save for their retirement (a distinction which was at the center of the two class models presented in earlier chapters); and between the owners of equity and the holders of debt instruments.[83] The two divisions are related: A central issue of wealth inequality is not just the proportion of overall wealth owned by the capitalists, but differences in portfolio composition.[84] If the two groups differ in their risk aversion—which one would expect, given the differences in their wealth—then their asset holdings will differ markedly, and policies affecting the returns on these different assets have large distributional effects. As we saw, it is the very wealthy that own disproportionately equities in the U.S.

Thus, the question of the critical distinctions and divisions in our society needs to be rethought.[85]

4.5 Distributive Effects of Monetary and Financial Policy

This is important because there can be large distributive effects of monetary, fiscal, and financial regulatory policy.[86] and these can be quite different from those reflected in traditional discussions and models (including the popular DSGE models). And except in models which assume away distributive effects (such as the representative agent models), the distributive effects have macroeconomic effects: in general, one cannot separate analyses of aggregative behavior from analyses of distribution.

[83] More accurately, all of these divisions are relevant, and as we have explained, these divisions are related.

[84] To repeat: these characterizations, while highly useful, obviously simplify. Large wage inequalities translate into large inequalities in life-cycle wealth, and there is some movement between the two categories we have defined. In Section 4 of Chapter 13 we provided a model where the groups and movements between the groups were defined endogenously.

[85] It is perhaps worth noting that it has been in the interests of "capitalists" to persuade life-cycle savers that they have now joined the capitalist class, and therefore their interests are coincident. In some instances, such as garnering support for reductions in the inheritance tax and capital gains taxes, they have been remarkably successful, in spite of the fact that their interests are in fact very divergent, as the analysis of Chapters 13 and 14 has demonstrated.

[86] Elsewhere, we have argued that these distributive effects can have especially large macro-economic consequences in economies operating at less than full capacity. (Central banks focus on the effects of their policies on aggregate demand; in all of the models examined here, the economy is at full employment.) See Stiglitz (2010a, 2013a, 2015c, 2018e) and UN (2010). Changes in factor shares also affect the direction of technological change, as Chapter 17 shows, and encourages more capital intensive investment, making the return to full employment all the more difficult, especially in real economies where ex post there is limited capital malleability (as in the putty-clay models; see Cass-Stiglitz, 1970).

With capitalists disproportionately controlling the *equity* in the economy, we have to ascertain how different policies affect bonds (T-bills) and equity differently. A lowering of the tax on capital gains benefits owners of equity—disproportionately capitalists, not the life-cycle savers[87]—and this increases inequality. Similarly, a land tax (a tax on rents) may disproportionately impact capitalists[88]—besides leading to more capital accumulation and thus increasing wages, as we noted in the previous chapter. A lowering of interest rates benefits holders of equity—again the capitalists—but hurts holders of government bonds, disproportionately life-cycle savers. Overall, these effects may be larger than the distributional effects between creditors and borrowers; at the very least, they mitigate the distributional benefits arising from creditor/debtor relationships that have been the subject of traditional distributional analyses.

4.6 The Three Critical Analytic Distinctions

The analysis of macroeconomics in this chapter differs from much of standard macroeconomics in three critical ways:

4.6.1 A Focus on Inequality

First is the focus on inequality, including how distribution affects savings and consumption—an old theme in economics which went out of fashion some four decades ago, but at last is beginning to get the attention it deserves. The discussion above highlighted, moreover, the importance of shifting the focus of analysis, away from just impacts on creditors vs. debtors towards impacts on workers/life-cycle savers vs. capitalists based on differing portfolio compositions.

4.6.2 Prices vs. Quantities

Second, is the focus on quantities rather than (just) prices. In the Arrow–Debreu world with perfect markets, prices play a critical role in ensuring economic efficiency. But in the real world in which we live, as Marty Weitzman (1974) explained long ago, it is often better not to just rely on prices—to try, as this framework does, to control the *quantity* of credit and to regulate the uses to which credit is put. There is a large literature showing under a variety of conditions when there is a departure from the first best world that such quantity controls are a better way of regulating the economy.[89] Moreover, economists have typically paid insufficient attention to instrument uncertainty, to the loose links between policy actions and outcomes.

These quantity effects are especially important because credit rationing and collateral constraints are central to the functioning of the financial system, and changes in policy thus

[87] Especially so, since most life-cycle savings of all but the rich had already been treated favorably, through the favorable tax treatment of pensions and IRA accounts.

[88] This may not always be the case, since in some countries, for those in the middle, real estate (home ownership) may represent a disproportionate share of wealth. Progressive land taxation may mitigate any adverse effects on those in the middle. One needs, in addition, to distinguish between impacts on *existing* middle-class workers and young middle-class workers. An unanticipated land tax may hurt existing middle-class property owners but help younger individuals by lowering overall housing costs.

[89] See also Dasgupta and Stiglitz (1977), Stiglitz (2019b), and the large literature that developed after Weitzman's original paper. This literature has been concerned with efficiency in the absence of a complete set of state-contingent markets.

affect the macroeconomy often more through their impact on these constraints (quantities) than through prices (interest rates).[90]

The management of the economy in the electronic monetary framework analyzed in this chapter relies, however, heavily on the use of market mechanisms, in particular, on credit auctions; there is no micro-management, but potentially better macro-management than exists today. The government plays an important role in setting the amount of credit to be auctioned and the rules governing credit allocation.[91] But, of course, under *any* monetary system there is extensive government intervention: In some, it attempts to set interest rates, in others, the money supply. The proposal contained in this chapter is an attempt to make use of the informational comparative advantages of the different agents in the economy: firms have better *micro* information, about the relative ability of different market participants to repay a loan, assuming that there is relative macro-stability; and the government is in a better position to engage in macro-management/coordination. (Interestingly, standard monetarism focused on a quantity mechanism—the amount of money—rather than a price.)

4.6.3 The Key Role of a Non-produced Asset

The third and crucial difference with standard macro/monetary theory is the introduction of a non-produced asset, and the recognition that money/credit can be used to buy non-produced assets, and that money is *not* needed to acquire produced goods.[92] Standard theory assumed that (a) the velocity of circulation (the ratio of the money supply to the value of transactions associated with *produced* goods) was fixed, or a stable function of the nominal interest rate, and finite; (b) money was only used to purchase produced goods; (c) money was required to purchase produced goods; and (d) that the government either controlled the money supply directly, affecting the level of economic activity through the impact of the money supply on the interest rate or controlled the interest rate directly (with the money supply adjusting to the required level to sustain that interest rate).[93] Each of these assumptions has been questioned.

We obtain contrasting results by making the alternative polar assumption that credit, the supply of which may be regulated, is used only to purchase a non-produced good.[94] This assumption means that an increase in credit or an improvement in the terms at which credit is made available (a lowering of the interest rate charged, a reduction in collateral constraints) is reflected in an increase in the value of land and wealth inequality but not

[90] When the economy is affected through these constraints, impacts can be larger, though the equilibrium is not in general Pareto efficient (Greenwald and Stiglitz, 1986).

[91] In the open economy, the government also sets the amount of trade chits (how many export chits are granted per dollar of exports). See Stiglitz (2017a).

[92] Equivalently, with electronic money, the velocity of circulation can be viewed as being infinite.

[93] In the classical dichotomy, monetary policy did not affect economic activity at all; it only affected the price level. A central theme of modern macroeconomics is to explain the channels through which monetary policy affects real economic activity.

[94] Though less relevant for the focus of our concern here on inequality, the channels by which monetary policy affects the economy and the instruments by which monetary authorities affect the credit supply under current arrangements differ too from the standard analysis. We have emphasized that it is not the money supply itself which matters so much as the supply of credit; monetary policy affects banks' ability and willingness to lend. It is not so much the T-bill interest rate that matters but the lending rate. It is not just interest rates that matter, but also the availability of credit and other terms besides the interest rate, such as collateral requirements. And it is not just open market operations and reserve requirements that affect the ability and willingness to lend, but a host of other regulations, such as capital adequacy standards, including those usually thought of as prudential regulations. See Stiglitz and Greenwald (2003a).

necessarily in wages, the level of economic activity, or the capital stock.[95] Indeed, an important aspect of our analysis is that greater credit creation (usually associated with looser monetary policy) actually reduces the level of capital accumulation (investment)—the opposite of the standard analyses in models with no non-produced asset.

This difference between the model presented here and more standard macroeconomic models can be described in still a different way: In standard Keynesian economics, the failure of Say's Law to hold—of supply to create its own demand—arises from the existence of a non-produced store of value, money. The increased income generated by increased production is not necessarily used to purchase produced goods. But Keynes ignored the existence of another store of value, land, and thus attributed too much importance to money in giving rise to the dysfunctions of the economy.[96]

4.6.4 Inflation

While we have focused on the link between asset price inflation and monetary policy, we have said little about the link between commodity price inflation (the price of produced goods) and monetary policy. This lacuna may seem especially glaring, since one of the main objectives of monetary policy seems to be to control the rate of inflation. An adequate treatment would, however, take us too far afield from the main subject of inquiry of this book. Here, we note that recent expansions of the money and credit supply have had, in fact, little effect on goods prices, but considerable impact on asset prices, suggesting the relevance of the models developed here.

Given the focus of this book on inequality, we comment further on the distributive consequences of inflation and anti-inflation monetary policies. Monetary authorities often justify tight monetary policies by claiming that "inflation is the cruelest tax," suggesting that its impacts are regressive, hurting the poor more (at least proportionately) than the rich. But this is almost surely not the case. Workers' wages (especially in standard market models) reflect their marginal revenue product (in competitive markets, the value of their marginal product), and this increases in tandem with prices. While there may be lags in adjustment, so long as the inflation rate is not excessively volatile, anticipated inflation is typically built into bargaining processes. When there is greater uncertainty about inflation, wage bargains typically include automatic cost of living adjustments. Similarly, poor and middle-income elderly depend on social security, which is indexed to inflation. Holders of long-term bonds which are not indexed—disproportionately the rich, but also including some life-cycle savers—are those who lose the most from unanticipated inflation, while debtors have the value of their debts diminished. When those from the financial sector thus

[95] Less extreme assumptions would still generate a disproportionate effect on land and equity prices and an increase in wealth inequality.

[96] For example, focusing on the liquidity trap, an excessively elastic demand for money.

As we have repeatedly noted, the models in this chapter and largely elsewhere in the book assume full employment; but it would be easy to adapt them, introducing wage and price rigidities (e.g., associated with efficiency wages or nominal rigidities) and/or supply side effects (as in Greenwald-Stiglitz, 1993a) where the perturbations we have described give rise to variations in employment and unemployment.

The influence of standard Keynesian economics has been so strong that central bankers have given short shrift to the impact of their actions on asset prices, and the impact of those prices on macroeconomic activity. In the 1990s, the seeming large impact of the collapse of real estate and stock prices in Japan led to a beginning of a re-examination. Almost buried in Alan Greenspan's famous "irrational exuberance" speech in 1996 was an argument that "evaluating shifts in balance sheets generally, and in asset prices particularly, must be an integral part of the development of monetary policy." Nonetheless, over the subsequent decade, the Fed paid little attention to the growth of either the tech or the real estate bubble. See Greenspan (1996).

claim that inflation is the cruelest tax, they are really just putting forward a self-serving argument; one should be suspicious when bankers suddenly seem to have a conscience, worrying about the poor and the impact of policy on inequality. A well-designed tax system could easily provide appropriate compensation for those of limited means who are hurt by the inflation tax.[97] In fact, there are large asymmetries in the costs of too little or too much stimulation of the economy—too little results in a waste of resources, with a large burden borne by those at the bottom and middle, too much results in inflation, the burden of which is felt disproportionately by the rich.[98]

5 Concluding Remarks: Toward Better Policy

That there is scope for a better macro/monetary theory and better instruments for managing the economy should be obvious: Decades ago, we learned that one could not let a market economy manage itself. That is why, for instance, every country has a central bank determining interest rates and/or the money supply, and regulatory authorities overseeing banking.

Anyone observing macroeconomic performance in recent years will see that things have not gone well in many countries around the world, even in advanced countries, with supposedly well-functioning markets and institutions and individuals who are supposedly well-informed about economics and presumably know how to manage the economy.

Part of the reason for the poor performance may in fact have been misguided ideas about how the economy functions, an underappreciation of the importance of macroeconomic externalities;[99] an overconfidence in self-regulation—which makes no sense in the presence of externalities—and a reliance on models which *assume* the economy magically is always on an equilibrium path, contrary to the analysis of this and the previous chapter, which suggest a presumption for instability.[100] Policies aimed at increasing economic efficiency—using misguided models—may have in the end imposed high costs on the economy, particularly on those in the bottom and middle. So too, policies focusing on *price* stability may have, in the end, contributed to higher levels of *real* instability.

Advances in technology in recent years has made construction of a fully electronic monetary system feasible. This chapter has shown that in such a fully electronic system, there are new and better ways in which macro management could be conducted. In particular, we analyzed the effects of a major institutional innovation, credit auctions among banks.[101]

[97] For instance, by allowing a loss-offset for the loss in real value of any bonds for low- and middle-income taxpayers.

[98] To reemphasize a qualification made at the beginning of the chapter: we have not developed here short run macro models, where there may be persistent unemployment, an obvious concern in any study of inequality. A major source of deep downturns is the breaking of asset bubbles, and this chapter has provided some insights into the creation of such asset bubbles.

[99] See Jeanne and Korinek (2010), Davila and Korinek (2018), and Korinek (2018b).

[100] The DSGE models have been particularly misleading in this regard. See Guzman and Stiglitz (2020) and Stiglitz (2018e). For a broader discussion of the role of economic ideas in creating the 2008 crisis, see Stiglitz (2010a).

[101] In Stiglitz (2017a) I discuss two further innovations, state-contingent loans, and trade chits for managing imports and exports, which can further enhance macro-stability. State-contingent loans might reduce the limitations confronting monetary policy in deep recession, facilitating the return of the economy to full employment, even when confronted by a liquidity trap created by banks' unwillingness to lend or the inability to lower T-bill rates because of a zero-lower bound. The efficiency of capital markets might increase by directly addressing the

Well-designed credit auctions can be used to control better both the quantity of credit created, the uses to which it is put, and the rents and inequality associated with credit creation in the current economic regime. It can help address the critical problems that we have identified: how excessive credit creation directed at the purchase of non-produced assets can create asset price inflation crowding out real capital accumulation, hurting overall long-term economic performance and workers in particular.

This and the last chapter have focused on two of the most important sources of rents in the economy—land and finance—and how they are intertwined. An equally important source of rent is monopoly rents, the subject of the next chapter.

problems posed by perceptions of excessive risk, rather than attempting to address such problems indirectly by changing intertemporal prices.

Trade-chits enable the government to better control the size of net exports, thereby stabilizing an important component of aggregate demand.

16

Monopoly, Rents, and Political Equilibrium

1 Introduction

Chapter 10 argued that the growth of rents is central to understanding the growth of inequality in the U.S. in recent decades.[1] Chapters 14 and 15 explained why one should expect an increase in land rents, both as a result of urban agglomerations and policy changes (including in monetary and financial policies) which contributed to the growth of the real estate bubble. The increase in monopoly and oligopoly rents is almost certainly as important, or more so.

Increased market power, for whatever reason, leads to greater monopoly rents, and the capitalized value of that leads to more "wealth." The increase in wealth will go to the residual claimants of the corporations—the owners of the equity—at the time the increased market power is recognized. As we have seen, it is those at the very top that own equities, that is, that gain from the (greater than expected)[2] increased market power.

Of course, if the increased rents were fully anticipated and there were no risks, the returns on all assets would have been the same. But neither condition is satisfied: The gains have not, and likely could not, have been fully anticipated. They arose in large measure out of hard-to-anticipate changes in politics, in the rules of the game, and in policies, sometimes in response to hard-to-anticipate events, like the Great Recession. The low interest rates and ample supply of liquidity helped fuel a stock market boom. Moreover, as we noted in the previous chapter, the rich have a much greater ability to bear risk, which explains why they disproportionately own risky assets like land and equities (illustrated by the figures in Chapter 4), and it is these assets which have disproportionately benefited from certain policy changes, like financial market deregulation, more lax enforcement of antitrust laws, and quantitative easing.

This chapter focuses on the consequences of the growth in monopoly and oligopoly rents, which is now well-documented (see Philippon, 2019 and Stiglitz, 2019a, and the references cited there). After a brief discussion of the explanations of this growth in market power (Section 2), we explain how it contributes to inequality through several distinct channels: ordinary citizens have to pay more for the goods they buy—lowering their income—while the rich owners of these firms with market power become still richer.

[1] Much of this chapter was originally presented as keynote at the Eighteenth World Congress of the International Economic Association, Mexico City, June 19–23, 2017. This work itself was a continuation of a long-term research program. Earlier results were reported in a paper originally presented as a Keynote address at the World Congress of the International Economic Association, Mexico City (Stiglitz, 2071b). At the World Congress, I dedicated this lecture in memory of my good friend and co-author, Anthony B. Atkinson (and a former President of the IEA), who worked tirelessly throughout his life to understand better the sources of inequality and what can be done about it. His enormous contributions have left an indelible mark on the profession.

[2] In informational efficient markets, an expectation of an increase in market power sometime in the future would be fully capitalized at the moment that it occurred. But Grossman and Stiglitz (1976, 1980a) explain why markets will never be fully informational efficient. Shiller's work (1981, 2002) confirms their theoretical prediction.

The Origins of Inequality, and Policies to Contain It. Joseph E. Stiglitz, Oxford University Press. © Joseph E. Stiglitz (2025).
DOI: 10.1093/oso/9780198799580.003.0017

Moreover, the growth in the capitalized value of monopoly rents discourages real capital accumulation—it provides an alternative store of value for those who want to save for the future, the subject of Section 3. This in turn leads to lower wages, and if the elasticity of substitution is less than unity, a smaller share of labor. Sections 4 and 5 explain how the growth in monopoly rents can help explain a number of the new stylized (macro and micro) facts of the economy, including the increased dispersion of wages.

Decisions about the legal framework for ensuring a competitive marketplace are, obviously, political; and especially in a money-driven democracy, inequalities in wealth affect such decisions: those who make their wealth through rent-seeking activities will use their wealth to ensure that they can continue to do so. Section 6 shows that, as a result, there may exist multiple political-economic equilibria, in particular a more competitive regime, with less inequality and less rent seeking, and a regime characterized by higher inequality and more rent seeking. The United States may have sunk into the latter.

Throughout the chapter, we explore the implications of changes in taxes, especially on corporate profits, a subject which has been a long-standing subject of contention. An increase in the corporate profits tax can (and is likely to) increase output and wages, both because it reduces the extent to which the rent-wealth associated with corporate profits crowds out savings and because it reduces incentives for rent-seeking.[3]

2 Explaining Increased Market Power

There are several reasons that changes in the structure of the economy and in technology over the past third of a century may have naturally been associated with an increase in corporate market power: (a) an increase in the importance of sectors with large network externalities, in which naturally there will be one or a few dominant platforms; (b) an increase in the importance of sectors with high fixed costs and low marginal costs (much of the digital and knowledge economy), where again there is a tendency for there to be a few dominant firms[4,5]—closely related to the growth of superstar firms in a winner-take-all economy; (c) an increase in knowledge about how to create, maintain, and extend market power,[6] including the design of contracts that help preclude entry;[7] along with learning

[3] See, for instance, Piketty, Saez, and Stantcheva (2014).

[4] See Stiglitz and Greenwald (2014). Schumpeter thought that competition for the market was an effective substitute for competition in the market (what later came to be called the contestability doctrine). This has, however, shown not to hold with any generality. See, for example, Farrell (1986) and Stiglitz (1987e).

[5] This explanation is not totally persuasive, since if it were true, one would expect to see an increase in the value of investment (e.g., relative to GDP). This has not occurred.

[6] For instance, Microsoft bundled its browser with its operating system, effectively killing its competitor Netscape. It was willing to do so—effectively to give away its browser—out of fear that a competitor browser might be used to undermine its market power in PC operating systems. It used other techniques to undermine competition—spreading fear that there would be problems of interoperability. Its actions were ruled to be anti-competitive in both U.S. and Europe. (For full disclosure, I was an expert witness in antitrust actions taken against Microsoft in Europe, U.S., and Korea.)

[7] These contracts have played an important role in many industries which have been called "two-sided," including credit cards and airline reservation systems. These contracts do not allow, for instance, merchants to pass on the high costs of using a credit card to their customers, effectively short-circuiting the price system, and creating an almost unsurmountable barrier to entry.

In fact, the alleged two-sided markets, like credit cards and airline reservation systems, are often not characterized by the externalities that are central to two-sided markets. A 2017 court ruling in the U.S. in a suit against Sabre by U.S. Airways, following a jury finding, held that Sabre's contract terms were anti-competitive (*U.S. Airways, Inc., vs. Sabre Holdings Corp., et al., 11 Civ. 2725* in the United States District Court for the Southern District of New York). On the other hand, a widely criticized 5 to 4 Supreme Court ruling held that analogous contract

about how to make goods more efficiently has come learning about how to create entry barriers; (d) an increase in the ability to engage in price discrimination, using big data and AI (an example of advances in technology "enabling" more market power); (e) the move to a knowledge economy, where intellectual property rights (IPR) play an important role; IPR has enhanced the market power of those who do make advances in knowledge—and sometimes by those whose comparative advantage is simply knowing how to take advantage of the intellectual property regime; and (f) the move from manufacturing to the service sector economy, one of the implications of which is an increase in (the average degree of) market power, since services are provided locally, and competition within each locale for the provision of these services may be limited.

But even given all of these changes, the magnitude of the increase in market concentration and market power that has been observed in the U.S. was not inevitable. There has, for instance, been a much less marked increase in market power and concentration in Europe. At least part of the difference is *law and policy.* It would, of course, be a challenge for antitrust law to keep up with all the changes in technology and the structure of the economy; some of these pose particularly large challenges to ensuring the maintenance of a reasonably competitive economy. However, competition authorities in the U.S. have not shown the same resolve in fighting for competition that some business leaders have shown in fighting against it—in establishing their market power. Making their task all the more difficult are numerous court decisions, influenced by the "Chicago School," holding that markets on their own are naturally competitive, so that the government should be wary about interfering. Courts have made it more difficult to bring cases involving predatory pricing and the use of contracts to strengthen and perpetuate market power. And so far, in the U.S., the political process has not been able to override these decisions to create a more competitive economy.[8]

So too, intellectual property rights have been strengthened, increasing IPR rents at a pace that is greater than can be accounted for simply by the shift toward a knowledge economy. (See Henry and Stiglitz, 2010.)

3 Links between Increased Rents and Decreased Real Wages and Capital Accumulation

3.1 Increases in Prices Relative to Marginal Costs of Production

The increases in market power leading to an increase in wealth (relative to income) also obviously lead to increased prices (relative to marginal costs) and thus decreased *real*

terms imposed on merchants by American Express were not anti-competitive. As a result, the Sabre decision was retried, with the jury again affirming that Sabre had engaged in wrongful behavior. The decision is being appealed as this book goes to press.

Some countries, Australia in particular, have prohibited these anti-competitive contracts, with a dramatic lowering of the costs of debit and credit card services. (At various times, I was an expert witness in competition proceedings in these cases.)

[8] There are many differences between competition laws in different countries. While the U.S. led the way in the adoption of antitrust laws late in the nineteenth century and early in the twentieth, since then it has lagged behind others. For instance, in Europe, it is not acceptable to abuse market dominance (e.g., by raising drug prices hundreds of times above costs); in the U.S., it is, so long as market dominance was legitimately acquired. We do not expand here on how to construct a more effective competition regime. See, for example, Wu (2018), Philipon (2019), and Stiglitz (2019a).

wages. There is, in effect, a transfer of wealth from consumers to monopolists. As we noted in Chapter 10, though we measure the increased wealth of the corporations, we don't measure that of consumers, so that it appears as if the wealth of the economy has increased. In fact, because market power introduces a distortion into the economy, there is a decrease in national wealth (e.g., as measured by the present discounted value of GDP).

3.2 Weakened Bargaining Power of Workers

Moreover, labor markets are typically only imperfectly competitive, and the increased market power of firms may enhance their market power not only relative to consumers but also relative to that of workers, again leading to decreased real wages, an increase in corporate wealth, more than offset by the decrease in the (unmeasured real) wealth of workers.[9]

There are other reasons for the weakening of workers' bargaining power: (a) an increase in the average unemployment rate, itself a consequence of changed macro-economic policies, in particular, monetary policies focusing on inflation; (b) a change in labor legislation and its enforcement, weakening unionization and changing the structure of collective bargaining;[10] (c) changing market structure, with a smaller share of employment in big factories and enterprises that may be easily be unionized; and (d) globalization—increasing the threat of firms to outsource and relocate.[11]

3.3 Changes in Corporate Governance

Moreover, changes in corporate governance laws and norms enable senior management in a company to increase the share of corporate revenues going to themselves. Their ability to enhance their own well-being at the expense of other stakeholders, combined with incentive structures which encourage short-sighted behavior, contribute to a decrease both in investment in the future of the company and workers' compensation. Indeed, in Chapter 4, we presented evidence of an enormous decrease in the share of the bottom 99% of workers, excluding effectively bankers, CEOs, and other senior management, from around 75% of GDP to 60%.

3.4 Decreased Capital Accumulation

Even if labor markets were competitive and deficiencies in corporate governance had not led to decreases in investment, the increased market power of firms can lead to lower wages as a result of a decrease in capital accumulation. The economy suffers on two accounts—the

[9] In this and the following subsections, we simply summarize the main arguments. For a more extended discussion with references, see Stiglitz (2019a).

[10] Indeed Stelzner (2015, 2017) argues that much of the increase in inequality can simply be explained by changes in the enforcement of labor legislation.

[11] Reinforced, for instance, be investment agreements which increase property rights protections of firms. (See Stiglitz, 2008c, 2018a, 2018d.) Even without this, globalization/trade liberalization would predictably lead to an increase in wage inequality within advanced countries, as a result of the factor price equalization theorem. See Stiglitz (2006a).

inefficiencies associated with the increase in market power and decreased capital accumulation. The mechanisms by which this happens are similar to those discussed in Chapter 14, where we saw than an increase in the value of land leads to a decrease in the long run capital–labor ratio.

3.4.1 Haig-Simons Savings Function

This adverse effect is seen most simply in a simple model where individual savings are a function of individual's income, in the Haig–Simons definition, including capital gains. But individuals also include the increased value of their assets in their savings. We thus have:

$$I + \Delta E = s(Y + \Delta E), \tag{16.1}$$

where I is investment, ΔE is the change in equity value as a result of the (anticipated) increase in market power, Y is national income in the national accounting sense (wage income, return to capital, and profits; in our simple model, national income in real terms equals national output, denoted by Q below) and s is the savings rate (for the moment assumed fixed.) Thus:

$$I = sY - (1 - s)\Delta E, \tag{16.2}$$

so that if macro-policy keeps the economy at, say, full employment, an increase in ΔE decreases investment. Those wishing to hold more wealth, do so in the form of an increased value of existing assets (ownership claims against existing corporations) rather than the creation of new assets. While there is some evidence that simple behavioral rules such as represented by Equation (16.1) may provide a better description of savings behavior than the standard intertemporal welfare maximization model, similar results may hold in such a model.[12]

The effect of the increase in the value of equities crowds out real capital accumulation, just as we saw to be the case in the life-cycle model of Chapter 14. More generally, an increase in what we call rent-wealth, the present discounted value of rents, crowds out real capital accumulation.

3.4.2 Life-Cycle Model

We now show this more formally in a life-cycle model of the kind discussed in previous chapters. Let $\alpha F(K)$ be the value of rents at any time, and assume that rents are permanent, a fraction of output Q, which is just a function of the capital stock, K: $Q = F(K)$. We assume that the fraction of output seized by rents, α, is fixed. In this book, we do not, for the most part, derive endogenously the degree of market power, as reflected in α. In a later section, we analyze the political/economic equilibrium that determines the toughness of antitrust policies, one of the major determinants of α, and we show how that may be affected both by changes in technology and in politics. And in Section 2, we discussed how changes in technology and market structure (the structure of the demand) affected the equilibrium degree of market concentration and market power. There is, moreover, a large

[12] As a result of the distortion of monopoly power, the marginal return to savings has decreased. Under reasonable preferences, this may reduce the savings rate and capital accumulation.

literature explaining how an increase in fixed costs relative to marginal costs may affect the equilibrium market power, both in monopolistically competitive markets and in dynamic oligopolies with innovation.[13] The basic intuition is simple: with large fixed costs, the equilibrium number of firms will be limited, and that results in high levels of monopoly rents, at least in Cournot models, where firms take the level of output of other firms as given.

We assume, moreover, as in earlier life-cycle models, for simplicity that the labor supply is fixed.[14] Thus rent-wealth, W_R, is given by

$$W_R = \alpha Q/[(1-\alpha)F'(K)], \tag{16.3}$$

where we have taken into account that market power has reduced the marginal return to investments in capital by the same proportion that it reduced the marginal return to labor. Life-cycle savers can hold either real wealth, K, or rent-wealth, W_R.[15]

$$K_{t+1} + W_{Rt+1} = sw(K_t, \alpha) = s(1-\alpha)(F(K_t) - K_tF'(K_t)). \tag{16.4}$$

An increase in W_R acts as a substitute for K in the portfolios of savers, leading to a decrease in K and wages. At the same time, an increase in market power reduces wages at any value of K, resulting in less savings. Thus, we can describe, for a fixed s, the dynamics by

$$K_{t+1} = s(1-\alpha)(F(K_t) - K_tF'(K_t)) - \alpha F(K_t)/[(1-\alpha)F'(K_t)] = \psi(K_t, \alpha). \tag{16.4'}$$

For instance, in the case of a Cobb–Douglas production function with share of capital equal to S_K, we have

$$K_{t+1} = sK_t\{(1-\alpha)(1-S_K) - \alpha\}/[(1-\alpha)S_K]. \tag{16.4''}$$

It immediately follows that for any K_t, next period's capital stock will be smaller the greater are rents, that is, $\psi_\alpha < 0$. (See Figure 16.1.) In steady state, we obtain[16]

$$K^* = s(F(K^*) - K^*F'(K^*))(1-\alpha) - \alpha F(K^*)/[(1-\alpha)F'(K^*)]. \tag{16.5}$$

implying that the equilibrium value of K (at any stable equilibrium) is decreased,[17]

[13] See, for instance, Dixit and Stiglitz (1977), Dasgupta and Stiglitz (1980a, 1980b), Stiglitz (1986c), Stiglitz and Greenwald (2014), and the references cited there.

[14] Similar results hold if market-power rents are temporary, say lasting only one period before they get dissipated through competition.

[15] This formulation assumes that savings come only out of wages. The rents generated by market power accrue to the owners of enterprises, last period's young people who are now retired. See the following subsection where we introduce a separate group of capitalists, who are naturally the owners of the oligopolies.

[16] Similar results obtain if monopoly power is only temporary.

[17] There may be multiple values of K^* satisfying (16.5), especially if the savings rate increases as r decreases (as K increases). Then stability requires the RHS of (16.4) to cut the 45-degree line from above, that is, an increase in K_t above K^* leads to a less than proportionate increase in K_{t+1}.

If the savings rate is a decreasing function of the expected return on capital and there are rational expectations (so the expected return is just $F'(K_{t+1})$), then for any K_t there may be multiple values of K_{t+1} satisfying (16.4′). See Hirano and Stiglitz (2022a, 2022b, 2022c).

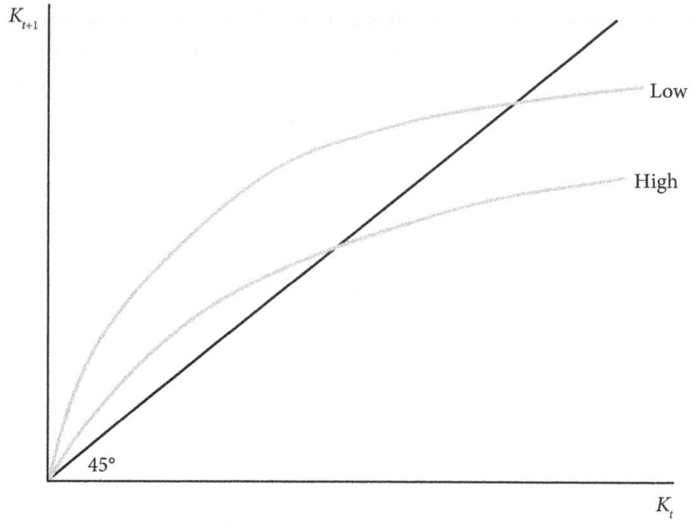

Figure 16.1 An increase in market power leads to a reduction in the equilibrium level of capital. (The equilibrium value of K is that where $K_{t+1} = K_t$).

3.4.2.1 The Impact of Taxation

Changes in taxes have a multiplicity of effects: they can capture some of the rents, returning them to workers, who then invest them, increasing the capital stock and wages; they can reduce the amount of rent-wealth, implying that more of savings goes into productive investments; but alternatively, they can lead to a lower discount rate, increasing the amount of rent-wealth, discouraging savings and hurting workers—even taking into account the redistribution of incomes toward them.

We focus on two possible taxes: a marginal tax on the return to capital, lowering the (after tax) discount rate to $(1 - \alpha)F'(K)(1 - \tau_i)$, where τ_i is the interest income tax; and a (pure) corporate profits tax at the rate τ_c, which is a tax just on the rent αF.

Then, with just the corporate profits tax:

$$W_R = \alpha F(K)(1 - \tau_c)/[(1 - \alpha)F'(K)]. \quad (16.6)$$

At any value of K, rent-wealth decreases. If the proceeds of the tax are redistributed to workers, then savings increases, and together, this means that *a tax on pure corporate profits increases K, GDP, and wages.* Because the corporate profits tax allows for a full deduction of the cost of capital goods (under current U.S. law) and/or the deduction of interest, plus depreciation (in most countries, and in the U.S. before 2017), the tax is close to a tax on pure profits. (See also Stiglitz, 1973e). In our life-cycle model, a pure corporate profits tax increases savings, and increases the fraction of that savings that goes into productive capital, and on both accounts, increases economic output and wages. These direct effects are reinforced by second round effects, as the increase in wages increases aggregate savings still further.[18]

[18] If the elasticity of substitution is less than one (rather than, as here, equal to one), the increase in the capital stock increases the share of labor, which further increases aggregate savings and wages.

On the other hand, an interest income tax leads to an increase (at each K) in the value of rent-wealth.

$$W_R = \alpha F(K)/[(1-\alpha)F'(K)(1-\tau_i)], \tag{16.7}$$

so the change in W_R is just

$$\Delta W_R = \{\alpha F(K)/[(1-\alpha)F'(K)]\}(\tau_i/(1-\tau_i)), \tag{16.7a}$$

while, if the proceeds are distributed to workers, and the savings rate is fixed, the increase in savings is

$$\Delta S = s\tau_i F'(K). \tag{16.8}$$

The increase in savings is greater than the increase in rent-wealth if and only if

$$sF'(K) > \alpha F(K)/[(1-\alpha)F'(K)(1-\tau_i)] \tag{16.9}$$

or

$$(1-\tau_i)\,sS_K > \frac{\alpha}{1-\alpha}, \tag{16.9a}$$

where $S_K = (F_K)^2/F$ i.e. *if the rent share α is small relative to sS_K, then a small tax on capital leads to an increase in capital accumulation, but if the rent share is large and/or the tax rate is high, an increase in the interest income tax decreases capital accumulation.*

If both a corporate profit tax and an interest income tax are imposed, then

$$W_R = \frac{\alpha F(K)(1-\tau_c)}{(1-\alpha)\,F'(K)(1-\tau_i)}, \tag{16.10}$$

from which it follows that so long as the corporate profits tax rate is greater than the interest income tax, rent-wealth decreases; and that implies that if the proceeds are distributed to workers, wages and output both increase in the long run. Only if the corporate profits tax rate is substantially below the interest income tax is it possible that the corporate profits tax reduces wages and GDP—and it has to be even lower for workers after transfer-income and welfare to be reduced.[19]

It is still the case, whether (16.9) is satisfied or not, however, that, fixing the tax on interest income, an increase in the corporate income tax decreases rent-wealth, and increases K, national output, and wages.

[19] For the purposes of this analysis, it is hard to ascertain the appropriate values of *c* and *i*. Effective tax rates can differ markedly from nominal tax rates. For life-cycle savers, for instance, much of interest income is tax exempt in the U.S., through IRA accounts. Returns on capital distributed as capital gains get preferential treatment.

Finally, we consider the effect of an imperfect corporate profits tax, where the imposition of a tax at the rate of τ_c lowers the marginal return on capital by $\phi\tau_c$, so now

$$W_R = \frac{\alpha F(K)(1 - \tau_c)}{(1 - \alpha)\ F'(K)(1 - \tau_i - \phi\tau_c)}. \tag{16.10a}$$

It should be clear that if ϕ is small enough, the results are the same as for a pure profits tax. Indeed, if τ_i is zero, rent-wealth is reduced no matter what the value of ϕ so long as $\phi < 1$, so that an increase in the corporate income tax increases K, output, and wages.

The analysis here focuses on steady states. Obviously, if the economy is in one steady state at a low corporate profits tax rate, and then the corporate profits tax is increased, in the process of moving to the new steady state, associated with a higher per capita income, the growth rate increases. But as in standard growth models, the long-run growth rate itself is determined by factors here assumed exogenous (the rate of growth of population and of labor augmenting technological change). We postpone until later chapters a discussion of endogenous growth.

3.4.3 A Two-Class Model

Similar results hold in the two-class model explored in Chapter 13. Assume capitalists allocate wealth intertemporally, so that the return on capital is δ, the pure rate of time preference (assuming, as earlier, no technological change):

$$(1 - \alpha)F_K = \delta. \tag{16.11}$$

Underlying (16.11) is the assumption that dynastic savers base their intergenerational savings on the intertemporal trade-off, as reflected in the marginal return to investment, which is diminishing by the rent-seekers ability to divert a fraction of output to themselves).[20] Workers, living two periods, working in the first, similarly maximize their lifetime utility. For simplicity, we assume a logarithmic utility function, giving rise to a fixed savings rate s_w.[21]

$$s_w(F - KF_K(1 - \alpha)) = W_w, \tag{16.12}$$

where W_w is workers' wealth, and

$$K + W_R = W_W + W_C, \tag{16.13}$$

where W_C is capitalists' wealth.[22]

[20] That is, they don't act collusively, thinking that if they save and invest more, they will also earn more rents. Those receiving the rents take them as given, fixed at a given fraction of output. Later sections will endogenize the share of rents.

[21] See Chapters 14 and 19 for the more general case.

[22] While it is natural to think of the rent-wealth as (largely) owned by the capitalists, since the returns on K and on rent-wealth are the same, nothing depends on to whom the monopoly returns actually accrue. This is because (in this model) monopoly rents are fully anticipated, and so all capital earns the same returns. More realistically, of course, it is the owners of equity, intellectual property, and those who exercise control over firms that benefit from especially (unanticipated) increases in market power.

As before, an increase in workers' savings rate leaves aggregate K and rent-wealth unchanged, increasing workers' wealth at the expense of capitalists' wealth.

More interesting, an increase in market power (rents, as reflected in an increase in α) leads to lower K (from (16.11)),

$$\frac{d\ln K}{d\ln\alpha} = \frac{\alpha}{1-\alpha}\frac{F_{KK}K}{F_K} = -\frac{\alpha}{1-\alpha}\frac{\sigma}{S_L} < 0, \tag{16.14}$$

where σ is the elasticity of substitution and S_L is $\frac{F_L L}{F}$ (what would have been the share of labor in the absence of market power). It follows that rent-wealth may increase or decrease depending on the elasticity of substitution:

$$W_R = \frac{\alpha F}{(1-\alpha)F_K} = \frac{\alpha F}{\delta}. \tag{16.15}$$

So (comparing long run equilibria with different degrees of market power):

$$\frac{d\ln W_R}{d\ln\alpha} = 1 - \frac{\alpha}{1-\alpha}\frac{\sigma(1-S_L)}{S_L} \tag{16.16}$$

$$\frac{d\ln W_R}{d\ln\alpha} > or < 0 \; as \; \sigma < or > \frac{(1-\alpha)S_L}{\alpha(1-S_L)}, \tag{16.17}$$

that is, so long as the elasticity of substitution is small enough relative to S_L, so the adverse effect on K is small, and the share of rents is small enough, an increase in market power increases rent-wealth. If $\alpha = 0.2$ and $S_L = 0.6$, for instance, all that is required is that the elasticity of substitution be less than 6.

A slight Kaldor-Passinetti variant of the model yields similar results. Let s_p be the savings rate out of capitalists' income, which includes both their rents, αF, and the return on their capital, rK_C, where K_C is capitalists' ownership of capital. Then, if the rate of growth of the population is n, then (expressing everything in per capita terms, in the usual notation):

$$s_p f'(k)(1-\alpha)w_c = (1+n)w_c,$$

where w_c is wealth per capita of the capitalists, yielding the result analogous to (16.11):

$$s_p f'(k)(1-\alpha) = (1+n).$$

The analysis proceeds in exactly the same manner (with δ being substituted for by $(1+n)/s_p$).

Still another variant has all the rents accruing to the capitalists, and they save, say, the same fraction s_p of those rents, so we now have

$$s_p\{f'(k)(1-\alpha)w_c + \alpha f\} = (1+n)\,w_c.$$

We can use (16.18) below to solve for w_c as a function of k: $w_c = k\left[1 + \frac{\alpha}{(1-\alpha)S_K}\right] - s(1-\alpha)(f - kf')$, enabling us to solve the above equation for k as a function of $s_p/(1+n)$ and α, as before. Note now, however, that an increase in market power leads to an increase in k, at least for small α: because more of capitalists' income is saved, a redistribution to capitalists through an increase in rents increases capital accumulation, benefitting workers. Their share of wealth, however, can be written

$$\frac{f' S_L}{S_K + \frac{\alpha}{1-\alpha}},$$

which decreases with an increase in market power unless the elasticity of substitution is sufficiently less than one.

While an increase in market power always leads to a decrease in K, if S_L is large enough relative to α, it leads to an overall increase in measured wealth because it leads to an increase in rent-wealth:

$$W^* = K + \frac{\alpha F}{(1-\alpha) F_K} = K\left\{1 + \frac{\alpha F}{\delta K}\right\}. \tag{16.18}$$

Notice that, not surprisingly, the fraction of wealth that is "real-wealth"—$\chi \equiv \frac{1}{1+\frac{\alpha F}{\delta K}}$ —decreases with market power. Overall wealth increases if rent-wealth increases enough and K decreases relatively little. Straightforward differentiation of (16.18) yields the result that

$$\frac{d \ln W^*}{d \ln \alpha} = \chi - \frac{\alpha}{1-\alpha}\frac{\sigma}{S_L}(\chi + (1-\chi) S_L)$$

so

$$\frac{d \ln W^*}{d \ln \alpha} > or < 0 \; as \; \sigma < or > \frac{(1-\alpha)\chi S_L}{\alpha(\chi + (1-\chi) S_L)}. \tag{16.19}$$

Thus, for the parameters introduced earlier, using (16.11), $\chi = \frac{1}{\left\{1+\frac{\alpha}{(1-\alpha)(1-S_L)}\cdot\right\}} = .62$ wealth increases so long as the elasticity of substitution is less than 1.7—there is a strong presumption that increases in market power will be associated with an increase in overall wealth, even as the level of the capital stock falls.

Note that the relative share of workers is particularly hurt with an increase in market power. Denote the share of labor in GDP by $\widehat{S_L} = (1-\alpha) S_L$, and similarly define $\widehat{S_K} = (1-\alpha) S_K$, then

$$\frac{d \ln \widehat{S_K}}{d \ln \alpha} = -\frac{\alpha}{(1-\alpha)} - \frac{\alpha}{1-\alpha}\frac{\sigma-1}{S_L}\frac{\alpha}{(1-\alpha)}\left(1 - \frac{1-\sigma}{S_L}\right) = \frac{\alpha}{(1-\alpha) S_L}(S_K - \sigma) < or > 0 \tag{16.20}$$

as

$$\sigma > \text{or} < S_K. \tag{16.20a}$$

For low elasticities, even though the capital stock doesn't change much, there is a large change in the distribution of income (S_K) as a result of the decrease in K, and this overpowers the fact that more rents are being extracted. It follows that since $S_L + S_K = 1$, that the share of labor will go down provided that the elasticity of substitution is not too large ($\sigma < 1 + \frac{S_L^2}{1-S_L}$). When the elasticity is very large, the decrease in K leads to an increase in the share of labor, offsetting the direct effect of the increase in rents.

3.4.3.1 *Impacts of Taxation*

We can now see how tax policy in this model can affect the distribution of income. An increase in the corporate profits tax decreases rent-wealth, but has no effect on K, since it doesn't decrease the marginal return to capital. Thus, if the proceeds of the tax are redistributed to workers, their wealth increases. And since overall wealth has decreased (K is unchanged and rent-wealth decreased), that means that capitalists' wealth has decreased: the tax unambiguously increases the well-being of workers and reduces wealth and income inequality.

On the other hand, the effects of an interest income tax are more complex, since it reduces the discount rate, increases rent-wealth at any value of K, reduces K, and thereby reduces wages.

The long run equilibrium condition for K is now

$$(1 - t_i)(1 - \alpha)F_K = \delta. \tag{16.21}$$

so that

$$\frac{d\ln K}{d\ln t_i} = \left(\frac{t_i}{1 - t_i}\right)\frac{\sigma}{S_L} < 0. \tag{16.22}$$

The interest income tax lowers the return to capital and hence the capital stock. Now rent-wealth is (using (16.21)):

$$W_R = \frac{\alpha F}{(1 - t_i)(1 - \alpha)F_K} = \frac{\alpha F}{\delta}. \tag{16.23}$$

Thus, if the capital stock is reduced, so will be rent-wealth. And unless the elasticity of substitution is small enough, the share of wealth owned by the workers increases. To see this, assume that the savings rate of workers is fixed at s, and that the share of labor S_L is fixed. Then the share of workers' life-cycle savings is just

$$\frac{K_w}{W^*} = \frac{s(1 - \alpha)S_L F}{K + \frac{\alpha F}{\delta}} = \frac{s(1 - \alpha)S_L}{\frac{K}{F} + \frac{\alpha}{\delta}}. \tag{16.24}$$

The denominator increases with K, and since the tax decreases K, it means that $\frac{K_w}{W^*}$ increases, unless S_L falls a great deal, which it will if the elasticity of substitution is low.

Even if, however, the workers' share of capital increases, the effect on workers is adverse. As in Chapter 13, the tax lowers wages, and even if the proceeds of the tax are redistributed to workers, they are still worse off. But as we noted there, these adverse effects can be more than mitigated if the proceeds are spent on public investments, either on human capital or public capital goods.

Finally, we consider the case where the interest income and corporate profits taxes are imposed at the same rate, i.e. $t = t_c = t_i$. Rent-wealth is now

$$W_R = \frac{\alpha F(1 - t)}{\delta}.$$

Rent-wealth is reduced in two ways: the interest income tax lowers K, and thus output (F), and the fraction of that wealth that is captured by rent-seekers is reduced.

It is still the case that K is lowered, by an amount given by (16.22), while transfer payments

$$T = tF'K + t\alpha F = tF(\alpha + S_K). \tag{16.25}$$

Thus an increase in the tax changes workers' total income, $w + T$, by

$$F[\alpha - t\{\frac{S_K}{S_L(1 - t)}\{\sigma(\alpha + S_K) + (\sigma - 1) + S_L\}\}]. \tag{16.26}$$

For small enough t, this is clearly positive provided $\alpha > 0$. (At $\alpha = 0$, we're back to the model of Chapter 13.)[23] A tax on interest income and corporate profits tax increases workers' income (and welfare, since the after-tax return on their investments remains unchanged) provided that there are rents in the economy. It also increases their wealth. Because rent-wealth has decreased and workers' wealth has increased, wealth inequality will be reduced.

4 Increased Rents as Explaining the Paradoxes of Modern Growth

In Chapter 10, I set forth a set of seeming paradoxes, aspects of modern growth that are hard to reconcile with standard theory. For instance, *if* capital and wealth were the same, then the observed increase in the wealth–income ratio should have been associated with a decreased share of capital, given the wealth of studies suggesting an aggregate elasticity of substitution less than unity; and it should have similarly been associated with increased wages. But if the productive capital decreased relative to GDP (as predicted by the above model and confirmed by national accounts data for the U.S. and some other advanced countries for which we have the data), then the paradox is potentially resolved. Much of the increase in wealth is an increase in the capitalized value of rents; the real capital–output ratio may have actually decreased.

Similarly, if capital stock decreased (relative to GDP), then a decrease in average wages is less of a surprise.[24]

Another seeming paradox: the average profit rate seems to have increased, yet investment (as a share of GDP) remains low. Again, an increase in market power provides an explanation: first, the average profit rate confounds the return to capital with monopoly rents; monopoly rents could have increased, while the return to capital has decreased—and a lower (marginal) return to capital *is* consistent with a decline in investment. An increase in market power will be associated with a larger gap between marginal and average returns.

[23] Equation (16.26) provides a simple formula for the optimal tax (where workers' income is maximized, putting no weight on the income of capitalists):

$$\frac{t^*}{1 - t} = \frac{S_K}{S_L\alpha} + S_K + (\sigma - 1) + S_L.$$

Using the parameters given above, and assuming the elasticity of substitution is unity, then the optimal tax rate is 44%.

[24] I say "less of a surprise" because one might still have expected technological progress to offset the effects of a lower level of capital.

Even if the average return to capital had increased, the marginal return to capital might have decreased.

Perhaps the greatest paradox is this: not only do real wages on average seem to be stagnating, at least in the U.S., the return to capital seems to be low, with a riskless rate that is negative in real terms. The factor-price frontier, the dual to the production function, implies that with technological change, in a competitive economy, the real wage corresponding to any given real interest rate (return on capital) should increase; but while the real interest rate has not increased (indeed, it seems to have decreased), neither has the real wage. One cannot account for this within a competitive framework; this paradox can be resolved simply: an increase in market power.[25]

4.1 The Paradox of Tobin's *Q* and the Level of Investment

The investment paradox that we have just discussed can be looked at another way—through Tobin's q. Tobin had argued that investment was driven not so much by the rate of interest as by the price of equity (the "demand" price of capital goods)—more precisely, the ratio of the market value of an additional unit of capital to its replacement cost.[26] If q is high—the market value is high relative to the cost of producing capital goods—then investment will be stimulated. The paradox is that in recent years q appears to be high, and yet the level of investment has not been. Of course, we don't observe directly the incremental market value; what we observe is the market value of a company relative to the replacement value of its capital stock.

In the absence of competition, there will be rents, and these rents will be reflected in the value of stocks, so that in a long run equilibrium where firms have optimally adjusted their capital stock, $q = \frac{K + W_R}{K} > 1$. An increase in market power results in an increase in rent-wealth, an increase in q, but not necessarily any increase in a firm's demand for capital (and hence an increase in its level of investment). Indeed, as we explained, it may lower the marginal return to sales, and thus reduce the level of investment.[27]

Similarly, any policy change that increases W_R (such as the tax changes described above), increases q. But such changes may or may not lead to more investment. For instance, we showed that a lowering of the corporate income tax rate increases rent-wealth and hence q, but may reduce the equilibrium value of the capital stock. (See Brun and Gonzalez, 2017) for a far more extensive discussion of these issues, with relevant empirical evidence on what has happened.)

[25] The standard neoclassical analysis ignores risk, but it is straightforward to incorporate risk into this analysis. In particular, improvements in risk management (affecting both the magnitude of overall risk and the sharing of risk within the economy) should have lowered the risk premium, implying that the average return should have been lowered.

[26] Somewhat earlier, Kaldor (1966) had put forward a similar idea to that developed by Tobin and Brainard (1977).

[27] This is perhaps one of the reasons that, in spite of the persuasiveness of the theory, empirically, investment is not well-explained by q. (Henwood, 1997). While even earlier, Branchard, Rhee and Summers (1993) had argued that profitability did a better job of explaining investment, our analysis has explained why observed profitability metrics, which typically incorporate rents, may not be a good indicator of the marginal return on investment.

5 Rents and Increased Dispersion in Productivity and Wages across Firms

It has been widely observed that there are large wage differences across firms, and some have suggested that changes in these across firm wage differences may be more important in explaining changes in wage inequalities than wage differences within firms, that is, between executives and workers (related to the problems in corporate governance noted in Section 3.3), and that the cross-firm wage differences are systematically related to productivity differences across firms.[28] The within-firm wage differentials have been the focus of those who see weaknesses in corporate governance as contributing to inequality. The cross-firm differentials suggest something else is going on. Why are there persistent differences in productivities across firms? And if there are, why would high productivity/profit companies pay workers of a given skill more? Why would they seemingly share some of their profits with their workers?[29]

5.1 Explaining Persistent Productivity/Profitability Differences

There is some evidence that there are *seemingly* large and persistent differences in productivities across firms. There are two explanations. One relates to the slow diffusion of knowledge, emphasized by Stiglitz and Greenwald (2014). Knowledge does not disseminate quickly across society. Some firms specialize in moving the frontier forward. Others let information diffuse to them. Because knowledge is costly to produce and acquire, it will be optimal for firms not to spend the resources to "catch up" (Stiglitz, 2015c). If the pace of innovation increases or the costs of innovation relative to the cost of imitation increases, then there will be greater productivity dispersion. It seems plausible that this has occurred, at least in some sectors.

The second explanation is an increase in market power. If an industry comes to be dominated by one or a couple of firms, those firms will have higher profitability; and the higher prices these firms receive for the goods relative to the cost of production will show up as higher productivity. But it is not that these firms are producing more or better "widgets per man hour," just that they use their market power to extract more from consumers for each widget sold. It is an improvement, as it were, in "marketing" rather than in "production," as we conventionally think of it. Earlier in this section, we provided several reasons why on average we might observe an increase in market concentration.

5.2 Rent Sharing

Regardless of the explanation of productivity and profitability differences across firms, the question remains, why are wages (of seemingly similar workers) in more profitable firms

[28] See, e.g. Furman and Orszag (2018a, 2018b) and the broader discussion in Stiglitz (2019a).

[29] One answer is that the analyses have not fully adjusted for worker quality. There are unobservable characteristics, which, try as one might, are impossible to fully correct for. The more profitable firms are also better at identifying these hard to observe characteristics; there are enough of these firms that workers can appropriate some of the returns from their hard-to-observe characteristics. We do not explore this explanation here, but note that it is consistent with the well-established theory of screening (Stiglitz 1975a). See Card other references for empirical evidence suggesting that at most this explains only part of the wage differences.

higher—something that would not occur in a perfectly competitive labor market, where wages are driven by opportunity costs?

Efficiency wage theory provides one possible explanation. In more productive firms it may be harder to measure any individual's contribution. Hence, it is more important to provide a strong incentive not to shirk (interpreting that in the broadest sense, including exerting due effort at the duties that have been assigned). If, moreover, there are higher turnover costs (workers are not replaceable parts in an assembly line, e.g., it is expensive to create a research team and to replace any member who has departed) then firms will pay higher wages to induce workers not to leave (e.g., for a firm with more attractive non-pecuniary attributes).[30]

There is a related reason that may be relevant for many such firms, especially those relying on intellectual property or engaged in borderline nefarious practices (umbrellas that brings within its ambit a large fraction of highly profitable firms). Even with non-compete clauses, information about what is going on inside the firm can leak out, and such information can be deleterious to the long-term well-being of the firm or its senior management. So too, many of the reasons that a firm is doing well are not "patentable." Departing personnel may carry this information with them and make use of it to profit themselves and their new employers, at the expense of their current employer. This is especially true of the mechanisms by which firms with market power exercise their market power and increase profits by exploiting consumers. Much of the market power in certain sectors of the economy is not so much related to patentable product innovation but to "innovations" in marketing and contracting. The greater the profitability of the firm, the more it stands to lose from turnover of key personnel, who carry with them this knowledge.

More broadly, morale is important in all firms, but it may be especially important in those firms attempting to strive to maintain a competitive edge over their rivals, and especially so in the more dynamic sectors of the economy. Morale is affected by perceptions of fairness (Akerlof and Yellen, 1990),[31] and that can be affected by relative wages—relative to profits and relative to that received by senior management.

On the other hand, if a firm is heading toward bankruptcy, the value of lower turnover or better morale is much lower. These firms thus pay lower wages not only because they cannot "afford" to pay higher wages, but also because it is not optimal for them to do so. The fact that they can retain labor while paying lower wages is as much testimony to labor market imperfections as the fact that profitable firms seem to be paying more than necessary.[32]

All of these arguments imply that, at the margin, it will pay for highly profitable firms to pay higher wages for worker, and less profitable firms lower wages.

[30] See Stiglitz (1974c, 1985b), Arnott and Stiglitz (1985).

[31] In my original working paper on efficiency wages, Institute of Development Studies, Nairobi, 1969, I laid out four explanations, going beyond nutrition: labor turnover, morale, incentives, and selection.

[32] It also reinforces the view that there may be measurement problems. A firm contemplating hiring a low paid worker that (on the basis of observable data) seems underpaid would naturally suspect that there is some hidden characteristic. A firm making such an offer knows that it will suffer from a winner's curse problem: it will only succeed in recruiting the worker when the wage offered exceeds his productivity; otherwise, the existing firm will match the offer. In short, adverse selection (lemons) problems are intrinsic in labor markets—all previously employed workers are "used" workers. See Greenwald (1979, 1986); Stiglitz (1982f), Nalebuff and Stiglitz (1985), and Nalebuff, Rodriguez, and Stiglitz (1993). Thus, labor market imperfections—immobility of labor—is an intrinsic consequence of information asymmetries of the adverse selection form.

These arguments are reinforced by managerial theories of the firm (theories in which managers have considerable discretion).[33] Life is easier for managers if workers are happier and well-motivated. It is executives that make the decisions about wages; shareholders bear the costs of higher wages; but much of the benefits of keeping workers happy—making the life of the manager easier—are received by executives.[34]

In short, in an economy marked by more monopoly power, firms will have higher profits, and some of those profits will be shared by workers—not just the top management, but throughout the firm. Workers lucky enough to work at those firms will wind up better off; and even more so for the executives in those firms.

Because of costly search and information-based imperfections in labor markets, those in low paying firms can't easily move to higher paying firms.[35] Wage differentials may persist (Stiglitz, 1985a).

5.3 Vertical Disintegration

Management, of course, may act to limit the extent of rent sharing, by engaging in vertical disintegration. Workers may be more sensitive to their pay relative to others in the same firm than to others in different firms. This may be partially because they may ascribe some of the differences in wages received by similar workers in other firms to unobservable variables that represent a fair basis of differentiation: the firm may be in a more difficult financial position, or the working conditions may be poorer or promotion possibilities weaker.

There is an old theory of the boundaries of firms, based on Coase's work on transactions costs (Coase, 1937). But our analysis provides another theory: creating distance through vertical disintegration between workers in different parts of the value-creation chain allows greater opportunities for wage differentiation, and for a larger fraction of the value added to be seized by "upstream" parts of the production process, including those involved in design, innovation, and the overall management of the production process.[36]

[33] Older formulations of these theories (Berle and Means 1932) were based on institutional analysis. More recent developments, including those of March and Simon (1958), Stiglitz (1985a), and Simon (1991), derived managerial delegation from theories of imperfect information.

[34] Of course, firms may establish countervailing incentives, e.g. paying executives on the basis of profits (though that is more a "narrative" sold by CEOs). The incentive pay schemes are not well designed. See Stiglitz (2012a).

[35] Not only may it be difficult for individuals to find these higher paying firms, there are important imperfections of information on both sides of the market: Efficiency wage arguments explain why, because of adverse selection problems, firms may rightly be suspicious of individuals who are willing to work at lower wages; and similarly, individuals may rightly be suspicious of firms who are willing to pay higher wages.

In the absence of these barriers to mobility, presumably firms where efficiency wage effects were more important would auction off jobs—workers would pay for the "right" to receive higher efficiency wages. The possibility (reflected not so much in a real auction, but a period in which workers get paid less than they might get elsewhere) emphasizes that one needs to take a lifetime perspective in assessing wage differences. More to the point, limitations in wealth (individuals may not have the resources to bid up front for jobs) and the double-moral hazard problem (firms may, after they receive the money up-front, fire the worker) mean that such job auctions cannot fully resolve the problem of wage differentials to which efficiency wages give rise, just as the provision of collateral cannot fully resolve the problems to which adverse selection and incentives give rise in credit markets. See Stiglitz and Weiss (1986),

[36] Stiglitz and Greenwald (2014) provide still another theory: that information moves more freely within a firm, and the optimal size of the firm balances these benefits with the diseconomies of scale and scope.

6 Political Equilibria

This book has emphasized that markets don't exist in a vacuum: the rules of the game are set in a political process, and these rules can have a large effect on the equilibrium level of inequality. But economic inequality gets translated into political inequality, implying that we have to analyze both simultaneously.

If we do this, we can again get multiple equilibria, as illustrated in Figure 16.2a. On the horizontal axis we have a measure of inequality. On the vertical axis we have a measure of some inequality increasing policy, such as the degree of regressivity of the tax system or the effectiveness of enforcement of antitrust laws, or the extent of trade liberalization. Since this chapter focuses on rents, it is natural for us to focus on the effectiveness of the enforcement of competition. There is considerable evidence that what matters in politics is not the median voter (the person in the middle), as in classical voting theory, where, say, half vote for more spending, half vote for less, half vote for more liberal policies, half vote for less.

There are two key ideas: money matters in politics (not only through campaign contributions, but through lobbying, revolving doors, control of the media, so they can better disseminate their views and influence public opinion); and the rich have both more incentive and more ability to spend money to get candidates and policies that advocate their interests. They have more to protect. Moreover, political action is a classical public good—policies that are pro-rich benefit all, or at least most, of the rich. But the magnitude of the collective action problem is less, since the benefits and costs are more concentrated.

Not surprisingly, then, even in democratic societies, politicians pay more attention to the concerns of the better off.[37] In more economically unequal societies, with more of the income and wealth at the top, the policies adopted reflect the perspectives and interests of the top (not always, but by and large). And in many arenas, there are marked differences in economic interests (again, on average, because beliefs matter as well as interests; some of the rich believe in a society with shared prosperity and are disturbed by excesses of inequality). Thus, the rich tend to support liberalization, because they benefit more from it and are better able to handle the resulting risk (because they are better able and more willing to bear risk, making the usual assumption that risk aversion declines with wealth), so when their voice is heard more loudly, the political process will enact greater liberalization on average. So too for issues like more progressive taxes or more effective enforcement of antitrust laws. We do not have to formalize precisely the political system. We only have to make the reasonable assumptions that political power is unequally distributed, with (i) the rich having *disproportionate* power and (ii) an increase in the income of the rich relative to the rest increases their power, so that in a polity with more inequality, outcomes reflect more the preferences of the rich.

[37] See Bartels (2008), McElwee (2016), and Gilens and Page (2016, 2017). This is hardly surprising: so much money could not rationally be spent on political activity if it didn't have *some* effect. That doesn't mean, of course, that the wealthy always get their way.

Figure 16.2a illustrates the two-sided relationship between inequality and antitrust enforcement. The weaker antitrust enforcement (measured along the vertical axis), the greater inequality (measured along the horizontal axis.)[38] Hence we can write:

$$G = \Phi(L), with\ \Phi' > 0. \tag{16.27}$$

where G is a measure of inequality (G stands for Gini coefficient, a standard measure of inequality) and the *weakness* of antitrust laws is given by L[39], that is, a higher value of L means a weaker set of antitrust laws.

On the other hand, the greater inequality, the greater the "effective demand" for weak enforcement. (That is, a transfer of wealth from the poor and middle class to the rich, leading to more inequality, implies a political equilibrium in which there is weaker enforcement of antitrust laws (more liberalization, less progressive taxation).)

$$L = \psi(G), \psi' > 0. \tag{16.28}$$

Equation (16.28) assumes that increasing inequality increases the power of the rich, so that the outcome that emerges is more attuned to their preferences. This may be particularly plausible if the rich are able to persuade the rest that the change will increase the incomes of all, either directly or through some version of trickle-down economics. (Large companies can serve as national champions from which all benefit; large companies can engage in more research from which all benefit; greater liberalization will lead to faster growth from which all will benefit, etc.)[40]

The political and economic equilibrium is the simultaneous solution to Equations (16.27) and (16.28). (See Figure 16.2a.) Since both $\psi' > 0$ and $\varphi' > 0$, with no strong a priori restrictions on the shape, there can exist multiple equilibria: a highly competitive economy, where there is a low level of inequality, and where the low level of inequality provides the necessary political support to sustain the high level of competition, and an economy with a low level of competition, where there is a high level of inequality, and where the high level of inequality provides the necessary political support to sustain the low level of antitrust enforcement. (In the previous sentence, one can substitute any inequality generating measure: a regressive tax system leads to more inequality (as we showed in Chapter 12), and that provides the political support for regressivity; while a progressive tax system leads to a low level of inequality, which generates the necessary political support for progressivity; a high level of liberalization leads to more inequality and that provides the political support for maintaining that level of liberalization.)

[38] Similar arguments apply to other inequality-increasing policies. Liberalization is associated with more volatility, and volatility increases the income of the rich disproportionately, as it increases the risk premium, which goes disproportionately to the rich.

[39] Again, a similar analysis applies to any other inequality-increasing policy. Thus L can also be thought of as referring to the level of liberalization,

[40] The benefits of weaker antitrust enforcement are concentrated among the rich, and the corporations which would benefit are likely to be very aware of these benefits; while the costs among the result of society are diffuse, with individuals much less aware of these costs. The higher the level of inequality, the more concentrated the benefits of weaker antitrust enforcement and the more diffuse the costs.

6.1 The Interaction between Changes in Economic Structure and Policies

Policies and circumstances interact. An exogenous change in the structure of the economy, such that at a given set of rules (e.g., concerning competition) inequality increases, for example because there is more market power the level of inequality will have increased; and that in turn means that the *equilibrium* level of inequality will have increased and the level of enforcement of antitrust laws will have decreased (see Figure 16.2b). One might have thought that the changed structure of the economy—where competition is weaker at any given set of rules—would have led to stronger rules. But politics dominates economics: the greater inequality that results means that the rich take advantage of this new situation to weaken the antitrust laws further, resulting in still more inequality.

So too, if beliefs (among the rich) about the benefits of trade liberalization or weaker antitrust enforcement for them increase, then at any level of inequality, their "demand" for such measures will increase, and the equilibrium level of inequality and inequality generating policies will increase. Moreover, the rich may be able to persuade others that antitrust laws are less necessary in a more open economy, so that at any level of inequality, the political "demand" for antitrust enforcement is weaker, and this too will lead to more inequality and weaker antitrust enforcement.[41] Figure 16.2c illustrates the converse situation where the political power of the rich has been diminished, so that the "effective

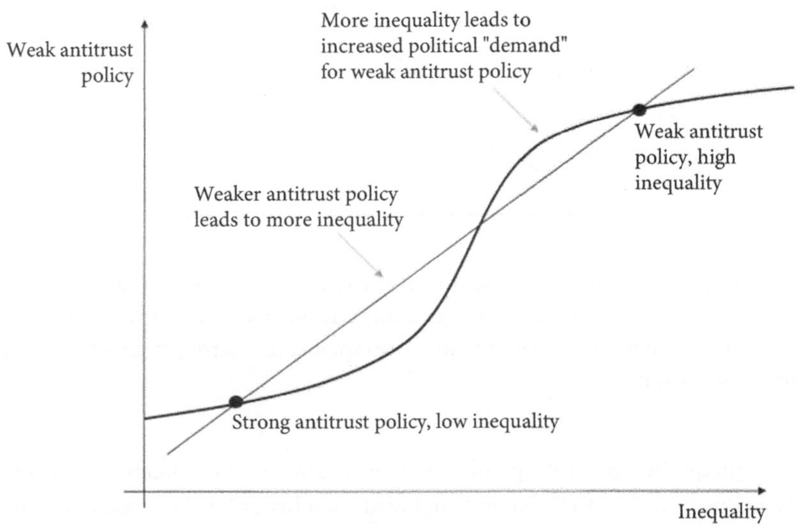

Figure 16.2a Endogenous Political Equilibria. On horizontal axis we have a measure of inequality. On the vertical axis we have a measure of the weakness of competition enforcement (or any other inequality increasing policy, such as the degree of regressivity of the tax system). With more inequality, the political equilibrium entails policies resulting in weaker antitrust enforcement (greater risk and a higher risk premium). But weaker antitrust enforcement is associated with more inequality. There may be multiple equilibria, where the two curves intersect.

[41] Mathematically, the level of inequality is a function of all of the policies, and each of the policies is themselves a function of the other policies and inequality. Changes in the structure of the economy or polity or beliefs about these relationships obviously affect the equilibrium which emerges.

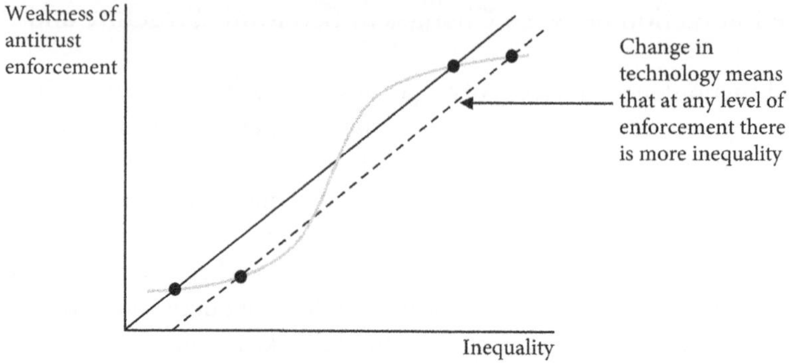

Figure 16.2b Impact of a change in the structure of the economy which results in more inequality (less competition) with any given set of competition rules. The rightward shift of the 'light' line leads to a new equilibrium with more inequality and weaker antitrust enforcement in the stable equilibrium.

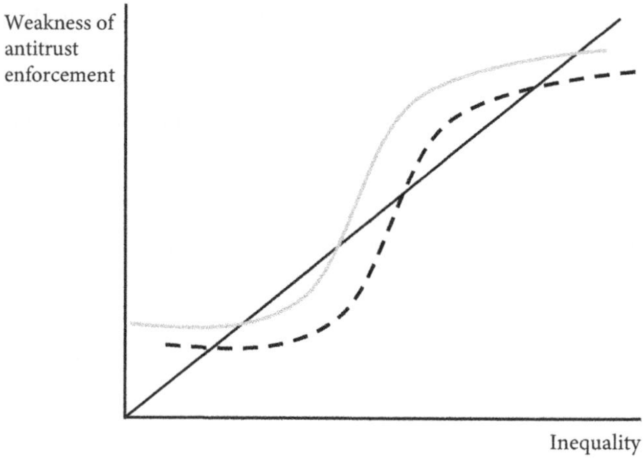

Figure 16.2c Impact of a change in the political structure—making money matter less—results in more equality and stronger competition laws. The leftward shift of the dashed line leads to a new equilibrium with more equality and stronger antitrust enforcement in the stable equilibrium.

demand" for inequality-generating policies (like lax anti-trust enforcement), at any level of inequality, is lowered. Not surprisingly, that leads to a lower level of inequality (in a stable equilibrium) and a higher level of antitrust enforcement (less of the inequality-generating policy). Democratization shifts the $\psi(I)$ curve down and makes it flatter, resulting in a more egalitarian, and a more competitive market economy.

6.2 The Economic Value of Democracy

The relationship between inequality and political support for competition policy depends, of course, on the nature of democracy. In a "true" one person one vote democracy, wealth doesn't matter, and accordingly, $\psi'(I)$ is small, and there may be a unique equilibrium—with a high level of competition and a low level of inequality.

This chapter has illustrated how there can be multiple economic and political equilibria. We have emphasized that these equilibria differ in the level of inequality. But they are likely to differ in many other ways. For instance, in the context of the transition from Communism to a market economy, Hoff and Stiglitz (2004) explored two different equilibria which might emerge, one with the rule of law and one without; GDP could be much higher in the former than the latter, and yet the inefficient system could persist. It was an equilibrium. In the no rule of law equilibrium, those who benefited from the lack of a rule of law prospered—those who are good at stealing (taking advantage of weaknesses in corporate governance law) do well, sufficiently well that they can predominate in the political process to ensure that, politically, the no rule of law equilibrium persisted. This was so in spite of the fact that there was another equilibrium with a rule of law, where those who had a comparative advantage in creating wealth under a rule of law prevailed, and they supported the rule of law political equilibrium.

In democracies where money matters, the moneyed interests may similarly support policies which lead to a less vibrant economy—lower taxes with less investment in education, infrastructure, and technology and more scope for rent-seeking. Here, we are particularly concerned with the stringency of antitrust laws and their enforcement.

A political equilibrium may emerge marked by high inequality and weak competition policies. The resulting monopoly-oligopolistic equilibrium may entail low levels of innovation[42] and weak aggregate demand, both because investment is low in such an equilibrium and so is consumption. This is especially so because the active fiscal and monetary policies that might restore the economy to full employment are opposed by the wealthy: a strong government might not just use its power to restore the economy to full employment, but also to redistribute. In short, capitalism, without a strong check from democracy, may prove itself less dynamic and less efficient, with both macroeconomic and microeconomic distortions.

6.3 Increased Political Rents (Including IPR)

The term rent seeking originated in a political context: domestic industries sought protection from foreign competition through tariffs and quotas. These trade interventions increased firm profits—but it seemed better to refer to these profits simply as "rents" that they received as a result of the protection. It paid firms to lobby: the higher the tariffs, the more the rents.

Recent literature has expanded the use of the term rents, to embrace virtually any return not related to "effort."[43] Rent seeking entails seeking a larger fraction of a given economic pie, as opposed to returns from increasing the size of the economic pie.

[42] While there is some debate about the exact relationship between the level of competition and the level of innovation, there is some presumption that when competition is particularly weak, innovation will be low. See Stiglitz and Greenwald (2014, 2015), Stiglitz (2019a) and the references cited there, and Fudenberg, Gilbert, Stiglitz, and Tirole (1983).

[43] Though admittedly, tariffs and quotas arise from lobbying efforts, there is an obvious distinction between these "efforts" and productive efforts. On the other hand, intellectual property rents arise, at least to some extent, from the efforts directed at innovation. Thus, the returns to intellectual property are sometimes referred to as quasi-rents. The distinction is important, because taxing land rents has no effect on the amount of land; taxing pure political rents discourages such rent-seeking (with positive social benefits); while taxing intellectual property rents could discourage innovation, with possibly adverse social consequences. There is a large literature noting how various changes in the intellectual property laws may have simultaneously increased rents and decreased societal welfare, in some cases even decreasing the pace of innovation. See, e.g. Henry and Stiglitz (2010) and Stiglitz (2014c).

Such rents take on many forms—from direct gifts (agricultural subsidies) and tax benefits (e.g., associated with preferential treatment of capital gains or depletion allowances for natural resources), to paying more than market prices for some goods (the prohibition of U.S. government from negotiating competitive prices for drugs) to selling assets (like natural resources) at below competitive prices. Many rents are hidden (e.g., in the tax code or through the provision of insurance at below market prices, or in banks' access to funds at low interest rates from the Federal Reserve) or arise from protection from competition afforded through regulation. Some rents are an inevitable byproduct of even good regulation, for example those that arise from zoning or the construction of public transport; but even then, the government could capture much or all of the rents through appropriate taxation or auctions.

Earlier, we described the multiple economic/political equilibria that can arise—public policy can be set as to lead to more inequality, and more inequality leads to such public policies. One key set of policies are those that give rise to rents. Since the wealthy are better able to lobby for such rents and are more likely to own the corporations which successfully do so, this rent seeking is typically inequality increasing. Thus, in a country like the U.S. where money has a large role in politics, it is not a surprise to see a large amount of rent seeking and rents play such a large role in the economy.

Again, there may be multiple equilibria: high levels of economic inequality result in high levels of political inequality, which result in pro-inequality economic and political systems, and pro-inequality economic and political systems result in higher levels of inequality and high rents. A country like the U.S. can be trapped in the bad equilibrium. Others have been fortunate to be in a good equilibrium.

6.4 General Equilibrium Effects

Such multiple equilibria are especially likely to arise once we take into account general equilibrium effects. Assume, for instance, that some effort is required to achieve a lower tax rate—expenditures which are themselves not tax deductible. Assume a tax benefit b for an industry could be achieved through the expenditure of e, $b(e)$, with $b' > 0$. Assume too that the industry acts cooperatively in setting that effort to maximize industry after tax profits (where π gives the maximized value of profits at any level of benefits b, and π is assumed to strictly increase with b, i.e., $\pi = \pi(b)$, with $\pi' > 0$):[44]

$$\Pi = (1 - \tau)\pi(b(e)) - e, \tag{16.29}$$

where Π is total "net" industry profits, after taxes (where the profits tax rate is τ) and taking account of lobbying, yielding:[45]

$$(1 - \tau)\pi' b' = 1. \tag{16.30}$$

Industries, in determining their lobbying efforts, take the tax rate τ as given. The solution is denoted by b^*. The equilibrium level of benefits b^* is a function of τ. Under plausible

[44] We assume further that π is concave in e, i.e. $\pi'' b'^2 + \pi' b'' < 0$.

[45] What is essential in our formulation is that the lobbying efforts are not fully tax deductible; if they were, the solution to (16.10) would not depend on the tax rate.

restrictions on the profit and benefit (as a function of effort), b^* is a decreasing function of τ, that is, $b^* = b^*(\tau)$, with $b^{*\prime} < 0$. *It pays to put less effort into getting benefits when the tax rate is higher.*

Rents can be defined as the difference between what profits would have been at $b = 0$ and at b^*.

$$R = \Pi(b^*(\tau)) - \Pi(0) = R(\tau), \tag{16.31}$$

with $R' < 0$. (The social costs typically exceed R, i.e., the rents are worse than pure transfers.) It follows that *the higher the tax rate, the lower the rents.*

Now imagine an economy with many similarly situated industries, and assume they collectively lobby for the level of corporate income tax τ. The strength of their lobbying effort is related to the marginal benefit that they get out of a lower tax rate. The expected corporate income tax rate with a corporate lobbying effort of E is $\tau(E)$, $\tau' < 0$, $\tau'' < 0$. The corporate sector cooperates to maximize its net income,

$$(1 - \tau)\Pi(b^*) - E.$$

The optimal lobbying (where each sector takes its own benefits b^* as fixed) is given by

$$-\tau'(E)\Pi^* = -\tau'(E)[R + \Pi(0)] = 1. \tag{16.32}$$

The level of effort put into reducing the corporate tax rate is a function of the level of corporate rents, R, and naturally increases with the level of rents:[46]

$$d \ln E / d \ln R = R/\xi(R + \Pi(0)) > 0, \tag{16.33}$$

where $\xi = -d \ln \tau' / d \ln E > 0$. Thus, the corporate tax which emerges falls as the level of rents increases:

$$\begin{aligned} d \ln \tau / d \ln R &= (d \ln \tau / d \ln E)(d \ln E / d \ln R) = -\eta\, d \ln E / d \ln R \\ &= -\eta R/\xi(R + \Pi(0)) < 0 \end{aligned} \tag{16.34}$$

where $\eta = -d \ln \tau / d \ln E > 0$. The lower the rents, the higher the equilibrium corporate income tax rate.

The equilibrium is the simultaneous solution to (16.32) and (16.30), the levels of sectoral lobbying for special benefits e and the level of corporate sector lobbying E for a low corporate tax rate, generating simultaneously the equilibrium level of special benefits $b(e^*)$ and corporate tax rate $\tau(E^*)$. Once again, there can be multiple equilibria. When rents are low, the corporate sector agitates less for low tax rates, so the political equilibrium entails higher taxes; and when tax rates are high, the corporate sector engages in less rent seeking.[47]

[46] This is especially so because, as we have noted earlier, the corporate profits tax is, to a first approximation, *just* a tax on pure corporate profits, i.e., rents.

[47] Similar results have been obtained, in the context of a quite different model, by Piketty, Saez, and Stantcheva (2011, 2014).

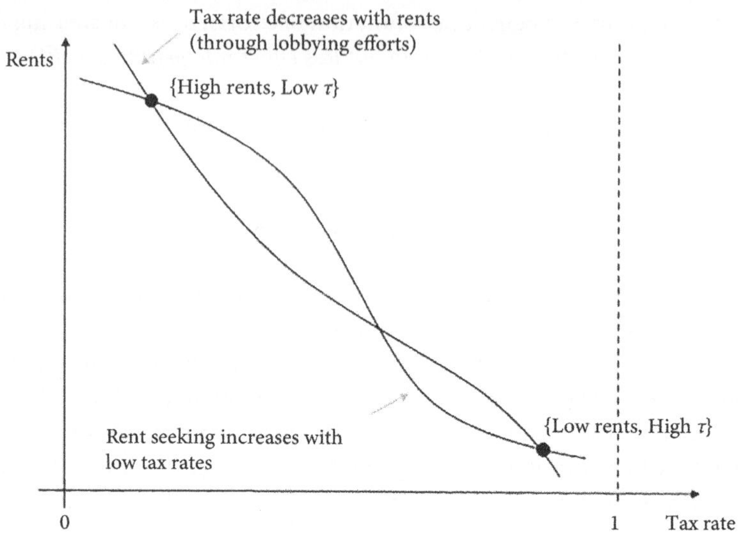

Figure 16.3 Endogenous Political Equilibria II. Higher tax rates lead to less lobbying for rents in each industry, and therefore lower rents. Higher rents lead to more lobbying for lower tax rates, and therefore lower tax rates. There can be multiple equilibria—a low tax rate, high rent equilibrium, and a high tax rate, low rent equilibrium.

And once again, the economy can be trapped in a bad equilibrium, with low (corporate) tax rates inducing high levels of rent seeking (Equation (16.30)); and high levels of rents inducing high levels of effort at lowering the corporate income tax—and achieving that (Equation (16.32)). Figure 16.3 illustrates.

Note that the same argument holds for strength of antitrust enforcement: if the corporate income tax rate is low, there will be a high level of lobbying for weak antitrust enforcement, which will give rise to high levels of monopoly rents, which will induce greater efforts at lobbying for low corporate income tax rates.

7 Concluding Comments

The fact that the capitalized value of rents accounts for much of the increase in wealth (at least relative to income) suggests that more attention should be given to the analysis of rents. Previous chapters analyzed land rents and showed how policies—like taxes on land rents—could lead to less inequality and higher incomes per capita. In a standard life-cycle model, land-wealth crowded out productive capital accumulation. Here, we focus on other sources of rents, and in particular those associated with market power, showing that they have even more adverse effects, both on living standards and inequality—more adverse than land-rents, and more adverse than suggested by traditional models of market power, because they combine the negative effects of both—a market distortion that lowers GDP and a crowding out of productive capital, so workers get a smaller share of a smaller pie. There are other sources of rents—most importantly, rents extracted from the public—and these have almost all surely played a role in the increase in inequality in the U.S. and other advanced countries. And these have also had adverse effects on standards of living, particularly of workers.

The models explored here are consistent with the stylized facts of Chapter 10—an increase in measured wealth per capita with relative stagnation or decreases in productive capital per capita (or per efficiency unit of labor) and in wages and an increase in inequality. Investment may be low even though (average) rates of return (especially if those include monopoly rents) are high.

We have explained why many of the changes in the structure of the economy in recent decades might naturally have led to an increase in market power and shown how some of the standard models of labor markets with imperfect information and contracting result in some of the resulting monopoly rents being shared with labor but shared inequitably. Competition within the labor market is sufficiently weak as to prevent the resulting "labor rents" from being competed away.

An underlying current in the models explored here is the role of policy. While there are economic forces at play which may be moving the economy toward an equilibrium with more inequality, there are changes in policies which could countervail these forces. Too often, changes in policy may, instead, have reinforced them.

We have explored the role that policies *could* play. In particular, we have presented models which show forcefully that the conventional wisdom of the Right (heard frequently in the debate over the 2017 corporate income tax cut in the U.S.) that reductions in the corporate profits tax stimulate investment and lead to increases in wages are wrong. An increase in corporate profits tax lowers rent-wealth, so there is *less* crowding out of productive capital. And the results obtained in Chapter 13, that in a two-class model with capitalists and life-cycle savers, a tax on capital redistributed to workers would hurt workers and could possibly increase inequality, because of an adverse incidence effect—capital accumulation and wages would be depressed—are reversed. At least for a small tax, workers are unambiguously better off, and wealth-inequality is unambiguously reduced. A fortiori, a tax on interest and on pure profits increases workers' well-being and reduces inequality.[48]

However, we have argued that one needs to see the policies themselves as part of the equilibrium. Policies are endogenous. There may be multiple political-economic equilibria—the economy can be caught in an equilibrium in which there is a high level of economic inequality, leading to politics which support economic rules which support the high level of economic inequality; but there is a "better" equilibrium in which there is a low level of

[48] We do not recapitulate all the central results of this chapter. Results for the standard life-cycle model are more complicated, because a tax on capital (interest) income reduces the discount rate, and thus at each value of capital, increases rent-wealth, displacing capital accumulation. If, however, market power is small enough then this effect is small enough, so that the standard result that a capital income tax distributed to workers increases capital accumulation holds (unless there is a very adverse effect on workers' savings rates). We also showed that if both an interest income and corporate profits tax are imposed, so long as the corporate profits tax rate is greater than the interest income tax, rent-wealth decreases; and that implies that if the proceeds are distributed to workers, wages and output both increase in the long run; or to put it slightly differently, capital accumulation and wages are increased, so long as the corporate profits tax rate is not too much less than the interest income tax rate.

inequality, and the politics supports policies which are consistent with this more egalitarian society. (We have not explored how one could move from the bad equilibrium to the good equilibrium.)

We have focused, in particular, on two policies which have a direct bearing on inequality. We have shown that economies with stronger competition laws may have a more equalitarian income distribution which supports these laws; and conversely for those with weaker competition laws and weaker enforcement. We have also shown that economies with more corporate rents (whether as a result of weak competition or of stronger lobbying for preferential benefits) will generate more lobbying for lower corporate tax rates; and that countries with low corporate tax rates will generate more lobbying for weak competition laws and more preferential benefits. There can again be multiple equilibria, one with a low corporate tax rate and low rents; another with a higher corporate tax rate and high rents. Obviously, inequality in the former will be greater than in the latter. In this perspective, low corporate tax rates help drive the increase in corporate rents.

Implicit in our analysis is the belief that perhaps, in those societies like the U.S. caught in an inequalitarian equilibrium, if members of society had a better understanding of what is occurring, they might take actions *within the given political rules of the game*, to move the economy toward economic rules that might succeed in moving society toward the good equilibrium. But, especially when inequality-increasing policies are concerned, it may take changes in the political rules of the game—decreasing the power of money in politics—to achieve an economic equilibrium with more competition and greater equality.

The consensus that emerged after the fall of the Berlin Wall, Fukuyama's "end of history" thesis (1992)—the belief that liberal democracies and a particular version of capitalism American style, the late twentieth variety with heavy doses of financialization and globalization and a limited role for government, would eventually triumph—has now eroded. The models of this chapter have helped explain why: that version of a market economy led, at least in some countries, to an economic and political equilibrium marked by increasing inequality and concentrations of market power. Overall growth rates fell. Large parts of society saw their incomes stagnate, as we saw in Chapter 4. Yet the growing inequality in a money-driven politics led to a politics that seemed to be inconsistent with anything that would emerge from a democratic one-person-one-vote system. Disillusion with the political and economic system grew.

Economists had long recognized that there were pervasive market failures, instances where markets on their own led to inefficiency. They had long recognized too that there was no presumption that the distribution of income that emerged from a market economy would be socially acceptable. Many have not, however, grasped that there are built-in dynamics in capitalism which might increase over time the extent of market failures, because as inequality grew, so too grew the ability of the state to correct these market failures. Firms could flourish not on the basis of being more efficient and innovative in producing products at lower cost and products that better met the needs of consumers, but on their ability to exploit others, including through the exercise of market power, whether that market power is a result of "natural" or man-made barriers to entry, or whether through taking advantage of natural or man-made asymmetries of information. For brevity, we refer to these enterprises as the rent-seekers.

But more telling, economists have typically taken the rules of the economic game as given, and haven't appreciated the potential consequences of the *interaction* of economic forces and politics: the increasing wealth of the rent seekers relative to the rest can lead to changes in the rules that favor these, over the rest of society, including the true wealth creators. The result is a less dynamic economy. Dynamic capitalism, on its own, may not be a stable system, and especially when combined with political regimes that don't actively curb the influence of money.[49] One way, perhaps the only way, of preventing this dystopia is creating a "true" democracy where money matters less: if those who are being exploited realize what is happening, they can then check these abusive practices, and restore a set of rules for the market economy that limits exploitation, thereby encouraging the success of the true wealth creators.[50] But better understandings may not be enough to move countries like the U.S. permanently away from their current situation. Wealth will inevitably matter to some extent, and if there is a high level of inequality, as in the U.S., it will somehow get reflected in the political process, and thus, over the long run, in the economic rules of the game. What may be required to move to a new, sustainable equilibrium with a lower level of inequality is *simultaneously* changing the economic rules—to curb, for instance, rent-seeking—*and* changing the political rules—to reduce the influence of money in politics—*and* reducing the current level of wealth inequality.

We have attempted to use the "benchmark models" of this and the previous five chapters to provide some insights into the marked increase in inequality in so many societies around the world. There are several general conclusions worth noting: There are multiple factors contributing to the growth of inequality; any attempt to reduce it significantly will accordingly have to be multi-faceted. Simplistic solutions often heard in political discourse, such as increasing education, while necessary, will not suffice. It will take major actions, significant changes to the economic system, including diminishing the role of rents and reducing the forces for intergenerational transmission of advantage and disadvantage. Because, as we have argued here, so much of the growth of inequality is associated with rents, policies aimed at reducing those rents and appropriating more of the rents for public purpose and redistribution (e.g., through taxation) will simultaneously increase growth and efficiency and reduce inequality.

The one "defense" of monopoly is that provided by Schumpeter—that it leads to higher levels of innovation. He argued that monopolies were only temporary, that competition for the market, not competition in the market, was what was crucial and that competition for the market spurred innovation. Each of these contentions has been questioned: indeed, monopolies may discourage innovation; the monopolist may put himself ahead of potential

[49] In a sense, Adam Smith recognized this, when he observed in the *Wealth of Nations* (1776) both the tendency of those in any business to try to collude to raise prices ("People of the same trade seldom meet together, even for merriment and diversion, but the conversation ends in a conspiracy against the public, or in some contrivance to raise prices") and their ability to use their political influence to maintain their monopoly rents ("This monopoly has so much increased the number of some particular tribes of them, that, like an overgrown standing army, they have become formidable to the government, and upon many occasions intimidate the legislature.")

[50] I present this interpretation more fully in Stiglitz (2019b). While conventional economists have, for the most part, ignored these interactions, they are, of course, at the center of discussions of political economy and economic sociologists. For an excellent parallel discussion, see Block (2018).

competitors just enough to ensure that they cannot leapfrog over him.[51] Innovators may create barriers to entry, including through use and abuse of the patent system,[52] that give rise to the monopoly rents which in turn are associated with inequality, as we have explored in this chapter.

But innovation may also give rise other sources of inequality, as it decreases the demand for labor, especially unskilled labor. This is the subject to which we turn in the next chapter.

[51] See Dasgupta and Stiglitz (1980b), Fudenberg, Gilbert, Stiglitz, and Tirole (1983), Stiglitz (2010e, 1987c), and Stiglitz and Greenwald (2014) and the references cited there.

[52] See, for example, Stiglitz (2008b), Henry and Stiglitz (2010), and Dosi and Stiglitz (2014).

17
Innovation and Inequality

1 Introduction

While there has long been a presumption among economists that innovations represent a societal Pareto improvement, historically, there have often been instances in which significant groups within societies have resisted innovation, and they have done so because they believe that these changes will make them worse off.[1] Most notable in this regard were the Luddites in the beginning of the nineteenth century, who saw modern machines as leading to unemployment and impoverishment.

While increases in productivity could *in principle* make everyone better off—the production possibilities curve moves out—in practice there are always winners and losers. The market equilibrium may change so that wages of certain classes of workers, such as the unskilled, fall, while other factor prices increases; some workers may face high costs in moving from one job to another, with extended periods of unemployment in the transition; some never recover their former wages; and still others never get a job.

More recently, it has been shown that with market imperfections and societal rigidities—including costs of workers moving from one location or one job to another, all (or at least most) groups in society can be worse off.[2] In the 1920s, productivity increases in agriculture were so large—especially given the inelasticity of demand for agricultural goods—that incomes in the sector declined. With perfect mobility, the surplus agricultural workers would have moved into the urban sector. But there are significant costs to the mobility of labor, and with wages in agriculture declining and the value of rural assets (like houses) declining as well, many in that sector couldn't afford to move to the city and obtain the skills that would make them productive there. Worse still, neither they nor the banks that provided credit anticipated these events. Hence, as incomes in the rural sector collapsed, those in that sector were left with a legacy of debt burdens and banks faced massive losses. The result was a marked decline in demand for urban goods—so great that incomes in the urban sector itself fell. Innovation may have helped precipitate the Great Depression.

[1] Much of this chapter is excerpted from Stiglitz (2006b). Other parts are drawn from Stiglitz (2014d); while a few results were presented at the AEA meetings in Philadelphia, in January 2018.

The former essay (Stiglitz 2006b) was written on the occasion of Paul Samuelson's 90th birthday. I had the good fortune of being asked to write a preface for *Paul Samuleson: On Being an Economist* (Szenberg, Gottesman, and Ramrattan 2015), in which I describe my days as a student of Paul Samuelson and my huge indebtedness to Paul—and the indebtedness of my fellow students and the entire economics profession.

One of the many topics in which Samuelson made important contributions was on the bias of technological progress—whether it was labor or capital augmenting. (Samuelson, 1965). In this work, he was much engaged in the on-going discussion of the time, with work by Kennedy (1964) and Von Weizsäcker (1966). These works had been preceded by other work, both theoretical and historical, on factor bias, for example by Salter (1960), Fellner (1961), and Habakkuk (1962).

[2] See Delli Gatti, Gallegati, Greenwald, et al., 2012a, 2012b.

The Origins of Inequality, and Policies to Contain It. Joseph E. Stiglitz, Oxford University Press. © Joseph E. Stiglitz (2025).
DOI: 10.1093/oso/9780198799580.003.0018

By the same token, more recently, improvements in productivity in manufacturing and increased imports of manufacturing goods produced by cheap labor—which in the standard theory should have made society better off—led to decreased employment and wages in that sector and contributed to economic weakness in the decades after 1980.

Innovation requires economic restructuring, and markets often do not manage such restructurings well. But as firms make decisions that affect the pace and direction of innovation, they do not take these general equilibrium consequences into account. Each small firm takes the course of wages and unemployment, for instance, as given; but collectively, as they make their innovation decisions, they affect the evolution of wages and unemployment. Unfettered and undirected markets may result in patterns of production and innovation that result in more inequality and higher unemployment than is socially desirable. There are other patterns that would enhance societal well-being.

These results should not come as a surprise, for they reflect the general proposition that there are marked discrepancies between private rewards and social returns, especially when it comes to innovation and/or when there are imperfections of information[3] and incomplete markets—that is, always (Greenwald and Stiglitz, 1986; Stiglitz and Greenwald, 2014).

In this chapter, I construct a simple model examining the factor bias of technological change (i.e., the extent to which it is labor- or capital-augmenting, or skilled- or unskilled-biased), to show that the market solution is not Pareto efficient. In the particular model examined here, we establish that there is excessive labor-saving technological change, and that the equilibrium unemployment rate that emerges is too high. We also demonstrate a fundamental instability in the equilibrium dynamics when the elasticity of substitution is greater than unity: while there is a steady state equilibrium, it is a saddle-point, and slight deviations from the convergence path can lead to extreme outcomes.

Economic historians, such as Salter (1962) and Habakkuk (1962), had discussed such issues earlier, arguing that it was a shortage of labor that motivated labor-saving innovations, for example, in America. Of course, in standard neoclassical economics, there is no such thing as a shortage—demand equals supply. One might be tempted to say what they meant to say was "high" wages. But what does that even mean? Of course, with productivity increases, wages are high, but not relative to productivity.

Once we get out of the neoclassical paradigm, of course, markets may be characterized by "tightness" or "looseness." There can be unemployment. Firms may have a hard time finding employees. Moreover, if the unemployment rate is low, workers are more likely to leave, so firms face high turnover costs; what matters is not just the wage, but total labor costs. Worse still, if the unemployment rate is low, workers may shirk—the penalty for getting caught is low. (Shapiro and Stiglitz, 1984). Some economies are plagued by labor strife, again increasing the total cost of labor. Management, in particular, may feel these costs. One of the motivations for the model below is to try to capture, even if imperfectly, what drives firms' decisions concerning the direction of innovation.

The rest of this chapter is divided into five sections. Section 2 introduces the basic model where production coefficients are fixed, and shows that endogenous changes in technology

[3] Information can be thought of as a particular form of knowledge, and virtually all the principles of the economics of information apply to the economics of knowledge, for example information and knowledge are public goods (in the sense defined by Samuelson (1954)). For an early exploration of the similarity between the two, see Stiglitz (1975c).

provide an alternative way of reconciling the conundrum presented by Harrod and Domar of the disparity between the warranted and natural rate of growth than that provided by Solow, based on adjustments in the techniques of production. We show that the dynamic path may be oscillatory, instead of the kind of smooth convergence obtained in most standard growth models. Section 3 extends the analysis to a standard neoclassical economy, with full employment, but where there is both a choice of technique today and a choice of the factor bias of technological change, showing that there may be multiple long run equilibria, and that if the elasticity of substitution is greater than unity, the "standard" long-run equilibrium will be unstable, while if the elasticity of substitution is less than unity, it is stable but convergence is oscillatory. Section 4 combines the analysis of the previous two sections showing in particular that the choice of the direction of technological change is not efficient, while Section 5 extends the analysis to incorporate skill-biased technological change. The concluding section provides alternative interpretations of the model and discusses the implications for inequality and policy.

2 A Simple Model of Innovation and Distribution

The dynamics of the economy—including savings, labor force growth, and the factor bias of technological change—clearly affect whether labor markets are tight; but this in turn affects the factor bias of technological change.[4] There is a complex simultaneity, which this chapter attempts to unravel. The early beginnings of growth theory derive from the basic model of Harrod and Domar, where there was a fixed capital–output ratio, *a*. With savings, *s*, a fixed fraction of output (income),[5]

$$I = sQ = \frac{dK}{dt}, \tag{17.1}$$

where Q is output and K is the capital stock, so the rate of growth of capital is

$$\frac{d\ln K}{dt} = \frac{sQ}{K} = \frac{s}{a}, \tag{17.2}$$

where a is the capital required per unit of output. Moreover, as machines become more efficient, each machine requires less labor, so the number of jobs created goes up more slowly than the capital stock. If

$$\frac{L}{Q} = b \tag{17.3}$$

is the labor requirement per unit output, then $\frac{b}{a}$ is the labor required per unit capital, and job growth is

$$\frac{d\ln L}{dt} = \frac{s}{a} - \beta - \alpha, \tag{17.4}$$

[4] Two parts of this nexus, that between wages and capital accumulation, are explored below in Chapter 29, based on Akerlof and Stiglitz (1969).

[5] As in the case of the other models explored in this book, it is easy to provide microfoundations for this assumption and to extend these results to more general savings functions.

where

$$-\frac{d\ln b}{dt} = \beta, \tag{17.5}$$

and

$$\frac{d\ln a}{dt} = \alpha. \tag{17.6}$$

$\frac{s}{a}$ is sometimes referred to as the warranted rate of growth, what the system would support in the absence of innovation. Once technological change is incorporated, the warranted rate of growth is modified to $\frac{s}{a} - \beta - \alpha$. By contrast, if labor is assumed to grow at an exogenous rate, n, there is a problem: In general, n is not equal to $\frac{s}{a} - \beta - \alpha$.

If (in the model without technological change), $\frac{s}{a} < n$, unemployment would grow continually; and if $\frac{s}{a} > n$, eventually the economy would reach full employment—after which it would be profitable to invest only enough to keep full employment, an amount less than $\frac{s}{a}$.

The "dilemma" was resolved by Solow (1956), who proposed that the capital–output ratio depended on the capital–labor ratio, $k : a(k)$, which could and would adjust. The micro-foundations are straightforward: if there were unemployment, wages would fall, inducing a lower value of k and hence a high value of a. In long-run equilibrium (upon which Solow focused) $s = a(k)\,n$, determining the equilibrium value of k.

The analysis with technological change was similar. The rate of technological change was assumed given and it was assumed that it was purely labor-augmenting—so one worker now could do what two workers used to do. In equilibrium

$$\frac{s}{a(k^*)} = n + \beta. \tag{17.7}$$

There is a capital–labor ratio such that capital and effective labor (the demand for jobs and the supply of labor) grow precisely at the same rate.

The problem with Solow's "solution" is that it does away with the very concept of a job; alternatively, if there were ever a job shortage, simply by lowering the wage, more jobs would be created until the economy reached full employment. In developing countries, this means there is never a capital shortage; if there is unemployment, it must simply be because wages are too high. By the same token, there is never "technological unemployment." Technology may reduce the demand for labor at a particular wage, but whatever technology does, wage adjustments can undo. In practice, of course, at least in the short run, there is not such flexibility.[6]

In this section of this chapter, we take seriously the notion of jobs (perhaps more seriously than the concept should be taken). Given today's technology and capital stock, wage adjustments will not lead to full employment. There is a maximum employment which they can support.

[6] Standard models have formalized this in the notion of putty-clay models in which after investments have been made, the ability to change its characteristics (the labor required to work it) is very limited. Dynamics of growth in putty-clay models are markedly different from those of standard neoclassical models. See Cass and Stiglitz (1969) and the references cited there. Unfortunately, the models were not easy to work with, and the distinction seems to have been lost in discussions of growth in recent decades.

In the model here, it is the combination of changes in capital stock and technology which drive changes in employment. Wages make a difference, through their effects on technology and possibly capital accumulation. In short, we construct a model where, over time, technological change leads to either increases or decreases in the capital–output ratio, so that *eventually*

$$\frac{s}{a^*} = n + \beta^*, \tag{17.8}$$

that is,

$$a = a^* = \frac{s}{n}. \tag{17.9}$$

It is technological change that ensures that jobs grow at the same rate as the labor force. The problem with standard versions of the fixed coefficients model (where, at any moment of time, a and b are fixed) is that the distribution of income is very fragile: if N is the supply of labor and L is the demand,

$$L = \left(\frac{L}{Y}\right)\left(\frac{Y}{K}\right)K = \left(\frac{b}{a}\right)K \tag{17.10}$$

$$\text{If } \left(\frac{b}{a}\right)K < N, \text{ then } w = 0$$

$$\text{If } \left(\frac{b}{a}\right)K > N, \text{ then } r = 0,$$

where w = (real) wage, r = (real) return on capital, or equivalently, the rental cost of machines. If $\left(\frac{b}{a}\right)K = N$, the distribution of income is indeterminate.

Here, however, we present an analysis based on an alternative theory of the determination of the distribution of income, based on agency theory (Shapiro and Stiglitz, 1984).[7] If workers are paid too low a wage, they prefer to shirk; there is the lowest wage which firms can pay at any unemployment rate to induce them not to shirk. That wage depends on the payment an unemployed worker receives, denoted w_{min}. We write this in simplified form as

$$w = f(v)\, w_{min}, \tag{17.11}$$

where v is the employment ratio,

$$v = \frac{L}{N} = \left(\frac{b}{a}\right)\left(\frac{K}{N}\right) \tag{17.12}$$

so

$$\frac{d \ln v}{dt} = \frac{s}{a} - n - \beta - \alpha. \tag{17.13}$$

[7] Similar results obtain in models where wages are determining through bargaining.

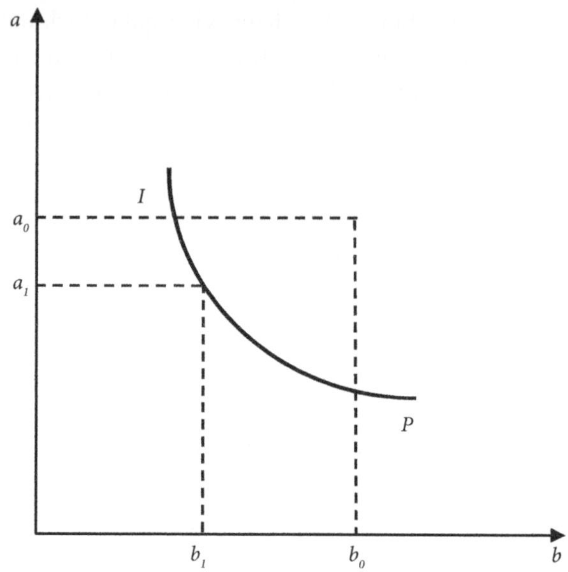

Figure 17.1a Given today's technology giving the labor and capital required per unit of output, $\{a_o, b_o\}$, the firm can choose how to innovate, whether to lower the labor or capital requirements more. Next period's possibilities are given by the curve IP. Of course, each of those points determines the possibilities for technologies the period after, and so on.

Finally, firms have a choice of innovations. (As in Solow, we assume the overall pace of innovation is fixed; here we simply endogenize the direction of innovation. It is straightforward to endogenize both the rate and direction of innovation, but little is added to the analysis here.[8]) Total cost of production per unit output, c, is

$$c = ar + bw. \tag{17.14}$$

The firm has a given technology today $\{a_0, b_0\}$. It can, however, decide on the nature of the technology by which it can produce next period, $\{a_1, b_1\}$, and from there, the period after, and on so. Focusing just on period 1, the firm can invest lowering either the capital or labor requirements per unit of output, that is, there is *an innovation frontier*, such that $a_1 = \psi(b_1)$, with $\psi' < 0$.

Figure 17.1a shows the original point, and its opportunity set, the locus of points which (given the *technology of change*) it can achieve next period.[9]

Assume, for simplicity, that the nature of technology diffusion is such that after one period, all knowledge is diffused—that is everyone knows the best technology available.[10]

[8] Since the early work of Salter (1960), Fellner (1961), Habakkuk (1962), Kennedy (1964), and Von Weizsäcker (1966), cited earlier, there have been a host of studies of induced innovation focusing on its factor bias, including Drandakis and Phelps (1966), Ahmad (1966), and Acemoglu (1998, 2002, 2010). While some of the more recent literature has deepened insights into the possible relationships between consumption and investment sectors and induced innovation, but at the cost of substantial increase in complexity, which in turn has necessitated the use of restrictive parameterizations. As always in modeling, there are trade-offs.

[9] Next period's technological opportunity set will, of course, depend on the choices made this year. History matters. This is, of course, the framework that Atkinson and I set forth in our 1969 paper.

[10] As noted earlier, at any point of time, the representative firm has a given technology, defined by {a, b}. Its choice is about its technology next period. Its choice is affected by wages prevailing then and in the future. Hence,

The firm forms expectations of the rental cost of machines r_1 and wages w_1, and seeks to minimize next period's costs

$$\min c = \{\psi(b_1) r_1 + b_1 w_1\},$$

taking r_1 and w_1 as given, unaffected by what it does. (Of course, the collective actions do affect next period's wages.)

Redoing this in continuous time, with wages and interest rates moving continuously, the rate of decrease in costs is given by

$$\frac{d \ln c}{dt} = \alpha m - \beta (1 - m), \tag{17.15}$$

where m is the share of capital in costs, or, equivalently in this model, the share of capital in income:

$$m = ar = \frac{rK}{Y}. \tag{17.16}$$

Now, the technology innovation frontier takes the form of specifying the trade-off between the *rate* of labor and capital augmenting progress (increases in the productivity of labor and capital),

$$\alpha = Z(\beta), Z' > 0, Z' < 0 \tag{17.17}$$

as depicted in Figure 17.1b. Then it is straightforward to show that the rate of cost reductions is maximized when

$$Z'(\beta) = \frac{1 - m}{m}, \tag{17.18}$$

where each firm takes factor prices as given. The slope of the cost function is equal to the relative shares. There is an increase in the growth of labor productivity when the labor share increases. For these purposes, the share of labor is the appropriate measure of the "scarcity" of labor. Of course, it is the total cost of labor *from the perspective of management* that matters, so that turnover costs and the costs of management of labor are included in the overall labor costs.

In the next two subsections, we analyze the dynamics of this simple model.

2.1 Steady State Equilibrium

We first describe the steady state equilibrium. We assume the unemployment compensation w_{min} increases with productivity. In the long run, we have argued that a must converge to a^*, which means that

in reality, what should matter for a firm is not just tomorrow's wage, but the entire wage profile. The full solution of this complicated dynamic programming problem is beyond the scope of this chapter. What emerges is identical to that described here, though the dynamics are somewhat more complicated. We avoid these complexities, however, by our assumption that information about technology becomes publicly available with a one period lag.

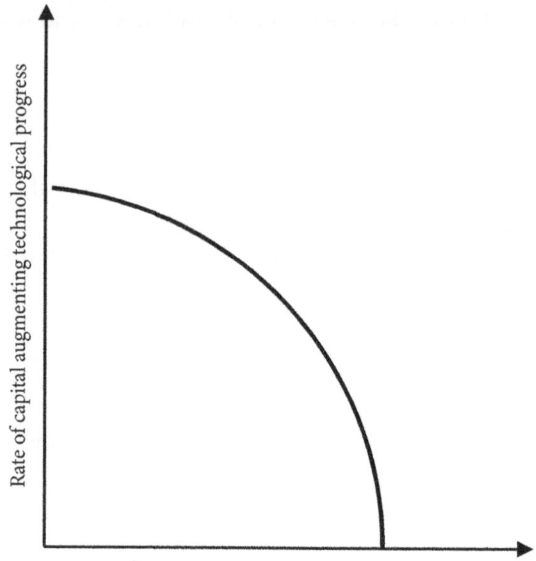

Figure 17.1b Innovation possibilities frontier. There is a trade-off between the rate of capital augmenting technological progress, α, and the rate of labor-augmenting technological progress, β. Throughout, we assume that the innovation possibilities curve cuts the horizontal axis, i.e. there is a value of β for which $\alpha = 0$. The value of β at which this occurs is denoted by β^*.

$$\alpha^* = 0, \tag{17.19}$$

which in turn means (using (17.18)) that β^* is such that

$$0 = Z(\beta^*) \tag{17.20}$$

and

$$Z(\beta^*) = \frac{1 - m^*}{m^*} \tag{17.21}$$

a^*, in turn, solves

$$\frac{s}{a^*} = n + \beta^* \tag{17.22}$$

We can similarly solve for the wage (conditional on productivity):

$$w^* b_0 = (1 - m^*) \tag{17.23}$$

Finally, we can use this to solve for the equilibrium unemployment rate:

$$\frac{w^*}{w_{\min}} = \left(\frac{w^* b_0}{b_0 w_{\min}}\right) = \left(\frac{1 - m^*}{b_0 w_{\min}}\right) = f(v^*). \tag{17.24}$$

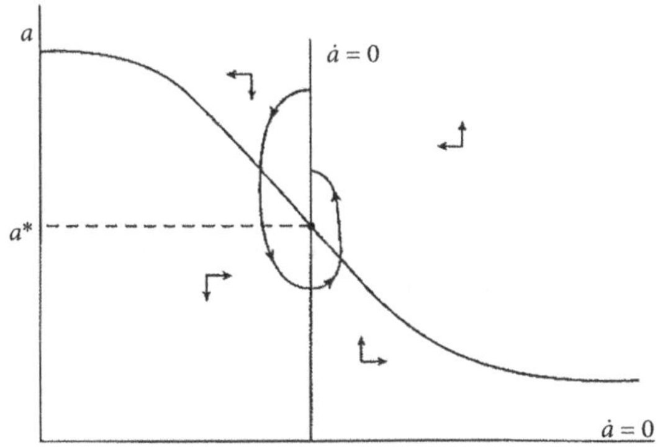

Figure 17.2 Dynamics of equilibrium. The economy converges to the unique steady state, but the convergence is oscillatory.

That is, once we set the unemployment compensation w_{min} relative to labor market productivity, then we know the unemployment rate and real wages.

2.2 Heuristic Dynamics

In this model, there is a simple adjustment process. If the capital–output ratio is too high, too few jobs will be created (given the savings rate) and unemployment grows. Growing unemployment means that wages will become depressed—in the story told here, firms can pay a lower wage without workers' shirking, but there are other stories (such as bargaining models) which yield much the same outcome. Lower wages mean, of course, that the return to capital is increased.

As wages get depressed, and labor becomes easier to hire, and the return (cost) of capital increases, firms seek ways of economizing on capital, and pay less attention to economizing on labor. The new technologies that are developed are capital saving and labor using. The capital–output ratio falls, and the labor–output ratio increases. Given the savings rate, more jobs are created, and the unemployment rate starts to fall.

2.3 Formal Dynamics

The convergence to equilibrium, however, may neither be direct nor fast. Figure 17.2 depicts the phase diagram, in $\{a, v\}$ space.

The locus of points for which $\frac{da}{dt} = 0$ is a vertical line, given by

$$v = v^*, \tag{17.25}$$

From Equations (17.24), (17.23), and (17.20), given $b_0 w_{min}$ (which we will take as set), there is a unique value of v^* for which $\alpha = 0$, that is, a is constant; and if

$$v > v^*, \frac{da}{dt} > 0.$$

$$v < v^*, \frac{da}{dt} < 0.$$

When employment is high, wages are high; firms economize on labor, and the capital–output ratio increases, and conversely when employment is low.

The locus of points for which $\frac{dv}{dt} = 0$ is the negatively sloped curve defined by

$$a = \frac{s}{n + \beta + \alpha}. \qquad (17.26)$$

And it is easy to show that below the curve, v is increasing, and above it, it is decreasing. We show a sample path converging through oscillations into the equilibrium.[11]

2.4 Microeconomics

As noted earlier, at any point of time, the representative firm has a given technology, defined by $\{a, b\}$. Its choice is about its technology next period. Under the assumptions we have set forth, the firm chooses the point on the feasibility locus that will minimize next period's cost, at expectations concerning next period's factor prices. Thus, what is relevant in the cost minimization described earlier are not current factor prices, but next period's factor prices; but in the continuous time formulation used here, there is no real difference.

In the more general case, where technology doesn't disseminate quickly, the firm will be concerned not only with how its choice of technology affects costs next period, but in subsequent periods. And of course, the costs of production in each of those subsequent periods are affected by wages prevailing then and in the future. Hence, when knowledge disseminates slowly, what should matter for a firm is not just tomorrow's wage, but the entire wage profile, and how this period's choices affect the technology opportunity sets in all subsequent periods. The full solution of this complicated dynamic programming problem is beyond the scope of this brief chapter. The steady state *equilibrium* which emerges is identical to that described here, though the dynamics are somewhat more complicated.

2.5 A Generalization

Earlier, we set forth the notion that what mattered in the choice of technology was not just factor prices, but the total cost of labor, including turnover costs, how hard it was to hire workers, etc. These variables too will, in general, be related to the unemployment rate, so that the point along the feasibility set chosen by the firm will depend not only on relative shares, which depend on v, but also on v directly:

[11] In the appendix to the original version of this paper (Stiglitz, 2006b), it is shown that cyclical convergence is the normal case.

$$\alpha = \phi(m(v), v). \tag{17.27}$$

Equilibrium still requires that

$$\alpha = 0, \beta = \beta^* = \beta(0) \tag{17.28}$$

and so $a = a^*$. Indeed, once we set the policy variable $(b_0 w_{min})$, the analysis is changed little, except now, using Equation (17.24), m^* is defined by

$$0 = \phi(m, v) = \phi(m^*, f^{-1}(1 - m^*)/b_0 w_{min})). \tag{17.29}$$

2.6 A Kaldorian Variant

Kaldor provided an alternative approach to reconciling the "warranted" and "natural" rate of growth, the disparity between $\frac{s}{a} - \beta - \alpha$, the rate at which jobs are created, and n, the rate at which the labor force grows. He suggested that the average savings rate depends on the distribution of income, and by changing the distribution of income, s can be brought into line. Thus, he posited (in simplified form) that none of the wages are saved, but a fraction s_p of profits, so

$$\frac{dK}{dt} = s_p rK. \tag{17.30}$$

Hence, we replace the differential equation for v, (17.13), with (17.13′)

$$\frac{d\ln v}{dt} = s_p r - n - \beta - \alpha = s_p\left(\frac{1}{a} - \frac{w(v)\,b}{a}\right) - n - \beta - \alpha. \tag{17.13′}$$

It is still the case that the steady state requires a to be constant, $\beta = \beta^*$, which implies that $m = m^*$ (defined by (17.21) as before. From (17.13′) we can calculate the rate of return on capital, r:

$$r^* = \frac{n + \beta^*}{s_p} = \frac{a^* - w(v^*)\,b}{a^*}. \tag{17.31}$$

Now, we can solve for a^* from the equation determining the distribution of income; from (17.16)

$$a^* = \frac{m^*}{r^*}. \tag{17.32}$$

These, together with (1.23) and (1.24), which continue to hold, completely define the equilibrium.

The dynamics are also modified only slightly, as we only replace (17.13) with (17.13′). As (17.13′) makes clear, it is still the case that above the locus $\frac{dv}{dt} = 0$ (i.e., for higher values of a), the rate of growth of capital is lower (as before), so v(the employment rate) is falling; below the curve, it is rising. Hence, the qualitative dynamics remains unchanged.[12]

[12] The stability conditions are of course changed. See the appendix to the original paper for details.

3 Two Way Causality: How Technology Drives Distribution and Distribution Drives Technology in a Model with Full Employment

The previous section explored a special case where capital and labor were not substitutes, and the distribution of income was determined in the short run by agency costs (by the wages required to induce individuals not to shirk) or bargaining. This distribution of income, in turn, drove the evolution of technology, and it was that that shaped the long run distribution of income. Marginal productivity theory, the cornerstone of distribution theory for two centuries, played no role. In this section, we reintroduce marginal productivity theory, allowing capital and labor to be substitutes. In this section, we assume full employment, dropping totally the concerns about agency costs and bargaining. In the next section, we combine the insights of Sections 2 and 3.

3.1 The Basic Model

We assume a simple aggregate production function with constant returns to scale of the form

$$Q = F\left(\mu^{t+1}K, \lambda^{t+1}L\right), \tag{17.33}$$

μK and λL are the effective capital and labor supply.[13] If we set μ^t and $\lambda^t = 1$, then μ^{t+1} and λ^{t+1} measure the level of capital and labor-augmenting technological progress respectively between period t and $t + 1$. In the following discussion, without ambiguity, we drop the superscript on λ and μ.

Because of constant returns to scale, we can write

$$\frac{Q}{\lambda L} = f\left(\frac{\mu k}{\lambda}\right) = f(\kappa), \tag{17.34}$$

where $k = \frac{K}{L}$, the capital–labor ratio, assumed for the moment as given, f is output per unit of effective labor, and $\kappa \equiv \frac{\mu k}{\lambda}$, the *effective* capital–labor ratio. Standard analyses yield

$$S_L = \frac{[f(k) - \kappa f(\kappa)]}{f(\kappa)}, S_K = \frac{f'(\kappa)\kappa}{f(\kappa)}, \tag{17.35}$$

where S_L and S_K are the share of labor and capital in national income, respectively. To relate more clearly the notation of this section to that of the previous: $m = S_L$, the share of labor, which without our agency theory, was indeterminate there (because of the fixed coefficients technology), while here, it's completely determined by the effective capital–labor ratio. $a = \frac{K}{Q}$, the capital–output ratio, which there was fixed, but here equals $\frac{K}{Q} = \frac{\kappa}{\mu f(\kappa)}$. Similarly, $b = \frac{L}{Q} = \frac{1}{f(\kappa)\beta}$.

[13] In terms of our earlier notation, $\mu = \frac{1}{a}$; $\lambda = \frac{1}{b}$.

As before, we postulate an innovation frontier with the rate of capital augmenting progress as a function of the rate of labor-augmenting progress:

$$\alpha = Z(\beta), Z' < 0. \tag{17.36}$$

where now $\alpha = \frac{d\ln\mu}{dt}$ and $\beta = \frac{d\ln\lambda}{dt}$.

We can rewrite the equilibrium condition for the determination of the factor bias of technological change, (17.18), as

$$z(\beta) \equiv -Z'(\beta) = \frac{S_L}{S_K}. \tag{17.37}$$

But the relative shares themselves are a function of the effective capital–labor ratio κ, so that the equilibrium "direction" (or bias) of innovation is given by the solution to

$$z(\beta^*) = \frac{S_L\kappa}{[1 - S_L(\kappa)]} \equiv \Phi(\kappa), \tag{17.38}$$

and

$$\Phi(\kappa) > or < 0 \, as \, \sigma < \text{ or } > 1. \tag{17.39}$$

where σ is the elasticity of substitution. Given our assumptions concerning the innovation possibilities curve, we can solve (17.37) for the rate of labor and capital augmenting technological change as a function of κ:

$$\beta = z^{-1}(\Phi(\kappa)) \equiv \theta(\kappa). \tag{17.40}$$

and

$$\frac{d\ln\mu}{dt} = \alpha = Z(\beta) = Z(\theta(\kappa)). \tag{17.41}$$

For any given κ, there is a unique value of β—a well-specified bias of technical change. But unless the elasticity of substitution is unambiguously greater or less than unity, β may not be monotonic in κ. If the elasticity of substitution is greater than unity, an increase in κ leads to an increased share of profits and therefore a decrease in β and conversely if the elasticity of substitution is less than unity.

3.2 Basic Differential Equations

In the previous section, we assumed that the capital stock was fixed, and technology was given. Over time, however, it increases. At the same time, technology also changes. In this section, we describe the long-run dynamics of the economy. Given the current technology and capital–labor ratio, the distribution of income is determined, and that in turn determines both savings and the evolution of technology.

When the elasticity of substitution is high, an increase in capital augmenting technological change increases the share of capital (other things being equal) leading to further increases in the rate of capital augmenting technological progress. It is well known from standard growth theory that a steady state requires that technological change be purely labor augmenting. This suggests that if the elasticity of substitution is greater than unity, the steady state equilibrium may be unstable. The analysis below shows that that is in fact the case, and that if the elasticity of substitution is less than unity, the equilibrium is stable, but that convergence to the equilibrium may not be monotonic.

We simplify, as before, by assuming a fixed savings rate s (this assumption can be generalized, at the cost of some complexity), so that

$$\frac{d\,ln}{dt} = \frac{sQ}{K} = \frac{s\mu f(\kappa)}{\kappa}. \tag{17.42}$$

Letting the rate of growth of the labor force be fixed, as before, at n, we can describe the dynamics of the economy by the pair of Equations (17.41) and

$$\frac{d\,ln\kappa}{dt} = s\mu + Z(\theta(\kappa)) - \beta(\kappa) - n = s\mu\left(\frac{f(\kappa)}{\kappa}\right) - \zeta(\kappa), \tag{17.43}$$

where

$$\zeta(\kappa) \equiv n + \beta(\kappa) - Z(\beta(\kappa)),$$

the difference between the rate of growth of the effective labor supply and the rate of capital augmenting technological change.

3.3 Dynamics

The steady state is given by the solution to, as before, $\alpha = 0$ and $\beta = \beta^*$, where $Z(\beta^*) = 0$. Now, however, knowing β^*, we know the distribution of income that supports it, which implies, from (17.39) that κ must be such that

$$\beta^* = \theta(\kappa^*). \tag{17.44a$'$}$$

Equation (17.44a′) may not necessarily be solved uniquely for κ^*, unless the elasticity of substitution is always greater than or less than unity. From (17.43), at $\kappa = \kappa^*$:

$$\mu^* = \frac{[n + \beta^*]\,\kappa^*}{sf(\kappa^*)}. \tag{17.44b}$$

But more generally, κ is constant along the locus

$$\mu = \frac{\zeta(\kappa)\,\kappa}{sf(\kappa)}. \tag{17.44c}$$

Given β^* and *any* corresponding κ^*, (17.44b) can be solved uniquely for μ^*.[14] (If there are multiple κ^*, for each possible κ^*, there is a corresponding equilibrium value of μ^* which sustains the steady state.)

Figure 17.3 provides the phase diagram. The $\frac{d\ln\mu}{dt} = 0$ locus is a vertical line at $\kappa = \kappa^*$.[15] Figure 17.3c illustrates a case where there are three multiple steady state values. In other cases, we assume only one such value. If the elasticity of substitution is less than unity (Panel a), to the right of κ^*, the share of labor is larger, so $\frac{d\ln\mu}{dt} < 0$; and conversely to the left. Just the opposite happens if the elasticity of substitution is greater than unity (Panel b).

On the other hand, from (17.44c) the shape of the $\frac{d\ln\kappa}{dt} = 0$ locus depends critically on whether the elasticity of substitution is greater or less than unity.

$$\frac{d\ln\mu}{d\kappa} = \left(\frac{\zeta(\kappa)\,\kappa}{\zeta}\right) + 1 - S_K, \tag{17.45a}$$

where

$$\zeta'(\kappa) > or < 0\; as\, \sigma < \text{or} > 1, \tag{17.45b}$$

that is, if the elasticity of substitution is less (greater) than unity, as κ increases, the share of labor increases (decreases), so $\beta - Z$, the difference between the rate of labor and capital augmenting progress, increases (decreases). On the other hand, above the $\frac{d\ln\mu}{dt} = 0$ locus (a higher value of μ), $\frac{d\ln\mu}{dt} > 0$, and this is true regardless of the elasticity of substitution.

The full dynamics is very sensitive to the elasticity of substitution, so we consider each of the cases in turn.

If the elasticity of substitution is less than unity, the $\frac{d\kappa}{dt} = 0$ locus is upward sloping, and if as κ goes to zero, $\frac{f(\kappa)}{\kappa}$ goes to infinity, $\mu = 0$ at $\kappa = 0$. Figure 17.3a illustrates this case. The phase diagram shows an oscillatory convergence to equilibrium (Illustrated in Figure 17.3a).

On the other hand, if the elasticity of substitution is greater than unity, then ζ is a negatively sloped function of κ. Consider the limiting case of an infinite elasticity of substitution, where $Q = h\mu K + e\lambda L$, h and e are constants, so at $\kappa = 0$, $\frac{f(\kappa)}{\kappa}$ is infinite and the share of capital is zero, so $\beta = \hat{\beta}$ where $\left(z\left(\hat{\beta}\right) = 0\right.$, and $\alpha = Z\left(\hat{\beta}\right)$, so μ along the $\frac{d\ln\kappa}{dt} = 0$ at $\kappa = 0$ equals zero.

On the other hand, the $\frac{d\ln\mu}{dt} = 0$ locus again hits the horizontal axis at $\kappa = \kappa^{**}$ where κ^{**} defined as the solution to

$$\zeta(\kappa^{**}) = 0, \tag{17.46a}$$

that is, where the rate of capital augmentation is very high, equal to the rate of growth of the effective labor supply. Obviously, that requires a much higher share of capital than that associated with zero capital augmentation, and that requires a much higher value of κ, $\kappa^{**} > \kappa^*$.

[14] Provided only that $n + \theta^* - Z(\theta^*) > 0$, which we assume to be the case.

[15] If there are multiple steady state values, at each such value, there is a vertical line for which $\frac{d\ln\mu}{dt} = 0$.

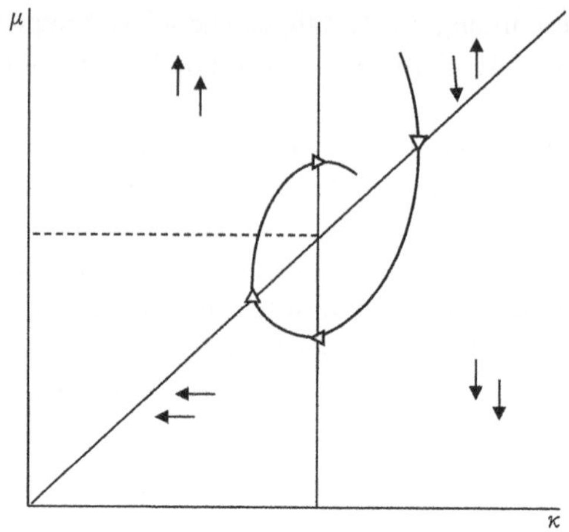

Figure 17.3a Steady states and dynamics with elasticity of substitution less than unity. The steady state is given by the intersection of the curves giving $\frac{d\mu}{dt} = 0$ and $\frac{d\kappa}{dt} = 0$. The former curve(s) is a vertical straight line. The $\frac{d\kappa}{dt} = 0$ locus is upward sloping. The equilibrium is stable, and the convergence is oscillatory.

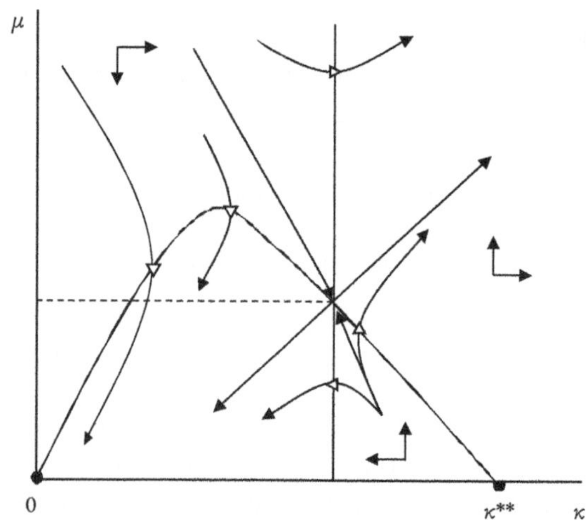

Figure 17.3b. Steady states and dynamics with elasticity of substitution greater than unity. The $\frac{d\mu}{dt} = 0$ is a vertical straight line, the $\frac{d\kappa}{dt} = 0$ locus is an inverted *U* shape (though it can actually be more complicated than that). There is a unique interior steady state, which is a saddle point. Above the convergent trajectory, μ and κ both go off to infinity; below, to zero.

Figure 17.3b shows the $\frac{d \ln \kappa}{dt} = 0$ locus as inverted U-shaped curve.[16]

The dynamics are complicated. The steady state is an unstable saddle point, with the economy normally converging either to a situation where $\kappa = 0$ or infinity (the asymptotic share of labor either is zero or one). If the economy gets into a situation where the effective capital–labor ratio is too high (above the trajectories going into (κ^*, μ^*), the

[16] The curve may actually have multiple peaks and exhibit more complicated dynamics that illustrated, and this is especially so if the elasticity of substitution varies between being greater or less than unity, depending on the value of .

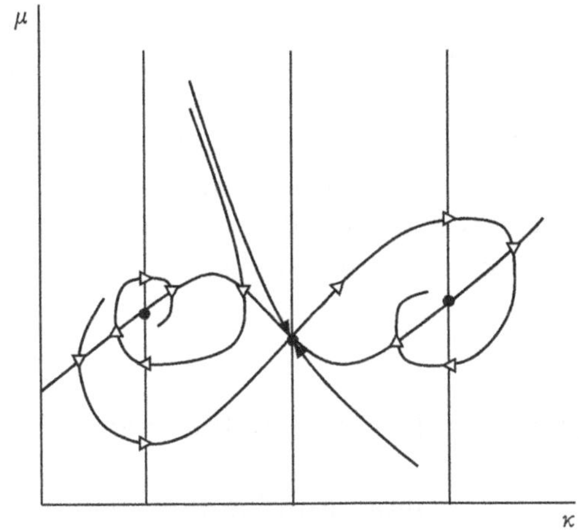

Figure 17.3c. Steady states and dynamics with the elasticity of substitution is both above and below unity (for different values of κ), then there can exist multiple steady states. Here, we illustrate a case with three, with the middle, E2, being unstable, and the other two (locally) stable.

share of capital is "too high,"), technology becomes capital augmenting, leading the effective capital–labor ratio to increase still further. On the other hand, if the economy is initially at any value of $\{\kappa, \mu\}$ below the equilibrium trajectories, μ and κ both approach zero.[17]

Figure 17.3c illustrates the case with multiple steady states as a result of the fact that the elasticity of substitution for low and high values of κ is less than unity, but for intermediate values of κ is greater than unity. In the case exhibited, there are three values of κ for which $\frac{d \ln \mu}{dt} = 0$.

Then for initial conditions below the trajectories AE_2 or BE_2 the economy converges to E_1, while for any set of initial conditions above those trajectories the economy converges to E_3. (In both cases, the convergence is oscillatory.)

Proposition 1. The economy with endogenous factor bias and full employment is stable if the elasticity of substitution is less than unity but convergence may not be monotonic; but the economy is dynamically unstable if the elasticity of substitution is greater than unity.

3.3.1 Qualifications

These instability results are a consequence of the strong assumption that the innovation frontier itself is invariant to the value of labor and capital augmentation previously achieved. If, for instance, the economy has increasingly focused on labor-augmenting

[17] In the case of an elasticity of substitution greater than unity, it is worth observing the limiting values of some of the relevant variables. When κ goes to zero (SL goes to 1), even as the effective capital–labor ratio is shrinking, per capital income, βf is increasing, at an asymptotic rate of max, which is considerably higher than the rate of increase in the steady state, where it is just *.

When κ goes to infinity (SK goes to 1), it can be shown that $d \ln \kappa dt$ may grow without bound. The limiting case of an infinite elasticity of substitution production function illustrates what can happen. κ increases super exponentially. While income per capita is increasing without bound, not only does the share of wages go to zero, but the income of workers' does too, if min < 0, which it well may be (the unbounded increase in capital productivity comes at the expense of a decrease in labor productivity). If min = 0, worker incomes stagnate.

technical progress because of the increasing share of labor, further labor augmentation might become more difficult. Thus, even at the high share of labor, there would be a shift toward capital-augmenting technological progress. By contrast, with the possibility of "learning to learn" (Stiglitz, 1987f), the process of factor biased technological change may feed upon itself, that is, as the economy engages in, say, labor-augmenting technological progress, it becomes more skilled at learning how to save labor (relative to saving capital). This would suggest an even greater dynamic instability than that in our model.

4 Unemployment Equilibrium and the Evolution of Technology

4.1 Short-Run Equilibrium

Now assume, as in Section 2 that as the level of unemployment decreases, the wage that firms must pay increases.

$$W = W(U; w_{\min}\ldots), W_U < 0, \tag{17.47}$$

where we have noted that the wage decreases as the unemployment rate increases, and depends on other variables, including the level of unemployment compensation, $w_{\min}$. (In a dynamic representation, as in Section 2, this will increase over time.)

Then an increase in productivity of labor (that is, a labor-augmenting technological change) may shift the demand curve for labor up or down, depending on the elasticity of substitution. The marginal return to an effective labor unit is $\frac{W}{\lambda} = f(\kappa) - \kappa f'(\kappa) \equiv g(\kappa)$.

Hence

$$L_d = \mu K/\lambda g^{-1}\left(\frac{W}{\lambda}\right). \tag{17.48}$$

The short-run equilibrium, where the labor force is given by N, and $UN + L = N$, is given by

$$\mu K/\lambda g^{-1}\left(\frac{W(U; w_{\min}\ldots)}{\lambda}\right) = N(1 - U). \tag{17.49}$$

An increase in λ shifts the demand curve for labor. Figure 17.4 shows how a shift in the demand curve for laborers affects the equilibrium unemployment.

Proposition 2a. If the demand for laborers decreases as a result of a change in technology (innovation is labor saving, in the sense that at any wage, the demand for workers decreases[18]) then unemployment increases.

It is easy to show that

Proposition 2b. If the elasticity of substitution is less (greater) than unity, then (at the equilibrium wage), an increase in productivity of each worker (a labor-augmenting technological change) leads to a reduced (increased) demand for workers.

[18] See Hicks (1932), for a discussion of a typology of innovation.

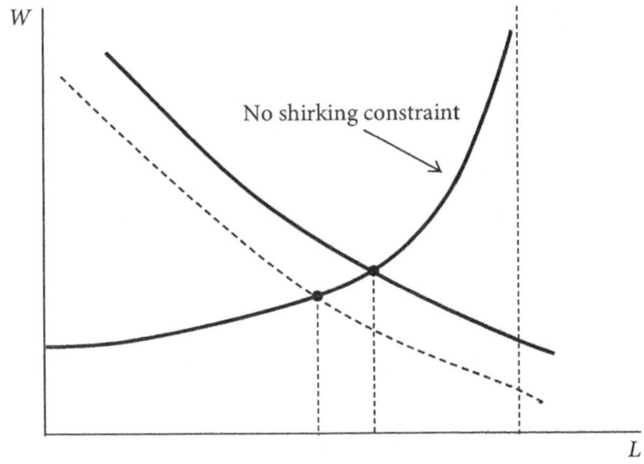

Figure 17.4 Effect of labor-augmenting innovation in Shapiro–Stiglitz model. If the demand curve for labor (L^d) shifts down, then labor-augmenting technological progress leads to more unemployment. The market does not take into account the social costs of this induced unemployment.

4.2 Social Welfare Maximization

Assuming that costless redistributions are possible, social welfare is maximized by maximizing national output with respect to λ, taking into account the effect of λ on the unemployment rate:

$$\max F(\mu K, \lambda(1-U)L), \tag{17.50}$$

where U is the unemployment rate, and now, we formulate the innovation frontier as we did earlier in Section 2, with $\mu = Z(\lambda)$, that is,

$$\begin{aligned}\frac{d\ln Q}{d\ln\lambda} &= \left\{F_1\lambda Z'K + F_2\left[(1-U)\lambda L\right] - w\lambda L\left(\frac{dU}{d\ln\lambda}\right)\right\}/Q \\ &= \left[r\mu K\left(\frac{d\ln\mu}{d\ln\lambda}\right) + (1-U)L\lambda w - w\lambda L\left(\frac{dU}{d\ln\lambda}\right)\right]/Q \\ &= S_K\left(\frac{d\ln\mu}{d\ln\lambda}\right) + (1-S_K)\left\{1 + \left(\frac{d\ln(1-U)}{d\ln\lambda}\right)\right\}.\end{aligned} \tag{17.51}$$

At the private sector optimization, this is < or > 0 as $\frac{dU}{d\ln\lambda} > or < 0$:

Proposition 3. There is excessive (insufficient) labor-augmenting innovation if the effect of innovation is to increase (decrease) the unemployment rate, i.e. if $\sigma < (>)1$.

Empirical estimates suggest that the elasticity of substitution is less than unity.[19] There is thus a presumption that (in the short run, with fixed K and L), innovation focuses excessively on increasing the productivity of labor. The market does not take into account the effects of labor-saving innovation in increasing unemployment.

Making matters worse, if social welfare is concerned with the distribution of income (inequality)—because redistributions are not costless—the market will also lead to excessively labor-augmenting innovation, if the elasticity of substitution is less than unity.[20]

5 Skill-Biased Innovation

The same kind of analysis applies if we extend the model to innovation that is "skill-biased." Assume, for instance that

$$Q = F(\lambda_s L_s, \lambda_u L_u), \tag{17.52}$$

where L_s is the input of skilled labor, L_u that of unskilled labor, and λ_s and λ_u is the level of skill-augmenting and unskilled-augmenting technological progress, with an innovation frontier

$$\lambda_u = Z(\lambda_s). \tag{17.53}$$

As before, the market allocation will pay no attention to distributive and unemployment effects of the choices it makes.

For instance, if employers can distinguish who is skilled and unskilled, there will be a different no-shirking curve (as in the Shapiro–Stiglitz model) for each group. A change in the skill bias of technological change will typically shift the demand curve for one group of workers up and the other down, leading to a reduction of one type of unemployment and an increase in the other. If monitoring is, say, more difficult for unskilled workers than for skilled workers, unskilled worker unemployment may be more important. (In the limit, if the performance of skilled workers was perfectly observable, then there would be no efficiency-wage unemployment of skilled workers, only of unskilled workers.) It follows then, from the same logic as used earlier, that if the elasticity of substitution between skilled and unskilled workers is less than unity, that the market equilibrium will be associated with excessively skill biased technological progress.

At the end of Section 3, we observed that if the elasticity of substitution is greater than unity, then the long-run equilibrium may be unstable. An increase in the share of capital leads to a bias toward further capital-augmenting technological progress, further increasing the share of capital. The same logic applies as well to innovation augmenting the

[19] See, among others, David and van de Klundert (1965), Kalt (1978), and Antràs (2004). Piketty (2014) criticizes the finding that the elasticity of substitution is always less than zero. He argues that the data used to draw this conclusion focuses on too narrow a time period. On the other hand, much of his analysis does not make an adequate distinction between wealth and capital (e.g., much of the increase in the value of wealth is related to an increase in the relative price of land; see the discussion in earlier chapters, particularly Chapter 10).

[20] Assuming, as is the case, that the income per capita of workers is less than that of "capitalists."

productivity of skilled and unskilled workers. In the case of a low elasticity of substitution, if productivity of the highly skilled workers increases relative to unskilled, the share of skilled workers goes down, and this then leads to reduced incentives for such innovation. But if the elasticity of substitution is large, then the share of income going to skilled workers increases, and the bias increases. The implication is that the ratio of income (wages) of skilled and unskilled workers increases (without bound), with increasing incentives for more skill-biased innovation.

There are peculiar long-run implications of such an analysis. The share of skilled labor would increase toward unity. It also means that the return to converting an unskilled worker into a skilled worker increases (again without bound). An increasingly large fraction of the labor force would thus become "educated"—further accelerating the pace of skilled bias technological change. If there are increasing costs associated with converting the marginal unskilled worker into a skilled worker, at each date there will be a residual of unskilled workers, suffering from increasing relative deprivation.

But again, there may be an equilibrating force: as skilled-labor-augmenting technological progress proceeds, further progress becomes increasingly difficult, especially relative to say capital or unskilled-biased technological change. And, if there is a distribution of innate talents, it may become increasingly difficult at the margin to convert an unskilled worker into a skilled worker—ensuring the persistence of extreme inequality.

6 Concluding Comments

6.1 Interpretations

In the standard neoclassical model, factor supplies (including the [given] relative productivities of different factors) determine the distribution of income. In the Solow (1956) growth model, however, the long-run rate of growth itself does not in any way depend on the distribution of income.[21] Moreover, there is always full employment. If there is unemployment, there is only one reason: wage rigidities. Conventional discourse attributes wage rigidities either to what the government does (minimum wages) or what it does not do (circumscribing unions). Eliminating such rigidities increases efficiency and eliminates unemployment. With a high elasticity of substitution, a relatively small change in the wage will return the economy to full employment, so that not even workers will suffer much. Though firms choose the technology to employ, factor prices always adjust so that the technology they choose is such that factors are fully employed. On the other hand, if the elasticity of substitution (ex post) is low, then to achieve full or even significantly *fuller* employment in the short run may require a large reduction in wages. Indeed, it may not even be possible to achieve full employment, as in the model of Section 2. The short-run effect of lowering wages on employment may be nil.

Here, the distribution of income matters a great deal for the dynamics of the economy (obviously, much more than in representative agent model where its effects are assumed away): it determines the pattern of innovation. Technology is *endogenous*, and the

[21] And this is even true in Kaldorian variants of that model, where the savings rate is dependent on the distribution of income, or on more neoclassical variants of that model, where the savings rate is determined endogenously.

distribution of income determines technology and possibly factor supply ratios as much as factor supply ratios and technology determine the distribution of income. And wage rigidities are a consequence of market forces—given imperfections of information, it benefits firms to pay wages above the market-clearing level. This model provides a far better interpretation of the pattern of unemployment than that which attributes unemployment either to minimum wages or unions; for we see high levels of unemployment both in non-unionized sectors and at skill levels far above those for which the minimum wage is relevant.

But these high wages provide firms with an incentive to innovate to augment the productivity of labor, with further impacts on both wages and unemployment that we have traced out in our dynamic analysis.[22]

Moreover, the market on its own is inefficient, both in the level of unemployment[23] and, importantly, in the pattern of innovation. When firms collectively engage in, say, (unskilled) labor-augmenting technological change which increases the level of unemployment, they take no account of the social costs of this unemployment. They think only of their own savings, in labor expenditures. We have presented a quite general argument establishing that there is excessive labor-augmenting technological change, and that innovation is likely to be excessively skill-biased.[24]

The efficiency wage model is the simplest within which to explore market distortions in the pattern of innovation, but similar results emerge in other models with (endogenous) market imperfections. Economic historians, such as Habakkuk (1962) and Salter (1962) have emphasized the role of "labor scarcity" as an inducement to labor-saving innovation. (Such explanations seem to have special relevance in particular historical periods, e.g., in the period of the rapid expansion of the United States in the nineteenth century.) Standard economic theory has had a hard time understanding what labor scarcity might mean, but the theory of endogenous innovation has provided a simple interpretation: when the share of labor increases, more efforts are devoted to augmenting the productivity of labor.[25] Models with costly information and highly differentiated labor extend this interpretation. It may take time and resources to recruit a new worker to replace a worker that leaves. Firms' inability to instantaneously hire workers of the particular type in which they are interested (there is, in this sense, a labor scarcity) can impose large costs: Even a relatively small gap in time in being able to fill a position may result in a significant reduction in profits. The shadow cost of labor will exceed the wage.

There are many other contexts in which this is true. From the perspective of the firm, what matters is not just the wage or interest rate, as these might show up in the system of national income accounts, but the *effective* total labor and capital costs, which can differ markedly from the recorded labor and capital shares, even apart from taxes and fringe benefits. Workers have to be managed. Strikes are costly. All of this requires scarce managerial time. On the other hand, if there is credit rationing, the "shadow" cost of capital may

[22] Barth, Moene, and Willumsen (2014) have explored this idea in greater depth. See also Stiglitz (2015f).

[23] As demonstrated in Shapiro and Stiglitz (1984).

[24] The effects that we have identified are examples of macroeconomic externalities, themselves the macroeconomic manifestation of pervasive inefficiencies which arise in the presence of imperfect and asymmetric information, incomplete risk markets, efficiency wage effects, and/or search. See Greenwald and Stiglitz (1986, 1988d), Jeanne and Korinek (2010), Dávila and Korinek (2018), and Korinek (2018b).

[25] There are other interpretations, discussed further briefly below. It seems, for instance, that at times wages did not fully adjust, and that at times, as a result, firms had difficult times hiring workers. This will result in the shadow wage exceeding the market wage.

well exceed the interest rate charged. By the same token, if machines are not fully reliable and cannot be easily replaced, a breakdown of a machine can be costly, and this risk is part of the shadow cost of capital. On the other hand, if the Central Bank provides access to funds at super-low rates, as in the years after the Great Recession, the cost of capital to those firms that can access these funds will be correspondingly low.

When a firm assesses whether to save on labor or capital, all of these costs are relevant. Labor-augmenting technological progress, for instance, may reduce not only the direct labor costs, but the indirect turnover (search and recruitment) costs and the managerial costs associated with labor.

6.2 Policy Implications

There are several important policy implications of this analysis. High wages do have an effect on unemployment, through the impact on the evolution of technology. This has two implications. First, it takes considerable time before any action to lower wages (even if it were successful—recall that in our model, high wages are a result of natural market forces, not of unions or government minimum wages) has any effect. The short-run effect on unemployment in the model with fixed coefficients (Section 2) is nil.[26] Second, there are other ways by which the government could affect the evolution of the system and the creation of jobs. There are, in particular, two ways by which this can be done in the medium run. First, policies that increase the national savings rate can be an effective way of increasing employment in the medium term.[27] (This is especially true in the model where there is zero ex post elasticity of substitution.)

Second, wage subsidies reduce the cost of labor, and it is the high cost of labor that induces firms to shift the direction of technological development toward excessive labor-saving and capital-using technologies. By the same token, when the Fed lowers the cost of capital dramatically (as it attempted to do after the Great Recession), it encourages labor-saving innovation. Thus, we observe the curious phenomenon of firms replacing unskilled labor (with presumably a low "social" shadow price, given the high unemployment rate among unskilled workers), such as checkout clerks with automatic tellers. While there are almost surely social benefits from the induced employment resulting from the increased aggregate demand from such investments, those benefits have to be set against the social costs of higher unemployment in the medium term as a result of the labor-saving innovation induced by the lowering of the cost of capital. A full analysis of the intertemporal trade-offs would take us beyond the confines of this discussion.

Third, increasing the price paid by firms for environmental impacts (e.g., as a result of carbon emissions) shifts innovation away from labor-saving (augmenting) innovation, again with positive effects on the distribution of income and employment.

[26] Early students of growth theory recognized that this would be true even within the neoclassical model; they focused on putty-clay models, as discussed earlier in this chapter. But even in those models, there is an extensive margin, that is, machines with higher labor requirements per unit of output, and so long as there are enough of such machines, the economy can reach full employment.

[27] This stands in sharp contrast to the implications of the standard neoclassical model, where there is always full employment.

6.3 Toward a More General Theory

By bringing together a plausible theory of wage determination with the theory of induced innovation, we have provided a general theory of growth and employment which makes sense of discussions of technological unemployment or job shortages—concepts that have no meaning in Solow's formulation. In this theory, we have emphasized, the distribution of income matters; it affects technology and the dynamics of the economy, and these in turn affect the distribution of income at later dates.[28] In our formulation, too, history matters: an episode of ultra-low interest rates, such as in the era after the 2008 financial crisis, encourages firms to explore labor-saving innovations—after all, capital was almost "free." The innovations made then provide the basis for subsequent explorations. There are thus important hysteresis effects.[29]

Recent discussions of persistent unemployment and growing inequality have centered around labor-saving innovations (such as labor-replacing robots, discussed more extensively in Chapter 18). Critics of such innovation are sometimes referred to as modern-day Luddites, and defenders of the market have claimed that one should not interfere with market processes. In the long run, they argue, everyone will be better off. Our analysis has suggested that such views may be Panglossian. Not only within their life span may workers *not* be better off—the benefits of the improvements may not trickle down—but additionally, the changes in factor demands may actually lead them to be worse off even in the longer run.[30]

We have shown not only that innovations may fail to improve the welfare of some groups in society—they may not result in a Pareto improvement—but also that market processes may lead to patterns of innovation that are not even output maximizing—they would not be Pareto efficient even if redistributions could be made costlessly.[31] Indeed, there is a presumption that unfettered markets will *not* be efficient in the choice of factor bias, and will lead to excessively high levels of unemployment and this in turn will lead to lower real wages and lower output than would otherwise be the case.

Chapter 18 takes a closer look at the effects of innovation on the distribution of income.

[28] We also note that the dynamics can be markedly different from those of the standard Solow model, where convergence to equilibrium is monotonic. As we noted, convergence is oscillatory. This is true both in models with full employment and unemployment induced by efficiency wage considerations. We have also uncovered a fundamental dynamic instability in the case of elasticity of substitution greater than unity. We should observe, however, that the smooth convergence to the steady state in the Solow model is a function of its extreme simplifying assumptions. Other slight modifications (vintage capital, savings depending on the distribution of income) can also lead to more complicated dynamics. See, for example, Stiglitz (1967), Akerlof and Stiglitz (1969), or Cass and Stiglitz (1969).

[29] Similarly, the Black Plague leading to high wages induces labor-saving innovations, that may have eventually heralded in the industrial revolution.

[30] This is consistent with the evidence on the stagnation of median and mean wages in the U.S. over a span of more than 40 years, and a decline in mean and median wages of unskilled workers (e.g., workers with only a high school education).

[31] The consequences of innovation on wages, output, and inequality are, of course, highly dependent on the presence of other imperfections in the economy. As we noted earlier, with imperfect labor mobility, not only are those in the sector experiencing innovation adversely affected, but, because of macroeconomic externalities, so may be those in other sectors.

PART II.C

RECENT PUBLISHED CONTRIBUTIONS

18

The Future of Inequality

Artificial Intelligence, Worker-Replacing Technological Progress and Income Distribution

With Anton Korinek

1 Introduction

The introduction of artificial intelligence (AI) is the continuation of a long process of automation.[1] Advances in mechanization in the late-nineteenth and early-twentieth century automated much of the physical labor performed by humans. Advances in information technology in the mid- to late-twentieth century automated much of the standardized data processing that used to be performed by humans. However, each of these past episodes of automation left large areas of work that could only be performed by humans.

Some propose that advances in AI are merely the latest wave in this long process of automation, and may in fact generate less economic growth than past technological advances (see e.g., Gordon, 2016). Others, by contrast, emphasize that AI critically differs from past inventions: as artificial intelligence draws closer and closer to human general intelligence, much of human labor runs the risk of becoming obsolete and being replaced by AI in all domains.

In this view, progress in artificial intelligence is not only a continuation but the culmination of technological progress—it could lead to a course of history that is markedly different from the implications of previous waves of innovation, and may even represent what James Barrat (2013) has termed "Our Final Invention."

No matter what the long-run implications of AI are, it has the potential to disrupt labor markets in a major way, even in the short and medium run, affecting workers across many professions and skill levels.[2] The magnitude of these disruptions will depend on two important factors: the speed and the factor bias of progress in AI.

[1] Co-authored with Anton Korinek. Slightly edited version of chapter 14 of Agrawal, A., J. Gans, and A. Goldfarb (eds.), 2019, *The Economics of Artificial Intelligence: An Agenda*, Chicago: NBER/ University of Chicago Press, pp. 349–90. Reprinted with permission. The chapter was prepared as a background paper for the NBER Conference "The Economics of Artificial Intelligence." Coauthored with Anton Korinek. We would like to thank our discussant Tyler Cowan as well as Jayant Ray and participants at the NBER conference for helpful comments. We also acknowledge research assistance from Haaris Mateen as well as financial support from the Institute for New Economic Thinking (INET) and the Rewriting the Rules project at the Roosevelt Institute, supported by the Ford, Open Society, and Bernard and Irene Schwartz Foundations.

[2] For example, Frey and Osborne (2017) warn that 47% of jobs in the U.S. economy are at risk of being automated by advances in AI-related fields. Areas in which human intelligence has recently become inferior to artificial intelligence include many applications of radiology, trading in financial markets, paralegal work, underwriting, driving, etc.

The Origins of Inequality, and Policies to Contain It. Joseph E. Stiglitz with Anton Korinek, Oxford University Press.
 DOI: 10.1093/oso/9780198799580.003.0019

On the first factor, measured productivity has increased rather slowly in recent years, even as the world seems to be captured by AI fever.[3] If AI-related innovations enter the economy at the same slow pace as suggested by recent productivity statistics, then the transition will be slower than, for example, the wave of mechanization in the 1950s–70s, and the resulting disruptions may not be very significant. However, there are three possible alternative interpretations of these statistics: First, some suggest that productivity is significantly under-measured, for example because quality improvements are not accurately captured. The best available estimates suggest that this problem is limited to a few tenth of a percentage point (see, e.g., the discussion in Groshen, Moyer, Aizcorbe, et al., 2017). Furthermore, there are also unmeasured deteriorations in productivity, for example declines in service quality as customer service is increasingly automated. Secondly, the aggregate implications of progress in AI may follow a delayed pattern, similar to what happened after the introduction of computers in the 1980s. Robert Solow (1987) famously quipped that "you can see the computer age everywhere but in the productivity statistics." It was not until the 1990s that a significant rise in aggregate productivity could be detected, after sustained investment in computers and a reorganization of business practices had taken place. Third, it is of course possible that a significant discontinuity in productivity growth occurs, as suggested, for example, by proponents of a technological singularity (see, e.g., Kurzweil, 2005).

On the second factor, the disruptions generated by AI-related innovations depend on whether they are labor-saving, using the terminology of Hicks (1932), that is, whether at a given wage, the innovations lead to less demand for labor. Some suggest that artificial intelligence will mainly *assist* humans in being more productive and refer to such new technologies as *intelligence assisting innovation, IA,* rather than AI. Although we agree that most AI-related innovations are likely to be complementary to at least some jobs, we believe that taking a broader perspective, progress in AI is more likely to substitute for human labor, or even to replace workers outright, as we will assume in some of our formal models below.

We believe that the primary economic challenge posed by the proliferation of AI will be one of income distribution. We economists set ourselves too easy a goal if we just say that technological progress *can make everybody better off*—we also have to say *how we can make this happen.* The following chapter is an attempt to do so by discussing some of the key economic research issues that this raises.[4]

In Section 2 we provide a general taxonomy of the relationship between technological progress and welfare. We first observe that in a truly first-best economy—in which complete risk markets are available before a veil of ignorance about innovations is lifted—all individuals will share in the benefits of technological progress. However, since the real world does not correspond to this ideal, redistribution is generally needed to ensure that technological progress generates Pareto improvements. If markets are perfect and redistribution is costless, it can always be ensured that technological progress makes everybody better off. The same result holds if the costs of redistribution are sufficiently low. In all these cases, there can be political unanimity about the desirability of technological progress. However, if redistribution is too costly, it may be impossible to compensate the losers of technological

[3] For example, Google Trends reveals that search interest in the topic "artificial intelligence" has quadrupled over the past four years.

[4] An important, and maybe even more difficult, complementary question, which is beyond the scope of this chapter, is to analyze the political issues involved.

progress, and they will rationally oppose progress. Even worse, if the economy suffers from market imperfections, technological progress may actually move the Pareto frontier inwards, that is, some individuals may necessarily be worse off. Finally, we observe that the first welfare theorem does not apply to the process of innovation, and as a result, privately optimal innovation choices may move the Pareto frontier inwards.

In Section 3, we decompose the mechanisms through which innovation leads to inequality into two channels. First, inequality rises because innovators earn a surplus. Unless markets for innovation are fully contestable, the surplus earned by innovators is generally in excess of the costs of innovation and includes what we call innovator rents. We discuss policies that affect the sharing of such rents, such as anti-trust policies and changes in intellectual property rights. The second channel is that innovations affect market prices; they change the demand for factors such as different types of labor and capital, which affects their prices and generates redistributions. For example, AI may reduce wages and generate a redistribution to entrepreneurs. From the perspective of our first-best benchmark with complete insurance markets, these factor price change represent pecuniary externalities. We discuss policies to counter the effects of the resulting factor price changes.

In Section 4, we develop a simple formal model of worker-replacing technological change, that is, we introduce a machine technology that acts as a perfect substitute for human labor. We study the implications for wages and discuss policy remedies. In the short run, an additional unit of machine labor that is added to the economy earns its marginal product, but also generates a zero-sum redistribution from labor to traditional capital because it changes the relative supply of the two. In the long run, the machine technology turns labor into a reproducible factor. Thus, in the long run, growth will likely be limited by some other irreproducible factor, and all the benefits of technological progress will accrue to that factor. However, since it is in fixed supply, it can be taxed and the proceeds can be redistributed without creating distortions. Hence a Pareto improvement is easily achieved.

In a second model, we demonstrate how changes in patent length and capital taxation can act as a second-best device to redistribute if lump sum transfers between workers and innovators are not available. A longer patent life both delays how quickly innovations enter the public domain, lowering consumer prices, and increases the incentives of innovators to produce worker-replacing machines. However, the resulting losses for workers can be made up for by imposing a distortionary tax on capital and providing transfers, so long as the supply elasticity of capital is sufficiently low.

We also discuss the implications of endogenous factor bias in technological change. Worker-replacing technological progress should make capital-saving innovations more desirable, providing some relief to workers. We also note that our economy is developing more and more into a service economy, and that the large role of government in many service sectors (e.g., education, healthcare, etc.) creates ample scope for interventions to support workers.

In Section 5, we observe two categories of reasons for why innovation may lead to technological unemployment. The first relates to wage rigidities, which may persist, even in the long run: efficiency wage theory implies that employers may find it efficient to pay wages above the market clearing level so that workers have incentives to exert proper effort. If technological progress lowers the marginal product of workers, and hence their real wage, decline below their cost of living, then classic nutritional efficiency wage theories apply: unemployment would result because (in the absence of government support) workers could not survive working for the market-clearing wage and it would pay employers to raise real wages above the market-clearing level because of the resulting increase in worker productivity. The second category of technological unemployment arises as a transition phenomenon, when jobs are replaced at a faster rate than workers can find new ones. We discuss a variety of factors that may slow down the adjustment process. Efficiency wage arguments may also play an important role as a transitional phenomenon, in particular if workers' notion of fair wages is sticky. Finally, we discuss the implications of the fact that jobs may not only provide wages but also meaning and note that, unless societal attitudes change with the proliferation of AI, it may be welfare enhancing to subsidize jobs rather than simply redistributing resources.

In Section 6, we take a longer-term perspective that is somewhat more speculative and discuss the potential implications of some humans using technology to enhance themselves and attain superhuman artificial intelligence.

2 Technological Progress and Welfare: A Taxonomy

In 1930, Keynes wrote an essay on the "Economic Possibilities of our Grandchildren," in which he described how an improvement in technological possibilities might not translate into an improvement in utility possibilities. He worried about the quality of life that would emerge in a world with excess leisure. But what has happened in recent years has raised another possibility: innovation could lead to a few very rich individuals—who may face this challenge—whereas the vast majority of ordinary workers may be left behind, with wages far below what they were at the peak of the industrial age.

So let us start by considering the arrival of a new technology that partially (or fully) replaces workers and let us ask the question: *would their standard of living necessarily decline*? We will consider this question in a number of different settings, providing a taxonomy for how technological progress might affect the welfare of different groups in society depending on the environment.

2.1 First Best

We start with a first-best scenario in which we assume that all markets are perfect. This includes risk markets that are free of adverse incentive effects and that allow individuals to insure against the advent of innovations "behind the veil of ignorance," that is, before they know whether they will be workers or innovators. The main purpose for considering this idealized setting is to demonstrate that from an ex ante perspective, compensating workers for the losses imposed by technological progress is a question of economic efficiency not redistribution.

If risk markets were perfect and accessible to all agents before they knew their place in the economy, then all agents would be insured against any risk that might affect their well-being, including the risk of innovation reducing the value of their factor endowment. For example, workers would be insured against the risk of declining wages.[5] This leads us to the following observation:

Observation 1. *Consider a first-best world in which all individuals have access to a perfect insurance market "behind the veil of ignorance," that is, before they know whether they will be innovators or workers. If an innovation occurs in such a world, the winners would compensate the losers as a matter of optimal risk sharing. As a result, technological progress always makes everybody better off, and there is political unanimity in supporting it.*

This is a powerful observation because it reminds us that if we had an ideal market, something that very much looks like redistribution would naturally emerge. In our first-best economy, there are no losers from technological progress. Losers only exist if risk markets are imperfect compared to this benchmark. In more technical language, worker-replacing technological progress imposes pecuniary externalities on workers, which lead to inefficiency when risk markets are imperfect (see, e.g., Stiglitz, 1982g; Greenwald and Stiglitz, 1986; Geanakoplos and Polemarchakis, 1986; or more recently Dávila and Korinek, 2018).

This implies that policy measures to mitigate or undo the pecuniary externalities arising from technological progress—for example redistribution programs—make the economy's allocation more efficient from an ex ante perspective, rather than "interfering" with economic efficiency. They bring us closer to the allocation that a well-functioning risk market would achieve. Policymakers who oppose redistribution to compensate the losers of innovation because it interferes with the free market seem to—inappropriately, in our view—take an ex post perspective, after an innovation has taken place and after individuals know their place in the economy. Even though they may pretend to preach about idealized free markets, they clearly have not understood the full implications of how an idealized free market would work, that is, that such a market would provide the kind of social protection that they are opposing.[6]

In practice, workers who might be replaced by technological progress cannot purchase insurance contracts against being replaced, so in the absence of adequate government assistance, they are in fact hurt by the innovation. Of course, there are good reasons for why such idealized risk markets are not present in the real world:

First, the limited lifespan of humans makes it difficult to write insurance contracts that stretch over multiple generations. Workers would have had to obtain the described insurance a long time ago, before AI was well-conceived and its implications were clear, when the associated insurance premium would have been commensurately low. Perhaps their far-sighted ancestors could have written state-contingent contracts on their behalf. Today, obtaining insurance against AI reducing wages would require workers to pay large amounts since the possibility is very real. In short, effective insurance would have had to take place behind a "veil of ignorance" about the likely advent of AI.

To put it another way, in this perspective, the first "insurable damage" to the individual occurs at the time that the probability of an innovation becomes non-negligible, for at that time, the insurance premium required for income smoothing becomes significant, and her welfare is lowered. The individual would have wanted to buy insurance against the risk

[5] We will discuss the reasons why this is typically not the case in practice below.

[6] There is a difference: first-best insurance is defined over the Arrow–Debreu states, and therefore generates no adverse incentive effects. See the discussion below for why such insurance contracts cannot be written.

that her insurance premium would go up. Thus, in a perfect market, insurance markets would have to go back at least to a date at which there was a negligible probability that the innovation occurs. This presents a problem: it may be that at the moment that the concept of AI is formulated precisely enough to be an insurable event (and therefore becomes an insurable event) it has a non-zero probability.

Second, even for more limited time periods, risk markets with respect to technological change are clearly not perfect. Among the main reasons are information problems: *Describing the State Space:* This starts with the basic problem, alluded to earlier, of how difficult it is to describe the future state space.[7] We cannot easily write a contract on something before it has been invented. Addressing this problem would require that an individual has to be insured against any technological event that leads to lower wages. But any such insurance contract would necessarily have adverse incentive effects.[8]

More broadly, the curse of asymmetric information which inhibits insurance markets is as prevalent here as it is elsewhere:

Adverse Selection: Innovation leads to important adverse selection problems. Some people in the market are more informed than others. In an ideal market, the winners of innovation would provide insurance to the losers, and the winners (e.g., entrepreneurs) would almost certainly be better informed than the losers (e.g., workers).[9]

Moral Hazard: Innovation may also be subject to moral hazard problems, that is, the presence of insurance may affect the likelihood that the insured event occurs. Full insurance—sharing the gains fully with workers—would obviously attenuate incentives; but the appropriate response, as in other areas where moral hazard is present, is to provide some redistribution.[10]

2.1.1 Insurance and Redistribution

A natural counterpart to observation 1 is that in the absence of perfect insurance markets "behind the veil of ignorance," ensuring that progress leads to a Pareto improvement generally requires redistribution. If workers have access to some insurance against the risk of AI but not perfect insurance, this doesn't remove the need for redistributions.

For example, obtaining AI insurance today (with AI so clearly in the offing) would require workers to pay a large premium. Of course, conceptually, if one went back in time, before AI was well-conceived and its implications clear, one might argue that the premium would be low. But even that might not be so, since premia for large events, even with small probability, can be high. In any case, at the very moment of conception of AI—the first possible moment that one could conceivably have written a policy—AI would

[7] Interestingly, this type of information problem is easy to deal with after innovation has occurred, because then we know what has been invented and in which state we are, but very difficult to capture in ex ante contracts.

[8] Interestingly, this type of information problem is easy to deal with after innovation has occurred, because then we know what has been invented and in which state we are, but very difficult to capture in ex ante contracts.

[9] See the previous note.

[10] The significance of these adverse effects is not clear. Innovators are at least partially driven by non-pecuniary motives. If Bill Gates had been told, ex ante, that government would take away 50% of his returns over $10 billion, there is little reason to believe that it would have had any significant effect on innovation and investment. Ex post, taxing the winners in "winner takes all" games may have only small incentive effects.

still have distributional consequences; workers would have to pay a premium to divest themselves of this risk, and thus they would be worse off compared to the innovators, the winners.

2.2 Perfect Markets Ex Post and No Costs of Redistribution

Our next case pertains to a world that may be described as a second-best world without the perfect insurance markets referred to earlier, but in which, ex post, all markets are functioning well *and* there can be costless redistributions. This case covers several critical results that, although obvious at some level, often get lost in the debate about AI and technological progress more generally.

Observation 2. *If redistribution is costless and appropriate redistributions are made, then technological progress is always desirable for all agents. In that case, there is political unanimity in supporting technological progress.*

For convenience, and in conformity to conventional usage, we will refer the world with costless redistribution but otherwise perfectly functioning markets, as first best ex post; though we remind the reader that the previous analysis suggested that in a true first best, workers would have insurance against the risks from AI, such that they would commensurately share any gains from innovation. If the world is first-best ex post in the sense thus defined, then the utility possibilities curve (or *Pareto* frontier) moves out. We provide an example in Figure 18.1, which depicts a utility possibilities frontier for two types of agents, workers and entrepreneurs. In the example, technological progress increases the maximum utility level of entrepreneurs for any given level of utility of workers.[11] Innovation has increased production possibilities, and with lump sum redistributions, an expansion in production possibilities automatically implies an expansion in utility possibilities, that is, that everybody could be better off.

The fact that they *could* be better off does not mean that they *will* be better off. That depends on institutional arrangements. In Figure 18.1, we denote the initial equilibrium by E_0 and the after-innovation equilibrium by E_1. We have deliberately not called it a competitive market equilibrium: markets don't exist in a vacuum (see, e.g., Stiglitz, Abernathy, Hersh, et al., 2015). They are structured by rules and regulations, e.g. concerning intellectual property rights and anti-trust policies, and there may be tax and other policies in place. We thus simply refer to E_0 and E_1 as the before and after innovation (institution-given) equilibrium given the existing set of institutions. Note that in the example drawn in the figure, workers are worse off. That would normally be the case with what Hicks referred to as labor-saving innovations, that is, innovations which at a given wage, lead to less demand for labor. AI appears to be a labor- saving innovation. In the simple formal models of worker-replacing innovations which we work out below, that is clearly the case.

[11] More generally, we could define a multi-dimensional utility possibilities frontier by adding any number of categories of individuals, or even naming the individuals.

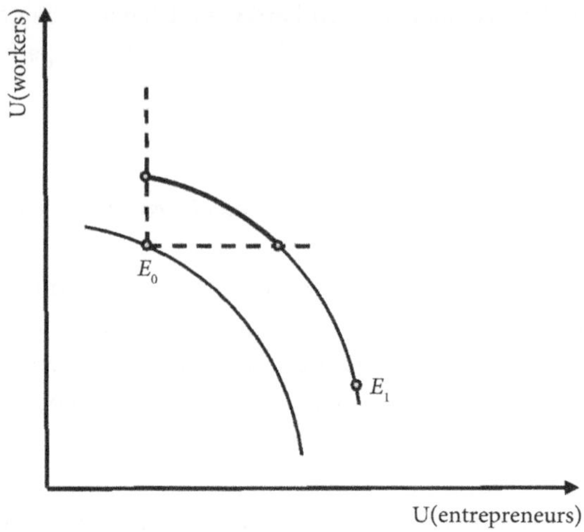

Figure 18.1 Pareto frontier before and after innovation with costless redistribution.

This in turn has two important implications:

First, without adequate redistribution, it makes sense for workers to resist the innovation. Luddism—the movement named after the possibly fictional character Ned Ludd that opposed automation in the textile sector in late-eighteenth-century and early-nineteenth-century England—is a rational response for workers who are made worse-off by automation and who are not sufficiently compensated.

Second, in a democracy in which workers are in a majority, it would make sense for enlightened innovators to support redistribution, to make sure that workers are at least not worse off. With redistribution, both innovators and workers *can* be better off. If appropriate redistribution is made so that everybody shares in the fruits of technological progress, there will again be political unanimity in supporting technological progress—progress will not be politically contentious.

There might be significant debate about how much compensation workers should receive, that is, where in the "northeast corner of E_0" society should be. On the one hand, this debate concerns the distribution of the surplus generated by innovation. On the other hand, labor-saving innovation reduces wages, which generates a redistribution from workers to other factor owners like rentiers and capitalists, for which workers may seek compensation. This redistribution represents a pecuniary externality from the innovation, as we will discuss in further detail in Section 3.2.

In Figure 18.1, we have marked in bold that part of the post-innovation Pareto frontier which represents a Pareto improvement and lies to the northeast of E_0. A range of philosophical principles can be adduced for determining what is a "just" division of the fruits of innovation. Behavioral economics may provide insights into what kinds of divisions might be acceptable.[12]

[12] Consider a model in which workers and innovators have to agree on whether the innovation is acceptable. The innovator has the power to set the division of the gains (i.e., where along the curve Northeast of E_0 the new equilibrium lies), but the workers have the power to accept or reject. This is the standard ultimatum game, for

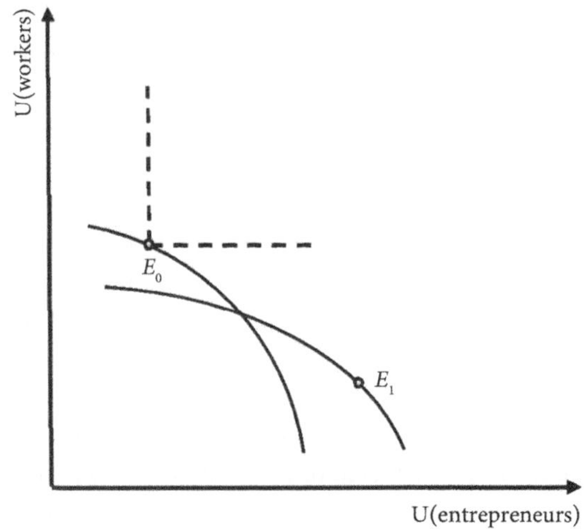

Figure 18.2 Potential Pareto frontier with costly redistribution.

Of course, the innovation may not be labor saving, and the equilibrium E_1 itself could be to the northeast of E_0. Although this case is easier, the distribution of the gains from innovation and any associated pecuniary externalities and rents may still be contentious, especially if they lead to large disparities in income. Distributive issues can also interact with production, as emphasized, for example, by the efficiency wage theories that we consider in greater depth in Section 5.

2.3 Perfect Markets but Costly Redistribution

There is another possibility—that as we try to redistribute, the new utility possibility curve may lie inside of the old utility possibilities frontier near the original equilibrium. This may be the case even in a world that is first-best ex post; in other words, in which all the conditions for Pareto efficiency would be satisfied ex post, after the innovation has taken place.

Observation 3. *If the world is first-best ex post, but redistribution is limited or costly, then a Pareto improvement may not be possible, and some groups in society may oppose technological progress. With a sufficiently inequality-averse social welfare function, societal welfare may be reduced.*

This case is illustrated in Figure 18.2. The utility possibilities frontier is constrained by the costs imposed by redistribution. Even though it might appear that innovation could make everyone better off technologically, given the existing set of institutions of that economy, it actually can't—there may not be scope for avoiding utility losses for workers *if the innovation is allowed.*

which there is a large body of literature suggesting that at least some of the fruits of innovation have to be shared with workers. If they perceive the allocation of benefits to be unfair, they would rather be worse off (e.g., at the original point without the innovation) rather than at the point that just makes them indifferent to where they were before. See Fehr and Schmidt (2003).

Some economists argue that the world looks like Figure 18.2, and that if we try to transfer from innovators to workers, so much output is lost that workers are still worse off. If that is the case, then one cannot say that the innovation is a Pareto improvement. One hesitates to use the word "innovation." It is a change, perhaps a technological change, which has had the effect of making some people better off and others worse off. It is a distribution-inducing change and will be contentious.

A social welfare function that places no weight on inequality—which treats a dollar to rich innovators the same as a dollar to a poor worker—would, of course, conclude that the innovation is desirable. But with a more natural, inequality averse social welfare function, the so-called innovation is welfare decreasing.

The workers who lose out would rationally oppose the innovation. If workers are in a majority and innovators wish to maintain their position, it would behoove the innovators to think harder about how to engage in redistribution. This is, of course, a collective action problem for innovators—for individual innovators, the contribution to economy-wide inequality is typically limited, even if their collective behavior makes workers worse off. As a result, innovators often devote effort to actions which enhance their market power—lowering *real* incomes of workers still further—and to not paying taxes (both via clever tax avoidance using the existing legal framework, and via political lobbying to provide special exemptions from taxation for their industries). Disregarding, in our view unwisely, that their actions may stir up political opposition to innovation, some innovators go further and argue for weakening the progressivity of the tax system and a smaller state, so there are less public resources to provide for the well-being of the workers who are hurt by innovation.

According to a long-run version of "trickle-down" economics, repeated innovations will eventually increase the wealth of innovators so much that the benefits will trickle down to regular workers. In this view, a Pareto improvement is always possible in the long run, as in Figure 18.1, even if an entire generation of workers is hurt in the short to medium run. This is a possibility and, in fact, the first industrial revolution may be an example. During the industrial revolution, workers eventually obtained enough human capital—which was publicly provided, as was then in the interests of the innovators—so that the wages of almost all increased. In the current context, however, once machines are smart enough, innovators may no longer have incentives to support the public financing of human capital accumulation, and it may well be that workers' standards of living decrease. In particular, in a political system dominated by money, the innovators, increasingly rich, may use their economic and political influence to resist redistribution. Furthermore, even if long-run trickle-down economics were correct, it may lead to tremendous suffering and social upheaval in the short run. It may also—understandably—not be very credible if innovators promise that once they are rich enough, they will support workers, but that they are not quite rich enough yet.

This leads to the important question: *How costly is redistribution in practice?* As we noted earlier, markets don't exist in a vacuum. They are structured by laws and regulations and by how those laws and regulations are enforced. The outcome is the so-called "market" distribution of income, which is then subject to taxes and transfer, leading to an after-tax distribution of income. But this conventional distinction may not be quite accurate: the rules of the game concerning redistribution affect the market income distribution, and are themselves endogenous, affected by the rules of the political game, which in turn are affected by the distribution of wealth. See Piketty, Saez, and Stantcheva (2014), Stiglitz (2018b), and Chapter 16 in this volume. The points that we have denoted E_0 and E_1 describe the initial outcome and the outcome after-technological change, *assuming that laws, regulations, institutions, etc. remain unchanged.* But, of course, it is not reasonable to expect that they would remain unchanged with the advent of a change as significant as AI.

Setting aside the endogeneity of the rules themselves, each set of (feasible) laws, regulations, institutions, etc. defines a feasible utility possibilities frontier. We can think of the second-best utility possibilities frontier as the outer envelope of all these frontiers. As the outer envelope, the second-best utilities possibilities frontier provides more flexibility for redistribution than does that associated with one particular set of rules, regulations, and institutions. This reflects that any changes in laws, regulations, or institutions etc. will also have redistributive effects. Given this additional flexibility, the likelihood that a Pareto improvement as in Figure 18.1 can be achieved is greater. We provide further arguments for why this is likely to be the case in Section 4 (although we cannot entirely rule out a situation like that depicted in Figure 18,2 in which a Pareto improvement is not feasible).

2.4 Imperfect Markets

Let us now consider a fourth case:

Observation 4. *If the economy is not first-best ex post, then the utility possibilities frontier may move inwards in response to an expansion of production possibilities. Furthermore, this may even be true with costless redistribution.*

When we speak about an economy that is not first-best, we mean an economy that deviates from the Arrow–Debreu benchmark, that is, that exhibits market imperfections such as information problems, missing markets, price and wage rigidities which can result in aggregate demand problems, monopolies and monopsonies, and so forth. Typically, these mean that the market equilibrium is not Pareto efficient. The utility possibilities frontier now represents the maximum utility of workers, given that of entrepreneurs, taking the market failures as given.

This case is illustrated in Figure 18.3. The initial equilibrium is E_0, but the innovation, which would have led to greater efficiency in the absence of these market imperfections, makes workers worse off—and even with costless redistributions, there is no way that both workers and entrepreneurs can be better off.

An example, elaborated on by Delli Gatti, Gallegati, Greenwald, et al. (2012a, 2012b), were the agricultural improvements at the end of the nineteenth century and beginning of the twentieth. The result was that agricultural prices plummeted, and so too did incomes on farms and in the rural sector. But mobility is costly—moving to the urban sector required capital, and many farmers saw their capital disappear as the value of their farms decreased. Those with loans often went bankrupt. Capital market imperfections (based on information asymmetries) meant that farmers couldn't borrow to move to the city to where the new jobs would be created. But as incomes in the rural sector plummeted, they couldn't buy the goods made by the manufacturing sector. Workers in both the rural and urban sector were

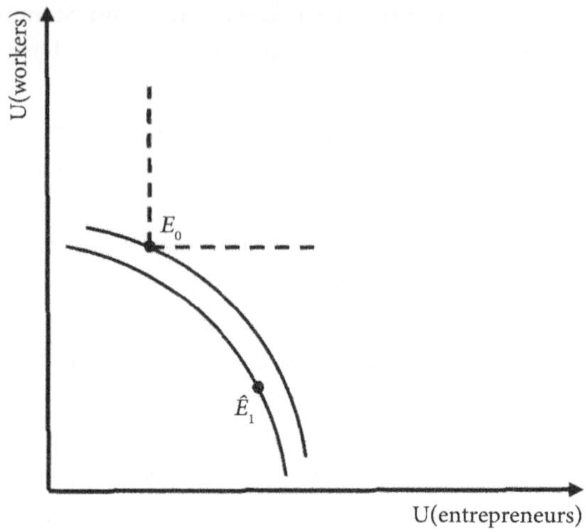

Figure 18.3 Potential Pareto frontier with market imperfections.

worse off.[13] This provides one interpretation of the Great Depression—in the short run, the innovations at the time proved Pareto inferior.

Another example is given by the now standard result that free trade may lead everyone to be worse off in the absence of good risk markets (Newbery and Stiglitz, 1984). That result can be interpreted as one involving technological progress. Assume that there were no way of transporting goods between two countries. A technological advance allows goods to be transported freely. Then, under the quite plausible conditions postulated by Newbery-Stiglitz, welfare (of everyone!) in both countries could decrease.

The theory of the second best (Meade, 1955; Lipsey and Lancaster, 1956) reminds us that in the presence of market imperfections, improving the functioning of one market may deteriorate overall welfare. There are reasons to believe that certain innovations in financial markets, for example, structured financial products and certain derivatives like credit default swaps, especially in the absence of appropriate regulations, contributed greatly to the Great Recession (Financial Crisis Inquiry Commission, 2011).[14]

It is important to appreciate the result described in Observation 4 to understand how crucial our institutions and our market imperfections are in determining whether and how large a benefit society will derive from innovation.

2.5 Endogenous Technological Progress

A fifth and last point to emphasize is that there is no first welfare theorem for endogenous innovation. Generally speaking, the private returns to innovation in an economy differ from the social returns.

[13] In the central Deli Gatti, Gallegati, Greenwald, et al. model, the agricultural sector has constant returns to scale and wages in the urban sector are rigid (e.g., because of efficiency wage considerations), so that the agricultural innovations are unambiguously welfare decreasing. In one variant of the model, where urban wages are flexible, wage decreases lead to still higher unemployment. Though it is possible that entrepreneurs gain more from the wage reductions than they lose from the loss of sales, social welfare is decreased with sufficiently inequality averse social welfare functions.

[14] At a theoretical level, Simsek (2013) and Guzman and Stiglitz (2016a, 2016b) have shown that opening up new markets—through financial innovation—can lead to greater volatility in consumption.

Observation 5. *The privately optimal choice of innovation may move the utility possibilities frontier inward, even if redistribution is costless and even if there were no other market failures.*

This implies that there may be benefits from intervening in the innovation process to generate Pareto improvements, for example, by making it less labor saving (see, e.g., Chapter 17 above). Again, this does not specifically refer to advances in artificial intelligence—it will probably not apply to most examples of innovation in AI—but it is easy to think of examples where privately optimal innovation may generate Pareto deteriorations, for example, in the context of high-frequency trading in financial markets (see, e.g., Stiglitz, 2014c).

2.6 Ascertaining Whether the Economy Is Best Described by Observation 1, 2, 3, 4, or 5

It is not always easy to ascertain which of the situations discussed in the four subsections above best describes the economy. Typically, the only thing that we can observe is that an innovation has made some individuals better off, some worse off. (In our analysis of AI, we assume that it has made workers worse off, entrepreneurs better off.) The presumption is that risk markets for innovation are highly imperfect (so Observation 1 does not apply), redistributions are costly (so Observation 2 does not strictly apply) and markets are imperfect (so Observation 3 does not strictly apply). But the costs of redistributions may be sufficiently low and the market imperfections sufficiently small that Figure 18.1 still applies: everyone could be made better off. Alternatively, redistributions may be so costly that Figure 18.2 applies. Or market failures may be sufficiently large and redistributions sufficiently costly that Figure 18.3 applies.

We emphasize that which situation we are in depends not just on the possibilities of ex post redistribution, but on the institutional flexibility, which determines the ex ante distribution. Moreover, when we see a technological innovation that has resulted in the worsening of some group's well-being, we can't infer much about which of the situations we are in: it may well be that there is a feasible redistribution that could have made all groups better off, but it was *politics* that determined the outcome. Indeed, if politics are driven by money, and the technological innovation leads to a new distribution marked by more inequality, the rich may use some of their increased wealth to invest in the adoption of an even more inequalitarian set of rules, including a more regressive tax system, as discussed in Chapter 16.

As we noted, the second-best utility possibilities frontier is the outer envelope of all conceivable constrained utility possibilities frontiers, which reflect all the conceivable institutional regimes in an economy and all the market imperfections that the economy may suffer from. By *institutional regimes* we mean all explicit tax and redistribution systems (from negative income tax systems to universal basic income to the regressive tax system currently in place), intellectual property regimes, job programs, education programs, but even social norms such as those related to charitable contributions. *Market imperfections* include all the market arrangements that differ from the Arrow–Debreu "optimal" benchmark, the conditions which ensure the Pareto efficiency of the market. As we noted earlier, the term embraces imperfections in information, competition, and risk and capital markets (including "missing" markets) but also rigidities in factor reallocation or in prices that determine how easily factors and products reallocate and which may be particularly important in the context of technological progress.

Changing any of these institutions or market imperfections affects workers' welfare. In general, it may be desirable to use a package of changes to all these institutions to ensure Pareto improvements after technological change has occurred. For instance, in Section 4.3, we show that a combination of a change in the intellectual property regime *and* a change in capital taxation can ensure that an innovation is a Pareto improvement.

Finally, we also note that the possibility of achieving a Pareto improvement depends on how broadly we define the classes of individuals which are affected by an innovation. Our earlier example differentiated society, for simplicity, into two categories, workers and entrepreneurs. More generally, different categories of workers, for example, skilled and unskilled workers, or workers in different sectors or tasks, are differentially affected by innovation. By the same token, different categories of entrepreneurs or innovators are differentially affected by innovation—for example, a given entrepreneur will generally be worse off if she is out-competed by another's innovation. In the limit, if we consider the welfare of every single agent in the economy, clear Pareto improvements in a strict sense will be very difficult to find. As a result, our scope of analysis has to be targeted at the level that is relevant for the question at hand.

From both a political and a macroeconomic perspective, it is desirable that our welfare analysis focuses on groups that are sufficiently broad so that they matter for the political or economic equilibrium. It may also be useful to focus on groups that can be targeted with specific policy measures. Having said that, there is also a useful role for social safety nets that insure single individuals that lose out—for example, an innovator who goes broke because he was outpaced by a competitor.

2.7 Relationship between Technological Progress and Globalization

Many of the effects of technological change in general and AI in particular are similar to those of globalization. Indeed, globalization can be viewed as a change in technology, that of trading with the rest of the world.

In particular, trade of advanced countries with developing countries is "labor saving" (in the sense of Hicks): the demand for unskilled workers, or workers in general, decreases, at any given wage, implying that while the production possibilities curve moves out, and the utility possibilities curve may move out, the new equilibrium entails workers being worse off, as in Figures 18.1 and 18.2. (In the absence of good risk markets, as we noted, everyone can be worse off, as in Figure 18.3.) Thus, the issue of whether globalization is welfare enhancing comes back to the question addressed in this chapter: is it possible to ensure, either through redistributive taxes or changes in institutions/rules, that workers are not made worse off. Again, there is a presumption that the gains to capital (or enterprises) could be taxed, to provide the requisite redistributions.[15]

[15] Although a given country that opens up to trade is always made better off in a first-best world, ensuring a global Pareto improvement after a country reduces its trade barriers may be even more difficult than after technological progress has occurred, since changes in trade barriers affect international terms of trade and lead to

As we discuss in greater detail below, one of the side effects of innovation and IPR is the creation of market power, resulting in ex post inefficient outcomes. Similarly, one of the consequences of globalization is to weaken the market power of workers. This is important because there is ample evidence that labor markets are far from perfectly competitive. The requisite compensation and/or offsetting changes in institutional rules to ensure that globalization represents a Pareto improvement may thus have to be all the greater.

3 Technological Progress and Channels of Inequality

There are two main channels through which technological progress may affect the distribution of resources and thus inequality: first, through the surplus earned by innovators and secondly, through effects on other agents in the economy.

3.1 Surplus Earned by Innovators

Technology is an information good, which implies that it is *non-rival*, but it may be *excludable*. Non-rival means that information can be used without being used up—in principle, many economic actors could use the same technology at the same time. If information about an innovation is widely shared, it can be used by all of society and provide welfare benefits to anybody who uses it. The excludable nature of information means, however, that others can be prevented from either obtaining or using a technology, for example by withholding it from the public (e.g., as a business secret) or by using social institutions such as intellectual property rights (e.g., copyrights or patents). This excludability may provide innovators with market power that enables them to charge a positive price for the innovation and earn a surplus.

Society faces a difficult trade-off in determining how to engineer the optimal level of innovation. In a first-best world, there are no agency problems in the process of innovation, and an optimal solution would be for the public to fund innovations and make them freely available to all (see, e.g., Arrow, 1962). In fact, this model of financing innovation is common for basic research and has given rise to some very significant innovations in history, including the invention of the Internet. A closely related solution is the production of innovations for non-pecuniary rewards, such as e.g. the prevalence of open-source technology, which is widespread in the context of software and even artificial intelligence.[16]

However, in many circumstances, private agents operating in a very decentralized way are superior in producing innovation, and when they fund innovation, they expect to earn a return, which they obtain by having some degree of monopoly power over the innovation, the ideas behind it, or both. The surplus earned by innovators then plays an important economic role because it rewards innovators for what they accomplish—it represents the

redistributions across all other countries that can only be undone via cross-country transfers. See, for example, Korinek (2016). Furthermore, within each country, gains from trade inherently require changes in relative prices, which means that large redistributions are even more likely than in the case of technological progress.

[16] This approach relies on individuals or companies that are willing to innovate in exchange for non-pecuniary rewards such as prestige or, alternatively, on a calculated decision that providing free technology will steer potential customers or employees toward an innovator's platform, as seems to be the case in the field of AI.

economic return to innovation activity. However, as a result there is generally some market power associated with innovations, especially when there is a system of IPR in place, and this generally leads to inefficiencies compared to the first-best allocation in which innovations are distributed as public goods.[17]

We distinguish the following two cases, which determine whether innovators earn rents, that is, payoffs in excess of the cost of their innovative activity:

First, if entry into innovation activity is restricted, then the surplus or net income earned by innovators is generally greater than the costs of innovation activity. A natural example of such restrictions is when only a small number of people are endowed with special skills that enable them to innovate. These innovators then earn rents based on their exclusive differential abilities.

Restrictions to innovative activity may also arise from market structure: in markets with Bertrand competition, the first entrant who develops a costly innovation may enjoy a monopoly position because any potential competitor knows that if she enters, the incumbent will cut prices to marginal cost so that she cannot recoup the investment into an innovation.[18]

Secondly, if innovative activity is contestable, that is, if there is a sufficiently large set of potential innovators with equal skills, then the expected rents to innovative activity are competed down to zero, that is, the marginal entrant into innovative activity is indifferent between innovating or not.[19] However, given that the payoffs to innovation are highly stochastic, there will be winners and losers ex post. In the context of new technologies, the distribution of payoffs seems to be increasingly skewed, with a small number of entrepreneurs earning gigantic payoffs and the vast majority earning little in return for their efforts. This gives rise to significant inequality even among innovators.[20]

In either case, the returns earned by an innovator may not correspond closely to the social returns to the innovation; in particular, some of the returns may reflect the capture of profits that would otherwise have gone to other entrepreneurs.

3.1.1 Policies to Share the Surplus of Innovators

There is a growing consensus that one of the sources of the growth of inequality is the growth of rents, including the rents that innovators earn in excess of the cost of innovation

[17] For discussions of the merits of alternative ways of funding and incentivizing innovation, see Stiglitz (2008), Dosi and Stiglitz (2014), Baker, Jayadev, and Stiglitz (2017), and Korinek and Ng (2017).

[18] See Stiglitz (1987e) and Dasgupta and Stiglitz (1988c). When the number of firms is limited and there is Cournot competition, there will also be rents associated with innovation. For more general theoretical discussions of industrial structure and innovation, see Dasgupta and Stiglitz (1980a, 1980b) and Stiglitz and Greenwald (2014). Note that even if the expected return to investments in R&D is just the opportunity cost of capital—there are no rents—the stochastic nature of returns to innovation means that large inequalities may be generated.

[19] Given the difficulty of predicting the success of innovative activity or of even assigning success probabilities, it is questionable how efficiently this mechanism works in practice. For example, there may be excessive entry because of over-optimism by some potential entrepreneurs, or there may be insufficient entry because of imperfect insurance markets for entrepreneurs.

[20] If there are diminishing returns to the allocation of resources to innovation, the efficient resource allocation will entail there being rents associated with innovation. Who captures these rents will be affected by the institutional (including tax) structure. In the absence of adequate mechanisms for the public capturing those rents, there may be excessive investments in innovation, a standard result in the economics of the commons.

Under some circumstances, well-designed contests can provide strong cost-effective incentives, but patent races may fail to incentivize the appropriate levels and nature of innovation. Incumbents may attempt to pre-empt rivals (Dasgupta and Stiglitz, 1980b). Those ahead may simply establish a sufficient lead over others to discourage other (Fudenberg, Gilbert, Stiglitz, and Tirole, 1983).

(see, e.g., Korinek and Ng, 2018). Taxing and redistributing such rents have an important role in ensuring that AI and other advances in technology are Pareto improving. Also, antitrust policies may lower such rents, ensuring that the benefits of innovations are more widely shared, as more competition lowers consumer prices from which all benefit. From the perspective of low-wage workers who lose from innovation, targeted expenditure programs financed by high rent taxes may be of greater benefit than the lowering of prices, the benefit of which will go disproportionately to those who have high spending power.

Moreover, changes in intellectual property rights (IPRs) affect who receives the benefits of innovation—and thus the "incidence" of innovation, since IPRs are instrumental in providing extended market power to innovators.[21]

Additionally, public research—with government or the public at large appropriating the returns, rather than allowing private firms to do so—together with stronger competition policies, might reduce the scope for monopolies capturing large fractions of the returns to innovation, and thus enhance the likelihood that AI will be Pareto improving.

Workers may also note that the innovations that ultimately led to AI—including those created by private entrepreneurs—build on significant public support. Society as a whole, but not necessarily this generation of innovators, paid for this knowledge, and should therefore share in the surplus generated by the innovation. One proposal to ensure that workers share in the benefits of innovation—and are less likely to lose from it—is to give workers shares in enterprises to ensure that their welfare goes up in tandem with that of shareholders/innovators as a whole.

3.2 Effects on Others

Innovation also leads to large redistributions among others in the economy who are not directly involved in the process of innovation, for example workers who experience a sudden increase or decline in the demand for their labor. These redistributions can thus be viewed as externalities from innovation, and they are one of the main reasons why innovation raises concerns about inequality. We distinguish two categories of such externalities, pecuniary and non-pecuniary externalities. We discuss both in detail in the following:

3.2.1 Pecuniary Externalities: Price and Wages Changes

Among the most prominent implications of technological change is that it affects the prices of factors of production (including wages) and of produced goods. Hicks (1932) already observed that innovations generally change the demand for factors and will, in equilibrium, lead to factor price changes, especially changes in wages. The price and wage changes that result from innovations represent pecuniary externalities. Traditional general equilibrium theory, following Arrow and Debreu, emphasized that pecuniary externalities are fully consistent with Pareto efficiency. However, the benchmark of Pareto efficiency is blind to the distribution of income. Even if the equilibrium reached after an innovation is Pareto efficient, the pecuniary externalities lead to redistributions and imply that there are winners and losers.

[21] Especially when there is Bertrand competition, the benefits of innovation may be quickly shared with consumers upon the termination of patents.

If—as many technologists predict—artificial intelligence directly replaces human labor, the demand for human labor will go down, and so will wages. More generally, innovations typically reduce demand for specific types of labor with specific human capital. For example, self-driving cars will likely depress the wages of drivers, or radiology-reading AI may lower the wages of traditional radiologists. Conversely, AI has certainly led to an increase in demand for computer scientists and has greatly increased their wages, in particular in sub-fields that are directly related to AI. Since AI is a general-purpose technology, there are reasons to believe that advances in AI will reverberate throughout many different sectors and lead to significant changes in wages throughout the economy in coming decades. Similar arguments can be made about the demand for and the value of different types of specific capital, as well as the demand for and prices of particular products.

Even though there are frequently losers, technological progress by definition shifts out the production possibilities frontier. This implies that the total dollar gain of the winners of progress exceeds the dollar loss of the losers.[22] In Section 4 below, we will use this property of technological progress to argue that, under relatively broad conditions, this should enable the redistribution that is necessary to ensure that innovation leads to a Pareto improvement: the gains that arise to some factor owners as a result of technological progress are excess returns that are like unearned rents and could be taxed away without introducing distortions into the economy.

Although we noted that pecuniary externalities are generally viewed as Pareto efficient, there are two reasons for why they are likely to be associated with inefficiency in practice. First, Geanakoplos and Polemarchakis (1986) and Greenwald and Stiglitz (1986) demonstrated that pecuniary externalities matter for efficiency when there are market imperfections such as imperfect information and incomplete risk markets—which there always are, and especially in the presence of innovation; market equilibrium will as a result not be Pareto efficient.

Second, if the pecuniary externalities from innovation give rise to the need for redistributive policies that are costly to perform, the policy response will generate additional inefficiencies.

3.2.2 Policies to Counter Wage Declines

Aside from lump-sum transfers, there are a range of further policies to counter the wage declines that are experienced by workers who are displaced by machines, even for low skilled jobs. These include wage subsidies and earned income tax credits. If bargaining power in labor markets is biased toward employers, an increased minimum wage can even increase employment and improve efficiency—and also help ensure that no one who works full time is in poverty. Furthermore, ensuring high aggregate demand—and thus a low unemployment rate—also increases the bargaining power of workers and leads to higher wages.

Other policies aimed at increasing the demand for labor, including those with low skills, include, for example, higher wages in the public sector as well as increases in public investments and other public expenditures; all of these policies help to drive up wages in the economy more generally.

[22] If lump sum transfers were feasible, the winners could compensate the losers. However, in the absence of such compensation, social welfare may be lower.

Policies that could be used to finance such measures include carbon taxes, which would encourage resource saving innovation, at the expense of labor-saving innovation. It would thus simultaneously address two of most serious global problems, global climate change and inequality.[23]

Furthermore, the elimination of tax deduction for interest and the imposition of a tax on capital would increase the cost of capital and induce more capital augmenting innovation rather than labor-saving innovation.[24]

3.2.3 Non-pecuniary Externalities

Innovation may also generate non-pecuniary externalities on agents other than the innovator. Classic examples for this are technological externalities—for example, if an innovation produces public goods, or generates or alleviates pollution. In markets that deviate from the Arrow–Debreu benchmark, a variety of non-pecuniary effects may arise: for example, innovation may affect quantities demanded, or the probability of buying or selling a good or factor, including the probability of being unemployed.

Some effects are such that they can be interpreted either as pecuniary or non-pecuniary externalities. For example, product innovations can be interpreted as a price changes—the price of the newly invented good changes from infinity to some positive value—or as a change in the price of the consumption services provided by the good. Alternatively, they can also be interpreted in a non-pecuniary manner by viewing a product (such as a smartphone) as providing a bundle of services to consumers which can only be bought in fixed proportion (e.g., since we cannot separately purchase different functions of the smartphone). In that view, an innovation represents a change in the structure of incomplete markets because it changes the bundle of consumption service available from a product. Similarly, changes in job quality can be interpreted by viewing each job as a vector of transactions that are only available in pre-determined bundles, and the innovation changes the elements in the bundle that are available. It is well-known, that changes in the degree of market incompleteness for such bundles give rise to externalities (a specific application of Greenwald and Stiglitz, 1986).

4 Worker-Replacing Progress and Redistribution

This section considers a stark form of technological progress that we term worker-replacing technological progress. We develop two simple models to analyze the two channels generating inequality that we discussed in the previous section. In Sections 4.1 and 4.2, we consider the pecuniary externalities (redistributions) generated by worker-replacing progress, both from a static and a dynamic perspective. In Section 4.3, we focus on the distribution of the surplus accruing to innovators in a model in which the surplus is determined by the level of patent protection. Furthermore, in Section 4.4 we discuss the implications of endogenous factor bias in technological progress.

[23] As we noted above, there is no first fundamental welfare theorem for innovation, and indeed, there is a presumption that the market is biased toward labor-saving innovation relative to innovations directed toward "saving the planet.". See Stiglitz (2014d).

[24] The allocation of resources to capital augmenting technological change depends on the after-tax share of capital. An increase in the relative cost of capital will increase the capital share if the elasticity of substitution is less than unity. Most of the empirical evidence suggests that this is the case.

4.1 Static Pecuniary Externalities of Worker-Replacing Progress

We assume a production technology that combines capital and labor in a constant- returns-to-scale (CRS) function, but where labor consists of the sum of human and machine labor. Assuming that human and machine labor enter the production function additively means that they are perfect substitutes for each other. The details of the baseline model are presented in Section 4.1.1. We analyze three questions: What does worker-replacing technological change do to wages in the short run and in the long run? And what can policy do about it?

First, we look exclusively at the short run before any of the other factors have adjusted:

Observation 6. ***Machine Labor and Factor Earnings (in the short run):*** *adding a marginal unit of machine labor reduces human wages but increases returns of complementary factors in a zero-sum manner.*

Intuitively, what happens if we add one unit of machine labor is that first, that unit will earn its marginal return, but secondly, there is also a redistribution from labor to capital, which now becomes relatively scarcer. The gains of capital are exactly the losses of the existing stock of labor.

The redistribution generated by technological progress can be thought of as a pecuniary externality, as we emphasized earlier. The owners of capital have obtained windfall gains but have not done anything to earn these higher returns. A compensatory transfer from capital owners to workers simply undoes these windfall gains and leaves them equally well off as they were before.

More generally, adding machine labor creates a redistribution away from human labor toward complementary factors. This result holds for any CRS production function no matter what the complementary factor, for instance, whether it is capital or land or unskilled versus skilled labor or entrepreneurial rents. Policy can undo these redistributions by taxing windfall gains while leaving the price system to work at the margin. The result also holds for decreasing-returns-to-scale production functions if we interpret the profits earned by the owner of the technology as compensation for the implicit as a factor "entrepreneurship," which takes part in the zero-sum redistribution. Taxes on previously accumulated factors that suddenly earn an unexpected excess return are, of course, non-distortionary. This means that at least in principle, there is a role for implementing costless redistribution and generating a Pareto improvement. (In practice, there are some natural caveats to this result. For example, it relies on the assumption that we can distinguish between previously installed capital that earns windfall gains and new capital that would confront distorted incentives if it were taxed.)

Let us also emphasize that taxes on previously accumulated factors that suddenly earn an unexpected excess return are non-distortionary. This means that at least in principle, there is a role for implementing costless redistribution and generating a Pareto-improvement. (In practice, there are some natural caveats to this result. For example, it relies on the assumption that we can distinguish between previously installed capital that earns windfall gains and new capital that would be distorted if it were taxed.)

4.1.1 A Simple Model of Machine Labor and Factor Earnings

The key insights can be seen in a simple model. Assume a constant-returns-to-scale production function that produces output Y by combining capital K with labor, consisting of the sum of human labor H and machine labor M:

$$Y = F(K, H + M).$$

In this formulation human labor and machine labor are perfect substitutes, so machine technology is what we call worker-replacing. In the competitive equilibrium, the wage is determined by the marginal product of labor,

$$w = F_L.$$

Proposition 1. ***Machine Labor and Factor Earnings:*** adding a marginal unit of machine labor reduces human wages but increases the returns to capital in a zero-sum manner, in addition to increasing output by the marginal product of labor, which is equal to the wage.

Proof: Using Euler's Theorem, we rewrite the production function:

$$(H + M)F_L + KF_K = F(K, H + M).$$

We can now ascertain the effect of an additional unit of M:

$$F_L + (H + M)F_{LL} + KF_{KL} = F_L.$$

or

$$(H + M)F_{LL} + KF_{KL} = 0.$$

KF_{KL} is the increase in returns to capital as a result of the increased supply of human-replacing robots. This gain comes at the expense of a decline in the wage bill.

4.2 Dynamic Implications of Worker-Replacing Progress

In the longer run, worker-replacing technological change will lead to significant economic change. It implies that the biggest constraint on output—the scarcity of labor—is suddenly relaxed. As a result, greater amounts of complementary factors, here capital, are accumulated.

Observation 7. ***Machine Labor and Abundance of Labor:*** *If not only capital but also labor is reproducible at sufficiently low cost, then the economy will grow exponentially in AK-fashion, driven purely by factor accumulation, even in the absence of further technological change.*

In Korinek and Stiglitz (2017), we describe the dynamics of this transition, as machines made by machines get increasingly efficient or equivalently, as the cost of producing machines decreases. We identify a singularity point at which it becomes cost-effective for machines to start to fully replace human labor.[25] In the simplest case, when complementary factors such as capital adjust without friction, the human wage may actually be unchanged because capital K grows in proportion to effective labor (H + M) so that the marginal productivity of labor and the wage remain unchanged. In other words, investment is allocated between conventional machines and human-replacing robots in such a way that the return is equal to the intertemporal marginal rate of substitution. Under the assumption that workers only care about their absolute income, not their relative income, this outcome would not be too bad: in absolute terms, even though the human labor share would go to zero as an increasing fraction of the labor in the economy is performed by machines, workers are no worse off as a result of AI.

When factors are slow to adjust, the pattern of transition can be complex, with demand for human labor typically going down temporarily.[26] In general, the pattern of adjustment depends on how fast the capital stock versus the stock of labor-cum-human-replacing machines adjust. (For example, if the capital stock rises in anticipation of an increased supply of machine labor in the future that has not yet materialized, then human wages may even go up at intermediate stages.[27])

However, the following observation describes that, in the long run, workers are actually worse off as a result of machine labor if there are non-reproducible complementary factors that are in scarce supply, such as land or other natural resources:

Observation 8. ***Machine Labor and Return of Scarcity*:** *if there are non-reproducible complementary factors, they eventually limit growth; human real wages fall, and the owners of non-reproducible factors absorb all the rents.*

Intuitively, as the supply of effective labor proliferates due to the introduction of machine labor, agents in the economy will compete for scarce non-reproducible resources like land, driving up their price.

A similar argument holds for non-reproducible consumption goods: even if all factors in the production process are reproducible so that productive output in the economy exhibits AK-style growth and workers' product wages remain unchanged, competition for fixed resources that are part of their consumption basket, such as land used for housing, may lead workers to eventually be worse off. This may be particularly important in urban settings where, say, economic activity occurs at the center. Rich rentiers may occupy the more desirable locations near the center, with workers having to obtain less expensive housing at the periphery, spending more time commuting. The advent of AI will thus lower their utility.

[25] This singularity captures the important economic aspects of what technologists such as Vernor Vinge (1993) or Ray Kurzweil (2005) call the technological singularity. A similar point is also made in Aghion, Jones, and Jones (2017).

[26] Berg, Buffie, and Zana (2018) shows that it may actually take decades for the economy's complementary capital stock to adjust after major revolutions in labor-saving technology.

[27] This assumes that capital is "putty-putty," that is, that capital investments made before AI arrives are equally productive after AI, as would be the case if humans and robots were in fact identical.

However, just as in the earlier case, at the margin, the redistribution from workers to non-reproducible factor owners is zero sum. Since taxes on non-reproducible factors are by definition non-distortionary, there is scope for non-distortionary redistribution.

Observation 9. ***Non-Reproducible Factors and Pareto Improvements:*** *So long as non-distortionary taxes on factor rents are feasible, labor-replacing innovation can be a Pareto improvement.*

4.3 Redistributing the Innovators' Surplus via Changes in Institutions

If outright redistribution is limited or infeasible, there may be other institutional changes which result in market distributions which are more favorable to workers. For example, intervention to steer technological progress may act as a second-best device.

In this section, we provide an example in which a change in intellectual property rights—a shortening of the term of patent protection—effectively redistributes some of the innovators' surplus to workers (consumers) to mitigate the pecuniary externalities on wages that they experience, with the ultimate goal that the benefits of the innovation are more widely shared. If an innovation results in a lower cost of production, then the innovator enjoys the benefits of the innovation in the form of higher profits during the life of the patent; but after the expiration of the patent, society enjoys the benefits in terms of lower prices. The trade-off is that shortening the life of the patent may reduce the pace of innovation. But in the spirit of the theory of the second-best, there is generally an "optimal" patent life, in which there is still some innovation, but in which the well-being of workers is protected.

With network externalities the innovator may be able to maintain a dominant position even after the end of the patent and may continue to earn the surplus from her innovation. With taxes on monopoly profits, it should be possible to ensure that the innovations are Pareto improving and that even human worker-replacing technological change can improve the well-being of workers.

4.3.1 Intellectual Property Regime and Redistribution

Consider an economy with a unit mass of workers $H = 1$, in which the capital stock supplied each period $K(\tau)$ is a function solely of a distortionary capital tax τ, the proceeds of which are distributed to workers, and the effective stock of machine labor $M(z)$ is an increasing function of patent life z.

A worker's total income I consists of her wage plus the revenue of the capital tax,

$$I = w + \tau K(\tau)$$

For any level of $M(z)$, we define $\tau(M)$ as the value of the capital tax that keeps workers just as well off as they were before the introduction of machine labor. ($\tau(M)$ can take into account both the adverse effect of the innovation on wages as a result of the increase in the supply of human-replacing machines and any increase in real wages as a result of a reduction in the costs of producing goods not captured by the innovator.)

Proposition 2. As long as elasticity of capital supply is not too large, we can always increase z from $z = 0$ and compensate workers by raising the capital tax τ.

4.3.1.1 Steady-State Dynamics

Consider an intertemporal setting in which the growth rate $g = g(z, \tau)$ is a function of the length of the patent z and the tax rate τ, by which we now denote the tax rate on innovators. Assume that the share of output that is invested is a function of the growth rate ($i(g)$) and that the fraction of output not spent on investment that is appropriated by the innovator is $b(z, \tau)$. In steady state, the present discounted value of the income of workers can be approximated as

$$PDV = (1 - i(g))[1 - (1 - \tau)\, b(z, \tau)] / (r - g)$$

where r is the discount rate. If we choose $\{z, \tau\}$ to maximize the PDV, in general, the optimum will not be a corner solution in which any innovation hurts workers.

Proposition 3. In general, the optimal $\{z^*, \tau^*\}$ entails $g > 0$.

It is easy to write down sufficient conditions under which Proposition 3 holds: setting τ^* equal to zero, all that we require is that $|gz|$ is not too large relative to $|bz|$.

4.4 Factor-Biased Technological Change

So far, we have simply assumed that technological change—the introduction of AI—is worker-replacing. But advances in technology also make some machines more productive, and others obsolete, affecting the marginal return to traditional capital.[28] It is thus useful to think of the world as having three groups: capitalists, workers, and innovators. Intellectual property rights (and anti-trust laws) determine the returns to innovators; but the nature of technological change in a competitive market determines the division between workers and capitalists.

A long-standing literature, going back to Kennedy (1964), Samuelson (1965), and Von Weizsäcker (1966), describes the endogenous determination of the factor bias of technological progress.[29] The central result is that as the share of labor becomes smaller, the bias shifts toward capital-augmenting technological progress. If the world works as these models suggest, this should limit the decline in the share of labor (at least in a stable equilibrium) and in inequality.[30] As the share of labor decreases, the incentive to produce worker-replacing innovation such as AI decreases. But the relevant discounted future wage share near the point of singularity—the point where it is cost-effective for machines to fully replace human

[28] As we noted earlier, IA (intelligence assisting) innovation may increase the productivity of humans, and thus increase the demand for humans, if the elasticity of substitution is less than unity.

[29] Important contributions were also made by Drandakis and Phelps (1966). More recently, there has been some revival of the literature, with work of Acemoglu (2002), Stiglitz (2006b, 2014d), and Acemoglu and Restrepo (2018), among others.

[30] One can describe dynamics with standard wage-setting mechanisms. The system is stable so long as the elasticity of substitution between factors is less than unity (Acemoglu, 1998; Stiglitz, 2006b, 2014d).

labor and produce more machines all by themselves—may be sufficiently great that there is nonetheless an incentive to pass the point of singularity.

Let us assume that land becomes the binding constraint once human labor is fully replaceable by machine labor. In that case, provided the elasticity of substitution between land and the other production factors—capital cum labor—is less than unity, the share of land increases over time, generating the result (analogous to that where labor is the binding constraint in the standard literature) that in the long run, all technological progress is land-augmenting. If the production function is constant returns to scale in land, labor (including machine labor) and traditional capital, then the long run rate of growth is determined by the pace of land-augmenting technological change.

4.4.1 Role of the Service Sector

Currently, progress in AI focuses on certain sectors of the economy, like manufacturing. Partly because of the resulting lower cost of manufacturing, partly because of the shape of preferences, the economy is evolving toward a service sector economy. (If there is differential productivity across sectors, and the elasticity of demand for the innovation sector is not too high, then production factors will move out of that sector into other sectors. This is even more so if preferences are non-homothetic, e.g., demand for food and many manufactured goods having an income elasticity less than unity.) Among the key service sectors are education, health, the military, and other public services. The value of those services is in large part socially determined, that is, by public policies not just a market process. If we value those services highly—pay good wages, provide good working conditions, and create a sufficient number of jobs—this will limit increases in the inequality of market income. Governments typically play an important role in these sectors, and their employment policies will thus play an important role in the AI transition. Many of these service sector jobs have limited skill requirements. However, higher public sector wages will—through standard equilibrium effects—also raise wages in the private sector, will improve the bargaining position of workers, and will result in such jobs having higher "respect." All of this will, of course, require tax revenues. If the elasticity of entrepreneurial services is low—for example, if entrepreneurs are driven partly by non-pecuniary motives—we can impose high taxes to finance these jobs and still maintain a high rate of innovation.

5 Technological Unemployment

Unemployment is one of the most problematic societal implications of technological progress—new technology often implies that old jobs are destroyed and workers need to find new jobs. Economists, of course, understand the "lump-of-labor fallacy"—the false notion that there is a fixed number of jobs, and that automating a given job means that there will forever be fewer jobs left in the economy. In a well-functioning economy, we generally expect that technological progress creates additional income, which in turn can support more jobs.

However, there are two sound economic reasons for why technological unemployment may arise: first, because wages do not adjust for some structural reason, as described, for example, by efficiency wage theories, and second as a transition phenomenon. The two phenomena may also interact in important ways, for example, when efficiency wage considerations slow down the transition to a new equilibrium. We discuss the two categories in turn in the following subsections.

The unemployment implications are especially problematic when technological progress is labor-saving, which—by definition—requires that either wages have to fall or that other complementary factors like capital have to adjust enough for labor market equilibrium to be restored, at or above the historic wage.

5.1 Efficiency Wage Theory and Nonadjustment of Wages

The first category of technological unemployment arises when wages do not adjust for structural reasons. Efficiency wage theory emphasizes that productivity depends on wages and so employers may have reasons to pay wages above the market clearing level. The original paper on efficiency wages (Stiglitz, 1969c) noted one of the reasons for this: that income disparities can weaken worker morale. Akerlof and Yellen (1990) have formalized this into the "fair wage hypothesis."

If fairness considerations are significant enough, and workers think that a decrease in their wages is "unfair" (for example because the income of entrepreneurs increases so entrepreneurs could easily "afford" pay increases), it means that the scope of labor-saving progress which shifts the utility possibilities curve out *without redistributions* is very limited. Similar results hold if workers' well-being and efforts are related to relative incomes. The new utility possibilities curve may lie outside the old one to the "north" of E_0, that is, there is scope for a Pareto improvement in principle; but it may lie inside of the old utility possibilities curve near E_1, that is, the utility possibilities of workers decrease for a given level of utility of entrepreneurs because workers reduce their effort so much that the effective labor supply declines—any gains from technology are more than offset by increased shirking. Shapiro and Stiglitz (1984) emphasize that paying a wage above the market-clearing level reduces shirking, leading to unemployment.

An even more daunting example of efficiency wages may arise if automation continues and the marginal product of labor for low-skill workers falls below their cost of living at what they view as their basic subsistence (even if they exert their best effort). Unless basic social services are provided to such workers, a nutritional efficiency wage model applies in that case, similar to what Stiglitz (1976d) described for developing countries: employers could not pay a market clearing wage because they know that this would be insufficient for their employees to provide for themselves and remain productive.[31]

In traditional efficiency wage models, the unemployment effects of efficiency wages are permanent, part of the long run equilibrium. For example, if technological change leads to greater inequality (or better information about the existing level of inequality), morale effects and the resulting efficiency wage responses imply that the equilibrium level of unemployment rises.

However, efficiency wage arguments may also contribute to slowing down the transition to a new equilibrium after an innovation, as we will explore below in Section 5.2.

[31] Even worse outcomes could emerge in the presence of imperfect capital markets if expenditures on health and nutrition at one date affect productivity at later dates.

5.1.1 Minimum Wages and Nonadjustment of Wages

An alternative reason why wages may not adjust to the market-clearing level are minimum wage laws. Basic economics implies that there will be unemployment if wages are set to an excessive level. Although this is a theoretical possibility, recent experience in the U.S. has repeatedly shown that modest increases in minimum wages from current levels have hardly any employment effects but raise the income of minimum wage workers, which may have positive aggregate demand effects since low-income workers have a high marginal propensity to consume (see, e.g., Schmitt, 2013). From an economic theory perspective, these observations are possible because wages are not determined in a purely Walrasian manner—there is a significant amount of bargaining involved when prospective employers and employees match—and increases in minimum wages substitute for the lacking bargaining power of workers (see, e.g., Manning, 2011). Indeed, in monoposonistic labor markets, a minimum wage may lower the marginal cost of hiring an additional worker, and even lead to increased employment.

5.2 Technological Unemployment as a Transition Phenomenon

The second category of technological unemployment is as a transition phenomenon, that is, when technological change makes workers redundant at a faster pace than they can find new jobs or that new jobs are created. This phenomenon was already observed by Keynes (1930). It is well understood that there is always a certain "natural" or "equilibrium" level of unemployment as a result of churning in the labor market. In benchmark models of search and matching to characterize this equilibrium level of unemployment (see Mortensen and Pissarides, 1994, 1998), employment relationships are separated at random, and workers and employers need to search for new matches to replace them. The random shocks in this framework can be viewed as capturing, in reduced form, phenomena such as life-cycle transitions but also technological progress in individual firms. In this view, an increase in the pace of technological progress corresponds to a higher job separation rate and results in a higher equilibrium level of unemployment.

The transition may be especially prolonged if technology implies that the old skills of workers become obsolete and they need to acquire new skills and/or find out what new jobs match their skills (see, e.g., Restrepo, 2015).

Even if in the long run, workers adjusted to AI, the transition may be difficult. AI will impact some sectors more than others, and there will be significant job dislocation. As a general lesson, markets on their own are not good at structural transformation. Often, the pace of job destruction is greater than the pace of job creation, especially as a result of imperfections in capital markets, inhibiting the ability of entrepreneurs to exploit quickly new opportunities as they are opened up.

5.2.1 The Great Depression as an Example of Transitional Unemployment

The Great Depression can be viewed as being caused by rapid pace of innovation in agriculture (see Delli Gatti, Gallegati, Greenwald, et al., 2012a, 2012b). Fewer workers were needed to produce the food that individuals demanded, resulting in marked decline in agriculture prices and income, leading to a decline in demand for urban products. In the late 1920s, these effects became so large that long standing migration patterns were reversed.

What *might* have been a Pareto improvement turned out to be an immiserizing technological change, as both those in the urban and rural sector suffered.

The general result is that noted earlier: with mobility frictions and rigidities (themselves partly caused be capital market imperfections, as workers in the rural sector couldn't obtain funds to obtain the human capital required in the urban sector and to relocate) technological change can be welfare decreasing. The economy can be caught, for an extensive period of time, in a low-level equilibrium trap, with high unemployment and low output.

In the case of the Great Depression, government intervention (as a by-product of World War II) eventually enabled a successful structural transformation: The intervention was not only a Keynesian stimulus, but facilitated the move from rural farming areas to the cities where manufacturing was occurring at the time; and facilitated the retraining of the labor force, helping workers acquire the skills necessary for success in an urban manufacturing environment, which were quite different from those that ensured success in a rural, farming environment. It was, in this sense, an example of a successful industrial policy.

There are clear parallels to the situation today in that a significant fraction of the workforce may not have the skills required to succeed in the age of AI.

5.2.2 Transitional Efficiency Wage Theory

Efficiency wage arguments may also slow down the transition to a new equilibrium after technological progress. For example, if worker morale depends on last period's wages, it may be difficult to reduce wages to the market-clearing level after a labor-saving innovation, and unemployment may persist for a long time.[32]

5.2.3 Jobs and Meaning

The potentially widespread destruction of jobs can have large human consequences that go beyond just economics because jobs provide not only income but also other mental services such as meaning, dignity, and fulfillment to humans. Whether this is a legacy of our past, and whether individuals could find meaning in other forms of activities, mental or physical, is a matter of philosophical debate.

If workers derive a separate benefit from work in the form of meaning, then job subsidies are a better way of ensuring that technological advances are welfare-enhancing than simply providing lump sum grants (e.g., through the provision a universal basic income), as some are suggesting in response to the inequalities created by AI.

This discussion is, of course, a departure from the usual neoclassical formulation, where work only enters negatively into individual's well-being. There are some that claim that individuals' deriving dignity and meaning from work is an artifact of a world with labor scarcity. In a workerless AI world, individuals will have to obtain their identity and dignity elsewhere, for example, through spiritual or cultural values. The fact that most humans can find a meaningful life after retirement perhaps suggests that there are good substitutes for jobs in providing meaning, but Keynes' (1931) concerns about the inabilities of England's wealthy classes to find meaningful uses for their leisure casts somewhat of a pall over this possibility. (See also Stiglitz, 2008d.)

[32] In the limiting case, employers may simply keep wages fixed to avoid negative morale effects, and unemployment would persist forever—or until some offsetting shock occurs.

6 Longer-Term Perspectives

There is a final point, related to a somewhat longer-term perspective, that is worth discussing in a chapter on the implications of artificial intelligence for inequality. Currently, artificial intelligence is at the stage where it strictly dominates human intelligence in a number of specific areas, for instance playing chess or Go, identifying patterns in x-rays, driving, etc. This is commonly termed *narrow* artificial intelligence. By contrast, humans are able to apply their intelligence across a wide range of domains. This capacity is termed *general* intelligence.

If AI reaches and surpasses human levels of general intelligence, a set of radically different considerations apply. Some techno-optimists predict the advent of general artificial intelligence for as early as 2029 (see Kurzweil, 2005), although the median estimate in the AI expert community is around 2040–50, with most AI experts assigning a 90% probability to human-level general artificial intelligence arising within the current century (see Bostrom, 2014). A minority believes that general artificial intelligence will never arrive. However, if human-level artificial general intelligence is reached, there is broad agreement that AI would soon after become super-intelligent, that is, more intelligent than humans, since technological progress would likely accelerate, aided by the intelligent machines. Given these predictions, we have to think seriously about the implications of artificial general intelligence for humanity and, in the context of this chapter, for what it implies for our economy as well as for inequality.

Assuming that our social and economic system will be maintained upon the advent of artificial general intelligence and superintelligence,[33] there are two main scenarios. One scenario is that man and machine will merge, that is, that humans will "enhance" themselves with ever more advanced technology so that their physical and mental capabilities are increasingly determined by the state of the art in technology and AI rather than by traditional human biology (see, e.g., Kurzweil, 2005). The second scenario is that artificially intelligent entities will develop separately from humans, with their own objectives and behavior (see, e.g., Tegmark, 2017). This scenario is explored more fully in Korinek (2018a).

The scenario that humans will enhance themselves with machines may lead to massive increases in human inequality, unless policymakers recognize the threat and take steps to equalize access to human enhancement technologies.[34] Human intelligence is currently distributed within a fairly narrow range compared to the distance between the intelligence of humans and that of the next-closest species. If intelligence becomes a matter of ability-to-pay, it is conceivable that the wealthiest (enhanced) humans will become orders of magnitude more productive—"more intelligent"—than the unenhanced, leaving the majority of the population further and further behind. In fact, if intelligence enhancement becomes possible, then—unless pre-emptive actions are taken—it is difficult to imagine

[33] Researchers who work on the topic of AI safety point out that there is also a risk of doomsday scenarios in which a sufficiently advanced artificial intelligence eradicates humanity because humans stand in the way of its goals. See, for example, Bostrom who elaborates on this using the example of a "paperclip maximizer"—an AI that has been programmed to produce as many paperclips as possible, without regard for other human goals, and who realizes that humans contain valuable raw materials that should better be transformed into paperclips.

[34] In many respects, the issues are parallel to those associated with performance enhancing drugs. In sports, these have been strictly regulated, but in other arenas, they have not.

how to avoid such a dynamic. For those who can afford it, the incentive to purchase enhancements is great, especially since they are in competition with other wealthy humans who may otherwise leapfrog them. This is even more so in an economy which is, or is perceived to be, a winner-take-all economy and/or in which well-being is based on relative income. Those who cannot afford the latest technology will have to rely on what is in the public domain, and if the pace of innovation increases, the gap between the best technology and what is publicly available will increase.

A useful analogy is to compare human enhancement technology to healthcare—technology to *maintain* rather than *enhance* the human body. Different countries have chosen significantly different models for how to provide access to healthcare, with some regarding it as a basic human right and others allocating it more according to ability to pay. In the U.S., for example, the expected life spans of the poor and the wealthy have diverged significantly in recent decades, in part because of unequal access to healthcare and ever more costly new technologies that are only available to those who can pay. The differences are even starker if we look at humanity across nations, with the expected life span in the richest countries being two-thirds longer than in the least developed countries (see, e.g., UN, 2015). Like with healthcare, it is conceivable that different societies will make significantly different choices about access to human enhancement technologies.

Once the wealthiest enhanced humans have separated sufficiently far from the unenhanced, they can effectively be considered as a separate species of artificially intelligent agents. To emphasize the difference in productivities, Yuval Harari (2017) has dubbed the two classes that may result "the gods" and "the useless."[35]

7 Conclusions

The proliferation of AI and other forms of worker-replacing technological change can be unambiguously positive in a first-best economy in which individuals are fully insured against any adverse effects of innovation, or if it is coupled with the right form of redistribution. In the absence of such intervention, worker-replacing technological change may not only lead to workers getting a diminishing fraction of national income but may actually make them worse off in absolute terms.

The scope for redistribution is facilitated by the fact that the changes in factor prices create windfall gains on the complementary factors, which should make it feasible to achieve Pareto improvements. If there are limits on redistribution, the calculus worsens and a Pareto improvement can no longer be ensured. This may lead to resistance from those in society who are losing. As a result, it is desirable to use as broad of a set of second-best policies as possible, including changes in intellectual property rights, to maximize the likelihood that AI (or technological progress more generally) generate a Pareto improvement.

[35] In the original version of this chapter, there was an extensive discussion of an alternative course, where artificially intelligent entities develop separately from regular (or unenhanced) humans, pursuing intermediate objectives or "basic drives," such as self-preservation, self-improvement, and resource accumulation, that are instrumental for any final objective (Omohundro 2008). In particular, we explored what happens if humans do not or cannot assert ownership rights over artificially intelligent or super-intelligent entities, a plausible outcome in which sufficiently advanced AI is to operate autonomously. See Korinek (2018a).

AI and other changes in technology necessitate large adjustments, and while individuals and the economy more broadly may be able to adjust to slow changes, this may not be so when the pace is rapid. Indeed, in such situations, outcomes can be Pareto inferior. The more willing society is to support the necessary transition and to provide support to those who are "left behind," the faster the pace of innovation that society can accommodate, and still ensure that the outcomes are Pareto improvements. A society that is not willing to engage in such actions should expect resistance to innovation, with uncertain political and economic consequences.

19

Pareto Efficient Taxation and Expenditures

Pre- and Re-distribution

1 Introduction

Beginning with my supervision of Tony Atkinson in Cambridge in 1965–66 while I was a junior research fellow at Gonville and Caius College, Tony and I enjoyed a close collaboration and friendship.[1] One of our early results that received a great deal of attention was that when there was separability in the utility function between consumption and leisure,[2] if there existed an optimal income tax, it was optimal to have no commodity taxation (Atkinson and Stiglitz, 1976). An immediate corollary of that result was that, under the stipulated conditions, there should be no tax on interest income—treating consumption at different dates as different commodities. This and similar results from optimal tax theory were seized upon as a basis of policy by those critical of capital taxation.[3] Those who did so typically did not understand (or did not want to understand) the limitations of the model. As always, one has to look carefully at the assumptions going into a model to judge whether they provide an appropriate basis for policy.

This chapter argues that *even within the confines of a model in which differences in labor productivity are the only source of differences in income, the conclusion that there should be no capital taxation is, in general wrong, even in the presence of separability, and that in a*

[1] Slighted edited version of a paper written for special issue of the *Journal of Public Economics in Honor of Sir Tony Atkinson (1944–2017)*, Vol. 162, pp. 101–19, Erzo Luttmer and Henrik Kleven (eds.), 2018, and the paper was dedicated to his memory.

This chapter develops ideas on which we worked jointly together, and I am greatly indebted to him. In particular, it elaborates ideas originally presented in Atkinson and Stiglitz (1972, 1976) and further developed in Atkinson and Stiglitz (1980) and Stiglitz (1982d, 1987a, 2009a.) In recent years, there has been marked progress on the issues raised in our 1976 paper. While this chapter presents a unifying approach addressing, for example, the circumstances in which a tax on interest income is desirable, deriving a number of new results and putting a new perspective on some earlier derived results, it does not intend to provide a comprehensive review of the literature that AS 1976 spawned.

The chapter includes revisions of ideas that I had developed earlier in "Inequality and Capital Taxation," (Stiglitz, 1985e) and "Pareto Efficient Taxation and Expenditure Policies, with Applications to the Taxation of Capital, Public Investment, and Externalities," (Stiglitz, 1998a) presented at conference in honor of Agnar Sandmo, Bergen, January 1998.

I am indebted to INET and the Roosevelt Institute, and the supporters of its Inequality Project for financial support; to Matthieu Teachout and to Haaris Mateen for research assistance; to Debarati Ghosh for editorial assistance; and to Simcha Barkai, Martin Guzman, Linus Mattauch, the editor, Henrik Kleven, and an anonymous referee for comments on an earlier draft.

[2] That is, utility U could be written $U = U(u(\mathbf{C}), L)$ where $\mathbf{C}$ is the vector of consumption goods and L is labor supply. We do not require additive separability.

[3] See, for instance, Atkeson, Chari, and Kehoe (1999) and Mankiw, Weinzierl, and Yagan (2009). Using a quite different framework, with individuals with infinite lives, Chamley (1986) has also concluded that the optimal tax rate on capital should be zero in the long run. In Section 3, we consider a social welfare maximization problem extending infinitely far into the future, but using an overlapping generations model, and show that his results obtains if and only if there is separability in the utility function between labor and consumption. Later sections, present still more general frameworks, showing that even with separability, results on asymptotic zero capital taxation are not general.

The Origins of Inequality, and Policies to Contain It. Joseph E. Stiglitz, Oxford University Press. © Joseph E. Stiglitz (2025).
DOI: 10.1093/oso/9780198799580.003.0020

plausible model where individuals differ as well in the amount of inherited capital, there is a presumption for a possibly quite high tax on income from capital.

The rest of the chapter is divided into seven parts. The first presents some general reflections on our 1976 paper, our motivations in writing it, what we saw as some of the limitations, and some of the important extensions of the result in the subsequent literature. The second presents the basic model, based on Stiglitz (1982e), including some straightforward but important extensions to Pigouvian taxation and the provision of public goods. In both cases, in the case of separability, results much more akin to those that arise when government can impose lump sum taxes than to those generated when government relies on distortionary Ramsey results obtain. For instance, the optimal provision of a pure public good entails the sum of the marginal rate of substitution equaling the marginal rate of transformation. In the standard Ramsey–Diamond–Mirrlees model with public goods with distortionary taxation, the Samuelson condition for optimal supply (1955, 1958), that the marginal rate of transformation (MRT) equal the sum of the marginal rates of substitution (MRS) is altered, and instead MRT $< \Sigma$ MRS, the marginal rate of transformation is less than the sum of the sum of the marginal rate of substitution.[4] Section 3 shows that the Samuelsonian condition is restored with optimal non-linear taxation, provided there is separability between labor and consumption goods.[5] Similarly, first best Pigouvian taxation is optimal with separability either between leisure and consumption, or between the externality on the one hand and consumption and labor on the other, though in the latter case, the Pigouvian tax has to be interpreted as the tax in excess of the optimal commodity tax (the shadow price).[6]

To analyze optimal interest taxation in general equilibrium, one has to construct a dynamic general equilibrium model. Section 4 does this, embedding optimal non-linear taxation in a general equilibrium overlapping generations model. While Atkinson and Sandmo (1980) had extended the Atkinson–Stiglitz (1972) model for excise taxation to a similar overlapping-generations setting, this chapter, a development of Stiglitz (1985e), provides the corresponding extension of Atkinson–Stiglitz (1976). The conclusion of Atkinson and Sandmo (1980) was that "it is difficult to make a strong case *either* for the expenditure tax *or* for taxing interest income at the same rate as wage income." By contrast, we find that the basic results of our static model extend to this dynamic framework: (a) With separability, there should be no taxation of capital income *provided that relative wages are either observable or unaffected by taxation or investment (by the consumption/labor supplies which they induce, which will be the case if there are fixed relative productivities)*; but (b) in the absence of separability between consumption and leisure, but with intertemporal separability, whether there should be an interest income tax or subsidy depends on whether first period consumption is a complement or substitute for leisure.[7] But both separability and the italicized proviso are crucial. While the latter result is reminiscent of that of Corlett and Hague (1953) (in a model with no income taxation and just commodity

[4] See Pigou (1947), Dasgupta and Stiglitz (1971), and Atkinson and Stern (1974). Atkinson and Stern make the important point that one cannot infer from the fact that the sum of the MRT $< \Sigma$ MRS the impact of distortionary taxation on the supply of public goods.

[5] Boadway and Kean (1993), using the Stiglitz (1982b) framework for the analysis of optimal taxation, had noted this result earlier. See also Kaplow (1996).

[6] Kaplow (2012) had noted the former result. Sandmo (1975) had established that one could obtain results that were closely akin to first best Pigouvian taxes even in a Ramsey–Diamond–Mirrlees model.

[7] Similar in spirit to the Corlett and Hague (1953) analysis.

taxation), we establish it in the presence of an optimal non-linear income tax. This is important, because in many cases, the presence of one tax—in particular an income tax—changes markedly the taxes that should be imposed elsewhere in the system; for reasons we explain, often with unconstrained non-linear taxes, results that hold only with lump sum taxes are restored. As a prelude to the later discussion of public investment in the next section, the section also shows that the standard result on the desirability of productive efficiency holds.

The rest of the chapter then provides a critique of the Atkinson–Stiglitz (1976) result and the extensions to it presented in Section 4, focusing particularly on capital taxation. The fifth section focuses on the case where relative wages are not fixed. Even with separability between labor and consumption, (a) it is in general desirable to impose distortionary commodity taxation, even on high ability individuals; (b) there should be a distortionary income tax, even on high ability individuals; (c) there should be an interest income tax (or subsidy), even on high ability individuals; (d) productive efficiency of the economy (where there is no production taxes and the marginal rate of transformation of all goods is the same among all firms) is not desirable;[8] (e) even asymptotically, the rate of return on public capital goods may not equal either the pure rate of time discount or the rate of return on private goods; the long run return to some kinds of public capital may be lower than the social discount rate.

Recent policy discussions have suggested the desirability of focusing on policies which improve the market distribution of income, leaving less of a burden on *redistribution*.[9] Our analysis establishes that this intuition is correct. In each of the cases listed above, taxes and expenditures are adjusted at the margin to increase wages of the low skilled relative to the high skilled.[10] Formally, the improvement in the distribution of income loosens the binding self-selection constraint, allowing for a Pareto improvement.

The optimal tax literature developed in the context of an economy of seemingly self-employed individuals, say making widgets. The only information problem was that of the government, who, seeing the output of widgets (or income from producing widgets) could not tell whether a high output was the result of hard work (long hours) or high ability. But most individuals in a modern economy work for others, and employers have an analogous information problem to that of government: they seek to differentiate among individuals, including by using self-selection mechanisms. But private screening is affected by public tax policy, and optimal taxation needs to take this into account. Section 6 does this, again showing that the Atkinson–Stiglitz (1976) result may not hold, even with separability.

Section 7 considers optimal taxation with inheritances. Inheritances mean that individuals differ not just in their labor productivity, and optimal taxation ought to take that into account. This is so even in a world with dynastic families optimally sharing their wealth

[8] One of the important results in Diamond–Mirrlees (1971) was establishing that optimal taxation entailed only consumption taxes, no production taxes, and that the economy was productively efficient. Dasgupta and Stiglitz (1971, 1972) had established this was not so in the standard Diamond–Mirrlees model, but with restricted taxation (i.e., the government could not impose 100% taxes on pure rents or profits and could impose taxes on all goods and services at differential rates). The result here generalizes that of Naito (1999), whose analysis built on Stiglitz (1982e).

[9] See Hacker and Pierson (2011) and Stiglitz, Abernathy, Hersh, et al. (2015).

[10] In Stiglitz (1982e), I showed that this was true for taxes on labor income, but did not explore the full range of issues examined here.

with their children. We show that the design of capital taxation is more nuanced than populist calls might suggest: careful attention has to be paid to incidence. A simplistic call for capital taxation with proceeds distributed to workers may actually leave workers worse off, as we showed in Chapter 13.

The real argument behind the taxation of capital almost surely is related to disparities in inherited capital and in disparities in the ability to obtain returns out of capital—and luck—than with differences in productivities among workers, the subject of our 1976 paper. Section 8 provides some concluding remarks, including putting the results presented here into some broader perspectives.

2 Reflections on the Atkinson–Stiglitz Theorem

Our analysis was motivated in part as a critique of Ramsey taxation (Ramsey, 1927), which seemed to justify not just high taxes on basic necessities like food (which had a low elasticity of demand) but also patterns of pricing by monopolies like AT&T.[11] Ramsey had established that optimal commodity taxes should be inversely related to the elasticity of demand and to the elasticity of supply in a model in which everyone was identical; hence there were no distributional concerns—and therefore a lump sum tax would have been presumably acceptable. Our 1972 paper (Atkinson and Stiglitz, 1972) had shown that *in the absence of an income tax*, optimal commodity taxes could be described by a simple Ramsey-like formula incorporating distributional effects, which suggested that when distributional concerns were given sufficient weight (for instance, in a society with a high level of both inequality and inequality aversion) goods like food with a low price elasticity of demand but a low-income elasticity of demand would not be taxed at a high rate, but rather, that luxuries like perfume might face high rates, even though they have a higher price elasticity than food. We were, however, never satisfied with that result, since it was obvious that we had an income tax, the intent of which was at least partly redistributive.[12] The question was, given the existence of such a redistributive income tax, was commodity taxation still desirable? Our 1976 paper yielded stronger results than we had anticipated.

Another of the motivations behind our paper was to demonstrate two general results in the general theory of screening in the context of optimal taxation:

(a) *In general*, the optimal commodity taxes depended on the set of *other* taxes that were available.[13] Ramsey (1927) and Diamond–Mirrlees (1971) analyses clearly depended on the absence of lump sum taxes. If it were feasible to levy lump sum taxes, they would be employed, and the optimal commodity taxes would be zero. Some of the Diamond–Mirrlees results, both on production efficiency (not using

[11] See, for example, Boiteux (1956) and Baumol and Bradford (1970). Elsewhere, Sappington and Stiglitz (1987) explained while there were some similarities between the two problems, there were also some critical differences.

[12] Our 1972 results would, presumably, still be relevant for developing countries and emerging markets in which income taxation played little role, though in many such economies other considerations (such as migration and rural/urban income differences) play an important role. See Sah and Stiglitz (1992).

[13] There are a set of parallel questions in the more general theory of incentives and selection with asymmetric information. For instance, the design of the optimal sharecropping contract is affected by the ability of the landlord to affect credit, the purchase of inputs, and the choice of technology. See Braverman and Stiglitz (1982, 1986a, 1986b).

producer taxes) and the structure of taxation were shown to be undermined if there were profits (rents) which could not be taxed directly at 100% (Dasgupta and Stiglitz, 1971, 1972).[14] Our 1976 paper thus explored the interaction between an (optimal) income tax and commodity taxation.

(b) The optimal income tax problem was at its heart a standard problem in asymmetric information with adverse selection. We assumed that individuals differed only in their abilities to perform work, and they all had the same endowment of time and the same utility functions. The Mirrlees' optimal tax problem could be thought of as extracting information about those differences efficiently as one raised tax revenues. Even though there was a single "dimension" in which individuals differed (ability), in general, it seemed possible that one could extract information about that difference more efficiently by looking not just at the individual's labor supply, but also at his consumption patterns. While that conjecture turned out to be true in general, in the special case of separability, Pareto efficient taxation required only an income tax; not surprisingly, there was no benefit to be had by using information about consumption patterns.

We never thought that the separability assumption was plausible. It meant that there were no goods that were complementary to leisure. Clearly, the marginal rate of substitution between skis and say food depends on the amount of leisure. Someone with no leisure time simply doesn't value skiing much. Thus, we never attached much weight to the result that there should be no tax on capital with separability.

But this was not the only, or even the most important, reason that our theorem did not provide the basis of policy for capital taxation. For instance, if individuals differed in other ways—as in fact they do, in their level of inherited capital and their ability to earn returns on capital—it was possible that capital taxation was desirable, even if the separability assumption held. Indeed, it is not hard to generate more general plausible models in which capital taxation is clearly desirable. Showing this is one of the main objectives of this chapter.

Thus, in Chapter 13, we considered a simple model, which perhaps captures key aspects of the sources of inequality which give rise to the desirability of capital taxation far better than generalizations of Atkinson–Stiglitz (1976) discussed earlier in the chapter. We assume that there are two classes of individuals—a group of capitalists with large endowments of capital who invest their capital, earn returns, consume, and leave bequests to their children, and workers—with the capitalists sufficiently richer than the workers that the social marginal utility of a dollar to the capitalists is negligible.[15] It is obvious that in such a situation the optimal utilitarian[16] tax on capitalists is close to a Rawlsian tax, maximizing

[14] See Dasgupta and Stiglitz (1971, 1972). They thus reconcile the Diamond–Mirrlees results, where supply elasticities play no role, and Ramsey's analysis, where they are central. Dasgupta and Stiglitz also show that other restrictions on taxation fundamentally change optimal tax structures, including the desirability of efficiency.

[15] This model is a generalization of Stiglitz (2015a), Mattauch, Edenhofer, Klenert, and Bénard (2016), and Mattauch et al. (2017). It many ways, it formalizes the model that is implicit in Piketty (2014), building on Stiglitz (1969b).

[16] In the discussion below, we often refer to results based on a utilitarian social welfare function, such as that employed by Mirrlees (1971). But virtually all of the results would hold for any individualistic inequality averse social welfare function, for example along the lines discussed in Rothschild and Stiglitz (1973), and indeed, for any Pareto efficient tax structure (Stiglitz, 1987a; Brito, Hamilton, Slutsky, and Stiglitz, 1990).

the revenue that one could obtain from a tax on capital.[17] The optimal capital tax is significantly greater than zero and may be far higher than the current tax on capital, especially the tax on capital gains.[18]

There are other "thought" experiments that help us understand the role of capital taxation, and why in general it should be positive. Consider, for instance, a simple model in which all members of a group of individuals have an equal endowment of capital, but some individuals are better at transforming a unit input of capital into output (i.e., they are better at selecting good projects). Assume that the more effort an individual exerts, the higher income; and that there is disutility associated with the exertion of effort.[19] Then the optimal tax structure for this group would be parallel to that which we analyzed in the chapter: with separability between the utility of goods and effort, then the optimal tax is *only* a tax on capital income. In the absence of separability, both goods taxes/subsidies and a capital tax are desirable.

With individuals having equal endowments of both capital and labor, with full separability (of consumption from effort and labor, and effort and labor from each other), but differing in both the ability to transform labor and capital into "income," if one can separately identify income from labor and from capital,[20] optimal taxation involves separate non-linear taxation of capital income and labor income, but no commodity taxation; but even with separability of consumption from effort and labor, but effort and labor not being separable from each other, then matters are far more complicated. While there would still be no indirect taxation, in general, taxes would not just be a function of total income.[21]

Of course, some individuals have larger endowments of wealth. If such wealth were observable, a utilitarian would want to impose a lump sum tax on it. If the supply of that wealth were elastic—parents' transfers to children could be affected by the taxes imposed

[17] It is easy to design capital taxes that effectively tax only the capital income of capitalists, for example, exempting life-cycle savings or taxing only the returns on capital above a certain level. (In this model, there is great inequality in the ownership and returns to capital.) The analytics sometimes turn out simpler for a general tax on capital.

[18] Especially in countries like the United States, where there is a step-up-in-basis at death, resulting in capital gains not being taxed at all. There are a wide range of ways by which through tax planning high income individuals can reduce their taxes, and especially their taxes on capital. See Stiglitz (1985f).

[19] Note that if the higher returns of some individuals is *just* a result of luck, then "excess" returns (i.e., returns above the average) should be fully taxed, since there is no adverse incentive effects. The same thing is true if the higher returns are a result of just inherited ability or better connections. (Such taxes could, of course, affect the incentives of those providing "connections," if it is costly to do so or if the benefit to the "gift" of the giver depends on the amount the recipient receives after tax. See Section 6 below.) In each of these cases, the desirability of a highly progressive capital tax is obvious. Here, we make the equally obvious point: if there is an unobservable variable, effort, that together with ability, determines returns to capital, there should be a progressive tax along the lines of that analyzed in the optimal (labor) income tax literature. There is one difference: If we assume that total returns, R, are a function of capital, K, ability, a, and effort, e, $R = R(e, K, a, \epsilon)$, where ϵ is a random variable, and Utility is a function of consumption and effort (but not of K), then there is an additional variable we have to deal with. (It is as if individuals had different endowments of time.) If K is observable, then taxes paid would be a function of $\{K, R\}$. This model is formally identical to the standard one when K is the same for all individuals, there is no variability (ϵ is fixed) and e is not fixed. If everyone had the same K and a, we would have the standard moral hazard model. With K fixed (observable), but ϵ variable, individuals' differing in a, and e not fixed, then we have the standard moral hazard cum adverse selection model, where both self-selection and incentive compatibility constraints have to be taken into account. This changes some of the standard results that have been obtained in models with pure adverse selection. See Stiglitz and Yun (2013).

[20] Note that for small businesses, tax authorities cannot separately identify income from capital and labor. At best they can impute income from capital.

[21] Let W = wage income, C = capital income, and T be total taxes paid. The optimal tax function $T(W, C)$ is not of the form $T = T(W + C)$.

on the transfer or assets or the after-tax income generated—then there might be a trade-off, with higher tax rates generating more tax revenue but leading to less accumulation and transfer of wealth. Even a Rawlsian would impose a tax that was less than 100%. It may be that the actual value of the wealth transfer is not observable, but only the income generated by it. Then there is no presumption that the optimal tax (whatever the social welfare function) on the income generated by that wealth would be taxed at zero. Quite the contrary: there is a presumption that it would be taxed, and possibly at high rates.

2.1 Taxing Capital Goods and Rents

Moreover, the result that one does not want to tax the returns to individuals is often confused with not taxing the returns to particular assets or corporations. If land is inelastically supplied, there is nothing in our analysis that undermines the conventional result that one would want to tax the returns on that asset at a very high rate (100%) (George, 1879).[22] The price of the asset would fall, to reflect the tax. Indeed, more recent results—extending the standard overlapping generations model include land as an asset—note that since land crowds out capital, a tax on land leads to a higher steady state level of capital (per capita) and thus to higher levels of income.[23] All that the Atkinson-Stiglitz theorem said was that (under the stipulated conditions) one should not tax the returns received by the individual.

2.2 Risk

We (along with most of the subsequent literature) ignored uncertainty. This was an important omission. In a world in which there are imperfect risk markets, Domar and Musgrave (1944)[24] had already shown that an income tax with appropriate loss offsets could encourage risk taking. With, say, expensing of capital goods, the government entered as a silent partner. The government was in a better position to absorb risk than the firm or individual: it could spread risk over all of society (Arrow and Linn, 1970, 2014).[25] If the tax rate was τ, the government picked up τ percent of the costs, taking in turn τ percent of the returns. The expected marginal return per dollar invested was thus unchanged. But taking account of risk, the tax actually led to more investment.[26] A utilitarian government would again want to impose a capital income tax. Indeed, it would be part of Pareto efficient taxation.

[22] For a more modern rendition, see Arnott and Stiglitz (1979, 1981).

[23] This is a result obtained earlier in models with money and capital accumulation (see, e.g., Shell, Sidrauski, and Stiglitz, 1969). For more recent and general results, see Stiglitz (2015a, 2017b) and Chapters 14 and 15 above.

[24] Their analysis was put into modern expected utility form by Stiglitz (1969a). See also Piketty and Saez (2013) who explain how if there is uninsurable uncertainty about future returns, capital taxation can be viewed as providing insurance against returns. (The older literature emphasized the importance of loss offsets.)

[25] A fuller analysis would address why the government is better able to spread risks than the market. Well-developed theories based on information asymmetries have explained imperfections in capital markets and their ability to share risk.

[26] Domar and Musgrave (1944) used mean variance analysis. Stiglitz (1969a showed that this was true more generally, for risk averse individuals.

2.3 Extending Atkinson-Stiglitz

There were two natural extensions to our analysis: to ask whether there were more general conditions under which commodity taxation was not necessary, and to ask whether the result remained true with an income tax that was not the optimal non-linear tax, for example, with an (optimal) linear income tax. Deaton (1979, 1981) showed that with an optimal *linear* income tax, weak separability between goods and leisure together with linear Engel curves for goods is a sufficient condition for no indirect taxation. But when these restrictive conditions are not satisfied, in general commodity taxation is required, even with an optimal linear tax (Stiglitz, 2009a, a revision and extension of Stiglitz 1976e).[27] Gauthier and Laroque (2009) provide a more general account of the role of separability in optimal taxation and expenditure.

Sections 3 and 4 explore some of the more general results (some, as we note, already in the literature) in which separability suffices to ensure that commodity taxation is not needed with an optimal income tax—and thus an interest income tax is not desirable. Later sections show that, in particular, an interest income tax is needed.

3 The Basic Model

We begin our discussion with the standard model, with two types of individuals, differing in ability, but having the same utility function, reviewing the results of Stiglitz (1982e), as a prelude to the subsequent analysis. The ith individual faces a before-tax wage (output per hour) of w_i, and thus, in the absence of taxation, his budget constraint is simply:

$$\sum_j C_{ij} = w_i L_i, \tag{19.1}$$

where C_{ij} = the ith individual's consumption of good j, all goods are normalized to have a price of unity, L_{ij} = number of hours worked by the ith individual. Neither w_i nor L_i is observable, but the product, the ith individual's income, $Y_i = w_i L_i$ is. The ith individual receives utility from consuming goods and disutility from work:

$$U^i = U^i(C_i, L_i), \tag{19.2}$$

[27] Itself a revision and extension of Stiglitz (1976e)). It is worth noting, though, that the structure of optimal commodity taxation with an optimal linear tax does not look like that described by Ramsey (1927) (where tax rates were simply related to elasticities of demand and supply) or Diamond and Mirrlees (1971). At the same time, one can still derive a simple formula, given the optimal commodity taxes, for the optimal linear tax rate, based on an appropriately weighted average of the labor supply elasticities. The optimal tax can be related to a measure of the *marginal* benefit associated with inequality reduction (this marginal measure differs from the Atkinson measure, which identified how much individuals would be willing to pay to get rid of all inequality. Obviously, at the *margin*, there is greater social cost of inequality. Stiglitz (1976e) relates this to a societal measure of inequality aversion, obtaining a remarkably simple approximation for the optimal tax: $\frac{\tau}{1-\tau} = \frac{Rs_Y{}^2}{{}_u\bar{n}_L(1-g)}$ where as usual τ is the (income) tax rate, R is the measure of risk (inequality) aversion, $s_Y{}^2$ is the variance of income inequality, g is the share of government revenue spent on public goods, and unL is a welfare weighted averaged compensated labor supply elasticity. (Earlier, Sheshinki (1972) analyzed the optimal income tax, but did not derive the above simple expression for the optimal tax rate. Subsequently, Piketty and Saez (2012) extended these earlier papers to provide tax formulae based on observable sufficient statistics.)

where $\frac{\partial U^i}{\partial C_i} > 0$, $\frac{\partial U^i}{\partial L_i} < 0$, U is quasi-concave, and C_i represents the ith individual's consumption vector: $C_i = (C_{i1}, \ldots, C_{ij}, \ldots)$. Assume the government imposes a tax, T, as a function of income: $T_i = T(Y_i)$. The individual's consumption now is his income minus his tax payment, $\sum C_{ij} = Y_i - T(Y_i)$. The individual maximizes his utility subject to his budget constraint:

$$U^i(C_i, L_i) \ s.t \sum_j C_{ij} \le w_i L_i - T(w_i L_i), \tag{19.3}$$

yielding the first-order condition (assuming differentiability, etc.):

$$\frac{dU^i/d_i}{dU^i/dC_{ij}} = -w_i(1 - T'). \tag{19.4}$$

The left-hand side is the individual's marginal rate of substitution. The right-hand side is the after-tax marginal return to working an extra hour.

The problem of the government concerned with Pareto efficiency[28] is to maximize the utility of, say, individuals of type 2, subject to (a) individuals of type 1 having at least a given level of utility and (b) raising a given amount of revenue. It does this by offering two $\{C, Y\}$ packages, one of which will be chosen by the first group, the other of which will be chosen by the second group.[29] We write $U^i(C_i, L_i) = U^i\left(C_i, \frac{Y_i}{w_i}\right) \equiv V^i(C_i, Y_i)$. The government thus solves the following program:

$$\begin{aligned} \max_{\{C, Y\}} V^2(C_2, Y_2) \quad s.t \quad & V^1(C_1, Y_1) \ge \overline{U}^1 \\ & V^2(C_2, Y_2) \ge V^2(C_1, Y_1) \\ & V^1(C_1, Y_1) \ge V^1(C_2, Y_2) \end{aligned} \tag{19.5}$$

And the revenue constraint

$$R = (Y_1 - C_1)N_1 + (Y_2 - C_2)N_2 \ge \overline{R}$$

where $C_i = \sum_j C_{ij}$, the ith consumer's aggregate consumption, R is government revenue; $\overline{R}$ is the revenue requirement, and N_i the number of individuals of type i. If we let μ be the shadow price associated with the utility constraint, λ_i be the shadow prices associated with the self-selection constraints, and γ be the shadow price associated with the revenue constraint, then without loss of generality, the Lagrangian can be written as:[30]

$$\begin{aligned} \Lambda = {} & N_2 V^2 + N_1 \mu \left(V^1 - \overline{U^1}\right) + N_2 \lambda_2 \left(V^2(C_2, Y_2) - V^2(C_1, Y_1)\right) \\ & + N_1 \lambda_1 \left(V^1(C_1, Y_1) - V^1(C_2, Y_2)\right) + \gamma\left((Y_1 - C_1)N_1 + (Y_2 - C_2)N_2 - \overline{R}\right) \end{aligned} \tag{19.6}$$

[28] The notion of Pareto efficient tax structure is a slight generalization of the "optimum" tax analysis of Mirrlees and Diamond and Mirrlees. Pareto efficient tax structures are those (given the admissible set of taxes and the required public revenue) which are such that no one can be better off without making someone worse off. We identify properties of Pareto efficient tax structures which hold regardless of the social welfare function. See, for example, Stiglitz (1982e, 1987a) and Brito, Hamilton, Slutsky, and Stiglitz (1990).

[29] Obviously, the government can offer a continuum of $\{C, Y\}$ packages (i.e., an entire tax function), but at most two will be chosen, and therefore we need be concerned with at most two.

[30] Recall that $\mathbf{C_i}$ represents the vector of consumption by the ith individual.

Then, the first order conditions are:

$$\frac{d\Lambda}{dC_{1j}} = N_2\mu\frac{dV^1}{dC_{1j}} - N_2\lambda_2\frac{dV^2}{dC_{1j}} + N_1\lambda_1\frac{dV^1}{dC_{1j}} - \gamma N_1 = 0 \tag{19.7a}$$

$$\frac{d\Lambda}{dC_{2j}} = N_2\frac{dV^2}{dC_{2j}} + N_2\lambda_2\frac{dV^2}{dC_{2j}} - N_1\lambda_1\frac{dV^1}{dC_{2j}} - \gamma N_2 = 0 \tag{19.7b}$$

$$\frac{d\Lambda}{dY_1} = N_1\mu\frac{dV^1}{dY_1} - N_2\lambda_2\frac{dV^2}{dY_1} + N_1\lambda_1\frac{dV^1}{dY_1} + \gamma N_1 = 0 \tag{19.7c}$$

$$\frac{d\Lambda}{dY_2} = N_2\frac{dV^2}{dY_2} + N_2\lambda_2\frac{dV^2}{dY_2} - N_1\lambda_1\frac{dV^1}{dY_2} + \gamma N_2 = 0. \tag{19.7d}$$

It is easy to show that at most one of the two self-selection constraints will be binding. We focus on the case where $\lambda_1 = 0$ and $\lambda_2 > 0$: only the second self-selection constraint is binding. Note that the standard case of *optimal utilitarian tax policy*, where the government maximizes $\sum_i N_i V^i$ implies that $\mu = 1$.[31]

From (19.7a–d) we obtain:

$$\frac{dV^2/dC_{2j}}{dV^2/dC_{2k}} = 1, \tag{19.8a}$$

$$\frac{dV^2/dC_{2j}}{dV^2/dY_2} = 1 \tag{19.8b}$$

$$\frac{dV^1/dC_{1j}}{dV^1/dC_{1k}} = \frac{\gamma + \lambda_2 dV^2/dC_{1j}}{\gamma + \lambda_2 dV^2/dC_{1k}} \tag{19.9a}$$

$$\frac{dV^1/dC_{1j}}{dV^1/dY_1} = \frac{\gamma + \lambda_2 dV^2/dC_{1j}}{\gamma + \lambda_2 dV^2/dY_1}. \tag{19.9b}$$

We have formulated the problem as a direct control problem on $\{C_i, L_i\}$, but the solution can be implemented by a simple non-linear tax system, that is, individual 1 is confronted with indirect taxes giving relative prices corresponding to the LHS of (19.9a), a marginal income tax rate given by the LHS of (19.9b), and a non-linear income tax giving the equivalent of a lump sum tax combined with a linear income tax with marginal rate given by (19.9b) yielding utility level for individual 1 of $\overline{U^1}$. Similarly, the high ability individual faces no marginal income tax or consumption tax but faces a non-linear income tax giving the equivalent of a lump sum tax yielding V^{2*}, where $\{V^{1*}, V^{2*}\}$ are the utility levels given by the solution to the optimal tax problem. Thus, we have the familiar result:

Proposition 1a. There should be no distortionary taxation on the individual with the highest ability while the labor supply of the less able is distorted.

This result goes beyond that of Mirrlees (1971) which said that the top marginal income tax rate should be zero.[32] (19.8a) says that there should be no commodity taxation on the high ability as well.

[31] With U1 becoming, in effect, an endogenous variable.

[32] See also Sadka (1976), Seade (1977), and (for an overview) Tuomala (1990). Saez (2001), following Mirrlees (1971), shows that these results are not robust to a distribution with no top income (e.g., a Pareto tail) and derives

Figure 19.1 provides a simple diagrammatic illustration with a single consumption good. In Figure 19.1a, the two types are quite different, so different that the high ability does not want to mimic the low ability if we impose non-distortionary taxation. Point E^{1*} is the point on the low ability indifference curve U^{1*} which maximizes revenues, that is, in which there is no distortionary taxation, so the slope of the indifference curve is unity. (Government revenue is just the difference between Y and C.) Knowing R_1, the revenue raised from the low ability individuals (or, as illustrated in this figure, the subsidy provided to them) and the required government revenue, $\overline{R}$, we know the revenue that has to be

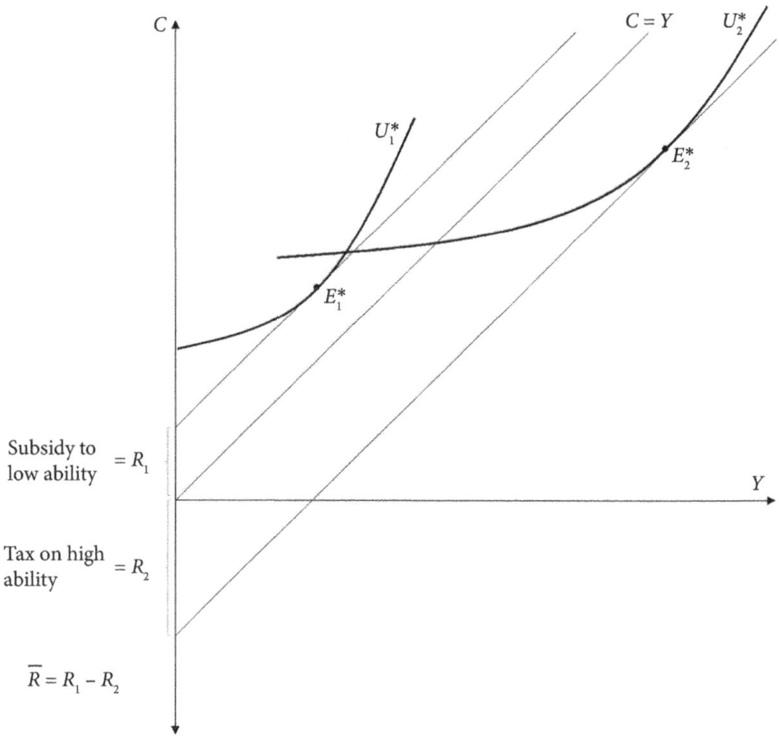

Figure 19.1a Non-distortionary self-selection equilibrium. At the lump sum taxes imposed, two types choose different {C, Y}.

The required revenue $\overline{R}$ can be raised in a Pareto efficient way which gives individual 1 utility $\overline{U}^1$ by a non-linear income tax (dotted line illustrated in Figure 19.1b) which confronts both types with zero marginal tax rates. At E_2^*, high ability individuals do not want to mimic low ability individuals. (The optimal tax schedule entails a lump sum grant to type 1, a zero tax rate on income up to some income in excess of that associated with E_1^*, then a very high marginal tax rate up to some level short of that associated with E_2^*, and a zero marginal tax rate beyond that.)

simple asymptotic results. See also Diamond (1998). But the Pareto tail is used as a good approximation of a *description* of the probability distribution of the tail. There is, in practice, an identifiable person with the top income. Thus, we would have no problem in the United States identifying who that person is (assuming honest reporting of income), and setting a top marginal tax rate for that individual at zero. That income will be going up over time—as the incomes of all individuals will be changing, implying a change in the optimal structure. But there is no reason to impose a distortionary tax on that individual simply because we could conceive of there being a higher income individual.

raised by from the high ability individuals, and V^{2*} is the highest level of utility of the high ability consistent with raising that revenue. It is clear that the high ability individual does not want to imitate the low ability individual. But Figure 19.1b shows the more typical case, where he would. For the revenue and self-selection constraints to be satisfied, E^{1*} now must entail lower levels of income and consumption (labor supply) and lower tax revenues from the low ability—a distortion in his labor supply—and hence a higher level of revenues raised from the high ability. At the optimum, the high ability is just indifferent to imitating the low. Figure 19.1c shows the Pareto efficient allocation generating the requisite revenue, and 19.1d illustrates how that tax revenue can be achieved through an optimal income tax.

The interpretation of (19.9a) is, however, somewhat more subtle. For simplicity, denote

$$\alpha^{i}_{jk} = MRS_{ijk}\,(C_1, Y_1)$$

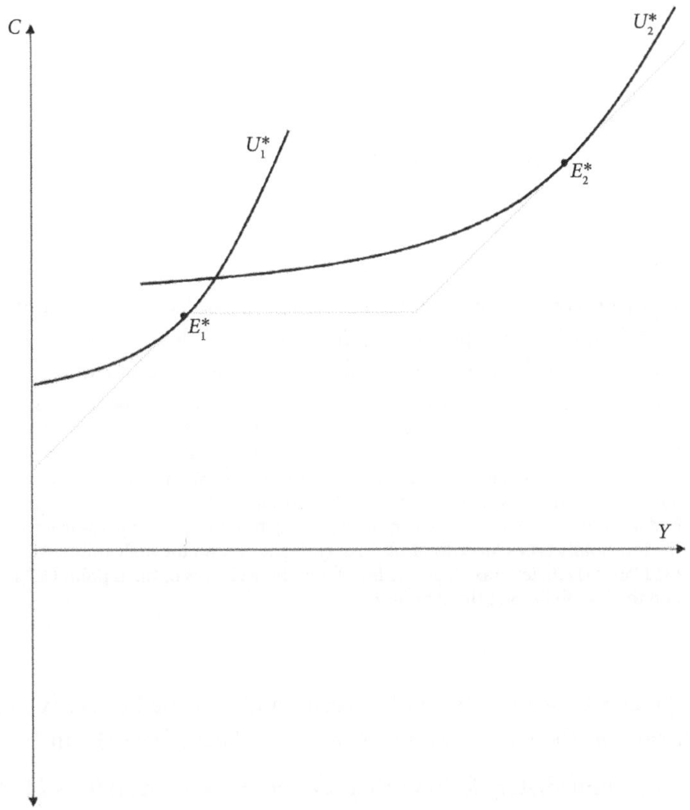

Figure 19.1b Implementing non-distortionary allocation through highly non-linear income tax.

The Pareto-efficient allocation can be implemented through a tax that is linear, with slope equal to that of type 1 at E_1^* (i.e., effectively a demi-grant plus a positive tax rate), then at some income level above Y_1^*, but below Y_2^*, a high (infinite) tax rate, and then above a critical threshold somewhat below Y_2^*, a zero marginal tax rate. (See Figure 19.1d.)

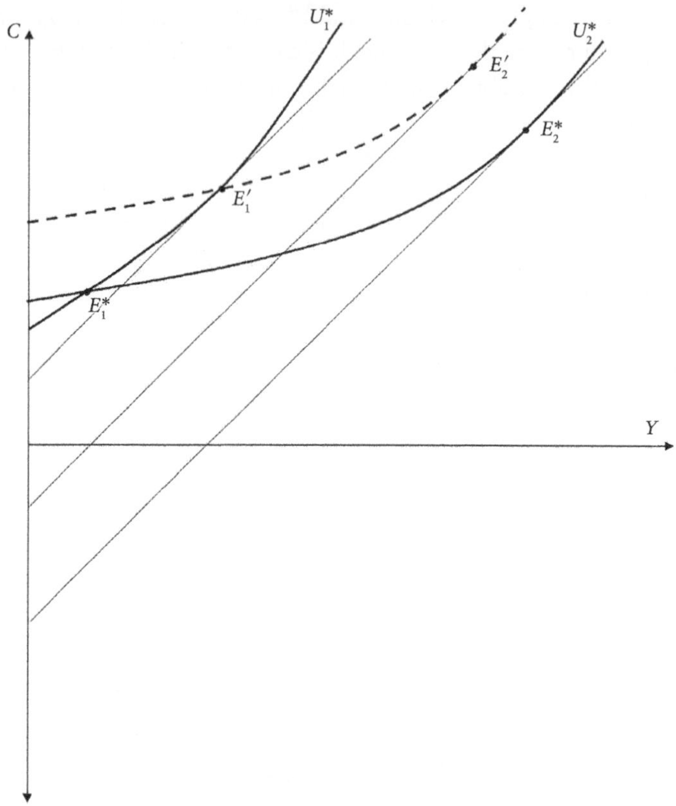

Figure 19.1c The more normal case: the self-selection constraint binds, and the self-selection equilibrium entails low ability individual working less than in full-information equilibrium.

The more normal case: at maximal revenue associated with U^1, point E'_1, we can identify the maximal revenue we can extract from high ability, by drawing type 2's indifference curve through E'_1. The maximal revenue corresponds to point E'_2. It is insufficient to raise required revenue $\overline{R}$. We thus have to impose a higher tax on 2, lowering his utility, which results in his mimicking 1 if we had left 1 at E_1. We force 1 to work less, moving him to E_1^*, raising less from the low-ability types, necessitating an even higher tax on the high ability. At the (Pareto) efficient tax, type 2 is indifferent between his optimal point (E^{2*}) and the low ability's optimal point E_1^*.

that is, i's marginal rate of substitution between j and k at the bundle $\{\mathbf{C}_i, Y_i\}$. Individual 1 and 2 differ only in their abilities. Let $\lambda_2 \frac{\partial V^2}{\partial C_{1k}} = b$. Then, (19.9a) can be rewritten as: $\alpha_{jk}^1 = \frac{\gamma + b\alpha_{jk}^2}{\gamma + b}$ and it immediately follows that $\alpha_{jk}^1 - \alpha_{jk}^2 = \{\gamma[1 - \alpha_{jk}^2]\}/\{\gamma + b\}$. The denominator of the preceding expression is positive. In the case of separability, the marginal rate of substitution between j and k is unaffected by the amount of leisure, so $\alpha_{jk}^1 = \alpha_{jk}^2$ which in turn implies $\alpha_{jk}^1 = \alpha_{jk}^2 = 1$, thus establishing:

Proposition 1b. There should be no commodity taxation on either high or low ability individuals if leisure and consumption are separable.

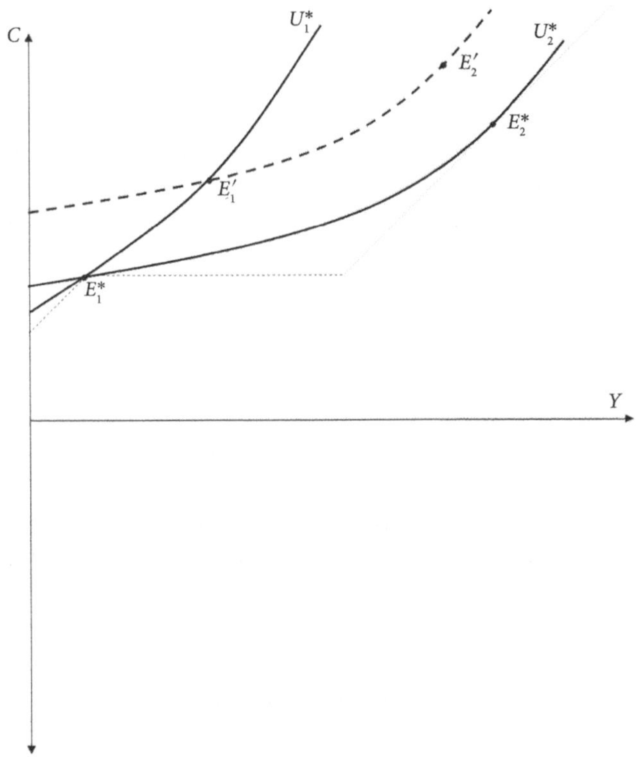

Figure 19.1d Implementing the optimal allocation through a distortionary income tax.

There are many tax schedules that can implement the Pareto efficient allocation. This is not so when there is a continuum of types, for then we have to be sensitive to marginal tax rates at every income level.

Whether commodity j should be taxed (relative to k) depends simply on the impact of an increase in leisure on the marginal rate of substitution between commodities j and k—a property that has nothing to do with Ramsey's focus on deadweight loss. The tax structure is related to the deadweight loss associated with the self-selection constraint which come into play if government needs to raise a given revenue, cares about distribution, but is in an environment in which governments cannot tell who is able and who is not. The self-selection constraints that the government employs to achieve fair taxation create first order distortions. Commodity taxation can, under certain conditions, reduce the force of those distortions.

The intuition is simple: consider a good which is complementary with leisure. If a high ability individual tries to mimic a low-level individual, he has more leisure, and his demand for that good will accordingly be higher. Hence, taxing that good and using the proceeds to subsidize a good which is a substitute for leisure will make mimicking the low ability individual less attractive. With a weakened self-selection constraint, the low ability individual can work more, moving along his indifference curve—and in doing so generate more revenue for the government. Thus, the utility of both individuals can be increased and still satisfy the revenue constraint: indirect taxation is a Pareto improvement. However, if there is separability, then the levels of consumption of the goods is identical when the high ability imitates the low ability, and hence there is no way to use differential taxation to weaken the self-selection constraint.

There is another intuition which may prove helpful. In the case of separability, where $V^i = V^i(\phi(C_i), L_i)$, one can think of ϕ itself as an aggregate consumption good. Individuals take their wage income and buy "ϕ." We know from Diamond and Mirrlees (1971) that we want production efficiency.[33] Productive efficiency in producing φ implies no commodity taxation.

3.1 Taxation of Interest Income

An immediate implication of these results is that *in the case where consumption in different periods is separable from leisure—typical of many of the simplified models explored in the macroeconomic literature—there should be no interest income taxation.*

There is no strong presumption whether in the absence of separability there should be an interest income tax or subsidy. Consider, for instance, the standard life-cycle formulation (dropping for the moment subscripts describing the individual and simplifying by assuming consumption is uni-dimensional).

$$U^t = u_t(C_t, L_t) + u_{t+1}(C_{t+1}), \tag{19.10}$$

where there is time separability, but not separability between consumption and leisure and where C_t is consumption of the individual when he is young and working and C_{t+1} is consumption in retirement. Then the marginal rate of substitution between second period consumption and first period consumption is $\frac{\partial u_t/\partial C_t}{\partial u_{t+1}/\partial C_{t+1}}$. It follows that:

Proposition 2. With the time separable utility function (19.10), if an increase in leisure increases the marginal utility of consumption in the first period, i.e. if leisure and consumption are complements, then there should be an interest income tax. Conversely, if an increase in leisure decreases the marginal utility of consumption in the first period, that is, if they are substitutes, then there should be an interest income subsidy. Either is plausible and individuals may differ.

The intuition provided earlier helps understand what is going on. We want to make it more expensive (less advantageous) for the high ability person to pretend to be the low ability person. In doing so, he increases his leisure. Skiing is a complement to leisure, so we want to tax skis; household help is a substitute for leisure, so we want to subsidize domestic help. High income people who work long hours with high savings rates, in anticipation of an enjoyable retirement, are evidencing complementarity between leisure and consumption; a subsidy on the return to savings increases the cost of cutting back on savings (as would happen if the high ability pretends to be a low ability).[34]

[33] Later, we will qualify this result. See also Dasgupta and Stiglitz (1971, 1972).

[34] It should be clear from the structure of the analysis that if individuals supplied labor at different dates, so $U^i = U^i(C_t, C_{t+1}, \ldots C_T, L_t, L_{t+1}, \ldots L_T)$, but the utility function remained separable between consumption and leisure (work) $U^i = u^i(C_t, C_{t+1}, \ldots C_T) + v^i(L_t, L_{t+1}, \ldots L_T)$ it would remain true that no interest income tax should

3.2 Atmospheric Externalities

Still another generalization that is easy to incorporate into the model is atmospheric externalities,[35] that is, there is some variable B (for Bad) which is a function of the aggregate consumption variables. Both production and utility can be adversely affected by B:

$$V^i = V^i(C_i, L, B) \text{ where } V^i_B < 0 \tag{19.11}$$

and $Q = F(K, L, B)$, where $F < 0$. It is useful if we reformulate our self-selection constraints:

$$V^2(C_2, L_2, B) \geq V^2\left(C_1, \hat{L}_2, B\right), \tag{19.12a}$$

where $\hat{L}_2$ is the labor a type 2 individual would have to put forth to imitate the income of a type 1 individual, that is,

$$\hat{L}_2 = \frac{w_1 L_1}{w_2} = \nu L_1, \tag{19.12b}$$

where ν is the ratio of the productivity of the low ability individual to the high ability individual, assumed for now fixed. Then we have:

$$\frac{d\Lambda}{dC_i} = [\ldots] + \left\{ \underbrace{\sum \mu_i \frac{dV^i}{dB}}_{A} + \underbrace{\gamma \frac{dF}{dB}}_{B} + \lambda_2 \left(\underbrace{V^2_B - \hat{V}^2_B}_{C} \right) \right\} \frac{dB}{dC_i}, \tag{19.13}$$

where [...] represents the derivative of the Lagrangian in the absence of externalities. There are three additional terms: {A} represents the direct consumption externality; {B} represents the production externality; and {C} represents the impact on the self-selection constraint.

In the case of a separable utility function, which can take on the form of:[36]

$$V^i = \nu(C, L) - Z(B), \tag{19.14a}$$

the third term disappears, and there are only the direct externality effects of the kind that have been analyzed by Pigou (1920) and Sandmo (1975). Because of the structure of preferences, the level of B can't affect any choices made by anyone, and therefore can't affect the structure of taxation. Moreover, the presence of atmospheric externalities (under 19.14a) does not affect choices, and so we can ignore the indirect income effects *arising from B*, though obviously, not those arising from the taxation of labor or goods. However, in the case of (19.14a), the very presence of self-selection constraints changes the social marginal valuation of consumption (in effect, the shadow price on different consumption goods).

be imposed, though, in general, the tax an individual would pay on wage income in one year would depend in wage income earned in other years.

[35] An atmospheric externality is an externality the value of which depends on aggregate consumption. In the notation below C, is the vector aggregate consumption of all commodities.

[36] Obviously, it can also be fully separable, and the analysis does not require additive separability.

The additional terms A and B represent alterations to these shadow prices, as opposed to the market prices.

Alternatively, separability could take the form of

$$V^i = v(C, B) - Z(L). \tag{19.14b}$$

The results for (19.14b) follow directly from our earlier analysis. A change in B simply shifts the common utility function for goods.

Proposition 3A. If labor is separable from consumption, then a straightforward Pigouvian tax/subsidy is optimal. If the externality is separable from consumption and labor (but consumption and labor are not necessarily separable), then a first-best Pigouvian tax/subsidy—over and above the shadow prices (prices with optimal commodity taxes/subsidies)—is desirable.

In other words, in these cases, the complicated formulae underlying the literature on corrective taxation that focus on interactions between the corrective taxes and other taxes are not relevant. What has been called "first best Pigouvian taxation"—where the tax is imposed to reflect marginal harm—is desirable (Kaplow 2012). On the other hand, if the utility functions are not separable, simple Pigouvian corrective taxation is not appropriate, but the deviations from simple Pigouvian corrective taxation do not depend (just) on indirect revenue effects, but (also) on the impacts on self-selection constraints.

Proposition 3B. With non-separable utility functions, Pigouvian corrective taxation has to be modified to take account not just of the effects on government revenue but of the first order effects on the self-selection restraints.[37]

In particular, if those with more leisure are more sensitive to the quality of the environment than those with less leisure, then the (Pareto) optimal level of consumption of negative externality generating consumption is higher, because by increasing the level of the atmospheric externality, it enhances the ease of separation.

[37] Sandmo (1975) provided the classic modern discussion of optimal taxation in the presence of externalities, but he conducted the analysis in the standard Ramsey–Diamond-Mirrlees framework with no income tax. The contribution here is simply to add the self-selection constraint. Kaplow (2012) analyzes the problem posed here, using a very clever approach which he applies to the analysis of public goods and to the general problem of indirect taxation discussed above (Kaplow (1996, 2006b)), which highlights the role of separability. He shows that if there were a differential tax on commodities, there would always exist a perturbation in the tax function that would lead to a Pareto improvement. In some respects, his result is stronger than that here, for he shows that differential commodity taxation is not desirable regardless of whether the imposed income tax is optimal or not, *so long as it is possible to make any perturbation in the income tax function.* The last observation, though, is critical. For instance, Stiglitz (1976e, 2009a) considers differential commodity taxation in the presence of an optimal linear income tax. There are both administrative, economic, and political reasons for a linear, or a piece-wise linear, tax system, implying that arbitrary deviations from (quasi-) linearity may not be feasible or will entail costs not incorporated into the analysis. Kaplow's analysis focuses on the case of separability between consumption and labor (19.14b).

3.3 Public Goods

The previous subsections' analysis can be directly applied to public goods. A public good, like a public bad, enters everyone's utility, and since we are assuming all individuals have the same preferences: $V^i = V^i(C_i, L, G)$. Assume the production function is of the form $\sum_i C_i + G = \sum_i w_i L_i$, and let γ now represent the overall resource constraint. Then optimal G entails:

$$\sum_i \mu_i N_i V^i_G + \lambda_2 \left(V^2_G - \hat{V}^2_G\right) = \gamma.$$

In the utilitarian formulation, $\mu_i = 1$, for all i. With separability (of either the form of (19.14a) or (19.14b), with G replacing B), the sum of the marginal utilities of the public good equals the marginal social cost, γ. But γ is normally itself influenced by the self-selection constraint. Consider first the case where neither self-selection constraint is binding (Figure 19.1a). Then we have $\lambda_2 = 0$ which implies that $(\mu_i/\gamma)\,\frac{dV^i}{dC_{ij}} = 1$ or $\sum_i (N_i V^i_G / \frac{dV^i}{dC_{ij}}) = 1$: we obtain the standard result that the sum of the marginal rate of substitution equals the marginal rate of transformation, here unity (Samuelson, 1954). But more generally, so long as we have separability, we have $\sum_i (N_i V^i_G / \frac{dV^i}{dC_{ij}}) = 1$: Even with distortionary taxation, the Samuelson rule holds. In a sense, the result should not be too surprising. With unconstrained optimal non-linear taxation, there is no distortion associated with the top person. Then there is, in effect, no *marginal* distortion arising from raising *additional* revenue—even though taxes are, as a whole, distortionary. In the absence of separability, the sum of the marginal rates of substitution may be either greater or less than the marginal rate of transformation.[38] Since different public goods enter into preferences differently, for some goods the sum of the MRSs may be less than the MRT, for others greater.

4 Extension to Many Periods with Overlapping Generations

If we are to analyze meaningfully the desirability of an interest income tax, we have to do so within a model in which the return to capital is determined endogenously. We do so in the standard overlapping generations model. Each generation is assumed to live for two periods, working in the first, and consuming in both periods. Within each generation, there are two types (the able and the less able), but the government does not know who is who. The utility function of the ith type in the t-th generation is denoted by

$$V^i_t(C_{it,t}, C_{it,t+1}, L_{i,t}),$$

[38] Boadway and Keen (1993) provider a fuller analysis of the optimal provision of public goods. Note that the question of whether the sum of the MRS's is greater or less than the marginal rate of transformation does not translate directly into whether the supply of public goods with distortionary taxation is less than or greater than with lump sum taxation, since this is a matter of general equilibrium, in which all the variables are endogenous. See Atkinson and Stern (1974) for a discussion of the matter in the context of the Ramsey–Diamond–Mirrlees model.

where $C_{it,\,t}$ is the t-th generation's vector of consumption during the first (working) period, and $C_{it,\,t+1}$ is the t-th generation's consumption during the second (retirement) period of this life. As before, the self-selection constraint can be written as:

$$V_t^2\left(C_{2t,\,t}, C_{2t,\,t+1}, L_{2,\,t}\right) \geq V_t^2\left(C_{1t,\,t}, C_{1t,\,t+1}, \hat{L}_{2,\,t}\right).$$

Output at the time t is given by a neo-classical production function of the form $Q_t = F(K_t, E_t)$, where $E_t = \nu N_1 L_{1,\,t} + N_2 L_{2,\,t}$ is the effective labor supply. If there are no constraints on the government's ability to use social security or debt policy to control the capital stock (see Atkinson and Stiglitz, 1980) then the only macro-constraint that needs to be taken into account are the period resource constraints, which we write as

$$Q_t = K_{t+1} + \sum_i N_i C_{it,\,t} + \sum_i N_i C_{it-1,\,t} + G = F_t(K_t, E_t), \tag{19.15}$$

where we have assumed that capital wears out each period. Forming the Lagrangian as before,[39] but with separate constraints for each period (including for the self-selection constraint and the resource constraint (19.15) which replaces the budget constraint), and differentiating with respect to the consumption vector and labor supply, we obtain:

$$\frac{dV^2/dC_{it,\,t}}{dV^2/dC_{it,\,t+1}} = \frac{\gamma_t}{\gamma_{t+1}} \tag{19.16a}$$

$$\frac{dV^1/dC_{it,\,t}}{dV^1/dC_{it,\,t+1}} = \frac{N_1\gamma_t + \lambda_{2,\,t} dV^2/dC_{1jt,\,t}}{N_1\gamma_t + \lambda_{2,\,t} dV^2/dC_{1jt,\,t+1}} \tag{19.16b}$$

$$\frac{dV^2/dC_{i,\,t,\,t}}{dV^2/dL_{2,\,t}} = 1 \tag{19.16c}$$

$$\frac{dV^1/dC_{it,\,t}}{dV^1/dL_{1,\,t}} = \frac{N_1\gamma_t + \lambda_{2,\,t} dV^2/dC_{it,\,t}}{N_1\gamma_t + \lambda_{2},\, t dV^2/dL_{1,\,t}}, \tag{19.16d}$$

where γ_t is the Lagrange multiplier associated with the t-th period government budget constraint (19.15). By differentiating the Lagrangian with respect to K_t, we obtain

$$\gamma_{t+1} F_K(K_{t+1}, E_{t+1}) = \gamma_t. \tag{19.17}$$

Thus $\frac{\gamma_t}{\gamma_{t+1}} = F_K(K_{t+1}, E_{t+1})$ = the (gross) marginal return on capital.

Proposition 4a. In the overlapping generations model with two types of labor at every t, there should be no interest income tax on the savings of the high ability individuals, a zero marginal income tax, and no commodity taxation; while, as in the static model, low ability individuals face distortionary taxation on labor, commodities, and savings. With separability between leisure and consumption, there should be no commodity or interest taxation on the low ability. Without separability, there should be commodity and interest income taxes (or subsidies).

[39] Where μ_{it} is the Lagrange multiplier associated with the constraint $V_t^i \geq \bar{V}_t^i$, $\mu_{1,\,0} = 1$.

Rather than focusing on Pareto optimality, we could have maximized intertemporal social welfare, say using a utilitarian social welfare function: $\max \sum_t \delta^t \left(N_1 V_t^1 + N_2 V_t^2\right)$, where the welfare of future generations are discounted at the rate δ (δ is the pure rate of social time preference). In steady state $\frac{\gamma_t}{\gamma_{t+1}} = F_K(K^*, E^*) = r^* = 1/\delta$. (19.16) and (19.17) then imply that the economy with distortionary taxation converges to the modified golden rule, where the rate of return equals the pure rate of social time preference. With separability, both individuals' MRS is equal to that rate, but in general, the low ability individual's may not be.

Proposition 4b. In the steady state of the overlapping generations utilitarian optimal tax problem, with, and, in general, only with separability, the rate of interest (both the producer and consumer rate of interest, for both the low and high ability individuals) equals the pure rate of social time preference.

4.1 Public and Private Investment

It is easy to extend the analysis to incorporate public as well as private investment. Let K_g represent public investment, K_p private investment, and let the production function now be $Q = C + K_g + K_p = F\left(K_g, K_p, E\right)$, where C is aggregate consumption. It immediately follows that $F_{K_g} = F_{K_p}$.

Proposition 4c. Pareto efficient taxation-cum-expenditures requires that the return on public capital equal the return on private capital, which asymptotically, is just equal to the pure rate of time preference.

These results are clearly parallel to those of Diamond and Mirrlees (1971), who argued for production efficiency.

5 Distributive Effects of Tax and Expenditure Policy

The analysis so far has established that the results derived earlier, both with respect to taxation and public production, in simple partial equilibrium models hold more generally in a dynamic, overlapping generations, general equilibrium model; it has shown that Ramsey's analysis provides little guidance either for the design of efficient or redistributive commodity taxation; it has confirmed that the Diamond–Mirrlees result on the desirability of efficiency holds in this setting; and it has shown that the analysis can be extended to incorporate externalities, with modifications from Pigouvian corrective taxation based not on Ramsey-like indirect impacts on tax revenues but on impacts on self-selection constraints.

Unfortunately, several of these results are not robust, if government tax or expenditure policies can affect the distribution of income in ways which cannot be directly offset by tax policy: in our model, relative wages, v. If the two types of labor are not perfect substitutes, then in general v will be affected by levels of consumption of each of the goods and labor supply of the two types of labor. Optimal tax theory is predicated on the inability to observe either output per hour or the number of hours worked, because if one could do so, one could infer ability, and thus impose lump sum taxation.[40] Thus, dropping the time subscripts (focusing on the basic model of Section 3), the first order condition for C_{2j} is:

$$\frac{d\Lambda}{dC_{2j}}/N_2 = \frac{\partial V^2}{\partial C_{2j}} + \lambda_2 \left\{ \frac{\partial V^2}{\partial C_{2j}} - \left(\frac{\partial V^2}{\partial L} \right) L_1 \left(\frac{\partial v}{C_{2j}} \right) \right\} - \gamma = 0.$$

Any tax or expenditure which changes v affects the self-selection constraint, and hence all of the previous conditions are altered. Note that $\frac{\partial V^2}{\partial L} < 0$. If follows directly that

Proposition 5. If relative wages are affected by consumption levels of different commodities by the high skilled, then there should be indirect taxation on the high skilled; if relative wages are affected by levels of different commodities by the low skilled, then there should be indirect taxation on the low skilled even with separability between consumption and labor; if labor supply by high skilled individuals affects relative wages, then high wage individuals should face a marginal income tax (or subsidy). Any change in C_{ij} or L_i that improves the distribution of income (i.e. increases the low ability individual's wage relative to that of the high ability) improves welfare, and hence taxes should be designed to reflect this.

This means that the consumption of unskilled labor-intensive goods should be encouraged (their consumption prices reduced). In particular, we know from Samuelson's (1948) analysis of the two-factor two good international trade model, where output in each sector is a function of skilled and unskilled labor, that a movement along the production possibilities schedule (with fixed inputs of skilled and unskilled labor) toward the production of the unskilled-intensive good leads to an increase in relative wages of unskilled workers. The implications for labor supply (taxation of labor income) are, in this model where there are no other factors of production, disquieting (Stiglitz, 1982e). Since in such a model, the two types of labor have to be complements ($F_{12} > 0$), an increase in skilled labor has to increase the relative wage of the unskilled. This means that we have to encourage more labor supply by the skilled (from what it would be in the absence of an effect on relative wages), that is, the top marginal income tax rate should be negative. This result, however, is not general: if we have a three-factor production function (output is a function of the two types of labor and land or capital), then skilled and unskilled labor can be substitutes, in which case the top marginal tax rate should be positive, in contrast to the standard result in optimal (income) taxation that it should be zero (see Mirrlees, 1971 and Saez, 2001).

Similarly, the optimal Pigouvian tax formulae for correction of externalities and the formulae for the optimal supply of public goods have to be corrected for induced wage effects: the externality or public good may have an effect on relative wages, and thus on the self-selection constraints. The required modifications in the optimal formulae are straightforward. Note, in particular, that the simplifying results that hold with separability (that the effects on self-selection constraints can be ignored) no longer hold.

[40] Of course, that would not be the case if output per hour was itself a function of some unobservable variable besides ability, for example, effort or education. We cannot pursue these ideas here.

5.1 Production Efficiency

Soon after Diamond and Mirrlees established their efficiency result—that optimal commodity taxation should ensure production efficiency—Dasgupta and Stiglitz (1971, 1972) showed that this would not be so in general, in particular if there were restricted taxation, for instance if there were rents (pure profits) that could not be taxed at 100%, or if there were some factors or goods that had to be taxed at the same rate. A direct implication of the Diamond–Mirrlees efficiency result was that it was not optimal to impose tariffs. Correspondingly, an implication of the Dasgupta–Stiglitz results was that it often was desirable to impose tariffs (Dasgupta and Stiglitz, 1975). Not surprisingly, the same result holds in the current context. Here, the critical issue is distribution. In the previous paragraphs, we assumed that government could not directly control v by the imposition of (optimal) indirect taxes on the labor supply of skilled and unskilled labor—an assumption we noted that was fully consistent with the standard optimal tax model, where only the product of hours worked and wages per hour is observable. (That is, the standard model unrealistically treats skilled and unskilled labor as two different factors, and hence different factor taxes can be imposed on each.) But even if the wages received by or paid to any individual are not observable to the government, the government can affect the relative wage paid to unskilled workers.

Thus, if the government imposes a tariff on the relative price of the unskilled labor intensive good, it increases v, relaxing the self-selection constraint.[41] The benefit of relaxing that constraint has to be compared with the cost of the resulting inefficiency, which is captured by the impact on the resource constraint of an increase in p, the domestic producer price, over the international price, which we assume is unity. With international trade[42], the resource constraint can be written $\sum_j X_j\,(p; L_1, L_2) = \sum_i \sum_j C_{ij}$, where X_j is the output of the jth commodity, a function of relative (producer) prices and the aggregate supplies of the two types of labor. Specifying $\{L_1, L_2\}$ determines the production possibilities curve. Specifying p determines where on the production possibilities curve the economy operates. In Figure 19.2, AB measures the inefficiency at the equilibrium of aggregate consumption of one good in terms of the other good: how much more aggregate consumption could have been had a tariff not been imposed. We impose a tariff on the unskilled labor intensive good, which increases unskilled relative wages. The optimal tariff is greater than zero and satisfies the first order condition:[43]

$$\lambda_2\left\{-\left(\frac{\partial V^2}{\partial L}\right)L_{1t}\left(\frac{\partial v}{\partial p}\right)\right\}+\frac{\gamma\partial X_1}{\partial p}(1-p)=0,$$

where $p = MRT = \frac{\partial X_2}{\partial p} / \frac{\partial X_1}{\partial p}$ (where MRT stands for the marginal rate of transformation). The first term is the benefit from the relaxation of the self-selection constraint; the second term the resource cost of the tariff.

There are similarly many ways within the closed economy to show the (potential) desirability of distortionary production taxation in a world where we cannot tax separately

[41] See also Naito (1999).
[42] Assuming all goods are tradable.
[43] The effect on the budget constraint is $X_1\partial p + X_2\partial p = X_1\partial p\,[1 - MRT]$.

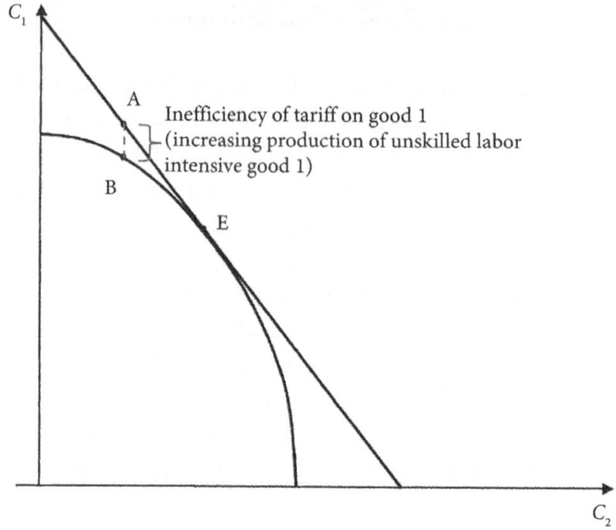

Figure 19.2 Measuring the inefficiency of a tariff.
By producing at *B* rather than at *E*, the economy can consume less than it otherwise could have. The effective loss in output in terms of good 1 is measured by *AB*

skilled and unskilled work. For instance, assume we have two sectors in the economy, each producing all the goods (a dual economy), one of which is more unskilled labor intensive. For each we have a transformation function $J^k\left(C_1^k + C_2^k,\ G^k,\ L_1^k, L_2^k\right) = 0$, where the *j*th element of C_1^k is output of consumption good *j* in the *k*th sector, so $C_{1j}^k + C_{2j}^k$ = total production of commodity *j* in the *k*th sector, which in equilibrium must be equal to the total consumption of that product. We can tax differently the consumption of good *j* depending on the producer. Doing so is equivalent to imposing a producer tax. In our direct control problem, where we specify the level of consumption of each good by each type of individual, we now specify the level of consumption of each good by sector. Since what we are concerned about is relative wages, what matters is aggregate consumption across the two individuals of output from the two sectors, which can variously be thought of as the advanced or large corporate sector, and the informal or SME sector. In equilibrium, there are additional constraints imposed by the fact that while the government cannot observe wages, individuals do, and they allocate themselves so that the wages in the two sectors for each type of labor are the same. (A more realistic model would incorporate labor market frictions.) The Lagrangian now needs to be rewritten, with additional terms representing resource constraints $\gamma_k J^k$; and the free labor mobility constraint, ensuring equal marginal products of labor in the two sectors relative to say the numeraire, 0: $\zeta_i\left[J_{L_i}^a/J_o^a - J_{L_i}^u/J_o^a\right]$, where the superscript *a* stands for the advanced sector, and *u* for the less advanced sector, and $J_{L_i}^k/J_o^k$ is the wage in the *k*th sector of type *i* labor in terms of the numeraire, denoted "o." The optimization equation (the derivative of the Lagrangian) for C_{ij}^k now contains an extra set of terms, one focusing on the effect of the consumption of the *j*th good from the *k*th production sector on the self-selection constraint, another embedding the resource constraints associated with each of the sectors, the third embedding the free movement of labor across sectors.

Production of a good in one production process may affect the self-selection constraint differently from that of the other.

$$\lambda_2\left\{-\left(\frac{\partial V^2}{\partial L}\right)L_{1t}\left(\frac{\partial v}{\partial C^k_{ij}}\right)\right\}+$$
$$\partial\left\{\sum\gamma_k\left[J^k\right]+\sum\zeta_i\left[J^a_{L_i}/J^a_o-J^u_{L_i}/J^a_o\right]\right\}/\partial C^k_{ij}=0.$$

With an increase in production in say good j in the advanced and SME sectors having different effects on the demand for unskilled labor, and thus affecting differently the value of v and thus the self-selection constraint, there is a strong presumption *against* production efficiency.[44]

Proposition 6. In general, production efficiency is not desirable. If there are two (or more) sectors of the economy with different production functions, and in particular, different responses of relative demands for different types of labor (and thus relative wages) to demands for different goods, then production efficiency is not desirable. In particular, distortionary tariffs are in general desirable.

Distortionary production tax in effect reduces the burden imposed on distortionary consumption taxes. The freedom that Diamond and Mirrlees had in setting taxes on skilled and unskilled labor—different factors of production that to them were observable—meant that these distributive effects could always be "undone" by changes in factor taxation. The assumption here is that this is not possible: if we could observe the type of labor (skilled or unskilled), we could observe who was providing that type of labor, and thus infer directly the type of the individual, and thus impose lump sum taxation.[45]

5.2 Extending the Life-Cycle Model

In this subsection, we extend the analysis of the previous sections to include distributive effects of taxation within a life-cycle model. As before, we assume that the two types of labor are not perfect substitutes, that is, the aggregate production is of the form $Q_t = F(K_t, L_{1t}, L_{2t})$ with $w_{i,t} = F_{L_{i,t}}$, where $Q_t = K_{t+1} + \sum_i\sum_j C_{ijt}$. Now, relative wages depend on investment. If we assume constant returns to scale, $v_t = \frac{w_{1t}}{w_{2,t}} = \Phi\left(\frac{L_{1t}}{K_t}, \frac{L_{2t}}{K_t}\right)$. Given

[44] Production efficiency requires that the marginal rate of transformation of all goods that are produced in both sectors be the same in the two sectors, i.e. $\mathfrak{J}^a_j/\mathfrak{J}^a_m = \mathfrak{J}^u_j/\mathfrak{J}^u_m$, where j and m are any two goods. It also entails

$$\frac{\frac{\partial\mathfrak{J}^a}{\partial C^a_{ij}}}{\frac{\partial\mathfrak{J}^a}{\partial C^a_{il}}}=\frac{\frac{\partial\mathfrak{J}^u}{\partial C^u_{ij}}}{\frac{\partial\mathfrak{J}^u}{\partial C^u_{il}}}$$

[45] It is *conceivable* that the government observe the type of labor input, but not the "name" of the individual providing that type of labor. Especially in the unincorporated sector, our assumption is more plausible; and so long as there are some sectors of the economy where the type of labor being provided is unobservable, our results on the desirability of distortionary production taxation hold.

this reformulation, we can again form the Lagrangian, obtaining the same first order conditions for $C_{it,\,t+1}$ and $C_{it,\,t+1}$ as before but now there is an extra term in each equation to reflect the effect of relative wages on the self-selection constraint through K, so

$$\gamma_{t+1}F_K = \gamma_t + \lambda^2_{t+1}L_{1t}\frac{dV^2}{dL_{it}}\left(C_{it+1,\,t+1}, C_{it+1,\,t+2}, \nu L_{it+1}\right)\frac{d\nu}{dK}. \tag{19.18}$$

In turn $\frac{d\ln\nu}{dK} = (F_{13}/F_1 - F_{23}/F_2)$. While constant returns to scale implies $F_{13}+F_{23}+F_{33}= 0$, there are no implications about $\frac{d\ln\nu}{dK}$. If, for instance, capital is a substitute for unskilled labor and a complement to skilled labor, then an increase in K decreases ν. Substituting into the first order conditions for consumption of the high ability at t and $t+1$, we obtain:

$$\frac{\frac{dV^2}{dC_{2jt,t}}}{\frac{dV^2}{dC_{2jt,\,t+1}}} = \frac{\gamma_t}{\gamma_{t+1}} = F_K - \lambda^2_{t+1}L_{1t}\frac{dV^2}{dL_{it}}\left(C_{it+1,\,t+1}, C_{it+1,\,t+2}, \nu L_{it+1}\right)\frac{d\nu}{dK}/\gamma_{t+1},$$

where $C_{2jt,t}$ is the high ability individual of generation t's consumption of commodity j in time t, $C_{2jt,t+1}$ is that at time $t+1$. A similar calculation applies to type 1 individuals. So too, consider two types of capital goods, say K_g and K_p using the same amount of resources to construct, $Q_t = K_{gt+1} + K_{pt+1} + \sum\sum C_{ijt}$, so production efficiency requires $F_{Kgt} = F_{Kpt}$, the marginal returns to these two types of capital should be the same. It thus immediately follows that:

Proposition 7a: If the level of capital affects relative wages, the marginal rate of substitution is in general not equal to the marginal rate of transformation even for the high ability individual; even in the presence of separability, it may be optimal to have an interest income tax or subsidy on both high and low ability individuals. Production efficiency is not desirable if different kinds of capital affect the distribution of income differently.

Increases in capital (and in different types of capital goods) change wage inequality. We impose a tax on interest income if an increase in K increases wage inequality, that is, if capital (like robots) lowers unskilled wage relative to skilled wages.[46] The reason we do so is related to how the self-selection constraints are affected. More generally, whether there should be a tax or subsidy on capital depends on whether an increase in the capital stock increases or decreases relative wages, that is, makes the self-selection constraint more or less binding.[47]

If we can differentiate among different kinds of capital, that is, **K** is a vector, with some components labor saving or using for different kinds of labor, then there should be a tax on those kinds of capital goods which are unskilled labor saving and a subsidy on those

[46] Hicks (1932) defined an innovation as labor saving if at the given levels of inputs the marginal return to labor is reduced. Labor saving innovations lead to a reduction in wages. The vocabulary extends directly to the context here: an increase in capital is unskilled labor saving if at the given levels of inputs, the marginal return to unskilled labor decreases. We are particularly concerned here how a change in K affects *relative* wages, v.

[47] Conditions under which either result obtains may easily be derived, simply by differentiating $\frac{F_{L_1}\left(\frac{N_1L_1}{K},\frac{N_2L_2}{K}\right)}{F_{L_2}\left(\frac{N_1L_1}{K},\frac{N_2L_2}{K}\right)}$ with respect to K.

which are unskilled labor using. The returns on different kinds of capital goods should, accordingly, differ. There is no reason that the effect on inequality of public and private capital goods will be the same. In general, government can have more control (directly) in the choice of the extent to which public capital goods are complementary to unskilled labor (i.e., increase v). If so, then public capital goods should be advantaged over private capital goods; the (average) marginal return ("F_K") to public investment goods should be less than that for private capital goods, and in a utilitarian dynamic optimal growth model, in steady state, F_{Kg} may thus be less than $1/\delta$.

More generally, the economy's transformation curve can be written as before as

$$J(C_1 + C_2, L_1, L_2, K_{t+1}, K_t) = 0, \text{ with } v = \frac{J_{L_2}}{J_{L_1}}. \tag{19.19}$$

Equation (19.19) describes an economy in which different consumption or capital goods are produced with different production functions. A movement along the transformation curve changes the relative demand for high and low skilled workers, that is, affects relative wages. It follows that

Proposition 7b: If relative wages depend on consumption or public expenditure patterns, then in general, even with separability (i) the rate of return should not equal the intertemporal marginal rate of substitution, (ii) the rate of return in the public sector should not equal that in the private one, and (iii) even asymptotically, with utilitarian intertemporal optimization, it will not equal the pure rate of time preference.[48] As before, the marginal rate of substitution is in general not equal to the marginal rate of transformation even for the high ability individual.

Consumption at date t affects the self-selection constraint at date t, while consumption at date $t + 1$ *of the same commodity* affects the self-selection constraint at $t + 1$. But individuals consume different commodity bundles; if the elderly on average consume more unskilled labor-intensive services (e.g., home care), then we want to encourage individuals to consume more later in life, because that drives up the relative wages of unskilled workers, reducing before tax inequality and the extent to which the self-selection constraint binds, that is, we would want to subsidize high income individual's savings. Conversely, if the elderly on average consume more skill-labor intensive goods and services, like complex medical procedures. (As we explain in the next section, we do not believe that this model captures accurately the most important aspects of capital taxation.)

Thus, in the utilitarian dynamic optimization problem, even with separability, the consumer rate of discount (for either high nor low ability individuals) may not converges to δ, and the producer rate of return is greater or less than δ as increasing K decreases or increases v, the relative wage. If an increase in capital accumulation increases the wage differential (if capital is a complement to high skill labor and a substitute for low skilled workers) the optimal level of F_k (assuming separability in consumption) is higher than the pure discount rate, that is, the optimal level of capital accumulation is lower.

[48] In contrast to the earlier result where $F_K = 1/\delta$.

5.3 Distortions in the Overlapping Generations Model with Unskilled Labor Replacing Robots

We have already seen that the level of investment in different kinds of investment goods, whether in the private or public sector, depends in part on the impact of that good (at the margin) on the distribution of income. Recently, there has been some controversy over the taxation of robots.[49] Assume we have robots which are perfect substitutes for unskilled labor.

Consider robots (a particular type of machine), each costing one unit of ordinary capital goods, replacing unskilled labor. Our production function is now $Q = F(L_1 + R, L_2, K - R)$. Production efficiency requires $F_{L_1} = F_K$. But maximizing social welfare entails:

$$\lambda_2 \left(\frac{\partial V^2}{\partial L}\right) L_{1t} \left(\frac{\partial v}{\partial R}\right) = \gamma (F_{L_1} - F_K) \tag{19.20}$$

where $\frac{\partial ln ln\, v}{\partial R_1} = \frac{F_{11} - F_{13}}{F_1} - \frac{F_{21} - F_{23}}{F_2}$. Equation (19.20) implies that when there is production efficiency ($F_{L1} = F_K$) there should be further investments in unskilled labor replacing robots if it increases ν; and if it decreases ν, the level of investment in robots should be decreased (there should be a tax on that kind of robot). Thus, so long as the direct effect of "competition" from robots driving down wages ($F_{11} < 0$) dominates any secondary effects from the decrease in K on wages of high skilled workers, it is desirable to tax unskilled labor replacing robots. It is easy to see that that is the case for the standard Cobb–Douglas production function $Q = L_1^{\alpha_1} L_2^{\alpha_2} K^{1-\alpha_1-\alpha_2}$.[50]

5.4 Central Message

The central message of this section of the chapter is simple: tax and expenditure policies can have effects on the distribution of income that cannot be fully offset by other tax and subsidy policies. Measures which improve the market distribution of income (here increase ν) are desirable. Heuristically, we can think of such measures as reducing the burden imposed on distortionary consumption taxation. This result provides theoretical underpinnings for recent policy perspectives, noted in the introduction, which have emphasized the importance of achieving greater equality of market incomes. Thus, tax and expenditure policies need to be sensitive to the general equilibrium distributional consequences. A tax which has the effect of reducing the demand for unskilled labor should be reduced from the level which it otherwise would have been; conversely if it increases the demand for skilled labor. Public investments should be targeted to increase the productivity of unskilled workers. Private expenditures aimed at replacing unskilled labor with machines should be discouraged (through taxation).

The mechanism by which the welfare benefits are generated in this model is not just the direct effect on, say unskilled workers. In the context of a government already engaged in welfare maximizing redistributions with lump sum taxes, all that would matter is what

[49] Bill Gates suggested that there should be such a tax (Delaney, 2017). There was the predictable backlash among those who thought that that was foolish, since it would interfere with efficiency and impede innovation. If there is learning by doing with spill-overs to other sector, there is a presumption that the government should be subsidizing robot development (see Stiglitz and Greenwald, 2014). The analysis here explains in effect how that subsidy has to be adjusted to reflect distributional consequences of robots.

[50] A similar analysis applies to skilled labor replacing robots.

happens to aggregate output. But such taxes and redistributions are not feasible. Hence, changes in relative wages also matter because they may affect the constraints on redistribution. Here, the central constraint is the self-selection constraint. In our model, an "improvement" in the distribution of income through an increase in the relative wage of unskilled workers loosens the self-selection constraint and thus enables the government to engage in further redistributions which improve societal welfare. Our analysis formalizes the notion that improving the before tax distribution of income makes it easier to get a better after-tax distribution of income.

More generally, there are a broad set of hard-to-model political constraints. It is apparent that tax policy does not quickly (if at all) act to offset changes in the market distribution of income. Thus, an improvement in the before tax distribution of income will typically lead to an improvement in the after-tax distribution of income and in societal welfare.

Perhaps the most striking result is that these concerns over distribution are so strong that they justify policies that lead to production inefficiency. In Diamond–Mirrlees, any distributive benefits achieved through production inefficiency could be achieved at lower cost simply by adjusting tax rates. But if there are restraints on the set of feasible taxes that go beyond just limitations on lump sum taxes, then government cannot necessarily achieve the general equilibrium effects on distribution that are obtained through distortionary production taxes (including tariffs).

6 Layered Self-Selection

There is one more important set of circumstances requiring significant modification of the Atkinson-Stiglitz (1976) framework. The standard Mirrlees model, of which our analysis can be viewed as an elaboration, is based on self-employed individuals producing widgets. The government can only observe the number of widgets produced, not the hours worked, and therefore it cannot infer abilities. But in fact, in modern economies, most individuals work for others, and their employers also need to identify abilities. Individuals too will seek to demonstrate to their employers that they are more able, so as to obtain higher wages.[51] While screening and signaling may be done in a number of ways, the government may be able to partially free ride on this information; and in any case, government has to take into account that tax policies affect screening and signaling.

Consider the simplest case where an employer cannot observe either an individual's output, Y, or his ability but can observe his level of education. But Y itself is a function of education, E, and ability, A. High and low ability individuals differ in the cost of education, so we can write utility as $V^i = V^i(w, E)$, with $i = 1, 2$, where w is the wage paid to the individual with education E, with a low ability individual's indifference curve in $\{E, w\}$ space being steeper: he requires a greater increase in wages to compensate him for getting more education. The standard competitive equilibrium entails a separating equilibrium, with $\{E_1^*, w_1^*\}$ being the point on the low ability production function (or more precisely, $w_1 = f_1(E_1)$) which maximizes V^1. $\{E_2^*, w_2^*\}$ is the point along the high ability's productivity curve $w_2 = f_2(E_2)$) satisfying the self-selection constraint: $V^1\{E_1^*, w_1^*\} \leq V^1\{E_2^*, w_2^*\}$. If w is observable *to the government*, even if E is not, the government knows the ability of the individual. It effectively free rides off of the private sector. By imposing a lump sum tax on

[51] See Stiglitz (1975a), where it is established that under certain conditions, there may exist a pooling equilibrium. The only competitive *self-selection* equilibria entail separation.

high wage individuals used to pay a lump sum subsidy to low wage individuals, the government can achieve another Pareto efficient self-selection equilibrium, one more in accord with its social welfare function.[52] In this case, optimal income taxation is far simpler than that modelled by Mirrlees.

But there is a more difficult case, where there are binding self-selection constraints where the outcomes of the private self-selection processes are not observable. Consider, in particular, the above education model, but where education affects individual's productivity. Firm's observe this, and pay a wage accordingly; but, as in Mirrlees, the government cannot observe the wage (output per hour) or education level. Individual's utility is a function of their wage (= productivity), E(education), and labor supply. $V^i = V^i(w, E)$, where now individuals can choose how much to work. We now need to embed the private self-selection constraint inside our social welfare maximization problem by adding a term to our Lagrangian $\zeta[V_1(C_1, L_1, E_1) - -V_1(C_2, L_2, E_2)]$. While the binding self-selection in the usual optimal tax problem entails the high ability pretending to be low ability—working less and getting a lower income—in the usual competitive market equilibrium, the binding self-selection constraint entails the low ability pretending to be high ability. Thus, as he increases his education level (to imitate the high ability) and so gets a high wage (w_2), he will have to work more. It is the fact that there are now two binding self-selection constraints which upsets the standard results of optimal tax theory.

The resource constraint also needs to be rewritten to include the costs and benefits of education:[53] $C_1 + C_2 + E_1 + E_2 = F(L_1 f(E_1) + L_2 f(E_2))$.

Focusing in particular on the first order conditions for L_2 and C_{2j}, there is an additional term $-\zeta V_L^1$ and $-\zeta V_{C_{2j}}^1$[54] so that

$$-\frac{dV^2}{dL_2} \Big/ \frac{dV^2}{dC_{2j}} = \{\gamma F' w_2 - \zeta V_L^1\} / \gamma + \zeta V_{C_{2j}}^1,$$

[52] The taxes will, of course, affect equilibrium wages and education levels, because of income effects. Assume, for instance, there were an equal number of individuals of the two types. Then Pareto efficiency entails maximizing $V^2(f_2(E_2) - T, E_2)$ s.t. $V^1(f_1(E_1) + T, E_1) \geq \bar{U}^1$ and the self-selection constraint $V^1\{w_1^* + T, E_1^*\} \leq V^1\{w_2^* - T, E_2^*\}$, where T is the lump sum tax. Each firm takes the lump sum taxes imposed on high wage workers (lump sum subsidies on low wage workers) as given, but of course the government knows that changing T changes the market's screening equilibrium.

[53] In this formulation, E and C occur simultaneously. A more natural formulation (especially in our dynamic model) is that there are three periods in an individual's life, in the first of which he gets educated, in the second of which he works, and in the third of which he is retired. None of the results are dependent on this formulation.

Moreover, this formulation assumes that skilled and unskilled labor are perfect substitutes. The more general case is considered in Section 5. It also assumes that the expenditures on education are "goods," not forgone leisure. The results hold for the more general case.

[54] In general, there are several self-selection constraints, all of which could be binding: (a) the low ability individual is indifferent between mimicking the high ability in the eyes of the firm; (b) the high ability individual who has obtained a high level of education is indifferent between mimicking the low ability individual who has obtained a low level of education in the eyes of the government; and (c) the low ability individual who has mimicked a high ability individual in obtaining a high level of education (and thus has become more productive) is indifferent between mimicking a low ability individual who has not obtained a high level of education. But in this model, if a high ability individual is indifferent between mimicking a low ability individual in the eyes of the government, then a low ability individual would not want to simultaneously pretend before his employer to be high ability (and thus get a high level of education) and pretend before the government to be low ability, for in doing so, he reduces the value of education, since in imitating the low ability, he must restrict the number of hours worked. Thus, here we can focus simply on the single additional self-selection constraint. Whether we have to include a still further self-selection constraint, the more general point that the addition of the new self-selection constraint means that only when certain separability conditions are satisfied will it be desirable not to impose distortionary taxation on the high ability individual, remains valid.

implying that in general, the MRS is not equal to the MRT: there should be intervention even in the labor market of high ability individuals. By the same token the marginal rate of substitution between two commodities j and k is given by $\frac{\gamma+\zeta V^1_{C_{2j}}}{\gamma+\zeta V^1_{C_{2k}}}$ which equals unity only if $\zeta V^1_{C_{2j}} = \zeta V^1_{C_{2k}}$, which is true if $\zeta = 0$ or if $V^1_{C_{2j}} = V^1_{C_{2k}}$. As earlier, we can write:

$$\text{MRS}^2 - \text{MRS}^1 = \gamma\left(\text{MRT} - \text{MRS}^1\right).$$

Thus, if the low ability is mimicking the high ability in the acquisition of education, he is spending more on, say, tutoring services and more time doing homework, leaving less income and less leisure. If, somehow, the result is that the marginal rate of substitution between good j and k is the same, that would mean that $MRS^1 = MRS^2$ and from the above equation, that would mean that $MRT = MRS^i = 1$, that is, there should be no consumption taxes; in the case of consumption at different dates, no interest income tax. But education takes away from "net" consumption and leisure when the individual is young, and thus inevitably changes the MRS between consumption at t and $t + 1$ and the MRS will differ between high ability and low ability individuals. Taxing interest income—making the future less valuable at the margin relative to today—discourages low ability individuals from imitating high ability, loosening the private self-selection constraint, and thus increasing welfare.

The general point is that tax structures affect private mechanisms for sorting individuals, and government needs to take into account these impacts. Greenwald and Stiglitz (1986) and Arnott, Greenwald, and Stiglitz (1994) established that, in general, whenever there are self-selection constraints, the competitive equilibrium is not (constrained) Pareto efficient. The distortions are first order. Small taxes have a second order deadweight loss associated with them but can have a first order effect in correcting distortions associated with self-selection constraints, for example in improving the efficiency of market sorting. Thus, we can think of optimal taxation as entailing two parts: (a) corrective taxation, to ensure that the market is Pareto efficient; (b) redistributive taxation, to move us toward a "better" Pareto efficient allocation. Not surprisingly, when both of these are taken into account, the presumption of AS 76 that there should not be intertemporal taxation no longer holds.

7 Inheritances

The most critical assumption underlying Atkinson and Stiglitz (1976) was that all individuals were identical except for their abilities. But there are huge differences in inherited wealth and in returns to capital of those with wealth.[55] Much of the argument for capital taxation is that taxation of capital and returns to capital can achieve greater equity at a lower cost (say in terms of the deadweight losses associated with the tax) than just reliance on an earned income tax. In Section 3, we commented on the taxation of capital in the context of a world in which individuals differ in their ability to generate returns on capital. Here, we focus on inheritances.

[55] In a world without uncertainty in returns, the taxation of capital and the return to capital are equivalent, but this is not so in general.

It is easy (in principle) to separate the taxation of inheritances and the return on inheritances from the life-cycle savings discussed in previous sections. The latter can be thought of as put into Income Retirement Accounts (IRAs), and the analysis of earlier sections argued that in the absence of, for example, distributive effects and with separability, there should be no taxation of returns in IRAs. But that says nothing about the taxation of capital in general, which we will argue should be taxed, and possibly at a high rate. If some inherited savings slips into IRAs and not all life-cycle savings is included in tax-exempt IRAs, there would be some presumption for taxing the return to capital in IRAs, but still taxing the return to capital not in IRAs.

An analysis of optimal/Pareto efficient taxation of inheritances entails two complications, beyond the general equilibrium distributive effects upon which Section 5 focused: (a) A full analysis of taxation and inequality in the presence of bequests has to come to terms with the drivers of financial and human capital bequests—the determinants of the intergenerational transmission of advantage and disadvantage.[56] (b) It is not obvious what the appropriate social welfare function should be.

7.1 Determinants of Inheritances and the Intergenerational Transmission of Advantages

Individual's lifetime income (wealth) is determined by their endowments—inherited ability, education provided by their parents and the State, and inherited financial wealth—and the returns on those endowments, itself a function of those endowments, effort and luck. Thus, there are three sources of high levels of lifetime wealth: children who have the good fortune of having parents who bequeath them good endowments, either high abilities or substantial amounts of financial and human capital; high levels of effort; and those who get high earnings on their endowments, often at least partially as a result of luck. The latter also include the inventors and entrepreneurs who earn outsized incomes, often through the exploitation of market power. Gates and Rockefeller are examples. The "successful" also include individuals who were particularly effective in receiving favors from the state, e.g. in the form of land grants. In many cases, wealth begets wealth through a variety of mechanisms, including the exercise of market and political power and returns to information asymmetries.

While some of the determinants are under the control of the individual, others are not: most importantly, inherited ability.[57] While some receive a high inheritance because of the luck of having parents with a high "taste" for bequests, others because of the luck of having very rich parents, others because they have fewer siblings among whom the wealth of the parents have to be divided, there is still a fourth source of differences in inherited wealth (more important among "life-cycle savers"): in the absence of good annuities and reverse mortgages, upper individuals who do not wish to turn to the government for support in their final years have to hold more than what they actuarially need to live; on average, they die before eating up all of their savings. The children of those who die early may receive a small fortune, especially if there are no siblings. While it is natural that economists begin

[56] See Stiglitz (1966, 1969b, and, most related to the discussion here, earlier chapters of this book) and Becker and Tomes (1979, 1986) for a more extensive discussion.

[57] A fuller analysis of the intergenerational transmission of wealth is contained in Chapter 12.

with a discussion of *choices and tastes* (some individuals or dynasties might give greater weight to their descendants than others),[58] almost surely, these other factors are as or more important.

In most of these cases there is little reason to believe that, in general, taxing transfers at the top at a high marginal rate would have significant adverse effects on economic activity. For instance, the amount of money that individuals hold for their old age as a result of the absence of annuity markets is likely determined largely by the individual's risk aversion, the extent of public support for the aged and expectations of support from one's children, and uncertainties about life expectancy. Fertility decisions are similarly unlikely to be significantly affected by inheritance taxation. The efforts of those like Gates and Rockefeller (either at innovative and entrepreneurial activities or at exerting market power) are unlikely to be affected much by high inheritance or capital taxation at levels of wealth and income exceeding some billions of dollars.[59] Indeed, there is some positive evidence and theory that high marginal tax rates might reduce incentives for rent seeking and exploitation, thereby increasing economic efficiency.[60]

Thus, there is some presumption that there should be high tax rates on very large bequests, the main concern being not that individuals won't work as hard, but that they would engage more in tax avoidance activities (in the extreme cases, changing residence to avoid taxation). Concern about inherited wealth inequality would center progressive taxation on inheritances, not bequests.

Whatever the reason, in practice, in most countries there is still substantial intergenerational transfer of wealth, implying that even with taxes on bequests and inheritances, there will be individuals with substantial incomes from inherited capital. Thus, (progressive) taxation on capital arises naturally within any utilitarian framework. It can be viewed as an indirect (and imperfect) way of taxing bequests, as a second-best response to an important source of inequality.[61]

7.2 Objectives

While Pareto efficiency and utilitarianism provide a natural framework for evaluating alternative taxes on wages, the welfare evaluation of inheritance taxes is more complicated. As Stiglitz (1987a) noted, bequests are doubly blessed: while they give utility to the giver, they also give utility to the receiver. There is a positive consumption externality. There is thus a presumption that there will be an undersupply of bequests, all else being equal, and that they should be subsidized.[62] In the context of models such as those considered in previous sections, apart from this externality effect—and possible general equilibrium distributive effects of the kind discussed in the previous section—bequests are just another form of

[58] See, for instance Piketty and Saez (2013).

[59] Obviously, their ability to engage in philanthropic activities, which absorbed so much of their energies after making their fortunes, would be affected.

[60] See Saez Piketty, and Stantcheva (2014) and Chapter 16 above.

[61] See Cremer and Pestieau (2006) and Cremer, Pesteiau, and Rochet (2003), Farhi and Werning (2010), Piketty and Saez (2013), and Stiglitz (2017b).

[62] This idea has been incorporated into and commented upon by many of the more recent models of inheritance taxation. See, for example, Kaplow (2001) and Piketty and Saez (2013). At the same time there is another important externality, that associated with an increase in inequality. Most of the economics literature on bequests has not incorporated these important externalities.

utility generating expenditure, and thus there should be no bequest taxation if (and, in general, only if) if there is separability between consumption (now including bequests) and labor (Kaplow, 2001).[63]

7.2.1 Trade-offs between Consumption Inequality and Wealth Inequality

But this analysis does not fully capture societal concerns about inequality, or the manner in which wealth inequalities arise.

Consider a model (such as Bevan and Stiglitz, 1979) where individuals themselves think about their children and, when they have good luck, either being born with high ability or getting an unusually large return on their investments, set aside an optimal amount to share with their descendants. Ignoring general equilibrium effects (impacts on the distribution of income and self-selection constraints), each individual is optimally smoothing income over generations. It might seem that so long as the family's intertemporal discount rate is the same as the social welfare function,[64] there is no reason for government to engage in intertemporal distribution. But that is not correct: it is still the case that *at this moment* some families have a larger endowment of "ability" and capital than others, and therefore a redistributive tax would be desirable. Moreover, each period, some individuals get a better roll of the dice—given their parents, they have higher wages or higher returns on their inherited capital. While they optimally share their good fortune with their descendants, they don't share their good fortune at all with other families (dynasties) who have had a bad roll of the dice, ending up with low wages or low returns on capital. A utilitarian would wish to redistribute income between the lucky and those who had a bad roll of the dice. (Indeed, so would an individual, behind a veil of ignorance, not knowing how the dice would roll. Moreover, because of limitations on indebtedness, even optimal intergenerational redistribution within a family cannot achieve outcomes as good as those that can be achieved through government redistribution.)

If the government can observe inherited wealth I_t, then, at time 0, there should obviously be a tax on the inheritance and on returns to inherited capital. Indeed, taxing past bequests (capital that individuals have already inherited) at 100% is non-distortionary and would thus be part of a utilitarian optimal tax program. Of course, this is just the standard paradox of capital taxation: in the absence of some form of commitment, savers (those providing bequests) would know this, and there would be no bequests. (The absence of all bequests would have general equilibrium incidence effects, unless government savings/investment could full compensate.) If the government could costlessly redistribute within and between generations, this would not be of concern. But while there is no deadweight loss associated with intergenerational redistribution within a family, there typically is with redistributions across families. Then, there has to be some way that governments can make a credible commitment not to impose confiscatory taxes. We do not answer the question of how such a commitment can be made here, but rather ask, if the government could make a credible commitment to say a fixed inheritance tax and/or return to capital, how would those

[63] Much of the literature models the utility of bequests in a reduced form, rather than as a result of increasing the utility of one's descendants, the benefits of which are incorporated into one's well-being. Standard structural modeling (e.g., a dynastic utility function) also typically entails separability between labor and bequests, though such analyses employ the separability hypothesis as a matter of analytical convenience; the empirical implications are typically not tested.

[64] And putting aside the fact noted above that in a utilitarian framework, a bequest gives utility to both the giver and the receiver.

taxes be determined?[65] The government must balance the benefits of greater equality across families with reduced intertemporal smoothing of consumption within the dynasty and the deadweight loss associated with distortionary taxation. In principle, the optimal tax function would relate the tax paid by individual at time t to all observables related to his current behavior and past history (i.e., to Y_t, I_t for all $t \leq t_0$, where t_0 is today's date), since such data (together with knowledge of the stochastic processes) convey information about relevant current period variables, in particular w_t (the individual's ability). For instance, if ability were perfectly inherited, information from previous periods' incomes of the parents perfectly conveys information about the individual's current ability. If there is a high correlation, past data would still convey considerable information. (Since the standard models assume Markovian processes for ability, in those models, only inherited wealth and the previous period income is relevant.[66])

Of course, individuals know this, and if they care about their descendants, as assumed here, their behavior would correspondingly adjust. This can have profound consequences, including that the equilibrium is not a separating equilibrium (as in the previous sections of this chapter) but a pooling one.[67] We thus have to compare the level of social welfare with the optimal tax of the form $T(Y_t, Y_{t-1}, I_t, I_{t-1})$ with that generated simply by a tax of the form: $T(Y_t, I_t)$ where, we assume, the government has made an additional commitment, not to use prior information about the individual (family) in setting current taxes.[68]

7.2.1.1 Societal Implications of Inequalities of Wealth and Inheritance

Should society be concerned with consumption inequalities within a generation, with inequalities in dynastic utility, or with inequalities in wealth? Societies with large wealth inequalities are different; large wealth inequalities are associated with inequalities in political power and access to privilege.

Moreover, several externalities have been associated with inequality. There is, for instance, a large literature emphasizing how inequality affects economic performance and society more generally (Stiglitz, 2012a; Ostry, Loungani, and Berg, 2019).[69]

If society is concerned with excessive inequalities in wealth—that is, if the social welfare function is not just a Benthamite utilitarian function adding up the utilities of each

[65] No democratic government can make such commitments, and it is apparent that different parties have different views about the appropriate tax rate. Much political campaigning centers around such issues. Each party *should* however take into account the likelihood that a successor government would change tax rates and the effect of perceptions that this might be so on behavior. One can reconcile observed behavior, for example of the Republican Party in the U.S., as they adopt regressive taxation—which are more likely to be reversed with the next Democratic period of control—with this perspective by assuming that they have become increasingly short sighted, perhaps because of a belief in declining probabilities of success in future elections; see Korinek and Stiglitz (2008, 2009).

[66] There is some evidence that the ability generating process is not so simple, for example that characteristics of the grandparents may affect the grandchildren independently of the state of the child.

[67] The self-selection constraints take into account that actions at t-1 affect taxes at t. See Roberts (1982) and Stiglitz (2009b).

[68] In our earlier analysis, we implicitly assumed that the government did not make use of the information implicit in the inheritability of ability. But while using such information would almost surely be viewed as politically unacceptable, inheritances are correlated with income of previous generations.

[69] This is especially so if preferences are endogenous, and inequality affects aspirations at the bottom or gives rise to a sense of entitlement at the top (See Demerritt, Hoff, and Stiglitz, forthcoming). Consumption externalities can also arise when preferences are interdependent, for example when individuals care about their relative position. See, for example, Frank (2005) and Stiglitz (2008d).

generation[70]—then progressive inheritance taxes may be desirable, even if they cause deadweight losses in utility, in inducing excessive consumption of an individual within his lifetime. Concerns about extremes of inequalities in lifetime consumption can then be addressed separately by a progressive lifetime consumption tax.

Bequests as a source of inequality may be viewed as particularly iniquitous, because such bequests mean that there is not a level playing field; there is no equality of opportunity.[71] While society cannot create a perfectly level playing field, there are some forms of inequality—those associated with the transmission of financial wealth—which can be redressed.

In Chapter 13, we developed a simple model in which we could evaluate, within a utilitarian context, the benefits of capital taxation, using a two-class model, with workers engaging in life-cycle savings, and capitalists passing on wealth from generation to generation. Life-cycle savers maximize utility over their lifetime, dynastic families maximize intertemporal utility in the standard fashion. The analysis there showed that, at first blush, concerns about trade-offs were justified: an inheritance tax discourages bequests, reducing capital accumulation, and hence wages. Even if all the proceeds of the tax are transferred to workers, and they save more, their additional savings won't compensate for the loss of savings by capitalists, so wages fall—so much that workers are worse off *even taking into account the transfers they receive.* But if tax revenues are invested in human capital (education) or public capital goods, under quite general conditions the adverse incidence effects are more than offset,[72] so that with an equalitarian social welfare function it is desirable to impose a tax on capitalists' return to capital, and with large disparities in income between capitalists and workers, strong equalitarianism, and high productivity of investments in human capital, the optimal tax on capital may be very high.

8 Concluding Remarks

It is remarkable that so much of the policy literature has focused on simplistic models in which differences among individuals were limited, arising mostly out of differences in wage incomes. The Atkinson-Stiglitz 1976 model was useful in reminding us that the role of commodity taxation had to be seen in conjunction with other taxes that were in place as well as taxes that we might have wanted to have in place, but which are not there—a general principle of considerable importance. When there was an optimal non-linear income tax, the role of commodity taxation was limited. Its role could be seen in two ways. First, as improving the before tax (market) distribution of income, putting less of a burden on distortionary redistributive taxes. Alternatively, it could be seen as part of the general theory of corrective taxation. Whenever there are self-selection constraints in an economy, there will be a first order distortion, and commodity taxation can be used to reduce the magnitude of that distortion. This is true whether the self-selection constraint arises purely from

[70] Or the slightly more general function $W = W\{U_t\}$, where social welfare function is any concave function of each generation's utility.

[71] It is worth noting that equality of opportunity is a distinctively different norm that that associated with, say, maximizing an inequality averse dynastic social welfare function. See Chapters 22 and 23 below.

[72] The result can be shown to hold with more general utility functions for capitalists (e.g., recursive Koopmans functions, so that the long run interest rate need not be invariant to tax policy). It also holds with different specifications of taxation, for example a wealth tax on capitalists, or a tax on their net income.

the government attempting to engage in redistributive taxation or also within the private sector—from the more-able individuals attempting to appropriate their ability rents. The presence of self-selection constraints represents a big wedge, a big distortion, in the economy. It is worth creating a small distortion elsewhere in the economy if it can reduce the size of this wedge.[73]

Public investment too needs to take into account its effects on the market distribution of income, and how it alters the distribution of income and self-selection constraints within the economy. In general, even asymptotically and even with separability, the rate of discount for public investment varies across public projects and may be greater or less than the social rate of discount.

There are many other limitations to the basic Atkinson–Stiglitz model that we have not explored here. We have, in particular, assumed the absence of tax evasion and avoidance, and in particular the ability to shift income from one category to another. In practice, it is often difficult to distinguish between capital and labor income, especially for self-employed individuals; and if that is the case, large differences in tax rates provides large incentives to convert wage income into capital income.[74]

This is perhaps related to one of the deepest criticisms of the literature on optimal non-linear taxes: in practice, there are many restraints. We have noted, for instance, if government is restrained to using a linear income tax, commodity taxation is still, in general, desirable. The rationale is somewhat different from that presented above. Such taxation may improve the before tax distribution of income, as we have emphasized, but even if does not do this, it may enable us, with little social deadweight loss, to improve the after-tax and transfer distribution of income, and thus social welfare. A tax on perfume may generate significant revenues from a subset of high-income individuals—individuals who are such that with even an optimal linear income tax have a much lower social marginal utility than poor individuals. Similarly, for a bread subsidy. Though as Deaton noted, with linear expenditure systems, one can't achieve improvements through perfume taxes and bread subsidies, there may be significant departures from those patterns of expenditure.

This leads to the question: why the restraints? There are obvious advantages to simplicity, but when one looks at the tax code, it is clear that simplicity itself was not the guiding principle. Making the tax system non-linear, with several brackets, adds virtually no cost in a modern computer driven tax system, raising a key point: what is costly or feasible depends on technology, and that changes over time—with some changes endogenously driven. When Vickrey advocated the use of congestion taxes, a good congestion tax could not have been implemented. But advances in technology now make the administrative

[73] Thus, it is desirable to introduce random taxation, even though all individuals are risk averse, if by doing so the self-selection constraints are relaxed. See Stiglitz (1982b), Arnott and Stiglitz (1988a), and Brito, Hamilton, Slutsky, and Stiglitz (1995).

[74] There are, of course, several other widely noted limitations on the model, which limit the direct applicability of the result: (a) Hours may be partially observable, in which case government would want to use that information; and (b) there may be large stochastic elements in the translation of labor, given an individual's ability and effort, into income. In dynamic models, as we noted earlier, observations of an individual in time t are relevant to inferences at subsequent dates (and this may even be true of observations of an individual's parents). Optimal taxation ought to make use of that information, but if individuals know this, it affects behavior. In effect, the models here entail a commitment on the part of government not to use such information. The models here are adverse selection models. There are also important incentive effects, for example, in effort and education. Thus, a full analysis would include both effects, with incentive compatibility constraints added to the self-selection constraints. (For a discussion of optimal taxation with moral hazard, see Arnott and Stiglitz, 1986.)

costs associated with imposing taxes low. Economists often refer to political costs, but my experience with "political constraints" is that they are soft and ambiguous. What seems like an insurmountable barrier at one time can be suddenly overcome, especially as economists explain the high costs of such a constraint. I had argued some quarter a century ago that there would be substantial benefits from substantially increasing the standard deduction, moving many individuals out of the income tax net and reducing the importance of many key distortionary deductions and credits; but it was claimed doing so was politically infeasible. Suddenly, in 2017, in the U.S., it happened. I would have thought that in a democracy, a tax cut for billionaires financed by tax increases for lower income individuals would be infeasible; again, in 2017, it happened.

There are two sets of constraints for which there are important rationale. One we have already noted: large differential tax rates, say between capital and labor, open up large opportunities for arbitrage. Similarly, for large differential rates among classes of similar activities. More broadly, there are limitations in what government can observe, and what it can define precisely, and those limitations provide openings for arbitrage and distortions. When there are large differences in marginal tax rates, money can be shifted from one person (say in a family) to another. Much of the complexity of the tax system arises from these forms of differentiation and from the attempts to prevent tax-shifting to which they give rise, and any tax structure needs to take this into account.[75]

Most importantly, there is a simple reason to tax the returns to capital of the very rich: it is equitable. With any equality-preferring social welfare function with sufficient weight on equity, the benefits in terms of social equity would outweigh the distortionary effects, given the disparities in incomes observed in advanced countries such as the United States. The intertemporal distortions in consumption patterns affect only the very rich, when the tax is levied only on very high incomes. If the proceeds of the tax are invested in ways which sufficiently enhance the productivity of workers and/or provide sufficiently highly valued public goods, workers are better off, and the gains to the workers more than offset the losses to the "capitalists" who bear the tax. In general, the adverse incidence effect on workers as a result of capitalists' reduced savings can be offset. With the standard utilitarian social welfare functions, with the degree of concavity conventionally assumed, there can be even considerable inefficiency in public investments, and still capital taxes would be desirable.

All of this has been predicated on individualistic inequality averse social welfare functions. But there is increasing awareness that inequality itself may have an adverse effect on societal well-being, and even productivity. There is an increasing awareness that living in an unequal society changes the nature of society and that of those that live within it, with effects on preferences and behavior of both those at the top and the bottom that would widely be agreed to be adverse. Indeed, inequality itself may affect productivity. Once we take these consequences of inequality into account, the case for a progressive tax on the income from capital, inheritances, and in particular, taxing the return to what we have identified as "capitalists' capital" at a high rate becomes even more compelling.

I believe that Tony would have agreed with these conclusions.

[75] In 1985f, I set out a general theory of tax avoidance. It is particularly difficult for the government to impose different taxes on things which are similar (but still different). Defining the relevant differences in ways that can be implemented at low costs and sustained in courts can be extraordinarily difficult, and thus it may be necessary to tax the different commodities at the same rate.

All of modern tax theory begins, of course, with the hypothesis that certain things (like ability) are not observable. In fact, different things are observed with different degrees of accuracy.

PART III
EARLIER CONTRIBUTIONS

Introduction to Part III

This part of the book contains a selection of 18 chapters written over the past five decades on a wide range of topics touching on inequality.

The first section focuses on issues of the *measurement of inequality*. We live in an age of metrics. While there is general agreement that inequality is increased, some believe that the increase is far more severe than others. The chapters here both highlight why it is so difficult—indeed impossible—to come up with a single, simple measure of inequality, and suggest a new measure that highlights the cost of inequality *at the margin*. This measure suggests that the costs of inequality (at the margin) may be much higher than indicated by one of the standard measures based on conventional welfare economics, the Atkinson measure. Our new measure reflecting the marginal cost of inequality turns out to be very useful in developing a general formula for the optimal (linear) income tax rate.

The second section is on *mobility and opportunity*. Both reflected the shift in attention in the latter part of the last century away from inequalities in outcomes—understandable, perhaps, as those inequalities were growing ever larger—to inequalities in opportunity. The mythology at the moment was that even though the United States might be the most unequal of the advanced countries in income and wealth, we were still the land of opportunity. Data (cited in Chapter 4) shows that that was, in a fundamental sense, not true. But the discussion of opportunity raised a number of fundamental questions to which economists had, up to that point, given little attention. The first chapter in the section is a continuation of the research agenda of the previous: when can we say that one economy has more opportunity than another. Comparing income distributions is hard enough. Comparing mobility matrices is even more difficult. Chapter 22 (written with Ravi Kanbur) provides a strong characterization theorem, showing the stringent conditions that have to be satisfied if we are to rank economies according to whether they provide more opportunity.

The second chapter in this part delves into some of the more philosophical questions associated with evaluating the extent to which different societies provide equality of opportunity and income.

The next two sections discuss the relationships between inequality and economic efficiency and growth, at the macro- and micro-level. The papers helped upend the earlier prevailing consensus that one could only obtain more equality by progressive taxation, which in turn would introduce a distortion in the economy, leading to lower growth and efficiency—what had been labeled the "Big Trade-off." The papers on which these chapters were based showed that greater equality could lead to better economic performance. Part

III.C explains why inequality may lead to inefficiencies and institutional arrangements that, in turn, lead to more inequality: there can be multiple equilibria. Part III.D shows, in turn, how more inequality can lead to more instability, lower aggregate demand, and lower growth; and these in turn can lead to greater inequality—another vicious circle.

The next two sections contain some of my earlier attempts to understand the origins of inequality, both at the top, through bequests, and at the bottom, through discrimination.

The final section explores two of the many dimensions of public policy which are affected by and directed at limiting inequality: taxation and the welfare state. The first chapter of the section describes some of my earlier work (with Tony Atkinson) "correcting" the prevailing theory of optimal taxation—Ramsey taxes, which argued to high taxes on commodities, like bread, the demand for which is inelastic; following that prescription would have worsened inequalities. The second argues for a "modern" reconceptualization of the welfare state, going beyond social protection, with expenditure programs that would help address inequalities of opportunity and ensure, in spite of persistent inequalities of income, decent lives for most citizens.

PART III.A

BASIC THEORY OF THE MEASUREMENT OF INEQUALITY

Introduction to Part III.A

The measurement of inequality, a topic that might seem only of interest to technical economists has become highly politically charged. Critics of a variety of conservative policies since the mid-1970s—under names such as "neoliberalism," "supply side economics," or "market fundamentalism"—have claimed that those policies, while having only a limited impact on growth (indeed, growth was even slower than in the decades after World War II), had led to enormous increases in inequality. The defenders of those policies argued that there were both theoretical and empirical problems with the standard measures of inequality.

The two chapters included here include two of my contributions to the pure theory. My objective was to answer two seemingly simple questions: when could we say one income distribution is more equal than another? And was there a simple measure that might capture well the *marginal* societal cost of inequality? In the final part of this introduction, I discuss some of the empirical issues in the measurement.

The Ranking of Income Distributions

Work on the ranking of income distributions grew naturally out of work I had done earlier on the ranking of probability distributions: when could we say that one probability distribution was riskier than another. (An income distribution is nothing more than the probability distribution of a particular variable—income.) The late 1950s and early 1960s marked the development of formal risk analysis in economics, spurred on by Savage's work on subjective expected utility (1954). Among the great achievements were the development of portfolio theory by Markowitz (1952), subsequently used by Tobin (1958) for developing a theory of the demand for money. But in these applications, it became conventional to use mean-variance analysis. In that framework, an increase in risk meant an increase in variance, and it was possible to obtain strong comparative statics results on the implications of an increase in risk. A natural question, discussed extensively in the papers in Volume 3 of *Selected Scientific Papers,* was ascertaining results that were not dependent on this stringent assumption, which had empirical implications that could clearly be rejected. Michael Rothschild and I addressed this question in two papers (Rothschild and Stiglitz,

1970, 1971). First, though, we had to answer the question: what did it mean for one situation to be riskier than another. The answer, we suggested, was that if every risk averse individual preferred probability distribution *A* to *B*, then *B* was unambiguously riskier than *A*; and then we were able to show two equivalent representations, one a condition on the integrals of the two distributions, the other on how *B* could be generated from A—through a set of mean preserving "spreads" (moving weight in the probability distribution from any point to points greater and smaller than that point in such a way that the average value of the variable remained unchanged).

Tony Atkinson, whom I had supervised when I was a research fellow at Cambridge, and who became a good friend and co-author, realized that the same logic applied to the comparison of two income distributions, but took the analysis one step further: he showed that our mean preserving spread condition was equivalent to a regressive transfer (transferring money from the poor to the rich) and that our integral condition could be expressed in a way that was familiar to students of inequality, that the Lorenz curve[1] of distribution A lay entirely within that of *B* (Atkinson, 1970). He then defined what has since come to be called the Atkinson–Dalton measure of inequality—how much society would be willing to give up—the percent of total income—if it could rid itself totally of inequality. He suggested that for plausible degrees of inequality aversion, given the level of inequality *then* prevailing, the amount was very large.

Generalizing the Social Welfare Function

The two chapters in this section expand on these issues in two different ways. The first, written with Michael Rothschild, generalizes our results and those of Atkinson and the further development by Dasgupta, Sen, and Starrett (1973) in several directions. First, in the analysis of risk, it is conventional to assume expected utility, that is, separability between consumption in different states. This assumption is less persuasive in the context of social welfare functions. Dropping the assumption of separability, and simply assuming quasi-concavity (which meant that an ordering was equality preferring if whenever it is indifferent between two income distributions, it prefers a distribution which is a weighted average of both to either one alone), we showed that the orderings provided by (a) Lorenz curves not crossing, (b) regressive transfers, and (c) quasi-concave preferences were all equivalent.

We then show that if the fact that two Lorenz curves, for *A* and *B*, never cross implies that $W(A) \geq W(B)$, then we can infer that *W* is a symmetric, monotone, and locally equality preferring social welfare function, that is, welfare is improved if we redistribute income between two individuals, keeping all other incomes unchanged. Such welfare functions need not be quasi-concave.[2]

Why the Gini Coefficient Is Not a Good Way of Measuring Inequality

Just as variance had become the standard measure in risk, the Gini coefficient has become the standard measure of inequality, and it is accordingly natural to ask, what is the class of social welfare functions which ranks income in the same way that the Gini coefficient

[1] The Lorenz curve arranges people from the poorest to the richest and plots the percentage of total income of the poorest *x* percent against that percent.

[2] We also introduce the concept of "globally equality preferring," showing that although every locally equality preferring function is globally equality preferring, the converse is not true.

does. We show that there is no strictly concave social welfare function that ranks income as the Gini coefficient does.

Limitations Posed by Multiple Commodities

Finally, we conclude by noting that these results on ranking distributions apply one if there is a single good (or if all individuals have the same homothetic preferences). In the more general case, there is an inherent index number problem. We comment in the final section of the introduction on some aspects of this.

These analyses note how difficult it is to unambiguously rank different income distributions, particularly when the Lorenz curves cross. This should not come as a surprise. Different distributions differ in how much income goes to the top, what fraction of the people are in poverty—and how deep their deprivations are—and the size and strength of the middle (including the extent to which the median income differs from the average income). Different societies might put different weights on different aspects of inequality. Many (including the World Bank, at the time I served as chief economist) focus on poverty; but there is now an understanding that extremes of income and wealth at the top can also adversely affect society—and it is not just a matter of envy. Today, there is also a great concern about the weakening of the middle. Changes in each of these parts of the income distribution raises its own concerns. In many countries, in recent decades the income distribution has worsened in every dimension: more and deeper poverty, an evisceration of the middle, with the middle having fewer people, and their average income moving down relative to the mean, and more money at the top.

A Theoretical Quandary

While these papers are consistent with the long-standing presumption (dating back to utilitarian/Benthamite analysis, arguing that the social marginal utility of a dollar to a rich person was less than that to a poor individual) that more equal distributions generate higher levels of social welfare, there is an important exception to this presumption. The insight is provided by the famous Donner Pass puzzle: ten people are stranded in the pass in a snowstorm. There is enough food to feed one. Equality means that all will die. Isn't social welfare enhanced by giving the available food to one individual: the other nine are no worse off. In this case, inequality seems to be Pareto dominant.

Equality is preferable as long as there is concavity in the relevant domain. Diminishing returns in production and diminishing marginal utility has been a touchstone of economics, reflected forcefully in Paul Samuelson's *Foundations of Economic Analysis* (1947). But there are some circumstances where those assumptions are not persuasive. The Donner Pass example is one. When there are large fixed costs and low marginal costs—increasingly characterizing the modern economy, and in particular the digital and information economy—there are fundamental non-convexities.[3] Indeed, the standard optimal tax problem (see Chapters 19 and 36) introduces a non-convexity such that it is often the case that the optimum entails *creating inequalities through random taxation*.[4]

Even earlier (Stiglitz, 1976d) I had noted that with the standard nutritional wage-efficiency model, where labor productivity increases with nutrition, it might be better

[3] See, for instance, Radner and Stiglitz (1984), Arnott and Stiglitz (1988b), Stiglitz and Greenwald (2014), and the discussions in Volumes I and II of *Selected Works*.

[4] See Stiglitz (1982b), Arnott and Stiglitz (1988a), and Brito, Hamilton, Slutsky, and Stiglitz 1995.

from the perspective of a utilitarian social welfare function to pay some individuals high wages (allocate more consumption to some members of the family), and leave others at a minimum wage (allocate just subsistence to others).

A Useful Measure of Inequality Reflecting its Marginal Cost

The point of departure of Chapter 21 is again Atkinson's 1971 paper. The first draft of the paper was written in the early 1970s,[5] but then revised for a festschrift in honor of my good friend Amartya Sen (who succeeded me in the Drummond Chair at All Souls College, Oxford, in 1979). Though I can't recall when I first met Sen—probably either at MIT or Cambridge—I do remember vividly visiting him in August 1967 in Delhi, on my first trip to India. He had already established himself as one of the leading intellectual gurus, and our interests in poverty, development, and inequality greatly overlapped.

Atkinson had asked, how much would individuals be willing to give up to get rid of all inequality. For most purposes, that was the wrong question, simply because we would never get rid of all inequality. We make decisions on the margin. The question is, how much would we be willing to give up *at the margin* for a marginal reduction in inequality. That number was, not surprisingly, much larger. Here, I construct this marginal measure, relating it to the underlying measure of inequality aversion.

One of the uses to which such a measure could be put was to ask, how much should we redistribute income through, say, a linear income tax. Such a tax imposes a cost, a loss in incentives. I derive a strikingly simple formula for the optimal tax, balancing the marginal cost of the tax with the marginal value of the increase in inequality.

On re-reading the paper, I am struck by the simple calculation of the benefits of the tax and the optimal tax rate that it includes. Subsequent research (e.g., by Diamond and Saez, 2011) suggest a much higher marginal tax rate at the top, and much greater benefits for redistributive taxation. These disparate results can, however, easily be reconciled: I had assumed a linear income tax, they a progressive income tax. Progressivity is essential. More generally, as Chapter 18 points out, the only source of inequality in this model is differences in labor productivity—there are no differences, for instance, in inherited wealth, or in "luck." And as inequality has increased, I have become more convinced of its broader deleterious effects on our society, our democracy, and our economy, as I lay out in *The Price of Inequality* (Stiglitz, 2012a).[6]

[5] And distributed as IMSSS Technical Report No. 215, Stanford University, August 1976.

[6] There are further technical issues. The calculated values depend on estimates of the degree of inequality aversion and on the (compensated) elasticity of labor supply.

20

Some Further Results on the Measurement of Inequality

With Michael Rothschild

1 Introduction

How should we measure inequality?[1] This old question has received much attention[2] since the appearance of Atkinson's paper "On the Measurement of Inequality" (1970). Drawing on recent work[3] in the theory of choice under uncertainty, Atkinson showed that many seemingly different procedures for evaluating income distributions are equivalent. The major purpose of the paper by Dasgupta, Sen, and Starrett (1973) is to prove a stronger version of Atkinson's theorem. In this chapter, we show how these results can be obtained as simple extensions of our earlier analysis.[4]

Another purpose of Atkinson's paper was to argue that comparisons of income distributions are most intelligently made when the social welfare function implicit in the use of any single summary measure of income distribution is made explicit. Following Dalton (1920), he restricted attention in his paper to additive social welfare functions. The stronger theorem of this chapter shows that this restriction is not necessary. But it does still leave open the question of whether additivity is a property which ethically defensible social welfare functions must have. We discuss this in Section 3 in the context of the debate between Newbery and Sheshinski about the reasonableness of the Gini coefficient as a measure of social welfare.

The social welfare functions in Atkinson's and most papers are proclaimed to be "individualistic." In the fourth section of this chapter we discuss briefly the nature and meaning of this statement. We argue that in the one good economy, which most discussions of income distribution assume, the requirement is equivalent to assuming that income is desired by all individuals and that there are no externalities. If there is more than one good,

[1] Written with Michael Rothschild. Originally published in 1973 as "Some Further Results on the Measurement of Inequality," *Journal of Economic Theory*, 6(2): 188–204. Republished with permission.

[2] Among the recent contributions are those of Newbery (1970), Allingham (1972), Schultz (1972), Sheshinski (1972), Dasgupta, Sen, and Starrett (1973), and Feldstein (1974). For a somewhat different exploitation of the relationship between uncertainty and income distribution see Hamada 1972, 1973.

[3] The papers in this area are those by Hadar and Russell (1969), Hanoch and Levy (1969), and Rothschild and Stiglitz (1970).

[4] The hard part of the proof of that paper was the extension of results obtained for discrete distributions to continuous distributions. Comparisons among income distributions are naturally confined to the discrete case; this fact makes the present proof quite simple. Another important difference between choice under uncertainty (evaluating probability distributions) and evaluating income distributions is that in the former case we naturally use additive (Von Neumann–Morgenstern) utility functions. It is not so clear that we should so restrict ourselves when comparing income distributions. This problem is discussed further below. Extension of these results to the continuous case along the lines of our 1965 paper or of the more sophisticated earlier statements of this result (see Strassen, 1965), should present no difficulty.

The Origins of Inequality, and Policies to Contain It. Joseph E. Stiglitz with Michael Rothschild, Oxford University Press.
 DOI: 10.1093/oso/9780198799580.003.0021

the implications are substantial. A consideration of them leads to a discussion of the index number problems inherent in any discussion of income distribution.

2 Ranking Income Distributions

In this section we give a simple self-contained proof of a stronger version of Atkinson's theorem.[5]

Suppose $X = (x_1, \ldots, x_n)$ and $Y = (y_1, \ldots, y_n)$ are different ways of distributing the same amount of income[6] ($\sum x_i = \sum y_i$) among n people. What do we mean by the statement: "X is a more equal distribution than Y?" Among the many possible answers, the following three are likely to command assent.

1. *The Lorenz Curve of X Is Inside That of Y*
   A common measure of the inequality of a particular distribution X, is the share of total income received by the poorest $\alpha \times 100\%$ of the population which we write as $s(\alpha, X)$. As α goes from 0 to 1, $s(\alpha, X)$ traces out the Lorenz curve associated with X. The Lorenz curve of a distribution X is inside that of Y if

$$s(\alpha, X) \geq s(\alpha, Y), \quad \text{for all} \quad \alpha \in [0, 1]. \tag{20.1}$$

   If (1) holds we shall write $X \geq_L Y$ Note that if X and Y are ordered,

$$x_1 \leq x_2 \leq \cdots \leq x_n; \quad y_1 \leq y_2 \leq \cdots \leq y_n, \tag{20.2}$$

   and (1) is equivalent to

$$\sum_{i=1}^{k} x_i \geq \sum_{i=1}^{k} y_i, \quad k = 1, \ldots, n. \tag{20.3}$$

2. *All Those Who Value Equality Prefer X to Y*
   Among the various possible ways of completely ranking income distributions, some exhibit a clear preference for equality and some do not. If all methods of ranking income distributions which valued equality chose X over Y then we would be prepared to say that X is more equal than Y. To implement this notion it is necessary to have a criterion for deciding whether or not a particular method of choosing among income distributions values equality or not. Finding such a criterion may seem at first glance more difficult than simply deciding which income distributions are more equal. Fortunately, it is not; the following weak, and, we think, appealing, condition is sufficient for our purposes: an ordering of income distributions is equality preferring if, whenever it is indifferent between two income distributions, it prefers a distribution which is a weighted average of both to either one alone. If we restrict our consideration, as we may do without loss, to orderings which are closed and

[5] Theorem 20.1 is, however, not the strongest possible extension of Atkinson's theorem. This is presented in Theorem 20.3.

[6] We consider rankings of distributions of different amounts of total income later in this chapter.

which, therefore, may be represented by a social welfare function, then our criterion is that the social welfare function be quasiconcave. A further requirement is that all persons be treated similarly or that the social welfare function be symmetric. Thus we shall write $X \geq_w Y$ if

$$W(X) \geq W(Y),$$

for all real valued, quasiconcave functions from R^n to R^1 which satisfy:

$$W(Z) = W(\pi(Z)),$$

for π any permutation of Z.

3. *Y is Obtained from X by Transfers from the Poor to the Rich*
   Suppose X is an ordered income distribution and $\hat{X}$ is another one obtained from X by transferring income d from individual j to the richer k. That is:
   (i) $x_i = \hat{x}_i, \quad i \neq j, k$;
   (ii) $x_k + d = \hat{x}_k$;
   (iii) $x_j - d = \hat{x}_j$;
   where $x_j \leq x_k$
   Then we shall say $\hat{X}$ differs from X by a single regressive transfer (RT).[7] Surely $\hat{X}$ is less equal than X. If Y can be obtained from X by a finite sequence of RTs then we shall write

$$X \geq_T Y.$$

We now show that for comparison of distributions of the same amount of income among the same number of people all three methods will lead to the same answer.

Theorem 20.1. *If X and Y are distributions of the same amount of income, then the following statements are equivalent:*

A. $X \geq_L Y$;
B. $X \geq_T Y$;
C. $X \geq_W Y$.

Proof The proof consists of demonstrating the chain of implications

$$A \Rightarrow B \Rightarrow C \Rightarrow A.$$

(i) $X \geq_L Y \Rightarrow X \geq_T Y$. Suppose $X \geq_L Y$, we show how to get Y from X by a sequence of RT. Let k be the first integer such that $x_k \neq y_k$. Since $X \geq_L Y$, $x_k > y_k$ and we may obtain a new distribution, $X(k)$ by an RT which lowers the income of the

[7] Atkinson first pointed out that regressive transfers (first discussed by Dalton (1920)) were similar to the mean preserving spreads of our earlier paper. Readers of that paper will observe that a particular kind of RT, one which would result from a wager between individuals of the same income level, corresponds to the partial ordering $\leq a$ of that paper.

kth individual to y_k and raises the income of the $k + 1$st by the same amount. The distribution, $X(k)$ has the properties:

$$x_i(k) = y_i, \quad i \leq k,$$
$$\sum_{i=1}^{k+1} x_i(k) = \sum_{i=1}^{k+1} x_i,$$
$$x_j(k) = x_j, \quad j > k + 1.$$

Thus $X(k) \geq_L Y$ and $X(k)$ agrees with Y in k places. We may use the same procedure to find an RT which when applied to $X(k)$ produces a distribution $X(k + j)$ which is $\geq_L$, Y and which agrees with Y in $k + j(\geq k + 1)$ places. Continuing, we produce Y from X by a sequence of less than n RTs.

(ii) $X \geq_T Y \Rightarrow X \geq_W Y$. Since $X \geq_T Y$ means that Y can be obtained from X by a finite sequence of RT's it will suffice to show that a single RT does not increase the value of $W(x_i, \ldots, x_n)$ where W is quasiconcave and symmetric. We may suppose without loss of generality that Y is obtained from X by an RT affecting the income of only the first two persons. Thus,

$$y_1 = x_1 - d$$
$$y_2 = x_2 + d,$$
$$y_i = x_i, \quad i \geq 3, \quad and$$
$$d \geq 0.$$

Consider

$$q(t) = W(x_1 - t,\ x_2 + t,\ x_3, \ldots, x_n).$$

Since W is quasiconcave so is $q(t)$. Because W is symmetric, $q(t) = q(t^*)$ where $t^* = x_1 - x_2 - t$. Thus $q(t)$ attains a maximum when $t = t^*$, i.e., $t = (x_1 - x_2)/2 < 0$. For $t > (x_1 - x_2)/2$, $q(t)$ is decreasing. Thus,

$$W(x_1, \ldots, x_n) = q(0) \geq q(d) = W(y_1, \ldots, y_n).$$

(iii) $X \geq_W Y \Rightarrow X \geq_L Y$. Consider

$$W^k(X) = \sum_{i=1}^{k} x_i.$$

$w^k(X)$ is symmetric,[8] nondecreasing, and quasiconcave. Thus,

$$W^k(X) \geq W^k(Y)$$

or

$$\sum_{i=1}^{k} x_i \geq \sum_{i=1}^{k} y_i.$$

[8] Symmetry follows from the fact that the distributions X and Y are ordered. $W^k(X)$ is the total income received by the k poorest people under distribution X.

This completes the proof of Theorem 20.1.

***Remark* 1.** Comparing distributions of different amounts of income.

It is not hard to define the partial orderings $\geq_L$, $\geq_T$, and $\geq_W$ so that they apply to distributions of different amounts of income. The criterion for $\geq_L$, given in (3) is unchanged. A distribution X is preferred to a distribution Y if the income received by the k poorest people is greater under X than under Y for all k. We write $X \geq_W Y$ if $W(X) \geq W(Y)$ whenever W is quasiconcave, symmetric, *and* monotone increasing. Define an inefficient regressive transfer, *IRT*, (the appropriateness of the symbolism will be apparent to all New Yorkers) as a redistribution of income in which a poor man gives up d while a richer man receives less than d. Then write $X \geq_T Y$ if Y could be obtained from X by a sequence of *IRT*s. With these definitions, Theorem 20.1 holds when applied to comparisons of distributions of different amounts of income. The proof given above goes through with trivial changes.

***Remark* 2.** *Other definitions of equality-preferring orderings.*

Atkinson originally suggested that social welfare functions should meet stronger criteria than those we have put forth, before they could classify as equality preferring. That is, he suggested that a reasonable criterion for X to be considered more equal than Y was that for all concave U.

$$\sum_{i=1}^{n} U(x_i) \geq \sum_{i=1}^{n} U(y_i), \tag{20.4}$$

If (20.4) holds, we shall write $X \geq_U Y$. Is $\geq_U$ a more appealing criterion than $\geq_W$? We would be inclined to say no. There seems no reason why a social welfare function should have to be additively separable for it to be equality preferring. However, arguments for additivity can be given, even though this may not seem a very persuasive answer to our query. Fortunately, the answer does not matter because $\geq_W$ and $\geq_U$ are equivalent. Since the social welfare function in (20.4) is quasiconcave and symmetric, $X \geq_W Y$ implies $X \geq_U Y$. The reverse implication follows from Theorem 20.1 and Atkinson's proof that $\geq_U$ implies $\geq_L$. An independent proof may be constructed by using the fact that $m_z(x) = \min(x - z, 0)$ is concave to prove that $X \geq_U Y$ implies
$X \geq_L Y$[9]

Dasgupta, Sen, and Starrett first suggested that it was not necessary to limit the scope of equality preferring orderings to additively separable ones. They suggested that a weaker

[9] If $X \geq_U Y$, then (i)

$$\sum_{x_i \leq z} (x_i - z) \geq \sum_{y_i \leq z} (y_i - z).$$

If it is not true that $X \geq_L Y$, then for some j,
(ii)

$$\sum_{i=1}^{j} x_i < \sum_{i=1}^{j} y_i.$$

For the first j for which (ii) holds, it must be that $x_j < y_j$, from which it follows that

and more appealing criterion was $W(X) \geq W(Y)$, for all social welfare functions which could be written

$$W(X) = S(U(x_1), \ldots, U(x_n)), \tag{20.5}$$

where S is symmetric and concave and U is concave. If this is true we shall write $X \geq_S Y$. Since the function W in (20.5) is quasiconcave, $X \geq_W Y$ implies $X \geq_S Y$. Furthermore, $\geq_U$ is obviously a special case of $\geq_S$ so that $X \geq_S Y$ implies $X \geq_U Y$. Since $X \geq_U Y$ implies $X \geq_L Y$, which is equivalent to $X \geq_W Y$ by Theorem 20.1, we have proved the following theorem.

Theorem 20.2. The following are equivalent:

A. $X \geq_W Y$;
B. $X \geq_U Y$;
C. $X \geq_S Y$.

As we have stated it, Theorem 20.2 applies only to comparisons of distributions of the same total income. If all functions used to define $\geq_S$, $\geq_U$, and $\geq_W$ are additionally required to be monotone increasing then Theorem 20.2 still holds and may be used to make comparisons of different income distributions.

The question naturally arises of whether this is the strongest theorem which can be proved. It is not. We would like to characterize the class of functions $W(\cdot)$ satisfying

$$X \geq_L Y \Rightarrow W(X) \geq W(Y). \tag{20.6}$$

It is trivial to show that if $W(\cdot)$ is continuous and $\geq_L$ is defined as in Remark 1, then (20.6) implies that $W(\cdot)$ is monotonic and symmetric. The following property completes the characterization of the set of functions which yield orderings which are equivalent to $\geq_L$ and $\geq_T$.

Definition. A function $W(X)$ is locally equality preferring if for every vector X,

$$W(X) \leq W(\alpha X' + (1 - \alpha)X) \text{ for } 0 \leq \alpha \leq 1,$$

(iii)

$$\sum_{i=1}^{j} (x_i - y_i) \geq \sum_{y_i \leq y_j} (x_i - y_j) \geq \sum_{i=1}^{j} (y_i - y_j).$$

(The last inequality is (i) with $z = y_i$.) Together, the inequalities of (iii) imply

$$\sum_{i=1}^{j} x_i \geq \sum_{i=1}^{j} y_i,$$

which contradicts (ii).

where

$$x_i' = x_i, \quad i \neq k, l,$$
$$x_k' = x_l' = (x_k + x_l)/2.$$

Welfare is improved if we redistribute income between k and l, keeping all other individuals' income unchanged.

We shall now write $X \geq_E Y$ if

$$W(X) \geq W(Y),$$

for all real valued, locally equality preferring monotonic functions which satisfy

$$W(Z) \geq W(\pi(Z))$$

for π any permutation of Z.

It is easy to establish the following theorem.

Theorem 20.3. The following are equivalent:

A. $\geq_L$,
B. $\geq_T$,
C. $\geq_E$.

(a) If $X \geq_L Y \Rightarrow W(X) \geq W(Y)$, then W is a symmetric, monotone, locally equality preferring function.

It is clear that local equality preferring is a weaker concept than quasiconcavity, for while every quasiconcave function is equality preferring the converse is not so, as is easily seen by examining the social welfare function whose indifference curves are illustrated in Figure 20.1. Clearly, that social welfare function is symmetric and monotone increasing, but it is not quasiconcave. This function is clearly locally equality preferring. (This is equivalent to the requirement that lines perpendicular to the 45° line cut the indifference curves exactly twice. Since the line segment $\overline{\alpha\beta\gamma\delta}$ is drawn to be perpendicular to the 45° line, this requirement is satisfied.) It would not be difficult to construct a "smooth" W satisfying (20.6) which was not quasiconcave.

The contrast between the notion of locally equality preferring and that of quasiconcavity is seen more clearly if we recall the definition of quasiconcavity.

Definition. A function $W(X)$ is quasiconcave if for any two vectors X and X', $W(X) \leq W(X')$,

$$W(X) \leq W(\alpha X' + (1-\alpha)X).$$

Thus, the definition of locally equality preferring restricts the vectors X' that we examine.

On the other hand, the notion of locally equality preferring is stronger than that of "globally equality preferring," which may be defined as follows.

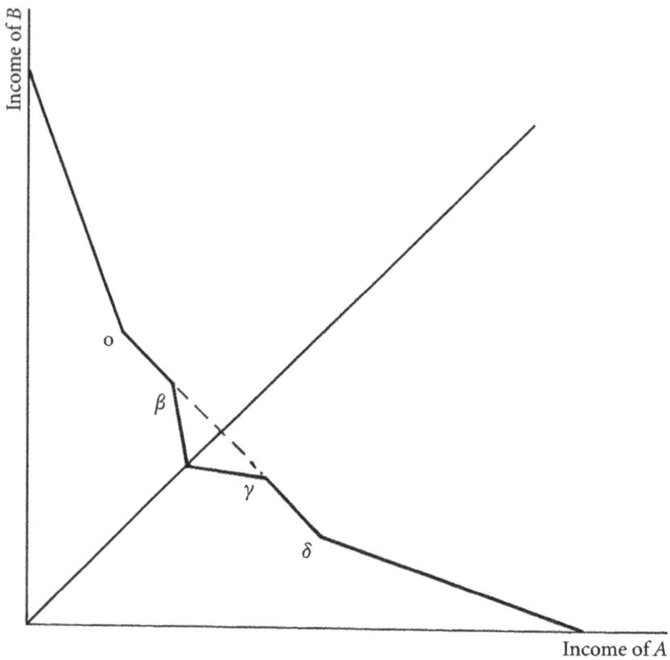

Figure 20.1 Non-quasi-concave symmetric and local equality preferring.

Definition. A function $W(X)$ is globally equality preferring if for every vector X,

$$W(X) \leq W(\alpha\overline{X} + (1-\alpha)X), \quad 0 \leq \alpha \leq 1,$$

where

$$\overline{x}_j = \Sigma x_i / n,$$

that is, the mean value of x.

Diagrammatically, the line joining any point to the point of equal total income and complete equality lies everywhere above the indifference curve through the given point.

In the case of two individuals, local and global equality preferring are equivalent. But if there are more than two individuals, although every locally equality preferring function is globally equality preferring, the converse is not true. This may be seen by examining a three person economy, with $x_1 < x_2 < x_3$,

$$\begin{aligned} x_1 &= z \\ x_2 &= z + d \\ x_3 &= 3 - 2z - d. \end{aligned}$$

Then $\overline{X} = (1, 1, 1)$. Define:

$$\varphi(\alpha, d) = W(\alpha\overline{X} + (1-\alpha)X),$$

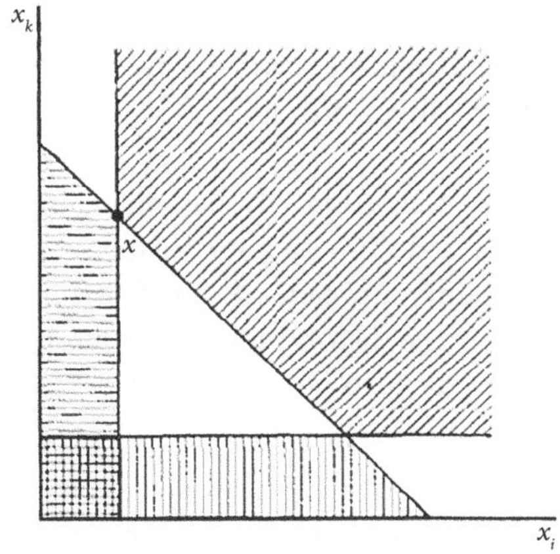

Figure 20.2 Set of values of $\{x_k, x_l\}$ where a locally monotone equality preferring function makes no statement about whether the rankings of such pairs in independent of x_i, I $\neq \neq l, k$ (white area).

for a locally equality preferring welfare function:

$$\varphi_d = W_2 - W_3 > 0;$$

while for a globally equality preferring welfare function:

$$\varphi_\alpha = W_1(1 - z) + W_2(1 - z - d) + W_3(2z - 2 + d) > 0.$$

It is easy to construct numerical examples for which $\varphi_\alpha > 0$ and $\varphi_d < 0$.

Finally, we note the close relationship between the concept of independence and that of locally equality preferring. A locally equality preferring function ranks (x_k, x_l) relative to (x_k', x_l') independently of the values of x_i, $i \neq k, l$, provided only that

$$[((x_k + x_l)/2) - ((x_k' + x_l')/2)]\,[\min(x_k, x_l) - \min(x_k', x_l')] \geq 0,$$

that is, if the average income has increased, the minimum income has increased. A locally monotone equality preferring function makes no comparisons between points for which the above condition is not satisfied, in particular makes no statements about whether the rankings of such points is independent of x_i, $i \neq k, l$. In Figure 20.2, we have shaded in the set of points for which the locally equality preferring function gives a ranking relative to the point X, independent of the levels of income enjoyed by everyone else. As we note in the next section, if we are willing to extend the principle of independence to the relatively small unshaded areas, then we obtain an additive utility function.

3 The Gini-Coeffient and Additivity

The status of additivity as a desideratum for a social welfare function is of some import since it bears directly on whether the Gini coefficient is an acceptable measure of inequality. Newbery (1970) proved that there was no additive social welfare function which ranked incomes in the same order as the Gini-coefficient. Sheshinski argued that "an additive welfare function has no particular significance" and exhibited a social welfare function which agreed with the Gini coefficient in its ordering of distributions of the same amount of income.[10]

We disagree with Sheshinski that additivity has no significance. Two quite separate interpretations of the meaning of additivity are available. First, drawing on the analogy between choice under uncertainty we can ask the following question: Given a complete transitive ordering, ≥, over the distribution of income $(x_1, \ldots, x_n)$ among n persons what conditions must ≥ satisfy for it to be the case that: (E) There exists a function U such that

$$(x_1, \ldots, x_n) \geq (y_1, \ldots, y_n) \quad \text{iff} \quad \Sigma U(x_i) \geq \Sigma U(yy_i).$$

If we examine Arrow's (1965) exposition of the expected utility theorem and make the appropriate translations we see that of the postulates which guarantee that (E) holds, the only one which a symmetric ordering, ≥, might not satisfy is what Arrow calls "dominance." In the language of income distribution the postulate means roughly the following: Suppose there were two islands, A and B. Of two distributions of income among the inhabitants of A, A_1 is preferred to A_2, or $A_1 \geq A_2$. Suppose the islands are now merged and B is any distribution of income among the inhabitants of island B, then

$$(A_1, B) \geq (A_2, B).$$

Second, if $W(x_1, \ldots, x_n)$ is a social welfare function, then there exist functions $U^i(i = 1, \ldots, n)$ such that

$$W(x_1, \ldots, x_n) = \sum_i U^i(X_i),$$

if $W(\cdot)$ satisfies the well known Leontief separability conditions. These conditions have a perfectly clear meaning in this case: Consider a benevolent dictator distributing income among his subjects according to his social welfare function. Additional income becomes available; he discovers that he may either give an additional dollar to individual A or an additional p dollars to individual B. There is a p for which the dictator is indifferent between giving an additional income to A or B. If p is independent of the income of everyone in society but A and B then his social welfare function is additive.

Both these arguments show that additivity is a defensible, even a reasonable, property for a social welfare function to have. It is not, however, compelling. To prove a social welfare function morally indefensible, one needs a stronger case than its failure to exhibit additive separability.

The question then naturally arises of what ethical properties a social welfare function which ranks income distributions by their Gini coefficient can and cannot have. We give part of an answer here. We show that no social welfare function which ranks income as

[10] See Sheshinski (1972). For different arguments against the use of the Gini index see Theil (1967) and Atkinson (1970).

does the Gini coefficient is *strictly* quasiconcave. However, if $G(X)$ is the Gini coefficient of an income distribution X, the function which Sheshinski discussed,

$$W(X) = \sum_{i=1}^{n} x_i (1 - G(X)) \tag{20.7}$$

is concave and is diminished by any *RT*. Thus, the Gini coefficient can be part of an equality preferring social welfare function. Both these results follow from the fact that if X is ordered ($x_1 \leq x_2 \leq \ldots \leq x_n$) and $T(X) = \sum_{i=1}^{n} x_i$ then

$$G(X) = (T(X)n)^{-1} \sum_{i=1}^{n} (2i - n - 1)x_i. \tag{20.8}$$

Thus, if X and Y are ordered distributions of the same income ($T(X) = T(Y)$), and if $G(X) = G(Y)$, then it follows from the linear form of (20.8) that

$$G(\lambda X + (1 - \lambda)Y) = \lambda G(X) + (1 - \lambda)G(Y) = G(X),$$

so that no function which ranks distributions of the same amount of income as does the Gini coefficient is strictly quasiconcave.

However, we may use (20.8) to rewrite (20.7) as

$$W(X) = T(X)\frac{2n + 1}{n} - \left(\sum_{i=1}^{n} 2ix_i\right)/n, \tag{20.9}$$

from which it is obvious that an *RT* diminishes $W(X)$. It is also easy to show that the function (20.9) is concave. To do so we must change notation slightly since we may no longer assume X and Y are ordered. Let $Z = \lambda X + (1 - \lambda)Y$. Let $x(i)$ be the ith smallest member of the distribution X and define $y(i)$ and $z(i)$ similarly. Since $T(Z) = \lambda T(X) + (1 - \lambda)T(Y)$ it is only necessary to show that

$$\sum_{i=1}^{n} 2iz(i) \leq \sum_{i=1}^{n} \lambda 2ix(i) + (1 - \lambda)\, 2iy(i). \tag{20.10}$$

We may write $z(k)$ as $z(k) = \lambda x(\rho(k)) + (1 - \lambda)\, y(\sigma(k))$, where ρ and σ are permutations of 1, 2,..., n. Thus the *LHS* of (10) is equal to

$$\sum_{i=1}^{n} \lambda 2ix(\rho(i)) + (1 - \lambda)\, 2iy(\sigma(i)).$$

Clearly

$$\sum_{i=1}^{n} 2ix(i) \geq \sum_{i=1}^{k} 2ix(\rho(i)),$$

$$\sum_{i=1}^{n} 2iy(i) \geq \sum_{i=1}^{k} 2iy(\sigma(i)),$$

4 Individualistic Social Welfare Functions

Economists often refer to "individualistic" social welfare functions. What restrictions are implicit in the term "individualistic?" There is no uniformity in usage, so the following represents one reasonable approach:

(A) No individual's utility depends on the utility or consumption of any other individual.
(B) Social welfare depends simply on the levels of utility of the different individuals and is an increasing function of each.

In the case of a single commodity economy of the kind we have been discussing so far, conditions (A) and (B) impose only one restriction on the set of functions $W(X)$ that may be called individualistic, namely,

$W_i > 0$. Since we are looking for increasing real valued functions: $R^n \to R^1$ and $U : R^1 \to R^1$ such that

$$\phi\left(U(x_1), \ldots, U(x_n)\right) = W(x_1, \ldots, x_n),$$

if we set $\phi = W$ and define U by $U(x) = x$, the result is immediate.

In the case of a many commodity economy, the restriction has a great deal of content, for it is a statement about separability, which in terms of the Leontief conditions can be expressed as

$$\frac{\partial\left[\partial W/\partial C_i(k)/\partial W/\partial C_i(l)\right]}{\partial C_j(m)} = 0 \quad \text{for} \quad j \neq i,$$

where $C_i(k)$ is the ith individual's consumption of the kth commodity.

Furthermore, the marginal rates of substitution between $C_j(l)$ and $C_j(k)$ for an individualistic social welfare function will be individual j's own marginal rate of substitution:

$$\frac{\partial W/\partial C_j(k)}{\partial W/\partial C_j(l)} = \frac{\partial U_j/\partial C_j(k)}{\partial U_j/\partial C_j(l)}.$$

Even if the social welfare function should satisfy these restrictive conditions, we still encounter many difficulties trying to apply the results of the previous sections in a many commodity world. Suppose that all individuals have identical utility functions. Then if the social welfare function is individualistic we may write

$$\begin{aligned} &W(U(C_1(1), \ldots, C_1(m)), \ldots, U(C_n(1), \ldots, C_n(m))) \\ &\qquad = W(V(x_1, P), \ldots, V(x_n, P)) \\ &\qquad = \hat{\Omega}(X, P), \end{aligned}$$

where $V(x, P)$ is the indirect utility function of all persons in society. We are certainly justified in concluding that if $X \geq_L Y$ then $\Omega(X; P) \geq \Omega(Y; P)$, but in general we will have difficulty making statements like:

$$X \geq_L Y \text{ implies } \Omega(X; P) \geq \Omega(Y; P^*).$$

Obviously, if we could get a measure of "real income" then we could make such inferences (but, of course, only between different distributions of real income; statements like $X \geq_L Y$ would have no meaning unless both X and Y were measured in real income or if prices were the same under both distributions). The conditions under which such a true cost of living index exists are both well known and very restrictive; individuals' utility functions must be homothetic. A consequence of this argument is that individualistic social welfare functions which rank income as the Gini coefficient does, even when prices change, exist only if all individuals' indifference curves are homothetic and real income is used to calculate the Gini-coefficient. It is hard to say what meaning can be ascribed to comparisons of Gini-coefficients calculated in economies with widely different relative price structures.

Far more serious problems arise when individuals differ. When individuals differ in tastes, a rise in the price of a commodity which is important for one person may not be of any concern to another. The distribution of money incomes will remain unchanged, but the distribution of real incomes may become more or less unequal. Again, we require that there exists a true cost of living index to convert money incomes to real incomes, which requires each individual to have a homothetic indifference curve. But even this does not resolve our difficulties. For what are we to mean by "equal levels of utility?" Assume all individuals had a homothetic indifference map and we were willing to adopt a cardinal utility function homogeneous of degree one for each individual. This still leaves us with one parameter to choose, which specifies in effect at which set of relative prices individuals are said to have the same level of utility.[11] This problem is illustrated in Figure 20.3. Do individuals A and

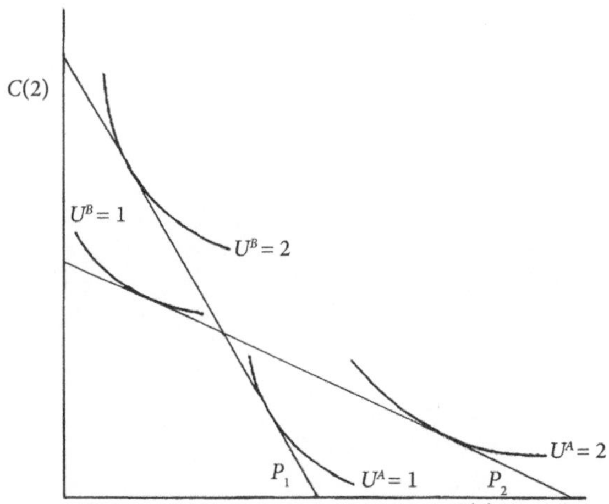

Figure 20.3 Problems associated with assessment of differences in real income with differences in preferences.

[11] A more satisfactory way to handle the problem of measuring equality in a multicommodity world could possibly be constructed by using the multi-dimensional versions of the theorems on choosing probability distributions on which Theorems 20.1 and 20.2 are modeled. These theorems make it possible to talk about more and less unequal distributions of 1 commodities thus permitting unambiguous orderings of distributions of consumption goods independent of prices. See Blackwell and Girshick (1954) and Strassen (1965) for generalizations of the results of Newbery (1970).

B have the same real income when prices are given by P_1 or when prices are given by P_2? The same sort of difficulty can arise when two individuals have the same shape indifference curves but may possibly vary in their ability to produce socially valued utility from the same amount of goods. However, the arbitrariness of scale seems much greater in the first case because the lack of symmetry between the individuals gives no clues as to how real income should be parameterized. When individuals have the same indifference curves it is natural to suppose they are the same in other respects. There is no such obvious solution to the problem presented by Figure 20.3. The point of these remarks is to emphasize that Theorems 20.1–20.3, although they help clarify the meaning of income inequality, do not resolve the index number problems inherent in comparing income distributions.

Acknowledgments

We are indebted to Partha Dasgupta and Amartya Sen for access to unpublished material (subsequently appearing in [Dasgupta, Sen, and Starett 1973]) which suggested to us our Theorem 20.1. Conversations with Kenneth Arrow, Alvin Klevorick, James Mirrlees, and Hajime Oniki were both stimulating and instructive. This research was supported by grants from the National Science Foundation and the Ford Foundation.

21

Simple Formulae for the Measurement of Inequality and the Optimal Linear Income Tax

1 Introduction

It is a pleasure to contribute this essay in honor of Amartya Sen, whose intellectual work has been an inspiration, and whose friendship I have valued, for more than four decades.[1] Amartya's interests, especially in inequality and development, have overlapped with mine. At a time when so many developmental economists were advocating Washington Consensus policies—almost completely ignoring the consequences for poverty and inequality—Amartya stood out as a lonely voice, at least within the West. Today many, if not most, of those who pushed these policies have recognized that the policies often have not promoted growth, and even when they have led to growth, not all have benefited. They now recognize the seriousness of the failure to pay attention to the distributive consequences of economic policies.[2]

For this festschrift, however, I want to focus on another area in which Sen has made an important contribution—the measurement of inequality. Some 35 years ago, Michael Rothschild and I asked when one can say that one distribution is "riskier" than another—for any risk-averse individual.[3] The same logic could be applied to income distributions: when can one say that one income distribution is more unequal than another—for any inequality-averse social welfare function? Atkinson noticed that our earlier results had a natural interpretation in terms of the standard Lorenz curve: an income distribution is more unequal than another (such that any inequality-averse Benthamite social welfare function prefers one distribution to the other) if and only if one Lorenz curve lies inside the other.[4] Dasgupta, Sen and Starrett, and Rothschild and I, then extended the analysis to more general inequality-averse social welfare functions.[5]

Sen made two even more important contributions to the policy and conceptual debate. The first was to emphasize that, in assessing the performance of the economy (or more

[1] Originally published in 1976 as "Simple Formulae for Optimal Income Taxation and the Measurement of Inequality," IMSSS Technical Report No. 215, Stanford University. A revised version was published in in 2009 in K. Basu and R. Kanbur (eds.), *Arguments for a Better World: Essays in Honor of Amartya Sen, Volume I, Ethics, Welfare, and Measurement*, Oxford: Oxford University Press pp. 535–66. Reprinted with permission. The author is indebted to Peter Diamond, James Mirrlees, Arjun Jayadev, Ravi Kanbur, and the late John Flemming for helpful discussions. This work was supported in part by the National Science Foundation, the MacArthur Foundation, and the Ford Foundation. This chapter is a revised and extended version of an earlier working paper of the same title, IMSSS 215, Stanford University, 1976. The earlier version provides alternative formulae.

[2] For a broader discussion, see Stiglitz (2008a).

[3] Rothschild and Stiglitz (1970, 1971).

[4] Atkinson (1970).

[5] See, for instance, Dasgupta, Sen, and Starrett (1973). Rothschild and I showed that Atkinson's results hold for a much more general class of social welfare functions than he had assumed—they hold for any symmetric,

The Origins of Inequality, and Policies to Contain It. Joseph E. Stiglitz, Oxford University Press. © Joseph E. Stiglitz (2025).
DOI: 10.1093/oso/9780198799580.003.0022

broadly, society), one should look not only at outcomes (the incomes or consumptions that individuals enjoy), but also at the freedom they give for human action, which in turn depends on the capabilities of individuals and the scope they have for participating in the decisions that affect their lives.

This emphasis on capabilities is congruent with the emphasis of modern political discourse on "opportunity."[6] If all individuals had the same opportunities, including education and access to basic necessities of life (e.g., health care or food, so that, for instance, they do not suffer the lifelong consequences of lack of medical care or malnutrition), inequalities in income or consumption would not be of great concern; in such circumstances, inequalities would simply reflect the fact that some individuals work harder and others do not.[7] The inequalities that are so marked in our societies are, however, only partly the result of differences in preferences; they reflect differences in opportunity sets and in "luck"—that is, even when individuals *on average* have the same opportunity set, even when individuals work just as hard, some win one of life's many lotteries and wind up wealthy, and others lose. Parsing out the relative importance of these different sources of inequality is not easy; but there are obviously fundamental differences in the appropriate policy responses.[8] The difficulties of ranking opportunity sets (when one opportunity set is "more equal" than another) are even greater than those we discussed earlier in ranking probability distributions of income. When focusing on just two commodities, it is easy to assess whether one individual's opportunity set is better than another's (see Figure 21.1): if it lies outside the other, it clearly is better. But even if one individual's opportunity set lies outside the other, the extent to which it does so depends on the axis (vertical or horizontal) on which we make our measurements.

However, the situation changes if budget constraints cross. Then some individuals might prefer one budget constraint, others the other. The point becomes particularly relevant when we think about the two goods as "consumption" and "leisure," for all individuals have the same endowment of leisure, though not necessarily the ability to use it well (see Figure 21.2).

One aspect whose importance can shift greatly over time is the provision of public goods. To the extent that public goods are truly public goods and are equally enjoyed by all individuals, societies where a greater fraction of GDP is spent on public goods will, in a fundamental sense, be more egalitarian; focusing on the inequality of *private consumption* may, accordingly, misrepresent the degree of inequality in society.[9] This highlights

monotone, locally equality-preferring social welfare function (i.e., separability is not required, nor even quasi-concavity). Our analysis also highlighted the problems in measuring inequality which arise when there is more than one commodity and relative prices are not fixed—one of the subjects on which this chapter focuses.

[6] It should be clear, however, that the focus on economic opportunity sets touches on only one aspect of Sen's broader conception, which includes participation rights and opportunities, seen as more than just instrumental in ensuring equality (or fairness) in outcomes.

[7] There are, of course, deeper concerns: do those individuals who "choose" not to work really have the freedom to make those choices, given their upbringing, their inherited psychological make-up, etc.?

[8] One of my own earliest papers was concerned with trying to understand the dynamics of inequality, the forces which give rise to its persistence. See Stiglitz (1969b).

Interestingly, it appears that many conservatives think that most inequality arises from differences in choices; "liberals" emphasize the importance of luck. See Mille (2003). Many successful individuals obviously attribute their success to their hard work and their insight (itself a result of self-determined investments in, say, education) rather than "luck," including the luck of being born with good brain power or parents who provide one with a good education.

[9] Of course, many goods provided by the public sector are really publicly provided private goods (in the terminology of Atkinson and Stiglitz), and there needs to be an independent assessment of how these are distributed

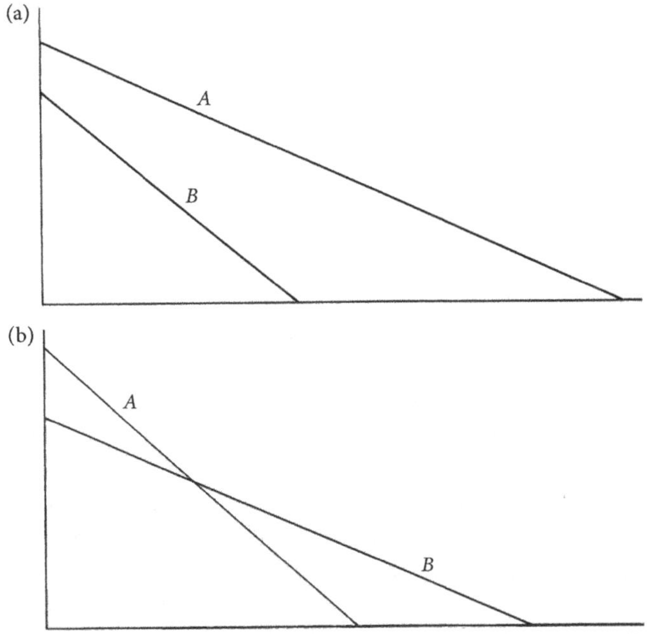

Figure 21.1 Ranking opportunity sets. (a) Opportunity set *A* is better than opportunity set *B*: all individuals (regardless of their preferences) would prefer *A* over *B*. (b) When the budget constraints cross, one cannot rank the opportunity sets: some individuals would prefer *A* to *B*; others would prefer *B* to *A*.

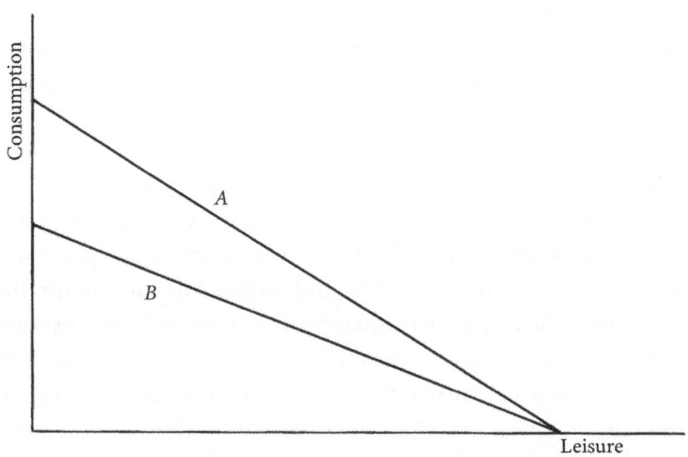

Figure 21.2 Measuring inequality with different wages when all individuals have the same endowment of leisure.

the fact that there are many dimensions to an individual's well-being or that of society. One of Sen's most important practical contributions was the role he played in the construction of the Human Development Index (HDI), a centerpiece of the annual *Human*

within a society. But even pure public goods can be goods that are more valued by the poor or by the rich, and therefore, in a fundamental sense, either reduce or increase the overall degree of inequality in society.

Development Report published by the UN Development Programme (UNDP). The HDI provides a metric of societal well-being that goes beyond GDP per capita and includes, for instance, measures of health and education. It is a metric which has made an enormous positive contribution to the policy debate by drawing attention to aspects of society which would receive inadequate attention were GDP the main metric of success. What you measure is what you strive for. By noting that some societies that may rank toward the top on GDP per capita (like the U.S.) score much more poorly in the HDI (more poorly, in particular, than all of the Scandinavian countries), it at least raises questions about the appropriate direction of policy.[10]

One of the dimensions of societal well-being that is not captured at all in measures of *average* GDP per capita is how access to goods is distributed among those in society Atkinson went on from his analysis of the question of when one society has a "better" distribution of income than another to construct a simple and powerful measure of inequality: how much a society would be willing to give up in order to eliminate inequality.[11] The amount was simply related to society's inequality aversion (a measure of the concavity of the social welfare function, analogous to the Arrow–Pratt measure of risk aversion) and the magnitude of the inequality itself. Just as Rothschild and Stiglitz's work highlighted that often one could not rank two distributions (one might be preferred by some risk-averse individual, and another by another risk-averse individual), so too Atkinson's work highlighted that whenever two Lorenz curves cross, some inequality-averse individual would prefer one distribution, another the other. And just as Rothschild and I highlighted that standard measures of risk (like variance) may be misleading, Atkinson's work highlighted that standard measures of inequality (like the Gini coefficient) may be misleading. These limitations in ranking were not the result of an incompleteness in the theory; they called attention to the fact that one could "improve" the distribution of income at one place (such as reducing poverty) and, at the same time, make it worse (transferring income from the middle class to the rich).

This measure (often referred to as the Atkinson–Dalton measure, because of its earlier use by Hugh Dalton[12]) may, however, not be the best measure of inequality, for several reasons.[13] There are two that I do not take up in this chapter. The first is that the Atkinson–Dalton measure is a static measure, a glimpse of inequality at one point in time. If there is individual variability of income over time, and individuals can smooth their consumption, then this overstates the degree of inequality of "well-being" (or consumption). If there is an increase in year-to-year income variability, it may seem as if there is an increase in inequality, but this may in reality be of little consequence. On the other hand, if capital markets are imperfect (as they are), so that individuals cannot effectively smooth consumption over time, and if there are imperfect insurance markets (as there are), so that individuals cannot insure against this variability, then the increased year-to-year variability will have adverse welfare consequences, though it is still the case that looking at income inequality

[10] There are broader objections to the use of GDP. It does not, for instance, take into account resource depletion or environmental degradation; it looks at the output produced within a country, not the well-being of the citizens of the country etc. See, for instance, Stiglitz (2006a).

[11] Corneo and Fong (2008) find, on the basis of survey data, that on average, individuals would be willing to sacrifice 20% of income to eliminate inequality.

[12] Dalton (1920).

[13] Sen himself provided a critique of the Atkinson measure in *Inequality Re-Examined* (1992).

(or even consumption inequality) at a certain point in time exaggerates the degree of lifetime inequality. Year-to-year variability gives rise to insecurity, which can be very costly to risk-averse individuals. Indeed, much of the political debate in recent years has focused on how to reduce various forms of insecurity.[14]

The second issue I do not discuss here is related, but in some sense has even more profound social consequences: the Atkinson–Dalton measure is not a measure of social mobility and therefore does not capture the dynamics of equality of opportunity, that is, to what extent the life chances of someone born at the bottom of the income distribution differ from someone born at the top. A society's social mobility is characterized by a mobility matrix, which describes, for instance, the probability distribution (measured by the decile of the population) of a person born in a particular decile. If the probability distributions of each decile were the same, there would be true equality of opportunity. One concern is that there is some evidence that opportunities for upward mobility in the U.S. may be decreasing.[15] Just as we can ask when one income distribution is more egalitarian than another, we can ask when one mobility matrix is more egalitarian than another (i.e., preferred by a society with an inequality-averse social welfare function). The difficulties noted by Rothschild, Stiglitz, and Atkinson in ranking income distributions (or probability distributions) are compounded in ranking mobility matrices.[16]

However, there are several limitations to the Atkinson–Dalton measure which this chapter does address. The Atkinson–Dalton measure illustrates the percentage of national income which society would be willing to sacrifice if all inequality were eliminated. It is, in other words, a measure of the total cost of inequality. We wish to develop a *marginal* measure of inequality, that is, a measure of how much society is willing to sacrifice to reduce inequality a given amount.

As in most aspects of economic analysis, it is marginal valuations, not total valuations, which are crucial to resource allocation. The question which is often of relevance is how society should trade off distribution and efficiency. That there is a trade-off between "distribution" and "efficiency" has long been recognized, for instance, in the literature on income taxation. More progressive tax structures have greater disincentive effects but, in principle at least, result in more egalitarian income distributions.

It has sometimes been suggested that some countries have gone too far in their attempts to obtain more egalitarian income distribution: that the cost in loss of efficiency and disincentives is too great relative to the benefits of attaining a "better" income distribution, at least at the margin. Such a statement involves judgments of two sorts:

(a) empirical judgments concerning the order of magnitude of the "costs," the disincentive effects, and benefits, that is, the change in the income distribution; and
(b) value judgments concerning one's attitudes toward inequality.

[14] That is, how to reduce various forms of insecurity without adverse incentive effects. The UN has promoted a "Human Security" agenda, in which Amartya Sen has played an important role. See the final report of the UN Commission on Human Security, chaired by Sadako Ogata and Amartya Sen (United Nations, 2003) emphasized the importance of insecurity among the poor.

[15] See, in particular, Fertig (2001), Mazumder (2001), McMurrer and Sawhill (1998), Bowles and Gintis (2002), Chadwick and Son (2002), Levine and Mazumder (2002), Hertz (2006), and Lee and Solon (2009).

[16] See, for instance Kanbur and Stiglitz (1982, 1986).

The Atkinson–Dalton measure addresses (b). But no one proposes eliminating all inequality—the Atkinson–Dalton measure tells us how much we would be willing to give up to achieve this, but such a number is not relevant for policy. Rather, the question is posed *at the margin*: what is the marginal cost of more progressivity, and what is the marginal benefit? There are standard ways of calculating the marginal costs, the increments in the dead-weight loss. But it would be useful to have a measure of the marginal benefit from reducing inequality; we need, in short, a *marginal measure* of inequality. This is what I provide here.

Since the marginal value of a reduction in inequality may, in some sense, exceed the total value, previous measures have understated the social cost of inequality, or perhaps more accurately, the social gain from reducing it. That is, intuitively, if, in the process of transferring money from the rich to the poor, one loses a proportion of the resources being transferred, and if society has a great deal of inequality, one might be willing to pay a great deal to reduce inequality a little bit, but the socially acceptable proportion of resources that could be lost would get smaller as the degree of inequality is reduced.

There is a second problem with these measures of inequality: they assume implicitly either that the supply of labor is inelastic or that the only source of inequality is in inherited income. In other words, differences in income arising out of differences in ability when labor is elastically supplied—and the consequent differences in leisure consumed—are not appropriately taken into account.

The first objective of this chapter, then, is to construct a new measure of inequality, a measure which focuses, on the one hand, on the value of marginal reductions in equality (rather than its total elimination), and on the other hand, on differences in abilities to earn. While focusing on the evaluation of marginal changes in inequality suggests that the Atkinson–Dalton measure understates the costs of inequality, my analysis of the consequences of wage inequality with an elastic labor supply suggests that the conventional measures overstate the cost of inequality.

There is a second objective of this chapter: to relate the optimal tax structure to some simple observable parameters and to my newly developed measure of inequality. My results provide a simple formula for determining the optimal tax rate.

The analysis proceeds within the utilitarian framework for analyzing the desirability of redistribution and the design of tax structures, a tradition dating back at least to Edgeworth and Bentham.[17] Whether this is an appropriate framework for analyzing these questions is an issue we discuss briefly in the concluding section of the chapter, which will bring us back to issues to which Sen has made fundamental contributions.

2 On the Cost of Inequality and the Benefits of Redistribution: A New Measure of Inequality

Social attitudes about the importance of inequality have varied greatly. At times, there has been a general consensus that economic growth, while not eliminating poverty itself, will increase the standard of living of the poor far more than would be possible under any

[17] See Edgeworth 1897, resuscitated in the "New Public Finance Literature" of Mirrlees, Diamond and Mirrlees, Stiglitz and Dasgupta, Atkinson and Stiglitz, Feldstein, and others.

redistributive scheme; this led to the belief that attention should be directed at growth rather than inequality. More recently, however, there has been a widespread feeling that some of the worst manifestations of poverty are a result of the *relative* position of the poor, and, if that is the case, growth which does not eliminate the degree of inequality will not alleviate the problems of poverty.[18]

What do statements such as "Inequality is a significant problem in the U.S." mean? We can measure the degree of inequality, say, by statistical measures such as the coefficient of variation. But how can we decide what is a large number and what is a small number? One way of attacking the problem is a suggestion originally put forward by Dalton, and developed by Kolm, Atkinson, and others. Assume you did not know where in the income distribution you were going to be. One could calculate the expected utility of income, $Eu(Y)$. If individuals are risk-averse, the expected utility is lower than that which individuals would have received if the same total income were distributed equally, that is,

$$Eu(Y) < u(E(Y)) \text{ if } u'' < 0. \tag{21.1}$$

Thus, to eliminate inequality, one would be willing to give up a fraction of total income, $\hat{\mu}$ where

$$Eu(Y) = u((1 - \hat{\mu})EY). \tag{21.2}$$

Thus, the measure of inequality is given by

$$\hat{\mu} = 1 - \frac{u^{-1}[Eu(Y)]}{EY}. \tag{21.3}$$

As an approximation, it is easy to show that

$$\hat{\mu} \approx \frac{Rs_Y^2}{2}, \tag{21.4}$$

where

$$R = -\frac{u''Y}{u'} \tag{21.5}$$

is the elasticity of marginal utility (sometimes referred to as the measure of inequality aversion), and

$$s_Y = \frac{\sqrt{E(Y - \bar{Y})^2}}{\bar{Y}} \tag{21.6}$$

is the coefficient of variation.[19]

[18] See, in particular, Citro and Michael (1995) and Ravallion (2007a, 2007b).

[19] For the lognormal distribution with a logarithmic utility function we can calculate $\hat{\mu}$ precisely:

$$\hat{\mu} = 1 - \frac{1}{(1 + s_Y^2)^{\frac{1}{2}}}.$$

If, for instance, $s_y = .5$, then $\hat{\mu} = .11$.

Thus, for example, if $R = 1$, and the coefficient of variation of income is 0.5, then one is willing to sacrifice approximately 12.5% of national income to eliminate inequality, a seemingly large figure (though still only equal to a few years' growth).

This provides a measure of the total gains to eliminating all inequality and is thus a measure of the total degree of inequality. But for many problems, a marginal notion is more useful. Assume we could take 1% of all incomes and redistribute a fraction of the amount collected equally to all individuals. The marginal measure of inequality is defined as the fraction which just leaves social welfare unaffected:

$$Eu'(Y)(\overline{Y} - Y) = \hat{m}\overline{Y}Eu' \tag{21.7}$$

or

$$\hat{m} = \frac{Eu'(\overline{Y} - Y)}{\overline{Y}Eu'}. \tag{21.8}$$

The LHS of (21.7) is the gain from the redistribution. $Eu'(Y)$ is the loss in expected utility in subtracting a dollar from each individual, $\hat{m}$ can be rewritten in a slightly different way:

$$\hat{m} = \frac{-E[u' - \overline{u}'][Y - \overline{Y}]}{\overline{Y}\overline{u}'},$$
$$\text{where } \overline{u}' \equiv Eu'$$

$\hat{m}$ is just the normalized covariance between the marginal utility of income and income. $\hat{m}$ is generally greater than $\hat{\mu}$, reflecting diminishing marginal returns to redistribution.

Although $\hat{m}$ and $\hat{\mu}$ are defined differently, for small variance $\hat{m} \approx 2\hat{\mu}$:

$$\hat{m} \approx \frac{u'(\overline{Y})E(\overline{Y} - Y) - u''(\overline{Y})E(Y - \overline{Y})^2}{\overline{Y}u'(\overline{Y})} \approx Rs_Y^2 = 2\hat{\mu}. \tag{21.8'}$$

This means, for instance, that if $R = 1$ and $s_Y = 0.5$, a redistribution scheme which took 1% of each person's income away and redistributed just over three-quarters of that amount back again, but this time equally to everyone, would increase social welfare.[20]

Of course, while all complete reductions of inequality are the same, every reduction of inequality is marginal in its own way. The amount society would be willing to pay to move a little bit of income from the very top to the very bottom is obviously much larger than it would be willing to pay to move a little bit of income from someone just above the median to someone just below the median. The particular marginal measure we have used is tailor-made for analyzing the optimal *linear* income tax. For greater progressivity in that context entails taking away a fraction of each individual's income and returning the proceeds as

[20] For the lognormal distribution with a logarithmic utility function,

$$\hat{m} = \frac{\overline{Y}E\frac{1}{Y} - 1}{\overline{Y}E\frac{1}{Y}} = \frac{e^{\sigma^2} - 1}{e^{\sigma^2}} = \frac{s_Y^2}{1 - s_Y^2}.$$

Thus, if $s_Y = .5$, $\hat{m} = 1/3$.

a uniform lump sum (demi-grant) to each individual. We know that there is a distortion as a result of the higher marginal tax rate—a dead-weight loss. Our marginal measure is designed to answer the question: how large can this dead-weight loss be (as a fraction of the revenue raised) before it is no longer worthwhile (at the margin) to raise the tax rate still further?

2.1 Measures of Inequality with Wage Differences

I have just developed a marginal measure of inequality; like the earlier Atkinson–Dalton measure, however, I ignored leisure. But individuals enjoy leisure, just as they enjoy goods; and individuals differ in their consumption of leisure, just as they differ in their consumption of goods.

The measurement of inequality when individuals "consume" goods and leisure poses a classical index-number problem. The natural question is: Can we develop measures of inequality analogous to Atkinson's total measure and our marginal measure which take leisure into account? What relationship would such a new measure have to the older measures?[21]

Intuitively, it would seem that ignoring leisure leads the Atkinson measure to overstate the significance of inequality. This may be seen in several ways. Clearly, if all individuals had the same ability (received the same wage) but differed with respect to their preferences for goods and leisure, the conventional measures of inequality, focusing just on difference in consumption of goods, would provide a gross overestimate of the significance of inequality in "welfare." If hours of leisure have increased generally, and particularly if they have increased more for low-wage workers than for high-wage workers, then the conventional measure may overstate the increase in inequality over time.

When the source of inequality is a difference in wages, the endowments of leisure are still the same. Hence, if we formulated a simple index of welfare consisting of a weighted average of leisure and consumption,

$$W = \delta(1 - \ell) + (1 - \delta)C,$$

where the time available is normalized at unity, ℓ is the percentage of time spent working, and C is consumption, then it is clear that if ℓ is, say, constant (zero elasticity of labor supply), then the coefficient of variation of W, s_W, is less than that of C,s_C:

$$s_W = \frac{(1 - \delta)\overline{C}}{\delta(1 - \overline{\ell}) + (1 - \delta)\overline{C}} s_C,$$

where $\overline{C}$ and $\overline{\ell}$ are the mean values or labor and consumption.

[21] We could also ask when one distribution of goods-cum-leisure will be more equal than another. This is a question Kolm (1969) has addressed. It is clear that looking at the distribution of each good (leisure) separately is not appropriate. If there were two goods (x_1, x_2), then in A, the distribution of x_1 could be more unequal (in the sense of Rothschild and Stiglitz, 1973) than in B, and the distribution of x_2 could be more unequal than in B. But if utility, $u = x_1 + x_2$, it is clear that u may be more equally distributed. If everyone has the same tastes, the utility function provides the natural basis for aggregation.

But even this exaggerates the magnitude of inequality. Inequality in wages affects the ability to transform leisure into consumption commodities. The more willing that individuals are to substitute leisure for consumption goods (i.e., the greater the elasticity of substitution) the less the "cost" of inequality. Moreover, if the elasticity of labor supply is positive, inequality in incomes will be greater than inequality in wages.[22]

The problem is highlighted in the case of a high elasticity of substitution, for which it is immediately apparent that a mean-preserving increase in the inequality of abilities[23] (which preserves the mean level of ability) actually *raises* expected utility (social welfare).[24] Consider what happens with an infinite elasticity of substitution. Assume originally that all individuals have the same productivity (= "unity") and that the marginal rate of substitution between leisure and consumption goods is unity. Then assume that one-half the population has a productivity of $1 + w$ and one-half the population has a productivity of $1 - w$. Obviously those who have a lowered productivity simply consume "leisure" and are no worse off than before, but those who have a higher productivity are better off. Thus, the cost of "productivity" inequality would appear to be negative.[25] As Figure 21.3 makes clear,

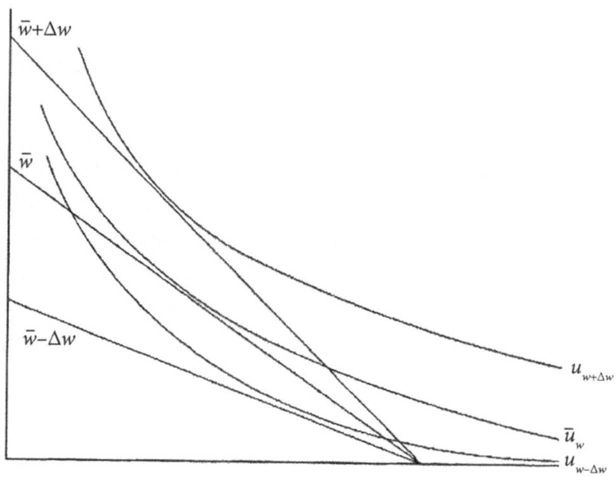

Figure 21.3 Increasing variability in wages may lead to an increase in welfare: the loss in welfare from a reduction in the wage is much smaller than the increase in welfare from a symmetric increase in the wage.

[22] This sounds like a proposition which could easily be verified. Unfortunately, this is not the case, for what we mean by the "wage" rate is the payment for a standard unit of effort for one hour.

Although differences in wages per hour are easy to observe, differences in effort are difficult, if not impossible, to observe and quantify.

[23] For a discussion of the concept of a mean-preserving increase in inequality, see Rothschild and Stiglitz, (1973).

[24] There have been numerous extensions to our understanding mean-preserving changes in distributions, notably in the literature on income polarization. These (like the writings on the role of relative deprivation cited earlier) highlight that there may be mean-preserving changes in distributions which raise inequality but which also increase, or decrease, polarization, or increase, or decrease, relative deprivation. These important dimensions of changes in income distribution are not captured in the standard utilitarian model, or in measures that are derived from that model. Esteban and Ray (1994) and Duclos, Esteban, and Ray (2004).

[25] It should be clear by now that the problem of ability inequality is much like the problem of price uncertainty, just as the problem of income inequality is much like the problem of income uncertainty. See, for instance, Stiglitz (1969d) and Rothschild and Stiglitz (1973).

the result is more general: the gain in utility when wages (productivity) are increased more than offsets the losses when they are decreased symmetrically.

For the remainder of this chapter I focus on inequalities arising from differences in ability. This is a very important assumption that has become conventional within the optimal income tax literature. Yet ironically, its implications for the measurement-of-inequality literature do not seem to have been explored. All workers are assumed to be perfect substitutes for one another; that is, they differ only in the number of "efficiency units of labor" which they embody. I choose my units so that an individual of "unit" efficiency receives a wage of unity. Hence, the before-tax income of somebody of efficiency w is

$$Y = wL.$$

where L is the amount of labor supplied. We again define the total measure of social loss to be that amount of consumption goods one would be willing to give up to obtain complete equality. To do this we let $U(C, L)$ be the level of utility as a function of consumption and work, and $U_1 > 0$ and $U_2 < 0$. We then define the indirect utility function:

$$V(w, I) = \max U(C, L)$$
$$\text{s.t. } C = wL + I, \tag{21.9}$$

giving the maximum level of utility attainable as a function of the wage rate and "exogenous" income, I. Then our new "total" measure of inequality, μ, is given by

$$EV(w, 0) = V(1, -\mu Y),$$

where we have normalized $Ew = 1$. I show (in Appendix 21.A) that

$$\mu \approx \frac{V_{11}}{2V_2} s_w^2 = \frac{s_w^2}{2(1 + n_L)^2} \left(R - n_L - \frac{\partial L}{\partial I} \right), \tag{21.10}$$

where
$[n_L = \frac{d \ln L}{d \ln w}]$, the supply elasticity of labor,

$$R = \frac{-V_{22}C}{V_2} \left(= \frac{-u'C}{u'} \text{ if the utility function is additive} \right),$$

the elasticity of marginal utility of income, where s_w is the coefficient of variation of abilities (wages), and where, in the conventional notation,

$$V_1 = \frac{\partial V}{\partial W}, \quad V_2 = \frac{\partial V}{\partial I}.$$

Note that if $n_L = 0$ and $\partial L/\partial I = 0$, then (21.10) is identical to (21.4), as we would have expected; otherwise, the measures differ. And as I noted intuitively earlier, if R is small (low measure of income-inequality aversion) but the labor supply is highly elastic, μ may be negative; wage variability increases expected utility.

More generally, the percentage of income that one would be willing to forgo to eliminate wage inequality is a function not only of R and the coefficient of variation of income, s_Y^2, but also of the wage elasticity of labor and the income elasticity of labor. The greater the wage elasticity, the greater the magnitude of the overestimate of the degree of inequality yielded by the Atkinson measure.

In the Appendices, two special cases are presented:

(a) additive utility function:

$$\mu \approx \frac{s_Y^2}{2(1+n_L)^2}\left[R - n_L\left(\frac{1-2R}{1-R}\right)\right], \quad R \neq 1 \tag{21.11'}$$

$$\mu \approx \frac{s_Y^2}{2}\left(1 - \frac{\partial L}{\partial I}\right), \quad R = 1 \tag{21.11'}$$

and

(b) homothetic indifference curves:

$$\mu \approx \frac{s_Y^2}{2(1+n_L)^2}\left[R + (1-L) - n_L\right], \tag{21.11''}$$

where L is to be interpreted here as the fraction of the time available that is worked.

If, in addition, we assume a constant elasticity utility function, we obtain:

$$\mu \approx \frac{s_W^2}{2}[R + (1-L)(2-\sigma)] = \frac{s_Y^2[R + (1-L)(2-\sigma)]}{2[1+(\sigma-1)(1-L)]^2}, \tag{21.11'''}$$

where σ is the elasticity of substitution.

In Table 21.1 I provide some estimates of μ and $\hat{\mu}$ for different values of the parameters. Notice that the measure may differ considerably from the Atkinson measure, even for small values of n_L. Indeed, as I suggested earlier, if n_L, is large and R small, $\hat{\mu}$ may be negative.

More generally, in a command economy (where the government assigns everyone a level of consumption and work) expected utility is always higher if abilities are unequally distributed than if all individuals have the same productivity, equal to the mean productivity

Table 21.1 Social losses from inequality (percent), $s_Y = 4$

	$R = 1, n_L = 0, {}_u n_L = \frac{1}{2}$	$R = \frac{3}{2}, n_L = \frac{1}{4} {}_u n_L = \frac{1}{2}$
Atkinson measure	8	12
No tax: relative to zero inequality	4	5.1
Optimal linear income tax rate	32	48
Gains from optimal linear tax	2.6	5.8
Egalitarian lump-sum tax: relative to zero inequality	−4	−2.6

in the situation with inequality. That is, each individual could work the same amount in the situation with inequality as without it, and then net output would be the same, so each individual could receive the same consumption goods. However, this will not in general be optimal for the economy with inequality, so that the attainable level of expected utility must be higher. Indeed, *everyone* can be made better off. Whether they are or not depends on what kinds of redistribution taxes are introduced. If we allow lump-sum taxes but insist on everyone remaining at the same level of utility, the social gain from inequality in abilities is approximately equal to (see Appendix 21.C)

$$\frac{1}{2}\left(\frac{\partial L}{\partial w}\right)_{\overline{w}} s_w^2.$$

With the linear income tax, there may be either a social gain or social loss, although for reasonable values of the relevant parameters the gain or loss appears to be small. To see this, we must first analyze the optimal linear income tax, to which I turn in Section 3.

Before that, however, we must define the analog to m, our marginal measure of inequality, for the case where there is an elastic labor supply. Two such measures will prove useful in the subsequent discussion. The first is

$$m_C \equiv \frac{EU_C(\overline{C} - C)}{ECEU_C} = \frac{E\left(U_C - \overline{U}_C\right)(\overline{C} - C)}{\overline{C}\,\overline{U}_C}, \tag{21.12}$$

the normalized covariance of consumption with marginal utility. If we had an additive (Benthamite) social welfare function and took 1% of consumption away from everyone and redistributed it equally to everyone, m_C tells us the fraction of consumption we could lose in the process and still be better off.

If there is an additive utility function,

$$m_C \approx R s_C^2. \tag{21.13}$$

A natural extension of this measure is to the case where the social welfare function is of the form (where $f(w)$ is the density distribution of abilities):

$$\int W(U(C, L)) f(w)\, dw,$$

in which case we obtain, instead of (21.12),

$$m_C = \frac{EW' U_C(\overline{C} - C)}{ECEW' U_C}. \tag{21.12$'$}$$

We define analogously

$$m_Y \equiv \frac{EW' U_C(\overline{Y} - Y)}{EYEW' U_C}. \tag{21.14}$$

For some purposes, however, these are not good measures: when we take income away from individuals or give it to them, individuals adjust their effort supply, and this affects tax revenue and the amount we can redistribute. Thus, the net social gain from giving an individual a dollar is not $W'U_C$, the social marginal utility of income, but $W'U_c + \lambda\tau w(dL/dI)$, where λ is the shadow price on government revenue and τ is the (marginal) tax rate. If we define:

$$\beta \equiv \frac{W'U_C}{\lambda} + \tau w\frac{\partial L}{\partial I}$$

as the marginal social utility of income to an individual of wage w then we can define:

$$m_\beta \equiv \frac{-E(\beta - \bar{\beta})(Y - \bar{Y})}{\bar{\beta}\bar{Y}}. \tag{21.15}$$

3 Optimal Linear Income Tax

In this section, I shall derive several simple alternative expressions for the optimal linear income tax rate, in terms of our measure of inequality and certain characteristics of individuals' behavior (in particular, the elasticity of supply of labor). It should be observed that although I shall write down expressions in which the tax rate appears explicitly on the left-hand side of an equation, it often appears implicitly on the right-hand side. For instance, the elasticity of supply of labor will in general not be constant. The alternative expressions may be useful in deriving the optimal tax rate, depending on what assumptions are made about what parameters in the system are constant (e.g., whether the compensated or the uncompensated demand curves have constant elasticity).[26]

A linear income tax rate is characterized by an equation of the form:

$$T = \tau Y - I, \tag{21.16}$$

where T is total tax payment, τ is the marginal tax rate, assumed to be constant, Y is before-tax income, and I is the value of the tax credit. The essential characteristic of the linear income tax is said to be progressive if $I > 0$, that is,

$$\frac{T}{Y} = \tau - \frac{I}{Y} \tag{21.17}$$

is an increasing function of income. It is regressive if $I < 0$.

Mirrlees (1971) shows some examples in which the optimal tax structure is approximately linear.[27] If this conclusion is correct more generally, then focusing on linear income taxes may not be too restrictive.

The national income identity takes on the form:

$$\int wL_w f(w)dw = (1 - \tau)\int wL_w f(w)dw + I + G, \tag{21.18}$$

[26] Saez (2001) calculates optimal tax formulas based on compensated and uncompensated elasticities of earnings with respect to taxes. Other recent theoretical explorations of the issue of optimal taxation include Kanbur and Tuomala (1994), Kanbur, Keen, and Tuomala (1994), and Diamond (1998).

[27] Mirrless (1971).

where $f(w)$ is the density function of the population by ability, G is per capita expenditure on government services, and L_w is the labor supplied by an individual of wage w.[28] Alternatively this can be written as

$$\tau = \frac{I + G}{\int wL_w f(w)dw}. \tag{21.19}$$

For given government revenue $(I + G)$ there are in general at least two values of τ satisfying (21.19). That is, government revenue is not a monotonic function of τ; at $\tau = 0$, government revenue equals zero, and at $\tau = 1$, revenue equals zero.[29] With multiple solutions, it is clear that the relevant solution is the one with the lowest value of τ.

For simplicity, I assume as I did in Section 2 that all individuals have the same utility function and that the utility from public goods is separable from that of private goods, that is, $U^* = U(C, L) + H(G)$. For this part of the analysis, I assume G is fixed.

Individuals maximize utility,

$$U = U(C, L), U_1 > 0, U_2 < 0, \tag{21.20}$$

where C = consumption, subject to the budget constraint:

$$\begin{aligned} C &= I + (1 - \tau)wL \\ &= \tau\bar{Y} - G + (1 - \tau)Y_1 \end{aligned}, \tag{21.21}$$

where $Y = wL$, so $\bar{Y} = \int wL_w f(w)dw$.

The maximized value of this, expressed as a function of after-tax wage and I, is, as I mentioned before, the indirect utility function, $V(w(1 - \tau), I)$.

The government has a social welfare function of the form:

$$\int W(U_w)f(w)dw \text{ with } W' > 0, W'' \leq 0.^{29} \tag{21.22}$$

The problem of the optimum income tax may be formulated as

$$\max \int W(V(w(1 - \tau), I))f(w)dw,$$

subject to the constraint (21.18). Thus, letting λ be the Lagrange multiplier associated with (21.18), we obtain:

$$EW'V_I = \lambda E\left(1 - \tau w\frac{\partial L}{\partial I}\right)$$

or

$$E\beta = 1$$

[28] We are thus assuming that all individuals of a given ability are identical alternatively, we could interpret L_w as the average labor supplied by individuals of wage level w.

[29] This obvious result, which I noted in the early 1970s, was popularized under President Reagan, in the 1980s, by Arthur Laffer, and came to be called the Laffer curve. It provided the basis of supply-side economics, featuring in arguments that lowering taxes could lead to more revenues and increased welfare.

and

$$EW'V_w w = \lambda E\left[wL - \tau w^2 \frac{\partial L}{\partial w}\right] \tag{21.23}$$

or

$$\tau = \frac{-E(\beta - \overline{\beta})(Y - \overline{Y})}{\overline{Y}\overline{\beta}} \times \frac{1}{{}_u\overline{n}_L} = \frac{m_\beta}{{}_u\overline{n}_L}, \tag{21.24}$$

where

$${}_u\overline{n}_L = \frac{EY_u n_L}{\overline{Y}} = \text{weighted average compensated labor supply elasticity.}$$

Equation (21.24) is the key result of this chapter, providing a remarkably simple formula for the optimal linear income tax. It relates the optimal tax rate to the normalized covariance between income and the marginal social utility of income—what I identified earlier as our marginal measure of inequality—and the weighted mean value of the compensated supply elasticity of labor. The greater the marginal measure of inequality, the greater the tax rate, and the smaller the elasticity of supply—the less the loss in welfare from the income tax—the greater the tax rate. This is just as one might expect, although the simplicity of the expression may be seen as somewhat surprising. The optimal tax rate is equal to the marginal measure of inequality divided by the (average) compensated supply elasticity of labor.

In some special cases, (21.24) might be a useful expression for obtaining some idea of the magnitude of the optimal tax rate. Assume, for instance, that we have an additive utility function with constant marginal utility of labor. Then, by taking an approximation to m_β, we obtain:

$$\tau \approx \left(1 + \overline{\eta}_L\right) s_w{}^2 / {}_u\overline{\eta}_L,$$

where $\overline{\eta}_L$ is the weighted average (uncompensated) elasticity of labor supply ($\equiv EY_{\eta L}/EY$). The tax rate is proportional to the coefficient of variation of wages and the ratio of (1 plus the uncompensated wage elasticity) to the compensated wage elasticity. Of course, for small variance, the weighted average elasticities are equal to the elasticities evaluated at $\{\tau = 1, w = 1\}$. If we assume further that $u(C) = ln\, C$, we can show that

$$\tau \approx s_w^2$$

For instance, if $s = 0.4$, the optimal tax rate is 0.16.

Note that in the case of an additive (Benthamite) social welfare function (and with government expenditures having no effect on labor supply or the marginal social utility of income), the tax rate does not depend at all on government expenditures; but this is obviously a limiting and special case.[30] Although (21.24) provides a simple and intuitively

[30] In a more general analysis, there are several effects going on. Assume that, at one extreme, public goods were a perfect substitute for private goods, that is, the utility function was of the form $U(C + G, L)$. Then an increase in G is equivalent to increasing the endowment of I by the same amount. More generally, a change in the supply of a public good can affect the marginal rate of substitution between private goods and leisure. (In the case of the separable utility function on which we focus, this effect is absent.)

appealing formula, it suffers from the tax rate being explicitly involved in the definition of m_β. An alternative formula is derived directly from (21.23):

$$-E\tau w^2 \frac{\partial L}{\partial w} = \frac{EW'V_I wL}{\lambda} - \overline{Y}$$
$$= \frac{EW'V_I wL}{EW'V_I}\left(1 - \tau E w \frac{\partial L}{\partial I}\right) - \overline{Y},$$

so

$$\tau = -\frac{EW'V_I(Y-\overline{Y})}{EW'V_I\overline{Y}}\left[\frac{1}{\overline{n}_L - \frac{EW'V_I Y}{EW'V_I EY} E\frac{dY}{dI}}\right]$$
$$= m_Y\left[\frac{1}{\overline{n}_L - (1-m_Y)\frac{d\overline{Y}}{dI}}\right]. \tag{21.25}$$

Equation (21.25) stresses one further aspect of the determination of the optimal tax rate; if total income is reduced as a result of the lump-sum payment (because of income effects), the optimal tax will be lower. The importance of this term depends on the degree of inequality; with a very high degree of inequality, this term is insignificant.

Notice that in (21.25) it is the uncompensated elasticity which is used. However, if the aggregate labor supply equation approximately satisfies the Slutsky equation, we can write:

$$u\overline{n}_L \approx \overline{n}_L - \frac{d\overline{Y}}{dI};$$

then (21.25) becomes

$$\tau \approx m_Y\left[\frac{1}{u\overline{n}_L + m_Y\frac{d\overline{Y}}{dI}}\right].$$

A third expression for the optimal tax formula is in terms of the marginal measure of inequality of C. Using (21.12), we obtain directly from (21.25):

$$\tau(1-\tau)\left[\overline{n}_L - \frac{d\overline{Y}}{dI}\right] + \tau m_C \frac{d\overline{Y}}{dI}(1-g) = m_C(1-g), \tag{21.26}$$

where g is the proportion of optimal income spent on government expenditures. This is a quadratic equation in τ which can be solved in a straightforward manner. If τ is small, the solution can be approximated by

$$\tau \approx \frac{m_C(1-g)}{\overline{n}_L - \frac{d\overline{Y}}{dI} + m_C(1-g)}. \tag{21.27}$$

A fourth expression relates the optimal tax rate to m_{ya}, when $G = o$:[31,32]

$$\tau = m_Y / d\,ln\bar{Y}/d\tau \tag{21.28}$$

$$\approx m_Y/_u\eta_L. \tag{21.29}$$

The optimal tax rate just depends on the marginal measure of income inequality divided by the percentage change in national income as a result of a change in tire tax rate, which in turn depends on the *total* wage elasticity. As the tax rate increases, the lump sum payment increases, further reducing labor supply.

The expressions derived so far have been either general expressions, valid for any utility function[33] and valid regardless of the magnitude of the degree of inequality, or valid so long as inequality is small and government expenditure is zero.

The expressions derived thus far have been general expressions, valid for any utility function and valid regardless of the magnitude of the degree of inequality, so long as inequality is small and government expenditure is zero. There are two approaches that one might take at this point. First, one could specify a particular utility function and distribution of abilities and then compute precisely the optimal tax rate (depending on the social welfare function posited, and the level of government expenditures). Alternatively, we can use the approximations derived earlier to obtain approximate numerical magnitudes for the optimal tax rate and to ascertain:

so

$$\frac{d\,ln\bar{Y}}{d\,ln\tau}\left(1-\tau\frac{d\bar{Y}}{dI}\right) = \tau\frac{\partial\bar{Y}}{\partial I} + \frac{\tau}{Y}\frac{\partial\bar{Y}}{\partial\tau}.$$

[31] Equation (21.29) can be derived directly from our maximization problem: substituting (21.21) into (21.22), we obtain:

$$\max \int W(U(1-\tau)wL + \tau(\bar{Y}-G), L))f(w)dw$$

or

$$-\int W'U_1(Y-\bar{Y})f(w)dw + \left(\tau\frac{d\bar{Y}}{d\tau} - G\right)\int W'U_1 f(w)dw = 0.$$

[32] Note, that

$$\frac{d\,ln\bar{Y}}{d\,ln\tau} = \frac{\partial\,ln\bar{Y}}{\partial\,lnI}\frac{d\,lnI}{d\,ln\tau} + \frac{\partial\,ln\bar{Y}}{\partial\,ln\tau};$$

and the national income identity,

$$\frac{dI}{d\tau} = \tau\frac{d\bar{Y}}{d\tau} + \bar{Y},$$

so

$$\frac{d\,ln\bar{Y}}{d\,ln\tau}\left(1-\tau\frac{d\bar{Y}}{dI}\right) = \tau\frac{\partial\bar{Y}}{\partial I} + \frac{\tau}{Y}\frac{\partial\bar{Y}}{\partial\tau}.$$

[33] Though in several cases, we have derived approximations, valid for small levels of inequality.

The expression to use is (21.25). We then obtain, for small[34] variance, with an additive utility function and assuming no government expenditure,

$$\frac{\tau}{1-\tau} \approx \frac{Rs_Y^2}{{}_u\overline{n}_L}. \qquad (21.30)$$

With government expenditures we obtain:

$$\frac{\tau}{1-\tau} = \frac{Rs_Y^2}{{}_u\overline{n}_L(1-g)}. \qquad (21.31)$$

(21.30) displays several of the properties which we would expect of an optimal tax rate: the greater the degree of equality or equality aversion, and the smaller the magnitude of the compensated price elasticity, the higher the tax rate. What this expression also makes clear is that the optimal tax rate will be extremely sensitive to estimates of the compensated price elasticity and the magnitude of inequality aversion (R).

Estimates of the compensated supply elasticity vary greatly, although the estimates are almost all small. Ashenfelter and Heckman (1974), for instance, estimate the compensated supply elasticity as 0.12, so that if $R = 1$, $s_Y = 0.4$, and $g = 0$, we obtain as our optimal tax rate 4/7. On the other hand, if we assume that the compensated price elasticity is approximately one-half, then the optimal tax rate is 0.4, while if the compensated price elasticity is unity, the optimal tax rate is 2/7. Higher degrees of inequality aversion will clearly result in much higher tax rates, making our approximations less valid.[35]

4 Concluding Comments[36]

It is always difficult to think rationally about a subject with all the political and moral overtones of inequality. This chapter has re-examined these issues, within the standard optimal tax (utilitarian) framework. Here, I want to call attention to some key limitations to that framework, which has emphasized differences in wages (abilities) as giving rise to inequalities. But to the extent that inequality is the result of other factors—"luck," the good fortune of a farmer having a good crop, of a real estate investor buying a plot of land next to where a road is constructed years later, of an entrepreneur coming up with the right product at the right time, or of an investor betting on the right stock—then the trade-offs on which

[34] Further expressions, in terms of the consumption elasticities, may be derived in a straightforward manner. Since, however, numerical estimates tend to be expressed in labor supply elasticities, I have chosen to express our formulae in those terms.

[35] There are several reasons for believing that conventional cross-section estimates of the supply elasticity of labor may not provide an accurate estimate of the magnitude of the elasticity. First, if real wages consist of a pecuniary and non-pecuniary component,

$$w^* = w + \epsilon,$$

with ϵ uncorrelated with w, then very high wages will on the average represent a lower real wage, and low wages will represent a higher real wage. Thus, for reasons analogous to those analyzed by Friedman in his analysis of the consumption function (1957), the estimated elasticity of the supply of labor will be biased downwards.

[36] In the original paper, I included an attempt to estimate how much good does the optimal linear income tax do. I have not reprinted that here, because I am not convinced that that exercise was very informative, both because of the limitations of the standard optimal tax framework, discussed further in this section, and because most countries have not limited themselves to linear taxes.

I have focused are not the key determinants of the optimal income tax. Analyses based on these determinants of inequality would suggest far higher optimal income tax rates within a utilitarian framework.

Sen's work, however, leads us to the conclusion that the desirability of progressivity in taxes probably should be justified on grounds other than just the individualistic utilitarian framework used by Edgeworth, Lerner, Samuelson, and others. We should focus our attention not so much on the distribution of income itself, but on the processes by which it is generated; our concern should be as much with equality of opportunity as with with equality of incomes; we should look at opportunities to participate in political processes as well, because the distribution of goods (economic power) has consequences for the distribution of political power, with further consequences for the outcomes of these political processes; and, finally, what is at stake is both the nature of society itself and the ability of individuals to live meaningful lives, living up fully to their potentials.

Appendix A Calculation of Social Loss from Inequality of Wages: No Redistribution

The measure of social loss is defined by

$$EV(w,0) = V(1,-\mu\bar{Y}). \tag{21.A1}$$

Taking a Taylor series expansion, we obtain:

$$V(w,0) \approx V(1,0) + V_1(w-1) + \frac{V_{11}}{2}(w-1)^2, \tag{21.A2}$$

$$EV(w,0) \approx V(1,0) + \frac{s_w^2}{2}V_{11} \tag{21.A3}$$

and

$$V(1,-\mu\bar{Y}) \approx V(1,0) - \mu YV_2(1,0). \tag{21.A4}$$

Thus,

$$\mu \approx -\frac{V_{11}}{2V_2}\frac{s_w^2}{\bar{Y}}. \tag{21.A5}$$

Our problem is to interpret V^{11}. Recall that

$$V_1 = LV_2, \tag{21.A6}$$

$$V_{12} = V_2\frac{\partial L}{\partial I} + LV_{22}, \text{ and} \tag{21.A7}$$

$$V_{11} = LV_{21} + V_2\frac{\partial L}{\partial w} = V_2\left(\frac{\partial L}{\partial w} + L\frac{\partial L}{\partial I}\right) + L^2V_{22}.$$

Defining

$$R = -\frac{V_{22}C}{V_2}, \quad n_L = \frac{\partial \ln L}{\partial \ln w}$$

we obtain:

$$\mu \approx \frac{1}{2}\left(R - \frac{dL}{dI} - n_L\right) s_w^2. \tag{21.A8}$$

Thus, since the coefficient of variation is

$$s_Y^2 = \frac{E(wL - EwL)^2}{(EwL)^2} = s_w^2 (1 + n_L)^2,$$

we obtain:

$$\mu \approx \frac{s_Y^2}{2} \frac{\left(R - n_L - \frac{dL}{dI}\right)}{(1 + n_L)^2}. \tag{21.A9}$$

If the individual has homothetic indifference curves between leisure goods and consumption and if we normalize the length of the day at unity, then (if $w = 1$),

$$-\left(\frac{dL}{dI}\right)_{I=0} = 1 - L.$$

If there is a constant elasticity-of-substitution utility function of the form:

$$\left[\delta C^{-\rho} + (1 - \delta)(1 - L)^{-\rho}\right]^{-\frac{1}{\rho}},$$

with $1/(1 + \rho) = \sigma$, the elasticity of substitution, then

$$\left[\frac{1 - L}{I + wL}\right]^{1+\rho} = \frac{1 - \delta}{\delta w}.$$

Straightforward differentiation of the above expression leads, when $I = 0$, to

$$n_L = -\frac{\rho}{1 + \rho}(1 - L) = (\sigma - 1)(1 - L).$$

Substituting this into (21.A8) we obtain (21.11‴).

If there is an additive utility function,

$$U = u(C) - Z(L)$$

$$u'w = Z'$$

$$\left(\frac{\partial L}{\partial w}\right)_{I=0} = -\frac{u''w + u''w}{u''w^2 - Z''}, \quad \text{and}$$

$$\frac{dL}{dI} = -\frac{u''}{u''w^2 - Z''}$$

Hence:

$$\left.\left(\frac{\partial L}{\partial w} + L\frac{dL}{dI}\right)\right|_{\substack{w=1\\ I=0}} = -\frac{u'}{u''w^2 - Z''}(1 - 2R)$$

$$= \left(\frac{\partial L}{\partial w}\right)\left(\frac{1 - 2R}{1 - R}\right) \text{if } R \neq 1.$$

Appendix B Calculation of Social Loss from Inequality: Linear Income Tax, Additive Utility Function

The measure of social loss is

$$EV((1 - \tau)w, I) = V(1, -\hat{\mu}\overline{Y}) \tag{21.B1}$$

where $\hat{\mu}$ is the fraction of national income that could be given away (required to be added) were there no variable in w (i.e., if $W^* = E_w = 1$)

or

$$max\, Eu((1 - \tau)wL + \tau\overline{Y}) - Z(L) = max\, U(L(1 - \hat{\mu})) - Z(L), \tag{21.B2}$$

where $Z(L)$ is the disutility of labor. The left-hand side can be approximated by

$$EV(w, 0) + \tau\left(\frac{dEV}{d\tau}\right)_{\tau=0} + \frac{\tau^2}{2}\left(\frac{d^2EV}{d\tau^2}\right)_{\tau=0}.$$

At $\tau = 0$,

$$\frac{dEV}{d\tau} = EU'(\overline{Y} - wL) + EU'\tau\frac{d\overline{Y}}{d\tau}$$

$$\approx -U''\left(\frac{dY}{dw}(1 - \tau)\right)\frac{dY}{dw}s_w^2$$

$$= \left[R(1 + n_L)^2 s_w^2\right] U'\overline{Y}(1 - \tau) \quad \text{and}$$

$$\tau^2\left(\frac{d^2EV}{d\tau^2}\right)_{\tau=0} \approx \tau^2\frac{d\overline{Y}}{d\tau}U' \approx -U'\tau_u^2 n_L\overline{Y}.$$

Thus

$$\hat{\hat{\mu}} = \hat{\mu} + \left(R(1+n_L)^2 s_w^2 \tau - \frac{\tau^2 U'' L}{2} \right).$$

Appendix C Calculation of Social Loss (Gain): Equal Utility

This appendix calculates the social loss (gain) from inequality on the assumption that the government can provide lump sum taxes/subsidies as a function of w to equalize utility.

We let the lump-sum subsidy (tax) $I(w)$ be such that

$$\frac{dV(w, I(w))}{dw} = V_1 + V_2 I' = 0 \tag{21.C1}$$

and

$$EI(w) = 0. \tag{21.C2}$$

Thus, using the standard result that $V_w = L v_L$,

$$I' = -L. \tag{21.C3}$$

We define the social loss (gain) as $I(1)$ since

$$EV(w, I(w)) = V(1, I(1)).$$

From (21.C2)

$$I(1) + \frac{I''}{2} s_w^2 \approx 0,$$

so

$$I(1) \approx -\frac{I''}{2} s_w^2.$$

While from (21.C3)

$$I'' = -\left(\frac{\partial L}{\partial w} \right)_{\bar{u}}.$$

Hence, the social "gain" is approximately:

$$\frac{1}{2} \left(\frac{\partial I}{\partial w} \right)_{\bar{u}} s_w^2.$$

Appendix D Quadratic Utility Function, with Constant Marginal Disutility of Labor

First we write the utility function,

$$U = -\frac{b(\hat{c} - c)^2}{2} - L.$$

Then we can solve for the optimal consumption as a function of the tax rate:

$$b(1 - \tau)w(\hat{c} - c) = 1.$$

Hence:

$$c = \hat{c} - \frac{1}{b(1 - \tau)w} = I + (1 - \tau)wL,$$

$$L = \frac{\hat{c} - I}{(1 - \tau)w} - \frac{1}{b((1 - \tau)w)^2},$$

$$Y = wL = \frac{\hat{c} - I}{1 - \tau} - \frac{1}{b(1 - \tau)^2 w}, \quad \text{and}$$

$$\bar{Y} = \frac{\hat{c} - I}{1 - \tau} - \frac{1}{b(1 - \tau)^2} \int \frac{1}{w} f(w)dw,$$

assuming that the distribution is sufficiently concentrated that everyone works. (The modifications in the general case are straightforward but tedious.) Hence the national income identity can be written:

$$\tau\bar{Y} = \frac{\tau(\hat{c} - I)}{1 - \tau} - \frac{\tau A}{(1 - \tau)^2} = I + G,$$

or

$$I = \tau\left(\hat{c} - \frac{A}{1 - \tau}\right) - G(1 - \tau),$$

where

$$A = \int \frac{1}{bw} f(w)dw.$$

The maximization problem thus becomes:

$$\max -\frac{1}{2b(1 - \tau)^2} E\frac{1}{w^2} - EL.$$

Since

$$L = \frac{\hat{c}}{(1 - \tau)w} - \frac{\tau}{(1 - \tau)w}\left(\hat{c} - \frac{A}{1 - \tau}\right) - \frac{1}{b((1 - \tau)w)^2} + \frac{G}{w},$$

it follows that

$$\overline{L} = bA(\hat{c} + G) + \frac{A^2\tau b}{(1-\tau)^2} - \frac{bB}{(1-\tau)^2},$$

where

$$B = \frac{1}{b^2}\int\left(\frac{1}{w}\right)^2 f(w)dw.$$

Thus optimality requires:

$$\max -A(G+\hat{c}) - \frac{\tau A^2}{(1-\tau)^2} + \frac{1}{2}\frac{B}{(1-\tau)^2}$$

that is,

$$-\tau A^2 + \frac{1}{2}B - \frac{(1-\tau)A^2}{2} = 0$$

or

$$\tau = \frac{1}{A^2} - 1.$$

Observe that

$$\frac{d\tau}{dG} = 0,$$

so

$$\frac{dI}{dG} = -1.$$

An increase in government expenditure reduces the progressivity of the tax.

Appendix E Cobb–Douglas Utility Function

First we write down the utility function,

$$U = \frac{ln\, C}{b} + ln\,(\hat{L} - L).$$

Then we derive the optimal level of consumption

$$\frac{(1-\tau)w}{bC} = \frac{1}{\hat{L} - L}$$

or

$$L = \hat{L} - \frac{bI}{(1-\tau)w} - bL$$
$$= \frac{\hat{L}}{1+b} - \frac{Ib}{(1+b)(1-\tau)w'}$$
$$\overline{Y} = \frac{\hat{L}}{1+b} - \frac{Ib}{(1+b)(1-\tau)}$$

(where we have used the fact that $Ew = 1$). Thus

$$\tau\overline{Y} = \frac{\tau\hat{L}}{1+b} - \frac{\tau Ib}{(1+b)(1-\tau)} = I + G$$

or

$$\frac{\tau\hat{L}}{1+b} = G + I\left(1 + \frac{\tau b}{(1+b)(1-\tau)}\right)$$

or

$$I = \frac{(\tau\hat{L} - G(1+b))}{(1+b-\tau)}(1-\tau).$$

Also

$$C = \frac{1}{1+b}(w\hat{L}(1-\tau) + I)$$
$$= \frac{(1-\tau)}{(1+b)(1+b-\tau)} \times [\hat{L}(w(1+b-\tau)+\tau) - G(1+b)].$$

Our problem is thus to maximize

$$\phi(\tau, G) \equiv E\ln\left[\hat{L}(w(1+b-\tau)+\tau) - G(1+b)\right] - \ln(1+b-\tau)$$
$$+ \frac{1}{1+b}\ln(1-\tau)\ \frac{d\tau}{dG} = -\frac{\phi_{\tau G}}{\phi_{GG}} > 0,$$

since

$$\phi_G = -E\frac{1+b}{\hat{L}(w(1+b-\tau)+\tau) - G(1+b)} \quad \text{and}$$
$$\phi_G = E\frac{(1+b)\hat{L}(1-w)}{[\hat{L}(w(1+b-\tau)+\tau) - G(1+b)]^2} > 0.$$

When $G = \tau\hat{L}/(1+b)$, $I = 0$. We can solve for the value of τ for which $\phi_\tau = 0$, when $G = 0$:

$$\phi_\tau = E\frac{1-w}{w(1+b-\tau)} + \frac{1}{1+b-\tau} - \frac{1}{(1+b)(1-\tau)} = 0$$

or

$$\frac{\tau}{1-\tau} = \frac{1+b}{b}\left(E\frac{1}{w} - 1\right).$$

If there is a lognormal distribution, and if individuals in the absence of taxation would have spent approximately half of the available time working (so $b = 1$), then

$$\frac{\tau}{1-\tau} = 2s_w^2.$$

If $s_w = 0.4$, $\tau \approx 0.24$.

PART III.B
MOBILITY

Introduction to Part III.B

One of the responses of conservatives to the evidence of growing inequality in the U.S. in the 1980s was that "we are concerned not with inequality of outcomes, but with equality of opportunity." This led naturally to a natural set of follow-on questions: for instance, how do we measure inequality of opportunity? What is the relationship between inequality of income and inequality of opportunity? Two economies could have the same distribution of income and wealth, but in one, there is stasis—the same families are always in the same position—and the other is marked by high levels of mobility.

As we noted in Part I, we care about opportunity, the ability of children at the bottom to make it. But if there is upward mobility, there has to be downward mobility. Explicit in the stochastic models of Champernowne (1953) and Chapters 22 and 23 below are assumptions about mobility. In the diffusion model, the question becomes: to what extent does the wage or wealth generating stochastic processes exhibit regression towards the mean? If not, the children of the rich will be rich.

Equality of Opportunity

As Ravi Kanbur and I note in Chapter 22, an often heard counter to the concern about rising income and wealth inequality is that what matters is not *outcomes* but *opportunities.* We should strive for equality of opportunity. But what does that mean?

An important question (discussed further in Part III.A) is, can we rank economies by their degree of inequality? We typically measure inequality by the Gini coefficient, and there is a widespread presumption that an economy with a higher Gini coefficient is more unequal. But is that necessarily so? Is that just a definition?

One of my earliest papers, co-authored with Michael Rothschild, asked a similar question: when is one probability distribution (say of portfolio returns) riskier than another. At the time, the common measure of risk was variance (or standard deviation). But unless individuals had a quadratic utility function, the variance might not be a good measure of risk *from that individual's perspective.* We asked: when can we rank probability distributions, such that all risk averse individuals would prefer distribution *A* over *B*. We were able to provide a complete characterization. There were some distributions that couldn't be so ranked (Rothschild and Stiglitz, 1970, 1971).[1]

[1] See also Diamond and Stiglitz (1974).

Tony Atkinson, whom I had tutored during 1965–6 in Cambridge, UK, and who then came as a visitor to MIT the next year (where I was then teaching) saw how these ideas could be used for ranking income distributions, and then pushed them further. He showed that the condition we had derived was equivalent in turn to the condition that one Lorenz curve lie inside the other: all equality preferring societies would prefer the distribution that was inside; and if the two Lorenz curves crossed,[2] there was some equality preferring society that would prefer one distribution, some other one that would prefer the other (Atkinson, 1970).[3]

The mobility matrix provides the natural framework for looking at equality of opportunity. Ranking mobility matrices (giving for instance the probability that the child of somebody in the *i*th decile of the income distribution will be in the *j*th decile) is an order of magnitude more difficult than ranking income distributions. In the 1980s, Ravi Kanbur (who did his thesis with me at Oxford) and I set about seeing if we could provide some ranking of matrices, some way of saying that one mobility matrix is preferred by all equality preferring societies.

If we looked at equality of opportunity strictly from the perspective of the individual, then the two extremes of no inequality of opportunity and full equality could easily be identified. The former is a diagonal matrix: the position of a child is totally determined by his parents. The latter is a mobility matrix where every row is the same, that is, everyone has equal chances, regardless of the position of his parents in the income distribution. But what happens if our normative framework looks at dynasties?

While we derived quite general results in two Princeton Working Papers (1982, 1986), we didn't get around to finalizing and publishing the results until 2016, published here as Chapter 22, where we succeed in providing a complete characterization. A general interpretation of our result is that when comparing two transition matrices, if one matrix is "further away" from the identity matrix then it will lead to lower dynastic inequality. The set of matrices that can be so ranked is limited. That raises the question, if we have more information about social preferences (other than that it is inequality averse), how can we refine our rankings?

One of the implications of our result is that what has been viewed as equal opportunity (described above) is not the most preferred matrix from a dynastic perspective: If we have intertemporal welfare functions associated with dynasties, then we might want an abnormally low wage income in the current generation to be offset by a greater prospect of a higher one later.

This chapter was originally delivered at a conference at the Interamerican Development Bank while I was still Chief Economist of the World Bank. It was a moment when there was optimism that we could (and were) reversing the increase in inequality in the U.S., but there was still much concern about poverty traps—that those at the bottom, especially African-Americans, had bleak economic prospects, with little chance of getting a college education or of joining the middle class. Of course, we now know that the small reductions in inequality that occurred in the 1990s would be quickly erased, and inequality would resume its upward trend.

[2] Arranging the population from the poorest to the richest, the Lorenz curve plots the percentage of wealth held against the percentage of the population.

[3] Rothschild and I later turned to the question of when one could rank income distributions in the absence of the standard separability assumption. See Rothschild and Stiglitz (1973), reprinted above as Chapter 20.

Subsequent research has, moreover, helped us see more clearly the close relationship between equality and mobility. Miles Corak (now Professor at City University of New York) established that countries with more inequality also had lower levels of mobility.[4] There are many reasons for this relationship, including that when there is more inequality, the rungs of the latter are further apart, and thus it's harder to climb up.[5] Moreover, in a meritocratic world, human capital matters, and access to both quality and quantity of education depends on money—on the income of one's parents. This is even true in countries with high quality publicly provided education with low university tuition, but is especially true in the U.S., where elementary and secondary education is local, where there is extensive economic segregation (with rich people living in their own enclaves), and where university tuition, even in state schools, can be very high.

Standard studies focus on a simple metric of mobility, the correlation between the income (or income and education) of the parent and that of the child. A fuller description is provided by a mobility matrix giving, for instance, the likelihood that an individual whose parents were in the *i*th decile would be in the *j*th decile.[6] There can be mobility in some parts of the distribution, but not in others; there can, for instance, be both a poverty trap—those born in the bottom decile(s) have a hard time moving up; and a wealth trap—those born at the top are likely to stay there, no matter how poorly they perform in school. We care not just about the average degree of mobility in society but also about such traps.

I began worrying about such issues in the 1980s, in work with Ravi Kanbur, presented here in Chapter 22. Just as I had sought to determine when could one say that one income distribution was more equal than another, we asked, when could one say that one mobility matrix exhibited more equality of opportunity than another. There, we pointed out that ranking mobility was of an order of difficulty greater than that of ranking income distributions. (See Part III.A.) In ranking probability distributions, we asked, when can we say probability distribution of income *A* would be preferred by *any* inequality averse society to probability distribution B; that is, would generate a higher level of social welfare with any concave social welfare function. As Chapter 21 and the introduction to Part III.A pointed out, we were able to obtain quite general results, even though one couldn't rank all distributions, that is to say, distribution *A* might be preferred by some inequality averse societies over *B*, and conversely for other social welfare functions, *B* might be preferred.

Our objective was to use the same methodology in ranking matrices: under what conditions would matrix *A* be preferred by all inequality averse societies? We were able to show several important results: With a utilitarian social welfare function with full separability in utilities between generations, and full separability in consumption over time by each individual, then (in steady state) all matrices generating the same probability distribution of income generate the same level of social welfare. The standard model used for welfare analysis by economists simply doesn't say anything about mobility.

Secondly, going beyond this full separability of the social welfare function, the usual view of full equality of opportunity—that the probability distribution of the child's income does

[4] Corak (2013). The relationship mentioned here was popularized by Obama's Chairman of the Council of Economic Advisers, Alan Krueger, under the name of the "Gatsby Curve." See Krueger (2012).

[5] For a fuller discussion, see Stiglitz (2012a).

[6] A fuller description is provided by the probability distribution of the income of the child, conditional on the income of the parent.

not depend at all on the income of the parent—was not in general welfare maximizing. For a simple social welfare function embracing dynastic utility over two generations, where the utility of the parent and child are not separable, we fully characterized the conditions under which one mobility matrix *A* could be said preferred to (generate a higher level of social welfare than that arising from, or, equivalently, to provide greater equality of opportunity than) mobility matrix B.

Clinton Policies and My Reflections on Mobility

Chapter 23 was intended to provide an intuitive summary of these results, to extend them, and to set the analysis within the broader policy discourse.

My longstanding interest in the economics of mobility were heightened further by the policy debates during the Clinton era in which I participated as a member, and then Chairman, of the Council of Economic Advisers. Distributive issues were at the center of the Clinton Administration from the beginning, with a modest increase in tax rates at the top and a substantial expansion of the earned income tax credit (substantially increasing incomes of the working poor with children) at the bottom. Bob Reich, secretary of labor, and I waged a war against "corporate welfare"—the huge subsidies, many embedded in our tax laws, that went to corporations, ultimately to the benefit of rich Americans—and were met with strong resistance from the head of the National Economic Council and later Secretary of Treasurer Robert Rubin, who accused us of fomenting class warfare.[7]

While the members of the Clinton Administration agreed on many policy issues, there were two that were particularly divisive: The first centered around what could we do to eliminate, or at least reduce the magnitude of the poverty trap. Since President Reagan had baited racism with his descriptions of the "welfare queen," welfare reform had been a subject of debate. Many in the Republican Party had wanted to use allegations of "free riding" to simply scale it back, leaving the poor to fend for themselves. In the early years of the Clinton Administration, we had struggled to find a way to use welfare reform as a way of breaking the poverty trap: as some put it, to ensure that it was a hand up, not a hand out. That would, however, require additional resources, a few billion dollars, for instance, to provide the education and training needed to increase the likelihood that those on welfare could get jobs paying well enough to support their families. But those limited funders simply seemed unavailable within the Clinton Administration's (successful) struggle to balance the budget. In retrospect, of course, these budget balancing efforts appeared to be foolish, perhaps even shortsighted, in light of subsequent tax reductions in both the Clinton and subsequent Bush and Trump administrations, the benefits of which went to the very rich. In the end, a welfare reform bill was passed in August 1996,[8] over the opposition of many in the Clinton Administration,[9] and without the funds necessary to break the

[7] For further discussions of the policy debates in that era, see Stiglitz (2003a).

[8] The official title of the act was "The Personal Responsibility and Work Opportunity Reconciliation Act of 1996 (P.L. 104–93).

[9] Three of the assistant secretaries of Department of Health and Human Services, Mary Jo Bane, Peter B. Edelman, and Wendell E. Primus, some of whom I had worked closely with, resigned in protest.

poverty trap:[10] President Clinton thought it a good beginning, and that these extra funds would be provided later. I was not so sanguine. They never were. And while it didn't turn out to be the utter disaster that its vehement critics had predicted, it did nothing to end poverty or the poverty trap. Indeed, for 15 years one out of seven Americans had to rely on food stamps to provide the food they needed to survive, and poverty rates continued to increase. The inability of the "new" welfare system to act as a safety net was demonstrated in both the economic downturns of 2001 and 2008.

The second focused on the other end of the spectrum, the very wealthy. Capital gains go disproportionately to the very wealthy, and capital gains already received favorable treatment. While an argument could have been made in the era of rapid inflation for ensuring that the tax system only taxed real rather than nominal capital gains, by the 1980s, inflation had been tamed. There was little justification for taxing workers at far higher rates than capital gains; indeed, there was a compelling case for taxing the capital gains on land at a far higher rate, since the supply of land was essentially inelastic. Nonetheless President Clinton proposed and got a significant lowering of the capital gains tax rate, which not surprisingly contributed to the increase in wealth inequality and the creation of America's "wealth trap," the perpetuation of wealth at the top.[11,12]

Further Reflections

The discussions surrounding these and other measures that might affect mobility and opportunity spurred many reflections on the economics and philosophy of policies directed at improving opportunity and mobility, discussed in the chapter reprinted here. It seemed that we care not only about the distribution of wealth but also the processes by which inequality of income and wealth are generated.

Roughly contemporaneous with my own work, John Roemer of Yale had proposed decomposing economic outcomes into those derived from "circumstances" and "efforts"—circumstances including, for instance, genetic and other endowments. Luck, of course, is a third critical factor. The underlying rationale for the separation into these categories is clear: individuals should be held responsible for their efforts—this is what incentives and individual responsibility is all about. But a society that believes in social justice should attempt to offset differences that arise from circumstances or mere luck.

The three are intertwined and are often hard to separate, in spite of all the hard statistical work that has been done in the subsequent decades. Some of the discussion of this chapter reflects on why these distinctions may not be as useful as they might seem at first: part of what we are endowed with are attitudes towards work, and a sense of efficacy of our

[10] The few billion necessary to transform welfare into an effective program seem paltry in comparison to the huge corporate welfare programs—$180 billion going to one company alone, AIG, whose reckless behavior was central in bringing about the global financial crisis.

[11] I strongly opposed this measure (see Stiglitz, 2003a), and argued that if there were to be a tax cut, it should not apply to capital gains from land or apply retrospectively, to investments that had already been made (since there obviously could be no incentive benefits from such a tax cut). While most of Clinton's economics team sided with me on this issue, Undersecretary of Treasury Larry Summers was a strong supporter.

[12] See the discussion of Chapters 12, 33, and 36 for how lowering taxes on the return to capital at the top leads to greater wealth inequality.

efforts. A legacy of discrimination—of not getting ahead no matter how hard one tries—has consequences for the exertion of effort.

The chapter goes beyond these philosophical questions to address analytical questions similar to those of Chapter 10, providing a fairly complete analysis of the conditions under which two-class mobility matrices can be ranked, and providing insights into the very restrictive conditions under which higher order mobility matrices can be ranked.

22
Dynastic Inequality, Mobility, and Equality of Opportunity

With Ravi Kanbur

1 Introduction

It is clear that global economic forces are now aligned to produce rising income and wealth inequality.[1] There is, of course, disagreement about the relative importance of the potential drivers of these changes. The direction of technical change appears to be favoring capital over labor and, within labor, skilled labor over unskilled labor. Globalization of trade and investment is transmitting these forces to all countries, and may itself be a contributor to growing inequality. Across a wide spectrum of countries, there has been an increase in market power at least in certain sectors, and arguably, more broadly in rent seeking.[2] In Latin America these underlying forces have been countered by pro-active policy. But elsewhere, including in Asia, Europe and the U.S., policy has not countered, and perhaps has even exacerbated, the forces for rising inequality. Not surprisingly, rising inequality is now of great concern to policy makers and the general public the world over. The phenomenal response to the book on inequality by Thomas Piketty (2014) is but one illustration of these concerns.

One often heard counter to the concern on rising inequality is that it is wrong to focus on inequality of outcome in a "snapshot." What is important is how income or wealth evolves over time, especially across generations.[3] Intergenerational mobility, so the argument goes, is what matters for normative evaluation. These arguments have resurfaced in the post-Piketty debates, but have actually been ever present in the discourse on inequality and public policy. Thus Friedman (1962) writes as follows in *Capitalism and Freedom*:

> Consider two societies that have the same annual distribution of income. In one there is great mobility and change so that the positions of particular families in the income hierarchy varies widely from year to year. In the other there is great rigidity so that each family

[1] Written with Ravi Kanbur. Originally published as "Dynastic Inequality, Mobility and Equality of Opportunity," *Journal of Economic Inequality*, 14(4): 419–34. Reprinted with permission. We first started thinking about this issue in Oxford more than 30 years ago (see Kanbur and Stiglitz, 1982, 1986). We have returned to that line of inquiry and are reviving our earlier work given the recent tendency to counter rising inequality concerns with the argument that what matters is not inequality but mobility.

[2] See Stiglitz (2012a).

[3] Some have argued that inequalities in lifetime incomes is much less than inequalities observed at any moment of time: in any particular year, some individuals may have a high income, others a low income, but these average out over time. Arguing that consumption is related to permanent income, some, looking at the variability of consumption, suggest that the variability of permanent income must be much lower than the variability in outcomes in any one year. Data before the crisis for the U.S. contaminates the analysis, since a large fraction of Americans in the bottom 80% seemingly *believed* that they had a much higher permanent income than they did. In any case, this theoretical chapter can be made to apply to either context, with an important distinction made below.

The Origins of Inequality, and Policies to Contain It. Joseph E. Stiglitz with Ravi Kanbur, Oxford University Press.
 DOI: 10.1093/oso/9780198799580.003.0023

stays in the same position year after year. The one kind of inequality is a sign of dynamic change, social mobility, equality of opportunity; the other, of a status society. The confusion between the two kinds of inequality is particularly important precisely because competitive free enterprise capitalism tends to substitute the one for the other.

Friedman (1962) uses the phrase "equality of opportunity" which has also received a great deal of attention in recent years. Roemer (1998), in particular, has attempted to formalize the concept by distinguishing between two types of factors to which snapshot inequality might be attributed—circumstances and effort. Circumstances are those factors which are outside the individual's control and effort is the term for those factors for which society holds the individual responsible. A move towards equality of opportunity would reduce the influence of circumstances on outcome.

Whether one can separate out circumstances from effort, empirically or even perhaps conceptually, is a live debate (see Arneson, 2014; Kanbur and Wagstaff, 2016).[4] But in an intergenerational context Roemer's (1998) concept has had many precursors. Thus Nancy Stokey (1998) writes as follows:

But we care about the sources of inequality as well as its extent, which is why we distinguish between equal opportunity and equal outcomes. To what extent is the claim that our society provides equal opportunity justified? How can we tell?... I am going to take the position that if economic success is largely unpredictable on the basis of observed aspects of family background, than we can reasonably claim that society provides equal opportunity. There still might be significant inequality in income across individuals, due to differences in ability, hard work, luck, and so on, but I will call these unequal outcomes.

On the other hand, if economic success is highly predictable on the basis of family background, then I think it is difficult to accept the claim that our society provides equal opportunity. In this case accidents of birth–unequal opportunity–are primary determinants of economic status.... Consequently, on a first pass we can judge whether there is equal opportunity by looking at parents and their children to see whether the economic success of the children is determined in large part by the success of their parents.

Whether current inequality in turn influences intergenerational mobility is an important question, as discussed in the recent review by Corak (2013), and by Roemer in applying his distinction between circumstances and effort to the intergenerational context (Roemer, 2004).[5] But the other side of the causal link is equally important: whether less mobility leads to more inequality *in the next generation*. There could be an adverse feedback process, where more inequality today leads to less mobility, and that in turn leads to still more inequality in the subsequent generation, and so forth. There is now considerable evidence of the existence of a correlation between a simple measure of mobility (intergenerational

[4] However, both at the theoretical and at the empirical level, both in normative and descriptive models, there is much discussion of the links between inequality of outcomes and inequality of opportunity. While the theoretical work describes mobility in terms of transition matrices (the likelihood of moving from one income level to another), empirical work focuses on correlations, typically simple correlations between the income of a child and the income of the parent(s).

[5] There is now a growing literature in this vein; see Aaberge, Mogstad, and Peragine (2011).

correlations) and a simple measure of inequality of outcomes (Gini coefficient); and there is some literature arguing that there is evidence for both parts of the causal structure.

This chapter, by contrast, focuses largely on normative issues, but underneath these normative issues are complicated relationships between mobility and observed outcomes. We wish to know whether, for instance, societies with more mobility *necessarily* have a higher level of social welfare, using the economists' standard welfare framework.[6] Within such a normative framework, Friedman (1962) and Stokey (1998) seem to suggest that societies with more mobility have higher levels of social welfare, *regardless of the degree of inequality in outcomes observed at any moment of time*. To evaluate such claims, one needs to have a more general understanding of both what we mean by more mobility and an explicit normative framework. Well before Stokey (1998), Atkinson (1981a, 1981b) had characterized equality of opportunity in terms an intergenerational transition probability matrix with identical rows, and Shorrocks (1978) had referred to this zero correlation between parents' income and children's prospects as "perfect mobility." Atkinson and Shorrocks, and others, had also noted an alternative type of transition matrix which might capture the notion of high mobility, namely one with strong negative correlation between parents' income and children's expected prospects, and Shorrocks (1978) noted that these two views—"equality of opportunity" and "negative correlation"—were not necessarily consistent with each other.

We can of course make a direct set of arguments favoring one of these views, and some of the literature does this.[7] But much of the literature relates views on intergenerational mobility to specific social welfare functions, on the grounds that this allows precision on the nature of the value judgments in play. Starting from the early work of Atkinson (1981a, 1981b), and Atkinson and Bourguignon (1982) there is now a very large literature in this vein. Our earlier working papers, Kanbur and Stiglitz (1982, 1986) were in this strand of literature, with a particular focus on dynastic inequality. Since those papers, the literature has seen tremendous growth.[8] However, the particular result and characterization we presented then has not been covered in this literature, and we are reviving our earlier work in this chapter to engage with the current debate on mobility as a normative counter to inequality. In particular, we wish to ask, what pattern of intergenerational mobility leads to lower inequality not between individuals but between the dynasties to which they belong? And how does this pattern in turn relate to commonly held views on what constitutes equality of opportunity?

The plan of the chapter is as follows. Section 2 introduces the notation of intergenerational transition matrices and reviews the basic literature to set up the analytical problem we are addressing. Section 3 presents a characterization result which allows a partial ordering on intergenerational mobility matrices with respect to dynastic inequality. Section 4

[6] Of course, many would claim that the economists' standard framework, generalizations of utilitarianism, is badly flawed. We care about *fairness*, and fairness is *defined* by equality of opportunity. In this view, equality of opportunity is a value in its own right. We will not have anything more to say on this alternative framework here.

[7] Thus "equality of opportunity" type characterizations have been appealed to directly by Roemer (1998) and by the earlier literature of which Dworkin (1981) is a prime example.

[8] Comprehensive surveys of the earlier literature include the one by Fields and Ok (1999). Examples of papers in this vein include Markandya (1984), Chakravarty, Dutta, and Weymark (1985), and Dardanoni (1993). More recent references are given in Amiel, Bernasconi, Cowell, and Dardanoni (2013) and in Corak (2013).

interprets and discusses the result through particular examples. Section 5 concludes with an agenda for future research.

2 The Model and a Standard Result

Let us specify the $n \times n$ transition matrix:

$$A = \|a_{ij}\|;\, a_{ij} \geq 0,\, \sum_{j=1}^{n} a_{ij} = 1, \tag{22.1}$$

whose typical element a_ij is the probability of movement from income category i to income category j. In our case the transition can best be thought of as intergenerational.[9] Let there be n categories of incomes with income levels:

$$y_1 \leq y_2 \leq y_3 \leq \ldots \leq y_n. \tag{22.2}$$

For simplicity, the transition matrix A will be assumed to be constant over time and, where appropriate, the probability that a particular income category is occupied will be identified with the proportion of people who actually end up in that category.

An oft-encountered view on what constitutes greater mobility may be characterized as the "diagonals view." Thus a transition matrix $A = ||a_{ij}||$ is said to exhibit greater mobility than a transition matrix $B = ||b_{ij}||$ if $a_{ii} \leq b_{ii}$ for all i with strict inequality for some i, in other words each diagonal element of A is no larger than the corresponding diagonal element of B. A "strong diagonals view" can be characterized as saying that $a_{ij} \geq b_{ij}$ for all $i \neq j$ with strict inequality for some $i \neq j$. Shorrocks (1978) called this property of a mobility matrix "monotonicity."

The extreme of immobility in the "diagonals view" is of course the case of the Identity matrix:

$$A = I;\, a_{ij} = \delta_{ij} = \begin{cases} 1 & \text{for} \quad i = j \\ 0 & \text{for} \quad i \neq j \end{cases}. \tag{22.3}$$

In this case, families' status remains unchanged generation after generation. Strong monotonicity simply means that there is a smaller probability of remaining in the same position, and a higher probability of going into *every other position.*

The other extreme is sometimes argued to be the matrix which has ones along the nonleading diagonal and zeros elsewhere:

$$A = K;\, a_{ij} = k_{ij} = \begin{cases} 1 & \text{for} \quad j = n + 1 - i \\ 0 & \text{for} \quad j \neq n + 1 - i \end{cases}. \tag{22.4}$$

[9] If the incomes are those of an individual in a particular year, and there were perfect capital markets, all that would matter is the present discounted value of income over his life, that is, if individuals lived for two periods and the interest rate were zero, it is the inequality in y_t, y_{t+1} that we would study. This is a very special case of the more general model that we formulate below, with a linear utility function. Implicitly, in our more general formulation, we do not allow intertemporal smoothing.

Atkinson (1981a) calls this the case of "complete reversal." Those at the bottom move to the top and vice versa. Atkinson contrasts this with another view of perfect mobility, namely that of "equality of opportunity" as indicated by independence of future prospects from the current situation. This is given by a matrix whose rows are identical:

$$E = \begin{bmatrix} \underset{\sim}{a'} \\ a' \\ \underset{\sim}{a'} \end{bmatrix}, \tag{22.5}$$

where a' represents the vector of transition probabilities.

Shorrocks (1978) also uses (22.5) to define his property PM ("perfect mobility"). As Shorrocks goes on to show, one cannot both hold the "diagonals view" and the "equality of opportunity view" simultaneously. For example, with

$$A = \begin{bmatrix} 0 & 1 \\ 1 & 0 \end{bmatrix} \text{and } B = \begin{bmatrix} 1/2 & 1/2 \\ 1/2 & 1/2 \end{bmatrix}, \tag{22.6}$$

it should be clear that A is better than B on the diagonals view while the reverse is true on the equality of opportunity view. This disjuncture came to be well appreciated in the technical literature which developed since the work of Shorrocks and Atkinson (see for example the survey by Fields and Ok, 1999), and yet one finds both views present in the discourse on intergenerational mobility.

There has been considerable development in the literature through specification of explicit dynastic social welfare functions. Consider a two-period world with dynasty i currently having income y_i. Thus income in the next period is y_j with probability a_ij, from (1). If $W(y_i, y_j)$ represents the welfare from incomes (y_i, y_j), then the expected welfare of dynasty i is[10]

$$V_i = \sum_{j=1}^{n} a_{ij} W(y_i, y_j). \tag{22.7}$$

If p_i° is the proportion of total units in category i, then social welfare will be some function of the V_is and the p_i^0s. If we suppose that social welfare S is additive in dynastic welfares, then

$$S = \sum_{i=1}^{n} p_i^0 \sum_{j=1}^{n} a_{ij} W(y_i, y_j). \tag{22.8}$$

This is, in fact, the social welfare function considered by Atkinson (1981a, b). Let us now impose the condition that income transitions are in a steady state, so that the snapshot

[10] Note that with individual risk neutrality and zero rate of pure time preference $V_i = y_i + \sum_{j=1}^{n} a_{ij} y_j$

distribution of income remains unchanged over time.[11] Then

$$p^0 = p^1 = p^*.$$

The class of bistochastic transition matrices, that is, those for which

$$a_{ij} \geq 0; \quad \sum_{j=1}^{n} a_{ij} = \sum_{i=1}^{n} a_{ij} = 1, \tag{22.9}$$

all have a steady state distribution of the form:

$$p^* = \left(\frac{1}{n}, \frac{1}{n}, \frac{1}{n}, \ldots, \frac{1}{n}\right), \tag{22.10}$$

that is, equal numbers in each category. The bistochastic assumption is made by Atkinson (1981a, 1981b) and the subsequent literature to focus on the pure consequences of mobility, independent of the impact on the long run snapshot distribution of income.[12]

Focusing then just on mobility, and by analogy with multivariate stochastic dominance, a condition is derived by Atkinson (1981a, 1981b) for one transition matrix to give a higher social welfare than another for a class of social welfare functions. If

$$A = \|a_{ij}\| \text{ and } B = \|b_{ij}\|$$

are the two transition matrices being compared and social welfare is given by (22.8) with $p_i^0 = p_i^* = \frac{1}{n} n$ for all i, then it can be shown that

$$S^A \geq S^B \text{ for all } W(\cdot,\cdot) \text{ such that } \frac{\partial^2 W}{\partial y_i \partial y_j} 0,$$

if and only if

$$M = \sum_{i=1}^{k} \sum_{j=1}^{m} (a_{ij} - b_{ij}) \leq 0 \text{ for all } k, m. \tag{22.11}$$

This condition on transition matrices is essentially equivalent to the cumulative of the bivariate distribution of (y_i, y_j) being nowhere greater in society A than in society B.

The result in (22.11) gives a specific method of comparing intergenerational transition matrices. Notice that according to this criterion although E dominates I, K dominates E. Thus equality of opportunity does not necessarily lead to higher social welfare as specified here.

[11] Kanbur and Stromberg (1988) is an example of a line of work which assesses the dominance properties of income distributions $p^0, p^1, \ldots, p^t$.

[12] This is also referred to as the distinction between "structural mobility" and "exchange mobility" the latter being the case where the snapshot distributions are held constant.

3 Mobility and Dynastic Inequality: A Characterization Result

We continue to assume a bistochastic transition matrix with the income distribution in steady state. The bistochastic assumption is restrictive but (i) it focuses attention on "pure" mobility or "exchange mobility" and (ii) as Atkinson (1981a) argues, if the income categories are quantiles then the transition matrix is by definition bistochastic.[13] Notice that since the steady state of a bistochastic transition matrix has equal numbers in each category, we can normalize to the situation where there is one person in each category. We will, however, need to be careful and not give a strict cardinal interpretation to income levels y_i associated with each category.

We will further simplify the dynasty's intertemporal utility to be the expected discounted value of a given instantaneous utility function with a constant discount rate.

Then for a two-period world dynasty i's lifetime expected welfare is given by

$$V_i = U(y_i) + \gamma \sum_{j=1}^{n} a_{ij} U(y_i) \quad ; \quad i = 1, 2, \ldots, n, \tag{22.12}$$

where γ is the discount factor (lying between 0 and 1) and $U(.)$ is the instantaneous utility function. In this case the condition on $W(.)$ in result (22.11) is satisfied with standard utility functions $U(.)$.

However, what happens in the case of dynasties which live more than two generations? In this case the two period results of Atkinson (1981a, 1981b), and the bivariate results of Atkinson and Bourguignon (1982), are no longer valid. Indeed, it is not exactly clear what the analogy would be for the condition on the social welfare function in the bivariate case, and how and whether even a similar class of results could be derived.

Thus the Atkinson (1981a, 1981b) results are somewhat limited in the long-lived dynasties case. In what follows we extend their analysis to the case of infinitely lived dynasties. If we define:[14]

$$\underset{\sim}{U} = (U(y_1), U(y_2), \ldots, U(y_n)) \tag{22.13}$$

as the column vector of utilities of income, then we can stack the expressions in (22.12) to give

$$\underset{\sim}{V} = \underset{\sim}{U} + \gamma A \underset{\sim}{U}, \tag{22.14}$$

where $\underset{\sim}{V}$ is the vector of dynastic expected welfares. For a T generations world (22.14) becomes:

$$\underset{\sim}{V} = \left[I + \gamma A + \gamma^2 A^2 + \ldots + \gamma^T A^T\right] \underset{\sim}{U}, \tag{22.15}$$

if we let $T \to \infty$ then under standard conditions we get

[13] Key papers in the literature make further restrictive assumptions, for example the assumption that a matrix is "monotone" in other words, the rows of the matrix from a sequence of stochastic domination (Dardanoni, 1993). Dardanoni, Fiorini, and Forcini (2010) argue that this assumption is borne out in reality. However, the income categories corresponding to say the deciles differ across societies, and we may also care a great deal about those.

[14] This approach from Kanbur and Stiglitz (1982, 1986) was also followed for example by Dardanoni (1993).

$$\underset{\sim}{V} = [I - \gamma A]^{-1}\underset{\sim}{U}. \tag{22.16}$$

Now it can be shown that

$$e'\underset{\sim}{V} = \frac{1}{1-\gamma}\, e'\underset{\sim}{U} \text{ where } e' = (1, 1, \ldots, 1), \tag{22.17}$$

so that the sum of dynastic welfare is the same for all transition mechanisms in this class. This allows us to focus purely on the inequality of dynastic welfare. Instead of simply taking the sum of $V_1, V_2, \ldots, V_n$, we will let social welfare be

$$S = S(V_1, V_2, \ldots, V_n), \tag{22.18}$$

where $S(\cdot, \cdot, \ldots \cdot, \cdot)$ is now a symmetric, quasi-concave function, assumptions which are meant to capture, respectively, anonymity and egalitarianism with respect to dynastic prospects.

Our object is to rank transition matrices according to the social welfare function (22.18). Denote $\underset{\sim}{V}^A$ and $\underset{\sim}{V}^B$ as the vector of lifetime utilities under two transition matrices A and B:

$$\begin{aligned} \underset{\sim}{V}^A &= [I - \gamma A]^{-1}\underset{\sim}{U} \\ \underset{\sim}{V}^B &= [I - \gamma B]^{-1}\underset{\sim}{U} \end{aligned} \tag{22.19}$$

and let

$$S^A = S\left(\underset{\sim}{V}^A\right); S^B = S\left(\underset{\sim}{V}^B\right), \tag{22.20}$$

we can now state the basic result of this section:

Proposition *$S^A \geq S^B$ for all symmetric, quasi-concave $S(.)$ for all $(y_1, y_2, \ldots . y_n)$ and all $U(.)$ which are unique up to a positive linear transformation, if and only if there exists a bistochastic matrix Q such that*

$$B = \frac{1}{\gamma}[I - Q] + AQ$$

Proof of Sufficiency

$$\begin{aligned} & B = \tfrac{1}{\gamma}[I - Q] + AQ \\ & \Rightarrow [I - \gamma B] = [I - \gamma A]Q \\ & \Rightarrow [I - \gamma A]^{-1} = Q\left[I - \gamma B^{-1}\right] \\ & \Rightarrow [I - \gamma A]^{-1} = Q[I - \gamma B]^{-1} \qquad \textit{for all } (y_1, y_2, \ldots y_n) \textit{ and all } U(.) \\ & \Rightarrow A = Q\underset{\sim}{V}^B \end{aligned}$$

Now if it is not the case that $V_1^A \leq V_2^A \leq \ldots \leq V_n^A$, simply permute them to give

$$\underset{\sim}{\hat{V}}^A = p_A \underset{\sim}{\hat{V}}^A,$$

where the vector $\hat{\underset{\sim}{V}}^A$ is ordered so that $\hat{V}_1^A \leq \hat{V}_2^A \cdots \leq \hat{V}_n^A$, and P_A is the appropriate permutation matrix. Similarly, use an appropriate permutation matrix P_B to reorder $\hat{\underset{\sim}{V}}^B$ and $\hat{\underset{\sim}{V}}^B$. The argument now continues as follows:

$$\begin{aligned}
&\hat{\underset{\sim}{V}}^A = Q\hat{\underset{\sim}{V}}^B \\
&\Rightarrow P_A\hat{\underset{\sim}{V}}^A = P_A Q\, P_B^{-1} P_B \hat{\underset{\sim}{V}}^B \\
&\Rightarrow \hat{\underset{\sim}{V}}^A = \left[P_A Q\, P_B^{-1}\right] \hat{\underset{\sim}{V}}^B \\
&\Rightarrow \hat{\underset{\sim}{V}}^A = \hat{Q}\hat{\underset{\sim}{V}}^B.
\end{aligned}$$

It is easy to check that the inverse of a permutation matrix is itself a permutation matrix and hence $\hat{Q} = P_A Q\, P_B^{-1}$ is also a bistochastic matrix. But from Dasgupta, Sen, and Starrett (1973, Theorem 1), $\hat{V}^A = \hat{Q}\hat{\underset{\sim}{V}}^B$ where $\hat{Q}$ bistochastic

$$\Rightarrow S\left(\hat{\underset{\sim}{V}}^A\right) \geq S\left(\hat{\underset{\sim}{V}}^B\right),$$

for all symmetric quasi-concave functions $S(.)$. Moreover, by symmetry of the $S(.)$ function,

$$\begin{aligned}
&S\left(\hat{\underset{\sim}{V}}^A\right) = S\left(\hat{\underset{\sim}{V}}^A\right);\; S\left(\hat{\underset{\sim}{V}}^B\right) = S\left(V^B\right); \quad \text{so that} \\
&S\left(\hat{\underset{\sim}{V}}^A\right) \geq S\left(\hat{\underset{\sim}{V}}^B\right) \text{ and sufficiency is proved.}
\end{aligned}$$

Proof of Necessity

$S\left(\underset{\sim}{V}^A\right) \geq S\underset{\sim}{V}^B$ for all symmetric quasi-concave functions $S(.)$, all $(y_1, y_2, \ldots, y_n)$, and all $U(.)$ unique up to a positive linear transformation

$\Rightarrow S\left(\hat{\underset{\sim}{V}}^A\right) \geq S\underset{\sim}{V}^B$ by symmetry of $S(.)$

$\Rightarrow$ there exists a bistochastic matrix $\hat{Q}$ such that

$\hat{\underset{\sim}{V}}^A \geq \hat{Q}\hat{\underset{\sim}{V}}^B$ from Dasgupta, Sen, and Starrett (1973), Theorem 1

$$\begin{aligned}
&\Rightarrow P_A^{-1}\hat{\underset{\sim}{V}}^A = P_A^{-1}\hat{Q}P_B P_B' \underset{\sim}{V}^B \\
&\Rightarrow \underset{\sim}{V}^A = \left[P_A^{-1}\hat{Q}P_B\right] \underset{\sim}{V}^B \\
&\Rightarrow \underset{\sim}{V}^A = Q\underset{\sim}{V}^B \\
&\Rightarrow [I - \gamma A]^{-1}\underset{\sim}{U} = Q[I - \gamma B]^{-1}\underset{\sim}{U} \\
&\Rightarrow [I - \gamma A]^{-1} = Q[I - \gamma B]^{-1}
\end{aligned}$$

Since the above equality is true for all $(y_1, y_2, \ldots, y_n)$ and all $U(.)$ unique up to a positive linear transformation:

$$\Rightarrow B = \frac{1}{\gamma}[I - Q] + AQ$$

and proof of necessity is completed.

We thus have a characterization result on intergenerational mobility—what two patterns must look like so that we can say with confidence that dynastic inequality is lower in one than the other.[15] How does the result relate to conventional views on "more mobility" or "equality of opportunity"? The next section interprets the result in light of this discourse.

4 Interpretations

It should be noted that the theorem of the previous section provides us with a necessary and sufficient characterization result. Within the class of bistochastic transition matrices and restricting ourselves to steady states; if we are not willing to specify the social welfare function in any greater detail than that it be symmetric and quasi-concave in dynastic expected welfares; and if we accept that lifetime utility is the present discounted sum of von-Neumann Morgenstern expected utility over an infinite horizon; then to say that social welfare is higher under transition matrix *A* than under transition matrix *B*, is equivalent to saying that *A* and *B* stand in the relation

$$B = \frac{1}{\gamma}[I - Q] + AQ, \tag{22.21}$$

where *Q* is a bistochastic matrix. Of course, this is a very strong requirement. But under the conditions stated this is all that can be said. One route for further research may be to relax some of these conditions, but here we will restrict ourselves to relating (22.21) to some conventional views on "greater mobility."

Given any two bistochastic transition matrices *A* and *B*, from (22.21) we simply have to check whether or not

$$Q = [I - \gamma A]^{-1}[I - \gamma B] \tag{22.22}$$

is a bistochastic matrix. Then, and only then, will *A*'s welfare ranking be higher than that of *B* for the class of social welfare functions being considered. Now using

$$[I - \gamma A]^{-1} = \sum_{t=0}^{\infty} \gamma^t A^t,$$

it can be seen that

$$\underset{\sim}{e}'Q = \underset{\sim}{e}' \ ; \ Q\underset{\sim}{e} = \underset{\sim}{e} \tag{22.23}$$

[15] Dardanoni (1993) also presents characterization results for the class of monotone matrices.

Thus all that remains to be checked is whether each element of the matrix in (22.22) is nonnegative, that is, whether $q_{ij} \geq 0$.

For any two matrices, calculation of (22.22) and checking if the resultant matrix is non-negative is the operational method of identifying social welfare dominance in our setting. It is the equivalent of the Lorenz curve comparison in the static case, and of the Atkinson criterion (22.11) in the case of measuring mobility for two-period dynasties.

Let us illustrate (22.22) with some examples. Start with an intuitively obvious case. How does the identify matrix compare to other bistochastic matrices? Let $B = I$ in (22.22) and let

A be any other bistochastic matrix, noting that from the many steady state distributions for I we choose $p^* = \left(\frac{1}{n}, \frac{1}{n}, \frac{1}{n}, \ldots, \frac{1}{n}\right)$ to maintain comparability. Then from (22.22):

$$Q = (1 - \gamma)[I - \gamma A]^{-1}, \tag{22.24}$$

all of whose elements are non-negative. Thus *any* matrix in the bistochastic class is ranked better than the identity matrix. Moreover, letting $A = I$ in (22.22) we get

$$Q = \frac{1}{1-\gamma}[I - \gamma B], \tag{22.25}$$

some of whose off-diagonal elements will always be negative if B is not itself the identity matrix. Thus I is not ranked better than any other bistochastic matrix. It is in this sense that I is the unique globally "worse" transition matrix in the bistochastic class if the objective is dynastic inequality.

Consider now the "equality of opportunity view," which would regard the matrix

$$E = \frac{1}{n}\begin{bmatrix} \underset{\sim}{e}' \\ \underset{\sim}{e}' \\ \cdot \\ \cdot \\ \cdot \\ \cdot \\ \underset{\sim}{e}' \end{bmatrix} = \begin{bmatrix} \frac{1}{n} & \frac{1}{n} & \cdots & \frac{1}{n} \\ \frac{1}{n} & \frac{1}{n} & \cdots & \frac{1}{n} \\ \cdot & \cdot & & \cdot \\ \cdot & \cdot & & \cdot \\ \cdot & \cdot & & \cdot \\ \cdot & \cdot & & \cdot \\ \frac{1}{n} & \frac{1}{n} & \cdots & \frac{1}{n} \end{bmatrix} \tag{22.26}$$

as the best in the class of bistochastic transition matrices. This is of course the matrix E in (22.5) for the bistochastic case. Let us compare this with the matrix K defined in (22.4), where correlation between one period's income and the next period's income is the most negative it can be. First of all, let $A = E$ and $B = K$ in (22.22). Noting that $E^2 = E$, it is easy to show (as in Kanbur and Mukerji, 1980) that:

$$[I - \gamma E]^{-1} = \left[I + \frac{\gamma}{1-\gamma}E\right] \tag{22.27}$$

So we have

$$Q = \left[I + \frac{\gamma}{1-\gamma}E\right][I - \gamma K]$$
$$= I - \gamma K + \gamma E. \tag{22.28}$$

In deriving the final form of (22.28) we have used the fact that $KE = E$. Now from (22.28) and the definition of K in (22.4),

$$\begin{aligned} i \neq j;\quad q_{ij} &= \gamma\left(\frac{1}{n} - k_{ij}\right) = \begin{cases} \gamma\left(\frac{1}{n} - 1\right) & \text{for } j = n - i + 1 \neq i \\ \frac{\gamma}{n} & \text{for } j \neq n - i + 1 = i \end{cases} \\ i = j;\quad q_{ij} &= 1 - \gamma\frac{1}{n} + \gamma\frac{1}{n} = \begin{cases} 1 - \gamma + \gamma\frac{1}{n} & \text{for } i = \frac{n+1}{2} (n \text{ odd}) \\ 1 + \gamma\frac{1}{n} & \text{for other } i \end{cases} \end{aligned} \tag{22.29}$$

Thus at least some elements of Q (those for which $j = n - i + 1 = i$) will be negative and E cannot be established as unambiguously better than K.

Can K be established an unambiguously better than E? Letting $A = K$, $B = E$ in (22.22), and noting that

$$[I - \gamma K]^{-1} = \frac{1}{1-\gamma^2}[I + \gamma K] \tag{22.30}$$

we get

$$Q = [I - \gamma K]^{-1}[I - \gamma E] \tag{22.31}$$
$$= \frac{1}{1-\gamma^2}\mathrm{I} + \frac{\gamma}{1-\gamma^2}\mathrm{K} - \frac{\gamma}{1-\gamma}E, \tag{22.31}$$

hence:

$$\begin{aligned} i \neq j;\quad q_{ij} &= \tfrac{\gamma}{1-\gamma^2}k_{ij} - \tfrac{\gamma}{1-\gamma}\cdot\tfrac{1}{n} = \begin{cases} \frac{\gamma}{1-\gamma^2} - \frac{\gamma}{1-\gamma}\cdot\frac{1}{n} & \text{for } j = n - i + 1 \neq i \\ \frac{\gamma}{1-\gamma}\cdot\frac{1}{n} & \text{for } j \neq n - i + 1 \neq i \end{cases} \\ i = j;\quad q_{ij} &= \tfrac{1}{1-\gamma^2} + \tfrac{\gamma}{1-\gamma^2}k_{ij} - \tfrac{\gamma}{1-\gamma}\cdot\tfrac{1}{n} = \begin{cases} \frac{n-\gamma(1+\gamma)}{n(1-\gamma^2)} + \frac{\gamma}{1-\gamma^2} & \text{for } i = \frac{n+1}{2} (n \text{ odd}) \\ \frac{n-\gamma(1+\gamma)}{n(1-\gamma^2)} & \text{for other } i. \end{cases} \end{aligned} \tag{22.32}$$

The only dimension for which the $j \neq n - i + 1$ and $j \neq i$ case is not a possibility is $n = 2$.

For $n = 3$, the element q_{23}, for example, satisfies $j \neq n - i + 1$ and $j \neq i$.

Thus in the 2×2 case K is unambiguously ranked better than E. However, more generally the two cannot be ranked without specifying the social welfare function further.

In fact in the 2×2 case if we let

$$A = \begin{bmatrix} \alpha & 1-\alpha \\ 1-\alpha & \alpha \end{bmatrix}; B = \begin{bmatrix} \beta & 1-\beta \\ 1-\beta & \beta \end{bmatrix} \tag{22.33}$$

then

$$Q = \begin{bmatrix} q & 1-q \\ 1-q & q \end{bmatrix}; \quad q = \frac{1+\frac{1}{\gamma}-(\alpha+\beta)}{1+\frac{1}{\gamma}-2\alpha}. \tag{22.34}$$

Clearly in this case q is always non-negative and

$$\beta \geq \alpha \Leftrightarrow q \leq 1 \tag{22.35}$$

so that if B is worse than A on the "diagonals view" then, and only then, is it unambiguously worse from the dynastic inequality point of view. Of course, it should be noted that in the 2×2 case the "diagonals view" and the "strong diagonals view" or "monotonicity," as Shorrocks (1978) called it coincide exactly. When presenting the incompatibility of the equality of opportunity view with monotonicity in the context of the 2×2 example. Shorrocks (1978) argued that "on balance monotonicity seems to be the less artificial restriction." The result here makes this intuition precise in the social welfare framework.[16]

Of course, no comparable general validation of the "diagonals view" is available for $n \geq 3$.

A counter example is easily presented using the result comparing K and E for $n = 4$.

$$K = \begin{bmatrix} 0 & 0 & 0 & 1 \\ 0 & 0 & 1 & 0 \\ 0 & 1 & 0 & 0 \\ 1 & 0 & 0 & 0 \end{bmatrix}; E = \begin{bmatrix} 1/4 & 1/4 & 1/4 & 1/4 \\ 1/4 & 1/4 & 1/4 & 1/4 \\ 1/4 & 1/4 & 1/4 & 1/4 \\ 1/4 & 1/4 & 1/4 & 1/4 \end{bmatrix}. \tag{22.36}$$

On the diagonals view K is superior to E for $n = 4$. But we already know from (22.32) that an unambiguous ranking on social welfare grounds is not available. More generally, for any two bistochastic matrices A and B, let

$$D = B - A \tag{22.37}$$

if B and A stand in the relation (22.21), then

$$d_{ij} = \frac{1}{\gamma}\left[\delta_{ij} - q_{ij}\right] + \sum_{\ell=1}^{n} a_{i\ell} q_{\ell j} - a_{ij}. \tag{22.38}$$

[16] Amiel, Bernasconi, Cowell, and Dardanoni (2013) argue that the negative correlation case is "only of theoretical interest since real world mobility data never show complete reversal between parents and children's economic positions." However, the issue is surely one of normative comparison rather than empirical regularity, in which case the negative correlation case is valid one to consider in the framework of minimizing dynastic inequality.

In particular,

$$d_{ii} = \sum_{\ell=1} a_{i\ell}q_{\ell i} + \left(\frac{1}{\gamma} - a_{ii}\right)(1 - a_{ii}) \geq 0. \tag{22.39}$$

Thus any two matrices which stand in the relation (22.21) satisfy the diagonals view. But the converse is not true: any two matrices which satisfy the diagonals view need not necessarily stand in the relation (22.21) to each other—the counter-example in (22.36) establishes that.

A general interpretation of (22.21) can be provided by writing it as

$$B = \left[\frac{1}{\gamma}I\right][I - Q + AQ],$$

B can thus be seen as a matrix-weighed sum of $\frac{1}{\gamma}I$ and A, the weights being Q and $[I - Q]$.

If there exists a Q such that B can be written as this weighted sum, in a general sense B is closer to the identity matrix than A. If interpreted in this wide sense, the "diagonals view" has a rationale in a social welfare function that is egalitarian with respect to dynastic prospects.

For a specific application, consider the matrices A, B, and C given below, which are taken from Atkinson (1981a).

$$A = \begin{bmatrix} 0.48 & 0.42 & 0.10 & 0.00 \\ 0.25 & 0.34 & 0.27 & 0.14 \\ 0.19 & 0.17 & 0.37 & 0.27 \\ 0.08 & 0.07 & 0.26 & 0.59 \end{bmatrix}$$

$$B = \begin{bmatrix} 0.35 & 0.24 & 0.27 & 0.14 \\ 0.26 & 0.30 & 0.27 & 0.17 \\ 0.19 & 0.17 & 0.37 & 0.27 \\ 0.20 & 0.29 & 0.09 & 0.42 \end{bmatrix}$$

$$C = \begin{bmatrix} 0.44 & 0.23 & 0.19 & 0.14 \\ 0.32 & 0.26 & 0.25 & 0.17 \\ 0.18 & 0.36 & 0.27 & 0.19 \\ 0.06 & 0.15 & 0.29 & 0.50 \end{bmatrix}$$

Matrix C is a father to son, quartile to quartile, transition matrix for hourly earnings in Britain, derived from the work of Atkinson, Maynard, and Trinder (1983). Matrices A and B are alternative specifications of father to son occupational transition matrices which are got by adjusting the Goldthorpe (1980) data from its seven classes into four and enforcing bistochasticity. Atkinson (1981a) provides a fuller discussion of the procedure, but essentially matrix A has been derived by shifting weight towards the diagonal and matrix B by shifting weight away from the diagonal. Atkinson compares C with A and C with B using his criterion (22.11) and finds that C and A cannot be so ranked, but that "the earnings transition matrix is welfare inferior to case B of the occupational status matrix."

Can the same be said of the matrices using our criterion? For $\gamma = 0.5$ (an intergenerational interest rate of 100%), we get the following Q matrices:

$$Q_{CA}^{-1} = [I - \gamma C]^{-1}[I - \gamma A]$$
$$= \begin{bmatrix} 0.978 & -0.111 & 0.051 & 0.082 \\ 0.035 & 0.953 & -0.009 & 0.021 \\ -0.002 & 0.095 & 0.947 & -0.040 \\ -0.011 & 0.063 & 0.011 & 0.938 \end{bmatrix}$$
$$Q_{BC}^{-1} = [I - \gamma B]^{-1}[I - \gamma C]$$
$$= \begin{bmatrix} 0.948 & -0.001 & 0.049 & 0.003 \\ -0.034 & 0.016 & 0.016 & 0.002 \\ 0.009 & -0.101 & 0.050 & -0.042 \\ 0.076 & 0.086 & -0.115 & 0.953 \end{bmatrix}$$

As in the case of Atkinson's criterion, C cannot be ranked as better than A. However, what is interesting is that B cannot be ranked as better than C, in contrast to the Atkinson finding. Thus while it should be clear that there are a number of empirical problems in comparing earnings transition matrices with occupational ones, our calculations nevertheless indicate that a stress on dynastic inequality could alter rankings which emphasize intertemporal non-separability.

5 Conclusion

The normative riposte to concerns about sharply rising inequality of income and wealth, that it is intergenerational mobility and equality of opportunity which really matter, need to be assessed with respect to specific social welfare functions which make explicit the value judgments underlying the claim. An earlier literature, starting with the work of Shorrocks (1978), Atkinson (1981a, 1981b), and Atkinson and Bourguignon (1982) attempted to do just this, and developed criteria for assessment of alternative patterns of intergenerational mobility. Our contribution is in this vein, focusing on the implications of intergenerational mobility for inequality among infinitely lived dynasties.

Restricting attention to bistochastic transition matrices in order to hold constant the steady state snapshot income distribution, we have developed an explicit partial ordering which ranks matrices on the criterion of dynastic inequality. A general interpretation of our result is that when comparing two matrices, if one matrix is "further away" from the identity matrix then it will lead to lower dynastic inequality. More specifically, the result presents a computational procedure to check if one matrix dominates another on dynastic inequality. We can also assess "equality of opportunity," defined as identical prospects irrespective of starting position, or identical rows of a transition matrix. We find that this is not necessarily the mobility pattern which minimizes dynastic inequality, which requires instead a degree of negative correlation between intergenerational outcomes.

Much remains to be done. At the theoretical level, we can sharpen our ordering by restricting the class of transition matrices, for example to those which satisfy stochastic monotonicity as suggested by Dardanoni, Fiorini and Forcini (2010). The criterion we have developed can be applied to intergenerational transition matrices which are now being estimated with newly available data. The earlier literature on normative measurement of mobility needs to be revisited and extended to address the revived concerns on inequality and mobility. Most importantly, the normative implications of the current inequality of income for intergenerational inequality need to be assessed again with respect to alternative sets of social welfare value judgments, perhaps bolstered by empirical investigation of people's views on mobility and inequality in its different dimensions, as developed by Amiel, Bernasconi, Cowell, and Dardanoni (2013). Specifically, if "equality of opportunity" as captured identical rows of a transition matrix (independence of future prospects from current income or wealth), does indeed have normative significance as the best transition matrix, how do we reconcile this with the outcome that it does not necessarily minimize dynastic inequality?

23

Reflections on Mobility and Social Justice, Economic Efficiency, and Individual Responsibility

1 Introduction

Although much of modern positive economics is concerned with dynamic issues, economists have tended to approach distributional issues from a static point of view.[1] Economists study the distribution of income at a single point in time or even how this distribution of wages or income changes over time. But they have paid less attention to the mobility of individuals, their prospects for advancement or the chances of a reversal of fortune.[2] Traditional welfare economics, including utilitarian social welfare functions and the related Rawlsian social welfare functions, look at the economy at a point in time.[3] As a result, they do not reflect well basic ideas of social justice. In particular, I will show that utilitarian social welfare functions can rank as equivalent two economies where intuitively one would seem clearly preferable to another. Not only can it be shown that certain widely accepted norms such as equality of opportunity cannot be derived from standard utilitarianism, but such norms may be inconsistent with utilitarianism; and utilitarian social welfare functions do not reflect many of the attributes of our social and economic systems that public rhetoric, at least, suggests are of first importance.

In addition to developing a broader framework for evaluating alternative economic systems and assessing alternative views of the role of the state, especially in the areas beyond pure public goods, this chapter also seeks to apply this framework to two specific problems, the provision of social insurance and the rationale for inheritance taxes.

This discussion is a continuation of the inquiry into the economic role of the state and the relationship between the government and markets.[4] In recent years that inquiry has begun by identifying ways markets fail to produce efficient outcomes, the special properties of

[1] Originally published as "Reflections on Mobility and Social Justice, Economic Efficiency, and Individual Responsibility," in N. Birdsall and C. Graham (eds.), *New Markets, New Opportunities? Economic and Social Mobility in a Changing World*, Washington, DC: Brookings Institution Press, pp. 36–65. Reprinted with permission.

I am greatly indebted to Ravi Kanbur and Jason Furman for helpful discussions. Some of the general theoretical ideas in this chapter reflect a joint research project with Kanbur, Jessica Seddon, and Maya Tudor provided excellent research assistance. I also thank the participants of the MacArthur Inequality and Economic Performance Research Network in Bellagio, Italy, and the Brookings Inter-American Development Bank meeting on economic mobility for helpful comments.

[2] More recently, there has been a resurgence of interest in interests in mobility, spurred on in part by the work of Corak (see, e.g., his 2013 *Journal of Economic Perspectives* article) and the wealth of data uncovered by Raj Chetty and the work of his research team (opportunityinsights.org).

[3] Even within the traditional framework, however, it is clear that one should look at the distribution of lifetime utilities or consumption.

[4] See Stiglitz (1989, 1991, 1994b, 1994c, 2001a).

The Origins of Inequality, and Policies to Contain It. Joseph E. Stiglitz, Oxford University Press. © Joseph E. Stiglitz (2025).
DOI: 10.1093/oso/9780198799580.003.0024

the state (in contrast with other market and non-market institutions), and the powers and limitations that are derived from that. There has been a switch from seeing markets and government as substitutes to seeing them as complements.[5]

But much of the activity of the public sector goes beyond correcting market failures. Governments are concerned with redistribution, promoting social justice, and helping change the nature of society from what it might otherwise be (for example, through discouraging the consumption of drugs and encouraging the consumption of education). Today, much of the expenditure of the public sector is associated with the provision of *publicly provided private goods*, like education and social insurance, in contrast to the pure *public goods* on which Paul Samuelson focused attention. Typically, the marginal cost of providing these services to an additional individual is close to the average cost (while for public goods, the marginal cost is close to zero) and exclusion is easy (while for public goods exclusion is prohibitively expensive). The shape of these public programs, if not their very existence, is motivated by concerns that are not well captured in the "market failure" paradigm. Distributional concerns are paramount.

I have titled this chapter "Reflections ..." because I am more concerned with presenting a set of issues than with providing definitive answers. Although I do not provide a comprehensive alternative framework here, these results should at least make us cautious about excessive reliance on the traditional concepts of welfare economics.

2 Criteria for Assessing Economic Systems: Outcomes versus Mobility

For almost a century the concept of Pareto efficiency has dominated the economic profession's evaluation of economic systems and policies. In this tradition, for a "desirable" economic system Pareto efficiency is a necessary condition and an individualistic, social welfare function can be used for a more complete evaluation of alternative economic systems. Although there is some controversy about the meaning or usefulness of social welfare functions, there are, except at the fringes of the profession, few misgivings about the Pareto principle.[6]

Economists have looked at the implications of fairly weak restrictions on social welfare functions in choosing among Pareto-efficient allocations—for example, what are the implications of some weak ideas of egalitarianism for rankings among income distributions?[7] The basic idea was provided by the concept of utilitarianism—measuring the sum of individual utilities—where the marginal utility is decreasing with income. As a result, a mean-preserving spread of the income distribution, which moves people from the middle to the extremes of the income distribution, would make society worse off (from an egalitarian perspective) because the losses of the people made poorer would be larger than the

[5] Or as "market enhancing." See, for example, Aoki, Murdock, and Okuno-Fujiwara (1997); or Hellman, Murdock, and Stiglitz (1998).

[6] The standard argument in favor of the competitive market system is that it is Pareto efficient; the analysis has been extended, for instance, to thinking about alternative tax structures, in the concept of Pareto-efficient tax structures. See Stiglitz (1987a).

[7] The classic paper in this area is that of Atkinson (1970) who showed how one could translate the Rothschild-Stiglitz (1971, 1972) orderings of probability distributions into orderings of income distributions. These ideas were subsequently generalized by Dasgupta, Sen, and Starrett (1973) and Rothschild and Stiglitz (1973).

gains of those made richer. Specifically, *an income distribution with a given mean is considered more egalitarian than another distribution with the same mean if the sum of individual utilities, for any utility function characterized by diminishing marginal utilities (for example, a concave function of income), is greater for the first distribution than for the second.*[8]

Anthony Atkinson (1970), Michael Rothschild and Joseph Stiglitz (1973), and Partha Dasgupta, Amartya Sen, and David Starrett (1973) then provided alternative characterizations of such rankings. There has been extensive discussion about the implications of further refinements—for example, utilitarian versus Rawlsian social welfare functions—and further generalizations—for example, separable versus non-separable social welfare functions.

As applied, these approaches have been fundamentally *individualistic*, *outcome oriented*, and *static*. It is each person's own assessment of his welfare that counts; there are no "interaction" effects, no envy; and the process by which the outcomes are arrived at is of no relevance. But it is clear that such a social welfare function does not fully capture widespread, broader views of social justice.

2.1 Ranking Transition Matrices

The belief that we care only about *outcomes* implies that if we are studying an economy with income mobility, the only property that we care about (at least in a steady state) is the steady-state distribution of income. In more formal terms, if an economy is characterized by a Markov transition matrix, which gives the probability that a person whose parents are in the *i*th income group will be in the *j*th income group, the only information relevant for standard social welfare rankings is the eigenvector of the transition matrix.[9]

That this ranking system is at variance with our basic concepts of egalitarianism is illustrated by the following example. Consider two societies; one has no mobility and the other has considerable mobility, but with the same asymptotic distribution. For simplicity, assume that there are only two income states: low income and high income. The first society is characterized by the following transition matrix:

$$\begin{pmatrix} 1 & 0 \\ 0 & 1 \end{pmatrix} \tag{23.1}$$

In other words, with probability 1 a low-income parent will have a low-income child and a high-income parent will have a high-income child. This transition matrix is consistent with any initial distribution of income, which will also become the steady-state distribution of income.

[8] In more formal terms, *An income distribution (with given mean) $P_1(Y)$ is preferred to another income distribution $P_2(Y)$ with the same mean (which I write as $P_1 >_E P_2$ and describe as P_1 is more egalitarian than P_2) if and only if $\int U(Y)dP_1(Y) > \int U(Y)dP_2(Y)$ for all concave U. This analysis assumes that utilities (well-being) of different individuals are comparable and can be compared using the same utility function.*

[9] If λA is the eigenvector of matrix *A*, then $A >_R B$ if $\lambda A >_R \lambda B$ where the symbol $>_R$ means "stochastically dominates in the sense of Rothschild–Stiglitz (1971) or Atkinson (1970)." Throughout the chapter 1 focus on Markovian income processes, but of course, there may be more complicated income dynamics.

Compare this to the mobile society whose transition matrix is

$$\begin{pmatrix} .5 & .5 \\ .5 & .5 \end{pmatrix} \tag{23.2}$$

In this society a person has a 50–50 chance of being rich or poor regardless of his or her parents' income. Regardless of the initial distribution of income, the distribution of income will rapidly evolve to (0.5, 0.5), where half the people have high incomes and half have low incomes. This distribution of income, however, is also a feasible steady-state distribution in the immobile society. Although they are equally desirable according to the egalitarian definition, clearly the more mobile society is preferable to the less mobile one.

2.1.1 Equality of Opportunity

The idea that we care not so much about outcomes but about opportunities has received increasing attention, especially in political dialogue. We at least pay lip service to the view that children from disadvantaged homes should have the same life chances that are afforded to children of the more advantaged. One of the reasons for the increased emphasis on education is that it promotes equality of opportunity, and the fact that children from lower-income households are much less likely to attend college is cited as evidence of a lack of equality of opportunity.[10]

Equality of opportunity may require compensatory actions. That is, if we define an individual's "opportunity set" by his wage, then for individuals of equal ability,

$$w = w(E, H). \tag{23.3}$$

The wage is a function of education and home "investment," which is controlled by parents, not the individual. Equalizing w requires undertaking higher levels of E to offset lower levels of H.[11]

Equality of opportunity is perfectly consistent with inequality of outcome. People could have the same opportunity set, but some seize the opportunities while others do not. Some work hard and others do not.

Many believe that society has no responsibility to undo the inequality arising from individual decisions, given that they have comparable opportunities. The principle of individual responsibility with equality of opportunity suggests that once we have truly equalized opportunities, any inequalities arising from the extent to which individuals take advantage of those opportunities are socially acceptable.

But there is another perspective: those from disadvantaged homes might be more inclined not to seize the opportunities that were afforded them, and public actions might be required to offset these differences in proclivities. Underlying these differences in views are fundamental differences in beliefs about the nature of individuals,

[10] There are some that argue that even if they were given the same or better opportunities (for instance, free education) they might not avail themselves of those opportunities to the same extent. Preferences arc molded by family background, raising the troublesome question of the extent to which one thinks of preferences in a way similar to other inheritances. However, at least in some cases, the evidence is that there are high returns to providing equal opportunity. Bleemer (2022) shows that the returns to free education for under-represented minorities attending elite UC schools is higher their white and Asian counterparts.

[11] For more extensive discussion of these issues, see Arrow (1973) and Stiglitz (1973a).

including their freedom to "choose" who they are and the extent to which their preferences are socially determined. Traditional economics has taken the individual as the basic unit of analysis, with his characteristics exogenously determined. We all recognize that the nature of the individual is influenced both by genetics and the social milieu in which he exists. But what are the differences for which society should take offsetting actions?[12]

3 The Limits of Utilitarianism

This section is devoted to technical issues of transition matrices and may be omitted on first reading without loss of content.

If we use a utilitarian social welfare function, even with time discounting, then (at least in steady state) all matrices with the same steady-state distribution of income yield the same level of social welfare. The same is true of Rawlsian social welfare functions. Evidently, neither of these social welfare functions fully captures our sense of social justice.[13]

The utilitarian social welfare function, where each individual has a Benthamite utility function ($\sum U(Y_t)$) is separable both at the individual level and at the level of society. Both of these may be questioned.[14]

Constructing simple non-separable social welfare functions that allow the ranking of matrices is, however, not an easy task. Rather than addressing the task directly, I first approach it indirectly by asking whether there are intuitive conditions that might allow matrices to be ranked.

3.1 Partial Orderings of Transition Matrices

One such condition is the following. If those currently in low-income categories have a higher probability of doing well enough to partially compensate (in expected value) for their current low income (and by implication, those in high-income categories have a higher probability of doing poorly) under transition matrix A than under transition matrix B, then A is more egalitarian. It should be obvious that this is a partial ordering: most matrices will have the property that while some persons with initially low incomes may prefer A to B, others may prefer B to A. For simplicity, I shall refer to this as the *egalitarian mobility ranking*.[15] A formal statement of this ranking, and proofs of some of the propositions in

[12] Roemer (1998) examines the boundaries of social intervention to create equality of opportunity.

[13] The result is even stronger: *social welfare functions that are of the form* $W = W(V_0(U_0), \ldots V_t(U_t) \ldots)$ *rank matrices with the same eigenvector the same (in steady state), even when the period-by-period social welfare functions are not separable themselves.*

[14] As the previous note makes clear, even rejecting time separability at the level of society does not fully resolve the paradox. Moreover, the axioms underlying time separability (Harsanyi, 1955) have a certain degree of persuasiveness. Should the marginal rate of substitution between the utility of generation t and $t+1$ depend on the utility levels of earlier or succeeding generations? Although one may be concerned about an individual's parents, should the grandparents, or great grandparents, be relevant?

[15] There is a possible objection to this approach. Although the poor may prefer B over A, they may be so much better off that, behind the veil of ignorance, under, for example, matrix B individuals who put some weight on the welfare of their descendants, they might actually prefer to begin life poor, given that poverty gives their descendants better opportunities later. We may wish to restrict ourselves to matrices such that there is sufficiently limited mobility that, behind the veil of ignorance, all individuals would prefer to be born rich rather than poor.

this section, are contained in appendix A, of Stiglitz (2000b). See also Chapter 22 in this volume.

Our sense of the circumstances in which one transition matrix is more egalitarian than another may be sharpened if we look at two special cases. Assume first there are only two income groups in the economy. Consider two transition matrices A and B. In this case it can be shown that A is more egalitarian than B (in the sense of the egalitarian mobility ranking) if and only if A and B have the same steady-state distribution (that is, the same eigenvector), and $a_{11} < b_{11}$ (fewer of the low-income people get stuck in the low equilibrium).

Most matrices cannot be compared by this criterion (if they have different levels of expected income they cannot even be ranked under the standard Atkinson and Rothschild–Stiglitz criteria). In some cases the comparison is trivial; assuming there is an equality-preferring social welfare function with positive marginal social utility of income, any matrix with both a higher mean income and a lower probability of staying poor would be preferred. In this case there is no trade-off. The more difficult case comes in comparing matrices where there is a trade-off between a better asymptotic distribution but less mobility.

In the 2×2 case, the criterion of *egalitarian mobility* provides a complete ranking of matrices that generate the same asymptotic distribution of income. In the $n \times n$ case, for $n > 2$, it does not. To provide a more complete ordering, we might want to impose further conditions, a task to which we shall turn shortly.

3.2 Alternative Approaches

There are, in fact, at least two distinct ideas of what might be meant by an "egalitarian" transition matrix. One is captured by the idea of equality of opportunity, that a person's lifetime chances are independent of his or her parents' income.[16] The other captures the idea of compensation, that those whose parents have a low income have a greater chance of doing well, so that "dynastic utility," some way of weighing the levels of utility of successive generations together, is less unequal.

In the 2×2 case, perfect equality (equality of opportunity) in the first sense is attained by the matrix

$$\begin{pmatrix} .5 & .5 \\ .5 & .5 \end{pmatrix} \tag{23.4}$$

or by the matrix

$$\begin{pmatrix} .2 & .8 \\ .2 & .8 \end{pmatrix}. \tag{23.5}$$

[16] In formal terms, $a_{ij} = a_{kj}$ for all i, k where a_{ij} is the probability of being in income group j, given that one's parent is in income group i. The probability of an individual's being in state j does not depend on his parents' state (socioeconomic condition).

The perfect equality in the second (compensation) sense is attained by the matrix

$$\begin{pmatrix} 0 & 1 \\ 1 & 0 \end{pmatrix}. \tag{23.6}$$

The children of the rich are poor, and the children of the poor are rich. In ranking matrices with the same steady-state income distribution, the second criterion prefers matrices with small $a_{11}(a_{22})$, while the first criterion prefers matrices in which $|a_{11} - a_{21}|$ is smaller. The two give quite different rankings.[17]

Standard individualistic, non-separable, quasi-concave (equality-preferring) dynastic utility functions possessing the usual properties of anonymity can be used to motivate the second criterion. Dynastic utility will be more equal if there is at least some degree of compensation.

3.3 Non-separable Utility Functions

More generally, one can use non-separable utility functions to provide a complete ranking of matrices. One simple non-separable utility function ranks $W[U(\sum \delta^t Y_t)]$, that is the utility of lifetime dynastic incomes generated by the stochastic process. (This is the same ranking that would emerge if the mobility matrix described an individual's income process, there were perfect capital markets, and we wished to rank matrices by a standard social welfare function.) Clearly, standard results of Rothschild and Stiglitz, Atkinson, and Dasgupta, Sen, and Starrett imply that matrix A will be preferred to B by all social welfare functions that are equality-preferring and anonymous (symmetric), if the Lorenz curve of the present discounted value of income associated with A lies inside that of B.[18]

This is, however, not the only plausible non-separable utility function. The marginal rate of substitution between income of generation t and $t+1$ should not depend on income of generations before $t-1$ or after $t+2$, that is, interdependence should be limited to at most four generations (one's great-grandfather matters, but not one's great-great-grandfather). Then the social welfare function will be of the form:[19]

$$W = W[\ldots V_t(Y_t, Y_{t+1})\ldots]. \tag{23.7}$$

Consider V taking on two limiting shapes. The first case I will call quasi-Rawlsian. In steady state the minimum income attained each period is the same, and so it is natural to assume

[17] For further discussion of the difference between these two concepts, see Atkinson (1971), Shorrocks (1978), and Kanbur and Stiglitz (1986).

[18] Atkinson (1970); Dasgupta, Sen, and Starrett (1973); and Rothschild and Stiglitz (1973). Kanbur and Stiglitz (1986) and Conlisk (1989) provide sufficient conditions for this to occur for monotone matrices (see the definition in appendix *A* of the original paper).

[19] With full separability, social welfare depends solely on each individual's utility, with no concern for the relationship between the income of a parent and a child. The equation below is the simplest symmetric social welfare function chat embodies direct interdependence between a parent and child. But one of the implications of this interdependence is that to evaluate the marginal rate of substitution of income between these two generations we need to have data concerning income (consumption) levels of *four* generations.

that society simply wants to minimize the number of people for whom either the parent or the child are in that minimum state. The ranking places all the weight on the likelihood that someone in the best-off state remains there.

The alternative extreme is given by $V = V(Y_t + \delta Y_{t+1})$. In this case, A will be preferred to B if

$$(I + \delta \mathrm{A})(I + \delta \mathrm{B})^{-1} \geq 0. \tag{23.8}$$

4 The Importance of Process over Outcomes

I have argued that we care not just about the distribution of income but also about income dynamics. A society in which people inherit their position is, at least in current views, less fair than a society in which they have a more equal chance to attain different positions within the income distribution.

More broadly, we care about the *process* by which inequality is generated, what generates the elements of the transition matrix. There seem to be at least two principles that affect our attitudes about the *process* generating inequality, *fairness* and *individual responsibility.* Neither concept is precisely defined, as some of the following discussion should make clear.

The idea of fairness is reflected in the value placed on equality of opportunity. One would prefer life choices not to be determined by the roll of dice, but if that is to be the case, one would prefer that the dice not be loaded. One implication of this is that inequality that arises out of luck seems more acceptable than inequality that arises out of inheritance (either of physical or human capital), so long as the chances are the same for everyone. I shall return later to this idea of equality of opportunity.

But not all inheritances are equivalent. For instance, it makes a difference whether the inheritance is an inheritance of ability rather than of physical capital. Why? Presumably because ability is an intrinsic property of the individual; it reflects the individual's own "worth" even if he received that "gift" through no action of his own, just as in the case of inherited physical capital.

Similarly, inequality that is a result of differences in people's willingness to work hard seems more acceptable than inequality that arises from either luck or inheritance. Again, this is because it is an intrinsic attribute of the individual. It reflects a sense of individual responsibility, a consequence of a person's own actions rather than gifts, either gifts of nature or gifts from parents. People who receive higher incomes from working harder "deserve" higher income.

But the line between inherited differences in incomes and inequalities arising from individuals' actions is more blurred. We pay some attention to the fact that willingness to work hard may be an inherited attribute (either genetically or through parental influence). We are more sympathetic, for instance, to those who succeed against all odds.

The principle of individual responsibility—by which inequalities that arise from people's own actions are more acceptable than inequalities that arise from other sources—extends beyond simply the decision about how hard or long to work. There are other choices, too, that give rise to inequality: individuals decide on a level of risk taking. Those who are willing to take more risk have a better chance of a high income but also a better chance of a low income.

The idea of fairness that underlies this discussion of the inequality generating process is markedly different from Rawls's idea, which focuses only on *outcomes*. In Rawls's view, a just society should be judged simply on how it treats its worst-off person. I would argue that our views of what is a just society are also affected by our perceptions of the rules of the game. It makes a difference whether the rules give each of us an equal chance of being the worst-off person.[20] We care that the rules are fair. But because we often cannot tell whether they are or are not fair, we also care about how they are determined.

Some might argue that I am confusing attitudes toward inequality with the trade-offs associated with more or less inequality. To be sure, one of the reasons we care about individual responsibility is that if people are not rewarded for working hard or for taking risks, there will be no incentives to work hard or take risks. If, for instance, government always offsets the gains and losses associated with risk taking, individuals would have no basis to make rational decisions concerning trade-offs between risks and rewards (total returns). Our views about the degree of acceptable inequality are affected by these trade-offs. Optimal tax theory is based on using a social welfare function to balance carefully these trade-offs.[21] I am, however, trying to make a somewhat different argument: that our feelings about inequality itself, like our feelings about individual responsibility, are not just instrumental; that is, our willingness to accept inequality is not just that, for example, it results in more resources for society, which (were I a Rawlsian) might enable an improvement of the welfare of the worst-off individual. Rather, it is that our attitudes toward inequality are mixed with other, primitive concepts concerning a desirable society, that our sense of fairness and individual responsibility goes beyond simply the more traditional "functional" view that has been emphasized in the economics literature. *Unequal outcomes that serve a social function, are arrived at fairly, or are a consequence of individual exercise of responsibility are more acceptable than those that are not.*

While Rawls may have focused on outcomes, Rawls' *method* provides a way of think about what are fair or just *processes* as well as outcomes: what are processes that would be chosen *behind a veil of ignorance.*

4.1 Ex Post versus Ex Ante Expected Utility and Societal Implications of Free Choice

The views presented here are not universally accepted. For instance Ravi Kanbur (1987) has argued that society cares about ex post inequality even when it is a result of risk that is voluntarily engaged in. Part of the reason for his argument is that he is concerned

[20] Rawls motivated his argument that the just society worried about the worst-off individual by thinking about infinitely risk-averse people focusing on outcomes behind a veil of ignorance. The question is, "In thinking about justice, do individuals think about outcomes or processes?" Would they prefer a system in which individuals have a fair chance of attaining different outcomes, but where there is, for instance, some scope for them to exercise individual responsibility to avoid the worst outcome, or a system in which the outcome of the worst-off individual is guaranteed to be slightly better, even though all other outcomes are worse? Rawls has been extensively criticized for implicitly assuming all individuals, behind the veil of ignorance, assume that they are infinitely risk averse, even though no person may actually exhibit that degree of risk aversion.

The focus on process implies that we do not even have to make judgments about what our utility function will be behind the veil of ignorance.

[21] For an exploration of this idea in a setting that shows that individuals may never extract from their experience what that trade-off is, see Piketty (1995).

that individuals may make *irrational* decisions based on misperceptions of probabilities. Clearly the work of Daniel Kahneman and Amos Tversky (1972, 1973) showing that there are systematic deviations between individual risk perceptions and objective probabilities provides support for those concerns. But to the extent that this provides a reason for redistribution (for a concern about the resulting inequality), it suggests a form of paternalism: we are concerned about the resulting inequality just as we are concerned about people taking drugs because they are taking actions that are not in accord with their own best interest.

How to deal with irrational risk perceptions is, in a sense, no different from how to deal with other kinds of misperceptions. People underestimate the return to investing in school or the consequences of taking some drug (for example, the dangers of addiction). A society that is based on the principle of individual responsibility says that individuals must bear the consequences of those decisions. A society based on paternalism says that people should not have the right to exercise their individual responsibility when someone else (the government) believes that they will not exercise it well in some important arena. The difficulty with the extreme version of individual responsibility is that it may generation levels of deprivation that a humane society cannot tolerate, and so the government feels forced to provide assistance; but this means that the individual's actions may impose external costs on others. The difficulty with the paternalistic doctrine is that it is often hard to draw the line: whose judgment and what criteria? There are innumerable instances of governments taking what, in retrospect, we view as overreaching actions—from prohibitions on alcohol to attempts to prohibit certain consensual relationships among adults. Should taking undue risk be added to those instances in which the government should exercise paternalistic powers? And if so, where are the bounds?

For analytic purposes we need to distinguish instances of such irrationality from those in which people have rational perceptions but perhaps differ in their attitudes toward risk (some people may be risk lovers) or in their human and physical capital. Then, if we believe in the Pareto principle, a society that allows individuals to engage in bets that may increase ex post inequality but increase everyone's ex ante expected utility must be preferable to one that restricts such trades. All people in one society are better off (or at least as well off) than in the other unless a compelling case can be made that there are significant externalities associated with the ex post inequality. Yet at the same time, just as we were concerned before about individual responsibility and how inequality was generated *because of the implications for the fundamental nature of society,* so too here. Ex post inequality—no matter how generated, even if a part of a Pareto-efficient resource allocation—may be of concern because of the consequences it has for the nature of society.[22]

Attention does accordingly have to be paid to ex post outcomes, although I still believe that we should focus more on the distribution of ex ante utilities than ex post outcomes.

There is a category of risks that requires special attention: those that are involuntarily undertaken. The argument before was that if people voluntarily engage in risk-taking activities, it increases their ex ante expected utility, and the Pareto principle, combined with a skepticism about paternalism, suggests that we should focus on their ex ante expected utility. But this argument does not apply to risks thrust upon a person. A society in

[22] The distribution of political power may depend on the distribution of wealth. Excessive wealth inequality may thus undermine democracy.

which companies release high levels of pollutants, so that there is a higher risk of cancer, imposes an additional risk (additional dispersion in ex post outcomes) without an offsetting increase in ex ante expected utility. The additional risk is not a result of individuals' exercise of individual responsibility.

I have tried to give some sense of ranking of different sources of inequality. It would be nice if one could give more precision to these ideas and be able to derive them from some higher-order principles. Such an approach might attempt, for instance, to provide some axiomatic basis to the concepts of fairness and individual responsibility and then formulate a social welfare function that places weight on the outcomes, the transitions, *and* the fairness of the process by which those transitions occurred.

5 The Nature of Society

One of the reasons that we care about inequality and the processes by which it is generated is that we believe it has a fundamental impact on society. A society in which people perceive themselves as facing a fair game in which there is equality of opportunity is fundamentally different from a society in which some people, simply by right of birth, have attained a position of privilege. The views of individuals—of themselves, of their responsibilities to themselves as well as to others—may be markedly different in the two situations, and these perceptions may well affect behavior, including social interactions.

There are some concerns that go beyond those raised so far, where I have taken "utility functions" (behavior) as given, not shaped by the environment in which people live. But we know that this assumption is not valid, and although we have great difficulties in formulating generally accepted approaches to welfare analysis with endogenous individuals, still our concept of a just society may well take into account how the *rules* of society themselves shape the people in it.

So far, my focus has been on showing that in ranking societies we look not only at *outcomes,* the distributions of income, but at the *dynamics* that determine those outcomes (the transition matrices) and the underlying forces, the *processes,* that determine the dynamics. Matters are still more complicated than the above discussion suggests. The mobility in the society as described by the transition matrix may itself be a function of the distribution of income. This may be because the transitional matrix is an expression of institutional arrangements, which are themselves endogenous. A plausible example of this comes from agriculture in developing countries. In circumstances of great inequality the institution of sharecropping will emerge, solidifying the unequal distribution. But when land is distributed in a more egalitarian manner, farms will be owner managed, resolving the agency costs and making it easier for small farmers to maintain or even extend their property. In this case there may be multiple equilibria land distributions: a highly unequal distribution would tend to perpetuate itself as would a highly equal distribution.[23]

Algebraically, we could define the transition matrix as a function of the income distribution $A(Y)$ and then a steady-state income distribution would be Y^*, satisfying $A(Y^*)$ $Y^* = Y^*$. In these circumstances there may exist multiple equilibrium distributions. Even

[23] For an early discussion of this, see Braverman and Stiglitz (1989). For an excellent example of such dynamics, see Banerjee and Newman (1993).

if economies were valued simply by their transition matrices, those matrices are now *functions* and the task is to rank not a matrix of numbers but a matrix of functions. The difficulties are highlighted by the fact that some of the equilibrium distributions associated with $A(Y)$ may be preferable to some of the equilibrium distributions associated with $B(Y)$, but other of the equilibrium distributions may be strictly less preferred, while still others may not be rankable.

The dependence of the stochastic process on the wealth distribution raises another set of issues: while traditionally economists have focused on trade-offs (for example, between inequality and average income), in the presence of agency costs more egalitarian distributions may actually lead to higher average incomes.[24] There may even be Pareto-efficient redistributions. Clearly, from the perspective of evaluating outcomes, such redistributions (as those associated with land reforms) should increase welfare; but once the *process* of redistribution is taken into account, critics might claim that such redistributions are not desirable. By contrast, advocates of such redistributions might argue that even if they lead to lower incomes, they may be desirable, especially if they undo inequalities that were created through unjust processes.

6 Application: Inheritance Taxes

Inheritance taxes provide an interesting context within which to explore views about inequality. Most advanced industrial countries have adopted inheritance taxes. Such taxes reflect broadly held views of ethical principles. I want to consider how such taxes can be interpreted through various models of equality.

In many standard utilitarian analyses, inheritances smooth consumption across generations, and thus appear desirable. But the resulting inequalities of wealth affect the nature of society. Inheritances do result in inequality of opportunity: those who inherit more have opportunities opened up for them that are not available to others.[25] We worry too that a society in which people attain positions of status (high income) as a result of inheritance is, in some fundamental way, different from societies in which position is attained on the basis of each individual's own work.

Indeed, even when inheritances are Pareto improvements, society may wish to discourage them. Allowing an individual to give money to his children *increases* his welfare and that of his children. In the absence of envy it has no direct adverse effects on anyone else. Yet such a transfer does result in inequalities of opportunity.

These conflicts between equality of opportunity, individual rights, and the Pareto principle in the context of inheritances of wealth are troublesome enough. But consider the problem of human capital. Some parents may "invest" more than others in their children. Such investments may lead to inequalities of opportunity. Should such investments be restricted simply because some parent decides he does not want to make these investments? To improve equality of opportunity, should society provide compensation to those who are unlucky enough to be born into families where parents are not willing to make

[24] See, for instance, Stiglitz (1993b, and the references cited there) and Hoff (1994, 1996).

[25] In the previous models, assume some parents care about their children and some do not. Then inheritances smooth consumption within one set but leave consumption in the other set unaffected. Thus inheritances still unambiguously reduce inequality of outcomes, even though they increase inequality of opportunities.

such investments? Should the parents be taxed to finance these investments so that parents who choose not to invest will not be better off than those who do?[26] But does that imply that the parents who want to invest more in their children effectively force others either to do so or to pay the price?

7 Concluding Remarks

Thinking about inheritance taxation provides a good testing ground for our views about social justice and the role of government.[27] The conflict between standard welfare approaches and generally held views concerning such taxes is apparent: utilitarianism suggests even large bequests might be desirable, while broader concepts of social justice are far less supportive of inheritances.

More generally, I have argued that our views of social justice are not well reflected in the standard approach, which focuses on outcomes that can be evaluated using a social welfare function. Widely held views concerning the desirability of social mobility and equality of opportunity and the processes by which inequality is generated cannot be derived from, and are sometimes inconsistent with, standard specifications of social welfare functions. Although I have attempted to articulate the ways in which the standard formulations are deficient, I have not succeeded here in formulating a general alternative. That must await another occasion.

[26] Or should we assume that the parents who choose to invest more must be getting sufficient pleasure out of doing so that in fact we do not need to tax the parents who do not—we should not just focus on direct consumption.

[27] In the original paper, I take up another application, social insurance.

PART III.C
INEQUALITY AND INEFFICIENCY

Introduction to Part III.C

The chapters in this section explore the interactions between inequality and efficiency, and how these in turn affect the dynamics of inequality.

Traditional economics basically ignored the consequences of the distribution of income and wealth for economic efficiency, or more accurately, suggested that *distribution doesn't matter*. The first welfare theorem asserted that the market economy is (Pareto) efficient—and this was true whatever the distribution of income and wealth. And the second welfare theorem said that one could separate issues of distribution from those of efficiency; if one didn't like the distribution of income yielded by the market economy, "all" one had to do was to engage in lump sum redistributions. Nobel Prize economist Robert E. Lucas (2004) put the matter strongly:

"Of the tendencies that are harmful to sound economics, the most seductive, and in my opinion the most poisonous, is to focus on questions of distribution."

Imperfections of information, however, meant that such lump sum redistributions were not possible. "Correcting" the distribution of income necessarily entailed distortionary taxation (see Chapters 19 above and 36 below). Moreover, the greater the degree of inequality, the greater the burden imposed through distortionary taxation.

In addition, with imperfections in information and incomplete markets, the presumption that the market economy was efficient was replaced with a presumption that it was not.

Both the first and second welfare theorems were thus of, at best, limited relevance.[1]

As we noted in the introduction to this volume, there has been a longstanding presumption that there is a "big trade-off"—one can only have more output at the expense of lower output or poorer economic performance. The reason is that to get more equality, one has to impose more progressive—and therefore more distortionary—taxation. But that conclusion is predicated on the efficiency of the market economy. If the market economy is not efficient, then there can be taxes and other interventions which actually increase economic efficiency as they increase equality. For instance, capital market imperfections mean that individuals on their own won't be able to invest sufficiently in human capital; as Chapter 19

[1] See Stiglitz (1989, 1994b) and the references cited there. On the first welfare theorem, see Greenwald and Stiglitz, 1986, 1988d; for an early demonstration of the failure of the second welfare theorem, which goes beyond the inability to impose lump sum taxes, see Shapiro and Stiglitz (1984). For a broader discussion of the first and second welfare theorem, see Stiglitz (1994b).

illustrated, welfare can be increased even by imposing distortionary taxes, when revenues are devoted to public investments.[2]

So too, if inequality itself has adverse economic consequences, then there can be economic benefits from redistribution.

There are two central theses in the chapters in this section: (1) inequality can have an adverse effect on economic efficiency; (2) some of the same forces that lead to inequality impairing efficiency lead to the creation and perpetuation of inequality; they are part of the *endogenous determination of the level of inequality both in the short term and the long (that is, the equilibrium level of inequality, one of the central foci of this book).*

The chapters in this section explore two of the main channels between inequality and inefficiency—that arising from "agency costs," the costs that arise when one individual has to delegate to another the responsibility of managing (or partially managing) an asset in which he has an interest; and capital market imperfections, which limit the ability of those with limited resources to invest sufficiently, either in themselves or in the enterprises in which they are involved, and which result in there not being insurance for many of the important risks that individuals face.

Our theoretical work and those of others in the economics of information has elucidated both of these channels, explaining the nature of these agency costs and how markets address them and why capital markets are inherently imperfect: it's not a little blemish that, as markets advance, will soon be dealt with.

In these introductory remarks, I summarize some of the main insights of this line of research and briefly broaden the discussion, to include some of the other channels through which inequality affects economic efficiency.

Some Personal Reflections

Well before it became politically fashionable to emphasize that extremes of inequality might undermine productivity (as articulated in my *Price of Inequality* (2012)),[3] I had become concerned about the relationship between inequality and efficiency. I suppose my awareness of the issue began as a child growing up in Gary, Indiana, as I saw bright talented people who never were able to live up to their potential because they had never had an adequate education, some because they were African-Americans growing up in a segregated South that persistently engaged in discrimination, some because they didn't have the funds to continue their education, and some because they grew up in a poor neighborhood without good public schools.

My economics training though seemed to suggest otherwise: we focused on competitive markets; we were taught that competitive markets were "normally" efficient, with a few exceptions; and that (as I noted in the beginning of this introduction) in any case issues of efficiency could be neatly separated from those of equity and distribution. Not only did distribution not matter; neither did institutions, like sharecropping. Somehow, in spite of their seeming inefficiencies, beneath the surface things worked out in the same way as they

[2] Similarly, corrective taxes trying to correct for externalities both generate revenue that can be used for redistribution and improve economic performance.

[3] See also the references cited earlier in this book, including in the Introduction to the volume.

would if those institutions did not exist and the compensation of labor were determined as it ordinarily is by the balancing of supply and demand.[4] And because institutions didn't matter, there was little attempt to explain the institutions.

It was my belief that market failures were pervasive and deep rooted with pervasive consequences,[5] and it was this belief that led to my work on information economics, showing that the economy is almost never (constrained Pareto) efficient, or as I put it, Adam Smith's invisible hand (arguing that the pursuit of self-interest led, as if by an invisible hand, to the well-being of society) was invisible because it was not there. I showed that this was true so long as information was imperfect and asymmetric (that is, some individuals knew something that others didn't) or markets were "incomplete" (that is, there were not a complete set of risk and futures markets)—that is, always.

While my Ph.D. thesis had focused on inequality, it was only after I returned from Cambridge, UK to take up a year appointment as an assistant professor at MIT that I began focusing on market failures, in particular those associated with imperfect information and imperfect risk markets. The following summer (1967), I spend several weeks in developing countries in Asia, and it was there that I began to think about what are now called "agency issues" and inequality, in the context of sharecropping, the prevalent institutional arrangement under which billions of farmers around the world toiled the soil. Of course, I had read about sharecropping as the system that prevailed in the South in the years after the Civil War. But seeing this institution through the lens of an economist shed new light on it. There seemed a prima facie case that something was wrong: as we have already noted, this prevailing and persistent economic arrangement seemed to greatly undermine incentives.

Insights into Agency Costs from Sharecropping

The chapters in this part focus on the inefficiencies associated with agency costs, that is, costs that arise in the presence of imperfect and costly monitoring, and illustrate what is at issue by looking at sharecropping, where workers are compensated for their efforts by receiving a fraction (usually half or one-third) of the output. With high inequality in land ownership, sharecropping (discussed more fully below) will be the prevailing form of rural organization. Conservative economists complain about the disincentive effects of even a 40% tax on rich Americans and Europeans. Yet sharecropping entails an effective tax rate of between 50% and 70%.[6] Evolutionary economists believe that inefficient institutional arrangements cannot survive. Yet this is an arrangement that has survived for centuries, and has been little criticized by those of the Right.

The institution itself is a manifestation of inequality: if land and labor were distributed in proportion, workers would generally work on their own land, and the "sharecropping tax" would be eliminated. Presumably, incomes would increase enormously. Another institutional arrangement in agriculture is the plantation, with workers working for fixed

[4] See, for example, Cheung (1969).

[5] In marked contrast to the standard theory, in which there was a short list of instances where markets failed to produce efficient outcomes and simple remedies for each (externalities, like pollution, where "corrective" taxes and regulations restored efficiency; monopolies, where anti-trust laws restored competition).

[6] If there were other taxes, their net return could be substantially less than a third or half of their marginal product.

wages—but here too there is a cost to the inequality: the cost of supervising workers to ensure that they exert adequate effort.

Moreover, with sharecropping (or in the plantation system), it is virtually impossible for ordinary farmers to accumulate sufficient wealth to become landowners. High levels of inequality persist. On the other hand, when land is more equitably distributed, then the more productive arrangement where workers till their own land prevails, and especially if there is some kind of communal social insurance—so those who fall on hardship, say from an illness, don't have to sell their land—the system can persist.[7]

Thus, any government, or international institution, concerned about increasing productivity should think about land reform: A land redistribution that gave sharecroppers their own land should, on this account, lead to a large increase in national output. Land reforms in Japan, Korea, and Taiwan preceded their economic miracles. Poor countries pay a high price for their wealth inequality.[8]

I focus on sharecropping for several reasons. First, it is an extraordinarily important institution, governing the economic relationships of literally hundreds of millions, perhaps even billions, an institutional arrangement that has persisted over the centuries around the world. Secondly, it was in this context that the economics of imperfect information—including what have come to be called agency costs—was most thoroughly analyzed.[9] It provides a pristine context to see the full general equilibrium consequences. But as I emphasized in my 1974 article, discussed more fully below, the insights provided by the analysis of sharecropping are equally applicable to a modern industrial economy, where production technologies and economic relations are more complex, but agency costs associated with inequality are as or even more important.[10]

Explaining Sharecropping

In much of my early work in the economics of information I had used sharecropping to study what happens when we depart from the perfect markets assumptions so beloved by economists. In my 1974 paper (Stiglitz, 1974b), I had formulated the core incentive model (what subsequently came to be known as the principal-agent problem (Ross, 1973)) and is described more broadly as the problem of *agency costs*: landlords cannot perfectly monitor their workers; while rental contracts provide workers with good incentives, with imperfect risk markets, they impose an inefficient risk burden on poor workers, and besides,

[7] Even without that, individuals may be sufficiently well off that they can put aside sufficient funds to enable them to weather even a series of bad harvests.

[8] While land redistribution *may* enable the economy to move from one equilibrium to another, it may not suffice: other inputs (capital in particular) are required, and unless capital markets are sufficiently perfect or land redistribution is accompanied by other wealth redistribution measures, or other measures giving access to finance, the more equalitarian land distribution may not be sustainable. Chapter 25 emphasizes the importance of these credit constraints.

[9] This is partly because of its simplicity, the easy identification of what is and is not observable, the simplicity of the production process, etc. Until the development of the economics of information, the persistence of this seemingly inefficient institution was a mystery—contradicting, as we have noted, economists' faith in market efficiency. See Stiglitz 1974b. The other pristine context in which the consequences of information asymmetries was analyzed was the market for insurance.

[10] Thus, the incentive model I had formulated provided a paradigm for the problems posed by incentivizing managers as well as workers. See Stiglitz (1975b).

workers might not have the resources to pay the contractual rent, especially in bad years. Sharecropping was an institutional arrangement balancing incentives and risk sharing.[11]

While sharecropping and, more generally, a broad range of incentive schemes—both the institution itself and the governing parameters (e.g., the share of output given to the landlord)—might seem optimal from the perspective of the landlord/tenant or employer/employee, it didn't mean that the system was optimal from a societal (general equilibrium) perspective, and, as I noted above, my work with Bruce Greenwald established the opposite presumption: that whenever there was imperfect information or incomplete markets, generically the economy was *not* constrained Pareto efficient, even taking into account the costs of creating markets or obtaining information.[12] A general implication of the Greenwald-Stiglitz (1986) theorem is that while one can easily specify the equilibrium contract between landlords and tenants—given the expected utility level of workers, say with a given price distribution among different commodities, it maximizes the expected utility of landlords—in an economy with more than one good, that contract is not in general (constrained) Pareto efficient.

Inequality gives rise to these information inefficiencies simply because in a world in which land was equally distributed, workers would till their own fields: the adverse incentives associated with sharecropping, the pareto inefficiency of markets, would not arise.[13]

Inequality, Capital Constraints, and Imperfections of Risk Markets

Sharecropping arises from a mismatch of endowments of labor and land. Some (the poor) have little land relative to their labor, while others (landlords) have a great deal. If capital markets were perfect, individuals could borrow or rent, avoiding the distortions of sharecropping. But theories of imperfect information have explained why capital markets are

[11] While one could easily specify what an optimal sharecropping contract might look like, actual sharecropping arrangements differed from these "ideal" arrangements: they were typically far simpler, for example they were linear contracts, with tenants typically receiving either half or a third of the output. And the terms typically did not vary with changing economic conditions. (See the more extensive discussion in Volume I of *Selected Works* (Stiglitz, 2009b.) While my 1974 paper is now widely cited and understood to be one of the founding papers in the literature in the economics of incentives/agency theory, it met considerable resistance in getting published (just as Akerlof's "Theory of Lemons" (Akerlof, 1970) did), testimony to the conservatism of the profession and the difficulties in accepting challenges to the dominant paradigm. In Akerlof's case, some referees even questioned whether it was economics. In my case, the critiques were narrower: why had I *assumed* linear sharecropping contracts (though that in fact appeared empirically to be the case). It would have been easy to use special utility functions for which sharecropping contracts would be linear, but it would have been wrong to do so, since empirically, these utility functions are inconsistent with a wide range of observed behavior. In later work, I and others did try to explain this linearity.

[12] Arrow (1951) and Debreu (1959) had established the efficiency of a competitive market economy *with perfect markets/perfect information*; sharecropping arose in the context of incomplete risk markets/imperfect information. While the problems with markets with imperfect and asymmetric information that Akerlof, Spence, Rothschild, and Stiglitz uncovered in the late 1960s and early 70s suggested that something might be amiss with the efficiency of markets, some had contended otherwise. For instance, Diamond (1967) suggested that an economy with a competitive stock market—without the full set of state-contingent securities—was still efficient, in a precise and particular sense. By the early 1970s, I had begun to disprove the generality of that conclusion. See the introduction to Stiglitz (2009b). See also Stiglitz (1972e, 1982g) and Newbery and Stiglitz (1982b).

[13] Equalization of wealth would, of course, not resolve all market inefficiencies: Risk markets would still be imperfect, and individuals would still want to buy some insurance, and these alone would result in the market being constrained Pareto inefficient. See Newbery and Stiglitz (1982b), Stiglitz (1982g), and Arnott and Stiglitz (1990).

imperfect.[14] Imperfect capital markets worsen the consequences of inequality: the poor not only can't afford to pay for the land they work; they can't afford to pay for other inputs, and this can introduce still other distortions.[15]

Imperfections in risk markets compound the problems. If farmers were to rent land, they would bear the entire brunt of fluctuations in weather. While the plantation system, where workers work for a fixed wage, shifts all the burden of risk to the landlord, who is in the best position to bear the risk, doing so gives rise to other costs—those of monitoring. Sharecropping represents a compromise, but one in which one can plainly see the costs of these informational and market imperfections in terms of attenuated incentives. And because workers are also forced to bear risk, it gives rise to inequalities in wealth, as described in earlier chapters of this book.

Imperfections of risk markets mean too that even if farmers could borrow money to finance inputs and land improvements, the extent to which they would be willing to do so is limited, since they are left to bear the residual risk.

As we note further below, capital constraints and imperfections of risk markets help explain the perpetuation of inequalities in poor agrarian economies—and help explain why land reform is so difficult. Poor farmers are often hit by an adverse event (bad weather or sickness). They can't purchase insurance to protect themselves, and, living hand to mouth they seldom have the savings necessary to manage their way through these calamities. (In many countries, financial institutions that would provide a safe and convenient way of savings do not reach into poor areas.) When these adverse events occur, they have to mortgage their land or sell it, unless there are restrictions on doing so (as there are in some countries). It is the wealthy that provide the funds in these times of need, and it is in this way that land reforms, redistributing land to the poor, are often undone.

Moreover, even in the absence of these extreme events, lack of access to capital at reasonable terms impedes the ability of poor farmers to make the investments in seeds and fertilizers that are desirable, so their yields will be lower than rich farmers.

Broader Perspectives on Why Inequality May Be Bad for Economic Performance

While agency costs associated with inequality are one of the main channels through which inequality hurts economic performance, it is not the only one.

Capital Market Imperfections Impair Opportunity

Of particular relevance here, information imperfections, for instance, led to capital market imperfections, and those in turn meant that the children of the poor could not get the funds

[14] See Stiglitz (2009b, 2013b) and the references cited there.

[15] At one level, in a standard, well-functioning market, there is but a single constraint: that on wealth. The individual could allocate his wealth between "land" and "capital" required for purchase of other inputs. In practice, there are distinct market failures associated with each of these, including the absence of risk markets and large transactions costs associated with each market, so in practice, inequalities in land and inequalities in capital have distinct and separate effects. Many of the issues discussed here are explored in Braverman and Stiglitz (1982, 1986a) and the papers in Hoff, Braverman, and Stiglitz (1993).

necessary to invest in their future, thereby leading to greater inequality and perpetuating inequalities across generations, in the absence of good public education.[16,17]

Efficiency Wage Theory

Another way in which inequality affected efficiency that became clear to me as I began to study development related to what are called *efficiency wage effects*: paying higher wages leads to higher productivity. Earlier, Leibenstein (1957) had focused on one aspect of these efficiency wage effects—when workers were paid too little, they were too weak to be fully productive. This was called the nutritional wage efficiency effect. In my next extensive trip to the developing world, to the Institute of Development Studies at the University of Nairobi (1969–71) I thought about the various economic forces affecting productivity, and how efficiency wage effects might arise even in developed countries—based not on the dependence of physical strength on wages but on other forces.[18] Thus, low wages might affect not only individual's ability to exert effort, as Leibenstein had suggested, but there willingness to exert effort—if employers tried to use their market power to squeeze workers too much, they would not care much if they were fired (the worker-incentive effective[19]). Higher wages could also affect the quality of workers a firm could recruit. I also explored here a set of ideas that would eventually blossom into *behavioral economics* (and more particularly behavioral development economics):[20] low wages, especially when seemingly not "justified" by differences in productivity (for instance, when wages differences are the result of discrimination) undermine morale, and that in turn undermines productivity.[21]

Still another channel through which *wage inequality* affected productivity through efficiency wage effects was search and labor turnover. The greater wage inequality (for workers of similar abilities), the greater aggregate expenditures on search, as those in low paying jobs continue to search for a better paying job. This entails not only greater dissipation of resources on search, but also on turnover costs (e.g., associated with specific training). In a series of papers contained in volume II of *Selected Papers* (2013b), I explain how the market equilibrium will be associated with wage dispersion (even when there is no intrinsic reason for wage differences) and how the market equilibrium will not, in general, be efficient, entailing excessive expenditures on search and turnover costs.[22]

[16] As we have emphasized elsewhere in this book, in particular in Chapter 10, the problem of intertemporal transmission of advantage and disadvantage was deeper than this; it extended to the provision of education in public schools and to cultural patterns that themselves could lead to differences in levels of investment in education.

[17] There are multiple other ways by which inequality in conjunction with capital constraints leads to inefficiencies and can perpetuate inequalities: the poor will not search sufficiently to find a job that best matches their skills; and even when they know of a job with higher productivity, the poor will be impeded from moving to more efficient jobs. See, for example, Delli Gatti, Gallegati, Greenwald, et al. (2012a, 2012b).

[18] I wrote a long paper while at the Institute of Development Studies of the University of Nairobi discussing various efficiency wage models, which I subsequently published in a series of papers (Stiglitz, 1974c, 1982f, 1987b, 1992b and Nalebuff, Rodriguez, and Stiglitz, 1993)

[19] Developed further with Carl Shapiro in (1984).

[20] The subject of a forthcoming book with Hoff and Demeritt.

[21] Subsequently, Akerlof and Yellen (1990) formalized this into a "fair wage" efficiency wage theory.

[22] There is a fundamental externality: firms in deciding on their wages look only at the consequences for their own profitability, not on the induced search and turnover costs of others. See Arnott and Stiglitz (1985), Stiglitz (1974c, 1985b), and Greenwald and Stiglitz (1988d). Most of the subsequent literature on search focused on how individual's search costs, not the corresponding costs imposed by turnover on firms; and largely took the wage

Inequality and Rent Seeking

It is not only the magnitude of inequality that matters, but also how it is generated. Much of inequality is associated with rent-seeking—whether as a result of exploitation of market power (discussed in Chapter 16 above), connections with the government, or taking advantage of those who are less informed. Accordingly, limiting rent-seeking can increase both growth, efficiency and equality.[23]

One particular form of rent-seeking, not normally thought as such, is "ability rent-seeking." When individuals differ in their abilities, and the more able know that they are more able, they will expend resources to appropriate their ability rents, through providing information, for instance, to employers. Providing this information lowers net national product (net of expenditures on information) *and* increases inequality.

That this is so is almost obvious: in the absence of information we treat individuals who are different the same; and that means high and low ability individuals are "pooled" together and get the same wage. Better information then leads to more inequality. This is not just a theoretical curiosity: it helps provide part of the explanation for the growth in inequality. First, the economy has been shifting from manufacturing to a service sector economy. In manufacturing, people work in teams, and it is difficult to identify anyone's individual productivity. Accordingly, they all receive the same pay. (Moreover, industrial unions have campaigned for wage compression.) In the service sector economy to which we are moving, production units are smaller and it is easier to identify individual contributions. There are now more workers in professional sports than in the extractive industries, and it is typically easy to assess the ability of each player. On this account alone there will be an increase in inequality.

Moreover, education plays a more important role in our complex society, and while education adds to "human capital," providing the skills necessary for a modern economy to function, at the same time it also provides information about individual's capacities, especially in certain key dimensions, and this information may enhance inequality.

This was an idea that I explored earlier on in my work in the economics of information. For instance, in Stiglitz (1975a), I analyzed the effect of education *as a screening device*, that is, as a mechanism which differentiates between those with greater and less abilities. I was able to show that the market equilibrium could be characterized by multiple equilibria—a high information equilibrium, where the more able expend considerable resources proving their abilities; and a low information one. The former thus has lower net GDP and more inequality; indeed all individuals could be worse off—it is Pareto inefficient.[24] I suggested that at least some, and perhaps a considerable proportion, of education expenditures were

distribution as given, while our analyses saw wages as being set by firms, maximizing (expected) profits, so that the wage distribution had to be viewed as endogenous. We showed that even if firms were identical, there could be an equilibrium wage distribution. (Obviously, differences in the circumstances of firms and the shocks they confronted would give rise to wage distributions.) Moreover, there are not only inefficiencies in the level of search and labor turnover, there may be inefficiencies in *who* searches.

[23] The incentive to invest and to engage in research of those with market power may be less than in more competitive markets. See Arrow (1962) and Stiglitz and Greenwald (2014). Moreover, as Chapter 16 emphasized, an increase in "rent-wealth" leads to less investment in real capital.

[24] These results do not depend on there initially existing any asymmetries of information—the high ability individuals may not know that they are high ability. There will be excessive expenditures in finding out about one's abilities, and then, if one is one of the higher ability individuals, in ensuring that this is known by the market. See Stiglitz (1984).

directed at this kind of differentiation, rather than the formation of human capital; and that to the extent that education performed this "screening" function, there would be a discrepancy between social and private returns.[25,26]

Whether education was socially productive or just screening, capital market imperfections meant that those who were borne of poor parents couldn't get access to as much education as those with better off parents, again implying the perpetuation of inequalities, especially at the top, across generations.

Inequality, Instability, and Growth

For a variety of reasons explored in the next part of the volume, greater inequality may be associated with greater instability, and greater instability (volatility) in turn may lead to poorer economic performance, including lower average levels of income, with even worse impacts on standards of living, especially once one takes into account the cost of insecurity.[27] The instability discourages investment, and induces firms and households to engage in various costly "protective" measures to help them cope with the volatility.[28] Moreover, instability itself can lead to more inequality—with especially adverse effects on those at the bottom of the income distribution.

Other Channels by Which Inequality Impedes Economic Performance: Political and Social Consequences

Political economy provides an additional set of explanations for how inequality may weaken economic performance.[29] Economic inequality leads to political inequality. Those with wealth often want to curb government spending on high return public investments in infrastructure, education, and technology and curb efficiency enhancing government regulations, with the result that the economy is less productive. This may be partly because of ideology—disproportionately, they may believe that unfettered markets with a small government works best—after all, it worked well for them. But it may also be simply self-interest. With large numbers earning their wealth as a result of rent-seeking, the last thing they want is for government to curb rent-seeking opportunities, for example by ensuring that markets are more competitive. Another reason may be that when there is a high level of inequality, the rich worry that too strong of a government will result in using its powers

[25] The idea of education as a screening device is closely related to Spence's analysis of education (1973) as a signalling device—where the more able stay in school longer to signal that they are more able. (While Spence suggests that his signalling model generates multiple equilibria, his conclusion is the result of his failure to pay due attention to certain boundary value conditions. See Stiglitz (2002a). See also Arrow (1973) and Stiglitz (1974h).) For empirical evidence in support of the screening vs. human capital hypotheses, see Weiss (1988, 1995).

[26] There are a host of other ways in which more information can lead to more inequality, contexts in which there are incentives to provide information, leading to lower net output and greater inequality: knowing that individuals have certain genes exposing themselves to a greater likelihood of certain genetic diseases will increase the premia that they pay in competitive insurance markets. In markets where there is persistent discrimination, as discussion in Part III.E, when direct discrimination is banned, discrimination may occur by identifying correlated variables. See Rothschild and Stiglitz (1997).

[27] Insecurity, and the stress which it generates, itself can have adverse effects on productivity.

[28] The consequences are particularly severe when there are credit constraints. Ignoring these constraints (as Lucas, 1987, does) can lead to a large underestimate of the costs of volatility.

[29] Still other aspects of the relationship between inequality and efficiency are discussed in Part III.D.

not just to provide public goods, but also to redistribute income and wealth; though they benefit from the former, they worry about the latter. Moreover, the rich may rely less on these publicly provided goods.

Inequality may also have social consequences—changing the nature of society in ways which impact (adversely) economic performance. As we have discussed elsewhere in this book, preferences are largely culturally determined, affected by our surroundings. Those at the top in a highly unequal society often have a sense of entitlement, those at the bottom a sense of disempowerment, both of which may contribute to undermining effort. Cooperation, so essential for a well-functioning society, may be more difficult in a more divided society.[30]

An important channel through which inequality affects economic performance is discussed more extensively in Part III.F: discrimination. Its effects on both inequality and productivity are obvious—though some economists seem to have challenged the obvious.

A Two-Way Relationship

The previous paragraphs have highlighted some of the ways in which inequality leads to inefficiencies or otherwise affected economic performance. But inequality itself is *endogenous*, a consequence of the functioning of the economic, political, and social system. Chapter 12, for instance, described the equilibrium income and wealth distribution, affected by key structural properties of the economic system and key policy variables.

There, and in other chapters, we noticed certain feedback mechanisms, leading wealth to beget wealth. This introduction, and the chapters included in this part, represent my exploration of several of these feedback mechanisms.

Sometimes, these feedbacks can be so strong that there are multiple societal (political/economic) equilibria—a high inequality, low performance economy; or a low inequality, high performance one. Previous chapters have outlined several examples of this; for instance, how high economic inequality translates into a high level of political inequality, resulting in turn in rules of the game which lead in turn to high levels of economic inequality (Chapter 16).

In the following paragraphs, I summarize some of the ways that information, information imperfections, and market failures more generally give rise to inequality.

Efficiency Wage Theory Can Give Rise to Inequality

As we explained, efficiency wage theory argued that firms would pay a wage higher than the minimum at which they could recruit workers—higher than the market clearing wage—either to ensure that workers did not shirk, or to lower turnover costs, or simply to ensure they had the physical strength to do their work. Even if all workers were ex ante equal, this creates inequality: between those with jobs and the unemployed (and there was, in these models, always an equilibrium level of unemployment). But there are other consequences: small differences in individuals' circumstances (e.g., ability) might lead to large differences in outcomes, with the more able individuals fully employed, the less able unemployed.

[30] For further elaboration of these points as well as evidence, see Demeritt, Hoff, and Stiglitz (forthcoming).

Workers in industries where shirking might be difficult to detect or where the consequences of shirking were great (the breakage of an expensive machine) might get paid much higher wages than otherwise similar workers in other industries or jobs.

Indeed, in Stiglitz (1976d) I showed that with the nutritional wage model, a landlord would pay some workers the efficiency wage, leaving others simply unemployed. He would feed them on the job, to make sure that they did not fully share their income with their families, which would attenuate the efficiency benefits of paying high wages.[31]

Inequality, Power, and Hierarchy

There were some troubling aspects of inequality and the mechanisms by which it was created and perpetuated, some of which were very much in the air in the 1960s when I began this work. One was related to power, a concept that economists at the time had a hard time coming to terms with, though in subsequent decades, game theory provided tools which enabled them to deal more formally with something that was clearly of importance. In the standard model, it made no difference whether workers hired (or rented) capital goods, or capitalists hired workers. There was perfect symmetry. "Control" didn't matter. In the standard model, what would be done would be exactly the same under alternative organizations. But that seemed nonsensical. There are huge fights over control.[32] As I was working on these papers, I was coming to an understanding of why control mattered—and again it came down to the existence of an incomplete set of markets and imperfections of information.[33] Later work would explicate the implications for the design of economic arrangements,[34] with there being a delegation of "residual" control of decision making to specific parties over certain aspects, and provisions for renegotiations and joint determination over others (with fall-back consequences in the event of a failure to reach agreement).[35]

In practice, in organizations control is organized hierarchically: managers control workers, not the other way around.[36] And that raises another aspect of inequality: inequalities in power and control, in decision making. Of course, if the decisions made didn't depend on

[31] Dasgupta and Ray (1986) develop further the nutritional efficiency wage model. This result is a reflection of a more general result noted earlier: with the usual assumptions concerning diminishing returns, social welfare is maximized by equality, but in the presence of non-convexities, social welfare is maximized by inequality, sometimes achieved through randomization (the expected utility of an individual is higher if confronted with a lottery). See Stiglitz (1982b), Arnott and Stiglitz (1988a), and Brito, Hamilton, Slutsky, and Stiglitz (1995).

[32] See Grossman and Stiglitz (1977, 1980b).

[33] See Stiglitz (1985a).

[34] Managerial incentive schemes, it was often argued, were designed to efficiently align the interests of mangers with those of the owners. In a series of papers, I tried to debunk that theory, showing that one could design much better incentives, with lower risk-bearing on the part of managers. See Stiglitz (1982c, 1987c) and Nalebuff and Stiglitz (1983a, 1983b).

[35] The theory of "residual control" was first developed by Grossman and Hart (1986). But, as some of the subsequent literature made clear, assigning residual control to one party (the "capitalists") is too simplistic: different agents may have residual control in different domains, and control rights may be partially restricted, with rights to renegotiate, and with often ambiguously defined consequences of an agreement is not reached. For a survey of the broader issue of the theory of the firm, see Holmstrom and Roberts (1998) and the introduction to Part V of Volume III of *Selected Works* and the works cited there (Stiglitz, 2019c).

[36] In my early work, I spent a great deal of time trying to understand the role of hierarchy in our society, as evidenced by the title of my 1975b paper, "Incentives, Risk, and Information: Notes Toward a Theory of Hierarchy." In work with Raj Sah (Sah and Stiglitz 1985, 1986, 1988a, 1988b, 1991) I tried to understand the advantages and disadvantages that hierarchy provided in decision making.

who made the decisions, this wouldn't make any difference for outcomes. But the outcomes do depend on who makes the decisions, and individuals care not just about outcomes, but about processes.[37]

Equally important, if, as we have suggested, who makes decisions does matter, then economic arrangements with inequalities in decision making will result in inequalities in outcomes: it makes a difference, for instance, if employers can determine the work-schedules of their employees, paying little attention to their concerns and needs.[38] Standard theory said that in a perfectly competitive economy, an employer who engaged in such practices would have to pay a compensating wage differential to attract workers. But this assumes that markets are far more perfect than in fact they are. "Imperfect" economies (without perfect information, perfect competition, etc.) are not, in general Pareto efficient: those exercising power look only to the benefits that they receive and the costs they pay, and those may have little to do with the costs borne by others. They will undertake actions which increase their bargaining power and hence the outcomes *they* receive. This is especially so in the presence of imperfections in reputation mechanisms in markets with high unemployment and/or a limited number of employers, where mistreating current workers may have limited effects on the wages that have to be paid for future workers.[39] It may also be true when there are imperfections in managerial incentive systems (as there always are), so that managers do not even fully take into account costs borne by firms, for example in the higher wages that they might later have to pay in the future. They only focus on the short run savings in profits that accrue from their managerial actions.

A particularly important aspect of managerial decision-making concerns the development and implementation of new technologies. Standard theories of induced innovation[40] argued that firms will focus more on, say, labor-saving innovation if the costs of labor (relative to other factors of production) are greater. But managers include in their assessment of costs their managerial costs, but do not include in their assessment the induced unemployment that might result from reducing labor inputs. Workers, on the other hand, aware that they might one day be back looking for a job, would be concerned about any induced unemployment, and so would society more generally. In Chapter 17 above I show, for instance that the market's decision about factor bias is not in general efficient.

There is one more potentially important consequence of decision-making power: decisions about how hierarchical the organization of production and other aspects of decision making should be, and associated decisions about technology, which affect the ease of implementing hierarchical decision-making structures. Those with power may decide to organize production in ways which enhance their power, and to pursue technologies which enhance their ability to control others. We may then end up with a structure of production which is more hierarchical than is socially desirable or efficient (in terms of production)—with greater inequality in power and incomes.[41]

[37] Though it may be that they care about processes partly because they know that the control of processes affects outcomes. Thus, arguing about "good processes" is but an indirect way of attempting to ensure "good outcomes."

[38] There has been enormous concern about on-call scheduling and other abuses of managerial discretion in the U.S. in recent years. See Stiglitz (2019b).

[39] Even more so if workers are short-sighted, and don't fully take on board fully the possibility of abuse of authority.

[40] See, for instance, Chapter 17 and the references cited there.

[41] I began pursuing these issues in the context of simple models of agency in the early 1970s. For instance, in my 1974 sharecropping model, I compared the efficiency of direct supervision in say plantations (a hierarchical

The Perpetuation of Inequality

My concern in these papers was thus not just the consequences of inequality on efficiency, but understanding better the processes which lead to the perpetuation of inequality, in its multiple dimensions: inequalities not just in wages, but in voice and power.[42] There are numerous links between the variables: Lack of power and voice may lead to less effort and lower efficiency, and especially through the political realm, to rules which reinforce the inequalities. We have noted too that the decisions managers make may be neither efficient nor socially desirable but serve to enhance their power and perpetuate inequalities.

Some Policy Implications

There are three important policy corollaries to the insights that markets on their own are not in general efficient, that the extent of inefficiency may be affected by inequality, and that there is an equilibrium level of inequality, itself affected by the structure of markets: government intervention may be desirable, some of the interventions should take the form of redistribution, but interventions should not be limited to the redistribution of income or assets; and without more pervasive interventions, inequalities, with their attendant costs, will rearise. It is accordingly important to distinguish between the short run effects of any intervention and the longer run consequences.

The research described here and elsewhere in this book has identified several types of inefficiencies, several ways in which government intervention can reduce the inefficiencies upon which we focus here.

In some cases, as we have noted, there may exist multiple equilibria—an equilibrium with a low level of inequality and another with a high level of inequality.[43] The high inequality equilibrium may generate lower output and a lower level of social welfare. A society can get trapped in a high inequality/low performance trap. In such cases, intervention can move the economy from a bad equilibrium to a good one. The intervention may be time-limited: once the government moves the economy from the bad to the good equilibrium, the good equilibrium is self-sustaining.

In other cases, the intervention is to *shift* the equilibrium. The interventions can take three forms: (a) When inequality gives rise to inefficiency, reducing the equilibrium level

structure) with sharecropping (a more decentralized production mode). The next year, I published a paper explicitly addressing these issues, with a subtitle: "Notes toward a Theory of Hierarchy" (Stiglitz, 1975b). Chapter 26 explicitly addresses the incentives of landlords (managers) in choosing technologies that advance their well-being, at the expense of society more generally, and workers in particular.

Later, while I was serving as chairman of the Council of Economic Advisers, looking at the evidence on how more participatory workplaces not only delivered greater worker satisfaction for many workers, but also increased productivity, I suggested that we should try to think about how we could encourage them and greater worker voice in firm decision-making. See Stiglitz (2000c, 2001b) and the papers cited there.

One of the reasons for these productivity effects is improved morale; another is that because workers may be "closer to the ground" and therefore may understand better how to increase productivity. Later, policies to encourage ESOPs (employee stock ownership plans) became standard fare, though I worried about the consequences for risk diversification, with an individual's human capital and retirement wealth excessively correlated.

[42] In an important study conducted while I was chief economist of the World Bank, called the *Voices of the Poor* (Narayan et al., 2000) thousands of poor were interviewed to ascertain the dimensions of poverty and inequality that they found most oppressive. Obviously, lack of income was one. But lack of voice was another.

[43] Similar to the multiple equilibria that we discussed in Chapter 16.

of *market* inequality improves economic performance. Rather than there being a *trade-off* between economic performance and equality, the two can be complementary. (b) Reducing after-tax and transfer inequality through redistribution. (c) There are a variety of interventions that reduce the economic consequences of the distortions associated with inequality—recall the Greenwald–Stiglitz (1986) theorem showing that whenever there are "agency costs," including those that arise as a result of inequality, the market is not (constrained) Pareto efficient, so there are interventions that can improve welfare, for example taxes and subsidies on particular goods and services.

Of course, with equalitarian social welfare functions, policies which reduce inequalities in income and wealth may be doubly blessed, when they simultaneously also increase economic efficiency.

Because redistribution is in general costly, reducing the equilibrium level of inequality—inequalities in market income, today often referred to a pre-redistribution—reduces the burden of redistributive taxation.

We can, accordingly, think of there being several sets of costs associated with inequality: (a) those associated with being trapped in a bad equilibrium; (b) those associated with the reduced output as a result of agency costs and capital constraints often associated with inequality—formally, the incentive compatibility, self-selection, collateral constraints, etc. that inevitably arise: the difference in output with and without such constraints; (c) relatedly, the costs associated with the interventions attempted to mitigate those distortions; (d) the losses that arise from the redistributive taxes and expenditure trying to limit the socially unacceptable inequities associated with inequality, or more generally, to promote higher social welfare.

Comments on Specific Chapters

In the following paragraphs, I provide comments on each of the chapters in this section.

An Overview of Agency Costs and Inequality

Chapter 24 (previously unpublished) was written for a conference at Stanford University just as I was entering the Clinton Administration to serve on the Council of Economic Advisers. In it I provided an overview of the relationship between inequality and "agency costs" (costs associated with monitoring and supervising) that I had been exploring during the previous two decades. I suggested that they are pivotal in understanding the structure of the economy. And my concerns about inequality shaped much of the advice I was to give in the subsequent eight years, in the Clinton Administration and at the World Bank. As I noted earlier in this introduction, it had not yet become conventional wisdom that inequality was bad for economic performance—the opposite view that there was a trade-off was more prevalent.

The chapter explores two sides of the issue. In the first part, I look at the impact of inequality on agency costs, in the second, on how agency costs give rise to inequality.

The relationship between inequality and agency costs is somewhat more complex than I described earlier. I have already explained how a more equalitarian distribution of income could reduce agency costs, as in the examples of sharecropping described above or "unemployment as a worker discipline device," where lack of wealth makes it impossible for individuals to post a bond that they will not shirk.

But there are also instances where greater wealth concentration seemingly might reduce agency costs: where there are large returns to scale, so that an entrepreneur with limited wealth, must get resources from others. Both debt and equity markets are characterized by agency costs. An individual obtaining capital from others may be tempted to cheat them, in one way or another, giving rise to inefficiencies which would not otherwise arise (individuals aren't tempted to cheat themselves).

As I reflect back on this part of the chapter, I think I put too much emphasis on the latter set of agency costs, for two reasons: In practice, decisions get made by *individuals*, and whether a company is owned by a single individual or by a large number of shareholders, these individuals have the ability to pursue their own interests at the expense of that of the organization—there are still agency costs, no matter how concentrated ownership.[44] All firms, regardless of whether ownership is concentrated or disperse, have to motivate their workers.

Moreover, large firms, by and large, resort to raising funds from multiple sources: no single individual, even in a society with high levels of inequality, can provide all the requisite finance, especially if she wants to divest herself of risk. Of course, the ability to cheat suppliers of capital adds an additional set of agency costs, but at least in some economies, government regulations (corporate governance) and market oversight, especially of listed companies, provides some check on abuses.[45]

The second set of issues relates to how agency costs give rise to inequality. There are several mechanisms at play. As just discussed, those with sufficient wealth don't have to bear the consequences of agency costs: total output is lower under share tenancy than under farms that are worked by their owners, and that means that workers with sufficient wealth to avoid these agency costs benefit from the greater efficiency with which land and labor are used.

There are also non-convexities associated with agency costs, resulting in small differences in circumstances giving rise to large differences in outcomes.

The existence of information imperfections (reflected in agency costs) provides managers and others with discretion; and this discretion can often be abused, giving rise to corruption and other rent seeking behavior (Edlin and Stiglitz, 1995). With perfect information, it is obvious that individuals simply could not get away with such behavior. Rent seeking, as we have argued, is one of the major sources of inequality around the world.[46]

Agency Costs: Sharecropping as a Paradigm

As I noted earlier in this introduction, sharecropping provides a "paradigm" for studying the implications of agency costs. The two following chapters in this section continue my

44 Herb Simon (1991) has emphasized this as well.

45 Still, there is evidence that having a single large owner contributes to efficiency, by partially resolving the problem of "the public good is a public good," that is, all shareholders benefit from the good management of a firm. See Stiglitz (1985a).

46 See Stiglitz (2012a, 2019b).

earlier exploration of the insights that sharecropping and thus agency costs more generally has for market economies,[47] here taking up the consequences of and for inequality, leading both to greater inefficiency and to the perpetuation of inequality. As we have already noted, sharecropping, with its attenuation of incentives, would not have occurred had wealth (land ownership) been more equally distributed. The chapters extend the standard analysis of sharecropping by adding capital and the choice of technology. The two chapters focus on two different market failures: Chapter 25 on imperfections of capital markets; Chapter 26 on the distortions in the labor market that arise in sharecropping (the agency costs to which we referred earlier).

In Chapter 25, I explore the consequences of the need for capital to buy, say, good seeds or fertilizer, or to make land improvements. Land redistribution itself, without access to capital, won't ensure efficiency. Thus, equalitarian land reforms will be partially "undone" as poor farmers sell some of their land to rich landowners to obtain the capital they need.

Poor families may, however, be particularly reluctant to sell their land, knowing the destitution that may follow from being landless workers. In the absence of good insurance markets and alternative stores of value, land ownership becomes particularly important. Thus, it may be only in extreme exigencies—when, for instance, the alternative is starvation in the face of a crop failure—that such land sales occur. But the capital shortage then means that the land (and labor) will not be as productive as they otherwise would be.

Chapter 25 extends the analysis in one further direction, on that has preoccupied me greatly since beginning my work on inequality, to consider simultaneously the equilibrium distribution of wealth and tenancy arrangements. If the land (per worker) of a family is close to the average for the economy as a whole, the land will be worked as a family farm—the efficient economic arrangement. But those with very little land or limited capital will effectively sell their labor services to those with a great deal of land and capital, and given the imperfections of risk markets and costly monitoring, the second-best efficient arrangement will be sharecropping.[48] Thus, heuristically, we can think of there being critical values of land and capital (per worker), such that those below the lower thresholds work (at least in part) as sharecroppers for those above the upper threshold.

The wealth (land) distribution at time t determines the prevalent institutional arrangements at that time (e.g., the mix of sharecropping and owner-tilled farms); and that in turn determines the wealth (land) distribution the next period. We describe a simple stochastic process in which land shifts from being tilled by its owner to being sold to a wealthy landowner who will rely on sharecropping, as adverse events occur which deplete the capital of the small farmer, and back again to the more efficient owner-managed land, as a series of good crops enables a farmer to buy back land. A few lucky sharecroppers are thus able to save enough to move into family farming, a few unlucky (e.g., because of a sickness) family farmers sink into sharecropping, and similarly at the top. Since the transition matrix A describing the transitions in land distribution, Ω_{t+1} as a function of Ω_t, is itself a function of Ω_t, (where Ω_1, the first element of the vector Ω is the fraction of those

[47] Beginning with my 1974 paper on sharecropping, inspired by my visits to developing countries, and continued with my 1982 paper with my former student, Avishay Braverman. In that paper, we showed that in the presence of agency costs, there were advantages of interlinking of markets, going against the longstanding presumption of market decentralization, anticipating the more general result of Greenwald and Stiglitz (1986).

[48] For some crops, there is an alternative—wage labor under a plantation system (in instances where the costs of supervision are relatively low, lower than the distortions associated with sharecropping.)

with land endowments so small that they become sharecroppers, and the third element, Ω_3 is the fraction that is so large that they take on sharecroppers), there may be multiple steady states, that is, multiple solutions to $\Omega^* = A(\Omega^*)\Omega^*$. The chapter describes how the inefficient sharecropping system may be an equilibrium, that is, self-perpetuating. A land reform, if accompanied by the appropriate other reforms (access to credit and technology) may lead to a new sustained equilibrium where owner managed farms predominate. Similarly, a change in policy—a government program to provide seed on credit—loosening the credit constraint would be expected to result in a land distribution in which less land is operated under sharecropping, and thus average productivity is increased. (As elsewhere in this Part, results obtained here for simple agrarian economies are suggestive of similar results in a more modern industrial or post-industrial economy.)

Thus, the chapter provides not only a framework for thinking about the distribution of wealth (land), but also about the distribution of institutional arrangements.

The general inefficiency of markets with agency costs and imperfect risk and capital markets means, of course, that we should not expect that the market would be efficient in the choice of technologies (including the crop mix, investments in irrigation, etc.) or the development of new technologies. Chapters 25 and 26 investigates these distortions in greater detail. Within this perspective, recognizing that at any moment of time neither the distribution of wealth or land nor that of tenancy arrangements is optimal (either from the perspective of Pareto efficiency or output maximization), one can see how innovations (or other changes, such as investments in infrastructure) may not be welfare or output maximizing, and long-run effects may be distinctly different from those in the short run.[49] For instance, an innovation that increased average output but increased tail risk might in the short run lead to an increase in average output, but because over the long run, more owners are forced to sell their land (when rainfall is low) and accordingly the fraction of land under share tenancy increases, the resulting loss of output from the increase in tenancy arrangements might exceed the benefits from the increased average productivity. There are, of course, economic reforms which might mitigate these downside risks—crop insurance which reduces risk or cooperatives which enhance the supply of credit.

These potential adverse effects will be strengthened as a result of technological changes which increase the returns to capital, because they too will shift tenancy arrangements towards sharecropping.

As we noted earlier in this introduction, landlords may control the choice of technology (or other choices, such as input choices[50]). Several strong results emerge: When the terms of the contract are fixed (as a result, for instance, of strong norms about "fair" share cropping shares)—seemingly the case in large parts of the world—if the landlord controls the choice of technology, he will obviously maximize output; but that may not be (Pareto) efficient. He may prefer technologies that induce workers to work hard (because of high marginal returns) and take no account of these social costs.

When the terms of the contract are adjustable, a single monopsony landlord will choose a Pareto efficient technology but adjust the terms so that the worker remains at his

[49] As we have noted elsewhere (see, in particular, Chapter 18 and Stiglitz and Greenwald, 2014) the direction of innovation is not in general efficient.

[50] Which they can either specify explicitly or affect indirectly through subsidies. See, for example, Braverman and Stiglitz (1986a).

subsistence (reservation utility) level. All the benefits of innovation go to the landlord—innovations increase inequality.[51]

Thirdly, in a competitive economy, with many landlords, each landlord will ignore the effect of his choice of technology on the equilibrium; accordingly, competition may result in landlords adopting innovations that make them worse off in equilibrium. We identify a simple condition under which this can occur: when the innovation, at the previous level of expected utility of farmers, leads to an increase in optimal plot size.

Fourthly, whether a new technology is adopted may depend on whether there is competition or monopoly; an innovation (or other technology change or investment) which might be desirable in a world with family farms may not be desirable or adopted in a world of sharecropping.[52]

Of course, the new technologies generate a new distribution of wealth, as we have described above; and this new distribution of wealth may well exacerbate the consequences of the market failures. It should be clear that each individual farmer, in making the choice of technology, does not take into account these long-run consequences. Changes that might increase efficiency in the short run could lead to adverse distributional effects, which lower efficiency in the long run.[53] These are among the central messages of Chapter 26.[54]

While the chapter focuses on the two polar cases, of perfect competition and monopoly, it notes that the distortions in the choice of technology may be even greater in the "real" world that lies between these extremes. Exploring the nature of these distortions and their consequences is part of the research agenda going forward.

[51] See, e.g., Hoff, Braverman, and Stiglitz (1993) and the references cited there.

[52] These results thus anticipated the discussion of Chapter 18.

[53] There are other long-run dynamic consequences that tend to be ignored. Technologies at subsequent dates are built on developments today (that is, technological change is "localized"; improvements in the machines producing textiles may have little impact on handlooms). See Atkinson and Stiglitz (1969) and Stiglitz and Greenwald (2014).

[54] Thus, the advances in technology that have led to large reductions in employment in manufacturing did not take into account the full social, political, and economic consequences, including to the health of the working force, leading potentially to a long-term decrease in productivity.

24

Remarks on Inequality, Agency Costs, and Economic Efficiency

1 Introduction

In traditional economic theory, there is a clear dichotomy between issues of economic efficiency and distribution.[1] This is the central message of the Fundamental Theorems of Welfare Economics. Every Pareto-efficient allocation can be attained through a competitive market process. All (!) the government has to do is to engage in a set of lump sum redistributions.

With the development of the economics of information, we now recognize that issues of economic efficiency and distribution cannot be so easily separated. These remarks set out what we know as well as major lines of ongoing theoretical research. In the background, however, are some empirical observations and policy issues, on which, it is hoped, this theoretical work will shed some light, In the concluding remarks, we briefly address these.

2 The Basic Insight

2.1 The Causes and Importance of Agency Costs

Agency costs arise when the owner of an asset has to delegate use of the asset to someone else. They can be seen most clearly in the context of a landlord, whose land is tilled by a tenant. Because tenants are risk averse, the optimal contractual arrangement entails some risk sharing; but the risk sharing attenuates workers' incentives. If the landlord could costlessly monitor the tenant, his contract would specify the amount of labor that the worker would provide. But monitoring is costly, and hence the worker typically provides less labor than he otherwise would have; and the landlord receives a lower expected return than he otherwise would have. Moreover, since the tenant may not bear the full costs of any deterioration in the quality of the land, he may not take sufficient care, for instance, to avoid erosion. Finally, while the landlord may be able to bear risks easily, the tenant may not; hence he may be inclined to grow a crop whose average yield is lower, but for which the risk is lower.

We have identified three separate ways that the interests of the landlord and those of the tenant may differ: in the level of effort exerted, in risk decisions, and in maintaining the value of the assets. These are all examples of *agency costs.*

[1] Originally presented at a workshop on "Economic Theories of Inequality" sponsored by Stanford Institute for Theoretical Economics (SITE), Stanford University, March 11–13, 1993c. This chapter has not previously been published.

The Origins of Inequality, and Policies to Contain It. Joseph E. Stiglitz, Oxford University Press. © Joseph E. Stiglitz (2025).
DOI: 10.1093/oso/9780198799580.003.0025

Let us look more closely at the essential ingredients that went into the creation of these agency costs. First, there must be two (or more) parties involved in an economic relationship. Secondly, the actions of at least one of the parties (called the agent) must affect the other (called for simplicity here the principal)[2] in some "ongoing" way. This should be distinguished from simple relationships, where one party say sells another party an asset. We can think of these as "clean" relationships. Thirdly, the principal cannot or does not directly control the action of his agent, either because (a) writing down a contract which would specify what the agent should do in every circumstance is essentially impossible; or (b) monitoring whether the agent has in fact executed such a contract correctly is essentially impossible. Such monitoring would require the principal to be fully informed concerning every state; it is precisely because the principal is not so informed that he must delegate so much. Fourth, the principal cannot perfectly directly *or* indirectly control the agent, for example, by observing output.[3]

Agency costs can be significant. Sharecropping contracts typically involve the worker receiving between half and two-thirds of his output; they are equivalent in their effect to the government imposing a tax rate of between a third and 50%. When actual government taxes production are added, the total tax rate can be very large indeed. Deadweight losses associated with taxes increase with the square of the tax rate, so that the resulting welfare losses can be significant.

While traditional agricultural settings provide the simplest examples of agency costs, we now recognize that they are endemic to modern industry. As Stiglitz (1974b) noted, the separation between landlord and tiller, with the tiller having substantial discretion over his efforts and what he does with his land, is analogous to the separation between capital (ownership) and control in modern industry, to which Knight (1921) drew attention. In that setting, agency costs manifest themselves not only in managers exerting too little effort,[4] but in a variety of other decisions which may not be in the interests of shareholders. There is widespread concern that they undertake insufficient risk—though arguments have also been put forward why they might undertake too much risk (in particular, in developing new products; if successful, their rewards may be considerable, while if they fail, the company foots the bill). In the rash of take-overs of the 1980s, there was widespread evidence that the firms taking over gained little if anything; a major explanation of this seemingly irrational behavior has been called the "hubris theory"—to put the matter crudely, the managers of the firms taking over got kicks out of a successful take-over, at the expense of their shareholders.

[2] Similar issues can arise in, say, partnerships.

[3] That is, if output were perfectly correlated with input, then by observing output, the principal could infer input, and thus in effect could make pay contingent upon input. It is, of course, not necessary that the principal monitor every state of nature perfectly. If the agent is risk-averse, if his actions have to be taken before the state of nature is known, and if there is a monotonic relation between his actions, and the probability distribution of outcomes, then by setting sufficiently high penalties on outcomes that fall below some threshold, the principal can induce any desired level of effort (the so-called Stalin scheme, discussed in Mirrlees, 1974b and Stiglitz, 1975b). Of course, if any of the assumptions listed above are not valid, such Stalin schemes cannot work perfectly.

[4] Jensen and Murphy (1990) have estimated that managers receive less than 0.3% of any increment in market value of the firm for which they are responsible. Bertrand and Mullainathan (2001) "find that CEO pay is as sensitive to a lucky dollar as to a general dollar," that is, this pay-for-performance may just as well be pay-for-luck, which would further induce inefficient low effort by CEOs. Further, according to Garvey and Milbourn (2003), pay-for-luck is asymmetric, in that CEOs lose less compensation from bad luck than they gain from good luck: "The average executive loses 25–45% less pay from bad luck than is gained from good luck."

More broadly, and rationally, recent theories have explained how managers can increase their expected income (their rents from being a manager) by a set of actions, called managerial entrenchment, which increase their value to the firm, though it may decrease the value of the firm (Shleifer and Vishny, 1986; Edlin and Stiglitz, 1995).

3 Wealth Inequality and Agency Costs

The common theme in all of these instances is a separation of decision making from ownership, that is, from bearing the full consequences of the actions. We need to ask, when does this occur? How can it be alleviated?

3.1 Inequality Gives Rise to Agency Costs

To see the answer, let us return to our original setting, that of agriculture. There, *if land were equally distributed agency costs would not arise.* Agency costs arise from the disparity in the ownership of "labor power" and the ownership of capital.[5]

It needs to be emphasized that it is really the disparity in the wealth ownership, not the land ownership, which is at issue. Moreover, the problem cannot be alleviated by having workers borrow to buy the land. That simply shifts the locus of the agency costs, so long as there is limited liability. For the worker-borrower faces a risk of not paying back the loan; and so long as that is the case, he does not bear the full consequences of his actions—there are agency costs. A large literature (Stiglitz and Weiss, 1981, 1983; Allen, 1983) has investigated the nature of these agency costs.

The agency costs associated with peasants not having capital—enough capital to buy their land—extend beyond those which we have discussed so far, which have focused on effort, risk taking, and care of land. They extend to the use of other inputs, which have to be applied prior to output being yielded. The temporal separation implies that capital is required. With an absence of capital, the tenant cannot supply these inputs. (The argument is even stronger when it comes to capital goods used as inputs, where the capital constraint may be even more binding.)[6] With credit rationing, the tenant simply may not be able to obtain the requisite capital; but even without credit rationing, the tenant has insufficient incentives, since he must share the output of the capital good with the landlord. By the same token, the landlord has insufficient incentives to supply the capital goods, because he

[5] This raises a subtle, but not particularly relevant, point: it is possible that redistributing land will not increase net national product. With their greater wealth, workers may decide not to supply as much labor as they do as landless peasants. Thus, it need not be the case that output is lower under sharecropping than it would be after a land reform. Though this is a theoretical possibility, the evidence of Korea and Taiway at least strongly support the view that land reforms are output enhancing.

[6] Matters are slightly more subtle than this discussion would suggest. So long as the capital good can be used as collateral, the individual can borrow to buy the capital good, with little risk to the lender. Alternatively, the capital good can be owned by a third party but rented out. Then, all that is at issue is the year's rental value, putting the capital good on par with other inputs. Upon further examination, it is clear that both solutions entail further agency costs. The tenant farmer may not take adequate care of the capital good, decreasing its value as collateral (in the case of a loan) or its future market value (in the case of a rental). A response to the latter problem is to have the owner of the capital good control its use, a practice common for bullocks in LDCs. But then a new agency cost arises, for the owner/manager of the bullocks may be more concerned with conserving the energy of his bullocks than with doing a thorough job of, say, ploughing.

too appropriates only a fraction of the marginal output. In general, it may not be possible to devise contractual arrangements that do as well as the farm would do in the absence of agency costs (for which output is as high as it would be without agency costs).[7]

Another aspect of agency costs are the expenditures used to try to mitigate them: the costs of supervision. Similarly, firms may formulate "standard operating practices," reducing the degree of discretion. While such SOPs reduce the possibility of agents abusing their powers, they also reduce the potential scope for adapting behavior to circumstances.

Agency costs may be massive, and in the case at hand, a simple land reform—effectively, a massive redistribution of wealth—can easily solve them. But that is not necessarily the case in other contexts.

3.2 Equality May Give Rise to Agency Costs

In modern manufacturing, there are often returns to scale. The optimal scale of a firm requires large investments, more than a single individual would have under an egalitarian distribution of wealth. Such a company requires gathering capital from a large number of investors. The central player in such a firm is the manager/financier who puts the firm together. There is again a separation of ownership and control. The *problem* of ownership now, however, is far more severe. In the previous case, when agency costs were severe, it paid the owner of the land to hire a supervisor. Now, each shareholder hopes that the other shareholders will make sure that the manager treats their (collective) capital well.

Now, *agglomerations* of capital may reduce the size of agency costs: if a single, extremely wealthy individual owns the entire enterprise, then he has an incentive to make sure that it is well run. There is no managerial free rider problem.

Some attribute the success of the Korean economy to the willingness of the government to allow enormous concentrations of wealth, which, at the same time, facilitated the efficient management of firms that were competitive at a world-wide level—a unusual achievement in an economy which had, but a few years before, been among the very underdeveloped.

If a single shareholder owns a significant fraction of the wealth of a firm, then he may have sufficient incentive, looking after his own interests, to ensure that the firm is well managed. The small shareholders free ride on his managerial efforts, but the difference between the "optimal" level of managerial effort and the actual level may be relatively small. There is some evidence that firms in which there is a single large shareholder do operate more efficiently.

But this opens up a new source of agency problem. When a single individual owned the entire firm, there was no minority shareholder that he could take advantage of. When there is a controlling shareholder, with say 20% of the shares, he can gain either from improved management, or from diverting the firm towards his own benefit; for example, it is more likely that he will be among the management team, and he can increase managerial pay;

[7] See Braverman and Stiglitz (1986a).

he can engage in non-arms-length contractual arrangements which benefit companies of which he is the principal owner.

In the early days of capitalism, this kind of behavior was not uncommon in joint stock companies, and it proved an impediment to establishing a viable equities market. Fraud laws, laws protecting minority shareholders, and auditing standards have greatly ameliorated, but far from eliminated, the problem.

These legal changes can be viewed as ways of lowering the costs and increasing the benefits of monitoring by non-control groups.

I have, perhaps, overstated the case that a single owner reduces agency costs. For the single owner must still delegate, and those to whom he delegates face an agency problem; and there are further agency problems in the further delegation which is inevitable in large corporations.

3.2.1 Does Ownership Really Matter?

This perspective led many to conclude that ownership (and thus the distribution of wealth) was not of central importance. Was there really any significant difference between BP and Texaco? Between Singapore Airlines and TWA? Is it obvious, in each of these cases, that the state-run enterprise, or the enterprise in which the state had a majority of shares, was less efficient than the privately owned enterprise?

It is sometimes argued that without the ultimate boss who has a large stake in the firm, the firm will not have an incentive to adopt incentive schemes that ensure that the agents behave efficiently (or to select good managers). But those who run state enterprises have incentives to do a good job—either through incentive pay structures, or through the kudos that come from good performance—and it is not obvious that it is that much more difficult to adopt good incentive structures than to adopt bad incentive structures.

Earlier literature stressed the importance of hierarchical structures to ensure good performance, so that even if *ownership* was not important, some degree of inequality (if only in position) was necessary. Someone had to supervise the worker, else he would shirk. (Alternatively, reputation mechanisms/efficiency wages might be employed, but even these required someone to monitor periodically worker performance; and these devices, though they economized in supervision, required that workers receive higher wages than their opportunity costs.) By recursion, someone had to supervise the supervisor. The chain ended in a boss: and since the boss, by definition, had no supervisor, he had to have strong incentives, of the kind provided by ownership.

3.2.2 Peer Monitoring

But we now recognize that there are non-hierarchical monitoring structures—peer monitoring—and that these can be just as effective as hierarchical monitoring. Each person on a team monitors the others; and if individual rewards depend on team performance, each has an incentive to monitor, provided the group is small enough. (Game theoretic formulations, such as Abreu–Milgrom–Pearce (1991), have been formulated ensuring that "cooperative" outcomes can be obtained.)

3.3 Technology and Agency Costs

Whether or not ownership is important for the resolution of agency costs—as the very magnitude of agency costs itself—depends, to some extent at least, on the nature of technology.

Some of the important innovations of the early twentieth century greatly reduced monitoring (and hence agency) costs. The assembly line was not only a better way of organizing production. It also facilitated monitoring. It was immediately detected whenever any individual fell behind the pace of the assembly line.

It has been argued that another of the great innovations of the early twentieth century was the modern corporation, an economic organization which could monitor production of commodities such as steel and automobiles on a massive scale.

There are recent innovations which have also reduced monitoring costs. Just-in-time inventory management not only saves on inventory costs, but it is a useful mechanism for detecting production problems.

Computer/video monitoring of plants allows a single supervisor to monitor many more workers than was previously the case. Electronic inspection devices reduce monitoring costs for errors (quality) for many products.

(It is important to recognize that the choice of technology for or extent of monitoring need not be (in general will not be) constrained Pareto efficient. To see this heuristically, consider the Shapiro–Stiglitz (1984) model. An increase in monitoring intensity allows a reduction in the (efficiency) wage. The firm will seek to minimize its total (present discounted value) of wages plus monitoring costs. But while monitoring expenditures use real resources, which could be used to produce more goods, the wage payments are nothing but transfers. Thus, there is a presumption that markets result in too much monitoring.)

To the extent that agency costs can be reduced, then I suspect that the view that ownership (inequality) is not important has considerable validity.

But some of the important changes in the economy that have occurred in recent years probably have increased agency costs. Thus, it has become a commonplace to remark that we have become a service economy. It has been argued that if the United States is to sustain its high standard of living, it must increasingly focus on R & D intensive industries. Monitoring/agency costs in each of these cases are frequently very large indeed. The techniques of monitoring that worked so well in manufacturing—such as assembly lines—often are ineffective or inapplicable in these sectors. Perhaps it was the change in the structure of the world economy, more than anything else, which is responsible for the demise of the socialist economies; had steel, coal, and railroads remained the center of production, then socialism *might* have worked. But as it was, that form of organization proved utterly incapable of competing in some of the central arenas of modern technology—just as many large American corporations have found the going rough. Small-scale enterprises seemed to have accounted for a disproportionately large share of innovations. Perhaps this is because these small enterprises do a more effective job of mitigating agency costs.

Though small in scale, these enterprises still require considerable capital, more than the amount the typical worker may have accumulated on his own account, even by the time of retirement. If new enterprises are to be established, either there must be individuals with enough capital to found them, or there must be financial markets in which they can raise capital.

Another of the important innovations of the twentieth century is the establishment of strong capital markets. But in spite of their strength, access to capital is still limited. This should not be surprising: there is an infinite supply of charlatans willing to take someone else's money to invest in some harebrained scheme, or worse, simply to walk off with it. Distinguishing between good borrowers and charlatans—and ensuring that funds, once granted, are used well—are costly, and imperfect processes. Information problems are endemic to capital markets, and we now recognize that necessarily, capital markets function "imperfectly." It is now also widely recognized that if a borrower has more collateral, or more equity of his own invested in the project, then it is more likely that the project will be a good project, and that the borrower will take actions which make it more likely that the loan will be repaid (see, e.g., Stiglitz, 1993c). These are, of course, nothing more than the agency costs associated with capital markets.

Thus, some degree of concentration of wealth may be necessary to reduce these capital-market agency problems. The extent of benefits which accrue from wealth concentration depend on (i) the importance of these agency costs; (ii) the correlation between wealth and those with good managerial abilities; and (iii) the magnitude of returns to scale. If the optimal scale of a firm were a single individual, then individuals would only have to have enough wealth to purchase the capital goods required for production. But in general, there are economies of scale and scope, suggesting that the optimal firm has many individuals. Whenever the optimal size of the firm exceeds one individual, there is some agency cost; but as the optimal size of the firm increases, the magnitude of the agency costs is likely to increase. One conjecture is that while some changes in modern technology have lowered the optimal scale of the firm (even as they have increased the monitoring costs, at any scale of the firm), they have not lowered the optimal scale to one individual: the optimal scale still involves a large enough number of individuals that agency costs remain significant.

4 The Effect of Agency Costs on the Inequality of Wealth

So far, we have emphasized the effect that the distribution of wealth has on agency costs. In simple, agricultural environments, it appears clear that an increase in inequality increases agency costs, but in more modern economies, the relationship between inequality and agency costs is not so simple.

I now want to turn to the converse side of the relationship between agency costs and inequality: the effect of the presence of agency costs on economic inequality.

I want to suggest that agency costs lead to greater inequality than would exist in a world in which information were perfect, and that an understanding of the relationship between agency costs and inequality may provide us some insights into recent changes in the degree of inequality in our society.

There are three broad reasons that agency costs lead to an increase in inequality.

4.1 Efficiency Wage and Reputation Effects

First, in the labor market, agency costs lead to the necessity of paying efficiency wages, wages in excess of the opportunity cost of labor. A major set of tests of the efficiency wage model has consisted of asking the question of whether the differences in wages across individuals and firms can be explained in terms of differences in individuals' skills and attributes and those required by different firms and industries. The consensus is that there is far greater wage inequality than can be explained by marginal productivity theory, with appropriate adjustments for non-pecuniary characteristics.[8] Moreover, sectors in which wages are higher are those in which efficiency wage effects would seem naturally to be higher, for instance, in capital intensive industries,[9] in which mistakes by individuals can be very costly, or jobs (such as in the financial sector) were malfeasance is particularly easy, or occupations in which there are high specific training costs.[10]

While it is by now widely recognized that, in the presence of efficiency wage effects, economically identical individuals may receive markedly different wages, depending on the magnitude of the agency effects in the jobs in which they are working, it is not so widely recognized that *slight* differences in individual attributes may lead systematically to large differences in wages. Thus, consider two jobs with different agency costs (e.g., associated with different costs of monitoring)[11] and two individuals, one of which has an epsilon greater productivity than the other. The central lesson of the efficiency wage theory is that wages are not set according to opportunity costs, but according to the cost to the worker of being caught shirking (and the damage to the firm if the worker does shirk).[12] The cost of being caught shirking in the Shapiro–Stiglitz model is the (present discounted value of the) lost wages during the period of unemployment following being caught shirking, plus the (present discounted value of the) possibly lowered level of wages in the new job. In the Shapiro–Stiglitz model, the latter effect disappeared, because individuals were identical and jobs were identical, so that when the individual was rehired, he was rehired at the same wage. By the same token, in a simple economy in which there were two types of jobs and two types of individuals (with the number of "good" jobs matching the number of "more productive" individuals) good people will, when they are rehired, be hired back into good jobs. Thus, again there will be no permanent wage effect from shirking. The only effect will be the temporary cost of unemployment; but this cost only depends on the difference between the current wage and the level of unemployment compensation. Thus, if firms believe that any worker will be rehired in a firm of the same type, then they will be forced to pay the same wage to the workers of the two types of productivity; and given that, it will pay the firm with the high agency costs to hire only the more productive workers. Slight differences in productivity can thus translate into large differences in incomes.[13]

[8] See, for instance, Katz and Summers (1989).

[9] In some instances, such as this, there are possible alternative explanations of high wages, for example associated with bargaining between firms and unions representing their workers. The unions are in a position to "confiscate" more wealth than in the case of an industry with little capital. See, for example, Dickens and Katz (1987).

[10] For models focusing on the relationship between wages, training costs, and labor turnover, see Salop (1973, 1979), Stiglitz (1974b, 1985c), and Arnott and Stiglitz (1985c).

[11] So that, say, in the Shapiro–Stiglitz formulation of the efficiency wage model (1984), the monitoring intensity in one job is higher than in the other.

[12] Though this factor was omitted from the simplest efficiency wage models.

[13] The argument as presented is not quite complete. Denote the firms with high agency costs by *A*, and the good individuals by *S*; and the firms with low agency costs by *B*, and the less productive individuals by *U*. We have postulated an equilibrium in which type A firms hire type *S* individuals, and type *B* firms hire type *U* individuals. We need to show that it does not pay any firm to deviate from this policy, for example, a type *A* firm to hire a type *U* workers. Such a firm knows that if it does, then the type *U* worker will believe that, should he be fired, he will be rehired only by a type *B* firm, resulting in a much lower wage. Thus, he would be willing to work (not shirk)

This basic point can be brought home even more forcefully if we think of the economy as consisting of two sectors, in one of which there are efficiency wage effects. The other sector is described by traditional neoclassical models. Assume that the number of good jobs is far fewer than the number of good workers, so that once any worker is fired, his expectation of being rehired is very low. In this model, the penalty of being fired is not being unemployed, but joining the competitive labor sector.[14] Then firms with efficiency wage concerns will only hire the more productive workers (parallel results were obtained by Dasgupta and Ray (1986) in their analysis of efficiency wage effects in less developed countries).

Similarly in the product market, firms receive prices in excess of the marginal cost of production. Reputation effects serve as barriers to entry. While in standard competitive models, profits are quickly bid away, in the presence of agency costs, firms may glean profits over long periods of time; and of course the owners of such firms can, as a result, accumulate large amounts of capital.

4.2 Wealth Begetting Wealth: Vicious or Virtuous Circles

In the previous discussion, we emphasized that there may be large differences in wages (incomes) associated with small differences in productivity. These differences in productivity may be related to differences in wealth (or the wealth of parents). Thus, in the Dasgupta–Ray analysis, focusing on efficiency wage effects in less developed countries, workers who own some land have higher non-wage incomes, and are thus, at any wage level, more productive than landless workers. With job rationing, they are the ones who become employed. By the same token, agency effects can be reduced by workers posting bonds, or obtaining an economic stake in the job. But this requires workers to have capital. Those who have inherited wealth are thus in a better position to obtain these "good" jobs.

Finally, differences in productivity have much to do with human capital, which, in turn, is correlated with parental wealth.

4.2.1 Imperfections of Capital Markets

In neoclassical theory, inherited wealth makes no difference for individual productivities. With perfect capital markets, each individual invests in human capital up to the point where the marginal return is equal to the cost of capital.

Observers of actual capital markets have always been particularly skeptical of this aspect of neoclassical doctrine. Modern theories, based on the recognition of imperfections of information and the costs of acquiring information, have provided a theoretical bases for this skepticism: with information asymmetries (both selection and incentive problems) capital markets are essentially always "imperfect." There is credit and equity rationing.

for the firm at a lower wage than a type *S* individual. How much smaller wage depends on the length of time that the individual will be unemployed. At high unemployment rates (and high discount rates) the present discounted value of the future wage differentials becomes small. This must be compared to the present discounted value of the difference in productivity. With relatively high expected job lengths, then the latter can be larger than the former. The important point is that there is no simple correspondence between differences in productivities and differences in wages.

[14] Throughout, we are assuming that differences in individuals are observable, so that there are no signaling effects associated say with accepting a job in this low wage sector. The analysis is more complicated when there are both incentive and selection effects.

These imperfections are particularly important with respect to non-collateralizable investments and investments with significant asymmetries of information (such as arise from limited knowledge both about individual's abilities and motivations)-attributes of investments in human capital. We can think of these problems as agency problems within the capital market. Thus, because of capital market agency problems, the level of investment in human capital, and thus workers' productivities, will depend on the wealth of an individual (and his parents).

Wealthier parents can and do invest more in their children, giving rise to higher incomes for their children. What makes this a particularly "vicious" cycle is that the increases in wages of children may be more than commensurate with the increase in *physical* productivity, as we saw in the previous section. Those with access to slightly more capital may earn much higher wages, and thus differential access may be perpetuated.

The same kind of analysis applies to investment opportunities more broadly. We noted before the large agency costs associated with investment. There may be credit rationing (just as we noted before that there may be job rationing in efficiency wage models). And just as small differences in productivity may result in large differences in wages (or access to good jobs), so too may small differences in wealth lead to large differences in lending. Those who have collateral, or can invest equity, so that they have a substantial stake in the investment, may obtain credit, when those without that stake are denied it.

In neoclassical theory, this would not be of much moment, since the marginal return to all investments (in equilibrium) is driven down to the interest rate. But in the presence of agency costs, interest rates may be substantially below the expected return to the investment; those who gain access to capital may earn large rents.

4.2.2 Differential Returns to Capital

Agency costs, combined with information costs, lead to further positive feedbacks in wealth accumulation. In neoclassical theory, all individuals receive the same return on their investment. In practice, we know this is not true. It often seems to be the case that those with higher wealth earn higher returns. Part of this may be due to their greater ability to leverage, as suggested in the previous paragraph.

But Arrow (1974b) has provided another explanation. It is widely recognized that information costs are essentially fixed costs. When information costs are large, there is, in effect, a return to scale. But the essential problem of investment is that of obtaining information: wealthier individuals "can afford" (or more accurately, it pays them) to buy better information, to obtain higher returns on their investment.

This problem would not arise in the absence of agency costs in the market for information, and if information were a conventional commodity, sold like other commodities at its marginal cost. Since the marginal cost of information is essentially zero, anyone could have access to the same information. (Sellers of information might act as discriminating monopolists, capturing some of the infra-marginal returns to pay for the costs of obtaining information.) But markets for information differ in fundamental ways from markets for ordinary commodities. For instance, a buyer of information about investments always worries, if the seller has such confidence in his information, why doesn't he invest his own money?

If, for this or other reasons, wealthier individuals have access to better information, so that the returns to capital increase with the amount of capital, then again wealth inequality is perpetuated and exacerbated.

4.2.3 Risk and Inequality

More generally, the presence of agency costs lead to institutional arrangements which exacerbate inequality. In this and the next section, we discuss two important aspects of this.

In many, if not most, economic situations, risk is important. With perfect markets, of the kind envisaged by the neoclassical doctrine, there is perfect risk sharing. Thus, "luck" does not itself give rise to inequality. A farmer's income need not depend on the weather, or even the price of the commodities which he sells. He could obtain perfect insurance against the risks which he faces.

But perfect insurance gives rise to huge agency costs. By definition, with perfect insurance, individuals do not bear the full costs of the actions which they undertake. These agency costs (moral hazard effects) would not, of course, arise if it were costless to monitor individuals.

Thus, the greater the agency costs, the more risks individuals themselves will have to bear, and thus the greater role that "luck"—or more formally, stochastic elements—will play in determining the distribution of income.

4.2.4 Incentives and Redistribution

The same arguments apply, of course, at the level of society. Lerner and Samuelson characterized redistributive taxation as a form of social insurance. Behind the Rawlsian veil of ignorance, individuals would prefer to have "equal incomes" rather than to take their chance at the lottery of life. But this ignores the importance of incentives; because of agency costs, just as insurance cannot eliminate the effects of idiosyncratic shocks, so too redistribution cannot eliminate the effects of inequality.

4.2.5 Contests

The previous sections explained how agency costs limit the markets and government's ability to reduce the inequality that arises from random events and endowments. But agency costs may actually lead directly to increases in inequality.

A consequence of the existence of agency costs is that firms must design effective incentive structures. One form of incentives that has been particularly stressed in recent years are contests, in which the winner gets a large prize, or the loser gets a large penalty. Contests have been shown to be a particularly effective incentive mechanism. More generally, Nalebuff and Stiglitz (1983a, 1983b) showed that contests, where individual's compensation depends on their "rank" performance (including the punishment of the worst performer), may provide efficient incentives, especially when there is a common but unobservable shock affecting the performance of all participants. Lazear and Rosen (1981) and Nalebuff and Stiglitz (1983a, 1983b) have argued that they can explain the very large payments that go to superstars, for instance, to those who succeed in becoming president of a company (where the differences between the salary of the president and vice president seem all out of line with differences in abilities, as indicated, for instance, by the great difficulties often encountered in choosing who should be the president).

5 Simultaneous Models

We have described how agency costs give rise to inequality and how inequality gives rise to agency costs. There are equilibrium distributions of income: given the distribution of income, there are a set of contractual arrangements (wages, lending patterns, sharecropping arrangements, etc.), which result in particular outcomes the following period; that is, given that an individual has a particular wealth (income) this period, there is a particular probability distribution of wealth next period. Given that, there is an overall distribution of income (wealth) the next period. In equilibrium, the distribution of income (wealth) each period is the same: the contractual arrangements are thus sustained.

Mathematically, what we have just said is that there is a transition matrix A and an initial wealth distribution, p (p_i is the fraction of individuals in the ith income category), such that

$$p^* = Ap^*.$$

This is standard. Our analysis has emphasized, however, that the nature of the contractual arrangements as well as the nature of the risks borne by different individuals depends, itself, on the degree of inequality in society. We can summarize this by saying that the matrix A itself is a function of p. It can be shown that under a variety of conditions there exists multiple solutions to the equation:

$$p^* = A(p^*)p^*.$$

That is, there are multiple steady state income distributions.

It would go beyond the scope of this chapter to provide an evaluation of these alternative equilibria. These equilibria differ not only in the degree of inequality, but in the nature of the contractual arrangements. These, in turn, may have profound effects on the nature of society. The differences between two societies, in one of which everyone works their own land, and in the other of which everyone works on a plantation, or works as a tenant, are not adequately summarized by statistics concerning the Gini coefficient.

It should be emphasized, however, that there are a variety of government policies which themselves affect both the nature of the risks and the equilibrium contractual arrangements, and which accordingly change the equilibrium distribution of income—and the equilibrium set of contractual arrangements.

6 Concluding Remarks

While earlier theoretical work, such as the marginal productivity theory and Kaldorian theory, focused on the distribution of income among *factors* of production, it has only been in the past 25 years that theoretical economists have turned their attention to the distribution of income and wealth among *individuals*, with the work of Becker (1967), Stiglitz

(1969b), and Meade (1972), among others. These earlier studies have identified a number of important factors in determining income inequality, such as inheritance policies, inheritability of ability, reproductive and marriage patterns, and savings behavior. This study has added one important factor to that list-agency costs. Agency costs are important, of course, in that they affect *both* the distribution of income among factors and the distribution of income among individuals. Indeed, in economies in which agency costs are important, the distribution of income among factors will not be determined by (at least simple versions) of marginal productivity theory. Most importantly, changes in the distribution of income may not be related in any simple way to changes in relative factor supplies. Movements in real interest rates in recent years seem far more in accord with theories based on agency costs than on traditional marginal productivity theories (see Stiglitz, 1992a and Greenwald, Salinger, and Stiglitz, 1990).

We have emphasized the two-way linkages associated with agency costs: the distribution of income affects the magnitude of agency costs, and agency costs affect the distribution of income.

High on the research agenda for the future should be a further elaboration and articulation of the links that we have described in this chapter, providing the basis for a better understanding of the effects of policy changes, not only on the short-run distribution of income and wealth, but on the long run, and not only on the distribution of income and wealth itself, but on the very design of the manner in which society's economic relations are organized.

25

Credit Rationing, Tenancy, Productivity, and the Dynamics of Inequality

With Avishay Braverman

1 Introduction

In earlier work, we argued that it was mistaken for economists to treat institutions as given: many institutions frequently found in market economies arise endogenously as a response to informational considerations and inequality in the distribution of wealth.[1] In particular, these considerations can explain the persistence and pervasiveness of sharecropping in LDCs (Stiglitz, 1974b; Braverman and Stiglitz, 1986a) and credit rationing in capital markets in both developed and less developed countries (Stiglitz and Weiss, 1981).

This chapter has three objectives: to show how sharecropping and capital market imperfections affect rural productivity; to sketch a general equilibrium theory of land tenancy; and, finally, to show how changes in technology and in publicly provided infrastructure may affect the equilibrium distribution of land and, hence, the prevalent tenancy relationships. These relationships are important because they influence the long-run increase in national income made possible by changes in technology or infrastructure.

Recent literature has considered the effect of inequality on technological change. Concern has been expressed, for instance, that the inequality within LDCs has impeded the adoption of certain innovations.[2] In an earlier paper (Braverman and Stiglitz, 1986b) we examined the validity of that contention and showed that, although the standard exploitation arguments may not be valid, there were indeed innovations that might increase output, for each level of input, that would not be adopted; these innovations, however, exacerbated the incentive problems (e.g., associated with sharecropping).

This chapter is concerned with the other side of the relationship between technological change and inequality: the effect of technical change on inequality, and the effect of inequality, in turn, on productivity. We shall show that an increase in inequality may have a deleterious effect on productivity. The effect of changes in technology and infrastructure is ambiguous. For some changes long-run inequality is reduced, and for these changes the long-run productivity gains are accordingly likely to be greater than those in the short run. On the other hand, for some changes long-run inequality is increased. These innovations, while increasing output in the short run, may—in the absence of countervailing actions

[1] Written with Avishay Braverman. Originally published in 1989 as "Credit Rationing, Tenancy, Productivity, and the Dynamics of Inequality," in P. Bardhan (ed.), *The Economic Theory of Agrarian Institutions*, Oxford: Clarendon Press, pp. 185–201. First disseminated as Princeton University Discussion Paper 23, 1988, and in revised form, as World Bank Policy Research Working Paper 176, May 1989. Reprinted with permission.

[2] See, for example, Bhaduri (1973, 1980), who contends that landlords will resist innovations that reduce their power to exploit the workers.

The Origins of Inequality, and Policies to Contain It. Joseph E. Stiglitz with Avishay Braverman, Oxford University Press.
 DOI: 10.1093/oso/9780198799580.003.0026

by the government—in the long run have a deleterious effect on the economy. It is important to recognize this possibility, so that attention can be drawn to institutional reforms designed to ameliorate these inequality-related long-run productivity effects.

The fact that technological change can have an adverse effect on inequality has long been recognized. Indeed, it is known that it is possible that a technological change would so reduce the demand for, say, unskilled labor that not only its share, but also the absolute value of the real wage of unskilled workers might fall. This might be the case, for instance, if the innovation is "labor-augmenting" (so that one worker can do what ten workers previously could) and the elasticity of substitution between unskilled labor and other factors is very low (so that, given the increase in the effective supply of labor, the wage per efficiency unit falls more than proportionately to the increase in the productivity of the workers).

The mechanism by which technological change can have an adverse effect on workers in our analysis is, however, quite different. It is based on two hypotheses:

1. Many forms of technological change are capital-using; that is, they require as complementary inputs additional capital. (Equivalently, at the original levels of the inputs of capital, the value of the marginal product of capital is increased.)
2. Capital markets are imperfect, so that poor farmers cannot easily borrow the additional required capital. Even if they could, of course, the technological change could have an adverse effect on the distribution of wealth (income); for it will increase the scarcity value of capital, and thus the return to capital. But our concern is not with this static or short-run effect, but rather with a long-run effect that is a consequence of credit rationing.

The lack of access to capital means that, after a technological change, land will be more valuable to someone who has the capital to use with it than to someone who does not. This, in turn, will induce some of the poorer farmers to sell their land to richer landlords. In the short run, this simply represents a change in the form in which wealth is held. But because the wealth distribution in one period depends not only on the distribution of wealth in the previous period, but also on the form in which different wealth-groups hold their wealth, this sale of land may have adverse long-run effects on the wealth distribution.

Finally, an adverse effect on wealth distribution has an adverse effect on productivity. The reason for this is that, as inequality increases, it is more likely that sharecropping arrangements will be employed;[3] and, although sharecropping arrangements may be "Pareto-efficient" (that is, given the constraints on monitoring the worker and the risk aversion of workers, there may not be an alternative contractual arrangement between workers and landlords that makes both of them better off), still, output may be significantly lower with sharecropping than it would be with owner-operated farms.[4]

Our contention then that certain changes in technology (certain governmental projects, such as irrigation projects) may have long-run adverse effects on the economy that partly

[3] There are, of course, other reasons why wealth inequality may give rise to a reduction in productivity. Dasgupta and Rey (1986), for instance, discuss the consequences of inequality in the context of an economy in which productivity depends on nutrition.

[4] Although sharecropping contracts are "pairwise efficient," in the sense that they maximize the welfare of the worker, given the expected rents of the landlord, they may not be "globally efficient"; that is, there may exist governmental interventions (say, taxes or subsidies) which make all individuals better off. This is a general result in the theory of imperfect information and incomplete markets; see Greenwald and Stiglitz (1986).

offset the short-run effects requires a number of steps to establish, each of which is of some interest in its own right. In the subsequent sections, we provide simple models establishing conditions under which each of the contentions we have put forward is valid.

2 Productivity and Sharecropping

The standard formulation of the sharecropping contractual arrangement (where the contract is chosen to maximize the expected utility of the worker, subject to a constraint on the expected return per acre of the landlord) makes it clear that such contracts are (at least pairwise-) efficient. But that does not mean that national income might not be higher—significantly higher—in the absence of sharecropping.

Here we ask the question, What would happen if the land that a sharecropper currently works were redistributed to the worker, so that he now received the rents? The classical argument against sharecropping was that, because the worker received only a fraction of his marginal return, he would work less than he would if he received his marginal product, and accordingly such contracts were inefficient. We have already argued that sharecropping contracts are at least pairwise-efficient. The former contention, that individuals would work less, is not obvious, either, since as we transfer resources to the worker he becomes better off, and because he is better off he may work less hard.

The question of whether output would be higher or lower under a land reform is thus close to the question of whether an increase in wages increases or decreases the labor supply (measured in terms of hours or effort). While an increase in the wage has a positive incentive (substitution) effect, it has a negative income effect, and the net effect is ambiguous. The question is close to, but not the same as, the question concerning whether the standard labor supply curve is backward-bending, because the marginal return to labor in the circumstances under examination here is a stochastic variable (see Braverman and Srinivasan, 1981). We can however show that, so long as workers are not too risk-averse (that is, so long as there is not a too strongly diminishing marginal utility of income), the substitution effect will outweigh the income effect, and a land reform will increase output.

To see this, we postulate that workers are risk-averse, with a utility function of the form[5]

$$U(Y, L) = u(Y) - v(L), \tag{25.1}$$

where

$$u' > 0,\ u'' < 0,\ v' > 0,\ v'' > 0,$$

and where Y is income and L is the worker's labor supply, measured in terms of effort.

[5] Implicitly, in this formulation we are assuming that the individual's utility depends on his current income; that is, there are not capital markets in which he can borrow or lend. This is obviously an extreme assumption, but it is far better than the opposite extreme, in which it is postulated that workers can borrow and lend at a fixed (low) real market rate of interest. Thus, the assumption of capital constraints appears as an implicit assumption even in the traditional models of sharecropping. This analysis could be extended to the case where borrowing and lending are feasible, in which case U becomes the lifetime utility function, and Y is interpreted as lifetime wealth.

We assume that the agricultural production function takes on the simple form of

$$Q = ag(\theta)f(L/a), \tag{25.2}$$

where f is output per acre, θ is a random variable, and a is the representative worker's plot size. For simplicity, we shall normalize a at unity.

We assume a simple sharecropping system, where the tenant worker gets a fraction α of the return. For simplicity, we assume that this is his entire income, so that

$$Y = \alpha gf. \tag{25.3}$$

Then the first-order condition for the level of effort is[6]

$$Eu'(\alpha gf') = v'. \tag{25.4}$$

We can depict the consequences of a land reform as turning over control of the land to the worker, that is as an increase in α to 1. Thus, differentiating (25.4), we immediately obtain

$$\text{sign } dL/d\alpha = \text{sign } Egf'u'(1 - R) \tag{25.5}$$

where $R = -u'' Y/u'$, the elasticity of the marginal utility of income, or the Arrow–Pratt measure of relative risk aversion. Thus, provided

$$R < 1, \tag{25.6}$$

that is, provided workers are not too risk-averse, a land reform will increase effort, and hence will increase mean national output. (The analogous condition for the deterministic case is in Braverman and Srinivasan, 1981.)

The magnitude of the response may be quite large: crop shares typically are in the order of magnitude of 50%; thus, a land reform has the same effect as the elimination of a 50% income tax.

2.1 Land Reform and Land Taxes

This analysis provides some suggestions concerning the longstanding issue of the desirability of land taxes, as opposed to output taxes. Land taxes provide fixed payments to the government, just as rental payments provide fixed payments to the landlord. Output taxes are equivalent to sharecropping agreements; the government shares in production risks (as well as price risks). Land taxes have preferable incentive properties, just as rental payments do. But, just as earlier analyses (e.g., Stiglitz, 1974a) argued that sharecropping contracts were preferable to fixed rents when tenants are risk-averse, so too are output taxes preferable to land taxes when landlords are risk-averse. Indeed, the case for the desirable risk-sharing properties of output taxes is even greater, for the government is able to diversify

[6] This formulation assumes that effort is exerted before the random variable θ is known.

the risks that it faces better than the typical landlord.[7] To put it another way, the assumption made in the literature that landlords are risk-neutral is a much closer approximation to describing the government than it is to describing the representative landlord, particularly in Asia and Africa. And, by switching from output taxes to land taxes, the feasible set of, say, mean and standard deviation of income of landlords and workers is made worse.

Moreover, in the more general case of linear sharecropping contracts, with

$$Y = \alpha g f + \beta,$$

the shift from an output tax to an equal-expected-revenue land tax may result in a rise in α, the crop share, and an offsetting change in β, the fixed rent or wage, as the landlord shifts some of his increased risk to the worker. Note that welfare may be reduced, even though average rural income may be increased (as a result of the greater effort exerted by workers because of the greater share provided by the equilibrium contract under the land tax). In the case where the landlord is risk-averse, expected utility of workers and/or landlords will be reduced. Only in the case where the landlord is risk-neutral will the switch from an output tax to an equal-expected revenue land tax leave the equilibrium unchanged.[8]

3 A Model of Land Valuation

To ascertain the effect of technical change on the distribution of land, we first need to construct a model of land valuation.

We will find it useful to distinguish between the value of land to a landlord who lets out his land, and the value of land to a farmer who works his own land. Moreover, we will need to extend the production model described in the previous section in order to incorporate the effects of technical change and capital availability. We thus postulate that the average output per acre of a plot of land is represented by a production function of the form

$$q = \bar{f}(k, \ell, t), \tag{25.7}$$

where k is capital per acre, ℓ is the amount of effort that each sharecropper supplies per acre of the sharecropping land (hence, $\ell \equiv L/a$), t is the state of technology, and $Eg(\theta) = 1$ (and so is suppressed). Changes in t can be thought of as reflecting not only technological changes, but also changes in the level of certain publicly provided services, such as irrigation and extension services.

[7] This discussion has, of course, ignored what may be the central criticism against land taxes, the administrative problems associated with levying such taxes in an equitable manner, and the abuse to which such taxes are subject. Moreover, in practice, such taxes are usually based not on the intrinsic value of the land, but on the "improved" value of land. Thus, they are, in effect, a tax on (the present discounted value of) land rents plus a tax on capital. Because they are a tax on the present discounted value of land rents, they serve to increase the risk borne by landlords, since the present discounted value of land rents is likely to be much less variable than the annual value of land rents (and besides, tax authorities usually revise the appraised value of land only periodically). Moreover, the fact that capital is taxed, while labor is not, introduces an important distortion. As is usually the case in the theory of the second-best, it is not obvious whether a uniform distortion (taxing labor, land, and capital) is better or worse than a selective distortion (taxing land and capital). This is a question we hope to investigate on another occasion.

[8] This follows from the fact that total expected payments to landlords and the government are fixed, and hence the solution to the problem of maximizing the worker's expected utility subject to that constraint is unaffected.

Under a sharecropping contract with a fixed share α, the present discounted value of the returns to the landlord of an acre worked at intensity ℓ with capital k is just[9]

$$V^s = (1 - \alpha)\bar{f}(k, \ell, t)/r, \tag{25.8}$$

where k and ℓ are both endogenously determined, and r is the rate of interest at which future income flows are discounted.[10] In principle, we should also make α an endogenous variable,[11] but in practice α seems to vary little, even over quite extended periods, and even in the presence of some significant changes in technology. Here we take α and the number of workers on each plot of land as fixed, leaving for a later occasion the extension to the more general case where both are endogenous.

From the first-order condition for effort (Equation (25.4) above), we can immediately derive the equilibrium level of effort of a worker as a function of the amount of capital per acre provided by the landlord, the state of technology, and the size of the plot of land that the worker works:[12]

$$\ell = \phi(k, a, t), \tag{25.9}$$

where, as before, a is the number of acres per worker engaged in sharecropping. (In the previous section, it will be recalled, we took a to be unity.) k is then chosen to maximize:

$$(1 - \alpha)\bar{f}\{k, \ell(k, a, t), t\} - rk; \tag{25.10}$$

that is,

$$(1 - \alpha)\left\{\bar{f}_k + \bar{f}_\ell(d\ell/dk)\right\} = r; \tag{25.11}$$

Note that in this formulation all the capital costs are borne by the landlord; this follows naturally from the assumption, which will play a central role in the subsequent analysis, that landlords have access to capital but workers do not.[13]

Equation (25.11) has some interesting implications: while the fact that the landlord can appropriate only a fraction of the marginal returns from his application of additional capital

[9] For simplicity, we assume that the rate of interest is constant (or that the market values assets as if the rate of interest were constant). We also assume, somewhat less plausibly, that the market ignores all future possibilities of technological change (or changes in government-provided facilities which affect productivity). This may not be a bad approximation if such changes occur only sporadically, and real interest rates used for discounting are relatively high.

[10] Clearly, if there were a perfect capital market, r would be the rate of interest at which landlords could borrow and lend. In an imperfect capital market, it is a more subtle matter to determine r. Although in principle r itself may be affected by changes in technology, t, for the purposes of this analysis, we treat r as fixed.

[11] And indeed, we should introduce more complicated sharecropping contracts, for example with a fixed (rental or wage) component, or with cost-sharing. Each of these terms should, in principle, also be endogenously determined, and thus vary with t. Introducing these extensions would, we suspect, considerably complicate the analysis without changing the basic qualitative results.

[12] For the moment, we assume that the worker engaged in sharecropping can work only on the sharecropping land. If the sharecropper has alternative opportunities, for example if he can work as a wage laborer or if he owns or rents a plot of land, then this will obviously affect the amount of labor that he supplies on the sharecropping land. The landlord, in such situations, would attempt to restrict the sharecropper's access to these opportunities.

[13] At the same time, Braverman and Stiglitz (1986a) show that, in the absence of an asymmetry of information concerning θ, it makes no difference whether the contract specifies that the landlord or the tenant supply capital, so long as the capital input is observable.

discourages the use of capital, the fact that additional capital may elicit greater effort on the part of workers may encourage the use of capital: $d\ell/dk$ will be positive if capital and labor are complements, that is, if an increase in the supply of capital increases the marginal return to labor[14] by enough to offset the reduction in effort supply resulting from the higher income provided by the increased input of capital.

We now derive the effect of a change in technology on the value of sharecropping land. Assuming that the landlords optimally adjust the level of k, we obtain (here, as in the remainder of this section, we drop the bar over f):

$$dV^s/dt = (1-\alpha)\{f_t + f_\ell(d\ell/dt)\}/r. \tag{25.12}$$

In words, the change in technology has a direct effect (at fixed levels of inputs of effort and capital) and an indirect effect (through the effect on the supply of effort). If the technological improvement increases the marginal productivity of effort, as in Figure 25.1a, then again there is a presumption that the supply of effort will be increased.[15] But if the technological improvement reduces the marginal productivity of effort in the relevant range ($\ell(t) > \bar{\ell}$, that is, at the old equilibrium level of inputs, in Figure 25.1b), then the supply of effort will fall. Indeed, if the technological improvement reduces the marginal productivity at the old level of output by enough, then the indirect effect of reduced effort will outweigh the direct productivity effect, and equilibrium output will be lower. There is, of course, no presumption that a technological change will, at a fixed level of labor and capital input, increase the marginal productivity of labor. Figures 25.1(a) and (b) illustrate two possibilities. The indirect effect of a small change in technology on the input of capital can be ignored, by the envelope theorem. But the indirect effect on k of a large change in technology cannot be ignored:[16]

$$\Delta V_s = \frac{1-\alpha}{r}[f\{k(t'), \ell(t'), t'\} - f\{k(t), \ell(t), t\}] - \{k(t') - k(t)\}, \tag{25.13}$$

[14] From the first-order condition for ℓ (taking α as given), we obtain

$$\text{sign } d\ell/dk = \text{sign } Eu'\{g(f_{\ell k} - Rf_k f_\ell/f)\}$$

The income effect (the increased capital increases income at a fixed effort level) discourages effort; but the substitution effect encourages it, provided $f_{k\ell} > 0$. The substitution effect will exceed the income effect, provided only that

$$R < ff_{k\ell}/f_k f_\ell = 1/\sigma,$$

that is, provided that the product of the elasticity of marginal utility (the Arrow–Pratt measure of risk aversion) and the elasticity of substitution are less than unity.

Note that, if there were a fixed fee element to the sharecropping contract, which the landlord could adjust to offset the increased income resulting from the increased capital (making, in effect, the tenant pay for the capital), or if the landlord could adjust the share downward, to compensate for the increased capital, then there would not be an income effect. The presumption then that an increase in capital will result in greater effort will be stronger; see Braverman and Stiglitz (1986a).

[15] Again, there is an income effect and a substitution effect. As in n. 14, we can show that sign $d\ell/dt$ = sign $Eu'\{g(f_{t\ell} - Rf_\ell f_t/f)\}$. For a more extended discussion of these issues, see Braverman and Stiglitz (1986b).

[16] This analysis assumes that sharecropping land is purchased with its workers, that is, that one cannot change the number of workers per acre. More generally, of course, the value of land is a function of the number of workers per acre, which itself is an endogenous variable. Obviously, if the landlord does not need to change the terms of the contract to offset a decrease in the acreage per worker, he would increase the number of workers per acre without bound, or at least until certain efficiency wage effects became significant.

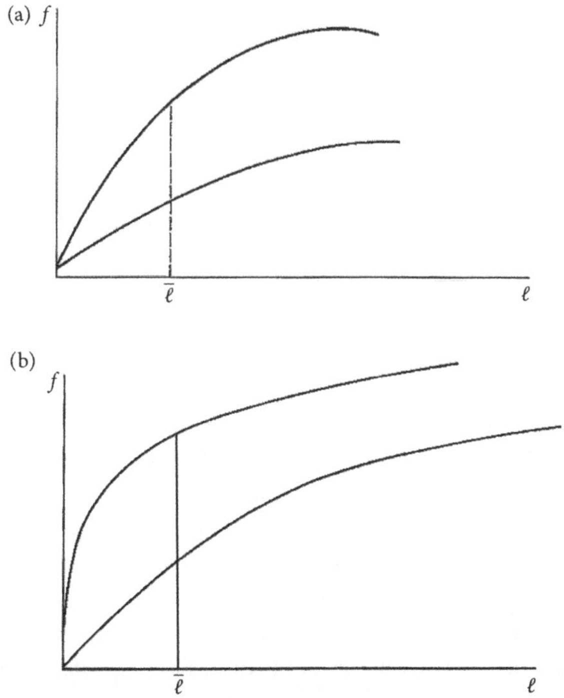

Figure 25.1 (a) At all levels of input, technical change increases the marginal productivity of labor. (b) At all levels of input above $\bar{\ell}$, technical change reduces the marginal productivity of labor.

where t is the original technology, t' the new technology, and $k(t)(k(t'))$ represents the capital input with the original (new) technology, and where $\ell(t) \equiv \phi\{k(t), a(t), t\}$ and $\ell(t') \equiv \phi\{k(t'), a(t'), t'\}$ are similarly defined.

We now turn to the effect of the technological change on the value of owner-worked land. We first express this value in terms of the present discounted value of utility generated by the land, under the hypothesis that the worker-owner does not have access to capital. Then the value of an a-acre farm is

$$V^0 = \max_{[\ell]} \frac{1}{r} E[u\{agf(0, \ell, t)\} - v(\ell)], \tag{25.14}$$

from which it follows that

$$\mathrm{d}V^0/\mathrm{d}t = (aEu'\{gf_t\})/r. \tag{25.15}$$

Again, because of the envelope theorem, we can ignore the induced change in the supply of effort; but for large changes in technology, we cannot, and we obtain:

$$\Delta V^0 = \frac{1}{r} Eu\,[af\{0, \ell\,(t'), t'\}g] - Eu\,[af\{0, \ell\,(t), t\}g] - v\{\ell\,(t')\} + v\{\ell\,(t)\}. \tag{25.16}$$

Comparing (25.16) and (25.13), it is apparent that a technological change can have quite different effects on land that is sharecropped and land that is worked by its owners. In the limiting case, for instance, where capital is required to take advantage of the new technology, there is no change in V^0. More generally, the technological improvement will have a larger effect on sharecropped land relative to owner-worked land,

1. the more the improvement depends on the level of capital;
2. the less the improvement depends on the level of labor effort; that is, the new technology may not increase output at very labor-intensive technologies as much as at less labor-intensive technologies.[17]

3.1 A Slight Generalization

The model presented above assumed that poor farmers who worked their own land had no access to capital. A better assumption might be that they can obtain capital only by selling their land. Assume that with the initial technology the owner-farmer uses no capital, and that in fact capital is not productive. The technological change alters this. Assume that he can now sell his land to a rich landowner for a price V^s per acre, and assume that his initial endowment of land is a^*. If he retains any land to farm himself, assume that it will be optimal for him to use the proceeds of the sale to buy capital equipment. Then he will choose a, the number of acres he retains, to maximize his expected utility:

$$\max_{\{\ell,a\}} Eu[gaf\{V^s(a^* - a), \ell, t\}] - v(\ell); \tag{25.17}$$

that is,

$$Eu'\{g(f - af_k V^s)\} = 0 \quad (\text{if } a < a^*) \tag{25.18}$$

or

$$f = af_k V^s. \tag{25.19}$$

or

$$\text{a} = \frac{r}{f_k(1-\alpha)}. \tag{25.20}$$

We can again consider the effects of technical change on the welfare of the owner-worker. Since, by assumption, with the original technology the owner employs no capital, by the envelope theorem, the effect of a small technological improvement is again described by Equation (25.15). But the effect of a larger technological improvement is now given by

$$\begin{aligned}\Delta V^0 = \tfrac{1}{r}\langle Eu\{ga(t')fV^s[a^* - a(t'), \ell(t'), t']\} - Eu[ga^*f[0, \ell(t), t]] \\ -[v\{\ell(t')\} - v\{\ell(t)\}]]\rangle,\end{aligned} \tag{25.21}$$

where it should be noted that the labor supply is now different from what is was earlier, because of the change in k and a.

[17] Recall from the earlier discussion of sharecropping that labor input will be lower with sharecropping, provided the income effects are not too large.

4 Technical Change and the Redistribution of Land

In the preceding section, we showed that a change in technology or infrastructure could have a markedly different effect on the value of sharecropped land (the welfare of landlords) and on the welfare of farmers working their own land. We now consider the effect of technical change on the distribution of land, and the effects that this in turn has.

Figure 25.2 shows the equilibrium in the land market under the assumption that the owner-workers can sell land to obtain capital. The curve *SS* is derived from Equation (25.19). It shows the amount of land that the owner-workers are willing to sell as a function of the market price, V^s. In the figure, we have depicted the case where, as V^s increases, they sell more, although this is not necessarily the case.[18]

The curve *DD* represents the "demand" for sharecropping land. If we assume that the number of available sharecroppers is fixed, then an increase in land under sharecropping tenancy will tend to decrease the value of each acre; V^s will normally fall. (Even if the substitution effect leads each worker to work harder, the effective labor supply per acre will fall.) Thus, the demand curve in Figure 25.2 is downward-sloping.

Now consider the effect of a technical change which increases the return to capital. This shifts the supply curve to the right, and may well shift the "demand curve" up. Thus, as depicted in Figure 25.2 land will be transferred from owner-operators to landlords as a result of the technical change: the technical change has resulted in an increase in the inequality of landownership.

In this static model, the change in the distribution of landownership is welfare (and productivity)-enhancing: it enables the poor farmers, who otherwise would not have access

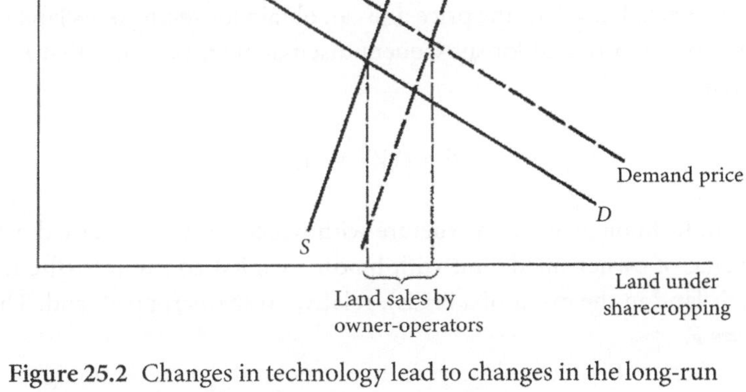

Figure 25.2 Changes in technology lead to changes in the long-run distribution of wealth and tenancy arrangements.

[18] We need to differentiate the first-order conditions with respect to V^s. From Equation (25.20) it is clear that, if we have a Cobb–Douglas production function, *a* is independent of V^s.

to capital, to take advantage of the new capital-using technology. But the productivity effects are more ambiguous in a dynamic context, as we shall now see.

5 A Dynamic Model

In spite of the enhanced productivity that might result from selling their land and using the proceeds to purchase capital, poor landowners may be reluctant to do so. They may feel that they are holding the land, which they inherited from their parents, in trust for their children. In any case, decisions to sell land may not be based solely on a rational calculation.

Land sales may occur in the event of certain stringencies, such as a crop failure or the need for funds for an emergency. Although it also maybe only under these circumstances that land sales might occur, this does not mean that economic factors do not affect the decision. How serious the crisis must be before land is sold may depend on how much could be obtained for the land, particularly relative to what is being obtained from it at present, and what would obtain if one became a sharecropper.

In this section, we develop a simple, stylized model to bring out the central issues. We assume that land sales do not occur simply on the basis of the kinds of considerations presented in the previous section. Changes in technology or infrastructure do not cause any instantaneous reorganization of land tenure arrangements. These occur only slowly. Individuals sell their land only in crises. For simplicity, we assume that all farms are of a fixed size, and that a farm is either tilled by its owner or under a sharecropping contract. The question then is, What fraction of land is tilled under sharecropping contracts?

We postulate that the probability that a farm that is owner-tilled will be sold, and thus become sharecropped, is

$$F = \tilde{F}(V^s, V^0, t).$$

The frequency of an owner-farmer selling his land depends on V^s and V^0, as well as on the technology itself, which may determine, for instance, the likelihood of a crop failure. What is perhaps more crucial than the absolute level of either the expected returns while owner-tilled (reflected in V^0) or the price one can obtain for selling one's land (reflected in V^s) is the ratio of the two; and for subsequent discussion we postulate that F takes on the simpler form of

$$F = F(V^0/V^s, t).$$

The changes in technology or infrastructure with which we are concerned here decrease V^0/V^s, the value of owner-tilled land with binding capital constraints (the farmers who must sell their land in the event of a crisis), relative to sharecropped land. This effect by itself increases F.

The direct effect on F of technological or infrastructural changes is ambiguous. It is often argued that the Green Revolution, while increasing mean returns, has increased the variance of the returns; the seeds are more sensitive to lack of rainfall, and thus the probability of a crisis is increased. If that is the case, then $F_t > 0$; the direct effect of the technological change is to increase the probability of a land sale. There are, of course, other changes in technology which reduce the likelihood of a crisis; irrigation projects, by making farmers less sensitive to the vagaries of weather, are likely to do this. It is even possible that this direct effect outweighs the indirect "market value" effect, so that the overall probability of an owner-tiller selling his land is decreased.

To derive an equilibrium distribution of landownership, we have to have a theory of how some land becomes converted back to owner-worked land; otherwise, the model would predict that eventually all land would be owned by large landowners. Any model in which there are some stochastic events that impinge on landowners, eventually converting a small fraction of tenancy land into owner-tilled land, will do. Since this is not the focus of our concern here, we simply postulate that there is a probability $\tau(t)$ of an acre of sharecropped land being converted into owner-worked land.[19]

The equilibrium pattern of landownership with a given technology is thus described by

$$S\tau = (1 - S)F$$

or

$$S = F/(F + \tau),$$

where S is the share of land that is sharecropped. Thus, if a change in technology increases F/τ, it will increase the proportion of land under sharecropping.

It is thus apparent that a technological change (or change in infrastructure) that induced more owner-farmers to sell their land (increased F) could, in the long run, lead to more inequality in land ownership and an increased proportion of land under sharecropping. This is true even though the productivity on both owner-run farms and sharecropped farms has increased, so long as the productivity on sharecropped farms has increased *relatively*, say because of the increased productivity of capital.[20] This change in the distribution of tenancy may have a deleterious effect on national productivity.[21]

By the same token, a technological change or change in infrastructure which reduces F/τ, that is, which induces fewer owner-farmers to sell their land, or which enables more sharecroppers to acquire the capital to make it possible (desirable) for them to be owner-tillers, has a long-run productivity effect that may be far in excess of the immediate, short-run, impact.

Similar results can be obtained in a more general model. The wealth distribution at time $v + 1$ depends on the wealth distribution at time v and the nature of the stochastic technology. Let $\Omega_i(v)$ be the fraction of the population with wealth i at time v. Let M_{ij} be the

[19] Clearly, we could make τ depend on the value of land under the alternative institutional arrangements. Moreover, the changes in the probability distribution of returns that affect the likelihood of owner-tilled land being converted to tenancy are also likely to affect the likelihood of tenancy land being converted to owner-tilled. For instance, if the variance of returns is large, then some sharecroppers will have large returns, enabling them to become owner-tillers. As we show below, what is crucial is the effect of technology on the ratio F/τ.

[20] Assuming that credit is rationed, and that credit constraints are more binding upon poor farmers than upon wealthier ones.

[21] The change in tenancy arrangements will have a more deleterious effect on productivity, the greater the difference in productivity on tenancy farms and on owner-run farms; this difference is likely to be larger the greater the elasticity of the supply of effort, and the smaller the extent to which an increase in capital increases the marginal product of effort. Note that what is driving the change in tenancy arrangements is capital constraints; with perfect risk markets and no capital controls, owner-run farms would of course, dominate, because of their advantages in providing incentives.

transition matrix, a function of t (both directly and indirectly, through the choices, say, of effort that it induces). Then in a steady state, in the obvious notation,

$$\Omega^* M(t) = \Omega^*.$$

Changes in technology will affect the distribution of outcomes at any given pattern of tenancy, and will affect the fraction of land under tenancy—see Figure 25.3. Hence changes in technology will affect the steady-state wealth distribution, and this in turn will have real productivity effects. Virtually all changes in technology that change the transition matrix M will lead to a change in long-run distribution of wealth, landholdings, and tenancy arrangements.

Three tasks now lie before us. First, we need to be able to show how particular changes in technology lead to particular changes in the transition matrix $M(t)$. We need to ascertain the precise conditions under which changes in technology are likely to change significantly the long-run equilibrium distributions, both positively and negatively. (Our discussion has suggested that adverse distribution effects are more likely to arise from changes in technology which increase the variance of output—or, more precisely, the likelihood of a serious crop failure, sufficiently serious that the farmer has to sell his land—Braverman and Guasch (1989)—and which increase the return to capital.)

Second, if there is an adverse distribution effect, we need to know the magnitude of the effect on productivity.

Third, the fact that the distribution of landholdings (tenancy arrangements) may have a significant impact on productivity suggests that institutional and other reforms which increase equality may have an important side-effect of increasing output. Economists have long focused on the tradeoff between inequality and output. This analysis suggests either that there may not be a trade-off in the long run, or that the amount of output that need be sacrificed for an improvement in equality may be less than previously thought.

Our analysis suggests particular institutional reforms that *might* either ameliorate any negative distribution effects or accentuate any positive distribution effects. We have emphasized the role of capital constraints. Credit rationing, we have argued, is the natural result of informational imperfections. Informational problems are no less important for the government than for private lenders. This is not a market failure for which there is an obvious

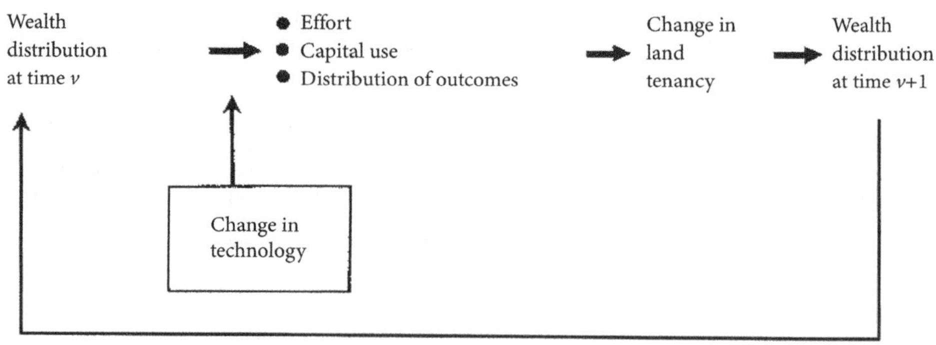

Figure 25.3 Changes in technology lead to changes in the long-run distribution of wealth and tenancy arrangements.

public remedy. On the other hand, our analysis points to the potential role of credit co-operatives in promoting rural development. Examples of successful co-operatives are found in Korea, Taiwan, and Kenya. Unfortunately, credit co-operatives in many other countries have failed. The reasons for the predominance of failures over successes and the analysis of effective enforcement mechanisms in credit co-operatives are the focus of other writings.

6 Concluding Remarks

We have argued here that even if share tenancy is Pareto-efficient, productivity with share tenancy may be lower than with owner-operated farms. The prevalence of share tenancy is directly related to the inequality in the distribution of wealth, and of land-holding in particular. But the degree of inequality should itself be viewed as an endogenous variable, affected by decisions by both large landholders and small peasants concerning the choice of technique and the forms in which to hold their wealth. Both these decisions and their consequences, in turn, are affected by changes in technology and in the rural infrastructure. In the presence of credit rationing, changes in technology or infrastructure may increase inequality in land-holdings, with a long-run increase in the prevalence of share tenancy. This in turn *may* have long-run deleterious effects on productivity at least partially off-setting the initial improvements. We have suggested that the development of small rural lending institutions would reduce the likelihood of these negative effects on equality and productivity.

Here, we have only sketched the outlines of a general theory. We have, however, provided a framework which should enable one to determine whether, in any particular case, changes in technology or infrastructure have the possible adverse effects we have noted.

26

Landlords, Tenants, and Technological Innovations

With Avishay Braverman

1 Introduction

There is a long-standing belief that landlords and capitalists have used their control over the means of production to direct the development and adoption of technologies which have increased their welfare at the expense of workers.[1] Although workers may be better off than they used to be, they are not as well-off as they might have been had they assumed control of the innovation process.

There is also a widespread belief that the interlinkage between credit and tenancy markets,[2] which seems so prevalent in LDCs, provides further impetus to the resistance of certain innovations: innovations which make tenants better off reduce their demand for loans, and thus make landlords (qua creditors) worse off.[3]

These contentions have typically been dismissed out of hand by standard welfare economics arguments. An innovation is defined as a shift outward in the production possibilities schedule, or equivalently, as an outward shift in the utility possibilities schedule. Then, if the economy is competitive, at the old equilibrium level of utility of workers, it pays each landlord to adopt the innovation. In doing so, landlords may increase their demand for tenants, and as a result, in the new equilibrium, they may be worse off. Still, it is in the interest of each competitive landlord to adopt the innovation. Alternatively, if the landlords act collusively, say as a single monopsonist, they will push the tenants to the

[1] Written with Avishay Braverman. Originally published in 1986 as "Landlords, Tenants and Technological Innovations," *Journal of Development Economics*, 23(2): 313–32. Reprinted with permission. We thank David Newbery, T. N. Srinivasan, Russ Krelove, In-Koo Cho, Erika Jorgensen, anonymous referees, and in particular D. Abreu for many helpful comments on earlier drafts of this chapter. An earlier version of this chapter was presented to the European Congress of the Econometric Society in Pisa, Italy, 1983.

[2] For an excellent survey of the phenomena of interlinked markets, see Bardhan (1980) and also Binswanger and Rosenzweig (1984). Elsewhere, we provide an economic rationale for interlinkage, derived from the general theory of moral hazard (Braverman and Stiglitz, 1982). For other theoretical discussions of interlinkage, see Bell and Zusman (1980), Braverman and Srinivasan (1981), Mitra (1983), and Braverman and Guasch (1984).

[3] See, for instance, Bhaduri (1973, 1980). Bhaduri, noting the interlinkage between credit, land, and labor markets to which we referred earlier, has argued that landlords resist innovations because these typically reduce the demand for tenants' credit, and hence landlords' profits. Newbery (1975), Braverman and Stiglitz (1982), and Mitra (1983) have questioned the exploitation explanation for interlinkage that Bhaduri has put forward. Srinivasan (1979), using Bhaduri's model, has argued against Bhaduri's contention that innovations lead to lesser demand for credit. As we show below the demand for credit may either increase or decrease as a result of an innovation, but whether landlords are better or worse off as a result of an innovation does not depend solely on the effect of the innovation on the demand for credit. A decrease in tenants' demand for credit is neither necessary nor sufficient for landlords to resist innovations. Newbery (1975) called attention to the need to focus on moral hazard issues in analyzing resistance to technological innovations. He provided an example in which technological innovation would be resisted by monopsonist landlords.

The Origins of Inequality, and Policies to Contain It. Joseph E. Stiglitz with Avishay Braverman, Oxford University Press.
 DOI: 10.1093/oso/9780198799580.003.0027

subsistence level. Again, it will always pay them to adopt the innovation. Thus, while in a perfect monopoly, innovations are never disadvantageous to an individual landlord; in perfectly competitive environments, innovations advantageous to an individual landlord, which when the general equilibrium effects are taken into account are disadvantageous to landlords as a group, cannot be effectively resisted.

The rural environment of most LDCs may not, however, be adequately described by the standard economic model on which this welfare analysis is based. In particular, in many LDCs, sharecropping contracts are widely employed; there is evidence of widespread unemployment, and there is not the full set of (risk and capital) markets required by the competitive paradigm.[4]

The objective of this chapter is to show under quite general conditions that the institutional structure of the economy may indeed be an important determinant of whether a particular innovation will or will not be adopted.[5] We show that:

(i) landlords may wish to—and can—resist innovations which unambiguously increase production whenever sharecropping contracts are employed;[6]

(ii) conversely, landlords may adopt innovations which not only lower the welfare of workers, but even lower net national product;

(iii) the presence of interlinkage may, indeed, affect the adoption of a new technology; however, the reason for this is only partly related to the effect of innovations on tenants' borrowing. Indeed, we show that innovations may increase as well as decrease the tenants' demand for borrowing.

2 Sharecropping and the Adoption of Technological Innovations

Traditional welfare analysis has equated an outward shift in the production possibilities schedule with an outward shift in the utility possibilities schedule. Under traditional economic assumptions, the two are, in fact, equivalent. But whenever factors do not get paid their full marginal product, the two may not be equivalent. Such is the case with sharecropping contracts.[7] The change in technology may increase output for each level of input; but at the same time, it may exacerbate the incentive problem. As a result, even a competitive landlord may not wish to adopt the innovation.

[4] The impact of innovations on the marginal costs of landlords and on the utilities of tenants and landlords has also been analyzed in the context of the economic history of the U.S. rural South; e.g., Reid (1979) and Alston (1981) discuss the impact of technology on southern landlords' attitude toward sharecropping.

[5] For most of the analysis, we do not discuss the costs of innovation. We envisage an invention which has occurred and ask under what conditions will the invention be adopted. It is straightforward to modify our analysis to take account of the costs of innovation, provided we have a well-defined theory of how those costs are to be shared.

[6] If landlords have monopsony power, then the possibility of their resisting an innovation which would be adopted in a competitive market is even greater, because as they assess the optimal input of labor, if it increases, they will take into account of the increased wages they will have to pay. These increased wages are, of course, distributive, a transfer from landlords to workers, particularly valued if we had an equalitarian social welfare function; but focusing just on output, the distributive effect would be ignored.

[7] The contract need not be a pure sharecropping contract; there may, for instance, be a fixed rent or wage component to the tenancy agreement. It should be clear that the argument applies to any principal–agent problem in which the principal (e.g., landlord) bears some of the risk and hence the agent (e.g., tenant) does not bear the full consequences of his actions.

The objective of this chapter is to identify circumstances in which, with sharecropping, innovations (in the *technological* sense) will not be adopted.

The analysis is divided into two stages:

(i) *Fixed contract.* Under what conditions will landlords be worse off when the terms of the contract between the landlord and tenant remain unchanged? The answer to this question determines whether, if landlords could resist an innovation, they would do so *if* the terms of the contract could not be altered (e.g., if they were fixed by social norms).

(ii) *Variable contracts: fixed expected utility.* The terms of the contract may, of course, change. The standard formulation of the competitive equilibrium with sharecropping (e.g., Stiglitz, 1974b) has the terms of the contract chosen to maximize the expected utility of the landlord, given a level of expected utility of the tenant.[8] The change in the technology will thus induce a change in the terms of the contract, and the question is, when these adjustments are taken into account, under what conditions will landlords still be worse off? The conditions derived in this section are important because they not only determine when innovations will not be adopted in competitive environments but they also show when innovations will not be adopted under noncompetitive conditions. A monopsony landlord may be modeled as maximizing his expected utility, subject to the subsistence constraint of his workers.

2.1 Partial vs. General Equilibrium Analysis

It is important to emphasize that even if landlords do not resist innovations, that is, each believes that his expected utility will be increased by its adoption, in the general equilibrium, landlords may be worse off. Under these circumstances, collusion may be required for landlords to resist innovation. In small villages with few landlords the possibility of collusion (tacit or explicit) is very plausible (e.g., Rudra, 1984). This collusion may be enforced by a variety of social and economic sanctions (see Akerlof, 1980). The conditions under which landlords will voluntarily adopt disadvantageous innovations are discussed in Section 2.5 below. The possibility of such innovations has, of course, long been recognized (see, e.g., Hicks 1932). What distinguishes our analysis from Hicks' is that we emphasize the implications of imperfect supervision technology and limited risk markets on the general equilibrium effects. Hicks deals only with perfectly competitive and perfectly monitored wage labor markets. Whether landlords can restrict the adoption of a new technique depends also on whether the tenants' use of the technique can be observed, and, if so, whether the contractual arrangements between the landlord and tenant allow the landlords to specify what technologies the tenant may employ.

Before using calculus we present a simple example illustrating why, with sharecropping, innovations may not be adopted.

[8] The landlord is an "expected utility" taker, rather than a price (wage) taker.

2.2 An Example

To make the example as simple as possible, we ignore uncertainty and, initially, assume that the terms of the contract are fixed.[9]

Consider the technological change represented by Figure 26.1. In the old technique, denoted by $f(e)$, the marginal return to effort was very high up to e^*, and that is the level of effort supplied by the tenant. The new technology, denoted by $\hat{f}(e)$, though unambiguously better than the old, has diminishing returns set in at a much lower level of effort and at a lower level of output. The tenant now operates at e^{**}. As a result, the landlord is worse off. (This may be true even when the share of the tenant, α, is lowered to leave the tenant just as well-off as before.)[10] Landlords, in this case, would like to restrict the adoption of the new technique. Note that *no collusive action is required* and in the particular instance drawn in Figure 26.1, *national output is increased* by this resistance to new technology, at the expense of tenants' welfare.[11]

This example shows that there may be improvements to the land which increase tenants' productivity but lower the net returns to land. These would clearly not be adopted by landlords. They would be if tenants owned their own land. Tenants might even be willing to pay for the improvements themselves, if their tenure on a particular plot of land was secure, but not otherwise (and the latter seems to be the prevalent situation in many LDCs).[12]

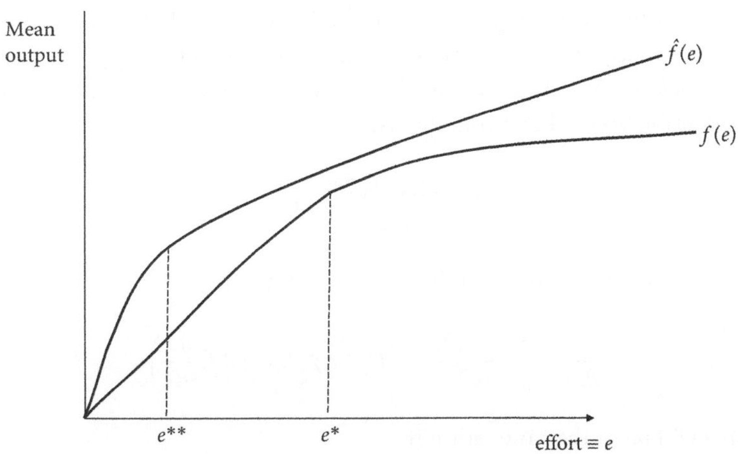

Figure 26.1 Comparison of the new technology, $\hat{f}$, with the old one, f.

[9] In the absence of uncertainty, it is hard to justify the employment of sharecropping relationships, so long as effort is variable. This assumption is employed to simplify the exposition; as the discussion below makes clear, nothing critical depends on this assumption.

[10] Other terms of the contract (such as plot size) might also adjust. See, for example, Stiglitz (1974b), Newbery and Stiglitz (1979a), Braverman and Srinivasan (1981), Braverman and Stiglitz (1982), and the discussion below.

[11] Ordinary national product measures evaluate only output and do not include effort evaluation which enters the tenant's utility.

[12] Alternatively, our analysis can be interpreted as showing that there is an important set of "welfare" enhancing innovations which it would never pay landlords to adopt.

2.3 A General Argument: Fixed Contract

More generally, with a sharecropping contract, the tenant's problem is

$$\max_{\{e\}} EU(\alpha f(e, T, \Omega, \theta), e) \equiv V(\Omega; \alpha, T), \tag{26.1}$$

where α = share of tenant, T = plot size, e = tenant's effort,[13] f = (value of) output[14] in state θ with technology Ω, effort e, and plot size T, and $U = U(Y^w, e)$ is the tenant's utility function, which depends on his income, $Y^w = \alpha f$, and his effort, e, with the usual properties.[15]

The equilibrium contract is described by $\{\alpha, T\}$.

The landlord is assumed to be sufficiently wealthy and provided with a sufficient number of alternatives to diversify his risk portfolio, so that he can be represented as risk-neutral; he maximizes his expected income,

$$\pi \equiv (1 - \alpha)Ef. \tag{26.2}$$

We shall be concerned with changes in technology which, in a purely technological sense, are unambiguous improvements, that is,

$$f_\Omega > 0 \text{ for all } \theta, e \text{ and } T. \tag{26.3}$$

In every state of nature, for any pre-specified level of effort and plot size, output is higher with the new technology than with the old, so that the new technology—in a *technological* sense—dominates the old. It is obvious that for such technologies, with a *fixed contract*, tenants are unambiguously better off, that is,

$$\frac{\partial V(\Omega; \alpha, T)}{\partial \Omega} > 0. \tag{26.4}$$

Straightforward differentiation of landlord profits shows that

$$\frac{\partial \pi}{\partial \Omega} = \frac{\partial (1 - \alpha)Ef}{\partial \Omega} = (1 - \alpha)\left(Ef_\Omega + Ef_e \frac{\partial e}{\partial \Omega}\right), \tag{26.5}$$

and landlords will resist the innovation if

$$\left|\frac{\partial e}{\partial \Omega}\right| > \frac{Ef_\Omega}{Ef_e}.^{16} \tag{26.6}$$

With a sufficiently large negative effort response on the part of tenants, landlords will be worse off at the old contract, and thus resist the innovation.

[13] e can represent a vector of inputs of the tenant.

[14] For most of the analysis we assume that the price of output of agricultural goods is fixed. Hence, we let it be equal to unity, and f becomes physical output.

[15] U is assumed to be quasi-concave, with $U_e < 0$ and $U_{ee} < 0$ and $U_Y > 0$ and $U_{YY} < 0$, where $Y = \alpha f$ (consumption).

[16] This formulation assumes that the effort decision is made before θ is known. It is straightforward to modify the analysis to the case where the effort decision is made after θ is known.

The magnitude of $\partial e/\partial\Omega$ depends both on the properties of the tenant's utility function and on how the innovation changes the technology. For instance, if the utility function is separable of the form

$$U = u(Y^w) - v(e), \tag{26.7}$$

then[17]

$$\frac{1}{e}\left(\frac{\partial e}{\partial\Omega}\right)\bigg|_\alpha = \frac{\{Em(f_{e\Omega}/f_e) - R(f_\Omega/f)\}}{\gamma + Em\{Ra - \eta\}}, \tag{26.8}$$

Where

$$m \equiv u'f \,|\, Eu'f_e, \quad a = \frac{f_e e}{f}, \quad \eta \equiv f_{ee}e/f.$$

$\gamma = v''e|v'$ denotes the elasticity of the marginal disutility of effort and $R \equiv -u''Y^w u'$ denotes the measure of relative risk aversion. The effect on effort depends not only on how the innovation affects output, f_Ω, but also on how the innovation affects the marginal return to effort, $f_{e\Omega}$, as our earlier example illustrated.[18] There are, as usual, two effects: an income effect, which if leisure is normal leads to a reduction in effort, and is greater the greater is the individual's risk aversion, R, and the greater is the proportionate upward shift in the production function, f_Ω/f; and a substitution effect, which can be of either sign. If the innovation reduces the marginal product of effort (as in our example), i.e., $f_{e\Omega} < 0$, then this too leads to a reduction in effort. Thus, landlords resist an innovation if it reduces the marginal return to effort by a sufficiently large amount.[19]

We now show that *landlords will adopt an innovation if and only if it increases national income* (taking into account the effort response of tenants).

The effect of an innovation on national income is simply given by

$$E\left(f_\Omega + f_e\frac{\partial e}{\partial\Omega}\right). \tag{26.9}$$

But this coincides precisely with condition (26.6), and the result is immediate. (Note that the level of landlord's share, $1 - \alpha$, affects the innovation adoption only indirectly.)

At the same time, it is apparent that landlords resist innovations which may decrease their welfare only slightly but increase that of tenants enormously; if the adoption of

[17] This follows by differentiating the tenant's first order condition for effort, $\alpha Eu'f_e = v'$.

[18] Note that the denominator of (26.8) is always positive from the second order condition.

[19] Alternative sufficient conditions for the landlord to resist innovation can also be derived. As R becomes large,

$$\frac{\partial e}{\partial\Omega} \approx \frac{-E\psi f_\Omega/f}{E\psi f_e/f} \text{ where } \psi \equiv Ru'f_e$$

This if $f = h(\theta)g(e, T, \Omega)$, then

$$\frac{\partial e}{\partial\Omega} \approx \frac{-f_\Omega}{f_e}$$

and the landlord is indifferent to the innovation.

the innovation were controlled by a government which maximizes national welfare, such innovations would be adopted, provided some weight is attached to the gain of tenants.[20]

2.4 Landlord's Profits at Fixed Expected Utility of Tenants

The argument above establishes that if the terms of the contract are fixed by law or custom (as they often are),[21] then, in the short run, landlords will resist the innovation, until appropriate adjustments can be made to the contract.

The relevant question for the longer run analysis, where the terms of the contract are adjustable, is whether, when the terms of the contract are adjusted to leave tenants indifferent, will landlords be better off. We established earlier that at the old terms, innovations always make tenants better off. Hence, if the expected utility of tenants is to remain unchanged, the share of tenants or the plot size must be lowered. The change in technology then has three effects on landlords: (a) the direct effect of an increase in output, which increases landlords' income, (b) the direct effect of the adjustment in the contract, which will make landlords better off, and (c) the effect of the adjustment of effort both to the change in technology and to the compensating adjustment in the contract. This is of ambiguous sign, the "substitution" effect from the lower share leads to lower levels of effort while the change in technology itself may increase the marginal return to effort. Since the landlord always adjusts the terms of the contract in such a way that the total effect of the adjustment is to make himself better off, the landlord is less likely to resist innovations if he is able to adjust the terms of the contract than if he is not.

Analytically, instead of (26.5) we obtain:

$$\left.\frac{d\pi}{d\Omega}\right|_{\overline{V}} = E\left\{(1-\alpha)\left[\underbrace{f_\Omega}_{\text{Direct effect of technology}} + \underbrace{f_T \left.\frac{dT}{d\Omega}\right|_{\overline{V}}\right] - f\left.\frac{d\alpha}{d\Omega}\right|_{\overline{V}}}_{\text{Direct effect of change of contract}} + \underbrace{(1-\alpha)f_e \left.\frac{de}{d\Omega}\right|_{\overline{V}}}_{\text{Effect of change in effort}}\right\}. \tag{26.10}$$

The general derivation of $d\alpha/d\Omega|_{\overline{V}}$, $dT/d\Omega|_{\overline{V}}$ and $de/d\Omega|_{\overline{V}}$ is complicated. For our present purpose, we limit ourselves to the special case where technology is such that there is an "efficient" plot size which remains unaltered by the change in Ω,[22] and where utility

[20] Since the terms of the contract are fixed, landlords will resist the adoption of some innovations which would be Pareto improvements if the terms of the contract could be adjusted, for example, if lump sum transfer payments may be made between workers and landlords.

[21] Output shares in LDCs are often found to be fixed at 50:50.

[22] Formally, the optimal contract is the solution to the problem

$$\max\,(1-x)Ef[e(x,T,\Omega),T,\Omega,\theta] \quad s.t. \quad V(\Omega;\alpha,T) \geq \overline{V},$$

that is, $\{\alpha, T\}$ solves the following pair of equations:

$$-Ef + (1-\alpha)\left[Ef_e\frac{\partial e}{\partial \alpha} - \left(f_e\frac{\partial e}{\partial T} + f_T\right)\frac{V_\alpha}{V_T}\right] = 0 \tag{i}$$

is separable. Then,

$$\left.\frac{d\alpha}{d\Omega}\right|_{\overline{V}} = -\frac{\alpha Eu'f_\Omega}{Eu'f} < 0 \tag{26.11}$$

and

$$\begin{aligned}\left.\frac{de}{d\Omega}\right|_{\overline{V}} &= \frac{\partial e}{\partial \Omega} + \left.\frac{\partial e}{\partial \alpha}\frac{d\alpha}{d\Omega}\right|_{\overline{V}} \\ &= \frac{\alpha\left[(Eu''f_\Omega f_e^\alpha + u'f_{e\Omega}) - (Eu'f_\Omega/Eu'f)\cdot E(u' + \alpha u''f)f_e\right]}{v' - \alpha E\{u''f_e^2\alpha + u'f_{ee}\}}.\end{aligned} \tag{26.12}$$

It is clear that there are changes in technology which have a large effect (locally) on the marginal return to effort ($f_{e\Omega}$ is large) but which, at the same time, have a small (positive) effect on output (f_Ω is small). These changes will thus induce a larger reduction in effort, cause only a small adjustment in the terms of the contract (note that $d\alpha/d\Omega$ depends only on the magnitude of f_Ω, not on $f_{e\Omega}$), and hence make landlords unambiguously worse off.

It should be noted that nowhere in the analysis so far have we made use of the competitive hypothesis. Hence our analysis is equally applicable to the competitive landlord who takes as given the expected utility which his contract must provide to tenants (in order to obtain tenants) as it does to monopsonist landlords, who push their tenants down to the subsistence expected utility level.

In this section we have established that when there are incentive problems (as arise in the context of sharecropping), an innovation which unambiguously increases output for each level of input may yet shift all or a segment of the utility possibilities schedule inward, that is, at certain prespecified levels of expected utility of tenants, landlords are worse off. In Figures 26.2 and 26.3 we provide two such examples. In the first example (Figure 26.2), the whole utility possibilities frontier shifts inward due to the new innovation. Therefore, the innovation will be rejected, both by a monopsonist landlord, who drives the workers down to their subsistence level, and in a competitive equilibrium.

Perhaps more interesting is the second example (Figure 26.3) where the new utility possibilities schedule crosses the old. In the case illustrated this innovation will be rejected by the monopsonist, but would be adopted in the competitive environment.

Finally, we note that in contrast to the results of Section 2.3 (compare (26.10) to (26.5) and (26.9)), if the terms of the contract are adjustable, the decision of the landlord to adopt an innovation does not coincide with whether the innovation increases national income (taking into account the adjustment of the terms of the contract). *There are innovations which lower national income but which still will be adopted because they enable the landlord to lower the share received by workers.*

and

$$V(\Omega; \alpha, T) \geq \overline{V}, \tag{ii}$$

$d\alpha/d\Omega$ and $dT/d\Omega$ are found by straightforward implicit differentiation of (i) and (ii).

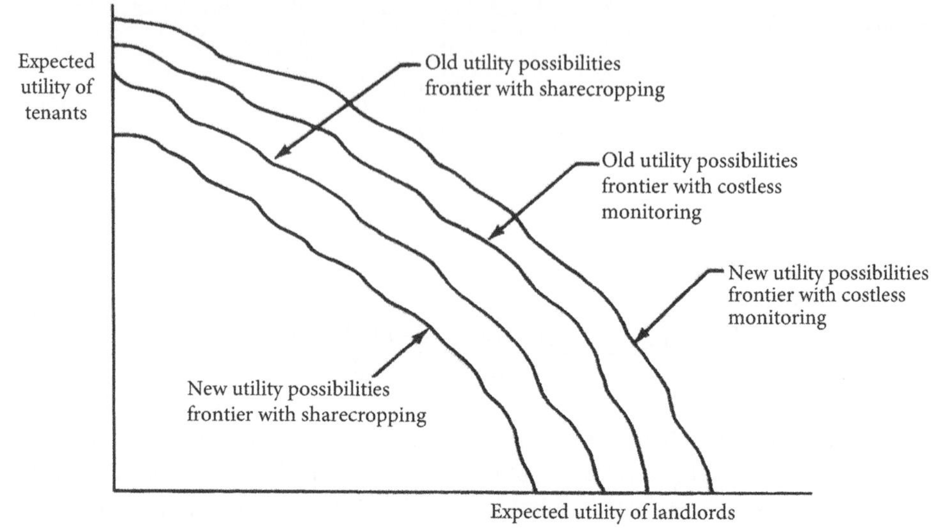

Figure 26.2 A case in which innovation under sharecropping shifts the whole utility possibilities frontiers inward.

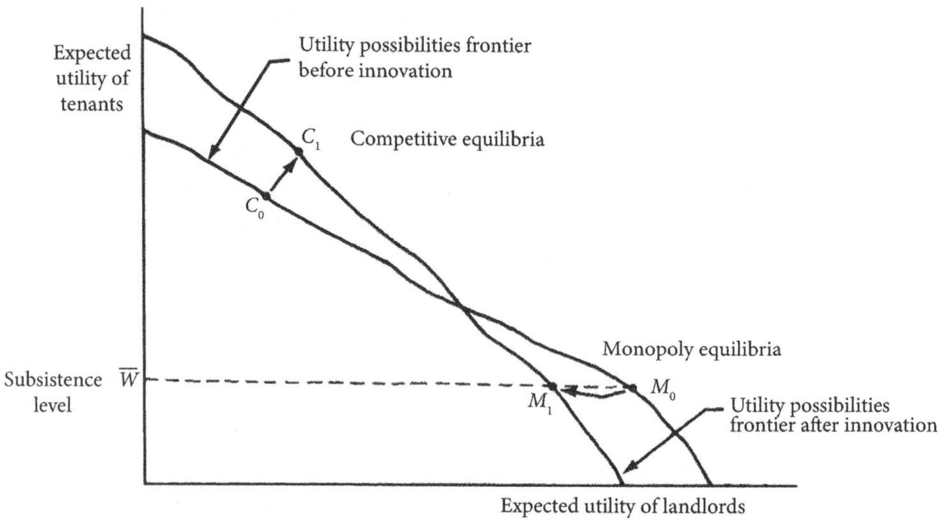

Figure 26.3 A case in which the utility possibilities frontiers cross; monopolist resists innovation which is adopted in competitive economy.

2.5 General Equilibrium Impact of Innovation

The fact that a landlord finds it in his interest to adopt the innovation in a competitive economy (where the landlord takes the level of expected utility of tenants as given) does not mean that when all landlords adopt the innovation, landlords will be better off. How the gains to an innovation are distributed between the landlords and tenants, in equilibrium, will depend on how the innovation affects the demand for tenants, or, equivalently, how the innovation affects the equilibrium plot size. If, at the old level of expected utility of tenants, the optimal plot size is increased, then demand for tenants will decrease, and tenants will be worse off with the innovation;[23] all the gains accrue to the landlords; if, in contrast, at the old level of expected income (utility) of landlords, the optimal plot size is reduced, then landlords will be worse off with the innovation. However, in a competitive environment, although they might wish to resist the innovation, they can only do so through collusive actions. Hence it will pay each landlord to adopt the new technology.

The conditions under which an innovation will lead to an increase in the demand for labor (smaller plot sizes) may be derived as a straightforward extension of the analysis of Braverman–Stiglitz (1982). For our purposes, it is sufficient to note that a critical determinant of the effect of the innovation on plot size is the magnitude of $f_{T\Omega}$, that is, whether the innovation increases or decreases the marginal return to (larger) plot size: while in the traditional analysis the sign of $f_{T\Omega}$ would be the sole determinant of the general equilibrium impact of the innovation on landlords, here the general equilibrium effect depends as well on how the innovation affects the marginal return to effort and the share compensated effort response from a change in plot size, that is, the technology of supervision and the contractual framework are also critical in assessing the general equilibrium effects.

3 Interlinkage and the Adoption of Innovations

In this section, we address the question of whether the fact that landlords are frequently also lenders to their tenants makes it more or less likely that landlords will wish, or be able, to resist innovations.[24] We argue here that the conclusion—that interlinkage of credit and tenancy markets (like other important aspects of the institutional organization of agriculture) has an important effect on innovation—is correct, but the lines of argument by which earlier studies reached that conclusion are either incorrect, or incomplete. In particular, we shall show:

(i) The earlier analyses of the effect of technological change on borrowing, though correct in noting that changes in technology could have a significant effect on borrowing by tenants, improperly treated the demand for loans by ignoring uncertainty; in contrast, we argue that the demand for loans which is a derived demand and which depends on the relationship between present and future income, is critically affected by the stochastic properties of future income. Thus, under quite plausible assumptions concerning the nature of the utility functions of tenants and the nature of the innovation, innovations may either increase or decrease the demand for borrowing. The basic line of the argument is provided below, while mathematical demonstration of sufficient conditions for results in both directions are presented in our earlier working paper (Braverman and Stiglitz, 1986b).

[23] This assumes that the supply of tenants is not perfectly elastic. If the supply is perfectly elastic, clearly, $\overline{V}$ remains unchanged, and the partial equilibrium and general equilibrium effects coincide. The change in plot size simply affects the number of tenant farmers (see Braverman and Srinivasan, 1981 for such a model).

[24] As we noted earlier Bhaduri (1973) argued that landlords-cum-lenders will be more resistant to innovation because it will lower the demand for their highly profitable lending. We also noted earlier that this result has been contest with Srinivasan (1979), demonstrating that Bhaduri's results require that loans be inferior goods. We will provide further qualification to Bhaduri's analysis below.

(ii) An analysis of the effect of the innovation on the demand for loans is neither necessary nor sufficient to determine the impact of interlinkage on the adoption of innovations. Elsewhere (Braverman and Stiglitz, 1982), we showed that one possible explanation for interlinkage is that, under sharecropping, the amount borrowed affects the landlord's return (through its effect both on the individual's effort and on his decisions concerning choices of technique), and conversely, the terms of the landlord's contract affect the returns to the lender (through its effect on the likelihood of default). Interlinkage was a method by which these "externalities" could be internalized. But if there are important interactions of the kind just described, then what is of concern to the landlord-cum-lender is the total impact of the innovation on his income; the decomposition of his income into return as a lender, or return as a landlord, has no particular significance. It is clear, however, that the impact of an innovation on a landlord-cum-lender may be quite different from the impact of the same innovation on a landlord who does not control the borrowing activities of his tenants.

We now turn to a more detailed examination of each of these points.

3.1 The Adoption of Innovations in Interlinked Markets

To ascertain the effect of an innovation on a landlord-cum-lender in an interlinked market, we employ an extension of the simple model developed in Section 2. There, we assumed that the landlord cannot control effort directly, and because tenants receive only a fraction of their marginal product, they will have insufficient incentives for exerting themselves. We assumed that effort was a function of the share they received.[25] Here, we assume (following Braverman and Stiglitz, 1982) that borrowing too has an effect on effort, while the amount tenants borrow, B, will, in turn, be affected by the terms of the loan contract. For simplicity, we shall assume that landlords have only one instrument in the capital market—the rate of interest which they charge on a loan.[26] Thus, if increased borrowing leads to increased effort, the landlord may attempt to encourage borrowing (by charging a lower interest rate) and conversely, if increased borrowing leads to reduced effort.

We thus write the income of the landlord-cum-lender as

$$\pi = (1 - \alpha)Ef(e, \Omega) + (r - \rho)B \tag{26.13}$$

and

$$\begin{aligned}\frac{d\pi}{d\Omega} &= (1 - \alpha)Ef_{\Omega} + (1 - \alpha)Ef_e\left(\frac{\partial e}{\partial \Omega} + \frac{\partial e}{\partial B}\frac{dB}{d\Omega} + \frac{\partial e}{\partial r}\frac{dr}{d\Omega}\right) \\ &\quad +(r - \rho)\frac{dB}{d\Omega} + B\frac{dr}{d\Omega},\end{aligned} \tag{26.14}$$

[25] Effort is also a function of the plot size, which, for simplicity, we take as fixed for purposes of the present analysis.

[26] In our earlier study, we showed that if the landlord could, he might wish to employ non-linear loan schedules.

where

$$\frac{dB}{d\Omega} = \frac{\partial B}{\partial \Omega} + \frac{\partial B}{\partial r}\frac{dr}{d\Omega} \tag{26.15}$$

and where ρ is the opportunity cost of funds to the landlord, r is the rate of interest charged,[27] and effort, e, is viewed as a function of the technology, Ω, the level of indebtedness, B, and the rate of interest charged, that is, $e(\Omega, B, r)$.

The effect of a change in technology now depends on whether the landlord can adjust the interest rate. We start by focusing our remarks on the case where the rate of interest charged is fixed so the terms in $dr/d\Omega$ are set at zero. The change in technology has (i) a direct effect, (ii) an indirect effect through an adjustment in effort (which again is ambiguous in sign), and (iii) an indirect effect through an adjustment in the demand for credit. The latter has two distinct effects. First, there is a direct effect, which may be positive or negative, both because the effect on the demand for loans is ambiguous, and because the interest rate charged may be greater or less than the opportunity cost of capital. Secondly, the level of indebtedness has an effect on effort which too is ambiguous in sign; elsewhere we have analyzed the determinants of this effect (Braverman and Stiglitz, 1982).

Because the landlord-cum-lender will always adjust the interest rate he charges so that the total effect (taking into account the adjustment of effort) will be to increase his profits, it is more likely that an innovation will be adopted if the interest rate can be varied than if it cannot. On the other hand, contrasting (26.14) and (26.5), it is clear that an innovation which increases a landlord's income might lower that of a landlord-cum-lender, and conversely.

Note, in particular that if the rate of interest charged on loans to tenants is the same as the rate of return which they can obtain elsewhere, then, of course, it makes no difference whether the technological innovation leads to an increase or decrease in borrowing, provided that borrowing does not have an indirect effect on effort. If the tenant borrows from the landlord because he gives him favorable terms (i.e., the terms of the typical tenancy contract do not restrict the tenant's rights to borrow elsewhere) the rate of interest charged by the landlord must be less than or equal to those charged elsewhere,[28] that is, $\rho > r$.

In short, a landlord's incentives for adopting innovations may be enhanced or diminished by interlinking.

[27] Equation (26.13) implicitly assumes the probability of default is zero. More generally, we write:

$$\Pi = (1 - \alpha)Ef(e, \Omega) + [\hat{r}(e, \Omega, \beta, r) - \rho]B,$$

where $\hat{r}$ is the expected return from a loan of size B bearing an interest rate r to individual exerting effort e, with technology Ω. Of course, e itself is a function of the terms of the other parameters of the problem. The share α and plot size T also actually affect both effort and the probability of default (and hence $\hat{r}$, given r) but we take α and T as given, and here suppress the dependence of $\hat{r}$ and e on α and T.

[28] This argument is not perfectly persuasive: if landlords are more informed concerning the risk characteristics of their tenants than others, and if the capital market is risk averse, then a tenant who borrows from the open market may have to pay a risk premium. Hence, it is possible that, the opportunity cost for the landlord, P, is less than r, the rate of interest charged by the landlord, even though r is less than the rate of interest which the tenant can obtain elsewhere.

Though we agree with Bhaduri that a reduction in the demand for loans is a real possibility, the *direct* effect of this reduction will increase the profits of a landlord-cum-lender if $r < p$.

Just as before, where we showed that a technological change with observability could shift the utility possibilities curve outward, but with costly monitoring, it could shift it inward, so too here: with interlinkage, the utility possibilities schedule might be shifted one way, without it, it could be shifted the other. Interlinking makes it more likely, however, that measured national income will be increased as a result of the adoption of any innovation. In the absence of interlinkage, there is always the possibility that innovations which increase the income of the landlord at the expense of lenders might be adopted.[29] Similarly, it is possible that innovations which increase the income of a lender-cum-landlord, decrease the income of landlords in non-interlinked markets, and thus will not be adopted. By internalizing these potential externalities, interlinking may be expected to result in a welfare gain.[30]

3.2 The Determination of Tenants' Borrowing

Equation (26.14) demonstrates that a critical determinant of the effect of an innovation on the profitability of the landlord-cum-lender was the effect of a change in technology on the demand for borrowing.[31] We asserted that, even for well behaved changes in technology and well-behaved utility functions, this could be of either sign. The basic argument is the following.

The objective of borrowing is to smooth income between different periods.

Consider a two-period model. If an individual has an abnormally low income in the first period, then he will borrow, in anticipation of having a higher income the next period. (Since there is uncertainty about next period's income, there is, of course, some chance that next period will be even worse than this.) Changes in the distribution of income affect both the likelihood of a low (say below mean) income this period, and the likelihood of that next period; they also have income effects, which affect the individual's willingness to accept different risks. Whether, on average, borrowing will be increased or decreased, depends both on the nature of the change in the probability distribution of output and on the tenant's utility function.[32] In our working paper (Braverman and Stiglitz, 1986b) we show that a uniform increase in output decreases borrowing if individuals have decreasing absolute risk aversion and the rate of interest exceeds the pure rate of time preference and if the variance of output is small; on the other hand, a mean-preserving spread in the distribution of output increases the level of borrowing if the utility function is quadratic, but, with other plausible utility functions, it may be decreased.[33]

[29] That is, we now need to expand the utility possibility schedule to include lenders as well as tenants and landlords.

[30] As always, in second best analysis internalizing one set of externalities may exacerbate other inefficiencies.

[31] We are concerned here mainly with borrowing for consumption credit, which is the focus of the Bhaduri–Srinivasan debate. However, Braverman and Stiglitz (1982) present a formulation which points out how the analysis can be extended to cover production credit.

[32] It depends on the value of the first *four* derivatives of the utility function, as well as on the nature of the change in the distribution of output.

[33] The formal procedure by which to analyze the effect of change in technology on the demand for credit is presented in the appendix to the original paper.

4 Concluding Comments

This chapter has shown that there may be some truth in the widespread view that landlords may wish to, and can, resist innovations, changes in technology which increase the amount of output that can be obtained from any given input. The institutional structure of the LDCs and the market power of landlords may, indeed, be an important determinant of whether a particular innovation is or is not adopted. Although such changes will, under the conventional assumptions concerning costless monitoring of workers, result in an unambiguous outward shift in the utility possibilities schedule, when monitoring is costly and contracts involve some form of sharecropping such innovations may result in segments of the utility possibilities schedule moving inward.

We have also argued that the presence of interlinkages between credit and land markets does not necessarily imply either resistance or encouragement to the adoption of technological innovations. Either case is possible. It might actually encourage the adoption of some technologies which otherwise would not be adopted, even though the effect of this innovation is to reduce tenants' demand for credit. Whether the demand for credit itself is increased or decreased turns out to depend critically both on how the technical change affects the probability distribution of yields and on tenants' utility functions.[34]

The analysis of this chapter suggests that the question of the adoption of new technologies is a far more complicated and subtle question than traditional welfare analyses might suggest.

Although we address here the issues of the adoption of innovation within the context of agriculture in a less developed country, it should be clear that very similar issues arise in developed industrialized countries as well. A slight variant of our model can be used to establish that there are certain systematic biases in the nature of the innovations which are adopted; in particular, one can construct a simple model which is consistent with the long-standing allegation that capitalism results in the adoption of innovations which entail "excessive" job routinization or "excessively" reduce the cost of monitoring.[35]

[34] A technological innovation such as the introduction of High Yield Varieties (HYV) is often associated not only with higher mean yield but also with higher spread of the distribution, the HYV being more susceptible to bad weather and pests. However, the introduction of HYV is also associated with increase in input of fertilizers and effort, additional "externalities." Landlords who internalize all these externalities by interlinking contracts are less likely to resist technological innovations. On the internalization of such externalities through cost sharing arrangements of inputs, see Braverman and Stiglitz (1986a).

[35] See Braverman and Stiglitz (1985).

PART III.D
INEQUALITY AND MACRO-DYNAMICS

Introduction to Part III.D

This part of the book presents some of my papers looking at the relationship between macro-dynamics and inequality (in contrast to the previous section which focused on microeconomics) Here, there are two essential questions: the impact of inequality on long-term growth and economic fluctuations, and the impact of economic fluctuations on inequalities of income and well-being. Two of the chapters are among my earliest papers, one was written in the aftermath of the 2008 financial crisis, while two others were written during the years that I was directly engaged in public policy, and reflect more directly matters of policy.

Long-Term Growth

Classical growth theory provided an unpleasant theory of the relationship between growth and inequality: it assumed that the rich, in particular capitalists, saved a larger fraction of their incomes than the poor, and that capital accumulation was critical to growth and standards of living.[1] Hence, societies with more inequality could (would) grow more rapidly.[2] If one redistributed income toward workers, one would pay a price in terms of future growth (or lower levels of steady state capital labor ratios, and therefore lower per capita income).

On the other hand, in situations where there is a lack of aggregate demand, an increase in inequality means, in effect, a transfer of income from those with a high marginal propensity to consume to those with a low marginal propensity to consume, lowering aggregate demand. If, for one reason or another, the economy doesn't automatically adjust, and there are no effective remediation policies, unemployment will increase and growth will slow.

For the most part, modern growth theory assumed away both issues: it *assumed* distribution had no effect on savings (it employed the representative agent model or, as in Solow (1956), that the aggregate savings rate did not depend on distribution) and *assumed* that the economy was always in a full employment equilibrium. What mattered were incentives to save, and in most formulations policies which supported a lower equilibrium (real)

[1] Solow's 1956 analysis clarified that higher savings led to faster growth only in the short run; in the long run, growth was driven by technological change (assumed in his analysis to be exogenous) and population growth. Savings rates affected the long run standard of living.

[2] At least in the short run. See the previous footnote.

interest rate supported a higher per capita income. Whether that increased or decreased the share of labor depended just on the elasticity of substitution, but with everyone being identical (being both a worker and a capitalist), the distribution of income wasn't of much moment.

By the time I had entered public service in 1993, I had become convinced that the first argument—that inequality was necessary for high levels of capital accumulation—was wrong. In the late 1980s, I had been asked by the World Bank (through a grant from the Japanese government) to join a study of the factors contributing to the East Asia miracle, the rapid growth of the countries of that region of the world. Our report[3] undermined support for the Washington Consensus policies which were the cornerstone of the Bank's advice at the time; but it also argued that more equalitarian policies had contributed to growth, rather than undermined it; and in spite of egalitarian policies, these countries had had extremely high savings rates. We explained how one could generate high savings even with high levels of equality.[4]

While these experiences showed that one could achieve high savings rate *without* inequality, the assumption that the aggregate savings rate did not depend at all on the distribution of income seemed badly wrong, and inconsistent with data showing a much higher savings rate among wealthy individuals than among poor individuals. Indeed, in the years prior to the 2008 crisis, the savings rate of lower income Americans was negative.[5]

Squaring the circle of how one could achieve higher savings without inequality *and* the fact that the rich saved more than the poor was easy: there were public policies that could encourage savings, like Japan's postal savings bank or devoting large fractions of government expenditures to investment.

Moreover, the assumption that the economy was always in full employment was also questionable: in practice, episodically, there has been a shortage of aggregate demand, and, in the aftermath of the 2008 crisis, growing inequality was widely viewed as one of the explanations for persistent deficiencies in aggregate demand (United Nations, 2010).

Chapter 27 was written while I was chief economist at the World Bank[6] and shortly after I left my position as Chairman of the Council of Economic Advisers. Inequality had just started to soar in the U.S. some 15–20 years earlier. The analysis of the forces driving the changes was not as developed as it is today. I did not believe it was just a matter of inevitable and unalterable market forces, a view I fleshed out more fully in subsequent writings (Stiglitz, 2012a; Stiglitz, Abernathy, Hersh, et al., 2015; and Stiglitz, Stetter, Dougherty, et al., 2019) and in this book. It was in this context that I came to the view that the big trade-off—that one could only achieve higher growth or greater efficiency at the expense of more inequality—was wrong, and that at least certain policies that advanced equality would enhance growth. Chapter 27 is thus my first articulation of the view of growth and equality being complementary, and that because taxation was distortionary, it made

[3] The published report, *The East Asia Miracle* (World Bank, 1993), was a toned-down version of our original report, more in line with standard World Bank policy.

[4] See also Birdsall, Ross, and Sabot (1995); Stiglitz (1996); Stiglitz and Uy (1996); and Hellman, Murdock, and Stiglitz (1996, 1997, 1998, 2000).

[5] My skepticism of the assumption that savings was unaffected by the distribution of income was surely affected by the time I spent at Cambridge. For instance, the growth models of Kaldor (1955a, 1957) and Pasinetti (1962) centered around differences in savings rates.

[6] And, like Chapter 23, it was presented at a conference at the Interamerican Bank. In the original paper, I devoted considerable time to issues specific to Latin America, which I have omitted from this volume.

sense to engage in pre-distribution—improving equality in market incomes, an idea I have elaborated on in greater detail in Chapter 19 above.[7] This chapter describes one set of policies that increases both equality and growth (education), but another that worsens both (the Reagan era supply-side measures (or what has come to be called neoliberalism)). It recognized that there are still other policies, like investments in technology, where trade-offs persist—growth may increase, but in ways which disadvantage unskilled workers. However, as we've explained elsewhere in this book (Chapters 17 and 18), one can shape technology policies and accompany them with additional measures so that the benefits of these investments are widely shared: it is not necessary that they result in increased inequality.

Many of these instances are associated with market failures. Capital market failures explain underinvestment in human capital, and public education can be seen as correcting this market failure—and since access to quality education is likely to be more restricted for the poor than the rich, it can do so in ways which reduce inequality. In later work,[8] I focused on another set of market failures, associated with market power: corporate market power distorts the economy, undermines efficiency, reduces investment and thus growth, at the same time that it leads to more inequality; curbing this and other forms of exploitation can thus lead to better economic performance and more equality.

Economic Fluctuations

The remainder of the chapters of this Part focus on economic fluctuations (instability). Market economies have been subject to large fluctuations since the beginning of capitalism. These chapters explore the two-way relationship between inequality and fluctuations—how inequality contributes to fluctuations and how fluctuations contribute to inequality. The final chapter of this part provides a connection between these papers and Chapter 27, exploring how fluctuations affect long-term growth.

Growth, Inequality, and Cyclical Behavior in Economies without Deficiencies in Aggregate Demand

Chapters 28 and 29, written 50 years ago, focus on the interaction between savings/investment and inequality in an economy where savings and investment depend on the distribution of income and in which there is never a deficiency in aggregate demand: high wages lower savings and investment, the lower capital stock eventually leads to lower wages. The lower wages, in turn, lead to higher investment. The question is: Does the economy *smoothly* converge to a unique long run equilibrium? These simple models suggest no.

In Chapter 28 we add one further complexity: there are two sectors to the economy, with different capital intensities. It has been well-known that in a two-sector model where savings depends on the distribution of income there can be multiple steady-state competitive

[7] Thus, my ideas in this period, when I was focusing on policy, built upon earlier theoretical work showing how tax policy can be used to change the before tax distribution of income (1982e, 1998a). The idea of pre-distribution (or changing the distribution of market incomes) has been highlighted in the work of Hacker and Pierson (2011).

[8] Chapter 16 above and Stiglitz (2012a, 2019a).

equilibria—sometimes called bootstrap equilibria. If capitalists save more than workers, when capitalists have a large share of the national income, then investment is high, and high investment increases the demand for capital goods, leading to a high share of national income going to capitalists. The unique equilibrium associated with standard aggregate models is an artifact of their extreme simplicity—only one of several reasons to take these models with a grain of salt. Of course, when there are multiple equilibria, typically, not all of them are stable.[9]

Here, we assume that the investment sector is labor intensive, so the problem just described does not arise. But we assume two classes of individuals, workers who receive income from previous savings as well as wages (and whose savings rate is lower than capitalists) and capitalists, who only receive capital income. When the aggregate capital labor–ratio is high, if the elasticity of substitution is low, the share of wages increases. The average savings rate falls, and so does the pace of aggregate capital accumulation. This leads to a lower share of labor and a higher savings rate. The higher savings rate then restores the wage and labor share. Thus, even if the economy converges to the steady state, there can be oscillations. The fluctuations are reinforced by the differential capital intensities in the two sectors: in the appendix to this introduction, we show that if there is only one sector, the unique two class balanced growth path is stable, though convergence is still oscillatory.

But in our two-sector model, the economy may not converge to a steady state—it may simply oscillate forever, converging to a limit cycle.

These results stand in marked contradistinction to the prevailing growth literature in the last third of a century, which not only ignored distribution, but concluded that the economy converged smoothly to the long run equilibrium. They were written not long after Kaldor (1940) and Goodwin (1967) had formulated models attempting to explain the cycles which seemed such a marked characteristic of capitalist economies. But the Kaldor and Goodwin models suffered from a lack of rational expectations: presumably, behavior would change if consumers and firms came to understand what was going on. For instance, in these cycles, investment expands in anticipation of future growth, and the turning point is reached when the economy hits labor market constraints, limiting growth, leading in turn to lower investment, leading in turn to an economic downturn. Anticipating these constraints would have induced firms to constrain investment *before* the bottleneck is reached. Whether the economy is well-described by a model of rational expectations has become almost ideological. To me, the evidence is overwhelming that it is not;[10] it is hard to reconcile, the economy's major fluctuations, for instance, the stock market crash of 1989 or the financial crisis of 2008, with rational expectations.[11]

[9] And there can in fact be an infinite number of rational expectations equilibrium. The problem of justifying a rational expectations equilibrium—how individuals can coordinate on the same equilibrium—in the absence of a complete set of markets extending infinitely far into the future has never be adequately addressed by the advocates of such models. See, for example, Hirano and Stiglitz (2020) and Stiglitz (2018e).

[10] See Shiller (2002).

[11] It is also obvious that the standard assumption of common knowledge—that all individuals have the same beliefs—should be rejected. The enormous trading volumes in financial asset markets can only be understood in terms of differences in beliefs. (See Milgrom and Stokey, 1982; Stiglitz, 1982a). The rational expectations model makes the most sense if the source of the perturbation to the economy were a random exogenous shock (such as a productivity shock) with a stationary distribution. The major shocks to the economy have been endogenous, and the major technology shocks (new discoveries, climate change) cannot be well described by a stationary distribution. There is a large literature on each of these topics. See, for example, Stiglitz (2016f, 2018e, and the references cited there) and Guzman and Stiglitz (2020).

But these objections do not apply to the cycles explored here. Though they invoke simple savings behavior (workers save a given fraction of their income, capitalists another), these models are almost more realistic than the more fashionable models based on utility maximization: advances in behavioral economics have shown that savings behavior is not well described by those models. Moreover, it is not difficult to write down utility functions (e.g., time separable logarithmic) which generate fixed savings behavior.

In the concluding paragraph of Chapter 28, I suggest that if we are to understand the true dynamics of the economy, we have to move beyond these simplistic models. Introducing more sectors and more heterogeneity in individuals will lead to more complex dynamics. At the time, we did not have either the mathematics or the computer technology to analyze such models. Now we do, and what I had suggested has turned out to be the case. We now know that the economy may even exhibit chaotic behavior. (In one model, even without introducing intra-generational issues, but with implications for distribution across generations, in a variant of the standard life-cycle model with rational expectations, the economy may "wobble" forever, neither converging nor diverging. See Hirano and Stiglitz [2020]).

In the appendix to this introduction, we provide an even simpler one-sector two-class model, showing that the two-class equilibrium is stable, but that, as in the two-sector model, the convergence is always oscillatory.

Unfortunately, the mainstream of the economics profession moved in the other direction, attempting to analyze the dynamics of the economic system by simplifying the structure of production and consumption, but introducing greater sophistication (and perhaps, as I have noted, unrealistic sophistication) in expectation formation, through rational expectations. But not even seemingly *more* sophisticated expectations formation (e.g., based on sophisticated econometric analysis of the kind that economists typically engage in) necessarily increases the stability of the economic system: quite the contrary, when there are large episodic shocks to the system, for example, associated with big technological revolutions which cannot be rationally anticipated. (See Dosi et al., 2020.)

In Chapter 29, written with my fellow student, George Akerlof,[12] we simplified by going to a one-sector model but added two more elements to the dynamics: (i) A generalized Phillips curve, letting wages or changes in wages be affected by the unemployment rate. (ii) Wages (including possibly the profile of future expected wages) affect not just savings but the capital intensity of newly installed machines. This model thus incorporates an important feature left out of most subsequent macro-models—once machines have been constructed, there is limited substitutability, limited flexibility in increasing output by increasing inputs. (Ex post there is less flexibility than ex ante. The so-called putty-clay models were just being formulated at the time we wrote the paper. Solow, 1962.) As subsequent work with David Cass (1972) showed, the dynamics of putty-clay models *even with the simplest of savings models* can be markedly different from that of the standard neoclassical model. Convergence to the equilibrium may well be oscillatory.

Indeed, here we show that if capital has a finite life (which it does—we explore the limiting case of capital that lives for only one period), even when aggregate savings does not depend on the distribution of income, there can be non-convergent oscillations.

[12] George Akerlof shared with me the 2001 Nobel Memorial Prize, awarded for our work on the economics of information (with Michael Spence).

We also show here that even when we drop the putty clay assumption the economy exhibits oscillatory behavior. In the limiting case where there is a fixed coefficients production function, there is a limit cycle. In the more general case, the economy eventually converges to an equilibrium.

We also show that for some specifications of the Phillips curve, it may be possible for the government by hiring workers directly to lower the equilibrium unemployment rate—anticipating recent interest in a government employment scheme (Stiglitz 2019a).

Economic Fluctuations in a Demand Constrained Economy

The final two chapters of this Part look at the relationship between inequality and business fluctuations in a demand constrained economy. In such an economy, inequality is both cause and consequence of fluctuations.

Chapter 30, written with Jason Furman,[13] later to be chairman of the Council of Economic Advisers, and presented at Jackson Hole, an annual gather of central bankers sponsored by the Kansas City Federal Reserve, explores empirically and theoretically the two-way relationship between inequality and fluctuations. It explains why downturns worsen inequality in labor income.[14] The reduction of hours worked is not well-distributed; if it were, it would not have the economic and social consequences that it does.[15] Some individuals lose their jobs, while others have only a mild reduction in hours worked. Worse: those who lose their jobs are disproportionately the poor. Moreover, the greater the initial level of inequality, before the downturn, the larger the impact on inequality. The chapter provides a theoretical explanation, using efficiency wage theory (see the discussion in the introduction to III.C), under which those with lower efficiency wage curves are excluded from the market; as demand shifts down, those who were marginally in the market become excluded. It also discusses other channels through which an economic downturn worsens inequality; in particular, it explores how differential search costs may lead to differential impacts, suggesting that economic and racial segregation may increase the magnitude of the differentials.

The 2008 crisis turned economists' attention to the causes of deep downturns. An international Commission appointed by the President of the UN General Assembly to look into the causes of the crisis and what could be done to prevent a recurrence concluded that the growth of inequality had played an important role.[16] Since the savings rate of the rich is so much higher than that of the poor and middle, an increase in inequality leads to reduced aggregate demand. The response to the decrease in aggregate demand by policy makers was to lower interest rates and to continue with the path of financial sector deregulation that had begun in the early 1980s with Reagan in the U.S. and Thatcher in the UK. These

[13] I recruited Jason as a graduate student to the Council of Economic Advisers (CEA). He demonstrated enormous economic insight and a real flair for policy. He moved with me to the World Bank, and then served as an adviser to presidential candidate Al Gore, before becoming deputy head of the National Economic Council and eventually CEA chair under President Obama.

[14] Economic downturns have an ambiguous effect on overall inequality, because profits often fall precipitously, and asset values decrease.

[15] This is just one of the reasons that Lucas's (1987) analysis of the costs of business fluctuations is so misguided. He also ignores the presence of credit constraints. If individuals could easily smooth consumption over their lives, again the adverse welfare impacts of unemployment would be greatly mitigated. See Stiglitz and Yun (2005).

[16] I chaired the Commission. See United Nations (2010).

created a credit boom and a housing bubble—which increased aggregate demand in an unsustainable demand. This was not the only way that government could have responded: it could, for instance, have increased government spending. It was, indeed, a particularly opportune time for investments in infrastructure, where there had been underinvestment for years. But as we have noted repeatedly, economic inequality translates into political inequality; and the same political forces that had led to rewriting the rules of the economy to favor the rich and to deregulate the financial sector inhibited fiscal stimulus.[17]

The chapter concludes with observing that since instability increases with inequality and inequality increases with instability, there may exist multiple equilibria—a low volatility economy with a high level of equality and a high volatility economy with a high level of inequality. Some of the changes in the "rules" of the economy—in particular, financial deregulation—have led to both more inequality and more instability.

In the original version of this chapter, I also discussed some aspects of the relationship between growth and inequality. While the cross-sectional empirical evidence at the time did not support the hypothesis that higher inequality was good for growth (because of its positive effects on savings), neither did it provide strong support for the contrary hypothesis. Part of the reason is that there are many factors affecting growth, and controlling for them well is difficult, especially because relationships may be very non-linear. For instance, some degree of financialization of the economy may improve stability, but excessive financialization may lead to instability. (Easterly et al., 2001a, 2001b). Moreover, the measure of inequality typically used in empirical analyses, the Gini coefficient of income, may not capture well the dimensions of inequality that are most relevant for economic performance.

The most relevant question is, are there policies which could both increase equality and growth, and on that, there is an emerging consensus that the answer is yes.

The Furman-Stiglitz results on how economic downturns lead to more inequality, and how more economic inequality leads to greater economic volatility, suggests a destructive feedback relationship, which the final chapter of this section (Chapter 31) explores more fully, at the same time discussing further the links between inequality and growth raised in Chapter 27. Greater inequality leads to greater volatility, and vice versa, and both impair economic growth.

Chapter 31 emphasizes too that the effects of volatility on well-being, and on inequalities in well-being, may be even greater than on income; and explains why there may be important hysteresis effects: the adverse consequences of a deep downturn may be long lasting.

At the same time, it addresses those who seek to blame unemployment on excessively rigid wages, explaining how more flexible wages may actually exacerbate economic fluctuations, through the Fisher–Greenwald–Stiglitz debt-deflation mechanism.[18]

Policy frameworks which lead to greater stability (less exposure to shocks—a more restrictive view on capital and financial market liberalization; and better automatic stabilizers—especially progressive taxation and a stronger welfare state) lead to greater equality, and to better economic performance, both directly (because greater volatility discourages investment, and leads to greater expenditures to cope with and adapt to the

[17] The alleged argument was a concern about the resulting fiscal deficit; but the willingness in 2017 to accept huge fiscal deficits *when the economy didn't need the stimulus* in order to get a large tax cut for corporations and upper income Americans suggested that this was mere rhetoric.

[18] See Fisher (1933); Greenwald and Stiglitz (1993a).

volatility) and indirectly, as a result of the lower inequality, which, for all the reasons cited in earlier chapters, enhances growth. At the same time, there are policies which lead to greater equality, that in turn lead to greater stability, and these too can lead to better growth on both accounts.

The chapter notes that there are several risks associated with current policy responses to economic downturns, which may unintentionally exacerbate impacts on inequality and even increase future volatility. Downturns lead to revenue losses, and if governments respond by cutting expenditures, it deepens the downturn. Even worse, if the expenditure cuts include education, health, and welfare benefits on which those at the bottom depend, the effects on inequality, properly measured, are compounded. If in response to the country's weakened fiscal position, there are cutbacks in the safety net, then the economy's automatic stabilizers are weakened, making the country more vulnerable to a future downturn. And, of course, if the weakened fiscal position means that in a subsequent downturn countercyclical cyclical measures are further weakened, then future downturns will be all the worse.

The potential adverse effects of prevalent monetary doctrines are also of concern. The chapter explains why a focus on inflation (such as with inflation targeting) leads to higher average levels of unemployment, increasing inequality both directly and indirectly, as a result of the downward pressure that the higher unemployment exerts on wages. Moreover, the focus on inflation shifted attention away from financial regulation, contributing to volatility—the 2008 crisis being the strongest manifestation. The response of U.S. monetary authorities to that crisis illustrates still another problem: cross-border externalities, a kind of beggar-thy-neighbor policy (much of the effect of the low interest rates was through lowering the exchange rate), which simultaneously lowered other countries' exports as the U.S. "exported" volatility, especially in the emerging markets, with the surges of capital flows into these markets.[19] Finally, the chapter raises the question of whether, by lowering interest rates, the Fed encouraged the use of more capital intensive technologies (and, following the analysis of Chapter 17, more labor-saving innovation), resulting in making the return to full employment all the more difficult.

While the causal links between inequality and volatility increasing policies are clear, the evidence of the reverse link, particularly between growth and inequality, is less so: growth may lead to poverty reduction, but evidence in the U.S. and elsewhere shows that that is not necessarily the case. As we noted earlier, Kuznets had hypothesized early stages of growth would lead to more inequality, but that would be reversed later; but experiences over the past half century have discredited this view too.

The argument that equality is good for growth and stability helps round out the argument for greater equality: it is not only a moral issue, but an economic one.

[19] For a broader discussion of these cross-border externalities, see Stiglitz (2015e).

Appendix: Dynamics of a One-Sector Two-Class Model

The dynamics of a one-sector two-class model are quite simple.

$$dk_c/dt = (s_c f' - n)\, k_c \tag{A.1}$$

$$dk_w/dt = s_w\,(f - k_c f') - nk_w, \tag{A.2}$$

where $f(k)$ is a standard aggregate production function, giving output per capita as a function of the capital–labor ratio, $k = K/L. f'' < 0,\ n > 0,\ s_c > s_w$ where $k = k_w + k_c$ and the other notation is as in Chapter 28.

$$dk_c/dt = 0 \text{ } \textit{if} \text{ either } k_c = 0, \textit{ or} \tag{A.3}$$

$$k_c + k_w = (f')^{-1}\,[n/s_c], \tag{A.4}$$

implying that $dk_c/dt = 0$ along the horizontal axis or along a line with slope -1, as depicted in Figures on p. 634. On the hand,

$$dk_w/dt = 0 \tag{A.5}$$

implies

$$s_w\,(f - k_c f') - nk_w = 0. \tag{A.6}$$

[Note: we know the two loci will intersect because they are both smooth continuous functions.] Using (A.4), we can solve for k_w^*, $dk_c/dt = 0$:

$$k_w^* = s_w\Big(f\big[(f')^{-1}[n/s_c]\big] - k_c n/s_c\Big)/n \tag{A.7}$$

and k_c^* follows accordingly.[20]

We can use the implicit value theorem on (A.6) to get the local slope around $dk_w/dt = 0$

$$dk_w/dk_c = -\,(s_w\,(f' - f' - k_c f''))\,/\,(s_w\,(f' - k_c f'') - n) = (s_w k_c f'')\,/\,(s_w\,(f' - k_c f'') - n).$$

Notice that the numerator is always negative.

$$\text{Case 1: } s_w\,(f' - k_c f'') - n > 0.$$

In this case, the slope is negative, and the diagram looks like the following:

[20] A two-class balanced growth path requires $k_c > 0$, that is, the parameters must be such that $s_w(f[(f')^{-1}[n/s_c]] < (f')^{-1}[n/s_c]$.
We assume that to be the case.

Case 1: $s_w(f' - k_c f'') - n > 0$

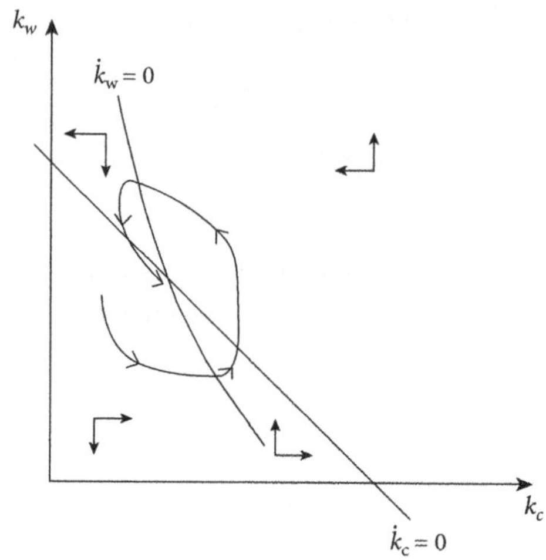

Case 2: $s_w(f' - k_c f'') - n < 0$

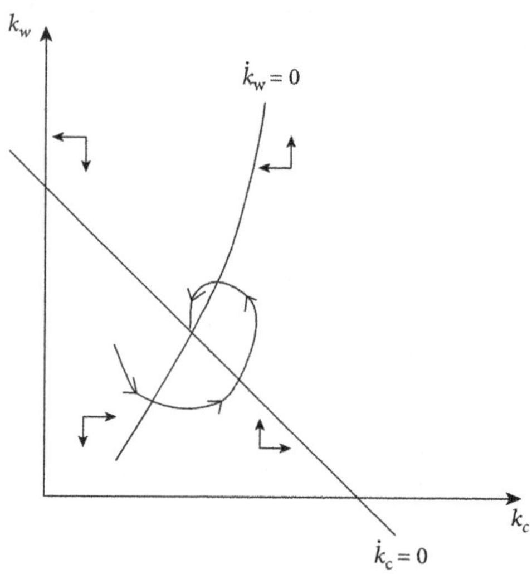

In either case, there are complex, negative real part eigenvalues that lead to a stable oscillating dynamic.

Two comments:

There is another solution that corresponds to $k_c = 0$. It is always unstable.

It is easy to establish that when the $dk_w/dt = 0$ locus is negatively sloped, it is steeper than the dk_c/dt locus, so long as $s_w < s_c$, so these are the only two possible cases.

27

Beyond Tradeoffs

Why Growth and Equality Can Be Complementary

1 Introduction

Economists once spoke about tradeoffs between equity and efficiency as if one were separate from the other.[1] That thinking was based on the first and second fundamental theorems of welfare economics, in particular the assumption that efficient redistribution could be carried out through lump-sum taxes and transfers.[2] Now developments in the real world, together with advances in the theory of public finance, have fundamentally altered this premise. One striking example is the East Asian miracle, which has demonstrated that more egalitarian distributions may be growth-enhancing. More recently, some Latin American countries have found that if reforms promote efficiency in several economic sectors, they can also have positive effects on equity.

There is much room for optimism regarding this. Our recent experience in the United States lends some insights into the possibilities of reforms, as well as the tradeoffs. Although we explicitly seek policies that promote both equality and growth, often those objectives cannot be simultaneously achieved. In these cases, additional policy measures are necessary to ensure that those at the bottom are not too disadvantaged by the tradeoffs many policies entail.

The first section of this chapter sets out the theoretical framework. The second explains the importance of public investments in education, an area where growth can be promoted at the same time that inequality is reduced. While this is a win–win situation, other situations can be double losses, where growth may be impaired and inequality increased. The third section of the chapter discusses how certain kinds of tax cuts fall into that category. The fourth section explains how trade liberalization is a policy area with real possibilities for an equity-efficiency tradeoff.

The final section concludes with a warning about excessive focus on win–win situations. Although there is considerable scope for these, the hardest questions involve hard choices. These choices have often been submerged in the political discourse. The United States may be embarking on a path of lower growth—and less inequality—than would have been chosen in a more open policy debate. Choices about public investments in Latin America, and the tradeoffs that result, are similarly affected by the nature of public debate.

[1] "Inequality and Growth: Implications for Public Finance and Lessons from Experience in the US," in N. Birdsall, C. Graham, and R. H. Sabot (eds.), *Beyond Tradeoffs: Market Reform and Equitable Growth in Latin America*," Inter-American Development Bank, 1998, pp. 305–19. Reprinted with permission.

[2] The fact that people thought the two could be separate, already suggests that certain elements of the theory were always remote from the *realpolitik* of policymaking.

The Origins of Inequality, and Policies to Contain It. Joseph E. Stiglitz, Oxford University Press. © Joseph E. Stiglitz (2025).
DOI: 10.1093/oso/9780198799580.003.0028

2 Distortionary Taxation and Enhancing Economic Growth

While it has long been recognized that income and other commonly used taxes are distortionary, recent theory has attempted to explain why taxation is essentially *always* distortionary.[3] We don't have lump-sum taxes that vary according to the ability and other immutable conditions of individuals. Taxes are distortionary because *real* governments have distributive objectives, and thus wish to impose different taxes on different individuals. However, the variables they can use for differentiating taxes are changeable. The instruments of tax policy that are required to implement distributive objectives are endogenous—that is, they entail *basing taxes on variables that are affected by tax policy.*

Tax policy cannot be implemented without impacts on individual behavior that go beyond the pure income effects. That is, lump-sum taxes, which individuals can do nothing to avoid, affect behavior because individuals have less to spend, must reduce their spending on some goods, and typically respond by reducing their expenditures on most, if not all, goods. Thus, all taxation has distortionary effects. The same can be said for all means-tested expenditure programs, including welfare and Medicaid. So long as benefits depend on variables that are affected by individual behavior, they will be distortionary; and since there is no way to assess eligibility other than by looking at such variables, distortions are unavoidable.

Because taxes are distortionary, it is important to consider how individuals will change their behavior *after* taxes. There always is a reaction to the tax system, whether it is to avoid or to exploit the tax regime. In the past we considered the before-tax earnings (or at least wage) distribution as given, or roughly given. Analyses of optimal taxation assessed the tradeoff between the after-tax distribution and the level of national income But, in fact, tax policy affects the *before-tax* distribution of income in a variety of ways. For instance, tax policy affects savings, thus capital accumulation. A more circuitous but potentially equally powerful effect is the impact of taxes on wage distribution. Taxes on capital (or profits), for instance, can affect the distribution of earnings. If we assume that skilled and unskilled labor have different degrees of complementarity with capital, then any tax that influences investment decisions will also alter the relative demand for skilled and unskilled labor, and thus the distribution of earnings as well. Not only are taxes distortionary, but changes in the tax system may affect the distribution of income in unexpected and complicated ways. (Again, the same can be said for direct government expenditures.)

The key question is: Given that taxes are distortionary, what measures would affect the *before-tax* distribution of income in ways that improve equity? For if there are such measures, we don't have to use distortionary redistributive taxes to the same extent to achieve a given income distribution. In general, it would be desirable to engage in policies that change the ex ante distribution—even if such policies are somewhat distortionary—to reduce the distortionary burden of the ex post redistributive policies.

[3] For a general discussion, see Stiglitz (1987a).

3 Efficiency with Equity: Policies to Increase Spending for Preschool Programs and College Education

The importance of education as a public investment priority in the United States is reflected in budgetary trends in recent years. The logic behind assigning such a high priority to education is that improved access to education can lead to lower inequality together with faster growth.

The growth effects of education are well documented.[4] A large body of evidence demonstrates that more educated workers are generally more productive, learn new things faster, and thus are better able to absorb new and changing technologies. All of this is reflected in a wage premium of 5% to 15% for each additional year of schooling.[5] For methodological reasons, the macroeconomic consequences of improving education are harder to identify. Correlations that emerge in cross-country regressions, however, support the claim that education increases a country's steady-state level of output.[6]

There are two sources of inequality in wages in a perfectly functioning labor market: differences in human capital and differences in ability. Among individuals of similar abilities, if some have more access to education than others, those with greater access will enjoy a higher income. Poor individuals may either lack the resources to invest in higher education, or may find their implicit cost of capital is so high that education is not a desirable investment. Moreover, elementary and secondary schools in poor neighborhoods may be less effective than schools in richer neighborhoods, and thus children in poorer neighborhoods get less "human capital" during those critical years. If elementary and secondary education complement tertiary education, then disadvantaged children will also derive a lower return to investments in tertiary education.[7] In addition, some children receive less human capital at home than do others, so that if home and school-based human capital are complementary, the returns to publicly provided schooling will be lowered.

There is evidence that all three sources of inequality are present in the United States: poorer children start school with educational disadvantages; the quality of education that they are provided in public schools is poorer; and they have less access to higher education.

Lack of access, in turn, means that the United States is not investing efficiently in its human resources. Consider the following evidence. In the United States the overall returns to education have increased substantially in the last 15 years.[8] For example, the income differential between a high school graduate and a college graduate has almost doubled.[9] Yet in spite of the fact that there are such high returns to college education, not everybody in our society has been responding in the same way. For children of upper- and middle-income individuals, enrollment rates in universities have been increasing substantially. This is not

[4] See Birdsall and Londoño (1997).

[5] For a general survey, see Willis (1986). More recently, see Ashenfelter and Krueger (1994) and Kane and Rouse (1995).

[6] See Barro (1991) and Mankiw, Romer, and Weil (1992).

[7] For present purposes, it matters little why these schools provide less human capital—whether it is lower expenditures, or, for instance, externalities arising from the mix of students in the classroom, or from less effective monitoring from parents.

[8] Psacharopoulos (1994).

[9] Council of Economic Advisers (1997a), p. 167.

the case with children of lower-income families: for them, the response has been relatively small. The result has been an increasing disparity in enrollment rates in college of children of upper- and lower-income families.[10] Why is it that some groups—such as the children of poor families or minorities—continue to invest so much less than others? Why, in particular, did some groups respond so differently to the huge changes in the returns to education? The answer to this question lies in three rather obvious factors.

First, there are no perfect capital markets, and over the last 20 years the mean income of families in the bottom income quintile has decreased in real terms.[11] Parents with low incomes cannot afford to send their children to college and, since people cannot borrow against their future income, neither they nor their children can borrow for it.

Second, the cost of going to college has increased. Over the last decade, tuition payments in public universities and colleges have increased by 50% in real terms.[12] It is not that the cost of education has increased that much. State subsidies have not kept pace with the increase in costs. As a result, the tuition charged in public two- and four-year colleges has increased at a much faster pace than the increase in the cost of education (i.e., faster than the increase in wages and salaries of educational workers).

Finally, between 1980 and 1994, the real value of the maximum Pell grant, the main federal program for low-income students, decreased by more than 25%.[13] The roughly 10% increase in real terms in the last three years has only partially reversed the erosion of this crucial program.[14]

The net result is underinvestment in higher education, particularly by children of poor families. The implication for policy is clear: a policy that supports investment in college education, particularly by the poor, would both promote economic growth and increase equality (by affecting the pretax distribution of income). This was the rationale for increases in federal support for college education during the Clinton administration, even in a period when there were cuts in overall fiscal expenditure. Two major programs provided support for college education: a new direct lending program[15] and a significant expansion of the

[10] Choy and Premo (1996).

[11] U.S. Census. *Historical Income and Poverty Tables.* The dispute over appropriate measure of inflation casts some doubt on the comparison of real income levels across time (http://www.centural.gov/hhem/income/histinc/ f03.html).

[12] U.S. Bureau of the Census, *Statistical Abstract of the United State;* 1996. Government Printing Office Washington, D.C. Table no. 290.

[13] Council of Economic Advisers (1996).

[14] Unpublished Office of Management and Budget data.

[15] One may ask, why choose to do directed credit instead of lending through the banking system? Why not use the private sector? These are good questions. But the problem is that, as it is implemented in the United States, the privately administered educational loan program leads to an inefficient use of resources. Under the program, the federal government maintains the residual risk and gives a large fee to the banks to administer the program. They bear no risk and get a high return. At the Council of Economic Advisors, we tried to suggest that if the private sector were to be engaged in this, it ought at least to face competition: to accept a competitive bidding process for the determination of the administrative fee. This idea was not well received. The banks in the program were only enthusiastic about private markets without competition. With competition, there would be no super-normal profits—and what would be the point of the whole exercise if profits were eroded!

Because we could not get a competitive private lending program, the Administration introduced a direct lending program with a lower cost of lending. More important than that, we also introduced a new lending instrument, one which it would have been hard for the private sector to administer. Among the options given students was one in which the amount that the student repays is related to his/her income. The design is a bit like the variable-rate mortgages that they have in England, where payments are fixed but the maturity of the debt is variable, and could be extended through capitalization of interest due. In the program, after 20 or 25 years, the loan is forgiven. If the student goes into a low-paying job like teaching, the amount paid back would essentially be subsidized. The view is that most children do not think about a 25-year horizon in their lives, so they won't choose to go into a

Pell grant program. In addition, a program of tax deductions and tax credits for going to college for lower- and middle-income individuals was proposed.[16]

This was coupled with efforts to improve the overall equality of educational opportunity at each point in the production process. The program of Goals 2000 sought to improve standards in all schools; and since there was particular concern about standards in the poorer schools, the students in these schools stood to benefit most.[17] It tried to redesign federal assistance to poor schools to target more of the money to the most needy through, for example, the school construction initiative, although those efforts were blunted by Congress.

Another area that was accorded considerable effort to improve educational equity is preschool education. Funding for Head Start (a program for disadvantaged preschool children to prepare them for going to regular school) by 1997 had increased 43% over its 1993 level.[18] The rationale was simple: students who are better prepared when they enter school will do better in school and are less likely to drop out. There is evidence that those enrolled in Head Start programs do have lower drop-out rates.

The concern about dropouts was motivated not just by economics. Evidence shows that, in the United States, there are large social costs to children not completing high school. The data available do not distinguish causal mechanisms, but there is a clear association between criminality and lack of high school education.[19] On any particular day, something like 25% of males between the ages of 18 and 35 who are not high school graduates are in the ambits of the criminal justice system. One out of four is either in prison or on parole or probation, whereas the corresponding number for high school graduates is 4%. A state like California spends more on the construction of prisons than on higher education, and it spends more per year to send a kid to prison than to college.

A number of studies have found a clear link between childhood poverty and failure in school; in fact, knowledge of this link was behind the idea of Head Start programs.[20] By the time they are ready for elementary school, children have accumulated a considerable amount of human capital—some more than others. And there is a threshold; a minimum level of private human capital is the necessary complement to the public capital provided by the elementary school. Middle-class children get that capital from their parents, but children that have grown up in poverty do not, and so they end up disadvantaged. The

low-paying profession just to avoid repaying the loan in full. In other words, our view was that the moral hazard created by the possible subsidy would not lead to a serious distortion in the labor market. (It will take 25 years, unfortunately, to find out whether there is a significant moral hazard effect.)

[16] These tax deductions and credits should, however, be viewed more as part of a program of tax reductions than a program of education expenditures. There is considerable doubt over the efficacy of these tax deductions and credits in increasing enrollments, and a general consensus that if increasing enrollment were the objective, it would have been better to spend the money in enhanced Pell grants, or in some other expenditure program. For political reasons, the Administration wanted to reduce taxes; given that taxes were to be reduced, the challenge was to find ways of doing so that might have some educational benefits, or more broadly improve the pretax distribution of income.

[17] There was some concern that the program could have adverse effects: if the poorest schools were not able to bring their students up to those standards, then the gap between them and the rest of the country could actually increase. Employers would have a legitimate reason not to hire students who failed to meet the standards, and thus children from these schools would face even more dismal employment opportunities. Advocates of Goals 2000 believed that increasing public attention—and support—would be provided to these schools, as the disparity in performance became increasingly visible.

[18] Office of Management and Budget (1997b).

[19] Freeman (1991).

[20] For a review of the literature, see Bamett (1992). See also Currie and Thomas (1995).

program, in providing that quantum of capital, increases the efficiency of learning and, ultimately, the quantity of learning. It has high returns and it also increases equity.

In sum, I have argued that educational policy may be used to reach both the efficiency and equity objectives of fiscal policy. Interestingly, in this case, both effects are produced through the labor market. In particular, the equity effect flows from an investment that increases the capacity to earn income; it does not flow from a post-tax income transfer.[21]

4 Inefficiency with Inequity, or Vice-Versa: Undesirable Tax Reforms

While educational reforms represented a win-win situation, where growth and equity could be increased, there was also considerable political pressure to enact lose-lose policies, which could lower growth and increase inequity. To be sure, the debate was not framed that way. Tax reform is also justified in terms of its benefits to growth and equity. But much of the impetus for tax reform came from upper-income individuals who pay a significant fraction of their income in taxes.

The "argument" for tax reform often begins with a legitimate source of concern: the low U.S. saving rate and its consequences for investment. A number of people have argued that we ought to encourage savings through a change in the tax structure. The argument for is simple: a lower tax on income from savings is equivalent to an increase in the effective interest rate, and higher interest rates lead to higher saving.

The argument, however, is disingenuous. The interest elasticity of savings is low. It would take a very large increase in the expected post-tax effective real interest rate to induce most Americans to save significantly more. Moreover, the American middle class already has much of its savings exempt from taxation (through Individual Retirement Accounts and, more importantly, through pensions).

The effect on aggregate savings may well be negative, as the lower tax revenue leads to an increase in the fiscal deficit (negative government savings) that is greater than the induced private savings. (This is the case for most reasonable estimates of the elasticity of supply of savings.) And as savings is decreased, growth will be decreased. At the same time, the primary beneficiaries will be upper-income individuals—those with significant savings.

In sum, the whole debate on tax relief on savings, while it was presented as in the "national interest of raising the American savings rate," was really one for tax breaks for the very rich. This is an example of a lose–lose reform: lose on growth, lose on equity.

5 Efficiency-Equity Tradeoffs: Trade Policy

The previous sections tackled a fairly easy target: find the win–win solutions and apply them, and avoid lose-lose reforms. What happens when there *are* tradeoffs? How do we deal with them in a world without neutral lump-sum taxes, where we no longer believe that government can satisfy everyone? The issue then is how to compensate losers.

[21] Of course, not all decisions about educational policy favor equity and efficiency. Consider the case of subsidies for R&D and for science and technology more broadly. There is considerable evidence that the rates of return on some of these investments are higher than on investments in college education. Yet, it is clearly going to another group in the population. These funds support the elite research institutions that are typically related to the upper-income groups. It may be, therefore, that by focusing on areas where there is a complementarity between efficiency and equity we are giving up things where the growth returns might be higher.

This problem is exemplified through the concurrent debate over another important policy issue in the United States: trade liberalization. As is well known, the push for open trade (e.g., the Uruguay Round, NAFTA) has been opposed by strong, well-organized groups. There is no question that many of these groups have lost or will lose with lower trade barriers; for example, imports have driven parts of the American textile industry into decline. (Interestingly, the United States has become a major *net exporter* of textiles. But this is due entirely to the high-tech and capital-intensive branches of the industry. The bottom end of the market has lost out to cheaper and better imports and, of course, consumers have gained.)

There are two clear implications for those concerned about equity: first, it is important to recognize that some may be adversely affected by trade—or by technological change. There is a market failure: individuals cannot buy insurance against these risks, and they often cannot borrow to buy the training required to move into a new job. But the rationale for government action goes beyond the market failures. The government has a responsibility for assisting individuals in the transition (through training or loans). The second implication is that the assistance should not be limited to those adversely affected by trade (indeed, ascertaining the cause of a job loss is often a hopeless exercise).

The public investment in the transition safety net could have high returns: by facilitating the transition, it reduces the time individuals spend being unproductive between jobs. But even if there were limited direct efficiency gains, the transition safety net would be desirable, and not just on arguments for "fairness"—that a few should not bear the costs of a reform that benefits society as a whole.

In addition to the efficiency and equity arguments, another rationale for building the transition safety net is based on political economy: Because we are convinced that the overall returns to trade are large, it is important to have this kind of assistance to build stronger constituencies *for trade reform.* This is an example where there can be a positive indirect interplay between efficiency and equity, if you have the right programs in place. Without those programs, political resistance will be greater, and it will be harder to effect an efficiency-enhancing move.

6 Conclusion

There are many opportunities for simultaneously improving equity and efficiency (growth). We should be actively engaged in looking for these opportunities. However, not all social and economic problems can be approached with win-win policies: there are hard tradeoffs that any society must face. Decisions are made all too often in a piecemeal way, without a hard look at their full implications.

Consider expenditures on science and technology. Under current budget proposals, these will be cut (in real terms) by about 20% over the next five years.[22] There is overwhelming evidence that investments in science and technology yield high returns, and that public and private expenditures are complementary. Over the years, investments in science and technology have contributed significantly to U.S. economic growth. Unlike expenditures on education, however, the distributional consequences of investment in technology are not clear. Improved technology has probably contributed to inequality by increasing the relative demand for skilled workers. Also, in a world with balanced budgets and roughly

[22] Office of Management and Budget (1997a).

constant taxes as a share of GDP, spending more in one area requires the government to spend less in other areas. Are there programs in which Americans would have been willing to accept a small cutback in order to ensure America's technological leadership in the next century?

The institutional changes that are still required, the political obstacles to making them, and the prospects for success, are the subject of this volume's final chapter.

28
A Two-Sector, Two-Class Model of Economic Growth

1 Introduction

This note examines the properties of a growth model with a consumption goods sector and a capital goods sector, in which there are two classes, one whose income is derived entirely from capital (the capitalists) and a second which derives its income from both wages and return on savings (the workers).[1]

In a one-sector version of this model, Meade (1963) and Samuelson and Modigliani (1966) have recently shown that Pasinetti's proposition (1962) that in such an economy the rate of profit is equal to the rate of growth divided by the savings propensity of capitalists is true only under certain restrictive conditions.[2]

2 The Model

The differential equations of capital accumulation are derived as in Samuelson and Modigliani (1966):

$$\dot{k}_c/k_c = s_c r - n \tag{28.1}$$

$$\dot{k}_w/k_w = s_w r - n + \frac{s_w(y - rk)}{k_w}, \tag{28.2}$$

where s_c is the propensity to save of capitalists, s_w that of workers, r the rate of profit, n the rate of growth of the labor force, k the aggregate capital per worker ratio, k_c the ratio of capital owned by the capitalists to the size of the labor force, k_w the ratio of capital owned by the workers to the size of the labor force, and y the output per man measured in machine goods numeraire. If we let λ be the proportion of the labor force in the capital goods industry (which we denote by a subscript 1), it is clear that

$$y = \lambda y_1 + (1 - \lambda)py_2 = w + rk,$$

where y_i is the output of machines per worker in the ith industry, p the price ratio and w the wage rate.

[1] Originally published in 1967 in the *Review of Economic Studies*, 34(2): 227–38. Reprinted with permission. This chapter is part of a Ph.D. thesis completed at the Massachusetts Institute of Technology. The author is indebted to his thesis advisors: Professors E. Kuh, P. A. Samuelson, and R. M. Solow; and to F. H. Hahn and C. Bliss of Cambridge for their comments and suggestions.

[2] This is not to say that these conditions may (or may not) be satisfied in some actual economies.

The Origins of Inequality, and Policies to Contain It. Joseph E. Stiglitz, Oxford University Press. © Joseph E. Stiglitz (2025).
DOI: 10.1093/oso/9780198799580.003.0029

We may write the savings equal investment equilibrium condition as

$$\lambda y_1 = s_w y + (s_c - s_w)\, rk_c \tag{28.3}$$

Finally, we have the usual production relations of a two-sector neoclassical model: factor payments equal to marginal products and full employment of labor and capital. Letting $y_i = f_i(k_i), i = 1, 2$, where k_i is the capital per worker in the ith industry, and ω be the wage–rentals ratio, we have

$$\omega = (f_i/f'_i) - k_i,\ f_i{}' > 0,\ f_i'' < 0 \quad i = 1, 2 \tag{28.4}$$

$$\lambda k_1 + (1 - \lambda)k_2 = k. \tag{28.5}$$

3 Uniqueness of Momentary Equilibrium

We shall explicitly assume throughout this chapter that momentary equilibrium is uniquely determined; that is, given k_c and k_w (and hence k), at any point of time, the path (that is, k_c and k_w) is determinate; in other words, specifying k_c and k_w uniquely specifies k_1 and k_2.

Sufficient conditions for this can easily be derived. If we define:

$$\bar{s}_c = s_w + (s_c - s_w)\, k_c/k > s_w,$$

our Equations (28.3)–(28.5) become identical in form to the corresponding equations in the usual two-sector growth models, with the savings-investment equilibrium condition:

$$\lambda y_1 = (s_w \underline{w} + \bar{s}_c k)\, r,$$

for which it is known that the following are sufficient conditions for uniqueness of momentary equilibrium: (1) the sum of the elasticities of substitution be greater than or equal to 1; or (2) the capital intensity of the capital goods sector be less than or equal to that of the consumption goods sector.

4 Existence of Balanced Growth Paths

If there is no capitalist class, the model presented above becomes simply the usual neoclassical model with a constant fraction of income (s_w) saved. Hence any balanced growth path of the Uzawa constant savings proportion model is a balanced growth path of our two-class model.

But the question we are really interested in is the existence (and uniqueness) of balanced growth paths for which $k_c \neq 0$. It is easy to see that if there exists a balanced growth path with both classes present, it is unique. A balanced growth path is one in which $\dot{k}_c = \dot{k}_w = 0$. Hence

$$r = n/s_c, \tag{28.6}$$

$$s_w y = s_w r(k - k_w) + nk_w = nk - nk_c + s_w rk_c, \quad \text{or} \tag{28.7}$$

$$s_w y = nk + k_c(s_w r - n). \tag{28.7$'$}$$

From (28.6), r is uniquely determined; hence from the marginal productivity equal factor price relations k_1 and k_2 are uniquely determined, and hence y_1 and y_2 are fixed. Substituting (28.7′) into the savings-investment equation, we have:

$$\lambda y_1 = nk + k_c(s_w r - n) + s_c k_c r - s_w k_c r = nk + k_c(s_c r - n) = nk. \tag{28.8}$$

Substituting into the full employment condition, we have:

$$\lambda = -k_2/(k_1 - k_2 - y_1/n), \tag{28.9}$$

from which it is clear that λ is fixed, and since $k = \lambda y_1/n$, k is uniquely determined Thus we have shown that there is at most one balanced growth path with both classes present.

There will exist such a balanced growth path if and only if the values of λ^*, y_1^*, y_2^*, k_1^*, k_2^*, and r^* (where the * variables are the solutions to Equations (28.3)–(28.9) are consistent with a positive value of k_c; that is, from (28.7′),

$$s_w y^* < nk^* = s_c r^* k^* \tag{28.10}$$

or

$$\frac{s_w}{s_c} < \frac{rk^*}{y^*}$$

or using (28.8) we have:

$$\lambda y_1^* > s_w y^*$$

or

$$\frac{I^*/L}{Y^*/L} > s_w \quad \text{(where } I \text{ is investment).} \tag{28.11}$$

Condition (28.10) states that the ratio of the savings propensity of workers to that of capitalists must be less than the share of capital (in balanced growth) while condition (28.11) states that the investment–output ratio must be greater than the savings propensity of workers.

What these restrictions imply may be seen in the following way. From (28.7), letting $k_c = 0$, we have:

$$\psi(k_1, k) = nk - s_w(w + rk). \tag{28.12}$$

Let us assume, for this model with $k_c = 0$, that there exists a unique value of k consistent with each value of k_1;[3] call this value $h(k_1)$. Let us assume moreover that

$$\phi(k_1) = \psi(k_1, h(k_1)) = 0 \tag{28.13}$$

at only one point (and $\phi'(k_1)_{\hat{\phi}=0} > 0$).[4] The question then is whether the solution to (28.13) gives k_1 greater or less than the solution to

$$s_c f_1'(k_1) - n = 0. \tag{28.14}$$

If the situation is as depicted below in Figure 28.1, then there exists an equilibrium with two classes, because at A, $s_w y < nk$ (see below for a detailed discussion of stability).

On the other hand, if the situation is as depicted below in Figure 28.2, then there cannot be a balanced growth path with both classes, because at A, $s_w y > nk$.

The important point to observe is that one cannot look at merely the values of, say, the savings propensity of workers and the investment–output ratio today to tell whether there exists a balanced growth path with both classes; note that this would be true even if the capital–output ratio of each sector were fixed (but different between the two sectors).[5]

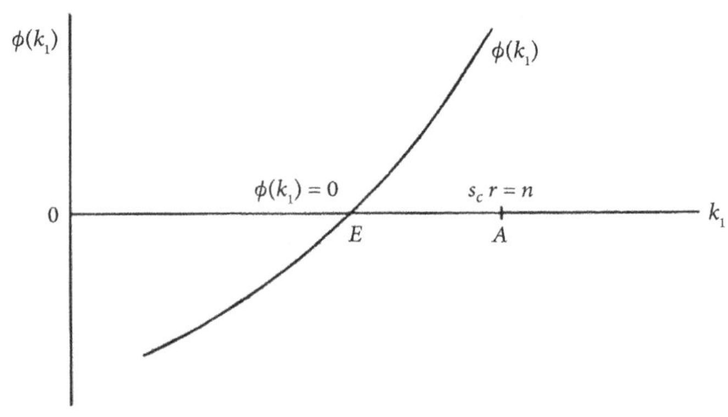

Figure 28.1 There exists an equilibrium with two classes when E lies to the left of A.

[3] This will be true, for instance, if $k_1 < k_2$, or the elasticity of substitution in each sector is greater than 1.

[4] This also will be true under the conditions stated in the previous footnote.

[5] For reference, we list the following well-known properties of the two-sector economy when $k_c = 0$, that is, there is a constant fraction of output saved: (*a*) Momentary equilibrium is always uniquely determined. (*b*) If the capital intensity of the capital goods sector is less than that of the consumption goods sector, or if the elasticity of substitution of each of the sectors is greater than or equal to one, then there exists a unique balanced growth path which the economy asymptotically approaches. Observe that the Pasinetti model is no "better behaved" than the two-sector growth model with a classical savings function (savings by type of income). As we have already indicated, the conditions for uniqueness of momentary equilibrium with $k_c \neq 0$, and the conditions for uniqueness of balanced growth and stability, with $k_c = 0$, are identical to those for a classical savings model with the savings ratio for profits greater than that for wages (but savings out of profits less than profits, and savings out of wages greater than zero).

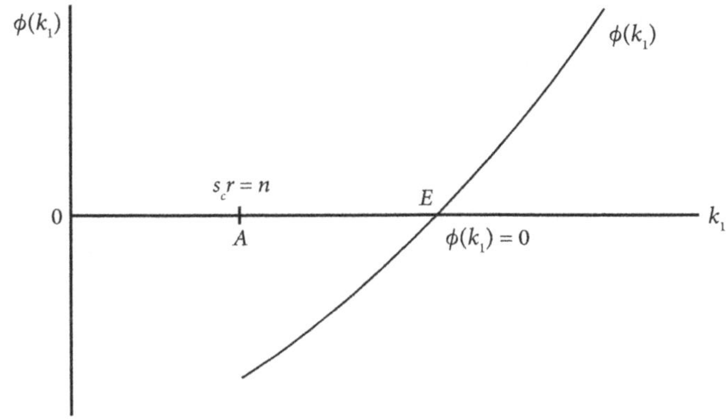

Figure 28.2 There does not exist a two-class equilibrium since *E* lies to the right of A.

5 Stability

If the only balanced growth path is the one-class balanced growth path (hereafter referred to as the OCBGP) then, of course, the stability properties of the model are exactly as Uzawa and Inada have analyzed them.

The interesting questions arise when there exists both a two-class and a one-class balanced growth path. In that case, we can ask two questions concerning the stability of the OCBGP:

(a) If k_c is constrained to be zero, is the OCBGP stable?
(b) In general, is the OCBGP stable?

The answer to the first question again is the same as provided by Uzawa and Inada. What we shall now show is that the answer to the second question is no: if k_c is ever positive, and there exists a balanced growth path with $k_c > 0$, then k_c will always be positive. But on the other hand, it cannot be shown that the economy will converge to the two-class balanced growth path (TCBGP); it may oscillate around it.

First, it can be shown that under the capital intensity hypothesis the system is always locally stable.

Observe, however, that since we are presently only interested in local stability, all we require is that, near the TCBGP, the consumption goods sector be more capital-intensive than the capital goods sector. This is, of course, a much weaker condition than the restriction that this holds for all wage-rentals ratios. What happens at interest rates other than those arbitrarily close to $r = n/s_c$ is completely irrelevant for local stability.

But the fact that the system is locally stable does not guarantee that there are not cyclical paths oscillating around the TCBGP; this can only be deduced from a complete analysis of the phase diagram, and it appears that such cyclical paths are a distinct possibility. But what it does exclude is the possibility of there being cyclical paths near the TCBGP, that is, there exists a region around the TCBGP in which all paths converge to it. This is what is meant by local stability; and how big this region is cannot be said without detailed information on the functions.

Secondly, it should be observed that if the OCBGP is unique and stable if k_c is constrained to equal zero, it is globally unstable if k_c is not so constrained (provided there exists a TCBGP). This follows from the fact that under the conditions stated, r must be greater than n/s_c, and hence $\dot{k}_c$ must be positive near the TCBGP. Moreover, since the minimum value of $\dot{k}_c$ is $-nk_c$, if k_c is ever positive, it will never become zero; hence if k_c is ever positive, k_c will always be positive when the economy enters a small neighborhood of the OCBGP (if it enters it). And clearly, once in the neighborhood, k_c increases until (k_w, k_c) is no longer arbitrarily close to the OCBGP.

The following theorem about the global stability of the system when there exists a two-class balanced growth path can be proven.[6]

(1) If the capital intensity of the consumption goods sector is not less than that of the capital goods sector, then the set of limit points (as $t \to \infty$) in (k_c, k_w) phase space for a path is either the TCBGP point or a limit cycle around it, or the capital–labor ratio of the path is unbounded. The Inada derivative conditions are sufficient to rule out the possibility of divergence.

(2) If the capital intensity of the capital goods sector is greater than that of the consumption goods sector, all of the above results obtain provided that there exists a unique OCBGP which, in the absence of capitalists, is stable. Moreover, if the Inada derivative conditions are satisfied, the TCBGP point cannot be a saddle-point.

(3) If, in addition to the conditions of (2), the TCBGP is unstable, then all paths oscillate around the TCBGP and at least one of the paths is perfectly periodic.[7]

We shall now investigate the properties of these cycles. First, any periodic trajectory must have a time-average value of the interest rate equal to the rate of growth divided by the savings propensity of capitalists.[8] Moreover, the average return on capitalists' capital

is equal to n/s_c.[9] Secondly, let IC be the closed curve representing the set of limit points for some path. Then any trajectory starting (or coming) sufficiently close to IC spirals around IC, in the sense that it is met an infinite number of times by a line through any point of IC, provided that the direction of the line is not the direction of the vector $\left(\dot{k}_w, \dot{k}_c\right)$.

Thirdly, since no two trajectories can intersect (because of uniqueness of momentary equilibria) successive limit cycles must be of unambiguously increasing amplitude.

[6] We ignore the case where k_c is ever zero, since our model is then identical to that investigated by Uzawa and Inada.

[7] Perhaps the difference between a general limit cycle and a periodic trajectory (as a special case) should be emphasized. A periodic orbit has itself as its limit; while a limit cycle has a closed curve (which in general is not identical to the orbit) as the set of its limit points.

[8] $\lim_{h\to\infty} \int_{2\pi h/z}^{2\pi(h+1)/z} d\ln k_c = s_c \int_{2\pi h/z}^{2\pi(h+1)/z} r dt - 2\pi n/z \to 0 \Rightarrow \lim_{h\to\infty} \frac{1}{2\pi/z} \int_{2\pi h/z}^{2\pi(h+1)/z} r dt \to n/s_c$.

[9] It should be clear that the first does not automatically imply the second. For instance, it cannot be shown that the average return on workers' capital is equal to n/s_c. To prove that for large h

$$\int_{2\pi h/z}^{2\pi(h+1)/z} rk_c dt \Big/ \int_{2\pi h/z}^{2\pi(h+1)/z} k_c dt \to n/s_c$$

observe that

$$\int_{2\pi h/z}^{2\pi(h+1)/z} s_c r k_c dt - n \int_{2\pi h/z}^{2\pi(h+1)/z} dt = \int_{2\pi h/z}^{2\pi(h+1)/z} d\dot{k}_c \to 0.$$

Fourthly, if C_{i+1} is a periodic trajectory, and C_i is the next smallest in amplitude, then at most one of them can be stable (under positive time).[10]

Fifthly, there are a finite number of limit cycles.

6 Concluding Remarks

These cycles do not constitute a business cycle, since full employment is an explicit assumption of the model. But the dynamics we describe may play into the generation of observed cyclical fluctuations. Indeed, many of the critical properties of the business cycle can be observed: fluctuations in the distribution of income, fluctuations in output per man, fluctuations in the rate of growth of output, fluctuations in the investment–output ratio, and constant average rates of profit for varying amplitudes of the cycle. In fact, the "story" of this cycle sounds very much like some of the capital-intensity versions found in the business cycle literature (minus, of course, the fluctuations in employment). But note that this cycle is generated without any rigidities or lags in the system.

In this chapter, we have shown that the dynamics are markedly different from those analyzed in earlier models assuming only one sector and one class: convergence to one of the balance growth paths, even under the restrictive Inada conditions, could not be guaranteed: oscillatory paths were found to be a definite possibility.[11] The analysis of stability with more classes and sectors is even more problematic, suggesting one should be cautious in using one sector one class models.

[10] See, for example, Coddington and Levinson (1955), p. 397.

[11] In the original, we provide two examples, one entailing Cobb–Douglas production functions, the other fixed coefficients. In the former case, we show that the TCBGP may exist and be locally stable even though the capital intensity hypothesis is not satisfied. In the case of fixed coefficients, we provide an example where the TCBGP is locally unstable.

29

Capital, Wages, and Structural Unemployment

With George A. Akerlof

1 Introduction

Of the "stylized facts" econometricians have uncovered in the last decade, one of the most interesting is the Phillips curve (Phillips, 1958; Samuelson and Solow, 1960), relating the rate of change of money wages to the level of employment.[1] It has led to a number of theoretical investigations into the role of wages in determining the behavior of the economy in the short run (Akerlof and Stiglitz, 1965; Solow and Stiglitz, 1968). The role of wages in determining the *long-run* behavior of the economy has, however, not been very extensively explored.[2] Most of the recent neoclassical growth models have treated wages essentially passively: in Solow's model (Solow, 1956) the savings rate and the rate of growth of labor determine the capital–output ratio, and given the capital–output ratio, the real wage is determined. The real wage has no further effect on the behavior of the economy. It is our view that the real wage is important and does play a more than passive role.[3]

High levels of employment are likely to lead to high wages. High wages lead to a decreased average savings rate for the economy (if the proportion of wages saved is smaller than that of profits) and, if the high wages are expected to continue, to more capital-intensive machines being constructed. Both of these lead to fewer jobs in the future, that is, to a low level of employment.[4] At very low levels of employment just the opposite occurs. In between there is some steady-state level of employment, but the economy is, as we shall see, likely to oscillate around this equilibrium (in damped cycles) rather than converge immediately to it. Our model is, accordingly, an attempt to relate the amount of unemployment (the number of jobs) and the wage-rate. It is a long-run theory, and does not account for unemployment caused by insufficient aggregate demand; rather this is closer to a model of structural unemployment.

To isolate the various interactions between wages and unemployment we shall employ a number of closely related models. In Section 2 we present the basic components of the

[1] Written with George Akerlof. Originally published in 1969 as "Capital, Wages and Structural Unemployment," *Economic Journal*, 79(314): 269–81. Reprinted with permission

[2] The authors would like to thank R. M. Solow, Eytan Sheshinski, and Gary Becker for valuable help and comments. The research was supported in part by the National Science Foundation.

[3] Important exceptions are the models of the neo-Keynesian or Cambridge economists (Kaldor, 1957; Pasinetti, 1962; Robinson, 1965); these have focused on the relation between savings and wages; we are interested in the interaction between wages, unemployment and choice of technique. Since this paper was written, the studies of Phelps (1967) and Rose (1967) have appeared; both of these authors, however, take quite different approaches and are interested in different questions.

[4] It is worth noting that in the 1930s and early 40s much attention was focused on wages; Hayek (1939) and Kaldor (1939), among others, built elaborate theories in which the behavior of real wages played a crucial role.

The Origins of Inequality, and Policies to Contain It. Joseph E. Stiglitz with George A. Akerlof, Oxford University Press.
 DOI: 10.1093/oso/9780198799580.003.0030

models. Section 3 is concerned with the dynamics. Section 4 is devoted to a brief discussion of attempts by the Government to alter the long-run equilibrium level of unemployment. Section 5 provides a theoretical justification for our long-run wage–unemployment relationship.

2 The Model

There are three basic relations in our models: the determination of the real wage, the choice of technique, and the accumulation of capital.

2.1 Choice of Technique

We shall consider two alternative assumptions about production. The assumption of ex-ante substitutability but ex-post fixed coefficients (putty-clay) is probably the more realistic, but the alternative assumption of malleable capital is analytically far simpler.

(1) *Putty-clay.* Ex-ante output is produced under neoclassical conditions:

$$Q = F(K, N),$$

where K is capital, N is employment, F is homogeneous of degree one, concave and satisfies the Inada conditions; both factors always have positive marginal products. But once machines are built, the capital hardens into hard-baked clay and the capital intensity is fixed forever after. Labor must work with capital of a given type in fixed proportions. In Figure 29.1 we depict an ex-ante isoquant as an envelope of ex-post isoquants. We denote the type of machine by its ex-post capital–employment ratio, $K/N = k$.

We shall assume that firms choose the technique of production to "maximize profits." If ex-post possibilities for substitution are limited, once the machine has been constructed, the firm will have to consider wages over the horizon of the machine's life. This becomes an extremely difficult problem (see Cass and Stiglitz, 1969), but can be simplified for our purposes. We assume that firms are myopic, and choose the technique which maximizes

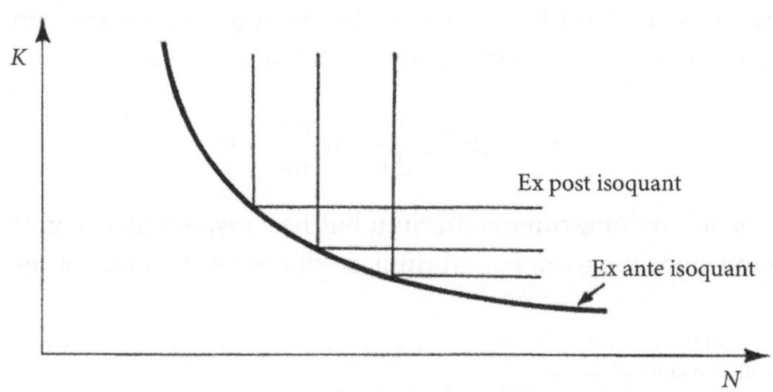

Figure 29.1 Isoquants—in putty clay models there is substitutability ex ante but not ex post.

profits on the assumption that wages are to remain constant.[5,6] Thus, if $f(k)$ gives the output per man on machines of different capital intensities, k, profits per machine are given by $f(k)/k - w/k$, where w is the real wage. The condition for maximum profit per machine is

$$w = f - kf',$$

so that, inverting, we obtain:

$$k = h(w) \quad h' = 1/-f'' > 0. \tag{29.1}$$

The capital intensity of the machine is an increasing function of the wage.

(2) *Malleable Capital.* In this case, the ex-ante and the ex-post production functions are identical. The firm need not form expectations about future factor costs. It simply hires labor up to the point where the real wage is equal to the marginal productivity of labor. The capital–employment ratio, k, is simply given by $h(w)$.

2.2 The Wage–Unemployment Relationship

There are several alternative formulations of a long-run Phillips curve. Because it is difficult to choose among them on a priori grounds and because the empirical evidence is far from unambiguous, we shall employ two different hypotheses.

The first is based on the presumption that in the long-run, individuals will not suffer from money illusion, so that the wage bargain will be made in effect in *real* rather than money terms. Hence, the rate of change of real wages is simply a function of the level of unemployment, u:

$$\frac{\dot{w}}{w} = Z(u), \quad Z' > 0, \quad Z(1) > 0, \quad Z(0) < 0. \tag{29.2}$$

The level of unemployment at which $\dot{w} = 0$, u^*, has been called the "natural" rate of unemployment by Friedman (1968).

More recent studies have suggested that the rate of change of wages is not so much a function of u as the change of u (Kuh, 1967; de Menil, 1968). These studies suggest that corresponding to any level of productivity and unemployment there is an equilibrium level of the real wage. Since in long-run equilibrium the average and marginal productivity of a worker is an increasing function of the capital–labor ratio, we have

$$w = w(u, k), \frac{\partial w}{\partial u} < 0, \frac{\partial w}{\partial k} > 0. \tag{29.3}$$

If the economy is not in long-run equilibrium but has, say, deviated slightly from it or is oscillating around some long-run equilibrium, so that we can identify a "normal" level of

[5] Here, as throughout the chapter, we ignore technical change. The reader can easily adapt the analysis for the case of Harrod–Neutral technical change.

[6] As Keynes argued "our usual practice [is] to take the existing situation and to project it into the future, modified only to the extent that we have more or less definite reasons for expecting a change" (Keynes 1936, p. 148). This assumption has been used by Akerlof (1967) and Sheshinski (1967) in analyzing the stability of the putty-clay model. For other discussions of the putty-clay model see Johansen (1959) and Solow (1962).

productivity, then it is this "normal" productivity that is relevant for the real wage determination (see Eckstein and Fromm, 1968, Hall and Hitch, 1939). In this situation, real wages are simply a function of the unemployment rate,

$$w = v(u) \quad v' < 0, \tag{29.3'}$$

and the rate of increase in the real wage is an increasing function of the rate of decrease in the unemployment rate.

2.3 Savings and Reproduction

We assume, as usual, that labor is growing exponentially at the rate λ. Savings consist of a fraction, s_w, of wage income, and s_p of profit income, with $s_w \leq s_p$. If $s_w = s_p = s$ we have the neoclassical savings assumption.

3 Dynamic Analysis

(*a*) We begin our dynamic analysis with an economy in which there is no choice of technique (*i.e.*, the ex-ante and ex-post production functions have fixed coefficients), but in which wages adjust to their equilibrium value only with a lag. The output–capital ratio, Q/K, is fixed at C, and the employment–capital ratio, N/K, at $b(= 1/k)$. We let $r = K/L$, where L is the size of the labor force.[7] $L = N$ if there is full employment, but otherwise $L > N$. We have, then,

$$\begin{array}{ll} \dot{r} = s_p Cr - (s_p - s_w)\, wbr - \lambda r & \text{if } N < L \\ \dot{r} = s_p C/b - (s_p - s_w)\, w - \lambda r & \text{if } N = L \end{array} . \tag{29.4}$$

Let the wage dynamics be given by (29.2), where $u = 1 - br$

$$\dot{w}/w = Z(1 - br).$$

In balanced growth, $\dot{w} = \dot{r} = 0$, so if $Z(u^*) = 0, u^* < 1, r^* = \frac{1-u^*}{b}$. Near the balanced growth path the economy oscillates in cyclical fluctuations which are neither damped nor undampened:

$$\begin{array}{l} \dot{r} = -(s_p - s_w)\, br^*\,(w - w^*) \\ \dot{w} = -w^* Z^* b\,(r - r^*) \end{array} . \tag{29.5}$$

The characteristic roots are accordingly purely imaginary:

$$\pm i\sqrt{-b^2 Z'^*\,(s_p - s_w)\, w^* r^*} = \pm i\sqrt{-(1 - u^*)\,(s_p C - \lambda)\, Z'^*},$$

[7] We assume that $s_p > s_w$ and $s_p C > \lambda$.

so the balanced growth path is a center. The periods of the cyclical fluctuations are approximately equal to

$$2\pi/\sqrt{|\,(1-u^*)\left(s_pC-\lambda\right)Z'^*|}.$$

If the capital–output ratio is around 2.5, the savings rate out of profits is 0.5–0.7 (Kaldor, 1966), $1 - u^*$ is around 0.97, λ is approximately 1%, and Z'^* around 3 (Dicks Mireaux, 1961), then the period is approximately 7.1–8.5 years, that is, well within the range of the "normal" 7–10 year cycle (Matthews, 1959).[8]

Two further properties of these cycles need to be noted:

1. The time average of the unemployment rate for all cycles is u^*. Integrating (29.5) over a period, m, we find:

$$\int_0^m w dt = 0 = \int_0^m brdt - (1-u^*)\,h$$

or

$$\frac{1}{m}\int_0^m (1-u)dt = 1 - u^*$$

2. Similarly, the time average wage is equal to w^* and the time average profit rate is equal to $C - w^*b$.

(*b*) If there is a choice of technique, but capital is malleable, then although there still may be cyclical oscillations, all cycles are damped. Capital accumulation is described by

$$\frac{\dot{r}}{r} = \frac{s_w f(h(w))}{h(w)} + \left(s_p - s_w\right)f' - \lambda. \tag{29.6}$$

The unemployment rate is simply $1 - (r/h(w))$, so

$$\frac{\dot{w}}{w} = Z(1 - (r/h(w))). \tag{29.7}$$

[8] The system of Equations (29.2) and (29.4) is simply a special case of the Volterra-Lotka prey-predator model, for which it is easy to establish that all paths are periodic. Dividing (29.2) by (29.4) and integrating, we obtain $P(r) + Q(w) =$ Constant (depending on initial conditions). Since $Q'' = -(s_pC - \lambda)/w^2 < 0$, and since we have shown that (w^*, r^*) is a center, all trajectories must be periodic. (Since $w < C/b$ and $0 \leq u \leq 1$, the paths cannot diverge. If the constraints are ever binding it can still be shown that (29.2) and (29.4), appropriately modified, generate periodic paths.) Goodwin (1967).

Balanced growth requires $\dot{r}/r = 0$, *i.e.*, $w = w^*$, where $\frac{s_w f(h(w^*))}{h(w^*)} + (s_p - s_w) f'(h(w^*)) - \lambda = 0$, and $\dot{w}/w = 0$, *i.e.*, $r = r^* = (1 - u^*)h(w^*)$, where $Z(u^*) = 0$. It is easy to show that the system (29.6) and (29.7) is locally stable, since the characteristic roots of the associated linear system have negative real parts.[9]

But if we take the simpler hypothesis, that the level of wages is a function of the unemployment rate (and the "normal" capital–labor ratio) the economy does not oscillate, but converges directly to its balanced growth state. From (29.3′), since $1 - u = r/h(w)$, we have (near balanced growth):

$$w = v(1 - r/h(w)),$$

which can be solved for w in terms of r for any value of r : $w = x(r)$,

$$dw/dr = -\frac{v'}{h - v'rh'/h} > 0.$$

Hence, we can write:

$$h(w) = h(x(r)) = \xi(r) \quad \xi' > 0.$$

Substituting into the capital accumulation equation with, for example, neoclassical savings, we obtain:

$$\dot{r}/r = sf(\xi(r))/\xi(r) - \lambda,$$

from which it immediately follows that the economy converges directly to its balanced growth trajectory.

(*c*) But even in the case of the simpler wage hypothesis (i.e., (29.3)), if capital is not malleable the economy may still oscillate. To see this, consider first the case where capital lives forever. The balanced growth paths look very similar to those with malleable capital. If $s(t)$ is savings and $k(t)$ the capital intensity on new machines at time t, the number of new jobs created, $\dot{N}(t)$, is $s(t)/k(t)$. In balanced growth, there is one type of capital, with capital intensity k^*. Since each worker produces an average product of $f(k^*)$ total output is $f(k^*)(1 - u^*) L(t)$. If the wage is w^*, then

$$\frac{s(t)}{L(t)} = s_w f(k^*)(1 - u^*) + (s_p - s_w)(1 - u^*)(f(k^*) - w^*).$$

Since $u = 1 - N(t)/L(t)$, for $\dot{u} = 0, -\frac{s(t)}{k(t)L(t)} + (1 - u)\lambda = 0$, or

$$s_w f(k^*) + (s_p - s_w)(f(k^*) - w^*) = \lambda k^*.$$

[9] The characteristic equation is $\lambda^2 - \frac{Z' rh'(w)}{h(w)^2} w\lambda - wrh' \frac{Z'}{h} \left(\frac{s_w w}{h^2} - (s_p - s_w) f''\right)$. Since the coefficients are all positive, the system is stable; there are damped oscillations if $Z' > 4f''(s_w \sigma/\alpha + s_p - s_w) h^3/rh'w$, where σ is the elasticity of substitution and α the share of capital.

If $s_p = s_w$, this reduces to the familiar Solow equilibrium. More generally, substituting (29.1) we have

$$s_w f(k^*) + (s_p - s_w)(f'(k^*)k^*) = \lambda k^*,$$

so k^* is identical to the value it would attain if capital were malleable. From (29.1), when k^* is uniquely determined,[10] so is w, * and from (29.2), u^* is therefore uniquely determined.

There is, however, one important difference between the malleable and non-malleable cases. In the former, in long-run equilibrium, the demand curve for labor looks as in Figure 29.2a. If wages today would fall, employment could rise. But in the latter the demand curve for labor looks as in Figure 29.2b; the capital is fully utilized. No new job would be created today by lowering wages today. Lowering wages today would lead to lower unemployment tomorrow, just as investment decisions in the past have led to the present level of unemployment.

The dynamics of the two cases are accordingly quite different. We consider, for simplicity, only the case where $s_w = 0$. Let $G(k, t)$ be the number of workers which can be employed on all machines of capital intensity k or less at time t (in *per capita* terms). Then it is easy to show that (see Cass and Stiglitz, 1969):

$$1 - u = \int_{\underline{k}}^{\infty} dG(k, t) \tag{29.8}$$

$$i = s_p \int_{\underline{k}}^{\infty} [f(k) - w]dG(k, t) \tag{29.9}$$

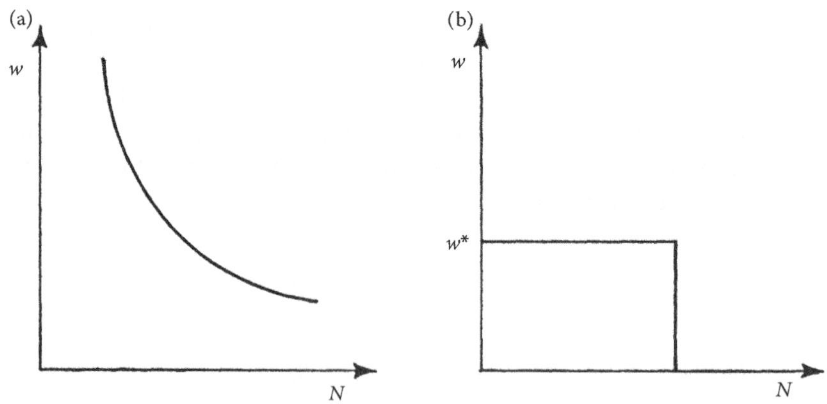

Figure 29.2 Demand curve for labor.

Panel (a) Normally, demand for labor declines smoothly with wages. Panel (b) With fixed coefficients technology, above w^* there is zero demand, and below w^* the demand is fixed at the economy's productive capacity.

[10] Sufficient conditions for k^* to be uniquely determined are (a) $s_p = s_w$ or (b) the elasticity of substitution is greater than or equal to unity.

where i is investment *per capita* and $\underline{k}$ is the lowest capital intensity used. (29.8) follows from the fact that the higher the capital intensity, the greater output per man, and hence the smaller variable costs. (29.9) follows from the fact that profits per man on a machine of type k are simply equal to output per man less the wage-rate. If firms hire workers up to the point where the quasi-rent on the marginal machine in use is zero,

$$w = f(\underline{k}) \tag{29.10}$$

(= $v(u)$ near balanced growth). Finally, if there were no investment the number of workers on any given type of machine in per capita terms would decline at the rate λ. With investment, we have

$$\frac{\partial G(k,t)}{\partial t} = \begin{cases} -\lambda G(k,t) + i/h(w) & k \geq h(w) \\ -\lambda G(k,t) & k < h(w) \end{cases}, \tag{29.11}$$

where, as noted earlier, $h(w(t))$ is the type of machine built at time t. Differentiation of (29.8) and (29.9) yields, after some simplification,[11]

$$\begin{aligned} \dot{w} &\sim -\left[\lambda\left(1 - v^{-1}(w)\right) - i/h(w)\right] \\ \dot{i} &\sim [f'(h(w)) - \lambda] \end{aligned} \tag{29.12}$$

("~" means "is of the same sign as"). As Figure 29.3 illustrates, this may give rise to cyclical oscillations. It can be proved (see Cass and Stiglitz, 1969), however, that all the cyclical oscillations are damped. Similar results obtain provided $s_w < s_p$.

(*d*) As we shall now see, the result that all cycles are damped depends crucially on the assumption that machines have an infinite life (or decay only exponentially). Consider, as the alternative polar case, an economy where machines live for one period only. In order to demonstrate that the cyclical oscillations generated arise not from the savings–wage relation but from the investment–wage interactions, we assume a constant fraction of income is saved. Then, in such an economy, letting n_t be the employment rate at time t,

$$n_{t+1} = n_t s f(k_t) / k_{t+1}(1 + \lambda). \tag{29.13}$$

The discrete analog of (29.2) may be taken to be

$$w_t / w_{t-1} = \phi(n_t). \tag{29.14}$$

Myopic expectations implies that

$$k_{t+1} = h(w_t) \text{ or } w_t = f(k_{t+1}) - k_{t+1} f'(k_{t+1}) \equiv g(k_{t+1}). \tag{29.15}$$

(29.13)–(29.15) define the dynamics of the economy. Given w_{t-1}, n_t, and k_t, (14) defines w_t. (29.15) then defines k_{t+1}. (29.13) then defines n_{t+1}. In balanced growth, $n_t = n_{t+1}$ and $w_t = w_{t+1}$; *i. e.*, $n = n^*$, where $\phi(n^*) = 1$, and $k = k^*$, where $sf(k^*) = (1 + \lambda)k^*$.[12]

[11] (29.12) can be shown to hold even if (29.8) and (29.9) are not differentiable. See Cass and Stiglitz 1969.

[12] To examine the stability properties of the balanced growth path, let $\eta = \ln n$ and $K = \ln k$, and take a linear expansion of (29.13) and (29.14):

$$\eta_{t+1} - \eta_t = \alpha K_t - K_{t+1} + d \tag{29.13'}$$

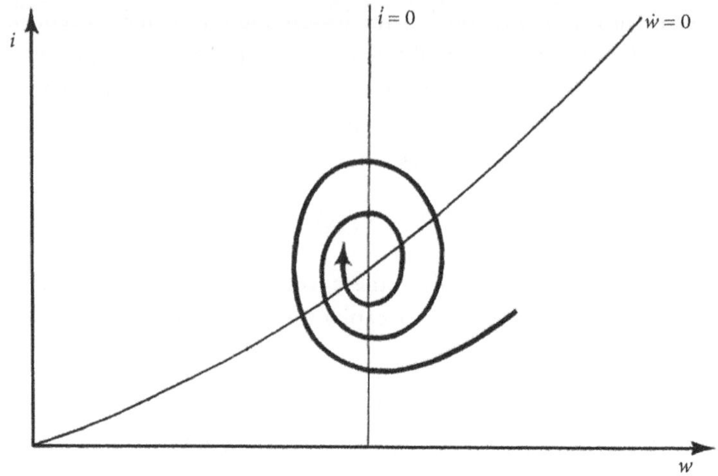

Figure 29.3 {wage, investment} dynamics: convergence to steady state is oscillatory.

It is easy to see that this model may give rise to periodic cycles. (In the originally published version of this chapter, we illustrate by solving for a two-period cycle, providing sufficient conditions for the existence of such cycles. What is crucial for the existence of cycles is the lag structure of expectations and wage adjustments, not the particular assumption of myopic expectations or the particular wage adjustment Equation (29.14).)

4 Governmental Attempts to Alter the Long-Run Equilibrium Level of Unemployment

In the previous section we have seen that in balanced growth there is some equilibrium level of unemployment, u^*. What happens if the Government wishes to change this level? If the long-run Phillips curve takes the form of (29.2), that is, $\dot{w}/w = Z(u)$, there is nothing it can do short of changing the $Z(u)$ function. If, however, the long-run Phillips curve is of the form (29.3), then if the Government wishes to attain a level of unemployment w^{**} we solve (29.1) and (29.2), for w^{**} and k^{**}, *i. e.*, $w^{**} = w(k^{**}, u^{**})$, $k^{**} = h(w^{**})$.[13] The question is, how can it ensure that the long-run capital intensity is k^{**}? If savings depend on the distribution of income, by redistributing income, it can change the savings rate and

$$K_{t+1} - K_t = (\sigma\beta/\alpha)\eta_t - \frac{\beta}{\alpha}\sigma\eta^*, \qquad (29.14')$$

where σ is the elasticity of substitution, α the share of capital, $\beta = \phi' n/\phi$ and $d = (1-\alpha)K^*$, all evaluated at n^*, k^*. Substituting (29.14') into (29.13'), we obtain:

$$K_{t+2} + (\sigma\beta/\alpha - 2)K_{t+1} + (1 - \sigma\beta)K_t = d. \qquad (29.16)$$

The roots of (29.16) are complex if, and only if, $\beta < 4(1-\alpha)\alpha/\sigma$ (if the roots are complex, it is easy to show that the modulus is less than one, so the oscillations are damped). If the roots are real the system is locally stable if, and only if, $\beta < 4\alpha/\sigma(1+a) = \beta^*$.

[13] We ignore the possibilities of multiple solutions, or no solutions.

hence k^{**}. If, on the other hand, $s_p = s_w$ redistribution taxes will have no effect. If the Government hires workers, engages them in jobs which require no capital and pays them the same wage as in industry there will be some steady-state proportion of the labor force hired by the Government g^{**}. From the savings-investment relation we have:

$$s(f(k^{**}) + w^{**}g) = \lambda k^{**}$$

or

$$g^{**} = \frac{\lambda k^{**} - sf^{**}}{sw^{**}}.$$

5 Theoretical Justification for Long-Run Wage–Unemployment Relationship

The purpose of this section is to provide a theoretical "justification" for our long-run real wage hypothesis (29.3). If we view the market wage as an outcome of bargaining between workers, either individually or collectively, then it is reasonable to assume that the wage will depend on the threats each can impose on the other (Luce and Raiffa, 1966; de Menil, 1968). Assume the wage is w, the unemployment rate is u and that a job lasts m years (on average). (If all jobs are homogeneous, then m would simply be the working lifetime of the individual.) Then an individual who quits his job can expect to stay in the unemployment pool for $\gamma(u, \lambda, m)$ years,[14] where $\partial\gamma/\partial u > 0$, that is, the larger the unemployment rate, the longer the duration in the pool, and hence the larger lost wages whose present discounted value is $w/r[1 - e^{-r\gamma}]$, where throughout this section, r stands for the rate of interest. On the other hand, even if individuals were homogeneous ex ante, there would still be some costs to the firm of hiring a replacement and of adapting him to the particular firm. We denote these costs by T. (T may depend on the capital intensity of the machines and the level of unemployment, increasing with k and decreasing with u.) Then

$$w = \Omega\left(\frac{w}{r}[1 - e^{-r\gamma}], T\right), \Omega_1 < 0, \Omega_2 > 0. \tag{29.17}$$

The greater the cost to the firm, the higher the wage; the greater the cost to the individual, the lower the wage; (29.17) defines an implicit relation between w, r and u (and the

[14] If the potential working life of the individual is n years, then $m + \gamma = n$. If the population is constant, the expected duration in the unemployment pool, γ, is the size of the pool, uL, divided by the outflow, $(L(1 - u)/m = L(1 - u)/n - \gamma : \gamma = un = mu/(1 - u)$, If the labor force is growing at the rate λ, and once the individual is employed, he remains on the job the rest of his life, then

$$\gamma = -\frac{ln(1 - u(1 - e^{-\lambda n}))}{\lambda} = \frac{ln}{\lambda}\left((1 - ue^{-\lambda m})/(1 - u)\right).$$

parameters λ, m, T). Since in long-run equilibrium $r = f'(k)$ we obtain $w = w(u, k)$, with

$$\frac{\partial w}{\partial u} = \frac{w\Omega_1 \frac{\partial \gamma}{\partial u} e^{-r\gamma}}{1 - \frac{\Omega_1}{r}(1 - e^{-r\gamma})} < 0$$

$$\frac{\partial w}{\partial k} = \frac{wf''\Omega_1 \int_0^{\gamma} te^{-rt}dt}{1 - \frac{\Omega_1}{r}\left(1 - e^{-r\lambda}\right)} > 0.$$

6 Concluding Comments

In conclusion, we note that this model suggests a partial answer to a fundamental question: why does unemployment in most capitalist countries most of the time shy away from both very low and very high levels? The answer, which may not be surprising, is that the number of jobs created depends upon the wage-rate, both because the level of savings and the capital intensity of machines depend on the wage, and the wage-rate in turn depends in part on the unemployment rate.

30

Inequality and the Business Cycle

With Jason Furman

1 Introduction

Economic fluctuations have large consequences for inequality.[1] For most workers and their families, the loss of a job can be cataclysmic. In the 2008 crisis, many lost their homes. High levels of unemployment put downward pressure on wages, especially of unskilled workers. This chapter explores the relationship between inequality and the business cycle. In particular, we are interested in the distributional consequences of changes in demand that affect unemployment or inflation.

2 Who Bears the Costs of Unemployment and Inflation?

2.1 Disparate Effects of Increases in Unemployment on Different Individuals

The business cycle and inequality are linked in a fundamental way through the indivisibility of employment and heterogeneity of economic agents. If a person's employment were continuous, then the economy could adjust to a negative shock by, say, reducing the number of hours that everyone worked by 5%. Given, however, that most jobs do not have continuous hours, in practice most of this adjustment is accomplished through, in the extreme case, 5% of the employed people losing their jobs while the other 95% continue to work normal hours. This is clear in the United States where three-quarters of the variation in total hours worked is explained by changes in the number of people employed, with the remainder accounted for by changes in hours. By imposing large adjustments on some people while others are relatively unaffected, this indivisibility means that temporarily increased unemployment increases earnings disparities and thus inequality.

2.2 Stronger Adverse Effects on Low-Income Individuals

This effect becomes even stronger when we take into account the initially unequal distribution of earnings. If, as is the case, the job losers are disproportionately drawn from the ranks of lower earners, then inequality will increase by even more. This gives rise to the

[1] Written with Jason Furman. Excerpted from a paper originally published in 1998 as "Economic Consequences of Income Inequality," with Jason Furman, in Symposium Proceedings—Income Inequality: Issues and Policy Options, Jackson Hole, Wyoming: Federal Reserve Bank of Kansas City, pp. 221–63. Originally presented at a meeting in Jackson Hole convened by the Federal Reserve Bank of Kansas, August 1998. We wish to thank Jessica Seddon and Dennis Tao for excellent research assistance.

The Origins of Inequality, and Policies to Contain It. Joseph E. Stiglitz with Jason Furman, Oxford University Press. © Joseph E. Stiglitz (2025). DOI: 10.1093/oso/9780198799580.003.0031

second result: the greater the initial degree of inequality, the more a given increase to the unemployment rate increases inequality.

Table 30.1 shows evidence on the strength of this effect for the United States. It shows data on unemployment rates and earnings for various race, occupational, and educational groups. There is a clear disparity between the unemployment rates of different groups, disparities that are almost perfectly correlated with the measure of usual weekly earnings.

We can look at the same effect in terms of changes in the unemployment rate. Specifically, we ask what happens to the unemployment rate of a particular group when the overall unemployment rate rises by 1 percentage point. This is measured by running the following regression for each group indexed by i:

$$\Delta URATE_{t,i} = \beta_0 + \beta_1 \Delta URATE_{t,total} + \epsilon_{t,i}$$

The results are shown in Table 30.2.[2]

Standard economic theory has little to say on these matters—simply because conventional competitive theory says that there should be no unemployment at all. Real business cycle economists might explain these patterns in terms of different utility functions (presumably those with lower income decide to "enjoy" more leisure in recessions, because of a greater complementarity between interest rates and labor supply!).

Efficiency wage theories and search theories both provide explanations for this phenomenon. In efficiency wage theory, different groups have different efficiency wage curves, as illustrated in Figure 30.1. In this simplified model, wages adjust so that the efficiency per wage unit is the same for all workers; those on a low efficiency wage curve are rationed out of the market. As the demand for labor falls, successive groups get rationed out of

Table 30.1 Unemployment and earnings in the United States (1992–7 average)

	Unemployment (percent)	Usual weekly earnings
Civilian (16+)	6.1	
Black	11.6	
Hispanic	9.7	
White	5.3	
<HS Diploma (25+ years)	9.6	
HS Diploma, no college (25+ years)	5.4	
<Bachelors degree (25+ years)	4.4	
College Graduates	2.6	
Farming, Forestry and Fishing	7.9	$282
Operators, Fabricators, and Laborers	9.0	$378
Technical, Sales & Administrative Support	4.9	$428
Precision, Production, Craft & Repair	6.6	$517
Managerial & Professional Specialty	2.6	$695

Source: Bureau of Labor Statistics and calculations by the authors

[2] The unemployment rates of different groups move very closely together, so that the fit in these equations is extremely good. The typical t-statistics are 20 or higher and the R2 s are almost all above 80%. These are simply regressions relating the macroeconomic variables as reported by the BLS.

Table 30.2 Percentage point change in the unemployment rate for a 1 percentage point change in the overall unemployment rate

Civilian (16+)	1.0
Black	1.5
Hispanic	1.4
White	0.9
<HS Diploma (25+ years)	1.3
HS Diploma, no college (25+ years)	1.1
<Bachelors degree (25+ years)	0.9
College Graduates	0.4

Source: Calculations by the authors based on Bureau of Labor Statistics data. Note the regressions use annual data from the first available period to 1997. All of the coefficients are significant at the 1% level.

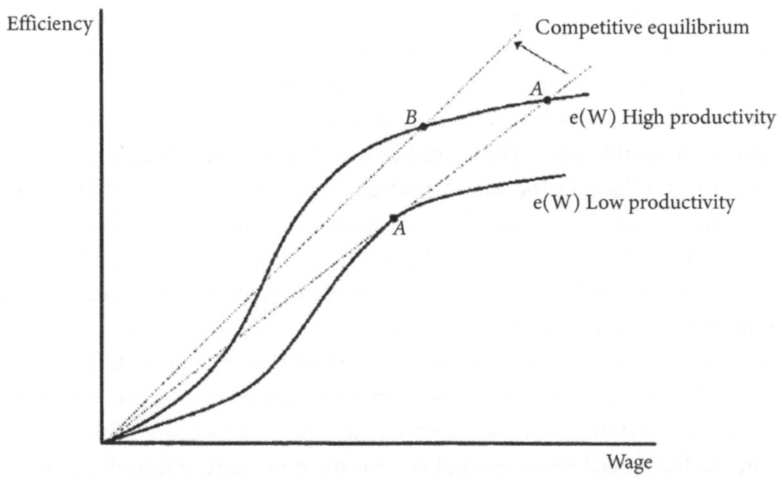

Figure 30.1 Efficiency Wage Theory: When the demand for labor decreases, low productivity workers may face job rationing (unemployment) while high productivity workers remain fully employed.

the market. More broadly, in an economic downturn, firms become more risk averse (see Greenwald and Stiglitz, 1993a); firms may feel that they have less information with which to judge the qualities of marginalized groups, and thus investments in hiring these workers are riskier. Moreover, the investment in higher productivity workers tends to be greater, so that laying off these workers involves greater risk. (There is less option value in retaining a low-skilled worker.) Thus, while hiring rates for marginalized workers are likely to be lower, the layoff rates are likely to be higher.

Similarly, search theory suggests that those with weaker search networks may be more adversely affected by a decrease in the density of jobs.[3]

[3] This explanation is elaborated in the original paper.

3 Efficiency Wages and Differential Unemployment

We have now traced out some of the elements of a vicious cycle between inequality and unemployment: high levels of unemployment lead to high levels of inequality, with some individuals losing their jobs while others having at most a limited reduction in hours. With higher levels of inequality, there may be more disparate effects on different groups of a decrease in aggregate demand. Since the marginal propensity to consume of the rich is so much lower than that of the poor, an increase in inequality leads to a decrease in aggregate demand, thus leading to higher levels of unemployment. This relationship between inequality and labor markets has implications for the persistence of unemployment, and thus for the dynamics of the business cycle.

3.1 The Distributional Consequences of Inflation

We have looked at some of the consequences of inequality, unemployment, and their relationship. For the sake of completeness, we need to look at the distributional consequences of inflation. We can separate this into several questions. First, what are the costs of inflation? Second, do these costs vary across different income groups? And finally, does the initial degree of inequality affect the magnitude or distribution of these costs?

First, the costs of inflation generally. Although no one doubts that high inflation is costly, studies have consistently shown that there are no significant adverse effects associated with low rates of inflation (see Fischer, 1993, Barro, 1997, and Bruno and Easterly, 1998), and some have even argued that problems may arise as the economy approaches a zero rate of inflation (Akerlof, Dickens, and Perry, 1996).

There is very little research on the distribution of the costs of inflation. The conventional wisdom, however, is that the costs of inflation are disproportionately borne by the better off. The lowest quintile of the income distribution gets more of their income from Federal benefits, like Social Security, that are, for the most part, indexed against changes in inflation. In contrast, the top quintile of the income distribution gets a larger fraction of its income from financial assets, which are an imperfect hedge against unexpected inflation. The intuition about the incidence of the costs of anticipated inflation is less clear. This is an important area for more research. It is clear, however, that the distributional costs of inflation are unlikely to be skewed as much toward the poor as the distributional costs of unemployment.

4 Other Aspects of Inequality and the Business Cycle

The relationship between inequality and labor markets also has implications for the persistence of unemployment, and thus for the business cycle. Furthermore, if inequality affects the extent of credit rationing, then it could also affect the degree of aggregate consumption smoothing and thus the volatility of output.

4.1 The Persistence of Unemployment

4.1.1 Search effectiveness and the stigma effects of long-term unemployment

One important factor in determining the hiring rate is how effective workers are in searching for jobs. The ability to learn about jobs, apply for them, and present oneself as a productive worker suited for a particular job can vary greatly across people. The large literature on hysteresis in European unemployment has documented evidence that people's search effectiveness declines over long spells of unemployment (see Layard and others, 1991, for an overview). It also seems that this process is nonlinear: a short spell does little to impair a worker's effectiveness in searching for jobs, but a long spell can have seriously adverse effects. In part this may be the result of the demoralization induced by long spells of unemployment.

Another complementary mechanism that explains the fact that the hiring rate declines over the length of unemployment is adverse selection. Employers do not fully know the productivity of a worker. If the worker has been unemployed for a long time, then this signals that they are not very productive and might make the employer averse to hiring them.[4]

Inequality could exacerbate the consequences of both of these mechanisms, sometimes collectively called the "outsider mechanism," for the search effectiveness of the average person. We have seen that both the level of unemployment and changes in unemployment are distributed very unevenly across races, educational levels, and occupations and that these rates are inversely correlated with earnings—the higher the wages in your group, the less likely you are to be unemployed.

Although these data do not show the gross flows of individuals into and out of employment, it is safe to infer that the disproportionate percentage of the people who lose their jobs in an adverse shock are from disadvantaged groups or have less education. If this observation is combined with the nonlinearities in the "outsider" mechanism, the result could be that the greater the degree of inequality, the more a given shock leads people to become less effective job searchers, demoralized, and stigmatized. This could lead to more persistent changes in unemployment and possibly even to higher equilibrium unemployment. Although we have not written down a formal model, we suspect that the nonlinearities in duration dependence would mean that adverse consequences for disadvantaged groups would more than offset the opposite effect on better-off groups, leading to a higher unemployment rate overall.

4.1.2 Hiring Networks

A similar effect could take place through hiring networks. One of the most important ways that people are matched with jobs is through their networks of friends, relatives, and associates. Informal communications can help people learn about job openings, figure out how best to apply for them, and even influence the chance that they are hired. To the extent that these networks are more extensive, the hiring rate will increase and the equilibrium

[4] Offsetting this effect is the fact that as the unemployment spell increases, the individual's reservation wage typically falls. There is evidence that beyond a certain point, this effect is dominated by the effects going in the opposite direction.

unemployment rate will decrease. If inequality results in greater segmentation of the labor force, it may have an adverse effect on these networks and thus on the ability to effectively get matched with jobs. The result could be a higher equilibrium unemployment rate.

The interaction between hiring networks and inequality could also lead to greater persistence of unemployment. To describe a heuristic model, take the earlier point that when worker-hours go down by, say, 5%, it is mostly due to 5% of people losing their jobs, with some adjustment in hours. Now imagine that rather than being spread evenly from across the population, these 5% are all drawn from a minority group. The result is that these people's hiring networks are seriously affected. Not only are many members of this minority group out of jobs, but they now know even fewer employed people who can help match them with jobs. The result is that their search effectiveness will be diminished, and their unemployment rate will only return to its equilibrium very slowly, if ever. This effect will be partially offset by the fact that the "advantaged" group was spared its share of job reductions. At least in a relatively stylized network hiring model, it can be shown that the former effect outweighs the latter effect and the persistence of unemployment is rising in the degree of inequality.[5]

4.2 Liquidity Constraints, Consumption, and Labor Participation

Elsewhere in this book (Chapter 25), we noted that inequality gives rise to agency costs and is related to credit rationing. Direct survey-based measures of aggregate wealth for the United States place it between $10 and $20 trillion in 1993.[6] These numbers represent a plausible range, given that they imply capital–output ratios of 1.5 and 3 respectively. If this wealth had been divided up evenly, the average household would have had somewhere between $100,000 and $200,000. This is a substantial multiple of the average household's income and would allow them to smooth shocks relatively easily.

The wealth, however, was distributed very unevenly. Only 42% of the lowest quintile of households (in terms of income) even had bank accounts; fewer than 5% had other interest-earning assets or stocks or mutual funds. Their median net worth in the lowest quintile, excluding home equity, was $949, less than two months' worth of income. The median wealth (excluding home equity) for the entire population was $8,283. Even within this group there is substantial heterogeneity of asset holdings, with 26% of households in the middle quintile of the income distribution reporting no assets at financial institutions. The median household in the top quintile had a net worth (excluding home equity) of $45,392—representing more than six months of income.

There are several explanations of the stylized facts that most households hold little wealth, and that the wealth–income ratio is rising with income. In addition, access to credit is also rising in wealth and income—a standard implication of equity and credit rationing.

[5] In this case it is "unemployment inequality"—either in terms of the means, the variances, or both, of the different groups. We have shown that this is strongly correlated with wage inequality and income inequality. The basic model assumes that unemployed people are matched randomly with one member of their network and get a job if the person they meet has a job. There is also an exogenous and possibly stochastic job separation rate that varies between groups. When there are two groups, it can be shown that as the difference between the job separation rates (or their variances) grows, the persistence of the unemployment rate rises.

[6] Bureau of the Census: Eller and Fraser (1995). All other figures on the distribution of wealth are from this source and, unless stated otherwise, refer to 1993.

As a result, the huge inequality of wealth in the United States and most other capitalist economies is associated with large fractions of the population having little or no savings to insulate themselves against negative income shocks, particularly against unemployment. For such families, the marginal propensity to consume remains close to 1 for negative shocks and for increases in income that restore them to their previous levels (to their view of their permanent income). The welfare costs of given fluctuations in income are correspondingly larger. This is exacerbated by the fact that much of the incidence of an economic downturn is borne by precisely those who are worst off.

The more people that are credit-rationed, and the more job loss is concentrated among credit-rationed people, the closer the economy's aggregate marginal propensity to consume is to 1, and thus demand shocks will result in greater fluctuations in output.[7] The effect of inequality on credit rationing is ambiguous. A mean-preserving spread of income moves some people up into less credit rationing and other people down into more credit rationing. It is plausible, but far from certain, that the increase in inequality in the United States over the past 20 years has resulted from income increases for the top of the distribution (those who were not credit constrained to start with) and decreases in income for the bottom half of the distribution, pushing some additional people into credit constraints. To the degree that inequality increases credit rationing, the economy will exhibit greater volatility than if there were less inequality; for instance, if more individuals had wealth they could use as collateral, there would be less credit rationing and more consumption smoothing.[8]

Credit constraints, and thus potentially inequality, may have a further effect on the cyclical behavior of the economy. As the economy goes into a recession, and the unemployment rate increases, families who do not have wealth to draw upon send their second member into the labor force to search (they "invest" more in search activities), increasing the observed level of unemployment.[9] This "added worker" effect can lead to greater fluctuations of observed unemployment for given fluctuations in output.

5 Concluding Remarks

An understanding of the nature and consequences of fluctuations must take into account the fact that reductions in hours worked are disproportionately borne by a few individuals (the unemployed), and that there are imperfections in capital markets, which mean that they cannot smooth the reduction in their lifetime income over their whole life. This leads to greater volatility in consumption than would be the case in a neoclassical model. (Similar issues arise at the level of the firm.)

We have seen in particular that business fluctuations do have disproportionately adverse effects on those with lower incomes. This observation itself has important implications.

[7] This is true, at least, in the simple Keynesian model where the demand multiplier is the reciprocal of the marginal propensity to consume.

[8] In the last decades the United States has also seen a huge increase in the access to and stock of consumer credit, in part as a result of improvements in risk scoring and securitization. The effects of this on the degree of liquidity constraints are, however, ambiguous. As consumers get larger credit lines, they also borrow more, and may not have any more of a buffer of assets plus potential credit to use in order to smooth fluctuations in their income. The rise in the personal bankruptcy rate is consistent with this hypothesis.

[9] For earlier discussions of this effect, see Woytinsky (1940). For a more recent theoretical analysis, see Basu, Genicot, and Stiglitz (2002).

Sometimes macroeconomic policy is posed as if there are no tradeoffs. Indeed, a major thrust of the new classical school has been to try to persuade us that there is a vertical Phillips curve and that there is nothing that can be done about the NAIRU. Posed that way, it would seem that macroeconomic management is indeed a technocratic subject, in which technocrats are simply hired to make sure that the economy stays at the NAIRU.

Even if the Phillips curve were vertical, however, there are issues of risk and tradeoffs: there is uncertainty about the level of the NAIRU, there is uncertainty about where the economy is going, and there is uncertainty about the consequences of different policies and their lags. Different groups have different attitudes toward these risks, different perceptions about the nature of these risks, and face different consequences from different policies. (Indeed, as Bayesians with different loss functions, it is not surprising that they have different perceptions about the nature of the tradeoffs.) Thus, macroeconomic policy should not be delegated to technocrats, but involves social choices: macroeconomic policy is an area of collective action, which in democratic societies requires democratic processes. Although there are legitimate issues concerning how best to combine expertise and democratic participation and how, whether, or to what extent, to insulate decision-making from the day-to-day political processes, it is important that it should be recognized that these are not just matters of technical expertise. Different policies impact different people differently. There is no single "Pareto" dominant policy.[10]

Because business fluctuations may increase inequality, and inequality may increase the magnitude of business fluctuations, there is the possibility of multiple equilibria. Governments that simultaneously pursue macroeconomic policies trying to maintain unemployment at low levels (a policy that probably has a more substantial effect on unemployment than microeconomic policies) and active redistributive policies (including through the support of education for disadvantaged groups) may push themselves into a better equilibrium, with sustained lower levels of unemployment, inequality, and instability.

These lower levels of inequality may, in turn, help support faster economic growth. While the econometric evidence on this proposition is not decisive, it is clear that the older view, that greater inequality is associated with faster growth, is not supported by the data.

While we have taken a narrow economic perspective on the consequences of inequality, it should be clear that there are broader concerns. We care about inequality because of its consequences for human well-being, and its broader consequences for the nature of society. Although it is probably true that inequality gives rise to social and political strife and such strife is not conducive to economic performance, we care about that strife not just because of these economic consequences, but for its own sake. Inequality in goods is, moreover, often translated into inequality in political power, especially in those societies that have political processes, which allow the rich and narrow but influential groups, like the media, to have undue influence in determining political outcomes. The sense that the political system is one in which, while each person may have one vote, some votes seem to count more, or are at least more effective in determining outcomes than others, leads to disillusionment with the democratic process and a decrease in participation by those who are effectively partially disenfranchised.

[10] Even if there were ex post redistributions, differences in attitudes toward risk would mean different individuals would prefer the government undertaking different policies.

One of the dramatic changes in the U.S. economy over the past quarter century is the marked increase in inequality. We have argued that there are good reasons to believe that there are adverse economic effects of this inequality, including on the magnitude and consequences of cyclical fluctuations, and that there would be economic gains from active policies, both microeconomic and macroeconomic, that explicitly take into account this increased inequality and try to reverse it. The positive broader benefits make a commitment to such policies all the more desirable.

31

Macroeconomic Fluctuations, Inequality, and Growth

1 Introduction

For years, the dominant paradigm in macroeconomics ignored inequality—both its role in *causing* crises and the effect of crises on inequality.[1] The dominant paradigm (particularly earlier variants with a representative agent) *assumed* that income distribution did not matter (at least for macroeconomic behavior).[2] Not surprisingly, then, the dominant paradigm had little to say about the impact of crises on inequality; or the converse, the impact of inequality on economic stability.

One of the few positive outcomes of the 2008 crisis is that, finally, these views are beginning to be questioned.[3] As Jayadev (2013) notes, citing data from Piketty and Saez (2003, with data updated to 2010), this crisis, like the Great Depression, was preceded by large increases in inequality.

Economists that had looked at the *average* equity of a homeowner—ignoring the distribution—felt comfortable that the economy could easily withstand a fall in housing prices of 20% or even more, because on average indebtedness was less than 80% of the market price. But such a fall has had disastrous effects, because it has meant that a large fraction of homeowners are "underwater," owing more on their homes than the value of the home, leading in turn to rates of foreclosure and widespread economic stress.

[1] Originally published in 2012 as "Macroeconomic Fluctuations, Inequality, and Human Development," *Journal of Human Development and Capabilities*, 13(1): 31–58. The paper was subsequently reprinted in 2012 in D. Nayyar (ed.), *Macroeconomics and Human Development*, New York: Taylor and Francis. Reprinted with permission. The paper has been shortened.

[2] For a critique of this paradigm, see, for instance, Stiglitz (2011a, 2011b) and the references cited there, including Stiglitz (2010a).

[3] In particular, the UN Commission on Reforms of the Global Monetary and Financial System (United Nations 2010) emphasized the role of inequality as a major contributing factor to the 2008 crisis. This work has spawned considerable research, including some cited elsewhere in this chapter. For an excellent survey, see Jayadev (2013) and the papers cited there. For a discussion of some empirical evidence, see Atkinson and Morelli (2010). Note that we are not claiming here that all financial crises are caused by inequality, or that inequality necessarily leads to a financial crisis. It is also important to note that the Gini coefficient may not adequately capture the appropriate notion of inequality for purposes of my discussion of economic fluctuations. If, for instance (as is in fact the case, see Dynan, Skinner, and Zeldes, 2004), there are marked differences in the marginal propensities to consume of the bottom 80% and the top 20%, then a better measure might be provided by the share of national income accruing to the top 20%. To the extent that fluctuations result from the ability of the financial elite to "capture" the political process, to strip away regulations, then what matters is the share of income of that sector, or the share of income at the very top. See Acemoglu (2011).

There is a much older literature relating economic fluctuations to the functional distribution of income (which in turn is broadly related to inequality), growing out of the Kaldorian tradition. Akerlof and Stiglitz (1969 (Chapter 29 of this volume)) show, for instance, in a simple model that this can give rise to fluctuations of regular periodicity. For a more comprehensive discussion of the Kaldorian literature and subsequent related developments, see Jayadev (2013).

The Origins of Inequality, and Policies to Contain It. Joseph E. Stiglitz, Oxford University Press. © Joseph E. Stiglitz (2025).
DOI: 10.1093/oso/9780198799580.003.0032

Policymakers too have finally come around to recognizing the role of inequality in this crisis—and in others. An April 2011 International Monetary Fund (IMF) report examining the effects of inequality on growth stated:

> We find that longer growth spells are robustly associated with more equality in the income distribution.... Over longer horizons, reduced inequality and sustained growth may thus be two sides of the same coin.[4]

In this brief chapter, I discuss the two-way relationship between inequality and economic fluctuations, and the implications for human development. Inequality can contribute to volatility and the creation of crises, and volatility can contribute to inequality.[5] As I note below, some of the changes in our economy—such as increased financialization—may have contributed to increased inequality and volatility both directly and indirectly. (For example, changes contributed directly to volatility, but also indirectly through effects on inequality; likewise, they contributed directly to inequality, and indirectly through effects on volatility.) The links between inequality and economic fluctuations are complex, involving both direct and indirect impacts; for example, volatility may adversely affect growth, and thereby the resources available for social expenditures.

A final prefatory remark: while I focus on the link between volatility and inequality *of income*, my real interest is on well-being, in a broader sense. I will note below adverse effects on health and education.[6] Volatility increases insecurity. Even in advanced industrial countries, insurance markets are far from perfect; most risks cannot be insured against. And even when insurance can be provided, there are significant transactions costs. Most developed countries rely on *social* insurance to mitigate these risks and do so only imperfectly.[7] But most developing countries provide at best very limited social insurance. Because individuals are risk-averse, the loss of well-being from high volatility is enormous.

Unemployment, however, has a direct adverse effect on individuals and families: work gives meaning to life and dignity to individuals. The social consequences of extended periods of unemployment cannot be compensated for simply by replacing the income that has been lost.[8]

The next section of the chapter lays out the basic two-way relationship between inequality and volatility. The third section then discusses a particular aspect of the inequality/volatility dynamics—hysteresis, the fact that the consequences of an economic downturn can be long-lived. The fourth section follows with an analysis of expenditure and that monetary policies can either mitigate or exacerbate the inequality consequences of economic downturns. The fifth section turns to one particular aspect of the policy response: how well-intentioned policies may actually turn out to have counterproductive effects on inequality.

[4] Berg and Ostry (2011).

[5] Breen and García-Peñalosa (2005) identified the cross-country linkage between inequality and volatility. They point out that their results are not driven by the high correlation of the two in Latin America.

[6] There is even evidence that America's foreclosure crisis had adverse effects on health. See Currie and Tekin (2011).

[7] The absence of good insurance markets for these risks—which are among the most important that individuals face—is a major market failure. The explanation of this market failure is only partially accounted for by information asymmetries. See Stiglitz (1993a).

[8] These are some of the reasons that GDP is not a good measure of societal performance. See Stiglitz, Sen, and Fitoussi (2010).

2 Inequality as a Cause and Consequence of Crises

The UN Commission on Reforms of the International Financial and Monetary System, which I chaired, argued that inequality played an important role in creating the 2008 crisis.[9] The link is simple and clear: increasing inequality[10] effectively redistributes income from those with a high marginal propensity to consume to those with a low marginal propensity to consume. This reduces aggregate demand. If the economy is to remain at full employment, the resulting reduced aggregate demand has to be compensated for somehow.[11] The route chosen by the United States (and, historically, by other countries) is low interest rates and lax regulation. This led to a bubble, which did sustain consumption *for a while*. But it was inevitable that the bubble would eventually break. And it was inevitable that when it broke, the economy would go into a downturn.

2.1 Political Economy

Of course, there are other ways by which the weaknesses in aggregate demand resulting from growing inequality might have been offset.[12] But the inequality itself made one of the key alternatives less likely: fiscal policy (say investments in education or infrastructure) could have been used to stimulate the economy, but the high inequality is often accompanied by a demand for a smaller government and more fiscal restraint. The well-off worry that a strong government might redistribute income away from them—the median voter's income is much less than the mean income, so he has much to gain from progressive taxation.[13]

In modern democracies, however, contrary to the standard theory, it does not appear that the median voter is pivotal (or at least that what emerges from the political process represents the informed interest of the median voter). Policies are affected by lobbying, campaign contributions, and revolving doors, so that the wealthy have disproportionate influence. Thus, as inequality grows, at least in many countries, so too do constraints on the government's fiscal space.

The problem is aggravated by the increase in debt and deficit that almost inevitably accompanies a severe economic downturn (such as the one in 2008). Conservative forces, always looking for an excuse to downsize government, seize upon the "unsustainable

[9] United Nations (2010).

[10] This analysis focuses on the impact of the change in inequality, and especially on the link through the accumulation of debt, which in turn is linked to credit crises. As we commented earlier, there are other links, such as that explored in Akerlof and Stiglitz (1969 (Chapter 29 of this volume)).

Although we do not pursue the question here, it may also be the case that the level of inequality is related to instability. For instance, at any given level of average income, more inequality may be associated with higher levels of consumption of durables, and purchases of durables are more volatile than purchases of food.

[11] Thus, the build-up in debt is based partially on the basis of policy and partially on the basis of irrationality (as is the case implicitly in the work of Minsky). Deregulation, in particular, did not prevent the irrational build-up of excessive risk. While it is true that the increased indebtedness enabled average Americans to avoid the decline in their standard of living that otherwise would have ensued, it is hard to reconcile the bubble itself with "rationality," and especially some of the extreme practices in the credit market.

For a recent paper attempting to construct an inequality induced credit cycle within a Dynamic Stochastic General Equilibrium (DSGE) framework, see Kumhof, Ranciere, and Winant (2015).

[12] For a more thorough discussion of these issues, see Jayadev (2013).

[13] See, for example, Atkinson and Stiglitz (1980), Besley (2004), and Besley and Persson (2009, 2010).

deficits" as grounds for cutbacks in government spending, even though such austerity measures may do little to improve the countries' long-term fiscal position—and in fact may have adverse effects. Austerity leads to lower gross domestic product (GDP), lower growth, and therefore lower tax revenues, and higher social expenditures. Experiences with IMF programs in East Asia and Latin America confirm these adverse effects. (So too do the more recent experiences in Latvia, Greece, and Spain.)

The burden is thus left to monetary policy to ensure that the economy operates somewhere near full employment.

Wage rigidities are not always the cause of unemployment: balance sheet effects and the risks of excessive flexibility. The evolution of the crisis has also made clear that inflexible labor markets are not (always) the cause of unemployment; quite the contrary, countries such as the United States with high degrees of labor market flexibility have at times experienced high unemployment.[14]

Indeed, there is an important tradition in macroeconomics, dating back to Fisher's debt deflation theories,[15] which suggests that greater wage and price flexibility, under certain circumstances, may be adverse not only for equality, but even for stability—and that the problems can arrive well before deflation sets in.[16] As wages fall, aggregate demand falls (as Keynes emphasized); but even if prices fall in tandem (meaning that *real wages* are not falling[17]), individuals and firms have *unindexed debt commitments.* Firms and households are forced into bankruptcy—with an increase in economic disruption, a loss of informational and organizational capital, and a downward shift in both aggregate demand and supply curves.

Such balance sheet effects can amplify an initial disturbance and, because firms are induced to contract their level of activity, net profits are reduced. With imperfections in equity markets, firms cannot simply go out to replace lost equity.[18] It takes time for balance sheets to be restored—thus adverse shocks are amplified and their effects are persistent as well.

Moreover, there are important asymmetries: while decreases in wages make firms better off (improve their balance sheets), they make households worse off. While increases in oil prices make oil producers better off, they make consumers worse off. Each of these (not fully anticipated) price changes has balance sheet effects, but in general the level of activities

[14] The U.S. unemployment rate hit a peak of 10.2% in October 2009, while the peak reached by Germany was 7.9% in July 2009 and Sweden 9% in April 2010. In April 2011, more than a year after the peak, the corresponding numbers were 9.0%, 6.2%, and 7.5%. Data are from Eurostat and the U.S. Bureau of Labor Statistics.

This is consistent with earlier empirical work based on cross-country regressions cited below showing that volatility is more associated with financial market problems than labor market rigidities.

[15] See Fisher (1933). Greenwald and Stiglitz (1987b, 1988a, 1988b, 1990b, 1993a) have revived and extended this theory, which has emphasized the adverse effects on balance sheets of unexpected price declines—or even price increases that are smaller than expected. In this crisis, considerable attention has been centered on these balance sheet effects. (For a review and extension to monetary policy, see Greenwald and Stiglitz, 1993b, 2003a.)

[16] There is a more general point: economic systems are not necessarily dynamically stable. The fall in wages that results from an increase in unemployment may move the economy away from the full employment equilibrium, rather than toward it. The implication is that it may be desirable for governments to intervene to prevent wage reductions; by contrast, policies of increasing wage flexibility may exacerbate this instability.

[17] See Solow and Stiglitz (1968).

[18] Theories of information asymmetries have explained why that is the case. See, for example, Greenwald and Stiglitz (1990a) for an analysis of the consequences and references.

are concave functions of balance sheets, so that those who wind up with improved balance sheets do not expand their activities as much as those who wind up with worsened balance sheets contract them (Greenwald and Stiglitz, 1993a).

2.2 Why Fluctuations May Have Adverse Effects on Inequality

We explained how inequality—and the attempt to maintain full employment in the face of increases in inequality by creating a bubble—may contribute to volatility. But the relationship is two-sided. Volatility contributes to inequality through several channels. Moreover, as the discussion of financialization below illustrates, some changes in the structure of the economy have contributed both directly to inequality and to volatility—and thereby indirectly to inequality as well.

One way that volatility contributes to inequality, which I have already noted, is that unemployment exerts downward pressure on wages.[19] Another is that in downturns governments cut back expenditures, and especially social expenditures that are of particular importance to the poor. (Later I will discuss how monetary policy may also exacerbate these effects.)

The adverse effects on inequality are all the greater because the incidence of unemployment is typically strongest among the least skilled (Furman and Stiglitz, 1998). This is not inevitable, but it is not surprising. Because of the high costs of training skilled workers and the difficulties of recruiting good workers, firms are more likely to retain these workers through a downturn, assigning them, if necessary, to jobs requiring fewer skills. Unskilled workers are more akin to "commodities" traded on spot markets.

But because skills decrease with unemployment, those at the bottom have, at the end of the crisis, less human capital (relative to their better-off peers), amplifying the effects on inequality and making them more persistent.

Just as there are policies that could mitigate the adverse effects of inequality on volatility—or exacerbate those effects—there are also policies that could mitigate (or exacerbate) the effects of volatility on inequality. Later, for instance, I will explain how, in the face of volatility, misguided policies of inflation targeting may have exacerbated both inequality and volatility.

Volatility may also have adverse effects through indirect channels. For instance, in a more volatile economy, firms may demand high-risk premiums. Thus, to achieve the same level of investment on average, the share of wages will be lower. Alternatively, the level of investment will be lower (at any given interest rate), and at least in the short to medium term this translates into lower growth—and less resources for the government, including less expenditures in public education and social protection.

[19] Because there is an upper bound on employment, economies with greater volatility typically have a higher average unemployment rate (a higher gap between actual and potential output.

While the notion that when unemployment is high, there is downward pressure on wages might seem obvious, in traditional neoclassical theory, lower employment (at a fixed level of capital) is associated with high real product wages. But such theories begin, in effect, by assuming full employment, and hence are of little relevance to the questions at hand. In efficiency wage theories (for example, Shapiro and Stiglitz, 1984) it is easy to see how increased unemployment is associated with lower wages. So too in bargaining theories.

2.3 Weakened Automatic Stabilizers

Policies in recent years have strengthened the nexus between inequality and volatility—in particular, leading not only to more inequality, but also to a greater sensitivity of inequality to economic fluctuations. The reductions in the progressivity of the income tax system, the shift of pension plans from defined benefit to defined contribution systems, and the broader undermining of social protections have weakened the economy's automatic stabilizers, making the economy more vulnerable to shocks—and, in particular, adversely affecting the poor in downturns.

In many countries (including the United States) the structure of government makes such cutbacks almost inevitable.[20] Delivery of education and health services is a local responsibility, and local governments' capacity to borrow is limited (in the United States, many states have balanced budget provisions in their constitutions, strictly limiting the extent to which they can borrow). Hence, an economic downturn translates directly into cutbacks in public services, including those on which the poor are dependent.

2.4 The Role of Financialization

Finally, financialization of the economy is an important component of the nexus between economic volatility and inequality; it is responsible both for increasing inequality and increasing fragility. A large fraction of economic crises are related to credit bubbles, and credit bubbles can more easily occur with an overdeveloped and under-regulated financial system.[21] Under-regulation contributes to the expansion of the financial sector, both because excessively risky and exploitive practices are not circumscribed, and because there is increased risk associated with an implicit increase in the "bailout" subsidy—evidenced over and over again in the last 30 years. Under-regulation/liberalization results in increased leverage (sometimes, as recently, hidden through "financial innovations") and a reliance on less stable sources of funding.

As elsewhere, politics and economics are intertwined: large financial sectors can exert influence to prevent effective enforcement of anti-trust laws, at least as they apply to the financial sector, again with adverse distribution effect, and to change regulations and laws in ways that give the financial sector more scope to exploit other parts of the economy. The 2005 creditor-friendly bankruptcy law is a case in point—which further contributed to the credit cycle by giving lenders confidence that they could recover money even from those who could not really afford to repay. There is thus a vicious circle: more profits in the financial sector increase their political influence to promote laws and regulations that advantage the sector over other parts of society; and at the same time, those laws and regulations increase the economy's fragility and the implicit subsidies those in the sector receive.

Within the financial sector, the same dynamic is at play: the too-big-to-fail institutions have an advantage over others, since their creditors are willing to supply them with funds at lower interest rates, *because* they know that they will be bailed out.

[20] Of course, the Federal government could, through a revenue sharing program, offset the impact of the reduction in state and local tax revenues.

[21] This is consistent with the empirical findings of Easterly, Islam, and Stiglitz (2001a, 2001b).

Thus, financialization directly and indirectly results in the economy being exposed to more (endogenous) shocks.[22] Financial and capital market liberalization has, in particular, exposed developing and emerging markets to external shocks—and, in most cases, the promised benefit of being able to smooth internally generated shocks has proved elusive. Capital flows have been procyclical, not countercyclical.[23]

But financialization has contributed to the vicious cycle of increasing inequality and volatility in another way. The "discipline" of short-term capital flows—the asymmetries between liberalization of capital and labor flows—has hurt the bargaining position of labor both within the private sector and the public. Employers threaten to leave, to go elsewhere, unless wages and taxes on capital are cut.

There is one more way that financial market globalization may have contributed not only to the depth of the crisis and its rapid spread, but also to its duration. In most economies, a major source of job creation is small and medium enterprises (SMEs), which typically rely on smaller, more local banks. There is some evidence, both from research at the IMF[24] and Columbia,[25] suggesting that financial market liberalization and the internationalization of banking has not been good for the access to credit of SMEs. So too, the way the bank rescue operation was conducted—rescuing the banks that were too big to fail but allowing smaller and community banks to go bankrupt—has meant that the credit channel remains clogged, with obvious implications for the effectiveness of the second round of quantitative easing, popularly known as QE2.

Empirical research using cross-country regressions to explain volatility and the likelihood of the occurrence of a recession has confirmed that wage rigidities are a less important source of economic "vulnerability" and fragility than an overextended financial system (see Easterly, Islam, and Stiglitz, 2001a, 2001b, 2003). These findings are consistent with more recent IMF research that suggests the duration of growth spurts is positively correlated with equality and the probability of financial crises, especially in countries with large financial sectors.[26] These results are also consistent with the theoretical perspectives advanced in this chapter.

3 Hysteresis—the Persistent Effects of Downturns

In the previous section, I explained both the role of increasing inequality in causing downturns, and the role of downturns in increasing inequality. In this section, I explain how these adverse effects can be long-lived, contributing to a weak and sometimes "jobless" recovery. The phenomena that I want to discuss here go under the broad rubric of hysteresis. Most importantly, policies—how we respond to the economic downturn—can not only affect the pace of recovery but also have effects that persist long after the downturn has officially come to an end.

[22] This is a fundamental way in which most of modern macroeconomics has gone astray: in the standard models, the shocks to the economy are assumed to be exogenous.

[23] For a broad discussion of these issues, see Ocampo and Stiglitz (2008) and the references cited therein.

[24] Detragiache, Tressel, and Gupta (2008) and Gupta, Kochhar, and Panth (2011). See also Gormley (2007, 2010).

[25] Rashid (2005).

[26] Kumhof, Ranciere, and Winant (2015).

While worries about a jobless recovery have been associated with virtually every recovery, analyses of data from the last few crises in the United States suggest that employment recovery has become slower. How governments responded to the 2008 crisis, especially in light of the looming concerns about debt, may both exacerbate these trends and compound the increasing problem of youth and long-term unemployment.

Increased unemployment is what follows from the difference between the flow into the unemployment pool and the flow out. Even in a deep downturn, individuals are being hired; the pace of hiring is simply less than the pace of job loss. Hence, in analyzing the dynamics of unemployment, we have to think carefully about the factors that contribute to these dynamics (Greenwald and Stiglitz, 1995). Measured unemployment typically does not include those who have dropped out of the labor force because they have been seeking employment so long without success that they have been discouraged. But in reality, such workers are unemployed—it would certainly be inaccurate to say they are employed. They would like a job, and they cannot get one. One of the reasons that unemployment rates fall so slowly in the process of recovery is that these "discouraged workers" return to the active labor market when job prospects improve.

One of the consequences of long-term unemployment is that workers' skills attenuate. The longer individuals are unemployed, the greater the loss in their "human capital," the skills required to make them productive in the labor market. The result is that the longer individuals are unemployed, the more difficult it is to re-employ them, at least at wages comparable with what they received in the past. (Formally speaking, the lower the probability that they will move from unemployment to employment in the next period, and the greater the difference between the wage they receive upon reemployment and the wage they previously received.) This is one of the reasons that it is important to do what can be done to have a speedy recovery.

It is worth noting that, aside from skills formation, which has been the focus of this discussion, there are other aspects of human development. Young people who see a society without good prospects—and good opportunities awarded disproportionately to those with connections—will become alienated from the rest of society. The sense of optimism and drive will be enervated, and with it their willingness to invest in themselves and in their communities.

This is an example of hysteresis—the path dependence of the economy.

In the United States and some other countries, there are other long-term effects that are likely to make a quick return to full employment particularly difficult. Here, I will note three.

Uncertainty—combined with large losses in pension wealth—has induced many elderly not to retire, reducing openings for young people, who are facing unemployment rates sometimes twice that of the average. These individuals may not retire quickly even after the economy recovers, partly because of the destruction of their retirement accounts, partly because the recession has permanently changed their risk perceptions, and partly because they may have changed their minds about the virtues of retirement versus work. (Unemployment increases when the flow into the labor market minus the flow out of the labor force exceeds the rate of new hires minus the rate of layoffs/job terminations. A decrease in the flow out of the labor force thus contributes as much to an increase in unemployment as a decrease in hiring or an increase in layoffs.)

Inadequacies in systems of social protection/safety nets imply that individuals are more reliant on their families for protection. This is especially so in countries (such as the United States and many developing countries) where health insurance is provided by the employer. In these circumstances, as the economy goes into a downturn, other family members may join the labor force—having a second member is then the best (or only) fall-back if the primary earner loses his job. This effect is called the *additional worker* effect (see Basu, Genicot, and Stiglitz, 2002). With more workers seeking jobs, it becomes more difficult for new entrants (with limited qualifications) to get a job.

The failure to restructure mortgages in the United States left many with large negative equity in their homes, impeding labor market mobility,[27] increasing both the unemployment rate and the decline in wages—in effect, an individual's job search is circumscribed.

3.1 Bankruptcy and Access to Credit

The 2008 crisis, like a large fraction of crises, entailed a collapse of credit markets and bankruptcies of large numbers of firms. Bankruptcies also provide examples of hysteresis: firms that go bankrupt when they cannot meet debt payments (either because of excessively high interest rates, as in the East Asia crisis, or because of deficiencies in demand, as in this crisis) are not "unbankrupted" when these circumstances are reversed; for example, when interest rates are lowered or demand is restored. This also constitutes a long-term loss of human capital—one of the most important elements, at least from the perspective of long-term economic development, is entrepreneurship.

In each of the instances described, the effects of the downturn are long-lived, making a quick recovery all the more difficult.

4 Policy and Inequality

The extent to which economic fluctuations lead to an increase in inequality (either in the short run or more permanently) critically depends, of course, on policy. My previous discussion highlighted how changes in automatic stabilizers (e.g., progressivity of the income tax, movements from defined-benefit to defined-contribution social security systems, changes in systems of unemployment compensation) can affect the extent to which GDP falls in response to an adverse shock, say to aggregate demand, and can affect the extent to which employment falls in responds to a decline in GDP. In the 2008 crisis, for instance, German policies managed to greatly limit the extent to which unemployment increased—it increased far more in America's allegedly "flexible" labor market. In this section, I focus more narrowly on two sets of policies—government expenditures and monetary policy.

[27] The empirical significance of this effect remains controversial. See Mike Konczal (2011). One of the reasons that the subject is so controversial is that some are using the argument of "housing lock" to suggest that there is a "new normal" with a higher natural unemployment rate.

4.1 Government Expenditures

Economic downturns lead to deficits, and pressures to bring deficits into control lead to cutbacks in public services, with particularly adverse effects on the poor. That this would be so is not inevitable: it is conceivable that government would protect social programs for the poor. But in practice that does not seem to be the case, at least in many instances.

The reason is obvious: the poor are the least politically powerful in most societies. They are the least able to protect themselves against cutbacks. As I noted earlier, the extent of inequality in a society may affect not only the size of the public sector, but also how it responds to cutbacks. Societies with greater inequality may not only have a smaller public sector, but the wealthy may be in a better position to ensure that government does not impose cutbacks on them.[28]

For some countries (such as those with high debt and deficits before the crisis), there is little choice but to cut back on spending. They lack access to capital markets to finance deficits to maintain pre-downturn levels of expenditure. Some political entities (such as the states in the United States) may face constitutional restrictions on their ability to borrow—although typically there are ways to circumvent these restrictions to a limited degree; for example, through infrastructure banks. Even with these restrictions, however, it is not *inevitable* that there be cutbacks on overall expenditures (most states and localities could increase their taxes) and that the incidence of the cutbacks fall disproportionately on the poor. These patterns are a result of the political economy considerations to which I referred earlier.

But other countries (such as the United States) face a more meaningful choice. They are able to borrow. Indeed, for the United States, there is an argument for increased spending, because the long-term cost of capital is low. We thus need to ask the following: why do they not sustain spending? And if there are spending cutbacks, why do they so often disproportionately affect social programs? The economic return to government spending may be even higher in the downturn, since the "shadow prices" of labor and other resources are diminished. The benefits of spending are increased by the multiplier, the fact that GDP increases by a multiple of what is spent, when there are underutilized resources. Indeed, in some cases the returns on increased government investment are so large that the increased government tax collections generated by the increased income (in the short run from the multiplier, and in the long run from the increased growth engendered) mean that the long-run national debt is lowered.

There are several possible explanations why, in spite of the increased net returns to government spending, there are typically pressures for cutbacks. First, even countries that are able to borrow may face significantly higher costs for doing so. They face worsened terms of intertemporal trade-offs. Income and substitution effects would naturally lead to cutbacks, even if "political economy" considerations were not at play. (As I noted above, this is not true for the United States, where real interest rates are close to zero.) Second, there is often a diminution of perceived national wealth, with the breaking of asset bubbles or, at least, the decline in asset prices. The persistent shortfall between actual and potential output is

[28] There is some recent research in the political science literature confirming this conjecture. The extent should depend on the nature of the political system. In democracies such as America where campaign contributions play a more important role, one might conjecture that the well-off are better able to resist cutbacks that would adversely affect them.

a waste of resources—a waste that is seldom anticipated in wealth assessments prior to the downturn. Finally, government receipts typically diminish markedly, with the decrease in GDP, and especially if, prior to the crisis, they were partially bloated with revenues from the bubble or boom that preceded it. It is politically contentious to increase resource transfers from the private to the public sector (e.g., through taxes).[29]

I think, however, that one of the real reasons for the cutbacks is a combination of misunderstandings of economics and of the forces of political economy. The analogy between government and households holds sway. If a household is spending beyond its means, it has to cut back. Otherwise, ruin lies in its future. Financial markets, with their focus on only one side of the ledger—the liability side, ignoring the asset side—contribute to these misunderstandings. And here ideology and interests intersect: many in the financial market have an agenda to downsize the government, and looming deficits and debts provide the rationale. (While money was pouring into the banks as part of the bailouts, they conveniently put these concerns aside.) Improved fiscal positions could lead to a lowering of long-term interest rates, which would lead them to realize large capital gains on their long-term bonds.

These arguments help explain the cutbacks. But why should cutbacks be disproportionately focused on social spending? My earlier discussions of political economy provide the explanation: Many areas of government are hard to cut (especially politically), such as defense; some areas, like disability pay, typically increase automatically. There is thus particularly strong downward pressure on discretionary social and educational expenditures (and other investments, for which the consequences of cutbacks will not be apparent for years[30]). The political constituencies of the poor are typically far weaker than, say, those calling for bank bailouts. And, again, conservative agendas that have long argued against social expenditures seize upon the opening provided by the downturn, arguing that we can no longer afford them.

In some countries, such as the United States, one could make an argument that income and substitution effects make ambiguous the question about whether social and educational expenditures should be cut or increased in an economic downturn. In the 2008 crisis, real interest rates (even long-term rates) were extraordinarily low, suggesting that it would have made sense to spend more, and that it would have made even more sense to invest more. Indeed, for those countries like the United States that have underinvested in the public sector in the last two decades, good public investments would lower the national debt in the long run. Increased public investments in infrastructure, technology, education, and job training programs promote growth and employment in both the short term and the long term—and thereby increase government revenues. Such investments, furthermore, crowd in private investment, with further benefits to growth, employment, and equality.

More broadly, there are careful restructurings of tax and expenditure programs that can simultaneously stimulate the economy, reduce the deficit in the short run, and lead to higher growth, employment, and improved equality. Because of differences in marginal propensities to consume, any increases in redistributive taxation can stimulate the economy

[29] The final point differs from the first in that the final point focuses on the "wealth" of the citizenry, and the first on the financial constraints facing government, recognizing that: shifting money from the private sector to the public is costly, because of the distortions associated with taxation; and changes in the rules governing the split between the public and private sector are politically contentious.

[30] This includes investments in R&D, with a consequent adverse effect on future growth. See, for example, Stiglitz (1994a).

and lower deficits. Because the unemployed typically have a very high marginal propensity to consume,[31] increased support for the unemployed (financed, say, by a tax on upper income individuals) will stimulate the economy. Because small firms are more likely to be finance-constrained than large firms,[32] government programs targeted to them may stimulate the economy (both in the short run and the long). Incremental investment tax credits financed by appropriately designed increases in the corporate income tax rate will stimulate the economy today and in the future. An increase in the estate/inheritance tax can encourage consumption today, lower the deficit, and improve equality of wealth and income.

In short, for many countries, there are policies that would strengthen the country's long-term fiscal position and promote growth and employment both in the short term and the long term—but these are often not the policies that are chosen. There are distributive consequences, which may make these policies conflict with the seeming interests of those who are richer. I say "seeming" because in some cases even their interests would be well-served. But here, ideology may play a role: these programs might lead to a stronger state, and they may worry that, while such a state might use its powers wisely to promote long-term economic growth from which they and the rest of society might benefit, there is no way of ensuring that the state will so limit its actions. It might use its powers to redistribute wealth away from them. The wealthier might even worry that any reforms could change the political processes, which allow their perspectives to have disproportionate weight (through campaign contributions, revolving doors, lobbying, and control of media), often resulting in policies that redistribute wealth *toward* the top (e.g., through lax enforcement of antitrust laws, giveaways of state resources, etc.).[33]

4.1.1 A Vicious Circle

Of particular concern is the possibility of adverse dynamics that result when putting together the results of this section and those of the preceding two: if societies with greater inequality adopt weaker measures of social protection and less progressive income tax structures, and act as if they face tighter fiscal constraints, then an economic shock will result in more adverse effects on inequality, weakening further the political weight of the poor, weakening further social protections, reducing tax progressivity, and tightening further fiscal constraints. Moreover, if the wealthier feel more able to cope with shocks—and even more so if they happened to be ideologically committed to free markets—then these societies characterized by greater inequality will deregulate and liberalize more, exposing them to more shocks, and will not respond as forcefully to economic downturns.

4.2 Monetary Policy

There is general consensus that monetary policy and financial regulations contributed to the creation of the 2008 crisis. Historically, flawed monetary policies have been a major source of volatility (e.g., in stepping on the brakes too strongly in response to worries about inflation).

[31] For example, see Dynarski and Sheffrin (1987) for a discussion of consumption and unemployment.
[32] See Beck, Demirguc-Kunt, and Maksimovic (2005) among others.
[33] See, for example, Besley (2004) and Besley and Persson (2009, 2010).

In this chapter, my focus is on how monetary policy has affected the inequality–volatility nexus. As I noted earlier, in the standard macroeconomic and monetary models that informed the policies that led to the crisis, there was little role for inequality. Not surprisingly, the policies predicated on those models have arguably increased both volatility and inequality.

4.2.1 Inflation-Targeting Monetary Policies as a Contributor to Inequality and Volatility

Doctrines focusing on inflation targeting, predicated on the mistaken belief that low inflation was necessary and almost sufficient for economic stability, shifted attention away from what has proved to be a far more costly source of instability—fragility in the financial sector.[34] (The models also supported deregulation; it was argued that banks, in their own self-interest, could and would manage risk well—far better than any outside regulator could. No note was made of the problems posed by agency and externalities—the interests of those making risk decisions did not coincide with those of the rest of society. No note was even made of the distorted incentive structures in the financial sector, designed to encourage excessive risk-taking and short-sighted behavior.) Moreover, stabilizing the price level meant, at least in some instances, more instability in *real* variables. Furthermore, there was no good argument for why, regardless of the source of the disturbance facing the economy, the best approach to adjustment should entail focusing on interest rates (rather than, say, exchange rates).[35] (See Stiglitz, Ocampo, Spiegel, et al., 2006.)

Inflation targeting also meant that, in practice, unemployment was often kept at a high level—at a higher level than may have been necessary for maintaining overall economic stability. Monetary policy in most countries reflects the perspectives of financial markets, and indeed, in most countries, those from the financial sector have a dominant role in the boards that determine policy. These doctrines serve their interests well, along with those of capital owners: high unemployment exerts downward pressure on real wages, increasing profits; and high real interest rates enhance incomes of creditors. The way such policies are implemented in practice may exacerbate these problems: when the economy is weak, real wages fail to keep up with productivity gains, and may even decline; when nominal wages subsequently start to grow, to make up for what happened during such periods, monetary authorities, worried about rising labor costs, tighten, ensuring that there is no "catch up."

Monetary authorities (in their role as financial regulator[36]) pushed deregulation of financial markets. As I have noted, this contributed to the financialization of the economy—and at least in some countries, much of the increased inequality was associated with this increased financialization, both directly and indirectly through the greater volatility to which it gave rise. Instability in cross-border capital flows, for instance, has been one of

[34] The models focused on second-order economic losses associated with intertemporal relative prices being misaligned, ignoring the first-order losses resulting from prolonged gaps between the economy's actual and potential output.

[35] Indeed, adjusting interest rates in response to inflation meant that when the inflation was "imported" (e.g., when it arose from international prices, say of energy or food), it risked vastly distorting the economy—putting all the burden of adjustment on non-traded sectors, and imposing an even greater burden on the poor, as a result of the increased unemployment and lower wages that resulted.

[36] In the United States, the Chairman of the Federal Reserve reportedly weighed in strongly against regulation of derivatives by the CFTC, supposedly an independent regulatory body. The heads of central banks often have influence that extends beyond the realm of their direct responsibility.

the major sources of volatility in many developing and emerging countries, and, as I noted earlier, capital market liberalization—the stripping away of regulations to control these flows—has thus contributed to economic instabilities. Capital market and financial market liberalization have facilitated the spread of a problem in one country (such as the United States) to others.[37]

In the response to the 2008 crisis, further inequalities were created, some of which are likely to contribute to the slow recovery. In the United States and Europe, interest rates were lowered to record levels. While the transfer helped recapitalize the banks, no conditions were put on the banks. Lending did not increase, as was hoped. But as interest-dependent retirees' incomes weakened, so did their consumption. Unemployment increased, both because of the resulting decrease in aggregate demand (there was little evident increase in investment in response to the low interest rate, although the low interest rate may have helped increase stock market values, which may have had some positive effect on consumption, to the extent that investors believed the effects were permanent[38]) and because the prospect of lower incomes from the only seemingly safe assets, T-bills, may have induced some workers to postpone retirement.

But for the poorest in the developing countries (and even the poor in the developed) the flood of liquidity generated by the Fed and other central banks may have had another adverse effect. With America's economy still weak and that part of its financial system that lends money to SMEs still not repaired, the money went to where it was not needed—the booming emerging markets—and not to where it was needed. It contributed to bubbles and exchange rate appreciation. The exchange rate appreciation threatened the stability of jobs and employment in export-competing and import-competing sectors.

In turn, higher interest rates and an appreciated currency lead to serious distortions in the structure of the economy. In those cases where export sectors are the source of long-term growth, the adverse effects on that sector (in the absence of government intervention) could be long-lived.[39] It is understandable why governments throughout the world have responded with a variety of capital account interventions. But these interventions are typically not costless.

5 How Well-Intentioned Responses to Downturns May Impede Recovery

So far, I have explained how: inequality contributes to economic downturns; economic downturns contribute to inequality; and governments' responses (both monetary and fiscal policies) may exacerbate adverse impacts on growth and human development both through actions that prolong the downturn and through cutbacks in government spending. I have argued that these effects are often long-lived.

In this section of the chapter, I want to explain how even well-intentioned policies to limit the extent of the downturn may at the same time prolong its duration—at least as far as workers are concerned.

[37] For a general theoretical discussion of these issues, see Stiglitz (2010c, 2010d).

[38] Analyses of the effects from monetary authorities were not always consistent. As the end of QE2 approached, they argued that there would be no market disruption, since the market had anticipated the end. But that raised the question, if they anticipated the end at the beginning, why should there have been much effect then?

[39] Stiglitz (2010a).

While there are often complaints about a jobless recovery, there is some evidence that the last recovery was indeed jobless. In the United States, the 2008 crisis was, I believe, the first instance where workers had not fully recovered from income losses suffered during a previous crisis. In 2010 the median income was lower than it was in 1997.[40] Making matters worse, as the economy went into recession in both 2001 and 2008, there is some evidence that there was more ruthless job cutting.[41]

It used to be that firms were reluctant to fire or lay off workers; there was a risk that they would find employment elsewhere, with a resulting loss of firm-specific human and organizational capital and individual-specific information.[42] With real interest rates in this and the previous downturns lower than in most other downturns, one might have thought that firms would be even more concerned to retain their workers. In fact, they have been more ruthless in cutting back.

There are two possible explanations of the seeming change in behavior. The first is that with increased emphases on quarterly returns, firms have become more myopic. Norms have changed to reflect this, with praise awarded to firms and managers that "bite the bullet" and quickly respond by firing workers or cutting costs.

Workers will, of course, respond to these changed norms. They will invest less in the firm, and more in "general human capital" that will increase their portability and malleability. This means, of course, that the cost to the firm of losing a worker will be less.

A change in norms also means that the adverse efficiency effects will be mitigated—a firm that mistreats its workers in this way is no longer viewed as a pariah. This is the new normal.

Of course, these changes do have adverse systemic effects. There is widespread recognition that systemic performance arising out of such myopic behavior is far from optimal.

There are policies the government could institute that might provide a check, and some policies may have exacerbated these problems. Giving more voting rights to long-term investors (called loyalty shares) might also encourage firms to think less myopically. So too would policies that encourage investment in human capital (as many countries do). Such policies would simultaneously act as automatic stabilizers through incentivizing firms to hang on to workers as the economy goes into a downturn.

The second set of explanations has to do with changes in cyclical patterns of interest rates and exchange rates, interacting with changes in technology.[43] Although standard models in economics use a simple aggregate production function, a more accurate depiction is provided by models with "vintage capital." In such models, capital goods produced at any date have a particular output and labor requirement, with relatively little substitutability. As demand increases, machines of lower output-per-unit labor are brought online. In a recession, if real interest rates become very low, firms have an incentive to buy capital-intensive machines requiring little labor. Wages may have fallen a little, but far less than

[40] U.S. Census income data, historical tables, Table H-9 [http://www.census.gov/hhes/www/ income/data/historical/household/index.html], accessed October 20, 2011.

[41] This is in contrast to earlier recessions that have been marked as "labor hoarding." A Boston Fed research paper by DeRemer, Fuhrer, Little, et al. (2004) finds that the period following the 2001 recession is even a "job-loss recovery."

[42] See, for example, Miller (1971), Clark (1973), and Fay and Medoff (1985).

[43] The discussion of this section is based on the highly innovative work of Miguel Morin (2011).

the cost of capital. Thus, as the economy recovers, there is less additional labor needed to increase output.

In the 2001 and 2008 recessions, real (T-bill) interest rates fell markedly. (Although the benefits of this were not universally felt—especially not by SMEs that faced persistent constraints on capital availability.) This stands in marked contrast to earlier downturns—in the Great Depression, short-term real interest rates actually increased.

6 Inequality, Volatility, and Growth

So far, I have focused on the nexus between economic fluctuations and inequality—and how policy can mitigate or exacerbate the adverse consequences that normally arise.

Volatility may also adversely affect growth.[44] For instance, greater volatility may adversely impact individuals' ability and willingness to invest in human capital, or firms' ability and willingness to invest in physical capital.[45] In economic downturns, financial constraints will impede long-term investments, including those in R&D. Greater volatility, especially in the absence of adequate safety nets or systems of social protection, discourages risk-taking.

Earlier I described the adverse effect of volatility on inequality. But increased inequality may have an adverse effect on growth. Successful growth requires heavy investments by government (public transportation, education, R&D, etc.), and support for such investments may weaken with greater inequality—as support for a strong government itself weakens. There is a vicious cycle—weak investments in human capital and human development more broadly weaken growth, increase volatility and inequality, and exacerbate the adverse effects of whatever volatility that occurs; but the weaker growth, greater volatility and inequality, and greater sensitivity to adverse shocks in turn lead to weaker investments in human capital.

The effects of volatility on human development can be long-lasting. There is a natural lifecycle to each individual, and events that happen at critical stages of their lives have lifelong effects. Prenatal and childhood malnutrition will impair productivity throughout an individual's life. It can stunt growth and impair mental development.[46] The damage cannot be undone in later years. That is one of the reasons that, in the absence of an adequate safety net, a severe economic downturn in a developing country can have such severe long-term effects. (There is a concern that, in somewhat diminished form, such effects can even arise

[44] The link between volatility and growth has been extensively discussed. There is a strong presumption that higher volatility raises the risk premium on investment and diminishes growth at least in the short to medium term. (In the standard Solow model, long-term growth is determined by the rate of population growth and the rate of technological progress. Volatility can affect long-term growth only by having an impact on those variables, which it may have.) See the discussion above and Ramey and Ramey (1995), Stiglitz, Ocampo, Spiegel, et al. (2006), and Imbs (2007).

[45] There is considerable evidence that firms act in a risk-averse way (Greenwald and Stiglitz, 1990a) and that, especially in downturns, investment is reduced as a result of financial constraints (Greenwald and Stiglitz, 1993a, 2003a; Greenwald, Levinson, and Stiglitz, 1993).

[46] The World Bank argues that ending malnutrition is crucial to human development, because of its irreversible effects on individuals' physical and intellectual development. See, for example, World Bank (2006) and the studies cited there.

in developed countries; in the United States, in the midst of the crisis, the incidence of food insecurity rose to more than 14%.[47])

Economic downturns also interrupt education—and the interruption has long-term effects. Large fractions of students never return; or if they do, they do not go as far. In the case of developing countries, children may not be able to afford even minimal school fees, or may be put to work. One of my most moving visits to Thailand during the East Asia crisis was to a slum community on the outskirts of Bangkok that had pooled its resources to ensure that its children's education would not be interrupted. Although there were other such examples, the statistics suggest these are exceptions, not the rule.[48]

While the broad economic forces that I have identified in this chapter that give rise to these links between volatility, inequality, and human development are present in all economies, whether developed or developing, there are some important differences. In developing countries, for instance, government-provided safety nets (social protection) are weaker, and that means that the social consequences (including the consequences for human development) are larger.

The combination of weaker social protections, tighter budget constraints, less access to international financial markets, and a weaker private-sector insurance system thus makes developing countries more vulnerable to adverse shocks and makes it more likely that these adverse shocks translate into adverse effects on human development—often with long-lasting effects.

7 Concluding Remarks

The years before the 2008 crisis saw an enormous increase in inequality—just as happened in the years before the 1929 crash. This naturally has led to the question: is there a connection between inequality and volatility? We have identified a complex two-way nexus—with volatility contributing to inequality and inequality contributing to volatility. The effect, in either direction, are not inevitable. They can be altered by economic policy.[49]

[47] US Department of Agriculture Economic Research Service figures, [http://www.ers.usda.gov/Briefing/FoodSecurity/stats_graphs.htm#food_secure].

[48] See, for example, Atinc and Walton (1998) and Knowles, Pernia, and Racelis (1999).

[49] I wish to acknowledge helpful conversations with Miguel Morin, Deepak Nayyar, Anton Korinek, and José Antonio Ocampo.

PART III.E
INHERITANCE

Introduction to Part III.E

The two chapters in this section, written in the 1970s, explore the role of bequests in generating inequality, focusing in particular on the impact of inheritance taxes.

There has been marked concern in recent years over the increased role of inheritances—whether, for instance, the U.S. is moving toward a plutocracy based on inheritance.[1] While with the new tech billionaires, it is evident that many of those at the top have made it on their own, a large fraction of the wealthiest are where they are at least partially as a result of inheritances. Some, like the Koch brothers, have augmented their inheritances, others like Trump would have been far richer than they are if they had simply put their money into an indexed fund of U.S. stocks.

These papers were part of the research agenda that I had begun in my Ph.D. thesis, striving to understand better the determinants of the distribution of income and wealth, and in particular, the role of the intergenerational transmission of wealth (or more broadly, advantages and disadvantages). Here, we explore the role of bequests, the potential importance of which was central to Chapters 12 and 13. I was particularly concerned with analyzing the effects of an inheritance tax (a tax focused on the amount of bequests received by an individual) or a bequest tax (focused on the amounts given). Such taxes seemingly played an important role in transforming some European countries in the years after World War II from societies where inherited wealth and privilege dominated into more egalitarian societies. At the time I wrote these papers, the U.S. and many other countries had a far more progressive tax structure than they do now: capital was not taxed at the favorable rates (with lower rates for dividends and capital gains than for other forms of income) that it is today, and inheritance taxes seemed more important. As I write this introduction in 2021, there

[1] It is, in fact, hard to calculate with any precision the proportion of total wealth attributable to inheritances and even more difficult to estimate the relative importance of bequests as wealth increases. Though the general consensus is that inheritances have, overall, become more important and the role of inheritances rises as wealth increases (Piketty, 2014; Piketty and Zucman, 2015), there are dissenting voices both about the role of inheritances in wealth inequality, what has been happening to wealth inequality, and changes in the role of inheritances in wealth inequality (Wolff and Gittleman, 2014; Boserup, Kopczuk, and Kramer, 2016). Part of the problem is methodological, for example, some of the studies require assumptions about the real return attributed to inherited wealth. If the wealthy own land or other assets yielding a higher return than assets in general (and there is evidence that the wealthy put their wealth into assets yielding higher than average returns, presumably partly because they can better bear risk, perhaps partly because they have inside information or because it pays them to be more informed, perhaps partly because their wealth allows them to engage in more leverage) then assuming that the real return on inheritances was the same as on life-cycle savings would greatly underestimate the relative role of inheritances.

is a renewed interest in increasing progressivity, imposing wealth taxes, and strengthening inheritance taxes in the U.S., as wealth inequality has increased, with the top 1% having more than 40% of the nation's wealth. (Remarkably, one of the two major American political parties has been striving to eliminate the estate tax, even though it is paid every year only by relatively few—in 2018, for instance, by some 1,700 estates.[2] Critics of the inheritance tax have labeled it as a tax on death.)

At the time I wrote these papers, I was very much under the influence of the traditional economist's mindset: if what matters ultimately is consumption, then we should be concerned about inequalities in consumption. Since inheritances *on average* spread consumption *within a family* from successful generations to less successful generations, and since on average, very successful generations will be followed by less successful generations (regression toward the mean), inheritances reduce consumption inequalities. It is clear that a 100% tax on inheritances would force a successful (high income) generation to consume fully its fortunate income, so consumption inequality would be higher than it is without such a tax. Stiglitz (1976b) (partially reprinted here as Chapter 32) showed under quite general conditions that *prohibiting* inheritances would unambiguously increase consumption inequality (at least in the sense that the *range* of outcomes would be increased).

The mathematical analysis was correct, as far as it went. But I worried at the time I wrote the paper about its policy relevance. In the intervening years, as inequality has grown so much worse, I have come to understand better what was left out from the analysis.

I had framed the question wrongly in two senses: I was wrong to focus so much on inequalities in consumption, and I had too narrowly limited the set of policy instruments. It should be obvious that if the money that had been left to an individual's heirs were spread instead progressively throughout society, inequalities in consumption would be reduced. If capital accumulation were not adversely affected, it would be a mean preserving increase in equality (Atkinson, 1970; Rothschild and Stiglitz, 1970). Thus the key questions were (a) what was the magnitude of the adverse effect on accumulation; and (b) could whatever the adverse effects on accumulation that occurred be offset by government policy—for example, by taking some of the tax revenues and investing them in public or human capital. Chapters 13 and 19 above show that in fact the potential adverse distributional effects can indeed be more than offset.

Perhaps more important was my excessive concern about consumption inequalities. In these earlier papers, when I stressed the importance of inequalities in consumption, I was following in a strong neoclassical tradition, in which social welfare is evaluated in terms of a Benthamite individualistic social welfare function, which each individual's welfare is only a function of his own consumption. *Relative* consumption and inequality were not directly relevant to the well-being of individuals, and therefore of society as a whole.

But once one departs from the neoclassical normative perspective, and once one realizes that the competitive model does not provide a good *description* of the workings of

[2] The 2017 tax bill increased the exemption from the tax to $22.4 million for couples, and it was estimated that total taxes paid under the tax in 2018 would be only $13.6 billion, according to the Tax Policy Center. https://www.taxpolicycenter.org/taxvox/only-1700-estates-would-owe-estate-tax-2018-under-tcja?mod=article_inline.

the economy and society, then one has to be concerned not just about the distribution of consumption, but also the distribution of wealth.

Reframing the Normative Analysis

Societies with large inherited wealth inequalities are different from those with less inequality in a number of ways.

Political Power and the Writing of the Economic Rules

Inherited wealth, especially large concentrations of wealth, leads to concentrations of economic and political power. In the competitive equilibrium model that was the reigning paradigm of the time, market power played no role, nor did politics. But as earlier chapters of this book have emphasized, there are large concentrations of market power, and economic power gets translated into political power, which is used to write the rules of the game in ways which favor those with economic and political power, enabling them to perpetuate their power. In *People, Power, and Profits* (Stiglitz, 2019a), I argued that systems of checks and balances, so necessary for the functioning of democracy, will never be fully effective if there is an excessive concentration of income and wealth; for those with that wealth will find some way or another to use their wealth to exercise power.

Americans may be especially attuned to the role of power in creating inequalities that have persisted across generations, for it was slavery that gave rise to some of the country's largest and most persistent social injustices and economic inequities.

Further Remarks about the Normative Framework: What Determines Individuals' Well-being?

Bequests represent a particular challenge for the standard economist's normally individualistic normative framework, for the fact that individuals *give* something to others shows that they care about others—others' well-being is relevant to their own. Indeed, bequests provide evidence that individuals are not as selfish as economists usually assume they are. But the most straightforward introduction of bequests into a standard Benthamite framework (say where parents care about the utility of their children, and their children about their children) implies that bequests are doubly blessed: the giver receives utility from giving, but the recipient is better off as well. Under plausible conditions, the Nash societal equilibrium will entail too little intergenerational transfers using a standard utilitarian social welfare function.

Of course, the government can effect the requisite additional intergenerational transfers (or could induce individuals to leave larger bequests), but that raises another normative question: do parents receive pleasure from the *act* of giving, or only from the actual level of consumption of their children (or their children's well-being)? If the former (a possibility again which is outside of the standard economics framework), then it makes a difference whether individuals are compelled by government to make a transfer (through general tax and social security policy) or if they are induced to do so individually, through incentives. But not only may the givers be affected by the act of giving, the receivers may be affected by the sources of their purchasing power: it may make a difference to them whether their income comes from their own work or as a result of an inheritance or as part of a grant given to all citizens (as in the case of a universal basic income).

Why a concern for inequality? Equality of outcomes or opportunities?

There are several different bases for the objection to inequality in inheritances that we noted briefly in the introduction.

There are many who believe that what matters is not so much equality of outcomes, but equality of opportunity, which speaks to the processes by which income and wealth gets generated and individual's initial endowments.[3] Even if we can't equalize abilities, we can equalize inherited wealth and human capital—what individuals can do with their inherited ability.

There are difficult questions, which we do not address here, involving trade-offs: if human capital and abilities are complementary, it is efficient (in terms of maximizing GDP) to provide those with more ability more human capital, but that increases inequality in market incomes. Compensatory education—providing additional human capital to those with less ability—could reduce disparities in wage incomes, but at a cost of GDP. If redistribution from high-income individuals to low-income individuals were costless, on standard efficiency grounds, it might be preferable to allocate human capital efficiently, and then redistribute. But such redistributions are not costless, and the costs are likely to increase the greater the magnitude of redistribution, so it would, overall, be more efficient to engage in "pre-distribution," i.e. to allocate human capital in ways that lead to less inequality in wage income, than to rely solely on redistribution.

Perhaps even more important though is that individuals care about the source of their income (consumption): an individual who believes he has earned his income, even if it is partially a result of public "overinvestment" in his education, has a higher sense of well-being than were he to have the same level of consumption, part of which is the result of a government transfer payment.

The sources of inequality. Not only do societies care about equality of opportunity as well as equality of outcomes, but they care about the origins of inequality. It is one thing if inequality results from an individual's efforts—working harder or saving more than others; it is quite another if inequality results from one individual exploiting another—whether the result of brute physical power, as in the case of slavery, or the abuse of market power. Neoclassical theory, of course, can be viewed as providing a justification of inequality based on social marginal contributions; Marxian analysis argued it was based on exploitation. Recent theory and evidence have placed increasing emphasis on the latter theories, as earlier chapters in this volume show. From such sources, it is natural that we be concerned with the perpetuation of those inequalities through inheritances.

[3] See Part III.B for some of the ambiguities in the meaning and measurement of equality of opportunity.

The Social and Political Dimensions of Inequality

In the introduction to this volume, we emphasized that, though this book is about the economics of inequality, a full assessment requires taking into account its political and social consequences, which we briefly described. These may be especially relevant in considering inheritances: a society marked by a hereditary plutocracy is the antithesis of a social democracy. The fear is that those who inherit wealth will use that wealth to create economic and political rules to perpetuate that inequality.

From Wealth Inequalities in One Generation to Wage Inequalities in the Next

In most of the analyses of this book, the only way that advantages get transmitted across generations is through the transfer of financial capital. But in reality there are many other mechanisms, some of which are far more invidious. Parents with higher education, wealth, and income give their children more education, and provide them with an abundance of connections, both of which lead to disparities in wage income and societal status and power, as we discussed in Chapter 12. Families with greater wealth may even use their wealth and connections to receive a higher return on their capital (as we saw in Chapter 11). All of this can result in a perpetuation of inequalities across generations. While government can't do much about some of these mechanisms by which advantages are transmitted across generations (such as the provision of "connections"), it can do something about others through tax and expenditure policies. These two chapters are about the use of capital and inheritance taxation.

As I note, however, the various approaches need to be approached holistically: increasing inheritance taxes may induce well-off parents to invest more in the education of their children, making it all the more important to have good public education.[4] Meritocratic reforms which reduce the importance of connections again increase incentives for the well-to-do to invest more in the education of their children, and some argue, in the absence of equalitarian public education, this can result in even less equality of opportunity.

Other Limitations

The analyses of these papers erred not just in the normative framework, but in the simplifying assumptions which did not capture many of the ways in which advantages and disadvantages were transmitted across generations. In the following paragraphs, I highlight a few other of the limitations of these papers.[5]

[4] In Stiglitz (1974h), I explored the interactions between public and private education.

[5] The list below is not meant to be exhaustive. Another important limitation is that I do not provide any empirical estimates of the magnitude of various effects. In modeling, one always makes judgments about what is or is not empirically relevant. On some of the key parameters of the economy, such as the supply elasticities of savings and labor supply, there are, unfortunately, widely disparate estimates, with a disturbing correlation between political views and estimates: those who argue for low taxes more worried about high elasticities and typically obtaining, when they do their econometric studies, higher estimates. I have implicitly put more emphasis on some things than others. I have not assumed, for instance, that the distribution of returns to capital would be significantly

Full Employment

At the time I wrote these papers, I was working very much within the neoclassical traditional where it was simply assumed that the economy was at full employment—wealth or inheritance taxes would have no effect on aggregate demand, and that wouldn't matter. But the decade following the 2008 crisis, like that following that 1929 stock market crash, showed that there can be persistent deficiencies in aggregate demand, and that (an increase in) inequality could weaken aggregate demand, simply because those at the top consumed less than those below.[6]

Credit Constraints and Other Capital and Product Market Imperfections

These chapters, like most of the work of the period, assumed perfect capital markets. It was only with Stiglitz and Weiss (1981) that theoretical foundations for the widely observed capital market imperfections were provided. Imperfections in capital markets mean that individuals cannot invest as much in human capital as they would like, to enable them to reach their full potential (or even to the level where the marginal return on investment would be equal to a "normal" cost of capital). Credit constraints are thus an important contributor to inequalities of opportunity and give rise to an important inefficiency. Moreover, because individuals cannot divest themselves of the risk of human capital, even if they could borrow, the amount they would be willing to borrow may be limited, again giving an advantage to those with wealthy parents, who can better absorb such risks.[7]

Imperfections in capital markets interact with other imperfections in information to give a real disadvantage to those without inherited capital. For instance, in labor markets, one of the ways that individuals can ensure employers that they will not shirk is to post a bond; those without wealth cannot do so. In capital markets, to get a loan, one often needs to put up some collateral; those without wealth cannot do so.[8] (See Chapter 15 above.) (Even when jobs don't formally require the posting of a bond, they may do so indirectly, through paying wages less than the marginal product in early years on the job, with vesting in a retirement program not occurring until the worker has worked a minimum number of years. Those from poorer families may find it more difficult to accept jobs in which compensation is thus effectively postponed.) Moreover, individuals who are well-off and confident in their skills can start their own businesses, supplementing their own capital with connection-based or collateral-based loans. But those without such capital and connections cannot do so. This is why several countries (including Mexico and China) have viewed making wider access to credit for small businesses, and especially for young entrepreneurs and entrepreneurs from marginalized groups, an important part of the equality of opportunity agenda.

affected by the taxes imposed (at least within the range of changes that are being contemplated.) Some of the possibilities that I (and others, such as Becker) have investigated are more a matter of pure theory than of empirical relevance. Thus, as I comment later, I am not sure that there is any significant effect of the inheritance tax on investments in human capital.

[6] See, for example, *Freefall* (Stiglitz (2010a)), *The Stiglitz Report* (United Nations, 2010) and Part III.D. above. As those analyses point out, the lack of aggregate demand could have been compensated for by an increase in public expenditures, but the "political economy" of the moment, circumscribing government spending—influenced by the inequalities of income—inhibited such a response.

[7] One of the objectives of income contingent education loans is to reduce risk. See Chapman, Higgins, and Stiglitz (2014), Stiglitz (2014g, 2016c).

[8] Some of these issues I addressed in Part III.C.

This suggests that there may be some efficiency benefits from having *some* intergenerational transfers, and some, such as Atkinson (2015) have proposed baby bonds—giving everyone at the time they reach say 18 or 21 a certain endowment. But ensuring that everyone has some wealth with which to begin their lives is a very different matter from the problems with which this chapter is concerned: large bequests giving rise to high levels of wealth inequality.[9]

The imperfections of capital markets just discussed have strong implications for how markets respond to capital taxation. In Chapter 33, we show that an increase in capital taxation leads to increased risk taking because the government is absorbing some of the risk when there are good loss offset provisions; the importance of this would obviously be reduced if markets did a better job in distributing risk.[10]

Perhaps the most important limitation of these models is that they begin with the assumption that the economy is competitive, so the return to capital is just its marginal product. But, as we have argued throughout this book, today's economy is not well-described by a competitive model, and much of what is called the taxation of capital is really a tax on rents. This is particularly true of the corporate profits tax, which to a first approximation is in fact a tax on pure profits, not a tax on capital.[11] The taxation of profits does not, of course, have any of the adverse incidence effects which are the focus of concern here:[12] indeed, in the life-cycle models explored earlier in this book, the reduced value of capitalized profits leads to more real investment, so that inequality is increased both *directly* (from the redistribution of the proceeds) and indirectly (from the general equilibrium incidence effect).

Why These Papers May Still Be Relevant

Analytically, in spite of the limitations just discussed, I still think these chapters are of interest for several reasons. First, many of the issues discussed in previous paragraphs and elsewhere in this book could be incorporated within our theoretical framework, especially if one abandons the aspiration of getting closed form analytic solutions.

Secondly, the analysis provides a series of warnings: if the objective of a more equalitarian society is to be achieved, policy has to be carefully designed. Good intentions are not enough. Economic systems are complex, and there are often unintended consequences of

[9] There are a set of assumptions under which even larger bequests might be justified, assumptions for which there is little empirical basis: if, for instance, capital markets were totally absent and if entrepreneurial ability were transmitted perfectly across generations, then from a perspective of efficiency alone, one would want more talented individuals to have access to more capital, and that is achieved by allowing large intergenerational wealth transfers. On the other hand, if the pace of regression toward the mean is rapid, then the children of good entrepreneurs who inherit wealth will likely not manage it well. Bequests provide a poor basis for societal wealth management. This is especially so given some of the observed behavioral/sociological implications of inherited privilege discussed above. (There may be a slightly stronger case for concern about the effect of *capital taxation* on entrepreneurship, given the importance of capital constraints for small and medium sized enterprises. See, e.g., Greenwald and Stiglitz (1989).) On the other hand, with well-designed loss offset provisions, capital taxation actually encourages risk-taking, as we have just noted.

There is a more recent literature exploring these issues further, significantly extending the kinds of models explored here. See Gabaix et al., 2016.

[10] See also as Domar and Musgrave (1944) and Stiglitz (1969a).

[11] This was always the case with interest deductibility (see Stiglitz, 1973e, but even more so in the U.S. after 2017 when capital investments could be fully expensed.

[12] See Stiglitz (1973e, 1976f).

policies. Chapter 13 already provided one such warning: a tax in capital (as recommended for instance by Piketty (2014)) may actually worsen the welfare of workers. And this is so even if the proceeds of the tax are redistributed to workers.[13] Only if the adverse effects on capital accumulation are offset, by public investments (in people, infrastructure, and technology) will workers' welfare be enhanced.[14]

Moreover, these chapters provide a framework for thinking about certain aspects of the design of capital and inheritance taxation. For instance, in one of the models explored here, we show that inequality in wealth at the extremes—in the upper tail—is directly related to the top marginal tax rate. This implies that if we are worried especially about extremes of inequality, we should have high top marginal tax rates, especially on capital—just the opposite of the view that comes out of standard optimal tax theory, which focuses only on the returns to labor (even though most of those with high incomes derive almost all of their income from capital).[15]

Similarly, if we are concerned about the intergenerational distribution of wealth, we should focus not on *bequests* but on *inheritances*. Adverse effects arise especially from large gifts to particular individuals.

The analysis of these chapters also shows that in some important cases—such as when there is risk that is imperfectly diversified by the market—capital taxation may actually increase risk taking.

This reinforces one of the main themes of this book: with appropriately designed tax and expenditure policies, overall economic efficiency can be enhanced (GDP can be increased) even as inequality is reduced, reinforcing the gains to those at the bottom and middle.

Further Remarks on Notes on Estate Taxes, Redistribution and the Concept of Balanced Growth Path Incidence (Chapter 32)

I first began thinking about the possibility of adverse incidence effects of capital and inheritance taxation in the late 1960s and early 70s, as reflected in Chapter 32, first presented at a conference at Stanford University. The standard argument for why a capital tax is progressive is that, since wealth inequality is so much greater than wage inequality, a tax on the return to capital redistributed as a lump sum payment or even a reduction in the income tax reduces inequality. But there can another effect: Capital taxation (whether wealth, inheritance, or interest taxation) could discourage savings and capital accumulation—and even without an incentive effect, the redistribution of income from the rich, who save a lot, to the poor, who save little, will lower savings and investment.[16] If that happens, the equilibrium aggregate capital–labor ratio would decline, and with that the wage rate. Inequality

[13] Another such example: better public pension programs lead those at the bottom to save less, and thus to exacerbate the extent of intergenerational transmission between them and the rich. But this is not an argument for cutting back on public pensions.

[14] This is one of the major messages of Chapter 19 above.

[15] As we noted earlier (Chapter 19) that view held that, with a finite population, the top marginal tax rate should be zero (in fact, negative, if skilled and unskilled labor are complements), and that if certain separability conditions on utility are satisfied, income from capital should not be taxed at all. Chapter 19 provided a critique of those conclusions.

[16] Recall the earlier caveat: we are focusing on full employment models.

in income, wealth, and consumption could increase—precisely the opposite of the intent of these measures.

I worried too that if there was a tax on the passing on financial wealth, parents would seek to give their children an advantage by passing on more human capital, and the resulting income inequalities could be even more invidious. (For a more extensive discussion of this point, see the discussion in the next chapter.)

At the time, I worried that these papers would be misinterpreted as an argument *against* an inheritance or wealth tax, and those fears proved to be correct.[17] It was really an argument about caution, that these taxes would have to be accompanied by other measures. In the chapter itself, I pointed out that there were measures available that could undo the adverse effects on capital accumulation.

Indeed, the simple models I used may have overestimated the adverse effects, even ignoring the fact that government policies can more than undo them.[18] Some individuals may be induced to save more to offset the effects of capital taxation. This is the case for those saving for a given target, for example, to smooth consumption between working years and retirement, or to have enough money for a down payment on a house or to pay college tuition. In the standard model, a lowering of the after-tax return on capital has both an income and a substitution effect, and as a matter of theory, either could dominate.

Moreover, some forms of capital taxation—that on pure rents, whether pure profits or land rents—may lead to more capital accumulation in a model with life-cycle savings, as we saw in Chapter 13).[19]

Further Remarks on "Equality, Taxation and Inheritance" (Chapter 33)

This paper represented my attempt to provide a general taxonomy of the effects of capital taxes (including inheritance taxes) on the distribution of income and wealth, and to explore in some detail several of the key mechanisms for the intergenerational transmission of wealth.

In this introduction, I want to comment on four aspects of this chapter.

Human Capital

At first blush, the taxation of inheritances of financial wealth (through, for example, the U.S. gift and estate taxes) would naturally be expected to induce more transfers of human capital—expenditures on education. Upon reflection, the effects are more ambiguous, for several reasons.

[17] For instance, in testimony before the Pennsylvania House Finance Committee on "The Economic Effects of the Estate Tax," David S. Logan of the conservative, business-friendly Tax Foundation said, citing this paper: "Another prominent study by Joseph Stiglitz concluded that taxes on wealth transfers may even cause an increase of income inequality." Testimony, October 17, 2011.

[18] However, in the two-class model of Chapter 13, there is full shifting: the after-tax return on capital is unaffected by the tax.

[19] Moreover, as I pointed out in Stiglitz (1973e), taxation of corporation income may not have adverse effects on investment, and indeed, in tax structures with accelerated depreciation, may even stimulate it.

First, the tax on the return to financial capital is actually lower in the United States (in 2019) than comparable wage income, so that the tax structure actually discourages investments in human capital.

Moreover, a large fraction of individuals borrow to fund especially their higher education. In this case, to the extent that tax policy affects decision making, it should reduce investments in human capital, because of limitations on interest deductibility. Those of higher ability will be taxed on their incremental income but will not be able (at the margin) to deduct the interest on student loans.

But even if a capital tax (a tax on inheritances) encourages investment in human capital, the effects on (wage) inequality are more ambiguous than a casual reading of the chapter suggests. In the chapter, I explore the consequences of a special wage function, giving wages, w, as a function of ability A and human capital c_h:

$$w = G(A, c_h) = Ag(c_h/A), \tag{1}$$

showing that inequality in human capital (say as measured by the coefficient of variation) is unaffected. In that case, we show that c_h is proportional to A. Here, we show that in the more general case, inequality may be increased or decreased.

In the more general case, c_h is not linear in A. To a second order of approximation, we let

$$c_h = k_o + k_1 A + k_2(A - \overline{A})^2. \tag{2}$$

where k_i are constants. Then the coefficient of variation of c_h is

$$(k_1 + k_2 - 2\overline{A})\sigma_A / k_o + k_1\overline{A} + k_2\sigma_A{}^2.$$

It is clear that so long as k_0, k_1, and k_2 can be affected by the interest rate that the coefficient of variation of c_h will also be. For instance, in the general case

$$dc_h/dA = -G_A c_h / G_{c_h} \equiv \beta(A, \hat{r}) = k_1, \tag{3}$$

and

$$d^2 c_h/dA^2 = \beta_A = -[G_{AAch} - \beta G_{c_h c_h A}]/G_{c_h c_h} = k_2. \tag{4}$$

At $\overline{A}$, a change in $\hat{r}$ will normally affect both k_1 and k_2 (through the effect on c_h). Note that the effects will depend on the *fourth* derivatives of G (e.g. $G_{AAc_hc_h}$, $G_{c_hc_hc_hA}$, etc.) about which there are, apart from special parameterizations, unlikely to be strong empirical hypotheses. *In short, it would appear that as a result of the lowering of the opportunity cost of capital the coefficient of variation of human capital could increase or decrease, and as a result so too could that of wages and income.*

The chapter shows, however, that whatever the initial effects, they may be exacerbated by wealth dynamics. In the analysis above, we had assumed that the amount of total capital that an individual has to divide between human and financial capital is fixed. But those with higher wages can and will pass on more human and financial capital to their children.

Inequality in one generation can affect that in the next. Earlier chapters explored these dynamics in terms of the intergenerational transmission of financial wealth, focusing in particular on the long run equilibrium, and this chapter extends that analysis to human capital.

A more realistic model introduces dispersion in the returns to capital, including human capital. More dispersion in wages and the returns to capital will lead to more dispersion in wealth, and higher after-tax interest rates will compound the effects. (See the discussion below.) Thus, higher inheritance and capital taxes will (provided that policy offsets any incidence effects, as described in the previous chapter) lower wealth and income inequality.

Education as a Screening Device

The chapter also considers education as a screening device (Arrow, 1973; Stiglitz, 1975a)—where the returns to investment in education are the private returns associated with being identified of as greater ability. Again, a lower opportunity cost of capital (a lower after-tax return on capital) will induce more screening, and thus more inequality. Unlike the human capital model, however, the returns to education are totally dissipative; that is, aggregate production is not increased at all.[20] In fact, the expenditures on education subtract from what is available to society for consumption.

Quantitative Insignificance of Effects of Inheritance Tax on Education

I suspect that the effect of the inheritance tax on education is a second order effect—less important today than I thought at the time—simply because the inheritance tax only affects very large estates. Most of such wealthy people would have invested as much in their children as would have been profitable in any case, so the estate tax rate has no effect.[21]

Public Education as an Antidote to Any Adverse Incidence Effects

A central message of the chapter, as I noted earlier, is that the government needs to be attentive to the potential adverse effects of taxation that I've described, and take countervailing measures. Probably the most important countervailing measure in this arena is stronger support for public education. This is especially important because in democratic societies, it is hard to proscribe private schools. Parents with enough wealth, wanting to give their children additional advantages, will—unless there are strong societal norms to the contrary—spend large amounts on private education. Countries that provide school vouchers, allowing parents to supplement those amounts with additional expenditures, induce higher levels of inequality in human capital. By contrast, forcing parents to give up all public subsidies when they withdraw their children from public schools, and requiring private schools to take in a minimum percentage of poor (scholarship) students will increase the income/wealth threshold below which parents will send their children to public schools.[22] Moreover, by increasing the quality/expenditures on public school, the threshold will be increased still further, while diminishing the gap between the human capital of lower and middle income individuals and the rich. (There is an important issue

[20] This is not true if screening identifies differences in comparative advantages. The earlier work on screening focused only on identifying differences in absolute abilities.

[21] There is still some effect: as a result of lower wealth inequality, fewer individuals will opt out of the public-school system. This in turn may lead to less wage inequality, reinforcing the original reduction in wealth inequality. The increased economic integration of schools may have large social benefits.

[22] These ideas are pursued at greater length in Stiglitz (1974h).

on the design of the public-school system—the extent to which there should be compensatory education for children who might otherwise be at a disadvantage, and the extent to which classes should be "streamed" or have students with mixed abilities, which we do not consider here.[23])

Diffusion Models

In the 1978 paper on which this chapter is based, I introduced diffusion models to study the long-run stochastic equilibrium, simultaneously explored in Bevan (1974, 1979), Bevan and Stiglitz (1979), and developed further in Chapter 12 in this volume. While today, it would be fairly easy to give numerical solutions to the Kolmogorov equations giving the asymptotic wealth distribution, at the time the only easily obtainable results relate to the asymptotic Pareto tail, obtaining a relatively simple expression for the tail.

We study variants of the model in which the only source of stochasticity is returns to capital, in which it is only wages that are variable, and in which both are variable.

The most interesting case is that where wages themselves are governed by a stochastic process with regression toward the mean, a model we discussed in Chapters 9 and 12. Those who are well off, either because they have inherited a lot of wealth or a high level of ability, know that their descendants will not be as well off, and if there is a dynastic utility function, where they care about their descendants, then they will save. Effectively, there is intergenerational smoothing—a standard (but difficult) optimization problem with a boundary condition that individuals cannot borrow, and more importantly, cannot pass on debts to their descendants.[24] Here, we don't solve the optimization problem, but rather explore what happens if families simply save a fraction of their lifetime income, but now, wage dispersion has the effect of increasing wealth dispersion. But still, the fatness of the tail of the distribution (the Pareto coefficient) is determined just by the (asymptotic) noise in the return to capital and the drift—the difference between the (average) net savings (s_r) and the division of wealth among the heirs (n).

It was only much later, as we noted in Part II, that the diffusion model was taken up by others to help understand inequality.[25] And it was more than three decades later that I returned to this model, embedding it into a more general equilibrium analysis where I solved simultaneously for the return to capital and labor—the analysis presented in Chapter 12.

Capital Taxation and Risk Sharing

In the presence of imperfect risk markets, redistributive taxation can be viewed as a form of risk sharing: those who are "lucky" share their good fortune with those who are not. Earlier, Domar and Musgrave (1944) and Stiglitz (1969a) showed that as a result, a capital tax

[23] See Stiglitz (1986b, 1973a).

[24] This was a problem that I was studying simultaneously in joint work with David Newbery in the context of optimal storage of agricultural commodities. See Newbery and Stiglitz (1981, 1982a).

[25] And as we noted there, there are large technical and economic differences. As we point out in Chapter 12, our analysis does not require a reflecting barrier, and key variables $\{w, r\}$ are endogenously determined. On the other hand, we only solve for the steady state solution, and we do not solve for the optimal bequest function.

with full loss offsets would actually induce more risk taking. Implicitly, they considered a situation where the risks were idiosyncratic; with the law of large numbers, each individual give up τe_j, where e_j is the random return on his own asset, and gets back (in the symmetric case) $\tau\bar{e}$, where $\bar{e}$ is the average return. Here, we consider the other polar case, where there is a single risky asset. Now, redistribution (from the rich to the poor, again with full loss offset) has no effect on aggregate risk taking. (Obviously, without full loss offset, a capital tax could discourage risk taking.)

This result has, I think, not received the attention it deserves in public policy debates. A standard argument of the Right against capital taxation is that it discourages risk taking and entrepreneurship. Again, it is an incidence argument: such taxes are counterproductive, because economic growth will slow and even those at the bottom and middle will be worse off. This analysis suggests that there is little merit to the argument. We should, of course, think carefully about tax structure, including provisions for loss offsets, just as we need to think carefully about how we spend tax proceeds—for instance on investments on infrastructure, technology, and education.

Imperfect Annuity Markets and Random Deaths

Another aspect of the analysis of the impact of capital taxation focuses on another capital market imperfection. Annuity markets are very imperfect, one of the reasons that social security (the public retirement program) has been so beneficial. Theories of imperfect and asymmetric information (that I was just formulating at the time I wrote this paper) help explain this market imperfection. But whatever the reason, if individuals have to save enough to deal with the risk of living a long time, when they have an untimely death, their children may inherit substantial amounts. Partly because of social security, there is only limited savings for retirement by low income individuals.[26] For those of higher income the amounts can be substantial. A succession of generations who die early in the retirement years will result in their heirs having increasing amounts of wealth. This can give rise to a Pareto tail wealth distribution. In the chapter, we assume that an increase in the inheritance tax rate (a lowering of the after-tax return) will discourage savings. (Part of the value of saving is that, if one should die early, one's children will enjoy the fruits of one's savings.) And it means that, at any savings rate (bequest rate), wealth compounds more slowly. If this is correct, then inheritance taxation will reduce wealth inequality.[27]

But there is a counterforce present with capital taxation, though not inheritance taxation: if individuals have a long retirement (longevity has increased substantially since this paper was written), and the return to capital is low, then individuals will have to save more to smooth consumption. If the real interest rate is 0, the outer bound of one's planning was 30 years in retirement, and one wanted annual consumption of $50,000, one would need $1.5 million at retirement, and if one died shortly thereafter, one's heirs would inherit

[26] Moreover, especially in the U.S., their life expectancy is shorter, so they have less need for retirement savings.
[27] Provided we take measures to offset any adverse general equilibrium incidence effect.

a great deal. If the real return to capital were 10%, a $1,500,000 account would generate $150,000 in perpetuity. These adverse effects can easily be offset by a corresponding increase in inheritance taxes.

The effects just described are, however, likely more than offset by the effects described in the previous two sections of this introduction, arguing that higher (and more progressive) taxation of capital results in more equality.

32

Notes on Estate Taxes, Redistribution, and the Concept of Balanced Growth Path Incidence

1 Introduction

The object of this chapter is to introduce a new kind of incidence analysis, which I refer to as balanced growth path incidence, and to apply this concept to the analysis of the effects of estate taxation on the distribution of wealth, income, and consumption.[1,2] I argue that using conventional approaches to the analysis of the effects of such a tax is likely to lead to misleading conclusions. More precisely, I argue that, because of capital accumulation effects, the estate tax may not achieve the objective to which it is presumably directed, that is, equalizing the distribution of income; if the government takes actions to offset these accumulation effects, the tax will lead to an increase in equality of income and wealth. The implication is that it will be important for the government to take offsetting actions, to ensure that there is not a decrease in the capital–labor ratio.

2 Capital Accumulation and Inequality

The reason that the estate tax may not increase the equality of income is the following:[3] the estate tax may reduce savings; the reduction in savings and capital accumulation will, in the long run, lead to a lower capital–labor ratio; and the lower capital–labor ratio will, if the elasticity of substitution between capital and labor is less than unity, lead to an increase in the share of capital. Since income from capital is more unequally distributed than is labor income, the increase in the proportion of income accruing to capital may increase the total inequality of income. This result hinges on three key assumptions (besides the assumption that the elasticity of substitution be less than unity).

3 Estate Taxes and Savings

The first assumption in the above argument is that the estate tax leads to a reduction in savings. There are two aspects to this. First, the estate tax can be thought of as a transfer

[1] Originally published in 1978 in the *Journal of Political Economy*, 86(2): S137–S150. Paper presented to NSF-NBER conference on income taxation, Stanford, California, January 1976. The basic results of Section 5 were presented at the San Francisco meeting of the Econometric Society, December 1967, as part of a more general study, "The Distribution of Income and Wealth among Individuals." My understandings of the issues discussed here has been greatly influenced by discussions with David Bevan. Reprinted with permission.

[2] My views on the subject have evolved markedly since I wrote this paper and that in the next chapter, as I discuss at greater length in the introduction to this part of the book. It is important for the remarks there to be read in conjunction with this chapter. This chapter has been shortened and edited, and several typographical and technical errors have been corrected.

[3] Further reasons why an estate tax might increase long-run wealth inequality are set forth in Stiglitz (1978).

The Origins of Inequality, and Policies to Contain It. Joseph E. Stiglitz, Oxford University Press. © Joseph E. Stiglitz (2025).
DOI: 10.1093/oso/9780198799580.003.0033

from the individuals who would have inherited the wealth to the population as a whole. The latter is effected, for instance, by the reduction in income tax which the revenues raised through the estate tax allows. The question is: What is the effect of this transfer?

The increased income to the population as a whole will have associated with it the conventional marginal propensity to consume out of income. The effect of the transfer depends on the magnitude of the marginal propensity to consume out of income relative to the marginal propensity to consume out of inheritances. If the latter is treated like any other wealth (rather than like any other income), as seems likely, then since the marginal propensity to consume out of wealth is much lower than that out of income, the estate tax has a significant effect on the aggregate consumption rate.

The second aspect is concerned with incentive effects. If bequests are treated like consumption the $n + 1st$] period of the individual's life (where the individual lives n periods), then there is an income effect and a substitution effect associated with the tax. The income effect leads the individual to consume less during his lifetime, the substitution effect to consume more. On a priori grounds it is not possible to say which effect is stronger. But even if the individual is induced to consume less to increase his gross bequest (so that his net bequest is reduced by less than the magnitude of the tax), it does not seem likely that this effect will overcome the transfer effect described above.

4 The Concept of Balanced Growth Incidence

The second assumption in the argument that the estate tax may lead to greater inequality because of reduced savings is that the government does not or cannot take countervailing actions. Presumably, the government through monetary policy could offset any effect on the pattern of capital accumulation.

The question raised here is of importance for more than just the analysis of the estate tax. A wide variety of taxes affect savings, and the question is, in a general equilibrium context, how are we to evaluate such taxes? The questions raised are analogous to how we are to evaluate the incidence of a tax in the context of the standard macroeconomic model, for the tax will have a deflationary effect on the economy so that the equilibrium level of national income will be reduced. There is now widespread agreement that the most meaningful comparisons are among policies which leave the level of output constant; for example, we substitute one tax for another tax.

Here it seems to me appropriate to introduce some notion of balanced growth path incidence, where we compare policy changes which leave the aggregate capital–labor ratio unchanged. There are a number of such policies: (a) an interest subsidy on savings (essentially substituting life-cycle savings for inheritance savings); (b) offsetting the reduced private savings by increased government savings; (c) reducing social security payments, which again would induce more life-cycle savings; (d) using monetary and debt policy to increase the rate of return on capital and thus increase savings.[4]

[4] Both the tax on inheritances (savings) and the policy measures designed to offset its effects have both income and substitution effects. Thus, a moderate inheritance tax could actually increase savings and capital accumulation. The simple models explored in later sections assume a fixed savings rate—where income and substitution effects just cancel. If that is true for both life-cycle and dynastic savers, then interest subsidies to induce life-cycle

5 The Distribution of Wealth

The third basic assumption in my argument that the estate tax might increase the inequality of income is that capital is more unequally distributed than labor. Although this is undoubtedly true at the present time, the question may legitimately be raised of whether this would be the case if we had larger inheritance taxes. The answer depends on the particular theory of the determination of the income and wealth distribution. I now show that, indeed, the inheritance tax may have an effect on the equilibrium distribution of wealth, but even if the estate tax has no effect on the aggregate capital–labor ratio, it may increase the inequality of consumption.

The argument is presented in a model which is a modification of that presented by Stiglitz (1969b). We assume that: (a) Individuals leave as a bequest to their children what they inherited plus an amount which is a linear function of their lifetime income, $B(t) = sY(t) - a + B(t-1)$, where B is the bequest and s is the marginal propensity to save out of lifetime income; $a \geq 0$ is the intercept of the consumption function (consumption at zero income). Lifetime income for the ith family is equal to their wage income plus interest income, that is, $\Upsilon_i = w_i L_i + rC_i$, where C_i is the amount of (inherited) capital of the family $[C_i(t) \equiv B_i(t-1)]$, w_i is the wage received, k the rate of interest, and L_i is the number of wage earners in the family; (b) Individuals differ in productivity, but the productivity of children is identical to the productivity of their parents (the assumption of perfect correlation of abilities); (c) All families reproduce at the same rate. In continuous time, we let n be the rate of increase in the size of the family; (d) Parents divide their wealth equally among their children.

If we let y_i be income per capita in the family and c_i be wealth per capita and represent the dynamics of capital accumulation of the family in continuous time, we obtain:

$$\dot{c}_i = sw_i - a + (sr - n)c_i \tag{32.1}$$

or, in equilibrium,

$$c_i = \frac{sw_i - a}{n - sr}. \tag{32.2}$$

We assume that a is small, that is, $a \ll sw_i \; \forall_i$ so that the numerator of (32.2) is positive.

Thus, the coefficient of variation of wealth, γ_c, is given by

$$\gamma_c^2 = \frac{E(c_i - \overline{c})^2}{\overline{c}^2} = \frac{s^2 \sigma_w^2}{(s\overline{w} - a)^2}, \tag{32.3}$$

where σ_w^2 is the variance of w, and $\overline{w}$ is the mean of w. To obtain this result, we observe that in equilibrium, if p_i is the proportion of the population in the ith group,

$$k \equiv \overline{c} \equiv \sum p_i c_i = \frac{s\overline{w} - a}{n - sr}, \tag{32.4}$$

savers to increase their savings rates won't be effective, but the income effects of reduced social security payments will be.

The conventional wisdom is that monetary policy, working in conjunction with tax policy, can achieve change in the composition of aggregate output to ensure any desired level of capital accumulation.

where $\bar{c}$ is the average per capita capital. (In this formulation, there is no capital arising from savings within a lifetime (life-cycle savings); the model can, however, easily be extended to that case.)

If we let γ_w be the coefficient of variation of (lifetime) wages, and if $a = 0$, $\gamma_c = \gamma_w$. The dispersion of capital and wages is identical. If $a > 0$, $\gamma_c > \gamma_w$, capital is distributed more unequally than wages. Since

$$y_i = w_i + rc_i = \frac{nw_i - ar}{n - sr}, \tag{32.5}$$

$$\begin{aligned} \gamma_y^2 &= \frac{n^2}{(n-sr)^2}\frac{\sigma_w^2}{\bar{y}^2} \\ &= \left(\frac{n}{n-sr}\right)^2 \gamma_w^2 \alpha^2 \\ &= \left[\frac{(sy-a)}{sw-a}\alpha\right]^2 \gamma_w^2 \\ &= \gamma_w^2 \text{ if } a = 0, \end{aligned} \tag{32.6}$$

where α = share of labor. If $a = 0$, inheritance has no effect on the inequality of consumption.

We now impose an inheritance or wealth tax[5] distributing the proceeds as income transfers which are uniform and lumpsum. If τ is the tax rate, the wealth-accumulation equation becomes

$$\dot{c}_i = (sw_i - a + src_i + s\tau k) - (n + \tau)c_i, \tag{32.7}$$

and

$$\dot{k} = s\overline{w} - a + s(r + \tau)k - (n + \tau)k. \tag{32.8}$$

Thus, in long-run equilibrium,

$$c_i = \frac{sw_i - a + s\tau k}{n + \tau - sr} \tag{32.9}$$

$$k = \frac{s\overline{w} - a}{n - sr + \tau(1 - s)'} \tag{32.10}$$

[5] In this particular model, a wealth tax is equivalent to an inheritance tax, since all wealth is continuously being passed on from one generation to another.

or $k[n + \tau(1 - s)] = sy(k) - a$, where $y \equiv w + rk = f(k)$ = output per capita, where f is the (per capita) production function, $f' > 0, f'' < 0$. Hence,

$$\frac{dk}{d\tau_{|s}} = \frac{(1-s)\,k}{sy' - (sy/k) + (a/k)} = -\frac{(1-s)\,k^2}{s\overline{w} - a} < 0. \tag{32.11}$$

Even if s were constant, capital accumulation would be reduced.[6]

As a consequence, even though if k were constant inequality of wealth would be reduced, k is not constant, so the effect of wealth taxation will depend on the elasticity of substitution.

Assume that individuals differ from each other in a Harrod neutral manner, so that $\gamma_w]$, the coefficient of variation of wages, is a constant, with taxation,

$$\gamma_c^2 = \frac{s^2\overline{w}^2\gamma_w^2}{(s\overline{w} - a + s\tau k)^2} = \frac{\gamma_w^2}{\left(1 - \frac{a}{s\overline{w}} + \frac{\tau k}{w}\right)^2}. \tag{32.12}$$

Since

$$\frac{d\ln\frac{k}{w}}{d\ln k} = 1 - \frac{1-\alpha}{\sigma} > \text{or } < 0 \text{ as } \sigma > \text{or } < (1-\alpha), \tag{32.13}$$

where σ is the elasticity of substitution, that is, as the elasticity of substitution is less than or greater than the share of capital, the coefficient of variation of consumption may increase with an increase in wealth taxation. This means that if $a = 0$, when the elasticity of substitution is very small (less than the share of capital), the adverse distribution effect resulting from the decrease in k is stronger than the direct redistribution effect of the wealth tax, and inequality is increased. This result holds more generally, so long as a is not too negative. Obviously, if the proceeds of the tax were redistributed more progressively, that is, only to those with very low incomes (wealth), the beneficial effects of the wealth tax would extend to even small elasticities of substitution.

Note that I have in this analysis ignored the possible decrease in the savings rate (s) as a result of the impositions of the tax. That is, the total effects with which we have been concerned are those arising from the reduction in the aggregate savings rate from transferring "capital" to "income"; if s is reduced, as it may well be, the possibility of an inheritance tax increasing inequality is even greater.

Assume, on the other hand, that s changes to keep k constant. From (32.11) we know that this requires

$$\frac{ds}{d\tau_{|k}} = \frac{(1-s)k}{y + \tau k}. \tag{32.14}$$

[6] Stability of (32.7) requires $n + \tau > sr$, and stability of (32.8) implies $n - sr + \tau(1 - s) > 0$, or, since $k > 0$, $s\overline{w} > a$.

Hence,

$$\frac{d\gamma_c}{d\tau_{|k}} \gtrless 0 \quad \text{as} \quad \frac{d[(\tau k/\overline{w}) - (a/s\overline{w})]}{d\tau|k} \gtrless 0, \tag{32.15}$$

but

$$\frac{d[(\tau k/\overline{w} - (a/s\overline{w})]}{d\tau|\overline{k}} = \frac{k}{\overline{w}} + \frac{a}{\overline{w}s^2}\frac{ds}{d\tau} > 0. \tag{32.15a}$$

Similarly,

$$\frac{d\gamma_y}{d\tau} \gtrless 0 \quad \text{as} \quad \frac{d\{[s\tau(1-\alpha)]/[(n+\tau)\alpha]\text{–ar}/[\overline{w}(n+\tau)]\}}{d\tau} \gtrless 0.$$

But

$$\frac{d\left[\frac{s\tau(1-\alpha)}{(n+\tau)\alpha} - \frac{ar}{\overline{w}(n+\tau)}\right]}{d\tau|k} = \frac{ns(1-\alpha)}{(n+\tau)^2\alpha} + \frac{ar}{\overline{w}(n+\tau)^2} + \frac{\tau(1-\alpha)}{(n+\tau)\alpha}\frac{ds}{d\tau_{|k}} > 0.$$

Thus the "balanced growth path" effects—keeping k constant—are as expected. Inheritance wealth taxation does reduce inequality of both consumption and income.

There are multiple ways by which the government might be able to achieve this kind of balance growth path, for example, through monetary or tax policies encouraging investment. Within the context of our analytic framework, assume that a fraction β of the tax revenue is allocated to (public) investment which is assumed a perfect substitute for private investment. If $\beta = \frac{1}{1+s}$, with the remaining tax proceeds being distributed uniformly as before, it is easy to show that the equilibrium value of k is unchanged, and Equation (32.12) for the coefficient of variation of consumption is now

$$\gamma_c^2 = \frac{\gamma_w^2}{\left(1 - \frac{a}{\overline{w}} + \frac{\tau(1-\beta)}{\overline{w}}\right)^2},$$

so that the increase in the tax unambiguously reduces wealth inequality.

6 Concluding Comments

In this chapter I have focused on several aspects of the economics of estate taxes that have received perhaps too little attention in recent discussions. These taxes may not lead to the reduction in inequality which their proponents desire, but rather may increase the degree of inequality—at least if the government does not take countervailing measures or does not use the proceeds of the taxes in ways which contravenes these effects. The important message of the chapter is that it may be necessary to accompany any inheritance taxes with other measures.

More broadly, the importance of these considerations depends not only on the values of certain economic parameters, which I have identified in my earlier discussion, but also on the importance ascribed to these economic considerations relative to the noneconomic considerations. Accumulations of wealth may, it is argued, lead to accumulations of political power and affect the nature of our political processes. Opponents of estate taxes are concerned with the ethical grounds for restricting this particular class of choices of individuals. They ask: Why should parents who do not wish to leave wealth to their children but prefer to consume it themselves restrict the ability of parents who do wish to leave wealth to their children? But there is an obvious answer: a society market by inherited inequalities with large differences in incomes, wealth, and opportunities—a hereditary plutocracy—is markedly different from a more egalitarian society.[7] Although these ethical and political questions may in the final analysis be more important in determining policies toward inheritances, it is at least worth noting the important economic effects of such policies.

[7] See the introduction to this part of the volume, and Stiglitz (2012a). There are economic, political, and social consequences arising from the intergenerational transmission of advantages and disadvantages, and from having a society marked by low levels of equality of opportunity. See also the Introduction to the volume.

33

Equality, Taxation, and Inheritance

1 Introduction

This chapter [1] is concerned with the determinants of the distribution of income, wealth, and consumption,[2] and the effect of taxation on these distributions. The chapter has a simple message: these distributions are endogenous, and are critically affected by taxation, but not always in the ways expected. As a result, many of the policies aimed at reducing inequality may, in the end, lead to an increase in wealth inequality. For instance, inheritance taxes and interest income taxes may, under some circumstances, increase the inequality of wealth.[3]

The error in the conventional reasoning concerning inheritance taxes is simple: it focusses on the direct effect—the heirs inherit less and, to the extent that wealth inequality is due to inheritance, wealth inequality is reduced. Our argument is that the before-tax distribution of wealth may change, and it may change so much as to actually increase the after-tax degree of inequality, unless government takes offsetting measures.

We are used to finding, in other areas of economic analysis, that such partial equilibrium analyses may be misleading. But generally, the general equilibrium effects, through reducing the magnitude of direct effects, do not reverse direction. But in the case of inheritance or capital taxation, the effects on inequality may, under quite plausible conditions, be reversed. This result is perhaps not intuitively obvious, and most of the chapter is devoted to explaining it.

Our basic strategy in formulating a theory of the income distribution is to first identify the exogenous variables which determine or define how individuals differ from one another. Individuals differ in three important respects:

(i) Endowments: different individuals inherit from their parents different amounts of capital, different abilities, and different amounts of human capital; these endowments are added to or subtracted from by the state, or by gifts from relatives and friends.

[1] The author is indebted to innumerable conversation on the topics of this paper with David Bevan. His study on closely related questions has greatly influenced my thinking about these questions. I am also indebted to John Flemming and Jim Mirrlees for discussions on these questions over the years. Financial support from the National Science Foundation is gratefully acknowledged. This chapter is a substantially shortened and revised version of a paper that was originally presented to an International Economic Association conference, Noordqijk aan Zee, Netherlands, April 1977, and published in W. Krelle and A.F. Shorrocks (eds.), 1978, *Personal Income Distribution*, Amsterdam: North-Holland Publishing Company, pp. 271–303. Reprinted with permission.

[2] We are concerned here with the personal distribution of income and wealth, not the distribution of factor shares.

[3] There is a long discussion of the appropriate measurement of wealth inequality (see, e.g., Atkinson, 1970 or Rothschild and Stiglitz, 1973) for a discussion of the measurement of income inequality; some additional complications are involved in developing measures of wealth inequality. For our purposes, however, we need not be particularly precise about what measure we use. In Section 3, we employ three measures: the coefficient of variation, the variance, and the Pareto coefficient of the tail of the distribution.

The Origins of Inequality, and Policies to Contain It. Joseph E. Stiglitz, Oxford University Press. © Joseph E. Stiglitz (2025).
DOI: 10.1093/oso/9780198799580.003.0034

(ii) Tastes: individuals differ in a number of ways which affect not only the temporal pattern and the probability distribution of their own income, but also affect the income and wealth of their children. Among the components of "tastes" which are important in determining the distribution of income are (a) attitudes toward work, leisure, and consumption; this clearly affects the income earned by different individuals with the same endowment; (b) attitudes toward risks; this affects decisions concerning job choices and portfolio allocation, and hence clearly affects the probability distribution of future income; (c) attitudes concerning consumption today versus consumption tomorrow; this affects the savings rate, lifetime consumption patterns, lifetime earnings patterns, and investments in human capital; (d) attitudes toward children, which affects the number of children, the size of bequests, and the form of bequest (human versus physical capital).

(iii) Luck: given a particular set of endowments and particular set of tastes, individuals may still differ, since the outcome of their decisions may well be random. Among the major stochastic elements involved in the distribution of the income and wealth are (a) "occupational luck": being a lawyer may be a risky occupation; some are lucky and make it, some are unlucky and don't; (b) "investment luck": some invest in risk securities and are lucky, others are not; (c) accidents and illnesses, which obviously affect the income and savings of individuals (although in a sense these can be incorporated into a comprehensive definition of endowments).

The endowments of one generation are related to the endowments, tastes, and luck of the previous generation; the relationship between the two involves both systematic and random components. Parents may differ in their attitudes about the number of children, and about the amount of human and non-human capital to transfer to their children; some, for instance, may wish to leave everything to the eldest son (primogeniture) while others may divide the inheritance equally among their heirs. Some may give a child of mediocre ability more than his brighter brother, to compensate for his poorer endowment, and some give him less, feeling that he can use it less well.

There are at least four important sources of randomness in the interaction of successive generations: (i) the ability of the child is not perfectly correlated with that of his parents; (ii) marriage: the ability of a child is related to that of both of his parents, but mating is, to some extent at least, random; (iii) births: the number of children is, to some extent at least, random; this affects the per capita inheritances of children of parents with a given wealth; (iv) death: so long as there are not perfect annuity markets[4] some individuals will have a positive net worth when they die; the exact amount depends on the date of death, which is random, and hence the amount inherited is random.

Of the variables listed, many have the property that they are exogenous in the short run, but endogenous in the long; for instance, the endowments of physical and human capital may be given in the short run, but in the long run, they depend on the level of capital accumulation, which depends on taxation. Moreover, the magnitude of the stochastic elements themselves are, to some extent, endogenous. The distribution of returns to a particular

[4] And the kinds of considerations discussed in Rothschild and Stiglitz (1976) suggest that so long as information is costly, there will never be perfect annuity markets.

risky asset may be exogenous, but, since the portfolio allocation is itself endogenous, the distribution of returns of investment as a whole is endogenous.

The theory of the distribution of income and wealth is concerned with how differences in endowments, tastes, and luck[5] become translated into an income and wealth distribution. For instance, if all individuals had the same endowments, if there were no random components in income determination, and if individuals differed only in their attitudes toward work and leisure, then the degree of inequality will depend simply on the distribution of those attitudes; and the effect of a change in the income tax rate on the distribution of income will depend simply on whether those who work more have a lower elasticity of labor with respect to the wage; in Figure 33.1, we have depicted a case where they do. The result that the income tax increases the degree of income inequality is immediate.

A full model, taking into account individual differences in tastes, endowments, and luck, seems intractable, and if we are to get anywhere we must simplify.

In this chapter, we focus on the distribution of lifetime income and wealth; as a consequence, we shall not be concerned with details concerning the lifetime pattern of income, including life-cycle savings. This simplifies matters considerably, but still leaves much to be done.

The basic model underlying our analysis is simple: we postulate that the ability of an individual is a stochastic function of the ability of his parents. The wage of an individual is a function of his ability, his human capital, the information about his ability which is available, and certain market aggregates (e.g., the aggregate capital–labor ratio). All of these except ability are endogenous variables, affected by government policy.

Similarly, the wealth of an individual is a function of his inheritance and his lifetime savings; the latter depends on his income, including the return he has earned on his capital

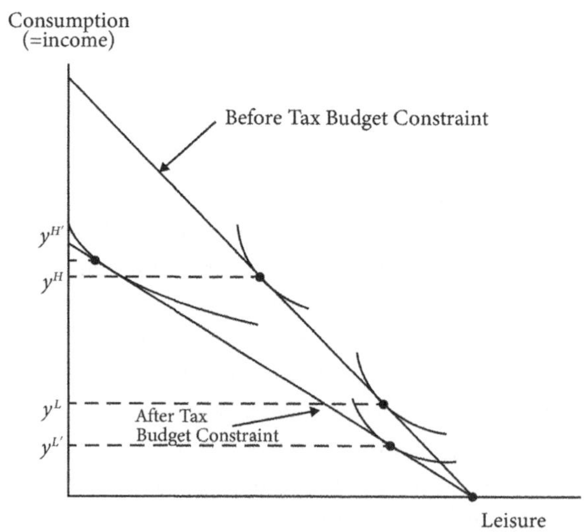

Figure 33.1 An example where an income tax *increases* the degree of income inequality.

[5] Monopoly power (including discrimination) and gifts from the government are sometimes suggested as further determinants of the distribution of income. We will not deal with these explicitly here, although formally, they perhaps should be included in the category of "endowments."

and his wages. His inheritance is a function of his parents' income, which depends on their inheritances, the return on their capital, and the tax rates on inheritance. The return he has earned on his capital depends on his portfolio allocation, which in turn depends on tax rates.

The distribution of lifetime income and wealth thus depends on certain underlying sources of randomness—in the above model, on the randomness associated with inherited ability, and on the randomness associated with returns to a particular security. But these underlying sources of randomness are translated into income and wealth inequality in a most complicated way, and are affected by the decisions of individuals with respect to savings, portfolio allocation, investment in human capital, the amount of screening, etc. Any change in the tax structure changes all of these decisions and hence changes the underlying distribution of income and wealth.

Note that even this model represents a considerable simplification, for example we have omitted several of the sources of randomness mentioned earlier.

There have, of course, been earlier stochastic models of income determination (see, for instance, Champernowne, 1953 and Mandelbrot, 1961); but these stochastic models have not been structural models; that is, they have not identified the determinants of the stochastic process describing income determination. There have also been earlier dynamic models of income determination (see, in particular, Stiglitz, 1969b), but these dynamic models, though focusing in an important way on the role of savings behavior, reproductive behavior, inheritance policy (e.g., primogeniture versus equal division among heirs), and ability differences in the determination of the income distribution, have not, for the most part, been stochastic,[6] and have had only limited scope for the adjustment of individual behavior to, say, changes in tax policy.

Our objective here is to formulate a dynamic, stochastic model in which the behavior of individuals is responsive to tax policy. We have attained only limited success in our objective. A number of "special models" which capture one or another aspect of the income determination process are formulated in the paper. But even the most general model treated does not capture as many of the important aspects as one would like. Hence, this chapter should be viewed as a preliminary exploration in an area which has been subjected to too little theoretical investigation. These preliminary results cast doubt on the efficacy and desirability of various government policies designed at redistributing income and wealth.

The chapter consists of two sections. Section 2 presents in a verbal and heuristic manner the argument that capital taxation may increase the degree of inequality. Section 3 presents a sequence of models designed to justify some of the assertions made in Section 2.

2 Why Might Capital Taxation Increase Inequality?

We present three sets of arguments for why capital taxation may increase inequality:

(i) Even if factor prices do not change, capital taxation may lead to individuals changing their behavior with respect to investment in human capital, screening, and portfolio allocation in such a way as to increase inequality.

[6] See, however, the brief discussion in Stiglitz (1969b).

(ii) Capital taxation may change the capital–labor ratio (it is likely to lower it); this changes factor prices, which may lead to an adverse change in the distribution of income and wealth.
(iii) In general, inheritances serve to decrease inequality[7] of consumption among the members of a single family.

2.1 Effects with Fixed Factor Prices

In this section, we consider the effect capital taxation has on the degree of observed inequality[8] in the economy when factor prices are fixed. The tax has a number of effects, on labor supply, human capital accumulation, screening life-cycle accumulation, risk taking, etc. Most of these may lead to an increase in inequality of income and/or wealth. Some of them would in fact normally be expected to. Other effects would normally be expected to reduce inequality. Our approach is basically taxonomic, that is, we list the various effects and trace out their implications. We are not able to construct a single, comprehensive model, and hence we are unable at this stage to make any judgment about whether "normally" one would expect the tax structure to increase or decrease inequality. Our purpose, as we noted earlier, is to show that there is a real possibility that inheritance and other capital taxes might increase inequality; by examining the particular mechanisms by which that is done, it may be possible to design the tax structure so as to reduce the likelihood of undesired consequences of the tax policy. And when that is not possible, there may be other measures to offset the adverse effects.

Of the arguments we present in this section, four relate to the effect of taxation on the distribution of lifetime wage income (two concern the level of wages (human, capital, screening), one concerns the effect on the distribution of wage income through the effect on labor supply, and the fourth concerns the effect on the distribution of lifetime incomes). The remaining three arguments relate to the effect of taxation on the distribution of inheritances.

2.1.1 Human Capital

Capital taxes may increase investment in human capital. Since "abilities" are unequally distributed, an increase in human capital expenditures may increase inequality of wage income. The simplest way to see this is to assume that the individual's wage is a function of his ability, A, and his human capital, c_h:

$$w = G(A, c_h)\,. \tag{33.1}$$

The individual invests in human capital (assuming a perfect capital market) to the point where the return is equal to the after-market tax rate of interest $\hat{r}$; that is,

[7] Obviously, primogeniture may serve to increase inequality. Throughout this chapter, we focus on "equal sharing" inheritance policies. The normative question of what aspects of inequality we should be most concerned with is addressed at greater length in the introduction to this section of the volume.

[8] By "observed inequality" we mean inequality in measured income, since differences in effort, leisure, etc. are difficult to observe. "Observed income" inequality and "real income" inequality may be markedly different.

individuals maximize their net income, y, where y is equal to the wage income plus capital income:[9]

$$y = w + \hat{r}(c - c_h), \tag{33.2}$$

where c is total capital. Hence $c - c_h$ is non-human capital. Hence:

$$G_{c_h} = \hat{r}. \tag{33.3}$$

Lowering the after-tax return on physical capital will, with diminishing returns, lead to an increase in c_h.

If everyone had equal total capital, but unequal abilities, this would tend to increase income inequality. Assume, for instance, that G had constant returns to scale; we can then write:

$$w = Ag\left(\frac{c_h}{A}\right), \tag{33.4}$$

so (3) becomes:

$$g'\left(\frac{c_h}{A}\right) = \hat{r} \tag{33.5}$$

or

$$\frac{c_h}{A} = g'^{-1}(\hat{r}).$$

So

$$\frac{d\ln\frac{c_h}{A}}{d\ln\hat{r}} = -1/\xi$$

where

$$\xi = -\frac{d\ln g'}{d\ln\frac{c_h}{A}}.$$

For all individuals, human capital is proportional to ability. This means that the variance of y, σ_y^2, can be simply related to the variance of A:

$$\sigma_y = \sigma_A\left[g - \frac{c_h}{A}\hat{r}\right],$$

[9] Alternatively, we might have assumed they maximized:

$$w + (1 + \hat{r})(c - c_h),$$

which would have yielded:

$$G_{c_h} = 1 + \hat{r}.$$

The analysis is identical with this formulation.

and similarly, the coefficient of variation of y, which we denote as

$$\hat{\sigma}_y \equiv \sigma_y/\bar{y},$$

where $\bar{y}$ is the mean of y, can be written as

$$\hat{\sigma} = \frac{\hat{\sigma}_A\left[g - \frac{c_h}{A}\hat{r}\right]}{g - \hat{r}\frac{c_h}{A} + \hat{r}\frac{c}{A}} = \frac{\hat{\sigma}_A}{1+\gamma},$$

where γ is just the ratio of the income from capital ($\hat{r}c$) to (net) income from wages (net of human capital), and where $\hat{\sigma}_A$ is the coefficient of variation of A. Hence:

$$\frac{d\ln\hat{\sigma}_y}{d\ln\hat{r}} = -\frac{\gamma}{1+\gamma}\left\{1 - \frac{\xi g}{g - \hat{r}c_h/A}\right\},$$

which is greater or less than zero as ξ is $<$ or $>$ $1 - \beta$, where $\beta \equiv \hat{r}(c_h/A)/g$, the share of total wage income attributable to human capital. When the elasticity of response of human capital to the interest rate is high, then lowering the cost of capital increases the coefficient of variation in income.[10]

The critical question is whether, on the whole, the tax structure encourages human capital. The inheritance tax does, since gifts of human capital are exempt from the estate and gifts tax. (Since that tax is paid by so few families, and those families may well have already invested in human capital to the point where diminishing returns to further education may have well set in, I suspect that the effect, if present at all, is negligible.[11]) On the other hand, a uniform wage and capital tax would reduce the return to human capital and its opportunity cost proportionately, so that there would be no effect on investment in human capital.

To the extent that, as a result of special provisions pertaining to capital (such as the special provisions for capital gains), capital is in fact taxed at an effective rate lower than wages, the tax structure may actually discourage human capital accumulation.

[10] This ignores the direct redistribution effects of the tax. A highly progressive inheritance tax will lead to little revenue from redistribution but could (as in the model just presented) have an incentive effect in encouraging investment in human capital. We have also ignored variations in initial endowments of c, constraints on human capital, and public provision of human capital. If, for instance, poor individuals are at a corner solution (they cannot borrow, and at $c_h = c, g'(c_h/A) > \hat{r}$), then lowering r increases human capital only among those with high levels of c. If, on average, these are individuals with high A, that will unambiguously increase inequality. On the other hand, if tax revenues are spent on public education, and public education expenditures are themselves equalize expenditures on human capital, then income inequality may be reduced.

[11] This chapter was originally written in the mid-1970s, when Gary Becker's 1964 book *Human Capital: A Theoretical and Empirical Analysis, with Special Reference to Education*, still had enormous influential. It was written before more own work with Andrew Weiss on credit rationing (1981). Becker implicitly assumed that capital markets were far more perfect than they are. With credit rationing, even within the human capital investment framework, changing tax rates may have no effect of investments in education among the credit constrained, but a lowering of the opportunity cost of capital leads to more investment in education about the wealth. This analysis would suggest that the lowering of the taxation of capital relative to wages that occurred between the decades after the war to the beginning of the twenty-first century should have led to a lowering of wage inequalities, as those at the top faced a greater increase in the opportunity cost of capital relative to the returns. See the discussion in the next paragraph.

This whole analysis needs to be taken with a grain of skepticism, such for the vast majority, education is publicly provided, with the levels of education provided a result of collective decisions. For a discussion of the determinants of those decisions, see Stiglitz (1974h, 1973a, 1986b) and Atkinson and Stiglitz (1980).

On the other hand, since higher education gives access to jobs with more non-pecuniary benefits, which are not taxed, it may be that, at the margin, the effective tax rate on the return to human capital is lower than that on physical capital.

This is still a partial analysis, for differences in the after-tax cost of capital are related to differences in parental income; thus, the increased inequality of wage income might lead to an increase in inequality of inherited income, and thus the total degree of inequality is magnified.

We postpone until Section 3 a detailed description of a dynamic model with human capital accumulation.

2.1.2 Screening

The above analysis assumed that education increased individuals' productivities. But the analysis only required that there be a private return to education—the return could be from screening; education provides information concerning individuals' relative abilities. Lowering the opportunity cost of capital encourages individuals to invest in more screening. By its very nature, screening increases inequality (see Stiglitz, 1975a).

2.1.3 Labor Supply

The labor supply elasticities of different incomes may be different; if the tax reduces the supply of labor less for high income individuals than low-income individuals, it will increase observed income inequality. Here we are concerned with capital taxes, so that the supply elasticity we are concerned with is the response of labor to a change in the after-tax rate of interest. If higher-income individuals retire at a later age, the rate of interest may play a smaller role in labor supply decisions. This effect is likely, however, to be weak, and we only mention it as a possibility.

2.1.4 Distribution of Lifetime Incomes

Individuals' wages differ from year to year, in a somewhat stochastic manner. In the long run, many of these stochastic elements even out, some individuals being lucky this year, others lucky next. When the after-tax rate of interest is low, the sequence of incomes, that is, whether one first has a good year followed by a bad year, or a bad year followed by a good year, makes no difference; but if the interest rate is high, the sequence is important. Thus, an interest income tax which lowers the after-tax rate of interest reduces the degree of inequality in the present discounted value of wage income. Consider a simple model in which the probability that an individual with income w_i has an income w_j next period a_{ij}. Assume the matrix $A = \{a_{ij}\}$ is indecomposable. Then in the limit, at a zero interest rate with infinite-lived individuals, average income is independent of initial income; there is complete equality. On the other hand, with an infinite rate of interest, in the steady state, the distribution of lifetime incomes is just equal to the eigenvector of A, that is, it is given by the vector w^*, where

$$w^*A = w^*.$$

The next three effects are directly concerned with the distribution of inheritances. In this subsection, we discuss a non-stochastic dynamic model, while in the next two we formulate stochastic models.

2.1.5 Dependence of Inheritances on Wage Income

If individuals bequeath to their children an amount which is a function of their own income, and if children's wages are perfectly correlated with parental wages, then it can easily be shown that the distribution of inherited wealth will be simply related to the distribution of wage income (including any governmental transfers). The greater the inequality of wage income, the greater the inequality of inherited wealth. Since redistributive capital taxes increase the equality of wage income (after taxes and transfers), they will increase the degree of equality of inheritances. This effect may be the most significant effect of those discussed. On the other hand, to the extent that the first three arguments presented above are applicable (concerning human capital accumulation, screening, and labor supply decision), so that wage income inequality is increased, there will be a "magnification effect," that is, capital income inequality will thereby also be increased.

2.1.6 Life-Cycle Accumulation and Unanticipated Deaths

This and the next argument are concerned with stochastic, dynamic models giving rise to inequality. The date of death of an individual is stochastic, and individuals cannot obtain complete life insurance (i.e., buy annuities which are actuarially fair). This is partly due to the fact that individuals are better informed concerning their health prospects than are firms, and hence there is a process of adverse selection at work: those who are the worst risk have the strongest incentive to purchase insurance (see Stiglitz, 1975c). The absence of perfect annuity markets means that individuals will normally have some wealth at the time of their death. The amount of wealth they have to leave to their heirs depends on how soon after retirement they die. Lowering the rate of interest implies that individuals have to save more to provide for an adequate income in their retirement. Thus, at the date of retirement, they may have more capital. This means that the degree of inequality of inherited wealth may be increased.

On the other hand, the lower after-tax rate of interest discourages lifetime saving, and if this effect dominates, the degree of inequality will be reduced.

The final important way that capital taxation changes the distribution of wealth in the long run is through its effect on risk taking. Elsewhere in the literature, there has been an extensive discussion of the effect of taxation on risk taking. In Section 3, we present a further analysis of this problem. The major conclusion of these studies is that, under not unreasonable conditions, the tax structure may lead to increased risk taking, and indeed to an increased (or unchanged) variance in after-tax income: to the extent that this is the case, inequality will be increased (or unchanged), not only directly, through its effect on the distribution of incomes, with given capital, but indirectly, through its effect on the inheritances of different individuals (this is analogous to the magnification effect discussed in connection with wage inequality in Section 2.1.5 above).[12]

[12] To the extent that there are limited loss offsets (which in most countries there are), higher capital taxation may reduce risk-taking, with the opposite effects of those just described (see Stiglitz, 1969a).

2.2 The Effect of Taxation on Factors Prices and the Effect of Changes in Factor Prices on the Distribution of Income

We wish to show here that:

(i) taxation may have an important effect on changes in factor supplies, and
(ii) the changes in factor supplies may, in turn, have a deleterious effect on the distribution of income and wealth.

There are two types of effects; one operating through the aggregate supply of factors, the other through the allocation of the factors.

2.2.1 Aggregate Factor Supplies

The argument here consists of three steps:

(i) The tax structure affects the aggregate supply of labor and capital. Here we focus entirely on the latter.
(ii) The changes in aggregate capital–labor ratio change the factor distribution of income.
(iii) The changes in the factor distribution of income in turn result in a change in the personal distribution of wealth.

We present three arguments for why capital and inheritance taxation may lower the supply of savings.

(a) The first, and perhaps most widely discussed effect arises from the differences in savings propensities of those who are taxed (the wealthy) and those who, in effect, receive the benefits of the tax (the poor). The magnitude of this depends on the magnitude of the differences in savings propensities.
(b) The second effect is the "incentive" effect; conventionally, it has been argued that its effects are ambiguous, with the substitution effect leading to less wealth left to one's heirs; but to leave that amount to one's heirs, one has to save more, so that if the elasticity of supply of net inheritances is less than unity, savings are actually increased.

But this analysis ignores the intergenerational redistributive nature of the tax. Individuals who receive (after tax) less in inheritances are likely to reduce the size of their bequests. It is simplest to analyze the net effect of the tax if we assume all individuals have identical, homothetic indifference maps between their consumption and consumption of their heirs. (Then the marginal propensities to save are identical, and, in the traditional discussions, focusing only on differences in saving propensities, there would accordingly be no effect on savings.) This assumption means that we can focus completely on a representative individual, ignoring—for the purpose of calculating the effect on savings—the distribution of wealth. We assume that the inheritance tax is levied at the end of the individual's life, and the proceeds are distributed uniformly in the population. For purposes of this analysis, we totally ignore life-cycle savings. The only wealth is assumed to be associated with bequests. For simplicity, we assume a constant population, though the analysis may be easily generalized.

The before-tax equilibrium (at fixed interest rate) can now be represented diagrammatically as in Figure 33.2. w_t is the wage, b_t is the bequest he receives, while b_{t+1} is the behest he gives $w_t + b_t$ is the lifetime "wealth" of the individual. His budget constraint is given by

$$C_t + \frac{b_{t+1}}{1 + r_t} = w_t + b_t, \tag{33.6}$$

where, for simplicity, we have assumed a zero rate of population growth (so all variables are per capita), and where r_t is the rate of interest, and C is his consumption. The budget constraint is given by the line BB in Figure 33.2.

By the homotheticity assumption we have:

$$b_{t+1} = s[1 + r_t](w_t + b_t)(1 + r_t), \tag{33.7}$$

where $s[1 + r_t]$ is the savings rate (or perhaps better, bequest rate), a function of r_t. Hence, in steady state

$$b = \frac{sw(1 + r)}{1 - s(1 + r)}, \tag{33.8}$$

b is just the capital stock per capita. Hence, if $f(b)$ is the output per man as a function of capital per man (assuming a constant return to scale technology), and if factors get paid their marginal product, we can rewrite (33.7) to read (assuming rational expectations, that is, individuals in making their savings decision at time t know the return at time $t + 1$ will be $f'(b_{t+1})$)

$$b_{t+1} = (f(b_t) - b_t f'(b_t) + b_t)\, s(1 + f'(b_{t+1}))(1 + f') \tag{33.9}$$

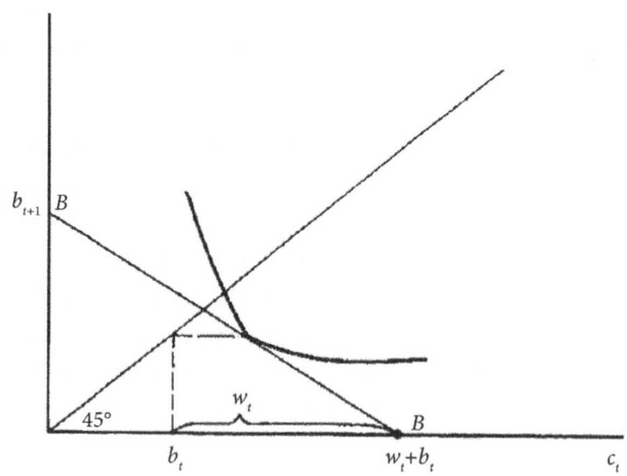

Figure 33.2 An individual inheriting b_t allocates his lifetime wealth between his own consumption and a bequest to his descendants.

or

$$\zeta(b_{t+1}) \equiv \frac{b_{t+1}}{s(1+f'(b_{t+1}))(1+f')} = f(b_t) - b_t f'(b_t) + b_t \equiv \varphi(b_t). \qquad (33.9')$$

Assuming that ζ is invertible (a sufficient condition for which is that $s' \geq 0$), we obtain:

$$b_{t+1} = \zeta^{-1}(\varphi(b_t)) \equiv \Phi(b_t). \qquad (33.9'')$$

The individual's choice decision (with utility a function of consumption and bequests) is illustrated in Figure 33.2, where consumption is along the horizontal axis. The maximum feasible consumption is the individual's wage plus the bequest he receives. In the steady state, of course, the bequest received must be equal to the bequest given, i.e. $b_{t+1} = b_t$, that is, the value of b for which $b^* = \Phi(b^*)$. (33.9′) is depicted in Figure 33.3.[13]

The imposition of an inheritance tax changes the dynamic equation to read

$$b_{t+1} = [f(b_t) - b_t f'(b_t) + b_t]\, s[b_t, \tau](1-\tau)(1+f') = \hat{\varphi}(b_t). \qquad (33.10)$$

It is immediate that b^* is lowered if (and only if) $\frac{d\,\ln s}{d\ln(1+r)} < 1$; the steady state capital stock is lowered and rate of interest increased.[14] If there are differences in marginal propensities

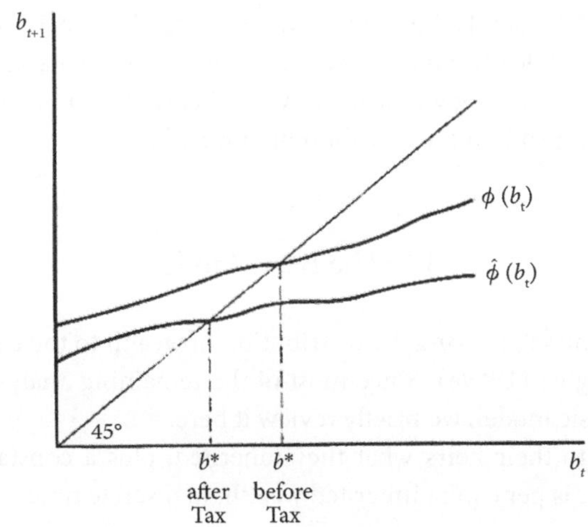

Figure 33.3 For each value of b_t there is an equilibrium b_{t+1}, with b_{t+1} increasing with b_t. Steady state entails $b_t = b_{t+1}$, i.e. where the curve crosses the 45 degree line. Changes in capital taxes (or inheritance taxes) shift the function up or down, and thus increase or decrease the steady state.

[13] We assume the stability condition:

$$\varphi' = (1 - bf'')(1+r)s + \left(\frac{s'}{s} + \frac{1}{1+r}\right) f''\varphi < 1$$

is satisfied.

[14] This assumes that the size of the bequest does not depend on the size of the redistributive payments provided to the next generation. If it does, then it is more likely that the equilibrium bequest will be reduced.

to save out of income the likelihood of a redistributive capital tax lowering the steady state capital stock is greater.

(c) The third way capital taxation may lower the rate of savings is through its effect on life-cycle savings; and because death is stochastic, different patterns of life-cycle savings will result in different levels of inherited wealth as we argued above (Section 2.1.6).

2.2.2 Implications of Reduced Savings for the Distribution of Income and Wealth

If the tax structure leads to a reduced level of savings, capital's share in input will increase when the elasticity of substation between capital and labor is less than unity. And since wealth is generally more unequally distributed than labor, this will increase the degree of inequality of income.

3 Models of Wealth and Income Distribution

In Section 3, we present some simple models explicitly showing the effect of taxation on the distribution of income and wealth. Section 3.1 presents the basic dynamic model; Sections 3.2 and 3.3 extend the basic model to include random interest income and random wages. Section 3.4 extends the analysis to screening. Section 3.5 analyzes the effect of the uncertain timing of death. Finally, Section 3.6 presents a general argument that with interest deductibility, a seemingly redistributive capital tax (with full loss offsets) will have no effect on risk taking and on the distribution of wealth.

3.1 The Basic Model

The basic dynamic model, relating the distribution of wealth to the distribution of wages, was presented in Stiglitz (1969a). Since most of the remaining analysis can be viewed as extensions of this basic model, we briefly review it here.

Individuals leave to their heirs what they inherited, plus a constant fraction of their lifetime income;[15] if c is per capita inherited wealth, in discrete time:

$$c_{t+1} = \frac{sy_t + c_t}{1+n}, \tag{33.11}$$

where s is the fraction of (lifetime) income, y_t, given to one's heirs, and n is the rate of growth of population. Income consists of wage income plus return on (inherited) capital:

$$y_t = w_t + rc_t, \tag{33.12}$$

[15] The analysis is little changed if, in instead, it is assumed that what individuals leave to their children is a function of $y_t + c_t$.

where the wage of a child is exactly equal to that of the parent. Thus, we obtain a simple difference equation relating c_{t+1} to c_t:

$$c_{t+1} = \frac{sw_t + src_t + c_t}{1+n} \tag{33.13}$$

or, in continuous time,

$$\dot{c} = sw + (sr - n)\, c, \tag{33.14}$$

yielding a steady state distribution of inherited wealth:

$$c^* = \frac{sw^*}{n - sr}, \tag{33.15}$$

which is a simple transformation of the wage distribution. Implicitly, we have assumed that the child's wage is perfectly correlated with the parent's wage. Later, we shall show how this assumption affects the analysis.

An immediate implication of (33.15) is that the coefficient of variation of per capita wealth is just equal to the coefficient of variation of w. Notice that one of the strong implications of this model is that if wages were equal, wealth would eventually be equalized. The fact that the rate of growth of population exceeds net savings out of interest income, sr, means that there is a strong equalizing force resulting from dividing one's wealth equally among one's heirs.

If individuals differ from one another in a pure labor augmenting way (i.e., one able individual is equivalent to λ less able individuals, where λ is independent of the capital–labor ratio), then the coefficient of variation of before-tax wages is a constant, unaffected by the capital–labor ratio.

The aggregate capital–labor ratio is simply the average per capita capital stock of the entire population, that is,

$$k \equiv Ec = \frac{sEw}{n - sr} = \frac{s\bar{w}}{n - sr},$$

where a bar over a variable represents its average value and E is the expectations operator.

In subsequent sections we shall modify and extend the model by allowing for (a) random return on capital; (b) random wage rates; (c) human capital accumulation.

3.2 Random Return on Capital

If we assume that the return on capital is random, then asymptotically, wealth will not be evenly distributed. Let $\rho(c)$ be the random distribution of returns; we assume that it may depend on c, perhaps because of the portfolio allocation decisions. Let

$$u = ln\, c$$

so

$$e^u = c.$$

Then, assuming returns are described by a simple diffusion process[16] we have (in the absence of taxation) the stochastic differential equation describing capital accumulation:

$$du = \left[swe^{-u} + (s\bar{\rho} - n) - \frac{s^2\alpha(u)}{2}\right]dt + s\sqrt{\alpha(u)}dW_t \tag{33.17}$$

where $\alpha(u)$ is the instantaneous variance of the rate of return, ρ, on wealth. Thus, if $a(u)$ is the proportion of wealth invested in a risky asset whose return is e, and if the safe return is r,

$$\rho \equiv a(u)(e - r) + r \tag{33.18a}$$

$$\bar{\rho} = a(u)(\bar{e} - r) + r \tag{33.18b}$$

then

$$\alpha(u) = a^2\sigma_e^2, \tag{33.19}$$

where σ_e^2 is the variance of e. The asymptotic wealth distribution $h(c)$ satisfies the differential equation:[17]

$$\frac{1}{2}\alpha s^2 h'' + \left[s^2\alpha' - (swe^{-u} + s\bar{\rho} - n) + \frac{s^2\alpha}{2}\right]h' + \left[\frac{1}{2}s^2\alpha'' + swe^{-u} - s \rightarrow \bar{\rho}' + \frac{s^2\alpha'}{2}\right]h = 0. \tag{33.20}$$

In particular, if

$$a \rightarrow a^* \text{ as } u \rightarrow \infty$$

$$a' \rightarrow 0 \text{ as } u \rightarrow \infty$$

then for large u

$$\frac{h''}{h'} \rightarrow \frac{2(s\bar{\rho} - n)}{a^2\sigma_e^2 s^2} - 1. \tag{33.21}$$

Now define

$$\hat{\sigma}_y = \sqrt{\frac{a^2\sigma_e^2 k^2}{\bar{y}^2}}$$

16 To our knowledge, this, along with the work of Bevan (1974) and Bevan and Stiglitz (1979) were the earliest known examples of the use of diffusion models to analyze income distribution. Since then, there have been many other examples. See the introduction to Part II.A above.

17 The distribution of u is given by the solution to the Kolmogorov equation:

$$\frac{\alpha}{2}h'' - \left(\beta - \frac{\alpha}{2} - \alpha'\right)h' + \left(\frac{\alpha''}{2} - \beta' + \frac{\alpha'}{2}\right)h = \frac{dh}{dt}. \tag{33.16}$$

Asymptotically, $[\frac{dh}{dt} = 0$. In this problem $\beta = swe^{-u} + (s\bar{\rho} - n)$ and $\beta' = -swe^{-u} + s\rho'$.

and

$$s\overline{w} = -s\overline{p}k + nk.$$

Hence:

$$-\frac{h''}{h'} \rightarrow \frac{2\overline{w}}{\overline{y}}\frac{k}{s\overline{y}}\frac{1}{\hat{\sigma}_y^2} + 1 = \frac{2\overline{w}}{n\overline{y}}\frac{1}{\hat{\sigma}_y^2} + 1 = \frac{2S_L}{n}\frac{1}{\hat{\sigma}_y^2} + 1, \tag{33.21'}$$

where S_L is the share of labor. The equation provides a simple formula relating the Pareto tail coefficient to the share of labor, the rate of growth, With redistributive taxation, the asymptotic degree of inequality (the coefficient of the Pareto tail) will be affected through the effect on $s, \overline{p}$ and $a\sigma_e$. Those changes, in turn, will lead to changes in k and w. For instance, later we show that a redistributive capital tax with full interest deductibility with the proceeds given uniformly to all individuals is fully shifted and has no effect on the coefficient of variation in y, so that the Pareto tail is unaffected. But that might not be true if (a) there are not full loss offsets; (b) the proceeds of the tax are redistributed progressively; or (c) savings rates are not constant. If there are not full loss offsets, then the tax reduces the average return to risk taking, because it leaves the investor with the downside but takes away the upside. Then there will be less risk taking, and the Pareto tail inequality would decrease as a result of the tax. Moreover, taxation has substitution and wealth effects; and the latter can, in general, affect both savings rates and portfolio composition.[18] There are also general equilibrium effects: if savings rates increase with income and wealth, redistribution will lead to a lower average savings rate, a lower asymptotic capital–labor ratio and wage and a higher average return to capital. This will weaken the restorative force in the economy, and hence on this account lead to increased tail inequality. One is, of course, concerned not just with tail inequality but also with broader measures of inequality, which we discuss in the next section.

3.3 A Stochastic Model of Wage and Capital Accumulation

In the models formulated thus far, the productivity of the child is identical to the productivity of the parent. This is inconsistent with the widely noted phenomenon of rags to riches in three generations. A more realistic model would involve the famous law of regression toward the mean; the purpose of this section is to formulate such a model. To obtain simple analytical results, we again shall use a diffusion model.

We define:

$$A = ln\, w \tag{33.22}$$

(where w is the wage). A is the "ability" of the individual. Without loss of generality, let $E[A] = 0$. We assume that the average ability of the immediate heirs lies between the ability

[18] If individuals exhibit decreasing relative risk aversion, as they become wealthier, they allocate a larger fraction of their wealth to the risky asset.

of the parent and the average ability in the population. On the other hand, there is considerable randomness in inheritance; some children are brighter than their parents (even if their parents are above average). Let $\alpha(A)$ be the instantaneous variance of inheritance, and $\beta(A)$ be the average rate of regression toward the mean; then

$$dA = -\beta(A)(A - E[A])\,dt + \sqrt{\alpha(A)}\sqrt{dt}. \tag{33.23}$$

The functions β and α completely determine the asymptotic distribution of income. In particular, if we assume that the instantaneous variance of A is constant (since A is the logarithm of wages, this is equivalent to a constant instantaneous coefficient of variation in w) and β is also constant (the average child's ability lies a constant fraction of the way between the parents' ability and the mean ability), then the asymptotic ability distribution is the normal distribution with variance equal to:[19]

$$\sigma_A^2 = \frac{\alpha}{2\beta}. \tag{33.24}$$

Note that since ability is the logarithm of wages, wages are lognormally distributed.

The effect of taxation on the asymptotic distribution of wages can easily be ascertained in terms of their effects on the functions α and β.

For instance, let us divide ability into natural ability ("nature") and "environmental" ability ("nurture")

$$A = A^n + A^e,$$

[19] The Kolmogorov equation (fn. 17 above) becomes:

$$\frac{1}{2}\alpha f'' + \beta A f' + \beta f = 0.$$

For the normal distribution

$$f = \frac{1}{2\pi\sigma_A}\exp\left(-\frac{A^2}{2\sigma_A^2}\right), \text{ when } E[A] = 0.$$

Hence

$$f' = f\frac{A^2}{2\sigma_A^2},$$

$$f'' = \frac{fA^2}{2\sigma_A^4} - \frac{f}{\sigma_A^4}.$$

Thus, we require:

$$\frac{1}{2}\alpha\left(\frac{A^2}{\sigma_A^4} - \frac{1}{\sigma_A^2}\right) - \beta\frac{A^2}{\sigma_A^2} + \beta = 0,$$

i.e.

$$\frac{\alpha}{2\sigma_A^2} = \beta \text{ or } {\sigma_A}^2 = \frac{\alpha}{2\beta}.$$

A follows what is known as an Ornstein-Uhlenbeck process.

where environmental ability is a function of human capital:

$$A^e = A^n v(c_w).$$

Then

$$A = \frac{A^n}{1 - v}. \tag{33.25}$$

If A^n is described by the diffusion process, so will A. If an inheritance tax encourages human capital transfers, v increases for all positive values of A (all A above average) and decreases all negative A (A below average), thus increasing inequality of wage income.

Regression toward the mean provides an explanation of why parents with above-average abilities leave money to their children; on average, their descendants will be less able than they are. If the parent's utility function includes descendants' utility functions with a discount factor, and children's utility functions are identical to those of parents, then the problem of deciding on the amount to leave to one's children is formally equivalent to the problem of determining the optimal savings rate with a stochastic wage described by a diffusion process with a drift. We shall not address ourselves to that question but will limit ourselves to the simpler one of describing the consequences of parents following certain simple rules of inheritance.

The natural extension of (33.14) would be to write:

$$dc = [s(w + \hat{r}c) - c]\, dt \tag{33.26}$$

(where $\hat{r}$ is the after-tax return on capital) or, letting

$$u = ln\, c.$$

And recalling that

$$A = ln\, w$$

$$\left[(s\hat{r} - n) + se^{A-u}\right] dt. \tag{33.27}$$

The pair of s.d.e. (33.23) and (33.27) need to be solved simultaneously, for the joint distribution of {A(t), u(t)}, or more relevantly, for {(w(t), c(t)}, and in particular for the joint equilibrium distribution. Analyzing the properties of the equilibrium distribution must await another occasion.[20]

3.4 Screening and Education

The private returns to education consist not only of the increased productivity, but also in the screening of individuals according to ability. It has been shown that screening may

[20] Some results are reported above in Chapter 12.

increase inequality of income (see Stiglitz, 1975a). Capital taxation, by lowering the after-tax rate of return (the opportunity cost of screening), encourages screening, and thus could lead to more inequality.

Consider the following slight modification of the model presented earlier. Let there be two groups in the population (A_1, A_2) with $A_1 > A_2$. Assume productivity (and A) are not easily observable, so firms use the education level as a screening device. Assume, moreover, that the cost of education, of staying in school (passing exams) through a particular education level is inversely proportional to A.[21] We let E be the educational level, $w = w(A, E)$, and c_w, the expenditure on education (in the previous example we did not distinguish between E and c_w) is $c_w = Em(A)$ where $m' > 0$.

The productivity curves for the two groups are depicted in Figure 33.4. With perfect information, each group would purchase education to the point where[22]

$$\frac{dw}{dE} = \hat{r}m(A). \tag{33.28}$$

With imperfect information, if there is an equilibrium, it is one in which the more able purchase enough education to separate themselves off from the less able, that is, they purchase a sufficiently large amount that the less able (lower A) decide not to try to become identified with the more able. The equilibrium is depicted in Figure 33.4 and is described analytically[23] by the values of $\{E_1, E_2\}$ that solve (33.29) and (33.30):

$$w(A_2, E_2) + m(A_2)\hat{r}(E_1 - E_2) = w(A_1, E_1). \tag{33.29}$$

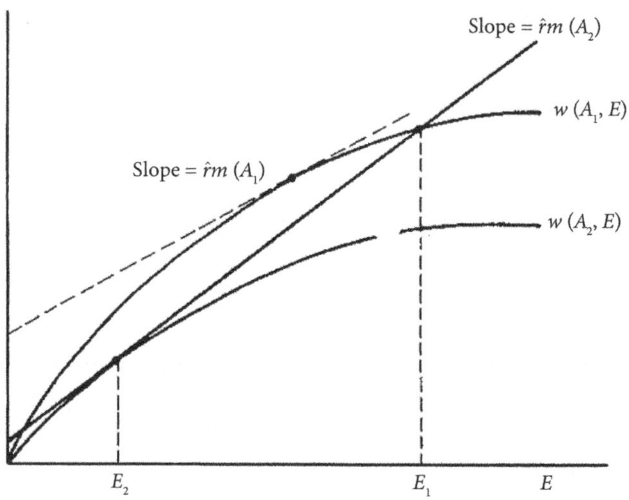

Figure 33.4 Education as a screening/signaling/sorting mechanism. A change in the interest rate affects the separating equilibrium.

21 We assume that the time and effort required by the more able is so much less than that required by the less able that it offsets the fact that the opportunity cost of time of the more able exceeds that of the less able.

22 Discounted income is $w(A, E) - rc_w = w(A, E) - rEm(A)$.

23 That is, the net wage of the less able if they stay with their own group, $w(A_2, E_2) - \hat{r}m(A_2)E_2$ is exactly the same as if they pretend to be able to be one of the more able, $w(A_1, E_1) - \hat{r}m(A_2)E_1$.

(Equation (33.29) is the self-selection constraint, which we assume is binding.)

$$\frac{dw(A_2, E_2)}{dE_2} = \hat{r}m(A_2). \tag{33.30}$$

The effect of a lowering of the after-tax return on physical capital may now be easily ascertained. In the figure, a lower after-tax return lowers the slope of $\hat{r}m(A_2)$ and hence leads to a higher level of education of the less able. That means the more able have to get a higher level of education to "separate." But the magnitude of the increase in w_1 depends on the global properties of $w(A_1, E_1)$. The ratio of wages (the extent of inequality) could either increase or decrease.

We can see this analytically. Let $w(A, E)$ take on the special form:

$$w = Ag(E). \tag{33.31}$$

Then

$$\frac{d\ln E_2}{d\ln\hat{r}} = \frac{1}{\frac{g''E_2}{g'}} \equiv -\frac{1}{\xi_2} < 0 \tag{33.32}$$

if the self-selection constraint is binding:

$$\frac{d\ln E_1}{d\ln\hat{r}} = \frac{m(A_2)\hat{r}(E_1 - E_2)}{(A_1 g' - \hat{r}m(A_2))E_1} < 0. \tag{33.33}$$

Using (33.29)–(33.31), we can rewrite (33.33) as

$$\frac{d\ln E_1}{d\ln\hat{r}} = \frac{w_2\eta_2(E_1 - E_2)/E_2}{w_1(\eta_1 - 1) - (\eta_2 - 1)w_2} < 0, \tag{33.34}$$

where

$$\eta_i = \frac{g'(E_i)E_i}{g(E_i)},$$

the elasticity of wages (productivity) with respect to education, which we assume is less than unity. An increase in $\hat{r}$ lowers the value of E_2 and the value of E_1 that separates.

Wages inequality can be measured in this case simply by w_1/w_2:

$$\begin{aligned}\frac{d\ln\frac{w_1}{w_2}}{d\ln\hat{r}} &= \frac{g'E_1}{g}\frac{d\ln E_1}{d\ln\hat{r}} - \frac{g'E_2}{g}\frac{d\ln E_2}{d\ln\hat{r}}\\ &= \frac{\eta_2}{\xi_2} - \frac{w_2\eta_2(E_1 - E_2)/E_2}{w_1(\eta_1 - 1) - (\eta_2 - 1)w_2}\end{aligned} \tag{33.35}$$

Clearly, if ξ_2 is large, this may be negative. In this case, lowering the after-tax return to capital increases inequality (and conversely for small ξ_2). The effects of capital taxation are ambiguous. But in the case of a constant elasticity function $g(E) = E^{\eta}$ with $\eta < 1$, $\xi_2 = \eta - 1$, and (33.35) becomes (in the obvious notation):

$$\frac{d\ln\frac{w_1}{w_2}}{d\ln\hat{r}} = \frac{\eta}{\eta - 1}\left\{1 - \frac{\frac{\Delta E}{E}}{\frac{\Delta w}{w}}\right\} > 0. \tag{33.35'}$$

Then the lowering of the cost of capital increases both E_1 and E_2, and thus both the wage of high and low ability individuals, as we have already noted; but the increase in the former is proportionately greater than that of the latter, so inequality increases.

What matters, of course, is after-tax incomes. An increase in taxes in both wages and capital, the effects on investments in education may be very limited. In fact, since much of the investment is "effort," and not affected by taxation (in the individual's youth, the individual does not face significant taxation so the opportunity cost of time or effort is not affected by taxation) but the return to education is taxed, the effect of taxation is just the opposite of that just depicted: E_2 is reduced, and this in turn reduces (screening induced) wage differences and the extent of inequality. Perhaps still more realistically, for the bulk of the populace, education levels are determined publicly. Hence E_2 is unchanged, and so is E_1 .

3.5 Stochastic Death and Imperfect Annuity Markets

We suggested earlier that an important source of inequality of inheritance is the stochastic nature of death; this means, if there are imperfect annuity markets, that the amount inherited depends on the "luck" of the timing of the death of one's parents; if it is shortly after retirement, one will inherit a considerable amount; if later, one will inherit much less.

The full formalization of this is quite complicated, and ought to take into account parents' concern for the welfare of their heirs. The following seems the simplest model which captures the effect.[24] In this model, parents obtain no explicit "utility" from giving bequests to their children. Assume individuals live for at most two periods. They work in the first for a wage w_0, and inherit capital, K_0, but choose a consumption rate to spread their consumption C evenly over their maximum life, that is, if r is the rate of interest:

$$C\left(1 + \frac{1}{1+r}\right) = w_0 + K_0 \tag{33.36}$$

or, letting $\lambda = 1/(1 + r)$,

$$C = \frac{w_0 + K_0}{1 + \lambda}. \tag{33.37}$$

The savings of workers for retirement are thus:

$$w_0 + K_0 - C_0 = \frac{\lambda}{1 + \lambda}(w_0 + K_0) = \frac{1}{2 + r}(w_0 + K_0), \tag{33.38}$$

[24] In the original paper, I presented a three-period model. The essence of the analysis can be presented more simply in the two-period rendition given here.

If a fraction $\frac{1}{2}$ of the individuals died at the end of their retirement, then $\frac{1}{2}$ of the individuals will have inherited zero wealth; of the remainder, $\frac{1}{2}$ will have parents who have inherited nothing, and so their inheritance is just $\hat{s}w_0$ where $\hat{s} \equiv \frac{1+r}{2+r}$ is the "marginal propensity of inheritances," that is, the marginal propensity to bequeath, times $1 + r$, since the bequests are received at the beginning of the next period, and include the return on capital; of the remainder, $\frac{1}{2}$ will have grandparents who have inherited nothing, and so their inheritance is just $(w_0 s + w_0)\hat{s} = (\hat{s} + \hat{s}^2) w_0$. More generally, $\left(\frac{1}{2}\right)^n$ of the population will inherit a wealth of

$$\frac{\hat{s} - \hat{s}^n}{1 - s} w_0. \tag{33.39}$$

This generates for large n a Pareto distribution with slope

$$\frac{d\,ln\,(1 - H)}{d\,ln\,c} \approx -\frac{ln\,2}{ln\,\hat{s}'}$$

where H is the wealth distribution function and c is the (per capita) inheritance.

What concerns us here is the effect of a change in the tax rate on inheritances on the wealth distribution. With interest income taxes at the rate t,

$$\hat{s} \equiv \frac{1 + r(1 - t)}{2 + r(1 - t)}$$

$$\frac{d\hat{s}}{dt} \geq 0.$$

The interest income tax increases the savings required to sustain consumption in retirement, and this effect more than offsets the reduction in bequests as a result of the reduced after-tax return. Hence inequality of inherited wealth increases.[25]

On the other hand, a bequest tax at the rate γ reduces the amount received by the descendant who is "lucky" enough to inherit, so now the wealth is given by

$$\frac{\hat{s\gamma} - \hat{s}^n \gamma^n}{1 - s\gamma} w_0. \tag{33.39'}$$

Implying that a bequest tax results in less inequality.

3.6 Effect of Redistributive Inheritance and Capital Taxation on Risk Taking

It has long been recognized (Domar and Musgrave, 1944; Stiglitz, 1976b; Mossin, 1968) that a proportional tax with full losses offset provisions would increase risk taking because the government acts as a partner in losses as well as gains, effectively sharing risk. These

[25] If individuals have an explicit bequest motive which affects the size of their bequest, the fact that individuals have a significant probability of giving a larger bequest (if they die early) will mitigate their bequest "savings," so that the overall increase in savings will be less than the above equation suggests, and therefore the increase in the degree of inequality will be smaller.

studies, however, ignored the effects of the proceeds of the tax. When these are taken into account, if interest is deductible, aggregate risk taking is completely unaffected, but there is complete shifting of the tax.

Let $H(W_0)$ denote a distribution function of initial wealth, W_0; $a(W_0)$ be the proportion allocated to the risky investment, which yields a return of e; r, the safe return; and t, the proportional tax rate. We assume full loss offset and interest deductibility.

Assume that the proceeds of the tax were redistributed as a lump sum payment. Let U be the utility function and we assume that the risk-averse individual maximizes $E[U(W)]$ where W is (terminal) wealth, and $U'' < 0$. Then the first order condition for portfolio allocation is

$$EU'\left\{W_0\left(a(e-r)(1-t)+r\right)+\overline{aW}(e-r)t\right\}(e-r)=0, \tag{33.40}$$

where

$$\overline{aW}=E[aW_0],$$

aggregate expenditure on risk taking, the expectation being taken on the entire population.

We need to calculate:

$$\begin{aligned}\frac{da}{dt}&=-\frac{E\left[U''\left(\overline{aW}-aW_0\right)(e-r)^2\right]}{E\left[U''(e-r)^2(1-t)W_0\right]} \\ &=-\frac{\overline{aW}-aW_0}{(1-t)W_0}.\end{aligned} \tag{33.41}$$

Hence the change in aggregate risk taking is

$$\int W_0\frac{da}{dt}dH(W_0)=-\frac{1}{1-t}\int\left(\overline{aW}-aW_0\right)dH(W_0)=0. \tag{33.42}$$

A capital tax with interest deductibility has absolutely no effect at all on aggregate risk taking. Indeed, letting W be the terminal wealth, with

$$W\equiv W_0\left[a(e-r)(1-t)+r\right]+\overline{aW}(e-r)t \tag{33.43}$$

and differentiating with respect to t, using (33.41), we immediately observe that proportional taxation with interest deductibility has no effect on the distribution of income. The redistributive effects of the tax are precisely offset by changes in the portfolio composition.

However, if there is not an interest deductibility provision, then the capital tax may either cause aggregate risk bearing to increase or decrease. There are income and substitution effects at work at each level of wealth, with the income (wealth) effects from the reduction in wealth partial (or more than) offsetting those arising from the increase in wealth below, but all groups experiencing a substitution effect.

4 Concluding Remarks

Progressive taxation may reduce inequality significantly. In the model of Section 3.3, for instance, tail inequality is related to the top marginal tax rate, and the regressive tax system in the U.S. (where the top marginal rate is so low and where inheritance taxation can be evaded) undoubtedly contributes to the extremes of wealth inequality.[26] But while there is some presumption that is the case, there is the possibility that general equilibrium incidence effects, or even responses of just wealthy individuals—if not offset by other government actions—could undo these benefits, and possibly even exacerbate inequality.

There are two other important issues, which seem to be the subject of much popular discussion: (i) political power: excessive concentration of wealth often, it is argued, leads to accumulation of political power, and this may affect the nature of our political processes; (ii) mobility and equal opportunity: we have focused on steady state distributions, not on differences in life chances of individuals born of different parents; much of the recent concern with income distribution has been concerned more with equalizing opportunity than with equalizing the distribution of income itself.

[26] The paper from which this chapter has been drawn was written before the large reductions in top marginal tax rates that occurred under President Reagan, the favorable tax treatment of capital gains, that occurred under Presidents George W. Bush and Bill Clinton, and the lowering of inheritance tax rates under Bush.

PART III.F
DISCRIMINATION

Introduction to Part III.F

Much of this book is about the extremes of inequality of income and wealth at the top. Equally or more troubling are the extremes of poverty at the bottom, and one of the major reasons for that, at least in the United States, is the massive racial discrimination which has long been part of American life.

I saw this discrimination as I was growing up in the 1940s and 50s in Gary, Indiana, a seemingly prosperous industrial town in what has sometimes been characterized as the golden era of capitalism—African-Americans living in slums and going to largely segregated schools. I felt it too more personally: when, at the age of 11, I discovered that the gentle, kind, and intelligent woman, Minnae Fae Ellis, who had helped care for me had only a sixth-grade education, I was dumbfounded. How could this be in a rich country like the U.S.? She had grown up in the South, and her experience was little different from so many others.

I switched from studying physics to economics because of my concerns about inequality, including and especially discrimination. It was the era of civil rights, and I was glad to be part of it. As President of the Amherst College Student Council, I organized an exchange program with one of America's premier Historical Black Colleges, Morehouse College, in Atlanta: it was both an education experience and a direct attack on segregation, as we lived in the dormitories of the College. We had no awareness of the dangers that would become more evident as the number of those killed in the civil rights movement mounted. I joined too Martin Luther King's March on Washington, at which he delivered the memorable "I have a Dream" speech.[1]

Thus, to me, one of the challenges of economics was to explain the persistence of discrimination which seemed so inconsonant with the alleged efficiency of a market economy—not to say those values, equality for all, that we were taught essentially defined the country. The book that helped define the subject was Gary Becker's 1957 book, *The Economics of Discrimination*. The thrust of the book was simple: in competitive markets, discrimination can't survive, as those with low wages relative to their productivity will be hired, driving up their demand and working to eliminate the effects of discrimination; market forces will force those with discriminatory preferences to pay a price in lower incomes or profits. (Consumers with discriminatory preferences too will have to pay a price—higher prices for the goods and services they consume.) This implies that, provided only there are

[1] In *The Great Divide* (Stiglitz, 2015h), I relate at greater length my thoughts concerning that March on its fiftieth anniversary.

enough firms and individuals without discriminatory preferences, if there are persistent differences in wages, they must reflect differences in ability. (Of course, as in any good academic book, it was cautioned with caveats and limitations.)

Wedded as he was to the competitive model, Becker could not explain the large differences in unemployment rates between say African Americans and whites (usually twice as high). In the competitive model, there is no unemployment. The implication is clear: if there is unemployment, it is either the government's fault, for example as a result of imposing minimum wages, or the fault of workers colluding together, in unions, from which African Americans were in earlier periods often excluded.

To me, this book symbolized what was wrong with the perfect markets, neoclassical economics that I had so assiduously studied. I knew there was massive discrimination. I had seen it first-hand. If discrimination was inconsistent with competitive markets, it was (another) proof that markets were not competitive or that something else was wrong with the model.[2] I was especially astounded that the argument would come from someone teaching at the University of Chicago, surrounded as it was by a massive ghetto, as bad as those I had seen growing up in Gary. (Gary is only 30 miles from Chicago, and as I was growing up, I often drove through and visited the area around the university.)

And anyone with a sense of history must be offended at the notion that what is currently observed is simply, or even largely, an outcome of competitive processes. Slavery employed markets—slaves were bought and sold—but more than that, it employed power, the power of one group to exploit another, often through the force of arms. Laws, such as those requiring the return of run-away slaves, ensured and enhanced the ability of one group to exploit another. So too, in other countries: in South Africa, the exclusion of Black Africans from agriculture was used to force them to work in the mines. One of the questions we ask in this chapter is how such past legacies lead to systemic differentiation and discrimination today, and what can be done about it.

The two papers in this section were written partly as a response to Becker, to show the ways in which his analysis was flawed and to explain how discrimination could persist. They were also written to frame policy discussions.

In spite of my and others' efforts to explain the limitations of Becker's analysis, it is remarkable how persistent its influence has been. A notable example was a speech before the NBER (the National Bureau of Economic Research) on January 14, 2005 made by Larry Summers, formerly secretary of Treasury under President Clinton and at the time president of Harvard, invoking Becker's reasoning to explain the dearth of women scientists. He suggested that it couldn't be (mostly) discrimination, and that accordingly, it had to be related to intrinsic differences, not necessarily in means, but in standard deviations, with the top scientists being drawn from the tails of the ability distribution.[3]

[2] A theme I take up more thoroughly in Stiglitz (2019a).

[3] The speech, "Remarks at NBER Conference on Diversifying the Science and Engineering Workforce" is available on Harvard's website https://www.harvard.edu/president/news-speeches-summers/2005/remarks-at-nber-conference-on-diversifying-the-science-engineering-workforce/ . Arguing against the role of discrimination, Summers said, almost paraphrasing Becker: "If it was really the case that everybody was discriminating, there would be very substantial opportunities for a limited number of people who were not prepared to discriminate to assemble remarkable departments of high quality people [sic] at relatively limited cost simply by the act of their not discriminating, because of what it would mean for the pool that was available. And there are certainly examples of institutions that have focused on increasing their diversity to their substantial benefit, but if there was really a pervasive pattern of discrimination that was leaving an extraordinary number of high-quality potential candidates behind, one suspects that in the highly competitive academic marketplace, there would be

It has been a big disappointment for me too how little progress there has been in reducing the scope of discrimination. On the occasion of the 50th anniversary of the Kerner Commission,[4] set up in response to the 1968 race riots, I was asked by the Eisenhower Foundation to contribute to a review of the progress that had occurred in the subsequent half century.[5] I concluded that their basic findings still ring true today:

> Our Nation is moving toward two societies, one black, one white—separate and unequal.
> (Kerner Report, p. 1)

The Kerner Commission went on to say[6] that underlying all of this was a diagnosis of the cause:

> the racial attitude and behavior of white Americans toward black Americans. Race prejudice has shaped our history decisively; it now threatens to affect our future.
> (Kerner Report, p. 203)

In my review, I concurred that it had accomplished this through power...

> deep seated and institutional racism [has] continued. New tests of discrimination in hiring and housing revealed the extent: blind resumes were sent, with the only difference being the name of the individual, giving a suggestion of race. Callbacks were markedly different (see Bertrand and Mullainathan, 2004).

Explanations

The key insight of these chapters—besides explaining the fallacies in Becker's analysis—is that there can be persistent differences even among groups that are intrinsically identical if there are imperfections of competition and information, and if preferences, behavior, and productivity are endogenous, affected by the environment in which one lives—including an

more examples of institutions that succeeded substantially by working to fill the gap." He identified several other factors: Differences in the distribution of abilities: "Even small differences in the standard deviation will translate into very large differences in the available pool substantially out." On differences in preferences: "there is reasonably strong evidence of taste differences between little girls and little boys that are not easy to attribute to socialization." On women in work: "The most prestigious activities in our society expect of people who are going to rise to leadership positions in their forties near total commitments to their work. They expect a large number of hours in the office, they expect a flexibility of schedules to respond to contingency, they expect a continuity of effort through the life cycle, and they expect—and this is harder to measure—but they expect that the mind is always working on the problems that are in the job, even when the job is not taking place. And it is a fact about our society that that is a level of commitment that a much higher fraction of married men have been historically prepared to make than of married women."

The speech was pivotal in a no-confidence vote by the faculty, which culminated in his leaving the Presidency of Harvard.

[4] Kerner et al. (1988).

[5] Some of the later sections of this introduction are excerpted from Stiglitz (2018c).

[6] For an earlier description, see Myrdal (1944). One of the striking aspects of the Kerner Commission report was the testimony of Dr. Kenneth B. Clark, reviewing reports on race riots that had occurred over the preceding half century (from 1919 on): "I must again in candor say to you members of this Commission—it is a kind of Alice in Wonderland—with the same moving pictures re-shown over and over again, the same analysis, the same recommendations and the same inaction."

environment of discrimination and exclusion.[7] This goes a step beyond "statistical discrimination" (Phelps, 1972), which suggested that differences in the wages of different groups rationally reflected differences in productivities, by showing that differences in those productivities could themselves be the result of discrimination—there was a vicious cycle at work.

Of course, there was discrimination not only in the marketplace: discrimination in the public provision of the quality and quantity of education meant that African-Americans began with a marked disadvantage. This is another arena in which history matters: past discrimination induces behavioral patterns which, unless contravened explicitly by policy, can be self-sustaining.[8]

There has been extensive segregation and discrimination in housing (still true, almost a half century after legislation banning it.[9]) With education largely locally provided and financed, this has contributed to inequalities in education opportunities.

When combined with poor public transportation—and discrimination in the provision of public transportation connecting African Americans residences with jobs—the consequence is markedly different opportunity sets.

Similarly, gender discrimination in schools, some quite subtle, has meant that women didn't have the same opportunities as men.

Imperfections of capital market have meant that African Americans, with so much less wealth than the rest of the population, were often constrained in how much they could invest in the education of their children. Wealth inequality—and especially poverty at the bottom—has, of course, many other pernicious effects.

Since so much education occurs within the family, discrimination in one generation adversely affects the opportunities of the next: another example of the intergenerational transmission of advantages and disadvantages.[10]

Discrimination has other manifestations, now well documented, in for instance access to housing and exposure to police brutality.

I took all of these inequities as given, and as almost surely providing much of the explanation for pervasive differences in, say, wages and incomes. These two chapters explore a narrower, but still important, question: how the market by itself could sustain discriminatory equilibria. Quite contrary to Becker, they show that an unregulated market economy can in fact exhibit discrimination—what our eyes show us so clearly is not a phantasm.

[7] Since these early papers, the literature has flourished, especially on the empirics. In the context of race, see O'Flaherty (2015).

[8] The endogenous determination of preferences (behavior)—and how preferences and behavior are affected by one's environment, including those among whom lives and interacts, and by history—is discussed below.

[9] Wells Fargo, for instance, paid a large fine to settle allegations that it discriminated in providing mortgages. See Stiglitz (2010a).

[10] There are many others discussed elsewhere in this book, for example the role of connections or just relevant information in access to good jobs.

Imperfections of Competition, Imperfections of Information, Labor Turnover and Other Vicious Circles

As I noted earlier, if it were true that discrimination were inconsistent with competition, the pervasive presence of discrimination would provide strong evidence against the competitive model. The key insights of the discussion here are:

(a) With imperfect competition, the marginal, not the average, costs of different types of labor (workers within different groups) is equated, and that is consistent with paying workers in different groups, even if they have the same productivities, different wages. If outside opportunities differ—if others discriminate against a certain group—then even those with no discriminatory preferences will discriminate.

(b) Discrimination—treating members of different groups differently, with different probabilities of being hired and/or paying those of different groups with the same ability different wages—leads to differences in opportunity sets.

(c) Discrimination—differences in opportunity sets—leads in turn to differences in investment in human capital, in screening, in search. There is thus a vicious circle. There can exist multiple equilibria—a discriminatory equilibrium, but also a non-discriminatory equilibrium. This is perhaps the most novel aspect of Chapter 35: in the absence of information about, say, the quality and quantities of investment in education (not just the number of years of schooling completed, but complementary inputs by the individual), race can convey information. If it is believed that the discriminated against group, at any observed level of education (E) are less productive, they will receive a lower wage; but because they receive a lower wage, it will not pay them to invest as much in education. Thus, the discriminatory equilibrium is self-fulfilling.

(d) Discrimination can have morale effects—those who are discriminated against work less hard because they feel they are being "cheated," and treated unfairly; but because they work less hard, and are accordingly are less productive, those discriminating against them feel justified in discriminating against them. Again, there are multiple equilibria: if one could move to a non-discriminatory equilibrium, it would be self-sustaining.[11]

(e) Social segregation affects information flows, and thus affects the relevant opportunity sets, reinforcing the perpetuation of discriminatory equilibria.

(f) In some cases, there can be no costs to the employer from discrimination, even if there are large social costs, With efficiency wages, there may be unemployment. If all individuals were identical, the employer could without cost select his employees from a favored group.

[11] This is an example of a broader range of issues, discussed under the rubric of "efficiency wages." (See vol. I, Selected Works), and the discussion earlier in this volume. I had originally developed this "morale" argument for the efficiency wage theory (where productivity depends on wages) in my 1969 working paper on "Alternative Theories of Wage Determination and Unemployment" written when I was a visitor at the University of Nairobi Institute for Development Studies in 1969. This idea has since been elaborated and formalized, for example by Akerlof and Yellen (1990).

"Social Capital"

There are two important advances since these chapters were originally written that have enhanced understandings of discrimination. The first is the development of game theory to analyze equilibria with imperfect competition. Critical is the insight that groups can engage in "cooperation" to discriminate against other groups, especially in repeated games with punishments. The "folk theorem" of repeated game theory holds that any Pareto efficient equilibrium can be sustained, including those which enhance the well-being of one group at the expense of others. It is thus easy using such models to explain the persistence of Jim Crow and other segregationist and discriminatory policies: Whites who violate the discriminatory norm are punished; and those who don't punish those who violate the norm are themselves punished, ad infinitum.[12] (This perhaps helps explain the violence against those from outside who were not part of this discriminatory equilibrium: in the absence of effective social sanctions, the only way to sustain the equilibrium was through violence. These models also help explain how, once the outside intervention was eliminated to promote equality of rights in the aftermath of the Civil War, there was a reversion to discriminatory policies, and especially those entailing disenfranchisement.)

Sustaining cooperation through a repeated game enforcing cooperation is sometimes referred to as social capital, but there is a dark side to social capital: the ability to sustain exploitive equilibrium.[13]

Endogenous Preferences

The second major advance since these papers was written is behavioral economics. There are two major strands of modern behavioral economics, one focusing incorporating insights from psychology and largely based on cognitive limitations (the inability to think fast, or fast enough, in many contexts); and the other focusing on incorporating insights from sociology and social psychology, and emphasizing in particular the endogeneity of preferences (see Hoff and Stiglitz, 2016).

The first strand of work has helped us understand better the depth and pervasiveness of implicit biases—biases that many individuals are not even aware of.

Here, however, I want to focus on the second strand. Becker in his analysis simply took the existence of preferences for discrimination as given. He made no judgment. He simply described the consequences. This was consistent with the prevailing view at the time. When I began my work as an economist, the standard assumption was that preferences were given, just as it was a standard assumption that information was perfect. I thought both of these amiss, but that changing the professions attitude about this would be extraordinarily difficult. Indeed, in 1977, three years after I published Chapter 35, in which I emphasize the endogeneity of preferences, George Stigler and Gary Becker wrote an influential paper, "De gustibus non est disputandum" (Stigler and Becker, 1977), essentially arguing that to question the origins of preferences was to go beyond the confines of economics.

[12] See, for instance, Abreu (1988) and Akerlof (1980).
[13] See Dasgupta (2005, 2012) and Stiglitz 2000b.

Today, there is a growing consensus that preferences are endogenous, determined by our culture and experience. Understanding how preferences and behavior are determined, influenced by others, including one's parents and those with whom one interacts, and transmitted across generations, is one of the important aspects of modern behavioral economics. This literature emphasizes that culture provides us a lens through which we see the world; race is a social construction; racism may in fact have been "convenient" for those wanting to justify slavery in a country which held that "we hold these truths to be self-evident. All men are created equal."[14]

It is, in this perspective, not an accident that so many growing up in the South, with its legacy of slavery and discrimination, have the prejudices they have, and that there are such differences in preferences not only across countries, but even between regions within a country, and between rural and urban areas.

Endogenous preferences enter, too, into the analytics of the discriminated against group. in Chapter 35, I postulate a simple reduced form of the intergenerational transmission of "values": those who choose more education today (or whose parents chose for them more education) put a greater value on education for their children. It is easy to see how there can be multiple equilibria, and that history matters: past discrimination which made investments in education unprofitable lead to preferences which put less value on education. (These results are also consistent with "learning by doing" and "learning by consuming." Those who spend more time in education get better at it, and transmit those skills and attitudes to their children.)[15]

Models of persistent racism have been developed, with equilibrium "fictions," that is, where because of confirmatory bias (one of the systematic biases that has been explored within behavioral economics) individuals may not accurately perceive the world as it is.[16] Perception—both of oneself and of others—affects performance (Fehr and Hoff, 2011); and because of confirmatory bias, one's perceptions of reality are biased by one's prior beliefs. Thus, seemingly rational fictions—where individuals' beliefs were in accord with reality as they perceived it—could persist, with again different groups which are intrinsically the same being treated differently, and leading to different behavior even when there were no intrinsic differences (Hoff and Stiglitz, 2010). But of course, given differences in education and the host of other factors affecting productivity, these processes amplify and further sustain the resulting wage differentials.[17]

Intergenerational Transmission of Advantages and Disadvantages and Equality of Opportunity

Earlier chapters in this book have emphasized the importance not just of inequalities in incomes and wealth (outcomes) but also opportunities, and the impact of discrimination

[14] See, for instance, the World Bank Policy Report version of Hoff and Stiglitz (2010).

[15] Elsewhere, I have used such a model to explain the growing differences in views about goods and leisure between Europe and the U.S. See Stiglitz (2008d).

[16] This literature emphasized (a) the cultural determination of preferences and beliefs; and (b) the role of identity and the effects of stereotyping. For the former, see, for example, DiMaggio (1997), Fehr and Hoff (2011), Hoff and Pandey (2006, 2014), and Hoff and Stiglitz (2016). For the latter see, for example, Steele (2010), Steele and Aronson (1995) and Akerlof and Kranton (2010).

[17] This paragraph is, with minor edits, from Stiglitz (2018c).

on opportunity may be among its most invidious effects. The chapters here emphasize how information networks and transportation, housing, and education systems all result in inequalities of opportunities. Inequalities are perpetuated too when race is used, even partially, as a basis of making employment decisions, even if in the short run, race conveys relevant information.

What I did not emphasize sufficiently is how poverty itself can be self-perpetuating, with those at the bottom, whether white or black, caught in a poverty trap. Recent research has documented both the extent of such poverty traps and the mechanisms through which they occur. Mobility matrices—tracing out the likelihood of someone at the bottom making it up to the middle or top—show how unlikely such transitions are for anyone of any race or color (Bhattacharya and Mazumder, 2011).

Most importantly, there is evidence that growing up in a family in poverty hurts future prospects, and not just through access to education. It affects learning and aspirations, determines the experiences one is exposed to, and shapes the individual's sense of identity and worth, all of which have been emphasized by work in behavioral economics.

Moreover, those in poverty, focusing on survival, have less ability to think long term, and thus are less likely to make the kinds of long-term investments that would help them get out of poverty (Mani, Mullainathan, Shafir, and Zhao, 2013).[18]

Policy

As I noted earlier, I wrote these chapters partly to help think through the consequences of alternative policies. In many of the models, for instance, addressing wage discrimination without simultaneously attacking hiring discrimination could be counterproductive. Indeed, several of the models explored here show that policies of not allowing race, or surrogates to race,[19] be used in employment can be useful in moving the economy to a non-discriminatory equilibrium. An interesting aspect of these models is that such interventions need only be temporary: once the economy has moved to the non-discriminatory equilibrium, it can be self-sustaining.[20]

These models thus had a great deal of influence on me when I served as a member and chair of the Council of Economic Advisers under President Clinton. A question which we confronted on several occasions was, what should our position be on affirmative action? These analyses had made clear the self-perpetuating nature of discriminatory equilibria, and that active policies, like affirmative action, would be required if there was to be any hope of moving away from such patterns of discrimination in any reasonable time. Other active policies, such as compensatory education,[21] including the pre-K education programs that James Heckman has done so much to show the effectiveness of,[22] are also necessary.

Were I to have written these chapters today, I would have emphasized four other matters.

[18] The previous two paragraphs are drawn from Stiglitz (2018c).

[19] Surrogates to race are variables which are correlated with race, but are not themselves of intrinsic relevance to the job at hand. See Rothschild and Stiglitz (1997).

[20] The point, though, is not to remove the prohibition; it is simply that the enforcement costs are likely to be low.

[21] See Stiglitz (1986b, 1973a).

[22] Heckman (2011, 2021).

First, there has to be a broadside attack against inequality and poverty in the United States. The most important policy is to maintain a very tight economy: the only time that marginalized groups were brought into the economy was when the unemployment rate fell to record lows in the late 90s under President Clinton. The benefits of this and the growth that it brings about far outweigh any deficits that might be experienced to support it or the inflation that might be engendered.

Secondly, there is an important interplay between laws, norms, and politics. Changing laws may not necessarily on its own be as effective as we would like unless we change attitudes and norms. Racism, as we have learned, is often subtle. Sometimes, those acting in a discriminatory manner are hardly aware of it. As the Kerner Report emphasized, racism is deeply ingrained in the country. But changing laws can help, for they do affect what is "expected" and thus affect norms. Changing norms though is difficult, and there needs to be a concerted effort in early education and in public discourse, through television, the media, and films (see, e.g., Jensen and Oster, 2009). Perhaps there should be a nationally mandated course in civil rights. At the very least, the federal government should provide massive funding for summer schools and research programs advancing a broader understanding of racism in America and what can be done about it.

Thirdly, there are many other important dimensions to well-being beside income, wealth, and opportunity in which there are large and persistent racial differences. The Covid-19 pandemic disproportionately affected people of color, partly because its most devastating effects were on those with pre-existing health conditions, and these were disproportionately in African American communities. Chapter 4 pointed out that there are large disparities in life expectancy and other indicators of health by income; and there are similarly large disparities by race and ethnicity. And even though white life-expectancy has been declining as a result of the "deaths of despair," while that of African Americans has been rising, that of whites remains higher than that of African Americans (Case and Deaton, 2017, 2020).

Fourthly, unequal access to justice is an important dimension of inequality, and America's criminal justice system and racial police brutality are a particularly damaging aspect of discrimination in the United States, with severe and long-lasting economic consequences.[23]

There are many who see neoclassical economics, claiming that the distribution of income reflects individuals' marginal social contribution, as serving to justify—and therefore perpetuate—the extremes of inequality that have marked capitalism. Much of this book has been devoted to exploring in detail how even a competitive economy can generate high levels of income and wealth inequalities which can persist. But this book has also shown that much of what is observed cannot be explained by that model, that "rents"—including those associated with exploitation of market power and abuses of information asymmetries—play an essential role in understanding today's inequality.

The role of the economist in perpetuating racism—and more broadly, inequalities generated through discrimination—may be even greater. Following the well-worn tradition of "blame the victim," differences in incomes were, as in the standard neoclassical theory, blamed on the failure to acquire skills or assets or to work hard, with little recognition of

[23] There is now a large literature on each of these topics. See, for example, Alexander (2010) and Roeder, Eisen, and Bowling. (2015), to which I wrote a forward. In this book, I have not discussed other aspects of unequal access to justice; these were particularly manifest in the foreclosure scandals associated with the Great Recession (see Stiglitz, 2010a, 2015h).

the enervating effects of discrimination, of the lack of opportunity, of how those discriminated against suffer from the abuses of power that are part of everyday life. By suggesting discrimination could not persist in a competitive economy—and by suggesting that we lived in a competitive economy—these economists suggested that strong public action and concerted civic action was not necessary to overcome the discrimination; and in doing so, they helped sustain the conditions in which discrimination persisted.

If the neoclassical competitive model says that discrimination cannot exist, if we had only opened our eyes, we would have been forced to conclude that that model provides at best an incomplete description of the American economy. These papers, written 50 years ago, were intended both to help us understand the nature of the discrimination which was pervasive then—and is still so today—and to help us understand our economy and society: what kind of an economic system and what kind of society allows such discrimination to persist?

34

Approaches to the Economics of Discrimination

1 Introduction

The object of this chapter is to see how much "conventional" economic theory can say about the problem of discrimination.[1] As in other areas, economists have more to say about questions of economic efficiency than about issues of equity; but because economists have less to say about the latter—or about the social and political implications of discrimination—does not mean that these are any the less important.

I shall limit myself to one aspect of the economics of discrimination, what I shall call wage discrimination.[2] There is wage discrimination if individuals with the same economic characteristics receive different wages and the differences are systematically correlated with certain noneconomic (racial, religious) characteristics of the individual. From an empirical point of view, defining what is an economic characteristic is no trivial matter; clearly education, absenteeism, physical strength, IQ are all economic characteristics, but, since our concern here is with conceptual approaches to the economics of discrimination, we can be satisfied by defining an economic characteristic as anything which affects the net marginal productivity of an individual (after paying training and hiring costs).

There are other kinds of occupational discrimination besides wage discrimination: individuals may be systematically excluded from one class of jobs or another. But, as we shall show later, such job exclusion does not necessarily entail wage discrimination.

By the same token, wage discrimination is not the same as segregation; the latter is concerned with how workers are organized into production units, that is, whether they are homogeneous with respect to some noneconomic characteristic or not, but neither implies nor is implied by wage discrimination. As we shall argue below, many of the conventional theories of discrimination explain segregation, but not wage discrimination.

The central problem posed by the economics of discrimination is the following: Under what circumstances is it possible for groups with identical economic characteristics to receive different wages in a competitive market equilibrium? If people of the same productivity receive different wages, then there are profits to be made by hiring the low-wage individual. If all firms are profit maximizers, then all will demand the services of the low-wage individuals, bidding their wages up until the wage differential is eliminated. Why does this not occur?

[1] Originally published in 1973 as "Approaches to the Economics of Discrimination," *American Economic Review* 63(2): 287–95. The research described in this paper was supported by grants from the National Science Foundation and the Ford Foundation. This is a much shorter version of an earlier paper. There is a danger of excess brevity that leads to misinterpretation; I hope that that does not arise here. Reprinted with permission. I wish to acknowledge helpful insights from Michael Rothschild.

[2] Space limitations do not allow me to give the customary detailed references to previous work. For these, the reader is referred to A. H. Pascal and in particular to the excellent articles by K.J. Arrow (1972a, 1972b). I shall only reference articles not cited in these works.

The Origins of Inequality, and Policies to Contain It. Joseph E. Stiglitz, Oxford University Press. © Joseph E. Stiglitz (2025).
DOI: 10.1093/oso/9780198799580.003.0035

There are two approaches to this problem. The first focuses on the consequences of discriminatory preferences, the second on market imperfections.

There is another set of explanations for wage differences between incomes of groups: groups may differ in some characteristic which is economically important.

There may be many explanations of such differences, but from an analytic point of view the interesting case is that where the groups are "innately" the same. The differences arise only because of differences in their economic treatment (present or past), although the differences in economic characteristics are at the same time the "explanation" of the differences in the economic treatment.

The first set of explanations is pursued in Section 2, the second in Section 3. Some of the models we present may be more appropriate to explaining racial discrimination, others to explaining sex discrimination, still others to religious or ethnic discrimination in one place or another. Our main concern here is not to judge the empirical validity of any particular model in explaining any particular kind of discrimination at any particular place and date, but rather to formulate alternative hypotheses which may be used to explain observed differences in wages. Accordingly, we shall refer to the group with the lower wage as the discriminated workers (*D*-workers for short) and the other group as the undiscriminated workers (*U*-workers), without prejudging the question of the explanation of the wage difference.

2 The "Discrimination-Preference Trade" Model

The most well-developed model is that originally presented by Gary S. Becker, and subsequently developed by Kenneth J. Arrow and A.O. Krueger, among others. It is a competitive equilibrium model which differs from the conventional model only in that some individuals of one group have a preference for working with individuals of the same group and are willing to sacrifice some income to satisfy these preferences.[3] Previous analyses have erred in not exploring the implications of discriminatory preferences in a general equilibrium framework with more than one sector.

To see why the model does not provide an adequate explanation of wage discrimination, we need only consider the extreme case where there is "infinite" aversion for working with members of the other group. For simplicity, assume we have only two factors of production, skilled laborers (employers and managers), and unskilled laborers. Then *U*-skilled workers will work with *U*-unskilled workers, *D*-skilled workers with *D*-unskilled workers. We have a conventional trade model, with no movement of factors. But trade in commodities is a perfect substitute for trade in factors, provided factor endowments are not too different;

[3] The focus on equilibrium is not that the economy is always in equilibrium, but (as in other areas of economic analysis) to ascertain whether there are market forces tending to equalize any differential treatment. The emphasis on competitive markets is based on the belief that here again, as in other areas of economic analysis, it is hard to accept conspiratorial theories in a decentralized economy such as ours. (This is not to say that political intervention may not be used to ensure discriminatory treatment.) The analyses do not, however, require perfect competition in the product markets.

As in the conventional model, we assume perfect information; the removal of this assumption plays an important role in the later discussion.

that is, from the factor price equalization theorem,[4] there will be complete equalization of factor price ratios, even if the relative factor supplies differ.[5] This, of course, requires that there be at least two commodities which are freely traded; although there is probably not "free trade" in the service sector, for most manufactured commodities the composition of the work force is unknown (and of no concern) to the purchaser of the commodity.[6] Thus, aversion by workers of working with others of the same skill of a different race can explain workplace segregation, but not wage discrimination.[7]

Moreover, if factor endowments differ so much that there is not complete factor-price equalization, the relatively scarce factor ought to receive the higher price, that is, the relative factor price of skilled to unskilled ought to be higher in the country (group) with the relative scarcity of skilled laborers. (This provides a testable implication of the model, a test which I suspect, in most cases, the model would fail.)

Consider now the case of between-factor (skilled vs. unskilled) discrimination. Consider the most extreme case where skilled individuals of one group have an infinite aversion to working with unskilled workers of the other group. Then establishments will consist only of members of a single group. But again this does not necessarily imply that there will be differences in factor prices, even if the ratio of skilled to unskilled workers differs in the two groups, because the group with a relatively high proportion of skilled workers will specialize in skilled-worker-intensive industries, and the group with a relatively high proportion of unskilled workers will specialize in unskilled worker intensive industries. As is well known from international trade theory, trade in commodities may be a perfect substitute for movements of factors. The Becker–Arrow analysis essentially assumes a single sector (or equivalently, that all sectors have the same factor intensities). It is obvious then that with infinite aversion, differences in factor supplies must result in differences in factor incomes.

We may, of course, not have complete factor price equalization, for example, if the differences in factor supplies (relative proportions of skilled and unskilled workers) in the two groups are sufficiently large.[8] This will provide an incentive for those individuals who are less than infinitely averse to working with members of the other group to do so. There will be some integration of establishments, and factor price differences will be reduced. If there are enough individuals who are indifferent with respect to the group with whom they work, there will again be complete factor-price equalization. Only a limited amount of factor movement is required to equalize factor prices—that is, to ensure that even with prejudice, wages in a competitive market will be equalized.[9]

[4] To guarantee factor-price equalization, we also need to assume constant returns to scale-production functions and no factor-intensity reversals. We are concerned only with establishing that even infinite aversion to working with other groups need not result in wage discrimination.

[5] Earlier studies assumed a single aggregate production function and, hence, differences in factor-supply ratios necessarily led to differences in factor-price ratios.

[6] That is, just as in the conventional trade model, the service sectors generally produce nontradeable commodities.

[7] Many individuals will object to this analysis, which sounds like a market justification of the old "separate but equal" doctrine, pointing out that, though jobs may be separate, they do not appear to be equal. This reflects the fact that, as we have argued throughout this section, these models do not adequately explain "discrimination."

[8] Of course, if both groups of unskilled workers prefer to work with. say, skilled workers of one of the groups, factor prices will not be equalized.

[9] In the case where all individuals are of identical productivities, a group which constitutes x percent of the population can be completely excluded from $1-x$ percent of the jobs without there being any wage discrimination.

Assume now that only unskilled workers have an aversion to working with members of the other group, but capital and skilled laborers do not. We have then a conventional "regional" trade model with mobile factors. As long as all but one of the factors are mobile, there will be complete factor-price equalization even in the absence of any commodity trade. We would again find all firms having completely segregated work forces, but there would be no wage discrimination.

This analysis is sometimes extended to a dynamic context, in two different directions. First, it has been argued by Arrow (1972a) that if there are costs of adjustment, and initially all firms are all white, then even asymptotically wage discrimination may persist, if, for instance, white workers require higher wages to compensate them for working with those of another race, and there are specific training costs associated with any job. Even if a firm could hire workers from the *D*-group at a lower wage, it will not do so, unless the wage is sufficiently low that it pays the firm either to pay the white workers the higher wage they demand or to let the white workers quit and hire a new labor force consisting just of workers from the *D*-group, paying for the additional training costs.

This analysis, however, assumes that there are fairly high specific training and hiring costs.[10] Moreover, it implies that no new plants, shops, departments, and so forth are established. Otherwise, the new production units (establishments) will hire only the workers in the lower-wage group, and this will continue until equality is attained—presumably in a fairly short time.

Secondly, it is argued that since the non-discriminatory firms are making higher profits, they will drive the discriminatory firms out of business, so in long-run steady state, only non-discriminatory firms will survive. Whether this is the case is ambiguous, because discriminatory firms are willing to accept a lower return to satisfy their prejudices. But if firms rely on internal profits (or if access to external funds is a function of observed internal profits) to expand and grow, then non-discriminatory firms can expand more rapidly, so that, asymptotically, they may dominate the market. This will not be true even asymptotically if the discriminatory firms can compensate for their lower returns by increasing their savings rate.

Even if there are dynamic forces, though, which eventually would eliminate wage discrimination in competitive markets, we have no evidence concerning the speed with which the economy converges to a non-discriminatory equilibrium. The broader spirit of Arrow is correct: There are lags in the adjustment of firms and imperfect mobility of factors: it is possible that discrimination could persist for a long time.

Previous discrimination may have an important impact on present wage differentials: if firms discriminated in the past, and firms today use past work experience to "screen" applicants, then there is indirect discrimination. If past work experience actually has increased productivity, then wage differentials will reflect these productivity differences. The differential is passed on over time and even across generations: (a) because of the apparent differential in returns to education, there will be less investment in it (in Chapter 35 we provide a precise model showing that this can occur in a persistent equilibrium); and

The group will simply find itself concentrated in the jobs from which it is not excluded, and since they have the same productivity, in equilibrium they will still receive the same wage.

[10] Presumably, if there were general training costs, in a competitive model, the individual himself would bear the costs.

(b) because of the differential information about job opportunities, children will have less access to the better jobs.

The evidence is that without government intervention, discrimination would not be simply a short-term transitory phenomenon. In particular, discrimination and inequities in housing and transportation may be important in restricting access to some jobs, for example, those outside of the urban center.

The basic argument of this section was that competitive forces strongly limit the extent to which individuals of the same productivity may receive different wages. The fact that discriminatory preferences cannot explain significant wage differences does not mean that the consequences of discriminatory preferences are any the less insidious. This is particularly important because the form in which the wage differentials are likely to show up is not in different wages for performing the same job, but rather in the assignment of individuals to different jobs. We can think in terms of a hierarchy of jobs by productivity requirements: individuals of the discriminated group may be assigned systematically to lower jobs in this hierarchy than individuals of the same productivity/qualifications belonging to the discriminating group. Thus, the discriminatory preferences result in differences in status and in advancement opportunities, which may be far more important to the individual—and to our sense of equal economic opportunity—than the simple differences in wages.

As we will see shortly, these problems arise even more strongly in the "disequilibrium" and non-competitive models discussed in the next section. And they imply that it is imperative that government not only take actions against wage discrimination but also against hiring discrimination.[11]

2.1 Market Failure

There are a number of different kinds of market failure which may be associated with discrimination.

2.1.1 Monopolies and Oligopolies

There are "monopolies" and "oligopolies" both in the product market and in the labor market (unions). We need to distinguish three separate aspects of the effects of these imperfections in competition: (1) If the ownership claims of the monopolies are not evenly distributed between the two groups, the two groups will not receive the same amount of monopoly rents and, hence, their incomes will differ.[12] (2) Unions might be able to obtain higher wages for their own members. However, the magnitude of the gains is open to some question. The standard estimates are too small to explain much of the racial wage differential. (3) Unions might be able to exclude workers of one group from membership. Whether the exclusion, by itself, will raise the wages of the excluding group and lower those of the excluded group is a moot question. It depends on the importance of "differential rents" to specific skills; that is, if some individuals have a particular ability for being a carpenter, then discrimination against *D* carpenters would presumably result in lowering the differential

[11] Presumably, if there were general training costs, in a competitive model, the individual himself would bear the costs.

[12] The intent of black empowerment legislation in South Africa was to help redress the massive inequalities in these entrepreneurial rents.

rent to this skill of D workers and raise that of U workers. On the other hand, if a carpenter is "raw labor" plus the specific training involved in being a carpenter, the differential rent to "carpenter's skill" is zero. Exclusion from carpentry simply diverts the "specific training" into other uses.

As in the competitive models, such exclusion behavior can have long run effects that lead to productivity and wage differences: if individuals acquire skills while on the job, the exclusion from certain jobs reduces the opportunity for obtaining higher paying jobs in the future. So too, if there is monopsony power in labor markets, and the two groups of workers differ in labor supply elasticities, then there will be discrimination against the firm with a lower labor supply elasticity: the firm knows it can discriminate and still hire the workers. What matters is not the average cost of workers but the marginal cost of hiring an additional worker. Two groups could have markedly different average costs (and average wages) and still present the firm with the same marginal costs.

Similarly, if firms differ in quit rates, the firm can offer a lower wage to the group with a lower response of quits to wages without worrying about labor turnover costs. Both labor supply and quit rate functions can, in turn, be related to discrimination: if the market systematically discriminates against a group, its opportunity set will be poorer, and it may exhibit lower labor supply and quit rate elasticities.

Elsewhere, we and others have described how labor supply and quit rate functions can be derived in simple models based on search and the relevant wage distribution confronting any individual. Search processes and the relevant wage distributions are, in turn, affected by workers' information networks and social and market discrimination.[13] If D-workers searching for a job only talk, say, to other D-workers who have jobs about job openings, their search will rationally concentrate on the jobs disproportionately held by D-workers, and if those jobs are low-paying jobs, that will affect D-workers' acceptance rates of offers. And this is even more so if the employer relies on recommendations of existing employees.[14] As a result, there can be markedly different wage distributions for the two groups, even though they are intrinsically identical.[15]

Although this may be part of the explanation of income differences, it is clearly not the whole story, for we still need to explain differences in wages in the nonunionized sector and in situations where firms have no monopoly power.

2.1.2 Disequilibrium in the Labor Market

Some economists have objected to the equilibrium framework implicit in the above analysis. The presence of queues means that firms can select among applicants and that wages do not—for one reason or another—adjust very quickly. In this world, it is hypothesized, the market forces leading to equalization of factor prices would not be present; that is, if there are two applicants, one D and one U, for the same job, and they both receive the same wage, then there is no market pressure for the firm not to exercise its prejudices. If, however, there is any flexibility in factor prices, then the group discriminated against would

[13] As this paper was being written, a large literature on equilibrium search models was developing. See, for example, Phelps (1970), Salop (1972), Stiglitz (1973a, 1973b, 1972f), and Mortenson (1970).

[14] This, in turn, makes sense in models where reputation matters (as in the Shapiro and Stiglitz, 1984 "shirking" model).

[15] This result can be obtained in an even simpler model, without differential information on the part of job-seekers, as we show in Section 3.

have its wage lowered, and all the market pressures of the kind described earlier would be brought to bear.

2.1.3 Minimum Wage Legislation

"Disequilibrium," where the labor market does not clear, can arise naturally, as a result of imperfections of information (a possibility discussed in the next section) or as a result of government intervention, the passage of minimum wage laws. If the minimum wage is effective in a competitive labor market, it means that the number of applicants for unskilled jobs exceeds the supply, so that the employer can, with no economic cost, indulge in his prejudices. If a worker is hired, he receives the same wage (in equilibrium) regardless of his group; but, because fewer members of one group are hired than of another, the average income of one group is lower than that of the other.

(Since this paper was published, important work by Card and Kruger (1994), and subsequent work supporting their conclusions, has shown that the passage of the minimum wage may not have the adverse employment effect predicted by the standard competitive model. There is imperfect competition in labor markets, and the minimum wage may increase the bargaining power of workers and/or lower the marginal cost of hiring a low skilled worker. With some monopsony power, the marginal cost of hiring an additional worker exceeds the wage, and in such a model, a minimum wage can both increase wages and employment.)

2.1.4 The Efficiency Wage Model

The same results obtain if the productivity of a worker is an increasing, initially convex then concave function of his wage.[16] This increased productivity may, as perhaps in some less developed countries, be due to nutrition, but in the more developed countries it is likely to be associated with psychological factors of the kind that Henry Ford recognized: Pay a worker more and he feels he ought to work harder. There is, then, a wage w^*, which minimizes labor costs. Firms then hire laborers up to the point where the marginal productivity of labor equals the wage. The cost-minimizing wage may be at a level above that which assures full employment; although all those working have a positive marginal product, there is no competitive pressure to lower the wage. In this world, firms can exercise their prejudices in selecting among the applicants with impunity. The model may be more appropriate to discrimination in earlier stages of development, but it may also have some applicability to individuals even in developed countries. Their "norms" concerning a reasonable wage are defined largely by the norms for the population as a whole and may not be very dependent on the distribution of wages for individuals performing comparable work requiring comparable skills to their own. In any case, the model makes an important point: one can construct perfectly competitive models with which there are no competitive pressures for the elimination of discrimination.

[16] See Stiglitz (1973b), subsequently published as Stiglitz (1974c). Since this paper was published, the literature on efficiency wages has identified not only the importance of nutritional and morale effects noted here and in Stiglitz (1969c) (see also Akerlof and Yellen, 1990), but also of labor turnover, adverse incentive, and adverse selection effects, all of relevance in developed countries. See Shapiro and Stiglitz (1984), Stiglitz (1982f, 1985b, 1987b, 1992b), and Nalebuff, Rodriguez, and Stiglitz (1993).

2.1.5 Disequilibrium (and Political Intervention) in the Housing and Transportation Markets

These may be important in restricting access to some jobs located out of the urban center. The presence of these restrictions has implications for inequalities not only in wages but more generally in wellbeing.

3 Explaining Income Differences across Groups in a World with no Intrinsic Group Differences

Among the economic characteristics by which individuals may differ, those which are likely to be important in explaining group differences in income are (a) differences in turnover rates, (b) differences in information about jobs, and (c) differences in education. There are a number of explanations for these differences which have been offered. Some of these have to do with within-group interactions; others have to do with the interaction between individuals and firms, particularly in economies with imperfect information.

We focus again on competitive market equilibrium. There are two categories of models: in one, there is discrimination on the part of government, for instance, in the provision of education. Then, markets respond by offering wages corresponding to the differences in productivities, in what has been called statistical discrimination (Phelps, 1972).

The more interesting case is that where the market itself gives rise to the differences in productivities. These are based on vicious cycle theories: discrimination against some group leads to behavioral responses which then justify the discriminatory behavior. (The next chapter develops one such model involving imperfect information and education.) Here, we explore the conditions under which such vicious cycles may be sustained in a long run equilibrium.

3.1 The Low-Wage High-Turnover Hypothesis

One common hypothesis is that workers of the *D*-group have low wages because they have high turnover rates, but that they have high turnover rates because they have poor jobs.[17] Assume that two groups had the same quit-rate function, that is, the percentage that quit per unit of time given the wage the firm pays and the alternative opportunities available to the individual would be the same for members of both groups. Loosely speaking, if the set of opportunities facing one group were better than that facing the other, then at any given wage the members of the former group would have a higher quit-rate. Firms attempt to minimize total labor costs, that is, direct wage costs plus turnover costs, which are just a function of the quit-rate. Hence, firms would hire only members of the group with the assumed poorer opportunity set.

[17] The analysis of this section is developed in Salop (1972). Although we focus our discussion in terms of turnover rates, the analysis is equally applicable to any job's characteristic the "supply" of which is determined by the wage and alternative job opportunities in a form similar to that here; later we shall present what appears to us to be a "correct" formulation of the hypothesis, in which imperfect information plays a central role.

This form of the "vicious cycle" hypothesis does not provide a consistent explanation. In later work, I showed that there can be equilibria where the costs to the firm are the same with different wage distributions, but because there is greater turnover, and therefore greater turnover costs, one wage distribution with its associated quit rate function may be associated with a lower average wage.[18]

Differential information on the part of entrants to the labor force can be shown to have very much the same effect, particularly when the sources of information are one's parents and associates in the same "group."

3.2 Implication of Group Differences

Individuals have different skills, work habits, etc., and it is important to firms to place individuals in the appropriate jobs. But firms have imperfect information of employees. And unfortunately, there do not exist any perfect predictors of job performance, and so firms must use whatever evidence they can bring to bear. If "race" or "sex" is correlated with the productive characteristics with which the firm is concerned, efficient job allocation—and competitive market forces—will, in general, entail the use of this information in the allocation of jobs. To see the implications of this, consider a simple case where, if the individual is placed in the correct job, output per man is proportional to some characteristic P which is unobservable before the individual begins to work.[19] If he is placed in the wrong job, he has a lower productivity (for any value of F). (See Figure 34.1.) There is a high fixed cost of training, and training is specific to the job, so that it is important to assign workers correctly before training. Before assigning workers to a job, a test is given, which gives an estimate of P with an error. If (the firm believes that) members of the two groups have different distributions of F, in forming an estimate of F, the firm clearly will take into account the group to which the individual belongs. This will affect the job assignment as well as the wage, w. The individual with characteristics F can calculate his expected wage (the wage he receives in a given job, times the probability of receiving that job, integrated over all jobs). The curve relating expected w to F will be lower for the group with the lower average value of P.

Now assume that increases in P can be purchased, but at a cost; for simplicity, we assume that the individual has a utility function relating P and expected wages, and that the two groups have the same indifference curves. Then, because their opportunity sets are different, they will choose different points; and their opportunity sets are different because they choose different points. This is an equilibrium with differential treatment: all firms are

[18] Assume, for instance, that one group has a wage distribution $\{w_1, w_2\}$, $w_1 < w_2$, with a fraction of Π_U paying the high wage, and the other group has a wage distribution $\{w_0, w_2\}$, $w_0 < w_1 < w_2$, with a fraction of $\Pi_D > \Pi_U$ paying the high wage. Assume that there is an exogenous quit rate at the high wage of μ and a search intensity of s, so that the quit rate from the low wage firm for group i is $\mu + s\Pi_i$. If training costs are T, wage costs are the same for all four groups (high and low wage Ds and Us) if $w_2 + \mu T = w_1 + \mu T + sT\,\Pi_U = w_o + \mu T + sT\,\Pi_D$. This analysis shows that two otherwise identical groups could in a long-run competitive discriminatory equilibrium receive different wages. It does not, however, provide a good explanation of race-based wage differences in the U.S. See Stiglitz (1985b).

[19] It may actually be unobservable after the individual begins to work as well as before, although average values of P for the group may be observable indirectly.

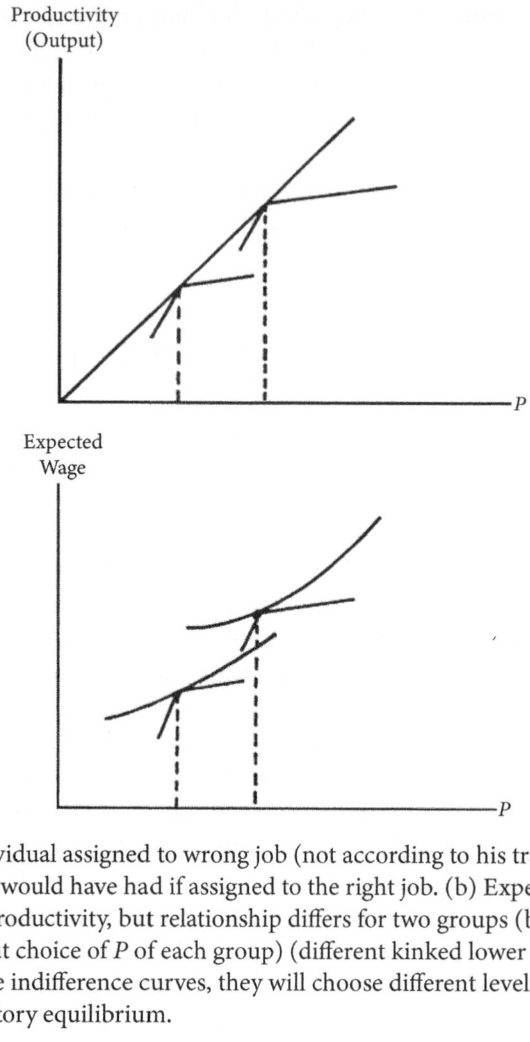

Figure 34.1 (a) Individual assigned to wrong job (not according to his training) has a lower productivity than he would have had if assigned to the right job. (b) Expected wage increases with investment in productivity, but relationship differs for two groups (because of prior (and rational) beliefs about choice of *P* of each group) (different kinked lower curves). Even if two groups have the same indifference curves, they will choose different levels of *P*, sustaining statistical discriminatory equilibrium.

maximizing profits at a zero level; if a firm did not engage in the discrimination, it would make lower profits. Moreover, all individuals are maximizing their (expected) utility given their opportunity sets.[20,21]

[20] Indeed, in the extreme case just described, there would be no need even to give the examination: since all individuals of a given group are identical, knowing the group to which the individual belongs is a perfect predictor of his value of *P*. In practice, individuals have different utility functions (and different native abilities, so different sacrifices of current resources are required to increase *P*), so there is a dispersion of *P* within each group, which means that an examination is required.

The assumption of costly movement from one job to another may be dropped if we also assume that observation on the job is also imperfect. All that we require is that for at least part of the working life of the individual, information about the group to which the individual belongs improves predictive performance on *P*. Firms which use that predictor can bid workers away from firms which do not and make a profit.

[21] If the individual had perfect knowledge of his production characteristics in relation to the job requirements, he would absorb the risk involved in misplacement; individuals do not, however, have perfect knowledge of their abilities, and they are risk averse.

These models have several interesting implications:

1. If firms are required to pay individuals the same wage, regardless of the "group" to which they belong, there will be hiring discrimination (just as in most of the other models examined).
2. If both hiring and wage discrimination are prohibited, then in the short-run (in the first model at least) national output will be lowered, since the allocation of labor will not be as efficient as before.
3. If firms are not allowed to differentiate between individuals according to the "group" to which they belong, firms may rely more heavily on other indices for the prediction of performance, e.g., test scores.[22,23] This may result in little change in the job opportunities facing the *D* and *U* workers from the original situation.

It is accordingly important, if de facto discrimination is to be attacked, that these indirect mechanisms for discrimination be prohibited.

In the long run, the prohibition on discrimination (both direct and indirect) will change investments in productivity. The discriminated against group will have incentives to invest more, and productivity will rise.

3.3 Self-Selection

In the previous discussion, the firm used information about the quit-rates or other economic characteristics of different groups of individuals to set wage rates. Individuals may have more knowledge about the likelihood of their quitting than firms, and firms accordingly attempt to design wage structures which make the individual reveal that information.[24] This can be done in a number of different ways; for instance, the firm may

[22] The argument is parallel to the discussion of discrimination in insurance. Assume that the average accident rate of *D*-workers is higher than for *U*-workers; the reason for the difference has to do with some unobservable factor *C* (cautiousness). If we could observe *C* directly, individuals with more *C* would pay a lower premium than those with less *C*; since we can't, the insurance firm attempts to find inexpensive predictors. Whether a worker is a member of the *D* or *U* groups may be one such predictor. If firms cannot differentiate premiums on that basis, they will rely more heavily on other predictors, like income (which may be correlated both with *C* and with the groups *D* and *U*). They may also rely more heavily on self-screening mechanisms (see below), for example, provide larger discounts for three-year premiums paid in advance (if individuals with lower income have to pay higher interest rates, and have less access to the capital market, this forces lower income individuals to pay higher premiums). They may also "discriminate" in more subtle ways, for example rewarding the individual insurance agent on the basis of premiums less claims; this would provide an incentive for the insurance agent to seek out individuals with less *C*. There will thus be a differential supply of "salesmanship" to the different groups.

[23] If the test were a perfect predictor of job performance, most individuals would agree that it would be "fair" to use that test. There is a feeling by some people that if the test is not a perfect predictor, it is "unfair." It is in the sense that some get a better job than they "ought to" and some a worse one. But as long as the test has some predictive power it means that the expected income of someone who would do a better job is higher than the expected income of someone who would do a poorer job. One might argue it would be unfair not to make use of the test, not to reward someone for being more productive (at least in the ex ante sense used here), particularly if the productive characteristics are not just innate endowments, but are acquired characteristics. There is a sense in which such tests could be "discriminatory." A given test score might be associated with a higher average level of productivity for *D*-workers than for *U*-workers, but because the firm is not allowed to differentiate on this basis individuals who perform the same on the tests must be treated the same.

[24] The role of wage structures in affecting quit-rates is set out in more detail in Stiglitz (1973b) and in Salop and Salop (1976).

confront individuals with two different wage schedules, one which starts high but does not increase with seniority, the other which starts lower, but increases more. Individuals with a higher quit-rate will choose the former schedule, individuals with a lower quit-rate the latter; the firm will accordingly assign the former individuals to jobs where quitting is not so important (i.e., training costs are low). In practice, the self-selection comes not in the form indicated, but in the kind of job for which individuals apply, for which the different wage structures obtain.

The difficulty arises in being able to ascertain whether the individual does not apply for the "better job" because (a) he has a higher propensity to quit or he has less of the characteristic *P* required for advancement; (b) he has misperceptions about his propensities to quit or the amount of *P* he has; (c) he is being discriminated against, so that his chances for advancement are less. The effects, however, are the same: the firm claims that it has fewer *D*-individuals in the "better jobs" not because the firm has excluded them, but because they have "screened themselves." This seems to put the "burden" for the elimination of differential incomes on the members of the *D*-group. It may be argued, however, on the contrary, that even if the reason for the self-screening is (a) or (b), affirmative action (quantitative guidelines) may be an effective policy instrument: they may be an effective way of changing individuals' perceptions of possibilities of advancement, propensities to quit, etc., and, if the reason that the members of the *D*-group have a different amount of *P* is related to one of the explanations provided in previous sections, an effective method of equalizing *P*.

4 Concluding Comments

These models do shed some light on the differential wages received by members of different groups. Which, if any, of these models is appropriate in any particular situation is a moot question. What is important to observe is that which model one believes to be the more appropriate has strong implications for the desirability (on economic grounds) of alternative policies. For instance, if one thinks of labor markets as fairly competitive, then minimum wage legislation not only results in unemployment of low-skilled workers, but eliminates the strong competitive forces that would naturally have led to the alleviation of economic discrimination among these workers. If one thinks of all capitalists conspiring together to exploit workers of low skills (many of whom may belong to particular groups in the population), then minimum wage legislation is an important element in the reduction of that exploitation. In many of the models, the elimination of differential treatment requires quantitative guidelines, or subsidies, for hiring D-workers, although in most of these models, in the long run, the quantitative guidelines or subsidies would become unnecessary.[25] In some of the models, the elimination of discrimination led to an increase in national output; in others to a decrease in the short run, but an increase in the long run.

[25] Individuals' expectations about the likelihood of quitting (or of not being fired, or of not advancing) are likely to be formed on the basis of the experience of other members of their group. If most of the members of the group are employed in jobs where there are not strong incentives against quitting (e.g., where possibilities of advancement are limited) they will have a higher quit-rate, and members of the group joining the labor force will take similar jobs. (If they were more sophisticated, they would not take the "average" quit-rate, but would ask, what is the likelihood that they would quit, given that they got the better job? Even in such a case, if individuals of one group are less certain about their abilities, if they believe that they may be discriminated against in advancement, or if they are more risk averse, then, if their estimates of ability are unbiased, they will not apply for the job requiring foregoing present wages in anticipation of future wages.)

We have, however, deliberately avoided taking positions on the desirability of alternative policies. First, it seems that more empirical evidence is required to select among the alternative hypotheses. Secondly, it is not clear that any of these models do very well. Attempts to explain differences between groups cannot be much more successful than attempts to explain difference within groups, and there appears to be much room for improvement on that score.[26] Thirdly, the economic consequences of alternative policies are probably less important in the assessment of their desirability than other political, social, and philosophical considerations.

[26] We have not addressed ourselves to the relative merits of guidelines versus subsidies.

35

Theories of Discrimination and Economic Policy

1 Introduction

It is now well established that different groups of workers—Blacks and whites, men and women, those with college education and those with less than college education—receive different incomes.[1] It is probably also true that in other categorizations of the population (e.g., by religion or ethnic origin), differences in incomes would be observed. The question is: How can we explain these differences?

To answer this question, we must have a theory of the determination of individuals' incomes. The theory which economists have generally accepted—and which will underly the discussion of this chapter—is the marginal productivity theory of distribution: factors get paid according to their marginal products. Differences in income can then be attributed to two sources: (1) Differences in endowments. Some individuals have more innate ability, or skills which are valued by the market, than do others. Some individuals inherit more capital than do others. Finally, some individuals receive—either as a gift of their parents or of the government—more human capital, more education, than do others. (2) Differences in tastes. Some individuals have a stronger relative preference for leisure over consumption goods than do others. Some individuals value certain non-pecuniary advantages associated with certain jobs more than do others. Some individuals have a greater aversion to risk than do others. And some individuals have a higher rate of time preference than do others (and hence save less for later years of their life than do others).

A number of the characteristics which we have mentioned as being potentially important in explaining differences in incomes are difficult to quantify, for example, the nonpecuniary characteristics associated with any job. Accordingly, it is perhaps not too surprising that attempts to use the "productivity model" to explain differences in income have met with only limited success.

The question in which we are interested here, however, is differences in incomes among groups of individuals. One's first inclination is to see how much of the difference in income can be attributed to differences in productivity. Unfortunately, we have few direct measures of productivity (apart from Rapping's study in the baseball industry) and accordingly we must use indirect methods. Specifically, we will attempt to see how much of the differences in income can be explained by differences in education and ability, as measured by test scores. Of course, such an approach fails to take into account some of the important explanations of differences in income discussed above, and for the most part, the data

[1] Originally published in 1974 in G. von Furstenberg, B. Harrison, and A. R. Horowitz (eds.), *Patterns of Racial Discrimination*, Lanham, MD: D.C. Heath and Company (Lexington Books), pp. 5–26. Chapter has been substantially edited and shortened from the original. Reprinted with permission.

The Origins of Inequality, and Policies to Contain It. Joseph E. Stiglitz, Oxford University Press.
DOI: 10.1093/oso/9780198799580.003.0036

used provides only a crude measure of the variables in which we are really interested. The underlying hypothesis, then, is that although such omissions limit the ability of the model to explain individual differences, there is no reason to believe that the groups under examination differ systematically with respect to those characteristics which affect productivity but which were not included in the analysis.

This hypothesis might, on the face of it, seem rather plausible; yet one might still be disturbed by the size of the unexplained income differences. These unexplained differences are so large that many individuals have concluded that individuals of equal productivity but belonging to different groups receive systematically different wages.

We have thus broken the problem of differences in income among groups into two parts: differences in productivity and differences in wage payments at the same productivity. We then face two further questions: (1) How is it possible in a competitive economy for individuals of the same productivity to receive different wages? Why will all competitive firms not hire only the worker with the lower wage, thereby bidding up his wage until wages are equalized? (2) If there are differences in productivity, how can we explain these differences?

The resolution of these issues is of some importance, for the policies which are appropriate to reduce such income differences depend critically on the answers.

In an earlier chapter (Chapter 26), we asked under what circumstances individuals of the same productivity might receive different wages.

The most extensively discussed theory is that originally due to Becker. Individuals have a preference for working with or employing members of a particular group; these preferences are sufficiently strong that individuals are willing to sacrifice income in order to work with individuals of their own group. Becker and the related literature assume competitive markets. In Chapter 34 (Stiglitz, 1973d) we explained why Becker's theory does not provide a plausible explanation of observed wage and income differences—at most it explains segregation in the workplace. We also showed how in models with imperfect markets—imperfect competition and imperfect information—groups with identical distributions of productivities could, in equilibrium, have different wage distributions. Discrimination could persist.

The policy implications of the competitive model are interesting, and some of them contrast markedly with those of the models to be presented here. First, the elimination of wage discrimination (if it exists), alone, without a prohibition on discrimination in hiring, will result in more hiring discrimination, and possibly in unemployment of the group of workers that was formerly discriminated against,[2] since it is only the fact that these workers are less expensive which induces the prejudiced firms to hire them. Second, if guidelines or quotas are imposed to ensure that job discrimination has not occurred, then national output may increase.

This chapter focuses on the question of how we can explain differences in productivities among groups. There may be explanations of such differences, but from an analytic point of view, the interesting case is that where the groups are, in some sense, "innately" the same. Is it possible that, in long-run equilibrium,[3] they have different productivities nonetheless? We shall argue that the answer is affirmative.

[2] Including assigning workers to less demanding jobs than their skills warrant—which is, of course, just another form of wage discrimination.

[3] The stress on long-run equilibrium is because there may be long lags of adjustment, during which income differences persist, even though in the long run, the groups have identical incomes. Although the difference is

In the discussion below, we shall discuss a number of factors leading to differences in productivities. Most of these will be related to considerations usually omitted from conventional economic analyses; for example, endogenous preferences, imperfect information, and the dependence of productivity on wages.

We will show how groups that are intrinsically the same, when confronted with a discriminatory equilibrium, make different decisions concerning investments in productivity. Thus, the differences in productivity are endogenous and a result themselves of discrimination. These differences can be sustained over time.

We consider two different models, in one of which the differences arise through the education system and the complementary output provided by families to formal education. We show that the perpetuation of differences may be strengthened as a result of endogeneity of preferences. The second model is based on imperfect information on the part of employers concerning employees. In both of these models, we do not need to invoke discriminatory preferences. Discrimination, however, may play a major role in understanding why the two groups end up in such different equilibria.

Since several of the arguments have a common mathematical structure, it is worthwhile to call attention to it here. Consider an economy with a single group of individuals. Under certain circumstances, it is clearly possible that there may be several long-run equilibria for this economy (with different levels of per capita income) which we denote by Equilibrium 1, Equilibrium 2, . .etc. . Assume that the given economy is in equilibrium in Equilibrium 1, and there is another economy in equilibrium in Equilibrium 2. Under certain circumstances it is possible that when they merge, the members of the first group remain distinct from members of the second group if discrimination is allowed.

2 Education

That there are differences in educational attainment among different groups in the population seems well established. These differences could be attributable to differences in demand or to differences in supply. Since education is primarily supplied by the government, a deliberate government policy in some states to provide differential education to Blacks and Whites would clearly result in differences in educational attainment, and this may be an important determinant of income differences. Numerous econometric studies have attempted to determine exactly how important these educational differences are in explaining income inequalities. Why don't educational differences appear to be more important than they are, and why, at least until recent years, was the white/Black wage ratio higher for more educated than for the less educated?

The most obvious answer, of course, is that the education variables commonly used do not appropriately measure the "quality" of education. The "real output," denoted by Q_i, is likely to be a function not only of the resources supplied by the school but also of the real investments and other resources—difficult to observe directly, and affected by the real educational attainment itself of parents and others in the family, another hard-to-observe

clearly important from an analytical point of view, it is not clear how important the difference is from a policy point of view.

variable—supplied by the individual and his family.[4] It is also a function of the inputs supplied to other children attending the same school (the externalities effect) and the homogeneity of the students (a kind of "returns to scale" effect), which we will refer to as the non-formal or informal education.[5] If E is the expenditure on formal education, I_i the level of informal education of the ith individual, $\bar{I}$ the mean level of informal education in the school,[6] and σ_I a measure of heterogeneity, then we postulate[7] (in simplified form):

$$Q_i = F(E, I_i, \bar{I}, \sigma_I). \tag{35.1}$$

The question of whether efficiency implies that we should allocate more or less resources to students with lower I_i hinges on whether E and I are substitutes or complements, that is, whether an increase in informal education increases or decreases the marginal returns to formal education. The question of whether students should (on "efficiency" grounds) be grouped homogeneously or heterogeneously depends on whether an individual's informal training is a complement or substitute for that of his peers (i.e., whether a high level of informal training in music is likely to increase or decrease the return to having a peer group with a high level of musical appreciation) and if a substitute, whether this spillover effect is stronger than the reduction in the "scale" effect produced by heterogeneity. The allocation of resources to education and of students to schools has important and obvious implications for the distribution of income as well.[8]

Consider any education system, with a particular rule for allocating students and educational dollars based on efficiency, equity, and discriminatory attitudes. We simplify by assuming all individuals in each group, D (the discriminated against group) and U (undiscriminated against group) are identical. We simplify two by assuming a school that allocates students to classes to achieve homogeneity of background, so that if students have different I, and I can be served, they will be assigned to different classes. This means that if the two groups choose different I, there will be de facto segregation (e.g., students are allocated on the basis of I_i and if the two groups differ in I_i, and therefore in $\bar{I}$ they will receive different amounts of E.

Assume that there were no racial discrimination, but schools could monitor I_i and so allocated E according to I_i. Family expenditures on I_i will take into account the impact of I_i on E, the two together on Q, and the effect of Q on wages. But now assume than the individual student's I_i cannot be monitored well, but the average value of a large group

[4] The ability (as opposed to the motivation) to supply these other factors is different in different groups, for instance, because of differences in wealth.

[5] That is, an education which is appropriate for one set of students, with one set of non-formal inputs may not be appropriate for another set. If a teacher prepares the same lesson plan for both groups, they would each be worse off than if he prepared a lesson plan directed at each group separately; if he prepares two lesson plans, one for each group. the quality of each will necessarily be lower than if he allocated the same time to developing a single lesson plan.

[6] We are not addressing ourselves to the issue of whether the externality is primarily internal to the classroom or internal to the school. The scale effect is internal to the classroom. Thus, if the externality effect is internal to the school, efficiency would require heterogenous schools with homogenous classrooms. For a more extensive discussion see Stiglitz (1973c).

[7] Without specifying clearly what we mean by output (value added) or how we measure it.

[8] It should also be noted that the efficiency and equity effects differ depending on whether private education is an alternative to public education. A policy of uniform allocation of students (regardless of the value of I_i) might increase national output and redistribute income from Whites to Blacks if there were no private schools; with private schools, it may increase the disparity of income between the groups (since the $\bar{I}$ of the students remaining in public schools could well be lower) and even lower overall output. See Stiglitz (1974h).

can be. Assume for simplicity that μ_I does not matter. Then if an individual is assigned to a group J, for whom $\overline{I_J}$ is given, and if $w_i = Q_i$, then, ignoring discounting, a family maximizing $w_i - I_i$ would set

$$\frac{\partial Q_i\left(E\left(\overline{I_J}\right), \overline{I_J}, I_i\right)}{\partial I_i} = 1.$$

Because each family knows that they will not get more E if they invest more in I_i, their optimal level of I_i is smaller. If there is discrimination, so that one group D gets less E than the other group, U, then the discriminated group will rationally invest less in I.

It is even possible for there to be "rational expectations" on the part of schools, i.e. the school's belief about the average value of I of each group could be accurate. Thus, the discriminatory equilibrium can persist even after discriminatory preferences no longer exist. Even if societal welfare were maximized by an allocation for both groups $\{E^*, I^*\}$ so $\bar{I} = I^*$, there can exist a Nash equilibrium where the D group invests in less than I^*, given its beliefs that others in the group will be doing similarly, and that they will be assigned to a school with a correspondingly less E. If the groups differ in other aspects of their cultural backgrounds, tests making references to those differences will demonstrate different levels of performance. If it is believed that efficiency is enhanced by homogeneity, then the argument for differential treatment is strengthened. (The opposite is the case if a value is placed on diversity.)

So far, we have assumed that everyone in the two groups is identical. If they are not, then variability matters in allocating students, and if because of background differences, there is greater variance in the tests attempting to ascertain $\overline{I_i}$ for one group relative to that of the other, for example because the tests measure true $\overline{I_i}$ less well for one group than the other, then again discriminatory education could persist even in a school system professing no preference for discrimination.

3 Endogenous Preferences

There is no doubt that many of our attitudes (preferences) are culturally determined: the food we eat, the clothes we wear, the design of the house we live in, all differ from country to country, and to a lesser extent, from group to group within a country. From our point of view, what is important are differences in attitudes which result in differences in incomes: differences in attitudes toward education, in the need for achievement, in attitudes toward job mobility, in intertemporal time preferences, in attitudes toward risks. These attitudes are likely to depend critically on the attitudes (income, socioeconomic status) of one's parents. Consider the following simple example. The percentage of one's income spent on education (a_t) depends on the current rate of return (ρ_t) and on the percentage of one's parents' income spent on education (a_{t-1}):

$$a_t = \phi\left(a_{t-1}, \rho_t\right). \tag{35.2}$$

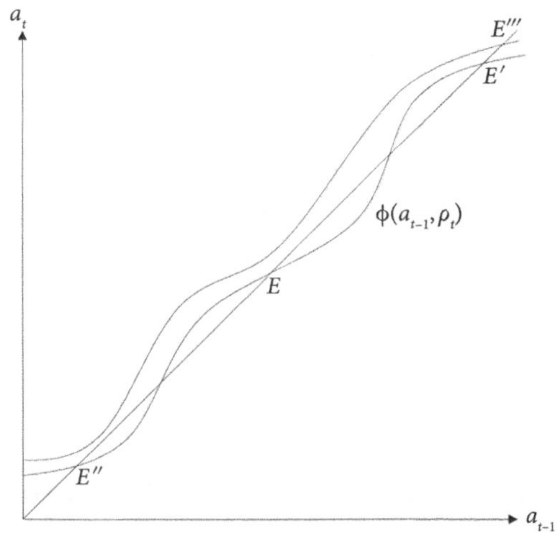

Figure 35.1 Endogenous preferences and demand for education: those with more education demand (at any level of pecuniary returns to education ρ) more education for their children. There may be multiple steady state equilibria.

(The excess of expenditure on education over that required to obtain the market rate of return may be thought of as "consumption.") Long-run equilibrium requires that

$$a_t = a_{t-1}. \tag{35.3}$$

Multiple equilibria are clearly possible, as illustrated in Figure 35.1. Consider a group which is discriminated against in such a way as to increase the return to education (by lowering the wages in activities not requiring high levels of education more than in activities requiring high levels). This shifts the curve upwards. Assume initially everyone is in the middle stable equilibrium. Then, the introduction of discrimination will move the group toward the upper equilibrium point E'''. If the discrimination is later removed, the historical effect remains: the group continues to obtain a high level of education E' and the associated high level of income. Conversely, if a group is discriminated against in such a way as to lower the return to education, and then subsequently the discrimination is removed, the group may now be in the lower equilibrium (E'').

Note that policies aimed at eliminating wage discrimination or job discrimination will not affect this outcome; reverse discrimination, raising temporarily the return to education leading to an increased consumption of it, may.

4 Education as a Screening Device

There is, however, another aspect to education: not all education is skill acquisition; some of it is "screening," that is, identifying individuals' abilities. One of the aspects in which poorer quality education is in fact poorer is that it screens less well. Thus, very able students are classified with students who are less able, and accordingly receive lower wages. The private returns to education of students with given abilities will be lower in a system with less screening at any given level of inputs in their education. (Even if no resources of their own were required, and even if the educational system had no effect on productivities, the "finer" screening system will tend to have wages rise more upon each stage of screening,[9] so those who manage to pass through the "screen" obtain a larger return to their "luck"; this private return is not directly related to any social return to education.[10]) There can be multiple equilibria with education-as-a-screening device. If the two groups believe that the market uses race even partially in making inferences about ability, then they can be sustained in different equilibria (one with less screening than the other), and accordingly, with fewer higher wage workers.[11]

5 Imperfect Information of Employer Concerning Employees

Individuals have different skills, work habits, and so forth, and it is important to firms to place individuals in the appropriate jobs. Unfortunately, there do not exist any perfect predictors of job performance, and so firms must use whatever evidence they can bring to bear. If "race" or "sex" is correlated with the productive characteristics with which the firm is concerned, then efficient job allocation—and competitive market forces—require the use of this information in the allocation of jobs. Under certain circumstances, these differences in economic treatment are themselves the cause of the differences in productive characteristics, that is, the difference in economic treatment on the basis of productivity characteristics is self-confirming. More precisely, we make the following assumptions: (1) There is, for any given vector of characteristics of the individual, a "best job" for the individual; at other jobs, he has a lower productivity. (2) Some elements of the vector are (a) not perfectly observable before the job placement and (b) can be "purchased" at a cost (e.g., foregone leisure). (3) Individuals are not perfectly certain of their vector and are risk averse. (4) There are specific training costs associated with each job and/or observation of productivity on the job is costly and imperfect. Then, if firms believe individuals of two groups have different distributions of the imperfectly observable characteristics, then they will in general use the group membership in job placements and hence in the determination of wages; and given that firms use group membership in job placement, the groups will have different incentives for acquiring the given characteristics and so will in fact differ in the distribution of these characteristics. There may exist a statistical discriminating equilibrium, where the distributions of partial observable characteristics assumed by the firms correspond to the actual distributions.

The importance of all but the third assumption should be obvious. The third assumption is required in order to avoid the possibility of the individual coming to the firm and offering to absorb the risk associated with hiring him (i.e., with the specific training costs). There are other reasons, particularly those associated with moral hazard, why the individual might

[9] The arguments of this section are developed at length in Stiglitz (1973c), subsequently published as Stiglitz (1975a).

[10] This may explain at the same time why the ratio of wages for the highly educated to the less educated may well differ between the two groups.

[11] In the Stiglitz (1973c, 1975a) model, the no screening equilibrium is, in a natural sense, more efficient: average income (net of education/screening costs) is higher.

not be willing to offer to insure the firm against the risk that he or she does not have the requisite skills.

We now consider an example,[12] in which, for analytic simplicity, individuals are assumed to be risk neutral, perfectly informed about their abilities, but unable to insure firms against the loss involved in training them if they do not have the requisite skills. The argument can be extended to the more general case. Assume we have two classes of jobs: the better job requires the individual to have acquired a value of productivity, P, at least equal to $\hat{P}$, and in addition demands an investment of T by the firm.[13] We assume the firm is risk neutral, and requires an expected return r on its investment, so that

$$r = \pi(M_2 - w_2)/T \tag{35.4}$$

where M_2 is the marginal return of an extra worker on the better job (which we shall assume to be constant), w_2 is the wage on the job, and π is the probability that the individual's value of $P \geq \hat{P}$. We assume that the firm can distinguish who has $\hat{P}$ immediately after training is completed, but not before, and that those with less that $\hat{P}$ then are assigned to the low skill/low wage job.[14]

Assume now that the individual is risk neutral. The cost of acquiring the given level of productivity $\hat{P}$ is a function of the individual's ability, (A), so if the return on the investment in acquiring the credential $\hat{P}$

$$(w_2 - w_1)/C(A) \tag{35.5}$$

(where w_1 is the wage in the lower job) is greater than say, ϕ (where ϕ reflects the individual's time value of money), then the individual undertakes the investment. For simplicity, we let C(A) = 1/cA, that is, costs are inversely related to A. Define $1/\hat{A} = A$. Let $F(\hat{A})$ be the distribution of $\hat{A}$, and $f(\hat{A})$ the density function. Then π, the proportion of individuals undertaking the investment, is defined as

$$\begin{aligned} \hat{\pi} &= F\left[\frac{c}{\phi}(w_2 - w_1)\right], \text{ and} \\ \frac{d\hat{\pi}}{dw_2} &= \frac{fc}{\phi}, \\ \frac{d^2\hat{\pi}}{dw_2^2} &= f'\left(\frac{c}{\phi}\right)^2. \end{aligned} \tag{35.6}$$

An equilibrium is where $\pi = \hat{\pi}$, and as Figure 35.2 makes clear, there may be multiple equilibria, so that one group could be in equilibrium at E and another E''. If there exists only

[12] This is an extension of an argument contained in Arrow (1972a) and related to Akerlof (1970); Spence (1973); and Phelps (1972).

[13] There is a "fixed coefficients technology" requiring 1 laborer, firm-specific training, T, and the individual's level of P.

[14] There is an alternative formulation with much the same result. Those of greater ability A not only face lower cost in getting the qualification P, but are more productive. Thus, the average productivity of those with qualification P is a decreasing function of the fraction of the group that gets the qualification, π. We replace Equation (35.4) with the equation $r = [M_2(\pi) - w_2]/T$. The average productivity of those who do not get the qualification is also a function of π, so we can write $w_1 = w_1(\pi)$. (In the model in the text, we assume that neither M_2 or the productivity of workers in the unskilled job depend on π: individuals differ only in the cost of getting the credential.) There can exist multiple equilibria in this model as well.

one interior equilibrium, it is unstable, as Figure 35.2 makes clear.[15] But from (35.4), if E is different, that is, if the fraction of the population who have obtained productivity $\hat{P}$ is different, the wages received will be different.[16]

There can be a discriminatory equilibrium, which can persist, in which employers assume that different proportions in the different groups have obtained the credentials, resulting in differences in average productivities for those with and without the credential. This kind of rational expectations multiple equilibria, while consistent with the persistence of discriminatory equilibria, cannot on its own explain observed patterns in the labor market.

These models have several interesting implications:

1. If firms are required to pay individuals the same wage, regardless of the group to which they belong, there will be hiring discrimination (just as in most of the other models examined).
2. If firms are not allowed to differentiate between individuals according to the group to which they belong, firms may rely more heavily on other indices for the prediction of performance, for example, on test scores. This may result in little change in the job opportunities facing workers of different groups, compared to the original situation. If individual investments have to occur before firm training (a natural assumption), and the change in the regime is not anticipated, then the short run equilibrium with no wage and hiring discrimination results in an adjustment of wages to ensure that (35.4) is satisfied, i.e. the new w without discrimination, w_{nd}, is given by M_2- $(rT/\bar{\pi})$, where $\bar{\pi}$ is the average proportion attaining the requisite productivity level *over the entire population.* w_{nd} is greater than the wage previously received by the "low" group and less than that received by the high group.
3. In the long run, all groups will converge to the same equilibrium, e.g., in Figure 35.2 either to E or E''. With expectations based on past wages, which will depend on whether wages after the elimination of discrimination is greater or less than that associated with E', which in turn will depend on the relative proportion of the two groups in the population. If the low wage (discriminated against) group is relatively small, the long-run equilibrium will be the high wage equilibrium associated with E''.
4. Net output is higher at the high wage equilibrium.[17]
5. Moreover, in the new, long-run equilibrium, quantitative restrictions will be unnecessary.[18]

[15] Conventional dynamic assumptions would imply that E and E' are stable, E' and E'' unstable. One objection that can be raised against this model is that there would be incentives for firms to offer contracts which paid the worker w_2 if, upon training, he turns out to be. successful (i.e., has invested enough to bring his productivity level up to $\overline{P}$), and zero otherwise. Then only the workers who had made the requisite investment would accept the job. This argument does make an important point which we elaborate in the next section; but in this context the possibility of multiple equilibria would remain, provided only that there is not perfect screening after training or that individuals do not have perfect knowledge of their own characteristics.

[16] In Stiglitz (1973d), I presented a slightly different model, with essentially the same results.

[17] Under our assumptions, net national product per capita is higher in the equilibrium where a larger fraction of the population attains the requisite productivity level.

[18] The same is true in the endogenous preference model.

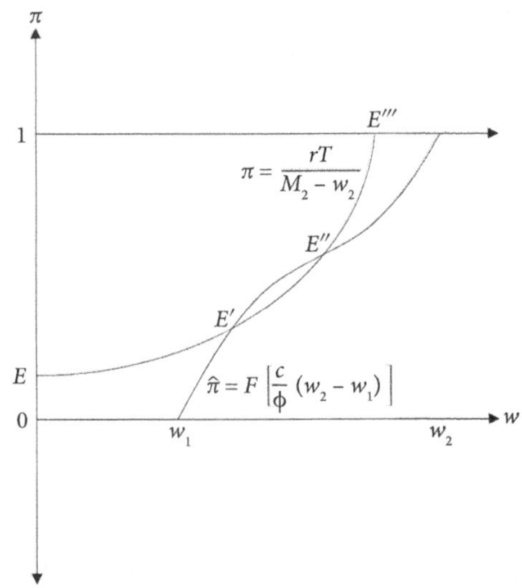

Figure 35.2 The proportion of workers (π) acquiring an education that enables them to be productive in a skilled job increases with the wage, and the wage paid in a skilled job increases with the proportion of the work force that has acquired the skills that enable them to be productive in a skilled job. There may be multiple equilibria.

6 Productivity Depending on Factor Payments

Conventional economic theory takes the productivity of the individual as given. Yet managers of rums have often recognized that individuals may work harder, and the labor force may have a lower turnover if the firm pays higher wages. Net productivity (productivity after paying for turnover costs) may be an increasing function of the wage.

Thus, the argument that individuals belonging to certain groups receive low wages because they have a low productivity is turned on its head: the reason that they have low productivity is that they have low wages.

The discussion of the preceding section provided an argument of why a wage schedule with a low return to increases in productivity will result in low productivity. But here we are concerned not with the wage schedule but with the level of wages. The argument must be put carefully, since in at least one of its common versions it is incorrect.

We shall first present an argument that, if the relationship between productivity and wages takes on a particular shape, then even without minimum-wage legislation there may be unemployment among the very unskilled even. in equilibrium, and this unemployment allows firms to discriminate (without cost) among different workers.

Assume that workers' productivity is an increasing initially convex and then concave function of his wage.[19] This increased productivity may, as perhaps in some LDCs, be due to nutrition, but in the more developed countries, it is likely be associated with psychological factors of the kind. that Henry Ford recognized: Pay a worker more and he feels he

[19] See Stiglitz (1974c).

ought to work harder. Then if a worker who receives a wage of w has an efficiency index of $\lambda(w)$, and the efficiency wage curve appears as in Figure 35.3, the firm minimizes labor costs:

$$w/\lambda(w) \tag{35.7}$$

by setting $\lambda' = \lambda/w$. Firms then hire laborers up to the point where the marginal productivity of labor equals the wage.

The equilibrium, that is, the cost minimizing wage, may be set at a level above that which assures full employment; although all those working have a positive marginal product, there is no competitive pressure to lower the wage. In this world, firms can exercise their prejudices in selecting among the applicants with impunity.

The model may be more appropriate to discrimination in earlier stages of development. but it may have some applicability to individuals who are very unskilled. Their "norms" concerning a reasonable wage are defined largely by the norms for the population as a whole and may not be very dependent on the distribution of wages for other individuals performing work requiring skills comparable to their own.

Thus, the discriminated against workers have low productivity because of the low morale from being discriminated against; and at the same time, their low productivity seems to justify paying them a low wage. The elimination of (both wage and hiring) discrimination would lead to a new equilibrium, where there is no difference in productivities between the two groups. As in the model given in the previous section, once discrimination is eliminated, competition in the market economy can sustain the non-discriminatory equilibrium.[20]

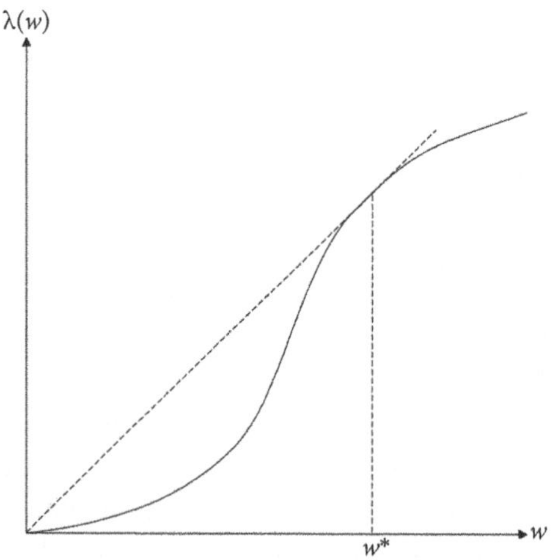

Figure 35.3 The efficiency wage curve as a function of the wage level. The adverse moral effect of discrimination lowers productivity and the lower productivity leads to low wages.

[20] In the original, there was an extended discussion of costly search can give rise to wage and employment discrimination, especially when economic and social segregation gives rise to different information networks.

7 Concluding Remarks

In this chapter, we have attempted to review the various arguments explaining differences in income between groups. We have divided them into two categories: differences in wages of individuals of the same productivity and differences in productivity between groups. We have suggested that at least the standard arguments advanced for explaining differences in the wages of individuals belonging to the same group are not convincing. We have attempted to put forth some arguments why group differences in productivity might be sustained in long-run equilibrium. Whether these are themselves very convincing is a moot question. What is clear, however, is that the effect of the various policies the government may undertake to reduce these income differences depends critically on the explanation of their origin.

PART III.G
INEQUALITY AND PUBLIC POLICY
Some Final Comments

Introduction to Part III.G

Almost every public policy has distributive consequences, and good public policy making seeks to take these into account, even if the effects are "unintended consequences": One needs to always ask, does the policy increase inequality? Are the benefits skewed to the top? Will it hurt those at the bottom or the middle? Of particular concern are policies that harm already disadvantaged groups, including groups that have long suffered from discrimination.

Take monetary policy, the stated objective of which is maintain macro stability, preventing excesses of unemployment and inflation. But as we have already noted, how monetary policy is conducted can have large distributive consequences. A focus on inflation results in a higher level of unemployment, which adversely affects workers and increases inequality. It is only when the U.S. economy has been run very tightly—with very low levels of unemployment—that marginalized groups have been brought (almost) fully into the labor force. On the other hand, the ultra-low interest rates associated with quantity easing hurt worker retirees, who had put their money into safe government bonds, and helped the very rich, who owned a disproportionate share of the country's equity, which increased in value as a result.[1] That monetary policy can have such large distributive effects has important institutional implications: it means that the conduct of monetary policy must be essentially part of a political process where decision makers are held accountable for the full consequences of their actions—including distributive consequences. It cannot be simply delegated to technocrats who are given simple mandates—like keeping inflation low—with no mention of differential impacts on different groups. Indeed, since monetary policy is always conducted in the context of considerable uncertainty, policy makers should be attentive to who bears the risks. It also means that it is especially problematic that conventional governance arrangements, where the governing boards of central banks disproportionately represent the financial sector and reflect the values and perspectives of that sector. Even if one argues for an independent central bank, its decisions should reflect

[1] In Stiglitz (2015c) and (2018f) I discussed these and other adverse distributional effects of monetary policy. Largely since that paper was originally written, there has developed a large literature on the effect of monetary policy on inequality, surveyed in Colciago, Samarina, and de Haan (2019).

not just the interests and perspectives of Wall Street and the financial community more generally.[2]

The chapters here discuss but two key public policies, taxation (Chapter 36) and the welfare state (Chapter 37).

Taxation

The first of these was written on the occasion of the 125th anniversary of the premier UK economics journal, *The Economic Journal.* Among the several articles selected as the most influential was one by Frank Ramsey on optimal taxation.[3] That paper focused on the design of a tax system which would minimize distortions ("deadweight loss") of taxation. Its prescription was to tax heavily commodities the demand for which was inelastic. When I read that result as a student, I was greatly disturbed, because it implied taxing, at a high rate, commodities like bread, and that would obviously be regressive. Ramsey had ignored distribution, but that was like leaving Hamlet out of the play: in the absence of distributional concerns, one could just impose lump sum taxes. This chapter (along with Chapter 19) summarizes research that I did with the late Anthony Atkinson and with others, beginning in the late 1960s, attempting to incorporate distributional concerns into a general theory of taxation. We were, for instance, able to derive simple formulae that made far more sense, that appropriately balanced concerns about deadweight loss with those of distribution.

The Key Role of Distribution in Designing Tax Structures

One of the central insights of my work with Atkinson and Dasgupta[4] was that distributional concerns played a first order role in shaping the design of optimal taxes, but so did the set of feasible taxes. Unless one had 100% rent/profits taxes, supply elasticities as well as demand elasticities were relevant in determining taxes—higher taxes on inelastically supplied commodities was an indirect way of extracting some of the rents. This contrasted with the result of Diamond and Mirrlees (1971), which seemed to suggest that optimal commodity taxes depended only on properties of the demand functions. Chapter 19 above explored how having a progressive income tax affected the desirability of commodity taxation—including a tax on interest income. It made clear that the presence of an (optimal) income tax drastically changed the structure of optimal commodity taxation.

Feasible Taxes

Assessing the set of feasible taxes is not always easy. Sometimes, there seems to be a political constraint, and these can vary across countries, having to do with the history and politics

[2] These are issues I raised in a lecture I gave in 1997 to the Netherlands Central Bank in honor of Jan Tinbergen, on the early winners of the Nobel Prize (Stiglitz, 1998b) and revisited several times after the 2008 financial crisis (Stiglitz, 2010a, 2012a, 2014d).

[3] Another article selected was Atkinson and Stiglitz (1969), reprinted in volume 5 of *Selected Works.*

[4] Both of whom I met when I went to Cambridge as a Fulbright scholar in 1965–6. Atkinson was in the first group of students I tutored in Cambridge, and Dasgupta was completing work on his Ph.D.

of the country. While most of the world has adopted value-added taxes, there is a taboo on even discussions of the tax in the U.S.: the worry is that it would make the overall tax system even less progressive (or more regressive.) My experience is that such political constraints sometimes can change almost overnight, with changing perceptions and political dynamics.[5] In other cases, the constraints related to administrability: many less developed countries do not have the capacity to impose non-linear capital and income taxes, so the original Ramsey formulation may be most relevant for these countries.[6]

The Taxation of Interest and Corporations

A specific application of the ideas discussed in this chapter concerns the taxation of interest and corporate profits, a topic discussed at greater length in Chapter 19. There is often confusion between taxing interest and broader taxes on corporations and capital. In the standard neoclassical model (including the models explored by most of the optimal tax literature) there are no rents or pure profits, but a major theme of this book is that such rents are significant, and the increase in rents plays an important role in the growth of inequality. Taxing these rents is desirable because it is non-distortionary; and earlier chapters explained that such taxes, by reducing what we called "rent-capital" led to more real capital accumulation, increasing national income and increasing in particular wages. Elsewhere (Stiglitz, 1973e), I have explained why the corporation tax—with its provisions of interest deductibility and accelerated depreciation (in some cases, full expensing of investment) is close to a tax on pure profits, and that increasing the tax rate accordingly has little if any effect on the level of investment for most firms.

Pre-distribution and General Equilibrium Incidence Effects

A theme we emphasized throughout this book is that tax and expenditure policies can have general equilibrium incidence effects, changing the *market* distribution of income. Much of the early work on optimal taxation employed models that explicitly excluded such effects, for example by assuming that the ratio of wages of skilled and unskilled workers was fixed. This chapter (along with Chapter 19) explains the advantages of "pre-distribution": by having a less unequal market distribution, less burden is place on distortionary redistribution.[7]

[5] Thus, for a long while, a tax on carbon, to discourage use of fossil fuels, was viewed as a non-starter, but then as many corporations perceived growing support for green policies, it received strong support even in conservative circles, as a lesser evil than regulation. But then the yellow vest movement in Paris called attention to the adverse distributive effects of a carbon tax and this reinvigorated opposition to the tax (see Stiglitz, 2019b).

Optimal tax theory calls for the use of any surrogate variable that might convey information about the individual, his social marginal utility, and the economic impact of taxes; but in practice, many variables that might convey information are unacceptable as a basis of taxation (such as gender or race). Similarly, optimal tax theory says that because of the non-convexities associated with self-selection and incentive compatibility constraints, it is in general optimal to employ random taxation. In most societies, such taxes would be viewed as unacceptable. See Arnott and Stiglitz (1988a), Brito, Hamilton, Slutsky, and Stiglitz, (1995), and Stiglitz (1982b).

[6] In the full version of the paper of which this chapter is an excerpt, this issue is discussed more extensively. See also Sah and Stiglitz (1987, 1992).

[7] Ideas I originally explored in Stiglitz (1982e).

Expenditure Policy and the Welfare State

The final chapter of the volume focuses on the expenditure side of public policy, and, in particular, on what I call a "twenty-first century welfare state"—one in which the government takes an active role in raising living standards for most citizens and creating greater equality. The origins of the welfare state are usually attribute to the nineteenth-century policies of the Prussian Otto Bismarck, with the introduction of social security (public old age pensions). The twentieth-century welfare state expanded the role of government to incorporate other elements of social protection, like disability and unemployment insurance.

During the second half of the twentieth century, economists provided an explanation for why government had to undertake these roles, in terms of the theory of market failures—instances where the market "failed" to deliver the efficiency associated with Adam Smith's invisible hand, including providing important goods and services, including insurance against important risks which individuals faced. The analysis of market failures implied that there was a presumption that government had a role, to remedy these market failures; and the early welfare state initiatives focused especially in providing insurance. It was more than a "safety net"—something that might prevent one from falling into extremes of deprivation. It was appropriately referred to as social insurance or social protection, and embraced unemployment insurance, disability, and the provision of old age pensions.

In spite of these advances in economic theory which explained why a welfare state was needed,[8] it came under attack by the proponents of neo-liberalism, of a market-oriented state in which the role of the state was minimal. They argued that it wasn't "affordable." Some even blamed the 2008 crisis on the welfare state. Others agreed that the level of inequality produced by the market was unacceptable—there was a role for government in redistributing income. But, these critics argue, it should not be involved in the details of what individuals consume—in, for instance, the provision of health or housing or even ensuring security in retirement. The role of government should be narrowly circumscribed.[9]

The chapter argues against these views: we should be concerned with inequalities not just in incomes but in well-being, and in access to the basic goods and services which are essential to individual well-being. Market imperfections, and limitations in the ability of governments to redistribute or to change the market distribution of income, mean that without a more active government role in the provision of certain essential goods and services large swaths of the population may face significant deprivations and there may be persistent large inequalities in well-being. It is not enough for governments just to provide cash.

Countries with strong welfare states have delivered higher standards of living to their citizens—and have done so in a relatively stable and sustainable way. It was the neoliberal

[8] In Stiglitz (1993a) I provide a somewhat different rationale for mandatory retirement insurance: A modern society cannot continence old individuals living in utter poverty, even if it is the result of their own failure to save for retirement. There will be a "bail-out," and that gives rise to a moral hazard problem. Compulsory pensions mitigate the moral hazard problem.

[9] Much along the lines suggested by the second welfare theorem—to lump sum redistributions. Earlier discussions have explained why such redistributions are not feasible.

policies, especially associated with deregulation, which brought on the 2008 crisis and have led to repeated crises around the world.

The chapter argues that both advances in our understandings of the limits of markets and the power of collective action, and changes in the structure of the economy, make it necessary to strengthen the welfare state and to broaden the range of what it does, going beyond social protection. It should, for instance, include programs to guarantee full access to the labor market and basic elements of a middle-class life to most citizens. (There are multiple justifications of such an assertion. Within the individualistic social welfare framework that has long been at the center of economic analysis, the market failures to which we have already alluded provide a rationale for government intervention—for instance, before government began to provide mortgages for ordinary families, they typically didn't have access to the finance they needed; and even now, prevalent mortgages are not well designed to enable individuals to withstand the risks that families face, and private issuers of mortgages often engage in exploitive behavior.[10] There are economic consequences of excesses of inequalities in income and wealth, and deprivations in housing and health to which we have referred in earlier chapters: economies marked by such inequalities perform more broadly. The presence of these externalities too provides a rationale for government intervention. Chapter 37 provides another justification of the welfare state, seeing society less narrowly than through the lens provided by an individualistic social welfare state. In particular, once it is recognized that preferences are endogenous and largely socially determined,[11] then the economists' standard approach to welfare analysis falls apart, and it is hard to escape asking deeper, and long-standing, philosophical questions, such as what constitutes a good society.)

But even in the area of social protection, there is a need for a broadened mandate, to deal with, for instance, the large groups in society suffering from significant deprivations—even in wealthy countries. The chapter argues that the neoliberal philosophy of putting the onus for deprivation among the elderly on the individual is questionable; but even most of those that believe that there should, in general, be reliance on markets agree that that simply cannot be done for children. One cannot claim that they should have done a better job at picking their parents.

The twenty-first-century welfare state entails both broader responsibilities and more instruments. Markets, on their own, fail not just in providing social protection (insurance), but in a host of other ways which are important to well-being. The chapter focuses in particular on those arising out of pervasive imperfections in capital markets and the presence of a broad range of externalities—for instance, individuals when they are young may not have the funds to invest in the education and health of their children, and society as a whole benefits from having a well-educated and healthy workforce and citizenry.

I emphasize here too the importance of the public option—government providing services like health care, retirement annuities, and mortgages in competition with the private sector. (The role of the public option is expanded in Stiglitz, 2019a.) In many areas, government has shown itself to have lower transactions costs and to provide products (like income contingent loans and inflation indexed annuities) that are highly valued but which

[10] This was especially evident in the run-up to the 2008 financial crisis. See Stiglitz (2010a) or the rash of books written about that crisis.

[11] As we have argued elsewhere in this book and in Hoff and Stiglitz (2016) and Demerritt, Hoff, and Stiglitz (forthcoming).

the private market has not provided.[12] The government may be able to not just broaden the range of choices confronting individuals, but through increased competition generate lower prices and more innovation.

The chapter ends with what may be a fitting conclusion for the entire book:

> Thus, the welfare state is not *just* a matter of social justice. Still, I believe the most compelling case for the welfare state goes beyond ... narrow economic arguments [such as that the welfare state leads to stronger growth]. It even goes beyond standard arguments for social justice.
>
> The questions are, what kind of society do we wish to live in, and what kind of individuals do we wish to be? For those who support the welfare state, its central role is in creating compassionate individuals with a social conscience and a sense of solidarity with their fellow citizens.

[12] See, for instance, Chapman, Higgins, and Stiglitz (2014). In many cases, as we have noted, the market failures are *inherent,* the almost inevitable consequence of imperfect and costly information. In some cases, the government has advantages arising out of economies of scale and scope; for instance, if the government collects income taxes, the marginal cost of collecting payments due on an income contingent loan are, with modern technology, minimal. See, for example, Stiglitz (2014g).

36
Inequality and Taxation

1 Introduction

Frank Ramsey's brilliant 1927 paper, modestly entitled, "A contribution to the theory of taxation," is a landmark in the economics of public finance.[1] Nearly a half century later, through the work of Diamond and Mirrlees (1971) and Mirrlees (1971), his paper can be thought of as launching the field of optimal taxation and revolutionizing public finance.[2]

Ramsey, in his short life, made pathbreaking contributions to two other fields, the theory of optimal growth (Ramsey, 1928) and the theory of subjective probability (Ramsey, 1931).[3] Here, he addresses a question which he says was posed to him by A. C. Pigou: Given that commodity taxes are distortionary, what is the best way of raising revenues, that is, what is the set of taxes to raise a given revenue which maximizes utility? The answer is now commonly referred to as Ramsey taxes. The basic insight was that taxes should be set so as to reduce the consumption of each good (along its compensated demand curve) equiproportionately. He establishes this result in two contexts:

(i) if the government needs to raise only a small amount of tax revenue; and
(ii) if utility functions are quadratic.

The analysis is beautiful, mathematically sophisticated, making use of all the artillery in the theory of consumer behavior, including the symmetry of the Slutsky relations. The conclusion overturned simplistic analyses that somehow continue to prevail in some quarters for decades after Ramsey's paper and, in some subfields of economics, continue to this day. Some economists argued against differential taxation on the grounds that it is best just to have a single tax (typically on wages). A wage tax introduces a single distortion—between the marginal rate of substitution between labor and consumption and the marginal rate of transformation. Interest income taxes and commodity taxes introduce additional distortions. (Interestingly, Ramsey's analysis has, wrongly, continued to be used by some economists to argue against the taxation of capital.)[4]

[1] Excerpted from a longer article, "In Praise of Frank Ramsey's Contribution to the Theory of Taxation," *Economic Journal*, March 2015, written on the occasion of the 125th anniversary of the *Economic Journal*.

I owe a great debt to my co-authors with whom I have written work that may be considered to follow in Ramsey's footsteps—Richard Arnott, Bob Brito, Shahe Emran, John Hamilton, Raaj Sah, Steve Slutsky, and most especially Tony Atkinson and Partha Dasgupta; and like all those who toil in these fields, I owe a debt to Peter Diamond and James Mirrlees, who not only shaped the modern theory of optimal taxation but also shaped my own thinking. I am indebted to Frederic Vermeulen and an anonymous referee for their helpful comments on an earlier draft and to Sandesh Dhungana and Eamon Kircher-Allen for research and editorial assistance. Financial support from INET is gratefully acknowledged.

[2] Given the huge number of papers that have been written in this field in the last half century, this chapter cannot even attempt a survey. Rather, I focus on the central themes raised by Ramsey in his paper. Textbook treatments are provided by Atkinson and Stiglitz (1980) and Salanié (2003).

[3] In addition, he made important contributions to mathematics, logic and philosophy, before dying at the young age of 26.

[4] See the discussion below and the references cited there.

The Origins of Inequality, and Policies to Contain It. Joseph E. Stiglitz, Oxford University Press. © Joseph E. Stiglitz (2025).
DOI: 10.1093/oso/9780198799580.003.0037

As another example of such simplistic economics, some macroeconomists continue to argue that monetary authorities should only interfere with the market in setting short-term interest rates.

Ramsey showed that efficient taxation required imposing a complete array of taxes—not just a single tax. A large number of small distortions, carefully constructed, is better than a single large distortion. And he showed precisely what these market interventions would look like. (He even explains that the optimal intervention might require subsidies—what he calls bounties—for some commodities. "A tax on sugar might reduce the consumption of damsons more than in proportion to the reduction in the total consumption of sugar and so require to be offset by a bounty on damsons" (Ramsey 1927, p. 54). Similar reasoning would suggest that if there are a variety of tools for managing the macroeconomy, in general, they should all be employed.

Ramsey's paper has been enormously influential, but its central policy recommendations—the desirability of taxing goods for which there is low demand elasticity—is fundamentally misguided, because it ignores distribution. As we emphasize below, if we didn't care about distribution, we could simply impose lump sum taxes. This chapter briefly describes Ramsey's basic insights (Section 2), before showing how they are fundamentally altered in the presence of distributional considerations (Sections 3 and 4). Section 5 puts the subject of the design of optimal taxation within a broader information-theoretic perspective, while Section 6 comments on how the analysis needs to be modified once general equilibrium considerations are taken into account.

2 Major Insights

One of the striking aspects of the paper is that he not only provides a general formulation of the set of optimal taxes but he also translates this into concrete results in the case of linear demand and supply functions (quadratic utility functions) and shows how the results can be extended to situations when there are restrictions on the set of feasible taxes. In particular, when there are a set of commodities with fixed taxes (including commodities that cannot be taxed at all), he shows that there should be an equi-proportionate reduction in the goods for which taxes can be freely set. In the case of linear and separable demand and supply curves (quadratic utility functions) and small taxes, he shows that optimal taxes are inversely related to the compensated elasticity of demand and supply.

$$t/p = 1/\text{elasticity of demand} + 1/\text{elasticity of supply}. \tag{36.1}$$

This implies, of course, raising all the requisite revenue from a good which is either inelastically demanded or supplied, because such a tax generates no distortions. This in turn has one other implication: if say labor is supplied inelastically, then optimal taxation requires imposing a tax on labor alone; but a proportionate tax on all commodities is equivalent to a tax on labor. This is hardly a surprising result—one for which one did not need Ramsey's apparatus (as Ramsey himself recognized): when there is an inelastic factor, it has long been recognized that there is no distortion associated with taxing it.[5]

[5] Henry (1886) focused on the taxation of land as the inelastic supply factor of production. Subsequent research by Vickrey (1977, 1999) and Arnott and Stiglitz (1979) identified conditions under which such a tax would provide

Ramsey's analysis can be viewed as the first successful exercise in second best economics. First best economics called for the imposition of lump sum taxes. Later, Meade (1955) and Lipsey and Lancaster (1956) would call attention to the fact that when some of the efficiency conditions are not satisfied, it may mean that others should not be satisfied. Their analysis would suggest that it would be very difficult indeed to characterize optimal resource allocations under such conditions. But Ramsey showed precisely how this could be done, when the reason for the distortion (the discrepancy between the marginal rate of substitution in preferences and the marginal rate of transformation in production) was to raise funds for the government.

Ramsey, however, went beyond this into an exploration of third best economics. He asked, what happens if there are some commodities that cannot be taxed, or whose tax rates are fixed. He argues that the same result (on the equi-proportionate reduction in consumption) holds for the set of goods that can be freely taxed.

3 Distributional Considerations

There was something distinctly unpleasant about Ramsey's recommendations: it suggested taxing the necessities of life, which tend to have low price elasticities (especially for the poor) at a high rate. If such a policy were pursued, it would imply that taxation should be regressive.[6]

Of course, Ramsey considered a model in which all individuals were identical, so distributional issues simply did not arise. But if all individuals were identical, there would be no problem imposing a lump sum tax. The only reason that we resort to distortionary commodity taxes is implicitly because we are concerned with the regressivity of a lump sum (per capita) tax. But that in turn means that we have to focus explicitly on the distributional consequences of commodity taxation.

When we do this, not surprisingly we obtain markedly different results. There is a tension between imposing high taxes on commodities with low (compensated) price elasticities (generating low dead weight loss) and imposing high taxes on commodities with high income elasticities—resulting in a more progressive tax system. (The precise formulas are given, for example, by Atkinson and Stiglitz (1972d, 1980), and depend on the weight given to equity.)[7]

But if we are concerned with equity, in general, there is no reason to limit ourselves to commodity taxation. Ramsey's analysis can, as we observed earlier, be viewed as the first

all the revenue that was required for financing public goods (in economies in which there was a local public good and congestion or other factors leading to decreasing returns to scale led to optimal sized communities).

[6] We focus on the implications tax formula (36.1) for the dependence of taxation on the elasticity of demand. In contrast to Diamond and Mirrlees, Ramsey also has the tax rate depend (inversely) on the elasticity of supply. As this paper emphasizes, the optimal set of commodity taxes depends heavily on what other set of taxes are in place. Dasgupta and Stiglitz (1971) show that with a profit tax at rate τ, the optimal tax formula is

$$t/p = 1/\text{elasticity of demand} + (1-\tau)/\text{elasticity of supply}. \tag{36.2}$$

With a 100% tax on pure profits or infinite supply elasticities, we get a result analogous to DM, where it is only properties of the demand function which affect tax rate. With a zero tax on pure profits, we get the original Ramsey result. Of course, there are important distributional concerns in the taxation of profits and rents, since these accrue disproportionately to the rich.

[7] See also Diamond (1975) and Mirrlees (1975c).

(and one of the best) examples of second-best welfare economics. He assumed that lump sum taxes were not feasible and asked what is the best set of distortionary commodity taxes. But in the theory of the second best, it is always necessary to be precise about what are the constraints: even if lump sum taxes are not feasible, other taxes may be. Most importantly, the government can impose redistributive income taxes, or even possibly redistributive wage taxes.

Going beyond the analysis of taxation with identical individuals, one faces a problem: how does one weigh the well-being of different individuals? The standard approach in the theory of optimal taxation developing out of Ramsey's work was to use a utilitarian social welfare function, that is, simply "add up" the utility of different individuals. But it turns out that many, if not most, of the qualitative results can be extended to Pareto efficient tax structures, tax structures such that no one (no group) can be made better off without making someone else—or some group—worse off.

Thus, the set of Pareto efficient tax structures depends explicitly on the set of feasible taxes.[8] If the number of hours worked is observable, then it is possible to have progressive wage taxes. If only income is observable (the product of wages per hour and the number of hours worked), then it is possible to have a progressive income tax but not a progressive wage tax.

But in the presence of a progressive income tax, the optimal set of commodity taxes looks markedly different from that suggested by Ramsey. In one polar case, where (the entire vector of) consumption is separable from leisure (work), Pareto efficient taxation implies no commodity taxation (Atkinson and Stiglitz 1976; Mirrlees 1976).

Kaplow (2006b) shows that under the separability condition, whenever there is distortionary commodity taxation, a distribution neutral Pareto improvement can be obtained through the income tax system. Without separability or in the presence of consumer heterogeneity, however, commodity taxation may be desirable: if richer individuals consume proportionately more chocolate, or if chocolate is a substitute for leisure, a chocolate tax may enable one to obtain a desired redistribution with less distortion in the income tax system.

Though the case of separability is very special, what the Atkinson–Stiglitz theorem illustrates is that in the presence of an (optimal) income tax, the optimal set of commodity taxes looks markedly different from that described by Ramsey.

In particular, commodity taxation can be viewed as a particular type of Pigouvian corrective tax.[9] The focus is not on the impact on tax revenues, or even directly on dead weight losses (as usually conceived), but on impacts on the self-selection constraints that are central to the design of the optimal income tax. "Loosening" the self-selection constraints has a first order effect on welfare, while the distortions associated with small commodity taxation have a second order effect on welfare.[10]

[8] The concept of Pareto efficient taxation is noted in Mirrlees (1976) and Stiglitz (1982e), and explored further in Stiglitz (1985e, 1987a, 1998a) and Brito, Hamilton, Slutsky, and Stiglitz (1990). See also Konishi (1995) and Saez (2002a).

[9] Pigouvian corrective taxes attempt to "correct" for market failures, such as environmental externalities. Greenwald and Stiglitz (1986) show that whenever there are asymmetries of information and/or an incomplete set of risk markets, there are pecuniary externalities that matter.

[10] This is the essential point of Greenwald and Stiglitz (1986) and Arnott, Greenwald, and Stiglitz, et al. (1994).

4 Non-linear Taxation and Heterogeneous Individuals

Moreover, once one admits the possibility of non-linear income taxes, should not one consider the possibility of non-linear commodity taxes? If so, the problem that Ramsey solved was a special case of a more general problem (just as the optimal linear income tax (Stiglitz, 2009a) is a special case of the optimal non-linear income tax (Mirrlees, 1971)). Of course, as we have already noted, the special case may be the more relevant case. For many commodities, the possibility of arbitrage means that taxes have to be linear; but there are some commodities, perhaps most importantly, electricity, for which arbitrage opportunities are typically limited.

Most of the work in the analysis of optimal taxation with heterogeneous individuals assumes that individuals differ in simple ways, for example, their productivity, but not their preferences. This enables us to elide the classical welfare question of interpersonal utility comparisons. There is a simple question that has to be answered for determining the optimal degree of progressivity: if (full) income increases by 1%, by what percentage does the marginal social utility of income decrease? A broad consensus has emerged within the fraternity of optimal tax economists that the answer (related to revealed individual behavior, e.g., in the context of risk taking) is by 1–2%. But if individuals have different indifference curves (curves that cross, perhaps even more than once), there is no such easy trick available. Changes in relative prices can have markedly different effects on different individuals, even with roughly similar income. In practice, we give considerable weight to the current set of consumer prices (affected as they may be by government policy) and assess the welfare impact by looking at the income equivalent changes arising from the proposed change in tax (or expenditure) policy.[11]

5 An Information Theoretic Perspective

There are many ways in which individuals differ that are easily observable, for example, age, gender, marital status, some of which (like age and gender) are not (easily) alterable. In principle, if the unobservable or imperfectly observable characteristics that we would like to base taxation on are correlated with observable characteristics or behavior, there is some presumption that we should differentiate taxes based on those observables—unless all the relevant information is contained in some other variable that might more easily be the basis of taxation.[12] Thus, with separability of utility (between consumption and leisure) and the only basis of individual differences being labor productivity, an optimal progressive income tax fully captures the relevant information. But if more productive individuals (and only more productive individuals) eat chocolate ice cream rather than vanilla ice cream, then it might be desirable to supplement the optimal income tax with a tax on chocolate

[11] Implicitly, the standard approach sets utility levels of two individuals with different preferences but the same income (at current wages and prices) as the same. The point is that we might come to very different views of the distributional impacts if we set the utility levels to be the same at different wages and prices, and assess the income equivalent impact of a change in a tax off of that different base.

[12] It is an open question why more extensive use of such variables is not made. In practice, some redistribution for the elderly is done through the social insurance system.

ice cream.[13] Similarly, we might feel that individuals have relatively little choice about how much they spend on heating—the main determinant is the weather—but it is not possible to observe the weather conditions under which each individual lives. But fuel consumption may be (imperfectly) correlated with the weather, especially for poor individuals. Of course, some individuals may consume more fuel because they like a warmer temperature, and it is inefficient to subsidize fuel consumption, because it leads to excessive consumption. Still, an optimal tax structure might include a fuel subsidy, at least for poor individuals. While economists have typically criticized these subsidies, the optimal tax theory growing out of Ramsey's seminal work provides a rationale.[14]

6 General Equilibrium Incidence

We have described how at the center of modern optimal tax theory and the work growing out of Ramsey lies a balancing of distributional and efficiency concerns. The early literature essentially took the before tax-and-transfer distribution of income, or more accurately, the relative wages of different individuals, as given. It worried about how an increase in taxes on the rich might affect their labor supply and thus the supply of funds available for redistribution. But government tax and expenditure policies can change the before tax and transfer distribution and, in particular, relative wages. This can reduce the burden imposed on distortionary redistribution policies. If it is possible to do so, governments should—again, even possibly if their doing so interferes with production efficiency.[15]

7 Concluding Comments

Ramsey's paper can be viewed as the seminal paper in what has become an immense literature on optimal taxation.[16] He focused narrowly on the question of how to minimize the deadweight losses associated with commodity taxation. His contributions—both methodological and in terms of insights into the design of tax structure—have been lasting.[17]

[13] For an early formal discussion of this point, see Mirrlees (1976); for a more recent discussion, see Saez (2002a).

[14] Much of the criticism though is based on political economy concerns that go well beyond the simple normative framework posited by Ramsey. The magnitude of the subsidies, once enacted, often go well beyond anything that could be justified by an optimal tax framework and are hard to reverse when circumstances change.

[15] See Chapter 19 of this volume for a more extensive discussion of both general equilibrium incidence and of the way taxation can act as a corrective tax, weakening the impact of self-selection, incentive compatibility, and collateral constraints.

[16] There are many other directions in which Ramsey's work has had great influence. Ramsey focused on a government needing to raise a fixed amount of revenue. The amount of revenue to be raised depends on the desirable level of public goods, itself a result of balancing out the marginal benefit of public goods and the marginal costs of raising the revenue—which in turn depends on the design of the tax structure. Much of the literature already referred to addresses these issues. In the absence of perfect redistributive taxation, the level and form of public expenditure needs to be sensitive to distributional consequences (Stiglitz, 1998a). This is a sub-theme within the huge literature in cost-benefit analysis.

[17] We have not been able to address many of the interesting and difficult questions that have been addressed in the huge literature that has grown out of Ramsey's work. For instance, natural formulations of optimal tax problems give rise to non-convexities, which in turn imply that optimal taxes should be random. See, for example, Stiglitz (1983b), Arnott and Stiglitz (1988a), and Brito, Hamilton, Slutsky, and Stiglitz (1995). Nor have we considered the costs of administering the tax system and compliance (Slemrod, 1990).

The subsequent literature took many turns and twists. The original suggestion, that inelastically demanded commodities like bread should face a high tax rate, was regressive enough; but Ramsey-like arguments were then used against any taxation of the income from capital, or even bequests. But even as those arguments were being formulated, deeper analyses suggested just the contrary—goods demanded by the poor should be taxed at lower rates, and interest income should be taxed. Though the pathbreaking work of DM showed that Ramsey's results could be generalized in some important ways, other work showed that the domain of applicability of Ramsey's original insights may be more limited: changes in assumptions about the set of feasible taxes (not allowing certain taxes, or allowing a progressive income tax or non-linear commodity taxes) and, in particular, about the taxation of pure rents, incorporating more explicitly distributional considerations, and/or recognizing the important ways in which our economy differs from the competitive model underlying Ramsey's analysis all change the optimal structure of commodity taxation in important ways.

Ramsey ended his 1927 essay by modestly observing that "the more complicated results" he had obtained might "well be valid under still wider conditions. But these are, in the general case, too complicated to be worth setting down in the absence of practical data to compare with them" (p. 60). We have noted that indeed many of the more complicated results described here require estimates of parameters about which there is little information. In the end, perhaps the most important contribution of the line of work growing out of Ramsey's seminal paper has been to force us to think carefully about the distortionary and the distributive effects of taxation and their interactions, and when we do that, our intuitions about what kind of a tax system is desirable are reinforced. If it were not for our concern about distribution—if we cared only about minimizing the dead-weight loss of our tax system—we would have imposed lump sum taxes. Moreover, tax structures are limited to making use of observable information, but there are distortionary consequences of imposing axes on observable but alterable variables. A (inequality averse) society concerned with maximizing societal welfare should implement progressive income taxes, complemented by well-designed indirect taxation, bequest taxes, capital and wealth taxes that enhance the progressivity of the overall tax structure. Each of these taxes makes use of different information—each imperfectly reflecting underlying variables of interest. While Ramsey was correct in his conclusion that the implementation of optimal taxation may depend on hard to estimate parameters, policy requires making judgments about the magnitudes of critical tradeoffs, and the line of research the Ramsey opened up has helped us identify what those critical tradeoffs are and how they can be best assessed.

37

The Welfare State in the Twenty-First Century

1 Introduction

Designing the twenty-first-century welfare state is part of a broader debate redefining the role of the market, the state, and "civil society"—non-state forms of collective action.[1]

One of the tenets of the Reagan–Thatcher revolution was questioning the welfare state. Some worried that the financial burdens of the welfare state would drag down growth. Some worried about the effect of the welfare state on the sense of individual responsibility, others that the welfare state provides an opportunity for the lazy and profligate to take advantage of hardworking citizens. A sense of social solidarity had united citizens around the world during World War II. Some 30 years after that global conflict, that solidarity was eroding, and economic arguments quickened its disintegration.

This chapter argues that these arguments criticizing the welfare state are for the most part fallacious and that changes in the global economy have even increased the importance of the system. It then describes some of the key elements of a twenty-first-century welfare state.

2 Basic Precepts of the Welfare State

To understand the principles and philosophy of the welfare state, it is useful to contrast it with the "neoliberal" or market-oriented state.[2]

The central economic doctrine of neoliberalism is that markets are efficient. Moreover, market advocates believe that every (Pareto-) efficient outcome can be supported by a free-market economy, with the appropriate (lump-sum) redistributions.[3] This implies that one can separate issues of efficiency and distribution, and that the task of economics is to maximize output (as reflected, say, in GDP), leaving the distribution to the political process. When the conditions required for these results to hold are not satisfied, the job of the economist is to advise governments on how to ensure that they are. For example, markets must be made competitive through effective enforcement of antitrust laws.

Of course, politicians who have argued against the welfare state typically do not frame their critique in the formal language of economics. Rather, they talk about how the provision of social insurance attenuates incentives, for example, through the taxes that are used

[1] This is a shortened version of the chapter "The Welfare State in the Twenty-First Century" in *The Welfare State Revisited*, Jose Antonio Ocampo and Joseph E. Stiglitz (eds.), New York: Columbia University Press, 2018, focusing particularly on inequality and the welfare state.

[2] As in any set of doctrines, there are large differences in views among the adherents of these market-based philosophies. I ignore those subtleties here and refer to doctrines that argue against the welfare state and for the reliance on markets as "neoliberalism."

[3] These are referred to as the first and second fundamental theorems of welfare economics. For further elaboration on these issues, see Stiglitz (1994b).

The Origins of Inequality, and Policies to Contain It. Joseph E. Stiglitz, Oxford University Press. © Joseph E. Stiglitz (2025).
DOI: 10.1093/oso/9780198799580.003.0038

to finance it. Many politicians go further, saying that the welfare state creates a culture of dependency, implicitly arguing that it changes the nature of the individual. This argument moves beyond standard welfare economics, which takes preferences as fixed and given. This is an important argument, to which I return shortly.

By contrast, the advocates of the welfare state believe that markets are not, in general, efficient; that market failures are pervasive and not easily correctable; and that as a result, government needs to take a more active role. Of course, government should do what it can to ensure that markets work well, more in accord with how they are described in standard textbooks—for example, making sure that there is strong competition and that firms do not exploit ordinary individuals through questionable practices.

Later in this chapter, I will briefly recount the theoretical research done over the past 40 years that helped us understand that pervasive market failures indicate that markets are often not efficient and that there is an important role for government, including those roles typically associated with the welfare state. The political debate was framed differently: the demand for the welfare state was driven by hard-to-ignore imperfections in markets that sometimes had a devastating effect on people's lives and well-being. It was obvious that markets were not providing insurance against many of the important risks that individuals faced, such as unemployment and inadequately financed retirement. The annuities that were available were expensive, and none had provisions against important risks, like the risk of inflation. The absence of these insurance markets had profound effects both on efficiency and individual well-being. Indeed, it can be shown that the provision of well-designed unemployment benefit programs can not only increase well-being but even increase GDP (Stiglitz and Yun, 2017).

So too, many individuals had substandard housing, suffered from hunger, and had inadequate access to medicine. Access to these necessities was declared a basic human right under the UN's 1948 Universal Declaration of Human Rights. Whether one framed these deprivations in terms of basic economic human rights or in other ways, there was a call for *specific equalitarianism*, focusing not just on income but on specific goods (Tobin, 1970). Economists might debate why individuals faced these specific deprivations—whether it was a result of market failures or individuals' poor decisions or the failure of the political process to make the necessary redistributions—but the fact of the matter is that the deprivations were deep and pervasive.

Of special concern were those deprivations confronting children, which were in no way a result of their own choices or behavior. Here again it was clear that such deprivations represented a social injustice but also led to lower GDP—these individuals would not be able to live up to their potential.

Thus, the creation of the welfare state was motivated by observed failures in the economy and society, outcomes that seemed socially unacceptable. Developments in economic theory only helped explain why these failures should have been expected.

Twenty-first-century advocates of the welfare state begin with the premise that something is not working when large sections of society face such deprivations and that government can and should do something about these failures. Moreover, ordinary individuals are having difficulty coping with unanticipated financial stresses. In the United States, what was once viewed as a basic middle-class life is no longer attainable for large swaths of society. The welfare state cannot remedy all of the ills facing our society, but the advocates of the welfare state believe it can make a difference. The traditional welfare state focuses on a particular set of "market failures" associated with the markets' ability to help individuals confront important risks that they face, such as providing for social protection, through, for instance, retirement insurance (annuities) and health insurance. Markets have also failed to provide insurance against unemployment and disability, and again the welfare state stepped in.[4]

Advocates of the twenty-first-century welfare state argue that it should go beyond the traditional welfare state model in several critical ways and it rooted in broader philosophical foundations. First, it is based on seeing the country as a community and promoting a broader sense of social solidarity. Think of a country as a large family. Family members take care of one another. That is one of the most important things they do. There is solidarity among the members of the family. National solidarity implies that those who can do so take care of those who are less fortunate. At the very least, they provide some form of social protection.

Within communities, concepts of social justice—a fair distribution of income—are important. The welfare state is essential to achieving social justice, broadly understood. Rawls (1971) provides a convincing case for thinking about social justice as choosing rules for society behind a veil of ignorance, before one knows one's ability, or one's station in life. I would add: and before one knows the risks that one will confront. Clearly, if individuals are averse to risk, and if markets fail to provide adequate insurance, one would want society to provide social protection. Social justice also entails government ensuring that all children, regardless of the wealth of their parents, had access to good health care and education.

There is another set of arguments for government provision of annuities (retirement) insurance and health insurance and other basic needs, like housing, which are essential at different stages of their lives. Neoliberalism simply assumed that markets provided the most efficient way of providing for these life-cycle needs, at least at a basic level. In some countries or circumstances that might be true. But it was also obviously not so in certain other circumstances. The largely private health sector in the United States is far less efficient than that of European countries with greater state involvement and delivers poorer outcomes with greater expenditures. Australia's system of public income-contingent student loan programs is far more equitable and efficient than America's privately based student loan system. The American public social security annuity program is far more efficient than any private annuity—with a smaller fraction of resources going into overhead.

While in principle the market *might* provide insurance annuities or health insurance, there are some forms of risk sharing in which the market cannot engage but the state can. Cross-generational risk sharing is one. Individuals within a generation can pool their risks, but it is not possible for an individual to make a contract with someone in a generation yet to be born. Society as a whole can, however, make such social contracts, and it does so all of the time. Some of the costs of fighting World War I and World War II were borne by later

[4] In some ways, there is a parallel between the welfare state and the developmental state. In the latter, it was recognized that markets on their own often did not succeed in the structural transformations that were required if countries were to achieve their developmental ambitions. As in the case of the welfare state, the rationale for state intervention was partly pervasive market failures of both the static and dynamic varieties. The developmental state corrected these market failures and had a catalytic role in promoting structural transformation. It helped change mind-sets—to understand that change was possible and to understand the scientific and technological bases of change.

generations. Of course, the societal expenditures occurred during the war. And aggregate consumption during that period was reduced. But later generations' effective transfer of goods to the working-age people of the 1940s—via social security and other society-wide expenditures—meant that the World War II–era generation's consumption was probably reduced by less than it would have been otherwise. Well-designed social security systems are in part structured to facilitate this intergenerational risk sharing.

The welfare state seeks not only to respond to these calls for solidarity, social justice, and intergenerational equity, but to shape society and the individuals in it. The construction of society—including the rules of the economic game—affects the nature of the individual—his or her beliefs, preferences, and behavior. Indeed, we noted that some critics of the welfare state emphasize that it may undermine its beneficiaries' sense of individual responsibility. Supporters make precisely the opposite argument: the welfare state encourages social solidarity, making the individual think more about the community of which he or she is a part and, in doing so, improving social behavior in a myriad of other ways.[5] Neoliberalism has encouraged selfishness and has led to pervasive moral depravities, evidenced so clearly by the bankers in the run-up to the Great Recession: a willingness to do almost anything that enhances profits, so long as one could get away with it.

2.1 Government and Market Failure

There are some who acknowledge the pervasiveness of market failures—such as the failure to provide insurance against critical risks that individuals face—and the ability of government, *in principle*, to correct them. But they argue that government failures are so deep and pervasive that, in practice, government interventions are unlikely to correct the market failures.

There is, of course, ample evidence of both government and market failure, without highlighting one and underestimating the other. How far the government should go in correcting market failures and with what instruments may depend on the capacities and capabilities of the state. The best-performing societies (using almost any measure) have created a well-functioning state—these societies have shown that the welfare state *can* work. It should be noted that in those societies that have achieved the best-functioning welfare states, such as those of Scandinavia, markets also work better. This is probably no accident: a well-functioning welfare state may contribute to the functioning of the market.[6]

2.2 A Variety of Practices

In the twenty-first-century welfare state, there is no ideological attachment as to the best way of addressing the failures with which the state is concerned. Whether the welfare state operates through government provision of services, government regulations,

[5] Hoff and Stiglitz (2016) emphasize the endogeneity of preferences and the role that society plays in structuring beliefs. See, in particular, their citations to evidence concerning the effects of banking on greed and dishonesty.

[6] In the original version of the paper, there is an extensive discussion of how a good welfare state can, for instance, encourage risk taking and entrepreneurship.

or interventions in markets is not important, so long as it is effective. In some circumstances, the evolution of the market—sometimes as a result of the catalytic effects of government—reduces the magnitude of the market failure and changes the nature of public-welfare-state-intervention. Thus, some might say that annuity markets are better today than they were at the time retirement social insurance programs were created (in the 1930s for the United States). Though this is true, they still do not provide insurance against critical risks like inflation. There are still unacceptably high transactions costs.

When we look around the globe, we see a range of practices. Some countries have retained the welfare state, modifying it here, strengthening it there, as they identify problems and opportunities for improvement. The Scandinavian countries are all thought to have a welfare state, but remarkably, there are also a few developing countries, like Namibia, Mauritius, and the Seychelles, that can be said to have a form of the welfare state, adapted to their (much) lower standards of living. These countries think of the welfare state as advancing a broad range of societal objectives—including economic growth. They have done well (well above the average for Africa), and many in these countries attribute at least part of that success to their having a welfare state. At the other extreme, some countries, including the United States, have at most limited social protection. The safety net is just something to prevent citizens from starving but is not designed to enable them to live a life with dignity or to give them the capabilities to be more self-supporting.

There are many institutions, laws, and programs that make up the welfare state, and many of these overlap with what occurs in governments that do not think of themselves as having a welfare state. I want to focus on those aspects of the role of government that are particularly associated with a twenty-first-century welfare state.

I begin with a discussion of the developments in ideas, especially in economic theory, that have influenced—or should have influenced—thinking about the welfare state. This is followed by a discussion of some of the changes in the world that also have had an effect on the evolution of the modern welfare state. Section 5 then analyzes the principles of a twenty-first-century welfare state. The chapter then turns to two particular issues, the welfare state and deprivations (Section 6) and a twenty-first-century American welfare state (Section 7).

3 Changes in Ideas and the Evolution of the Welfare State

There have been large changes in the world—and in our understanding of the world—that have affected views of the welfare state.

The welfare state came into its own in the aftermath of World War II and the social solidarity to which it gave rise. This was a period of rapid economic growth in both Europe and America, and it was a period of shared prosperity. Every group grew, but those at the bottom saw their incomes grow faster than those at the top.

A third of a century later, this sense of solidarity seemed to wane, and neoliberalism seemed to triumph. It is worth noting that neoliberalism did not come into fashion as a result of the failure of the welfare state. There were many problems that did smooth the way for neoliberalism's growing popularity. The United States, for instance, was beset by inflation, as it tried to fight a war in Vietnam without having anyone pay the price. This macro-mismanagement was then aggravated by the oil price shocks. But these problems were not *caused* by the welfare state, and abandoning the welfare state was not the solution. Still, they provided an opportunity for the ever-present critics of the welfare state to push for another model, neoliberalism, or as it was called at the time, supply side economics, which promised faster growth—so much faster that all would benefit. The pie would increase so much that even though those in the middle and bottom would be receiving a smaller proportion, the size of their piece would increase. But the reforms did not pan out: the economies grew more slowly, rather than faster; inequality was even greater than "promised." Similar, but less extreme changes occurred in Europe. The welfare state, weakened but not gone, softened the consequences, especially in Europe, but did not reverse them: inequality grew in most countries around the world.

The irony was that this seeming faith in markets grew just as economists were beginning to understand the limits of markets and why market failures were so pervasive. Many of these have been highlighted elsewhere in this book, so I will be brief. Adam Smith's presumption—that markets would lead the economy, as if by an invisible hand, to societal well-being—was reversed. Greenwald and Stiglitz (1986, 1988d) showed that even competitive economies were almost always inefficient, so long as there were imperfections (asymmetries) of information and incomplete risk markets—that is, always.[7] Diamond (1971) and Rothschild and Stiglitz (1976) showed that even a little bit of imperfection of information could have very large consequences. These advances also meant that one could not separate issues of distribution from issues of efficiency, as we explained more fully in Part III.C.[8]

Not only has there been greater understanding of the inefficiency of markets, there has also been greater understanding of the origins and adverse effects of inequality, illustrated in earlier chapters. In particular, nineteenth-century justifications of inequality ("just deserts," based on marginal productivity) are increasingly unpersuasive. Developments in game theory and markets with information imperfections provided understandings of why imperfections of competition were so pervasive, as well as understandings of the links among this market power, inequality, and the precariousness felt by so many ordinary citizens. Market power was often exercised by the rich (often through corporations) to exploit the disadvantaged, or even ordinary individuals. Because markets do not exist in a vacuum, they have to be structured: how they are structured affects efficiency and distributions. The rules of the game are set through political processes. But economic power too often gets translated into political power. The political power of the rich enabled them to write the rules of the game to enhance their market power and incomes—and to exploit workers and consumers. A vicious circle emerged.

One of the most profound implications of this new understanding of inequality was that we pay a high price for inequality and that, especially once we take into account what gave rise to this inequality, we could get better economic performance if we reduced inequality

[7] In particular, they showed that the economy was not constrained Pareto efficient, that is, there exist interventions within the given market structure that would make some individuals better off without making anyone else worse off. See also Geanakoplos and Polemarchakis (1986) and Arnott, Greenwald, and Stiglitz (1994b).

[8] Our own research showed that the second welfare theorem, which said in effect that one could separate out distribution and efficiency issues, was true only under restrictive and unrealistic conditions. Distribution effected, for instance, the magnitude of agency costs in a society. Moreover, imperfections of information meant that lump-sum taxes targeted at correcting distributional inequities could not exist. Greater inequalities in market incomes put a greater burden on redistribution through the tax and transfer system, and such redistributions were not costless.

from the extremes to which it was rising in the United States and many other Western countries.[9]

The research just described explained how it was that even with most of the standard assumptions of conventional economics—including fully rational individuals—market outcomes were inefficient and inequitable. But in recent decades not only have assumptions such as perfect information, perfect risk markets, and perfect competition that underlie the neoliberal model been questioned, the rational actor model itself has also been discredited thanks to the development of behavioral economics. Firms have ruthlessly exploited these irrationalities.[10] Among those who are most vulnerable to such exploitation are the poorest.

All of these increases in our understanding of the economy, the limitations of markets, the limitations of individual rationality, and the importance of equality should lead to a renewed focus on the welfare state—a reexamination of what it should do and how it should do it. We now have a better understanding, for instance, for why the government has to take a large role in social protection—failures in private insurance markets are endemic. But we also have a better understanding of why advancing well-being requires more than just social protection. Twenty-first-century welfare states should and will be different from those of the mid-twentieth century.

4 Changes in the World

While changes in ideas provide a renewed interest in the welfare state and the role it can play in improving societal well-being, changes in the world have increased the imperative for reconstructing the welfare state.

For instance, there have been marked changes in the labor market—there are no longer lifetime jobs, implying less incentive for firms to invest in their workers and less loyalty between workers and firms. Workplace-based welfarism of the mid-twentieth-century variety won't work today.[11] Matters have been made even worse because of the "sharing economy" and "innovations" in worker–employer relations—converting workers into "independent contractors." Many firms that have embraced these new models are motivated in part by the desire to avoid taxes and circumvent employer regulations.

At the same time, the enormous growth in inequality makes it clear that the market on its own, at least as it has been structured under neoliberalism, won't achieve anything approaching something that is socially acceptable, let alone any higher ambition, such as the just society. At the bottom, those in the United States confront the same real wages as they did 60 years ago. In the middle, the income of a full-time male worker—and it is increasingly difficult for those without a college education to get a full-time job—is comparable to what it was more than four decades ago.

There is an especially strong consensus that something needs to be done about childhood poverty—with approximately one in five people in the United States growing up in families in poverty. While the United States committed itself to the elimination of

[9] This was the central point of Stiglitz (2012a). There have been a rash of empirical studies from the IMF (Ostry, Berg, and Tsangarides, 2014; Dabla-Norris, Kochhar, Suphaphiphat, et al., 2015), the OECD (Cingano, 2014), and elsewhere corroborating this perspective.

[10] Evidenced so strongly in the Great Recession. See chapter 10 in Stiglitz (2010a). See also Akerlof and Shiller (2015).

[11] Just as earlier, the decline in the extended family and urbanization, with the weakening of the sense of community and the decreased role of religion placed increasing burdens on the state for social protection.

discrimination, the large gaps in gender, race, and ethnicity are evidence that discrimination still abounds. (The financial crisis of 2008 provided further evidence of racial and ethnic discrimination in lending.) Not only do the changes in the economy make it clear that the corporation cannot play the role in social protection that it once did, changes in the structure of our society limit the role of social institutions. Changes in demography mean that we have gone from the extended family to the nuclear family and, increasingly, to the non-family, as marriage becomes increasingly unpopular, especially among low-income individuals. As urbanization has progressed, social bonds have weakened, and with that the kind of social protection provided by communal solidarity (Putnam, 2000, 2015).

Finally, there have been a number of changes that have weakened the bargaining power of workers—including poorly managed globalization—and increased the market power of firms. Some of these have led to weakened unionization, and weakened unionization has led in turn to workers' weakened bargaining power. Rents have taken on greater importance: the competitive model provides an increasingly poor description of many (or even most) sectors of the economy (Council of Economic Advisers, 2016).

This means that without the protection of the state, there will be more individuals at the bottom, and the deprivations they suffer will only be addressed by state action, providing further impetus for a twenty-first-century welfare state.

5 Principles and Practices of a Twenty-First-Century Welfare State

The twenty-first-century welfare state is about achieving a just society and improving the well-being of ordinary citizens, recognizing that markets on their own won't necessarily do this and that corporate interests and national interests (interests of ordinary citizens) are often markedly different. It focuses on inequalities in initial distribution of assets, asymmetries of market power (including those arising from asymmetries of information and associated with discrimination, past and present), and market failures, with special attention to those least able to fend for themselves, especially children; and with ensuring that the basic prerequisites of a middle-class life (appropriate to the country's GDP) are accessible for most citizens.

Similarly, the modern welfare state does more than just providing a safety net, a subsistence floor and social protection. It is also a system of consumer, investor, and worker protection, including trying to increase competitiveness and transparency of markets, in the belief that more competitive and transparent markets enhance the welfare of society.

A central tenet of a twenty-first-century welfare state is ensuring equality of opportunity, and that, of course, entails a particular focus on children and their health and education, fighting against the intergenerational transmission of advantages and disadvantages and against discrimination in all its forms. And there is increasing recognition that one can't have equality of opportunity in a society with large disparities in income and wealth.

5.1 Multiple Instruments

Earlier we observed that the twenty-first-century welfare state is focused on creating opportunities and improving outcomes but is not wedded to any particular mechanism for achieving these. It sometimes employs market mechanisms but rejects income fetishism—the idea that well-being is necessarily enhanced by "cashing" out benefits—and allows individuals to make choices of their own. This rejection is not a matter of paternalism, though it is partially motivated by a concern about children who are not allowed to make choices for themselves and may not be in good positions to make good decisions. Behavioral economics has shown that individuals may make short-run choices that are not in their long-run interests, and persistent irrationalities can and are exploited by profit-maximizing firms. But even absent these, pervasive market failures may make access to certain basic necessities difficult at best for those of modest income. Private sector firms have shown the willingness and capacity to engage in broad and deep exploitation, including of those who are less informed. This means, at a minimum, that relying on the private sector necessitates tight monitoring and regulation; but both monitoring and regulation can be difficult—and once a private sector has been established, a political economy process is set in play to weaken regulation and its enforcement.

Moreover, there can be social consequences from the way the private sector works, which in turn have important societal consequences. In education, for instance, it can result in segregation by income or ability.[12] Again, one can imagine regulation to prevent this, but the design and implementation of such regulation is difficult. Further, education has shown itself to be one of the areas where exploitation is particularly easy: those from poor backgrounds may be in a weak position to judge what is being "sold," and in the United States, private for-profit colleges have proved particularly adept at taking advantage of this. The industry has also proved to be particularly adept at fighting off attempts to regulate it—even attempts to force disclosure of information (such as graduation rates, employment rates, and average salaries for degree holders) that would facilitate good choices on the part of potential enrollees.

There are, moreover, important social externalities, with the education of one child being affected by who else is in the classroom. But it is more than that: the provision of public education, with children from all backgrounds sharing similar experiences, helps shape society, providing an example of the endogeneity of preferences and attitudes discussed earlier in this chapter.[13]

While market power and asymmetries of bargaining power can arise in any market, the consequences can be particularly important in the provision of basic necessities. Here, if the market is relied upon, a welfare-state government has to be particularly sensitive to the importance of the rules of the game; changing the rules of the game can change relative bargaining positions. For instance, in a twenty-first-century welfare state, most jobs will be provided by the private sector, but there must be rules that facilitate workers engaging in

[12] For instance, if the rich prefer having their children go to school with the rich, profit-maximizing schools for the rich will be economically segregated.

[13] Given the centrality of education to our society, it is not surprising that there is a large literature on these subjects—the effects of choice on the quality of education and on educational segregation; the consequences of particular market and market-like mechanisms, such as vouchers and charter schools; the political economy of private education; and market failures in education, particularly once one sees education not just as part of the formation of human capital but as at the center of how society screens individuals, differentiating among those with different abilities. Stiglitz (1973a) discussed social externalities and the efficient provision of education; Stiglitz (1974h) discussed the interactions between private and public educational systems, with a majoritarian political economy model; Stiglitz (1977b) analyzed more broadly the inefficiencies associated with the provision of public goods by local authorities; Stiglitz (1975a) discussed the inefficiencies of the market provision of education, when there is screening; and Stiglitz (1988a) analyzed how market inefficiencies even extended to the market provision of textbooks.

collective bargaining. And the government will need to impose constraints on the market processes, setting minimum wages, maximum hours, minimum overtime pay, minimum family leave benefits, and so on.

All of the instruments relevant to reducing inequality might be considered part of "welfare policies," going well beyond the usual tax and transfer policies. Antitrust and consumer protection policies may be especially important in preventing exploitation. Changes in corporate governance and bankruptcy laws over the last 30 years in the United States have played an important role in the increase in extremes of inequality at the top and have even contributed to the increase in poverty. Creditor-friendly bankruptcy laws encouraged, for instance, predatory lending, with lenders knowing that it would be more difficult for individuals to discharge their debts.

5.2 Government as Producer and Regulator (and Entrepreneur)

The neoliberal agenda attempted to discredit government in many of its roles, except perhaps in providing a safety net for corporations, as was evident in the aftermath of the 2008 crisis. The oft-noted irony is that an agenda focused on minimizing the role of the state had resulted in the largest intervention of the state up to that point. But while corporations were provided with social protection, much more limited social protection was provided to those losing their homes and jobs.[14]

In fact, however, government-run programs can play an important role in the twenty-first-century welfare state. The next section will illustrate the role they can play through income-contingent loan programs; and our previous discussion has noted problems associated with the private provision of education.

Government has marked advantages in information, transactions cost, risk pooling, and the avoidance of exploitation. There at least needs to be strong government oversight in areas like insurance, education, and health, recognizing not only market failures but also the opportunities for exploitation.

As we noted earlier, in some areas government has proved to be an effective catalyst and entrepreneur.[15]

At the same time, a better understanding of economics has enabled an improvement in the design of the programs provided by the welfare state. Behavioral economics, for instance, has provided insights into how "nudges" can increase retirement security (see Sunstein and Thaler, 2008). Combining income-contingent loan programs with standard unemployment insurance can lead to more efficient provision of insurance (Stiglitz and Yun, 2014, 2017), as can the integration of various social insurance programs (Stiglitz and Yun, 2005).[16]

[14] In the United States, of the hundreds of billions of dollars that went to "saving the economy," a very small fraction went to helping homeowners. Many conservatives opposed providing bankruptcy relief or extending unemployment insurance, even as many reached even the extended time limits for support.

[15] See Mazzucato's book, *The Entrepreneurial State* (2015), describing the central role that government has played in the big innovations in recent decades.

Public social insurance for retirement spurred the development of the private annuity markets, though private annuities remain imperfect and expensive, partly because of the large profits, sales costs, and other transactions costs, and, like all insurance markets, they face problems of adverse selection.

[16] Research has also made us more aware of why private provision of, say, insurance, can have large externalities on public programs, that can sometimes be addressed, at least in part, by appropriate taxation, but also may

6 Deprivations

The growth of the welfare state was associated with the recognition that there were large groups in society suffering from significant deprivations—even in wealthy countries. For simplicity, we can divide them into three groups: youth, the elderly, and the poor of working age.

6.1 The Elderly

The distinction between neoliberalism and the welfare state is perhaps clearest in the context of the treatment of the elderly. If the elderly have insufficient income to live a decent life, the neoliberal response is: they should have saved for their retirement. Those that did not save enough are getting the just deserts of their profligacy, of their failure to save and manage risk appropriately. The nanny state undermines incentives for individuals to take care of themselves.

By contrast, the welfare state recognizes that there may be multiple reasons that individuals might end up in poverty in their old age, and whatever the reason, it is intolerable to allow them to suffer. Realizing that individuals might not save enough, and that our humane society is too soft not to bail out an elderly person who hadn't saved adequately, there needs to be a *minimal* compulsory savings program with minimal or no discretion over the management of funds.[17] And because some individuals have so low an income during their lifetimes that there was no way their savings could finance a retirement with a minimum of human decency, there is a need for supplementing what these workers would receive on an actuarial fair basis.

This twentieth-century perspective ignores multiple failures in the market for annuities and retirement products which calls forth a broader role for government: (1) Before social security, the market did not provide adequate annuities; and indeed, the market for annuities has been very slow to develop. (2) Even as it developed, premiums were high, partly because of high administrative costs compared with the government, which could take advantage of certain economies of scale and scope, including lower transactions costs in collecting and dispersing funds. (3) Even today, those who manage retirement accounts are often not required to obey fiduciary standards, resulting in large transfers of wealth from retirees to those managing the funds. (4) Even today, markets do not provide adequate insurance against some of the important risks, which are sometimes hard to anticipate. Private annuities do not provide insurance against inflation. Those buying safe government bonds can't buy insurance against the risk that the government will push interest rates down to zero for an extended period of time.

Modern theory has explained why, with adverse selection, important insurance markets (like the market for annuities) may not exist. Government can force pooling and risk sharing in ways that the private sector cannot.

require regulation. See Arnott and Stiglitz (1986, 1990) and Stiglitz and Yun (2013). In the context of education, see the discussion above.

[17] See Stiglitz (1993a).

Ironically, much of the interest in privatization of social security arose from the desire of the financial sector to increase its profits: they wanted to increase transactions costs, and they knew that there were huge opportunities for them to "phish for phools"[18]—to find individuals who were relatively financially unsophisticated and could be exploited.

Thus, in the low interest rate economy that emerged after 2008, many elderly in the United States who prudently put their savings into government bonds were bereft of income. They acted responsibly: who could have anticipated a decade of zero interest rates? Neoliberalism simply accepts that they were unlucky. The welfare state says that societal well-being can be improved by providing social protection—social insurance—against the vagaries of markets.

6.2 Children

We have argued that the neoliberal philosophy of putting the onus for deprivation among the elderly on the individual is questionable; but even most of those who believe that there should, in general, be reliance on markets agree that the same approach cannot be adopted for children. One cannot claim that they should have done a better job at picking their parents.

Admittedly, there are real concerns with state paternalism. What happens, for instance, if parental views about education differ from those of the government? But such issues arise with or without the welfare state. The welfare state is concerned about access to resources—including educational resources.

Advocates of the welfare state put primacy on the well-being of the child and the long-run consequences of the child facing deprivations. Though this is an ethical stance, from a long-run efficiency view, the economic benefits of ensuring that each child lives up to his or her potential are enormous.[19]

There is one more philosophical issue: many parents may believe that they have a fundamental right to advantage their children over others. This conflicts with a principle of equality of opportunity. In some societies, such inequities would be viewed as intolerable. In others, circumscribing them would be viewed as intolerable. The welfare state begins with the premise that *at a minimum* every child should have the opportunity to live up to his or her potential. This entails access to good preschool education and to affordable higher education, either through low tuition (subsidized by the state) or income-contingent loans (as in Australia).[20] And most of those subscribing to welfare-state principles, while not proscribing individuals from attempting to give some advantage to their children—how could one even imagine doing that—want to tilt the scale at least slightly toward equality. Thus, there is free public education, and parents wishing to send their children to private school forgo this benefit. But the charter school movement is

[18] In the words of Akerlof and Shiller (2015). The financial sector has engaged in extensive and well-documented fraud, but what we are talking about here is more subtle—selling products to individuals with higher fees that cannot be justified by performance.

[19] These almost surely outweigh any adverse incentive effect that might arise from parents may not working as hard knowing that the state will provide some support.

[20] See Chapman, Higgins, and Stiglitz (2014).

in part an attempt at circumvention of this attempt at creating a more egalitarian educational system, unless strict regulations are imposed on the socioeconomic and racial mix of students. Local education in the United States suffers from a similar problem: with increasing economic segregation, rich parents move to rich suburbs to get their children a "private-school quality" education. If one is committed to maintaining a modicum of equality of opportunity, one has to ensure more economic integration and less dispersion in spending.

6.3 The Working-Age Population

Neoliberalism and the welfare state have the greatest conflict when it comes to the working-age population. The young cannot be held accountable for their state. The elderly can be, but it's too late to lecture them that they should have saved more. But what about those who are able to work but do not. Should one let them suffer?

Here, the advocates of the welfare state again emphasize the presence of market failures. With high levels of unemployment, it may be hard to get jobs. India has made an important contribution to the welfare state agenda: the rural guaranteed-employment scheme, which guarantees a job for everyone willing to work in a public works project, at a wage at or slightly below the minimum wage.

Even a full-time worker may be in poverty, if market wages are too low. Neoliberals and welfare state advocates often agree that if someone works full time, he or she should not be in poverty; there needs to be an earned income tax credit to ensure that all full-time workers deserve to live above the poverty level and/or a minimum wage.

Welfare state advocates are typically concerned not just with income but with access to certain basic goods, like food, medical care, and shelter. Presumably, if everyone had an income large enough to guarantee adequate access to these basic goods, then there would not be such a concern about these goods. But no country has achieved that ideal, and in its absence, welfare state advocates argue that some attention must be paid to ensuring that individuals have access to adequate amounts of these basic necessities. But there is another reason for their focus on these markets: the belief that they often do not work well, in ways that lead to large numbers of the poor and middle-class facing deprivation. Direct intervention is needed. Today, as our understanding of market failures has improved, there is a better grasp of why the markets for these goods often fail, and this knowledge can be used either to design ways of correcting the market failure and/or to create better systems of public provision.

With the growing concern about labor-saving technological progress—the notion that robots may replace humans, and that jobs for all but the highly skilled will be scarce—has led to growing support for a universal basic income (UBI), a grant given to everyone. This proposal also has the support of many who believe that targeted welfare programs (aimed at the "needy") are sufficiently cumbersome and inefficient that they often do not reach those in need, and when they do, they do so in ways that undermine human dignity. While recognizing the merits of these arguments, I still believe that work is an essential part of human dignity and a meaningful life, and that our economic system must be designed to provide work that pays a livable income to any who are able and willing to engage in it. Besides, we are far from the point, even in our richest countries, where there is a public willingness to tax at a level that would ensure that the UBI benefit would be sufficient to sustain a decent life. And for the foreseeable future, there is ample work that needs to be done, including the investments required for a green transition.

7 Elements of a Twenty-First-Century System for the United States

Any welfare state program has to be tailored to the country and its history, institutions, and problems. In advanced countries like the United States, the scope for tax evasion is limited, and most transactions now occur digitally. Indeed, it would be easy to move to a completely digital system (see Stiglitz 2016d, 2016f, 2017a). By contrast, in Latin America, where there is a strong welfare state tradition, many people still fall within the informal sector—those small-scale economic activities that the government often does not fully monitor or tax and which typically provide few of the fringe benefits and job security associated with the formal sector. Much of the social protection is directed at those in the formal sector—who are typically better off than those in the informal sector—and the worry is that, if there is a fiscal deficit in these programs to be made up for by support from general revenues, the beneficiaries of such state support are those who are better off on average. The response is to make more of the schemes universal and less contingent on income (because income is not accurately observable for large portions of the population). But moves in that direction result in the programs providing less social insurance—evening out income across good and bad "events." Income-contingent public loan programs (described in greater detail later) may be one way of squaring the circle.

In many quarters, there has been resistance to the notion of the welfare state, with even Democratic presidents justifying the strength of our corporate welfare system (but not the weakness of our system of social protection for the rest of society) by saying that we're different from Scandinavia.[21] That puts a special onus on those proposing public programs. Yet, while there is widespread skepticism of public programs, there is very strong support for both Social Security and Medicare. Indeed, in a famous incident at a 2009 town hall meeting with a congressman from South Carolina, an audience member shouted for the representative to "keep your government hands off my Medicare": evidently, because the program was so successful, it was presumed it must be a private program.

In the following sections, I briefly describe elements of a twenty-first-century welfare state for the United States.

7.1 Programs Aimed at the Elderly

Medicare and Social Security should continue to be at the center of programs for the elderly. These programs have elements of both intergenerational and intragenerational distribution.[22]

But there are at least three important extensions that should be considered:

[21] This was Obama's defense for his bank bailout, when it was pointed out that there were far better ways of dealing with banks in trouble—ways that are more consistent with the "rules" of capitalism. See Stiglitz (2010a).

[22] It is not clear that the design of these programs takes into account differences in life expectancy and retirement ages across income classes to the extent it should. These differences may be becoming even more important.

7.1.1 Public Option for Supplementary Coverage for Medicare, Stronger Fiduciary Regulations for Private Supplementary Coverage, and Taxes on Certain Types of Supplemental Coverage

The provision of private supplemental insurance interacts with the public provision of base coverage. Again there is an irony: neoliberals consistently worry about the moral hazard effect, the effect of coverage on the likelihood of the insured-against event occurring. They worry that people will not take as good care of themselves if they have health insurance or that they will overuse medical care. Yet when it comes to advocating for private supplemental coverage, these concerns are suddenly forgotten. If such coverage were provided by a competitive, there would be excessive coverage, because the private-sector firms would ignore the additional costs their coverage imposes on the public sector. But the sector is often far from perfectly competitive, charging prices higher than they should; and there is ample opportunity to exploit the elderly, especially given the complexities of the coverage, that is, describing what is and is not covered.

That is why it may be desirable to have a public option, one that enables consumers to know they are not being exploited. The public option would likely be less expensive (more value per dollar premium), simply because it can take advantage of economies of scale and scope—the government is already providing Medicare coverage to everyone. Moreover, because so much of private insurance companies costs are associated with marketing, cream skimming (efforts to ensure that one is insuring only good risks), and collecting insurance premium and other charges, overall "transactions costs"—dollars that go to running the insurance system rather than to providing health care benefits—would be lower with the public option than under the current regime. Finally, prices could be lower simply because there is no "market power profit" built into the charges—prices would simply reflect the costs of providing the insurance.

The pervasive incentive of private providers to engage in cream skimming, the attempt to recruit as customers only the healthiest—imposing a kind of externality on others—provides a rationale for either forbidding private coverage, regulating it to ensure that it does not engage in cream skimming, or taxing it in a way that reduces the incentives for cream skimming.

7.1.2 Retirement Insurance

The United States has created a multitiered system—an efficient, universal basic coverage provided by government; corporate pensions for those lucky enough to work for a corporation providing these tax-preferenced benefits; and a supplemental retirement program that, up to a point, also receives tax preferences. In these programs, individuals are left to invest in the market, with the individual drawing down his or her savings postretirement or purchasing annuities. Corporate programs have switched from defined benefits to defined contributions, and thus both corporate and individual supplementary programs leave huge risks on the shoulders of ordinary citizens; and as we have noted, market annuities leave much to be desired. Criticism of the basic universal coverage is not based on

See Case and Deaton (2015, 2017). Changing the structure of retirement income with retirement age can rectify existing inequities, at least on average.

its lack of efficiency but on the fact that, in some central forecasting models of the evolution of the economy over the next 75 years, its expenditures will exceed its revenues. Critics argue, moreover, that political economy considerations make it difficult to bring the public program back into balance.

The fact of the matter is that the deficit is relatively small, sufficiently small that reasonable alternative estimates of, say, migration would bring it back into balance. Alternatively, small adjustments either to taxes to finance it or to the design of the program itself would bring it back into balance. Part of the reluctance to make large changes now in the anticipation that fiscal gaps would appear later is that the models on which the projections of fiscal deficits depend are highly sensitive to the assumptions.

Prior to the 2008 financial crisis, there was a big push, especially by those in the private financial sector, to at least partially privatize social security. The argument was that the private sector was more efficient; the reality was just the opposite. It was simply an attempt by the private sector to grab more rents for itself; the incomes of those selling the annuities increase as transaction costs increase—all at the expense of retirees. Results from the partial privatization of social security in the United Kingdom suggested that retirement benefits might be reduced by as much as 40% (Orszag and Stiglitz, 2001).

A further critique of private programs is that, here again, there is an incentive to "phish for phools" (Akerlof and Shiller, 2015)—profits can be increased more readily by developing better ways of exploiting the unwary than by lowering transactions costs or "beating the market" in one's investments, both extremely difficult. Indeed, the resistance the financial sector put up against fiduciary standards to prevent conflicts of interest was remarkable. They seemed to argue that they could not function if they were not allowed to continue with practices rife with conflicts of interest.

Again, a public option provides effective competition to the private sector and security against exploitation: the government would simply allow individuals to make contributions to social security, treating such contributions as if they were received as a result of employment. That is, what a retiree receives is based on contributions made into his account over the many years before his retirement, both by himself and by his employer on his behalf. Those with greater contributions receive more back in their social security benefits. Now, there is a cap, because contributions are limited; in 2017, individuals and their employers only made contributions on incomes up to $127,200. The "public option" would allow individuals to choose to make contributions beyond that—and to put aside, in their social security account, more of their income than the 6.2% they currently contribute.

7.1.3 Nursing Home Care

The facts that individuals are living longer, families are getting smaller, and the cost of housing is high in the urban areas where an increasingly large proportion of families live mean that increasingly large numbers of the elderly are left to themselves in their old age. They have to turn to nursing homes, which they cannot afford. Through Medicare, the government is picking up a large fraction of these costs. Over the years, there have been discussions of adding nursing home care to the Social Security program. Private insurance again has proven very costly. Such insurance could be provided by a modest increase in the Medicare or Social Security contributions.

7.2 Programs for Children

There is an increasing recognition of the inequities faced by children from poor families and that investing in these children can pay large social dividends. There is a need for stronger prenatal and preschool programs. Earlier programs aimed at ensuring nutrition and health for all children have proven their worth.

Reducing inequities at birth requires not just equal access to education but compensatory education systems.

Children live in families, and income support for low-income parents redounds to the benefit of children. That, of course, is part of the philosophy of the earned income tax credit. That program has to be extended and strengthened.

Children from poor families get off to an unfair start even when compensations are attempted, but when it comes to tertiary education, they are again placed at a disadvantage. America used to be the leader in the fraction of the population that goes on to college; it no longer is, because it is more difficult for a young American of modest means to go to college or get access to a quality education enabling him or her to live up to his or her potential than is the case in other developed countries. President Obama recognized this, but he proposed only universal access to community colleges. While these institutions have played an important role in extending access, the quality is sometimes not the same as in the country's better schools. Some critics say that we cannot afford even this much. But somehow, at the end of World War II, as we emerged with an enormous debt—130% of GDP—the country said that it could afford to provide education to all who had fought in the war, essentially every young man and many women, for as many years at as good a school as the person was qualified to attend. The country is much richer now; anyone who says the country can't afford this is making a statement about *choices* and *preferences*—that he or she thinks there are better ways of spending that money, such as leaving it in the pockets of the very wealthy or the banks or the corporations and letting them determine how it is spent. By contrast, anyone committed to a twenty-first-century welfare state would argue that one must ensure affordable access to college for *all*.

Around the world, there are two approaches: low tuition (financed by government subsidies) or income-contingent loans. The latter have proven particularly effective in Australia. With the government providing the loans, the transaction costs will be low. Repayment can be done through the tax system, and the cost of capital for the government is far lower than for the private sector.

This is another area where more regulation is required—both on those providing finance and those providing higher education.

7.3 Programs to Guarantee Full Access to the Labor Market

The poor, workers of color, and even many middle-class Americans, do not have equal access to labor markets. Discrimination is pervasive. America has done less to make it easy for women to participate in the labor market and get ahead—which is why female labor force participation rates in the United States trail those of the best performing countries. Public transportation systems are weak, and when they exist, they often do not provide connections between the locations where low- and middle-income Americans live and where the jobs are situated.

Furthermore, an excessive focus on inflation and an unwillingness to engage in sufficiently large and effective fiscal policies has meant that the economy is often at less than full employment. Unemployment puts downward pressure on wages, especially when combined with provisions that have weakened workers' bargaining position.

The remedies for these problems are clear: stronger antidiscrimination laws more effectively enforced; active labor market policies to help those who lose a job get the skills needed for the new jobs being created; childcare and family leave policies; public transportation policies focused on connecting people and jobs; and a renewed commitment to full-employment policies. While many of these policies are not traditionally viewed as part of the Welfare State, they are among the most important in advancing the well-being and welfare of the country, and the most successful welfare states have embraced this broader agenda.

7.4 Basic Elements of a Middle-Class Life

The basic elements of a middle-class life seem increasingly out of reach for many Americans. Among those requisites are health care, housing, education for one's children, and a modicum of security, including retirement security and social protection in case one loses a job. I have already discussed several aspects of these. Here, I identify programs that might address other deficiencies in current arrangements.

7.4.1 Health

The Affordable Care Act (ACA) made great strides in increasing access to health care, but 26 states refused to extend Medicaid so that more of the previously uninsured were covered. This extension was a central part of the "design" of ACA, so there are still large gaps in coverage, though the numbers without insurance are, at the same time, markedly lower than before ACA. (This fact was brought home forcefully in 2017, as Republicans attempted to "repeal and replace" ACA. They simply could not come up with a new program that didn't leave some 20 million Americans who now have health insurance coverage without coverage. While many Americans still did not fully recognize access to medical care as a basic human right, the vast majority believed that millions *more* should not be left uninsured. The assault on the ACA has continued, resulting in an increase in the uninsured; but the system has not been broken, as those trying to undermine it had hoped.) Beyond ensuring that *everyone* has health insurance, there are three further reforms needed. First is to recognize that health and access to health care are basic rights, as other countries have done.

Second is to improve competition in health care provision. There has been disappointment in the level of competition in many of the so-called exchanges that the ACA mandated, which are supposed to be marketplaces where consumers can compare plans. In some cases, there may be scope for stronger antitrust enforcement. In many cases, though, it may not be easy to prove collusion, and thus competition laws will not suffice.

What is required for competition is a public option, which can simply be provided by extending access to Medicare to everyone. (This had been originally proposed as part of the

ACA, but got scuttled as the law was debated.) The presence of the public option will lead to more competitive pricing by private firms, more innovation, and higher quality service.

Thirdly and finally, there must be policies aimed at behavioral changes and ensuring the availability of good nutrition. An increasing proportion of health problems are associated with social diseases, like obesity. The market has left large parts of the country as "food deserts," places, for instance, where it is hard to access fresh fruits and vegetables. In New York, former mayor Michael Bloomberg showed how public policy could remedy such shortcomings.

Many of these social diseases are in part the result of corporate avarice—corporations that enrich themselves by selling unhealthy foods, including to children, or, as in the case of cigarettes, making their products more addictive. What is required are strong regulations curbing these purveyors of disease and death.

7.4.2 Housing

Many Americans face inadequate housing and obtain housing finance only at excessively high costs. The private-sector model of providing housing finance proved its inadequacies in the 2008 crisis, in which the housing bubble played such a large role. But as the practices of the private sector came under scrutiny, it became clear that they were more focused on exploitation—exploiting both consumers and investors—than on risk management and prudential lending. Remarkably, more than a decade after the crisis, the private-sector model is still broken; the government provides more than 90% of all housing finance.

While there is an open question about how best to provide housing for low-income individuals, there is a simple solution for providing housing finance, which I call the public option for housing finance. There are two pieces of information that are critical in determining an individual's eligibility for a mortgage—the value of the house and the individual's income—and both of these pieces of information exist in public records. Transferring this information from the public sector to the private sector is costly. This would become unnecessary under the public option. Moreover, the cost of collection would be greatly reduced; there are economies of scope in using the tax-collection system. Repayment could even be made on an income-contingent basis. Thus, a better product could be provided at a lower cost. The loan could be provided at just a little more than the rate at which the government borrows.

7.4.3 Social Protection Systems

Individuals are averse to risk; they care about the risks they face, and security has a value. The market overcharges for—or simply doesn't provide—the security that individuals want and, as has been suggested, government could provide. Much of what we have already discussed is part of society's social protection system. Here, I want to make two observations.

Most individuals are unemployed for periods that represent a small fraction of their working lives. Unemployment, especially for the young or average wage earners, has a high cost, because they cannot engage in intertemporal smoothing. Providing unemployment loans would enable individuals to smooth their incomes without the adverse incentive effects sometimes associated with unemployment insurance. It would allow them to continue to search for jobs appropriate to their skills and preferences, thus increasing GDP (Stiglitz and Yun, 2005).

But there are some individuals who face repeated and/or extended bouts of unemployment; thus "interstate insurance"—insurance against this risk—is important. But the risk of future unemployment decreases the unattractiveness of a conventional loan (even if one could get one) to tide one over a short bout of unemployment, since it lowers consumption in some states where the marginal utility of income is very high. There is an easy solution: income-contingent unemployment loans. The optimal unemployment benefit program thus consists of a combination of income-contingent unemployment loans and unemployment insurance. The optimal design looks markedly different from that of the U.S. unemployment system (Stiglitz and Yun, 2014, 2017).

More broadly, the design of optimal systems of social protection entails maximizing risk mitigation while minimizing market distortions (adverse incentive effects), and this can be done by pooling risks, that is, having a single individual lifetime account addressing a variety of risks, along the lines of Singapore or Malaysia's provident fund. It provides for a high level of individual responsibility—because of the risk pooling, individuals can themselves take care of most of the risks they face—while allowing social insurance against large cumulative calamities.

8 Concluding Remarks

Many critics of the welfare state believed it would bring down the economy, as the weight of social obligations and the security provided by social insurance both eroded incentives. It turned out that none of the major crises have been related to the welfare state but were instead brought on by the excesses of the financial sector (a sector that employs many of the welfare state's critics). After the crisis, some in the financial sector found seized the opportunity to warn against the dangers of the welfare state, even though countries with the strongest welfare states were among those with the strongest recoveries.

The question is sometimes posed: Is a welfare state viable today? Globalization has in many ways increased the need for a modern welfare state but at the same time reduced the fiscal capacity to provide it, because of tax competition.[23]

There are two responses. The first is that we must reform globalization, limit the scope for tax competition, and design effective systems of taxation of multinational corporations. In Europe, this is an especially important issue, because of the ease with which goods, money, and people can move. On the Continent, there is a need for a progressive Europe-wide income tax, the revenues from which could in part be used to provide some basic social protection.

The second is to note that a well-designed welfare state would actually *increase* overall economic performance. As we noted, there is now a large body of theory and a wealth of evidence that societies that are more equal perform better, having both higher growth and more stability.[24] Karl Ove Moene and his co-authors (Moene, 2013; Barth, Moene, and Willumsen, 2014) have also noted the benefits in creating a politics that supports openness: with a modicum of social protection, individuals are more willing to accept

[23] This is a theme I analyzed in Stiglitz (2013d). See also the other papers in that volume, in particular Moene (2013).

[24] Good systems of social protection, for instance, can lead to more innovative societies, because individuals are more willing to take risks. See Stiglitz (2015f), and the papers by Moene and his co-authors.

change and openness. The evident growth in protectionist sentiments among Americans and Europeans who have been left behind bears testimony to this insight.

Thus, the welfare state is not *only* a matter of social justice. Still, I believe the most compelling case for the welfare state goes beyond these narrow economic arguments. It even goes beyond standard arguments for social justice. We must ask ourselves: What kind of society do we wish to live in, and what kind of individuals do we wish to be? For those who support the welfare state, its central role is in creating compassionate individuals with a social conscience and a sense of solidarity with their fellow citizens.

References

Aaberge, R., M. Mogstad, and V. Peragine, 2011. "Measuring Long-Term Inequality of Opportunity," *Journal of Public Economics*, 95(3): 193–204.

Abreu, D. 1988. "On the theory of infinitely repeated games with discounting," *Econometrica: Journal of the Econometric Society* (1988): 383–96.

Abreu, D., P. Milgrom, and D. Pearce, 1991. "Information and Timing in Repeated Partnerships," *Econometrica*, 59(6): 1713–33.

Acemoglu, D., 1998. "Why Do New Technologies Complement Skills? Directed Technical Change and Wage Inequality," *Quarterly Journal of Economics*, 113(4): 1055–89.

Acemoglu, D., 2002. "Directed Technical Change," *Review of Economic Studies*, 69(4): 781–809.

Acemoglu, D., 2010. "When Does Labor Scarcity Encourage Innovation?," *Journal of Political Economy*, 118(6): 1037–78.

Acemoglu, D., 2011. "Thoughts on Inequality and the Financial Crisis," presentation at the AEA meeting in Denver, January 8. Available at: http://econ-www.mit.edu/files/6348.

Acemoglu, D. and P. Restrepo, 2018. "The Race between Machine and Man: Implications of Technology for Growth, Factor Shares and Employment," *American Economic Review*, 108(6): 1488–1542.

Acemoglu, D. and A. Wolitzky, A., 2011. "The Economics of Labor Coercion," *Econometrica*, 79: 555–600. https://doi.org/10.3982/ECTA8963

Acemoglu, D., D. Autor, D. Dorn, G. Hanson, and B. Price, 2016. "Import Competition and the Great US Employment Sag of the 2000s," *Journal of Labor Economics*, 34(S1, Part 2, January): S141–S198.

Achdou, Y., F. J. Buera, J. M. Lasry, and P.L. Lions, B. Moll, 2014. "Partial Differential Equation Models in Macroeconomics," *Philosophical Transactions of the Royal Society A: Mathematical, Physical and Engineering Sciences*, 372(2028): 20130397.

Achdou, Y., J. Han, J. M. Lasry, and P.L. Lions, B. Moll, 2022. "Income and Wealth Distribution in Macroeconomics: A Continuous-Time Approach," *The Review of Economic Studies*, 89(1) (2022): 45–86.

AFL-CIO, 2013. "CEO-to-Worker Pay Ratios around the World," available at http://www.aflcio.org/Corporate-Watch/Paywatch-Archive/CEO-Pay-and-You/CEO-to-Worker-PayGap-in-the-United-States/Pay-Gaps-in-the-World (accessed December 22, 2015).

Aghion, P., B. F. Jones, and C. I. Jones, 2017. "Artificial Intelligence and Economic Growth" NBER Working Paper No. w23928,

Aguiar, M., M. Bils, K. K. Charles, and E. Hurst, 2017. "Leisure Luxuries and the Labor Supply of Young Men," NBER Working Paper 23552

Ahmad, S., 1966. "On the Theory of Induced Innovation," *Economic Journal*, 76, June, 344–57.

Aitchison, J. and J. A. C. Brown, 1957. "The Lognormal Distribution," *The Economic Journal*, 67(268): 713–15.

Akee, R. K. Q., W. E. Copeland, G. Keeler, et al. 2010 "Parents' Incomes and Children's Outcomes: A Quasi-experiment Using Transfer Payments from Casino Profits," *American Economic Journal: Applied Economics*, 2(1): 86–115.

Akerlof, G. A., 1967. "Stability, Marginal Products, Putty and Clay," in K. Shell (ed.), *Essays in the Theory of Optimal Economic Growth*, Cambridge, Mass.: M.I.T. Press, 281–94.

Akerlof, G. A., 1969. "Capital, Wages and Structural Unemployment," *Economic Journal*, 79(314): 269–81.

Akerlof, G. A., 1970. "The Market for Lemons: Qualitative Uncertainty and the Market Mechanism," *Quarterly Journal of Economics*, 84(3): 488–500.

Akerlof, G. A., 1978. "The Market for "Lemons": Quality Uncertainty and the Market Mechanism," in Peter Diamond and Michael Rothschild, (eds.), *Uncertainty in Economics*, Cambridge, MA: Academic Press, 235–51.

Akerlof, G. A., 1980. "A Theory of Social Custom, of Which Unemployment May Be One Consequence," *Quarterly Journal of Economics*, 94(4): 749–75.

Akerlof, G. A. and R. E. Kranton, 2010. *Identity Economics*, Princeton: Princeton University Press.

Akerlof, G. A. and R. J. Shiller, 2015. *Phishing for Phools: The Economics of Manipulation and Deception*, Princeton, NJ: Princeton University Press.

Akerlof, G. A. and J. E. Stiglitz, 1965. "Investment and Wages," paper read at New York meetings of Econometric Society, December.

Akerlof, G. and J. E. Stiglitz, 1969. "Capital, Wages and Structural Unemployment," Economic Journal, vol. 79, issue 314, 269–81

Akerlof, G. A. and J. Yellen, 1990. "The Fair Wage-Effort Hypothesis and Unemployment," *Quarterly Journal of Economics*, 105(2): 255–83.

Akerlof, G. A., W. Dickens, and G. Perry, 1996. "The Macroeconomics of Low Inflation," *Brookings Papers on Economic Activity*, 1996(1): 1–76.

Alesina, A. and D. Rodrik, 1994. "Distributive Politics and Economic Growth," *Quarterly Journal of Economics* 109(2): 465–90.

Alesina, A., S. Ozler, N. Roubini, and P. Swagel, 1996. "Political Instability and Economic Growth," *Journal of Economic Growth*, 1(2): 149–87.

Alexander, M., 2010. *The New Jim Crow: Mass Incarceration in the Age of Colorblindness*, New York: The New Press.

Allen, D., 2014. *Our Declaration: A Reading of the Declaration of Independence in Defense of Equality*, New York: W. W. Norton.

Allen, F. 1983. "Credit Rationing and Payment Incentives," *Review of Economic Studies*, 50(4): 639–46.

Allingham, M.G., 1972. "The Measurement of Inequality," *Journal of Economic Theory*, 5(1): 163–9.

Alstadsæter, A., N. Johannesen, and G. Zucman, 2019. "*Tax Evasion and Inequality*," *American Economic Review*, 109(6): 2073–2103.

Alston, L. J., 1981. "Tenure Choice in Southern Agriculture, 1930–1960," *Explorations in Economic History*, 18(3): 211–32.

Alvaredo, F., A. B. Atkinson, T. Piketty, and E. Saez, 2013. "The Top 1 Percent in International and Historical Perspective," *Journal of Economic Perspectives*, 27(3): 3–20

Alvaredo, F., B. Garbinti, and T. Piketty, 2017. "On the Share of Inheritance in Aggregate Wealth: Europe and the USA, 1900–2010," *Economica*, 84(334): 239–260.

Amiel, Y., M. Bernasconi, F. Cowell, and V. Dardanoni, 2013. "Do We Value Mobility?" London School of Economics STCERD Discussion Paper, Number PEP 17.

Anderson, S. T., R. Kellogg, and S. W. Salant, 2018. "Hotelling under Pressure," *Journal of Political Economy*, 126(3): 984–1026.

Andronov, A. A. and C. E. Chakin, 1949. *Theory of Oscillations*, Princeton, N.J.: Princeton University Press.

Annan, K. and N. Mousavizadeh, 2012. *Interventions: A Life in War and Peace*, New York: Penguin.

Antràs P., 2004. "Is the US Aggregate Production Function Cobb–Douglas? New Estimates of the Elasticity of Substitution," *Berkeley Electronic Journals in Macroeconomics: Contributions to Macroeconomics*, 4(1): article 4.

Aoki, M., K. Murdock, and M. Okuno-Fujiwara, 1997. "Beyond the East Asian Miracle: Introducing the Market-Enhancing View," in M. Aoki, H. Kim, and M. Okuno-Fujiwara, (eds.), *The Role of Government in East Asian Development*, Oxford: Clarendon Press, 1–2.

Aoki, S., and M. Nirei, 2015. "Zipf's Law, Pareto's Law, and the Evolution of Top Incomes in the U.S.," Working Paper, Hitotsubashi University.

Apps, P., 1981. *A Theory of Inequality and Taxation*. Cambridge: Cambridge University Press.

Apps, P. and J. E. Stiglitz, 1979. "Individualism, Inequality, and Taxation," unpublished mimeo.

Arneson, R., 2014. "Four Conceptions of Equal Opportunity," working paper.

Arnott, R., B. Greenwald, and J. E. Stiglitz, 1994. "Information and economic efficiency," *Information Economics and Policy*, Elsevier, 6(1): 77–82.

Arnott, R. and R. C. Lind, 1970. "Uncertainty and the Evaluation of Public Investment Decisions," *American Economic Review*, 60: 364–78.

Arnott, R. and J. E. Stiglitz, 1979. "Aggregate Land Rents, Expenditure on Public Goods and Optimal City Size," *Quarterly Journal of Economics*, 93(4): 471–500.

Arnott, R. and J. E. Stiglitz, 1981. "Aggregate Land Rents and Aggregate Transport Costs," *Economic Journal*, 91(362): 331–47.

Arnott, R. and J. E. Stiglitz, 1985. "Labor Turnover, Wage Structure and Moral Hazard: The Inefficiency of Competitive Markets," *Journal of Labor Economics*, 3(4): 434–62 (reprinted as Chapter 25, *Selected Works*, Volume II).

Arnott, R. and J. E. Stiglitz, 1986. "Moral Hazard and Optimal Commodity Taxation," *Journal of Public Economics*, 29(1): 1–24.

Arnott, R. and J. E. Stiglitz, 1988a. "Randomization with Asymmetric Information," *Rand Journal of Economics*, 19(3): 344–62.

Arnott, R. and J. E. Stiglitz, 1988b. "The Basic Analytics of Moral Hazard," *Scandinavian Journal of Economics*, 90(3): 383–413.

Arnott, R. and J. E. Stiglitz, 1990. "The Welfare Economics of Moral Hazard," in H. Louberge (ed.), *Risk, Information and Insurance: Essays in the Memory of Karl H. Borch*, Norwell, MA.: Kluwer Academic, 91–122.

Arnott, R. and J. E. Stiglitz, 2014. "Uncertainty and the Evaluation of Public Investment Decisions," *Journal of Natural Resources Policy Research*, 6(1): 29–44.

Arnott, R., B. Greenwald, and J. E. Stiglitz, 1994. "Information and Economic Efficiency," *Information Economics and Policy*, 6(1): 77–88.

Arrow, K., 1951. "An Extension of the Basic Theorems of Classical Welfare Economics," *Proceedings of the Second Berkeley Symposium on Mathematical Statistics and Probability*, Berkeley: University of California Press, 507–32.

Arrow, K., 1962. "Economic Welfare and the Allocation of Resources for Invention," in R. R. Nelson (ed.), *The Rate and Direction of Inventive Activity: Economic and Social Factors*, Princeton, NJ: Princeton University Press, 609–26.

Arrow, K., 1963. *Social Choice and Individual Values*, New York: Wiley.

Arrow, K., 1965. *Aspects of the Theory of Risk-Bearing*, Yrjo Jahnsson Lectures.

Arrow, K., 1972a. "Models of Job Discrimination," in A. H. Pascal (ed.), *Racial Discrimination in Economic Life*, Lexington, Mass: Lexington Books, 83–102.

Arrow, K., 1972b. "Some Mathematical Models of Race in the Labor Market," in A. H. Pascal (ed.), *Racial Discrimination in Economic Life*, Lexington, Mass: Lexington Books, 187–204.

Arrow, K., 1973. "Higher Education as a Filter," *Journal of Public Economics*, 2(3): 193–216.

Arrow, K., 1974. *The Limits of Organization*, New York: W. W. Norton.

Arrow, K. J. and P. Dasgupta, 2009. "Conspicuous Consumption, Inconspicuous Leisure," *Economic Journal*, 119(541): F497–F516.

Arrow, K. J., H. B. Chenery, B. S. Minhas, and R. M. Solow, 1961. "Capital-Labor Substitution and Economic Efficiency," *The Review of Economics and Statistics*, 43(3): 225–50.

Ashenfelter, O., and J. Heckman, 1974. "The Estimation of Income and Substitution Effects in a Model of Family Labor Supply," *Econometrica*, 42(1): 73–85. https://doi.org/10.2307/1913686.

Ashenfelter, O. and A. Kruefer, 1994. "Estimates of the Economic Return to Schooling from a New Sample of Twins," *American Economic Review*, 84(5): 1157–73.

Asquith, P. and D. Mullins, 1986. "Equity Issues and Offering Dilution," *Journal of Financial Economics*, 15(1): 61–89.

Atinc, T. M. and M. Walton, 1998. "Responding to the Global Financial Crisis: Social Consequences of the East Asian Financial Crisis," World Bank Working Paper 31041.

Atkeson, A., V. V. Chari, and P. J. Kehoe, 1999. "Taxing Capital Income: A Bad Idea," *Federal Reserve Bank of Minneapolis Quarterly Review*, 23(3): 3–17.

Atkinson, A. B., 1970. "On the Measurement of Inequality," *Journal of Economic Theory*, 2(3): 244–63.

Atkinson, A. B., 1971. "The Distribution of Wealth and the Individual Life-Cycle," *Oxford Economic Papers*, 23(2): 239–54.

Atkinson, A. B., 1980. "Inheritance and the Redistribution of Wealth," in G.M. Heal and G.A. Hughes (eds.), *Public Policy and the Tax System*, London: Allen and Unwin, 26–66.

Atkinson, A. B., 1981a. "On Intergenerational Income Mobility in Britain," *Journal of Post Keynesian Economics*, 3(2): 194–218.

Atkinson, A. B., 1981b. "The Measurement of Economic Mobility," in P.J. Eigjelshoven and L.J. van Gemerden (eds.), *Inkomensverdeling en openbare financien – Essays in Honour of Jan Pen*, Utrecht: Het Spectrum, 9–24.

Atkinson, A. B., 1983. *The Economics of Inequality*, Second Edition, Oxford: Clarendon Press.

Atkinson, A. B., 2015. *Inequality: What Can Be Done?*, Cambridge, MA: Harvard University Press.

Atkinson, A. B. and F. Bourguignon, 1982. "The Comparison of Multi-Dimensional Distributions of Economic Status," *Review of Economic Studies*, 49(2): 183–201.

Atkinson, A. B. and S. Morelli, 2010. "Inequality and Banking Crises: A First Look," Oxford University working paper.

Atkinson, A. B. and A. Sandmo, 1977. "The Welfare Implications of Personal Income and Consumption Taxes," University College, London discussion paper.

Atkinson, A. B. and A. Sandmo 1980. "Welfare Implications of the Taxation of Savings," *Economic Journal*, 90: 529–49.

Atkinson, A. B. and N. Stern, 1974. "Pigou, Taxation and Public Goods," *Review of Economic Studies*, 41(1): 119–28.

Atkinson, A. B. and J. E. Stiglitz, 1969. "A New View of Technological Change," *Economic Journal*, 79(315): 573–78.
Atkinson, A. B. and J. E. Stiglitz, 1972. "The Structure of Indirect Taxation and Economic Efficiency," *Journal of Public Economics*, 1(1): 97–119.
Atkinson, A. B. and J. E. Stiglitz, 1976. "The Design of Tax Structure: Direct versus Indirect Taxation," *Journal of Public Economics*, 6(1): 55–75.
Atkinson, A. B. and J. E. Stiglitz, 1980. *Lectures on Public Economics*, New York: McGraw-Hill. Reprinted by Princeton University Press, 2015.
Atkinson, A. B., A. K. Maynard, and C. G. Trinder, 1983. *Parents and Children: Incomes in Two Generations*, London: Heinemann Educational Books.
Auten, G., and David Splinter. 2019. *"Top 1 Percent Income Shares: Comparing Estimates Using Tax Data", AEA Papers and Proceedings*, 109: 307–11.
Autor, D., 2002. "Skill Biased Technical Change and Rising Inequality: What is the Evidence? What are the Alternatives?" Working paper, MIT and NBER.
Autor, D. and D. Dorn, 2013. "The Growth of Low-Skill Service Jobs and the Polarization of the US Labor Market," *American Economic Review*, 103(5): 1553–97.
Autor, D., F. Levy, and R. J. Murnane, 2003. "The Skill Content of Recent Technological Change: An Empirical Investigation," *Quarterly Journal of Economics*, 118: 4.
Autor, D., L. F. Katz, and M. S. Kearney, 2008. "Trends in U.S. Wage Inequality: Revising the Revisionists," *Review of Economics and Statistics*, 90(2): 300–23.
Autor, D., D. Dorn, and G. H. Hanson, 2013. "The China Syndrome: Local Labor Market Effects of Import Competition in the United States," *American Economic Review*, 103(6): 2121–68.
Autor, D., D. Dorn, and G. H. Hanson, 2016. "The China Shock: Learning from Labor-Market Adjustment to Large Changes in Trade," *Annual Review of Economics*, 8: 205–40.
Autor, D., et al., 2020. "Importing Political Polarization? The Electoral Consequences of Rising Trade Exposure," *American Economic Review*, 110(10): 3139–83.
Baker, D. and T. McArthur, 2009. "The Value of the 'Too Big to Fail' Big Bank Subsidy," Center for Economic and Policy Social Research issue Brief, September.
Baker, D., A. Jayadev, and J. E. Stiglitz, 2017. "Innovation, Intellectual Property, and Development: A Better Set of Approaches for the 21st Century," AccessIBSA: Innovation & Access to Medicines in India, Brazil & South Africa.
Bakija, J., A. Cole, and B. T. Heim, 2012. "Job and Income Growth of Top Earners and the Causes of Changing Income Inequality: Evidence from U.S. Tax Return Data," 2012, available at http://web.williams.edu/Economics/wp/BakijaColeHeimJobsIncomeGrowthTopEarners.pdf (accessed July 10, 2019).
Baltensperger, E., 1978. ""Credit Rationing: Issues and Question," *Journal of Money, Credit and Banking*, 10(2): 170–83.
Baltensperger, E. and T. Devinney 1985. "Credit Rationing Theory: A Survey and Synthesis," *Zeitschrift Fur Die Gesamte Staatswissenschaft/Journal of Institutional and Theoretical Economics*, 141(4): 475–502.
Banerjee, A. and S. Mullainathan, 2010. "The Shape of Temptation: Implications for the Economic Lives of the Poor," NBER Working Paper 15973.
Banerjee, A. and A. F. Newman, 1993. "Occupational Choice and the Process of Development," *Journal of Political Economy*, 10(21): 274–98.
Baran, P. A. and P. M. Sweezy, 1966. *Monopoly Capital: An Essay on the American Economic and Social Order*," New York: Monthly Review Press.
Baranzini, Mauro, 1991. *A Theory of Wealth Distribution and Accumulation*. Oxford; online edn, Oxford Academic, 31 Oct. 2023; https://doi.org/10.1093/oso/9780198233138.001.0001.
Barba, A. and M. Pivetti, 2009. "Rising Household Debt: Its Causes and Macroeconomic Implications—a Long Period Analysis," *Cambridge Journal of Economics*, 33(1): 113–37.
Bardhan, P. K., 1980. "Interlocking Factor Markets and Agrarian Development: A Review of Issues," *Oxford Economic* Papers, 32(1): 82–98.
Barkai, S., 2020. "Declining Labor and Capital Shares," *Journal of Finance*, *75*(5): 2421–63.
Barnett, W.S., 1992. "Benefits of Compensatory Preschool Education," *Journal of Human Resources*, 27(2): 279–312.
Barrales, J., and R. von Arnim, 2017. "Longer-run distributive cycles: Wavelet decompositions for the US, 1948–2011," *Review of Keynesian Economics*, 5(2): 196–217.
Barrales-Ruiz J., I. Mendieta-Muñoz, C. Rada, D. Tavani, and R. von Arnim, 2022. "The Distributive Cycle: Evidence and Current Debates," *Journal of Economic Surveys*, Wiley Blackwell, 36(2): 468–503, April.
Barrat, J., 2013. *Our Final Invention: Artificial Intelligence and the End of the Human Era*, New York: St. Martin's Press.

Barro, R. J., 1974. "Are Government Bonds Net Wealth?" *Journal of Political Economy*, 82(6): 1095–117
Barro, R. J., 1991. "Economic Growth in a Cross-Section of Countries," *Quarterly Journal of Economics*, 106(2): 407–43.
Barro, R. J., 1996. "Democracy and Growth," *Journal of Economic Growth*, 1(1): 1–28.
Barro, R. J., 1997. *The Determinants of Economic Growth*, Cambridge, Mass.: MIT Press.
Bartels, L., 2008. *Unequal Democracy*, Princeton, N.J.: Princeton University Press.
Barth, E., K. O. Moene, and F. Willumsen, 2014. "The Scandinavian Model—An Interpretation," *Journal of Public Economics* 117(C): 60–72.
Basu, K., 2010. *Beyond the Invisible Hand: Groundwork for a New Economics*, Princeton, NJ: Princeton University Press.
Basu, K., G. Genicot, and J. E. Stiglitz, 2002. "Minimum Wage Laws and Unemployment Benefits, When Labor Supply is a Household Decision," in K. Basu, P. Nayak, and R. B. Ray (eds.), *Markets and Governments*, Oxford: Oxford University Press, 38–59.
Battiston, S., D. Delli Gatti, M. Gallegati, B. Greenwald, and J. E. Stiglitz, 2012. "Liaisons Dangereuses: Increasing Connectivity, Risk Sharing, and Systemic Risk," *Journal of Economic Dynamics and Control*, 36(8): 1121–41.
Baumol, W. J. and D. F. Bradford, 1970. "Optimal Departures from Marginal Cost Pricing," *American Economic Review*, 60(3): 265–83.
Bebchuk, L., and J. Fried, 2006. *Pay without Performance: The Unfulfilled Promise of Executive Compensation*, Cambridge, MA: Harvard University Press.
Bebchuk, L. and Y. Grinstein, 2005. "The Growth of Executive Pay," *Oxford Review of Economic Policy*, 21(2): 283–303.
Bebchuk, L., A. Cohen, and H. Spamann 2010. "The Wages of Failure: Executive Compensation at Bear Stearns and Lehman 2000–2008," *Yale Journal on Regulation*, 27: 257–82.
Beck, T., A. Demirguc-Kunt, and V. Maksimovic, 2005. "Financial and Legal Constraints to Growth: Does Firm Size Matter?" *Journal of Finance*, 60(1): 137–77.
Becker, G. S., 1957. *The Economics of Discrimination*, Chicago: University of Chicago Press.
Becker, G. S., 1967. "Human Capital and the Personal Distribution of Income: An Analytical Approach," Woytinsky Lecture No. 1 University of Michigan, Institute of Public Administration, Ann Arbor.
Becker, G. S. and N. Tomes, 1979. "An Equilibrium Theory of the Distribution of Income and Intergenerational Mobility," *Journal of Political Economy*, 87(6): 1153–89.
Becker, G. S. and N. Tomes, 1986. "Human Capital and the Rise and Fall of Families," *Journal of Labor Economics*, vol. 4(3): S1–S39.
Becker, G. S. and N. Tomes, 1994. "Human Capital and the Rise and Fall of Families," in Gary S. Becker (ed.), *Human Capital: A Theoretical and Empirical Analysis with Special Reference to Education*, Third Edition, Chicago: University of Chicago Press, 257–98.
Bell, C., and P. Zusman, 1980. "On the Interrelationship of Credit and Tenancy Contracts," World Bank Development Research Center.
Belluz, J., 2018 "What the Dip in US life Expectancy Is Really About: Inequality," *Vox*, November 30, 2018, https://www.vox.com/science-and-health/2018/1/9/16860994/life-expectancy-us-income-inequality.
Benabou, R., 1996. "Inequality and Growth," in B. Bernanke and J. Rotemberg (eds.), *NBER Macroeconomics Annual 1996*, Volume 11, Cambridge, Mass.: MIT Press, 11–92.
Benhabib, J. and A. Bisin, 2018. "Skewed Wealth Distributions: Theory and Empirics," *Journal of Economic Literature*, 56(4): 1261–91.
Benhabib, J., A. Bisin and S. Zhu, 2011. "The Distribution of Wealth and Fiscal Policy in Economies with Finitely Lived Agents," *Econometrica*, 79(1) (2011): 123–57.
Benhabib, J., A. Bisin, and S. Zhu, 2015. "The Wealth Distribution in Bewley Economies with Capital Income Risk," *Journal of Economic Theory* 159 (September 1): 489–515. https://doi.org/10.1016/j.jet.2015.07.013.
Benhabib, J., A. Bisin and S. Zhu, 2016. "The Distribution of Wealth in the Blanchard–Yaari Model," *Macroeconomic Dynamics*, 20(2): 466–81.
Beraja, M., A. Fuster, E. Hurst, J. J Vavra, 2019. "Regional Heterogeneity and the Refinancing Channel of Monetary Policy," *The Quarterly Journal of Economics*, 134(1): 109–183, https://doi.org/10.1093/qje/qjy021
Berg, A. and J. Ostry, 2011. "Inequality and Unsustainable Growth: Two Sides of the Same Coin?" IMF Staff Discussion Note No. 11/08.
Berg, A. and J. Ostry, and J. Zettelmeyer, 2012. "What Makes Growth Sustained?" *Journal of Development Economics*, 98(2): 149–66.

Berg, A., E. F. Buffie, and L.-F. Zanna, 2018. "Should We Fear the Robot Revolution? (The Correct Answer Is Yes)," *Journal of Monetary Economics*, 97: 117–48.

Berle, A.A., Jr., and G. C. Means, 1932. *The Modern Corporation and Private Property*, New York: Macmillan.

Bernanke, B. S., 1983. "Non-Monetary Effects of the Financial Collapse in the Propagation of the Great Depression," *American Economic Review*, 73(3): 257–76.

Bernanke, B. S., 1984. "Permanent Income, Liquidity, and Expenditure on Automobiles: Evidence from Panel Data," *Quarterly Journal of Economics*, 99(3): 587–616.

Bernanke, B. S., 2005. "The Global Saving Glut and the U.S. Current Account Deficit," The Sandridge Lecture, Virginia Association of Economists, Richmond.

Bernanke, B. S. and M. Gertler, 1987. "Financial Fragility and Economic Performance," *Quarterly Journal of Economics*, 105(1): 87–114.

Bertrand, M. and S. Mullainathan, 2001. "Are ceos rewarded for luck? The ones without principals are,"* *The Quarterly Journal of Economics*, August 2001: 901–932.

Bertrand, M., and S. Mullainathan, 2004. "Are Emily and Greg More Employable than Lakisha and Jamal? A Field Experiment on Labor Market Discrimination," *American Economic Review*, 94(4): 991–1013.

Besley, T., 2004. "The New Political Economy," paper based on Keynes lecture delivered at the British Academy on October 13, 2004, available at http://econ.lse.ac.uk/staff/tbesley/papers/keyneslecturetext.pdf (accessed March 29, 2011).

Besley, T. and T. Persson, 2009. "The Origins of State Capacity: Property Rights, Taxation and Politics," *American Economic Review*, 99(4): 1218–44.

Besley, T. and T. Persson, 2010. "State Capacity, Conflict and Development," *Econometrica*, 78(1): 1–34.

Bestor, H., 1985. "Screening versus Rationing in Credit Markets with Imperfect Information," *American Economic Review*, 75(4): 850–5.

Bevan, D. L., 1974. "Savings, Inheritance and Economic Growth in the Presence of Earnings Inequality," Oxford University mimeo.

Bevan, D. L., 1979. "Inheritance and the Distribution of Wealth," *Economica*, 46(184): 381–402.

Bevan, D. L. and J. E. Stiglitz, 1979. "Intergenerational Transfers and Inequality," *Greek Economic Review*, 1(1): 8–26.

Bhaduri, A., 1973. "A Study in Agricultural Backwardness under Semi-Feudalism," *Economic Journal*, 83(329): 120–37.

Bhaduri, A., 1980. "Agricultural Backwardness under Semi-Feudalism: A Rejoinder," *Economic Journal*, 89(354): 420–1.

Bhattacharya, D. and B. Mazumder, 2011. "A Nonparametric Analysis of Black–White Differences in Intergenerational Income Mobility in the United States," *Quantitative Economics*, 2(3): 335–79.

Binder, A. J., and J. Bound, 2019. "The Declining Labor Market Prospects of Less-Educated Men," *Journal of Economic Perspectives*, 33(2): 163–90.

Binswanger, H. P., and M. R. Rosenzweig (eds.), 1984. *Contractual Arrangements, Employment and Wages in Labor Markets in Asia*, New Haven, CT: Yale university Press.

Birdsall, N., D. Ross, and R. Sabot, 1995. "Inequality and Growth Reconsidered: Lessons from East Asia," *World Bank Economic Review*, 9(3): 477–508.

Birdsall, N., & Londoño, J. L. (1997). *Asset inequality does matter: Lessons from latin america*. St. Louis: Retrieved from http://ezproxy.cul.columbia.edu/login?url=https://www.proquest.com/working-papers/asset-inequality-does-matter-lessons-latin/docview/1941866122/se-2

Bischoff, C. W., B. Bosworth, and R. Hall. 1971. "Business Investment in the 1970s: A Comparison of Models," *Brookings Papers on Economic Activity*, 1971(1): 13–58.

Bivens, J., and L. Mishel, 2013. "The Pay of Corporate Executives and Financial Professionals as Evidence of Rents in the Top 1 Percent Incomes," *Journal of Economic Perspectives*, 27(3): 57–78.

Bivens, J., L. Mishel, and H. Shierholz, 2015. "Understanding the Historic Divergence Between Productivity and a Typical Worker's Pay," Economic Policy Institute Briefing Paper No. 406, September 2.

Black, D. A., N. Kolesnikova, S. G. Sanders, and L.J. Taylor, 2013. "Are Children 'Normal?'," *Review of Economics and Statistics*, 95(1): 21–33.

Blackstone, B., M. Karnitschnig, and R. Thomson, 2012. "Europe's Banker Talks Tough—Draghi Says Continent's Social Model Is 'Gone', Won't Backtrack on Austerity," *Wall Street Journal*, February 4.

Blackwell, D., and M. A. Girshick, 1954. *Theory of Games and Statistical Decisions*, New York: John Wiley & Sons.

Blanchard, O. and L. Summers, 1986. "Hysterisis and the European Unemployment Problem," in Stanley Fischer (ed.), *NBER Macroeconomics Annual 1986*, Volume 1, Cambridge, Mass.: MIT Press, 15–90.

Blanchard, O., C. Rhee, and L. Summers, 1993. "The Stock Market, Profit, and Investment," *Quarterly Journal of Economics*, 108(1): 115–36.
Bleemer, Z., 2002. "Affirmative Action, Mismatch, and Economic Mobility after California's Proposition 209*," *The Quarterly Journal of Economics* 137, no. 1: 115–60. https://doi.org/10.1093/qje/qjab027.
Blinder, A., 1987. "Credit Rationing and Effective Supply Failure," *Economic Journal*, 97(386): 327–52.
Blinder, A., 1998. *Central Banking in Theory and Practice*, Cambridge, Mass. and London: MIT Press.
Blinder, A. and J. E. Stiglitz, 1983. "Money, Credit Constraints, and Economic Activity," *American Economic Review*, 73(2): 297–302.
Block, F. L., 2018. *Capitalism: The Future of an Illusion*, Berkeley: University of California Press.
Boadway, R. and M. Keen, 1993. "Public Goods, Self-Selection and Optimal Income Taxation," *International Economic Review*, 34: 463–78.
Boiteux, M., 1956. "Sur la gestion des monopoles publics astreints à l'équilibre budgetaire," *Econometrica*, 24(1): 22–40.
Boiteux, M., 1971. "On the Management of Public Monopolies Subject to Budgetary Constraints," *Journal of Economic Theory*, 3(3): 219–40.
Borkovec, M. and C. Klüppelberg, 1998. "Extremal Behavior of Diffusion Models in Finance," *Extremes*, 1(1): 47–80.
Boserup, S. H., W. Kopczuk, and C. T. Kreiner, 2016. "The Role of Bequests in Shaping Wealth Inequality: Evidence from Danish Wealth Records," *American Economic Review: Papers & Proceedings*, 106(5): 656–61.
Boshara, R., W. Emmons, and B. Noeth, 2014. "The Great Recession Casts a Long Shadow on Family Finances," *On the Economy*, a blog of the Federal Reserve Bank of St. Louis, St. Louis, MI.
Bostrom, N., 2014. *Superintelligence: Paths, Dangers, Strategies*, Oxford: Oxford University Press.
Bourguignon, F., 2012. *La mondialisation de l'inégalité*, Editions Le Seuil, Paris, France.
Bourguignon, F. and T. Scott-Railton, 2015. *The Globalization of Inequality* (Princeton, NJ: Princeton University Press).
Bowden, R., 1978. The Econometrics of Disequilibrium, Amsterdam: North-Holland.
Bowles, S. and H. Gintis, 2002. "The Inheritance of Inequality," *Journal of Economic Perspectives*, 16(3): 3–30.
Bowles, S. and A. Jayadev, 2006. "Guard Labor," *Journal of Development Economics*, 79(2): 328–48
Boyle, J., 2003. "The Second Enclosure Movement and the Construction of the Public Domain," *Law and Contemporary Problems*, 66(1): 33–74.
Braverman, A., and J. L. Guasch, 1984. "Capital Requirements, Screening and Interlinked Sharecropping and Credit Contracts," *Journal of Development Economics*, 14(3): 359–74.
Braverman, A., and J. L. Guasch, 1989. "Institutional Analysis of Credit Cooperatives," in P. Bardhan (ed.), *The Economic Theory of Agrarian Institutions*, Oxford: Clarendon Press, 340–55.
Braverman, A. and T. N. Srinivasan, 1981. "Credit and Sharecropping in Agrarian Societies," *Journal of Development Economics* 9(3): 289–312.
Braverman, A. and J. E. Stiglitz, 1982. "Sharecropping and the Interlinking of Agrarian Markets," *American Economic Review*, 72(4): 695–715.
Braverman, A. and J. E. Stiglitz, 1985. "Unemployment, Supervision Technology, and Employers' Resistance to Technological Innovations," mimeo, Princeton, NJ: Princeton University).
Braverman, A. and J. E. Stiglitz, 1986a. "Cost Sharing Arrangement under Sharecropping: Moral Hazard, Incentive Flexibility and Risk," *Journal of Agricultural Economics*, 68(3): 642–52.
Braverman, A. and J. E. Stiglitz, 1986b. "Landlords, Tenants and Technological Innovations," *Journal of Development Economics*, 23(2): 313–32.
Braverman, A. and J. E. Stiglitz, 1989. "Credit Rationing, Tenancy, Productivity and the Dynamics of Inequality," in P. Bardhan (ed.), *The Economic Theory of Agrarian Institutions*, Oxford: Clarendon Press, 185–201.
Breen, R. and C. García-Peñalosa, 2005. "Income Inequality and Macroeconomic Volatility: An Empirical Investigation," *Review of Development Economics*, 9(3): 380–98.
Bricker, J., L. J. Dettling, A. Henriques, J. W. Hsu, K. B. Moore, J. Sabelhaus, J. Thompson, and R. A. Windle, 2014. "Changes in U.S. Family Finances from 2010 to 2013: Evidence from the Survey of Consumer Finances," *Federal Reserve Bulletin*, 100(4): 1–41.
Bricker, J., R. Ramcharan, and J. Krimmel, 2014. "Signaling Status: The Impact of Relative Income on Household Consumption and Financial Decisions," Federal Reserve Board, Washington, D.C.
Bricker J., Krimmel J., Ramcharan R., 2020. "Signaling Status: The Impact of Relative Income on Household Consumption and Financial Decisions," *Management Science*, 67(4): 1993–2009.

Brito, D. L., J. H. Hamilton, S. M. Slutsky, and J. E. Stiglitz, 1990. "Pareto Efficient Tax Structures," *Oxford Economic Papers*, 42: 61–77.
Brito, D. L., J. H. Hamilton, S. M. Slutsky, and J. E. Stiglitz, 1995. "Randomization in Optimal Income Tax Schedules," *Journal of Public Economics*, 56(2): 189–223.
Brun, L. and I. González, 2017. "Tobin's Q and Inequality," available at https://papers.ssrn.com/sol3/papers.cfm?abstract_id=3069980.
Brunner, B. and A. Kuhn, 2010. "The Impact of Labor Market Entry Conditions on Initial Job Assignment, Human Capital Accumulation and Wages, IZA Discussion Paper 5360.
Bruno, M., 1993. *Crisis, Stabilization, and Economic Reform: Therapy by Consensus*, Oxford: Clarendon Press.
Bruno, M. and W. Easterly, 1998. "Inflation Crises and Long-Run Growth," *Journal of Monetary Economics*, 41(1): 3–26.
Calomiris, C., R. Hubbard, and J. Stock, 1986. "The Farm Debt Crisis and Public Policy," *Brookings Papers on Economic Activity*, 1986(2): 441–79.
Campbell, J. Y. and G. Mankiw, 1987. "Are Output Fluctuations Transitory?" *Quarterly Journal of Economics*, 102(4): 857–80.
Campbell, J. Y. and G. Mankiw, 1990. "Permanent Income, Current Income, and Consumption," *Journal of Business & Economic Statistics*, 8(3): 265–79.
Card, D. and J. E. DiNardo, 2002. "Skill-Biased Technological Change and Rising Wage Inequality: Some Problems and Puzzles," *Journal of Labor Economics*, 20(4): 733–83.
Card, D. and A. B. Krueger 1994. "Minimum Wages and Employment: A Case Study of the Fast-Food Industry in New Jersey and Pennsylvania," *American Economic Review*, 84(4): 772–93.
Carroll, C. D., 1998. "Why Do the Rich Save So Much?" NBER Working Paper 6549.
Case, A., and A. Deaton, 2015. "Rising Morbidity and Mortality in Midlife among White Non-Hispanic Americans in the 21st Century," *Proceedings of the National Academy of Sciences*, 112(49): 15078–83.
Case, A., and A. Deaton, 2017. "Mortality and Morbidity in the 21st Century," *Brookings Papers on Economic Activity*, Spring.
Case, A., and A. Deaton, 2020. *Deaths of Despair and the Future of Capitalism*. Princeton, NJ: Princeton University Press.
Cass, D. and J. E. Stiglitz, 1969. "The Implications of Alternative Saving and Expectations Hypotheses for Choices of Technique and Patterns of Growth," *Journal of Political Economy*, 77(4): 586–627.
Cass, D. and J. E. Stiglitz, 1972 "Risk Aversion and Wealth Effects on Portfolios with Many Assets," with D. Cass, *Review of Economic Studies*, 39(3): 331–54 (reprinted as Chapter 6 in *Selected Works*, Volume III).
Cederman, L.-E., N. B. Weidmann, and K. S. Gleditsch, 2011. "Horizontal Inequalities and Ethnonationalist Civil War: A Global Comparison," *American Political Science Review*, 105(3): 487–89.
Center for Responsible Lending, 2015. "The State of Lending in America and Its Impact on U.S. Households: The Cumulative Costs of Predatory Practices," Available at: http://www.responsiblelending.org/sites/default/files/uploads/13-cumulative-impact.pdf.
Chadwick, L. and G. Solon, 2002. "Intergenerational Income Mobility among Daughters," *American Economic Review*, 92(1): 335–44.
Chakravarty, S. R., B. Dutta and J. A. Weymark, 1985. "Ethical Indices of Income Mobility," *Social Choice and Welfare*, 2(1): 1–21.
Chamley, C., 1986. "Optimal Taxation of Capital Income in General Equilibrium with Infinite Lives," *Econometrica*, 54(3): 607–22.
Champernowne, D. G., 1937. "The Theory of Income Distribution," *Econometrica* 5(4): 379–81.
Champernowne, D. G., 1953. "A Model of Income Distribution," *Economic Journal*, 63(250): 318–51.
Chang, H.-J., 1999. "The Economic Theory of the Developmental State," in Meredith Woo-Cumings (ed.), *The Developmental State*, Ithaca, NY: Cornell University Press, 192–99.
Chapman, B., T. Higgins, and J. E. Stiglitz (eds.), 2014. *Income Contingent Loans: Theory, Practice and Prospects*, Houndmills, UK and New York: Palgrave Macmillan.
Chen, H., V. Cúrdia, and A. Ferrero, 2012. "The macroeconomic effects of large-scale asset purchase programmes," *The Economic Journal*, 122(564: F289–F315.
Chetty, R., N. Hendren, P. Kline, and E. Saez, 2014. "Where Is the Land of Opportunity? The Geography of Intergenerational Mobility in the United States," *Quarterly Journal of Economics*, 129(4): 1553–623.
Chetty, R., M. Stepner, S. Abraham, S. Lin, B. Scuderi, N. Turner, A. Bergeron, and D. Cutler, 2016. "The Association between Income and Life Expectancy in the United States, 2001–2014," *Jama*, 315(16): 1750–66.,
Chetty, R., D. Grusky, M. Hell, et al., 2017. "The fading American dream: Trends in absolute income mobility since 1940," *Science* 356: 398–406. DOI:10.1126/science.aal4617.

Chetty, R., J. N. Friedman, E. Saez, et al., 2020. "Income Segregation and Intergenerational Mobility Across Colleges in the United States" (previously titled "Mobility Report Cards"), *Quarterly Journal of Economics*, 135(3): 1567–1633.

Cheung, S. N. S., 1969. "Transaction Costs, Risk Aversion and the Choice of Contractual Arrangements," *Journal of Law and Economics*, 19(1): 377–99.

Chirinko, R. S., 2008. "σ: The Long and Short of It," *Journal of Macroeconomics*, 30(2): 671–86.

Chiswick, B. R., 1974. "Racial Discrimination in the Labor Market: A Test of Alternative Hypotheses," in G. von Furstenberg, B. Harrison, and A. R. Horowitz (eds.), *Patterns of Racial Discrimination, Volume II*, Lanham, MD: D.C. Heath and Company (Lexington Books), 101–19.

Choy, S. and M. Premo, 1996. *How Low-Income Undergraduates Financed Postsecondary Education: 1992–93*, Washington, DC: National Center for Education Statistics.

Christiansen, V., 1984. "Which Commodity Taxes Should Supplement the Income Tax?" *Journal of Public Economics*, 24(2): 195–220.

Cingano, F., 2014. "Trends in Income Inequality and Its Impact on Economic Growth," OECD Social, Employment and Migration Working Papers, No. 163, December.

Citro, C. and R. Maichael (eds.), 1995. *Measuring Poverty: A New Approach*, Washington, DC: National Academies Press.

Clarida, R., J. Galí, and M. Gertler, 2000. "Monetary Policy Rules and Macroeconomic Stability: Evidence and Some Theory," *Quarterly Journal of Economics*, 115(1): 147–80.

Clark, C. S., 1973. "Labor Hoarding in Durable Goods Industries," *American Economic Review*, 63(5): 811–24.

Clark, P., 1979. "Investment in the 1970s: Theory, Performance, and Prediction," *Brookings Papers*, 1979(1): 73–113.

Clemenz, G., 1986. Credit Markets with Asymmetric Information, Lecture Notes in Economics and Mathematical Systems 27, Berlin: Springer-Verlag.

Coase, R. H., 1937. "The Nature of the Firm," *Economica*, 4(16): 386–405

Coase, R. H., 1960. "The Problem of Social Cost," *Journal of Law and Economics*, 3: 1–44.

Coase, R. H., 1992. "The Institutional Structure of Production," Nobel Prize Lecture (originally delivered in 1991), *American Economic Review*, 82(4): 713–19.

Coase, R. H., 1998. "The New Institutional Economics," *American Economic Review*, 88(2): 72–4.

Cobham, A., and A. Sumner, 2013a. "Putting the Gini Back in the Bottle? 'The Palma' as a Policy-Relevant Measure of Inequality," King's College working paper, London, March 15. Available at: www.kcl.ac.uk/aboutkings/worldwide/initiatives/global/intdev/people/Sumner/Cobham-Sumner-15March2013.pdf.

Cobham, A., and A. Sumner, 2013b. "Is It All About the Tails? The Palma Measure of Income Inequality," Center for Global Development Working Paper 343, September.

Coddington, E. A. and H. Levinson, 1955. *Theory of Differential Equations*, New York: McGraw-Hill.

Colciago, A., A, Samarina, and H. de Haan, 2019. "Central Bank Policies and Income and Wealth Inequality: A Survey," *Journal of Economic Surveys*, 33(4): 1199–31.

Commons, J. R., 1931. "Institutional Economics," *American Economic Review*, 21: 648–57.

Congressional Budget Office, 2013. *The Distribution of Major Tax Expenditures in the Individual Income Tax System*, May, 31, available at http://cbo.gov/sites/default/files/cbofiles/attachments/TaxExpenditures_One-Column.pdf (accessed July 16, 2019).

Conlisk, J., 1989. "Ranking Mobility Matrices," *Economics Letters*, 29(3): 231–35.

Corak, M., 2013. "Income Inequality, Equality of Opportunity, and Intergenerational Mobility," *Journal of Economic Perspectives*, 27(3): 79–102.

Corlett, W. J. and D. C. Hague, 1953. "Complementarity and the Excess Burden of Taxation," *Review of Economic Studies*, 21(1): 21–30.

Corneo, G. and C. M. Fong, 2008. "What's the Monetary Value of Distributive Justice?" *Journal of Public Economics*, 92(1): 289–308.

Council of Economic Advisers, 1996. *Economic Report of the President 1996*, Washington DC: Government Printing Office.

Council of Economic Advisers, 1997a. *Economic Report of the President 1997*, Washington DC: Government Printing Office.

Council of Economic Advisers, 1997b. *Economic Indicators*, June, Washington, DC: Government Printing Office.

Council of Economic Advisers, 2016. *Economic Report of the President (2016)*, Executive Office of the President, www.gpo.gov/fdsys/pkg/ERP-2016/pdf/ERP-2016.pdf (accessed February 14, 2020).

Council on Foreign Relations, 2013. "Remedial Education: Federal Education Policy," updated in January 2016. Available at: http://i.cfr.org/content/publications/attachments/RA-RemedialEducation.pdf

Cremer, H., and P. Pestieau, 2006. "Wealth Transfer Taxation: A Survey of the Theoretical Literature," in S.C. Kolm and J. Mercier Ythier (eds.), *Handbook of the Economics of Giving, Altruism, and Reciprocity*, Elsevier 2(2): 1107–34. https://www.sciencedirect.com/science/article/abs/pii/S1574071406020161?via%3Dihub.

Cremer, H., P. Pestieau, J.-C. Rochet, 2003. "Capital income taxation when inherited wealth is not observable," *Journal of Public Economics*, 87(11): 2475–90.0

Currie, J. and E. Tekin, 2011. "The Effect of Foreclosure Crisis on Health," George Mason University, May.

Currie, J. and D. Thomas, 1995. "Does Head Start Make a Difference?" *American Economic Review*, 85(3): 341–64.

Dabla-Norris, M. E., M. K. Kochhar, M. N. Suphaphiphat, M. F. Ricka, and E. Tsounta, 2015. "Causes and Consequences of Income Inequality: A Global Perspective," IMF Staff Discussion Note 15/13.

Dalton, H., 1920. "The Measurement of the Inequality of Incomes," *Economic Journal*, 3(119): 348–61.

Dardanoni, V., 1993. "Measuring Social Mobility," *Journal of Economic Theory*, 61(2): 372–94.

Dardanoni, V., M. Fiorini, and A. Forcina, 2010. "Stochastic Monotonicity in Intergenerational Mobility Tables," *Journal of Applied Econometrics*, 27(1): 85–107.

Dasgupta, P., 2005. "The Economics of Social Capital," *Economic Record*, 81(S1): S2–S21.

Dasgupta, P., 2012. "Dark Matters: Exploitation as Cooperation," *Journal of Theoretical Biology*, 299: 180–87.

Dasgupta, P. and G. M. Heal, 1974. "The Optimal Depletion of Exhaustible Resources," *Review of Economic Studies*, 41(5): 3–28.

Dasgupta, P. and D. Ray, 1986. "Inequality as a Determinant of Malnutrition and Unemployment," *Economic Journal*, 96(384): 1011–34.

Dasgupta, P. and J. E. Stiglitz, 1971. "Differential Taxation, Public Goods, and Economic Efficiency," *Review of Economic Studies*, 38(2): 151–74.

Dasgupta, P. and J. E. Stiglitz, 1972. "On Optimal Taxation and Public Production," *Review of Economic Studies*, 39(1): 87–103.

Dasgupta, P. and J. E. Stiglitz, 1975. "Benefit-Cost Analysis and Trade Policies," *Journal of Political Economy*, 82(1): 1–33.

Dasgupta, P. and J. E. Stiglitz, 1977. "Tariffs vs. Quotas as Revenue Raising Devices Under Uncertainty," *American Economic Review*, 67(5): 975–81.

Dasgupta, P. and J. E. Stiglitz, 1980a. "Industrial Structure and the Nature of Innovative Activity," *Economic Journal*, 90(358): 266–93.

Dasgupta, P. and J. E. Stiglitz, 1980b. "Uncertainty, Industrial Structure and the Speed of R&D," *Bell Journal of Economics*, 11(1): 1–28.

Dasgupta, P. and J. E. Stiglitz, 1988c. "Potential Competition, Actual Competition, and Economic Welfare," *European Economic Review*, 32: 569–77.

Dasgupta, P., A. Sen, and D. Starett, 1973. "Notes on the Measurement of Inequality," *Journal of Economic Theory*, 6(2): 180–87.

David, P.A. and Van de Klundert, T. 1965. "Biased Efficiency Growth and Capital-Labor Substitution in the U.S., 1899–1960," *American Economic Review*, 55(3): 357–93.

Dávila, E., and A. Korinek, 2018. "Pecuniary Externalities in Economies with Financial Frictions," *The Review of Economic Studies*, 85(1): 352–95.

De Loecker, Jan and Jan Eeckhout, 2017. "The Rise of Market Power and the Macroeconomic Implications," NBER Working Paper 23687.

De Loecker, Jan and G. Unger, 2020. "The Rise of Market Power and the Macroeconomic Implications," *Quarterly Journal of Economics*, 135(2): 561–644.

de Menil, G., 1968. "Three Essays on Wage Determination in U.S. Manufacturing," M.I.T. doctoral dissertation, February.

Deaton, A., 1979. "Optimally Uniform Commodity Taxes," *Economics Letters*, 2(4): 357–61.

Deaton, A., 1981. "Optimal Taxes and the Structure of Preferences," *Econometrica*, 49(5): 1245–59.

Debreu, G., 1959. *The Theory of Value: An Axiomatic Analysis of Economic Equilibrium*, New York: Wiley.

Deininger, K. and L. Squire, 1996. "A New Data Set Measuring Income Inequality," World Bank *Economic Review*, 10(3): 565–91.

Delaney, K. J., 2017. "The Robot That Takes Your Job Should Pay Taxes, Says Bill Gates," *Quartz*, February 17.

Delli Gatti, D., M. Gallegati, B. C. Greenwald, A. Russo, and J. E. Stiglitz, 2012a. "Mobility Constraints, Productivity Trends, and Extended Crises," *Journal of Economic Behavior & Organization*, 83(3): 375–93.

Delli Gatti, D., M. Gallegati, B. C. Greenwald, A. Russo, and J. E. Stiglitz, 2012b "Sectoral Imbalances and Long Run Crises," in F. Allen, M. Aoki, J.-P. Fitoussi, N. Kiyotaki, R. Gordon, and J. E. Stiglitz (eds.), *The Global Macro Economy and Finance*, IEA Conference Volume No. 150-III, Houndmills, UK and New York: Palgrave, 61–97.

Demeritt, A. and K. Hoff, 2018. "The Making of Behavioral Development Economics," *History of Political Economy*, 50(annual supplement): 303–22.

Demeritt, A., K. Hoff, and J. E. Stiglitz, forthcoming, *Malleable Minds: A Psychological, Sociological, and Anthropological Perspective on What Makes Economic Progress Possible*, New York: Columbia University Press.

DeRemer, D., J. C. Fuhrer, J. S. Little, R. Raykov, S. Schuh, G. M. B. Tootell, R. Triest, and A. van Grondelle, 2004. "Understanding the 'Job-Loss Recovery'," Federal Reserve Bank of Boston public policy brief, Issue No. 1, January-August

Detragiache, E., T. Tressel, and P. Gupta, 2008. "Foreign Banks in Poor Countries: Theory and Evidence," *Journal of Finance*, 63(5): 2123–60.

Desilver, D., 2018. "For Most U.S. Workers, Real Wages Have Barely Budged in Decades," Pew Research Center, August 7.

Dewey, J., 1889. "Galton's Statistical Methods," *Publications of the American Statistical Association*, 1(7): 331–34.

Diamond, D. and P. Dybvig, 1983. "Bank Runs, Deposit Insurance, and Liquidity," *Journal of Political Economy*, 91(3): 401–19

Diamond, P. A., 1967. "The Role of a Stock Market in a General Equilibrium Model with Technological Uncertainty," *American Economic Review*, 57(4): 759–76.

Diamond, P. A., 1971. "A Model of Price Adjustment," *Journal of Economic Theory*, 3(2): 156–68.

Diamond, P. A., 1975. "A Many-Person Ramsey Tax Rule," *Journal of Public Economics* 4(4): 335–42.

Diamond, P. A., 1982. "Aggregate Demand Management in Search Equilibrium," *American Economic Review*, 90(5): 881–94.

Diamond, P. A., 1998. "Optimal Income Taxation: An Example with a U-Shaped Pattern for the Optimal Marginal Rates," *American Economic Review*, 88(1): 83–95.

Diamond, P. A. and J. A. Mirrlees, 1971. "Optimal Taxation and Public Production," *American Economic Review*, 61(1): 8–27 and 261–78.

Diamond, P. A. and J. A. Mirrlees, 2011. "The Case for a Progressive Tax: From Basic Research to Policy Recommendations," *Journal of Economic Perspectives*, 25(4): 165–90.

Diamond, P. A. and E. Saez, 1978. "A Model of Social Insurance with Variable Retirement," *Journal of Public Economics*, 10(3): 295–336.

Diamond, P. A, and E. Saez, 2011. "The case for a progressive tax: From basic research to policy recommendation," *Journal of Economic Perspectives*, 25(4): 165–90.

Diamond, P. A. and J. E. Stiglitz, 1974. "Increases in Risk and in Risk Aversion," *Journal of Economic Theory*, 8(3): 337–60.

Dickens, W. and L. F. Katz, 1987. "Inter-Industry Wage Differences and Industry Characteristics," in K. Lang (ed.), *Unemployment and the Structure of Labor Markets*, New York and Oxford: Blackwell, 48–89.

Dicks-Mireaux, L.A., 1961. "The Interrelationship between Cost and Price Changes, 1946–59," *Oxford Economic Papers*, 13(3): 267–92.

DiMaggio, P., 1997. "Culture and Cognition," *Annual Review of Sociology*, 23(1): 263–87.

Dixit, A. and J. E. Stiglitz, 1977. "Monopolistic Competition and Optimum Product Diversity," *American Economic Review*, 67(3): 297–308.

Domar, E. D. and R. A. Musgrave, 1944. "Proportional Income Taxation and Risk-Taking," *Quarterly Journal of Economics*, 58(3): 388–422.

Domar, E. D. and J. E. Stiglitz. 2014. "The Role of Intellectual Property Rights in the Development Process, with Some Lessons from Developed Countries: An Introduction," in M. Cimoli et al. (eds.), *Intellectual Property Rights: Legal and Economic Challenges for Development*, Oxford and New York: Oxford University Press, 1–53.

Domar, E. D., et al., 2017. "Rational Heuristics? Expectations and Behaviors in Evolving Economies with Heterogeneous Interacting Agents," *Economic Inquiry*, 58(2): 1487–1516

Domar, E. D., et al., 2020. "The Distribution of Wealth and Fiscal Policy in Economies with Finitely Lived Agents," *Economic Inquiry*, 58(3): 1487–516.

Dosi, Giovanni, and Joseph E. Stiglitz, 2014. "The Role of Intellectual Property Rights in the Development Process, with Some Lessons from Developed Countries: An Introduction," in Mario Cimoli, and others (eds), *Intellectual Property Rights: Legal and Economic Challenges for Development*, Initiative for Policy Dialogue (Oxford, 2014; online edn, Oxford Academic, 21 Aug. 2014).

Dosi, Giovanni, Mauro Napoletano, Andrea Roventini, Joseph E. Stiglitz, and Tania Treibich, 2020. "Rational Heuristics? Expectations and Behaviors in Evolving Economies with Heterogeneous Interacting Agents," *Economic Inquiry*, 58(3): 1487–1516.

Doyle, M., 2012. "Dialectics of a Global Constitution: The Struggle over the UN Charter," *European Journal of International Relations*, 18(4): 601–24.

Drandakis, E. and E. Phelps, 1966. "A Model of Induced Invention, Growth and Distribution," *Economic Journal*, 76(304): 823–40.

Dreier, P., 2014. "What Housing Recovery?," *New York Times*, May 8, 2014, available at http://www.nytimes.com/2014/05/09/opinion/what-housing-recovery.html?ref=opinion&_r=0 (accessed January 8, 2019).

Duca, J., 1986. "Trade Credit and Credit Rationing: A Theoretical Model," Research Papers in Banking and Financial Economics, Board of Governors of the Federal Reserve System.

Duca, J. and S. Rosenthal, 1988. "Mortgage Rationing in the Post-Disintermediation Era: Does FHA Make a Difference?" Economic Activity Working Paper 83, Board of Governors of the Federal Reserve System.

Duclos, J. Y., J.-M. Esteban, and D. Ray, 2004. "Polarization: Concepts, Measurement, Estimation," *Econometrica*, 72(6): 1737–72.

Duesenberry, J. S., 1949. *Income, Saving and the Theory of Consumer Behavior*, Cambridge: Harvard University Press.

Dworkin, R., 1981. "What Is Equality? Part 2: Equality of Resources," *Philosophy and Public Affairs*, 10(4): 283–345.

Dynan, K., J. Skinner, and S. P. Zeldes, 2004. "Do the Rich Save More?" *Journal of Political Economy*, 112(2): 397–444.

Dynarski, M. and S. M. Sheffrin, 1987. "Consumption and Unemployment," *Quarterly Journal of Economics*, 102(2): 411–28.

Easterly, W., 2007. "Inequality Does Cause Underdevelopment: Insights from a New Instrument," *Journal of Development Economics*, 84(2): 755–76.

Easterly, W., R. Islam, and J. E. Stiglitz, 2001a. "Shaken and Stirred: Explaining Growth Volatility," in *Annual Bank Conference on Development Economics 2000*, Washington: World Bank, 191–212.

Easterly, W., R. Islam, and J. E. Stiglitz, 2001b. "Shaken and Stirred: Volatility and Macroeconomic Paradigms for Rich and Poor Countries," in J. Dreze (ed.), *Advances in Macroeconomic Theory*, IEA Conference Volume, 133, Houndsmills, UK: Palgrave, 353–72. (Speech given for Michael Bruno Memorial Lecture, 12th World Congress of IEA, Buenos Aires, August 27, 1999.)

Easterly, W., R. Islam, and J. E. Stiglitz, 2003. "Volatility and macroeconomic paradigms for rich and poor countries," in Jacques H. Drèze (ed.). Advances in Macroeconomic Theory: Volume 1, Palgrave MacMillian, Basingstoke, 352–372.

Eaton, J., 1986. "Lending with Costly Enforcement of Repayment and Potential Fraud," *Journal of Banking and Finance*, 10(2): 281–93.

Eaton, J. and M. Gersovitz, 1981. "Debt with Potential Repudiation: Theoretical and Empirical Analysis," *Review of Economic Studies*, 48(2): 289–309.

Eaton, J.and J. E. Stiglitz, 1986. "The Pure Theory of Country Risk," *European Economic Review*, 30(3): 481–513.

Eckstein, O. and G. Fromm, 1968. "The Price Equation," *American Economic Review*, 58(5): 1159–83.

Economic Policy Institute, 2015. "Hourly Wages by Education, 1973–2011 (2011 Dollars)," available at http://www.stateofworkingamerica.org/chart/swa-wages-table-4-14-hourly-wages-education/ (accessed January 8, 2020).

Edgeworth, F. Y., 1897. "The Pure Theory of Taxation," *Economic Journal*, 7(28): 550–71.

Edlin, A. and J. E. Stiglitz, 1995. "Discouraging Rivals: Managerial Rent-Seeking and Economic Inefficiencies," American Economic Review, 85(5): 1301–12.

Eisner, R. and M. Nadiri, 1968. "Investment Behavior and Neoclassical Theory," *Review of Economics and Statistics*, 50(3): 369–82.

Elinder, M., O. Erixson, and D. Waldenström, 2018. "Inheritance and Wealth Inequality: Evidence From Population Registers" *Journal of Public Economics* 165: 17–30

Eller, T. J. and W. Fraser, 1995. *Asset Ownership of Households: 1993*, US Department of Commerce, Economics and Statistics Administration, Bureau of the Census, 1995.

Esteban, J.-M. and D. Ray, 1994. "On the Measurement of Polarization," *Econometrica*, 62(4): 819–51.

Fagereng, A., et al., 2019. "Heterogeneity and Persistence in Returns to Wealth" April, https://drive.google.com/file/d/1TC3tjL_X9qmRJVSS74WRF7DvgybxJWbx/view.

Fair, R. and D. Jaffee, 1972. "Methods of Estimations for Markets in Disequilibrium," *Econometrica*, 40(3): 497–514.

Farhi, E. and I. Werning, 2010. "Progressive Estate Taxation," *Quarterly Journal of Economics*, 125(2): 635–73.

Farrell, J. M., 1970. "The Magnitude of 'Rate of Growth' Effects on Aggregate Savings," *Economic Journal*, 80(320): 873–94.

Farrell, J. M., 1986. "How Effective Is Potential Competition?" *Economic Letters*, 20(1): 67–70.

Fay, J. and J. Medoff, 1985. "Labor and Output over the Business Cycle: Some Direct Evidence," *American Economic Review*, 75(4): 638–55.

Fazzari, S., R. Hubbard, and B. Petersen, 1988. "Financing Constraints and Corporate Investment," *Brookings Papers on Economic Activity*, 1988(2): 141–95.

Fehr, E., and K. Hoff, 2011. "Tastes, Castes and Culture: The Influence of Society on Preferences," *Economic Journal*, 121(556): F291–F493.

Fehr, E., and K. M. Schmidt, 2003. "Theories of Fairness and Reciprocity—Evidence and Economic Applications," in M. Dewatripont, L. P. Hansen, and S. J. Turnovsky (eds.), *Advances in Economics and Econometrics*, Econometric Society Monographs, Eighth World Congress, Volume 1, Cambridge: Cambridge University Press, 208–57.

Feiveson, L., and J. Sabelhaus, 2019. "Lifecycle Patterns of Saving and Wealth Accumulation," Finance and Economics Discussion Series 2019-010. Washington: Board of Governors of the Federal Reserve System, https://doi.org/10.17016/FEDS.2019.010r1.

Feldstein, M., 1974. "Distributional Preferences in Public Expenditure Analysis," in H. M. Hochman and G. D. Peterson (eds.), *Redistribution through Public Choice*, New York: Columbia University Press. https://scholar.harvard.edu/feldstein/publications/distributional-preferences-public-expenditure-analysis.

Feldstein, M., 1998. "Savings Grace," *The New Republic*, April 6, 19.

Feldstein, M., 2014. "Piketty's Numbers Don't Add Up," *Wall Street Journal*, May 14.

Feller, W., 1950. *An Introduction to Probability Theory, Volume I* (New York: John Wiley and Son).

Ferguson, N., 2009. *The Ascent of Money: A Financial History of the World*, London: Penguin.

Fertig, A., 2001. "Trends in Intergenerational Mobility," Center for Research on Child Well-Being Working Paper 01-23.

Fellner, W., 1961. "Two Propositions in the Theory of Induced Innovations," *Economic Journal*, 71(282): 305–8.

Fields, G. S. and Ok, E. A., 1999. "The Measurement of Income Mobility: An Introduction to the Literature," in J. Silber (ed.), *Handbook on Income Inequality Measurement*, Norwell, Mass.: Kluwer Academic Publishers, 557–96.

Financial Crisis Inquiry Commission (2011). "The Financial Crisis Inquiry Report," Final Report of the National Commission, available at https://www.govinfo.gov/content/pkg/GPO-FCIC/pdf/GPO-FCIC.pdf (accessed July 23, 2019).

Fischer, S., 1993. "The Role of Macroeconomic Factors in Growth," *Journal of Monetary Economics*, 32(3): 485–512.

Fisher, I., 1933. "The Debt-Deflation Theory of Great Depressions," *Econometrica*, 1(4): 337–57.

Flavin, M. A., 1981. "The Adjustment of Consumption to Changing Expectations about Future Income," *Journal of Political Economy*, 89(5): 974–1009.

Flemming, J. S., 1976. Selected Evidence submitted for Report No. 1 Royal Commission on the Distribution of Income and Wealth, London: HMSO.

Flemming, J. S., 1979. "The Effects of Earnings Inequality, Imperfect Capital Markets, and Dynastic Altruism on the Distribution of Wealth in Life-cycle Models," *Economica*, 46(184): 363–80.

Florini, A. (ed.), 2007. *The Right to Know: Transparency for an Open World*, New York: Columbia University Press, 2007.

Frank, R. H., 2005. "Positional Externalities Cause Large and Preventable Welfare Losses," *American Economic Review Papers and Proceedings*, 95(2): 137–41.

Freeland, C., 2000. *Sale of the Century: Russia's Wild Ride from Communism to Capitalism*, New York: Crown Books.

Freeman, R., 1991. "Crime and the Unemployment of Disadvantaged Youths," NBER Working Paper 3875.

Freimer, M. and M. Gordon, 1965. "Why Bankers Ration Credit," *Quarterly Journal of Economics*, 79(3): 397–410.

Frey, C. B., and M. A. Osborne, 2017. "The Future of Employment: How Susceptible Are Jobs to Computerisation?," *Technological Forecasting and Social Change*, 114: 254–80.

Fried, J. and P. Howitt, 1980. "Credit Rationing and Implicit Contract Theory," *Journal of Money, Credit and Banking*, 12(3): 471–87.

Friedman, B., 1981. "The Roles of Money and Credit in Macroeconomic Analysis," NBER Working Paper 831.

Friedman, M., 1957. *A Theory of the Consumption Function*, National Bureau of Economic Research, Princeton, N.J.: Princeton University Press.

Friedman, M., 1962. *Capitalism and Freedom*, Chicago: University of Chicago Press.

Friedman, M., 1968. "The Role of Monetary Policy," *American Economic Review*, 58(1): 1–17.

Fudenberg, D., R. Gilbert, J. E. Stiglitz, and J. Tirole, 1983. "Preemption, Leapfrogging and Competition in Patent Races," *European Economic Review*, 22(1): 3–32.

Fujita, M., P. Krugman and A. Venables, 1999. *The Spatial Economy: Cities, Regions and International Trade*, MIT Press.

Fukuyama, F., 1992, *The End of History and the Last Man*, New York: Free Press.

Furman, J. and P. Orszag, 2018a. "A Firm-Level Perspective on the Role of Rents in the Rise in Inequality," in M. Guzman (ed.), *Toward a Just Society: Joseph Stiglitz and Twenty-First Century Economics*, New York: Columbia University Press, 2018, 19–47.

Furman, J. and P. Orszag, 2018b. "Slower Productivity and Higher Inequality: Are They Related?," Peterson Institute for International Economics Working Paper no. 2018-4.

Furman, J. and J. E. Stiglitz, 1998. "Economic Consequences of Income Inequality," in *Symposium Proceedings – Income Inequality: Issues and Policy Options*, Jackson Hole, Wyoming: Federal Reserve Bank of Kansas City, 221–63.

Gabaix, X., 2009 "Power Laws in Economics and Finance,"; *Annual Review of Economics, Annual Reviews*, 1(1): 255–94, 05.

Gabaix, X., J. M. Lastry, P. L. Lions, and B. Moll, 2016. "The Dynamics of Inequality," *Econometrica*, 84(6): 2071–2111.

Galbraith, K., 2012. *Inequality and Instability: A Study of the World Economy Just Before the Great Crisis*, New York and Oxford: Oxford University Press.

Gale, I. and J. E. Stiglitz, 1989. "The Informational Content of Initial Public Offerings," *Journal of Finance*, 44(2): 469–78 (reprinted as Chapter 6, *Selected Works*, Volume II).

Galton, F., 1886. "Regression towards Mediocrity in Hereditary Stature," *Journal of the Anthropological Institute of Great Britain and Ireland*, 15: 246–63.

Garvey, G., and T. Milbourn, 2003. "Incentive Compensation When Executives Can Hedge the Market: Evidence of Relative Performance Evaluation in the Cross Section," *The Journal of Finance*, 58: 1557–82.

Gauthier, S., and G. Laroque, 2009. "Separability and Public Finance," *Journal of Public Economics*, 93(11): 1168–74.

Geanakoplos, J., and H. Polemarchakis, 1986. "Existence, Regularity, and Constrained Suboptimality of Competitive Allocations When the Asset Market Is Incomplete," in W. Heller, R. Starr, and D. Starrett (eds.), *Uncertainty, Information and Communication: Essays in Honor of K. J. Arrow*, Cambridge, UK: Cambridge University Press, 65–96.

George, H., 1879. *Progress and Poverty: An Inquiry into the Cause of Industrial Depressions and of Increase of Want with Increase of Wealth*, Book VI, New York: D. Appleton & Company.

Gilens, M., and B. I. Page, 2016. "Critics Argued with Our Analysis of U.S. Political Inequality. Here Are 5 Ways They're Wrong," *Washington Post*, May 23, available at https://www.washingtonpost.com/news/monkey-cage/wp/2016/05/23/critics-challenge-our-portrait-of-americas-political-inequality-heres-5-ways-they-are-wrong/.

Gilens, M., and B. I. Page, 2017. *Democracy in America?: What Has Gone Wrong and What We Can Do about It*, Chicago: University of Chicago Press.

Giovannoni, O. G., 2014. "What Do We Know about the Labor Share and the Profit Share?—Part III: Measures and Structural Factors," Working Paper No. 805, Levy Economics Institute of Bard College.

Giovannoni, O. G., 2015. "Inequality: Challenge of the Century?" Paper presented at The Preliminary Program of the Allied Social Science Association, Boston, January 3.

Glaeser, E. L., and J. D. Gottlieb, 2009. "The Wealth of Cities: Agglomeration Economies and Spatial Equilibrium in the United States," *Journal of Economic Literature*, 47(4): 983–1028.

Godoy, S., and J. E. Stiglitz, 2007. "Growth, Initial Conditions, Law and Speed of Privatization in Transition Countries: 11 Years Later," in S. Estrin et al. (eds.), *Transition and Beyond*, Hampsire England: Palgrave Macmillian, 89–117.

Goldberger, A. S., 1989. "Economic and Mechanical Models of Intergenerational Transmission," *American Economic Review*, 79(3): 504–13.

Goldfeld, S. and R. Quandt, 1975. "Estimation in a Disequilibrium Model and the Value of Information," *Journal of Econometrics*, 3(4): 325–48.

Goldin, C. and L. F. Katz, 2008. *The Race between Education and Technology*, Cambridge: Harvard University Press.

Goldthorpe, J. H., 1980. *Social Mobility and Class Structure in Modern Britain*, Oxford: Oxford University Press.

Goodwin, R., 1967. "A Growth Cycle," in C. H. Feinstein (ed.), *Socialism, Capitalism and Economic Growth*, Cambridge: Cambridge University Press, 54–58.

Gordon, R., 2016. *The Rise and Fall of American Growth: The U.S. Standard of Living since the Civil War*, Princeton, NJ: Princeton University Press.

Gormley, T. A., 2007. "Banking Competition in Developing Countries: Does Foreign Bank Entry Improve Credit Access?" University of Pennsylvania working paper.

Gormley, T. A., 2010. "The Impact of Foreign Bank Entry in Emerging Markets: Evidence from India," *Journal of Financial Intermediation*, 19(1): 26–51.

Greenspan, A., 1996. "Remarks at the Annual Dinner and Francis Boyer Lecture of the American Enterprise Institute for Public Policy Research," Washington, D.C. December 5, available at https://www.federalreserve.gov/boarddocs/speeches/1996/19961205.htm.

Greenstone, M. and A. Looney, 2012. "The Marriage Gap: The Impact of Economic and Technological Change on Marriage Rates," The Hamilton Project. Available at: http://www.hamiltonproject.org/files/downloads_and_links/020312_jobs_greenstone_looney.pdf."

Greenwald, B., 1979 *Adverse Selection in the Labor Market*, New York: Garland Press.

Greenwald, B., 1986. "Adverse Selection in the Labor Market," *Review of Economic Studies*, 53(3): 325–47.

Greenwald, B. and J. Kahn, 2009. *Globalization: The Irrational Fear that Someone in China Will Take Your Job*, Hoboken, N.J.: John Wiley & Sons.

Greenwald, B. and J. E. Stiglitz, 1984. "Pecuniary and Market Mediated Externalities: Towards a General Theory of the Welfare Economics of Economies with Imperfect Information and Incomplete Markets," NBER Working Paper 1304.

Greenwald, B. and J. E. Stiglitz, 1986. "Externalities in Economies with Imperfect Information and Incomplete Markets," *Quarterly Journal of Economics*, 101(2): 229–64 (reprinted as Chapter 23, Selected Works, Volume I).

Greenwald, B. and J. E. Stiglitz, 1987a. "Imperfect Information, Credit Markets and Unemployment," *European Economic Review*, 31(1): 444–56.

Greenwald, B. and J. E. Stiglitz, 1987b. "Keynesian, New Keynesian and New Classical Economics," *Oxford Economic Papers*, 39(1): 119–33.

Greenwald, B. and J. E. Stiglitz, 1988a. "Examining Alternative Macroeconomic Theories," *Brookings Papers on Economic Activity*, 1988(1): 207–70. Reprinted in Edmund Phelps (ed.), Recent Developments in Macroeconomics, Edward Elgar, 1991, 335–88.

Greenwald, B. and J. E. Stiglitz, 1988b. "Imperfect Information, Finance Constraints and Business Fluctuations," in M. Kohn and S.C. Tsiang (eds.), *Finance Constraints, Expectations, and Macroeconomics*, Oxford: Oxford University Press, 103–40.

Greenwald, B. and J. E. Stiglitz, 1988c. "Money, Imperfect Information and Economic Fluctuations," in M. Kohn and S.C. Tsiang (eds.), *Finance Constraints, Expectations and Macroeconomics*, Oxford: Oxford University Press, 141–65.

Greenwald, B. and J. E. Stiglitz, 1988d. "Pareto Inefficiency of Market Economies: Search and Efficiency Wage Models," *American Economic Review*, 78(2): 351–5.

Greenwald, B. and J. E. Stiglitz, 1990a. "Asymmetric Information and the New Theory of the Firm: Financial Constraints and Risk Behavior," *American Economic Review*, 80(2): 160–5.

Greenwald, B. and J. E. Stiglitz, 1990b. "Macroeconomic Models with Equity and Credit Rationing," in R. B. Hubbard (ed.), *Asymmetric Information, Corporate Finance, and Investment*, Chicago: University of Chicago Press, 15–42.

Greenwald, B. and J. E. Stiglitz, 1991. "Toward a Reformulation of Monetary Theory: Competitive Banking," *Economic and Social Review*, 23(1): 1–34. (Paper prepared for the Irish Economic Association Annual Conference, Dublin, May 1991, and Caffee Lectures presented to the University of Rome and the Bank of Italy, Rome, April 1991.)

Greenwald, B. and J. E. Stiglitz, 1993a. "Financial Market Imperfections and Business Cycles," *Quarterly Journal of Economics*, 108(1): 77–114.

Greenwald, B. and J. E. Stiglitz, 1993b. "New and Old Keynesians," *Journal of Economic Perspectives*, 7(1): 23–44.

Greenwald, B. and J. E. Stiglitz, 1993c. "Monetary Policy and the Theory of the Risk-Averse Bank," prepared for the conference "Macroeconomic Stabilization Policy: Lessons for the Future," CEPR, Stanford University and the Federal Reserve Bank of San Francisco, March 5.

Greenwald, B. and J. E. Stiglitz, 1995. "Labor Market Adjustments and the Persistence of Unemployment," *American Economic Review*, 85(2): 219–25.

Greenwald, B. and J. E. Stiglitz, 2003a. *Towards a New Paradigm in Monetary Economics*, Cambridge, UK: Cambridge University Press.

Greenwald, B. and J. E. Stiglitz, 2003b. "Macroeconomic Fluctuations in an Economy of Phelps-Winter Markets," in P. Aghion, R. Frydman, J. E. Stiglitz, and M. Woodford (eds.), *Knowledge, Information, and Expectations in Modern Macroeconomics: In Honor of Edmund S. Phelps*, Princeton, N.J.: Princeton University Press, 123–36.

Greenwald, B., A. Levinson, and J. E. Stiglitz, J. E., 1993. "Capital market imperfections and regional economic development," in A. Giovannini (Ed.) Finance and Development: Issues and Experience, Cambridge University Press, Cambridge, 65–93.

Greenwald, B., M. Kohn, and J. E. Stiglitz, 1990. "Financial Market Imperfections and Productivity Growth," *Journal of Economic Behavior and Organization*, 13(3): 321–45.

Greenwald, B., M. Salinger, and J. E. Stiglitz, 1990. "Imperfect Capital Markets and Productivity Growth," paper presented at NBER Conference in Vail, CO, April 1990, revised March 1991 and April 1992.

Greenwald, B., J. E. Stiglitz, and A. Weiss, 1984. "Informational Imperfections in the Capital Market and Macroeconomic Fluctuations," *American Economic Review*, 74(2): 194–205.

Greider, W., 1987. *Secrets of the Temple*, New York: Simon & Schuster.

Greiner, A., J. Rubart, and W. Semmler, 2004. "Economic Growth, Skill-Biased Technical Change and Wage Inequality: A Model and Estimations for the U.S. and Europe," *Journal of Macroeconomics*, 26(4): 597–621.

Griliches, Z., 1969. "Capital-Skill Complementarity," *Review of Economics and Statistics*, 51(4): 465–68.

Groshen, E. L., B. C. Moyer, A. M. Aizcorbe, R. Bradley, and D. M. Friedman, 2017. "How Government Statistics Adjust for Potential Biases from Quality Change and New Goods in an Age of Digital Technologies: A View from the Trenches," *Journal of Economic Perspectives*, 31(2): 187–210.

Grossman, S. J. and O. D. Hart, 1986. "The Costs and Benefits of Ownership: A Theory of Vertical and Lateral Integration," *Journal of Political Economy*, 94(4): 691–719.

Grossman, S. and J. E. Stiglitz, 1976. "Information and Competitive Price Systems," *American Economic Review*, 66(2): 246–53.

Grossman, S. and J. E. Stiglitz, 1977. "On Value Maximization and Alternative Objectives of the Firm," *Journal of Finance*, 32(2): 389–402.

Grossman, S. and J. E. Stiglitz, 1980a. "On the Impossibility of Informationally Efficient Markets," *American Economic Review*, 70(3): 393–408.

Grossman, S. and J. E. Stiglitz, 1980b. "Stockholder Unanimity in the Making of Production and Financial Decisions," *Quarterly Journal of Economics*, 94(3): 543–66.

Guesnerie, R., 1992. "An Exploration of the Eductive Justifications of the Rational-expectations Hypothesis," *The American Economic Review*, 82(5): 1254–78.

Gupta, P., Kochhar, K. and Panth, S., 2011. "Bank Ownership and the Effects of Financial Liberalization: Evidence from India," International Monetary Fund Working Paper 11/50.

Gurley, J. and E. Shaw, 1960. *Money in a Theory of Finance*, Washington: The Brookings Institution.

Guttentag, J., 1960. "Credit Availability, Interest Rates, and Monetary Policy," *Southern Economic Journal*, 26(3): 219–28.

Guzman, M. and J. E. Stiglitz, 2014. "Pseudo-Wealth and Consumption Fluctuations," Columbia University working paper.

Guzman, M. and J. E. Stiglitz, 2016a. "A Theory of Pseudo-Wealth," in J. E. Stiglitz and M. Guzman (eds.), *Contemporary Issues in Macroeconomics: Lessons from The Crisis and Beyond*, IEA Conference Volume, No.155-II, New York: Palgrave Macmillan, 21–33.

Guzman, M. and J. E. Stiglitz, 2016b. "Pseudo-Wealth and Consumption Fluctuations," NBER Working Paper 22838.

Guzman, M. and J. E. Stiglitz, 2020. "Towards a Dynamic Disequilibrium Theory with Randomness," *Oxford Review of Economic Policy*, 621–674.

Habakkuk, H. J., 1962. *American and British Technology in the Nineteenth Century*, London: Cambridge Univ. Press.

Hacker, J. and P. Pierson, 2011. *Winner-Take-All Politics: How Washington Made the Rich Richer—and Turned its Back on the Middle Class*, New York: Simon and Schulster.

Hadar, J. and W. R. Russell, 1969. "Rules for Ordering Uncertain Prospects," *American Economic Review*, 59(1): 25–34.

Hahn, F. H., 1966. "Equilibrium Dynamics with Heterogeneous Capital Goods," *Quarterly Journal of Economics*, 80(321): 633–46.

Haig, R. M., 1921. "The Concept of Income—Economic and Legal Aspects," *The Federal Income Tax*, 1(7): 1–28.

Hall, R. E., 1978. "Stochastic Implications of the Life Cycle-Permanent Income Hypothesis: Theory and Evidence," *Journal of Political Economy*, 86(6): 971–88.

Hall, R. E. and D. Jorgenson, 1967. "Tax Policy and Investment Behavior," *American Economic Review*, 57(3): 391–414.

Hall, R. E. and F. Mishkin, 1982. "The Sensitivity of Consumption to Transitory Income: Estimates from Panel Data on Households," *Econometrica*, 50: 461–82.

Hall, R. L. and C. J. Hitch, 1939. "Price Theory and Business Behaviour," *Oxford Economic Papers*, 2(2): 12–45.

Hamada, K., 1972. "Ability Spread and the Optimal Linear Income Tax," presented at the 1972 NSF-NBER Conference on Decision Rules and Uncertainty, Iowa City, Iowa.

Hamada, K., 1973. "A Simple Majority Rule on the Distribution of Income," *Journal of Economic Theory*, 6(3): 243–64.

Hamilton, W. H., 1919. "The Institutional Approach to Economic Theory," *American Economic Review*, 9(1), Supplement: 309–18.

Hanoch, G., and H. Levy, 1969. "The Efficiency Analysis of Choices Involving Risk," *Review of Economic Studies*, 36(3): 335–46.

Hanson, R., 2016. *The Age of Em: Work, Love, and Life When Robots Rule the Earth*, Oxford: Oxford University Press.

Harari, Y. N., 2017. *Homo Deus: A Brief History of Tomorrow*, New York: Harper.

Harkinson, J. "The Walmart Heirs Are Worth More than Everyone in Your City Combined," *Mother Jones*, October 3, 2015, available at http://www.motherjones.com/politics/2014/10/walmart-walton-heirs-net-worth-cities (accessed January 8, 2020).

Harris, D., 1974. "Credit Rationing at Commercial Banks," *Journal of Money, Credit and Banking*, 6(2): 227–40.

Harris, B. H, and S. Block (eds.), 2021. *Inequality and the Labor Market: The Case for Greater Competition*, Washington, D.C: Brookings Institution Press.

Harris, F. R., and A. Curtis (eds.). 2018. *Healing Our Divided Society: Investing in America Fifty Years after the Kerner* Report, Philadelphia: Temple University Press.

Harsanyi, J. C. 1955. "Cardinal Welfare, Individualistic Ethics, and Interpersonal Comparisons of Utility," *Journal of Political Economy*, 63(4): 309–71.

Haushofer J, E. Fehr, 2014. "On the psychology of poverty," *Science*, May 23; 344(6186): 862–7. doi: 10.1126/science.1232491. PMID: 24855262.

Haveman, R., G. Sandefur, B. Wolfe, and A. Voyer. 2004. "Trends in Children's attainments and their determinants as family income inequality has increased," in K.M. Neckerman (ed.), *Social Inequality*. New York: Russell Sage 149–188.

Hawtrey, R., 1919. *Currency and Credit*, New York: Longmans, Green & Co.

Hayashi, F., 1985a. "The Effect of Liquidity Constraints on Consumption: A Cross-Sectional Analysis," *Quarterly Journal of Economics*, 100(1): 183–206.

Hayashi, F., 1985b. "Tests for Liquidity Constraints: A Critical Survey," NBER Working Paper 1720.

Hayek, F., 1939. *Profits, Interest, and Investment*, London: George Routledge and Sons.

Heckman, J., 2011. "The Economics of Inequality: The Value of Early Childhood Education," *American Educator*, 35(1): 31–47.

Heckman, J., 2021. "The Economics of Human Potential," https://heckmanequation.org/

Heckman, J. and S. Mosso, 2014. "The Economics of Human Development and Social Mobility," *Annual Review of Economics*, 6(1): 689–733.

Heckman, J., R. Pinto, and P. Savelyev, 2013. "Understanding the Mechanisms through Which an Influential Early Childhood Program Boosted Adult Outcomes," *American Economic Review*, 103(6): 2052–86.

Hellman, T., K. Murdock, and J. E. Stiglitz, 1996. "Deposit Mobilisation through Financial Restraint," in N. Hermes and R. Lensink (ed.), *Financial Development and Economic Growth*, New York: Routledge, 219–46.

Hellman, T., K. Murdock, and J. E. Stiglitz, 1997. "Financial Restraint: Toward a New Paradigm," in M. Aoki, H. Kim, and M. Okuna-Fujiwara (eds.), *The Role of Government in East Asian Economic Development*, Oxford: Clarendon Press, 163–207.

Hellman, T., K. Murdock, and J. E. Stiglitz, 1998. "Financial Restraint and the Market Enhancing View," in Y. Hayami and M. Aoki (eds.), *The Institutional Foundations of East Asian Economic Development*, London: Macmillan, 255–84.

Hellman, T., K. Murdock, and J. E. Stiglitz, 2000. "Liberalization, Moral Hazard in Banking and Prudential Regulation: Are Capital Requirements Enough?," *American Economic Review*, 90(1): 147–65.

Hellwig, M., 1977. "A Model of Borrowing and Lending with Bankruptcy," *Econometrica*, 45(8): 1879–906.

Henry, C. and J. E. Stiglitz, 2010. "Intellecutal Property, Dissemination of Innovation, and Sustainable Development," *Global Policy*, 1(1): 237–51.

Henry, G., 1886. *Progress and Poverty*, London: Kegan Paul, Tench & Co.

Henwood, D., 1997. *Wall Street: How It Works and for Whom*, London and New York: Verso.

Hertz, T., 2006. "Understanding Mobility in America," Center for American Progress and American University Working Paper, April.

Hicks, J., 1932. *The Theory of Wages*. London: Macmillan.

High-Level Panel of Eminent Persons on the Post-2015 Development Agenda, 2013. *A New Global Partnership: Eradicate Poverty and Transform Economies through Sustainable Development*, New York: United Nations.

Hodgman, D., 1960. "Credit Risk and Credit Rationing," *Quarterly Journal of Economics*, 74(2): 258–78.

Hirano, T., and J. E. Stiglitz, 2022a. "Land Speculation and Wobbly Dynamics with Endogenous Phase Transitions,", NBER Working Paper No. 29745, February, 2022.

Hirano, T. and J. E. Stiglitz, 2022b. "The Wobbly Economy: Global Dynamics with Phase and State Transitions," NBER Working Paper No. 29806, February, 2022.Tomohiro

Hirano, T. and J. E. Stiglitz, 2022c. "Land Speculation, Booms, and Busts with Endogenous Phase Transitions: A Model of Economic Fluctuations with Rational Exuberance," VoxEU, June 28, 2022. Accessible at: https://voxeu.org/article/land-speculation-booms-and-busts-endogenous-phase-transitions

Hodgman, D., 1963. *Commercial Bank Loan and Investment Policy*, Champaign-Urbana: Bureau of Economic and Business Research, University of Illinois.

Hoff, K., 1994. "The Second Theorem of the Second Best," *Journal of Public Economics*, 54(2): 223–42.

Hoff, K., 1996. "Market Failures and the Distribution of Wealth: A Perspective from the Economics of Information," *Politics and Society*, 24(4): 411–32.

Hoff, K. and P. Pandey, 2006. "Discrimination, Social Identity, and Durable Inequalities," *American Economic Review*, 96(2): 206–11.

Hoff, K. and P. Pandey, 2014. "Making Up People—The Effect of Identity on Performance in a Modernizing Society, *Journal of Development Economics*, 106(C): 118–31.

Hoff, K. and J. E. Stiglitz, 2004. "After the Big Bang? Obstacles to the Emergence of the Rule of Law in Post-Communist Societies," *American Economic Review*, 94(3): 753–63.

Hoff, K. and J. E. Stiglitz, 2008. "Exiting a Lawless State," *Economic Journal*, 118(531): 1474–97.

Hoff, K. and J. E. Stiglitz, 2010. "Equilibrium Fictions: A Cognitive Approach to Societal Rigidity," *American Economic Review*, 100(2): 141–46. Shortened version of a World Bank Policy Research Paper 5219 of the same title, The World Bank Development Research Group, February 2010, available at http://elibrary.worldbank.org/docserver/download/5219.pdf?expires=1304012730&id=id&accname=guest&checksum=5428C2B3013CF8ECBB54953BAC3F328C.

Hoff, K. and J. E. Stiglitz, 2016. "Striving for Balance in Economics: Towards a Theory of the Social Determination of Behavior," *Journal of Economic Behavior and Organization*, Iss. 126 (June): 25–57.

Hoff, K. and J. E. Stiglitz, 2017. "How Inequality Weakens Our Economy and Divides Our Society," paper presented to the American Sociological Association Annual Meeting, Montreal.

Hoff, K., A. Braverman, and J. E. Stiglitz (eds.), 1993. *The Economics of Rural Organization: Theory, Practice, and Policy*, New York: Oxford University Press.

Holmström, B., and J. Roberts, 1998. "The Boundaries of the Firm Revisited," *Journal of Economic Perspectives*, 12(4): 73–94.

Hotelling, H., 1931. "The Economics of Exhaustible Resources," *Journal of Political Economy*, 39(2): 137–75.

Hubbard, R. (ed.), 1990. *Asymmetric Information, Corporate Finance, and Investment*, Chicago: University of Chicago Press.

Hubbard, R. and K. Judd, 1986. "Liquidity Constraints, Fiscal Policy, and Consumption," *Brookings Papers on Economic Activity*, 1986(1): 1–51.

Hussain, A., N. Stern, and J. E. Stiglitz, 2000. "Chinese Reforms from a Comparative Perspective," in P. J. Hammond and G. D. Myles (eds.), *Incentives, Organization, and Public Economics: Papers in Honour of Sir James Mirrlees*, Oxford: Oxford University Press, 243–77.

Imbs, J., 2007. "Growth and Volatility," *Journal of Monetary Economics*, 54(7): 1848–62.

Inada, K., 1963. "On a Two-Sector Model of Economic Growth: Comments and a Generalization," *Review of Economic Studies*, 30(2): 119–27.

International Monetary Fund, 2014. "Is It Time for an Infrastructure Push? The Macroeconomic Effects of Public Investment," in *World Economic Outlook*, Chapter 3, 75–114, available at http://www.imf.org/external/pubs/ft/weo/2014/02/pdf/c3.pdf.

Jaffee, D., 1971. *Credit Rationing and the Commercial Loan Market*, New York: Wiley.
Jaffee, D. and F. Modigliani, 1969. "A Theory and Test of Credit Rationing," *American Economic Review*, 59(5): 850–72.
Jaffee, D. and T. Russell, 1976. "Imperfect Information, Uncertainty, and Credit Rationing," *Quarterly Journal of Economics*, 90(4): 651–66.
Jaffee, D. and J. E. Stiglitz, 1990. "Credit Rationing," in B. Friedman and F. Hahn (eds.), *Handbook of Monetary Economics*, Amsterdam: Elsevier Science Publishers, 837–88.
Jaffee, D., K. Rosen, B. Friedman, and L. Klein, 1979. "Mortgage Credit Availability and Residential Construction," *Brookings Papers on Economic Activity*, 1979(2): 333–86.
Jäntti, M., B. Bratsberg, K. Røed, O. Raaum, R. Naylor, E. Österbacka, A. Björklund, and T. Eriksson, 2006. "American Exceptionalism in a New Light: A Comparison of Intergenerational Earnings Mobility in the Nordic Countries, the United Kingdom and the United States," IZA Discussion Paper No. 1938.
Jayadev, A., 2013. "Distribution and Crisis: Reviewing Some of the Linkages," in ed. G. Epstein and M. Wolfson (eds.), *The Oxford Handbook on the Political Economy of the Financial Crisis*, 95–112.
Jeanne, O. and A. Korinek, 2010. "Excessive Volatility in Capital Flows: A Pigouvian Taxation Approach," *American Economic Review*, 100(2): 403–7.
Jensen, M. and K. Murphy, 1990. "Performance Pay and Top Management," *Journal of Policital Economy*, 98(2): 225–64.
Jensen, R. and E. Oster, 2009. "The Power of TV: Cable Television and Women's Status in India," *Quarterly Journal of Economics*, 124(3): 1057–94.
Johansen, L., 1959. "Substitution Versus Fixed Production Co-efficients in the Theory of Economic Growth: A Synthesis," *Econometrica*, 27(2): 157–76.
Johnson, S. and J. Kwak, 2010. *13 Bankers: The Wall Street Takeover and the Next Financial Meltdown*, New York: Pantheon Books.
Jones, C. and P. Romer, 2010. "The New Kaldor Facts: Ideas, Institutions, Population, and Human Capital," *American Economic Journal: Macroeconomics*, 2(1): 224–45.
Judd, K., 1985. "Redistributive Taxation in a Simple Perfect Foresight Model," *Journal of Public Economics*, 28(1): 59–83.
Kahneman, D. and A. Tversky, 1972. "Subjective Probability: A Judgment of Representativeness," *Cognitive Psychology* 3(3): 430–54.
Kahneman, D. and A. Tversky, 1973. "On the Psychology of Prediction," Psychological Review, 80(4): 237–51.
Kaldor, N., 1939. "Capital Intensity and the Trade Cycle," *Economica*, 6(21): 40–66.
Kaldor, N., 1940. "A Model of the Trade Cycle," *Economic Journal*, 50(197): 78–92.
Kaldor, N., 1955a. "Alternative Theories of Distribution," *Review of Economic Studies*, 23(2): 83–100.
Kaldor, N., 1955b. *An Expenditure Tax*, London: Allen and Urwin.
Kaldor, N., 1957. "A Model of Economic Growth," *Economic Journal*, 67(268): 591–624.
Kaldor, N., 1961. "Capital Accumulation and Economic Growth," in F. A. Lutz and D. C. Hague (eds.), *The Theory of Capital*, London: St. Martins Press, 177–222.
Kaldor, N., 1966. "Marginal Productivity and the Macro-economic Theories of Distribution," *Review of Economic Studies*, 33(4): 309–20.
Kalt, J. P., 1978. "Technological Change and Factor Substitution in the United States: 1929–1967," *International Economic Review*, 19(3): 761–75.
Kanbur, R., 1987. "The Standard of Living: Uncertainty, Inequality and Opportunity" in G. Hawthorn (ed.), *The Standard of Living: The Tanner Lectures, Clare Hall, Cambridge, 1985*, Cambridge, New York and Melbourne: Cambridge University Press, 59–69.
Kanbur, R., 2012. "Does Kuznets Still Matter?" in S. Kochhar (ed.), *Policy-Making for Indian Planning: Essays on Contemporary Issues in Honor of Montek S. Ahluwalia*, Delhi: Academic Foundation Press, 115–28.
Kanbur, R. and V. Mukerji, 1980. "Probabilistic Equity and Equality of Opportunity in a Stochastic Framework," *Arthaniti*, XX: 1–9.
Kanbur, R. and J. E. Stiglitz, 1982. "Mobility and Inequality: A Utilitarian Analysis," University of Cambridge Economic Theory Discussion Paper 57, May.
Kanbur, R. and J. E. Stiglitz, 1986. "Intergenerational Mobility and Dynastic Inequality," Princeton University Economic Research Program Research Memorandum 324, April.
Kanbur, R. and J. E. Stiglitz, 2015. "Wealth and Income Distribution: New Theories Needed for a New Era" *Vox*, August 18, 2015 (reprinted as chapter 6 in this volume).
Kanbur, R. and J. E. Stiglitz, 2016. "Dynastic Inequality, Mobility and Equality of Opportunity," *Journal of Economic Inequality*, 14(4): 419–34 (reprinted as Chapter 18 in this volume).

Kanbur, R. and J. O. Stromberg, 1988. "Income Transitions and Income Distribution Dominance," *Journal of Economic Theory*, 45(2): 408–17.

Kanbur, R. and M. Tuomala, 1994. "Inherent Inequality and the Optimal Graduation of Marginal Tax Rates," *Scandinavian Journal of Economics*, 96(2): 275–82.

Kanbur, R. and A. Wagstaff, 2014. "How Useful is Inequality of Opportunity as a Policy Construct?" World Bank Policy Research Working Paper 6980.

Kanbur, R., M. Keen, and M. Tuomala, 1994. "Optimal Non-Linear Income Taxation for the Alleviation of Income Poverty," *European Economic Review*, 38(8): 1613–32.

Kane, E. and B. Malkiel, 1965. "Bank Portfolio Allocation, Deposit Variability and the Availability Doctrine," *Quarterly Journal of Economics*, 79(1): 113–34.

Kane, T. and C. Rouse, 1995. "Labor Market Returns to Teo- and Four-Year College Degrees: Is a Credit a Credit and Do Degrees Matter?" *American Economic Review*, 85(3): 600–14.

Kaplan, G., B. Moll, and G. L. Violante, 2018. "Monetary Policy According to HANK," *American Economic Review*, 108(3): 697–743.

Kaplow, L., 1996. "The Optimal Supply of Public Goods and the Distortionary Cost of Taxation," *National Tax Journal*, 49: 513–33.

Kaplow, L., 2001. "A Framework for Assessing Estate and Gift Taxation," in W. Gale, J. Hines, and J. Slemrod (eds.), *Rethinking Estate and Gift Taxation*, Washington, D.C.: Brookings Institution Press, 164–204.

Kaplow, L., 2006a. "Optimal Control of Externalities in the Presence of Income Taxation," NBER Working Paper 12339.

Kaplow, L., 2006b. "On the Undesirability of Commodity Taxation Even When Income Taxation Is Not Optimal," *Journal of Public Economics*, 90(6–7): 1235–50.

Kaplow, L., 2012. "Optimal Control of Externalities in the Presence of Income Taxation," *International Economic Review*, 53(2) (2012): 487–509.

Katz, L. F. and L. Summers, 1989. "Industry Rents: Evidence and Implications," *Brookings Papers on Economic Activity*, 1989(Special Issue): 209–75.

Katz, M. L. and C. Shapiro, 1994. "Systems Competition and Network Effects," Journal of Economic Perspectives, 8(2): 93–115.

Kaur, S., S. Mullainathan, S. Oh, and F. Schilbach, 2019. "Does Financial Strain Lower Productivity?"_working paper, available at https://www.semanticscholar.org/paper/Does-Financial-Strain-Lower-Worker-Productivity%E2%88%97-Kaur/c6d2478fed81a0fd97d4d0f1ebb8449fc1de0a5b.

Kay, J., 2015. *Other People's Money: The Real Business of Finance*, New York: PublicAffairs

Keaton, W., 1979. *Equilibrium Credit Rationing*, New York: Garland Publishing Company.

Keilson, J. and A. Kester, 1977. "Montone Matrices and Monotone Markov Processes," *Stochastic Processes and Their Applications*, 5(3): 231–41.

Kennedy, C., 1964. "Induced Bias in Innovation and the Theory of Distribution," *Economic Journal*, 74(295): 541–47.

Kennedy, J. F., 1963. "Remarks in Heber Springs, Arkansas, at the Dedication of Grers Ferry Dam," October 3.

Kerner, O., et al., 1988. *The Kerner Report: The 1968 Report of the National Advisory Comm. on Civil Disorders*, New York: Pantheon Books.

Kevei, P., 2016. "A Note on the Kesten–Grincevičius–Goldie Theorem," *Electronic Communications in Probability*, 21: 1–12.

Keynes, J. M., 1930. *A Treatise on Money*, London: Macmillan.

Keynes, J. M., 1931. "Economic Possibilities for Our Grandchildren," in J. M. Keynes, *Essays in Persuasion*, San Diego, CA: Harcourt Brace, 358–73.

Keynes, J. M., 1936. *The General Theory of Employment, Interest, and Money*, London: Macmillan.

Khan, L. B., 2010. "The Long-Term Labor Market Consequences of Graduating from College in a Bad Economy," *Labour Economics*, 17(2): 303–16.

Kindleberger, Charles, 1978. *Manias Panics and Crashes: A History of Financial Crises*. First Edition. New York: Basic Books.

Kindleberger, C. P., and R. Z. Aliber, 1978. *Manias, Panics and Crashes: A History of Financial Crises*, New York: Basic Books.

King, M., 1986. "Capital Market 'Imperfections' and the Consumption Function," *Scandinavian Journal of Economics*, 88(1): 59–80.

Klasen, S., 1996. "Nutrition, Health, and Mortality in Sub-Saharan Africa: Is There a Gender Bias?" *Journal of Development Studies*, 32(6): 913–32.

Klenert, D., L. Mattauch, O. Edenhofer, and K. Lessmann, 2018. Infrastructure and inequality: Insights from incorporating key economic facts about household heterogeneity. Macroeconomic Dynamics, 22: 864–895.

Knight, F., 1921. *Risk, Uncertainty, and Profit*, Boston: Houghton-Mifflin.

Knoblach, M., M. Roessler, and P. Zwerschke, 2016. "The Elasticity of Factor Substitution between Capital and Labor in the U.S. Economy: A Meta-Regression Analysis," CEPIE Working Paper Series 03/16.

Knoblach, M. and Stöckl, F. (2020). "What Determines The Elasticity Of Substitution Between Capital And Labor? A Literature Review," *Journal of Economic Surveys*, 34: 847–75. https://doi.org/10.1111/joes.12366

Knolly, K., M. Schularickz, and T. Steger, 2014. "Home Prices since 1870: No Price Like Home," *Vox*, November 1. Available at: http://voxeu.org/article/home-prices-1870.

Knolly, K., M. Schularickz, and T. Steger, 2015. "No Price Like Home: Global House Prices, 1870–2012," working paper.

Knowles, J. C., E. M. Pernia, and M. Racelis, 1999. "Social Consequences of the Financial Crisis in Asia," Economic Staff Paper Number 60, Asian Development Bank.

Kolm, S. C., 1969. "The Optimal Production of Social Justice," in J. Margolis and H. Guitton (eds.), *Public Economics*, London: Macmillan, 145–200.

Konczal, M., 2011. "Housing Lock Is Not a Major Part of This Crisis, Plus Scatterplots of Deleveraging!" (blog post). Available at: http://rortybomb.wordpress.com/2011/04/11/housing-lock-is-not-a-major-component-of-this-crisis-plus-scatterplots-of-deleveraging/.

Konishi, H., 1995. "A Pareto-Improving Commodity Tax Reform under a Smooth Nonlinear Income Tax," *Journal of Public Economics*, 56(3): 413–46.

Koopmans, T.C., 1960. "Stationary Ordinal Utility and Impatience," *Econometrica*, 28, 287.

Kopczuk, W., 2015. "What Do We Know about the Evolution of Top Wealth Shares in the United States?" *Journal of Economic Perspectives*, 29(1): 47–66.

Kopczuk, W., and J. Lupton, 2007. "To Leave or Not to Leave: The Distribution of Bequest Motives," *Review of Economic Studies*, 74(1): 207–35.

Kopczuk, W., and J. Slemrod, 2001. "The Impact of the Estate Tax on Wealth Accumulation and Avoidance Behavior," in W. Gale, J. R. Hines, and J. Slemrod (eds.), *Rethinking Estate and Gift Taxation*, Washington, D.C.: Brookings Institution Press, 299–349.

Korinek, A., 2016. "Currency Wars or Efficient Spillovers? A General Theory of International Policy Cooperation," NBER Working Paper 23004.

Korinek, A., 2018a. "Humans, Artificially Intelligent Agents, and the Return of Malthus," working paper.

Korinek, A., 2018b. "Regulating Capital Flows to Emerging Markets: An Externality View," *Journal of International Economics*, 111: 61–80.

Korinek, A. and D. X. Ng, 2017. "The Macroeconomics of Superstars," working paper.

Korinek, A. and J. E. Stiglitz, 2008. "Political Economy in a Contestable Democracy: The Case of Dividend Taxation," 2008 Meeting Papers, Society for Economic Dynamics.

Korinek, A. and J. E. Stiglitz, 2009. "Dividend Taxation and Intertemporal Tax Arbitrage," *Journal of Public Economics*, 93(1–2): 142–59.

Korinek, A. and J. E. Stiglitz, 2017. "Worker-Replacing Technological Progress," working paper.

Koskela, E., 1976. *A Study of Bank Behavior and Credit Rationing*, Helsinki: Academiae Scientarum Fennicae.

Koskela, E., 1979. "On the Theory of Rationing Equilibrium with Special Reference to Credit Markets: A Survey," *Zeitschrift fur Nationalokonomie/Journal of Economics*, 39(1/2): 63–82.

Kosse, F., et al., 2020. "The Formation of Prosociality: Causal Evidence on the Role of Social Environment," *Journal of Political Economy* 128(2): 434–67.

Kotlikoff, L. and L. Summers, 1981. "The Role of Intergenerational Transfers in Aggregate Capital Accumulation," *Journal of Political Economy*, 89(4): 706–32.

Kreamer, J., 2015. "Credit and Liquidity in the Macroeconomy," doctoral dissertation, University of Maryland, College Park.

Krueger, A., 2012. "The Rise and Consequences of Inequality," presentation made to the Center for American Progress, Washington, DC. Available at: http://www.americanprogress.org/events/%20/2012/01/12/17181/the-rise-and-consequences-of-inequality/.

Krueger, A., 2013. "Land of Hope and Dreams: Rock and Roll, Economics, and Rebuilding the Middle Class," remarks, Rock and Roll Hall of Fame and Museum, Cleveland, Ohio, June 12.

Krueger, A. B. and O. Ashenfelter, 2018 "Theory and Evidence on Employer Collusion in the Franchise Sector," NBER Working Paper 24831.

Krugman, P., 1991. "Increasing Returns and Economic Geography," Journal of Political Economy, 99(3): 483–99.

Krugman, P., 1994. "Past and Prospective Causes of High Unemployment," *Economic Review—Federal Reserve Bank of Kansas City*, 79(4): 23.

Krusell, P., L. E. Ohanian, J.-V. Rìos-rull, and G. L. Violante, 2000. "Capital-Skill Complementarity and Inequality: A Macroeconomic Analysism" *Econometrica*, 68(5): 1029–54.

Kuh, E., 1967. "A Productivity Theory of Wage Levels—An Alternative to the Phillips Curve," *Review of Economic Studies*, 34(4): 333–60.

Kumhof, M., R. Ranciere, and Winant, 2015. "Inequality, Leverage, and Crises," *American Economic Review*, 105(3): 1217–45.

Kurzweil, R., 2005. *The Singularity Is Near: When Humans Transcend Biology*, New York: Viking.

Kuznets, S., 1955. "Economic Growth and Income Inequality," *American Economic Review*, 45(1): 1–28.

Laffont, J. and R. Garcia, 1977. "Disequilibrium Econometrics for Business Loans," *Econometrica*, 45(5): 1187–204.

Lampman, R. J., 1962. *The Share of Wealth-Holders in National Wealth*, National Bureau of Economic Research, Princeton, N.J.: Princeton University Press.

Layard, R., S. Nickell, and R. Jackman, 1991. *Unemployment*, Oxford: Oxford University Press.

Lazear, E. P. and S. Rosen 1981. "Rank-Order Tournaments as Optimum Labor Contracts," *Journal of Political Economy*, 89(5): 841–64.

Lebergott, S., 1959. "The Shape of the Income Distribution," *American Economic Review*, 49(3): 328–47.

Lee, C.-I. and G. Solon 2009. "Trends in Intergenerational Income Mobility," *Review of Economics and Statistics*, 91(4): 766–72.

Leibenstein, H., 1957. *Economic Backwardness and Economic Growth*, New York: Wiley.

Leiserowitz, A., E. Maibach, C. Roser-Renouf, G. Feinberg, and S. Rosenthal, 2015. "Climate Change in the American Mind," Yale Project on Climate Change Communication, available at http://environment.yale.edu/climate-communication/files/Climate-Beliefs-November-2013.pdf (accessed July 24, 2019).

Leland, H. E., and D. H. Pyle, 1977. "Informational Asymmetries, Financial Structure and Financial Intermediation," *Journal of Finance*, 32(2): 371–87.

Levine, D. I. and B. Mazumder, "Choosing the Right Parents: Changes in the Intergenerational Transmission of Inequality between 1980 and the Early 1990s," Federal Reserve Bank of Chicago Working Paper 2002–08, June.

Lewis, M., 2014. *Flash Boys: A Wall Street Revolt*, New York: W. W. Norton.

Lindahl, M., M. Palme, M. Sandgren-Massih, and A. Sjögren, 2014. "A Test of the Becker-Tomes Model of Human Capital Transmission Using Microdata on Four Generations," *Journal of Human Capital*, 8(1): 80–96.

Lindbeck, A., 1962. *The "New" Theory of Credit Control in the United States*, 2nd edition, Stockholm: Stockholm Economic Studies.

Lipsey, R., and K. Lancaster, 1956. "The General Theory of Second Best," *Review of Economic Studies*, 24(1): 11–32.

Londegran, J. and K. Poole, 1991. "Poverty, the Coup Trap, and the Unconstitutional Seizure of Power," *World Politics*, 92: 1–24.

Lovenheim, M. F. and K. J. Mumford, 2013. "Do Family Wealth Shocks Affect Fertility Choices? Evidence from the Housing Market," *Review of Economics and Statistics*, 95(2) (May): 464–75.

Lucas, R., 1987. *Models of Business Cycles*, Cambridge, Mass.: MIT Press.

Lucas, R., 2004. "The Industrial Revolution: Past and Future," Federal Reserve Bank of Minneapolis, 2003 Annual Report Essay, available at https://www.minneapolisfed.org/article/2004/the-industrial-revolution-past-and-future (accessed January 22, 2020).

Luce, R. D., and H. Raiffa, 1966. *Games and Decisions*, New York: Wiley.

Maddala, G. S., 1983. *Limited-Dependent and Qualitative Variables in Econometrics*, Cambridge: Cambridge University Press.

Mallick, D., 2012. "The Role of the Elasticity of Substitution in Economic Growth: A Cross-Country Investigation," *Journal of Labor Economics*, 19(5): 682–94.

Mallick, S.K. and Mohsin, M., 2007. "On the Effects of Inflation Shocks in a Small Open Economy," *Australian Economic Review*, 40: 253-266. https://doi.org/10.1111/j.1467-8462.2007.00450.x

Malthus, T. R., 1798. *An Essay on the Principle of Population*, Project Gutenberg.

Manchester, J., J. Song, and T. von Wachter, 2009. "Long-Term Earnings Losses due to Job Separation During the 1982 Recession: An Analysis Using Longitudinal Administrative Data from 1974 to 2004," Columbia University Economics Discussion Paper 0708-16.

Mandelbrot, B., 1961. "Stable Paretian Random Functions and the Multiplicative Variation of Income," *Econometrica*, 29(4): 517–43.
Mani, A., S. Mullainathan, E. Shafir, and J. Zhao, 2013. "Poverty Impedes Cognitive Function," *Science*, 341(6149): 976–80.
Mankiw, N. G., 2013. "Defending the One Percent," *Journal of Economic Perspectives*, 27(3): 21–34.
Mankiw, N. G., D. Romer, and D. Weil, 1992. "A Contribution to the Empirics of Economic Growth," *Quarterly Journal of Economics*, 107(2): 407–37.
Mankiw, N. G., M. Weinzierl, and D. Yagan, 2009. "Optimal Taxation in Theory and Practice," NBER Working Paper 15071.
Manning, A., 2011. "Imperfect Competition in Labour Markets," in O. Ashenfelter and D. Card (eds.), *Handbook of Labor Economics*, Volume 4: 973–1041, Amsterdam: North-Holland.
March, J. G., and H. A. Simon, 1958. *Organizations*, New York: John Wiley & Sons.
Markandya, A., 1984. "The Welfare Measurement of Changes in Economic Mobility," *Economica*, 51(204): 457–71.
Markovits, D., 2019. *The Meritocracy Trap: How America's Foundational Myth Feeds Inequality, Dismantles the Middle Class, and Devours the Elite*, New York: Penguin.
Markowitz, H. M., 1952. "Portfolio Selection," *Journal of Finance*, 7(1): 77–91.
Mason, J. W., 2014. "Three Essays in Macroeconomic History," doctoral dissertaion, University of Massachusetts, Amherst.
Mason, J. W., 2015. "Disgorge the Cash," Roosevelt Institute working paper.
Mattauch, L., O. Edenhofer, D. Klenert, and S. Bénard, 2016. "Distributional Effects of Public Investment when Wealth and Classes Are Back," *Metroeconomica*, 67(3): 603–29.
Mattauch, L., J. Siegmeier, O. Edenhofer, and F. Creutzig, 2018. "Financing public capital when rents are back: a macroeconomic henry george theorem," *FinanzArchiv/Public Finance Analysis*, 74(3).
Mattauch, L., D. Klenert, J. E. Stiglitz, and O. Edenhofer, 2019. "Overcoming Wealth Inequality: When Can Capital-Tax Financed Public Investment Help?," updated version of NBER Working Paper 25126, October 2018.
Mattauch, L., D. Klenert, J. E. Stiglitz, and O. Edenhofer, 2022. "Overcoming Wealth Inequality by Capital Taxes that Finance Public Investment," *Structural Change and Economic Dynamics*, Vol. 62, June 6, 2022
Matthews, R., 1959. *The Business Cycle*, Chicago: University of Chicago Press.
Mazumder, B., 2001. "Earnings Mobility in the US: A New Look at Intergenerational Inequality," Federal Reserve Bank of Chicago Working Paper 2001–19, March.
Mazumder, B., 2012. "Is Intergenerational Economic Mobility Lower Now than in the Past," *Chicago Fed Letter*, April 2012.
Mazzucato, M. 2015, *The Entrepreneurial State: Debunking Public vs. Private Sector Myths*, London: Anthem.
Mazzucato, M. and M. Jacobs (eds.), 2016. *Rethinking Capitalism, Rethinking Capitalism*, Hoboken, New Jersey: Wiley-Blackwell.
McClellan, M. B. and J. S. Skinner, 1997. "The Incidence of Medicare," NBER Working Paper No. w6013.
McElwee, S. C., 2016. "To Influence Policy, You Have to Be More than Rich," *Washington Monthly*, February 16, available at https://washingtonmonthly.com/2016/02/16/to-influence-policy-you-have-to-be-more-than-rich/.
McMurrer, D. P. and I. V. Sawhill, 1998. *Getting Ahead: Economic and Social Mobility in America*, Washington, DC: Urban Institute Press.
Meade, J. E., 1955. *Trade and Welfare*, Oxford: Oxford University Press.
Meade, J. E., 1963. "The Rate of Profit in a Growing Economy," *Economic Journal*, 74(294): 667–74.
Meade, J. E., 1972. "Poverty in the Welfare State," *Oxford Economic Papers*, 24(3): 289–326.
Meltzer, A., 1960. "Mercantile Credit, Monetary Policy, and the Size of Firms," *Review of Economics and Statistics*, 42(4): 429–37.
Meyer, J. R. and E. Kuh, 1957. *The Investment Decision: An Empirical Study*, Cambridge: Harvard University Press.
Michl, T. R., 2009. *Capitalists, Workers, and Fiscal Policy: A Classical Model of Growth and Distribution*, Cambridge, MA and London, England: Harvard University Press.
Milanovic, B., 2010. *The Haves and the Have-Nots: A Brief and Idiosyncratic History of Global Inequality*, New York: Basic Books.
Milanovic, B., 2016. *Global Inequality: A New Approach for the Age of Globalization*, Cambridge, MA: Harvard University Press.
Milevsky, M. A. and Huaxiong, H., 2011. "Spending Retirement on Planet Vulcan: The Impact of Longevity Risk Aversion on Optimal Withdrawal Rates," *Financial Analysts Journal*, 67(2): 45–58.

Milgrom, P. and N. Stokey, 1982. "Information, Trade, and Common Knowledge," *Journal of Economic Theory*, 26(1): 17–27.
Miller, R., 1971. "The Reserve labor Hypothesis: Some Tests of Its Implications," *Economic Journal*, 81(321): 17–35.
Miller, M., 2003. *The Two-Percent Solution: Fixing America's Problems in a Way that Conservatives and Liberals Can Love*, New York: Public Affairs Books.
Minorsky, N. 1962. *Nonlinear Oscillations*, Princeton, N.J.: Van Nostrand.
Minsky, H. P., 1992. "The Financial Instability Hypothesis," Jerome Levy Economics Institute of Bard College, Working Paper No. 74.
Mirrlees, J., 1971. "An Exploration in the Theory of Optimum Income Taxation," *Review of Economic Studies*, 38(2): 175–203.
Mirrlees, J., 1974. "Notes on Welfare Economics, Information, and Uncertainty," in M. Balon, D. McFadden and S. Wu (eds.), *Essays on Economic Behavior under Uncertainty*, Amsterdam: North-Holland, 243–61.
Mirrlees, J., 1975a. "The Theory of Moral Hazard and Observable Behavior: Part 1," Working Paper, Nuffield College."
Mirrlees, J., 1975b. "A Pure Theory of Underdeveloped Economies," in L. A. Reynolds (ed.), Agriculture in Development Theory, New Haven: Yale University Press, 84–106.
Mirrlees, J., 1975c. "Optimal Commodity Taxation in a Two-Class Economy," *Journal of Public Economics* 4(1): 27–33.
Mirrlees, J., 1976. "Optimal Tax Theory: A Synthesis," *Journal of Public Economics*, 6(4): 327–58.
Mishel, L., and N. Sabadish, 2012. "CEO Pay and the Top 1%," Economic Policy Institute Brief 332.
Mitra, P. K., 1983. "A Theory of Interlinked Rural Transactions," *Journal of Public Economics*, 20(2): 167–91.
Modigliani, F., 1963. "The Monetary Mechanism and Its Interaction with Real Phenomena: A Review of Recent Developments," *Review of Economics and Statistics*, 45(1, part 2): 79–107.
Moene, K. O., 2013. "Scandinavian Equality: A Prime Example of Protection without Protectionism," in J. E. Stiglitz and M. Kaldor (eds.), *The Quest for Security: Protection without Protectionism and the Challenge of Global Governance*, New York: Columbia University Press, 48–74.
Moore, G. E., 1965. "Cramming More Components onto Integrated Circuits," *Electronics*, 38(8): 114:ff.
Morin, M., 2011. "Jobless Recoveries," Columbia University working paper.
Mortenson, D., 1970. "A Theory of Wage and Employment Dynamics," in E. S. Phelps et al., *Microeconomic Foundations of Employment and Inflation Theory*, New York: W. W. Norton, 167–211.
Mortenson, D., 1986. "Job Search and Labor Market Analysis," in O. Ashenfelter and R. Layard (eds.), Handbook of Labor Economics Volume II, Amsterdam: North Holland, 849–919.
Mortenson, D., 2005. *Wage Dispersion: Why Are Similar Workers Paid Differently?*, Cambridge, MA: MIT Press.
Mortenson, D. and C. A. Pissarides, 1994. "Job Creation and Job Destruction in the Theory of Unemployment," *Review of Economic Studies*, 61(3): 397–415.
Mortenson, D. and C. A. Pissarides, 1998. "Technological Progress, Job Creation, and Job Destruction," *Review of Economic Dynamics*, 1(4): 733–53.
Mossin, J., 1968. "Taxation and Risk Taking: An Expected Utility Approach," *Econometrica*, 35(1): 74–83.
Mroz, T. A. and T. Savage, 2006. "The Long-Term Effects of Youth Unemployment," *Journal of Human Resources*, 41(2): 259–93.
Mullainathan, S., and E. Shafir, 2009. "Savings Policy and Decisionmaking in Low-Income Households," in R. M. Blank, and M. S. Barr (eds.), *Insufficient Funds: Savings, Assets, Credit, and Banking among Low-Income Households*, New York: Russell Sage Foundation, 121–46.
Mullainathan, S. and E. Shafir, 2013. *Scarcity: Why Having Too Little Means So Much*, New York: Henry Holt.
Myers, S., 1977. "Determinants of Corporate Borrowing," *Journal of Financial Economics*, 5(2): 147–75.
Myers, S. and N. Majluf, 1984. "Corporate Financing Decisions When Firms Have Investment Information that Investors Do Not Have," *Journal of Financial Economics*, 13(2): 187–220.
Myrdal, G., 1944. *An American Dilemma: The Negro Problem and Modern Democracy*, New York: Harper Brothers.
Nadiri, M., 1969. "The Determinants of Trade Credit in the U.S. Total Manufacturing Sector," *Econometrica*, 37(3): 408–23.
Naidu S., 2010. "Recruitment restrictions and labor markets: Evidence from the Postbellum US South," *Journal of Labor Economics*
Naidu, S., 2014. "Capital Eats the World," Jacobin, May 30. Available at: https://www.jacobinmag.com/2014/05/capital-eats-the-world/.

Naidu, S., and N. Yuchtman. 2013. "Coercive Contract Enforcement: Law and the Labor Market in Nineteenth Century Industrial Britain," *American Economic Review*, 103(1): 107–44.

Naito, H., 1999. "Re-Examination of Uniform Commodity Taxes under a Non-Linear Income Tax System and Its Implications for Production Efficiency," *Journal of Public Economics*, 71(2): 168–88.

Nakamura, L., 1984. "Bankruptcy and the Informational Problems of Commercial Bank Lending," Financial Research Center Memorandum 54, Princeton University.

Nalebuff, B. and J. E. Stiglitz, 1983a. "Information, Competition, and Markets," *American Economic Review*, 73(2): 278–84.

Nalebuff, B. and J. E. Stiglitz, 1983b. "Prizes and Incentives: Towards a General Theory of Compensation and Competition," *Bell Journal of Economics*, 14(1): 21–43.

Nalebuff, B. and J. E. Stiglitz, 1985. "Unemployment as a Worker Selection Device," Princeton University, (Revision of "Quality and Prices," Princeton University Econometric Research Memorandum No. 297, May 1982).

Nalebuff, B., A. Rodriguez, and J. E. Stiglitz, 1993. "Equilibrium Unemployment as a Worker Screening Device," NBER Working Paper 4357 (reprinted as Chapter 23 in *Selected Works*, Volume II).

Narayan, D., R. Patel, K. Schafft, et al., 2000. *Can Anyone Hear Us?*, Oxford: Oxford University Press for the World Bank.

Nationalbanken, 2016. "Report on the Role of Cash in Society," August 13, 2016. https://www.nationalbanken.dk/en/news-and-knowledge/publications-and-speeches/archive-publications/2016/report-on-the-role-of-cash-in-society.

Newbery, D., 1970. "A Theorem on the Measurement of Inequality," *Journal of Economic Theory*, 2(3): 264–66.

Newbery, D., 1975. "Tenurial Obstacles to Innovation," *Journal of Development Studies*, 11(4): 263–77.

Newbery, D. and J. E. Stiglitz 1979a. "Sharecropping: Risk Sharing and the Importance of Imperfect Information," with D. Newbery, in, J.A. Roumasset, et al. (eds.), *Risk, Uncertainty and Agricultural Development*, Southeast Asian Regional Center for Graduate Study and Research in Agriculture (SEARCA) and Agricultural Development Council, 1979, 311–41. New York, N.Y. : Agricultural Development Council. https://searchworks.stanford.edu/view/756414.

Newbery, D. and J. E. Stiglitz, 1979b. "The Theory of Commodity Price Stabilization Rules: Welfare Impacts and Supply Responses," *Economic Journal*, 89(356): 799–817.

Newbery, D. and J. E. Stiglitz, 1981. *The Theory of Commodity Price Stabilization*, Oxford: Oxford University Press.

Newbery, D. and J. E. Stiglitz, 1982a. "Optimal Commodity Stock-Piling Rules," *Oxford Economic Papers*, November 1982, 403–27.

Newbery, D. and J. E. Stiglitz, 1982b. "The Choice of Techniques and the Optimality of Market Equilibrium with Rational Expectations," with D. Newbery, *Journal of Political Economy*, 90(2): 223–46.

Newbery, D. and J. E. Stiglitz, 1982c. "Risk Aversion, Supply Response, and the Optimality of Random Prices: A Diagrammatic Analysis," *Quarterly Journal of Economics*, 97(1): 1–26.

Newbery, D. and J. E. Stiglitz 1984. "Pareto Inferior Trade," *Review of Economic Studies*, 51(1): 1–12.

Nichols, A. L., and R. J. Zeckhauser, 1982. "Targeting Transfers through Restrictions on Recipients," *American Economic Review*, 72(2): 372–77.

Nirei, M. and S. Aoki, 2016. "Pareto Distribution of Income in Neoclassical Growth Models," *Review of Economic Dynamics*, 20(April): 25–42.

Noah, T., 2012. *The Great Divergence: America's Growing Inequality Crisis and What We Can Do about It*, New York: Bloomsbury.

North, D. C. 1990. *Institutions, Institutional Change and Economic Performance*, Cambridge: Cambridge University Press.

North, D. C 2006. *Understanding the Process of Economic Change*, Princeton, NJ: Princeton University Press.

Obama, B., 2011. "Remarks by the President on the Economy in Osawatomie, Kansas," Osawatomie High School, Osawatomie, Kansas, December 6.

Obama, B., 2013. "Remarks by the President on Economic Mobility," December 4, The White House, Washington.

Obama, B., 2014. "President Barack Obama's State of the Union Address," January 28.

Ocampo, J. A. and J. E. Stiglitz (eds.), 2008. *Capital Market Liberalization and Development*, New York: Oxford University Press.

Office of Management and Budget, 1997a. *Analytical Perspectives FY 1998*, Washington, DC: Government Printing Office.

Office of Management and Budget, 1997b. *Budget of the United States Government, Fiscal Year 1998*, Washington, DC: Government Printing Office.

O'Flaherty, B., 2015. *The Economics of Race in the United States*, Cambridge: Harvard University Press.

Okun, A., 1975. *Equality and Efficiency: The Big Trade Off*, Washington, DC: Brookings Institution Press.

Omohundro, S. M., 2008. "The Basic AI Drives," in P. Wang, B. Goertzel, and S. Franklin (eds.), *Artificial General Intelligence 2008: Proceedings of the First AGI Conference*, Amsterdam: IOS, 483–92.

Organisation for Economic Co-operation and Development, 2011. *Divided We Stand: Why Inequality Keeps Rising*, Paris: OECD Publishing.

Organisation for Economic Co-operation and Development, 2013. *Pension Markets in Focus 2013*. Available at: https://www.oecd.org/finance/PensionMarketsInFocus2013.pdf.

Organisation for Economic Co-operation and Development, 2014. "Focus on Inequality and Growth," http://www.oecd.org/els/soc/Focus-Inequality-and-Growth-2014.pdf (accessed July 10, 2019).

Organisation for Economic Co-operation and Development, 2015. *In It Together: Why Less Inequality Benefits All*, Paris: OECD Publishing.

Orszag, P., and J. E. Stiglitz, 2001. "Rethinking Pension Reform: Ten Myths About Social Security Systems," in R. Holman and J. E. Stiglitz (eds.), *New Ideas About Old Age Security*, Washington, DC: World Bank, 17–56.

Østby, G., 2008. "Inequalities, the Political Environment and Civil Conflict: Evidence from 55 Developing Countries," in F. Stewart (ed.), *Horizontal Inequalities and Conflict: Understanding Group Violence in Multiethnic Societies*, Basingstoke: Palgrave Macmillan, 136–57.

Østby, G. and H. Strand 2013. "Horizontal Inequalities and Internal Conflict: The Impact of Regime Type and Political Leadership Regulation," in K. Kalu, U. O. Uzodike, D. Kraybill, and J. Mool *Territoriality, Citizenship, and Peacebuilding: Perspectives on Challenges to Peace in Africa*, Pietermaritzburg, South Africa: Adonis & Abbey.

akkattu (eds.), *Territoriality, Citizenship, and Peacebuilding: Perspectives on Challenges to Peace in Africa*, Pietermaritzburg, South Africa: Adonis & Abbey, 139–190.

Ostrom, E., 2005. "Doing Institutional Analysis: Digging Deeper than Markets and Hierarchies," in C. Ménard and M. Shirley (eds.), *Handbook of New Institutional Economics* (New York: Springer), 819–48.

Ostry, J. D., M. A. Berg, and M. C. G. Tsangarides, 2014. "Redistribution, Inequality, and Growth," IMF Staff Discussion Notes, 14/2, available at https://www.imf.org/external/pubs/ft/sdn/2014/sdn1402.pdf (accessed July 19, 2019).

Ostry, J. D., P. Loungani, and A. Berg, 2019. *Confronting Inequality: How Societies Can Choose Inclusive Growth*, New York: Columbia University Press.

Otsuka, K., H. Chuma, and Y. Hayami, 1992. "Land and Labor Contracts in Agrarian Economies: Theories and Facts," *Journal of Economic Literature*, 30(4): 1965–2018.

Owens, A., S. F. Reardon, and C. Jencks, 2016. "Income Segregation Between Schools and School Districts," *American Educational Research Journal*, 53(4): 1159–1197.

Oxfam, 2020. *Time to Care*, UK: Oxford. DOI:10.21201/2020.5419.

Palley, T. I., 2008. "The Relative Income Theory of Consumption: A Synthetic Keynes-Duesenberry-Friedman Model," University of Massachusetts at Amherst WORKINGP APER SERIES Number 170, April.

Palma, J. G., 2011. "Homogeneous Middles vs. Heterogeneous Tails, and the End of the 'Inverted-U': the Share of the Rich Is What It's All About," Cambridge Working Papers in Economics (CWPE) 1111, January.

Park, W-S, B. Y. Cheon, et al., 2018. *Rewriting the Rules of the Korean Economy*, Seoul: The Seoul Institute.

Pascal, A. H. (ed.), 1972. *Racial Discrimination in Economic Life*, Lexington, Mass.: Lexington Books.

Pasinetti, L. L., 1962. "The Rate of Profit and Income Distribution in Relation to the Rate of Economic Growth," *Review of Economic Studies*, 29(4): 267–79.

Patman Hearings, 1952. "Hearings before the Subcommittee on General Credit Control and Debt Management of the Joint Committee on the Economic Report," *82nd Congress, 2nd Session*, Washington: Government Printing Office.

Perlin, R., 2011. *Intern Nation*, London: Verso.

Perotti, R., 1996. "Growth, Income Distribution, and Democracy: What the Data Say," *Journal of Economic Growth*, 1(2): 149–88.

Pew Research Center, 2013. "Public's Views on Human Evolution," Pew Research Center, December 30, 2013, available at http://www.pewforum.org/2013/12/30/publics-views-on-human-evolution/ (accessed July 24, 2019).

Phelps, E. S., 1967. "Phillips Curves, Expectations of Inflation and Optimal Unemployment over Time," *Economica*, 34(135): 254–81.

Phelps, E. S. (ed.), 1970. *The Microeconomic Foundations of Employment and Inflation Theory*, New York: W. W. Norton.
Phelps, E. S., 1972. "The Statistical Theory of Racism and Sexism," *American Economic Review*, 62(4): 659–61.
Phelps, E. S., and S. G. Winter, 1970. "Optimal Price Policy under Atomistic Competition," in G. C. Archibald, A. A. Alchian, and E. S. Phelps, eds., *Microeconomic Foundations of Employment and Inflation Theory*, New York: Norton.
Philippon, T., 2019. *The Great Reversal: How America Gave Up on Free Markets*, Cambridge: Harvard University Press.
Philippon, T. and A. Reshef, 2012. "Wages and Human Capital in the US Financial Industry: 1909–2006," *Quarterly Journal of Economics*, 127(4): 1551–609.
Phillips, A. W., 1958. "The Relation between Unemployment and the Rate of Change of Money Wage Rates in the United Kingdom, 1861–1957," *Economica*, 25(100): 283–99.
Piff, P., D. M. Stancato, S. Côté, et al., 2012. "Higher Social Class Predicts Increased Unethical Behavior," *Proceedings of the National Academy of Sciences*, 109(11): 4086–91.
Pigou, A. C., 1920 *The Economics of Welfare*, London (4th edition 1932).
Pigou, A. C., 1947. *A Study in Public Finance*, London: Macmillan.
Piketty, T., 1995. "Social Mobility and Redistributive Politics," *Quarterly Journal of Economics*; 110(3): 551–84.
Piketty, T., 2014. *Capital in the Twenty-First Century*, Cambridge, Mass.: The Belknap Press of Harvard University Press.
Piketty, T., 2019. *Capital and Ideology* (Cambridge, MA: Harvard University Press).
Piketty, T. and E. Saez, 2003. "Income Inequality in the United States, 1913–1998," *Quarterly Journal of Economics*, 118(1): 1–39. (Tables and figures updated to 2013, as of January 2015.)
Piketty, T. and E. Saez, 2012. "Optimal Labor Income Taxation," NBER Working Paper 18521.
Piketty, T. and E. Saez, 2013. "A Theory of Optimal Inheritance Taxation," *Econometrica*, 81(5): 1851–86.
Piketty, T. and G. Zucman, 2014. "Capital Is Back: Wealth-Income Ratios in Rich Countries 1700–2010," *Quarterly Journal of Economics*, 129(3): 1255–310.
Piketty, T. and G. Zucman, 2015. "Wealth and Inheritance in the Long-Run," in A. Atkinson and F. Bourguignon (eds.), *Handbook of Income Distribution*, vol. 2, London: Elsevier, 1303–68.
Piketty, T., E. Saez, and S. Stantcheva, 2011. "Taxing the 1%: Why the Top Tax Rate Could Be over 80%," VoxEU.org, December 8. Available at: http://voxeu.org/article/taxing-1-why-top-tax-rate-could-be-over-80.
Piketty, T., E. Saez, and G. Zucman, 2018. "Distributional National Accounts: Methods and Estimates for the United States," *Quarterly Journal of Economics*, 133(2): 553–609.
Piketty, T., E. Saez, and S. Stantcheva, 2014. "Optimal Taxation of Top Labor Incomes: A Tale of Three Elasticities," *American Economic Journal: Economic Policy*, 6(1): 230–71.
Pissarides, C., 1990. *Equilibrium Unemployment Theory*, Oxford: Basil Blackwell.
Pogge, T. and S. Reddy, 2010. "How Not to Count the Poor," in S. Anand, P. Segal, and J. E. Stiglitz (eds.), *Debates in the Measurement of Poverty*, Oxford and New York: Oxford University Press, 42–115.
Pope F., 2013. "WYD 2013: Full Text of Pope Francis's Address in Rio Slum," *Catholic Herald*, July 25.
Psacharopoulos, G., 1994. "Returns to Investment in Education: A Global Update," *World Development*, 22(9): 1325–43.
Putnam, R. D. 2000. *Bowling Alone: The Collapse and Revival of American Community*. New York: Simon & Schuster.
Putnam, R. D., 2015. *Our Kids: The American Dream in Crisis.* New York: Simon & Schuster.
Radner, R. and J. E. Stiglitz, 1984. "A Nonconcavity in the Value of Information," in M. Boyer and R. Khilstrom (eds.), *Bayesian Models in Economic Theory*, New York: Elsevier, 33–52.
Ramey, G. and V. Ramey, 1995. "Cross-country Evidence on the Link between Volatility and Growth," *American Economic Review*, 85(5): 1138–51.
Ramsey, F. P., 1927. "A Contribution to the Theory of Taxation," *Economic Journal*, 37(145): 47–61.
Ramsey, F. P., 1928. "A Mathematical Theory of Saving," *Economic Journal*, 38(152): 543–59.
Ramsey, F. P., 1931. "Truth and Probability," in R. B. Braithwaite (ed.), *Foundations of Mathematics and other Logical Essays*, 156–98, New York: Harcourt Brace.
Ranaldi, M. and B. Milanovic, 2020. "Capitalist Systems and Income Inequality," *Vox EU*, December 3. https://cepr.org/voxeu/about-voxeu.
Rao, G., 2019. "Familiarity Does Not Breed Contempt: Diversity, Discrimination, and Generosity in Delhi Schools," *American Economic Review*, 109(3): 774–809.

Rashid, H., 2005. "Evidence of Financial Disintermediation in Low Income Countries: Are the Foreign Banks Responsible?" thesis, Columbia University.
Ravallion, M., 2002. "How Not to Count the Poor? A Reply to Reddy and Pogge," World Bank Development Research Group, available at https://www.researchgate.net/publication/252553786_How_not_to_Count_the_Poor_A_Reply_to_Reddy_and_Pogge/citation/download.
Ravallion, M., 2007a. "Inequality Is Bad for the Poor," in J. Micklewright and S. Jenkins (eds.), *Inequality and Poverty Re-Examined*, Oxford: Oxford University Press.
Ravallion, M., 2007b. "Economic Growth and Poverty Reduction: Do Poor Countries Need to Worry about Inequality?" 2020 Focus Brief on the World's Poor and Hungry People, IFPRI.
Rawls, J., 1971. *A Theory of Justice*, Cambridge, MA: Belknap Press of Harvard University Press.
Reardon, S. F., and K. Bischoff, 2011. "Income Inequality and Income Segregation," *American Journal of Sociology*, 116(4): 1092–53.
Reich, R., 2015. *Saving Capitalism: For the Many, Not the Few* (New York: Knopf).
Reid, J. D., Jr., 1979. "White Land, Black Labor, and Agricultural Stagnation: The Causes and Effects of Sharecropping in the Postbellum South," *Explorations in Economic History*, 16(1): 31.
Reifschneider, D., W. L. Wascher, and D. Wilcox, 2013. "Aggregate Supply in the United States: Recent Developments and Implications for the Conduct of Monetary Policy," 14th Jacques Polak Annual Research Conference, November.
Reinhart, C. and K. Rogoff, 2009. *This Time Is Different: Eight Centuries of Financial Folly*, Princeton, NJ: Princeton University Press.
Restrepo, P., 2015. "Skill Mismatch and Structural Unemployment," Massachusetts Institute of Technology Job Market Paper.
Riley, J., 1987. "Credit Rationing: A Further Remark," *American Economic Review*, 77(1): 224–7.
Robbins, J. A. 2019. "Capital Gains and the Distribution of Income in the United States," December, available at https://rooseveltinstitute.org/author/jacobrobbins/.
Roberts, K., 1982. "Long-Term Contracts," mimeo.
Roberts, S., 2014. "Why Are Rockefellers Moving from 30 Rock? 'We Got a Great Deal,'" *New York Times*, November 24.
Robinson, J., 1933. *The Economics of Imperfect Competition*, London: Macmillan.
Robinson, J., 1965. *The Accumulation of Capital*, London: Macmillan.
Rodrik, D., 1999. "Where Did All the Growth Go? External Shocks, Social Conflict, and Growth Collapses," *Journal of Economic Growth*, 4(4): 385–412.
Roeder, O., L.-B. Eisen, and J. Bowling, 2015. "What Caused the Crime Decline?," report of the Brennan Center for Justice at the New York University School of Law.
Roemer, J. E., 1998. *Equality of Opportunity*, Cambridge, Mass. and London: Harvard University Press.
Roemer, J. E., 2004. "Equal Opportunity and Intergenerational Mobility: Going Beyond Intergenerational Income Transition Matrices," in M. Corak (ed.), *Generational Income Mobility in North America and Europe*, Cambridge, UK: Cambridge University Press, 48–57.
Roemer, J. E. and A. Trannoy, 2014. "Equality of Opportunity," in A. B. Atkinson and F. Bourguignon (eds.), *Handbook of Income Distribution*, Volumes 2A–2B, Amsterdam: Elsevier, 217–300.
Roemer, J. E. and A. Trannoy, 2016. "Equality of Opportunity: Theory and Measurement," *Journal of Economic Literature*, 54(4): 1288–332.
Rognlie, M., 2015. "Deciphering the Fall and Rise in the Net Capital Share: Accumulation or Scarcity?" *Brookings Papers on Economic Activity*, 2015(1): 1–69.
Rogoff, K. S., 2017. *The Curse of Cash: How Large-Denomination Bills Aid Crime and Tax Evasion and Constrain Monetary Policy*, Princeton, NJ: Princeton University Press, 2017.
Romer, C. D. and D. H. Romer, 1989. "Does Monetary Policy Matter? A New Test in the Spirit of Friedman and Schwartz," *NBER Macroeconomics Annual*, 4, 121–184.
Romer, T., 1975. "Individual Welfare, Majority Voting, and the Properties of a Linear Income Tax," *Journal of Public Economics*, 4(2): 163–85.
Roosa, R., 1951. "Interest Rates and the Central Bank," in *Money, Trade and Ecnomic Growth: Essays in Honor of John H. Williams*, New York: The Macmillan Company, 270–95.
Rose, H., 1967. "On the Non-Linear Theory of the Employment Cycle," *Review of Economic Studies*, 34(2): 153–74.
Rosenthal, S., J. Duca, and S. Gabriel, 1991. "Credit Rationing and the Demand for Owner-Occupied Housing," *Journal of Urban Economics*, 30(1): 48–63.
Ross, S., 1973. "The Economic Theory of Agency: The Principal's Problem," *American Economic Review*, 63(2): 134–39.

Ross, S., 1977. "The Determination of Financial Structure: The Incentive Signalling Approach," *Bell Journal of Economics*, 8(1): 23–40.

Rothschild, M. and J. E. Stiglitz, 1970. "Increasing Risk I: A Definition," *Journal of Economic Theory*, 2(1): 225–43.

Rothschild, M. and J. E. Stiglitz, 1971. "Increasing Risk II: Its Economic Consequences," *Journal of Economic Theory*, 3(1): 66–84.

Rothschild, M. and J. E. Stiglitz, 1972. "Addendum to Increasing Risk: I. A Definition," *Journal of Economic Theory*, 5(2): 306.

Rothschild, M. and J. E. Stiglitz, 1973. "Some Further Results on the Measurement of Inequality," *Journal of Economic Theory*, 6(2): 188–204 (reprinted as Chapter 15 in this volume).

Rothschild, M. and J. E. Stiglitz, 1976. "Equilibrium in Competitive Insurance Markets: An Essay on the Economics of Imperfect Information," *Quarterly Journal of Economics*, 90(4): 629–49 (reprinted as Chapter 5, Selected Works, Volume I).

Rothschild, M. and J. E. Stiglitz, 1982. "A Model of Employment Outcomes Illustrating the Effect of the Structure of Information on the Level and Distribution of Income," *Economic Letters*, 10(3–4): 231–36 (reprinted as Chapter 4 in *Selected Works*, Volume I).

Rothschild, M. and J. E. Stiglitz, 1997. "Competition and Insurance Twenty Years Later," *Geneva Papers on Risk and Insurance Theory*, 22(2): 73–79. Reprinted in *Selected Works of Joseph E. Stiglitz, Volume I: Information and Economic Analysis*, Oxford: Oxford University Press, 2009, 160–67.

Rudra, A., 1984. "Local Power and Farm Level Decision-Making," *Agrarian Power and Agricultural Productivity in South Asia*, 1984: 251–80.

Sadka, E., 1976. "On Income Distribution, Incentive Effects and Optimal Income Taxation," *Review of Economic Studies*, 42: 261–68.

Saez, E., 2001. "Using Elasticities to Derive Optimal Income Tax Rates," *Review of Economic Studies*, 68(1): 205–29.

Saez, E., 2002a. "The Desirability of Commodity Taxation under Non-Linear Income Taxation and Heterogeneous Tastes," *Journal of Public Economics*, 83(2): 217–30.

Saez, E., 2004. "Direct or Indirect Tax Instruments for Redistribution: Short-Run Versus Long-Run," *Journal of Public Economics*, 88(3–4): 503–18.

Saez, E. and G. Zucman, 2014. "Wealth Inequality in the United States since 1913: Evidence from Capitalized Income Tax Data," NBER Working Paper No. 20625.

Saez, E. and G. Zucman, 2019a. "Progressive Wealth Taxation," Brookings Papers on Economic Activity, https://www.brookings.edu/wp-content/uploads/2019/09/Saez-Zucman_conference-draft.pdf (accessed January 22, 2020).

Saez, E. and G. Zucman, 2019b. *The Triumph of Injustice: How the Rich Dodge Taxes and How to Make Them Pay*, New York: W. W. Norton

Sah, R. and J. E. Stiglitz, 1985. "Human Fallibility and Economic Organization," *American Economic Review*, 75(2): 292–96.

Sah, R. and J. E. Stiglitz, 1986. "The Architecture of Economic Systems: Hierarchies and Polyarchies," *American Economic Review*, 76(4): 716–27. Also a shortened version in AEA Papers and Proceedings, also published in *Personnel Economics*, Edward P. Lasear and Robert NcNabb (eds.) 2002.

Sah, R. and J. E. Stiglitz, 1987. "Taxation and Pricing of Agricultural and Industrial Goods in Developing Economies," in D. Newbery and N. Stern (eds.), *The Tax Theory for Developing Countries*, Oxford: Oxford University Press, 1987, 430–58.

Sah, R. and J. E. Stiglitz, 1988a. "Committees, Hierarchies and Polyarchies," *The Economic Journal*, 98(391): 451–470.

Sah, R. and J. E. Stiglitz, 1988b. "Qualitative Properties of Profit-Maximizing K-out-of-N Systems Subject to Two Kinds of Failure," *IEEE Transactions on Reliability*, 37(5): 515–20.

Sah, R. and J. E. Stiglitz, 1992. *Peasants versus City-Dwellers: Taxation and the Burden of Economic Development*, Oxford and New York: Oxford University Press, 1992.

Sah, R. and J. E. Stiglitz, Peasants versus City-Dwellers: Taxation and the Burden of Economic Development, Oxford and New York: Oxford University Press, 1992.

Salanié, B., 2003. *The Economics of Taxation*, Cambridge, MA: MIT Press.

Salop, S., 1972. "Wage Differentials and Unemployment," Yale Ph.D. thesis.

Salop, S., 1973. "Systematic Job Search and Unemployment," *Review of Economic Studies*, 40(2): 191–201.

Salop, S., 1979. "A Model of the Natural Rate of Unemployment," *American Economic Review*, 69(1): 117–25.

Salop, J. and S. Salop, 1976. "Self Selection and Turnover in the Labor Market," *Quarterly Journal of Economics*, 90(4): 619–27.

Salter, W. E. G., 1960. Productivity and Technical Change. University of Cambridge, Department of Applied Economics, Monographs n° 6. Cambridge, At the University Press, XI, 198, 22/6.
Salter, W. E. G., 1962. *Productivity and Technical Change*, Cambridge: Cambridge University Press (second edition, 1966).
Samans, R., J. Blanke, G. Corrigan, and M. Drzeniek, 2015. "Benchmarking Inclusive Growth and Development," World Economic Forum Discussion Paper, January.
Samuelson, P., 1947. *Foundations of Economic Analysis*, Cambridge, MA: Harvard University Press.
Samuelson, P., 1948. "International Trade and the Equalization of Factor Prices," *Economic Journal*, 58(230): 163–84.
Samuelson, P., 1954. "The Pure Theory of Public Expenditure," *Review of Economics and Statistics*, 36(4): 387–89.
Samuelson, P.A. 1955. "Diagrammatic exposition of a theory of public expenditure," *Review of Economics and Statistics* 37, November, 350–56.
Samuelson, P. A. 1958. "Aspects of Public Expenditure Theories," *Review of Economics and Statistics*, 40(4): 332–38.
Samuelson, P., 1965. "A Theory of Induced Innovation along Kennedy-Weisäcker Lines," *Review of Economics and Statistics*, 1965: 343–56.
Samuelson, P. A., and F. Modigliani, 1966. "The Pasinetti Paradox in Neoclassical and More General Models," *Review of Economic Studies*, 33(4): 269–302.
Samuelson, P. A., and R. M. Solow, 1960. "Analytical Aspects of Anti-Inflation Policy," *American Economic Review*, 50(2): 174–94.
Sandmo, A., 1975. "Optimal Taxation in the Presence of Externalities," *Swedish Journal of Economics*, 77(1): 86–98.
Saporta, B., 2004. "Etude de la Solution Stationnaire de l'Equation Yn+1 = anYn + bn, a Coefficients Aléatoires," thesis, Université de Rennes I.
Saporta, B., 2005. "Tail of the Stationary Solution to the Stochastic Equation Yn+1== anYn + bn With Markovian Coefficients," *Stochastic Processes and Their Applications*, 115, 1954–78.
Sappington, D., and J. E. Stiglitz, 1987. "Information and Regulation," in E. Bailey (ed.), *Public Regulation*, London: MIT Press, 3–43.
Sargan, J. D., 1964. "Wages and Prices in the United Kingdom: A Study in Econometric Methodology," in P. E. Hart, G. Mills, and J. K. Whitaker (eds.), *Econometric Analysis for Economic Planning: Sixteenth Symposium of the Colston Research Society*, 16: 25–54.
Savage, L. J., 1954. *The Foundations of Statistics*, New York: Wiley.
Sawhill, I., 1994. "Income Inequality and the Underclass," in D. B. Papadimitriou (ed.), *Aspects of Distribution of Wealth and Income*, Jerome Levy Economics Institute Series, New York: St. Martin's Press; London: Macmillan Press, 194–8.
Scheinkman, J. A., and W. Xiong, 2003. "Overconfidence and Speculative Bubbles," *Journal of Political Economy*, 111(6): 1183–220.
Schmidt-Hebbel, K. and L. Servén, 1997. *Income Inequality and Aggregate Saving: the Cross-Country Evidence*, Washington, DC: World Bank Publications.
Schmitt, J., 2013. *Why Does the Minimum Wage Have No Discernible Effect on Employment?*, Washington, DC: Center for Economic and Policy Research.
Schultz, T. P., 1972. "Long-Term Changes in Personal Income Distribution: Theoretical Approaches, Evidence, and Explanations," *American Economic Review*, 62(2): 361–2.
Schumpeter, J., 1934. *The Theory of Economic Development*, Cambridge: Harvard University Press.
Schwartz, R. and D. Whitcomb, 1980. "The Trade Credit Decision," in J. Bicksler (ed.), *Handbook of Financial Economics*, Amsterdam: North-Holland.
Seade, J. K., 1977. "On the Shape of Optimal Tax Schedules," *Journal of Public Economics*, 7(2): 203–36.
Sealey, C., 1979. "Credit Rationing in the Commercial Loan Market: Estimates of a Structural Model under Conditions of Disequilibrium," Journal of Finance, 34(3): 689–702.
Semega J, M. Kollar, J. Creamer, and A. Mohanty, 2019. "Income and Poverty in the United States: 2018. Report" # P60-266. *Current Population Reports*, (September), 1–88.
Sen, A., 1989. "Women's Survival as a Development Problem," *Bulletin of the American Academy of Arts and Sciences*, 43(2): 14–29.
Sen, A., 1992. *Inequality Re-Examined*, Cambridge, Mass.: Harvard University Press.
Senior, N. W., 1836. *An Outline of the Science of Political Economy*, London: W. Clowes and Sons.
Shah, A. K., S. Mullainathan, and E. Shafir, 2012. "Some Consequences of Having Too Little," *Science*, 338(6107): 682–5.

Shang-Jin W. and X. Zhang, 2011. "The Competitive Saving Motive: Evidence from Rising Sex Ratios and Savings Rates in China," *Journal of Political Economy*, 119(3): 511–564.
Shapiro, C., 1983. "Premiums for High Quality Products as Returns to Reputation," *Quarterly Journal of Economics*, 98(4): 659–79.
Shapiro, C. and J. E. Stiglitz, 1984. "Equilibrium Unemployment as a Worker Discipline Device," *American Economic Review*, 74(3): 433–44 (reprinted as Chapter 11, Selected Works, Volume I).
Shear, M. and P. Baker, 2013. "Obama Focuses on Economy, Vowing to Help Middle Class," *New York Times*, July 24.
Sheifer, A., and R. Vishny, 1986. "Large Shareholders and Corporate Control," *Journal of Political Economy*, 34(3): 461–88.
Shell, K., and J. E. Stiglitz, 1967. "The Allocation of Investment in a Dynamic Economy," *Quarterly Journal of Economics*, 81(4): 592–609.
Shell, K., M. Sidrauski, and J. E. Stiglitz, 1969. "Capital Gains, Income and Savings," *Review of Economic Studies*, 36(1): 15–26.
Sheshinski, E., 1967. "Balanced Growth and Stability in the Johansen Vintage Model," *Review of Economic Studies*, 34(2): 239–48.
Sheshinski, E., 1972. "Relation between a Social Welfare Function and the Gini Index of Income Inequality," *Journal of Economic Theory*, 4(1): 98–100.
Shierholz, H. and L. Mishel, 2013. "A Decade of Flat Wages," Economic Policy Institute, available at https://www.epi.org/publication/a-decade-of-flat-wages-the-key-barrier-to-shared-prosperity-and-a-rising-middle-class/.
Shierholz, H., L. Mishel, and J. Schmitt, 2013. "Don't Blame the Robots: Assessing the Job Polarization Explanation of Growing Wage Inequality," Economic Policy Institute, available at https://www.epi.org/publication/technology-inequality-dont-blame-the-robots/.
Shiller, R. J., 1981. "Do Stock Prices Move Too Much to be Justified by Subsequent Changes in Dividends?" *The American Economic Review*, 71(3): 421–36.
Shiller, R., 2002. *Irrational Exuberance*, Princeton, N.J.: Princeton University Press.
Shleifer, A. and R. W. Vishny 1989. "Industrialization and the Big Push," *Journal of Political Economy*, 97(5): 1003–26.
Shorrocks, A. F., 1978. "The Measurement of Mobility," *Econometrica*, 46(5): 1013–24.
Simon, H. A., 1955. "On a Class of Skew Distribution Functions," *Biometrika*, 42(3/4): 425–40.
Simon, H. A., 1991. "Organizations and Markets," *Journal of Economic Perspectives*, 5(2): 25–44.
Simons, H., 1938. *Personal Income Taxation: The Definition of Income as a Problem of Fiscal Policy*, Chicago: University of Chicago Press.
Simsek, A., 2013. "Speculation and Risk Sharing with New Financial Assets," *Quarterly Journal of Economics*, 128(3): 1365–96.
Slemrod, J., 1990. "Optimal Taxation and Optimal Tax Systems," *Journal of Economic Perspectives*, 4(1): 157–78.
Smith, A., 1776. *An Inquiry into the Nature and Causes of the Wealth of Nations*, London: W. Strahan and T. Cadel.
Smith, B., 1983. "Limited Information, Credit Rationing, and Optimal Government Lending Policy," *American Economic Review*, 73(3): 305–18.
Smith, W. L. and R. F. Mikesell, 1957. "The Effectiveness of Monetary Policy: Recent British Experience," *Journal of Political Economy*, 65(1): 18–39.
Solow, R. M., 1956. "A Contribution to the Theory of Economic Growth," *Quarterly Journal of Economics*, 70(1): 65–94.
Solow, R. M., 1957. "Technical Change and the Aggregate Production Function," *Review of Economics and Statistics*, 1957: 312–20.
Solow, R. M., 1961. "Note on Uzawa's Two-Sector Model of Economic Growth," *Review of Economic Studies*, 29(1): 48–50.
Solow, R. M., 1962. "Substitution and Fixed Proportions in the Theory of Capital," *Review of Economic Studies*, 29(3): 207–18.
Solow, R. M., 1987. "We'd Better Watch Out," *New York Times Book Review*, July 12, 36.
Solow, R. M. and J. E. Stiglitz, 1968. "Output, Employment and Wages in the Short Run," *Quarterly Journal of Economics*, 82(4): 537–60.
Spence, M., 1973. "Job Market Signalling," *Quarterly Journal of Economics*, 10(2): 659–61.
Spence, M., 1974. *Market Signalling*, Cambridge, Mass.: Harvard University Press.
Sraffa, P., 1960. *Production of Commodities by Means of Commodities: Prelude to a Critique of Economic Theory*, Cambridge, England: Cambridge University Press.

Srinivasan, T. N., 1979. "Agricultural Backwardness under Semi-Feudalism—Comment," *Economic Journal*, 89(354): 416–19.

Starr, E. 2019. "Consider This: Training, Wages, and the Enforceability of Covenants Not to Compete," *ILR Review*, 72(4): 783–817.

Steele, C. M., 2010. *Whistling Vivaldi: How Stereotypes Affect Us and What We Can Do*, New York: W. W. Norton.

Steele, C. M. and J. Aronson, 1995. "Stereotype Threat and the Intellectual Test Performance of African Americans," *Journal of Personals Social Psychology*, 69(5): 797–811.

Stelzner, M., 2015. *Economic Inequality and Policy Control in the United States*, New York: Springer.

Stelzner, M., 2017. "The New American Way—How Changes in Labour Law Are Increasing Inequality," *Industrial Relations Journal*, 48(3): 231–55.

Stigler, G., 1967. "Imperfections in the Capital Market," *Journal of Political Economy*, 75(3): 287–93.

Stigler, G. and G. Becker, 1977. "De Gustibus Non Est Disputandum," *American Economic Review*, 67(2): 76–90.

Stiglitz, J. E., 1966. "The Distribution of Income and Wealth among Individuals," presented at the December 1966 meetings of the Econometric Society, San Francisco, December 29 (MIT, mimeo).

Stiglitz, J. E., 1967. "A Two-Sector, Two Class Model of Economic Growth," *Review of Economic Studies*, 34(2): 227–38 (reprinted as Chapter 28, this volume).

Stiglitz, J. E., 1969a. "The Effects of Income, Wealth and Capital Gains Taxation on RiskTaking," *Quarterly Journal of Economics*, 83(2): 263–83.

Stiglitz, J. E., 1969b. "Distribution of Income and Wealth among Individuals," *Econometrica*, 37(3): 382–97.

Stiglitz, J. E., 1969c "Alternative Theories of Wage Determination and Unemployment in LDC's," Institute for Development Studies, University of Nairobi, August.

Stiglitz, J. E., 1969d. "Behavior toward Risk with Many Commodities," *Econometrica*, 37(4): 660–67.

Stiglitz, J. E., 1970. "A Consumption Oriented Theory of the Demand for Financial Assets and the Term Structure of Interest Rates," *Review of Economic Studies*, 37(3): 321–51 (reprinted as Chapter 4, Selected Works, Volume III).

Stiglitz, J. E., 1972a. "Portfolio Allocation with Many Risky Assets," in G.P. Szego and K. Shell (eds.), *Mathematical Methods in Investment and Finance*, Amsterdam and New York: North-Holland Publishing/ American Elsevier, 76–108.

Stiglitz, J. E., 1972b. "On Some Aspects of the Pure Theory of Corporate Finance: Bankruptcies and Takeovers," *Bell Journal of Economics*, 3(2): 458–82 (reprinted as Chapter 22, *Selected Works*, Volume III).

Stiglitz, J. E., 1972c. "Optimal Wage Structure," Yale University mimeo.

Stiglitz, J. E., 1972d. "Taxation, Risk Taking, and the Allocation of Investment in a Competitive Economy," in M. Jensen, (ed.), *Studies in the Theory of Capital Markets*, New York: Praeger, 294–361.

Stiglitz, J. E., 1972e. "On the Optimality of the Stock Market Allocation of Investment," *The Quarterly Journal of Economics*, 86(1): 25–60.

Stiglitz, J. E., 1972f. "Equilibrium Wage Distributions," Yale University mimeo.

Stiglitz, J. E., 1973a. "Education and Inequality," *Annals of the American Academy of Political and Social Sciences*, 409(1): 135–45.

Stiglitz, J. E., 1973b. "Labor Turnover and Wage Structure," mimeo.

Stiglitz, J. E., 1973c. "Education as a Screening Device and the Distribution of Income," Yale University working paper.

Stiglitz, J. E., 1973d. "Approaches to the Economics of Discrimination," *American Economic Review*, 62(2): 287–95 (reprinted as Chapter 24, this volume).

Stiglitz, J. E., 1973e. "Taxation, Corporate Financial Policy and the Cost of Capital," *Journal of Public Economics*, 2(1): 1–34.

Stiglitz, J. E., 1973f. "The Badly Behaved Economy with the Well Behaved Production Function," in J. Mirrlees (ed.), *Models of Economic Growth*, New York: Macmillan, 118–37. (Presented at the International Economic Association Conference on Growth Theory, Jerusalem, 1970.)

Stiglitz, J. E., 1974a. "The Cambridge-Cambridge Controversy in the Theory of Capital; A View from New Haven: A Review Article," *Journal of Political Economy*, 82(4): 893–904.

Stiglitz, J. E., 1974b. "Incentives and Risk Sharing in Sharecropping," *Review of Economic Studies*, 41(2): 219–56 (reprinted as Chapter 13, *Selected Works*, Volume I).

Stiglitz, J. E., 1974c. "Alternative Theories of Wage Determination and Unemployment in L.D.C.'s: The Labor Turnover Model," *Quarterly Journal of Economics*, 88(2): 194–227 (reprinted as Chapter 21, *Selected Works*, Volume II).

Stiglitz, J. E., 2014g. "Remarks on Income Contingent Loans: How Effective Can They Be at Mitigating Risk?," in J. E. Stiglitz, B. Chapman, and T. Higgins (eds.), *Income Contingent Loans: Theory, Practice and Prospects*, Houndmills, UK and New York: Palgrave Macmillan, 31–38.

Stiglitz, J. E., 2015a. "New Theoretical Perspectives on the Distribution of Income and Wealth among Individuals: Parts I-IV," NBER Working Papers 21189-21192.

Stiglitz, J. E., 2015b. "Inequality in America: A Policy Agenda for a Stronger Future," *Annals of the American Academy of Political and Social Science*, 657(1): 8–20.

Stiglitz, J. E., 2015c. "Fed Policy, Inequality, and Equality of Opportunity," in A. Brown et al. (eds.), *Economic Mobility: Research & Ideas on Strengthening Families, Communities & the Economy*, St. Louis and Washington, DC: Federal Reserve Bank of St. Louis and the Board of Governors of the Federal Reserve System, 77–94. Originally presented as a keynote address to The Ninth Biennial Federal Reserve System Community Development Research Conference, April 3; also disseminated as a report by the Roosevelt Institute, August 27.

Stiglitz, J. E., 2015d. "In Praise of Frank Ramsey's Contribution to the Theory of Taxation," *Economic Journal*, 125(583): 235–68.

Stiglitz, J. E., 2015e. "Monetary Policy in a Multi-Polar World," in J. E. Stiglitz and R. F. Gürkaynak (eds.), *Taming Capital Flows: Capital Account Management in an Era of Globalization*, International Economic Association Series, London: Palgrave Macmillan, 124–70.

Stiglitz, J. E., 2015f. "Leaders and Followers: Perspectives on the Nordic Model and the Economics of Innovation," *Journal of Public Economics*, 127(July): 3–16.

Stiglitz, J. E., 2015g. "The Origins of Inequality, and Policies to Contain It," *National Tax Journal*, 68(2): 425–48 (reprinted as Chapter 2 of this volume).

Stiglitz, J. E., 2015h. *The Great Divide: Unequal Societies and What We Can Do About Them*, New York: W. W. Norton. Published in paperback in 2016.

Stiglitz, J. E., 2016a. "New Theoretical Perspectives on the Distribution of Income and Wealth among Individuals," in K. Basu and J. E. Stiglitz (eds.), *Inequality and Growth: Patterns and Policy, Volume I: Concepts and Analysis*, IEA Conference Volume No. 156-I, Houndsmills, UK and New York: Palgrave Macmillan (excerpted in Chapter 14 of this volume).

Stiglitz, J. E., 2016b. "The Measurement of Wealth: Recessions, Sustainability and Inequality," in J. E. Stiglitz and M. Guzman (eds.), Contemporary Issues in Macroeconomics: Lessons from The Crisis and Beyond, IEA Conference Volume, No.155-II, New York: Palgrave Macmillan, 63–76.

Stiglitz, J. E., 2016c. "Income Contingent Loans: Some General Theoretical Considerations, with Applications," in J. E. Stiglitz and M. Guzman (eds.), *Contemporary Issues in Microeconomics*, IEA Conference Volume, No. 155-III, Houndmills, UK and New York: Palgrave Macmillan.

Stiglitz, J. E., 2016d. *The Euro: How a Common Currency Threatens the Future of Europe*, New York: W. W. Norton. Reissued as a paperback in 2017, with a new introduction.

Stiglitz, J. E., 2016e. "In Praise of Frank Ramsey's Contribution to the Theory of Taxation," *Economic Journal*, 125(583): 235–68 (excerpted in Chapter 36 of this volume).

Stiglitz, J. E., 2016f. *Towards a General Theory of Deep Downturns*, IEA Conference Volume, 155-VI, Houndmills, UK and New York: Palgrave Macmillan. Also NBER Working Paper 21444, August 2015. Originally presented as Presidential Address to the 17th World Congress of the International Economic Congress, Dead Sea, Jordan, June, 2014.

Stiglitz, J. E., 2017a. "Macro-Economic Management in an Electronic Credit/Financial System," NBER Working Paper 23032.

Stiglitz, J. E., 2017b. "Wealth and Income Inequality in the Twenty-First Century," keynote lecture delivered at the Eighteenth World Congress of the International Economic Association, Mexico City, June 19–23.

Stiglitz, J. E., 2018a. *Globalization and Its Discontents Revisited: Anti-Globalization in the Age of Trump*, New York: W. W. Norton.

Stiglitz, J. E., 2018b. "Pareto Efficient Taxation and Expenditures: Pre- and Re-Distribution," *Journal of Public Economics*, 162: 101–19.

Stiglitz, J. E., 2018c. "Economic Justice in America: Fifty Years after the Kerner Report," in F. Harris and A. Curtis (eds.), *Healing Our Divided Society: Investing in America Fifty Years after the Kerner Report*, Philadelphia: Temple University Press, 127–38.

Stiglitz, J. E., 2018d. "Towards a Twenty-First Century Investment Agreement," in L. Johnson and L. Sachs (eds.), *Yearbook on International Investment Law and Policy 2015–2016*, xiii–xxviii, Oxford University Press.

Stiglitz, J. E., 2018e. "Where Modern Macroeconomics Went Wrong," *Oxford Review of Economic Policy*, 34(1–2): 70–106. Originally NBER Working Paper 23795.

Stiglitz, J. E., 2018f. "The Theory of Credit and Macroeconomic Stability," in A. Ghosh Dastidar, R. Malhotra, and V. Suneja (eds.), *Economic Theory and Policy Amidst Global Discontent: Essays in Honour of Deepak Nayyar*, London: Routledge India, 127–83.

Stiglitz, J. E., 2019a. *People, Power, and Profits: Progressive Capitalism for an Age of Discontent*, New York: W. W. Norton.

Stiglitz, J. E., 2019b. "Addressing Climate Change Through Price and Non-Price Interventions," *European Economic Review*, 119: 594–612.

Stiglitz, J. E., 2019c. *The Selected Works of Joseph E. Stiglitz, Volume III: Rethinking Microeconomics*, Oxford: Oxford University Press.

Stiglitz, J. E., 2020 "GDP Is the Wrong Tool for Measuring What Matters," *Scientific American*, 323 (August 1).

Stiglitz, J. E., 2021. "Fostering More-Competitive Labor Markets," in B. H. Harris, and S. Block (eds.) *Inequality and the Labor Market: The Case for Greater* Competition (Washington, D.C: Brookings Institution Press), 1–16.

Stiglitz, J. E., and L. Bilmes, 2008. *The Three Trillion Dollar War: The True Cost of the Iraq Conflict* (New York: W. W. Norton).

Stiglitz, J. E. and A. Charlton, 2005. *Fair Trade for All*, New York: Oxford University Press.

Stiglitz, J. E. and P. Dasgupta, 1981. "Market Structure and Resource Extraction under Uncertainty," *Scandinavian Economic Journal*, 83(2): 318–33.

Stiglitz, J. E. and B. Greenwald, 2014. *Creating a Learning Society: A New Approach to Growth, Development, and Social Progress*, New York: Columbia University Press. Reader's Edition published 2015.

Stiglitz, J. E. and M. Uy, 1996. "Financial Markets, Public Policy, and the East Asian Miracle," *World Bank Research Observer*, 11(2): 249–76.

Stiglitz, J. E. and H. Uzawa (eds.), 1969. *Readings in Modern Theory of Economic Growth*, Cambridge, MA: MIT Press.

Stiglitz, J. E. and A. Weiss, 1981. "Credit Rationing in Markets with Imperfect Information," *American Economic Review*, 71(3): 393–410 (reprinted as Chapter 9, *Selected Works*, Volume I).

Stiglitz, J. E. and A. Weiss, 1983. "Incentive Effects of Termination: Applications to the Credit and Labor Markets," *American Economic Review*, 73(5): 912–27 (reprinted as Chapter 8, *Selected Works*, Volume II).

Stiglitz, J. E. and A. Weiss, 1986. "Credit Rationing and Collateral," in J. Edwards, J. Franks, C. Mayer, and S. Schaefer (eds.), *Recent Developments in Corporate Finance*, Cambridge: Cambridge University Press, 101–35. Reprinted as Chapter 9, *Selected Works*, Volume II.

Stiglitz, J. E. and A. Weiss, 1987a. "Macroeconomic Equilibrium and Credit Rationing," NBER Working Paper 2164.

Stiglitz, J. E. and A. Weiss, 1987b. "Credit Rationing: Reply," *American Economic Review*, 77(1): 228–31.

Stiglitz, J. E. and A. Weiss, 1990. "Banks as Social Accountants and Screening Devices for the Allocation of Credit," *Greek Economic Review*, 12(Supplement): 85–118. Reprinted in M. K. Lewis (ed.), *Financial Intermediaries*, Aldershot, UK: Elgar, 1995, 297–330. Also NBER Working Paper 2710, September 1988. Reprinted as Chapter 12 in *Selected Works*, Volume II.

Stiglitz, J. E. and A. Weiss, 1992. "Asymmetric Information in Credit Markets and Its Implications for Macro-Economics," *Oxford Economic Papers*, 44(4): 694–724.

Stiglitz, J. E. and J. Yun, 2005. "The Integration of Unemployment Insurance with Retirement Insurance," *Journal of Public Economics*, 89(11–12): 2037–67.

Stiglitz, J. E. and J. Yun, 2013. "Optimality and Equilibrium in a Competitive Insurance Market under Adverse Selection and Moral Hazard," NBER Working Paper 19317.

Stiglitz, J. E. and J. Yun, 2014. "Income Contingent Loans for the Unemployed: A Prelude to a General Theory of the Efficient Provision of Social Insurance," in J. E. Stiglitz, B. Chapman, and T. Higgins (eds.), *Income Contingent Loans: Theory, Practice and Prospects*, New York: Palgrave Macmillan, 180–204.

Stiglitz, J. E., and J. Yun, 2017. "Income Contingent Loan as an Unemployment Benefit," Columbia University Working Paper.

Stiglitz, J. E. with N. Abernathy, A. Hersh, S. Holmberg, and M. Konczal, 2015. *Rewriting the Rules of the American Economy: An Agenda for Growth and Shared Prosperity*, New York: W. W. Norton.

Stiglitz, J. E., J.-P. Fitoussi, and M. Durand, 2018. *Beyond GDP: Measuring What Counts for Economic and Social Performance*, OECD Publishing, Paris. https://doi.org/10.1787/9789264307292-en.

Stiglitz, J. E., J.-P. Fitoussi, and M. Durand, 2019a. *Measuring What Counts: The Global Movement for Well-Being*, New York: The New Press. Originally published as *Measuring What Counts for Economic and Social Performance*, Paris: OECD, November 2018.

Stiglitz, J. E., J.-P. Fitoussi, and M. Durand, 2019b. *For Good Measure: An Agenda for Moving Beyond GDP Report of the OECD High Level Expert Group on the Measurement of Economic Performance and Social Progress*, New York: New Press, 2019. Originally published as *For Good Measure: Advancing Research and Well-being Metrics Beyond GDP*, Paris: OECD, 2018.

Stiglitz, J. E., D. McFadden, and S. Peltzman, 1988. "Technological Change, Sunk Costs and Competition," *Brookings Papers on Economic Activity* 3: 883–947.

Stiglitz, J. E., J. A. Ocampo, S. Spiegel, R. French-Davis, and D. Nayyar, 2006. *Stability with Growth: Macroeconomics, Liberalization, and Development*, The Initiative for Policy Dialogue Series, Oxford: Oxford University Press.

Stiglitz, J. E., P. Segal, and S. Ananda (eds.), 2010. *Debates on the Measurement of Global Poverty*, New York: Oxford University Press.

Stiglitz, J. E., A. Sen, and J.-P. Fitoussi, 2010. *Mismeasuring Our Lives: Why GDP Doesn't Add Up*, New York: The New Press.

Stiglitz, J. E. with E. Stetter, C. Dougherty, S. Griffith-Jones, I. Ortiz, J. Capaldo, D. Gabor, and M. Schratzenstaller-Altzinger, 2019. "Rewriting the Rules of the European Economy," Foundation for European Progressive Studies, available at https://www.feps-europe.eu/attachments/publications/book_stiglitz-rewriting_rules.pdf (accessed January 8, 2020).

Stokey, N., 1998. "Shirtsleeves to Shirtsleeves: The Economics of Social Mobility," in N. L. Schwartz, D. Jacobs, and E. Kalai (eds.), *Frontiers of Research in Economic Theory: The Nancy L. Schwartz Memorial Lectures 1983–1997*, Cambridge: Econometric Society Monographs, 210–41.

Stolper, W. F. and P. A. Samuelson, 1941. "Protection and Real Wages," *The Review of Economic Studies*, 9(1): 58–73.

Strassen, V., 1965. "The Existence of Probability Measures with Given Marginals," *Annals of Mathematical Statistics*, 36(2): 423–39.

Sufi, A. and A. Mian, 2015. *House of Debt: How They (and You) Caused the Great Recession, and How We Can Prevent It from Happening Again* (Chicago: University of Chicago Press).

Sunstein, C., 2016. "People Prefer System 2 Nudges (Kind Of)," *Duke Law Journal* 66: 121.

Sunstein, C. and R. Thaler, 2008. *Nudge: Improving Decisions about Health, Wealth, and Happiness*, New Haven, CT: Yale University Press.

Svedborg, P., 1990. "Undernutrition in Sub-Saharan Africa: Is There a Gender Bias?" *Journal of Development Studies*, 32(4): 933–43.

Sweezy, P. M., 1990. "Monopoly Capitalism," in J. Eatwell, M. Milgate, and P. Newman (eds.), *Marxian Economics*, London: Palgrave Macmillan, 297–303.

Szenberg, M., A. A. Gottesman, and L. Ramrattan (eds.), 2015. *Paul Samuelson: On Being an Economist*, New York: Jorge Pinto Books.

Taylor, M., 2013. "The Labour Market Impacts of Leaving Education when Unemployment Is High: Evidence from Britain," ISER Working Paper Series, 2013–12.

Taylor, P. and R. Fry, 2012. "The Rise of Residential Segregation by Income," Pew Center, https://www.pewresearch.org/social-trends/2012/08/01/the-rise-of-residential-segregation-by-income/

Taylor, P., R. Kochhar, R. Fry, G. V Elasco, and S. Motel, 2011. "Wealth Gaps Rise to Record Highs between Whites, Blacks and Hispanics," Pew Research Center report, available at http://www.pewsocialtrends.org/files/2011/07/SDT-Wealth-Report_7-26-11_FINAL.pdf (accessed January 8, 2020).

Tegmark, M. 2017. *Life 3.0: Being Human in the Age of Artificial Intelligence*, New York: Knopf.

Theil, H., 1967. *Economics and Information Theory*, Chicago: Rand McNally.

Thomas, H., A. Jain, and M. Angus, 2013. The global journey from cash to cashless. MasterCard Advisors Cashless Journey, 1–15.

Tobin, J., 1958. "Liquidity Preference as Behavior Towards Risk," *Review of Economic Studies*, 25(2): 65–86.

Tobin, J., 1967. "Life Cycle Saving and Balanced Growth," in W. J. Fellner (ed.), *Ten Economic Stuides in the Tradition of Irving Fisher*, New York: John Wiley & Sons, 231–56.

Tobin, J., 1970. "On Limiting the Domain of Inequality," *Journal of Law and Economics*, 13(2): 263–77.

Tobin, J. and W. C. Brainard, 1977. "Asset Markets and the Cost of Capital," in Richard Nelson and Bela Balassa (eds.), *Economic Progress: Private Values and Public Policy (Essays in Honor of William Fellner)*, Amsterdam: North-Holland, 235–62.

Tobin, J. and W. Dolde, 1971. *Wealth, Liquidity, and Consumption*, Federal Reserve Bank of Boston, Conference Series No 5.

Tuomala, M., 1990. *Optimal Income Tax and Redistribution*, Oxford: Clarendon Press.

Turing, A. M., 1950. "Computing Machinery and Intelligence," *Mind*, 59(236): 433–60.

Turner, A., 2015. Between Debt and the Devil: Money, Credit, and Fixing Global Finance, Princeton, NJ: Princeton University Press.

U.S. Treasury, 1977. *Blueprints for Basic Tax Reform*, Washington, DC: Government Printing Office.

United Nations, 2003. *Human Security Now: Protecting and Empowering People*, New York: United Nations.

United Nations, 2010. *The Stiglitz Report: Reforming the International Monetary and Financial Systems in the Wake of the Global Crisis*, Members of the Commission of Experts on Reforms of the International Monetary and Financial System appointed by the President of the United Nations General Assembly, chaired by J. E. Stiglitz, New York: The New Press, 2010.

United Nations, 2013a. *The Millennium Development Goals Report 2013*, New York: United Nations.

United Nations, 2013b. World Population Prospects: The 2012 Revision, New York: United Nations.

United Nations Department of Economic and Social Affairs, 2015. "United Nations World Population Prospects: 2015 Revision."

United States Government Accountability Office, 2014. "Large Bank Holding Companies: Expectations of Government Support," GAO-14-621, United States General Accounting Office.

Uzawa, H., 1961. "On a Two-Sector Model of Economic Growth," *Review of Economic Studies*, 29(1): 40–47.

Uzawa, H., 1963. "On a Two-Sector Model of Economic Growth, II," *Review of Economic Studies*, 30(2): 105–18.

Valenti, J. and E. Schultz, 2016. "How Predatory Debt Traps Threaten Vulnerable Families," *Center for American Progress*, October 6, 2016. https://www.americanprogress.org/article/how-predatory-debt-traps-threaten-vulnerable-families/

Veblen, T., 1899. *The Theory of the Leisure Class*, New York: Macmillan.

Venables, T., 2006. "Shifts in economic geography and their causes," *Economic Review, Federal Reserve Bank of Kansas City*, 91(Q IV): 61–85.

Venables, T., 2012. *The Spatial Economy: Cities, Regions and International Trade*, Oxford: Oxford University Press.

Vickrey, W., 1947. Agenda for Progressive Taxation, New York: Ronald Press.

Vickrey, W., 1977. "The City as a Firm," in M.S. Feldstein and R. P. Inman (eds.), *The Economics of Public Services*, London: Macmillan, 334–43.

Vickrey, W., 1999. "Henry George, Economies of Scale, and Land Taxation," in K. C. Wenzer (ed.), *Land Value Taxation*, New York: M. E. Sharpe, 24–37.

Viner, J., 1937. *Studies in the Theory of International Trade*, New York: Harper and Brothers.

Vinge, V., 1993. "The Coming Technological Singularity: How to Survive in the Post-Human Era," in *Proc. Vision 21: Interdisciplinary Science and Engineering in the Era of Cyberspace*, Lewis Research Center, NASA, 11–22.

Violante, G. L., 2008. "Skill-Biased Technical Change," in L. Blume and S. Durlauf (eds.), *The New Palgrave Dictionary of Economics*, New York: Macmillan, 2.

Von Weizsäcker, C. C., 1966. "Tentative Notes on a Two-Sector Model with Induced Technical Progress," *Review of Economic Studies*, 33(3): 245–51.

Watkins, G. C., and S. Streifel, 1997. Policy Research Report, *Private Capital Flows to Developing Countries: The Road to Financial Integration*, Washington, DC: World Bank.

Weiss, A., 1988. "High School Graduation, Performance, and Wages," *Journal of Political Economy*, University of Chicago Press, 96(4): 785–820.

Weiss, A., 1995. "Human Capital vs. Signalling Explanations of Wages," *Journal of Economic Perspectives*, American Economic Association, 9(4): 133–54, Fall.

Weitzman, M. L., 1974. "Prices vs. Quantities," *Review of Economic Studies*, 41(4): 477–91.

Wette, H., 1938. "Collateral in Credit Rationing in Markets with Imperfect Information: Note," *American Economic Review*, 73(3): 442–45.

Weatherford, J., 2010. *The History of Money*. New York: Crown, 1997.

Wilkinson, R. and K. Pickett, 2010. *The Spirit Level: Why More Equal Societies Almost Always Do Better*, New York: Bloomsbury Press.

Williams, H., 2010. "Intellectual Property Rights and Innovation: Evidence from the Human Genome," *Journal of Political Economy*, 121(1): 1–27.

Williamson, O. E., 2000. "The New Institutional Economics: Taking Stock, Looking Ahead," *Journal of Economic Literature*, 38(3): 595–613.

Willis, R., 1986. "Wage Determinants: A Survey and Reinerpretation of Human Capital Earnings Functions," in O. Ashenfelter and R. Layard (eds.), *Handbook of Labor Economics, Volume I*, San Diego: Elsevier Science & Technology Books, 525–602.

Wilse-Samson, Laurence H., 2013. Structural Change and Democratization: Evidence from Rural Apartheid (November 22). Available at http://dx.doi.org/10.2139/ssrn.2479681

Wojnilower, A., 1980. "The Central Role of Credit Crunches in Recent Financial History," *Brookings Papers on Economic Activity*, 1980(2): 277–340.
Wold, H. O. A., and P. Whittle. 1957. "A Model Explaining the Pareto Distribution of Wealth," *Econometrica*, 25(4): 591–95.
Wolff, E.N. and M. Gittleman, 2014. "Inheritances and the Distribution of Wealth or Whatever Happened to the Great Inheritance Boom," *Journal of Economic Inequality*, 12: 439–68.
Woodford, M., 2016. "Quantitative Easing and Financial Stability," Working Paper. Working Paper Series. National Bureau of Economic Research, May 2016. https://doi.org/10.3386/w22285.
World Bank, 1993. *The East Asian Miracle: Economic Growth and Public Policy* (World Bank Policy Research Report), Oxford: Oxford University Press.
World Bank, 1999. *Knowledge for Development: World Development Report: 1998/9*, Washington, DC: World Bank.
World Bank, 2001. World Development Report, 2000, Washington, DC: World Bank.
World Bank, 2006. *Repositioning Nutrition as Central to Development: A Strategy for Large-Scale Action*, Washington: The World Bank.
World Bank, 2014. *World Development Report 2015: Mind, Society, and Behavior*, Washington, DC: World Bank Publications.
Woytinsky, W. 1940. "Additional Workers and the Volume of Unemployment," Washington, DC: Committee on Social Security, Social Science Research Council.
Wray, L. R., and Y. Nersisyan, 2016. "Understanding Money and Macroeconomic Policy," in M. Mazzucato and M. Jacobs (eds.), *Rethinking Capitalism*, Hoboken, New Jersey: Wiley-Blackwell, 47–65.
Wu, T., 2018. *The Curse of Bigness: Antitrust in the New Gilded Age*. Columbia Global Reports. https://doi.org/10.2307/j.ctv1fx4h9c
Yellen, J., 1984. "Efficiency Wage Model of Unemployment," *American Economic Review*, 74(2): 200–5.
Young, A. T., 2013. "US Elasticity of Substitution and Factor-Augmentation at the Industry Level," *Macroeconomic Dynamics*, 17(4): 861–97.
Zucman, G., 2013. "The Missing Wealth of Nations: Are Europe and the U.S. Net Debtors or Net Creditors?" *Quarterly Journal of Economics*, 128(3): 1321–64.
Zucman, G., 2015. *The Hidden Wealth of Nations*, Chicago: University of Chicago Press.
Zucman, G., 2019. "Global Wealth Inequality," *Annual Review of Economics*, 11(1): 109–138.

Index

Tables and figures are indicated by an italic *t* and *f* following the page number.